OCA

Oracle® Database 11*g*
Administrator
Certified Associate
Study Guide

Exam specifications and content are subject to change at any time without prior notice and at Oracle's sole discretion. Please visit Oracle's website (http://education.oracle.com) for the most current information on their exam content.

Sybex®
An Imprint of
WILEY

1Z0-052 Exam Objectives

Sybex®
An Imprint of
WILEY

OCA: Oracle Database 11g Administrator Certified Associate Study Guide

1Z0-051 Exam Objectives

NOTE Exam specifications and content are subject to change at any time without prior notice and at Oracle's sole discretion. Please visit Oracle's website (http://education.oracle.com) for the most current information on their exam content.

Sybex®
An Imprint of
WILEY

Sybex®
An Imprint of
WILEY

OCA
Oracle® Database 11*g*
Administrator
Certified Associate
Study Guide

Biju Thomas

Wiley Publishing, Inc.

Acquisitions Editor: Jeff Kellum
Development Editor: Denise Santoro Lincoln
Technical Editors: Arup Nanda and Bob Bryla
Production Editor: Eric Charbonneau
Copy Editor: Kim Wimpsett
Production Manager: Tim Tate
Vice President and Executive Group Publisher: Richard Swadley
Vice President and Publisher: Neil Edde
Media Project Manager 1: Laura Moss-Hollister
Media Associate Producer: Josh Frank
Media Quality Assurance: Kit Malone
Book Designer: Judy Fung
Compositor: Craig Johnson, Happenstance Type-O-Rama
Proofreader: Candace English
Indexer: Ted Laux
Project Coordinator, Cover: Lynsey Stanford
Cover Designer: Ryan Sneed

Copyright © 2009 by Wiley Publishing, Inc., Indianapolis, Indiana

Published simultaneously in Canada

ISBN: 978-0-470-39512-7

No part of this publication may be reproduced, stored in a retrieval system or transmitted in any form or by any means, electronic, mechanical, photocopying, recording, scanning or otherwise, except as permitted under Sections 107 or 108 of the 1976 United States Copyright Act, without either the prior written permission of the Publisher, or authorization through payment of the appropriate per-copy fee to the Copyright Clearance Center, 222 Rosewood Drive, Danvers, MA 01923, (978) 750-8400, fax (978) 646-8600. Requests to the Publisher for permission should be addressed to the Permissions Department, John Wiley & Sons, Inc., 111 River Street, Hoboken, NJ 07030, (201) 748-6011, fax (201) 748-6008, or online at http://www.wiley.com/go/permissions.

Limit of Liability/Disclaimer of Warranty: The publisher and the author make no representations or warranties with respect to the accuracy or completeness of the contents of this work and specifically disclaim all warranties, including without limitation warranties of fitness for a particular purpose. No warranty may be created or extended by sales or promotional materials. The advice and strategies contained herein may not be suitable for every situation. This work is sold with the understanding that the publisher is not engaged in rendering legal, accounting, or other professional services. If professional assistance is required, the services of a competent professional person should be sought. Neither the publisher nor the author shall be liable for damages arising herefrom. The fact that an organization or Web site is referred to in this work as a citation and/or a potential source of further information does not mean that the author or the publisher endorses the information the organization or Web site may provide or recommendations it may make. Further, readers should be aware that Internet Web sites listed in this work may have changed or disappeared between when this work was written and when it is read.

For general information on our other products and services or to obtain technical support, please contact our Customer Care Department within the U.S. at (877) 762-2974, outside the U.S. at (317) 572-3993 or fax (317) 572-4002.

Wiley also publishes its books in a variety of electronic formats. Some content that appears in print may not be available in electronic books.

Library of Congress Cataloging-in-Publication Data

Thomas, Biju.
  OCA : Oracle database 11g administrator certified associate study guide (1Z0-051 and 1Z0-052) / Biju Thomas. — 1st ed.
    p. cm.
  ISBN 978-0-470-39512-7 (paper/cd-rom)
  1. Electronic data processing personnel—Certification. 2. Database management—Examinations—Study guides. 3. Oracle (Computer file) I. Title.
  QA76.3.T5136 2009
  005.75'75—dc22
                        2008052085

TRADEMARKS: Wiley, the Wiley logo, and the Sybex logo are trademarks or registered trademarks of John Wiley & Sons, Inc. and/or its affiliates, in the United States and other countries, and may not be used without written permission. Oracle is a registered trademark of Oracle Corporation and/or its affiliates. All other trademarks are the property of their respective owners. Wiley Publishing, Inc., is not associated with any product or vendor mentioned in this book.

10 9 8 7 6 5

Dear Reader,

Thank you for choosing *OCA: Oracle Database 11g Administrator Certified Associate Study Guide* (1ZO-051 and 1ZO-052). This book is part of a family of premium-quality Sybex books, all of which are written by outstanding authors who combine practical experience with a gift for teaching.

Sybex was founded in 1976. More than thirty years later, we're still committed to producing consistently exceptional books. With each of our titles we're working hard to set a new standard for the industry. From the paper we print on, to the authors we work with, our goal is to bring you the best books available.

I hope you see all that reflected in these pages. I'd be very interested to hear your comments and get your feedback on how we're doing. Feel free to let me know what you think about this or any other Sybex book by sending me an email at nedde@wiley.com, or if you think you've found a technical error in this book, please visit http://sybex.custhelp.com. Customer feedback is critical to our efforts at Sybex.

Best regards,

Neil Edde
Vice President and Publisher
Sybex, an Imprint of Wiley

To the loving memory of my father

To Joshua and Jeanette

Acknowledgments

Thanks first to Jeff Kellum and to Sybex for their faith in me to write this book. I would also like to thank the following wonderful people at Sybex for their support, patience with my slipping schedules, and good work: Denise Santoro Lincoln (developmental editor) for her valuable comments, thoughtful edits, patience, and making sure the chapters have a smooth flow; Eric Charbonneau (production editor) for making sure the various pieces of the book tie together; Candace English for proofreading; and Pete Gaughan for managing the project.

I thank Kim Wimpsett (copy editor) for her edits and making sure the same standard is followed across the book. I'm sure her edits made a difference to the look and feel of the chapters. I also thank Sybex and authors of the *Introduction to Oracle9i SQL* and *Oracle Database 10g Administration I* study guides for letting me reuse content from their books.

I am very fortunate and honored to have Arup Nanda as the technical editor. Thank you very much for all your valuable suggestions and for pointing out the errors and inaccuracies in the book. Your comments are invaluable. Thank you, Bob Bryla, for tech-reviewing the book and making sure the chapters are technically accurate.

I could not have completed this book without the endless support and love of my wife, Shiji. Thank you for engaging and taking care of the kids while I spent nights and weekends in front of the computer.

Last but not least, I thank all my colleagues and management at OneNeck IT Services for their friendship and support. My special thanks to Joe Hanna for all the encouragement.

About the Author

Biju Thomas   is an Oracle 7.3, Oracle8, Oracle8*i*, Oracle9*i*, Oracle 10*g*, and Oracle 11*g* OCP certified professional. He is also a certified Oracle Database SQL Expert. Biju has been developing and administering Oracle databases since 1993, starting with Oracle version 6. He is a senior database consultant at OneNeck IT Services Corporation (`www.oneneck.com`) and resides in Keller, Texas. He maintains a website for DBAs at `www.bijoos.com/oracle`.

Contents at a Glance

Contents

Introduction

There is high demand for professionals in the information technology (IT) industry, and Oracle certifications are the hottest credential in the database world. You have made the right decision to pursue certification, because being Oracle Database 11g certified will give you a distinct advantage in this highly competitive market.

Many readers may already be familiar with Oracle and do not need an introduction to Oracle databases. Oracle, founded in 1977, sold the first commercial relational database and is now the world's leading database company and second-largest independent software company with annual revenues of more than $22 billion, and is headquartered in Redwood City, California.

Oracle databases are the de facto standard for large Internet sites and mission-critical enterprise applications. Oracle advertisers are boastful but honest when they proclaim, "The Internet runs on Oracle." Almost all the big Internet sites run on Oracle databases. Oracle's penetration of the database market runs deep and is not limited to Internet implementations. Enterprise resource planning (ERP) application suites, data warehouses, and custom applications at many large and medium companies rely on Oracle. The demand for DBA resources remains higher than others during weak economic times.

This book is intended to help you on your exciting path toward becoming an Oracle Database 11g Administrator Certified Associate (OCA), which is the first step on the path toward the Oracle Certified Professional (OCP) and Oracle Certified Master (OCM) certifications. This book covers the two exams required for the OCA certification. Using this book and a practice database, you can start learning Oracle 11g and pass the Oracle Database 11g: SQL Fundamentals I (1Z0-051) and Oracle Database 11g: Administration I (1Z0-052) exams.

Why Become Oracle Certified?

The number-one reason to become OCA or OCP certified is to gain more visibility and greater access to the industry's most challenging opportunities. Oracle certification is the best way to demonstrate your knowledge and skills in Oracle database systems.

Certification is proof of your knowledge and shows that you have the skills required to support Oracle core products. The Oracle certification program can help a company identify proven performers who have demonstrated their skills and who can support the company's investment in Oracle technology. It demonstrates that you have a solid understanding of your job role and the Oracle products used in that role.

The certification tests are scenario-based, which is the most effective way to assess your hands-on expertise and critical problem-solving skills. OCPs are among the best paid in the IT industry. Salary surveys consistently show the OCP certification to yield higher salaries than the other certifications, including Microsoft, Novell, and Cisco.

So, whether you are beginning a career, changing careers, securing your current position, or seeking to refine and promote your position, this book is for you!

Oracle Certifications

Oracle certifications follow a track that is oriented toward a job role. The certification tracks are Database, Middleware, Applications, and Linux. Within each track, Oracle has a tiered certification program of OCA and OCP. Only the Database track has OCM.

The Database track is clearly for the database administrator job role. The Middleware track has certifications on many products, such as Oracle 10g Application Server, Oracle Essbase, Oracle Forms, Oracle PL/SQL, Oracle WebLogic, and Service-Oriented Architecture (SOA) and is intended for application developers, system administrators, consultants, and architects.

The Applications track is for ERP administrators and functional consultants. This track covers the Oracle E-Business Suite, Siebel, Hyperion, and PeopleSoft applications. The Linux track is for Linux administrators.

> For the latest certification information on all of Oracle certification paths, please visit the Oracle website at http://education.oracle.com/pls/web_prod-plq-dad/db_pages.getpage?page_id=39&p_org_id=1001&lang=US.

The role of database administrator (DBA) has become a key to success in today's highly complex database systems. The best DBAs work behind the scenes but are in the spotlight when critical issues arise. They plan, create, maintain, and ensure that the database is available for the business. They have tools to proactively monitor the database for performance issues and to prevent unscheduled downtime. The DBA's job requires a broad understanding of the architecture of Oracle Database and an expertise in solving problems.

Sybex has Oracle certification study guides for the Database track. In the following sections, I'll introduce you to the different tiers in the Oracle Database 11g certification track.

Oracle Database 11g Administrator Certified Associate

The Oracle Certified Associate (OCA) credential is the first step toward achieving the Oracle Certified Professional (OCP) certification. OCA shows that you have the fundamental knowledge and skills to support an Oracle 11g database. This certification requires you to pass two exams that demonstrate your Oracle basics:

- 1Z0-051: Oracle Database 11g: SQL Fundamentals I
- 1Z0-052: Oracle Database 11g: Administration I

If you have already passed any one of the following tests, you need not take the 1Z0-051 test; you need to pass only 1Z0-052:

- 1Z0-001: Introduction to Oracle: SQL and PL/SQL
- 1Z0-007: Introduction to Oracle9i SQL
- 1Z0-047: Oracle Database SQL Expert

You can take the 1Z0-051 exam at a testing location or from your home using the Internet. The 1Z0-052 test is offered only at a Prometric facility.

> To register for the test or find the location of a testing center, visit Prometric at www.prometric.com/oracle, or call 1-800-891-3926. At the time of writing this book, the exam fee was $95 USD for the online exam and $125 USD for the in-facility exam.

Oracle Database 11*g* Administrator Certified Professional

The Oracle Certified Professional credential shows that you have the skill and technical expertise to manage and implement enterprise databases. The OCP tier challenges you to demonstrate your continuing experience and knowledge of Oracle technologies. The Oracle Database 11*g* Administrator Certified Professional certification requires you to have the OCA certification as well as to pass the following exam at a Prometric facility.

- 1Z0-053: Oracle Database 11*g* Administration II

In addition, the OCP candidate must take one instructor-led Oracle University hands-on requirement class from the following list:

- Oracle Database 11*g*: Advanced PL/SQL
- Oracle Database 11*g*: Data Guard Administration
- Oracle Database 11*g*: Performance Tuning
- Oracle Database 11*g*: Administration Workshop I
- Oracle Database 11*g*: Administration Workshop II
- Oracle Database 11*g*: Introduction to SQL
- Oracle Database 11*g*: New Features for Administrators
- Oracle Database 11*g*: Program with PL/SQL
- Oracle Database 11*g*: Develop PL/SQL Program Units
- Oracle Database 11*g*: Implement Streams
- Oracle Database 11*g*: SQL Tuning Workshop
- Oracle Spatial 11*g*: Essentials
- Oracle Database 11*g*: RAC Administration
- Oracle Database 11*g*: SQL Fundamentals I

> You should verify the list of approved hands-on course at the Oracle University website at http://education.oracle.com/pls/web_prod-plq-dad/db_pages.getpage?page_id=244#5. This list may change without notice.

Oracle Database 11g Administrator Certified Master

The highest level of certification available in any track is the Oracle Certified Master. The OCM certification credential shows that you have the highest level of expertise in an Oracle product. To become an Oracle Certified Master, you must first achieve OCP status and then complete two advanced instructor-led classes at an Oracle University facility. You must also pass a hands-on examination at an Oracle University facility. At the time of writing this book, the Oracle Database 11g Certified Master exam has not been released yet.

More Information and Resources

You can find most current information about Oracle certifications at www.oracle.com/global/us/education/certification. You may be asked to choose your country of residence before being directed to the site. Follow the links under Certifications to choose the track and learn more.

Choose the Database track to view the different certification versions available. Choose Oracle 11g Administrator Certified Associate, and then click the test to learn more about the test contents, the objectives covered on the test, and the passing score. You can also register for the test here.

Oracle also provides sample practice questions for the OCA and OCP exams. You can find Oracle Database 11g SQL Fundamentals I exam practice questions at www.oracle.com/global/us/education/certification/sample_questions/exam_1z0-051.html. You can find the sample questions for the Oracle Database 11g Administration I exam at www.oracle.com/global/us/education/certification/sample_questions/exam_1z0-052.html.

The Oracle documentation is available online at http://tahiti.oracle.com. The Oracle documentation contains a wealth of information, which can be used to supplement what you learn from this book.

Oracle provides training series with step-by-step instructions to perform a variety of Oracle Database 11g tasks. You can find the Oracle by example (OBE) tutorial at www.oracle.com/technology/obe/11gr1_db/otn_all_db11gr1.html.

The Oracle Technology Network (www.oracle.com/technology/index.html) is also a great resource for database administrators and developers. You can read articles, view sample code, access documentation, participate in forums, and, most important, download a trial version of Oracle Database 11g and other Oracle products.

OCA/OCP Study Guides

The Oracle Database 11g administration certification consists of three tests: two for OCA and one for OCP. Sybex offers study guides to help you achieve OCA and OCP certification:

- *OCA: Oracle Database 11g Administrator Certified Associate Study Guide* (ISBN 9780470395127) covers the exams Oracle Database 11g: SQL Fundamentals I (1Z0-051) and Oracle Database 11g: Administration I (1Z0-052).

- *OCP: Oracle Database 11g Administrator Certified Professional Study Guide* (ISBN 9780470395134) covers the exam Oracle Database 11g: Administration II (1Z0-053).

These two books are offered in a boxed set as *OCP: Oracle Database 11g Administrator Certified Professional Certification Kit* (ISBN 9780470395141).

Oracle Exam Requirements

The Oracle Database 11g Database Administrator Certified Associate certification tests your basic SQL skills for the SQL exam and your database architecture and administration skills for the DBA exam. The SQL exam tests your knowledge of writing SQL and using the functions available in Oracle 11g. The Administration I exam concentrates on the architecture and the basic administration of Oracle 11g database. The following sections detail the skills needed to pass the SQL Fundamentals I and Administration I exams.

OCA SQL (1Z0-051) Requirements

To pass the Oracle Database 11g SQL Fundamentals I exam, you must have the following skills:

- Write SQL SELECT statements that display data from one or more tables.
- Join tables using ANSI syntax and Oracle traditional syntax.
- Restrict, sort, and aggregate data using single-row, conversion, and group functions.
- Write subqueries and queries using SET operators.
- Manipulate data via insert, update, and delete.
- Create and manage tables, indexes, views, synonyms, and sequences.

OCA Admin I (1Z0-052) Requirements

To pass the Oracle Database 11*g* Administration I exam, you must have the following skills:

- Understand the Oracle server architecture (database and instance).

- Be able to install the Oracle 11*g* software and create a database.

- Use the Database Configuration Assistant and Enterprise Manager Database Control tools.

- Understand the physical and logical storage of the database and be able to manage space allocation and growth.

- Use the data dictionary views and set database parameters.

- Manage and manipulate data, including its storage, loading, and reorganization.

- Create and manage tables, constraints, and indexes.

- Manage redo logs, archive logs, and automatic undo.

- Configure Oracle Net on the server side and the client side.

- Understand the backup and recovery architecture.

- Secure the database and audit database usage.

- Use advisors to tune and manage the database.

- Be able to contact Oracle Support for problem resolution and patches.

Tips for Taking the OCA Exams

The following tips will help you prepare for and pass each exam:

- Each OCP test consists of about 70 questions to be completed in 90 (120 for the SQL exam) minutes. Answer the questions you are sure of first, before you run out of time. Mark the difficult questions or the ones you are not sure of and return to them later.

- Many questions on the exam have answer choices that at first glance look identical. Read the questions carefully. Do not jump to conclusions. Make sure you clearly understand what each question asks.

- Most questions are based on scenarios. Some of the scenarios contain nonessential information and exhibits. You need to be able to identify what's important and what's not.

- Do not leave any questions unanswered. There is no negative scoring.

- When answering questions you are not sure about, use a process of elimination to get rid of the obviously incorrect answers first. Doing this greatly improves your odds if you need to make an educated guess.

- If you are not sure of your answer, mark it for review, and then look for other questions that may help you eliminate any incorrect answers. At the end of the test, you can review the questions you marked earlier.

You should be familiar with the exam objectives, which are included at the beginning of each chapter. Please check the objectives listing on the Oracle University website (http://education.oracle.com/pls/web_prod-plq-dad/db_pages.getpage?page_id=244#5) for any changes or updates. The detail page for each exam shows the passing score, the number of questions, the minutes allocated, and any exam fees or other requirements.

What Is Covered in This Book

This book covers everything you need to pass the Oracle Database 11*g* Certified Associate exams. Part I includes the first eight chapters that cover the objectives for the Oracle Database 11*g* SQL Fundamentals I exam. Part II of the book includes the remaining 10 chapters that cover the objectives for the Oracle Database 11*g* Administration I exam.

Part I: Oracle Database 11*g* SQL Fundamentals I

Chapter 1: Introducing SQL introduces you to writing simple queries using the SELECT statement. It also introduces you to filtering and sorting data.

Chapter 2: Using Single-Row Functions discusses the single-row functions and conversion functions available in Oracle 11*g*, with details on how and where to use them.

Chapter 3: Using Group Functions explains data aggregations, Oracle's built-in group function, and how to nest functions.

Chapter 4: Using Joins and Subqueries explains how data from multiple tables can be related via joins, subqueries, and SET operators.

Chapter 5: Manipulating Data explores how to manipulate data—adding, removing, and updating data. The chapter also covers how transaction control works.

Chapter 6: Creating Tables and Constraints explains how to create and manage tables and constraints. It also discusses the various data types available in Oracle 11*g* to store data.

Chapter 7: Creating Schema Objects introduces you to creating and managing views, sequences, and synonyms.

Part II: Oracle Database 11*g* Administration I

Chapter 8: Introducing Oracle Database 11g Components and Architecture is the first chapter to read if you're studying for the Administration I exam. This chapter introduces you to the Oracle 11*g* database architecture and how to install the Oracle 11*g* software.

Chapter 9: Creating an Oracle 11g Database explains how you can create an Oracle 11g database. It discusses the initialization parameters, stages of database startup and shutdown, where to find log and trace files, and how to use the data dictionary.

Chapter 10: Allocating Database Storage and Creating Schema Objects explores the logical and physical storage of the database. You will learn space management and the various types of tablespaces. This chapter also talks about creating and managing tables and constraints, but does not repeat what was covered in Chapter 6.

Chapter 11: Understanding Network Architecture introduces you to the Oracle Net configuration and setup. You will learn to set up network architecture on the server and client.

Chapter 12: Implementing Security and Auditing shows how you can secure your database using privileges, profiles, and roles. You will also learn how to audit database usage.

Chapter 13: Managing Data and Undo shows you how you can add, update, and remove data from tables as well as how transactions work. It also introduces you to undo data and undo management. Be sure to read Chapter 5 before you read this chapter.

Chapter 14: Maintaining the Database and Managing Performance explores the tools available in Oracle 11g to manage the performance of the database. You will learn about optimizer statistics, Automatic Workload Repository, various advisors, and Automatic Memory Management.

Chapter 15: Implementing Database Backups introduces you to the backup architecture concepts. It discusses the various backup modes and how to use RMAN.

Chapter 16: Recovering the Database explores the various recovery scenarios and how best to get the data back. It introduces you to the Data Recovery Advisor, a new tool in Oracle 11g that helps in finding the recovery-related errors in the database, gives you advice, and helps you recover the database.

Chapter 17: Moving Data and Using EM Tools introduces you to two tools available in Oracle 11g to move and load data: Data Pump and SQL*Loader. This chapter also covers the intelligent infrastructure of Enterprise Manager that helps DBAs manage patches and contact Oracle Support.

Each chapter ends with review questions that are specifically designed to help you retain the knowledge presented. To really nail down your skills, read and answer each question carefully.

How to Use This Book

This book provides a solid foundation for the serious effort of preparing for the Oracle 11*g* Certified Associate exams. To best benefit from the book, use the following study method:

1. Take the assessment test immediately following this introduction (the answers are at the end of the test). Carefully read the explanations for any questions you get wrong, and note in which chapters the material is covered. This information should help you plan the study strategy.

2. Study each chapter carefully, making sure you fully understand the information and the test objectives listed at the beginning of each chapter. Pay close attention to any chapter related to questions you missed on the assessment test.

3. Complete all examples in the chapter, referring to the chapter so that you understand the reason for each step you take. It is best to have an Oracle 11*g* database available to try the examples and code provided in the book. Answer the review questions related to that chapter.

4. Note the review questions that confuse or trick you, and study those sections of the book again.

5. Two bonus exams for each exam are included on the accompanying CD. They will give you a complete overview of what you can expect to see on the real test.

6. Answer all the flashcard questions on the CD.

 Remember to use the products on the CD included with this book. The electronic flashcards and Sybex test engine exam-preparation software have been specifically designed to help you study and pass your exams.

To learn all the material covered in this book, you will need to apply yourself regularly and with discipline. Try to set the same time period every day to study, and select a comfortable and quiet place to do so. If you work hard, you will be surprised at how quickly you learn this material. All the best!

 The companion CD is home to all the demo files, samples, and bonus resources mentioned in the book. See the CD appendix for more details on the contents and how to access them.

How to Contact the Author

I welcome feedback from you about this book or about books you'd like to see from me in the future. You can reach me by writing to biju.thomas.sybex@gmail.com. For more information about database administration and Oracle 11g, please visit my website at www.bijoos.com/oracle.

Sybex strives to keep you supplied with the latest tools and information you need for your work. Please check the website at www.sybex.com, where we'll post additional content, errata, and updates that supplement this book if the need arises. Enter **OCA Oracle 11g** in the Search box (or type the book's ISBN—**9780470395127**), and click Go to get to the book's update page.

SQL Fundamentals I Assessment Test

1. Which operator will be evaluated first in the following SELECT statement?
   SELECT (2+3*4/2-5) FROM dual;
   - **A.** +
   - **B.** *
   - **C.** /
   - **D.** –

2. Which two of the following statements are true?
   - **A.** A view can be created before creating the base table.
   - **B.** A view cannot be created before creating the base table.
   - **C.** A view will become invalid if the base table's column referred to in the view is altered.
   - **D.** A view will become invalid if any column in the base table is altered.

3. Which function can return a non-NULL value if passed a NULL argument?
   - **A.** NULLIF
   - **B.** LENGTH
   - **C.** CONCAT
   - **D.** INSTR
   - **E.** TAN

4. The following statement will raise an exception on which line?
   ```
   select dept_name, avg(all salary)
          ,count(*) "number of employees"
   from emp , dept
   where deptno = dept_no
     and count(*) > 5
   group by dept_name
   order by 2 desc;
   ```
   - **A.** select dept_name, avg(all salary), count(*) "number of employees"
   - **B.** where deptno = dept_no
   - **C.** and count(*) > 5
   - **D.** group by dept_name
   - **E.** order by 2 desc;

5. Review the code segment. Which line has an error?

```
1  INSERT INTO salaries VALUES (101, 23400, SYSDATE);
2  UPDATE salaries
3  SET salary = salary * 1.1
4  AND effective_dt = SYSDATE
5  WHERE empno = 333;
```

   A. 2

   B. 4

   C. 5

   D. There is no error.

6. Review the following SQL, and choose the most appropriate option.
```
SELECT job_id, COUNT(*)
FROM employees
GROUP BY department_id;
```
   A. The statement will show the number of jobs in each department.

   B. The statement will show the number of employees in each department.

   C. The statement will generate an error.

   D. The statement will work if the GROUP BY clause is removed.

7. Which datatype stores data outside Oracle Database?

   A. UROWID

   B. BFILE

   C. BLOB

   D. NCLOB

   E. EXTERNAL

8. The DEPT table has the following data:

```
SQL> SELECT * FROM dept;


   DEPTNO DNAME          LOC
---------- -------------- ----------
       10 ACCOUNTING     NEW YORK
       20 RESEARCH       DALLAS
       30 SALES          CHICAGO
       40 OPERATIONS     BOSTON
```

Consider this INSERT statement, and choose the best answer:

```
INSERT INTO (SELECT * FROM dept WHERE deptno = 10)
VALUES (50, 'MARKETING', 'FORT WORTH');
```

  A. The INSERT statement is invalid; a valid table name is missing.

  B. 50 is not a valid DEPTNO value, since the subquery limits DEPTNO to 10.

  C. The statement will work without error.

  D. A subquery and a VALUES clause cannot appear together.

9. Which two of the following queries are valid syntax that would return all rows from the EMPLOYEES and DEPARTMENTS tables, even if there are no corresponding/related rows in the other table?

  A.
```
SELECT last_name, first_name, department_name
FROM    employees e FULL JOIN departments d
ON      e.department_id = d.department_id;
```

  B.
```
SELECT last_name, first_name, department_name
FROM    employees e OUTER JOIN departments d
ON      e.department_id = d.department_id;
```

  C.
```
SELECT e.last_name, e.first_name, d.department_name
FROM    employees e
LEFT OUTER JOIN departments d
ON      e.department_id = d.department_id
RIGHT OUTER JOIN employees f
ON      f.department_id = d.department_id;
```

  D.
```
SELECT e.last_name, e.first_name, d.department_name
FROM    employees e
CROSS JOIN departments d
ON      e.department_id = d.department_id;
```

  E.
```
SELECT last_name, first_name, department_name
FROM    employees
FULL OUTER JOIN departments USING (department_id);
```

10. Which of the following statements could use an index on the columns PRODUCT_ID and WAREHOUSE_ID of the OE.INVENTORIES table? (Choose all that apply.)

    A. `select count(distinct warehouse_id)`
        `from oe.inventories;`

    B. `select product_id, quantity_on_hand`
        `from oe.inventories`
        `where product_id = 100;`

    C. `insert into oe.inventories values (5,100,32);`

    D. None of these statements could use the index.

11. The following statements are executed:

```
create sequence my_seq;
select my_seq.nextval from dual;
select my_seq.nextval from dual;
rollback;
select my_seq.nextval from dual;
```

What value will be returned when the last SQL SELECT statement is executed?

    A. 0

    B. 1

    C. 2

    D. 3

    E. NULL

12. Which of the following statements are true? (Choose two.)

    A. Primary key constraints allow NULL values in the columns.

    B. Unique key constraints allow NULL values in the columns.

    C. Primary key constraints do not allow NULL values in the columns.

    D. A nonunique index cannot be used to enforce primary key constraints.

13. The current time in Dubai is 04-APR-2008 08:50:00, and the time in Dallas is 03-APR-2008 23:50:00. A user from Dubai is connected to a session in the database located on a server in Dallas. What will be the result of his query?

`SELECT TO_CHAR(SYSDATE, 'DD-MON-YYYY HH24:MI:SS') FROM dual;`

    A. 04-APR-2008 08:50:00

    B. 03-APR-2008 23:50:00

    C. 03-APR-2008 2324:50:00

    D. None of the above

14. The FIRED_EMPLOYEE table has the following structure:

```
EMPLOYEE_ID  NUMBER (4)
FIRE_DATE DATE
```

How many rows will be counted from the last SQL statement in the code segment?

```
SELECT COUNT(*) FROM FIRED_EMPLOYEES;
COUNT(*)
--------
     105

INSERT INTO FIRED_EMPLOYEE VALUES (104, TRUNC(SYSDATE);
SAVEPOINT A;
INSERT INTO FIRED_EMPLOYEE VALUES (106, TRUNC(SYSDATE);
SAVEPOINT B;
INSERT INTO FIRED_EMPLOYEE VALUES (108, TRUNC(SYSDATE);
ROLLBACK TO A;
INSERT INTO FIRED_EMPLOYEE VALUES (104, TRUNC(SYSDATE);
COMMIT;
SELECT COUNT(*) FROM FIRED_EMPLOYEES;
```

A. 109

B. 106

C. 105

D. 107

15. At a minimum, how many join conditions should be there to avoid a Cartesian join if there are three tables in the FROM clause?

A. 1

B. 2

C. 3

D. There is no minimum.

16. Why does the following statement fail?

```
CREATE TABLE FRUITS-N-VEGETABLES
(NAME VARCHAR2 (40));
```

A. The table should have more than one column in its definition.

B. NAME is a reserved word, which cannot be used as a column name.

C. Oracle does not like the table name.

D. The column length cannot exceed 30 characters.

17. Which two statements are true about NULL values?

   A. You cannot search for a NULL value in a column using the WHERE clause.

   B. If a NULL value is returned in the subquery or if NULL is included in the list when using a NOT IN operator, no rows will be returned.

   C. Only = and != operators can be used to search for NULL values in a column.

   D. In an ascending-order sort, NULL values appear at the bottom of the result set.

   E. Concatenating a NULL value to a non-NULL string results in a NULL.

18. Table CUSTOMERS has a column named CUST_ZIP that could be NULL. Which of the following functions include the NULL rows in its result?

   A. COUNT (CUST_ZIP)

   B. SUM (CUST_ZIP)

   C. AVG (DISTINCT CUST_ZIP)

   D. None of the above

19. Using the following EMP table, you need to increase everyone's salary by 5 percent of their combined salary and bonus. Which of the following statements will achieve the desired results?

Column Name	emp_id	name	salary	bonus
Key Type	pk	pk		
NULLs/Unique	NN	NN	NN	
FK Table				
Datatype	VARCHAR2	VARCHAR2	NUMBER	NUMBER
Length	9	50	11,2	11,2

   A. UPDATE emp SET salary = (salary + bonus)*1.05;

   B. UPDATE emp SET salary = salary*1.05 + bonus*1.05;

   C. UPDATE emp SET salary = salary + (salary + bonus)*0.05;

   D. A, B, and C will achieve the desired results.

   E. None of these statements will achieve the desired results.

20. Which option is not available in Oracle when modifying tables?

   A. Adding new columns

   B. Renaming existing columns

   C. Dropping existing columns

   D. None of the above

21. The following data is from the EMPLOYEES table:

```
DEPARTMENT_ID      EMPNO FIRST_NAME
-------------- ---------- -------------
           30        119 Karen
           50        124 Kevin
           50        135 Ki
           80        146 Karen
                      178 Kimberely
           50        188 Kelly
           50        197 Kevin
```

Which EMPNO will be returned last when the following query is executed?

```
select department_id, employee_id empno, first_name
from employees
order by 1, 2
```

  A. 188

  B. 178

  C. 146

  D. 119

22. INTERVAL datatypes store a period of time. Which components are included in the INTERVAL DAY TO SECOND datatype column? (Choose all that apply.)

  A. Years

  B. Quarters

  C. Months

  D. Days

  E. Hours

  F. Minutes

  G. Seconds

  H. Fractional seconds

23. The primary key of the STATE table is STATE_CD. The primary key of the CITY table is STATE_CD/CITY_CD. The STATE_CD column of the CITY table is the foreign key to the STATE table. There are no other constraints on these two tables. Consider the following view definition:

```
CREATE OR REPLACE VIEW state_city AS
SELECT a.state_cd, a.state_name, b.city_cd, b.city_name
FROM   state a, city b
WHERE  a.state_cd = b.state_cd;
```

Which of the following operations are permitted on the base tables of the view? (Choose all that apply.)

A. Insert a record into the CITY table.

B. Insert a record into the STATE table.

C. Update the STATE_CD column of the CITY table.

D. Update the CITY_CD column of the CITY table.

E. Update the CITY_NAME column of the CITY table.

F. Update the STATE_NAME column of the STATE table.

24. The table CUSTOMERS has the following data:

```
ID    NAME                  ZIP  UPD_DATE
----  ----------------  ----------  ---------

L921  LEEZA                 75252 01-JAN-00
B023  WILLIAMS              15215
K783  KATHY                 75252 15-FEB-00
B445  BENJAMIN              76021 15-FEB-00
D334  DENNIS                12443
```

You issue the following command to alter the table. Which line of code will cause an error?

```
1  ALTER TABLE CUSTOMERS
2  MODIFY
3  (UPD_DATE DEFAULT SYSDATE NOT NULL,
4  ZIP NOT NULL);
```

A. Line 2 will cause an error.

B. Line 3 will cause an error.

C. Line 4 will cause an error.

D. There will be no error.

25. In ANSI SQL, a self-join can be represented by using which of the following? (Choose the best answer.)

A. NATURAL JOIN clause

B. CROSS JOIN clause

C. JOIN...USING clause

D. JOIN...ON clause

E. All of the above

26. What will be result of `trunc(2916.16, -1)`?

A. 2916.2

B. 290

C. 2916.1

D. 2900

E. 2910

27. The table ADDRESSES is created using the following syntax. How many indexes will be created automatically when this table is created?

```
CREATE TABLE ADDRESSES (
NAME    VARCHAR2 (40) PRIMARY KEY,
STREET VARCHAR2 (40),
CITY    VARCHAR2 (40),
STATE   CHAR     (2) REFERENCES STATE (ST_CODE),
ZIP     NUMBER   (5) NOT NULL,
PHONE   VARCHAR2 (12) UNIQUE);
```

A. 0

B. 1

C. 2

D. 3

28. Which line of the following code has an error?
```
SELECT *
FROM emp
WHERE comm = NULL
ORDER BY ename;
```

A. SELECT *

B. FROM emp

C. WHERE comm = NULL

D. There is no error in this statement.

29. Which of the following statements will raise an exception?

A. `alter sequence emp_seq nextval 23050;`

B. `alter sequence emp_seq nocycle;`

C. `alter sequence emp_seq increment by -5;`

D. `alter sequence emp_seq maxvalue 10000;`

30. What order does Oracle use in resolving a table or view referenced in a SQL statement?

    A. Table/view within user's schema, public synonym, private synonym

    B. Table/view within user's schema, private synonym, public synonym

    C. Public synonym, table/view within user's schema, private synonym

    D. Private synonym, public synonym, table/view within user's schema

31. Which two options are not true when you execute a COMMIT statement?

    A. All locks created by DML statements are released in the session.

    B. All savepoints created are erased in the session.

    C. Queries started before COMMIT in other sessions will show the current changes after COMMIT.

    D. All undo information written from the DML statements is erased.

32. Which two operators are used to add more joining conditions in a multiple-table query?

    A. NOT

    B. OR

    C. AND

    D. Comma (,)

33. What is wrong with the following SQL?

```
SELECT department_id, MAX(COUNT(*))
FROM employees
GROUP BY department_id;
```

    A. Aggregate functions cannot be nested.

    B. The GROUP BY clause should not be included when using nested aggregate functions.

    C. The department_id column in the SELECT clause should not be used when using nested aggregate functions.

    D. The COUNT function cannot be nested.

34. Which types of constraints can be created on a view?

    A. Check, NOT NULL

    B. Primary key, foreign key, unique key

    C. Check, NOT NULL, primary key, foreign key, unique key

    D. No constraints can be created on a view.

35. Which two declarations define the maximum length of a CHAR datatype column in bytes?

    A. CHAR (20)

    B. CHAR (20) BYTE

    C. CHAR (20 BYTE)

    D. BYTE (20 CHAR)

    E. CHAR BYTE (20)

36. A view is created using the following code. Which of the following operations are permitted on the view?

```
CREATE VIEW USA_STATES
AS SELECT * FROM STATE
WHERE  CNT_CODE = 1
WITH READ ONLY;
```

- **A.** SELECT
- **B.** SELECT, UPDATE
- **C.** SELECT, DELETE
- **D.** SELECT, INSERT

37. You query the database with the following:

```
SELECT PRODUCT_ID FROM PRODUCTS
WHERE PRODUCT_ID LIKE '%S\_J\_C' ESCAPE '\';
```

Choose the two PRODUCT_ID strings that will satisfy the query.

- **A.** BTS_J_C
- **B.** SJC
- **C.** SKJKC
- **D.** S_J_C

38. The EMPLOYEE table is defined as follows:

```
EMP_NAME   VARCHAR2(40)
HIRE_DATE  DATE
SALARY     NUMBER (14,2)
```

Which query is most appropriate to use if you need to find the employees who were hired before January 1, 1998 and have a salary greater than 5,000 or less than 1,000?

- **A.** SELECT emp_name FROM employee
    WHERE hire_date > TO_DATE('01011998','MMDDYYYY')
    AND SALARY < 1000 OR > 5000;
- **B.** SELECT emp_name FROM employee
    WHERE hire_date < TO_DATE('01011998','MMDDYYYY')
    AND SALARY < 1000 OR SALARY > 5000;
- **C.** SELECT emp_name FROM employee
    WHERE hire_date < TO_DATE('01011998','MMDDYYYY')
    AND (SALARY < 1000 OR SALARY > 5000);
- **D.** SELECT emp_name FROM employee
    WHERE hire_date < TO_DATE('01011998','MMDDYYYY')
    AND SALARY BETWEEN 1000 AND 5000;

39. What happens when you issue the following command? (Choose all that apply.)

```
TRUNCATE TABLE SCOTT.EMPLOYEE;
```

    A.   All the rows in the table EMPLOYEE owned by SCOTT are removed.

    B.   The storage space used by the table EMPLOYEE is released (except the initial extent).

    C.   If foreign key constraints are defined to this table using the ON DELETE CASCADE clause, the rows from the child tables are also removed.

    D.   The indexes on the table are dropped.

    E.   You cannot truncate a table if triggers are defined on the table.

40. Which two statements will drop the primary key defined on table EMP? The primary key name is PK_EMP.

    A.   ALTER TABLE EMP DROP PRIMARY KEY;

    B.   DROP CONSTRAINT PK_EMP;

    C.   ALTER TABLE EMP DROP CONSTRAINT PK_EMP;

    D.   ALTER CONSTRAINT PK_EMP DROP CASCADE;

    E.   DROP CONSTRAINT PK_EMP ON EMP;

Answers to SQL Fundamentals I Assessment Test

1. **B.** In the arithmetic operators, unary operators are evaluated first, then multiplication and division, and finally addition and subtraction. The expression is evaluated from left to right. For more information about order of evaluation, see Chapter 1.

2. **A, C.** The `CREATE FORCE VIEW` statement can be used to create a view before its base table is created. In versions prior to Oracle 11g, any modification to the table will invalidate the view. In Oracle 11g, the view will be invalidated only if the columns used in the view are modified in the base table. Use the `ALTER VIEW <view name> COMPILE` statement to recompile the view. See Chapter 7 to learn more about views.

3. **C.** `CONCAT` will return a non-`NULL` if only one parameter is `NULL`. Both `CONCAT` parameters would need to be `NULL` for `CONCAT` to return `NULL`. The `NULLIF` function returns `NULL` if the two parameters are equal. The `LENGTH` of a `NULL` is `NULL`. `INSTR` will return `NULL` if `NULL` is passed in and the tangent of a `NULL` is `NULL`. For more information about `NULL` values, see Chapter 2.

4. **C.** Group functions cannot appear in the `WHERE` clause. To learn more about group functions, see Chapter 3.

5. **B.** When updating multiple columns in a single `UPDATE` statement, the column assignments in the `SET` clause must be separated by commas, not `AND` operators. To read more about DML statements (`INSERT`, `UPDATE`, and `DELETE`), refer to Chapter 5.

6. **C.** Since `job_id` is used in the `SELECT` clause, it must be used in the `GROUP BY` clause also. To learn more about the rules of using the `GROUP BY` clause and aggregate functions, read Chapter 3.

7. **B.** The BFILE datatype stores only the locator to an external file in the database; the actual data is stored as an operating system file. BLOB, NCLOB, and CLOB are the other large object data types in Oracle 11g. UROWID is Universal ROWID datatype and EXTERNAL is a not a valid datatype. See Chapter 6 for information about datatypes.

8. **C.** The statement will work without error. Option B would be correct if you used the `WITH CHECK OPTION` clause in the subquery. See Chapter 4 for more information about subqueries.

9. **A, E.** An outer join on both tables can be achieved using the `FULL OUTER JOIN` syntax. You can specify the join condition using the `ON` clause to specify the columns explicitly or using the `USING` clause to specify the columns with common column names. Options B and D would result in errors. In option B, the join type is not specified; `OUTER` is an optional keyword. In option D, `CROSS JOIN` is used to get a Cartesian result, and Oracle does not expect a join condition. To learn more about joins, read Chapter 4.

10. A, B. The index contains all the information needed to satisfy the query in option A, and a full-index scan would be faster than a full-table scan. A subset of index columns is specified in the WHERE clause of option B; hence, Oracle 11*g* can use the index. For more information on indexes, see Chapter 7.

11. D. The CREATE SEQUENCE statement will create an increasing sequence that will start with 1, will increment by 1, and will be unaffected by the rollback. A rollback will never stuff vales back into a sequence. See Chapter 7 to learn more about sequences.

12. B, C. Primary and unique key constraints can be enforced using nonunique indexes. Unique constraints allow NULL values in the columns, but primary keys do not. Read Chapter 6 to learn more about constraints.

13. B. The SYSDATE function returns the date and time on the server where the database instance is started. CURRENT_DATE returns the local date and time. For information on the built-in date functions, read Chapter 2.

14. D. The first INSERT statement and last INSERT statement will be saved in the database. The ROLLBACK TO A statement will undo the second and third inserts. To know more about transaction control and ROLLBACK, read Chapter 5.

15. B. There should be at least *n*-1 join conditions when joining *n* tables to avoid a Cartesian join. To learn more about joins, see Chapter 4.

16. C. The table and column names can include only three special characters: #, $, and _. No other characters are allowed in the table name. You can have letters and numbers in the table name. To learn more about table and column names, read Chapter 6.

17. B, D. You can use the IS NULL or IS NOT NULL operator to search for NULLs or non-NULLs in a column. Since NULLs are sorted higher, they appear at the bottom of the result set in an ascending-order sort. See Chapter 1 for more information about sorting NULL values.

18. D. COUNT (<column_name>) does not include the NULL values, whereas COUNT (*) includes the NULL values. No other aggregate function takes NULL into consideration. To learn more about aggregate functions, read Chapter 3.

19. E. These statements don't account for possible NULL values in the BONUS column. For more information about NULL values, see Chapter 2.

20. D. Using the ALTER TABLE statement, you can add new columns, rename existing columns, and drop existing columns. To learn more about managing tables, read Chapter 6.

21. B. Since DEPARTMENT_ID is NULL for employee 178, NULL will be sorted after the non-NULL values when doing an ascending-order sort. Since I did not specify the sort order or the NULLS FIRST clause, the defaults are ASC and NULLS LAST. Read Chapter 1 for more information on SELECT and sort orders.

22. D, E, F, G. The INTERVAL DAY TO SECOND datatype is used to store an interval between two datetime components. See Chapter 6 for more information on the INTERVAL and TIMESTAMP datatypes.

23. D, E. In the join view, CITY is the key-preserved table. You can update the columns of the CITY table, except STATE_CD, because STATE_CD is not part of the view definition (the STATE_CD column in the view is from the STATE table). Since I did not include the STATE_CD column from the CITY table, no INSERT operations are permitted (STATE_CD is part of the primary key). If the view were defined as follows, all the columns of the CITY table would have been updatable, and new records could be inserted into the CITY table.

```
CREATE OR REPLACE VIEW state_city AS
SELECT b.state_cd, a.state_name, b.city_cd, b.city_name
FROM   states a, cities b
WHERE  a.state_cd = b.state_cd;
```

See Chapter 7 for more information about views.

24. B. When altering an existing column to add a NOT NULL constraint, no rows in the table should have NULL values. In the example, there are two rows with NULL values. Creating and modifying tables are discussed in Chapter 6.

25. D. NATURAL JOIN and JOIN…USING clauses will not allow alias names to be used. Since a self-join is getting data from the same table, you must include alias names and qualify column names. To learn more about ANSI join syntax, read Chapter 4.

26. E. The TRUNC function used with a negative second argument will truncate to the left of the decimal. To learn more about TRUNC and other numeric functions, read Chapter 2.

27. C. Oracle creates unique indexes for each unique key and primary key defined in the table. The table ADDRESSES has one unique key and a primary key. Indexes will not be created for NOT NULL or foreign key constraints. Constraints are discussed in Chapter 6.

28. D. Although there is no error in this statement, the statement will not return the desired result. When a NULL is compared, you cannot use the = or != operator; you must use the IS NULL or IS NOT NULL operator. See Chapter 1 for more information about the comparison operators.

29. A. You cannot explicitly change the next value of a sequence. You can set the MAXVALUE or INCREMENT BY value to a negative number, and NOCYCLE tells Oracle to not reuse a sequence number. See Chapter 7 for more information.

30. B. Private synonyms override public synonyms, and tables or views owned by the user always resolve first. To learn more about synonyms, see Chapter 7.

31. C, D. When COMMIT is executed, all locks are released, all savepoints are erased, and queries started before the COMMIT will constitute a read-consistent view using the undo information. To learn more about COMMIT, read Chapter 5.

32. B, C. The operators OR and AND are used to add more joining conditions to the query. NOT is a negation operator, and a comma is used to separate column names and table names. Read more about joins and join conditions in Chapter 4.

33. C. Since you are finding the aggregate of the aggregate, you should not use nonaggregate columns in the SELECT clause. To read more about nesting of aggregate functions, see Chapter 3.

34. B. You can create primary key, foreign key, and unique key constraints on a view. The constraints on views are not enforced by Oracle. To enforce a constraint, it must be defined on a table. Views can be created with the WITH CHECK OPTION and READ ONLY attributes during view creation. Read Chapter 7 to learn more.

35. A, C. The maximum lengths of CHAR and VARCHAR2 columns can be defined in characters or bytes. BYTE is the default. To learn more about CHAR and VARCHAR2 datatypes, read Chapter 6.

36. A. When the view is created with the READ ONLY option, only reads are allowed from the view. See Chapter 7 to learn more about creating views as read-only.

37. A, D. The substitution character % can be substituted for zero or many characters. The substitution character _ does not have any effect in this query because an escape character precedes it, so it is treated as a literal. Read Chapter 1 to learn more about substitution characters.

38. C. You have two main conditions in the question: one on the hire date and the other on the salary. So, you should use an AND operator. In the second part, you have two options: the salary can be either more than 5,000 or less than 1,000, so the second part should be enclosed in parentheses and should use an OR operator. Option B is similar to option C except for the parentheses, but the difference changes the meaning completely. Option B would select the employees who were hired before January 1, 1998 *or* have a salary greater than 5,000 or less than 1,000. Read Chapter 1 to learn more about writing queries using filtering conditions.

39. A, B. The TRUNCATE command is used to remove all the rows from a table or cluster. By default, this command releases all the storage space used by the table and resets the table's high-water mark to zero. No indexes, constraints, or triggers on the table are dropped or disabled. If there are valid foreign key constraints defined to this table, you must disable all of them before truncating the table. Chapter 5 includes a comparison between using TRUNCATE and the DELETE statement to remove rows.

40. A, C. Since there can be only one primary key per table, the syntax in option A works. Any constraint (except NOT NULL) can be dropped using the syntax in option C. Learn more about constraints in Chapter 6.

Administration I Assessment Test

1. Which of the following is not considered part of Oracle Database?

    A. Data files

    B. Redo logs

    C. Pfile and spfile

    D. Control files

2. The following are the steps required for relocating a data file belonging to the USERS tablespace. Order the steps in their proper sequence.

    A. Copy the `file /disk1/users01.dbf` to `/disk2/users01.dbf` using an OS command.

    B. `ALTER DATABASE RENAME FILE '/disk1/users01.dbf' TO '/disk2/users01.dbf'`

    C. `ALTER TABLESPACE USERS OFFLINE`

    D. `ALTER TABLESPACE USERS ONLINE`

3. You manage one non-Oracle Database and several Oracle Databases. An application needs to access the non-Oracle database as if it were part of the Oracle database. What tool allows you to do this? (Choose the best answer.)

    A. Oracle Advanced Security

    B. Oracle Connection Manager

    C. Heterogeneous Services

    D. Oracle Net

    E. None of the above

4. Choose two utilities that can be used to apply CPU patches on an Oracle 11*g* database.

    A. Oracle Universal Installer

    B. OPatch

    C. EM Database Control

    D. DBCA

5. The loss of a data file in which two tablespaces requires an instance shutdown to recover the tablespace?

    A. TEMP

    B. SYSTEM

    C. UNDO

    D. SYSAUX

6. Which of the following statements is not always true? (Choose two.)

    A. Every database should have at least two tablespaces.

    B. Every database should have at least two data files.

    C. Every database should have at least three multiplexed redo logs.

    D. Every database should have at least three control files.

7. Which statement about the initialization-parameter files is true?

    A. The pfile and spfile can be modified using the ALTER SYSTEM statement.

    B. You cannot have both an spfile and a pfile under the $ORACLE_HOME/dbs directory.

    C. The pfile is used only to read by the Oracle instance, whereas the spfile is used to read and write to.

    D. On Windows systems, pfile and spfiles are not used because parameters are modified using the system registry.

8. Which initialization parameter determines the location of the alert log file?

    A. DIAGNOSTIC_DEST

    B. BACKGROUND_DUMP_DEST

    C. ALERT_LOG_DEST

    D. USER_DUMP_DEST

9. Which parameter is used to set up the directory for Oracle to create data files if the DATAFILE clause does not specify a filename when creating or altering tablespaces?

    A. DB_FILE_CREATE_DEST

    B. DB_CREATE_FILE_DEST

    C. DB_8K_CACHE_SIZE

    D. USER_DUMP_DEST

    E. DB_CREATE_ONLINE_LOG_DEST_1

10. Which component of the SGA has the dictionary cache?

    A. Buffer cache

    B. Library cache

    C. Shared pool

    D. Program global area

    E. Large pool

    F. Result cache

11. A constraint is created with the DEFERRABLE INITIALLY IMMEDIATE clause. What does this mean?

A. Constraint checking is done only at commit time.

B. Constraint checking is done after each SQL, but you can change this behavior by specifying SET CONSTRAINTS ALL DEFERRED.

C. Existing rows in the table are immediately checked for constraint violation.

D. The constraint is immediately checked in a DML operation, but subsequent constraint verification is done at commit time.

12. You have just made changes to the listener.ora file for the listener called listener1 using Oracle Net Manager. Which of the following commands or combinations of commands would you use to put the changes into effect with the least amount of client disruption?

A. lsnrctl stop listener1 followed by lsnrctl start listener1

B. lsrnctl restart listener1

C. lsnrctl reload listener1

D. lsnrctl reload

13. What is the prefix for dynamic performance views?

A. X$

B. V$

C. ALL_

D. DBA_

14. If you are updating one row in a table using the ROWID in the WHERE clause (assume that the row is not already in the buffer cache), what will be the minimum amount of information copied to the database buffer cache?

A. The entire table is copied to the database buffer cache.

B. The extent is copied to the database buffer cache.

C. The block is copied to the database buffer cache.

D. The row is copied to the database buffer cache.

15. When you are configuring Shared Server, which initialization parameter would you likely need to modify?

A. DB_CACHE_SIZE

B. DB_BLOCK_BUFFERS

C. LARGE_POOL_SIZE

D. BUFFER_SIZE

E. None of the above

16. To grant the SELECT privilege on the table HR.CUSTOMERS to all users in the database, which statement would you use?

A. `GRANT SELECT ON HR.CUSTOMERS TO ALL USERS;`

B. `GRANT SELECT ON HR.CUSTOMERS TO ALL;`

C. `GRANT SELECT ON HR.CUSTOMERS TO ANONYMOUS;`

D. `GRANT SELECT ON HR.CUSTOMERS TO PUBLIC;`

17. Which of the following commands is most likely to generate an error message? (Choose two.)

A. `ALTER SYSTEM SET UNDO_MANAGEMENT=AUTO SCOPE=MEMORY;`

B. `ALTER SYSTEM SET UNDO_MANAGEMENT=AUTO SCOPE=SPFILE;`

C. `ALTER SYSTEM SET UNDO_MANAGEMENT=MANUAL SCOPE=MEMORY;`

D. `ALTER SYSTEM SET UNDO_MANAGEMENT=MANUAL SCOPE=SPFILE;`

E. `ALTER SYSTEM SET UNDO_TABLESPACE=RBS1 SCOPE=BOTH;`

18. The Automatic Workload Repository (AWR) is primarily populated with performance statistics by which Oracle 11g background process?

A. MMNL

B. QMN1

C. MMON

D. MMAN

19. You performed a SHUTDOWN ABORT on the database. What happens when you issue the STARTUP command?

A. Startup will fail because you have not completed the instance recovery.

B. Oracle automatically performs recovery; all committed changes are written to data files.

C. During instance recovery you have the option to selectively commit uncommitted transactions.

D. After the database starts, you have to manually clean out uncommitted transactions from the transaction table.

20. Which storage parameter is used to make sure that each extent is a multiple of the value specified on dictionary-managed tablespaces?

A. MINEXTENTS

B. INITIAL

C. MINIMUM EXTENT

D. MAXEXTENTS

21. Which of the following is the utility that you can use to test the network connections across TCP/IP?

   A. `trcasst`

   B. `lsnrctl`

   C. `namesctl`

   D. `ping`

   E. None of the above

22. What is the difference between a unique key constraint and a primary key constraint?

   A. A unique key constraint requires a unique index to enforce the constraint, whereas a primary key constraint can enforce uniqueness using a unique or nonunique index.

   B. A primary key column can be `NULL`, but a unique key column cannot be `NULL`.

   C. A primary key constraint can use an existing index, but a unique constraint always creates an index.

   D. A unique constraint column can be `NULL`, but the primary key column(s) cannot be `NULL`.

23. Which of the following conditions prevents you from being able to insert into a view?

   A. A `TO_NUMBER` function on one of the base table columns

   B. A `CONNECT BY` clause in the view definition

   C. A column of type `RAW`

   D. All of the above

24. Which parameter is used to enable the Automatic Memory Management feature of the Oracle 11g database?

   A. `MEMORY_MANAGEMENT`

   B. `MEMORY_TARGET`

   C. `SGA_TARGET`

   D. `MEMORY_SIZE`

25. Undo data in an undo tablespace is *not* used for which of the following purposes?

   A. Providing users with read-consistent queries

   B. Rolling forward after an instance failure

   C. Flashback queries

   D. Recovering from a failed transaction

   E. Restoring original data when a `ROLLBACK` is issued

26. Which initialization parameter determines the window of flashback database operation?

   A. DB_RECOVERY_FILE_DEST_SIZE

   B. DB_FLASHBACK_RETENTION_TARGET

   C. FAST_START_MTTR_TARGET

   D. No initialization parameter; the window is determined by the RMAN backups.

27. When you started the Oracle 11g database, you got an "ORA-01157: cannot identify data file..." error. After invoking RMAN, which command would you use before performing REPAIR FAILURE?

   A. RECOVER FAILURE

   B. ADVISE FAILURE

   C. LIST FAILURE

   D. CHANGE FAILURE

28. Who is the owner of a directory object?

   A. SYSTEM

   B. SYSMAN

   C. SYS

   D. The user who creates the directory

29. Which of the following types of statements can use a temporary tablespace?

   A. An index creation

   B. SQL statements with a GROUP BY clause

   C. A hash join operation

   D. All of the above

30. Which of the following is false about shared servers?

   A. Shared servers can process requests from many users.

   B. Shared servers receive their requests directly from dispatchers.

   C. Shared servers place completed requests on a dispatcher response queue.

   D. The SHARED_SERVERS parameter configures the number of shared servers to start at instance startup.

31. What is accomplished when you issue the following statement?
ALTER USER JOHN DEFAULT ROLE ALL;

   A. John is assigned all roles created in the database.

   B. Existing roles remain the same, but future roles created will be enabled.

   C. All of John's roles are enabled except the roles with passwords.

   D. All of John's roles are enabled, including the roles with passwords.

32. Which initialization parameter determines the location of the alert log file?

    A. LOG_ARCHIVE_DEST

    B USER_DUMP_DEST

    C. BACKGROUND_DUMP_DEST

    D. DIAGNOSTIC_DEST

33. The highest level at which a user can request a lock is the _____ level.

    A. schema

    B. table

    C. row

    D. block

34. How can you prevent someone from using an all-numeric password?

    A. Set the initialization parameter PASSWORD_COMPLEXITY to ALPHANUM.

    B. Alter that user's profile setting PASSWORD_COMPLEXITY to ALPHNANUM.

    C. Alter the user's profile to use a password-verify function that performs comparisons to validate the password.

    D. There is no mechanism that lets you prevent an all-numeric password.

35. Which of the following advisors is used to determine whether the database read-consistency mechanisms are properly configured?

    A. Undo Management Advisor

    B. SQL Access Advisor

    C. SQL Tuning Advisor

    D. Memory Advisor

36. Where does Oracle Database record all changes made to the database that can be used for recovery operations?

    A. Control files

    B. Redo log files

    C. Alert log file

    D. Parameter file

37. In the Disk Settings section of EM Database Control's Configure Backup Settings page, which of the following backup settings is not configurable?

    A. Disk Backup Type

    B. Control File Autobackup Format

    C. Disk Backup Location

    D. Parallelism

38. You need to copy the GL schema from production to qa_test, changing the tablespace for indexes from gl_index to fin_indx. What is the best way to satisfy these requirements?

    A. First, use Data Pump to copy the schema without indexes. Then, change the default tablespace for user GL in qa_test to fin_indx. Next, use Data Pump to copy the indexes. Finally, change the default tablespace for user GL back to gl_data.

    B. Use the dbms_metadata package to extract table and index DDL. Then, use Notepad (or sed) to edit this DDL, changing the tablespace for the indexes. Finally, run the DDL in the qa_test database.

    C. Use Data Pump import, specifying a remap_datafile parameter to change the data file location for indexes.

    D. Use Data Pump import, specifying a remap_tablespace parameter to change the tablespace location for indexes.

39. Identify the statement that is not true about checkpoints.

    A. Instance recovery is complete when the data from the last checkpoint up to the latest SCN in the control file has been written to the data files.

    B. A checkpoint keeps track of what has already been written to the data files.

    C. The redo log group writes must occur before a Commit complete is returned to the user.

    D. The distance between the checkpoint position in the redo log file and the end of the redo log group can never be more than 90 percent of the size of the largest redo log group.

    E. How much the checkpoint lags behind the SCN is controlled by both the size of the redo log groups and by setting the parameter FAST_START_MTTR_TARGET.

40. The STATUS column of the dynamic performance view V$LOG contains what value if the redo log file group has just been added?

    A. INVALID

    B. STALE

    C. UNUSED

    D. NULL

41. When performing Data Pump import using impdp, which of the following options is not a valid value to the TABLE_EXISTS_ACTION parameter?

    A. SKIP

    B. APPEND

    C. TRUNCATE

    D. RECREATE

42. What would you do to reduce the time required to start the instance after a database crash?

    A.   Multiplex the redo log files.

    B.   Increase the size of the redo log files.

    C.   Set the FAST_START_MTTR_TARGET parameter to 0.

    D.   All of the above.

    E.   None of the above.

Answers to Administration I Assessment Test

1. C. Although pfiles and spfiles are physical files used to configure the Oracle instance, they are not considered part of the database. To learn more about Oracle Database structure, read Chapter 8.

2. C, A, B, D. To rename a data file, you need to make the tablespace offline so that Oracle does not try to update the data file while you are renaming. Using OS commands, copy the data file to the new location, and using the ALTER DATABASE RENAME FILE command or the ALTER TABLESPACE RENAME FILE command, rename the file in the database's control file. To rename the file in the database, the new file should exist. Bring the tablespace online for normal database operation. See Chapter 10 for more information.

3. C. Heterogeneous Services is the correct answer because these services provide cross-platform connectivity to non-Oracle databases. Oracle Advanced Security would not solve this application problem because it addresses security and is not accessibility to non-Oracle databases. Oracle Net would be part of the solution, but another Oracle Network component is necessary. Connection Manager would also not be able to accommodate this requirement on its own. Read Chapter 11 to learn more.

4. B, C. CPU patches and interim patches can be applied using the OPatch utility or using EM Database Control. EM Database Control also includes patch search and download options. See Chapter 17 for more information.

5. B, C. Only the SYSTEM and UNDO tablespaces require the instance to be shut down when their data files need recovery. Read Chapter 16 to learn about database recovery.

6. C, D. Every database must have at least two redo log files, which may or may not be multiplexed. Every database must have one control file. It is a good idea to have more than one control file for redundancy. Since SYSTEM and SYSAUX are mandatory tablespaces in Oracle 11*g*, there will be at least two data files. See Chapter 8 for more information.

7. C. A pfile is a read-only file, and no database changes are written to the pfile. There is no harm in having both an spfile and a pfile in the $ORACLE_HOME/dbs directory; Oracle will only read the spfile when starting the database. On Windows systems also, you will need a parameter-initialization file; the registry is not used. Read more about parameter files in Chapter 9.

8. A. Oracle 11*g* uses the Automatic Diagnostic Repository to maintain the alert log and other diagnostic information. In pre–Oracle 11*g* databases, the BACKGROUND_DUMP_DEST parameter determined the alert log location; in Oracle 11*g*, this parameter value is ignored. To learn more about the alert log and its contents, read Chapter 9.

9. B. DB_CREATE_FILE_DEST specifies the directory to create data files and temp files. This directory is also used for control files and redo log files if the DB_CREATE_ONLINE_LOG_DEST_1 parameter is not set. Learn more in Chapter 10.

10. C. The shared pool has three components: the library cache, the result cache, and the dictionary cache. Read Chapter 8 to learn more about SGA and Oracle instances.

11. B. DEFERRABLE specifies that the constraint can be deferred using the SET CONSTRAINTS command. INITIALLY IMMEDIATE specifies that the constraint's default behavior is to validate the constraint for each SQL. Constraints are discussed in Chapters 7 and 10.

12. C. Although you can use option A to stop and start the listener, doing so temporarily disrupts clients attempting to connect to the database. Option D is fine if you are starting and stopping the default listener called LISTENER, but you are using a nondefault listener here. Option B is not valid because RESTART is not a valid command-line argument for lsnrctl. Therefore, the best method is to use the lsnrctl reload listener1 command to load the new set of values in for the listener without disrupting connection service to the databases that the listener is servicing. For more information, read Chapter 11.

13. B. Dynamic performance views begin with V$. The actual views have a prefix of V_$, and the synonyms have a prefix of V$. The V$ views are based on the X$ tables, known as dynamic performance tables. To learn more about dynamic performance views and tables, read Chapter 9.

14. C. The block is the smallest unit that can be copied to the buffer cache. Information in the dictionary cache is copied as rows. To learn about buffer cache and dictionary cache, read Chapter 8.

15. C. Shared Server requires a shift of memory away from individual session processes to the SGA. More information has to be kept in the SGA (in the UGA) within the shared pool. A large pool is configured and is responsible for most of the SGA space allocation. Option C is the correct answer. The cache size and block buffers settings do not affect Shared Server. Read Chapter 11 for more information.

16. D. PUBLIC is the group or class of database users where all existing and future database users belong. See Chapter 12 for more information.

17. A, C. You cannot dynamically change the parameter UNDO_MANAGEMENT after the instance has started. You can, however, change the UNDO_TABLESPACE parameter to switch to another undo tablespace while the instance is up and running. Read Chapter 13 to learn more.

18. C. The Manageability Monitor (MMON) process gathers performance statistics from the system global area (SGA) and stores them in the AWR. Manageability Monitor Light (MMNL) also does some AWR-related statistics gathering, but not to the extent that MMON does. QMN1 is the process that monitors Oracle advanced queuing features. Memory Manager (MMAN) is the process that dynamically manages the sizes of each SGA component when directed to make changes by the Automatic Database Diagnostic Monitor (ADDM). For more information, see Chapter 14.

19. B. Oracle automatically performs instance recovery after a database crash or SHUTDOWN ABORT. All uncommitted changes are rolled back, and committed changes are written to data files during instance recovery. Read Chapter 9 for more information.

20. C. The MINIMUM EXTENT parameter is used to make sure each extent is a multiple of the value specified on dictionary-managed tablespaces. This parameter is useful to reduce fragmentation in the tablespace. Oracle discourages the use of dictionary-managed tablespaces. You should use locally managed tablespaces. Read Chapter 10 for more information.

21. D. Protocols come with tools that allow you to test network connectivity. One such utility for TCP/IP is ping. The user supplies either an IP address or a hostname to the ping utility. It then searches the network for this address. If it finds one, it displays information on data that is sent and received and how quickly it found this address. The other choices are Oracle-supplied utilities. Read Chapter 11 for more information.

22. D. Columns that are part of the primary key cannot accept NULL values. Read Chapters 7 and 10 to learn more.

23. B. You cannot insert into a view that contains a CONNECT BY, ORDER BY, or GROUP BY clause. Read Chapter 13 to learn more.

24. B. A nonzero value for the MEMORY_TARGET parameter enables Automatic Memory Management. SGA_TARGET enables Automatic Shared Memory Management. Automatic Memory Management tunes both SGA and PGA components of the memory. To learn more, read Chapter 14.

25. B. The online redo log files are used to roll forward after an instance failure; undo data is used to roll back any uncommitted transactions. Read Chapter 13 to learn more.

26. B. The DB_FLASHBACK_RETENTION_TARGET parameter determines the window for the flashback database operation. The value is specified in minutes. So, a value of 1440 specifies that the flashback database window is 1 day. To learn more, read Chapter 15.

27. B. REPAIR FAILURE works only after ADVISE FAILURE. Option A, RECOVER FAILURE, is invalid. CHANGE FAILURE can be used to lower or raise the priority of a failure. To learn more about automatically recovering from failures, read Chapter 16.

28. C. SYS is always the owner of directory object. You can grant read and write privileges on the directory to users. See Chapter 17 to learn more.

29. D. Any operation that requires a large sort or other creation of temporary segments will create, alter, and drop those temporary segments in the TEMPORARY tablespace. See Chapter 12 for more information.

30. B. Shared servers can process requests from many users. The completed requests are placed into the dispatchers' response queues. The servers are configured with the SERVERS parameter. However, shared servers do not receive requests directly from dispatchers. The requests are taken from the request queue. Read Chapter 11 to learn more.

31. D. Default roles are enabled when a user connects to the database, even if the roles are password-protected. See Chapter 12 for more information.

32. D. DIAGNOSTIC_DEST is new to Oracle 11g, and it determines the location of the alert log file and trace files. Read Chapter 14 to learn more about alert log and trace file locations.

33. B. The highest level at which a user can request a lock is the table level; the only other lock level available to a user is a row-level lock. Users cannot lock at the block or schema level. Read Chapter 13 to learn more.

34. C. There are no standard password-complexity settings in either the initialization parameters or the profiles. A password-verify function can validate new passwords against any rules that you can code in PL/SQL, including regular-expression comparisons. See Chapter 12 for more information.

35. A. You can use the Undo Management Advisor to monitor and manage the undo segments to ensure maximum levels of read consistency and minimize occurrences of "ORA-01555: Snapshot Too Old" error messages. For more information, see Chapter 14.

36. B. Redo log files record all the changes made to Oracle Database, whether the changes are committed or not. To learn more about redo log files and database recovery, read Chapters 15 and 16.

37. B. Settings such as the control file autobackup filename format and the snapshot-control file destination filename must be configured using the RMAN command-line interface. To learn more, read Chapter 15.

38. D. Options A and B are a lot of work. The `remap_datafile` parameter applies only to `CREATE TABLESPACE` and `CREATE DIRECTORY` statements, not indexes. The `remap_tablespace` parameter tells Data Pump import to change the tablespace that objects are stored in between the source and the target database. See Chapter 17 for more information.

39. D. The distance between the checkpoint position in the redo log file and the end of the redo log group can never be more than 90 percent of the size of the *smallest* redo log group. Read Chapter 16 to learn more about checkpoints and instance recovery.

40. C. If the redo log file group has never been used, the value of `STATUS` is `UNUSED` until the log file member is used to record redo information. Read Chapter 16 for more information.

41. D. `REPLACE` is the valid value; it drops the existing table and creates the table using the definition from the dump file. `SKIP` leaves the table untouched. `APPEND` inserts rows to the existing table. `TRUNCATE` leaves the structure but removes all existing rows before inserting rows. See Chapter 17 to learn more.

42. E. To tune the instance-recovery time, configure the `FAST_START_MTTR_TARGET` parameter to a nonzero value. The default is 300 seconds. A lower value will reduce the instance-recovery time but may cause frequent checkpoints. A value of 0 turns off MTTR tuning. To learn more, read Chapter 15.

Oracle Database 11g: SQL Fundamentals I

Chapter

1

Introducing SQL

ORACLE DATABASE 11*g*:
SQL FUNDAMENTALS I EXAM OBJECTIVES
COVERED IN THIS CHAPTER:

✓ **Retrieving Data Using the SQL SELECT Statement**

- List the capabilities of SQL SELECT statements

- Execute a basic SELECT statement

✓ **Restricting and Sorting Data**

- Limit the rows that are retrieved by a query

- Sort the rows that are retrieved by a query

- Use ampersand substitution to restrict and sort output at runtime

Oracle 11g is a very powerful and feature-rich relational database management system (RDBMS). SQL has been adopted by most RDBMSs for the retrieval and management of data, schema creation, and access control. The American National Standards Institute (ANSI) has been refining standards for the SQL language for more than 20 years. Oracle, like many other companies, has taken the ANSI standard of SQL and extended it to include much additional functionality.

SQL is the basic language used to manipulate and retrieve data from the Oracle Database 11g. SQL is a nonprocedural language, meaning it does not have programmatic constructs such as loop structures. PL/SQL is Oracle's procedural extension of SQL, and SQLJ allows embedded SQL operations in Java code. The scope of the Oracle Database 11g SQL Fundamentals I test includes only SQL.

In this chapter, I will discuss Oracle SQL fundamentals such as the various types of SQL statements, introduce SQL*Plus and a few SQL*Plus commands, and discuss SELECT statements.

You will learn how to write basic SQL statements to retrieve data from tables. This will include coverage of SQL SELECT statements, which are used to query data from the database-storage structures, such as tables and views. You will also learn how to limit the information retrieved and to display the results in a specific order.

Exam objectives are subject to change at any time without prior notice and at Oracle's sole discretion. Please visit Oracle's Training and Certification website at http://education.oracle.com/pls/web_prod-plq-dad/db_pages.getpage?p_exam_id=1Z0_051 for the most current exam objectives.

SQL Fundamentals

SQL is the standard language to query and modify data as well as manage databases. SQL is the common language used by programmers, database administrators, and users to access and manipulate data as well as to administer databases. To get started with SQL in this chapter, I will show how to use the sample HR schema supplied with the Oracle Database 11g.

When you install Oracle software, you can choose the Basic Installation option and select the Create Starter Database check box. This database will have the sample schemas used in this book. The password you specify will be applicable to the SYS and SYSTEM accounts. The account SYS is the Oracle dictionary owner, and SYSTEM is a database administrator (DBA) account. Initially, the sample schemas are locked. You need to log in to the database using SQL*Plus as the SYSTEM user and then unlock the account using the ALTER USER statement. To unlock the HR schema, use `ALTER USER hr IDENTIFIED BY hrpassword ACCOUNT UNLOCK;`. Now you can log in to the database using the hr user with the password hrpassword. Remember, the password is case sensitive.

For detailed information on installing Oracle 11*g* software and creating Oracle Database 11*g*, please refer to the Oracle Technology Network at `www.oracle.com/technology/obe/11gr1_db/install/dbinst/windbinst2.htm`.

To install the sample schemas in an existing Oracle Database 11*g*, please follow the instructions in the Oracle document "Oracle Database Sample Schemas 11*g* Release 1" at `http://download.oracle.com/docs/cd/B28359_01/server.111/b28328/toc.htm`.

Chapter 2 of the "Oracle Database Sample Schemas 11*g* Release 1" manual on the Oracle Technology Network will provide instructions on how to install the sample schemas using Database Configuration Assistant (DBCA) as well as running scripts. The same chapter also gives you steps to reinitialize the sample schema data.

SQL statements are like plain English but with specific syntax. SQL is a simple yet powerful language used to create, access, and manipulate data and structures in the database. SQL statements can be categorized as listed in Table 1.1.

TABLE 1.1 SQL Statement Categories

SQL Category	Description
Data Manipulation Language (DML)	Used to access, create, modify, or delete data in the existing structures of the database. DML statements include those to query information (SELECT), add new rows (INSERT), modify existing rows (UPDATE), delete existing rows (DELETE), perform a conditional update or insert operation (MERGE), see an execution plan of SQL (EXPLAIN PLAN), and lock a table to restrict access (LOCK TABLE). Including the SELECT statement in the DML group is debatable within the SQL community, since SELECT does not modify data.

TABLE 1.1   SQL Statement Categories *(continued)*

SQL Category	Description
Data Definition Language (DDL)	Used to define, alter, or drop database objects and their privileges. DDL statements include those to create, modify, drop, or rename objects (CREATE, ALTER, DROP, RENAME), remove all rows from a database object without dropping the structure (TRUNCATE), manage access privileges (GRANT, REVOKE), audit database use (AUDIT, NOAUDIT) and add a description about an object to the dictionary (COMMENT).
Transaction Control	Used to group a set of DML statements as a single transaction. Using these statements, you can save the changes (COMMIT) or discard the changes (ROLLBACK) made by DML statements. Also included in the transaction-control statements are statements to set a point or marker in the transaction for possible rollback (SAVEPOINT) and to define the properties for the transaction (SET TRANSACTION).
Session Control	Used to control the properties of a user session. (A session is the point from which you are connected to the database until you disconnect.) Session-control statements include those to control the session properties (ALTER SESSION) and to enable/disable roles (SET ROLE).
System Control	Used to manage the properties of the database. There is only one statement in this category (ALTER SYSTEM).

Table 1.1 provides an overview of all the statements that will be covered in this book. Do not worry if you do not understand certain terms, such as *role*, *session*, *privilege*, and so on. I will cover all the statements in the coming chapters with many examples. In this chapter, I will begin with writing simple statements to query the database (SELECT statements). But first I'll go over some fundamentals.

SQL Tools: SQL*Plus

The Oracle Database 11*g* software comes with two primary tools to manage data and administer databases using SQL. SQL*Plus is a character-based command-line utility. SQL Developer is a graphical tool that has the capability to browse, edit, and manage database objects as well as to execute the SQL statements. On Windows platforms, these tools are located under the Application Development subfolder in the Oracle 11*g* program group.

On Linux and Unix platforms, you can find these tools in the bin directory under the Oracle software installation ($ORACLE_HOME/bin).

Since the test is on SQL and the tool used throughout the book for executing SQL is SQL*Plus, I will discuss some fundamentals of SQL*Plus in this section.

SQL*Plus, widely used by DBAs and developers to interact with the database, is a powerful tool from Oracle. Using SQL*Plus, you can execute all SQL statements and PL/SQL programs, format results from queries, and administer the database.

SQL*Plus is packaged with the Oracle software and can be installed using the client software installation routine on any machine. This tool is automatically installed when you install the server software.

On Unix/Linux platforms, you can invoke SQL*Plus using the `sqlplus` executable found in the `$ORACLE_HOME/bin` directory. On Windows and Unix/Linux platforms, when you start SQL*Plus, you will be prompted for a username and password, as shown in Figure 1.1.

FIGURE 1.1   SQL*Plus screen

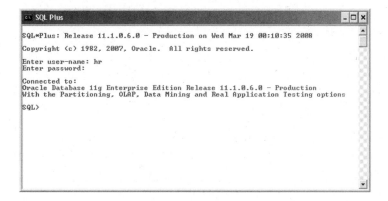

Once you are in SQL*Plus, you can connect to another database or change your connection by using the CONNECT command, with this syntax:

```
CONNECT <username>/<password>@<connectstring>
```

The slash separates the username and password. The connect string following @ is the database alias name. If you omit the password, you will be prompted to enter it. If you omit the connect string, SQL*Plus tries to connect you to the local database defined in the ORACLE_SID variable.

You can invoke and connect to SQL*Plus using the `sqlplus` command, with this syntax:

```
sqlplus <username>/<password>@<connectstring>
```

If you invoke the tool with just `sqlplus`, you will be prompted for a username and password. If you invoke SQL*Plus with a username, you will be prompted for a password.

Once you are connected to SQL*Plus, you get the SQL> prompt. This is the default prompt, which can be changed using the SET SQLPROMPT command. Type the command you want to execute at this prompt. With SQL*Plus, you can enter, edit, and execute SQL statements; perform database administration; and execute statements interactively by accepting user input. You can also format query results and perform calculations.

> `sqlplus -help` displays a help screen to show the various options available with starting SQL*Plus.

To exit from SQL*Plus, use the EXIT command. On platforms where a return code is used, you can provide a return code while exiting. You can also use the QUIT command to complete the session. EXIT and QUIT are synonymous.

Entering SQL Statements

A SQL statement can spread across multiple lines, and the commands are case insensitive. The previously executed SQL statement will always be available in the *SQL buffer*. The buffer can be edited or saved to a file. You can terminate a SQL statement in any of the following ways:

- End with a semicolon (;): The statement is completed and executed.
- Enter a slash (/) on a new line by itself: The statement in the buffer is executed.
- Enter a blank line: The statement is saved in the buffer.

You can use the RUN command instead of a slash to execute a statement in the buffer. The SQL prompt returns when the statement has completed execution. You can enter your next command at the prompt.

> Only SQL statements and PL/SQL blocks are stored in the SQL buffer; SQL*Plus commands are not stored in the buffer.

Entering SQL*Plus Commands

SQL*Plus has its own commands to perform-specific tasks on the database, as well as to format the query results. Unlike SQL statements, which are terminated with a semicolon or a blank line, SQL*Plus commands are entered on a single line. Pressing Enter executes the SQL*Plus command.

If you want to continue a SQL*Plus command onto the next line, you must end the current line with a hyphen (-), which indicates command continuation. This is in contrast to SQL statements, which can be continued to the next line without a continuation operator. For example, the following SQL statement gives an error, because SQL*Plus treats the hyphen operator (-) as a continuation character:

```
SQL> SELECT 800 -
> 400 FROM dual;
```

```
SELECT 800   400 FROM dual
                *
ERROR at line 1:
ORA-00923: FROM keyword not found where expected
SQL>
```

You need to put the hyphen in the next line for the query to succeed:

```
SQL> SELECT 800
  2  - 400 FROM dual;


  800-400
----------
       400
SQL>
```

Getting Information with the DESCRIBE Command

You can use the DESCRIBE command to get information about the database objects. Using DESCRIBE on a table or view shows the columns, its datatypes, and whether each column can be NULL. Using DESCRIBE on a stored program such as procedure or function shows the parameters that need to be passed in/out, their datatype, and whether there is a default value. You can abbreviate this command to the first four characters or more—DESC, DESCR, and DESCRIB are all valid.

If you're connected to the HR schema and need to see the tables and views in this schema, use the following query:

```
SQL> SELECT * FROM tab;


TNAME                          TABTYPE  CLUSTERID
------------------------------ -------  ----------
COUNTRIES                      TABLE
DEPARTMENTS                    TABLE
EMPLOYEES                      TABLE
EMP_DETAILS_VIEW               VIEW
JOBS                           TABLE
JOB_HISTORY                    TABLE
LOCATIONS                      TABLE
REGIONS                        TABLE

8 rows selected.
SQL>
```

Editing the SQL Buffer

The most recent SQL statement executed or entered is stored in the SQL buffer of SQL*Plus. You can run the command in this buffer again by simply typing a slash or using the RUN command.

SQL*Plus provides a set of commands to edit the buffer. Suppose you want to add another column or add an ORDER BY condition to the statement in the buffer. You do not need to type the entire SQL statement again. Instead, just edit the existing statement in the buffer.

One way to edit the SQL*Plus buffer is to use the EDIT command to write the buffer to an operating-system file named afiedt.buf (this is the default filename, which can be changed) and then use a system editor to make changes.

 You can use your favorite text editor by defining it in SQL*Plus. For example, to make Notepad your favorite editor, just issue the command DEFINE _EDITOR = NOTEPAD. You need to provide the entire path if the program is not available in the search path.

Another way to edit the buffer is to use the SQL*Plus editing commands. You can make changes, delete lines, add text, and list the buffer contents using the commands described in the following sections. Most editing commands operate on the current line. You can change the current line simply by typing the line number. All commands can be abbreviated except DEL (which is already abbreviated).

LIST

The LIST command lists the contents of the buffer. The asterisk indicates the current line. The abbreviated command for LIST is L.

```
SQL> L
  1  SELECT empno, ename
  2* FROM emp
SQL> LIST LAST
  2* FROM emp
SQL>
```

The command LIST *m n* displays lines from *m* through *n*. If you substitute * for *m* or *n*, it implies the current line. The command LIST LAST displays the last line.

APPEND

The APPEND *text* command adds text to the end of line. The abbreviated command is A.

```
SQL> A  WHERE empno <> 7926
  2* FROM emp WHERE empno <> 7926
SQL>
```

CHANGE

The CHANGE */old/new* command changes an old entry to a new entry. The abbreviated command is C. If you omit *new*, *old* will be deleted.

```
SQL> C /<>/=
  2* FROM emp WHERE empno = 7926
SQL> C /7926
  2* FROM emp WHERE empno =
SQL>
```

INPUT

The INPUT *text* command adds a line of text. Its abbreviation is I. If *text* is omitted, you can add as many lines you want.

```
SQL> I
  3   7777 AND
  4   empno = 4354
  5
SQL> I ORDER BY 1
SQL> L
  1   SELECT empno, ename
  2   FROM emp WHERE empno =
  3   7777 AND
  4   empno = 4354
  5* ORDER BY 1
SQL>
```

DEL

The DEL command used alone or with * deletes the current line. The DEL *m n* command deletes lines from *m* through *n*. If you substitute * for *m* or *n*, it implies the current line. The command DEL LAST deletes the last line.

```
SQL> 3
  3* 7777 AND
SQL> DEL
SQL> L
  1   SELECT empno, ename
  2   FROM emp WHERE empno =
  3   empno = 4354
  4* ORDER BY 1
SQL> DEL 3 *
```

```
SQL> L
  1   SELECT empno, ename
  2*  FROM emp WHERE empno =
SQL>
```

CLEAR BUFFER

The CLEAR BUFFER command (abbreviated CL BUFF) clears the buffer. This deletes all lines from the buffer.

```
SQL> L
  1   SELECT empno, ename
  2*  FROM emp WHERE empno =
SQL> CL BUFF
buffer cleared
SQL> L
No lines in SQL buffer.
SQL>
```

Using Script Files

SQL*Plus provides commands to save the SQL buffer to a file, as well as to run SQL statements from a file. SQL statements saved in a file are called a *script file*.

You can work with script files as follows:

- To save the SQL buffer to an operating-system file, use the command SAVE *filename*. If you do not provide an extension, the saved file will have an extension of .sql.

- By default, the SAVE command will not overwrite an existing file. If you want to overwrite an existing file, you need to use the keyword REPLACE.

- To add the buffer to the end of an existing file, use the SAVE *filename* APPEND command.

- You can edit the saved file using the EDIT *filename* command.

- You can bring the contents of a *script file* to the SQL buffer using the GET *filename* command.

- If you want to run a script file, use the command START *filename*. You can also run a script file using @*filename*.

- An @@*filename* used inside a script file looks for the filename in the directory where the parent *script file* is saved and executes it.

Exercise 1.1 will familiarize you with the script file commands, as well as the other topics I have covered so far.

EXERCISE 1.1

Practicing SQL*Plus File Commands

In this exercise, you will learn how to edit the SQL*Plus buffer using various buffer edit commands.

1. Enter the following SQL; the third line is a blank line so that the SQL is saved in the buffer:

```
SQL> SELECT employee_id, first_name, last_name
  2  FROM    employees
  3
SQL>
```

2. List the SQL buffer:

```
SQL> L
  1  SELECT employee_id, first_name, last_name
  2* FROM    employees
SQL>
```

3. Save the buffer to a file named myfile; the default extension will be .sql:

```
SQL> SAVE myfile
Created file MYFILE.sql
SQL>
```

4. Choose to edit the file:

```
SQL> EDIT myfile
SQL>
```

5. Add WHERE EMPLOYEE_ID = 106 as the third line to the SQL statement.

6. List the buffer:

```
SQL> LIST
  1  SELECT employee_id, first_name, last_name
  2* FROM    employees
SQL>
```

The buffer listed is still the old buffer. The edited changes are not reflected because you edited the file MYFILE, which is not yet loaded to the buffer.

7. Bring the file contents to the buffer:

```
SQL> GET myfile
  1  SELECT employee_id, first_name, last_name
```

```
  2   FROM    employees
  3*  WHERE employee_id = 106
SQL>
```

8. List the buffer to verify its contents:

```
SQL> LI
  1   SELECT employee_id, first_name, last_name
  2   FROM    employees
  3*  WHERE employee_id = 106
SQL>
```

9. Change the employee number from 106 to 110:

```
SQL> C/106/110
  3*  WHERE employee_id = 110
SQL>
```

10. Save the buffer again to the same file:

```
SQL> SAVE myfile
SP2-0540: File "MYFILE.sql" already exists.
Use "SAVE filename[.ext] REPLACE".
SQL>
```

An error is returned, because SAVE will not overwrite the file by default.

11. Save the file using the REPLACE keyword:

```
SQL> SAVE myfile REPLACE
Wrote file MYFILE.sql
SQL>
```

12. Execute the file:

```
SQL> START myfile


EMPLOYEE_ID FIRST_NAME           LAST_NAME
----------- -------------------- ---------
        110 John                 Chen
SQL>
```

13. Change the employee number from 110 to 106, and append this SQL to the file; then execute it using @:

```
SQL> C/110/106
  3*  WHERE employee_id = 106
```

```
SQL> SAVE myfile APPEND
Appended file to MYFILE.sql
SQL> @MYFILE
EMPLOYEE_ID FIRST_NAME          LAST_NAME
----------- -------------------- ---------
        110 John                 Chen

EMPLOYEE_ID FIRST_NAME          LAST_NAME
----------- -------------------- ---------
        106 Valli                Pataballa
SQL>
```

Saving Query Results to a File

You can use the SPOOL *filename* command to save the query results to a file. By default, the SPOOL command creates an .lst file extension. SPOOL overwrites an existing file by default. If you include the APPEND option as in SPOOL *filename* APPEND, the results are added to an existing file. A new file will be created if the file does not exist already.

SPOOL OFF stops writing the output to the file. SPOOL OUT stops the writing of output and sends the output file to the printer.

Adding Comments to a Script File

Having comments in the script file improves the readability and understandability of the code. You can enter comments in SQL*Plus using the REMARKS (abbreviated REM) command. Lines in the script file beginning with the keyword REM are comments and are not executed. You can also enter a comment between /* and */. Comments can also be entered following -- (double hyphen), all characters following -- in the line are treated as comment by Oracle.

While executing a script file with comments, the remarks entered using the REMARKS command are not displayed on the screen, but the comments within /* and */ are displayed on the screen with the prefix DOC> when there is more than one line between /* and */. You can turn this off by using SET DOCUMENT OFF.

This section provided an overview of SQL*Plus, the tool you will be using to enter and execute SQL statements in Oracle Database 11*g*. In the next sections, I will discuss some of the Oracle 11*g* SQL fundamentals before showing you how to write your first SQL query (a SELECT statement).

Oracle Datatypes

The basic structure of data storage in the Oracle Database 11*g* is a table. A table can be considered as a spreadsheet with columns and rows. Data is stored in the table as rows. Each column in the table has storage characteristics such as the type of data contained in the column. Oracle has several built-in datatypes to store different kinds of data. In this section, I will go over the built-in datatypes available in Oracle 11g. Detailed discussion on datatypes as well as creating and maintaining tables are discussed in Chapter 6, "Creating Tables and Constraints."

When you create a table to store data in the database, you need to specify a datatype for all the columns you define in the table. Oracle has many datatypes to suit application requirements. Oracle 11g also supports ANSI and DB2 datatypes. The Oracle built-in datatypes can be broadly classified as shown in Table 1.2.

TABLE 1.2   Oracle Built-in Datatypes

Category	Datatypes
Character	CHAR, NCHAR, VARCHAR2, NVARCHAR2
Number	NUMBER, FLOAT, BINARY_FLOAT, BINARY_DOUBLE
Long and raw	LONG, LONG RAW, RAW
Date and time	DATE, TIMESTAMP, TIMESTAMP WITH TIME ZONE, TIMESTAMP WITH LOCAL TIME ZONE, INTERVAL YEAR TO MONTH, INTERVAL DAY TO SECOND
Large object	CLOB, NCLOB, BCLOB, BFILE
Row ID	ROWID, UROWID

In the following sections, I will discuss only a few of the built-in datatypes to get you started with SQL. I discuss all the datatypes and their usage in detail in Chapter 6.

CHAR(<size>)

The *CHAR* datatype is a fixed-length alphanumeric string, which has a maximum length in bytes (to specify length in characters, use the CHAR keyword inside parentheses along with a size; see Chapter 6). Data stored in CHAR columns is space-padded to fill the maximum length. Its size can range from a minimum of 1 byte to a maximum of 2,000 bytes. The default size is 1.

When you create a column using the CHAR datatype, the database will ensure that all data placed in this column has the defined length. If the data is shorter than the defined length, it is space-padded on the right to the specified length. If the data is longer, an error is raised.

VARCHAR2(<size>)

The *VARCHAR2* datatype is a variable-length alphanumeric string, which has a maximum length in bytes (to specify the length in characters, use the CHAR keyword inside parentheses along with a size; see Chapter 6). VARCHAR2 columns require only the amount of space needed to store the data and can store up to 4,000 bytes. There is no default size for the VARCHAR2 datatype. An empty VARCHAR2(2000) column takes up as much room in the database as an empty VARCHAR2(1) column.

> The default size of a CHAR datatype is 1. For a VARCHAR2 datatype, you must always specify the size.

The VARCHAR2 and CHAR datatypes have different comparison rules for trailing spaces. With the CHAR datatype, trailing spaces are ignored. With the VARCHAR2 datatype, trailing spaces are not ignored, and they sort higher than no trailing spaces. Here's an example:

CHAR datatype: 'Yo' = 'Yo   '

VARCHAR2 datatype: 'Yo' < 'Yo   '

NUMBER (<p>, <s>)

The *NUMBER* datatype stores numbers with a precision of *<p>* digits and a scale of *<s>* digits. The precision and scale values are optional. Numeric datatypes are used to store negative and positive integers, fixed-point numbers, and floating-point numbers. The precision can be between 1 and 38, and the scale has a range between −84 and 127. If the precision and scale are omitted, Oracle assumes the maximum of the range for both values.

You can have precision and scale digits in the integer part. The scale rounds the value after the decimal point to *<s>* digits. For example, if you define a column as NUMBER(5,2), the range of values you can store in this column is from −999.99 to 999.99; that is, 5 − 2 = 3 for the integer part, and the decimal part is rounded to two digits. Even if you do not include the decimal part for the value inserted, the maximum number you can store in a NUMBER(5,2) definition is 999.

Oracle will round numbers inserted into numeric columns with a scale smaller than the inserted number. For example, if a column were defined as NUMBER(4,2) and you specified a value of 12.125 to go into that column, the resulting number would be rounded to 12.13 before it was inserted into the column. If the value exceeds the precision, however, an Oracle error is returned. You cannot insert 123.1 into a column defined as NUMBER(4,2). Specifying the scale and precision does not force all inserted values to be a fixed length.

If the scale is negative, the number is rounded to the left of the decimal. Basically, a negative scale forces *<s>* number of zeros just to the left of the decimal.

If you specify a scale that is greater than the precision value, the precision defines the maximum number of digits to the right of the decimal point after the zeros. For example, if a column is defined as NUMBER(3,5), the range of values you can store is from −0.00999 to 0.00999; that is, it requires two zeros (*<s>-<p>*) after the decimal point and rounds the decimal part to three digits (*<p>*) after zeros. Table 1.3 shows several examples of how numeric data is stored with various definitions.

TABLE 1.3   Precision and Scale Examples

Value	Datatype	Stored Value	Explanation
123.2564	NUMBER	123.2564	The range and precision are set to the maximum, so the datatype can store any value.
1234.9876	NUMBER(6,2)	1234.99	Since the scale is only 2, the decimal part of the value is rounded to two digits.
12345.12345	NUMBER(6,2)	Error	The range of the integer part is only from −9999 to 9999.
123456	NUMBER(6,2)	Error	The precision is larger than specified; the range is only from −9999 to 9999.
1234.9876	NUMBER(6)	1235	The decimal part is rounded to the next integer.
123456.1	NUMBER(6)	123456	The decimal part is rounded.
12345.345	NUMBER(5,-2)	12300	The negative scale rounds the number $<s>$ digits left to the decimal point. −2 rounds to hundreds.
1234567	NUMBER(5,-2)	1234600	Rounded to the nearest hundred.
12345678	NUMBER(5,-2)	Error	Outside the range; can have only five digits, excluding the two zeros representing hundreds, for a total of seven digits: $(s-(-p)=s+p=5+2=7)$.
123456789	NUMBER(5,-4)	123460000	Rounded to the nearest 10,000.
1234567890	NUMBER(5,-4)	Error	Outside the range; can have only five digits, excluding the four trailing zeros.
12345.58	NUMBER(*, 1)	12345.6	The use of * in the precision specifies the default limit (38).
0.1	NUMBER(4,5)	Error	Requires a zero after the decimal point $(5-4=1)$.
0.01234567	NUMBER(4,5)	0.01235	Rounded to four digits after the decimal point and zero.

TABLE 1.3   Precision and Scale Examples *(continued)*

Value	Datatype	Stored Value	Explanation
0.09999	NUMBER(4,5)	0.09999	Stored as it is; only four digits after the decimal point and zero.
0.099996	NUMBER(4,5)	Error	Rounding this value to four digits after the decimal and zero results in 0.1, which is outside the range.

DATE

The *DATE* datatype is used to store date and time information. This datatype can be converted to other forms for viewing, but it has a number of special functions and properties that make date manipulation and calculations simple. The time component of the DATE datatype has a resolution of one second—no less. The DATE datatype occupies a storage space of 7 bytes. The following information is contained within each DATE datatype:

- Century
- Year
- Month
- Day
- Hour
- Minute
- Second

Date values are inserted or updated in the database by converting either a numeric value or a character value into a DATE datatype using the function TO_DATE. Oracle defaults the format to display the date as DD-MON-YY. This format shows that the default date must begin with a two-digit day, followed by a three-character abbreviation for the month, followed by a two-digit year. If you specify the date without including a time component, the time is defaulted to midnight, or 00:00:00 in military time. The SYSDATE function returns the current system date and time from the database server to which you're currently connected.

TIMESTAMP [<precision>]

The TIMESTAMP datatype stores date and time information with fractional precision for seconds. The only difference between the DATE and TIMESTAMP datatypes is the ability to store fractional seconds up to a precision of nine digits. The default precision is 6 and can range from 0 to 9. Similar to the SYSDATE function, the SYSTIMESTAMP function returns the current system date and time, with fractional precision for seconds.

Operators and Literals

An *operator* is a manipulator that is applied to a data item in order to return a result. Special characters represent different operations in Oracle (+ represents addition, for example). Operators are commonly used in all programming environments, and you should already be familiar with the following operators, which may be classified into two types:

Unary operator   A unary operator has only one operand. Examples are +2 and –5. They have the format <operator><operand>.

Binary operator   A binary operator has two operands. Examples are 5+4 and 7*5. They have the format <operand1><operator><operand2>. You can insert spaces between the operand and operator to improve readability.

I'll now discuss the various types of operators available in Oracle.

Arithmetic Operators

Arithmetic operators operate on numeric values. Table 1.4 shows the various arithmetic operators in Oracle and how to use them.

TABLE 1.4   Arithmetic Operators

Operator	Purpose	Example
+ –	Unary operators: Use to represent positive or negative data item. For positive items, the + is optional.	–234.44
+	Addition: Use to add two data items or expressions.	2+4
–	Subtraction: Use to find the difference between two data items or expressions.	20.4-2
*	Multiplication: Use to multiply two data items or expressions.	5*10
/	Division: Use to divide a data item or expression with another.	8.4/2

WARNING   Do not use two hyphens (--) to represent double negation; use a space or parentheses in between, as in -(-20). Two hyphens represent the beginning of a comment in SQL.

Concatenation Operator

The *concatenation operator* is used to concatenate or join two character (text) strings. The result of concatenation is another character string. Concatenating a zero-length string (' ')

or a NULL with another string results in a string, not a NULL (NULL in Oracle 11*g* represents unknown or missing data). Two vertical bars (||) are used as the concatenation operator.

Here are two examples:

`'Oracle11g' || 'Database'` results in `'Oracle11gDatabase'`.

`'Oracle11g ' || 'Database'` results in `'Oracle11g Database'`.

Operator Precedence

If multiple operators are used in the same expression, Oracle evaluates them in the *order of precedence* set in the database engine. Operators with higher precedence are evaluated before operators with lower precedence. Operators with the same precedence are evaluated from left to right. Table 1.5 lists the precedence.

TABLE 1.5 SQL Operator Precedence

Precedence	Operator	Purpose
1	– +	Unary operators, negation
2	* /	Multiplication, division
3	+ - ||	Addition, subtraction, concatenation

Using parentheses changes the order of precedence. The innermost parenthesis is evaluated first. In the expression 1+2*3, the result is 7, because 2*3 is evaluated first and the result is added to 1. In the expression (1+2)*3, 1+2 is evaluated first, and the result is multiplied by 3, giving 9.

Literals

Literals are values that represent a fixed value (constant). There are four types of literals:

- Text (or character)
- Numeric (integer and number)
- Datetime
- Interval

You can use literals within many of the SQL functions, expressions, and conditions.

Text Literals

A *text literal* must be enclosed in single quotation marks. Any character between the quotation marks is considered part of the text value. Oracle treats all text literals as though they were CHAR datatypes for comparison (blank padded). The maximum length of a text literal is 4,000 bytes. Single quotation marks can be included in the literal text value by preceding it with another single quotation mark. Here are some examples of text literals:

```
'The Quick Brown Fox'
'That man''s suit is black'
'And I quote: "This will never do." '
'12-SEP-2001'
```

Alternatively, you can use Q or q quoting, which provides a range of delimiters. The syntax for using the Q/q quoting with a quote-delimiter text literal is as follows:

```
[Q|q]'<quote_delimiter> <text literal> <quote_delimiter>'
```

<quote_delimiter> is any character except a space, tab, or carriage return. The quote delimiter can be a single quotation mark, but make sure inside the text literal a single quotation mark is not immediately followed by another single quotation mark. If the opening quote delimiter is [or { or < or (, then the closing quote must be the corresponding] or } or > or). For all other quote delimiters, the opening quote delimiter must be the same as the closing quote delimiter. Here are some examples of text literals using the alternative quoting mechanism:

```
q'<The Quick Brown Fox>'
Q'#The Quick Brown Fox#'
q'{That man's suit is black}'
Q'(And I quote: "This will never do." )'
Q'"And I quote: "This will never do." "'
q'[12-SEP-2001]'
```

Numeric Literals

Integer literals can be any number of numerals, excluding a decimal separator and up to 38 digits long. Here are two examples:

- 24
- −456

Number and *floating-point literals* can include scientific notation, as well as digits and the decimal separator. E or e represents a number in scientific notation; the exponent can be in the range of −130 to 125. If the literal is followed by an f or F, it is treated as a BINARY_FLOAT datatype. If the literal is followed by a d or D, it is treated as a BINARY_DOUBLE datatype. Here are some examples:

- 24.0
- −345.65
- 23E-10

- 1.5f
- −34.567D
- −4d
- −4.0E+0

Datetime Literals

You can specify a date value as a string literal using the *datetime literals*. The most common methods to represent the datetime values are to use the conversion function TO_DATE or TO_TIMESTAMP with the appropriate format mask. For completeness of literals, I will discuss the datetime literals briefly.

The DATE literal uses the keyword DATE followed by the date value in single quotes, and the value must be specified in *YYYY-MM-DD* format with no time component. The time component will be defaulted to midnight (00:00:00). The following are examples of the DATE literal:

```
DATE '2008-03-24'
DATE '1999-12-31'
```

Similar to the TIMESTAMP datatype, the TIMESTAMP literal can be used to specify the year, month, date, hour, minute, second, and fractional second. You can also include time-zone data along with the TIMESTAMP literal. The time zone information can be specified using the UTC offset or using the time zone region name. The literal must be in the format YYYY-MM-DD HH24:MI:SS TZ. Here are some examples of the TIMESTAMP literal:

```
TIMESTAMP '2008-03-24 03:25:34.123'
TIMESTAMP '2008-03-24 03:25:34.123 -7:00'
TIMESTAMP '2008-03-24 03:25:34.123 US/Central'
TIMESTAMP '2008-03-24 03:25:34.123 US/Central CDT'
```

Interval Literals

Interval literals specify a period of time in terms of years and months or in terms of days and seconds. These literals correspond to the Oracle datatypes INTERVAL YEAR TO MONTH and INTERVAL DAY TO SECOND. I'll discuss these datatypes in more detail in Chapter 6.

Writing Simple Queries

A *query* is a request for information from the database tables. Queries do not modify data; they read data from database tables and views. Simple queries are those that retrieve data from a single table or view. A table is used to store data and is stored in rows and columns. The basis of a query is the SELECT statement. The SELECT statement can be used to get data from a single table or from multiple tables. Queries using multiple tables are discussed in later chapters.

Using the SELECT Statement

The SELECT statement is the most commonly used statement in SQL. It allows you to retrieve information already stored in the database. The statement begins with the keyword SELECT, followed by the column names whose data you want to query. You can select information either from all the columns (denoted by *) or from name-specific columns in the SELECT clause to retrieve data. The FROM clause provides the name of the table, view, or materialized view to use in the query. These objects are discussed in detail in later chapters. For simplicity, I will use tables for the rest of this chapter.

Let's use the JOBS table defined in the HR schema of the Oracle 11*g* sample database. You can use SQL*Plus tool to connect to the database as discussed earlier in the chapter. The JOBS table definition is provided in Table 1.6.

TABLE 1.6   JOBS Table Definition

Column Name	Datatype	Length
JOB_ID	VARCHAR2	10
JOB_TITLE	VARCHAR2	35
MIN_SALARY	NUMBER	6,0
MAX_SALARY	NUMBER	6,0

The simple form of a SELECT statement to retrieve all the columns and rows from the JOBS table is as follows (only part of output result set is shown here):

```
SQL> SELECT * FROM jobs;
```

```
JOB_ID      JOB_TITLE                         MIN_SALARY MAX_SALARY
----------  ------------------------------    ---------- ----------
AD_PRES     President                              20000      40000
AD_VP       Administration Vice President          15000      30000
AD_ASST     Administration Assistant                3000       6000
FI_MGR      Finance Manager                         8200      16000
FI_ACCOUNT  Accountant                              4200       9000
... ... ... ... ...
IT_PROG     Programmer                              4000      10000
```

MK_MAN	Marketing Manager	9000	15000
MK_REP	Marketing Representative	4000	9000
HR_REP	Human Resources Representative	4000	9000
PR_REP	Public Relations Representative	4500	10500

19 rows selected.

 The keywords, column names, and table names are case insensitive. Only literals enclosed in single quotation marks are case sensitive in Oracle.

How do you list only the job title and minimum salary from this table? If you know the column names and the table name, writing the query is simple. Here, the column names are JOB_TITLE and MIN_SALARY, and the table name is JOBS. Execute the query by ending the query with a semicolon. In SQL*Plus, you can execute the query by entering a slash on a line by itself or by using the RUN command.

```
SQL> SELECT job_title, min_salary FROM jobs;
```

JOB_TITLE	MIN_SALARY
President	20000
Administration Vice President	15000
Administration Assistant	3000
Finance Manager	8200
Accountant	4200
Accounting Manager	8200
Public Accountant	4200
... ...	
Programmer	4000
Marketing Manager	9000
Marketing Representative	4000
Human Resources Representative	4000
Public Relations Representative	4500

19 rows selected.

Notice that the numeric column (MIN_SALARY) is aligned to the right and the character column (JOB_TITLE) is aligned to the left. Does it seem that the column heading MIN_SALARY should be more meaningful? Well, you can provide a *column alias* to appear in the query results.

Column Alias Names

The column alias name is defined next to the column name with a space or by using the keyword AS. If you want a space in the column alias name, you must enclose it in double quotation marks. The case is preserved only when the alias name is enclosed in double quotation marks; otherwise, the display will be uppercase. The following example demonstrates using an alias name for the column heading in the previous query:

```
SELECT job_title AS Title, min_salary AS "Minimum Salary"
FROM jobs;
```

```
TITLE                                  Minimum Salary
----------------------------------     --------------
President                                      20000
Administration Vice President                  15000
Administration Assistant                        3000
Finance Manager                                 8200
Accountant                                      4200
Accounting Manager                              8200

... ... ... ...
Programmer                                      4000
Marketing Manager                               9000
Marketing Representative                        4000
Human Resources Representative                  4000
Public Relations Representative                 4500
```

19 rows selected.

In this listing, the column alias name Title appears in all capital letters because I did not enclose it in double quotation marks.

The asterisk (*) is used to select all columns in the table. This is useful when you do not know the column names or when you are too lazy to type all the column names.

Ensuring Uniqueness

The DISTINCT keyword (or UNIQUE keyword) following SELECT ensures that the resulting rows are unique. Uniqueness is verified against the complete row, not the first column. If you need to find the unique departments in the EMPLOYEES table, issue this query:

```
SELECT DISTINCT department_id
FROM employees;
```

```
DEPARTMENT_ID
-------------
          100
           30

           20
           70
           90
          110
           50
           40
           80
           10
           60
```

12 rows selected.

   To demonstrate that uniqueness is enforced across the row, let's do one more query using the SELECT DISTINCT clause. Notice DEPARTMENT_ID repeating for each JOB_ID value in the following example:

```
SELECT DISTINCT department_id, job_id
FROM employees;

DEPARTMENT_ID JOB_ID
------------- ----------
          110 AC_ACCOUNT
           90 AD_VP
           50 ST_CLERK
           80 SA_REP
          110 AC_MGR
... ... ...
           10 AD_ASST
           20 MK_REP
           40 HR_REP
           30 PU_MAN
```

20 rows selected.

SELECT * FROM TAB; shows all the tables and views in your schema. Don't be alarmed if you see a table name similar to BIN$PJV23QpwQfu0zPN9uaXw+w==$0. These are tables that belong to the Recycle Bin (or dropped tables). The tasks of creating tables and managing tables are discussed in Chapter 6.

The DUAL Table

The DUAL table is a dummy table available to all users in the database. It has one column and one row. The DUAL table is used to select system variables or to evaluate an expression. Here are few examples. The first query is to show the contents of the DUAL table.

```
SQL> SELECT * FROM dual;

DUMMY
-----
X

SQL> SELECT SYSDATE, USER FROM dual;

SYSDATE     USER
---------   -----------------------------
18-SEP-07 HR

SQL> SELECT 'I''m ' || user || ' Today is ' || SYSDATE
  2  FROM dual;

'I''M'||USER||'TODAYIS'||SYSDATE
------------------------------------------------------
I'm HR Today is 18-SEP-07
```

SYSDATE and USER are built-in functions that provide information about the environment. These functions are discussed in Chapter 2, "Using Single-Row Functions."

Limiting Rows

You can use the WHERE clause in the SELECT statement to limit the number of rows processed. Any logical conditions of the WHERE clause use the comparison operators. Rows are returned or operated upon where the data satisfies the logical condition(s) of the WHERE clause. You can use column names or expressions in the WHERE clause, but not column alias names. The WHERE clause follows the FROM clause in the SELECT statement.

How do you list the employees who work for department 90? The following example shows how to limit the query to only the records belonging to department 90 by using a WHERE clause:

```
SELECT first_name || ' ' || last_name "Name", department_id
FROM    employees
WHERE   department_id = 90;
```

```
Name                                        DEPARTMENT_ID
----------------------------------------    -------------
Steven King                                            90
Neena Kochhar                                          90
Lex De Haan                                            90
```

 You need not include the column names in the SELECT clause to use them in the WHERE clause.

You can use various operators in Oracle 11*g* in the WHERE clause to limit the number of rows.

Comparison Operators

Comparison operators compare two values or expressions and give a Boolean result of TRUE, FALSE, or NULL. The comparison operators include those that test for equality, inequality, less than, greater than, and value comparisons.

= (Equality)

The = operator tests for equality. The test evaluates to TRUE if the values or results of an expression on both sides of the operator are equal.

```
SELECT first_name || ' ' || last_name "Name", department_id
FROM    employees
WHERE   department_id = 90;
```

```
Name                                        DEPARTMENT_ID
----------------------------------------    -------------
Steven King                                            90
Neena Kochhar                                          90
Lex De Haan                                            90
```

!=, <>, or ^= (Inequality)

You can use any one of these three operators to test for inequality. The test evaluates to TRUE if the values on both sides of the operator do not match.

```
SELECT  first_name || ' ' || last_name "Name", commission_pct
FROM    employees
WHERE   commission_pct != .35;
```

Name	COMMISSION_PCT
John Russell	.4
Karen Partners	.3
Alberto Errazuriz	.3
Gerald Cambrault	.3
... ...	
Jack Livingston	.2
Kimberely Grant	.15
Charles Johnson	.1

32 rows selected.

< (Less Than)

The < operator evaluates to TRUE if the left side (expression or value) of the operator is less than the right side of the operator.

```
SELECT  first_name || ' ' || last_name "Name", commission_pct
FROM    employees
WHERE   commission_pct < .15;
```

Name	COMMISSION_PCT
Mattea Marvins	.1
David Lee	.1
Sundar Ande	.1
Amit Banda	.1
Sundita Kumar	.1
Charles Johnson	.1

6 rows selected.

> (Greater Than)

The > operator evaluates to TRUE if the left side (expression or value) of the operator is greater than the right side of the operator.

```
SELECT first_name || ' ' || last_name "Name", commission_pct
FROM    employees
WHERE   commission_pct > .35;
```

```
Name                                      COMMISSION_PCT
----------------------------------------- --------------
John Russell                                          .4
```

<= (Less Than or Equal to)

The <= operator evaluates to TRUE if the left side (expression or value) of the operator is less than or equal to the right side of the operator.

```
SELECT first_name || ' ' || last_name "Name", commission_pct
FROM    employees
WHERE   commission_pct <= .15;
```

```
Name                                      COMMISSION_PCT
----------------------------------------- --------------
Oliver Tuvault                                       .15
Danielle Greene                                      .15
Mattea Marvins                                        .1
David Lee                                             .1
Sundar Ande                                           .1
Amit Banda                                            .1
William Smith                                        .15
Elizabeth Bates                                      .15
Sundita Kumar                                         .1
Kimberely Grant                                      .15
Charles Johnson                                       .1
```

```
11 rows selected.
```

>= (Greater Than or Equal to)

The >= operator evaluates to TRUE if the left side (expression or value) of the operator is greater than or equal to the right side of the operator.

```
SELECT first_name || ' ' || last_name "Name", commission_pct
FROM    employees
WHERE   commission_pct >= .35;
```

Name	COMMISSION_PCT
John Russell	.4
Janette King	.35
Patrick Sully	.35
Allan McEwen	.35

ANY or SOME

You can use the ANY or SOME operator to compare a value to each value in a list or subquery. The ANY and SOME operators always must be preceded by one of the following comparison operators: =, !=, <, >, <=, or >=.

```
SELECT first_name || ' ' || last_name "Name", department_id
FROM    employees
WHERE   department_id <= ANY (10, 15, 20, 25);
```

Name	DEPARTMENT_ID
Jennifer Whalen	10
Michael Hartstein	20
Pat Fay	20

ALL

You can use the ALL operator to compare a value to every value in a list or subquery. The ALL operator must always be preceded by one of the following comparison operators: =, !=, <, >, <=, or >=.

```
SELECT first_name || ' ' || last_name "Name", department_id
FROM    employees
WHERE   department_id >= ALL (80, 90, 100);
```

Name	DEPARTMENT_ID
Nancy Greenberg	100
Daniel Faviet	100
John Chen	100
Ismael Sciarra	100
Jose Manuel Urman	100
Luis Popp	100
Shelley Higgins	110
William Gietz	110

```
8 rows selected.
```

For all the comparison operators discussed, if one side of the operator is NULL, the result is NULL.

Logical Operators

Logical operators are used to combine the results of two comparison conditions (compound conditions) to produce a single result or to reverse the result of a single comparison. NOT, AND, and OR are the logical operators. When a logical operator is applied to NULL, the result is UNKNOWN. UNKNOWN acts similarly to FALSE; the only difference is that NOT FALSE is TRUE, whereas NOT UNKNOWN is also UNKNOWN.

NOT

You can use the NOT operator to reverse the result. It evaluates to TRUE if the operand is FALSE, and it evaluates to FALSE if the operand is TRUE. NOT returns NULL if the operand is NULL.

```
WHERE   !(department_id >= 30)
        *
ERROR at line 3:
SELECT first_name, department_id
FROM    employees
WHERE   not (department_id >= 30);


FIRST_NAME          DEPARTMENT_ID
-------------------- -------------
Jennifer                       10
Michael                        20
Pat                            20
```

AND

The AND operator evaluates to TRUE if both operands are TRUE. It evaluates to FALSE if either operand is FALSE. Otherwise, it returns NULL.

```
SELECT first_name, salary
FROM    employees
WHERE   last_name = 'Smith'
AND     salary    > 7500;


FIRST_NAME          SALARY
-------------------- ----------
Lindsey                   8000
```

OR

The OR operator evaluates to TRUE if either operand is TRUE. It evaluates to FALSE if both operands are FALSE. Otherwise, it returns NULL.

```
SELECT first_name, last_name
FROM   employees
WHERE  first_name = 'Kelly'
OR     last_name  = 'Smith';
```

```
FIRST_NAME               LAST_NAME
-------------------- -------------------------

Lindsey              Smith
William              Smith
Kelly                Chung
```

Logical Operator Truth Tables

The following tables are the truth tables for the three logical operators.

Table 1.7 is a truth table for the AND operator.

TABLE 1.7   AND Truth Table

AND	TRUE	FALSE	UNKNOWN
TRUE	TRUE	FALSE	UNKNOWN
FALSE	FALSE	FALSE	FALSE
UNKNOWN	UNKNOWN	FALSE	UNKNOWN

Table 1.8 is the truth table for the OR operator.

TABLE 1.8   OR Truth Table

OR	TRUE	FALSE	UNKNOWN
TRUE	TRUE	TRUE	TRUE
FALSE	TRUE	FALSE	UNKNOWN
UNKNOWN	TRUE	UNKNOWN	UNKNOWN

Table 1.9 is the truth table for the NOT operator.

TABLE 1.9   NOT Truth Table

NOT	
TRUE	FALSE
FALSE	TRUE
UNKNOWN	UNKNOWN

Other Operators

In the following sections, I will discuss all the operators that can be used in the WHERE clause of the SQL statement that were not discussed earlier.

IN and NOT IN

You can use the IN and NOT IN operators to test a membership condition. IN is equivalent to the =ANY operator, which evaluates to TRUE if the value exists in the list or the result set from a subquery. The NOT IN operator is equivalent to the !=ALL operator, which evaluates to TRUE if the value does not exist in the list or the result set from a subquery. The following examples demonstrate how to use these two operators:

```
SELECT first_name, last_name, department_id
FROM    employees
WHERE   department_id IN (10, 20, 90);
```

```
FIRST_NAME            LAST_NAME                DEPARTMENT_ID
-------------------- ------------------------ ----------
Steven                King                                90
Neena                 Kochhar                             90
Lex                   De Haan                             90
Jennifer              Whalen                              10
Michael               Hartstein                           20
Pat                   Fay                                 20
```

6 rows selected.

```
SELECT first_name, last_name, department_id
FROM    employees
WHERE   department_id NOT IN
        (10, 30, 40, 50, 60, 80, 90, 110, 100);
```

FIRST_NAME	LAST_NAME	DEPARTMENT_ID
Michael	Hartstein	20
Pat	Fay	20
Hermann	Baer	70

SQL>

WARNING   When using the NOT IN operator, if any value in the list or the result returned from the subquery is NULL, the NOT IN condition is evaluated to FALSE. For example, last_name not in ('Smith', 'Thomas', NULL) evaluates to last_name != 'Smith' AND last_name != 'Thomas' AND last_name != NULL. Any comparison on a NULL value results in NULL. So, the previous condition does not return any row even through there may be some rows with LAST_NAME as Smith or Thomas.

BETWEEN

You can use the BETWEEN operator to test a range. BETWEEN A AND B evaluates to TRUE if the value is greater than or equal to *A* and less than or equal to *B*. If NOT is used, the result is the reverse. The following example lists all the employees whose salary is between $5,000 and $6,000:

```
SELECT first_name, last_name, salary
FROM    employees
WHERE   salary BETWEEN 5000 AND 6000;
```

FIRST_NAME	LAST_NAME	SALARY
Bruce	Ernst	6000
Kevin	Mourgos	5800
Pat	Fay	6000

EXISTS

The EXISTS operator is always followed by a subquery in parentheses. EXISTS evaluates to TRUE if the subquery returns at least one row. The following example lists the employees who work for the administration department. Here is an example of using EXISTS. Don't worry if you do not understand the SQL for now; subqueries are discussed in detail in Chapter 4, "Using Joins and Subqueries."

```
SELECT last_name, first_name, department_id
FROM    employees e
WHERE   EXISTS (select 1 FROM departments d
```

```
    WHERE  d.department_id = e.department_id
    AND    d.department_name = 'Administration');
```

```
LAST_NAME              FIRST_NAME            DEPARTMENT_ID
---------------------  --------------------  -------------
Whalen                 Jennifer                         10
SQL>
```

IS NULL and IS NOT NULL

To find the NULL values or NOT NULL values, you need to use the IS NULL operator. The = or
!= operator will not work with NULL values. IS NULL evaluates to TRUE if the value is NULL.
IS NOT NULL evaluates to TRUE if the value is not NULL. To find the employees who do not
have a department assigned, use this query:

```
SELECT last_name, department_id
FROM    employees
WHERE  department_id IS NULL;
```

```
LAST_NAME                 DEPARTMENT_ID
------------------------  -------------
Grant

SQL>
SELECT last_name, department_id
FROM employees
WHERE department_id = NULL;
```

```
no rows selected
```

LIKE

Using the LIKE operator, you can perform pattern matching. The pattern-search character %
is used to match any character and any number of characters. The pattern-search character
_ is used to match any single character. If you are looking for the actual character % or _ in the
pattern search, you can include an escape character in the search string and notify Oracle
using the ESCAPE clause.

The following query searches for all employees whose first name begins with *Su* and last
name does not begin with *S*:

```
SELECT first_name, last_name
FROM    employees
WHERE  first_name LIKE 'Su%'
AND    last_name NOT LIKE 'S%';
```

```
FIRST_NAME           LAST_NAME
-------------------- -------------------------
Sundar               Ande
Sundita              Kumar
Susan                Mavris
```

The following example looks for all JOB_ID values that begin with *AC_*. Since _ is a pattern-matching character, you must qualify it with an escape character. Oracle does not have a default escape character.

```
SELECT job_id, job_title
FROM   jobs
WHERE  job_id like 'AC\_%' ESCAPE '\';
```

```
JOB_ID     JOB_TITLE
---------- -----------------------------------
AC_MGR     Accounting Manager
AC_ACCOUNT Public Accountant
```

Table 1.10 shows more examples of pattern matching.

TABLE 1.10 Pattern-Matching Examples

Pattern	Matches	Does Not Match
%SONI_1	SONIC1, ULTRASONI21	SONICS1, SONI315
_IME	TIME, LIME	IME, CRIME
\%SONI_1 ESCAPE '\'	%SONIC1, %SONI91	SONIC1, ULTRASONIC1
%ME_ _ _LE ESCAPE '\'	CRIME_FILE, TIME_POLE	CRIMESPILE, CRIME_ALE

Sorting Rows

The SELECT statement may include the ORDER BY clause to sort the resulting rows in a specific order based on the data in the columns. Without the ORDER BY clause, there is no guarantee that the rows will be returned in any specific order. If an ORDER BY clause is specified, by default the rows are returned by ascending order of the columns specified. If you need to sort the rows in descending order, use the keyword DESC next to the column name. You can specify the keyword ASC to explicitly state to sort in ascending order, although it is the default. The ORDER BY clause follows the FROM clause and the WHERE clause in the SELECT statement.

To retrieve all employee names of department 90 from the EMPLOYEES table ordered by last name, use this query:

```
SELECT first_name || ' ' || last_name "Employee Name"
FROM    employees
WHERE   department_id = 90
ORDER BY last_name;


Employee Name
------------------------------------------------
Lex De Haan
Steven King
Neena Kochhar
SQL>
```

You can specify more than one column in the ORDER BY clause. In this case, the result set will be ordered by the first column in the ORDER BY clause, then the second, and so on. Columns or expressions not used in the SELECT clause can also be used in the ORDER BY clause. The following example shows how to use DESC and multiple columns in the ORDER BY clause:

```
SELECT first_name, hire_date, salary, manager_id mid
FROM    employees
WHERE   department_id IN (110,100)
ORDER BY mid ASC, salary DESC, hire_date;


FIRST_NAME            HIRE_DATE   SALARY      MID
--------------------- ---------   ----------  ----------
Shelley              07-JUN-94    12000       101
Nancy                17-AUG-94    12000       101
Daniel               16-AUG-94     9000       108
John                 28-SEP-97     8200       108
Jose Manuel          07-MAR-98     7800       108
Ismael               30-SEP-97     7700       108
Luis                 07-DEC-99     6900       108
William              07-JUN-94     8300       205

8 rows selected.
SQL>
```

You can use column alias names in the ORDER BY clause.

If the DISTINCT keyword is used in the SELECT clause, you can use only those columns listed in the SELECT clause in the ORDER BY clause. If you have used any operators on columns in the SELECT clause, the ORDER BY clause also should use them. Here is an example:

```
SELECT DISTINCT 'Region ' || region_id
FROM    countries
ORDER BY region_id;


ORDER BY region_id
         *
ERROR at line 3:
ORA-01791: not a SELECTed expression

SELECT DISTINCT 'Region ' || region_id
FROM    countries
ORDER BY 'Region ' || region_id;


'REGION'||REGION_ID
-----------------------------------------------
Region 1
Region 2
Region 3
Region 4
```

Not only can you use the column name or column alias to sort the result set of a query, but you can also sort the results by specifying the position of the column in the SELECT clause. This is useful if you have a lengthy expression in the SELECT clause and you need the results sorted on this value. The following example sorts the result set using positional values:

```
SELECT first_name, hire_date, salary, manager_id mid
FROM    employees
WHERE   department_id IN (110,100)
ORDER BY 4, 2, 3;


FIRST_NAME           HIRE_DATE   SALARY        MID
-------------------- --------- ---------- ----------
Shelley              07-JUN-94    12000        101
```

Nancy	17-AUG-94	12000	101
Daniel	16-AUG-94	9000	108
John	28-SEP-97	8200	108
Ismael	30-SEP-97	7700	108
Jose Manuel	07-MAR-98	7800	108
Luis	07-DEC-99	6900	108
William	07-JUN-94	8300	205

8 rows selected.

WARNING   The ORDER BY clause cannot have more than 255 columns or expressions.

Sorting NULLs

By default, in an ascending-order sort, the NULL values appear at the bottom of the result set; that is, NULLs are sorted higher. For descending-order sorts, NULL values appear at the top of the result set—again, NULL values are sorted higher. You can change the default behavior by using the NULLS FIRST or NULLS LAST keyword, along with the column names (or alias names or positions). The following examples demonstrate how to use NULLS FIRST in an ascending sort:

```
SELECT last_name, commission_pct
FROM    employees
WHERE   last_name LIKE 'R%'
ORDER BY commission_pct ASC, last_name DESC;
```

```
LAST_NAME                  COMMISSION_PCT
------------------------   --------------
Russell                                .4
Rogers
Raphaely
Rajs
```

```
SELECT last_name, commission_pct
FROM    employees
WHERE   last_name LIKE 'R%'
ORDER BY commission_pct ASC NULLS FIRST, last_name DESC;
```

```
LAST_NAME                  COMMISSION_PCT
------------------------   --------------
Rogers
Raphaely
Rajs
Russell                              .4
SQL>
```

Why Do You Limit and Sort Rows?

The power of an RDBMS and SQL lies in getting exactly what you want from the database. The sample tables you considered under the HR schema are small, so even if you get all the information from the table, you can still find the specific data you're seeking. But what if you have a huge transaction table with millions of rows?

You know how easy it is to look through a catalog in the library to find a particular book or to search through an alphabetical listing to find your name. When querying a large table, make sure you know what you want.

The WHERE clause lets you query for exactly what you're looking for. The ORDER BY clause lets you sort rows. The following steps can be used as an approach to query data from single table:

1. Know the columns of the table. You can issue the DESCRIBE command to get the column names and datatype. Understand which column has what information.

2. Pick the column names you are interested in including in the query. Use these columns in the SELECT clause.

3. Identify the column or columns where you can limit the rows, or the columns that can show you only the rows of interest. Use these columns in the WHERE clause of the query, and supply the values as well as the appropriate operator.

4. If the query returns more than a few rows, you may be interested in having them sorted in a particular order. Specify the column names and the sorting order in the ORDER BY clause of the query.

Let's consider a table named PURCHASE_ORDERS. First, use the DESCRIBE command to list the columns:

```
SQL> DESCRIBE purchase_orders

Name                     Null?     Type
---------------------    --------  --------------
ORDER#                   NOT NULL  NUMBER (16)
ORDER_DT                 NOT NULL  DATE
```

```
CUSTOMER#                NOT NULL VARCHAR2 (12)
BACK_ORDER                        CHAR (1)
ORD_STATUS                        CHAR (1)
TOTAL_AMT                NOT NULL NUMBER (18,4)
SALES_TAX                         NUMBER (12,2)
```

The objective of the query is to find the completed orders that do not have any sales tax. You want to see the order number and total amount of the order. The corresponding columns that appear in the SELECT clause are ORDER# and TOTAL_AMT. Since you're interested in only the rows with no sales tax in the completed orders, the columns to appear in the WHERE clause are SALES_TAX (checking for zero sales tax) and ORD_STATUS (checking for the completeness of the order, which is status code C). Since the query returns multiple rows, you want to order them by the order number. Notice that the SALES_TAX column can be NULL, so you want to make sure you get all rows that have a sales tax amount of zero or NULL.

```
SELECT order#, total_amt
FROM   purchase_orders
WHERE  ord_status = 'C'
AND    (sales_tax IS NULL
OR      sales_tax = 0)
ORDER BY order#;
```

An alternative is to use the NVL function to deal with the NULL values. This function is discussed in Chapter 2.

Using Expressions

An *expression* is a combination of one or more values, operators, and SQL functions that result in a value. The result of an expression generally assumes the datatype of its components. The simple expression 5+6 evaluates to 11 and assumes a datatype of NUMBER. Expressions can appear in the following clauses:

- The SELECT clause of queries
- The WHERE clause, ORDER BY clause, and HAVING clause
- The VALUES clause of the INSERT statement
- The SET clause of the UPDATE statement

I will review the syntax of using these statements in later chapters.

You can include parentheses to group and evaluate expressions and then apply the result to the rest of the expression. When parentheses are used, the expression in the innermost

parentheses is evaluated first. Here is an example of a compound expression: ((2*4)/
(3+1))*10. The result of 2*4 is divided by the result of 3+1. Then the result from the division operation is multiplied by 10.

The CASE Expression

You can use the CASE expression to derive the IF...THEN...ELSE logic in SQL. Here is the syntax of the simple CASE expression:

```
CASE <expression>
WHEN <compare value> THEN <return value> ... ... ...
[ELSE <return value>]
END
```

The CASE expression begins with the keyword CASE and ends with the keyword END. The ELSE clause is optional. The maximum number of arguments in a CASE expression is 255. The following query displays a description for the REGION_ID column based on the value:

```
SELECT country_name, region_id,
       CASE region_id WHEN 1 THEN 'Europe'
                      WHEN 2 THEN 'America'
                      WHEN 3 THEN 'Asia'
                      ELSE 'Other' END Continent
FROM    countries
WHERE   country_name LIKE 'I%';


COUNTRY_NAME              REGION_ID CONTINE
-------------------- ---------- -------
Israel                      4 Other
India                       3 Asia
Italy                       1 Europe
SQL>
```

The other form of the CASE expression is the searched CASE, where the values are derived based on a condition. Oracle evaluates the conditions top to bottom; when a condition evaluates to true, the rest of the WHEN clauses are not evaluated. This version has the following syntax:

```
CASE
WHEN <condition> THEN <return value> ... ... ...
[ELSE <return value>]
END
```

The following example categorizes the salary as Low, Medium, and High using a searched CASE expression:

```
SELECT first_name, department_id, salary,
       CASE WHEN salary < 6000 THEN 'Low'
            WHEN salary < 10000 THEN 'Medium'
            WHEN salary >= 10000 THEN 'High' END Category
FROM   employees
WHERE department_id <= 30
ORDER BY first_name;
```

FIRST_NAME	DEPARTMENT_ID	SALARY	CATEGO
Alexander	30	3100	Low
Den	30	11000	High
Guy	30	2600	Low
Jennifer	10	4400	Low
Karen	30	2500	Low
Michael	20	13000	High
Pat	20	6000	Medium
Shelli	30	2900	Low
Sigal	30	2800	Low

```
9 rows selected.
```

Oracle uses the & (ampersand) character to substitute values at runtime. In the next section, I will discuss how to create SQL statements that can be used to get a different set of results based on values passed during execution time.

Finding the Current Sessions and Program Name

As a DBA you may have to query the V$SESSION dictionary view to find the current sessions in the database. This view has several columns that show various information about the session; often the DBA is interested in finding out the username and which program is connecting to the database. If the DBA wants to find out what SQL is executed in the session, the SID and SERIAL# columns can be queried to enable tracing using the DBMS_TRACE package.

I'll review in this example how to query the V$SESSION view using the simple SQL statements you learned in this chapter.

The following query may return several rows depending on the activity and number of users connected to the database:

```
SELECT username, sid, serial#, program
FROM v$session;
```

If you're using SQL*Plus, you may have to adjust the column width to fit the output in one line:

```
COLUMN program FORMAT a20
COLUMN username FORMAT a20
SELECT username, sid, serial#, program
FROM v$session;
```

```
USERNAME                    SID    SERIAL# PROGRAM
-------------------- ---------- ---------- -----------------
                            118       6246 ORACLE.EXE (W000)
BTHOMAS                     121        963 sqlplus.exe
DBSNMP                      124      23310 emagent.exe
DBSNMP                      148        608 emagent.exe
                            150          1 ORACLE.EXE (FBDA)
                            152          7 ORACLE.EXE (SMCO)
                            155          1 ORACLE.EXE (MMNL)
                            156          1 ORACLE.EXE (DIA0)
                            158          1 ORACLE.EXE (MMON)
                            159          1 ORACLE.EXE (RECO)
                            164          1 ORACLE.EXE (MMAN)
... ... ... (Output truncated)
```

As you can see, the background processes do not have usernames. To find out only the user sessions in the database, you can filter out the rows that do no have valid user-names:

```
SELECT username, sid, serial#, program
FROM v$session
WHERE username is NOT NULL;
```

If you're looking for specific information, you may want to add more filter conditions such as looking for a specific user or a specific program. The following SQL returns the rows in order of their session login time, with the most recent session on the top:

```
SELECT username, sid, serial#, program
FROM v$session
```

```
WHERE username is NOT NULL
ORDER BY logon_time;

USERNAME                    SID     SERIAL# PROGRAM
------------------- ---------- ---------- ---------------

DBSNMP                      148         608 emagent.exe
DBSNMP                      124       23310 emagent.exe
BTHOMAS                     121         963 sqlplus.exe
SCOTT                       132          23 TOAD.EXE
SJACOB                      231          32 discoverer.exe
```

Accepting Values at Runtime

To create an interactive SQL statement, you can define variables in the SQL statement. This allows the user to supply values at runtime, further enhancing the ability to reuse the SQL scripts. An ampersand (&) followed by a variable name prompts for and accepts values at runtime. For example, the following SELECT statement queries the DEPARTMENTS table based on the department number supplied at runtime.

```
SELECT department_name
FROM    departments
WHERE   department_id = &dept;

Enter value for dept: 10
old   3: WHERE  DEPARTMENT_ID = &dept
new   3: WHERE  DEPARTMENT_ID = 10

DEPARTMENT_NAME
---------------
Administration

1 row selected.
```

Using Substitution Variables

Suppose that you have defined DEPT as a variable in your script, but you want to avoid the prompt for the value at runtime. SQL*Plus prompts you for a value only when the variable is undefined. You can define a *substitution variable* in SQL*Plus using the DEFINE command to provide a value. The variable will always have the CHAR datatype associated with it. Here is an example of defining a substitution variable:

```
SQL> DEFINE DEPT = 20
SQL> DEFINE DEPT
DEFINE DEPT              = "20" (CHAR)
SQL> LIST
  1   SELECT department_name
  2   FROM    departments
  3*  WHERE   department_id = &DEPT
SQL> /
old    3: WHERE  DEPARTMENT_ID = &DEPT
new    3: WHERE  DEPARTMENT_ID = 20


DEPARTMENT_NAME
---------------
Marketing


1 row selected.
SQL>
```

Using the DEFINE command without any arguments shows all the defined variables.

A . (dot) is used to append characters immediately after the substitution variable. The dot separates the variable name and the literal that follows immediately. If you need a dot to be part of the literal, provide two dots continuously. For example, the following query appends _REP to the user input when seeking a value from the JOBS table:

```
SQL> SELECT job_id, job_title FROM jobs
  2* WHERE  job_id = '&JOB._REP'
SQL> /
Enter value for job: MK
old    2: WHERE  JOB_ID = '&JOB._REP'
new    2: WHERE  JOB_ID = 'MK_REP'


JOB_ID     JOB_TITLE
---------- -----------------------
MK_REP     Marketing Representative


1 row selected.
SQL>
```

The old line with the variable and the new line with the substitution are displayed. You can turn off this display by using the command SET VERIFY OFF.

Saving a Variable for a Session

Consider the following SQL, saved to a file named ex01.sql. When you execute this script file, you will be prompted for the COL1 and COL2 values multiple times:

```
SQL> SELECT &COL1, &COL2
  2   FROM    &TABLE
  3   WHERE   &COL1 = '&VAL'
  4   ORDER BY &COL2
  5
SQL> SAVE ex01
Created file ex01.sql
SQL> @ex01
Enter value for col1: FIRST_NAME
Enter value for col2: LAST_NAME
old   1: SELECT &COL1, &COL2
new   1: SELECT FIRST_NAME, LAST_NAME
Enter value for table: EMPLOYEES
old   2: FROM    &TABLE
new   2: FROM    EMPLOYEES
Enter value for col1: FIRST_NAME
Enter value for val: John
old   3: WHERE   &COL1 = '&VAL'
new   3: WHERE   FIRST_NAME = 'John'
Enter value for col2: LAST_NAME
old   4: ORDER BY &COL2
new   4: ORDER BY LAST_NAME


FIRST_NAME            LAST_NAME
--------------------  ---------
John                  Chen
John                  Russell
John                  Seo

3 rows selected.
SQL>
```

The user can enter different or wrong values for each prompt. To avoid multiple prompts, use && (double ampersand), where the variable is saved for the session.

To clear a defined variable, you can use the UNDEFINE command. Let's edit the ex01.sql file to make it look like this:

```
SELECT &&COL1, &&COL2
FROM    &TABLE
WHERE   &COL1 = '&VAL'
ORDER BY &COL2
/
Enter value for col1: first_name
Enter value for col2: last_name
old    1: SELECT &&COL1, &&COL2
new    1: SELECT first_name, last_name
Enter value for table: employees
old    2: FROM &TABLE
new    2: FROM employees
Enter value for val: John
old    3: WHERE &COL1 = '&VAL'
new    3: WHERE first_name = 'John'
old    4: ORDER BY &COL1
new    4: ORDER BY first_name


FIRST_NAME            LAST_NAME
-------------------- -------------------------
John                 Chen
John                 Russell
John                 Seo


UNDEFINE COL1 COL2
```

Using Positional Notation for Variables

Instead of variable names, you can use positional notation, where each variable is identified by &1, &2, and so on. The values are assigned to the variables by position. Do this by putting an ampersand (&), followed by a numeral, in place of a variable name. Consider the following query:

```
SQL> SELECT department_name, department_id
  2  FROM    departments
  3  WHERE   &1 = &2;
Enter value for 1: DEPARTMENT_ID
Enter value for 2: 10
old    3: WHERE  &1 = &2
new    3: WHERE  DEPARTMENT_ID = 10
```

```
DEPARTMENT_NAME                DEPARTMENT_ID
------------------------------ -------------
Administration                            10
```

```
1 row selected.
SQL>
```

If you save the SQL as a script file, you can submit the substitution-variable values while invoking the script (as command-line arguments). Each time you run this command file, START replaces each &1 in the file with the first value (called an *argument*) after START *filename*, then replaces each &2 with the second value, and so forth. Here is an example of saving and running the previous query:

```
SQL> SAVE ex02
Created file ex02.sql
SQL> SET VERIFY OFF
SQL> @ex02 department_id 20
```

```
DEPARTMENT_NAME                DEPARTMENT_ID
------------------------------ -------------
Marketing                                 20
```

```
1 row selected.
SQL>
```

Although I did not specify two ampersands for positional substitution variables, SQL*Plus keeps the values of these variables for the session (since we passed the values as parameters to a script file). Next time you run any script with positional substitution variables, Oracle uses these values to execute the script.

Summary

This chapter started off with reviewing the fundamentals of SQL. You also saw an overview of SQL*Plus in this chapter. SQL*Plus is Oracle's native tool to interact with the database. You got a quick introduction to the Oracle datatypes, operators, and literals. You learned to write simple queries using the SELECT statement. You also learned to use the WHERE clause and the ORDER BY clause in this chapter.

The CHAR and VARCHAR2 datatypes are used to store alphanumeric information. The NUMBER datatype is used to store any numeric value. Date values can be stored using the DATE or TIMESTAMP datatypes. Oracle has a wide range of operators: arithmetic, concatenation, comparison, membership, logical, pattern matching, range, existence, and NULL checking. The CASE expression is used to bring conditional logic to SQL.

SQL*Plus supports all SQL statements and has its own formatting and enhancement commands. Using this tool, you can produce interactive SQL statements and formatted reports. SQL*Plus is the command-line interface to the database widely used by DBAs. SQL*Plus has its own buffer where SQL statements are buffered. You can edit the buffer using SQL*Plus editing commands. The DESCRIBE command is used to get information on a table, view, function, or procedure. Multiple SQL and SQL*Plus commands can be stored in a file and can be executed as a unit. Such files are called script files.

Data in the Oracle database is managed and accessed using SQL. A SELECT statement is the basic form of querying or reading records from the database table. You can limit or filter the rows using the WHERE clause. You can use the AND and OR logical operators to join multiple filter conditions. The ORDER BY clause is used to sort the result set in a particular order. You can use an ampersand (&) character to substitute a value at runtime.

Exam Essentials

Understand the operators.   Know the various operators that can be used in queries. The parentheses around an expression change the precedence of the operators.

Understand the WHERE clause.   The WHERE clause specifies a condition to limit the number or rows returned. You cannot use column alias names in this clause.

Understand the ORDER BY clause.   The ORDER BY clause is used to sort the result set from a query. You can specify ascending order or descending order for the sort. Ascending order is the default. Also know that column alias names can be used in the ORDER BY clause. You can also specify columns by their position.

Know how to specify string literals using the Q/q operator.   You can use the Q or q operator to specify the quote delimiters in string literals. Understand the difference between using the (, <, {, and [characters and other delimiters.

Know the order of clauses in the SELECT statement.   The SELECT statement must have a FROM clause. The WHERE clause, if it exists, should follow the FROM clause and precede the ORDER BY clause.

Know the use of the DUAL table.   The DUAL table is a dummy table in Oracle with one column and one row. This table is commonly used to get the values of system variables such as SYSDATE or USER.

Know the characters used for pattern matching.   The % character is used to match zero or more characters. The _ character is used to match one, and only one, character. The SQL operator used with a pattern-matching character is LIKE.

Know the sort order of NULL values in queries with ORDER BY clause.   By default, in an ascending-order sort, the NULL values appear at the bottom of the result set; that is, NULLs are sorted higher. For descending-order sorts, NULL values appear at the top of the result set—again, NULL values are sorted higher.

Review Questions

1. You issue the following query:

   ```
   SELECT salary "Employee Salary"
   FROM employees;
   ```

   How will the column heading appear in the result?
   A. EMPLOYEE SALARY
   B. EMPLOYEE_SALARY
   C. Employee Salary
   D. employee_salary

2. The EMP table is defined as follows:

Column	Datatype	Length
EMPNO	NUMBER	4
ENAME	VARCHAR2	30
SALARY	NUMBER	14,2
COMM	NUMBER	10,2
DEPTNO	NUMBER	2

   You perform the following two queries:

   ```
   1. SELECT empno enumber,  ename
      FROM emp ORDER BY 1;
   2. SELECT empno,  ename
      FROM emp ORDER BY  empno ASC;
   ```

   Which of the following is true?
   A. Statements 1 and 2 will produce the same result in data.
   B. Statement 1 will execute; statement 2 will return an error.
   C. Statement 2 will execute; statement 1 will return an error.
   D. Statements 1 and 2 will execute but produce different results.

3. You issue the following SELECT statement on the EMP table shown in question 2.

```
SELECT (200+((salary*0.1)/2)) FROM emp;
```

What will happen to the result if all the parentheses are removed?

A. No difference, because the answer will always be NULL.

B. No difference, because the result will be the same.

C. The result will be higher.

D. The result will be lower.

4. In the following SELECT statement, which component is a literal? (Choose all that apply.)

```
SELECT 'Employee Name: ' || ename
FROM emp where deptno = 10;
```

A. 10

B. ename

C. Employee Name:

D. ||

5. When you try to save 34567.2255 into a column defined as NUMBER(7,2), what value is actually saved?

A. 34567.00

B. 34567.23

C. 34567.22

D. 3456.22

6. What is the default display length of the DATE datatype column?

A. 18

B. 9

C. 19

D. 6

7. What will happen if you query the EMP table shown in question 2 with the following?

```
SELECT empno, DISTINCT ename, salary FROM emp;
```

A. EMPNO, unique values of ENAME, and then SALARY are displayed.

B. EMPNO and unique values of the two columns, ENAME and SALARY, are displayed.

C. DISTINCT is not a valid keyword in SQL.

D. No values will be displayed because the statement will return an error.

8. Which clause in a query limits the rows selected?

A. ORDER BY

B. WHERE

C. SELECT

D. FROM

9. The following listing shows the records of the EMP table:

EMPNO	ENAME	SALARY	COMM	DEPTNO
7369	SMITH	800		20
7499	ALLEN	1600	300	30
7521	WARD	1250	500	30
7566	JONES	2975		20
7654	MARTIN	1250	1400	30
7698	BLAKE	2850		30
7782	CLARK	2450	24500	10
7788	SCOTT	3000		20
7839	KING	5000	50000	10
7844	TURNER	1500	0	30
7876	ADAMS	1100		20
7900	JAMES	950		30
7902	FORD	3000		20
7934	MILLER	1300	13000	10

When you issue the following query, which value will be displayed in the first row?

```
SELECT empno
FROM emp
WHERE deptno = 10
ORDER BY ename DESC;
```

A. MILLER

B. 7934

C. 7876

D. No rows will be returned because ename cannot be used in the ORDER BY clause.

10. Refer to the listing of records in the EMP table in question 9. How many rows will the following query return?

```
SELECT * FROM emp WHERE ename BETWEEN 'A' AND 'C'
```

A. 4

B. 2

C. A character column cannot be used in the BETWEEN operator.

D. 3

11. Refer to the EMP table in question 2. When you issue the following query, which line has an error?

```
1. SELECT empno "Enumber", ename "EmpName"
2. FROM emp
3. WHERE deptno = 10
4. AND   "Enumber" = 7782
5. ORDER BY "Enumber";
```

A. 1

B. 5

C. 4

D. No error; the statement will finish successfully.

12. You issue the following query:

```
SELECT empno, ename
FROM emp
WHERE empno = 7782 OR empno = 7876;
```

Which other operator can replace the OR condition in the WHERE clause?

A. IN

B. BETWEEN .. AND ..

C. LIKE

D. <=

E. >=

13. The following are clauses of the SELECT statement:

```
1. WHERE
2. FROM
3. ORDER BY
```

In which order should they appear in a query?

A. 1, 3, 2

B. 2, 1, 3

C. 2, 3, 1

D. The order of these clauses does not matter.

14. Which statement searches for PRODUCT_ID values that begin with DI_ from the ORDERS table?

A. SELECT * FROM ORDERS
WHERE PRODUCT_ID = 'DI%';

B. SELECT * FROM ORDERS
WHERE PRODUCT_ID LIKE 'DI_' ESCAPE '\';

C. SELECT * FROM ORDERS
WHERE PRODUCT_ID LIKE 'DI_%' ESCAPE '\';

D. SELECT * FROM ORDERS
   WHERE PRODUCT_ID LIKE 'DI_' ESCAPE '\';

E. SELECT * FROM ORDERS
   WHERE PRODUCT_ID LIKE 'DI_%' ESCAPE '\';

15. COUNTRY_NAME and REGION_ID are valid column names in the COUNTRIES table. Which one of the following statements will execute without an error?

A. SELECT country_name, region_id,
   CASE region_id = 1 THEN 'Europe',
        region_id = 2 THEN 'America',
        region_id = 3 THEN 'Asia',
        ELSE 'Other' END Continent
   FROM   countries;

B. SELECT country_name, region_id,
   CASE (region_id WHEN 1 THEN 'Europe',
                   WHEN 2 THEN 'America',
                   WHEN 3 THEN 'Asia',
                   ELSE 'Other') Continent
   FROM   countries;

C. SELECT country_name, region_id,
   CASE region_id WHEN 1 THEN 'Europe'
                  WHEN 2 THEN 'America'
                  WHEN 3 THEN 'Asia'
                  ELSE 'Other' END Continent
   FROM   countries;

D. SELECT country_name, region_id,
   CASE region_id WHEN 1 THEN 'Europe'
                  WHEN 2 THEN 'America'
                  WHEN 3 THEN 'Asia'
                  ELSE 'Other' Continent
   FROM   countries;

16. Which special character is used to query all the columns from the table without listing each column by name?

A. %

B. &

C. @

D. *

17. The EMPLOYEE table has the following data:

EMP_NAME	HIRE_DATE	SALARY
SMITH	17-DEC-90	800
ALLEN	20-FEB-91	1600
WARD	22-FEB-91	1250
JONES	02-APR-91	5975
WARDEN	28-SEP-91	1250
BLAKE	01-MAY-91	2850

What will be the value in the first row of the result set when the following query is executed?

```
SELECT hire_date FROM employee
ORDER BY salary, emp_name;
```

A.   02-APR-91

B.   17-DEC-90

C.   28-SEP-91

D.   The query is invalid, because you cannot have a column in the ORDER BY clause that is not part of the SELECT clause.

18. Which SQL statement will query the EMPLOYEES table for FIRST_NAME, LAST_NAME, and SALARY of all employees in DEPARTMENT_ID 40 in the alphabetical order of last name?

A.
```
SELECT first_name last_name salary
FROM    employees
ORDER BY last_name
WHERE   department_id = 40;
```

B.
```
SELECT first_name, last_name, salary
FROM    employees
ORDER BY last_name ASC
WHERE   department_id = 40;
```

C.
```
SELECT first_name last_name salary
FROM    employees
WHERE   department_id = 40
ORDER BY last_name ASC;
```

D.
```
SELECT first_name, last_name, salary
FROM    employees
WHERE   department_id = 40
ORDER BY last_name;
```

E.
```
SELECT first_name, last_name, salary
FROM    TABLE employees
WHERE   department_id IS 40
ORDER BY last_name ASC;
```

19. When doing pattern matching using the LIKE operator, which character is used as the default escape character by Oracle?

A. |

B.   /

C.   \

D.   There is no default escape character in Oracle.

20. Column alias names cannot be used in which clause?

   A. SELECT clause

   B. WHERE clause

   C. ORDER BY clause

   D. None of the above

21. What is wrong with the following statements submitted in SQL*Plus?

```
DEFINE V_DEPTNO = 20
SELECT LAST_NAME, SALARY
FROM    EMPLOYEES
WHERE DEPARTMENT_ID = V_DeptNo;
```

   A. Nothing is wrong. The query lists the employee name and salary of the employees who belong to department 20.

   B. The DEFINE statement declaration is wrong.

   C. The substitution variable is not preceded with the & character.

   D. The substitution variable in the WHERE clause should be V_DEPTNO instead of V_DeptNo.

22. Which two statements regarding substitution variables are true?

   A. &*variable* is defined by SQL*Plus, and its value will be available for the duration of the session.

   B. &&*variable* is defined by SQL*Plus, and its value will be available for the duration of the session.

   C. &*n* (where *n* is a any integer) variables are defined by SQL*Plus when values are passed in as arguments to the script, and their values will be available for the duration of the session.

   D. &&*variable* is defined by SQL*Plus, and its value will be available only for every reference to that variable in the current SQL.

23. Look at the data in table PRODUCTS. Which SQL will list the items on the BL shelves? (Show the result with the most available quantity at the top row.)

```
PRODUCT_ID PRODUCT_NAME          SHELF   AVAILABLE_QTY
---------- --------------------  ------  -------------
      1001 CREST                 BL36              354
      1002 COLGATE               BL36               54
      1003 AQUAFRESH             BL37               43
      2002 SUNNY-D               LA21               53
      2003 CAPRISUN              LA22               45
```

A. SELECT * FROM products
   WHERE shelf like '%BL'
   ORDER BY available_qty SORT DESC;

B. SELECT * FROM products
   WHERE shelf like 'BL%';

C. SELECT * FROM products
   WHERE shelf = 'BL%'
   ORDER BY available_qty DESC;

D. SELECT * FROM products
   WHERE shelf like 'BL%'
   ORDER BY available_qty DESC;

E. SELECT * FROM products
   WHERE shelf like 'BL%'
   ORDER BY available_qty SORT;

24. The EMP table has the following data:

EMPNO	ENAME	SAL	COMM
7369	SMITH	800	
7499	ALLEN	1600	300
7521	WARD	1250	500
7566	JONES	2975	
7654	MARTIN	1250	1400
7698	BLAKE	2850	
7782	CLARK	2450	
7788	SCOTT	3000	
7839	KING	5000	
7844	TURNER	1500	0
7876	ADAMS	1100	
7900	JAMES	950	
7902	FORD	3000	
7934	MILLER	1300	

Consider the following two SQL statements:

1. SELECT empno, ename, sal, comm
   FROM emp WHERE comm IN (0, NULL);

2. SELECT empno, ename, sal, comm
   FROM emp WHERE comm = 0 OR comm IS NULL;

A. 1 and 2 will produce the same result.

B. 1 will error; 2 will work fine.

C. 1 and 2 will produce different results.

D. 1 and 2 will work but will not return any rows.

Answers to Review Questions

1. C. Column alias names enclosed in quotation marks will appear as typed. Spaces and mixed case appear in the column alias name only when the alias is enclosed in double quotation marks.

2. A. Statements 1 and 2 will produce the same result. You can use the column name, column alias, or column position in the ORDER BY clause. The default sort order is ascending. For a descending sort, you must explicitly specify that order with the DESC keyword.

3. B. In the arithmetic evaluation, multiplication and division have precedence over addition and subtraction. Even if you do not include the parentheses, salary*0.1 will be evaluated first. The result is then divided by 2, and its result is added to 200.

4. A, C. Character literals in the SQL statement are enclosed in single quotation marks. Literals are concatenated using ||. Employee Name: is a character literal, and 10 is a numeric literal.

5. B. Since the numeric column is defined with precision 7 and scale 2, you can have five digits in the integer part and two digits after the decimal point. The digits after the decimal are rounded.

6. B. The default display format of DATE column is DD-MON-YY, whose length is 9.

7. D. DISTINCT is used to display a unique result row, and it should follow immediately after the keyword SELECT. Uniqueness is identified across the row, not a single column.

8. B. The WHERE clause is used to limit the rows returned from a query. The WHERE clause condition is evaluated, and rows are returned only if the result is TRUE. The ORDER BY clause is used to display the result in certain order.

9. B. There are three records belonging to DEPTNO 10: EMPNO 7934 (MILLER), 7839 (KING), and 7782 (CLARK). When you sort their names by descending order, MILLER is the first row to display. You can use alias names and columns that are not in the SELECT clause in the ORDER BY clause.

10. D. Here, a character column is compared against a string using the BETWEEN operator, which is equivalent to ename >= 'A' AND ename <= 'C'. The name CLARK will not be included in this query, because 'CLARK' is > 'C'.

11. C. Column alias names cannot be used in the WHERE clause. They can be used in the ORDER BY clause.

12. A. The IN operator can be used. You can write the WHERE clause as WHERE empno IN (7782, 7876);.

13. B. The FROM clause appears after the SELECT statement, followed by WHERE and ORDER BY clauses. The FROM clause specifies the table names, the WHERE clause limits the result set, and the ORDER BY clause sorts the result.

14. C. Since _ is a special pattern-matching character, you need to include the ESCAPE clause in LIKE. The % character matches any number of characters including 0, and _ matches a single character.

15. C. A CASE expression begins with the keyword CASE and ends with the keyword END.

16. D. An asterisk (*) is used to denote all columns in a table.

17. B. The default sorting order for a numeric column is ascending. The columns are sorted first by salary and then by name, so the row with the lowest salary is displayed first. It is perfectly valid to use a column in the ORDER BY clause that is not part of the SELECT clause.

18. D. In the SELECT clause, the column names should be separated by commas. An alias name may be provided for each column with a space or using the keyword AS. The FROM clause should appear after the SELECT clause. The WHERE clause appears after the FROM clause. The ORDER BY clause comes after the WHERE clause.

19. D. There is no default escape character in Oracle for pattern matching. If your search includes pattern-matching characters such as _ or %, define an escape character using the ESCAPE keyword in the LIKE operator.

20. B. Column alias names cannot be used in the WHERE clause of the SQL statement. In the ORDER BY clause, you can use the column name or alias name, or you can indicate the column by its position in the SELECT clause.

21. C. The query will return an error, because the substitution variable is used without an ampersand (&) character. In this query, Oracle treats V_DEPTNO as another column name from the table and returns an error. Substitution variables are not case sensitive.

22. B, C. When a variable is preceded by double ampersands, SQL*Plus defines that variable. Similarly, when you pass values to a script using START *script_name arguments*, SQL*Plus defines those variables. Once a variable is defined, its value will be available for the duration of the session or until you use UNDEFINE *variable*.

23. D. % is the wild character to pattern-match for any number of characters. Option A is almost correct, except for the SORT keyword in the ORDER BY clause, which will produce an error since it is not a valid syntax. Option B will produce results but will sort them in the order you want. Option C will not return any rows because LIKE is the operator for pattern matching, not =. Option E has an error similar to Option A.

24. C. In the first SQL, the comm IN (0, NULL) will be treated as comm = 0 OR comm = NULL. For all NULL comparisons, you should use IS NULL instead of = NULL. The first SQL will return only one row where comm = 0, whereas the second SQL will return all the rows that have comm = NULL as well as comm = 0.

Chapter

2

Using Single-Row Functions

ORACLE DATABASE 11*g*: SQL FUNDAMENTALS I EXAM OBJECTIVES COVERED IN THIS CHAPTER:

✓ **Using Single-Row Functions to Customize Output**

- Describe various types of functions available in SQL

- Use character, number, and date functions in SELECT statements

✓ **Using Conversion Functions and Conditional Expressions**

- Describe various types of conversion functions that are available in SQL

- Use the TO_CHAR, TO_NUMBER, and TO_DATE conversion functions

- Apply conditional expressions in a SELECT statement

Functions are programs that take zero or more arguments and return a single value. Oracle has built a number of functions into SQL, and these functions can be called from SQL statements. The functions could be classified into many groups:

- Single-row functions
- Aggregate functions (also known as *group functions*)
- Analytical functions and regular expression functions
- National-language functions
- Object-reference functions
- Programmer-defined functions

The certification exam focuses on single-row and aggregate functions, so only those types are covered in this book. Single-row functions are covered in this chapter, and aggregate functions are covered in Chapter 3, "Using Group Functions."

Single-row functions operate on expressions derived from columns or literals, and they are executed once for each row retrieved. In this chapter, I will cover which single-row functions are available, the rules for how to use them, and what to expect on the exam regarding single-row functions.

Single-row functions also include conversion functions. Conversion functions are used to convert the datatype of the input value to a different datatype. The Oracle database has conditional expressions and functions. I discussed the conditional expression CASE in Chapter 1, "Introducing SQL." In this chapter, I will discuss the conditional function DECODE.

Single-Row Function Fundamentals

Many types of single-row functions are built into SQL. These include character, numeric, date, conversion, and miscellaneous single-row functions, as well as programmer-written stored functions.

All single-row functions can be incorporated into SQL (and PL/SQL). You can use these single-row functions in the SELECT, WHERE, and ORDER BY clauses of SELECT statements. For example, the following query includes the TO_CHAR, UPPER, and SOUNDEX single-row functions:

```
SELECT first_name, TO_CHAR(hire_date,'Day, DD-Mon-YYYY')
FROM employees
```

```
WHERE UPPER(first_name) LIKE 'AL%'
ORDER BY SOUNDEX(first_name);
```

Single-row functions also can appear in other types of statements, such as the SET clause of an UPDATE statement, the VALUES clause of an INSERT statement, and the WHERE clause of a DELETE statement. The certification exam tends to focus on using functions in SELECT statements, so I will use examples of SELECT statements in this chapter.

The built-in functions presented in this chapter are grouped by topic (character functions, date functions, and so on), and within each topic they appear in alphabetical order. Before I get into the different types of functions, I'll start with the functions that are used to handle NULL values.

 Functions can be nested so that the output from one function is used as input to another. Nested functions can include single-row functions nested within group functions or group functions nested within either single-row functions or other group functions.

Functions for NULL Handling

One area in which beginners frequently have difficulty and where even veterans sometimes stumble is the treatment of NULLs. You can expect at least one question on the exam to address the use of NULLs, but it probably won't look like a question on the use of NULLs.

NULL values represent unknown data or a lack of data. Any operation on a NULL results in a NULL. This NULL-in/NULL-out model is followed for most functions, as well. Oracle 11g has five NULL-handling functions; I'll give special attention to the NVL, NVL2, and COALESCE functions because these are commonly used.

NVL

The NVL function is used to replace a NULL value with a literal value. NVL takes two arguments, NVL(*x1*, *x2*), where *x1* and *x2* are expressions. The NVL function returns *x2* if *x1* is NULL. If *x1* is not NULL, then *x1* is returned. The arguments x1 and x2 can be of any datatype. If *x1* and *x2* are not of the same datatype, Oracle tries to convert them to the same datatype before performing the comparison.

For example, suppose you need to calculate the total compensation in the EMPLOYEES table, which contains SALARY and COMMISSION_PCT columns:

```
SELECT first_name, salary, commission_pct,
       salary + (salary * commission_pct) compensation
FROM employees
WHERE first_name LIKE 'T%';
```

FIRST_NAME	SALARY	COMMISSION_PCT	COMPENSATION
TJ	2100		
Trenna	3500		
Taylor	9600	.2	11520
Timothy	2900		

You see that only Taylor had the total compensation calculated in the SQL; all others have their total compensation as NULL. This is because any operation on NULL results in a NULL.

You can use the NVL function to substitute a zero in place of any NULL you encounter, like this:

```
SELECT first_name, salary, commission_pct,
       salary + (salary * NVL(commission_pct,0)) compensation
FROM employees
WHERE first_name LIKE 'T%';
```

FIRST_NAME	SALARY	COMMISSION_PCT	COMPENSATION
TJ	2100		2100
Trenna	3500		3500
Tayler	9600	.2	11520
Timothy	2900		2900

When you used the NVL function to substitute zero for NULL, you got the total compensation calculated correctly. For the employees who do not have a commission, the salary and compensation are the same.

NVL2

The function NVL2 is a variation of NVL. NVL2 takes three arguments, NVL2(*x1, x2, x3*), where *x1*, *x2*, and *x3* are expressions. NVL2 returns *x3* if *x1* is NULL, and *x2* if *x1* is not NULL.

For the example presented in the previous section, you could also use the NVL2 function and write the code a bit differently:

```
SELECT first_name, salary, commission_pct, NVL2(commission_pct,
       salary + salary * commission_pct, salary) compensation
FROM employees
WHERE first_name LIKE 'T%';
```

FIRST_NAME	SALARY	COMMISSION_PCT	COMPENSATION
TJ	2100		2100
Trenna	3500		3500
Tayler	9600	.2	11520
Timothy	2900		2900

Using the NVL2 function, if COMMISSION_PCT is not NULL, then salary + salary * commission_pct is returned. If COMMISSION_PCT is NULL, then just SALARY is returned.

The NVL function allows you to perform some value substitution for NULLs. The NVL2 function, on the other hand, allows you to implement an IF...THEN...ELSE construct based on the nullity of data. Both are useful tools to deal with NULL values.

Be prepared for a possible exam question that tests your knowledge of when to use an NVL function in a calculation. Such a question probably won't mention NVL and may not look like it is testing your knowledge of NULLs. If sample data is given as an exhibit, be sure to look for data columns with NULL values and whether they are used in the SQL presented to you.

COALESCE

COALESCE is a generalization of the NVL function. COALESCE(*exp_list*) takes more than one argument, where *exp_list* is a list of arguments separated by comma. This function returns the first non-NULL value in *exp_list*. If all expressions in *exp_list* are NULL, then NULL is returned. Each expression in *exp_list* should be the same datatype, or else Oracle tries to convert them implicitly.

For example, COALESCE(x1, x2, x3) would be evaluated as the following:

- If x1 is NULL, check x2, or else return x1. Stop.

- If x2 is NULL, check x3, or else return x2. Stop.

- If x3 is NULL, return NULL, or else return x3. Stop.

Consider the following example. The objective is to find the total salary based on COMMISSION_PCT. If COMMISSION_PCT is not NULL, calculate SALARY using COMMISSION_PCT. If COMMISSION_PCT is NULL, then give $100 as commission. If SALARY is not defined (NULL) for an employee, give the minimum salary of $900.

```
SELECT last_name, salary, commission_pct AS comm,
       COALESCE(salary+salary*commission_pct,
                salary+100, 900) compensation
FROM employees
WHERE last_name like 'T%';
```

LAST_NAME	SALARY	COMM	COMPENSATION
Taylor	8600	.2	10320
Taylor	3200		3300
Tobias			900
Tucker	10000	.3	13000
Tuvault	7000	.15	8050

As you can see in the example, using the COALESCE function helps you avoid writing several IF...THEN conditions. You could write the same SQL using the CASE statement you learned about in Chapter 1 as follows:

```
SELECT last_name, salary, commission_pct AS comm,
       (CASE WHEN salary IS NULL THEN 900
          WHEN commission_pct IS NOT NULL
             THEN salary+salary*commission_pct
          WHEN commission_pct IS NULL THEN salary+100
          ELSE 0 END) AS compensation
 FROM employees
 WHERE last_name like 'T%';
```

LAST_NAME	SALARY	COMM	COMPENSATION
Taylor	8600	.2	10320
Taylor	3200		3300
Tobias			900
Tucker	10000	.3	13000
Tuvault	7000	.15	8050

Try using WHEN salary IS NULL as the third condition in the CASE statement (instead of the first condition), and find out whether you see any difference in the result.

Using Single-Row Character Functions

Single-row character functions operate on character data. Most have one or more character arguments, and most return character values. Character functions take the character input value and return a character or numeric value. If the input to the function is a literal, be sure to enclose it in single quotes. The exam focuses on many commonly used character functions such as SUBSTR, INSTR, and LENGTH. When reading about these functions, pay particular attention to the commonly used functions. Even experienced programmers get confused with the REPLACE and TRANSLATE functions. In the following sections, I will review the single-row character functions in detail.

Character Function Overview

Table 2.1 summarizes the single-row character functions. I will cover each of these functions in the "Character Function Descriptions" section.

TABLE 2.1   Character Function Summary

Function	Description
ASCII	Returns the ASCII decimal equivalent of a character
CHR	Returns the character given the decimal equivalent
CONCAT	Concatenates two strings; same as the operator ||
INITCAP	Returns the string with the first letter of each word in uppercase
INSTR	Finds the numeric starting position of a string within a string
INSTRB	Same as INSTR but counts bytes instead of characters
LENGTH	Returns the length of a string in characters
LENGTHB	Returns the length of a string in bytes
LOWER	Converts a string to all lowercase
LPAD	Left-fills a string to a set length using a specified character
LTRIM	Strips leading characters from a string
REPLACE	Performs substring search and replace
RPAD	Right-fills a string to a set length using a specified character
RTRIM	Strips trailing characters from a string
SOUNDEX	Returns a phonetic representation of a string
SUBSTR	Returns a section of the specified string, specified by numeric character positions
SUBSTRB	Returns a section of the specified string, specified by numeric byte positions
TRANSLATE	Performs character search and replace
TRIM	Strips leading, trailing, or both leading and trailing characters from a string
UPPER	Converts a string to all uppercase

The functions ASCII, INSTR, LENGTH, and REGEXP_INSTR return number values, though they take character datatype as the input.

Character Function Descriptions

Over the years, Oracle has added several functions to its library to make the lives of developers easy so that they do not have to write built-in functions. Oracle has a function for most of the day-to-day programming needs. Before you write your own custom-developed piece of code, it is always a good idea to scan the Oracle documentation on built-in functions.

The character functions in the following sections are arranged in alphabetical order, with descriptions and examples of each one.

ASCII

ASCII(*c1*) takes a single argument, where *c1* is a character string. This function returns the ASCII decimal equivalent of the first character in *c1*. See also CHR() for the inverse operation.

```
SELECT ASCII('A') Big_A, ASCII('z') Little_Z, ASCII('AMER')
FROM dual;


     BIG_A    LITTLE_Z ASCII('AMER')
---------- ---------- --------------
        65         122            65
```

CHR

CHR(*i* [USING NCHAR_CS]) takes a single argument, where *i* is an integer. This function returns the character equivalent of the decimal (binary) representation of the character. If the optional USING NCHAR_CS is included, the character from the national character set is returned. The default behavior is to return the character from the database character set.

```
SELECT CHR(65), CHR(122), CHR(223)
FROM dual;


CHAR65 CHAR122 CHAR233
------ ------- -------
A      z       ß
```

CONCAT

CONCAT(*c1*, *c2*) takes two arguments, where *c1* and *c2* are both character strings. This function returns *c2* appended to *c1*. If *c1* is NULL, then *c2* is returned. If *c2* is NULL, then *c1* is returned. If both *c1* and *c2* are NULL, then NULL is returned. CONCAT returns the same results as using the concatenation operator: *c1*||*c2*. In the following example, notice the use of the nested function—a function inside a function—as an argument:

```
SELECT CONCAT(CONCAT(first_name, ' '), last_name) employee_name,
       first_name || ' ' || last_name AS alternate_method
FROM employees
WHERE department_id = 30;
```

```
EMPLOYEE_NAME              ALTERNATE_METHOD
------------------------   -------------------
Den Raphaely              Den Raphaely
Alexander Khoo            Alexander Khoo
Shelli Baida             Shelli Baida
Sigal Tobias             Sigal Tobias
Guy Himuro               Guy Himuro
Karen Colmenares         Karen Colmenares
```

INITCAP

INITCAP(*c1*) takes a single argument, where *c1* is a character string. This function returns *c1* with the first character of each word in uppercase and all others in lowercase. Words are delimited by white space or characters that are not alphanumeric.

```
SELECT data_value, INITCAP(data_value) initcap_example
FROM sample_data;
```

```
DATA_VALUE            INITCAP_EXAMPLE
--------------------  --------------------
THE three muskETeers  The Three Musketeers
ali and*41*thieves    Ali And*41*Thieves
mississippi           Mississippi
mister INDIA          Mister India
```

INSTR

INSTR(*c1*, *c2*[, *i*[, *j*]]) takes four arguments, where *c1* and *c2* are character strings and *i* and *j* are integers. This function returns the numeric character position in *c1* where the *j* occurrence of *c2* is found. The search begins at the *i* character position in *c1*. INSTR returns a 0 when the requested string is not found. If *i* is negative, the search is performed backward, from right to left, but the position is still counted from left to right. Both *i* and *j* default to 1, and *j* cannot be negative.

The following example finds the first occurrence of i in the string starting from the fourth position of the string:

```
SELECT data_value, INSTR(data_value,'i',4,1) instr_example
FROM sample_data;
```

```
DATA_VALUE              INSTR_EXAMPLE Comment
--------------------    ------------- ---------------------------------------------
THE three muskETeers              0 There is no "i" in the data value; so "0"
ali and*41*thieves               14 The first "i" is skipped, since we start
                                    at the 4th position. So the "i" in the 14th
                                    position is picked
mississippi                       5 the first i in 2nd position is skipped
mister INDIA                      0 INDIA has an "I" (upper case); so no
                                    match for "i"
```

Here is another example using a negative argument for the beginning character position. The search for the is string will start at the fourth position from the end and move to the left.

```
SELECT data_value, INSTR(data_value,'is',-4,1) instr_example
FROM sample_data;
```

```
DATA_VALUE              INSTR_EXAMPLE
--------------------    -------------
THE three muskETeers              0
ali and*41*thieves               0
mississippi                      5
mister INDIA                     2
```

INSTRB

INSTRB(c1,c2[,i[,j]]) is the same as INSTR(), except it returns bytes instead of characters. For single-byte character sets, INSTRB() is equivalent to INSTR().

LENGTH

LENGTH(c) takes a single argument, where c is a character string. This function returns the numeric length in characters of c. If c is NULL, a NULL is returned.

```
SELECT data_value, LENGTH(data_value) length_example
FROM sample_data;
```

DATA_VALUE	LENGTH_EXAMPLE
THE three muskETeers	20
ali and*41*thieves	18
mississippi	11
mister INDIA	12

LENGTHB

LENGTHB(c) is the same as LENGTH(), except it returns bytes instead of characters. For single-byte character sets, LENGTHB() is equivalent to LENGTH().

LOWER

LOWER(c) takes a single argument, where c is a character string. This function returns the character string c with all characters in lowercase. See also UPPER for the inverse operation.

```
SELECT data_value, LOWER(data_value) lower_example
FROM sample_data;
```

DATA_VALUE	LOWER_EXAMPLE
THE three muskETeers	the three musketeers
ali and*41*thieves	ali and*41*thieves
mississippi	mississippi
mister INDIA	mister india

LPAD

LPAD(c1, i [,c2]) takes three arguments, where c1 and c2 are character strings and i is an integer. This function returns the character string c1 expanded in length to i characters, using c2 to fill in space as needed on the left side of c1. If c1 is more than i characters, it is truncated to i characters. c2 defaults to a single space. See also RPAD.

The following example adds * to the SALARY column toward the left side. Since it does not specify a fill-in character when LPAD is applied to last_name, Oracle uses the default space as the fill-in character.

```
SELECT LPAD(last_name,10) lpad_lname,
       LPAD(salary,8,'*') lpad_salary
FROM employees
WHERE last_name like 'J%';
```

```
LPAD_LNAME LPAD_SAL
---------- --------
   Johnson ****6200
     Jones ****2800
```

LTRIM

LTRIM(*c1* [,*c2*]) takes two arguments, where *c1* and *c2* are character strings. This function returns *c1* without any leading characters that appear in *c2*. If no *c2* characters are leading characters in *c1*, then *c1* is returned unchanged. *c2* defaults to a single space. See also RTRIM and TRIM.

```
SELECT LTRIM('Mississippi','Mis') test1
      ,LTRIM('Rpadded         ') test2
      ,LTRIM('         Lpadded') test3
      ,LTRIM('     Lpadded', 'Z') test4
FROM dual;
```

```
TES TEST2             TEST3   TEST4
--- ----------------- ------- ------------
ppi Rpadded           Lpadded     Lpadded
```

In the previous example, all occurrences of the trimmed characters M, i, and s are trimmed from the input string Mississippi, beginning on the left (with M) and continuing until the first character that is not an M, i, or s is encountered. Note that the trailing i is not trimmed; only the leading characters are removed. In TEST4, there is no occurrence of Z, so the input string is returned unchanged.

REPLACE

REPLACE(*c1*, *c2* [,*c3*]) takes three arguments, where *c1*, *c2*, and *c3* are character strings. This function returns *c1* with all occurrences of *c2* replaced with *c3*. *c3* defaults to NULL. If *c3* is NULL, all occurrences of *c2* are removed. If *c2* is NULL, then *c1* is returned unchanged. If *c1* is NULL, then NULL is returned.

```
SELECT REPLACE('uptown','up','down') FROM dual;
```

```
REPLACE(
--------
downtown
```

This function can come in handy when you need to do some dynamic substitutions. For example, suppose you have a number of indexes that were created in the _DATA tablespace instead of in the _INDX tablespace:

```
SELECT index_name, tablespace_name
FROM user_indexes
WHERE tablespace_name like '%DATA%';


INDEX_NAME          TABLESPACE_NAME
---------------     ----------------
PK_DEPT             HR_DATA
PK_PO_MASTER        PO_DATA
```

You can generate the Data Definition Language (DDL) to rebuild these misplaced indexes in the correct location. In this scenario, you know your tablespace naming convention has an INDX tablespace for every DATA tablespace. You use the REPLACE function to generate the new tablespace name, replacing DATA with INDX. So, the HR index is rebuilt in the HR_INDX tablespace, and the PO index is rebuilt in the PO_INDX tablespace.

```
SELECT 'ALTER INDEX '||index_name||
                    ' rebuild tablespace '||
REPLACE(tablespace_name, 'DATA', 'INDX')|| '; ' DDL
FROM user_indexes
WHERE tablespace_name LIKE '%DATA%';


DDL
-----------------------------------------------------
ALTER INDEX PK_DEPT rebuild tablespace HR_INDX;
ALTER INDEX PK_PO_MASTER rebuild tablespace PO_INDX;
```

RPAD

RPAD(*c1*, *i* [, *c2*]) takes three arguments, where *c1* and *c2* are character strings and *i* is an integer. This function returns the character string *c1* expanded in length to *i* characters, using *c2* to fill in space as needed on the right side of *c1*. If *c1* is more than *i* characters, it is truncated to *i* characters. *c2* defaults to a single space. See also LPAD.

```
SELECT RPAD(first_name,15,'.') rpad_fname, lpad(job_id,12,'.') lpad_jid
FROM employees
WHERE first_name like 'B%';


RPAD_FNAME          LPAD_JID
---------------     ------------
Bruce..........     .....IT_PROG
Britney........     ....SH_CLERK
```

RTRIM

RTRIM(*c1* [,*c2*]) takes two arguments, where *c1* and *c2* are character strings. This function returns *c1* without any trailing characters that appear in *c2*. If no *c2* characters are trailing characters in *c1*, then *c1* is returned unchanged. *c2* defaults to a single space. See also LTRIM and TRIM.

```
SELECT RTRIM('Mississippi','ip') test1
      ,RTRIM('Rpadded         ') test2
      ,RTRIM('Rpadded    ', 'Z') test3
      ,RTRIM('        Lpadded') test4
FROM dual;


TEST1   TEST2   TEST3       TEST4
------- ------- ----------- ----------------
Mississ Rpadded Rpadded              Lpadded
```

SOUNDEX

SOUNDEX(*c1*) takes a single argument, where *c1* is a character string. This function returns the Soundex phonetic representation of *c1*. The SOUNDEX function is usually used to locate names that sound alike. The example returns the records with first names that sound like "Stevan."

```
SELECT first_name, last_name
FROM employees
WHERE SOUNDEX(first_name) = SOUNDEX('Stevan');


FIRST_NAME           LAST_NAME
-------------------- -------------------------
Steven               King
Steven               Markle
Stephen              Stiles
```

SUBSTR

SUBSTR(*c1*, *x* [, *y*]) takes three arguments, where *c1* is a character string and both *x* and *y* are integers. This function returns the portion of *c1* that is *y* characters long, beginning at position *x*. If *x* is negative, the position is counted backward (that is, right to left). This function returns NULL if *y* is 0 or negative. *y* defaults to the remainder of string *c1*.

```
SELECT SUBSTR('The Three Musketeers',1,3) Part1
      ,SUBSTR('The Three Musketeers',5,5) Part2
```

```
       ,SUBSTR('The Three Musketeers',11)  Part3
       ,SUBSTR('The Three Musketeers',-5)  Part4
FROM dual;


PAR PART2 PART3      PART4
--- ----- ---------- -----
The Three Musketeers teers
```

 Real World Scenario

Parsing the Filename from the Whole Path

Let's look at a real example from the life of a DBA. Suppose you want to extract only the filename from dba_data_files without the path name; you could use the following SQL. Here the INSTR function is nested inside a SUBSTR function. Single-row functions can be nested to any level. When functions are nested, the innermost function is evaluated first. The INSTR function is used to find the character position where the last \ appears in the filename string (looking for the first occurrence from the end). This position is passed into the SUBSTR function as the start position.

```
SELECT file_name,
       SUBSTR(file_name, INSTR(file_name,'\', -1,1)+1) name
FROM dba_data_files;


FILE_NAME                                NAME
---------------------------------------- -------------
C:\ORACLE\ORADATA\W11GR1\USERS01.DBF     USERS01.DBF
C:\ORACLE\ORADATA\W11GR1\UNDOTBS01.DBF   UNDOTBS01.DBF
C:\ORACLE\ORADATA\W11GR1\SYSAUX01.DBF    SYSAUX01.DBF
C:\ORACLE\ORADATA\W11GR1\SYSTEM01.DBF    SYSTEM01.DBF
C:\ORACLE\ORADATA\W11GR1\EXAMPLE01.DBF   EXAMPLE01.DBF
```

To perform the same operation on Unix or Linux databases, replace \ in the INSTR function with / because / is used on Linux/Unix to separate directories.

Let's review another example using the Linux or Unix platform. Suppose you want to find out all the file systems (mount points) used by your database; you could use the following SQL:

```
SELECT DISTINCT
       SUBSTR(file_name, 1, INSTR(file_name,'/', 1,2)-1) fs_name
FROM dba_data_files;
```

```
FS_NAME
----------------------------
/u01
/u05
/ora_temp
/ora_undo
```

In this example, you started looking for the second occurrence of / using the INSTR function and used SUBSTR to extract only the characters from 1 through the location before the second occurrence of / in the filename (hence the −1).

SUBSTRB

SUBSTRB(*c1*, *i*[, *j*]) takes three arguments, where *c1* is a character string and both *i* and *j* are integers. This function is the same as SUBSTR, except *i* and *j* are counted in bytes instead of characters. For single-byte character sets, they are equivalent.

TRANSLATE

TRANSLATE(*c1*, *c2*, *c3*) takes three arguments, where *c1*, *c2*, and *c3* are character strings. This function returns *c1* with all occurrences of characters in *c2* replaced with the positionally corresponding characters in *c3*. A NULL is returned if any of *c1*, *c2*, or *c3* is NULL. If *c3* has fewer characters than *c2*, the unmatched characters in *c2* are removed from *c1*. If *c2* has fewer characters than *c3*, the unmatched characters in *c3* are ignored. TRANSLATE is similar to the REPLACE function. REPLACE substitutes a single string from another string, whereas TRANSLATE makes several single-character one-to-one substitutions.

The following example substitutes * for a, # for e, and $ for i, and it removes o and u from the last_name column:

```
SELECT last_name, TRANSLATE(last_name, 'aeiou', '*#$') no_vowel
FROM employees
WHERE last_name like 'S%';
```

```
LAST_NAME                NO_VOWEL
------------------------ --------------
Sarchand                 S*rch*nd
Sciarra                  Sc$*rr*
Seo                      S#
Smith                    Sm$th
Sullivan                 Sll$v*n
Sully                    Slly
```

Here is another example, where the case is reversed; uppercase letters are converted to lowercase, and lowercase letters are converted to uppercase:

```
SELECT data_value, TRANSLATE(data_value,
'abcdefghijklmnopqrstuvwxyzABCDEFGHIJKLMNOPQRSTUVWXYZ',
'ABCDEFGHIJKLMNOPQRSTUVWXYZabcdefghijklmnopqrstuvwxyz')
FROM sample_data;


DATA_VALUE           TRANSLATE(DATA_VALUE
-------------------- --------------------
THE three muskETeers the THREE MUSKetEERS
ali and*41*thieves   ALI AND*41*THIEVES
mississippi          MISSISSIPPI
mister INDIA         MISTER india
```

TRIM

TRIM([[c1] c2 FROM] c3) can take three arguments, where c2 and c3 are character strings. If present, c1 can be one of the following literals: LEADING, TRAILING, or BOTH. This function returns c3 with all c1 (leading, trailing, or both) occurrences of characters in c2 removed. A NULL is returned if any of c1, c2, or c3 is NULL. c1 defaults to BOTH. c2 defaults to a space character. c3 is the only mandatory argument. If c2or c3 is NULL, the function returns a NULL. It's equivalent to applying both LTRIM and RTRIM on the string c3.

```
SELECT TRIM('   fully padded   ') test1
      ,TRIM('   left padded') test2
      ,TRIM('right padded   ') test3
FROM dual;


TEST1        TEST2        TEST3
------------ ------------ ------------
fully padded left padded right padded
```

UPPER

UPPER(c) takes a single argument, where c is a character string. This function returns the character string c with all characters in uppercase. UPPER frequently appears in WHERE clauses, when you're not sure of the case of the data in the table. See also LOWER.

```
SELECT first_name, last_name
FROM employees
WHERE UPPER(first_name) = 'JOHN';
```

```
FIRST_NAME           LAST_NAME
-------------------- --------------------
John                 Chen

SELECT data_value, UPPER(data_value) upper_data
FROM sample_data;

DATA_VALUE           UPPER_DATA
-------------------- --------------------
THE three muskETeers THE THREE MUSKETEERS
ali and*41*thieves   ALI AND*41*THIEVES
mississippi          MISSISSIPPI
mister INDIA         MISTER INDIA
```

Using Single-Row Numeric Functions

When you think of numeric functions, the tasks that come to mind are finding a total, finding the average, counting the number of records, and so on. These numeric functions are group functions that operate on one or more rows. I'll discuss group functions in Chapter 3, "Using Group Functions."

In the following sections, I will review the numeric functions used on single rows. Single-row numeric functions operate on numeric data and perform some kind of mathematical or arithmetic manipulation. When using a literal in a numeric function, do not enclose it in single quotes. Literals in single quotes are treated as a character datatype.

Numeric Function Overview

Table 2.2 summarizes the single-row numeric functions in Oracle 11g. I will cover each of these functions in the "Numeric Function Descriptions" section.

TABLE 2.2   Numeric Function Summary

Function	Description
ABS	Returns the absolute value
ACOS	Returns the arc cosine
ASIN	Returns the arc sine
ATAN	Returns the arc tangent

TABLE 2.2   Numeric Function Summary *(continued)*

Function	Description
ATAN2	Returns the arc tangent; takes two inputs
BITAND	Returns the result of a bitwise AND on two inputs
CEIL	Returns the next higher integer
COS	Returns the cosine
COSH	Returns the hyperbolic cosine
EXP	Returns the base of natural logarithms raised to a power
FLOOR	Returns the next smaller integer
LN	Returns the natural logarithm
LOG	Returns the logarithm
MOD	Returns the modulo (remainder) of a division operation
NANVL	Returns an alternate number if the value is Not a Number (NaN) for BINARY_FLOAT and BINARY_DOUBLE numbers
POWER	Returns a number raised to an arbitrary power
REMAINDER	Returns the remainder in a division operation
ROUND	Rounds a number
SIGN	Returns an indicator of sign: negative, positive, or zero
SIN	Returns the sine
SINH	Returns the hyperbolic sine
SQRT	Returns the square root of a number
TAN	Returns the tangent
TANH	Returns the hyperbolic tangent
TRUNC	Truncates a number
WIDTH_BUCKET	Creates equal-width histograms

Numeric Function Descriptions

Numeric functions have numeric arguments and return numeric values. The trigonometric functions all operate on radians, not degrees.

The numeric functions are arranged in alphabetical order, with descriptions and examples of each one.

SIGN, ROUND, and TRUNC are most commonly used numeric functions—pay particular attention to them. FLOOR, CEIL, MOD, and REMAINDER are also important functions that can appear in the test. TRUNC and ROUND functions can take numeric input or a datetime input. These two functions are discussed in the "Using Single-Row Date Functions" section to illustrate their behavior with a datetime datatype input.

ABS

ABS(n) takes a single argument, where n is a numeric datatype (NUMBER, BINARY_FLOAT or BINARY_DOUBLE). This function returns the absolute value of n.

```
SELECT ABS(-52) negative, ABS(52)  positive
FROM dual;


  NEGATIVE    POSITIVE
---------- ----------
        52          52
```

ACOS

ACOS(n) takes a single argument, where n is a numeric datatype between –1 and 1. This function returns the arc cosine of n expressed in radians, accurate to 30 digits of precision.

```
SELECT ACOS(-1) PI, ACOS(0) ACOSZERO,
       ACOS(.045) ACOS045, ACOS(1) ZERO
FROM dual;


        PI    ACOSZERO    ACOS045        ZERO
---------- ---------- ---------- ----------
3.14159265 1.57079633 1.52578113          0
```

ASIN

ASIN(n) takes a single argument, where n is a numeric datatype between –1 and 1. This function returns the arc sine of n expressed in radians, accurate to 30 digits of precision.

```
SELECT ASIN(1) high, ASIN(0) middle, ASIN(-1) low
FROM dual;
```

```
     HIGH    MIDDLE       LOW
---------- ---------- ----------
1.57079633          0 -1.5707963
```

ATAN

ATAN(*n*) takes a single argument, where *n* is a numeric datatype. This function returns the arc tangent of *n* expressed in radians, accurate to 30 digits of precision.

```
SELECT ATAN(9E99) high, ATAN(0) middle, ATAN(-9E99) low
FROM dual;
```

```
     HIGH    MIDDLE       LOW
---------- ---------- ----------
1.57079633          0 -1.5707963
```

ATAN2

ATAN2(*n1*, *n2*) takes two arguments, where *n1* and *n2* are numbers. This function returns the arc tangent of *n1* and *n2* expressed in radians, accurate to 30 digits of precision. ATAN2(*n1,n2*) is equivalent to ATAN(*n1/n2*), if *n1* and *n2* are positive integers.

```
SELECT ATAN2(9E99,1) high, ATAN2(0,3.1415) middle, ATAN2(-9E99,1) low
FROM dual;
```

```
     HIGH    MIDDLE       LOW
---------- ---------- ----------
1.57079633          0 -1.5707963
```

BITAND

BITAND(*n1*, *n2*) takes two arguments, where *n1* and *n2* are number data type. This function performs a bitwise AND operation on the two input values and returns the results, also an integer. It is used to examine bit fields.

Here are two examples of BITAND. The first one performs a bitwise AND operation on 6 (binary 0110) and 3 (binary 0011). The result is 2 (binary 0010). Similarly, the bitwise AND between 8 (binary 1000) and 2 (binary 0010) is 0 (0000).

```
SELECT BITAND(6,3) T1, BITAND(8,2) T2
FROM dual;
```

```
        T1         T2
---------- ----------
         2          0
```

CEIL

CEIL(*n*) takes a single argument, where *n* is a numeric datatype. This function returns the smallest integer that is greater than or equal to *n*. CEIL rounds up to a whole number. See also FLOOR.

```
SELECT CEIL(9.8), CEIL(-32.85), CEIL(0), CEIL(5)
FROM dual;


CEIL(9.8)  CEIL(-32.85)    CEIL(0)    CEIL(5)
---------- ------------ ---------- ----------
       10          -32          0          5
```

COS

COS(*n*) takes a single argument, where *n* is a numeric datatype in radians. This function returns the cosine of *n*, accurate to 36 digits of precision.

```
SELECT COS(-3.14159) FROM dual;


COS(-3.14159)
-------------
           -1
```

COSH

COSH(*n*) takes a single argument, where *n* is a numeric datatype. This function returns the hyperbolic cosine of *n*, accurate to 36 digits of precision.

```
SELECT COSH(1.4) FROM dual;


 COSH(1.4)
----------
2.15089847
```

EXP

EXP(*n*) takes a single argument, where *n* is a numeric datatype. This function returns e (the base of natural logarithms) raised to the *n* power, accurate to 36 digits of precision.

```
SELECT EXP(1) "e" FROM dual;


         e
----------
2.71828183
```

FLOOR

FLOOR(*n*) takes a single argument, where *n* is a numeric datatype. This function returns the largest integer that is less than or equal to *n*. FLOOR rounds down to a whole number. See also CEIL.

```
SELECT FLOOR(9.8), FLOOR(-32.85), FLOOR(137)
FROM dual;


FLOOR(9.8) FLOOR(-32.85) FLOOR(137)
---------- ------------- ----------
         9           -33        137
```

LN

LN(*n*) takes a single argument, where *n* is a numeric datatype greater than 0. This function returns the natural logarithm of *n*, accurate to 36 digits of precision.

```
SELECT LN(2.7) FROM dual;


   LN(2.7)
----------
.993251773
```

LOG

LOG(*n1*, *n2*) takes two arguments, where *n1* and *n2* are numeric datatypes. This function returns the logarithm base *n1* of *n2*, accurate to 36 digits of precision.

```
SELECT LOG(8,64), LOG(3,27), LOG(2,1024), LOG(2,8)
FROM dual;


 LOG(8,64)  LOG(3,27) LOG(2,1024)   LOG(2,8)
---------- ---------- ----------- ----------
         2          3          10          3
```

MOD

MOD(*n1*, *n2*) takes two arguments, where *n1* and *n2* are any numeric datatype. This function returns *n1* modulo *n2*, or the remainder of *n1* divided by *n2*. If *n1* is negative, the result is negative. The sign of *n2* has no effect on the result. If n2 is zero, the result is n1. See also REMAINDER.

```
SELECT MOD(14,5), MOD(8,2.5), MOD(-64,7), MOD(12,0)
FROM dual;
```

```
MOD(14,5) MOD(8,2.5) MOD(-64,7) MOD(12,0)
---------- ---------- ---------- ---------
        4         .5         -1        12
```

NANVL

This function is used with BINARY_FLOAT and BINARY_DOUBLE datatype numbers to return an alternate value if the input is NaN.

The following example defines the NULL display as ? to show NULL value. The TO_BINARY_FLOAT function (discussed later in the chapter) is used to convert input to a BINARY_FLOAT datatype number.

```
SET NULL ?
SELECT NANVL(TO_BINARY_FLOAT('NaN'), 0) T1,
       NANVL(TO_BINARY_FLOAT('NaN'), NULL) T2
FROM dual;


        T1         T2
---------- ----------
         0 ?
```

POWER

POWER(*n1*, *n2*) takes two arguments, where *n1* and *n2* are numeric datatypes. This function returns *n1* to the *n2* power.

```
SELECT POWER(2,10), POWER(3,3), POWER(5,3), POWER(2,-3)
FROM dual;

POWER(2,10) POWER(3,3) POWER(5,3) POWER(2,-3)
----------- ---------- ---------- -----------
       1024         27        125        .125
```

REMAINDER

REMAINDER(*n1*, *n2*) takes two arguments, where *n1* and *n2* are any numeric datatype. This function returns the remainder of *n1* divided by *n2*. If *n1* is negative, the result is negative. The sign of *n2* has no effect on the result. If *n2* is zero and the datatype of *n1* is NUMBER, an error is returned; if the datatype of *n1* is BINARY_FLOAT or BINARY_DOUBLE, NaNis returned. See also MOD.

```
SELECT REMAINDER(13,5), REMAINDER(12,5), REMAINDER(12.5, 5)
FROM dual;
```

```
REMAINDER(13,5) REMAINDER(12,5) REMAINDER(12.5,5)
--------------- --------------- -----------------
            -2               2               2.5
```

The difference between MOD and REMAINDER is that MOD uses the FLOOR function, whereas REMAINDER uses the ROUND function in the formula. If you apply MOD function to the previous example, the results are the same except for the first column:

```
SELECT MOD(13,5), MOD(12,5), MOD(12.5, 5)
FROM dual;


 MOD(13,5)   MOD(12,5) MOD(12.5,5)
---------- ---------- -----------
         3          2         2.5
```

Here is another example of using REMAINDER with a BINARY_FLOAT number, having *n2* as zero:

```
SELECT REMAINDER(TO_BINARY_FLOAT('13.0'), 0) RBF
from dual;


       RBF
----------
       Nan
```

ROUND

ROUND(*n1* [,*n2*]) takes two arguments, where *n1* is a numeric datatype and *n2* is an integer. This function returns *n1* rounded to *n2* digits of precision to the right of the decimal. If *n2* is negative, *n1* is rounded to the left of the decimal. If n2 is omitted, the default is zero. This function is similar to TRUNC.

```
SELECT ROUND(123.489), ROUND(123.489, 2),
       ROUND(123.489, -2), ROUND(1275, -2)
FROM dual;

ROUND(123.489) ROUND(123.489,2) ROUND(123.489,-2) ROUND(1275,-2)
-------------- ---------------- ----------------- --------------
           123           123.49               100           1300
```

SIGN

SIGN(*n*) takes a single argument, where *n* is a numeric datatype. This function returns –1 if *n* is negative, 1 if *n* is positive, and 0 if *n* is 0.

```
SELECT SIGN(-2.3), SIGN(0), SIGN(47)
FROM dual;
```

```
SIGN(-2.3)    SIGN(0)    SIGN(47)
---------- ---------- ----------
       -1          0           1
```

SIN

SIN(*n*) takes a single argument, where *n* is a number in radians. This function returns the sine of *n*, accurate to 36 digits of precision.

```
SELECT SIN(1.57079) FROM dual;
```

```
SIN(1.57079)
------------
           1
```

SINH

SINH(*n*) takes a single argument, where *n* is a number. This function returns the hyperbolic sine of *n*, accurate to 36 digits of precision.

```
SELECT SINH(1) FROM dual;
```

```
  SINH(1)
----------
1.17520119
```

SQRT

SQRT(*n*) takes a single argument, where *n* is a numeric datatype. This function returns the square root of *n*.

```
SELECT SQRT(64), SQRT(49), SQRT(5)
FROM dual;
```

```
 SQRT(64)   SQRT(49)    SQRT(5)
---------- ---------- ----------
        8          7 2.23606798
```

TAN

TAN(*n*) takes a single argument, where *n* is a numeric datatype in radians. This function returns the tangent of *n*, accurate to 36 digits of precision.

```
SELECT TAN(1.57079633/2) "45_degrees"
FROM dual;


45_Degrees
----------
         1
```

TANH

TANH(*n*) takes a single argument, where *n* is a numeric datatype. This function returns the hyperbolic tangent of *n*, accurate to 36 digits of precision.

```
SELECT TANH( ACOS(-1) ) hyp_tan_of_pi
FROM dual;


HYP_TAN_OF_PI
-------------
   .996272076
```

TRUNC

TRUNC(*n1* [,*n2*]) takes two arguments, where *n1* is a numeric datatype and *n2* is an integer. This function returns *n1* truncated to *n2* digits of precision to the right of the decimal. If *n2* is negative, *n1* is truncated to the left of the decimal. See also ROUND.

```
SELECT TRUNC(123.489), TRUNC(123.489, 2),
       TRUNC(123.489, -2), TRUNC(1275, -2)
FROM dual;


TRUNC(123.489) TRUNC(123.489,2) TRUNC(123.489,-2) TRUNC(1275,-2)
-------------- ---------------- ----------------- --------------
           123           123.48               100           1200
```

WIDTH_BUCKET

You can use WIDTH_BUCKET(*n1*, *min_val*, *max_val*, *buckets*) to build histograms of equal width. The first argument *n1* can be an expression of a numeric or datetime datatype. The second and third arguments, *min_val* and *max_val*, indicate the end points for the histogram's range. The fourth argument, *buckets*, indicates the number of buckets.

The following example divides the salary into a 10-bucket histogram within the range 2,500 to 11,000. If the salary falls below 2500, it will be in the underflow bucket (bucket 0), and if the salary exceeds 11,000, it will be in the overflow bucket (*buckets* + 1).

```
SELECT first_name, salary,
       WIDTH_BUCKET(salary, 2500, 11000, 10) hist
FROM employees
WHERE first_name like 'J%';
```

FIRST_NAME	SALARY	HIST
Jennifer	4400	3
John	8200	7
Jose Manuel	7800	7
Julia	3200	1
James	2400	0
James	2500	1
Jason	3300	1
John	2700	1
Joshua	2500	1
John	14000	11
Janette	10000	9
Jonathon	8600	8
Jack	8400	7
Jean	3100	1
Julia	3400	2
Jennifer	3600	2

Using Single-Row Date Functions

Single-row date functions operate on *datetime* datatypes. A datetime is a coined word to identify datatypes used to define dates and times. The datetime datatypes in Oracle 11*g* are DATE, TIMESTAMP, and INTERVAL. Most have one or more date arguments, and most return a datetime value. Date data is stored internally as numbers. The whole-number portion is the number of days since January 1, 4712 BC, and the decimal portion is the fraction of a day (for example, 0.5=12 hours).

Date-Format Conversion

National-language support (NLS) parameters and arguments allow you to internationalize your Oracle database system. NLS internationalizations include date representations, character sets, alphabets, and alphabetical ordering.

Oracle will implicitly or automatically convert its numeric date data to and from character data using the format model specified with NLS_DATE_FORMAT. The default format is *DD-MON-RR* (see Table 2.7). You can change this date-format model for each session with the ALTER SESSION SET NLS_DATE_FORMAT command. Here's an example:

```
SQL> SELECT SYSDATE FROM dual;

SYSDATE
---------
31-MAR-08

SQL> ALTER SESSION SET NLS_DATE_FORMAT='DD-Mon-YYYY HH24:MI:SS';

Session altered.

SQL> SELECT SYSDATE FROM dual;

SYSDATE
--------------------
31-Mar-2008 10:19:11
```

This ALTER SESSION command will set the *implicit conversion* mechanism to display date data in the format specified, such as 12-Dec-2002 15:45:32. This conversion works both ways. If the character string '30-Nov-2002 20:30:00' were inserted, updated, or assigned to a date column or variable, the correct date would be entered.

If the format model were *DD/MM/YY* or *MM/DD/YY*, there could be some ambiguity in the conversion of some dates, such as 12 April 2000 (04/12/00 or 12/04/00). To avoid problems with implicit conversions, Oracle provides explicit date/character-conversion functions: TO_DATE, TO_CHAR, TO_TIMESTAMP, TO_TIMESTAMP_TZ, TO_DSINTERVAL, and TO_YMINTERVAL. These explicit conversion functions are covered in the "Using Single-Row Conversion Functions" section later in this chapter.

Date-Function Overview

Table 2.3 summarizes the single-row date functions. I will cover each of these functions in the "Date-Function Descriptions" section.

TABLE 2.3   Date-Function Summary

Function	Description
ADD_MONTHS	Adds a number of months to a date
CURRENT_DATE	Returns the current date and time in a DATE datatype
CURRENT_TIMESTAMP	Returns the current date and time in a TIMESTAMP datatype
DBTIMEZONE	Returns the database's time zone
EXTRACT	Returns a component of a date/time expression
FROM_TZ	Returns a timestamp with time zone for a given timestamp
LAST_DAY	Returns the last day of a month
LOCALTIMESTAMP	Returns the current date and time in the session time zone
MONTHS_BETWEEN	Returns the number of months between two dates
NEW_TIME	Returns the date/time in a different time zone
NEXT_DAY	Returns the next day of a week following a given date
ROUND	Rounds a date/time
SESSIONTIMEZONE	Returns the time zone for the current session
SYS_EXTRACT_UTC	Returns the UTC (GMT) for a timestamp with a time zone
SYSDATE	Returns the current date and time in the DATE datatype
SYSTIMESTAMP	Returns the current timestamp in the TIMESTAMP datatype
TRUNC	Truncates a date to a given granularity
TZ_OFFSET	Returns the offset from UTC for a time zone name

Date-Function Descriptions

The date functions are arranged in alphabetical order except the first three, with descriptions and examples of each one. SYSDATE, SYSTIMESTAMP, and LOCALTIMESTAMP are used in many examples, and hence I'll discuss them first.

SYSDATE

SYSDATE takes no arguments and returns the current date and time to the second for the operating-system host where the database resides. The value is returned in a DATE data-type. The format that the value returned is based on NLS_DATE_FORMAT, which can be altered for the session using the ALTER SESSION SET NLS_DATE_FORMAT command. The format mask for dates and timestamps are discussed later in the chapter.

```
ALTER SESSION SET NLS_DATE_FORMAT='DD-MON-YYYY HH:MI:SS AM';
Session altered.

SELECT SYSDATE FROM dual;

SYSDATE
----------------------
31-MAR-2008 12:00:13 PM
```

SYSDATE is one of the most commonly used Oracle functions. There's a good chance you'll see it on the exam. Since the SYSDATE value is returned based on the time of the host server where the database resides, the result will be the same for a user sitting in New York or one in Hong Kong.

SYSTIMESTAMP

SYSTIMESTAMP takes no arguments and returns a TIMESTAMP WITH TIME ZONE for the current database date and time (the time of the host server where the database resides). The fractional second is returned with six digits of precision. The format of the value returned is based on NLS_TIMESTAMP_TZ_FORMAT, which can be altered for the session using the ALTER SESSION SET NLS_TIMESTAMP_TZ_FORMAT command.

```
SQL> SELECT SYSDATE, SYSTIMESTAMP FROM dual;

SYSDATE
SYSTIMESTAMP
------------------------------------
31-MAR-08
31-MAR-08 12.01.49.280000 PM -05:00

ALTER SESSION SET NLS_DATE_FORMAT='DD-MON-YYYY HH24:MI:SS';
Session altered.
```

```
ALTER SESSION SET
    NLS_TIMESTAMP_TZ_FORMAT='YYYY-MON-DD HH:MI:SS.FF TZR';
Session altered.

SELECT SYSDATE, SYSTIMESTAMP FROM dual;

SYSDATE
SYSTIMESTAMP
------------------------------------
31-MAR-2008 12:09:51
2008-MAR-31 12:09:51.429000 -05:00
```

LOCALTIMESTAMP

LOCALTIMESTAMP([p]) returns the current date and time in the session's time zone to p digits of precision. p can be 0 to 9 and defaults to 6. This function returns the value in the datatype TIMESTAMP. You can set the client time zone using the ALTER SESSION SET TIME_ZONE command.

The following example illustrates LOCALTIMESTAMP and how to change the time zone for the session. The database is in U.S./Central time zone, and the client is in U.S./Eastern time zone. See also CURRENT_TIMESTAMP.

```
SELECT SYSTIMESTAMP, LOCALTIMESTAMP FROM dual;

SYSTIMESTAMP
LOCALTIMESTAMP
-----------------------------------------------------
31-MAR-08 01.02.49.272000 PM -05:00
31-MAR-08 02.02.49.272000 PM

ALTER SESSION SET TIME_ZONE = '-8:00';
```

ADD_MONTHS

ADD_MONTHS(d, i) takes two arguments, where d is a date and i is an integer. This function returns the date d plus i months. If i is a decimal number, the database will implicitly convert it to an integer by truncating the decimal portion (for example, 3.9 becomes 3). If <d> is the last day of the month or the resulting month has fewer days, then the result is the last day of the resulting month.

```
SELECT SYSDATE, ADD_MONTHS(SYSDATE, -1) PREV_MONTH,
    ADD_MONTHS(SYSDATE, 12) NEXT_YEAR
FROM dual;
```

```
SYSDATE    PREV_MONT NEXT_YEAR
--------- --------- ---------
31-MAR-08 29-FEB-08 31-MAR-09
```

CURRENT_DATE

CURRENT_DATE takes no arguments and returns the current date in the Gregorian calendar for the session's (client) time zone. This function is similar to SYSDATE, whereas SYSDATE returns the current date for the database's (host's) time zone. You can set the client time zone using the ALTER SESSION SET TIME_ZONE command.

The following example illustrates CURRENT_DATE and how to change the time zone for the session. The database is in U.S./Central time zone, and the client is in U.S./Mountain time zone.

```
ALTER SESSION SET NLS_DATE_FORMAT='DD-Mon-YYYY HH24:MI:SS';
Session altered.

SELECT SYSDATE, CURRENT_DATE FROM dual;

SYSDATE              CURRENT_DATE
-------------------- --------------------
31-Mar-2008 10:52:34 31-Mar-2008 09:52:35

ALTER SESSION SET TIME_ZONE = 'US/Eastern';
Session altered.

SELECT SYSDATE, CURRENT_DATE FROM dual;

SYSDATE              CURRENT_DATE
-------------------- --------------------
31-Mar-2008 10:53:46 31-Mar-2008 11:53:47
```

CURRENT_TIMESTAMP

CURRENT_TIMESTAMP([*p*]) returns the current date and time in the session's time zone to *p* digits of precision. *p* can be an integer 0 through 9 and defaults to 6. See also LOCALTIMESTAMP. This function is similar to CURRENT_DATE. CURRENT_DATE returns result in the DATE datatype, whereas CURRENT_TIMESTAMP returns the result in the TIMESTAMP WITH TIME ZONE datatype.

```
SQL> SELECT CURRENT_DATE, CURRENT_TIMESTAMP FROM dual;

CURRENT_DATE
CURRENT_TIMESTAMP
--------------------------------------
31-Mar-2008 12:23:43
31-MAR-08 12.23.43.305000 PM US/EASTERN
```

DBTIMEZONE

DBTIMEZONE returns the database's time zone, as set by the latest CREATE DATABASE or ALTER DATABASE SET TIME_ZONE statement. Note that after changing the database time zone with the ALTER DATABASE statement, the database must be bounced (restarted) for the change to take effect. The time zone is a character string specifying the hours and minutes offset from UTC (Coordinated Universal Time, also known as GMT, or Greenwich mean time) or a time zone region name. The valid time zone region names can be found in the TZNAME column of the view V$TIMEZONE_NAMES. The default time zone for the database is UTC (00:00) if you do not explicitly set the time zone during database creation.

```
SQL> SELECT DBTIMEZONE FROM dual;

DBTIME
------
+00:00
```

EXTRACT

EXTRACT(c FROM dt) extracts and returns the specified component c of date/time or interval expression dt. The valid components are YEAR, MONTH, DAY, HOUR, MINUTE, SECOND, TIMEZONE_HOUR, TIMEZONE_MINUTE, TIMEZONE_REGION, and TIMEZONE_ABBR. The specified component must exist in the expression. So, to extract a TIMEZONE_HOUR, the date/time expression must be a TIMESTAMP WITH TIME ZONE datatype.

Though HOUR, MINUTE, and SECOND exist in the DATE datatype, you can extract only YEAR, MONTH, and DAY from the DATE dataype expressions.

```
SELECT SYSDATE, EXTRACT(YEAR FROM SYSDATE) year_d
FROM dual;

SYSDATE               YEAR_D
--------------------  ----------
31-MAR-2008 12:29:02      2008
```

You can extract YEAR, MONTH, DAY, HOUR, MINUTE, and SECOND from the TIMESTAMP datatype expression. You can extract all the components from the TIMESTAMP WITH TIMEZONE datatype expression.

```
SELECT LOCALTIMESTAMP,
       EXTRACT(YEAR FROM LOCALTIMESTAMP) YEAR_TS,
       EXTRACT(DAY FROM LOCALTIMESTAMP) DAY_TS,
       EXTRACT(SECOND FROM LOCALTIMESTAMP) SECOND_TS
FROM dual;

LOCALTIMESTAMP                  YEAR_TS DAY_TS  SECOND_TS
------------------------------  ------- ------- ---------
31-MAR-08 02.09.32.972000 PM       2008      31    32.972
```

FROM_TZ

FROM_TZ(*ts*, *tz*) returns a TIMESTAMP WITH TIME ZONE for the timestamp *ts* using time zone value *tz*. The character string *tz* specifies the hours and minutes offset from UTC or is a time zone region name. The valid time zone region names can be found in the TZNAME column of the view V$TIMEZONE_NAMES.

```
SELECT LOCALTIMESTAMP, FROM_TZ(LOCALTIMESTAMP, 'Japan') Japan,
FROM_TZ(LOCALTIMESTAMP, '-5:00') Central
FROM dual;

LOCALTIMESTAMP
JAPAN
CENTRAL
--------------------------------------
31-MAR-08 03.17.38.447000 PM
31-MAR-08 03.17.38.447000 PM JAPAN
31-MAR-08 03.17.38.447000 PM -05:00
```

LAST_DAY

LAST_DAY(*d*) takes a single argument, where *d* is a date. This function returns the last day of the month for the date *d*. The return datatype is DATE.

```
SELECT SYSDATE,
       LAST_DAY(SYSDATE)  END_OF_MONTH,
       LAST_DAY(SYSDATE)+1 NEXT_MONTH
FROM dual;

SYSDATE     END_OF_MONTH NEXT_MONTH
----------- ------------ -----------
09-SEP-2007 30-SEP-2007  01-OCT-2007
```

MONTHS_BETWEEN

MONTHS_BETWEEN(*d1*, *d2*) takes two arguments, where *d1* and *d2* are both dates. This function returns the number of months that *d2* is later than *d1*. A whole number is returned if *d1* and *d2* are the same day of the month or if both dates are the last day of a month.

```
SELECT MONTHS_BETWEEN('31-MAR-08', '30-SEP-08') E1,
       MONTHS_BETWEEN('11-MAR-08', '30-SEP-08') E2,
       MONTHS_BETWEEN('01-MAR-08', '30-SEP-08') E3,
       MONTHS_BETWEEN('31-MAR-08', '30-SEP-07') E4
FROM dual;

        E1         E2         E3         E4
---------- ---------- ---------- ----------
        -6 -6.6129032 -6.9354839          6
```

NEW_TIME

NEW_TIME(*d>*, *tz1*, *tz2*) takes three arguments, where *d* is a date and both *tz1* and *tz2* are one of the time zone constants. This function returns the date in time zone *tz2* for date *d* in time zone *tz1*.

```
SELECT SYSDATE Dallas, NEW_TIME(SYSDATE, 'CDT', 'HDT') Hawaii
FROM dual;

DALLAS               HAWAII
-------------------- --------------------
31-MAR-2008 14:34:03 31-MAR-2008 10:34:03
```

Table 2.4 lists the time zone constraints.

TABLE 2.4 Time Zone Constants

Code	Time Zone
GMT	Greenwich mean time
NST	Newfoundland standard time
AST	Atlantic standard time
ADT	Atlantic daylight time
BST	Bering standard time

TABLE 2.4   Time Zone Constants *(continued)*

Code	Time Zone
BDT	Bering daylight time
CST	Central standard time
CDT	Central daylight time
EST	Eastern standard time
EDT	Eastern daylight time
MST	Mountain standard time
MDT	Mountain daylight time
PST	Pacific standard time
PDT	Pacific daylight time
YST	Yukon standard time
YDT	Yukon daylight time
HST	Hawaii-Alaska standard time
HDT	Hawaii-Alaska daylight time

NEXT_DAY

NEXT_DAY(*d*, *dow*) takes two arguments, where *d* is a date and *dow* is a text string containing the full or abbreviated day of the week in the session's language. This function returns the next *dow* following *d*. The time portion of the return date is the same as the time portion of *d*.

```
SELECT SYSDATE, NEXT_DAY(SYSDATE,'Thu') NEXT_THU,
       NEXT_DAY('31-OCT-2008', 'Tue') Election_Day
FROM dual;


SYSDATE              NEXT_THU             ELECTION_DAY
-------------------- -------------------- --------------------
31-MAR-2008 14:53:54 03-APR-2008 14:53:54 04-NOV-2008 00:00:00
```

ROUND

ROUND(<*d*> [,*fmt*]) takes two arguments, where *d* is a date and *fmt* is a character string containing a date-format string. This function returns *d* rounded to the granularity specified in *fmt*. If fmt is omitted, d is rounded to the nearest day.

```
SELECT SYSDATE, ROUND(SYSDATE,'HH24') ROUND_HOUR,
       ROUND(SYSDATE) ROUND_DATE, ROUND(SYSDATE,'MM') NEW_MONTH,
       ROUND(SYSDATE,'YY') NEW_YEAR
FROM dual;


SYSDATE                ROUND_HOUR            ROUND_DATE
NEW_MONTH              NEW_YEAR
-------------------- -------------------- --------------------
31-MAR-2008 14:59:58 31-MAR-2008 15:00:00 01-APR-2008 00:00:00
01-APR-2008 00:00:00 01-JAN-2008 00:00:00
```

SESSIONTIMEZONE

SESSIONTIMEZONE takes no arguments and returns the database's time zone offset as per the last ALTER SESSION statement. SESSIONTIMEZONE will default to DBTIMEZONE if it is not changed with an ALTER SESSION statement.

```
SELECT DBTIMEZONE, SESSIONTIMEZONE
FROM dual;


DBTIMEZONE  SESSIONTIMEZONE
----------- ---------------
US/Central  -05:00
```

SYS_EXTRACT_UTC

SYS_EXTRACT_UTC(*ts*) takes a single argument, where *ts* is a TIMESTAMP WITH TIME ZONE. This function returns the UTC (GMT) time for the timestamp *ts*.

```
SELECT CURRENT_TIMESTAMP local,
       SYS_EXTRACT_UTC(CURRENT_TIMESTAMP) GMT
FROM dual;


LOCAL
GMT
----------------------------------------
31-MAR-08 04.06.53.731000 PM US/EASTERN
31-MAR-08 08.06.53.731000 PM
```

TRUNC

TRUNC(d [, fmt]) takes two arguments, where d is a date and fmt is a character string containing a date-format string. This function returns d truncated to the granularity specified in fmt. See also ROUND.

```
SELECT SYSDATE, TRUNC(SYSDATE,'HH24') CURR_HOUR,
       TRUNC(SYSDATE) CURR_DATE, TRUNC(SYSDATE,'MM') CURR_MONTH,
       TRUNC(SYSDATE,'YY') CURR_YEAR
FROM dual;


SYSDATE              CURR_HOUR            CURR_DATE
CURR_MONTH           CURR_YEAR
-------------------- -------------------- --------------------
31-MAR-2008 15:04:21 31-MAR-2008 15:00:00 31-MAR-2008 00:00:00
01-MAR-2008 00:00:00 01-JAN-2008 00:00:00
```

TZ_OFFSET

TZ_OFFSET(tz) takes a single argument, where tz is a time zone offset or time zone name. This function returns the numeric time zone offset for a textual time zone name. The valid time zone names can be obtained from the TZNAME column in the V$TIMEZONE_NAMES view.

```
SELECT TZ_OFFSET(SESSIONTIMEZONE) NEW_YORK,
       TZ_OFFSET('US/Pacific') LOS_ANGELES,
       TZ_OFFSET('Europe/London') LONDON,
       TZ_OFFSET('Asia/Singapore') SINGAPORE
FROM dual;


NEW_YOR LOS_ANG LONDON  SINGAPO
------- ------- ------- -------
-04:00  -07:00  +01:00  +08:00
```

Using Single-Row Conversion Functions

Single-row *conversion functions* operate on multiple datatypes. The TO_CHAR and TO_NUMBER functions have a significant number of formatting codes that can be used to display date and number data in a wide assortment of representations.

You can use the conversion functions to convert a numeric value to a character or a character value to a numeric or datetime value. Character datatypes in Oracle 11*g* are CHAR, VARCHAR2, NCHAR, NVARCHAR2, and CLOB. Numeric datatypes in Oracle

11*g* are NUMBER, BINARY_DOUBLE, and BINARY_FLOAT. Datetime datatypes in Oracle 11*g* are DATE, TIMESTAMP, and INTERVAL.

Datatype conversion are required and used extensively in day-to-day SQL use. When a user enters data, it may be in character format, which you may need to convert to a date or number. Sometimes the data is in a specific format and you have to tell Oracle how to treat the data using conversion functions and format codes. In the following sections, you will learn the various conversions and how to use them.

 The exam may include a question that tests your recollection of some of the nuances of these formatting codes. General usage in a professional setting would afford you the opportunity to look them up in a reference. In the test setting, however, you must recall them on your own.

Conversion-Function Overview

Table 2.5 summarizes the single-row conversion functions. I will cover each of these functions in the "Conversion-Function Descriptions" section.

TABLE 2.5   Conversion-Function Summary

Function	Description
ASCIISTR	Converts characters to ASCII
BIN_TO_NUM	Converts a string of bits to a number
CAST	Converts datatypes
CHARTOROWID	Casts a character to the ROWID datatype
COMPOSE	Converts to Unicode
CONVERT	Converts from one character set to another
DECOMPOSE	Decomposes a Unicode string
HEXTORAW	Casts a hexadecimal to a raw
NUMTODSINTERVAL	Converts a number value to an interval day to second literal
NUMTOYMINTERVAL	Converts a number value to an interval year to month literal
RAWTOHEX	Casts a raw to a hexadecimal

TABLE 2.5   Conversion-Function Summary *(continued)*

Function	Description
ROWIDTOCHAR	Casts a ROWID to a character
SCN_TO_TIMESTAMP	Converts an SCN to corresponding timestamp of the change
TIMESTAMP_TO_SCN	Converts timestamp to an SCN
TO_BINARY_DOUBLE	Converts input into a BINARY_DOUBLE number
TO_BINARY_FLOAT	Converts input into a BINARY_FLOAT number
TO_CHAR	Converts and formats a date into a string
TO_CLOB	Converts character input or NCLOB input to CLOB
TO_DATE	Converts a string to a date, specifying the format
TO_DSINTERVAL	Converts a character string value to an interval day to second literal
TO_LOB	Converts LONG or LONG RAW values to CLOB or BLOB datatype
TO_MULTIBYTE	Converts a single-byte character to its corresponding multibyte equivalent
TO_NUMBER	Converts a string to a number, specifying the format
TO_SINGLE_BYTE	Converts a multibyte character to its corresponding single-byte equivalent
TO_TIMESTAMP	Converts character string to a TIMESTAMP value
TO_TIMESTAMP_TZ	Converts character string to a TIMESTAMP WITH TIME ZONE value
TO_YMINTERVAL	Converts a character string value to an interval year to month literal
UNISTR	Converts UCS2 Unicode

Conversion-Function Descriptions

The conversion functions are arranged in alphabetical order, with descriptions and examples of each one. Oracle 11*g* includes functions to convert from one datatype to another datatype. Most of the functions have only one argument. Many functions used to convert to/from numeric or datetime datatypes have three arguments; the second argument will tell Oracle what format the input given in the first argument should be. The third argument may be to specify an NLS string. You can use NLS parameters to tell Oracle what character set or language should be used when performing the conversion. The format mask and NLS parameters are always optional.

Pay particular attention to the TO_CHAR, TO_NUMBER, and TO_DATE functions. The format codes associated with numbers and dates are always a favorite on OCP certification exams.

ASCIISTR

ASCIISTR(*c1*) takes a single argument, where *c1* is a character string. This function returns the ASCII equivalent of all the characters in *c1*. This function leaves ASCII characters unchanged, but non-ASCII characters are returned in the format *xxxx* where *xxxx* represents a UTF-16 code unit.

```
SELECT ASCIISTR('cañon') E1, ASCIISTR('faß') E2
FROM dual;


E1          E2
---------   -------
ca\00F1on   fa\00DF
```

BIN_TO_NUM

BIN_TO_NUM(*b*) takes a single argument, where *b* is a comma-delimited list of bits. This function returns the numeric representation of all the bit-field set *b*. It essentially converts a base 2 number into a base 10 number. Bit fields are the most efficient structure to store simple yes/no and true/false data. You can combine numerous bit fields into a single numeric column. Using bit fields departs from a normalized relational model, since one column represents more than one value, but this encoding can enhance performance and/or reduce disk-space usage. See also BITAND.

To understand the number returned from the BIN_TO_NUM function, recall from base 2 (binary) counting that the rightmost digit counts the 1s, the next counts the 2s, the next counts the 4s, then the 8s, and so on. Thus, 13 is represented in binary as 1101. There are one 1, zero 2s, one 4, and one 8, which add up to 13 in base 10.

```
SELECT BIN_TO_NUM(1,1,0,1) bitfield1,
       BIN_TO_NUM(0,0,0,1) bitfield2,
       BIN_TO_NUM(1,1) bitfield3
FROM dual;


BITFIELD1  BITFIELD2  BITFIELD3
---------- ---------- ----------
       13          1          3
```

CAST

CAST(c AS t) takes two arguments, where c is an expression, subquery, or MULTISET clause and t is a datatype. This function converts the expression c into the datatype t. The *CAST* function is most frequently used to convert data into programmer-defined datatypes, but it can also be used to convert data to built-in datatypes. No translation is performed; only the datatype is converted. Table 2.6 shows the datatypes that can be converted using CAST.

TABLE 2.6 CAST Datatype Conversions

Convert From/To	BINARY_ FLOAT, BINARY_ DOUBLE	CHAR, VARCHAR2	NCHAR, NVARCHAR2	DATE, TIMESTAMP, INTERVAL	NUMBER	RAW	ROWID, UROWID
BINARY_ FLOAT BINARY_ DOUBLE	Yes	Yes	Yes	No	Yes	No	No
CHAR, VARCHAR2	Yes	Yes	No	Yes	Yes	Yes	Yes
NCHAR, NVARCHAR2	Yes	No	Yes	Yes	Yes	Yes	Yes
DATE, TIMESTAMP, INTERVAL	No	Yes	No	Yes	No	No	No
NUMBER	Yes	Yes	No	No	Yes	No	No
RAW	No	Yes	No	No	No	Yes	No
ROWID, UROWID	No	Yes	No	No	No	No	Yes

The following example shows datatype conversion using the CAST function.

```
SELECT CAST(SYSDATE AS TIMESTAMP WITH LOCAL TIME ZONE) DT_2_TS
FROM dual;


DT_2_TS
----------------------------
31-MAR-08 04.43.43.000000 PM
```

CHARTOROWID

CHARTOROWID(c) takes a single argument, where c is a character string. This function returns c as a ROWID datatype. No translation is performed; only the datatype is converted.

```
SELECT rowid, first_name
FROM employees
WHERE first_name = 'Sarath';


ROWID               FIRST_NAME
------------------ --------------------
AAARAgAAFAAAABYAA9 Sarath

SELECT first_name, last_name
FROM employees
WHERE rowid = CHARTOROWID('AAARAgAAFAAAABYAA9');


FIRST_NAME          LAST_NAME
------------------- -------------------------
Sarath              Sewall
```

Each row in the database is uniquely identified by a ROWID. ROWID shows the physical location of the row stored in the database. The pseudocolumn ROWID shows the address of the row.

COMPOSE

COMPOSE(c) takes a single argument, where c is a character string. This function returns c as a Unicode string in its fully normalized form, in the same character set as c. The COMPOSE and DECOMPOSE functions support Unicode 3.0. The Unicode 3.0 standard allows you to combine, or *compose*, a valid character from a base character and a modifier.

CONVERT

CONVERT(c, *dset* [,*sset*]) takes three arguments, where c is a character string and *dset* and *sset* are character-set names. This function returns the character string c converted from the source character set *sset* to the destination character set *dset*. No translation is performed. If the character does not exist in both character sets, the replacement character for the character set is used. *sset* defaults to the database character set.

```
select convert ('vis-à-vis','AL16UTF16','AL32UTF8')
from dual;
```

```
CONVERT('VIS-?-VIS','AL16UTF
------------------------------------------
 v i s -?? - v i s
```

DECOMPOSE

DECOMPOSE(*c*) takes a single argument, where *c* is a character string. This function returns *c* as a Unicode string after canonical decomposition in the same character set as *c*. The COMPOSE and DECOMPOSE functions support Unicode 3.0.

HEXTORAW

HEXTORAW(*x*) takes a single argument, where *x* is a hexadecimal string. This function returns the hexadecimal string *x* converted to a RAW datatype. No translation is performed; only the datatype is changed.

NUMTODSINTERVAL

NUMTODSINTERVAL(*x* , *c*) takes two arguments, where *x* is a number and *c* is a character string denoting the units for *x*. This function converts the number *x* into an INTERVAL DAY TO SECOND datatype. Valid units are DAY, HOUR, MINUTE, and SECOND. *c* can be uppercase, lowercase, or mixed case.

```
SELECT SYSDATE,
       SYSDATE+NUMTODSINTERVAL(2,'HOUR') "2 hours later",
       SYSDATE+NUMTODSINTERVAL(30,'MINUTE') "30 minutes later"
FROM dual;


SYSDATE               2 hours later        30 minutes later
-------------------   ------------------   -------------------
31-MAR-2008 23:06:23  01-APR-2008 01:06:23 31-MAR-2008 23:36:23
```

NUMTOYMINTERVAL

NUMTOYMINTERVAL(*x* , *c*) takes two arguments, where *x* is a number and *c* is a character string denoting the units for *x*. This function converts the number *x* into an INTERVAL YEAR TO MONTH datatype. Valid units are YEAR and MONTH. *c* can be uppercase, lowercase, or mixed case.

```
SELECT SYSDATE,
       SYSDATE+NUMTOYMINTERVAL(2,'YEAR') "2 years later",
       SYSDATE+NUMTOYMINTERVAL(5,'MONTH') "5 months later"
```

```
FROM dual;

SYSDATE              2 years later       5 months later
-------------------- -------------------- --------------------
31-MAR-2008 23:13:07 31-MAR-2010 23:13:07 31-AUG-2008 23:13:07
```

RAWTOHEX

RAWTOHEX(*x*) takes a single argument, where *x* is a raw string. This function returns the raw string *x* converted to hexadecimal. No translation is performed; only the datatype is changed.

ROWIDTOCHAR

ROWIDTOCHAR(*x*) takes a single argument, where *x* is a character string in the datatype ROWID. This function returns the ROWID string *x* converted to a VARCHAR2 datatype. No translation is performed; only the datatype is changed. The resulting string is always 18 characters long.

```
SELECT ROWIDTOCHAR(ROWID) Char_RowID, first_name
FROM employees
WHERE first_name = 'Sarath';

CHAR_ROWID          FIRST_NAME
------------------  --------------------
AAARAgAAFAAAABYAA9 Sarath
```

SCN_TO_TIMESTAMP

SCN_TO_TIMESTAMP (*n*) takes a single argument, where *n* is a numeric datatype representing a system change number (SCN) in the database. This function returns the timestamp associated with the SCN. The return datatype is TIMESTAMP.

```
SELECT SCN_TO_TIMESTAMP(8569432113130) UPD_TIME
from dual;

UPD_TIME
----------------------------------------------------
25-MAR-08 12.16.49.000000000 PM
```

An SCN is a number that gets incremented when a commit occurs in the database. The SCN identifies the state of the database uniquely, is recorded in the redo log files, and will be used in case instance recovery is needed. Please see Chapter 8, "Introducing Oracle 11*g* Components and Architecture," for more information.

Oracle provides the ORA_ROWSCN pseudocolumn to identify the SCN when the block containing the row was last modified. Using the ORA_ROWSCN pseudocolumn, you can identify the approximate time when the row was last modified. I say *approximate* because the SCN is associated with a block, and all the rows in the block will have the same SCN associated with them. This is useful in identifying the last modified time of a table, because a block can belong to only one table. Please see Chapter 10, "Allocating Database Storage and Creating Schema Objects," for more information on blocks.

```
SELECT SCN_TO_TIMESTAMP(ORA_ROWSCN) mod_time, last_name
FROM employees
WHERE first_name = 'Lex';


MOD_TIME                              LAST_NAME
----------------------------------    -----------
27-MAR-08 10.20.56.000000000 AM       De Haan
```

TIMESTAMP_TO_SCN

TIMESTAMP_TO_SCN (<ts>) is used to identify the SCN associated with a particular timestamp. The function takes one argument, *ts*, which is of datatype TIMESTAMP. The return datatype is NUMBER.

```
SELECT TIMESTAMP_TO_SCN('25-MAR-08 09.52.20') DB_SCN
FROM dual;


        DB_SCN
---------------
  8569432102308
```

TO_BINARY_DOUBLE

TO_BINARY_DOUBLE(<*expr*> [,<*fmt*> [,<*nlsparm*>]]) takes three arguments, where *expr* is a character or numeric string, *fmt* is a format string specifying the format that *c* appears in, and *nlsparm* specifies language- or location-formatting conventions. This function returns a binary double-precision floating-point number of datatype BINARY_DOUBLE represented by *expr*. The *fmt* and *nlsparm* arguments are valid only if *expr* is a character expression. You can also use 'INF', '-INF' and 'NaN' to represent positive infinity, negative infinity, and NaN in *expr*.

The valid *fmt* numeric format conventions are listed in Table 2.9.

```
SELECT TO_BINARY_DOUBLE('1234.5678','999999.9999') CHR_FMT_DOUBLE,
       TO_BINARY_DOUBLE('1234.5678') CHR_DOUBLE,
       TO_BINARY_DOUBLE(1234.5678) NUM_DOUBLE,
       TO_BINARY_DOUBLE('INF') INF_DOUBLE
FROM dual;


 CHR_FMT_DOUBLE      CHR_DOUBLE       NUM_DOUBLE       INF_DOUBLE
--------------- --------------- --------------- ---------------
  1.2345678E+003  1.2345678E+003  1.2345678E+003             Inf
```

TO_BINARY_FLOAT

TO_BINARY_FLOAT(<*expr*> [,<*fmt*> [,<*nlsparm*>]]) takes three arguments, where *expr* is
a character or numeric string, *fmt* is a format string specifying the format that *c* appears in,
and *nlsparm* specifies language- or location-formatting conventions. This function returns
a binary single-precision floating-point number of datatype BINARY_FLOAT represented by
expr. The *fmt* and *nlsparm* arguments are valid only if *expr* is a character expression. You
can also use 'INF', '-INF' and 'NaN' to represent positive infinity, negative infinity, and
NaN in *expr*.

```
SELECT TO_BINARY_FLOAT('1234.5678','999999.9999') CHR_FMT_FLOAT,
       TO_BINARY_FLOAT('1234.5678') CHR_FLOAT,
       TO_BINARY_FLOAT(1234.5678) NUM_FLOAT,
       TO_BINARY_FLOAT('INF') INF_FLOAT
FROM dual;


 CHR_FMT_FLOAT       CHR_FLOAT        NUM_FLOAT        INF_FLOAT
--------------- --------------- --------------- ---------------
1.23456775E+003 1.23456775E+003 1.23456775E+003             Inf
```

Converting from a character or NUMBER to BINARY_FLOAT and BINARY_
DOUBLE may not be exact since BINARY_FLOAT and BINARY_DOUBLE
use binary precision, whereas NUMBER uses decimal precision. Converting from BINARY_FLOAT to BINARY_DOUBLE is always exact; converting
BINARY_DOUBLE to BINARY_FLOAT may lose precision if BINARY_DOUBLE
uses more bits of precision.

TO_CHAR

TO_CHAR(<*expr*> [,<*fmt* >[,<*nlsparm*>]]) takes three arguments, where *expr* is a date or a number or a character datatype, *fmt* is a *format model* specifying the format that expr will appear in, and *nlsparm* specifies language- or location-formatting conventions. This function returns *expr* converted into a character string (the VARCHAR2 datatype).

You can use the TO_CHAR function to convert a datetime or numeric datatype value to character. When the input is not in the default format expected by the database, you have to provide the format of the input data as the second argument. In this section I'll show how a datetime datatype value and a numeric datatype value can be converted to a character datatype.

Date Conversion

If *expr* is a date or timestamp value, *fmt* is a date-format code, and *nlsparm* is an NLS_DATE_LANGUAGE specification, if included. Note that the spelled-out numbers always appear in English, while the day or month may appear in the NLS language.

```
SELECT TO_CHAR(SYSDATE,'Day Ddspth,Month YYYY'
              ,'NLS_DATE_LANGUAGE=German') Today_Heute
FROM dual;


TODAY_HEUTE
----------------------------------------
Dienstag   First,April     2008


SELECT TO_CHAR(SYSDATE
              ,'"On the "Ddspth" day of "Month, YYYY') Today
FROM dual;


TODAY
--------------------------------------------
On the First day of April    , 2008
```

Table 2.7 lists the date-format codes.

TABLE 2.7   Date-Format Codes

Date Code	Format-Code Description
AD or BC	Epoch indicator.
A.D. or B.C.	Epoch indicator with periods.
AM or PM	Meridian indicator.
A.M. or P.M.	Meridian indicator with periods.
DY	Day of week abbreviated.
DAY	Day of week spelled out.
D	Day of week (1–7).
DD	Day of month (1–31).
DDD	Day of year (1–366).
DL	Long date format.
DS	Short date format.
TS	Time in short format.
FF	Fractional seconds.
J	Julian day (days since 4712 BC).
W	Week of the month (1–5).
WW, IW	Week of the year, ISO week of the year.
MM	Two-digit month.
MON	Month name abbreviated.
MONTH	Month name spelled out.
Q	Quarter.

TABLE 2.7   Date-Format Codes *(continued)*

Date Code	Format-Code Description
RM	Roman numeral month (I–XII).
YYYY, YYY, YY, Y	Four-digit year; last 3, 2, 1 digits in the year.
YEAR	Year spelled out.
SYYYY	If BC, year is shown as negative.
RR	Used for data input with only two digits for the year to store 20th-century dates in the 21st century.
RRRR	Used for data input. If a two-digit year is entered, this works like RR. If a four-digit year is entered, it works like YYYY.
CC, SCC	Century.
HH, HH12	Hour of the half-day (1–12).
HH24	Hour of the day (0–23).
MI	Minutes of the hour (0–59).
SS	Seconds of the minute (0–59).
SSSSS	Seconds of the day (0–86399).
TZD	Time zone daylight savings; must correspond to TZR.
TZH	Time zone hour, together with TZM is time zone offset.
TZM	Time zone minute, together with TZH is time zone offset.
TZR	Time zone region.
, . / - ; :	Punctuation.
'text'	Quoted text.
FM	Returns value with no leading or trailing blanks (fill mode).
FX	Requires exact match for the format model.

The RR code is used for data input with only two digits for the year. It is intended to deal with two-digit years before and after 2000. It rounds the century based on the current year and the two-digit year, entered as follows:

- If the current year is greater than or equal to 50 and the two-digit year is less than 50, the century is rounded up to the next century.

- If the current year is greater than or equal to 50 and the two-digit year is greater than or equal to 50, the century is unchanged.

- If the current year is less than 50 and the two-digit year is less than 50, the century is unchanged.

- If the current year is less than 50 and the two-digit year is greater than or equal to 50, the century is rounded down to the previous century.

So if the current year is 2009 (less than 50) and the two-digit year is entered as 62 (greater than or equal to 50), the year is interpreted as 1962.

For any of the numeric codes, the ordinal and/or spelled-out representation can be displayed with the modifier codes th (for ordinal) and sp (for spelled out). Here is an example:

```
SELECT SYSDATE,
       TO_CHAR(SYSDATE,'Mmspth') Month,
       TO_CHAR(SYSDATE,'DDth') Day,
       TO_CHAR(SYSDATE,'Yyyysp') Year
FROM dual;


SYSDATE    MONTH    DAY  YEAR
---------  -------- ---- -------------------
01-APR-08  Fourth   01ST Two Thousand Eight
```

For any of the spelled-out words or ordinals, case follows the pattern of the first two characters in the code. If the first two characters are uppercase, the spelled-out words are all uppercase. If the first two characters are lowercase, the spelled-out words are all lowercase. If the first two characters are uppercase and then lowercase, the spelled-out words have the first letter in uppercase and the remaining characters in lowercase.

```
SELECT TO_CHAR(SYSDATE,'MONTH') upperCase,
       TO_CHAR(SYSDATE,'Month') mixedCase,
       TO_CHAR(SYSDATE,'month') lowerCase
FROM dual;


UPPERCASE MIXEDCASE LOWERCASE
--------- --------- ---------
APRIL     April     april
```

Table 2.8 shows several examples of using the different date-format models with the TO_CHAR function. Please pay close attention to the format model and result to understand the format-model characteristics. The format model is applied to the date Tuesday 01-APR-2008.

TABLE 2.8   Date-Format Examples for Tuesday 01–APR–2008

Format Model	Result
`'CCth "Century" BC'`	21ST Century AD
`'"On the "DDSpth" Day of "MONTH", "YYYY'`	On the FIRST Day of APRIL, 2008
`'"On the "DdSpth" Day of "FMMonth", "YYYY'`	On the First Day of April, 2008
`'DS TS'`	4/1/2008 01:41:32 PM
`'"Today is week" WW "and day" DDD'`	Today is week 14 and day 092
`'Year'`	Two Thousand Eight
`'W WW WW D DD DDD Y YY YYY YYYY'`	1 14 14 3 01 092 8 08 008 2008

Number Conversion

If *expr* is a number, *fmt* is a numeric format code. Table 2.9 lists these codes.

TABLE 2.9   Numeric Format Codes

Numeric Code	Format-Code Description
9	Numeric digits with a leading space if positive and a leading – (minus) if negative.
0	Leading and/or trailing zeros.
,	Comma, for use as a group separator. It cannot appear after a period or decimal code.
G	Local group separator; could be comma (,) or period (.).
.	Period, for use as the decimal character. It cannot appear more than once or to the left of a group separator.
D	Local decimal character; could be comma (,) or period (.). Only one D is allowed in the format model.
$	Dollar-sign currency symbol.
C	ISO currency symbol (USD for $).
L	Local currency symbol.
FM	No leading or trailing blanks.

TABLE 2.9   Numeric Format Codes *(continued)*

Numeric Code	Format-Code Description
EEEE	Scientific notation.
MI	Negative as a trailing minus. Can appear only in the last position of the format model.
PR	Negative in angle brackets (< >). Can appear only in the last position of the format model.
S	Negative as a leading minus. Can appear only in the first or last position of the format model.
RN	Uppercase Roman numeral.
rn	Lowercase Roman numeral.
X	Hexadecimal
V	Returns value multiplied by 10^n, where n is the number of 9s after the V.
B	Returns blanks for a fixed-point number if the integer part is zero.

nlsparm can include NLS_NUMERIC_CHARACTERS for specifying decimal and grouping symbols (format symbols D and G, respectively), NLS_CURRENCY for specifying the currency symbol (format symbol L), and NLS_ISO_CURRENCY for specifying the ISO international currency symbol (format symbol C). The NLS_CURRENCY symbol and the NLS_ISO_CURRENCY mnemonic are frequently different. For example, the NLS_CURRENCY symbol for U.S. dollars is $, but this symbol is not uniquely American, so the ISO symbol for U.S. dollars is USD.

```
SELECT TO_CHAR(-1234.56,'L099G999D99MI',
               'NLS_NUMERIC_CHARACTERS='',.''
               NLS_CURRENCY=''DM''
               NLS_ISO_CURRENCY=''GERMANY''
               ') Balance
FROM dual;

BALANCE
-----------------
    DM001.234,56-
```

Table 2.10 shows several examples of using the different numeric format models. Please pay close attention to the format model and result to understand the format-model characteristics.

TABLE 2.10   Numeric Format Examples

Numeric Format	Source Value	Result Value
'CO99G999D99'	-1234.56	-USD001,234.56
'O99.99'	1234.56	#######
'09G999V99'	1234.56	01,23456
'09G999D99'	1234.56	01,234.56
'09G999D99PR'	-1234.56	<01,234.56>
'999.99EEEE'	-1234.56	-1.23E+03
'$9999.999S'	-1234.56	$1234.560-
'$9999.999S'	1234.56	$1234.560+
'RN'	141	CXLI
'L99G999D99MI'	1234	$1,234.00

TO_CLOB

TO_CLOB ('<x>') converts input value to a CLOB datatype value. The argument x can be of type CHAR, VARCHAR2, NCLOB, NCHAR, NVARCHAR2, or CLOB. CLOB datatypes are discussed in Chapter 6, "Creating Tables and Constraints."

TO_DATE

TO_DATE(<c> [,<fmt> [,<nlsparm>]]) takes three arguments, where c is a character string, fmt is a format string specifying the format that c appears in (refer to Table 2.7, "Date-Format Codes"), and nlsparm specifies language- or location-formatting conventions. This function returns c converted into the DATE datatype.

If you omit fmt, c should be in the default date format (as defined in NLS_DATE_FORMAT or derived from NLS_TERRITORY). It is always a good practice to specify the format mask when using the TO_DATE function.

```
alter session set nls_date_format = 'DD-MON-RR HH24:MI:SS';
Session altered.

SELECT TO_DATE('30-SEP-2007', 'DD/MON/YY') DateExample
FROM dual;
```

```
DATEEXAMPLE
------------------
30-SEP-07 00:00:00


SELECT TO_DATE('SEP-2007 13', 'MON/YYYY HH24') DateExample
FROM dual;


DATEEXAMPLE
------------------
01-SEP-07 13:00:00
```

When you use the TO_DATE function and specify a format mask, Oracle will try some additional formats if the data in the input string does not match the original format. For the MM format, Oracle will try the MON and MONTH formats. The MON or MONTH formats can be used interchangeably. For the YY and RR formats, Oracle will try YYYY and RRRR.

Adding the FX format model to the TO_DATE function will require the input be given in the exact format, including spaces and punctuation characters.

Table 2.11 shows examples of the TO_DATE function and their resulting dates.

TABLE 2.11   Date-Conversion Examples

Function	Resulting Date
TO_DATE('01-01-08','DD-MM-RR')	01-JAN-2008
TO_DATE('01-01-1908','DD-MM-RR')	01-JAN-1908
TO_DATE('01-MAR-1998','DD-MONTH-YY')	01-MAR-1998
TO_DATE('01-01-98','DD-MM-YY')	01-JAN-2098
TO_DATE('01-01-98','DD-MM-YYYY')	01-JAN-0098
TO_DATE('01-01-98','DD-MM-RRRR')	01-JAN-1998
TO_DATE('01-MARCH-98','DD-MM-RRRR')	01-MAR-1998
TO_DATE('01-MAR-08','DD-MONTH-RRRR')	01-MAR-2008
TO_DATE('01-MAR-1998','fxDD/MON/YYYY')	ORA-01861 error
TO_DATE('13 MAY 2003','fxDD MON YYYY')	ORA-01841 error

Real World Scenario

Converting Numbers to Words

Once I had to debug a PL/SQL function developed by a programmer to convert numeric input to words. His program unit was very lengthy; basically, it defined the numbers from 1 through 20, tens, hundreds, thousands, and millions in words. He was using a complicated logic to split each digit from the input and was assigning a word for each digit. I told him there is a neat single-line SQL function that could replace his tens of lines of PL/SQL code. When I showed him the SQL, he was amazed with the power of simple SQL functions. I don't remember exactly where I came across this piece of magic code in my career to convert a number to words.

Using the J format along with the TO_CHAR and TO_DATE functions, you can display any number between 1 and 5,373,484 in words. The limit is because Oracle supports dates between January 1, 4712 BC, and December 31, 9999 AD.

The J format is used to display the date in Julian numbers.

```
SELECT SYSDATE, TO_CHAR(SYSDATE, 'J') Julian
FROM dual;


SYSDATE    JULIAN
---------  -------
06-APR-08  2454563
```

The SP format will spell the date. By combining the J and JSP formats, you call spell a number. Notice the use of & in the SQL. You run the SQL multiple times to input different values. Negative numbers cannot be converted to Julian dates.

```
SQL> SET VERIFY OFF
SQL> SELECT TO_CHAR(TO_DATE(&NUM, 'J'), 'jsp') num_to_spell
  2  FROM dual;
Enter value for num: 346


NUM_TO_SPELL
----------------------
three hundred forty-six


SQL> /
Enter value for num: 5023456


NUM_TO_SPELL
-----------------------------------------------------------
five million twenty-three thousand four hundred fifty-six
```

```
SQL> /
Enter value for num: -456
SELECT TO_CHAR(TO_DATE(-456, 'J'), 'jsp') num_to_spell
                        *
ERROR at line 1:
ORA-01854: julian date must be between 1 and 5373484
```

TO_DSINTERVAL

TO_DSINTERVAL(<*c*> [,<*nlsparm*>]) takes two arguments, where *c* is a character string and *nlsparm* specifies the decimal and group separator characters. This function returns *c* converted into an INTERVAL DAY TO SECOND datatype.

```
SELECT SYSDATE,
       SYSDATE+TO_DSINTERVAL('007 12:00:00') "+7 1/2 days",
       SYSDATE+TO_DSINTERVAL('030 00:00:00') "+30 days"
FROM dual;


SYSDATE            +7 1/2 days        +30 days
----------------- ----------------- -----------------
01-APR-08 14:45:34 09-APR-08 02:45:34 01-MAY-08 14:45:34
```

TO_LOB

TO_LOB (<long>) converts a LONG or LONG RAW datatype to a CLOB or BLOB datatype. LONG values are converted to a CLOB datatype, and LONG RAW values are converted to a BLOB datatype. To learn more about CLOB and BLOB datatypes, see Chapter 6.

TO_MULTI_BYTE

TO_MULTI_BYTE(<*c*>) takes a single argument, where *c* is a character string. This function returns a character string containing *c* with all single-byte characters converted to their multibyte counterparts. This function is useful only in databases using character sets with both single-byte and multibyte characters. See also TO_SINGLE_BYTE.

TO_NUMBER

TO_NUMBER(<*expr*> [,<*fmt*> [,<*nlsparm*>]]) takes three arguments, where *expr* is a character or numeric string, *fmt* is a format string specifying the format that *expr* appears in, and *nlsparm* specifies language- or location-formatting conventions. This function returns the numeric value represented by *expr*. Table 2.9 lists all the format models that can be used with the TO_NUMBER function. The return datatype is NUMBER.

```
SELECT TO_NUMBER('234.89'), TO_NUMBER(1E-3) FROM dual;
```

```
TO_NUMBER('234.89')  TO_NUMBER(1E-3)
-------------------  ----------------
          234.89                 .001
```

TO_SINGLE_BYTE

TO_SINGLE_BYTE(<c>) takes a single argument, where c is a character string. This function returns a character string containing c with all multibyte characters converted to their single-byte counterparts. This function is useful only in databases using character sets with both single-byte and multibyte characters. See also TO_MULTI_BYTE.

TO_TIMESTAMP

TO_TIMESTAMP(<c> [,<fmt> [,<nlsparm>]]) takes three arguments, where c is a character string, fmt is a format string specifying the format that c appears in, and nlsparm specifies language- or location-formatting conventions. If c is in default timestamp format (as defined in NLS_TIMESTAMP_FORMAT or derived from NLS_TERRITORY), then fmt need not be specified. The return value is of the TIMESTAMP datatype.

```
SELECT TO_TIMESTAMP('30-SEP-2007 08:51:23.456',
                    'DD-MON-YYYY HH24:MI:SS.FF')
FROM dual;

TO_TIMESTAMP('30-SEP-200708:51:23.456','DD-MON-YYYYHH24:MI:SS.FF')
------------------------------------------------------------------
30-SEP-07 08.51.23.456000000 AM
```

TO_TIMESTAMP_TZ

TO_TIMESTAMP(<c> [,<fmt> [,<nlsparm>]]) takes three arguments, where c is a character string, fmt is a format string specifying the format that c appears in, and nlsparm specifies language- or location-formatting conventions. This function has the same behavior as the TO_TIMESTAMP function, except you can specify a time zone. The return datatype is TIMESTAMP WITH TIME ZONE.

```
SELECT TO_TIMESTAMP_TZ('30-SEP-2007 08:51:23.456',
                    'DD-MON-YYYY HH24:MI:SS.FF') TS_TZ_Example
FROM dual;

TS_TZ_EXAMPLE
----------------------------------------
30-SEP-07 08.51.23.456000000 AM -05:00
```

TO_YMINTERVAL

TO_YMINTERVAL(<c>) takes a single argument, where c is a character string. This function returns c converted into an INTERVAL YEAR TO MONTH datatype.

```
SELECT SYSDATE,
       SYSDATE+TO_YMINTERVAL('01-03') "+15 months",
       SYSDATE-TO_YMINTERVAL('00-03') "-3 months"
FROM dual;


SYSDATE   +15 month -3 months
--------- --------- ---------
01-APR-08 01-JUL-09 01-JAN-08
```

Table 2.12 shows examples to demonstrate the difference between using the ADD_MONTHS function and the TO_YMINTERVAL function.

TABLE 2.12 Compare ADD_MONTHS and TO_YMINTERVAL

Expression	Result
TO_DATE('28-FEB-2007')+ TO_YMINTERVAL('01-00')	28-FEB-2008
ADD_MONTHS('28-FEB-2007',12)	29-FEB-2008
TO_DATE('29-FEB-2008')+ TO_YMINTERVAL('01-00')	Error: ORA-01839
ADD_MONTHS('29-FEB-2008',12)	28-FEB-2009
TO_DATE('30-APR-2008')+ TO_YMINTERVAL('00-04')	30-AUG-2008
ADD_MONTHS('30-APR-2008',04)	31-AUG-2008
TO_DATE('31-JAN-2008')+ TO_YMINTERVAL('00-03')	Error: ORA-01839

UNISTR

UNISTR(<c>) takes a single argument, where c is a character string. This function returns c in Unicode in the database Unicode character set. Include UCS2 characters by prepending a backslash (\) to the character's numeric code. Include the backslash character by specifying two backslashes (\\).

```
SELECT UNISTR('\00A3'), UNISTR('\00F1'), UNISTR('ca\00F1on')
FROM dual;
```

```
UN UN UNISTR('CA
-- -- ----------
 £  ñ  c a ñ o n
```

Using Other Single-Row Functions

This is the catchall category to include all the single-row functions that don't fit into the other categories. Some are incredibly useful, such as DECODE. DECODE is a very special function and the most widely used function. Most likely, you'll see a question on the certification exam about the DECODE function.

The NULLIF function is included in this category and not with other NULL-related functions. The NULLIF function returns a NULL value, whereas the NULL-related functions I discussed earlier take NULL as one of the inputs and give a value as a result.

Miscellaneous-Function Overview

Table 2.13 summarizes the single-row miscellaneous functions. I will cover each of these functions in the "Miscellaneous-Function Descriptions" section.

TABLE 2.13   Miscellaneous-Function Summary

Function	Description
BFILENAME	Returns the BFILE locator for the specified file and directory
DECODE	Acts as an inline CASE statement (emulating IF...THEN...ELSE logic)
DUMP	Returns a raw substring in the specified encoding (octal/hex/character/decimal)
EMPTY_BLOB	Returns an empty BLOB locator
EMPTY_CLOB	Returns an empty CLOB locator
GREATEST	Sorts the arguments and returns the largest
LEAST	Sorts the arguments and returns the smallest
NULLIF	Returns NULL if two expressions are equal
ORA_HASH	Returns the hash value for an expression

TABLE 2.13   Miscellaneous-Function Summary *(continued)*

Function	Description
SYS_CONTEXT	Returns various session attributes, such as IP address, terminal, and current user
SYS_GUID	Generates a globally unique identifier as a RAW value
UID	Returns the numeric user ID for the current session
USER	Returns the username for the current session
USERENV	Returns information about the current session
VSIZE	Returns the internal size in bytes for an expression

Miscellaneous-Function Descriptions

The miscellaneous functions are arranged in alphabetical order, with descriptions and examples of each one.

BFILENAME

BFILENAME(*dir, file*) takes two arguments, where *dir* is a directory and *file* is a filename. This function returns an empty BFILE locator. This function is used to initialize a BFILE variable or BFILE column in a table. When this function is used, the BFILE is instantiated. Neither *dir* nor *file* needs to exist at the time BFILENAME is called, but both must exist when the locator is used. I'll discuss the BFILE datatype in Chapter 6.

DECODE

DECODE is a conditional function. I discussed the CASE conditional expression in Chapter 1.

    DECODE(*x* ,*m1*, *r1* [,*m2* ,*r2*]…[,*d*]) can use multiple arguments. *x* is an expression. *m1* is a matching expression to compare with *x*. If *m1* is equivalent to *x*, then *r1* is returned; otherwise, additional matching expressions (*m2*, *m3*, *m4*, and so on) are compared, if they are included, and the corresponding result (*r2*, *r3*, *r4*, and so on) is returned. If no match is found and the default expression *d* is included, then *d* is returned. This function acts like a case statement in C, Pascal, or Ada. DECODE is a powerful tool that can make SQL very efficient—or very dense and nonintuitive. Let's look at some examples to help clarify its use.

    The following example queries the COUNTRIES table and displays a region name based on the region_id column value. If the region_id column value does not match the values in the list, you want to display Other. To limit the rows in the output, you use the SUBSTR function to identify the country codes that begin with I or end with R.

```
SELECT country_id, country_name, region_id,
       DECODE(region_id, 1, 'Europe',
                         2, 'Americas',
                         3, 'Asia',
                         'Other') Region
FROM countries
WHERE SUBSTR(country_id,1,1) = 'I'
   OR SUBSTR(country_id,2,1) = 'R';


CO COUNTRY_NA      REGION_ID REGION
-- ----------- ---------------- --------
AR Argentina           2 Americas
BR Brazil              2 Americas
FR France              1 Europe
IL Israel              4 Other
IN India               3 Asia
IT Italy               1 Europe
```

DECODE does not have to return a value; it can return NULL if the optional *d* argument is not provided. In the previous example, if Other is omitted, the region name for Israel will be NULL.

```
SELECT country_id, country_name, region_id,
       DECODE(region_id, 1, 'Europe',
                         2, 'Americas',
                         3, 'Asia') Region
FROM countries
WHERE SUBSTR(country_id,1,1) = 'I'
   OR SUBSTR(country_id,2,1) = 'R';
```

In the DECODE function, Oracle treats two NULL values as equal. Hence, you can represent the NVL function using DECODE, as in DECODE(<string>, NULL, <new_value>, <string>).

DUMP

DUMP(*x* [,*fmt* [,*n1* [,*n2*]]]) can take four arguments, where *x* is an expression. *fmt* is a format specification for octal (8), decimal (10), hexadecimal (16), or single characters (17). Decimal is the default. If you add 1000 to the format specification, the character set name is also returned (for example, 1008 for octal). *n1* is the starting byte offset within *x*, and *n2* is the length in bytes to dump. This function returns a character string containing the data-type of *x* in numeric notation (for example, 2=number, 12=date), the length in bytes of *x*, and the internal representation of *x*. This function is mainly used for troubleshooting data problems.

```
SELECT last_name, DUMP(last_name) DUMP_EX
FROM employees
WHERE last_name like 'J%';


LAST_NAME    DUMP_EX
------------ ------------------------------------------------
Johnson      Typ=1 Len=7: 74,111,104,110,115,111,110
Jones        Typ=1 Len=5: 74,111,110,101,115


SELECT last_name, DUMP(last_name, 1017, 3, 3) DUMP_EX
FROM employees
WHERE last_name like 'J%';


LAST_NAME    DUMP_EX
------------ ------------------------------------------------
Johnson      Typ=1 Len=7 CharacterSet=WE8MSWIN1252: h,n,s
Jones        Typ=1 Len=5 CharacterSet=WE8MSWIN1252: n,e,s
```

EMPTY_BLOB

EMPTY_BLOB() takes no arguments. This function returns an empty BLOB locator. This function is used to initialize a BLOB variable or BLOB column in a table. When used, the BLOB is instantiated but not populated.

EMPTY_CLOB

EMPTY_CLOB() takes no arguments. This function returns an empty CLOB locator. This function is used to initialize a CLOB variable or CLOB column in a table. When used, the CLOB is instantiated but not populated.

GREATEST

GREATEST(*exp_list*) takes one argument, where *exp_list* is a list of expressions. This function returns the expression that sorts highest in the datatype of the first expression. If the first expression is any of the character datatypes, a VARCHAR2 is returned, and the comparison rules for VARCHAR2 are used for character-literal strings. A NULL in the expression list results in a NULL being returned.

The following example shows you that the list was treated as a character list and not a date, even though you had all date values as input:

```
SELECT GREATEST('01-ARP-08','30-DEC-01','12-SEP-09')
FROM dual;

GREATEST(
---------
30-DEC-01
```

In the following example, since the first argument is numeric, Oracle tries to convert the rest of the list to numeric and encounters an error:

```
SELECT GREATEST(345, 'XYZ', 2354) FROM dual;
ERROR at line 1:
ORA-01722: invalid number
```

In the next example, I changed the order to have the character string as the first entry in the list; hence, Oracle considers the rest of the list to be characters and does not produce an error:

```
SELECT GREATEST('XYZ', 345, 2354) FROM dual;

GRE
---
XYZ
```

LEAST

LEAST(*exp_list*) takes one argument, where *exp_list* is a list of expressions. This function returns the expression that sorts lowest in the datatype of the first expression. If the first expression is any of the character datatypes, a VARCHAR2 is returned.

```
SELECT LEAST(SYSDATE,'15-MAR-2002','17-JUN-2002') oldest
FROM dual;

OLDEST
---------
15-MAR-02
```

The following SQL is used to calculate a bonus of 15 percent of salary to employees, with a maximum bonus at 500 and a minimum bonus at 400:

```
SELECT last_name, salary,
       GREATEST(LEAST(salary*0.15, 500), 400) bonus
FROM employees
WHERE department_id IN (30, 10)
ORDER BY last_name;
```

LAST_NAME	SALARY	BONUS
Baida	2900	435
Colmenares	2500	400
Himuro	2600	400
Khoo	3100	465
Raphaely	11000	500
Whalen	4400	500

The comparison rules used by GREATEST and LEAST on character literals order trailing spaces higher than no spaces. This behavior follows the nonpadded comparison rules of the VARCHAR2 datatype. Note the ordering of the leading and trailing spaces: trailing spaces are greatest and leading spaces are least.

```
SELECT GREATEST(' Yes','Yes','Yes ')
       ,LEAST(' Yes','Yes','Yes ')
FROM dual;


GREA LEAST
---- -----
Yes  Yes
```

 To remember the comparison rules for trailing and leading space in character literals, think "leading equals least."

NULLIF

NULLIF(*x1* , *x2*) takes two arguments, where *x1* and *x2* are expressions. This function returns NULL if *x1* equals *x2*; otherwise, it returns *x1*. If *x1* is NULL, NULLIF returns NULL.

To facilitate visualizing a NULL, the following example has the NULL indicator set to ?. So, a ? in the query results that follow represents a NULL:

```
SET NULL ?
SELECT ename, mgr, comm
       NULLIF(comm,0) test1,
       NULLIF(0,comm) test2,
       NULLIF(mgr,comm) test3
FROM scott.emp
WHERE empno IN (7844,7839,7654,7369);
```

ENAME	MGR	COMM	TEST1	TEST2	TEST3
SMITH	7902	?	?	0	7902
MARTIN	7698	1400	1400	0	7698
KING	?	?	?	0	?
TURNER	7698	0	?	?	7698

ORA_HASH

ORA_HASH (expr [,max_bucket [,seed]]) can take three arguments. The first argument, *expr*, is an expression whose hash value will be calculated and assigned to a bucket. The maximum bucket value is determined by the second argument, *max_bucket*; the default and maximum is 4,294,967,295. The *seed* argument enables Oracle to generate many different results for the same sets of data. The hash function is applied to *expr* and *seed*. The *seed* can be between 0 and 4,294,967,295.

This function is useful for getting a random sample of rows from table. In the following example, you can get few random rows from the EMPLOYEES table. Notice the difference in result for each run and with different seed values. The rows in the table are divided into 20 buckets (0 through 19) based on the hash value, and you are selecting the rows from bucket 0.

```
SELECT department_id, last_name, salary
FROM employees
WHERE ORA_HASH(last_name || first_name, 19, 2) = 0;
```

DEPARTMENT_ID	LAST_NAME	SALARY
80	Errazuriz	12000
80	Tuvault	7000
50	Feeney	3000

```
SELECT department_id, last_name, salary
FROM employees
WHERE ORA_HASH(last_name || first_name, 19, 5) = 0;
```

DEPARTMENT_ID	LAST_NAME	SALARY
90	Kochhar	17000
100	Sciarra	7700
80	Vishney	10500
	Grant	7000
50	Chung	3800

```
SELECT department_id, last_name, salary
FROM employees
WHERE ORA_HASH(last_name || first_name, 19) = 0;


   DEPARTMENT_ID LAST_NAME              SALARY
---------------- ------------ ----------------
             70 Baer                    10000
             30 Colmenares               2500
             50 Mallin                   3300
             50 Taylor                   3200
```

SYS_CONTEXT

SYS_CONTEXT(*n* , *p* [, *length*]) can take three arguments, where *n* is a namespace, *p* is a parameter associated with namespace *n*, and *length* is the length of the return value in bytes. *length* defaults to 256. The built-in namespace in Oracle is called USERENV, which describes the current session. The return datatype is VARCHAR2.

```
SELECT SYS_CONTEXT('USERENV','IP_ADDRESS')
FROM dual;


SYS_CONTEXT('USERENV','IP_ADDRESS')
-----------------------------------
192.168.1.100
```

Table 2.14 lists the parameters available in the USERENV namespace for the SYS_CONTEXT function.

TABLE 2.14 Parameters in the USERENV Namespace

Parameter	Description
ACTION	Returns the position in the module (application).
AUDITED_CURSORID	Returns the cursor ID of the SQL that triggered the auditing.
AUTHENTICATED_IDENTITY	Returns the identity used in the authentication.
AUTHENTICATION_DATA	Returns the data used to authenticate a logged-in user.
AUTHENTICATION_METHOD	Returns the method used to authenticate a user. The return value can be DATABASE for database-authenticated accounts, OS for externally identified accounts, NETWORK for globally identified accounts, and so on.

TABLE 2.14   Parameters in the USERENV Namespace *(continued)*

Parameter	Description
BG_JOB_ID	Returns the job ID (that is, DBA_JOBS) if the session was created by a background process. Returns NULL if the session is a foreground session. See also FG_JOB_ID.
CLIENT_IDENTIFIER	Returns the client session identifier in the global context. It can be set with the DBMS_SESSION built-in package.
CLIENT_INFO	Returns the 64 bytes of user session information stored by DBMS_APPLICATION_INFO.
CURRENT_BIND	Returns bind variables for fine-grained auditing.
CURRENT_SCHEMA	Returns the current schema as set by ALTER SESSION SET CURRENT_SCHEMA or, by default, the login schema/ID.
CURRENT_SCHEMAID	Returns the numeric ID for CURRENT_SCHEMA.
CURRENT_SQL	Returns the SQL that triggered fine-grained auditing (use only within scope inside the event handler for fine-grained auditing).
CURRENT_SQL_LENGTH	Returns the length of the current SQL that triggered fine-grained auditing.
DB_DOMAIN	Returns the contents of the DB_DOMAIN init.ora parameter.
DB_NAME	Returns the contents of the DB_NAME init.ora parameter.
DB_UNIQUE_NAME	Returns the contents of the DB_UNIQUE_NAME init.ora parameter.
ENTRYID	Returns the auditing entry identifier
ENTERPRISE_IDENTITY	Returns OID DN for enterprise users, for local users NULL.
FG_JOB_ID	Returns the job ID of the current session if a foreground process created it. Returns NULL if the session is a background session. See also BG_JOB_ID.
GLOBAL_CONTEXT_MEMORY	Returns the number in the SGA by the globally accessible context.
GLOBAL_UID	Returns the global user ID from OID.
HOST	Returns the hostname of the machine from where the client connected. This is not the same terminal in V$SESSION.

TABLE 2.14   Parameters in the USERENV Namespace *(continued)*

Parameter	Description
IDENTIFICATION_TYPE	Returns how the user is set to authenticate in the database: LOCAL, EXTERNAL, or GLOBAL.
INSTANCE	Returns the instance number for the instance to which the session is connected. This is always 1 unless you are running Oracle Real Application Clusters.
INSTANCE_NAME	Returns the name of the instance.
IP_ADDRESS	Returns the IP address of the machine from where the client connected.
ISDBA	Returns TRUE if the user connected AS SYSDBA.
LANG	Returns the ISO abbreviation for the language name.
LANGUAGE	Returns a character string containing the language and territory used by the session and the database character set in the form language_territory.characterset.
MODULE	Returns the application name set through DBMS_APPLICATION_INFO.
NETWORK_PROTOCOL	Returns the network protocol being used as specified in the PROTOCOL= section of the connect string or tnsnames.ora definition.
NLS_CALENDAR	Returns the calendar for the current session.
NLS_CURRENCY	Returns the currency for the current session.
NLS_DATE_FORMAT	Returns the date format for the current session.
NLS_DATE_LANGUAGE	Returns the language used for displaying dates.
NLS_SORT	Returns the binary or linguistic sort basis.
NLS_TERRITORY	Returns the territory for the current session.
OS_USER	Returns the operating-system username for the current session.
POLICY_INVOKER	Returns the invoker of row-level security-policy functions.
PROXY_ENTERPRISE_IDENTITY	Returns OID DN when the proxy user is an enterprise user.

TABLE 2.14   Parameters in the USERENV Namespace *(continued)*

Parameter	Description
PROXY_GOLBAL_UID	Returns the global user ID from OID for Enterprise User Security proxy users.
PROXY_USER	Returns the name of the database user who opened the current session for the session user.
PROXY_USERID	Returns the numeric ID for the database user who opened the current session for the session user.
SERVER_HOST	Returns the hostname of the machine where the instance is running.
SERVICE_NAME	Returns the name of the service where the session is connected.
SESSION_USER	Returns the database username for the current session.
SESSION_USERID	Returns the numeric database user ID for the current session.
SESSIONID	Returns the auditing session identifier AUDSID. This parameter is out of scope for distributed queries.
SID	Returns the session number (same as the SID from V$SESSION).
STATEMENT_ID	Returns the auditing statement identifier.
TERMINAL	Returns the terminal identifier for the current session. This is the same as the terminal in V$SESSION.

Here are few more examples of SYS_CONTEXT in the USERENV namespace:

```
SELECT SYS_CONTEXT('USERENV', 'OS_USER'),
       SYS_CONTEXT('USERENV', 'CURRENT_SCHEMA'),
       SYS_CONTEXT('USERENV', 'HOST'),
       SYS_CONTEXT('USERENV', 'NLS_TERRITORY')
FROM dual;

SYS_CONTEXT('USERENV','OS_USER')
SYS_CONTEXT('USERENV','CURRENT_SCHEMA')
SYS_CONTEXT('USERENV','HOST')
SYS_CONTEXT('USERENV','NLS_TERRITORY')
-------------------------------------------
```

```
oracle
HR
linux04.mycompany.corp
AMERICA
```

SYS_GUID

SYS_GUID() generates a globally unique identifier as a RAW value. This function is useful for creating a unique identifier to identify a row. SYS_GUID() returns a 32-bit hexadecimal representation of the 16-byte RAW value.

```
SELECT SYS_GUID() FROM DUAL;

SYS_GUID()
--------------------------------
CDA78A020D6E43A6AB743A5CE8CB8C55


SELECT SYS_GUID() FROM DUAL;

SYS_GUID()
--------------------------------
DC7C19A3AD264CE184C64194E65F83E5
```

UID

UID takes no parameters and returns the integer user ID for the current user connected to the session. The user ID uniquely identifies each user in a database and can be selected from the DBA_USERS view.

```
SQL> SHOW USER
USER is "BTHOMAS"

SELECT username, account_status
FROM dba_users
WHERE user_id = UID;

USERNAME          ACCOUNT_STATUS
----------------  ----------------
BTHOMAS           OPEN
```

USER

USER takes no parameters and returns a character string containing the username for the current user.

```
SELECT default_tablespace, temporary_tablespace
FROM dba_users
WHERE username = USER;


DEFAULT_TABLESPACE              TEMPORARY_TABLESPACE
------------------------------  ---------------------
USERS                           TEMP
```

USERENV

USERENV(*opt*) takes a single argument, where *opt* is one of the following options:

- ISDBA returns TRUE if the SYSDBA role is enabled in the current session.

- SESSIONID returns the AUDSID auditing session identifier.

- ENTRYID returns the auditing entry identifier if auditing is enabled for the instance (the init.ora parameter AUDIT_TRAIL is set to TRUE).

- INSTANCE returns the instance identifier to which the session is connected. This option is useful only if you are running the Oracle Parallel Server and have multiple instances.

- LANGUAGE returns the language, territory, and database character set. The delimiters are an underscore (_) between language and territory and a period (.) between the territory and character set.

- LANG returns the ISO abbreviation of the session's language.

- TERMINAL returns a VARCHAR2 string containing information corresponding to the operating system identifier for the current session's terminal.

The option can appear in uppercase, lowercase, or mixed case. The USERENV function has been deprecated since Oracle 9*i*. It is recommended to use the SYS_CONTEXT function with the built-in USERENV namespace instead.

VSIZE

VSIZE(*x*) takes a single argument, where *x* is an expression. This function returns the size in bytes of the internal representation of the *x*.

```
SELECT last_name, first_name,
       VSIZE(last_name) ln_size, VSIZE(first_name) fn_size
FROM employees
WHERE last_name like 'K%';
```

LAST_NAME	FIRST_NAME	LN_SIZE	FN_SIZE
Kaufling	Payam	8	5
Khoo	Alexander	4	9
King	Janette	4	7
King	Steven	4	6
Kochhar	Neena	7	5
Kumar	Sundita	5	7

Since the database character set is single-byte, the byte used for each character is 1; hence, the size shown here is actually the number of characters in the input. For multibyte characters, this would be different.

Summary

This chapter introduced single-row functions. It started by discussing the functions available in Oracle 11g to handle NULLs. Then it discussed the single-row functions available in Oracle 11g by grouping them into character, numeric, date, and conversion functions.

You learned that single-row functions return a value for each row as it is retrieved from the table. You can use single-row functions to interpret NULL values, format output, convert datatypes, transform data, perform date arithmetic, give environment information, and perform trigonometric calculations.

You can use single-row functions in the SELECT, WHERE, and ORDER BY clauses of SELECT statements. I covered the rich assortment of functions available in each datatype category and some functions that work on any datatype.

The NVL, NVL2, and COALESCE functions interpret NULL values.

The single-row character functions operate on character input. The INSTR function returns the position of a substring within the string. The SUBSTR function returns a portion of the string. INSTR and SUBSTR are great for extracting part of the input string. REPLACE and TRANSLATE transform the input.

Single-row numeric functions operate on numeric input. FLOOR, CEIL, ROUND, and TRUNC get the nearest number. FLOOR, CEIL, and ROUND return the nearest integer, whereas ROUND returns a value rounded to certain digits of precision. REMAINDER and MOD are similar functions.

Date functions operate on datetime values. SYSDATE and SYSTIMESTAMP values return the current date and time. MONTHS_BETWEEN finds the number of months between two date values. ADD_MONTHS is a commonly used function and can add months to or subtract months from a date. You can use ROUND and TRUNC on datetime values to find the nearest date, month, or year.

Of the conversion functions, TO_CHAR and TO_DATE are the most commonly used. I also reviewed the format codes that can be used with numeric and datetime values.

The DECODE function evaluates a condition, and you can easily build IF...THEN...ELSE logic into SQL using the DECODE function.

Exam Essentials

Understand where single-row functions can be used.   Single-row functions can be used in the SELECT, WHERE, and ORDER BY clauses of SELECT statements.

Know the effects that NULL values can have on arithmetic and other functions.   Any arithmetic operation on a NULL results in a NULL. This is true of most functions as well. Use the NVL, NVL2, and COALESCE functions to deal with NULLs.

Review the character-manipulation functions.   Understand the arguments and the result of using character-manipulation functions such as INSTR, SUBSTR, REPLACE, and TRANSLATE.

Understand the numeric functions.   Know the effects of using TRUNC and ROUND with -n as the second argument. Also practice using LENGTH and INSTR, which return a numeric result, inside SUBSTR and other character functions.

Know how date arithmetic works.   When adding or subtracting numeric values from a DATE datatype, whole numbers represent days. Also, the date/time intervals INTERVAL YEAR TO MONTH and INTERVAL DAY TO SECOND can be added or subtracted from date/time datatypes. You need to know how to interpret and create expressions that add intervals to or subtract intervals from dates.

Know the datatypes for the various date/time functions.   Oracle has many date/time functions to support the date/time datatypes. You need to know the return datatypes for these functions. SYSDATE and CURRENT_DATE return a DATE datatype. CURRENT_TIMESTAMP and SYSTIMESTAMP return a TIMESTAMP WITH TIME ZONE datatype. LOCALTIMESTAMP returns a TIMESTAMP datatype.

Know the format models for converting dates to/from character strings.   In practice, you can simply look up format codes in a reference. For the certification exam, you must have them memorized.

Understand the use of the DECODE function.   DECODE acts like a case statement in C, Pascal, or Ada. Learn how this function works and how to use it.

Review Questions

1. You want to display each project's start date as the day, week, number, and year. Which statement will give output like the following?

   Tuesday Week 23, 2008

   A. SELECT proj_id, TO_CHAR(start_date, 'DOW Week WOY YYYY') FROM projects;

   B. SELECT proj_id, TO_CHAR(start_date,'Day'||' Week'||' WOY, YYYY') FROM projects;

   C. SELECT proj_id, TO_CHAR(start_date, 'Day" Week" WW, YYYY') FROM projects;

   D. SELECT proj_id, TO_CHAR(start_date, 'Day Week# , YYYY') FROM projects;

   E. You can't calculate week numbers with Oracle.

2. What will the following statement return?

   ```
   SELECT last_name, first_name, start_date
   FROM employees
   WHERE hire_date < TRUNC(SYSDATE) - 5;
   ```

   A. Employees hired within the past five hours

   B. Employees hired within the past five days

   C. Employees hired more than five hours ago

   D. Employees hired more than five days ago

3. Which assertion about the following statements is most true?

   ```
   SELECT name, region_code||phone_number
   FROM customers;
   SELECT name, CONCAT(region_code,phone_number)
   FROM customers;
   ```

   A. If REGION_CODE is NULL, the first statement will not include that customer's PHONE_NUMBER.

   B. If REGION_CODE is NULL, the second statement will not include that customer's PHONE_NUMBER.

   C. Both statements will return the same data.

   D. The second statement will raise an error if REGION_CODE is NULL for any customer.

4. Which single-row function could you use to return a specific portion of a character string?

   A. INSTR

   B. SUBSTR

   C. LPAD

   D. LEAST

5. The data in the PRODUCT table is as described here. The bonus amount is calculated as the lesser of 5 percent of the base price or 20 percent of the surcharge.

sku	name	division	base_price	surcharge
1001	PROD-1001	A	200	50
1002	PROD-1002	C	250	
1003	PROD-1003	C	240	20
1004	PROD-1004	A	320	
1005	PROD-1005	C	225	40

Which of the following statements will achieve the desired results?

A. SELECT sku, name, LEAST(base_price * 1.05, surcharge * 1.2)
FROM products;

B. SELECT sku, name, LEAST(NVL(base_price,0) * 1.05, surcharge * 1.2)
FROM products;

C. SELECT sku, name, COALESCE(LEAST(base_price*1.05, surcharge * 1.2),
base_price * 1.05)
FROM products;

D. A, B, and C will all achieve the desired results.

E. None of these statements will achieve the desired results.

6. Which function(s) accept arguments of any datatype? (Choose all that apply.)

A. SUBSTR

B. NVL

C. ROUND

D. DECODE

E. SIGN

7. What will be returned by SIGN(ABS(NVL(-32,0)))?

A. 1

B. 32

C. -1

D. 0

E. NULL

8. The SALARY table has the following data:

LAST_NAME	FIRST_NAME	SALARY
Mavris	Susan	6500
Higgins	Shelley	12000
Tobias	Sigal	
Colmenares	Karen	2500
Weiss	Matthew	8000
Mourgos	Kevin	5800
Rogers	Michael	2900
Stiles	Stephen	3200

Consider the following SQL, and choose the best option:

```
SELECT last_name, NVL2(salary, salary, 0) N1,
       NVL(salary,0) N2
FROM salary;
```

A. Column N1 and N2 will have different results.

B. Column N1 will show zero for all rows, and column N2 will show the correct salary values, and zero for Tobias.

C. The SQL will error out because the number of arguments in the NVL2 function is incorrect.

D. Columns N1 and N2 will show the same result.

9. Which two functions could you use to strip leading characters from a character string? (Choose two.)

A. LTRIM

B. SUBSTR

C. RTRIM

D. INSTR

E. STRIP

10. What is the result of MOD(x1, 4), if x1 is 11?

A. −1

B. 3

C. 1

D. REMAINDER(11,4)

11. Which SQL statement will replace the last two characters of *last_name* with 'XX' in the employees table when executed? (Choose two.)

A. SELECT RTRIM(last_name, SUBSTR(last_name, LENGTH(last_name)-1)) || 'XX' new_col FROM employees;

B. SELECT REPLACE(last_name, SUBSTR(last_name, LENGTH(last_name)-1), 'XX') new_col FROM employees;

C. SELECT REPLACE(SUBSTR(last_name, LENGTH(last_name)-1), 'XX') new_col FROM employees;

D. SELECT CONCAT(SUBSTR(last_name, 1,LENGTH(last_name)-2), 'XX') new_col FROM employees;

12. Which date components does the CURRENT_TIMESTAMP function display?

A. Session date, session time, and session time zone offset

B. Session date and session time

C. Session date and session time zone offset

D. Session time zone offset

13. Using the SALESPERSON_REVENUE table described here, which statements will properly display the TOTAL_REVENUE (CAR_SALES + WARRANTY_SALES) of each salesperson?

Column Name	salesperson_id	car_sales	warranty_sales
Key Type	pk		
NULLs/Unique	NN	NN	
FK Table			
Datatype	NUMBER	NUMBER	NUMBER
Length	10	11,2	11,2

A. SELECT salesperson_id, car_sales, warranty_sales, car_sales + warranty_sales total_sales
FROM salesperson_revenue;

B. SELECT salesperson_id, car_sales, warranty_sales, car_sales + NVL2(warranty_sales,0) total_sales
FROM salesperson_revenue;

C. SELECT salesperson_id, car_sales, warranty_sales, NVL2(warranty_sales, car_sales + warranty_sales, car_sales) total_sales
FROM salesperson_revenue;

D. SELECT salesperson_id, car_sales, warranty_sales, car_sales + COALESCE(car_sales, warranty_sales, car_sales + warranty_sales) total_sales
FROM salesperson_revenue;

14. What will be the result of executing the following SQL, if today's date is February 28, 2009?

```
SELECT ADD_MONTHS('28-FEB-09', -12) from dual;
```

    A. 28-FEB-10

    B. 28-FEB-08

    C. 29-FEB-08

    D. 28-JAN-08

15. Consider the following two SQL statements, and choose the best option:

```
1. SELECT TO_DATE('30-SEP-07','DD-MM-YYYY')  from dual;
2. SELECT TO_DATE('30-SEP-07','DD-MON-RRRR') from dual;
```

    A. Statement 1 will error; 2 will produce result.

    B. The resulting date value from the two statements will be the same.

    C. The resulting date value from the two statements will be different.

    D. Both statements will generate an error.

16. What will the following SQL statement return?

```
SELECT COALESCE(NULL,'Oracle ','Certified') FROM dual;
```

    A. NULL

    B. Oracle

    C. Certified

    D. Oracle Certified

17. Which expression will always return the date one year later than the current date?

    A. SYSDATE + 365

    B. SYSDATE + TO_YMINTERVAL('01-00')

    C. CURRENT_DATE + 1

    D. NEW_TIME(CURRENT_DATE,1,'YEAR')

    E. None of the above

18. Which function will return a TIMESTAMP WITH TIME ZONE datatype?

    A. CURRENT_TIMESTAMP

    B. LOCALTIMESTAMP

    C. CURRENT_DATE

    D. SYSDATE

19. Which statement would change all occurrences of the string 'IBM' to the string 'SUN' in the DESCRIPTION column of the VENDOR table?

   A. SELECT TRANSLATE(description, 'IBM', 'SUN') FROM vendor

   B. SELECT CONVERT(description, 'IBM', 'SUN') FROM vendor

   C. SELECT EXTRACT(description, 'IBM', 'SUN') FROM vendor

   D. SELECT REPLACE(description, 'IBM', 'SUN') FROM vendor

20. Which function implements IF...THEN...ELSE logic?

   A. INITCAP

   B. REPLACE

   C. DECODE

   D. IFELSE

Answers to Review Questions

1. C. Double quotation marks must surround literal strings like `"Week"`.

2. D. The TRUNC function removes the time portion of a date by default, and whole numbers added to or subtracted from dates represent days added or subtracted from that date. `TRUNC(SYSDATE) -5` means five days ago at midnight.

3. C. The two statements are equivalent.

4. B. SUBSTR returns part of the string. INSTR returns a number. LPAD adds to a character string. LEAST does not change an input string.

5. C. Options A and B do not account for NULL surcharges correctly and will set the bonus to NULL where the surcharge is NULL. In option B, the NVL function is applied to the base_price column instead of the surcharge column. In option C, the LEAST function will return a NULL if surcharge is NULL, in which case BASE_PRICE * 1.05 would be returned from the COALESCE function.

6. B, D. ROUND does not accept character arguments. SUBSTR accepts only character arguments. SIGN accepts only numeric arguments.

7. A. The functions are evaluated from the innermost to outermost, as follows:
   `SIGN(ABS(NVL(-32,0))) = SIGN(ABS(-32)) = SIGN(32) = 1`

8. D. The NVL function returns zero if the salary value is NULL, or else it returns the original value. The NVL2 function returns the second argument if the salary value is not NULL. If NULL, the third argument is returned.

9. A, B. RTRIM removes trailing (not leading) characters. INSTR returns a number. STRIP is not a valid Oracle function. SUBSTR with second argument greater than 1 removes leading characters from a string.

10. B. MOD returns the number remainder after division. The REMAINDER function is similar to MOD but will use the ROUND function in the algorithm; hence, the result of `REMAINDER(11,4)` would be -1. MOD uses FLOOR in the algorithm.

11. D. The SUBSTR function in option A would return the last two characters of the last name (ul). These two characters are right trimmed using the RTRIM function, including all repeating occurrences at the end. The result would be first portion of the last name concatenated with XX, only if the last two characters are not repeating (for example "Paululul" will result in "PaXX" and "PaulSulul" will result in "PaulSXX"). Option B would replace all the occurrences of the last two characters ("Paululul" will result in "PaXXXXXX" and "PaulSulul" will result in "PaXXSXXXX"). Option C would return only the last two characters of the last name. The SUBSTR function in option D would return the first character through last -2 characters, XX is concatenated to the result.

12. A. The CURRENT_TIMESTAMP function returns the session date, session time, and session time zone offset. The return datatype is TIMESTAMP WITH TIME ZONE.

13. C. Option A will result in NULL TOTAL_SALES for rows where there are NULL WARRANTY_
SALES. Option B is not the correct syntax for NVL2, because it requires three arguments.
With option C, if WARRANTY_SALES is NULL, then CAR_SALES is returned; otherwise, CAR_
SALES+WARRANTY_SALES is returned. The COALESCE function returns the first non-NULL
argument and could be used to obtain the desired results, but the first argument here is
CAR_SALES, which is not NULL, and therefore COALESCE will always return CAR_SALES.

14. C. The ADD_MONTHS function returns the date *d* plus *i* months. If <*d*> is the last day of the month
or the resulting month has fewer days, then the result is the last day of the resulting
month.

15. C. Statement 1 will result in 30-SEP-0007, and statement 2 will result in 30-SEP-2007.
The RR and RRRR formats derive the century based on the current date if the century is not
specified. The YY format will use the current century, and the YYYY format expects the century in the input.

16. B. The COALESCE function returns the first non-NULL parameter, which is the character
string 'Oracle '.

17. E. Option A will not work if there is a February 29 (leap year) in the next 365 days. Option
B will always add one year to the present date, except if the current date is February 29
(leap year). Option C will return the date one day later. NEW_TIME is used to return the
date/time in a different time zone. ADD_MONTHS (SYSDATE,12) can be used to achieve the
desired result.

18. A. LOCALTIMESTAMP does not return the time zone. CURRENT_DATE and SYSDATE return neither fractional seconds nor a time zone; they both return the DATE datatype.

19. D. CONVERT is used to change from one character set to another. EXTRACT works on date/
time datatypes. TRANSLATE changes all occurrences of each character with a positionally
corresponding character, so 'I like IBM' would become 'S like SUN'.

20. C. The INITCAP function capitalizes the first letter in each word. The REPLACE function
performs search-and-replace string operations. There is no IFELSE function. The DECODE
function is the one that implements IF...THEN...ELSE logic.

Chapter

3

Using Group Functions

**ORACLE DATABASE 11*g*:
SQL FUNDAMENTALS I EXAM OBJECTIVES
COVERED IN THIS CHAPTER:**

✓ **Reporting Aggregated Data Using the Group Functions**

- Identify the available group functions

- Describe the use of group functions

- Group data by using the GROUP BY clause

- Include or exclude the grouped rows by using the HAVING clause

As explained in the previous chapter, *functions* are programs that take zero or more arguments and return a single value. The exam focuses on two types of functions: single-row and aggregate (group) functions. Single-row functions were covered in Chapter 2, "Using Single-Row Functions." Group functions are covered in this chapter.

Group functions differ from single-row functions in how they are evaluated. Single-row functions are evaluated once for each row retrieved. Group functions are evaluated on groups of one or more rows at a time.

In this chapter, you will explore which group functions are available in SQL, the rules for how to use them, and what to expect on the exam about aggregating data and group functions. You will also explore nesting function calls together. SQL allows you to nest group functions within calls to single-row functions, as well as nest single-row functions within calls to group functions.

Group-Function Fundamentals

Group functions are sometimes called *aggregate functions* and return a value based on a number of inputs. The exact number of inputs is not determined until the query is executed and all rows are fetched. This differs from single-row functions, in which the number of inputs is known at parse time—before the query is executed. Because of this difference, group functions have slightly different requirements and behavior than single-row functions.

Group functions do not consider NULL values, except the COUNT(*) and GROUPING functions. You may apply the NVL function to the argument of the group function to substitute a value for NULL and hence be included in the processing of the group function. If the dataset contains all NULL values or there are no rows in the dataset, the group function returns NULL (the only exception to this rule is COUNT—it returns zero).

Most of the group functions can be applied either to ALL values or to only the DISTINCT values for the specified expression. When ALL is specified, all non-NULL values are applied to the group function. When DISTINCT is specified, only one of each non-NULL value is applied to the function. If you do not specify ALL or DISTINCT, the default is ALL.

To better understand the difference of ALL vs. DISTINCT, let's look at a few rows from the EMPLOYEES table:

```
SELECT first_name,  salary
FROM employees
WHERE first_name LIKE 'D%'
ORDER BY salary;
```

```
FIRST_NAME               SALARY
--------------------  ----------
Donald                     2600
Douglas                    2600
Diana                      4200
David                      4800
David                      6800
Daniel                     9000
David                      9500
Danielle                   9500
Den                       11000
```

The SALARY column contains nine values. Two employees have 2,600 and 9,500 each. When you count unique entries in the SALARY column, there are seven, since two are duplicates. The following SQL shows a few examples. The COUNT function is used to get a count, and the SUM function is used to find the total. (I'll discuss these functions later in the chapter.) When the UNIQUE keyword is used, the 2,600 and 9,500 are included in the result only once.

```
SELECT COUNT(salary) cnt_nu, COUNT(DISTINCT salary) cnt_uq,
       SUM(salary) sum_nu, SUM(DISTINCT salary) sum_uq
FROM employees
WHERE first_name LIKE 'D%';
```

```
    CNT_NU     CNT_UQ     SUM_NU     SUM_UQ
---------- ---------- ---------- ----------
         9          7      60000      47900
```

Unlike with single-row functions, you cannot use programmer-written functions on grouped data.

Utilizing Aggregate Functions

As with single-row functions, Oracle offers a rich variety of aggregate functions. These functions can appear in the SELECT, ORDER BY, or HAVING clauses of SELECT statements. When used in the SELECT clause, they usually require a GROUP BY clause as well. If no GROUP BY clause is specified, the default grouping is for the entire result set. Group functions cannot appear in the WHERE clause of a SELECT statement. The GROUP BY and HAVING clauses of SELECT statements are associated with grouping data. I'll discuss the GROUP BY clause before you learn about the various group functions.

You almost certainly will encounter a certification-exam question that tests whether you will incorrectly put a group function in the WHERE clause.

Grouping Data with GROUP BY

As the name implies, group functions work on data that is grouped. You tell the database how to group or categorize the data with a GROUP BY clause. Whenever you use a group function in the SELECT clause of a SELECT statement, you must place all nongrouping/nonconstant columns in the GROUP BY clause. If no GROUP BY clause is specified (only group functions and constants appear in the SELECT clause), the default grouping becomes the entire result set. When the query executes and the data is fetched, it is grouped based on the GROUP BY clause, and the group function is applied.

The basic syntax of using a group function in the SELECT statement is as follows:

```
SELECT [column names], group_function (column_name), … … …
FROM table
[WHERE condition]
[GROUP BY column names]
[ORDER BY column names]
```

In the following example, you find the total number of employees from the EMPLOYEES table:

```
SELECT COUNT(*) FROM employees;
```

```
  COUNT(*)
----------
       107
```

Since you did not have any other column in the SELECT clause, you didn't need to specify the GROUP BY clause. Suppose you want to find out the number of employees in each department; you can include department_id in the SELECT clause:

```
SELECT department_id, COUNT(*) "#Employees"
FROM employees;
SELECT department_id, COUNT(*) "#Employees"
       *
ERROR at line 1:
ORA-00937: not a single-group group function
```

Since you used an aggregate function and nonaggregated column, Oracle gave an error and is telling you to group the data. Here you have to use the GROUP BY clause. If you include a group function in the SELECT clause, you cannot select individual results unless you use the GROUP BY clause. Make sure all the columns in the SELECT clause that are not part of a group function are included in the GROUP BY clause. The following SQL lists the number of employees by their department:

```
SELECT department_id, COUNT(*) "#Employees"
FROM employees
GROUP BY department_id;
```

```
DEPARTMENT_ID #Employees
------------- ----------
          100          6
           30          6
                       1
           20          2
           70          1
           90          3
          110          2
           50         45
           40          1
           80         34
           10          1
           60          5
```

Notice that the rows are returned in no specific order. If you want the rows to be arranged in the order of the number of employees, you can either specify the aggregate function in the ORDER BY clause or use the position of the column, like so:

```
SELECT department_id, COUNT(*) "#Employees"
FROM employees
GROUP BY department_id
ORDER BY count(*) DESC, department_id;
```

```
SELECT department_id, COUNT(*) "#Employees"
FROM employees
GROUP BY department_id
ORDER BY 2 DESC, department_id;
```

```
DEPARTMENT_ID #Employees
------------- ----------
           50         45
           80         34
           30          6
          100          6
           60          5
           90          3
           20          2
          110          2
           10          1
           40          1
           70          1
                       1
```

You cannot use a column alias name or column position in the GROUP BY clause (as you can in the ORDER BY clause). The following SQL is using the column position in the GROUP BY clause and hence is giving an error:

```
SELECT department_id, COUNT(*) "#Employees"
FROM employees
GROUP BY 1;
SELECT department_id, COUNT(*) "#Employees"
       *
ERROR at line 1:
ORA-00979: not a GROUP BY expression
```

The following is another invalid SQL statement. In this example, the GROUP BY clause is using a column alias, which is not supported. Pay particular attention to GROUP BY questions on the certification exam, because you might see one with a column alias or column position used.

```
SELECT department_id di, COUNT(*) emp_cnt
FROM employees
GROUP BY di;
GROUP BY di
         *
ERROR at line 3:
ORA-00904: "DI": invalid identifier
```

The GROUP BY column does not have to be in the SELECT clause. In most cases, the result may not make much sense, but you might need it. In the following example, you are calculating the average salary of employees in each department; you do not want to share which department the average salary belongs to, and all you are interested in is knowing the average salaries in the company by department:

```
SELECT AVG(salary) average_salary
FROM employees
GROUP BY department_id;
```

```
AVERAGE_SALARY
--------------
          8600
          4420
          7000
          9500
         10000
    19333.3333
         10150
    3475.55556
          6500
    8955.88235
          4400
          5760
```

If you have more than one column in the GROUP BY clause, Oracle creates groups within groups. The order of columns in the GROUP BY clause determines the grouping. Multiple columns in the GROUP BY clause are required when you have more than one nonaggregate column in the SELECT clause. In the following example, the rows are grouped by the department_id, and within each department they are grouped by the job_id. The SQL shows the number of different jobs within each department:

```
SELECT department_id, job_id, COUNT(*)
FROM employees
GROUP BY department_id, job_id
ORDER BY 1, 2;
```

```
DEPARTMENT_ID JOB_ID       COUNT(*)
------------- ---------- ----------
           10 AD_ASST             1
           20 MK_MAN              1
           20 MK_REP              1
           30 PU_CLERK            5
           30 PU_MAN              1
           40 HR_REP              1
           50 SH_CLERK           20
           50 ST_CLERK           20
           50 ST_MAN              5
           60 IT_PROG             5
           70 PR_REP              1
           80 SA_MAN              5
           80 SA_REP             29
```

90	AD_PRES	1
90	AD_VP	2
100	FI_ACCOUNT	5
100	FI_MGR	1
110	AC_ACCOUNT	1
110	AC_MGR	1
	SA_REP	1

> The GROUP BY clause groups data, but Oracle does not guarantee the order of the result set by the grouping order. To order the data in any specific order, you must use the ORDER BY clause.

Group-Function Overview

Tables 3.1 and 3.2 summarize the group functions discussed in this chapter. I will cover each of these functions in the "Group-Function Descriptions" sections. Table 3.1 summarizes the group functions that are most likely to appear on the OCP certification exam.

TABLE 3.1   Group-Function Summary: Part 1

Function	Description
AVG	Returns the statistical mean
COUNT	Returns the number of non-NULL rows
MAX	Returns the largest value
MEDIAN	Returns a middle value
MIN	Returns the smallest value
STDDEV	Returns the standard deviation
SUM	Adds all values and returns the result
VARIANCE	Returns the sample variance, or 1 for sample size 1

Table 3.2 summarizes the group functions available in Oracle Database 11g that are not included in Table 3.1. Although they are less likely to appear on the certification exam, they are still important to review.

TABLE 3.2   Group-Function Summary: Part 2

Function	Description
CORR	Returns the coefficient of correlation of number pairs
COVAR_POP	Returns the population covariance of number pairs
COVAR_SAMP	Returns the sample covariance of number pairs
CUME_DIST	Returns the cumulative distribution of values within groupings
DENSE_RANK	Returns the ranking of rows within an ordered group, without skipping ranks on ties
FIRST	Modifies other aggregate functions to return expressions based on the ordering of the second-column expression
GROUP_ID	Returns a group identifier used to uniquely identify duplicate groups
GROUPING	Returns 0 for nonsummary rows or 1 for summary rows
GROUPING_ID	Helps determine group by levels when CUBE or ROLLUP is used.
KEEP	Modifies other aggregate functions to return the first or last value in a grouping
LAST	Modifies other aggregate functions to return expressions based on ordering of the second-column expression
PERCENTILE_CONT	Returns the interpolated value that would fall in the specified percentile position using a continuous model
PERCENTILE_DISC	Returns the interpolated value that would fall in the specified percentile position using a discrete model
PERCENT_RANK	Returns the percentile ranking of the specified value
RANK	Returns the ranking of rows within an ordered group, skipping ranks when ties occur
STDDEV_POP	Returns the population standard deviation
STDDEV_SAMP	Returns the sample standard deviation
VAR_POP	Returns the population variance
VAR_SAMP	Returns the sample variance

Group-Function Descriptions: Part 1

I divided the group functions into two sections. The group functions included in the following sections are commonly used in everyday SQL and are most likely to appear on the OCP certification exam. I discuss each of these functions and include descriptions and examples of each.

For the certification exam, concentrate more on the group functions covered in the Part 1 discussion than those in the Part 2 discussion.

AVG

This function has the syntax AVG([{DISTINCT | ALL}] *n*), where *n* is a numeric expression. The AVG function returns the average of the expression *n*.

```
SELECT job_id, AVG(salary)
FROM employees
WHERE job_id like 'AC%'
GROUP BY job_id;


JOB_ID      AVG(SALARY)
----------  -----------
AC_ACCOUNT         8300
AC_MGR            12000
```

You can use an expression or formula in the group functions. In the following example, the average compensation including commission is calculated for department 30 from the SCOTT.EMP table. The expression will be evaluated first, and its result will be used to calculate the mean. The data in department 30 is listed for understanding the example better.

```
SELECT deptno, sal, comm
FROM scott.emp
WHERE deptno = 30;


    DEPTNO        SAL       COMM
----------  ---------- ----------
        30       1600        300
        30       1250        500
        30       1250       1400
        30       2850
        30       1500          0
        30        950
```

```
SELECT deptno, AVG(sal + NVL(comm,0)) avg_comp
FROM scott.emp
WHERE deptno = 30
GROUP BY deptno;


    DEPTNO   AVG_COMP
---------- ----------
        30 1933.33333
```

Remember that group functions ignore NULL values. If the NVL function is not used, the employees with no commission are not included in the mean calculation. See the result difference in the following example without the NVL use:

```
SELECT deptno, AVG(sal + comm) avg_comp
FROM scott.emp
WHERE deptno = 30
GROUP BY deptno;


    DEPTNO   AVG_COMP
---------- ----------
        30       1950
```

COUNT

This function has the syntax COUNT({* | [DISTINCT | ALL] <x>}), where x is an expression. The COUNT function returns the number of rows in the query. If an expression is given and neither DISTINCT nor ALL is specified, the default is ALL. The asterisk (*) is a special quantity—it counts all rows in the result set, regardless of NULLs.

In the example that follows, you can count the number of rows in the EMPLOYEES table (the number of employees), the number of departments that have employees in them (DEPT_COUNT), and the number of employees that have a department (NON_NULL_DEPT_COUNT). You can see from the results that one employee is not assigned to a department, and the other 106 are assigned to one of 11 departments.

```
SELECT COUNT(*) emp_count,
       COUNT(DISTINCT department_id) dept_count,
       COUNT(ALL department_id) non_null_dept_count
FROM hr.employees;

 EMP_COUNT DEPT_COUNT NON_NULL_DEPT_COUNT
---------- ---------- --------------------
       107         11                  106
```

This next example looks at the number of employees drawing a commission, as well as the distinct number of commissions drawn. You can see that 35 out of 107 employees draw a commission and that 7 different commission levels are in use.

```
SELECT COUNT(*),
       COUNT(commission_pct) comm_count,
       COUNT(DISTINCT commission_pct) distinct_comm
FROM hr.employees;


  COUNT(*) COMM_COUNT DISTINCT_COMM
---------- ---------- -------------
       107         35             7
```

MAX

This function has the syntax MAX([{DISTINCT | ALL}] <x>), where x is an expression. This function returns the highest value in the expression x. x can be a datetime, numeric, or character value. The result of the MAX operation on the three groups of datatypes is as follows:

- If the expression x is a datetime datatype, it returns a DATE. For dates, the maximum is the latest date.
- If the expression x is a numeric datatype, it returns a NUMBER. For numbers, the maximum is the largest number.
- If the expression is a character datatype, it returns a VARCHAR2. For character strings, the maximum is the one that sorts highest based on the database character set.

Although the inclusion of either DISTINCT or ALL is syntactically acceptable, their use does not affect the calculation of a MAX function; the largest distinct value is the same as the largest of all values.

```
SELECT MAX(hire_date),
       MAX(salary),
       MAX(last_name)
FROM hr.employees;


MAX(HIRE_DA MAX(SALARY) MAX(LAST_NAME)
----------- ----------- --------------
21-APR-2000       24000 Zlotkey
```

MIN

This function has the syntax MIN([{DISTINCT | ALL}] <x>), where x is an expression. This function returns the lowest value in the expression x. Similar to the MAX function, the x in MIN can also be a numeric, datetime, or character datatype.

- If the expression x is a datetime datatype, it returns a DATE. For dates, the minimum is the earliest date.

- If the expression *x* is a numeric datatype, it returns a NUMBER. For numbers, the minimum is the smallest number.
- If the expression is a character datatype, it returns a VARCHAR2. For character strings, the minimum is the one that sorts lowest based on the database character set.

Although the inclusion of either DISTINCT or ALL is syntactically acceptable, their use does not affect the calculation of a MIN function: the smallest distinct value is the same as the smallest value.

```
SELECT job_id, MIN(hire_date) oldest, MIN(salary) low_sal,
       MAX(salary) high_sal
FROM hr.employees
WHERE job_id like '%CLERK'
GROUP BY job_id;
```

JOB_ID	OLDEST	LOW_SAL	HIGH_SAL
PU_CLERK	18-MAY-95	2500	3100
SH_CLERK	27-JAN-96	2500	4200
ST_CLERK	14-JUL-95	2100	3600

SUM

This function has the syntax SUM([{DISTINCT | ALL}] <*x*>), where *x* is a numeric expression. This function returns the sum of the expression *x*.

```
SELECT SUBSTR(phone_number, 1,3) area_code,
       SUM(salary) total_sal, ROUND(AVG(salary)) avg_sal
FROM employees
GROUP BY SUBSTR(phone_number, 1,3);
```

ARE	TOTAL_SAL	AVG_SAL
515	185900	9295
590	28800	5760
603	6000	6000
011	311500	8900
650	156400	3476

MEDIAN

MEDIAN (<*x*>) is an inverse distribution function that returns a middle value after the values in the expression are sorted. The argument *x* is an expression of numeric or datetime value.

```
SELECT job_id, MEDIAN(Salary) median, AVG(salary) average,
       MIN(salary) low_sal, MAX(salary) high_sal
```

```
FROM hr.employees
WHERE job_id like '%CLERK'
GROUP BY job_id;
```

JOB_ID	MEDIAN	AVERAGE	LOW_SAL	HIGH_SAL
PU_CLERK	2750	2775	2500	3100
SH_CLERK	3100	3215	2500	4200
ST_CLERK	2700	2785	2100	3600

STDDEV

This function has the syntax STDDEV([{DISTINCT | ALL}] <x>), where x is a numeric expression. The STDDEV function returns the numeric standard deviation of the expression x.

The standard deviation is calculated as the square root of the variance:

```
SELECT department_id,
       COUNT(salary) emp_cnt,
       MIN(salary) minimum,
       MAX(salary) maximum,
       AVG(salary) mean,
       STDDEV(salary) deviation
FROM employees
GROUP BY department_id
ORDER BY department_id;
```

DEPARTMENT_ID	EMP_CNT	MINIMUM	MAXIMUM	MEAN	DEVIATION
10	1	4400	4400	4400	0
20	2	6000	13000	9500	4949.74747
30	5	2500	11000	4420	3686.0548
40	1	6500	6500	6500	0
50	45	2100	8200	3475.55556	1488.00592
60	5	4200	9000	5760	1925.61678
70	1	10000	10000	10000	0
80	34	6100	14000	8955.88235	2033.6847
90	3	17000	24000	19333.3333	4041.45188
100	6	6900	12000	8600	1801.11077
110	2	8300	12000	10150	2616.29509
	1	7000	7000	7000	0

VARIANCE

This function has the syntax VARIANCE([{DISTINCT | ALL}] <*x*>), where *x* is a numeric expression. This function returns the variance of the expression *x*.

```
SELECT department_id,
       COUNT(*),
       VARIANCE(salary)
FROM hr.employees
GROUP BY department_id
ORDER BY department_id;
```

DEPARTMENT_ID	COUNT(*)	VARIANCE(SALARY)
10	1	0
20	2	24500000
30	6	13587000
40	1	0
50	45	2214161.62
60	5	3708000
70	1	0
80	34	4135873.44
90	3	16333333.3
100	6	3244000
110	2	6845000
	1	0

Exploring DBA Queries Using Aggregate Functions

As a DBA, you often need to find out the space allocated for a schema and how much is free. You are not interested in seeing the space used by all the tables or indexes used in the schema, but it would be nice to have the summary broken down into tablespace-wise schema storage space. Let's write few SQL statements using the group functions that you can use to calculate space usage in a database.

The DBA_SEGMENTS dictionary view shows the segments allocated in the database—each table or index created in the database must have at least one segment created. The columns you are interested in for the query are tablespace_name, owner (or the schema name), and bytes (allocated space in bytes).

The first SQL just gives the total space used by all the objects in the database. This is a simple SQL statement, on all the rows in the view:

```
SELECT SUM(bytes)/1048576 size_mb
FROM dba_segments;
```

```
   SIZE_MB
----------
 1564.8125
```

Now, let's break down this space into the next level; see the space used in each tablespace. Since you are not interested in any aggregate function over the entire database but want to break it down by tablespaces, you must have the GROUP BY clause:

```
SELECT tablespace_name, SUM(bytes)/1048576 size_mb
FROM dba_segments
GROUP BY tablespace_name;
```

```
TABLESPACE_NAME                       SIZE_MB
------------------------------    ----------
SYSAUX                                716.375
UNDOTBS1                               48.25
USERS                                  21.25
SYSTEM                                701.625
EXAMPLE                               77.3125
```

To find out the space allocated to each schema owner within the tablespaces, all you have to do is add the owner column to the query. Remember, since you are not performing any aggregate function on owner, that column also should be part of the GROUP BY clause. You will also include an ORDER BY clause so that the rows returned are in the order of tablespace name.

```
SELECT tablespace_name, owner, SUM(bytes)/1048576 size_mb
FROM dba_segments
GROUP BY tablespace_name, owner
ORDER BY 1, 2;
```

```
TABLESPACE_NAME                   OWNER                              SIZE_MB
------------------------------    ------------------------------    ----------
EXAMPLE                           HR                                  1.5625
EXAMPLE                           IX                                   1.625
EXAMPLE                           OE                                    6.25
EXAMPLE                           PM                                  11.875
EXAMPLE                           SH                                      56
SYSAUX                            CTXSYS                              5.4375
... ... ...
USERS                             HR                                   .1875
USERS                             OE                                   2.625
```

```
USERS                    SCOTT                        .375
USERS                    SH                              2
```

If you want to know the space allocated to the objects owned by each schema, you can run the following query:

```
SELECT owner, SUM(bytes)/1048576 size_mb
FROM dba_segments
GROUP BY owner
ORDER BY 1;


OWNER                          SIZE_MB
------------------------------ ----------
BTHOMAS                        16.0625
CTXSYS                          5.4375
DBSNMP                             1.5
EXFSYS                           3.875
FLOWS_030000                  100.6875
FLOWS_FILES                      .4375
HR                                1.75
... ... ...
```

Group-Function Descriptions: Part 2

The group functions discussed in the following sections are included in this chapter for completeness of the group-functions discussion. The likelihood of these appearing in the OCP certification exam is minimal, but it helps to know these functions to write better SQL queries.

Many group functions discussed in this group (and AVG, COUNT, MAX, MIN, STDDEV, SUM, and VARIANCE) can be used as analytic functions. Analytic functions are commonly used in data-warehouse environments. They compute an aggregate based on a group of rows, called a *window*. Since the OCP certification exam does not include analytic functions, I won't discuss them in this chapter.

CORR

CORR(y, x) takes two arguments, where y and x are numeric expressions representing the dependent and independent variables, respectively. This function returns the coefficient of the correlation of a set of number pairs.

The coefficient of correlation is a measure of the strength of the relationship between the two numbers. CORR can return a NULL. The coefficient of the correlation is calculated from those *x*, *y* pairs that are both not NULL using the formula COVAR_POP(*y*,*x*) / (STDDEV_POP(*y*) * STDDEV_POP(*x*)).

```
SELECT CORR(list_price,min_price) correlation,
       COVAR_POP(list_price,min_price) covariance,
       STDDEV_POP(list_price) stddev_popy,
       STDDEV_POP(min_price) stddev_popx
FROM oe.product_information
WHERE list_price IS NOT NULL
AND  min_price IS NOT NULL;


CORRELATION   COVARIANCE STDDEV_POPY STDDEV_POPX
----------- ------------ ----------- -----------
  .99947495   206065.903  496.712198  415.077696
```

The previous output shows that there is a 99.947 percent change that the list price depends on the minimum price. So when the minimum price moves by *x* percent, there is a 99.947 percent chance that the list price will also move by *x* percent.

COVAR_POP

COVAR_POP(*y*, *x*) takes two arguments, where *y* and *x* are numeric expressions. This function returns the population covariance of a set of number pairs, which can be NULL.

The covariance is a measure of how two sets of data vary in the same way. The population covariance is calculated from those *y*, *x* pairs that are both not NULL using the formula (SUM(*y**x) - SUM(*y*) * SUM(*x*) / COUNT(*x*)) / COUNT(*x*).

```
SELECT category_id,
       COVAR_POP(list_price,min_price) population,
       COVAR_SAMP(list_price,min_price) sample
FROM oe.product_information
GROUP BY category_id;


CATEGORY_ID POPULATION     SAMPLE
----------- ---------- ----------
         22         45       67.5
         25   27670.25 31623.1429
         13  25142.125 26465.3947
         11 92804.9883 98991.9875
         29    3446.75 3574.40741
         14 17982.9924 18800.4012
         21 21.5306122 25.1190476
         31 1424679.17    1709615
         24 109428.285 114639.156
         32    4575.06 4815.85263
```

```
17 5466.14286    5739.45
33        945       1134
12 26472.3333  29781.375
15 7650.84375     8160.9
16     431.38 479.311111
19 417343.887 426038.551
39 1035.14059 1086.89762
```

COVAR_SAMP

COVAR_SAMP(*y*, *x*) takes two arguments, where *y* and *x* are numeric expressions representing the dependent and independent variables, respectively. This function returns the sample covariance of a set of number pairs, which can be NULL.

The covariance is a measure of how two sets of data vary in the same way. The sample covariance is calculated from those *x*, *y* pairs that are both not NULL using the formula (SUM(*y*x*) - SUM(*y*) * SUM(*x*) / COUNT(*x*)) / (COUNT(*x*)-1).

```
SELECT SUM(list_price*min_price) sum_xy,
       SUM(list_price) sum_y,
       SUM(min_price) sum_x,
       COVAR_SAMP(list_price,min_price) COVARIANCE
FROM oe.product_information;
```

```
   SUM_XY      SUM_Y       SUM_X COVARIANCE
---------- ---------- ---------- ----------
 73803559      71407       60280 206791.488
```

CUME_DIST

This function has the syntax

```
CUME_DIST(<val_list>) WITHIN GROUP (ORDER BY col_list
[ASC|DESC] [NULLS {first|last}])
```

where *val_list* is a comma-delimited list of expressions that evaluate to numeric constant values and *col_list* is the comma-delimited list of column expressions. CUME_DIST returns the cumulative distribution of a value in *val_list* within a distribution in *col_list*.

The cumulative distribution is a measure of ranking within the ordered group and will be in the range 0 < CUME_DIST <= 1. See also PERCENT_RANK.

```
SELECT department_id,
       COUNT(*) emp_count,
       AVG(salary) mean,
       PERCENTILE_CONT(0.5) WITHIN GROUP
           (ORDER BY salary DESC) Median,
       CUME_DIST(10000) WITHIN GROUP
```

```
        (ORDER BY salary DESC) Cume_Dist_10K
FROM hr.employees
GROUP BY department_id;
```

DEPARTMENT_ID	EMP_COUNT	MEAN	MEDIAN	CUME_DIST_10K
10	1	4400	4400	.5
20	2	9500	9500	.666666667
30	6	4420	2900	.428571429
40	1	6500	6500	.5
50	45	3475.55556	3100	.02173913
60	5	5760	4800	.166666667
70	1	10000	10000	1
80	34	8955.88235	8900	.342857143
90	3	19333.3333	17000	1
100	6	8600	8000	.285714286
110	2	10150	10150	.666666667
	1	7000	7000	.5

DENSE_RANK

This function has the syntax

```
DENSE_RANK(val_list) WITHIN GROUP (ORDER BY col_list
[ASC|DESC] [NULLS {first|last}])
```

where *val_list* is a comma-delimited list of numeric constant expressions (expressions that evaluate to numeric constant values) and *col_list* is the comma-delimited list of column expressions. DENSE_RANK returns the row's rank within an ordered group. The ranks are consecutive integers starting with 1. The rank values are the number of unique values returned by the query. When there are ties, ranks are not skipped. For example, if there are three items tied for first, then second and third will not be skipped. See also RANK.

```
SELECT department_id,
       COUNT(*) emp_count,
       AVG(salary) mean,
       DENSE_RANK(10000) WITHIN GROUP
          (ORDER BY salary DESC) dense_rank_10K
FROM hr.employees
GROUP BY department_id;
```

DEPARTMENT_ID	EMP_COUNT	MEAN	DENSE_RANK_10K
10	1	4400	1
20	2	9500	2
30	6	4420	3
40	1	6500	1
50	45	3475.55556	1
60	5	5760	1
70	1	10000	1
80	34	8955.88235	7
90	3	19333.3333	3
100	6	8600	2
110	2	10150	2
	1	7000	1

To understand this ranking, let's look closer at department 80. You can see that 10,000 is the 7th-highest salary in department 80. Even though there are 11 employees that make 10,000 or more, the duplicates are not counted for ranking purposes.

```
SELECT salary, COUNT(*)
FROM hr.employees
WHERE department_id=80
GROUP BY salary
ORDER BY salary DESC;
```

SALARY	COUNT(*)
14000	1
13500	1
12000	1
11500	1
11000	2
10500	2
10000	3
9600	1

… … … (output truncated)

FIRST

See KEEP.

GROUP_ID

GROUP_ID( ) takes no arguments and requires a GROUP BY clause. GROUP_ID returns a numeric identifier that can be used to uniquely identify duplicate groups. For i duplicate groups, GROUP_ID will return values 0 through i-1.

GROUPING

GROUPING(x) takes a single argument, where x is an expression in the GROUP BY clause of the query. The GROUPING function is applicable only for queries that have a GROUP BY clause and a ROLLUP or CUBE clause. The ROLLUP and CUBE clauses create summary rows (sometimes called *superaggregates*) containing NULL in the grouped expressions. The GROUPING function returns a 1 for these summary rows and a 0 for the nonsummary rows, and it is used to distinguish the summary rows from the nonsummary rows.

GROUPING is discussed in detail in the section "Creating Superaggregates with CUBE and ROLLUP" later in this chapter.

GROUPING_ID

This function has the syntax GROUPING_ID (<col_list>) and is applicable only in SELECT statements with a GROUP BY clause with CUBE or ROLLUP. If the query contains many expressions in the GROUP BY clause, determining the GROUP BY level will require many GROUPING functions. The GROUPING_ID eliminates such a need. See the section "Creating Superaggregates with CUBE and ROLLUP" later in this chapter for a more detailed discussion on GROUPING_ID.

KEEP

The KEEP function has the syntax

```
agg_function KEEP(DENSE_RANK {FIRST|LAST}
ORDER BY col_list [ASC|DESC] [NULLS {first|last}]))
```

where agg_function is an aggregate function (COUNT, SUM, AVG, MIN, MAX, VARIANCE, or STDDEV) and col_list is a list of columns to be ordered for the grouping.

This function is sometimes referred to as either the FIRST or LAST function, and it is actually a modifier for one of the other group functions, such as COUNT or MIN. The KEEP function returns the first or last row of a sorted group. It is used to avoid the need for a self-join, looking for the minimum or maximum.

```
SELECT department_id,
       MIN(hire_date) earliest,
       MAX(hire_date) latest,
       COUNT(salary) KEEP
            (DENSE_RANK FIRST ORDER BY hire_date) FIRST,
       COUNT(salary) KEEP
            (DENSE_RANK LAST ORDER BY hire_date) LAST
FROM hr.employees
GROUP BY department_id;
```

DEPARTMENT_ID	EARLIEST	LATEST	FIRST	LAST
10	17-Sep-1987	17-Sep-1987	1	1
20	17-Feb-1996	17-Aug-1997	1	1
30	07-Dec-1994	10-Aug-1999	1	1
40	07-Jun-1994	07-Jun-1994	1	1
50	01-May-1995	08-Mar-2000	1	1
60	03-Jan-1990	07-Feb-1999	1	1
70	07-Jun-1994	07-Jun-1994	1	1
80	**30-Jan-1996**	**21-Apr-2000**	**1**	**2**
90	17-Jun-1987	13-Jan-1993	1	1
100	16-Aug-1994	07-Dec-1999	1	1
110	**07-Jun-1994**	**07-Jun-1994**	**2**	**2**
	24-May-1999	24-May-1999	1	1

You can see from the previous query that department 80's earliest and latest anniversary dates are 30-Jan-1996 and 21-Apr-2000. The FIRST and LAST columns show us that there was one employee hired on the earliest anniversary date (30-Jun-1996) and two hired on the latest anniversary date (21-Apr-2000). Likewise, you can see that department 110 has two employees hired on the earliest anniversary date (07-Jun-1994) and two on the latest anniversary date (07-Jun-1994). If you look at the following detailed data, this becomes clearer:

```
SELECT department_id,hire_date
FROM hr.employees
WHERE department_id IN (80,110)
ORDER BY 1,2;
```

```
DEPARTMENT_ID HIRE_DATE
------------- -----------
           80 30-Jan-1996
           80 04-Mar-1996
           80 24-Jan-2000
           80 29-Jan-2000
... … … (output truncated)
           80 23-Feb-2000
           80 24-Mar-2000
           80 21-Apr-2000
           80 21-Apr-2000
          110 07-Jun-1994
          110 07-Jun-1994
```

LAST

See KEEP.

PERCENT_RANK

The PERCENT_RANK function has the syntax

PERCENT_RANK(<*val_list*>) WITHIN GROUP (ORDER BY *col_list*
[ASC|DESC] [NULLS {first|last}])

where *val_list* is a comma-delimited list of expressions that evaluate to numeric constant values and *col_list* is the comma-delimited list of column expressions. PERCENT_RANK returns the percent ranking of a value in *val_list* within a distribution in *col_list*. The percent rank x will be in the range $0 <= x <= 1$.

The main difference between PERCENT_RANK and CUME_DIST is that PERCENT_RANK will always return a 0 for the first row in any set, while the CUME_DIST function cannot return a 0. You can use the PERCENT_RANK and CUME_DIST functions to examine the rankings of employees with salaries of more than 10,000 in the HR.EMPLOYEES table. Notice the different results for departments 40 and 70.

```
SELECT DEPARTMENT_ID DID,
       COUNT(*) emp_count,
       AVG(salary) mean,
       PERCENTILE_CONT(0.5) WITHIN GROUP
           (ORDER BY salary DESC) median,
       PERCENT_RANK(10000) WITHIN GROUP
           (ORDER BY salary DESC)*100 pct_rank_10K,
       CUME_DIST(10000) WITHIN GROUP
           (ORDER BY salary DESC)*100 cume_dist_10K
FROM hr.employees
GROUP BY department_id;
```

DID	EMP_COUNT	MEAN	MEDIAN	PCT_RANK_10K	CUME_DIST_10K
10	1	4400	4400	0	50
20	2	9500	9500	50	66.6666667
30	6	4420	2900	33.3333333	42.8571429
40	1	6500	6500	0	50
50	45	3475.55	3100	0	2.17391304
60	5	5760	4800	0	16.6666667
70	1	10000	10000	0	100
80	34	8955.88	8900	23.5294118	34.2857143
90	3	19333.3	17000	100	100
100	6	8600	8000	16.6666667	28.5714286
110	2	10150	10150	50	66.6666667
	1	7000	7000	0	50

PERCENTILE_CONT

PERCENTILE_CONT has the syntax

PERCENTILE_CONT(<x>) WITHIN GROUP (ORDER BY col_list
[ASC|DESC])

where *x* is a percentile value in the range 0 < *x* < 1 and *col_list* is the sort specification. PERCENTILE_CONT returns the interpolated value that would fall in percentile position *x* within the sorted group *col_list*.

This function assumes a continuous distribution and is most useful for obtaining the median value of an ordered group. The median value is defined to be the midpoint in a group of ordered numbers—half of the values are greater than the median, and half of the values are less than the median.

 The median together with the mean or average are the two most common measures of a central tendency used to analyze data. See the AVG function for more information on calculating the mean.

For this example, you will use the SCOTT.EMP table, ordered by department number:

```
SELECT ename ,deptno ,sal
FROM scott.emp
ORDER BY deptno ,sal;
```

ENAME	DEPTNO	SAL
MILLER	10	1300
CLARK	10	2450
KING	10	5000
SMITH	20	800
ADAMS	20	1100
JONES	20	2975
SCOTT	20	3000
FORD	20	3000
JAMES	30	950
WARD	30	1250
MARTIN	30	1250
TURNER	30	1500
ALLEN	30	1600
BLAKE	30	2850

You can see that for department 10, there are three SAL values: 1300, 2450, and 5000. The median would be 2450, because there is one value greater than this number and one value less than this number. The median for department 30 is not so straightforward, since there are six values and the middle value is actually between the two data points 1250 and 1500. To get the median for department 30, you need to interpolate the midpoint.

Two common techniques are used to interpolate this median value: one technique uses a continuous model, and one uses a discrete model. In the continuous model, the midpoint is assumed to be the value halfway between the 1250 and 1500, which is 1375. Using the discrete model, the median must be an actual data point, and depending on whether the data is ordered ascending or descending, the median would be 1250 or 1500.

```
SELECT deptno,
       PERCENTILE_CONT(0.5) WITHIN GROUP
            (ORDER BY sal DESC) "CONTINUOUS",
       PERCENTILE_DISC(0.5) WITHIN GROUP
            (ORDER BY sal DESC) "DISCRETE DESC",
       PERCENTILE_DISC(0.5) WITHIN GROUP
            (ORDER BY sal ASC) "DISCRETE ASC",
       AVG(sal) mean
FROM scott.emp
GROUP BY deptno;
```

DEPTNO	CONTINUOUS	DISCRETE DESC	DISCRETE ASC	MEAN
10	2450	2450	2450	2916.66667
20	2975	2975	2975	2175
30	1375	1500	1250	1566.66667

PERCENTILE_DISC

PERCENTILE_DISC has the syntax

```
PERCENTILE_DISC(<x>) WITHIN GROUP (ORDER BY col_list
[ASC|DESC])
```

where x is a percentile value in the range $0 < x < 1$ and col_list is the sort specification. PERCENTILE_DISC returns the smallest cumulative distribution value from the col_list set that is greater than or equal to value x.

This function assumes a discrete distribution. Sometimes data cannot be averaged in a meaningful way. Date data, for example, cannot be averaged, but you can calculate the median date in a group of dates. For example, to calculate the median hire date for employees in each department, you could run the following query:

```
SELECT department_id did,
       COUNT(*) emp_count,
       MIN(HIRE_DATE) first,
       MAX(HIRE_DATE) last,
```

```
        PERCENTILE_DISC(0.5) WITHIN GROUP
            (ORDER BY HIRE_DATE) median
FROM hr.employees
GROUP BY department_id;
```

```
  DID  EMP_COUNT FIRST      LAST       MEDIAN
  ---- ---------- ---------- ---------- ---------
   10          1 17-SEP-87  17-SEP-87  17-SEP-87
   20          2 17-FEB-96  17-AUG-97  17-FEB-96
   30          6 07-DEC-94  10-AUG-99  24-JUL-97
   40          1 07-JUN-94  07-JUN-94  07-JUN-94
   50         45 01-MAY-95  08-MAR-00  15-MAR-98
   60          5 03-JAN-90  07-FEB-99  25-JUN-97
   70          1 07-JUN-94  07-JUN-94  07-JUN-94
   80         34 30-JAN-96  21-APR-00  23-MAR-98
   90          3 17-JUN-87  13-JAN-93  21-SEP-89
  100          6 16-AUG-94  07-DEC-99  28-SEP-97
  110          2 07-JUN-94  07-JUN-94  07-JUN-94
              1 24-MAY-99  24-MAY-99  24-MAY-99
```

RANK

RANK has the syntax

```
RANK(<val_list>) WITHIN GROUP (ORDER BY col_list
[ASC|DESC] [NULLS {first|last}])
```

where *val_list* is a comma-delimited list of numeric constant expressions (expressions that evaluate to numeric constant values) and *col_list* is the comma-delimited list of column expressions. RANK returns the row's rank within an ordered group.

When there are ties, ranks of equal value are assigned equal rank, and the number of tied rows is skipped before the next rank is assigned. For example, if there are three items tied for first, the second and third items will be skipped, and the next will be the fourth.

```
SELECT department_id DID,
       COUNT(*) emp_count,
       AVG(salary) mean,
       DENSE_RANK(10000) WITHIN GROUP
           (ORDER BY salary DESC) dense_rank_10K
FROM hr.employees
GROUP BY department_id;
```

DID	EMP_COUNT	MEAN	DENSE_RANK_10K
10	1	4400	1
20	2	9500	2
30	6	4420	3
40	1	6500	1
50	45	3475.55556	1
60	5	5760	1
70	1	10000	1
80	34	8955.88235	7
90	3	19333.3333	3
100	6	8600	2
110	2	10150	2
	1	7000	1

To understand this ranking, let's look closer at department 80. You can see that 10,000 is the 7th-highest salary in department 80. But since there are 8 employees who make more than 10,000, the rank of 10,000 is 9. The duplicates are counted for ranking purposes.

```
SELECT salary, COUNT(*)
FROM hr.employees
WHERE department_id=80
 AND  salary > 9000
GROUP BY salary
ORDER BY salary DESC;
```

SALARY	COUNT(*)
14000	1
13500	1
12000	1
11500	1
11000	2
10500	2
10000	3
9600	1
9500	3

STDDEV_POP

STDDEV_POP(<x>) takes a single argument, where x is a numeric expression. This function returns the numeric population standard deviation of the expression x. The population standard deviation is calculated as the square root of the population variance VAR_POP.

```
SELECT department_id DID,
       STDDEV(salary) STD,
       STDDEV_POP(salary) STDPOP,
       STDDEV_SAMP(salary) STDSAMP
FROM hr.employees
GROUP BY department_id;


  DID        STD     STDPOP    STDSAMP
----- ---------- ---------- ----------
  100 1801.11077 1644.18166 1801.11077
   30  3686.0548 3296.90764  3686.0548
                 0          0
   20 4949.74747       3500 4949.74747
   70          0          0
   90 4041.45188 3299.83165 4041.45188
  110 2616.29509       1850 2616.29509
   50 1488.00592 1471.37963 1488.00592
   40          0          0
   80  2033.6847 2003.55437  2033.6847
   10          0          0
   60 1925.61678 1722.32401 1925.61678
```

STDDEV_SAMP

STDDEV_SAMP(<x>) takes a single argument, where x is a numeric expression. This function returns the numeric sample standard deviation of the expression x.

The sample standard deviation is calculated as the square root of the sample variance VAR_SAMP. *STDDEV* is similar to the STDDEV_SAMP function, except STDDEV will return 1 when there is only one row of input, while STDDEV_SAMP will return NULL.

See the description of STDDEV_POP for an example.

VAR_POP

VAR_POP(<x>) takes a single argument, where x is a numeric expression. This function returns the numeric population variance of x. The population variance is calculated with the formula (SUM(x*x) − SUM(x) * SUM(x) / COUNT(x)) / COUNT(x).

```
SELECT department_id,
       VARIANCE(salary),
       VAR_POP(salary),
       VAR_SAMP(salary)
FROM hr.employees
GROUP BY department_id;
```

DEPARTMENT_ID	VARIANCE(SALARY)	VAR_POP(SALARY)	VAR_SAMP(SALARY)
100	3244000	2703333.33	3244000
30	13587000	10869600	13587000
	0	0	
20	24500000	12250000	24500000
70	0	0	
90	16333333.3	10888888.9	16333333.3
110	6845000	3422500	6845000
50	2214161.62	2164958.02	2214161.62
40	0	0	
80	4135873.44	4014230.1	4135873.44
10	0	0	
60	3708000	2966400	3708000

VAR_SAMP

VAR_SAMP(<x>) takes a single argument, where x is a numeric expression. This function returns the numeric sample variance of x. The sample variance is calculated with the formula (SUM(x*x) – SUM(x) * SUM(x) / COUNT(x)) / (COUNT(x)-1). When the number of expressions (COUNT(x)) = 1, VARIANCE returns a 0, whereas VAR_SAMP returns NULL. When (COUNT(x)) = 0, they both return NULL. See the description of VAR_POP for an example.

Limiting Grouped Data with HAVING

A SELECT statement includes a HAVING clause to filter the grouped data. I discussed the GROUP BY clause and various group functions earlier in this chapter. The group functions cannot be used in the WHERE clause. For example, if you want to query the total salary by department excluding department 50 and return only those rows with more than 10,000 in total salary column, you would have trouble with the following query:

```
SELECT department_id, sum(salary) total_sal
FROM employees
WHERE department_id != 50
AND SUM(salary) > 10000

GROUP BY department_id;
```

The database doesn't know what the sum is when extracting the rows from the table—remember that the grouping is done after all rows have been fetched. You get an exception when you try to use SUM in the WHERE clause. The correct way to get the requested information is to instruct the database to group all rows and then limit the output of those grouped rows. You do this by using the HAVING clause. The HAVING clause is used to restrict the groups of returned rows to those groups where the specified condition is satisfied.

```
SELECT department_id, sum(salary) total_sal
FROM employees
WHERE department_id != 50
GROUP BY department_id
HAVING SUM(salary) > 10000;
```

```
DEPARTMENT_ID  TOTAL_SAL
-------------  ----------
          100      51600
           30      22100
           20      19000
           90      58000
          110      20300
           80     304500
           60      28800
```

As you can see in the previous query, a SQL statement can have both a WHERE clause and a HAVING clause. WHERE filters data before grouping; HAVING filters data after grouping.

> If the SELECT statement includes a WHERE clause and a GROUP BY clause, the GROUP BY (and HAVING) clause should come after the WHERE clause. HAVING and GROUP BY clauses can appear in any order.

Creating Superaggregates with CUBE and ROLLUP

The CUBE and ROLLUP modifiers to the GROUP BY clause allow you to create aggregations of aggregates, or *superaggregates*. These superaggregates or summary rows are included with the result set in a way similar to using the COMPUTE statement on control breaks in SQL*Plus; that is, they are included in the data and contain NULL values in the aggregated columns:

- ROLLUP creates hierarchical aggregates.
- CUBE creates aggregates for all combinations of columns specified.

The key advantages of CUBE and ROLLUP are that they will allow more robust aggregations than COMPUTE and they work with any SQL-enabled tool.

These superaggregations can be visualized with a simple example using the OE.CUSTOMERS table. For this example, say you are interested in two columns —MARITAL_STATUS, which has value single or married, and GENDER, which has the value M or F. Let's write some SQL to find the total number or rows by GENDER and MARITAL_STATUS:

```
SELECT gender, marital_status, count(*) num_rec
FROM oe.customers
GROUP BY gender, marital_status;
```

G MARITAL_STATUS	NUM_REC
- ----------------------	----------
M married	117
M single	92
F single	47
F married	63

But suppose you want subtotals for each gender—a count of all female customers regardless of marital status and a count of all male customers regardless of marital status. You could remove the MARITAL_STATUS column from the previous query, which would give you the desired result, but what if you want to display the subtotals along with the original query? Oracle introduced the ROLLUP modifier to accomplish this task.

Using ROLLUP

ROLLUP is used in SELECT statements with GROUP BY clauses to calculate multiple levels of subtotals. It also provides a grand total. The ROLLUP extension adds only minimal overhead to the overall query performance. ROLLUP creates subtotals from the most detailed level to a grand total based on the grouping list provided with the ROLLUP modifier. It creates subtotals moving left to right using the columns provided in ROLLUP. The grand total is provided only if the ROLLUP modifier includes all the columns in the GROUP BY clause.

Using the previous example, you could use the ROLLUP modifier to roll up the MARITAL_STATUS column, leaving subtotals on the grouped column GENDER. Here we have not included GENDER in the ROLLUP; hence, the grand total is not provided:

```
SELECT gender, marital_status, count(*) num_rec
FROM oe.customers
GROUP BY gender, ROLLUP(marital_status);
```

G MARITAL_STATUS	NUM_REC	
- ----------------------	----------	
F single	47	
F married	63	
F	110	<- Subtotal
M single	92	
M married	117	
M	209	<- Subtotal

In the previous example, you do not have any NULL value in the MARITAL_STATUS column. If you add another record with GENDER = 'F' and a NULL value for MARITAL_STATUS, the result would be as follows:

```
SELECT gender, marital_status, count(*) num_rec
FROM oe.customers
GROUP BY gender, ROLLUP(marital_status);
```

```
G MARITAL_STATUS          NUM_REC
- -------------------- ----------
F single                      47
F married                     63
F                              1    <- Null Marital_Status
F                            111    <- Subtotal
M single                      92
M married                    117
M                            209    <- Subtotal
```

On the OCA certification exam, this can appear as a trick question to confuse you about which line is the subtotal. You may use an NVL function to display meaningful data in the result.

Now, if you want to add an aggregation for all genders as well, you put the GENDER column into the ROLLUP modifier, as follows:

```
SELECT gender, marital_status, count(*) num_rec
FROM oe.customers
GROUP BY  ROLLUP(gender, marital_status);
```

```
G MARITAL_STATUS          NUM_REC
- -------------------- ----------
F single                      47
F married                     63
F                            110    <- Subtotal
M single                      92
M married                    117
M                            209    <- Subtotal
                             319    <- Grand total
```

The order of the columns in the ROLLUP modifier is significant, because this order determines where Oracle produces subtotals. ROLLUP creates hierarchical aggregations, so the order of the expressions in the ROLLUP clause is significant. The ordering follows the same conventions used in the GROUP BY clause—most general to most specific. When you reverse the order in the example, you get different subtotals:

```
SELECT gender, marital_status, count(*) num_rec
FROM oe.customers
GROUP BY  ROLLUP(marital_status, gender);
```

```
G MARITAL_STATUS          NUM_REC
- -------------------- ----------
F single                      47
M single                      92
  single                     139    <- Subtotal
F married                     63
M married                    117
```

```
    married                       180    <- Subtotal
                                  319    <- Grand total
```

Suppose you want all these subtotals, both by GENDER and by MARITAL_STATUS. This requirement calls for the CUBE modifier, which will produce all possible aggregations, not just those in the hierarchy of columns specified.

Using CUBE

The CUBE modifier in the GROUP BY clause creates subtotals for all possible combinations of grouping columns. Let's try the previous example using the CUBE modifier:

```
SELECT gender, marital_status, count(*) num_rec
FROM oe.customers
GROUP BY  CUBE(gender, marital_status);


G MARITAL_STATUS            NUM_REC
- -------------------- ----------
                            319    <- Grand total
  single                    139    <- Subtotal Marital_Status
  married                   180    <- Subtotal Marital_Status
F                           110    <- Subtotal Gender
F single                     47
F married                    63
M                           209    <- Subtotal Gender
M single                     92
M married                   117
```

The number of aggregations created by the CUBE modifier is the number of distinct combinations of data values in all the columns that appear in the CUBE clause. CUBE creates aggregations for all combinations of columns, so unlike ROLLUP, the order of expressions in a CUBE is not significant. As you can see, the result set is the same, but the order of rows (grouping) is different:

```
SELECT gender, marital_status, count(*) num_rec
FROM oe.customers
GROUP BY  CUBE(marital_status, gender);


G MARITAL_STATUS            NUM_REC
- -------------------- ----------
                            319
F                           110
M                           209
  single                    139
```

```
F single                  47
M single                  92
  married                180
F married                 63
M married                117
```

More DBA Queries

In the "Exploring DBA Queries Using Aggregate Functions" sidebar, you saw some queries written to find out the space allocated by tablespace, the space allocated by schema, and the space allocated by tablespace and schema. These were written using three different SQL statements. You can see the power of CUBE in the following SQL. The results from all the three SQL statements you tried before are in this summary report, showing the different levels of aggregation.

```
SELECT tablespace_name, owner, SUM(bytes)/1048576 size_mb
FROM dba_segments
GROUP BY CUBE (tablespace_name, owner);


TABLESPACE_NAME   OWNER            SIZE_MB
----------------- ---------------- ----------
                                   1564.8125  <- Grand Total
                  HR                    1.75  <- Subtotal HR schema
                  IX                   1.625  <- Subtotal IX schema
                  OE                   8.875
... ... ...
                  FLOWS            100.6875  <- Subtotal FLOWS schema
USERS                                21.25  <- Subtotal USERS tablespace
USERS             HR                  .1875  <- HR schema in USERS
tablespace
USERS             OE                  2.625  <- OE schema in USERS
tablespace
USERS             SH                      2
USERS             SCOTT                .375
USERS             BTHOMAS           16.0625
SYSAUX                             716.375  <- Subtotal SYSAUX tablespace
... ... ...
SYSAUX            FLOWS            100.6875
SYSTEM                             701.625  <- Subtotal SYSTEM tablespace
SYSTEM            SYS              685.1875
```

SYSTEM	OUTLN	.5625
SYSTEM	SYSTEM	15.875
EXAMPLE		77.3125
EXAMPLE	HR	1.5625

... ...

As you can see in the result, the space used by each schema in each tablespace is shown as well as the total space used in each tablespace and the total space used by each schema. The total space used in the database (including all tablespaces) is also shown in the very first line.

Three functions come in handy with the ROLLUP and CUBE modifiers of the GROUP BY clause—GROUPING, GROUP_ID, and GROUPING_ID.

In the examples you have seen using the ROLLUP and CUBE modifiers, there was no way of telling which row is a subtotal and which row is a grand total. You can use the GROUPING function to overcome this problem. Review the following SQL example:

```
SELECT gender, marital_status, count(*) num_rec,
       GROUPING (gender) g_grp, GROUPING (marital_status) ms_grp
FROM oe.customers
GROUP BY  CUBE(marital_status, gender);
```

G	MARITAL_STATUS	NUM_REC	G_GRP	MS_GRP
		319	1	1
F		110	0	1
M		209	0	1
	single	139	1	0
F	single	47	0	0
M	single	92	0	0
	married	180	1	0
F	married	63	0	0
M	married	117	0	0

The G_GRP column has a 1 for NULL values generated by the CUBE or ROLLUP modifier for GENDER column. Similarly, the MS_GRP column has a 1 when NULL values are generated in the MARITAL_STATUS column. Using a DECODE function on the result of the GROUPING function, you can produce a more meaningful result set, as in the following example:

```
SELECT DECODE(GROUPING (gender), 1, 'Multi-Gender',
            gender) gender,
       DECODE(GROUPING (marital_status), 1,
```

```
                   'Multi-MaritalStatus', marital_status) marital_status,
        count(*) num_rec
FROM oe.customers
GROUP BY  CUBE(marital_status, gender);
```

GENDER	MARITAL_STATUS	NUM_REC
Multi-Gender	Multi-MaritalStatus	319
F	Multi-MaritalStatus	110
M	Multi-MaritalStatus	209
Multi-Gender	single	139
F	single	47
M	single	92
Multi-Gender	married	180
F	married	63
M	married	117

 You can use the GROUPING function in the HAVING clause to filter out rows. You can display only the summary results using the GROUPING function in the HAVING clause.

The GROUPING_ID function returns the exact level of the group. It is derived from the GROUPING function by concatenating the GROUPING levels together as bits, and gives the GROUPING_ID. Review the following example closely to understand this:

```
SELECT gender, marital_status, count(*) num_rec,
        GROUPING (gender) g_grp, GROUPING (marital_status) ms_grp,
        GROUPING_ID (gender, marital_status) groupingid
FROM oe.customers
GROUP BY  CUBE(gender, marital_status);
```

G	MARITAL_STATUS	NUM_REC	G_GRP	MS_GRP	GROUPINGID
		319	1	1	3
	single	139	1	0	2
	married	180	1	0	2
F		110	0	1	1
F	single	47	0	0	0
F	married	63	0	0	0
M		209	0	1	1
M	single	92	0	0	0
M	married	117	0	0	0

In this example, you can clearly identify the level of grouping using the GROUPING_ID function. The GROUP_ID function is used to distinguish the duplicate groups. In the following example, the GROUP_ID() value is 1 for duplicate groups. When writing complex aggregates, you can filter out the duplicate rows by using the HAVING GROUP_ID = 0 clause in the SELECT statement.

```
SELECT gender, marital_status, count(*) num_rec,
       GROUPING_ID (gender, marital_status) groupingid,
       GROUP_ID() groupid
FROM oe.customers
GROUP BY  gender, CUBE(gender, marital_status);
```

G	MARITAL_STATUS	NUM_REC	GROUPINGID	GROUPID
F	single	47	0	0
F	married	63	0	0
M	single	92	0	0
M	married	117	0	0
F	single	47	0	1
F	married	63	0	1
M	single	92	0	1
M	married	117	0	1
F		110	1	0
M		209	1	0
F		110	1	1
M		209	1	1

Nesting Functions

Functions can be *nested* so that the output from one function is used as input to another. Operators have an inherent precedence of execution such as * before +, but function precedence is based on position only. Functions are evaluated innermost to outermost and left to right. This nesting technique is common with some functions, such as DECODE (covered in Chapter 2), where it can be used to implement limited IF...THEN...ELSE logic within a SQL statement.

For example, the V$SYSSTAT view contains one row for each of three interesting sort statistics. If you want to report all three statistics on a single line, you can use DECODE combined with SUM to filter out data in the SELECT clause. This filtering operation is usually done in the WHERE or HAVING clause, but if you want all three statistics on one line, you can issue this command:

```
SELECT SUM (DECODE
       (name,'sorts (memory)',value,0)) in_memory,
```

```
    SUM (DECODE
     (name,'sorts (disk)',  value,0)) on_disk,
    SUM (DECODE
     (name,'sorts (rows)',  value,0)) rows_sorted
FROM v$sysstat;


IN_MEMORY ON_DISK ROWS_SORTED
--------- ------- -----------
    728       12      326714
```

What happens in the previous statement is a single pass through the V$SYSSTAT table. The presummary result set would have the same number of rows as V$SYSSTAT (232, for instance). Of these 232 rows, all rows and columns have zeros, except for one row in each column that has the data of interest. Table 3.3 shows the data that was used in this example. The summation operation then adds all the zeros to your interesting data and gives you the results you want.

TABLE 3.3   Presummarized Result Set

in_memory	on_disk	rows_sorted
0	0	0
0	12	0
0	0	0
0	0	326714
728	0	0
0	0	0

Nesting Single-Row Functions with Group Functions

Nested functions can include single-row functions nested within group functions, as you've just seen, or group functions nested within either single-row functions or other group functions. For example, suppose you need to report on the departments in the EMP table, showing either the number of jobs or the number of managers, whichever is greater. You would enter the following:

```
SELECT deptno, GREATEST(
       COUNT(DISTINCT job),
       COUNT(DISTINCT mgr)) cnt,
       COUNT(DISTINCT job) jobs,
```

```
      COUNT(DISTINCT mgr) mgrs
FROM scott.emp
GROUP BY deptno;
```

```
   DEPTNO        CNT        JOBS       MGRS
---------- ---------- ---------- ----------
       10          3          3          2
       20          4          3          4
       30          3          3          2
```

Nesting Group Functions

You can also nest group functions within group functions. Only one level of nesting is allowed when nesting a group function within a group function. To report the maximum number of jobs in a single department, you would query the following:

```
SELECT MAX(COUNT (DISTINCT job_id))
FROM employees
GROUP BY department_id;
```

```
MAX(COUNT(DISTINCTJOB_ID))
-------------------------
                        3
```

Group functions can be nested only one level. If you try to nest more than one level of nested group functions, you will encounter an error. Also, there is no reason to do so. Here is an example to show the error, though the SQL does not mean much:

```
SELECT MIN (MAX (COUNT (DISTINCT job_id)))
FROM employees
GROUP BY department_id;
```

```
SELECT MIN (MAX (COUNT (DISTINCT job_id)))
                  *
ERROR at line 1:
ORA-00935: group function is nested too deeply
```

Summary

Though this chapter is small in terms of OCA certification exam content, this chapter is very important for the test. It is important to understand the concept of grouping data, where GROUP BY and HAVING clauses can be used, and the rules associated with using these clauses. I started this chapter by discussing the group-function fundamentals and reviewed the group functions by concentrating on the functions that are important for the test.

I also discussed how group functions can be used in the SELECT, HAVING, and ORDER BY clauses of SELECT statements. Most group functions can be applied to all data values or only to the distinct data values. Except for COUNT(*), group functions ignore NULLs. Programmer-written functions cannot be used as group functions. COUNT, SUM, and AVG are the most commonly used group functions.

When using group functions or aggregate functions in a query, the columns that do not have any aggregate function applied to them must appear in the GROUP BY clause of the query. The HAVING clause is used to filter out data after the aggregates are calculated. Group functions cannot be used in the WHERE clause.

You can create superaggregates using the CUBE and ROLLUP modifiers in the GROUP BY clause.

Exam Essentials

Understand the usage of DISTINCT in group functions.   When DISTINCT is specified, only one of each non-NULL value is applied to the function. To apply all non-NULL values, the keyword ALL should be used.

Know where group functions can be used.   Group functions can be used in GROUP BY, ORDER BY, and HAVING clauses. They cannot be used in WHERE clauses.

Know how MIN and MAX sort date and character data.   Older dates evaluate to lower values, while newer dates evaluate to higher values. Character data, even if it contains numbers, is sorted according to the NLS_SORT specification.

Know which expressions in a SELECT list must appear in a GROUP BY clause.   If any grouping is performed, all nongroup function expressions and nonconstant expressions must appear in the GROUP BY clause.

Know the order of precedence for evaluating nested functions.   You may need to evaluate an expression containing nested functions. Make sure you understand the left-to-right order of precedence used to evaluate these expressions.

Review Questions

1. How will the results of the following two statements differ?
   Statement 1:
   ```
   SELECT MAX(longitude), MAX(latitude)
   FROM zip_state_city;
   ```

   Statement 2:
   ```
   SELECT MAX(longitude), MAX(latitude)
   FROM zip_state_city
   GROUP BY state;
   ```

   A. Statement 1 will fail because it is missing a GROUP BY clause.

   B. Statement 2 will return one row, and statement 1 may return more than one row.

   C. Statement 2 will fail because it does not have the columns used in the GROUP BY clause in the SELECT clause.

   D. Statement 1 will display two columns, and statement 2 will display two values for each state.

2. Using the SALES table described here, you need to report the following:
   - Gross, net, and earned revenue for the second and third quarters of 1999
   - Gross, net, and earned revenue for sales in the states of Illinois, California, and Texas (codes IL, CA, and TX)

Column Name	state_code	sales_date	gross	net	earned
Key Type	PK	PK			
Nulls/Unique	NN	NN	NN	NN	NN
FK Table					
Datatype	VARCHAR2	DATE	NUMBER	NUMBER	NUMBER
Length	2		11,2	11,2	11,2

   Will all the requirements be met with the following SQL statement?
   ```
   SELECT state_code, SUM(ALL gross), SUM(net), SUM(earned)
   FROM sales_detail
   WHERE TRUNC(sales_date,'Q') BETWEEN
                    TO_DATE('01-Apr-1999','DD-Mon-YYYY')
                AND TO_DATE('01-Sep-1999','DD-Mon-YYYY')
    AND  state_cd IN ('IL','CA','TX')
   GROUP BY state_code;
   ```

A. The statement meets all three requirements.

B. The statement meets two of the three requirements.

C. The statement meets one of the three requirements.

D. The statement meets none of the three requirements.

E. The statement will raise an exception.

3. Which line in the following SQL has an error?
```
1  SELECT department_id, SUM(salary)
2  FROM employees
3  WHERE department_id <> 40
4  ORDER BY department_id;
```
   A. 1

   B. 3

   C. 4

   D. No errors in SQL

4. John is trying to find out the average salary of employees in each department. He noticed that the SALARY column can have NULL values, and he does not want the NULLs included when calculating the average. Identify the correct SQL that will produce the desired results.

   A. SELECT department_id, AVG(salary)

      FROM employees

      GROUP BY department_id;

   B. SELECT department_id, AVG(NVL(salary,0))

      FROM employees

      GROUP BY department_id;

   C. SELECT department_id, NVL(AVG(salary), 0)

      FROM employees

      GROUP BY department_id;

   D. SELECT department_id, AVG(salary)

      FROM employees

      GROUP BY department_id

      HAVING salary IS NOT NULL;

5. Review the following two SQL statements, and choose the appropriate option.

    ```
    1.    SELECT department_id, COUNT(*)
    FROM employees
    HAVING COUNT(*) > 10
    GROUP BY department_id;
    2.    SELECT department_id, COUNT(*)
    FROM employees
    WHERE COUNT(*) > 10
    GROUP BY department_id;
    ```

    A. Statement 1 and statement 2 will produce the same results.

    B. Statement 1 will succeed, and statement 2 will fail.

    C. Statement 2 will succeed, and statement 1 will fail.

    D. Both statements fail.

6. Read the following SQL carefully, and choose the appropriate option. The JOB_ID column shows the various jobs.

    ```
    SELECT  MAX(COUNT(*))
    FROM employees
    GROUP BY  job_id, department_id;
    ```

    A. Aggregate functions cannot be nested.

    B. The columns in the GROUP BY clause must appear in the SELECT clause for the query to work.

    C. The GROUP BY clause is not required in this query.

    D. The SQL will produce the highest number of jobs within a department.

7. Identify the SQL that produces the correct result.

    A.
    ```
    SELECT department_id, SUM(salary)
    FROM employees
    WHERE department_id <> 50
    GROUP BY department_id
    HAVING COUNT(*) > 30;
    ```

    B.
    ```
    SELECT department_id, SUM(salary) sum_sal
    FROM employees
    WHERE department_id <> 50
    GROUP BY department_id
    HAVING sum_sal > 3000;
    ```

    C. SELECT department_id, SUM(salary) sum_sal

        FROM employees

        WHERE department_id <> 50

        AND sum_sal > 3000

        GROUP BY department_id;

    D. SELECT department_id, SUM(salary)

        FROM employees

        WHERE department_id <> 50

        AND SUM(salary) > 3000

        GROUP BY department_id;

8. Consider the following SQL, and choose the most appropriate option.

    SELECT COUNT(DISTINCT SUBSTR(first_name, 1,1))

    FROM employees;

    A. A single-row function nested inside a group function is not allowed.

    B. The GROUP BY clause is required to successfully run this query.

    C. Removing the DISTINCT qualifier will fix the error in the query.

    D. The query will execute successfully without any modification.

9. The sales order number (ORDER_NO) is the primary key in the table SALES_ORDERS. Which query will return the total number of orders in the SALES_ORDERS table?

    A. SELECT COUNT(ALL order_no) FROM sales_orders;

    B. SELECT COUNT(DISTINCT order_no) FROM sales_orders;

    C. SELECT COUNT(order_no) FROM sales_orders;

    D. SELECT COUNT(NVL(order_no,0) FROM sales_orders;

    E. All of the above

    F. A and C

10. Sheila wants to find the highest salary within each department of the EMPLOYEES table. Which query will help her get what she wants?

    A. SELECT MAX(salary) FROM employees;

    B. SELECT MAX(salary BY department_id) FROM employees;

    C. SELECT department_id, MAX(salary) max_sal FROM employees;

    D. SELECT department_id, MAX(salary) FROM employees GROUP BY department_id;

    E. SELECT department_id, MAX(salary) FROM employees USING department_id;

11. Which assertion about the following queries is true?
    ```
    SELECT COUNT(DISTINCT mgr), MAX(DISTINCT salary)
    FROM emp;

    SELECT COUNT(ALL mgr), MAX(ALL salary)
    FROM emp;
    ```
    A. They will always return the same numbers in columns 1 and 2.
    B. They may return different numbers in column 1 but will always return the same number in column 2.
    C. They may return different numbers in both columns 1 and 2.
    D. They will always return the same number in column 1 but may return different numbers in column 2.

12. Which clauses in the SELECT statement can use single-row functions nested in aggregate functions? (Choose all that apply.)
    A. SELECT
    B. ORDER BY
    C. WHERE
    D. GROUP BY

13. Consider the following two SQL statements. Choose the most appropriate option.
    1. `select substr(first_name, 1,1) fn, SUM(salary) FROM employees GROUP BY first_name;`
    2. `select substr(first_name, 1,1) fn, SUM(salary) FROM employees GROUP BY substr(first_name, 1,1);`

    A. Statement 1 and 2 will produce the same result.
    B. Statement 1 and 2 will produce different results.
    C. Statement 1 will fail.
    D. Statement 2 will fail, but statement 1 will succeed.

14. How will the results of the following two SQL statements differ?
    ```
    Statement 1:
    SELECT COUNT(*), SUM(salary)
    FROM hr.employees;

    Statement 2:
    SELECT COUNT(salary), SUM(salary)
    FROM hr.employees;
    ```

A. Statement 1 will return one row, and statement 2 may return more than one row.

B. Both statements will fail because they are missing a GROUP BY clause.

C. Both statements will return the same results.

D. Statement 2 may return a smaller COUNT value than statement 1.

15. Why does the following SELECT statement fail?

```
SELECT colorname Colour, MAX(cost)
FROM itemdetail
WHERE UPPER(colorname) LIKE '%WHITE%'
GROUP BY colour
HAVING COUNT(*) > 20;
```

A. A GROUP BY clause cannot contain a column alias.

B. The condition COUNT(*) > 20 should be in the WHERE clause.

C. The GROUP BY clause must contain the group functions used in the SELECT list.

D. The HAVING clause can contain only the group functions used in the SELECT list.

16. What will the following SQL statement return?

```
select max(prod_pack_size)
from sh.products
where min(prod_weight_class) = 5;
```

A. An exception will be raised.

B. The largest PROD_PACK_SIZE for rows containing PROD_WEIGHT_CLASS of 5 or higher

C. The largest PROD_PACK_SIZE for rows containing PROD_WEIGHT_CLASS of 5

D. The largest PROD_PACK_SIZE in the SH.PRODUCTS table

17. Why will the following query raise an exception?

```
select dept_no, avg(distinct salary),
       count(job) job_count
from emp
where mgr like 'J%'
  or  abs(salary) > 10
having count(job) > 5
order by 2 desc;
```

A. The HAVING clause cannot contain a group function.

B. The GROUP BY clause is missing.

C. ABS() is not an Oracle function.

D. The query will not raise an exception.

18. Which clause will generate an error when the following query is executed?

```
SELECT department_id, AVG(salary) avg_sal
FROM employees
GROUP BY department_id
HAVING TRUNC(department_id) > 50;
```

    A. The GROUP BY clause, because it is missing the group function.

    B. The HAVING clause, because single-row functions cannot be used.

    C. The HAVING clause, because the AVG function used in the SELECT clause is not used in the HAVING clause.

    D. None of the above. The SQL statement will not return an error.

19. Which statements are true? (Choose all that apply.)

    A. A group function can be used only if the GROUP BY clause is present.

    B. Group functions along with nonaggregated columns can appear in the SELECT clause as long as a GROUP BY clause and a HAVING clause are present.

    C. The HAVING clause is optional when the GROUP BY clause is used.

    D. The HAVING clause and the GROUP BY clause are mutually exclusive; you can use only one clause in a SELECT statement.

20. Read the following two statements, and choose the best option.

    1. HAVING clause should always appear after the GROUP BY clause.

    2. GROUP BY clause should always appear after the WHERE clause.

    A. Statement 1 and 2 are false.

    B. Statement 1 is true, and statement 2 is false.

    C. Statement 1 is false, and statement 2 is true.

    D. Statements 1 and 2 are true.

Answers to Review Questions

1. **D.** Though you do not have a `state` column in the SELECT clause, having it in the GROUP BY clause will group the results by state, so you end up getting two values (two columns) for each state.

2. **A.** All requirements are met. The gross-, net-, and earned-revenue requirements are satisfied with the SELECT clause. The second- and third-quarter sales requirement is satisfied with the first predicate of the WHERE clause—the sales date will be truncated to the first day of a quarter; thus, `01-Apr-1999` or `01-Jul-1999` for the required quarters (which are both between `01-Apr-1999` and `01-Sep-1999`). The state codes requirement is satisfied by the second predicate in the WHERE clause. This question is intentionally misleading, but so are some exam questions (and, unfortunately, some of the code in some shops).

3. **C.** Since the `department_id` column does not have any aggregate function applied to it, it must appear in the GROUP BY clause. The ORDER BY clause in the SQL must be replaced with a GROUP BY clause to make the query work.

4. **A.** Since group functions do not include NULL values in their calculation, you do not have to do anything special to exclude the NULL values. Only COUNT(*) includes NULL values.

5. **B.** An aggregate function is not allowed in the WHERE clause. You can have the GROUP BY and HAVING clauses in any order, but they must appear after the WHERE clause.

6. **D.** The SQL will work fine and produce the result. Since group functions are nested, a GROUP BY clause is required.

7. **A.** It is perfectly alright to have one function in the SELECT clause and another function in the HAVING clause of the query. Options B and C are trying to use the alias name, which is not allowed. Option D has a group function in the WHERE clause, which is also not allowed.

8. **D.** The query will return how many distinct alphabets are used to begin names in the EMPLOYEES table. You can nest a group function inside a single-row function, and vice versa.

9. **E.** All the queries will return the same result. Since ORDER_NO is the primary key, there cannot be NULL values in the column. Hence, ALL and DISTINCT will give the same result.

10. **D.** Option A will display the highest salary of all the employees. Options B and E use invalid syntax keywords. Option C does not have a GROUP BY clause.

11. **B.** The first column in the first query is counting the distinct MGR values in the table. The first column in the second query is counting all MGR values in the table. If a manager appears twice, the first query will count her one time, but the second will count her twice. Both the first query and the second query are selecting the maximum salary value in the table.

12. **A, B.** A group function is not allowed in GROUP BY or WHERE clauses, whether you use it as nested or not.

13. B. Both statements are valid. The first statement will produce the number of rows equal to the number of unique first_name values. The second statement will produce the number of rows equal to the unique number of first characters in the first_name column.

14. D. COUNT(*) will count all rows in the table. COUNT(salary) will count only the number of salary values that appear in the table. If there are any rows with a NULL salary, statement 2 will not count them.

15. A. A GROUP BY clause must contain the column or expressions on which to perform the grouping operation. It cannot use column aliasing.

16. A. You cannot place a group function in the WHERE clause. Instead, you should use a HAVING clause.

17. B. There is at least one column in the SELECT list that is not a constant or group function, so a GROUP BY clause is mandatory.

18. D. The HAVING clause filters data after the group function is applied. If an aggregate function is not used in the HAVING clause, the column used must be part of the SELECT clause.

19. C. The HAVING clause can be used in a SELECT statement only if the GROUP BY clause is present. The optional HAVING clause filters data after the rows are summarized.

20. C. The GROUP BY and HAVING clauses can appear in any order in the SELECT clause. If a WHERE clause is present, it must be before the GROUP BY clause.

Chapter

4

Using Joins and Subqueries

ORACLE DATABASE 11*g*: SQL FUNDAMENTALS I EXAM OBJECTIVES COVERED IN THIS CHAPTER

✓ **Displaying data from multiple tables**

- Write SELECT statements to access data from more than one table using equijoins and nonequijoins

- Join a table to itself by using a self-join

- View data that generally does not meet a join condition by using outer joins

- Generate a Cartesian product of all rows from two or more tables

✓ **Using subqueries to solve queries**

- Define subqueries

- Describe the types of problems that the subqueries can solve

- List the types of subqueries

- Write single-row and multiple-row subqueries

✓ **Using the Set operators**

- Describe set operators

- Use a set operator to combine multiple queries into a single query

- Control the order of rows returned

A database has many tables that store data. In Chapter 1, "Introducing SQL," you learned how to write simple queries that select data from one table. Although this information is essential to passing the certification exam, the ability to join two or more related tables and access information is the core strength of relational databases. Using the SELECT statement, you can write advanced queries that satisfy user requirements.

This chapter focuses on querying data from more than one table using table joins and subqueries. When you use two or more tables or views in a single query, it is a join query. You'll need to understand how the various types of joins and subqueries work, as well as the proper syntax, for the certification exam.

Set operators in Oracle let you combine results from two or more SELECT statements. The results of each SELECT statement are considered a set, and Oracle provides UNION, INTERSECT, and MINUS operators to get the desired results. You will learn how these operators work in this chapter.

Writing Multiple-Table Queries

In relational database management systems (RDBMSs), related data can be stored in multiple tables. You use the power of SQL to relate the information and query data. A SELECT statement has a mandatory SELECT clause and FROM clause. The SELECT clause can have a list of columns, expressions, functions, and so on. The FROM clause tells you in which table(s) to look for the required information. In Chapter 1, you learned to query data using simple SELECT statements from a single table. In this chapter, you will learn how to retrieve data from more than one table.

To query data from more than one table, you need to identify common columns that relate the two tables. Here's how you do it:

1.	In the SELECT clause, you list the columns you are interested in from all the related tables.

2.	In the FROM clause, you include all the table names separated by commas.

3.	In the WHERE clause, you define the relationship between the tables listed in the FROM clause using comparison operators.

You can also specify the relationship using a JOIN clause instead of the WHERE clause. The JOIN clause introduced by Oracle in Oracle 9i was then added to conform to the ISO/ANSI

SQL1999 standard. Throughout this section, you'll see examples of queries using the Oracle native syntax as well as the ISO/ANSI SQL1999 standard. A query from multiple tables without a relationship or common column is known as a Cartesian join or cross join and is discussed later in this chapter.

A *join* is a query that combines rows from two or more tables or views. Oracle performs a join whenever multiple tables appear in the query's FROM clause. The query's SELECT clause can have the columns or expressions from any or all of these tables.

> If multiple tables have the same column names, the duplicate column names should be qualified in the queries with their table name or table alias.

Inner Joins

Inner joins return only the rows that satisfy the join condition. The most common operator used to relate two tables is the equality operator (=). If you relate two tables using an equality operator, it is an *equality join*, also known as an *equijoin*. This type of join combines rows from two tables that have equivalent values for the specified columns.

Simple Inner Joins

A simple inner join has only the join condition specified, without any other filtering conditions. For example, let's consider a simple join between the DEPARTMENTS and LOCATIONS tables of the HR schema. The common column in these tables is LOCATION_ID. You will query these tables to get the location ID, city name, and department names in that city:

```
SELECT locations.location_id, city, department_name
FROM   locations, departments
WHERE  locations.location_id = departments.location_id;
```

Here, you are retrieving data from two tables—two columns from the LOCATIONS table and one column from the DEPARTMENTS table. These two tables are joined in the WHERE clause using an equality operator on the LOCATION_ID column. It is not necessary for the column names in both tables to have the same name to have a join. Notice that the LOCATION_ID column is qualified with its table name for every occurrence. This is to avoid ambiguity; it is not necessary to qualify each column, but it increases the readability of the query. If the same column name appears in more than one table used in the query, you must qualify the column name with the table name or table alias.

To execute a join of three or more tables, Oracle takes these steps:

1. Oracle joins two of the tables based on the join conditions, comparing their columns.

2. Oracle joins the result to another table, based on join conditions.

3. Oracle continues this process until all tables are joined into the result.

Complex Inner Joins

Apart from specifying the join condition in the WHERE clause, you may have another condition to limit the rows retrieved. Such joins are known as *complex joins*. For example, to continue with the example in the previous section, if you are interested only in the departments that are outside the United States, use this query:

```
SELECT locations.location_id, city, department_name
FROM   locations, departments
WHERE  locations.location_id = departments.location_id
AND    country_id != 'US';
```

```
LOCATION_ID CITY                 DEPARTMENT_NAME
----------- -------------------- -----------------
       1800 Toronto              Marketing
       2400 London              Human Resources
       2700 Munich              Public Relations
       2500 Oxford              Sales
```

Using Table Aliases

Like columns, tables can have alias names. Table aliases increase the readability of the query. You can also use them to shorten long table names with shorter alias names. Specify the *table alias name* next to the table, separated with a space. You can rewrite the query in the previous section using alias names, as follows:

```
SELECT l.location_id, city, department_name
FROM   locations l, departments d
WHERE  l.location_id = d.location_id
AND    country_id != 'US';
```

When tables (or views or materialized views) are specified in the FROM clause, Oracle looks for the object in the schema (or user) connected to the database. If the table belongs to another schema, you must qualify it with the schema name. (You may avoid this by using synonyms, which are discussed in Chapter 7, "Creating Schema Objects.") You can use the schema owner to qualify a table; you can also use the table owner and schema owner to qualify a column. Here is an example:

```
SELECT locations.location_id, hr.locations.city
     ,department_name
FROM   hr.locations, hr.departments
WHERE  locations.location_id = departments.location_id;
```

Keep in mind that you can qualify a column name with its schema and table only when the table name is qualified with the schema. In the previous SQL, you qualified the column

CITY with the schema HR. This is possible only if you qualify the LOCATIONS table with the schema. The following SQL will produce an error:

```
SELECT locations.location_id, hr.locations.city
       ,department_name
FROM   locations, hr.departments
WHERE  locations.location_id = departments.location_id;


SELECT locations.location_id, hr.locations.city
                              *
ERROR at line 1:
ORA-00904: "HR"."LOCATIONS"."CITY": invalid identifier
```

When you use table alias names, you must qualify the column names with the alias name only; qualifying the columns with the table name will produce an error, as in this example:

```
SELECT locations.location_id, city, department_name
FROM   locations l, hr.departments d
WHERE  locations.location_id = d.location_id;


WHERE  locations.location_id = d.location_id
       *
ERROR at line 3:
ORA-00904: "LOCATIONS"."LOCATION_ID": invalid identifier
```

The correct syntax is to replace locations.location_id with l.location_id in the SELECT and WHERE clauses.

If there are no common column names between the two tables used in the join (the FROM clause), you don't need to qualify the columns. However, if you qualify the columns, you are telling the Oracle database engine where exactly to find the column; hence, you are improving the performance of the query.

If there are column names common to multiple tables used in a join query, you must qualify the column name with a table name or table alias. This is true for column names appearing in SELECT, WHERE, ORDER BY, GROUP BY, and HAVING clauses. When using the ANSI syntax, the rule is different. The ANSI syntax is discussed in the next section.

NOTE   When joining columns using the traditional syntax or ANSI syntax, if the column datatypes are different, Oracle tries to perform an implicit datatype conversion. This may affect your query performance. It is better if the columns used in the join condition have the same datatype or if you use the explicit conversion functions you learned in Chapter 2, "Using Single-Row Functions."

Using the ANSI Syntax

The difference between traditional Oracle join syntax and the ANSI/ISO SQL1999 syntax is that in ANSI, the join type is specified explicitly in the FROM clause. Using the ANSI syntax is clearer and is recommended over the traditional Oracle syntax. Simple joins can have the following forms:

```
<table name> NATURAL [INNER] JOIN <table name>
```

```
<table name> [INNER] JOIN <table name> USING (<columns>)
```

```
<table name> [INNER] JOIN <table name> ON <condition>
```

The following sections discuss each of the syntax forms in detail. In all three syntaxes, the keyword INNER is optional and is the default.

NATURAL JOIN

The NATURAL keyword indicates a *natural join*, where the join is based on all columns that have same name in both tables. In this type of join, you should not qualify the column names with the table name or table alias name. Let's return to the example of querying the DEPARTMENTS and LOCATIONS tables using LOCATION_ID as the join column. The new Oracle syntax is as follows:

```
SELECT location_id, city, department_name
FROM   locations NATURAL JOIN departments;
```

The common column in these two tables is LOCATION_ID, and that column is used to join the tables. When specifying NATURAL JOIN, the columns with the same name in both tables should also have same datatype. The following query will return the same results:

```
SELECT location_id, city, department_name
FROM   departments NATURAL JOIN locations;
```

Notice that even though the LOCATION_ID column is in both tables, you did not qualify this column in the SELECT clause. You cannot qualify the column names used for the join when using the NATURAL JOIN clause. The following query will result in an error:

```
SELECT l.location_id, city, department_name
FROM   departments NATURAL JOIN locations l;
SELECT l.location_id, city, department_name
       *
ERROR at line 1:
ORA-25155: column used in NATURAL join cannot have qualifier
```

The following query will not return an error because the qualifier is used on a column that's not part of the join condition:

```
SELECT location_id, city, d.department_name
FROM   departments d NATURAL JOIN locations l;
```

If you use SELECT *, common columns are listed only once in the result set. The following example demonstrates this. The common column in the COUNTRIES table and the REGIONS table is the REGION_ID.

```
SQL> DESCRIBE regions
 Name                       Null?    Type
 ----------------------     -------- ------------
 REGION_ID                  NOT NULL NUMBER
 REGION_NAME                         VARCHAR2(25)


SQL> DESCRIBE countries
 Name                       Null?    Type
 ----------------------     -------- ------------
 COUNTRY_ID                 NOT NULL CHAR(2)
 COUNTRY_NAME                        VARCHAR2(40)
 REGION_ID                           NUMBER


SELECT *
FROM    regions NATURAL JOIN countries;


 REGION_ID REGION_NAME         CO COUNTRY_NAME
 ---------- ---------------    -- ------------------
         1 Europe              UK United Kingdom
         1 Europe              NL Netherlands
         1 Europe              IT Testing Update
         1 Europe              FR France
... ... ...
```

Here is another example, which joins three tables:

```
SELECT region_id, region_name, country_id, country_name,
       location_id, city
FROM    regions
NATURAL JOIN countries
NATURAL JOIN locations;
```

When specifying more than two tables using NATURAL JOIN syntax, it is a good idea to use parentheses to increase readability. The previous SQL can be interpreted in two ways:

- Join the REGIONS table and the COUNTRIES table, and join the result to the LOCATIONS table.

- Join the COUNTRIES table to the LOCATIONS table, and join the result to the REGIONS table.

If you do not use parentheses, Oracle uses left associativity by pairing the tables from left to right (as in the first scenario). By using parentheses, you can make the query less ambiguous, as shown here:

```
SELECT region_id, region_name, country_id, country_name,
       location_id, city
FROM   locations
NATURAL JOIN (regions
NATURAL JOIN countries);
```

The same query written in traditional Oracle syntax is as follows:

```
SELECT regions.region_id, region_name, countries.country_id, country_name,
       location_id, city
FROM   regions, countries, locations
WHERE  regions.region_id = countries.region_id
AND    countries.country_id = locations.country_id;
```

Though NATURAL JOIN syntax is easy to read and use, its usage should be discouraged in good coding practice. Since NATURAL JOIN joins the tables by all the identical column names, you could end up having a wrong join condition if you're not careful. It is always better to explicitly specify the join condition using the syntaxes available.

JOIN...USING

If there are many columns that have the same names in the tables you are joining and they do not have the same datatype, or you want to specify the columns that should be considered for an equijoin, you can use the JOIN...USING syntax. The USING clause specifies the column names that should be used to join the tables. Here is an example:

```
SELECT location_id, city, department_name
FROM   locations JOIN departments USING (location_id);
```

The column names used in the USING clause should not be qualified with a table name or table alias. The column names not appearing in the USING clause can be qualified. If there are other common column names in the tables and if those column names are used in the query, they must be qualified.

Let's consider this syntax with joining more than two tables:

```
SELECT region_name, country_name, city
FROM   regions
JOIN   countries USING (region_id)
JOIN   locations USING (country_id);
```

Here, the REGIONS table is joined with the COUNTRIES table using the REGION_ID column, and its result is joined with the LOCATIONS table using the COUNTRY_ID column.

The following query will result in an error because there is no common column between the REGIONS and LOCATIONS tables:

```
SELECT region_name, country_name, city
FROM    regions
JOIN    locations USING (country_id)
JOIN    countries USING (region_id);


JOIN    locations USING (country_id)
                          *
ERROR at line 3:
ORA-00904: "REGIONS"."COUNTRY_ID": invalid identifier
```

You can add a WHERE clause to limit the number of rows and an ORDER BY clause to sort the rows retrieved along with any type of join operation:

```
SELECT region_name, country_name, city
FROM    regions
JOIN    countries USING (region_id)
JOIN    locations USING (country_id)
WHERE   country_id = 'US'
ORDER BY 1;
```

Remember that you cannot use alias or table names to qualify the column names on the columns used in the join operation anywhere in the query when using the NATURAL JOIN or JOIN USING syntax. You may see questions in the certification exam testing this rule.

JOIN...ON

When you do not have common column names between tables to make a join or if you want to specify arbitrary join conditions, you can use the JOIN...ON syntax. This syntax specifically defines the join condition using the column names. You can qualify column names with a table name or alias name. If the column name is common to multiple tables involved in the query, those column names must be qualified.

Using the JOIN ON syntax over the traditional join method separates the table joins from the other conditions. Since this syntax explicitly states the join condition, it is easier to read and understand. Here is the three-table example you used in the previous section, written using the JOIN...ON syntax. Notice the use of qualifier on the COUNTRY_ID column; this is required because COUNTRY_ID appears in COUNTRIES and LOCATIONS tables.

```
SELECT region_name, country_name, city
FROM    regions r
JOIN    countries c ON r.region_id = c.region_id
JOIN    locations l ON c.country_id = l.country_id
WHERE   c.country_id = 'US';
```

Multitable Joins

A *multitable join* is a join of more than two tables. In the ANSI syntax, joins are performed from left to right. The first join condition can reference columns from only the first and second tables; the second join condition can reference columns from the first, second, and third tables; and so on. Consider the following example:

```
SELECT first_name, department_name, city
FROM    employees e
JOIN    departments d
ON (e.department_id = d.department_id)
JOIN    locations l
ON (d.location_id = l.location_id);
```

The first join to be performed is EMPLOYEES and DEPARTMENTS. The first join condition can reference columns in EMPLOYEES and DEPARTMENTS but cannot reference columns in LOCATIONS. The second join condition can reference columns from all three tables.

 Real World Scenario

How Do You Specify Join Conditions When You Have More Than One Column to Join?

Company XYZ was keeping detailed information about customer geography in its purchase-orders database. Consider the tables and data shown here. For simplicity, I've reduced the number of columns in the tables to the interesting ones for this example. For this demonstration, say you are interested in three tables: COUNTRY, STATE, and CITY.

```
SQL> SELECT * FROM country;

  CNT_CODE CNT_NAME               CONTINENT
---------- ---------------------- ----------
         1 UNITED STATES          N.AMERICA
        91 INDIA                  ASIA
        65 SINGAPORE              ASIA

SQL> SELECT * FROM state;

  CNT_CODE ST ST_NAME
---------- -- ---------------
         1 TX TEXAS
         1 CA CALIFORNIA
         1 TN TENNESSE
        91 TN TAMIL NADU
        91 KL KERALA
```

```
SQL> SELECT * FROM city;

  CNT_CODE ST    CTY_CODE CTY_NAME
---------- -- ---------- --------------------
         1 TX        1001 DALLAS
         1 CA        8099 LOS ANGELES
        91 TN        2243 CHENNAI

SQL>
```

The CNT_CODE column relates the COUNTRY table and the STATE table. The ST_CODE and CNT_CODE columns relate the STATE table and CITY table. The following examples show how to join the STATE and CITY tables to get information on the country code, state name, and city name.

Traditional Oracle Join

```
SQL> SELECT s.cnt_code, st_name, cty_name
  2  FROM    state s, city c
  3  WHERE   s.cnt_code = c.cnt_code
  4  AND     s.st_code  = c.st_code
  5  AND     s.cnt_code = 1;
  CNT_CODE ST_NAME              CTY_NAME
---------- -------------------- -------------
         1 CALIFORNIA           LOS ANGELES
         1 TEXAS                DALLAS
SQL>
```

ANSI Natural Join

```
SQL> SELECT cnt_code, st_name, cty_name
  2  FROM    state NATURAL JOIN city
  3  WHERE   cnt_code = 1;
  CNT_CODE ST_NAME              CTY_NAME
---------- -------------------- --------------
         1 TEXAS                DALLAS
         1 CALIFORNIA           LOS ANGELES
SQL>
```

ANSI Using JOIN...USING

```
SQL> SELECT cnt_code, st_name, cty_name
  2  FROM    state JOIN city USING (cnt_code, st_code)
  3  WHERE   cnt_code = 1;
```

```
    CNT_CODE ST_NAME             CTY_NAME
---------- -------------------- -----------------
         1 TEXAS                DALLAS
         1 CALIFORNIA           LOS ANGELES
SQL>

ANSI Using JOIN...ON
SQL> SELECT s.cnt_code, s.st_name, c.cty_name
  2  FROM    state s
  3  JOIN    city c ON s.cnt_code = c.cnt_code
  4  AND     s.st_code  = c.st_code
  5* WHERE   s.cnt_code = 1;
    CNT_CODE ST_NAME             CTY_NAME
---------- -------------------- -----------------
         1 CALIFORNIA           LOS ANGELES
         1 TEXAS                DALLAS
SQL>
```

Cartesian Joins

A *Cartesian join* occurs when data is selected from two or more tables and there is no common relation specified in the WHERE clause. If you do not specify a join condition for the tables listed in the FROM clause, Oracle joins each row from the first table to every row in the second table. If the first table has 3 rows and the second table has 4 rows, the result will have 12 rows. If you add another table with 2 rows without specifying a join condition, the result will have 24 rows.

For the most part, Cartesian joins happen when there are many tables in the FROM clause and developers forget to include the join condition or they specify a wrong join condition. You should therefore avoid them. To avoid a Cartesian join, there should be at least $n-1$ join conditions when joining n tables. Sometimes you intentionally use Cartesian joins to generate large amounts of data, especially when testing applications.

Consider the following example:

```
SELECT region_name, country_name
FROM   regions, countries
WHERE  countries.country_id LIKE 'I%';

REGION_NAME              COUNTRY_NAME
------------------------ -------------
Europe                   Israel
Americas                 Israel
```

Asia	Israel
Middle East and Africa	Israel
Europe	India
Americas	India
Asia	India
Middle East and Africa	India
Europe	Italy
Americas	Italy
Asia	Italy
Middle East and Africa	Italy

Although there is a WHERE clause, you did not specify a join condition between the COUNTRIES and REGIONS tables. The query returns all the matching rows from the COUNTRIES table based on the WHERE clause and retrieves one row from the REGIONS table for every row from the COUNTRIES table. There are four rows in the REGIONS table and three rows in the COUNTRIES table with a country name beginning with *I*.

 If a Cartesian join is made between a table having *m* rows and another table having *n* rows, the resulting query will have *m×n* rows.

Using the ANSI Syntax

A Cartesian join in ANSI syntax is known as a *cross join*. A cross join is represented in ANSI/ISO SQL1999 syntax using the CROSS JOIN keywords. You can code the previous example using the ANSI syntax as follows:

```
SELECT region_name, country_name
FROM   countries
CROSS JOIN regions
WHERE  countries.country_id LIKE 'I%';
```

REGION_NAME	COUNTRY_NAME
Europe	Israel
Americas	Israel
Asia	Israel
Middle East and Africa	Israel
Europe	India
Americas	India
Asia	India
Middle East and Africa	India
Europe	Italy

```
Americas              Italy
Asia                  Italy
Middle East and Africa  Italy
```

Outer Joins

So far, you have seen only inner joins, which return just the matched rows. Sometimes, however, you might want to see the data from one table, even if there is no corresponding row in the joining table. Oracle provides the *outer join* mechanism for this. An outer join returns results based on the inner join condition, as well as the unmatched rows from one or both of the tables.

In traditional Oracle syntax, the plus symbol surrounded by parentheses, (+), denotes an outer join in the query. Enter (+) beside the column name of the table in the WHERE clause where there may not be a corresponding row. For example, to write a query that performs an outer join of tables A and B and returns all rows from A, apply the outer join operator (+) to all columns of B in the join condition. For all rows in A that have no matching rows in B, the query returns NULL values for the columns in B.

Consider an example using the COUNTRIES and LOCATIONS tables. Say you want to list the country name and location city, and you also want to see all the countries in the COUNTRIES table. To perform this outer join, you place an outer join operator beside all columns referencing LOCATIONS in the WHERE clause:

```
SELECT c.country_name, l.city
FROM   countries c, locations l
WHERE  c.country_id = l.country_id (+);
```

```
COUNTRY_NAME                            CITY
--------------------------------------- --------------------
Australia                               Sydney
Brazil                                  Sao Paulo
Canada                                  Toronto
Canada                                  Whitehorse
Switzerland                             Geneva
Switzerland                             Bern
China                                   Beijing
Germany                                 Munich
India                                   Bombay
Italy                                   Rome
Italy                                   Venice
Japan                                   Tokyo
Japan                                   Hiroshima
Mexico                                  Mexico City
Netherlands                             Utrecht
```

Singapore	Singapore
United Kingdom	London
United Kingdom	Oxford
United Kingdom	Stretford
United States of America	Southlake
United States of America	South San Francisco
United States of America	South Brunswick
United States of America	Seattle
Argentina	
Israel	
Nigeria	
Egypt	
Kuwait	
France	
Hong Kong	
Belgium	
Zimbabwe	
Zambia	
Denmark	

The order of tables in the query's FROM clause determines whether the join is a left outer join or a right outer join. In the previous example, you are selecting all the rows from the table appearing on the left (COUNTRIES); hence this query is using a left outer join.

If tables A and B are outer-joined (FROM A, B) and you need all rows from B, the outer join operator is placed beside all columns of A. This is a right outer join, because you are retrieving all rows from the table on the right side (table B). In outer-join syntax using the (+) operator, the placement of the outer join operator, (+), is what determines the table from where all the rows are retrieved, not the order of tables; the order of tables determines whether it is a left or right outer join. When using the ANSI syntax, the left outer join and right outer join syntaxes depend on the table order.

The outer join operator, (+), can appear only in the WHERE clause. If there are multiple join conditions between the tables, the outer join operator should be used against all the conditions. Consider the following query:

```
SELECT c.country_name, l.city
FROM   countries c, locations l
WHERE  c.country_id = l.country_id (+)
AND    l.city LIKE 'B%';
```

COUNTRY_NAME	CITY
China	Beijing
India	Bombay
Switzerland	Bern

Even though you included the outer join operator, Oracle just ignored it, and did not provide unmatched rows in the query result. This is because you did not place the outer join operator beside all the columns from the LOCATIONS table. The following query will return the desired result:

```
SELECT c.country_name, l.city
FROM   countries c, locations l
WHERE  c.country_id = l.country_id (+)
AND    l.city (+) LIKE 'B%';
```

An outer join (containing the (+) operator) cannot be combined with another condition using the OR or IN logical operators. For example, the following query is not valid:

```
SELECT c.country_name, l.city
FROM   countries c, locations l
WHERE  c.country_id = l.country_id (+)
OR     l.city (+) LIKE 'B%';


OR     l.city (+) LIKE 'B%'
                    *
ERROR at line 4:
ORA-01719: outer join operator (+) not allowed in operand of OR or IN
```

The following query works because the outer join operator is used on the LOCATIONS table and the IN condition is used on the column from the COUNTRIES table:

```
SELECT c.country_name, l.city
FROM   countries c, locations l
WHERE  c.country_id = l.country_id (+)
AND    c.country_name IN ('India','Israel');


COUNTRY_NAME                         CITY
---------------------------------- --------
Israel
India                                Bombay
```

Using the ANSI Syntax

The ANSI syntax allows you to specify three types of outer joins:

- Left outer join
- Right outer join
- Full outer join

Left Outer Joins

A *left outer join* is a join between two tables that returns rows based on the matching condition, as well as unmatched rows from the table to the left of the JOIN clause. For example, the following query returns the country name and city name from the COUNTRIES and LOCATIONS tables, as well as the entire country names from the COUNTRIES table.

```
SELECT c.country_name, l.city
FROM   countries c LEFT OUTER JOIN locations l
ON  c.country_id = l.country_id;
```

The keyword OUTER between LEFT and JOIN is optional. LEFT JOIN will return the same result, as in the following example:

```
SELECT country_name, city
FROM   countries LEFT JOIN locations
USING (country_id);
```

The same query can be written using NATURAL JOIN, since COUNTRY_ID is the only column common to both tables.

```
SELECT country_name, city
FROM   countries NATURAL LEFT JOIN locations;
```

In traditional Oracle outer join syntax, the query is written as follows:

```
SELECT c.country_name, l.city
FROM   countries c, locations l
WHERE  l.country_id (+) = c.country_id;
```

Right Outer Joins

A *right outer join* is a join between two tables that returns rows based on the matching condition, as well as unmatched rows from the table to the right of the JOIN clause. Let's rewrite the previous example using RIGHT OUTER JOIN:

```
SELECT country_name, city
FROM   locations NATURAL RIGHT OUTER JOIN countries;
```

or:

```
SELECT c.country_name, l.city
FROM   locations l RIGHT JOIN countries c
ON  c.country_id = l.country_id;
```

You cannot specify the traditional outer join operator, (+), in a query when the ANSI JOIN syntax is used.

Full Outer Joins

A *full outer join* is possible when using the ANSI syntax. It is not available using the (+) operator. This is a join between two tables that returns rows based on the matching condition, as well as unmatched rows from the table on the right and left of the JOIN clause. Suppose you want to list all the employees' last names with their department names. You want to include all the employees, even if they have not been assigned a department. You also want to include all the departments, even if no employees are working for that department. Here's the query:

```
SELECT  e.employee_id, e.last_name,
        d.department_id, d.department_name
FROM    employees e FULL OUTER JOIN departments d
ON      e.department_id = d.department_id;
```

Trying to perform a similar query with the outer join operator will produce an error:

```
SELECT  e.employee_id, e.last_name, d.department_name
FROM    employees e, departments d
WHERE   e.department_id (+) = d.department_id (+);


WHERE   e.department_id (+) = d.department_id (+)
                         *
ERROR at line 3:
ORA-01468: a predicate may reference only one outer-joined table
```

You can achieve the full outer join using the UNION operator and the outer join operator, as in the following query:

```
SELECT  e.employee_id, e.last_name, d.department_name
FROM    employees e, departments d
WHERE   e.department_id (+) = d.department_id
UNION
SELECT  e.employee_id, e.last_name, d.department_name
FROM    employees e, departments d
WHERE   e.department_id = d.department_id (+);
```

If you do not specify a join type before the JOIN keyword, Oracle assumes the default value of INNER. To specify an outer join, you must use the LEFT, RIGHT, or FULL keyword.

Other Multiple-Table Queries

In this section, you will consider other methods used to retrieve data from more than one table. These methods include using self-joins and using nonequality joins. Using set operators in queries can also retrieve rows from multiple tables. Set operators are discussed in the next section.

Self-Joins

A *self-join* joins a table to itself. The table name appears in the FROM clause twice, with different alias names. The two aliases are treated as two different tables, and they are joined as you would join any other tables, using one or more related columns. The following example lists the employees' names and their manager names from the EMPLOYEES table:

```
SELECT e.last_name Employee, m.last_name Manager
FROM    employees e, employees m
WHERE   m.employee_id = e.manager_id;
```

When performing self-joins in the ANSI syntax, you must always use the JOIN...ON syntax. You cannot use NATURAL JOIN and JOIN...USING. In the following example, the keyword INNER is optional. The certification example also includes an additional WHERE clause to filter the records.

```
SELECT e.last_name Employee, m.last_name Manager
FROM    employees e INNER JOIN employees m
ON      m.employee_id = e.manager_id
WHERE   e.last_name like 'R%';
```

```
EMPLOYEE                 MANAGER
------------------------ -------------------------
Russell                  King
Raphaely                 King
Rogers                   Kaufling
Rajs                     Mourgos
```

Nonequality Joins

If the query is relating two tables using an equality operator (=), it is an equality join, also known as an *inner join* or an *equijoin*, as discussed earlier in this chapter. If any other operator is used to join the tables in the query, it is a *nonequality join*. Let's consider an example of a nonequality join. The EMPLOYEES table has a column named SALARY; the GRADES table has the range of salary values that correspond to each grade.

```
SELECT * FROM grades;
```

GRADE	LOW_SALARY	HIGH_SALARY
P5	0	3000
P4	3001	5000
P3	5001	7000
P2	7001	10000
P1	10001	

To find out which grade each employee belongs to, use the following query. You limit the rows returned by using `last_name LIKE 'R%'`.

```
SELECT last_name, salary, grade
FROM    employees, grades
WHERE   last_name LIKE 'R%'
AND     salary >= low_salary
AND     salary <= NVL(high_salary, salary);
```

```
LAST_NAME                     SALARY GRADE
------------------------- ---------- ------
Raphaely                       11000 P1
Rogers                          2900 P5
Rajs                            3500 P4
Russell                        14000 P1
```

You can write the same query using the ANSI syntax as follows:

```
SELECT last_name, salary, grade
FROM    employees JOIN grades
ON      salary >= low_salary
AND     salary <= NVL(high_salary, salary)
WHERE   last_name LIKE 'R%';
```

Using Set Operators

You can use *set operators* to select data from multiple tables. Set operators basically combine the result of two queries into one. These queries are known as *compound queries*. All set operators have equal precedence. When multiple set operators are present in the same query, they are evaluated from left to right, unless another order is specified by using parentheses. The datatypes of the resulting columns, as well as the number of columns, should match in both queries. Oracle has four set operators, which are listed in Table 4.1.

TABLE 4.1 Oracle Set Operators

Operator	Description
UNION	Returns all unique rows selected by either query
UNION ALL	Returns all rows, including duplicates selected by either query

TABLE 4.1   Oracle Set Operators *(continued)*

Operator	Description
INTERSECT	Returns rows selected from both queries
MINUS	Returns unique rows selected by the first query but not the rows selected from the second query

I'll discuss all of these in a bit, but let's first consider the EMPLOYEE table and the following two queries to illustrate the use of set operators:

```
SELECT last_name, hire_date
FROM    employees
WHERE   department_id = 90;
```

```
LAST_NAME                HIRE_DATE
------------------------ ---------
King                     17-JUN-87
Kochhar                  21-SEP-89
De Haan                  13-JAN-93
```

```
SELECT last_name, hire_date
FROM    employees
WHERE   last_name LIKE 'K%';
```

```
LAST_NAME                HIRE_DATE
------------------------ ---------
King                     17-JUN-87
Kochhar                  21-SEP-89
Khoo                     18-MAY-95
Kaufling                 01-MAY-95
King                     30-JAN-96
Kumar                    21-APR-00
```

The UNION Operator

The UNION operator is used to return rows from either query, without any duplicate rows.

```
SELECT last_name, hire_date
FROM    employees
WHERE   department_id = 90
```

```
UNION
SELECT last_name, hire_date
FROM   employees
WHERE  last_name LIKE 'K%';
```

```
LAST_NAME                HIRE_DATE
------------------------ ---------
De Haan                  13-JAN-93
Kaufling                 01-MAY-95
Khoo                     18-MAY-95
King                     17-JUN-87
King                     30-JAN-96
Kochhar                  21-SEP-89
Kumar                    21-APR-00
```

Notice that even though there is a total of nine rows in both queries, the UNION query returned only unique values. The employees with the last name King appear twice, but their hire dates are different.

The UNION ALL Operator

The UNION ALL operator does not sort or filter the result set; it returns all rows from both queries. Let's consider this SQL:

```
SELECT last_name, hire_date
FROM   employees
WHERE  department_id = 90
UNION ALL
SELECT last_name, hire_date
FROM   employees
WHERE  last_name LIKE 'K%';
```

```
LAST_NAME                HIRE_DATE
------------------------ ---------
King                     17-JUN-87
Kochhar                  21-SEP-89
De Haan                  13-JAN-93
King                     17-JUN-87
Kochhar                  21-SEP-89
Khoo                     18-MAY-95
Kaufling                 01-MAY-95
King                     30-JAN-96
Kumar                    21-APR-00
```

The INTERSECT Operator

The INTERSECT operator is used to return the rows returned by both queries. Let's find the employees common to both queries:

```
SELECT  last_name, hire_date
FROM    employees
WHERE   department_id = 90
INTERSECT
SELECT  last_name, hire_date
FROM    employees
WHERE   last_name LIKE 'K%';
```

```
LAST_NAME                  HIRE_DATE
------------------------   ---------
King                       17-JUN-87
Kochhar                    21-SEP-89
```

The MINUS Operator

Now, let's find the employees from the first query but not in the second query. You can use the MINUS operator here:

```
SELECT  last_name, hire_date
FROM    employees
WHERE   department_id = 90
MINUS
SELECT  last_name, hire_date
FROM    employees
WHERE   last_name LIKE 'K%';
```

```
LAST_NAME                  HIRE_DATE
------------------------   ---------
De Haan                    13-JAN-93
```

Putting It All Together

Each query appearing with the set operators is an independent query and will work by itself. You can have join conditions and all the SQL options and functions in these independent queries. There can be only one ORDER BY clause in the query at the very end; you cannot specify an ORDER BY clause for each query appearing with the set operators. For example, the following query will produce an error:

```
SELECT last_name, hire_date
FROM    employees
WHERE   department_id = 90
ORDER BY last_name
UNION ALL
SELECT first_name, hire_date
FROM    employees
WHERE   first_name LIKE 'K%'
ORDER BY first_name;


UNION ALL
*
ERROR at line 5:
ORA-00933: SQL command not properly ended
```

You can use the column name or alias name used in the first query or positional notation in the ORDER BY clause. Here are two examples (the result is the same for both queries):

```
SELECT last_name, hire_date "Join Date"
FROM    employees
WHERE   department_id = 90
UNION ALL
SELECT first_name, hire_date
FROM    employees
WHERE   first_name LIKE 'K%'
ORDER BY last_name, "Join Date";


SELECT last_name, hire_date "Join Date"
FROM    employees
WHERE   department_id = 90
UNION ALL
SELECT first_name, hire_date
FROM    employees
WHERE   first_name LIKE 'K%'
ORDER BY 1, 2;


LAST_NAME                 Join Date
------------------------- ---------
De Haan                   13-JAN-93
Karen                     05-JAN-97
```

Karen	10-AUG-99
Kelly	14-JUN-97
Kevin	23-MAY-98
Kevin	16-NOV-99
Ki	12-DEC-99
Kimberely	24-MAY-99
King	17-JUN-87
Kochhar	21-SEP-89

 When using set operators, the number of columns in the SELECT clause of the queries appearing on either side of the set operator should be the same. The column datatypes should be compatible. If the datatypes are different, Oracle tries to do an implicit conversion of data.

Subqueries

A *subquery* is a query within a query. A subquery answers the queries that have multiple parts; the subquery answers one part of the question, and the parent query answers the other part. When you nest many subqueries, the innermost query is evaluated first. Subqueries can be used with all Data Manipulation Language (DML) statements.

Using subqueries in the FROM clause of a top-level query is known as an *inline view*. You can nest any number of such queries; Oracle does not have a limit. Using the inline view, you can write queries to find top-*n* values. This is possible because Oracle allows an ORDER BY clause in the inline view. See Chapter 7 for details.

There are three types of subqueries:

- A subquery in the WHERE clause of a query is called a *nested subquery*. You can have 255 levels of nested subqueries.

- When a column from the table used in the parent query is referenced in the subquery, it is known as a *correlated subquery*. For each row processed in the parent query, the correlated subquery is evaluated once.

- A *scalar subquery* returns a single row and a single column value. Scalar subqueries can be used anywhere a column name or expression can be used.

If the columns in the subquery have the same name as the columns in the containing SQL statement, it is a good idea to qualify the column names with table names or table aliases to avoid ambiguity. A subquery must be enclosed in parentheses and must be placed on the right side of the comparison operator when used in the WHERE clause.

Single-Row Subqueries

Single-row subqueries return only one row of result. A single-row subquery uses a single-row operator; the common operator is the equality operator (=). Consider an example using the tables from the HR schema. To find the name of the employee with the highest salary, you first need to find the highest salary using a subquery. Then you can execute the parent query with the result from the subquery.

```
SELECT last_name, first_name, salary
FROM    employees
WHERE   salary = (SELECT MAX(salary) FROM employees);
```

LAST_NAME	FIRST_NAME	SALARY
King	Steven	24000

The parent query of a single-row subquery can return more than one row. For example, to find the names and salaries of employees who work in the accounting department, you need to find the department number for accounting in a subquery and then execute the parent query:

```
SELECT last_name, first_name, salary
FROM    employees
WHERE   department_id = (SELECT department_id
        FROM    departments
        WHERE   department_name = 'Accounting');
```

LAST_NAME	FIRST_NAME	SALARY
Higgins	Shelley	12000
Gietz	William	8300

All single-row comparison operators can be used in the single-row subquery (=, >, >=, <, <=, or <>). The following example uses two subqueries. So, there are three query blocks in total. The two inner query blocks (subqueries) are executed first, and their result is passed on to the outer query (parent query) to complete its processing.

```
SELECT last_name, first_name, department_id
FROM employees
WHERE department_id < (SELECT MAX(department_id)
                       FROM departments
                       WHERE location_id = 1500)
AND hire_date >= (SELECT MIN(hire_date)
                  FROM employees
                  WHERE department_id = 30);
```

Similar to the WHERE clause, a subquery can be used in the HAVING clause. The following query lists the latest hire dates by departments that have hired an employee after the first employee was hired in department 80:

```
SELECT department_id, MAX(hire_date)
FROM employees
GROUP BY department_id
HAVING MAX(hire_date) > (SELECT MIN(hire_date)
                        FROM employees
                        WHERE department_id = 80);
```

```
DEPARTMENT_ID MAX(HIRE_
------------- ---------
          100 07-DEC-99
           30 10-AUG-99
              24-MAY-99
           20 17-AUG-97
           50 08-MAR-00
           80 21-APR-00
           60 07-FEB-99
```

Multiple-Row Subqueries

Multiple-row subqueries return more than one row of results from the subquery. It is safer to provide the multiple-row operators in the subqueries if you are not sure of the results. In the previous query, if there is more than one department ID with the name accounting, the query will fail.

The following query returns three rows from the subquery. It lists all the employees who work for the same department as John does.

```
SELECT last_name, first_name, department_id
FROM    employees
WHERE   department_id = (SELECT department_id
        FROM    employees
        WHERE   first_name = 'John');
```

```
WHERE  department_id = (SELECT department_id
                           *
ERROR at line 3:
ORA-01427: single-row subquery returns more than one row
```

The query failed because you used a single-row operator with a multiple-row subquery. Change the = to a multiple-row operator to make the query work:

```
SELECT  last_name, first_name, department_id
FROM    employees
WHERE   department_id IN (SELECT department_id
        FROM    employees
        WHERE   first_name = 'John');
```

IN is the most commonly used multiple-row subquery operator. Other operators are EXISTS, ANY, SOME, and ALL. You may use NOT with the IN and EXISTS operators.

ANY and SOME are synonymous operators. ANY, SOME, and ALL operators must always be preceded by any of the single-row conditional operators (=, >, >=, <, <= or <>) and are used to compare a value to each value returned by the subquery. Table 4.2 lists the meaning of the ANY and ALL operators when used with different conditional operators.

TABLE 4.2   ANY and ALL Operator Meaning

Operation	Meaning
<ANY	Less than the maximum
<=ANY	Less than or equal to the maximum
>ANY	More than the minimum
=ANY	Equivalent to the IN operator
<ALL	Less than the minimum
>ALL	More than the maximum
<>ALL	Equivalent to the NOT IN operator

Let's review the ANY and ALL operators using examples. The following query will be used in the next subquery using the ANY operator. The subquery returns the 12000 and 8300 values. The minimum is 8,300. The second query returns salaries equal to or above 8,300 that do not belong to department 80.

```
SELECT salary FROM employees WHERE department_id = 110;
```

```
     SALARY
----------
     12000
      8300
```

```
SELECT last_name, salary, department_id
FROM employees
WHERe salary >= ANY (SELECT salary FROM employees
                WHERE department_id = 110)
AND department_id != 80;
```

LAST_NAME	SALARY	DEPARTMENT_ID
King	24000	90
De Haan	17000	90
Kochhar	17000	90
Hartstein	13000	20
Higgins	12000	110
Greenberg	12000	100
Raphaely	11000	30
Baer	10000	70
Faviet	9000	100
Hunold	9000	60
Gietz	8300	110

The following example lists only the salaries that are more than the maximum (12,000) returned from the subquery:

```
SELECT last_name, salary, department_id
FROM employees
WHERe salary > ALL (SELECT salary FROM employees
                WHERE department_id = 110)
AND department_id != 80;
```

LAST_NAME	SALARY	DEPARTMENT_ID
Hartstein	13000	20
De Haan	17000	90
Kochhar	17000	90
King	24000	90

You can use the DISTINCT keyword in the subquery when using ANY or ALL operators to prevent rows from being selected multiple times.

Subquery Returns No Rows

If the subquery returns no rows, a NULL value is returned to the parent query. Since NULL is not equal to another NULL, the parent query may not return any row even if there are NULL values in the column used in the WHERE clause of the subquery.

As shown in the following SQL, there is one record in the EMPLOYEES table where you have a NULL DEPARTMENT_ID:

```
SQL> SELECT last_name, first_name, salary
  2  FROM employees
  3  WHERE department_id IS NULL;
```

LAST_NAME	FIRST_NAME	SALARY
Grant	Kimberely	7000

Let's use this column in the subquery and see what happens:

```
SQL> SELECT last_name, first_name, salary
  2  FROM employees
  3  WHERE department_id = (SELECT department_id
  4                         FROM departments
  5                         WHERE department_name = 'JustDummy');


no rows selected


SQL>
```

In the previous example, the outer query will return a value only if the DEPARTMENT_ID column matches some value. Although the inner query returned NULL, the outer query will not match for NULL, since NULL ≠ NULL. Let's review another example. In the following query, only Tobias has a NULL salary value:

```
SQL> SELECT last_name, salary
  2  FROM employees
  3  WHERE department_id = 30;
```

LAST_NAME	SALARY
Raphaely	11000
Khoo	3100
Baida	2900
Tobias	
Himuro	2600
Colmenares	2500

   When you use this subquery, you expect to see some results, because you know the EMPLOYEES table has more than the five different salary values:

```
SQL> SELECT first_name, last_name, salary
  2  FROM employees
  3  WHERE salary NOT IN (
  4         SELECT salary
  5         FROM employees
  6         WHERE department_id = 30);


no rows selected


SQL>
```

   The SQL does not return any rows because one of the rows returned by the inner query is NULL. So, be careful when using NOT IN conditions with subqueries that could have a NULL value. This is not a problem when you use the IN operator. The IN operator is equivalent to =ANY, and the NOT IN operator is equivalent to <> ALL. If you include one more condition in the WHERE clause of the inner query, the SQL would work as expected:

```
SELECT first_name, last_name, salary
FROM employees
WHERE salary NOT IN (
       SELECT salary
       FROM employees
       WHERE department_id = 30
       AND salary is NOT NULL);
```

Correlated Subqueries

Oracle performs a *correlated subquery* when the subquery references a column from a table referred to in the parent statement. A correlated subquery is evaluated once for each row processed by the parent statement. The parent statement can be a SELECT, UPDATE, or DELETE statement. In the following example, the highest-paid employee of each department is selected. The subquery is executed for each row returned in the parent query. Notice that the parent table column is used inside the subquery.

```
SELECT department_id, last_name, salary
FROM    employees e1
WHERE   salary = (SELECT MAX(salary)
        FROM employees e2
        WHERE e1.department_id = e2.department_id)
ORDER BY 1, 2, 3;
```

DEPARTMENT_ID	LAST_NAME	SALARY
10	Whalen	4400
20	Hartstein	13000
30	Raphaely	11000
40	Mavris	6500
50	Fripp	8200
60	Hunold	9000
70	Baer	10000
80	Russell	14000
90	King	24000
100	Greenberg	12000
110	Higgins	12000

The following example shows a correlated subquery using the EXISTS operator. The EXISTS operator checks for the existence of a row in the subquery based on the condition. The column results of the SELECT clause in the subquery are ignored when using the EXISTS operator. The query lists the names of employees who work with John (in the same department). The subquery selects a dummy value of 'x', which is ignored.

```
SELECT last_name, first_name, department_id
FROM   employees e1
WHERE  EXISTS (SELECT 'x'
       FROM   employees e2
       WHERE  first_name = 'John'
       AND    e1.department_id = e2.department_id);
```

> The column names in the parent queries are available for reference in subqueries. The column names from the tables in the subquery cannot be used in the parent queries. The scope is only the current query level and its subqueries.

Scalar Subqueries

A *scalar subquery* returns exactly one column value from one row. You can use scalar subqueries in most places where you would use a column name or expression, such as in a single-row function as an argument, in the VALUES clause of an INSERT statement, in an ORDER BY clause, in a WHERE clause, and in a SELECT clause. You can also use scalar subqueries in CASE expressions. Scalar subqueries cannot be used in GROUP BY or HAVING clauses. The following sections review a few examples of using scalar subqueries.

A Scalar Subquery in a CASE Expression

To list the city name, the country code, and whether the city is in India, you use a CASE expression with a subquery to return the country code for India from the COUNTRIES table. To limit the rows, let's select only the cities that begin with *B*:

```
SELECT city, country_id, (CASE
        WHEN country_id IN (SELECT country_id
                  FROM    countries
                  WHERE   country_name = 'India')
        THEN 'Indian'
        ELSE 'Non-Indian'
        END) "INDIA?"
FROM    locations
WHERE   city LIKE 'B%';
```

```
CITY                            CO INDIA?
------------------------------- -- ----------
Beijing                         CN Non-Indian
Bombay                          IN Indian
Bern                            CH Non-Indian
```

A Scalar Subquery in a SELECT Clause

To report the employee name, the department, and the highest salary in that department, you use a subquery in the SELECT clause. This is also a correlated subquery.

```
SELECT last_name, department_id,
    (SELECT MAX(salary)
     FROM   employees sq
     WHERE  sq.department_id = e.department_id) HSAL
FROM    employees e
WHERE   last_name like 'R%';
```

```
LAST_NAME                 DEPARTMENT_ID       HSAL
------------------------- ------------- ----------
Raphaely                             30      11000
Rogers                               50       8200
Rajs                                 50       8200
Russell                              80      14000
```

A Scalar Subquery in SELECT and WHERE Clauses

The following query may be confusing, but pay close attention to the flexibility of using subqueries to solve your queries. A scalar subquery is used in the SELECT clause as well as in the WHERE clause. A multiple-row subquery is also used in the WHERE clause, after the IN operator. The purpose of the query is to find the department names and their manager names for all departments that are in the United States or Canada. Since the country information is not available in the DEPARTMENTS table, you need to get this information from the LOCATIONS table. Also, you do not know the country IDs of the United States and Canada, so you use a subquery to get them. The query also limits the number of rows retrieved by checking whether a manager is assigned to the department (d.manager_id IS NOT NULL).

```
SELECT department_name, manager_id, (SELECT last_name
    FROM employees e
    WHERE e.employee_id = d.manager_id) MGR_NAME
FROM   departments d
WHERE ((SELECT country_id FROM locations l
    WHERE  d.location_id = l.location_id)
    IN (SELECT country_id FROM countries c
    WHERE  c.country_name = 'United States of America'
    OR     c.country_name = 'Canada'))
AND    d.manager_id IS NOT NULL;
```

```
DEPARTMENT_NAME        MANAGER_ID MGR_NAME
-------------------- ---------- --------------
Administration              200 Whalen
Marketing                   201 Hartstein
Purchasing                  114 Raphaely
Shipping                    121 Fripp
IT                          103 Hunold
Executive                   100 King
Finance                     108 Greenberg
Accounting                  205 Higgins
```

A Scalar Subquery in an ORDER BY Clause

You can also use scalar subqueries in the ORDER BY clause. The following example sorts the city names by their country-name order. Notice that the country name is not included in the SELECT clause.

```
SELECT country_id, city, state_province
FROM    locations l
ORDER BY (SELECT country_name
        FROM    countries c
        WHERE   l.country_id = c.country_id);
```

If the scalar subquery returns more than one row, the query will fail. If the scalar subquery returns no rows, the value is NULL.

Finding Total Space and Free Space Using Dictionary Views

The following dictionary views are best friends of a DBA. They show the most critical aspect of the database from the user perspective—the space allocated and free. If the DBA is not monitoring the growth and free space available in the database, it is likely that they might get calls from the user community that they ran out of space in the tablespace. Let's build a query using four dictionary views (you may need the SELECT_CATALOG_ROLE privilege to query these views).

- DBA_TABLESPACES: Shows the tablespace name, type, and so on.

- DBA_DATA_FILES: Shows the data files associated with a permanent or undo tablespace and the size of the data file. The total size of all data files associated with a tablespace gives the total size of the tablespace.

- DBA_TEMP_FILES: Shows the temporary files associated with a temporary tablespace and their size.

- DBA_FREE_SPACE: Shows the unallocated space (free space) in each tablespace.

The query to get the tablespace names and type of tablespace would be as follows:

```
column tablespace_name format a18
SELECT tablespace_name, contents
FROM dba_tablespaces;


TABLESPACE_NAME     CONTENTS
------------------  ---------
SYSTEM              PERMANENT
SYSAUX              PERMANENT
UNDOTBS1            UNDO
TEMP                TEMPORARY
USERS               PERMANENT
EXAMPLE             PERMANENT
```

To find the total space allocated to each tablespace, you need to query DBA_DATA_FILES and DBA_TEMP_FILES. Since you are using a group function (SUM) along with a nonaggregated column (tablespace_name), the GROUP BY clause is a must. Notice the use of an arithmetic operation on the aggregated result to display the bytes in megabytes.

```
SELECT tablespace_name, SUM(bytes)/1048576 MBytes
FROM dba_data_files
```

```
GROUP BY tablespace_name;

TABLESPACE_NAME        MBYTES
------------------ ----------
UNDOTBS1                  730
SYSAUX              800.1875
USERS                201.75
SYSTEM                   710
EXAMPLE                  100


SELECT tablespace_name, SUM(bytes)/1048576 MBytes
FROM dba_temp_files
GROUP BY tablespace_name;

TABLESPACE_NAME        MBYTES
------------------ ----------
TEMP               50.0625
```

You can find the total free space in each tablespace using the DBA_FREE_SPACE view.
Notice that the free space from temporary tablespace is not shown in this query.

```
SELECT tablespace_name, SUM(bytes)/1048576 MBytesFree
FROM dba_free_space
GROUP BY tablespace_name;

TABLESPACE_NAME    MBYTESFREE
------------------ ----------
SYSAUX                  85.25
UNDOTBS1            718.6875
USERS               180.4375
SYSTEM                8.3125
EXAMPLE               22.625
```

Let's now try to display the total size of the tablespaces and their free space side-by-side
using a UNION ALL query. UNION ALL is used to avoid sorting. UNION will produce the
same result.

```
SELECT tablespace_name, SUM(bytes)/1048576 MBytes, 0 MBytesFree
FROM dba_data_files
GROUP BY tablespace_name
UNION ALL
SELECT tablespace_name, SUM(bytes)/1048576 MBytes, 0
FROM dba_temp_files
```

```
GROUP BY tablespace_name
UNION ALL
SELECT tablespace_name, 0, SUM(bytes)/1048576
FROM dba_free_space
GROUP BY tablespace_name;
```

TABLESPACE_NAME	MBYTES	MBYTESFREE
UNDOTBS1	730	0
SYSAUX	800.1875	0
USERS	201.75	0
SYSTEM	710	0
EXAMPLE	100	0
TEMP	50.0625	0
SYSAUX	0	85.25
UNDOTBS1	0	718.6875
USERS	0	180.4375
SYSTEM	0	8.3125
EXAMPLE	0	22.625

You got the result, but it's not exactly as you expected. You want to see the free-space information beside each tablespace. Let's join the results of the total space with the free space and see what happens. Here you are creating two subqueries (inline views `total-space` and `freespace`) and joining them together using the `tablespace_name` column.

```
SELECT tablespace_name, MBytes, MBytesFree
FROM
 (SELECT tablespace_name, SUM(bytes)/1048576 MBytes
  FROM dba_data_files
  GROUP BY tablespace_name
  UNION ALL
  SELECT tablespace_name, SUM(bytes)/1048576 MBytes
  FROM dba_temp_files
  GROUP BY tablespace_name) totalspace
JOIN
 (SELECT tablespace_name, 0, SUM(bytes)/1048576 MBytesFree
  FROM dba_free_space
  GROUP BY tablespace_name) freespace
USING (tablespace_name);
```

```
TABLESPACE_NAME        MBYTES MBYTESFREE
------------------ ---------- ----------
SYSAUX               800.1875      85.25
UNDOTBS1                  730    718.6875
USERS                 201.75    180.4375
SYSTEM                   710      8.3125
EXAMPLE                  100     22.625
```

You are almost there; the only item missing is information about the temporary tablespace. Since the temporary-tablespace free-space information is not included in the freespace subquery and you used an INNER join condition, the result set did not include temporary tablespaces. Now if you change the INNER JOIN to an OUTER JOIN, you get the desired result:

```
SELECT tablespace_name, MBytes, MBytesFree
FROM
 (SELECT tablespace_name, SUM(bytes)/1048576 MBytes
  FROM dba_data_files
  GROUP BY tablespace_name
  UNION ALL
  SELECT tablespace_name, SUM(bytes)/1048576 MBytes
  FROM dba_temp_files
  GROUP BY tablespace_name) totalspace
LEFT OUTER JOIN
 (SELECT tablespace_name, 0, SUM(bytes)/1048576 MBytesFree
  FROM dba_free_space
  GROUP BY tablespace_name) freespace
USING (tablespace_name)
ORDER BY 1;


TABLESPACE_NAME        MBYTES MBYTESFREE
------------------ ---------- ----------
EXAMPLE                  100     22.625
SYSAUX               800.1875    85.0625
SYSTEM                   710      8.3125
TEMP                 50.0625
UNDOTBS1                 730    718.6875
USERS                 201.75    180.4375
```

Another method to write the same query would be to use the query you built earlier and aggregate its result using an outer query, as shown here:

```
SELECT tsname, sum(MBytes) MBytes, sum(MBytesFree) MBytesFree
FROM (
  SELECT tablespace_name tsname, SUM(bytes)/1048576 MBytes, 0 MBytesFree
  FROM dba_data_files
  GROUP BY tablespace_name
  UNION ALL
  SELECT tablespace_name, SUM(bytes)/1048576 MBytes, 0
  FROM dba_temp_files
  GROUP BY tablespace_name
  UNION ALL
  SELECT tablespace_name, 0, SUM(bytes)/1048576
  FROM dba_free_space
  GROUP BY tablespace_name)
GROUP BY tsname
ORDER BY 1;


TSNAME                          MBYTES MBYTESFREE
------------------------------ ---------- ----------
EXAMPLE                            100     22.625
SYSAUX                        800.1875    85.0625
SYSTEM                             710     8.3125
TEMP                           50.0625          0
UNDOTBS1                           730   718.6875
USERS                          201.75    180.4375
```

Multiple-Column Subqueries

A subquery is multiple-column when you have more than one column in the SELECT clause of the subquery. *Multiple-column subqueries* are generally used to compare column conditions or in an UPDATE statement. Let's consider a simple example using the STATE and CITY tables shown here:

```
SQL> SELECT * FROM state;

  CNT_CODE  ST_CODE   ST_NAME
---------- -------   ------------
        1  TX        TEXAS
        1  CA        CALIFORNIA
```

```
        91  TN          TAMIL NADU
         1  TN          TENNESSE
        91  KL          KERALA
SQL> SELECT * FROM city;

  CNT_CODE ST_CODE   CTY_CODE  CTY_NAME
---------- -------   --------  --------------
         1 TX            1001  DALLAS
        91 TN            2243  MADRAS
         1 CA            8099  LOS ANGELES
```

List the cities in Texas using a subquery on the STATE table:

```
SELECT cty_name
FROM   city
WHERE  (cnt_code, st_code) IN
       (SELECT cnt_code, st_code
        FROM   state
        WHERE  st_name = 'TEXAS');

CTY_NAME
----------
DALLAS
```

Subqueries in Other DML Statements

You can use subqueries in DML statements such as INSERT, UPDATE, DELETE, and MERGE. DML statements and their syntax are discussed in Chapter 5, "Manipulating Data." The following are some examples of subqueries in DML statements:

- To update the salary of all employees to the maximum salary in the corresponding department (correlated subquery), use this:

```
UPDATE employees e1
SET  salary = (SELECT MAX(salary)
      FROM   employees e2
      WHERE e1.department_id = e2.department_id);
```

- To delete the records of employees whose salary is less than the average salary in the department (using a correlated subquery), use this:

```
DELETE FROM employees e
WHERE salary < (SELECT AVG(salary) FROM employees
      WHERE  department_id = e.department_id);
```

- To insert records to a table using a subquery, use this:

  ```
  INSERT INTO employee_archive
  SELECT * FROM employees;
  ```

- To specify a subquery in the VALUES clause of the INSERT statement, use this:

  ```
  INSERT INTO departments
          (department_id, department_name)
  VALUES ((SELECT MAX(department_id)
              +10 FROM departments), 'EDP');
  ```

You can also have a subquery in the INSERT, UPDATE, and DELETE statements in place of the table name. Here is an example:

```
DELETE FROM
(SELECT * FROM departments
 WHERE department_id < 20)
WHERE department_id = 10;
```

The subquery can have an optional WITH clause. WITH READ ONLY specifies that the subquery cannot be updated. WITH CHECK OPTION specifies that if the subquery is used in place of a table in an INSERT, UPDATE, or DELETE statement, Oracle will not allow any changes to the table that would produce rows that are not included in the subquery. Let's look at an example:

```
INSERT INTO (SELECT department_id, department_name
      FROM departments
      WHERE department_id < 20)
VALUES (35, 'MARKETING');

1 row created.

INSERT INTO (SELECT department_id, department_name
      FROM departments
      WHERE department_id < 20 WITH CHECK OPTION)
VALUES (45, 'EDP')
SQL> /
      FROM departments
          *
ERROR at line 2:
ORA-01402: view WITH CHECK OPTION where-clause violation
SQL>
```

Summary

In this chapter, you learned to retrieve data from multiple tables. I started off discussing table joins. You also learned how to use subqueries and set operators.

Joins are used to relate two or more tables (or views). In a relational database, it is common to have a requirement to join data. The tables are joined by using a common column in the tables in the WHERE clause of the query. Oracle supports ISO/ANSI SQL1999 syntax for joins. Using this syntax, the tables are joined using the JOIN keyword, and a condition can be specified using the ON clause.

If the join condition uses the equality operator (= or IN), it is known as an equality join. If any other operator is used to join the tables, it is a nonequality join. If you do not specify any join condition between the tables, the result will be a Cartesian product: each row from the first table joined to every row in the second table. To avoid Cartesian joins, there should be at least *n*-1 join conditions in the WHERE clause when there are *n* tables in the FROM clause. A table can be joined to itself. If you want to select the results from a table, even if there are no corresponding rows in the joined table, you can use the outer join operator: (+). In the ANSI syntax, you can use the NATURAL JOIN, CROSS JOIN, LEFT JOIN, RIGHT JOIN, and FULL JOIN keywords to specify the type of join.

A subquery is a query within a query. Writing subqueries is a powerful way to manipulate data. You can write single-row and multiple-row subqueries. Single-row subqueries must return zero or one row; multiple-row subqueries return zero or more rows. IN and EXISTS are the most commonly used subquery operators. Subqueries can appear in the WHERE clause or in the FROM clause. They can also replace table names in SELECT, DELETE, INSERT, and UPDATE statements. Subqueries that return one row and one column result are known as scalar subqueries. Scalar subqueries can be used in most places where you would use an expression.

Set operators are used to combine the results of more than one query into one. Each query is separate and will work on its own. Four set operators are available in Oracle: UNION, UNION ALL, MINUS, and INTERSECT.

Exam Essentials

Understand joins.   Make sure you know the different types of joins. Understand the difference between natural, cross, simple, complex, and outer joins.

Know the different outer join clauses.   You can specify outer joins using LEFT, RIGHT, or FULL. Know the syntax of each type of join.

Be sure of the join syntax.   Spend time practicing each type of join using the ANSI syntax. Understand the restrictions of using each ANSI keyword in the JOIN and their implied column-naming conventions.

Know how to write subqueries.   Understand the use and flexibility of subqueries. Practice using scalar subqueries and correlated subqueries.

Understand the use of the ORDER BY clause in the subqueries.   You can use the ORDER BY clause in all subqueries, except the subqueries appearing in the WHERE clause of the query. You can use the GROUP BY clause in the subqueries.

Know the set operators.   Understand the set operators that can be used in compound queries. Know the difference between the UNION and UNION ALL operators.

Understand where you can specify the ORDER BY clause when using set operators.   When using set operators to join two or more queries, the ORDER BY clause can appear only at the very end of the query. You can specify the column names as they appear in the top query or use positional notation.

Review Questions

1. Which line of code has an error?

   A. SELECT dname, ename

   B. FROM   emp e, dept d

   C. WHERE   emp.deptno = dept.deptno

   D. ORDER BY 1, 2;

2. What will be the result of the following query?

   ```
   SELECT c.cust_id, c.cust_name, o.ord_date, o.prod_id
   FROM    customers c, orders o
   WHERE   c.cust_id = o.cust_id (+);
   ```

   A. List all the customer names in the CUSTOMERS table and the orders they made from the ORDERS table, even if the customer has not placed an order.

   B. List only the names of customers from the CUSTOMERS table who have placed an order in the ORDERS table.

   C. List all orders from the ORDERS table, even if there is no valid customer record in the CUSTOMERS table.

   D. For each record in the CUSTOMERS table, list the information from the ORDERS table.

3. The CUSTOMERS and ORDERS tables have the following data:

   ```
   SQL> SELECT * FROM customers;


   CUST_ CUST_NAME               PHONE            CITY
   ----- -------------------- ---------------- -----------
   A0101 Abraham Taylor Jr.                     Fort Worth
   B0134 Betty Baylor         972-555-5555     Dallas
   B0135 Brian King                            Chicago


   SQL> SELECT * FROM orders;


   ORD_DATE     PROD_ID CUST_ID  QUANTITY      PRICE
   --------- ---------- ------- ---------- ----------
   20-FEB-00       1741 B0134            5       65.5
   02-FEB-00       1001 B0134           25    2065.85
   02-FEB-00       1001 B0135            3      247.9
   ```

   When the following query is executed, what will be the value of PROD_ID and ORD_DATE for the customer Abraham Taylor Jr.?

   ```
   SELECT c.cust_id, c.cust_name, o.ord_date, o.prod_id
   FROM    customers c, orders o
   WHERE   c.cust_id = o.cust_id (+);
   ```

   A. NULL, 01-JAN-01

   B. NULL, NULL

   C. 1001, 02-FEB-00

   D. The query will not return customer Abraham Taylor Jr.

4. When using ANSI join syntax, which clause is used to specify a join condition?

   A. JOIN

   B. USING

   C. ON

   D. WHERE

5. The EMPLOYEES table has EMPLOYEE_ID, DEPARTMENT_ID, and FULL_NAME columns. The DEPARTMENTS table has DEPARTMENT_ID and DEPARTMENT_NAME columns. Which two of the following queries return the department ID, name, and employee name, listing department names even if there is no employee assigned to that department? (Choose two.)

   A.
```
SELECT d.department_id, d.department_name, e.full_name
FROM    departments d
NATURAL LEFT OUTER JOIN employees e;
```

   B.
```
SELECT department_id, department_name, full_name
FROM    departments
NATURAL LEFT JOIN employees;
```

   C.
```
SELECT d.department_id, d.department_name, e.full_name
FROM    departments d
LEFT OUTER JOIN employees e
USING (d.department_id);
```

   D.
```
SELECT d.department_id, d.department_name, e.full_name
FROM    departments d
LEFT OUTER JOIN employees e
ON  (d.department_id = e.department_id);
```

6. Which two operators are not allowed when using an outer join operator in the query? (Choose two.)

   A. OR

   B. AND

   C. IN

   D. =

7. Which SQL statements do not give an error? (Choose all that apply.)

   A.
```
SELECT last_name, e.hire_date, department_id
FROM employees e
JOIN (SELECT max(hire_date) max_hire_date
        FROM employees ORDER BY 1) me
ON (e.hire_date = me.max_hire_date)
```

B. SELECT last_name, e.hire_date, department_id
FROM employees e
WHERE hire_date =
(SELECT max(hire_date) max_hire_date
        FROM employees ORDER BY 1)

C. SELECT last_name, e.hire_date, department_id
FROM employees e
WHERE (department_id, hire_date) IN
(SELECT department_id, max(hire_date) hire_date
        FROM employees GROUP BY department_id)

D. SELECT last_name, e.hire_date, department_id
FROM employees e JOIN
(SELECT department_id, max(hire_date) hire_date
FROM employees GROUP BY department_id) me
USING (hire_date)

8. The columns of the EMPLOYEES, DEPARTMENTS, and JOBS tables are shown here:

Table	Column Names	Datatype
EMPLOYEES	EMPLOYEE_ID	NUMBER (6)
	FIRST_NAME	VARCHAR2 (25)
	LAST_NAME	VARCHAR2 (25)
	SALARY	NUMBER (8,2)
	JOB_ID	VARCHAR2 (10)
	MANAGER_ID	NUMBER (6)
	DEPARTMENT_ID	NUMBER (2)
DEPARTMENTS	DEPARTMENT_ID	NUMBER (2)
	DEPARTMENT_NAME	VARCHAR2 (30)
	MANAGER_ID	NUMBER (6)
	LOCATION_ID	NUMBER (4)
JOBS	JOB_ID	VARCHAR2 (10)
	JOB_TITLE	VARCAHR2 (30)

Which assertion about the following query is correct?

```
1  SELECT e.last_name, d.department_name, j.job_title
2  FROM    jobs j
3  INNER JOIN employees e
4  ON (e.department_id = d.department_id)
5  JOIN departments d
6  ON (j.job_id = e.job_id);
```

A. The query returns all the rows from the EMPLOYEE table, where there is a corresponding record in the JOBS table and the DEPARTMENTS table.

B. The query fails with an invalid column name error.

C. The query fails because line 3 specifies INNER JOIN, which is not a valid syntax.

D. The query fails because line 5 does not specify the keyword INNER.

E. The query fails because the column names are qualified with the table alias.

9. The columns of the EMPLOYEES and DEPARTMENTS tables are shown in question 8. Consider the following three queries using those tables.

```
1. SELECT last_name, department_name
FROM    employees e, departments d
WHERE   e.department_id = d.department_id;
2. SELECT last_name, department_name
FROM    employees NATURAL JOIN departments;
3. SELECT last_name, department_name
FROM    employees JOIN departments
USING (department_id);
```

Which of the following assertions best describes the results?

A. Queries 1, 2, and 3 produce the same results.

B. Queries 2 and 3 produce the same result; query 1 produces a different result.

C. Queries 1, 2, and 3 produce different results.

D. Queries 1 and 3 produce the same result; query 2 produces a different result.

10. The data in the STATE table is as shown here:

```
SQL> SELECT * FROM state;

  CNT_CODE ST_CODE ST_NAME
---------- ------- ------------
         1 TX      TEXAS
         1 CA      CALIFORNIA
        91 TN      TAMIL NADU
         1 TN      TENNESSE
        91 KL      KERALA
```

Consider the following query.

```
SELECT cnt_code
FROM    state
WHERE   st_name = (SELECT st_name FROM state
                        WHERE   st_code = 'TN');
```

Which of the following assertions best describes the results?

A.   The query will return the CNT_CODE for the ST_CODE value 'TN'.

B.   The query will fail and will not return any rows.

C.   The query will display 1 and 91 as CNT_CODE values.

D.   The query will fail because an alias name is not used.

11. The data in the STATE table is shown in question 10. The data in the CITY table is as shown here:

```
SQL> SELECT * FROM city;
```

CNT_CODE	ST_CODE	CTY_CODE	CTY_NAME
1	TX	1001	DALLAS
91	TN	2243	MADRAS
1	CA	8099	LOS ANGELES

What is the result of the following query?

```
SELECT st_name "State Name"
FROM    state
WHERE   (cnt_code, st_code) =
        (SELECT cnt_code, st_code
          FROM    city
          WHERE   cty_name = 'DALLAS');
```

A.   TEXAS

B.   The query will fail because CNT_CODE and ST_CODE are not in the WHERE clause of the subquery.

C.   The query will fail because more than one column appears in the WHERE clause.

D.   TX

12. Which line of the code has an error?

```
1   SELECT department_id, count(*)
2   FROM    employees
3   GROUP BY department_id
4   HAVING COUNT(department_id) =
5   (SELECT max(count(department_id))
6     FROM employees
7     GROUP BY department_id);
```

A. Line 3

B. Line 4

C. Line 5

D. Line 7

E. No error

13. Which of the following is a correlated subquery?

    A.
    ```
    select cty_name from city
      where  st_code in (select st_code from state
      where st_name = 'TENNESSEE'
      and  city.cnt_code = state.cnt_code);
    ```

    B.
    ```
    select cty_name
      from   city
      where  st_code in (select st_code from state
      where st_name = 'TENNESSEE');
    ```

    C.
    ```
    select cty_name
      from city, state
      where  city.st_code = state.st_code
      and    city.cnt_code = state.cnt_code
      and    st_name = 'TENNESSEE';
    ```

    D.
    ```
    select cty_name
      from city, state
      where  city.st_code = state.st_code (+)
      and    city.cnt_code = state.cnt_code (+)
      and    st_name = 'TENNESSEE';
    ```

14. The COUNTRY table has the following data:
    ```
    SQL> SELECT * FROM country;

     CNT_CODE CNT_NAME           CONTINENT
    ---------- ------------------ ----------
             1 UNITED STATES      N.AMERICA
            91 INDIA              ASIA
            65 SINGAPORE          ASIA
    ```

    What value is returned from the subquery when you execute the following?
    ```
    SELECT CNT_NAME
    FROM    country
    WHERE   CNT_CODE =
    (SELECT MAX(cnt_code) FROM country);
    ```

A. INDIA

B. 65

C. 91

D. SINGAPORE

15. Which line in the following query contains an error?

```
1  SELECT deptno, ename, sal
2  FROM    emp e1
3  WHERE   sal = (SELECT MAX(sal) FROM emp
4                    WHERE  deptno = e1.deptno
5                    ORDER BY deptno);
```

A. Line 2

B. Line 3

C. Line 4

D. Line 5

16. Consider the following query:

```
SELECT deptno, ename, salary salary, average,
       salary-average difference
FROM    emp,
(SELECT deptno dno, AVG(salary) average FROM emp
 GROUP BY deptno)
WHERE   deptno = dno
ORDER BY 1, 2;
```

Which of the following statements is correct?

A. The query will fail because no alias name is provided for the subquery.

B. The query will fail because a column selected in the subquery is referenced outside the scope of the subquery.

C. The query will work without errors.

D. GROUP BY cannot be used inside a subquery.

17. The COUNTRY table has the following data:

```
SQL> SELECT * FROM country;
```

CNT_CODE	CNT_NAME	CONTINENT
1	UNITED STATES	N.AMERICA
91	INDIA	ASIA
65	SINGAPORE	ASIA

What will be result of the following query?

```
INSERT INTO (SELECT cnt_code FROM country
             WHERE continent = 'ASIA')
VALUES (971, 'SAUDI ARABIA', 'ASIA');
```

A. One row will be inserted into the COUNTRY table.

B. WITH CHECK OPTION is missing in the subquery.

C. The query will fail because the VALUES clause is invalid.

D. The WHERE clause cannot appear in the subqueries used in INSERT statements.

18. Review the SQL code, and choose the line number that has an error.

```
1  SELECT DISTINCT department_id
2  FROM employees
3  ORDER BY department_id
4  UNION ALL
5  SELECT department_id
6  FROM departments
7  ORDER BY department_id
```

A. 1

B. 3

C. 6

D. 7

E. No error

19. Consider the following queries:

```
1. SELECT last_name, salary,
        (SELECT (MAX(sq.salary) - e.salary)
        FROM    employees sq
        WHERE   sq.department_id = e.department_id) DSAL
FROM    employees e
WHERE   department_id = 20;
2. SELECT last_name, salary, msalary - salary dsal
FROM    employees e,
        (SELECT department_id, MAX(salary) msalary
        FROM    employees
        GROUP BY department_id) sq
WHERE e.department_id = sq.department_id
AND   e.department_id = 20;
```

```
3. SELECT last_name, salary, msalary - salary dsal
FROM    employees e INNER JOIN
        (SELECT department_id, MAX(salary) msalary
         FROM    employees
         GROUP BY department_id) sq
ON      e.department_id = sq.department_id
WHERE   e.department_id = 20;
4. SELECT last_name, salary, msalary - salary dsal
FROM    employees INNER JOIN
        (SELECT department_id, MAX(salary) msalary
         FROM    employees
         GROUP BY department_id) sq
USING   (department_id)
WHERE   department_id = 20;
```

Which of the following assertions best describes the results?

A. Queries 1 and 2 produce identical results, and queries 3 and 4 produce identical results, but queries 1 and 3 produce different results.

B. Queries 1, 2, 3, and 4 produce identical results.

C. Queries 1, 2, and 3 produce identical results; query 4 will produce errors.

D. Queries 1 and 3 produce identical results; queries 2 and 4 will produce errors.

E. Queries 1, 2, 3, and 4 produce different results.

F. Queries 1 and 2 are valid SQL; queries 3 and 4 are not valid.

20. The columns of the EMPLOYEES and DEPARTMENTS tables are shown in question 8. Which query will show you the top five highest-paid employees in the company?

A.
```
SELECT last_name, salary
FROM    employees
WHERE ROWNUM <= 5
ORDER BY salary DESC;
```

B.
```
SELECT last_name, salary
FROM (SELECT *
FROM    employees
WHERE ROWNUM <= 5
ORDER BY salary DESC )
WHERE ROWNUM <= 5;
```

C.
```
SELECT * FROM
(SELECT last_name, salary
FROM    employees
ORDER BY salary)
WHERE ROWNUM <= 5;
```

D.
```
SELECT * FROM
(SELECT last_name, salary
FROM    employees
ORDER BY salary DESC)
WHERE ROWNUM <= 5;
```

Answers to Review Questions

1. C. When table aliases are defined, you should qualify the column names with the table alias only. In this case, the table name cannot be used to qualify column names. The line in option C should read WHERE e.deptno = d.deptno.

2. A. An outer join operator (+) indicates an outer join and is used to display the records, even if there are no corresponding records in the table mentioned on the other side of the operator. Here, the outer join operator is next to the ORDERS table, so even if there are no corresponding orders from a customer, the result set will have the customer ID and name.

3. B. When an outer join returns values from a table that does not have corresponding records, a NULL is returned.

4. C. The join condition is specified in the ON clause. The JOIN clause specifies the table to be joined. The USING clause specifies the column names that should be used in the join. The WHERE clause is used to specify additional search criteria to restrict the rows returned.

5. B, D. Option A does not work because you cannot qualify column names when using a natural join. Option B works because the only common column between these two tables is DEPARTMENT_ID. The keyword OUTER is optional. Option C does not work, again because you cannot qualify column names when specifying the USING clause. Option D works because it specifies the join condition explicitly in the ON clause.

6. A, C. OR and IN are not allowed in the WHERE clause on the columns where an outer join operator is specified. You can use AND and = in the outer join.

7. A, C. Options A and B have an ORDER BY clause used in the subquery. An ORDER BY clause can be used in the subquery appearing in the FROM clause, but not in the WHERE clause. Options C and D use the GROUP BY clause in the subquery, and its use is allowed in FROM as well as WHERE clauses. Option D will give an error because the DEPARTMENT_ID in the SELECT clause is ambiguous and hence doesn't need to be qualified as e.DEPARTMENT_ID. Another issue with option D is that since you used the USING clause to join, the column used in the USING clause cannot be qualified; e.hire_date in the SELECT clause should be hire_date.

8. B. The query fails because the d.DEPARTMENT_ID column is referenced before the DEPARTMENTS table is specified in the JOIN clause. A column can be referenced only after its table is specified.

9. D. Since DEPARTMENT_ID and MANAGER_ID are common columns in the EMPLOYEES and DEPARTMENTS tables, a natural join will relate these two tables using the two common columns.

10. B. There are two records in the STATE table with the ST_CODE value as 'TN'. Since you are using a single-row operator for the subquery, it will fail. Option C would be correct if it used the IN operator instead of = for the subquery.

11. A. The query will succeed, because there is only one row in the CITY table with the CTY_NAME value 'DALLAS'.

12. E. There is no error in the statement. The query will return the department number where the most employees are working and the number of employees in that department.

13. A. A subquery is correlated when a reference is made to a column from a table in the parent statement.

14. C. The subquery returns 91 to the main query.

15. D. You cannot have an ORDER BY clause in the subquery used in a WHERE clause.

16. C. The query will work fine, producing the difference between the employee's salary and average salary in the department. You do not need to use the alias names, because the column names returned from the subquery are different from the column names returned by the parent query.

17. C. Because only one column is selected in the subquery to which you are doing the insert, only one column value should be supplied in the VALUES clause. The VALUES clause can have only CNT_CODE value (971).

18. B. When using set operators, the ORDER BY clause can appear only on the SQL at the very end. You can use the column names (or aliases) appearing in the top query or use positional columns.

19. B. All four queries produce the same result. The first query uses a scalar subquery in the SELECT clause. The rest of queries use an inline view. All the queries display the last name, salary, and difference of salary from the highest salary in the department for all employees in department 20.

20. D. To find the top *n* rows, you can select the necessary columns in an inline view with an ORDER BY DESC clause. An outer query limiting the rows to *n* will give the result. ROWNUM returns the row number of the result row.

Chapter

5

Manipulating Data

ORACLE DATABASE 11*g*: SQL FUNDAMENTALS I EXAM OBJECTIVES COVERED IN THIS CHAPTER:

✓ **Manipulating Data**

- Describe each data manipulation language (DML) statement

- Insert rows into a table

- Update rows in a table

- Delete rows from a table

- Control transactions

In this chapter, I will cover how to manipulate data. In an Oracle Database, this means using SQL data manipulation language (DML) statements. You will also learn how to coordinate multiple changes using transactions. I will discuss how to insert new data into a table, update existing data, and delete existing data from a table.

Because Oracle is a multiuser database and more than one user or session can change data at the same time, I will also need to cover locks and how they are used to control this concurrency. I will also cover another effect of a multiuser database, which is that data can change during the execution of statements. You can exercise some control over the consistency or visibility of these changes within a transaction, which is covered later in the chapter.

The certification exam will assess your knowledge of how to change data and control these changes. This chapter will solidify your understanding of these concepts in preparation for the certification exam.

Using DML Statements

DML is a subset of SQL that is employed to change data in a database table. Since SQL is English-like, meaning it's not cryptic like C or Perl, the statements used to perform data manipulation are easy to remember. The INSERT statement is used to add new rows to a table. The UPDATE statement is used modify rows in a table, and the DELETE statement is used to remove rows from a table.

Oracle also has the MERGE statement to perform an insert or update on the table from an existing source of data (table or view). MERGE also can include an optional clause to delete rows when certain conditions are met. At the time of publishing this book, however, MERGE is not part of the Oracle Database 11g SQL Fundamentals I test. Table 5.1 summarizes the DML statements that Oracle supports.

TABLE 5.1   DML Statements Supported by Oracle

Statement	Purpose
INSERT	Adds rows to a table
UPDATE	Changes the value stored in a table
DELETE	Removes rows from a table
MERGE	Updates or inserts rows from one table into another

Inserting Rows into a Table

The INSERT statement is used to add rows to one or more tables. The syntax for a simple INSERT statement is as follows:

```
INSERT INTO [schema.]table_name [(column_list)]
VALUES (data_values)
```

In the syntax, *table_name* is the name of the table where you want to add new rows. *table_name* may be qualified with the schema name. *column_list* is the name of the columns in the table, separated by commas, that you want to populate. *data_values* is the corresponding values separated by commas. Using this syntax, you can add only one row at a time.

column_list is optional. If *column_list* is not included, Oracle includes all columns in the order specified when creating the table. *data_values* in the VALUES clause must match the number of columns and datatype in *column_list* (or the number of columns and datatype in the table if *column_list* is omitted). For clarity, it is a good practice to include *column_list* when using the INSERT statement.

If you omit columns in *column_list*, those columns will have NULL values if no default value is defined for the column. If a default value is defined for the column, the column will get the default value. You can insert the default value using the DEFAULT keyword. The SQL statements in the following example show two methods to insert the default value into the MYACCOUNTS table if a default value of C is defined on the DR_CR column:

```
DESCRIBE MYACCOUNTS
Name          Null?    Type
------------- -------- -------------------
ACC_NO        NOT NULL NUMBER(5)
ACC_DT        NOT NULL DATE
DR_CR                  CHAR
AMOUNT                 NUMBER(15,2)


INSERT INTO myaccounts (acc_no, acc_dt, amount)
VALUES (120003, TRUNC(SYSDATE), 400);


INSERT INTO myaccounts (acc_no, acc_dt, dr_cr, amount)
VALUES (120003, TRUNC(SYSDATE), DEFAULT, 400);
```

When specifying *data_values*, enclose character and datetime values in single quotes. For date values, if the value is not in the default date format, you may have to use the TO_DATE function. When you enclose a value in single quotes, Oracle considers it character data and performs an implicit conversion if the column datatype is not a character; hence, do not enclose numeric values in single quotes.

> You can find out the order of columns in a table by using the USER_TAB_ COLUMNS view. The COLUMN_ID column shows the order of columns in the table. When you use the DESCRIBE command to list the table columns, the columns are listed in that order.

I'll use the ACCOUNTS table to demonstrate the INSERT statements. The column names, their order, and their datatype can be displayed using the DESCRIBE statement, as shown here:

```
SQL> DESCRIBE accounts
 Name                       Null?    Type
 ---------------------      -------- -------------
 CUST_NAME                           VARCHAR2(20)
 ACC_OPEN_DATE                       DATE
 BALANCE                             NUMBER(15,2)
```

To insert rows into the ACCOUNTS table, you can use the INSERT statement in its simplest form, as shown here:

```
SQL> INSERT INTO accounts VALUES ('John', '13-MAY-68', 2300.45);
1 row created.
```

The following are some more examples of using INSERT statements. When you use the column list, they can appear in any order. If the DATE value is not in the default date format specified by NLS_DATE_FORMAT parameter, you should use the TO_DATE function with the format mask. The examples also include some errors generated from INSERT to help you understand the statement rules. Notice that you can explicitly insert a NULL value, or if you omit a column in the column list, a NULL value is inserted into that column, provided the column is nullable—in other words, NOT NULL constraint is not defined on the column.

```
SQL> INSERT INTO hr.accounts (cust_name, acc_open_date)
  2   VALUES (Shine, 'April-23-2001');
VALUES (Shine, 'April-23-2001')
        *
ERROR at line 2:
ORA-00984: column not allowed here

SQL> INSERT INTO hr.accounts (cust_name, acc_open_date)
  2   VALUES ('Shine', 'April-23-2001');
VALUES ('Shine', 'April-23-2001')
               *
ERROR at line 2:
ORA-01858: a non-numeric character was found where a numeric was expected

SQL> INSERT INTO hr.accounts (cust_name, acc_open_date)
  2   VALUES ('Shine', TO_DATE('April-23-2001','Month-DD-YYYY'));
1 row created.
```

```
SQL> INSERT INTO accounts VALUES ('Jishi', '4-AUG-72');
INSERT INTO accounts VALUES ('Jishi', '4-AUG-72')
            *
ERROR at line 1:
ORA-00947: not enough values
```

You can also use functions like SYSDATE or USER in the INSERT statement. See these examples:

```
SQL> SHOW USER
USER is "HR"
SQL> INSERT INTO accounts VALUES (USER, SYSDATE, 345);
1 row created.

SQL> SELECT * FROM accounts;
CUST_NAME            ACC_OPEN_   BALANCE
-------------------- --------- ----------
John                 13-MAY-68   2300.45
Shine                23-APR-01
Jishi                12-SEP-99
HR                   23-APR-08        345
```

You can add rows with specific data values, as you have seen in the examples, or you can create rows from existing data using a subquery.

Inserting Rows from a Subquery

You can insert data into a table from an existing table or view using a subquery. To perform the subquery insert, replace the VALUES clause with the subquery. You cannot have both a VALUES clause and a subquery. The columns in the column list should match the number of columns selected in the subquery as well as their datatype. Here are a few examples:

```
SQL> INSERT INTO accounts
  2  SELECT first_name, hire_date, salary
  3  FROM hr.employees
  4  WHERE first_name like 'R%';
3 rows created.

SQL> INSERT INTO accounts (cust_name, balance)
  2  SELECT first_name, hire_date, salary
  3  FROM hr.employees
  4  WHERE first_name like 'T%';
```

```
INSERT INTO accounts (cust_name, balance)
          *
ERROR at line 1:
ORA-00913: too many values

SQL> INSERT INTO accounts (cust_name, acc_open_date)
  2   SELECT UPPER(first_name), ADD_MONTHS(hire_date,2)
  3   FROM hr.employees
  4   WHERE first_name like 'T%';
4 rows created.

SQL> SELECT * FROM accounts;
CUST_NAME                ACC_OPEN_    BALANCE
--------------------     ---------    ----------
John                     13-MAY-68    2300.45
Shine                    23-APR-01
Jishi                    04-AUG-72
Renske                   14-JUL-95       3600
Randall                  15-MAR-98       2600
Randall                  19-DEC-99       2500
TJ                       10-JUN-99
TRENNA                   17-DEC-95
TAYLER                   24-MAR-98
TIMOTHY                  11-SEP-98
10 rows selected.
```

You can use SELECT * FROM if the source and destination table have the same structure, as shown in the following example:

```
INSERT INTO old_employees
SELECT * FROM employees;

107 rows created.
```

Inserting Rows into Multiple Tables

You can also use the INSERT statement to add rows to more than one table at a time. This multiple-table insert is useful for efficiently loading data, because you can add the data to multiple target tables via a single pass through the source table, with a minimum of database calls. The syntax for the multiple-table INSERT statement is as shown here:

```
INSERT [ALL | FIRST] {WHEN <condition> THEN INTO <insert_clause> … … …} [ELSE
<insert_clause>}
```

The keyword ALL tells Oracle to evaluate each and every WHEN clause, whether or not any evaluate to TRUE. In contrast, the FIRST keyword tells Oracle to stop evaluating WHEN clauses after encountering the first one that evaluates to TRUE. The WHEN clause and the INTO clause can be repeated.

Suppose that your company, Sales Inc., sells books, videos, and audio CDs. You have a SALES_DETAIL table that contains information about all the sales and is used by the selling system. You need to load this information into three other tables that focus specifically on the three product categories: Book, Audio, and Video. These category-specific tables are used by the analysis systems. Here are the structure and contents of the source SALES_DETAIL table:

```
Name                          Null?      Type
----------------------------- --------   -------------
TXN_ID                        NOT NULL   NUMBER
PRODUCT_ID                               NUMBER
PROD_CATEGORY                            VARCHAR2(2)
CUSTOMER_ID                              VARCHAR2(10)
SALE_DATE                                DATE
SALE_QTY                                 NUMBER
SALE_PRICE                               NUMBER
```

```
SELECT * FROM sales_detail;
```

TXN_ID	PRODUCT_ID	PR	CUST	SALE_DATE	SALE_QTY	SALE_PRICE
1	304329743	B	43	17-JUN-02	2	19.1
2	304943209	B	22	17-JUN-02	1	8.95
3	211524098	A	16	17-JUN-02	1	11.4
4	413354981	V	41	17-JUN-02	1	12.95
5	304957315	B	48	17-JUN-02	1	38.5
6	304183648	B	32	17-JUN-02	2	17.9
7	211681559	A	32	18-JUN-02	1	11.4
8	211944553	A	21	18-JUN-02	1	11.4
9	304155687	B	26	18-JUN-02	1	8.95
10	304776352	B	18	18-JUN-02	3	48.45
11	413753861	V	30	18-JUN-02	1	12.95
12	413159654	V	29	18-JUN-02	1	19.99
13	304357689	B	11	18-JUN-02	2	72.3
14	211153246	A	14	18-JUN-02	2	26.4
15	304852369	B	44	18-JUN-02	1	15.95

The target table structures are described in the following output:

```
DESC book_sales
```

Name	Null?	Type
PROD_ID	NOT NULL	NUMBER
CUST_ID	NOT NULL	VARCHAR2(10)
QTY_SOLD	NOT NULL	NUMBER
AMT_SOLD	NOT NULL	NUMBER
ISBN		VARCHAR2(24)

```
DESC video_sales
```

Name	Null?	Type
PROD_ID	NOT NULL	NUMBER
CUST_ID	NOT NULL	VARCHAR2(10)
QTY_SOLD	NOT NULL	NUMBER
AMT_SOLD	NOT NULL	NUMBER
RATING		VARCHAR2(5)
YEAR_RELEASED		NUMBER

```
DESC audio_sales
```

Name	Null?	Type
PROD_ID	NOT NULL	NUMBER
CUST_ID	NOT NULL	VARCHAR2(10)
QTY_SOLD	NOT NULL	NUMBER
AMT_SOLD	NOT NULL	NUMBER
ARTIST		VARCHAR2(64)

The multiple-table insert that follows selects from the SALES_DETAIL table and, based on the value of PROD_CATEGORY, inserts a row into the BOOK_SALES, VIDEO_SALES, or AUDIO_SALES table:

```
INSERT ALL
WHEN prod_category='B' THEN
   INTO book_sales(prod_id,cust_id,qty_sold,amt_sold)
      VALUES(product_id,customer_id,sale_qty,sale_price)
WHEN prod_category='V' THEN
   INTO video_sales(prod_id,cust_id,qty_sold,amt_sold)
      VALUES(product_id,customer_id,sale_qty,sale_price)
```

```
WHEN prod_category='A' THEN
  INTO audio_sales(prod_id,cust_id,qty_sold,amt_sold)
      VALUES(product_id,customer_id,sale_qty,sale_price)
SELECT prod_category ,product_id ,customer_id ,sale_qty
      ,sale_price
FROM sales_detail;
```

This multiple-table insert will create eight rows in the BOOK_SALES table, four rows in the AUDIO_SALES table, and three rows in the VIDEO_SALES table.

In most SQL statements, you can prefix column names with a table alias. In fact, this aids readability even if it's not strictly required for parsing. If you try to use an alias for the table name and then prefix the column names with either this alias or the schema-qualified table name in a multiple-table insert, you may raise an exception.

Updating Rows in a Table

The UPDATE statement is used to modify existing rows in a table. The basic syntax for the UPDATE statement is as follows:

```
UPDATE <table_name>
SET <column> = <value>
  [,<column> = <value> … … …]
[WHERE <condition>]
```

You can update more than one row at a time. If the WHERE clause is omitted, all the rows in the table are updated.

If an employee named Jennifer got transferred to another department, you can change the department_id column in the employees table for that employee. Since you know the employee ID for Jennifer, you can use the employee ID to identify Jennifer's row in the table.

```
SELECT first_name, last_name, department_id
FROM employees
WHERE employee_id = 200;
```

```
FIRST_NAME           LAST_NAME                  DEPARTMENT_ID
-------------------- -------------------------- -------------
Jennifer             Whalen                                10
```

```
UPDATE employees
SET department_id = 20
WHERE employee_id = 200;


1 row updated.


SELECT first_name, last_name, department_id
FROM employees
WHERE employee_id = 200;
```

FIRST_NAME	LAST_NAME	DEPARTMENT_ID
Jennifer	Whalen	20

You can update more than one column in the same row by including the columns and values in the SET clause separated by commas. To remove a value from the column, you can update the column as NULL. The following example demonstrates how to update more than one column of the same row as well as update using NULL. Since no WHERE clause is included, all rows in the table are updated.

```
UPDATE old_employees
SET manager_id = NULL,
    commission_pct = 0;


107 rows updated.
```

Updating Rows Using a Subquery

When updating a column in the table, the value can be derived using a subquery. In the following example, the job_id values of all employees in department 30 are changed to match the job_id of employee 114:

```
SELECT first_name, last_name, job_id
FROM employees
WHERE department_id = 30;
```

FIRST_NAME	LAST_NAME	JOB_ID
Den	Raphaely	PU_MAN
Alexander	Khoo	PU_CLERK
Shelli	Baida	PU_CLERK
Sigal	Tobias	PU_CLERK

```
Guy                     Himuro                     PU_CLERK
Karen                   Colmenares                 PU_CLERK
```

6 rows selected.

```
UPDATE employees
SET job_id = (SELECT job_id
              FROM employees
              WHERE employee_id = 114)
WHERE department_id = 30;
```

6 rows updated.

```
SELECT first_name, last_name, job_id
FROM employees
WHERE department_id = 30;
```

```
FIRST_NAME              LAST_NAME                  JOB_ID
-------------------     ------------------------   ----------
Den                     Raphaely                   PU_MAN
Alexander               Khoo                       PU_MAN
Shelli                  Baida                      PU_MAN
Sigal                   Tobias                     PU_MAN
Guy                     Himuro                     PU_MAN
Karen                   Colmenares                 PU_MAN
```

6 rows selected.

You may have more than one column in the SET clause to update more than one column of the same row using a subquery. If you specify more than one column, they must be enclosed in parentheses, and the subquery should have the same number of columns in the SELECT clause.

```
UPDATE order_rollup
SET (qty, price) = (SELECT SUM(qty), SUM(price)
                    FROM order_lines
                    WHERE customer_id = 'KOHL')
WHERE customer_id = 'KOHL'
 AND  order_period = TO_DATE('01-Oct-2001');
```

 **Real World Scenario**

Using a Correct WHERE Clause in UPDATE

Once a developer came to me with a problem—he was trying to update one row in a table, and it was taking forever. He was sure he was using the primary key of the table in the WHERE clause and was expecting the result to come back in seconds.

The table he was updating had the following columns (some columns have been omitted):

ORDER_HEADER

```
ORDER#  VARCHAR2 (20) - Primary Key
ORDER_DT DATE
CUSTOMER# VARCHAR2 (12)
TOTAL_AMOUNT NUMBER
```

The update was performed using the value derived from another table named ORDER_ TRANSACTIONS. It had the following structure:

ORDER_TRANSACTIONS

```
ORDER# VARCHAR2 (20) - Primary Key
ITEM# VARCHAR2 (20) - Primary Key
SHIP_DATE DATE
ITEM_AMOUNT NUMBER
```

The developer was trying to update the total_amount column in the ORDER_HEADER table with the sum of all the order items from the ORDER_TRANSACTIONS table using a subquery. This was the SQL he used:

```
UPDATE order_header oh
SET total_amount = (SELECT SUM(item_amount)
                    FROM order_transactions ot
                    WHERE oh.order# = ot.order#
                    AND oh.order# = 'W2H3004FU');
```

Can you see what is wrong with this statement? By the way, the table has about 2 million rows.

Though the developer thought he was updating only one row in the ORDER_HEADER table and querying only three rows from the ORDER_TRANSACTIONS table, Oracle was in fact updating all the 2 million rows in the table. Why?

Look carefully at the UPDATE statement; it is missing a WHERE clause for the UPDATE statement. The WHERE clause is present as part of the correlated subquery. So, the result of this update would have been the TOTAL_AMOUNT column updated to NULL for all rows except for order W2H3004FU. When executing the correct SQL statement, the update completed in less than one second.

```
UPDATE order_header oh
SET total_amount = (SELECT SUM(item_amount)
                    FROM order_transactions ot
                    WHERE oh.order# = ot.order#
                    AND ot.order# = 'W2H3004FU')
WHERE oh.order# = 'W2H3004FU';
```

Since we are updating a specific order# in the table and we are using the order number in the WHERE clause, it is safe to remove the join condition inside the subquery as in the following code.

```
UPDATE order_header oh
SET total_amount = (SELECT SUM(item_amount)
                    FROM order_transactions ot
                    WHERE ot.order# = 'W2H3004FU')
WHERE oh.order# = 'W2H3004FU';
```

The moral of this story is to be careful when updating tables using subqueries. Always make sure you have the correct WHERE clause for the UPDATE statement.

Deleting Rows from a Table

The DELETE statement is used to remove rows from a table. The syntax for a basic DELETE statement is as follows:

```
DELETE [FROM] <table>
[WHERE <condition>]
```

The FROM keyword is optional, included to add readability to the statement. Similar to the UPDATE statement, if the WHERE clause is omitted, all the rows in the table will be deleted.

Here are some examples of the DELETE statement. The two hyphens (--) are used as comments.

```
--Remove old orders shipped to some states
DELETE FROM po_lines
WHERE ship_to_state IN ('TX','NY','IL')
 AND  order_date < TRUNC(SYSDATE) - 90
```

```
--Remove customer Gomez
DELETE FROM customers
WHERE customer_id = 'GOMEZ';

--Remove duplicate line_detail_ids
--Note keyword FROM is not needed
DELETE line_details
WHERE rowid NOT IN (SELECT MAX(rowid)
                    FROM line_detail
                    GROUP BY line_detail_id)

--Remove all rows from the table order_staging
DELETE FROM order_staging;
```

Removing all rows from a large table can take a long time and require significant roll-back segment space. If you are deleting all rows from a table, consider using the TRUNCATE statement, as described in the next section. TRUNCATE is not included in the Oracle Database 11g SQL Fundamentals I exam, but I've included it here for completeness.

Truncating a Table

Truncating a table can accomplish the same task as deleting if you're deleting all rows from the table, although it is sometimes a better choice. If you want to empty a table of all rows, consider using the Data Definition Language (DDL) statement TRUNCATE. Like a DELETE statement without a WHERE clause, TRUNCATE will remove all rows from a table. However, TRUNCATE is not DML—it is DDL, and therefore, it has different characteristics from the DELETE statement. DDL is the subset of SQL that is employed to define database objects. One of the key differences between DML and DDL is that DDL statements will implicitly perform a commit, not only affecting the change in object definition but also committing any pending DML. A DDL statement cannot be rolled back; only DML statements can be rolled back.

For example, to remove all rows from the ORDER_STAGING table, truncate the table as follows:

```
TRUNCATE TABLE order_staging;
```

TRUNCATE vs. DELETE

The TRUNCATE statement is similar to a DELETE statement without a WHERE clause, except for the following:

- TRUNCATE is very fast on both large and small tables. DELETE will generate undo information if a rollback is issued, but TRUNCATE will not generate undo information.

- TRUNCATE is DDL and, like all DDL, performs an implicit commit—you cannot roll back a TRUNCATE. Any uncommitted DML changes within the session will also be committed with the TRUNCATE operation.

- TRUNCATE resets the high-water mark in the table and all indexes. Since full-table scans and index fast-full scans read all data blocks up to the high-water mark, full-scan performance after a DELETE will not improve; after a TRUNCATE, it will be very fast.

- TRUNCATE does not fire any DELETE triggers.

- There is no object privilege that can be granted to allow a user to truncate another user's table. The DROP ANY TABLE system privilege is required to truncate a table in another schema. See Chapter 12, "Implementing Security and Auditing," for more information about getting around this limitation.

- When a table is truncated, the storage for the table and all indexes can be reset to the initial size. A DELETE will never shrink the size of a table or its indexes.

- You cannot truncate the parent table from an enabled referential integrity constraint. You must first disable the foreign key constraints that reference the parent table, and then you can truncate the parent table.

Merging Rows

Though the MERGE statement is not part of the test, to complete the DML discussion I will give you an introduction to the MERGE statement.

MERGE is a very powerful statement available in Oracle 11*g* (it was introduced in Oracle 9*i*) that can insert or update rows based on a condition. The statement also has an option to delete rows when certain conditions are met. The MERGE statement has a join specification that describes how to determine whether an update or insert should be executed. MERGE is a convenient way to combine multiple operations in one statement instead of writing a complex PL/SQL program.

The basic syntax of the MERGE statement is as follows:

```
MERGE INTO <table_or_view>
USING <table_or_view_or_subquery>
ON <join_condition>
WHEN MATCHED THEN UPDATE SET <update_clause> [<where clause>] [DELETE
where_clause]
WHEN NOT MATCHED THEN INSERT <insert_columns> VALUES <insert_columns>
```

The INTO clause specifies the target table where the update/insert/delete operation will be performed. The USING clause specifies the data source. The ON clause has the join condition between the source and target tables. The WHEN MATCHED THEN UPDATE clause specifies which columns to update when the ON condition is matched. You can also include an optional WHERE clause. The optional DELETE clause can delete the row if the WHERE condition specified in the DELETE clause is met. The WHEN NOT MATCHED THEN INSERT clause is used to add rows to the target table from the source table.

Let's look at a few examples. Consider two tables, ORDERS1 and ORDERS2. The rows in the tables are listed using the following SQL statements:

```
SQL> SELECT * FROM orders1;
```

ORDER_ID	ORDER_MO	CUSTOMER_ID	ORDER_TOTAL
2414	channel	102	10794.6
2397	direct	102	42283.2
2432	channel	102	10523
2431	direct	102	5610.6
2454	direct	103	6653.4
2415	direct	103	310
2433	channel	103	78
2437	direct	103	13550

8 rows selected.

```
SQL> SELECT * FROM orders2;
```

ORDER_ID	CUSTOMER_ID	ORDER_TOTAL
2414	102	35982
2397	102	140944
2432	102	35076.67
2431	102	0
2450	147	1636
2425	147	1500.8
2385	147	295892
2451	148	10474.6
2386	148	21116.9

9 rows selected.

```
SQL>
```

The task before you is to merge the rows in ORDERS2 to ORDERS1. If ORDER_ID and CUSTOMER_ID match between the two tables, you need to update the ORDER_TOTAL value with the value from the ORDERS2 table and update the ORDER_MODE value to modified. For the rows in ORDERS2 where ORDER_ID and CUSTOMER_ID do not match with existing rows in ORDERS1, you need to insert the values from ORDERS2 to ORDERS1. For such rows, the ORDER_MODE value should be merged. You also want to delete the row from ORDERS1 if the new order's total value is zero. The following SQL can accomplish all these tasks using the MERGE statement:

```
MERGE INTO orders1 o1
USING orders2 o2
```

```
ON (o1.order_id = o2.order_id
    AND o1.customer_id = o2.customer_id)
WHEN MATCHED THEN UPDATE SET o1.order_total = o2.order_total,
                             o1.order_mode = 'modified'
    DELETE WHERE o2.order_total = 0
WHEN NOT MATCHED THEN INSERT
    VALUES (o2.order_id, 'merged', o2.customer_id, o2.order_total);


9 rows merged.

select * from orders1;

  ORDER_ID ORDER_MO CUSTOMER_ID ORDER_TOTAL
---------- -------- ----------- -----------
      2414 modified         102       35982
      2397 modified         102      140944
      2432 modified         102    35076.67
      2454 direct           103      6653.4
      2415 direct           103         310
      2433 channel          103          78
      2437 direct           103       13550
      2450 merged           147        1636
      2385 merged           147      295892
      2386 merged           148     21116.9
      2451 merged           148     10474.6
      2425 merged           147      1500.8

12 rows selected.
```

As you can see from the result, Oracle updated four rows that matched the ON condition and inserted five new rows that did not match the ON condition, which is why you get the "9 rows merged" feedback. Since you had the DELETE clause to delete any rows that had order total zero (of the four rows that matched the ON condition), one of them matched the DELETE condition and hence was removed from the table.

Understanding Transaction Control

Transaction control involves coordinating multiple concurrent accesses to the same data. When one session is changing data that another session is accessing, Oracle uses *transactions* to control which users have visibility to changing data and when they can see the changed data. Transactions represent an atomic unit of work. All changes to data in a transaction are applied together or rolled back (undone) together. Transactions provide data consistency in the event of a user-process failure or system failure.

A transaction can include one or more DML statements. A transaction ends when you save the transaction (COMMIT) or undo the changes (ROLLBACK). When DDL statements are executed, Oracle implicitly ends the previous transaction by saving the changes. It also begins a new transaction for the DDL and ends the transaction after the DDL is completed. Hence, DDL statements cannot be undone.

A number of statements in SQL let the programmer control transactions. Using transaction-control statements, the programmer can do the following:

- Explicitly begin a transaction, choosing statement-level consistency or transaction-level consistency

- Set undo savepoints and undo changes back to a savepoint

- End a transaction by making the changes permanent or undoing the changes

Table 5.2 summarizes the transaction-control statements.

TABLE 5.2 Transaction-Control Statements

Statement	Purpose
COMMIT	Ends the current transaction, making data changes permanent and visible to other sessions
ROLLBACK	Undoes all data changes in the current transaction
ROLLBACK TO SAVEPOINT	Undoes all data changes in the current transactions going chronologically backward to the optionally named savepoint
SAVEPOINT	Set an optional marker in within the transaction to be able to go back to this position if needed
SET TRANSACTION	Enables transaction or statement consistency

Throughout this section, I will use a banking example to clarify transactional concepts and the control statements used to ensure data is changed as designed. In this example, say you have a banking customer named Sara who has a checking account and a brokerage account with her bank.

When Sara transfers $5,000 from her checking account to her brokerage account, the balance in her checking account is reduced by $5,000, and the cash balance in her brokerage account is increased by $5,000. You cannot allow only one account to change—either both must change or neither must change.

Consider the following statements to complete the transaction. All the statements in the group must be completed, or no changes should be recorded in the database. The INSERT statements are used to log the transaction in the log table.

```
UPDATE checking
SET balance = balance - 5000
WHERE account = 'SARA1001';
```

```
INSERT INTO checking_log (action_date, action, amount)
VALUES (SYSDATE, 'Withdrawal', 5000);

UPDATE brokerage
SET balance = balance + 5000
WHERE account = 'SARA1001';

INSERT INTO brokerage_log (action_date, action, amount)
VALUES (SYSDATE, 'Deposit', 5000);
```

You issued the two UPDATE statements and the two INSERT statements in a single transaction. If there is any failure in one of these four statements (say, perhaps, the CHECKING_LOG table ran out of room in the tablespace), then none of the changes should go through. When all the previous statements are successful, you can issue a COMMIT statement to save the work to the database. The changes will be committed and made permanent only if all four statements succeed. If only part of the SQL statements were successful, you can issue a ROLLBACK statement to undo the changes.

A transaction will implicitly begin with a DML statement. The transaction will always end with either an implicit or explicit COMMIT or ROLLBACK statement. A ROLLBACK TO SAVE-POINT statement will not end a transaction. The following actions will end a transaction:

- A COMMIT or ROLLBACK statement is issued.

- A DDL statement, such as TRUNCATE or CREATE, is issued (an implicit COMMIT is performed).

- Exit out of a SQL*Plus (an implicit COMMIT is performed).

- Abnormal termination of a SQL*Plus session, such as closing the window (the transaction is rolled back).

- Machine failure or database crash (the transaction is rolled back).

 If a DML statement fails, the transaction is not rolled back. The changes made from the successful DML statements before the failed statement are still valid. To undo those changes, you have to explicitly execute a ROLLBACK statement.

Savepoints and Partial Rollbacks

A ROLLBACK statement will undo all the changes made in the transaction. If you have to undo part of the changes in a transaction, you can set up savepoints or markers in the transaction and go back to a savepoint when needed. Savepoints are intermediate fallback positions in SQL code. The ROLLBACK TO SAVEPOINT statement is used to undo changes chronologically back to the last savepoint or to the named savepoint. Savepoints are not labels for goto statements, and ROLLBACK TO SAVEPOINT is not a goto. The code after a savepoint does not get reexecuted after a ROLLBACK TO SAVEPOINT—only the data changes made since that savepoint are undone.

Savepoints are not used extensively by programmers. However, you must understand them because there will likely be a question related to savepoints on the certification exam.

Consider a transaction with various DML statements and savepoints, as in Figure 5.1.

FIGURE 5.1 Transaction control

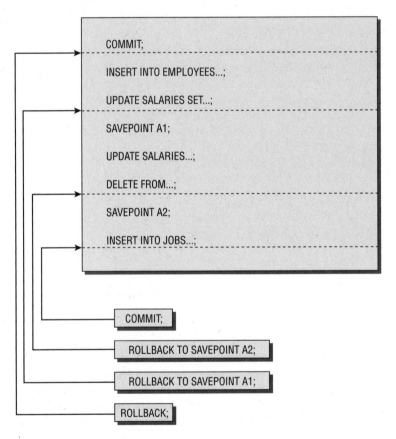

A new transaction begins after a COMMIT statement. Various DML statements are executed in the transaction. You have also set savepoints in between. After all the statements are successfully executed, the user has the option to issue the ROLLBACK TO SAVEPOINT, ROLLBACK, or COMMIT statement. The arrows in the figure show the effect of issuing the transaction-control statements.

 If you create a second savepoint with the same name as an earlier savepoint, the earlier savepoint is deleted, and Oracle keeps only the later savepoint.

Again, an example will help clarify. Sara tries to withdraw $100 from her checking account. You want to log her request in the ATM activity log, but if she has insufficient funds, you don't want to change her balance and will deny her request (part of a PL/SQL block is shown here; the IF statement is PL/SQL).

```
INSERT INTO ATM_LOG(who, when, what, where)
  VALUES('Kiesha', SYSDATE, 'Withdrawal of $100','ATM54');
SAVEPOINT ATM_logged;

UPDATE checking
  SET balance = balance - 100
  WHERE account = 'SARA1001';

SELECT balance INTO new_balance
  FROM checking
  WHERE account = 'SARA1001';

IF new_balance < 0
THEN
  ROLLBACK TO ATM_logged; -- undo update
  COMMIT; -- keep changes prior to savepoint (insert)
  RAISE insufficient_funds; -- Raise error/deny request
END IF;
COMMIT; -- keep insert and update
```

The keyword SAVEPOINT is optional, so the following two statements are equivalent:

```
ROLLBACK TO ATM_logged;
ROLLBACK TO SAVEPOINT ATM_logged;
```

 Because savepoints are not frequently used, always include the keyword SAVEPOINT in any ROLLBACK TO SAVEPOINT statement. That way, anyone reading the code will be reminded of the keyword SAVEPOINT, making it easier to recognize that a partial rollback has occurred.

Data Visibility

When DML operations are performed in a transaction, the changes are visible only to the session performing the DML operations. The changes are visible to other users in the database only when a COMMIT is issued (or a DDL statement causes an implicit commit).

All data changes made in a transaction are temporary until the transaction is committed. The Oracle Database has a read-consistency mechanism to ensure that each user sees the data as it existed at the last commit.

When DML operations are performed on existing rows (through UPDATE, DELETE, or MERGE operations), the affected rows are locked by Oracle, and hence no other user can perform a DML operation on those rows. The rows updated or deleted by a transaction can be queried by another session.

When changes are committed, they are made permanent to the database. All locks on the affected rows are released, and all savepoints are removed. The previous state of the data is lost (the undo segments may be overwritten). All users can view the changed data.

When changes are rolled back, data changes are undone and the previous state of data is restored. All locks on the affected rows are released.

Oracle uses read consistency to make sure you do not see the changes made to data after your query is started. Also, Oracle uses a locking mechanism to make sure that no two users are modifying data in the same row at the same time. Data consistency and the locking mechanism are discussed in the next sections.

Consistency and Transactions

Data consistency is one of the key concepts underlying the use of transaction-control statements. Understanding Oracle's consistency model will enable you to employ transaction control appropriately and answer exam questions about transaction control correctly. Oracle implements consistency to guarantee that the data seen by a statement or transaction does not change until that statement or transaction completes. This support is germane only to multiuser databases, where one database session can change (and commit) data that is being read by another session.

Oracle always uses statement-level consistency, which ensures that the data visible to a statement does not change during the life of that statement. Transactions can consist of one or more statements. When used, transaction-level consistency will ensure that the data visible to all statements in a transaction does not change for the life of the transaction. The banking example will help clarify.

Matt starts running a total-balance report against the checking account table at 10 a.m.; this report takes five minutes. During those five minutes, the data he is reporting on changes when Sara transfers $5,000 from her checking account to her brokerage account. When Matt's session gets to Sara's checking-account record, it will need to reconstruct what the record looked like at 10 a.m. Matt's session will examine the *undo segment* that Sara used during her account-transfer transaction and re-create the image of what the checking-account table looked like at 10 a.m.

Next, at 10:05 a.m., Matt runs a total balance report on the cash in the brokerage account table. If he is using transaction-level consistency, his session will re-create what the brokerage account table looked like at 10 a.m. (and exclude Sara's transfer). If Matt's session is using the default statement-level consistency, his session will report on what the brokerage account table looked like at 10:05 a.m. (and include Sara's transfer).

Oracle never uses locks for reading operations, since reading operations will never block writing operations. Instead, the undo segments (also known as *rollback segments*) are used to re-create the image needed. Undo segments are released for reuse when the transaction writing to them commits or if undo_management is set to auto and the undo_retention period is exceeded, so sometimes a consistent image cannot be re-created. When this happens, Oracle raises a "snapshot too old" exception. Using this example, if Matt's transaction can't locate Sara's transaction in the rollback segments because it was overwritten, Matt's transaction will not be able to re-create the 10 a.m. image of the table and will fail.

Oracle implements consistency internally through the use of system change numbers (SCNs). An SCN is a time-oriented, database-internal key. The SCN only increases, never decreases, and represents a point in time for comparison purposes. So, in the previous example, Oracle internally assigns Matt's first statement the current SCN when it starts reading the checking-account table. This starting SCN is compared to each data block's SCN. If the data-block SCN is higher (newer), then the rollback segments are examined to find the older version of the data.

Undo segments, concurrency, and SCN are discussed in detail in Chapter 13, "Managing Data and Undo."

Locking Mechanism

Locks are implemented by Oracle Database to prevent destructive interaction between concurrent transactions. Locks are acquired automatically by Oracle when a DML statement is executed; no user intervention or action is needed. Oracle uses the lowest level of restrictiveness when locking data for DML statements—only the rows affected by the DML operation are locked.

Locks are held for the duration of the transaction. A commit or rollback will release all the locks. There are two types of locks: explicit and implicit.

The locks acquired by Oracle automatically when DML operations are performed are called *implicit locks*. There is no implicit lock for SELECT statements.

If the user locks data manually, it is called *explicit locking*. The LOCK TABLE statement and SELECT...FOR UPDATE statements are used for explicitly locking the data.

The SELECT...FOR UPDATE statement is used to lock specific rows, preventing other sessions from changing or deleting those locked rows. When the rows are locked, other sessions can select these rows, but they cannot change or lock these rows. The syntax for this statement is identical to a SELECT statement, except you append the keywords FOR UPDATE to the statement. The locks acquired for a SELECT FOR UPDATE will not be released until the transaction ends with a COMMIT or ROLLBACK, even if no data changes.

```
SELECT product_id, warehouse_id, quantity_on_hand
FROM   oe.inventories
WHERE  quantity_on_hand < 5
FOR UPDATE;
```

The LOCK statement is used to lock an entire table, preventing other sessions from performing most or all DML on it. Locking can be in either shared or exclusive mode. Shared mode prevents other sessions from acquiring an exclusive lock but allows other sessions to acquire a shared lock. Exclusive mode prevents other sessions from acquiring either a shared lock or an exclusive lock. The following is an example of using the LOCK statement:

```
LOCK TABLE inventories IN EXCLUSIVE MODE;
```

Oracle employs both table and row locks. Table locks can be obtained in either share or exclusive mode. *Share locks* prevent other exclusive locks but allow other share locks. Exclusive locks prevent both other share locks and other exclusive locks. However, no DML locks prevent read access. To change data, Oracle must acquire an exclusive row-level lock on the rows that are changed. INSERT, UPDATE, DELETE, MERGE, and SELECT FOR UPDATE statements implicitly acquire the necessary row locks. Even if the DML operation affects all the rows in a table, Oracle Database never escalates the row-level lock to a table-level lock; and furthermore, users or developers shouldn't explicitly lock unless there is a very good reason—Oracle handles it automatically 99.9% of the time.

Summary

I started this chapter discussing DML statements in Oracle. I reviewed the INSERT, UPDATE, DELETE, and MERGE statements to add, modify, and delete data in tables. You also learned how transactions and locking work in Oracle.

The INSERT statement is used to add new rows to the table. The VALUES clause in the INSERT statement is used to add a single row at a time. Subqueries can be used to add rows to a table from an existing row source.

The UPDATE statement is used to change existing data in a table. The DELETE statement is used to remove rows from a table. Both the UPDATE and DELETE statements can have WHERE clauses to limit the data changes to specific rows. The MERGE statement allows you to insert or update rows based on a condition.

When an update or delete operation is performed on a table, the previous state of data is written to undo segments to build a read-consistent image of data. Oracle shows only committed data to users.

DML operations lock the affected rows of the table. The locks are held until the transaction is either committed or rolled back. Until the changes are committed, data changes are not visible to other users in the database.

Exam Essentials

Know the syntax for the INSERT statement.   When a subquery is used to add rows to a table, the VALUES clause should not be used.

Practice UPDATE statements   The UPDATE statement can update multiple columns in the same row using a subquery. Multiple subqueries can also be used to update columns in a single row.

Understand what will begin and end a transaction. A transaction will begin with an INSERT, UPDATE, DELETE, MERGE, or SELECT FOR UPDATE statement. A COMMIT or ROLLBACK will end a transaction. A DDL statement can also end a transaction.

Know how to set and roll back to savepoints. Savepoints are set with the SAVEPOINT statement. Data changes made after a savepoint are undone when a ROLLBACK TO SAVEPOINT statement is executed. ROLLBACK TO SAVEPOINT is a partial undo operation.

Understand the scope of data changes and consistency. Statement-level consistency is automatic and will ensure that each SELECT will see an image of the database consistent with the beginning of the statement's execution. Transaction-level consistency will ensure that all SELECT statements within a transaction will see an image of the database consistent with the beginning of the transaction.

Review Questions

1. Jim is trying to add records from the ORDER_DETAILS table to ORDER_DETAIL_HISTORY for orders placed before the current year. Which insert statement would accomplish his task?

   A. ```
   INSERT INTO ORDER_DETAIL_HISTORY
   VALUES (SELECT * FROM ORDER_DETAIL
   WHERE ORDER_DATE < TRUNC(SYSDATE,'YY'));
   ```

   **B.** ```
   INSERT FROM ORDER_DETAIL
   INTO ORDER_DETAIL_HISTORY
   WHERE ORDER_DATE < TRUNC(SYSDATE,'YY');
   ```

   C. ```
   INSERT INTO ORDER_DETAIL_HISTORY
   FROM ORDER_DETAIL
   WHERE ORDER_DATE < TRUNC(SYSDATE,'YY');
   ```

   **D.** ```
   INSERT INTO ORDER_DETAIL_HISTORY
   SELECT * FROM ORDER_DETAIL
   WHERE ORDER_DATE < TRUNC(SYSDATE,'YY');
   ```

2. Which of the following statements will not implicitly begin a transaction?

   A. INSERT

   B. UPDATE

   C. DELETE

   D. SELECT FOR UPDATE

   E. None of the above; they all implicitly begin a transaction, if not started already.

3. Consider the following UPDATE statement. Which UPDATE statements from the options will accomplish the same task? (Choose two.)

   ```
   UPDATE ACCOUNTS
   SET LAST_UPDATED = SYSDATE,
       UPDATE_USER = USER;
   ```

   A. ```
   UPDATE ACCOUNTS
   SET (LAST_UPDATED, UPDATE_USER) =
           (SYSDATE, USER);
   ```

   **B.** ```
   UPDATE ACCOUNTS
   SET LAST_UPDATED =
       (SELECT SYSDATE FROM DUAL),
   UPDATE_USER = (SELECT USER FROM DUAL);
   ```

C. UPDATE ACCOUNTS

　　SET (LAST_UPDATED, UPDATE_USER) =

　　(SELECT SYSDATE, USER FROM DUAL);

D. UPDATE ACCOUNTS

　　SET LAST_UPDATED = SYSDATE

　　AND UPDATE_USER = USER;

4. Which of the following statements do not end a transaction? (Choose two.)

A. SELECT

B. COMMIT

C. TRUNCATE TABLE

D. UPDATE

5. Sara wants to update the SALARY column in the OLD_EMPLOYEES table with the value from the EMPLOYEES table for employees in department 90. Which SQL will accomplish the task?

A. UPDATE old_employees a

　　SET salary = (SELECT salary FROM employees b

　　　　　　　　WHERE a.employee_id = b.employee_id)

　　WHERE department_id = 90;

B. UPDATE old_employees

　　SET salary = (SELECT salary FROM employees)

　　WHERE department_id = 90;

C. UPDATE old_employees a

　　FROM employees b

　　SET a.salary = b.salary

　　WHERE department_id = 90;

D. UPDATE old_employees a

　　SET salary = (SELECT salary FROM employees b

　　　　　　　　WHERE a.employee_id = b.employee_id

　　AND department_id = 90);

6. Review the following code snippet. Which line has an error?

```
1  UPDATE EMPLOYEES
2  WHERE EMPLOYEE_ID = 127
3  SET SALARY = SALARY * 1.25,
4  COMMISSION_PCT = 0
```

A 1

B. 2

C. 4

D. There is no error

7. Jim executes the following SQL statement. What will be the result?

```
DELETE salary, commission_pct
FROM employees
WHERE department_id = 30;
```

A. The `salary` and `commission_pct` columns for all records with `department_id` 30 are deleted (changed to NULL).

B. All the rows belonging to `department_id` 30 are deleted from the table.

C. The `salary` and `commission_pct` columns are deleted from the `employees` table.

D. The statement will produce an error.

8. Consider the following three SQL statements. Choose the most appropriate option.

```
1.  DELETE FROM CITY WHERE CNT_CODE = 1;
2.  DELETE CITY WHERE CNT_CODE = 1;
3.  DELETE (SELECT * FROM CITY WHERE CNT_CODE = 1);
```

A. Statements 1 and 2 will produce the same result, statement 3 will error out.

B. Statements 1 and 2 will produce the same result; statement 3 will produce a different result.

C. Statements 1, 2, and 3 will produce the same result.

D. Statements 1, 2, and 3 will produce different results.

9. Consider the following code segment. How many rows will be in the CARS table after all these statements are executed?

```
SELECT COUNT(*) FROM CARS;
COUNT(*)
--------
      30


DELETE FROM CARS WHERE MAKE = 'TOYOTA';
2 rows deleted.
```

```
SAVEPOINT A;
Savepoint creted.

INSERT INTO CARS VALUES ('TOYOTA','CAMRY',4,220);
1 row created.

SAVEPOINT A;

INSERT INTO CARS VALUES ('TOYOTA','COROLLA',4,180);
1 row created.

ROLLBACK TO SAVEPOINT A;
Rollback complete.
```

A. 30

B. 29

C. 28

D. 32

10. Jim noticed that the HIRE_DATE and START_DATE columns in the EMPLOYEES table had date and time values, and hence when he is trying to find employees hired on a certain date, he is not getting the desired result. Which SQL statement will update all the rows in the EMPLOY-EES table with no time portion in the HIRE_DATE and START_DATE columns (00:00:00).

A. UPDATE EMPLOYEES SET HIRE_DATE = TRUNC(HIRE_DATE) AND START_DATE = TRUNC(START_DATE);

B. UPDATE TABLE EMPLOYEES SET TRUNC(HIRE_DATE) AND TRUNC(START_DATE);

C. UPDATE EMPLOYEES SET HIRE_DATE = TRUNC(HIRE_DATE), START_DATE = TRUNC(START_DATE);

D. UPDATE HIRE_DATE = TRUNC(HIRE_DATE), START_DATE = TRUNC(START_DATE) IN EMPLOYEES;

11. Sara wants to update the SALARY column in the EMPLOYEE table from the SALARIES table, based on the JOB_ID value for all employees in department 22. The SALARIES table and the EMPLOYEE table have the following structure. Which is the correct UPDATE statement of the following options?

```
DESC EMPLOYEE
EMPLOYEE_ID    NUMBER (3),
EMP_NAME       VARCHAR2 (40),
JOB_ID         VARCHAR2 (4),
DEPT_ID        NUMBER
SALARY         NUMBER
```

```
DESC SALARIES
JOB_ID          VARCHAR2 (4),
SALARY          NUMBER
```

A. UPDATE SALARIES A SET SALARY = (SELECT SALARY FROM EMPLOYEES B WHERE A.JOB_ID = B.JOB_ID WHERE DEPT_ID = 22);

B. UPDATE EMPLOYEE E SET SALARY = (SELECT SALARY FROM SALARIES S WHERE E.JOB_ID = S.JOB_IB AND DEPT_ID = 22);

C. UPDATE EMPLOYEE E SET SALARY = (SELECT SALARY FROM SALARIES S WHERE E.JOB_ID = S.JOB_IB) AND DEPT_ID = 22;

D. UPDATE EMPLOYEE E SET SALARY = (SELECT SALARY FROM SALARIES S WHERE E.JOB_ID = S.JOB_IB) WHERE DEPT_ID = 22;

12. The FIRED_EMPLOYEE table has the following structure:

```
EMPLOYEE_ID  NUMBER (4)
FIRE_DATE DATE
```

How many rows will be counted from the last SQL statement in the code segment?

```
SELECT COUNT(*) FROM FIRED_EMPLOYEES;
COUNT(*)
--------
     105


INSERT INTO FIRED_EMPLOYEE VALUES (104, TRUNC(SYSDATE);
SAVEPOINT A;
INSERT INTO FIRED_EMPLOYEE VALUES (106, TRUNC(SYSDATE);
SAVEPOINT B;
INSERT INTO FIRED_EMPLOYEE VALUES (108, TRUNC(SYSDATE);
ROLLBACK TO A;
INSERT INTO FIRED_EMPLOYEE VALUES (104, TRUNC(SYSDATE);
COMMIT;
SELECT COUNT(*) FROM FIRED_EMPLOYEES;
```

A. 109

B. 106

C. 105

D. 107

13. The following table describes the DEPARTMENTS table:

Column Name	dept_id	dept_name	mgr_id	location_id
Key Type	pk			
Nulls/Unique	NN			
FK Table				
Datatype	NUMBER	VARCHAR2	NUMBER	NUMBER
Length	4	30	6	4
Default Value	None	None	None	99

Which of the following INSERT statements will raise an exception?

A. `INSERT INTO departments (dept_id, dept_name, location_id)`
`VALUES(280,'Security',1700);`

B. `INSERT INTO departments`
`VALUES(280,'Security',1700);`

C. `INSERT INTO departments`
`VALUES(280,'Corporate Giving',266,1700);`

D. None of these statements will raise an exception.

14. Refer to the DEPARTMENTS table structure in question 13. Two SQL statements are shown here. Choose the best option that describes the SQL statements.

`1.INSERT INTO departments (dept_id, dept_name, mgr_id)`
`VALUES(280,'Security',1700);`

`2.INSERT INTO departments (dept_id, dept_name, mgr_id, location_id)`
`VALUES(280,'Security',1700, NULL);`

A. Statements 1 and 2 insert the same values to all columns in the table.

B. Statements 1 and 2 insert different values to at least one column in the table.

C. The `location_id` column must be included in the column list of statement 1.

D. A NULL value cannot be inserted explicitly in statement 2.

15. The SALES table contains the following data:

```
SELECT channel_id, COUNT(*)
FROM sales
GROUP BY channel_id;


C    COUNT(*)
-    ----------
T      12000
I      24000
```

How many rows will be inserted into the NEW_CHANNEL_SALES table with the following SQL statement?

```
INSERT FIRST
 WHEN channel_id ='C' THEN
    INTO catalog_sales (prod_id,time_id,promo_id
                        ,amount_sold)
        VALUES (prod_id,time_id,promo_id,amount_sold)
 WHEN channel_id ='I' THEN
    INTO internet_sales (prod_id,time_id,promo_id
                        ,amount_sold)
        VALUES (prod_id,time_id,promo_id,amount_sold)
 WHEN  channel_id IN ('I','T') THEN
    INTO new_channel_sales (prod_id,time_id,promo_id
                        ,amount_sold)
        VALUES (prod_id,time_id,promo_id,amount_sold)
SELECT channel_id,prod_id,time_id,promo_id,amount_sold
FROM sales;
```

A. 0

B. 12,000

C. 24,000

D. 36,000

16. How many rows will be counted in the last SQL statement that follows?

```
SELECT COUNT(*) FROM emp;
120 returned

INSERT INTO emp (emp_id)
    VALUES (140);
SAVEPOINT emp140;
```

```
INSERT INTO emp (emp_id)
   VALUES (141);
INSERT INTO emp (emp_id)
   VALUES (142);
INSERT INTO emp (emp_id)
   VALUES (143);
TRUNCATE TABLE employees;
INSERT INTO emp (emp_id)
   VALUES (144);

ROLLBACK;

SELECT COUNT(*) FROM emp;
```

A. 121

B. 0

C. 124

D. 143

17. Which is the best option that describes the following SQL statement?

    1.UPDATE countries

    2.CNT_NAME = UPPER(CNT_NAME)

    3.WHERE country_code BETWEEN 1 and 99;

    A. The statement is missing the keyword SET, but the statement will work just fine because SET is an optional keyword.

    B. The BETWEEN operator cannot be used in the WHERE clause used in an UPDATE statement.

    C. The function UPPER(CNT_NAME) should be changed to UPPER('CNT_NAME').

    D. The statement is missing keyword SET; hence, the statement will fail.

18. The table ORDERS has 35 rows. The following UPDATE statement updates all 35 rows. Which is the best option?

    ```
    UPDATE orders
    SET ship_date = TRUNC(ship_date)
    WHERE ship_date != TRUNC(ship_date)
    ```

    A. When all rows in a table are updated, the LOCK TABLE orders IN EXCLUSIVE MODE statement must be executed before the UPDATE statement.

    B. No other session can query from the table until the transaction ends.

    C. Since all rows are updated, there is no need for any locking, and hence Oracle does not lock the records.

    D. The statement locks all the rows until the transaction ends.

19. Which of the following INSERT statements will raise an exception?

   A. `INSERT INTO EMP SELECT * FROM NEW_EMP;`

   B. `INSERT FIRST WHEN DEPT_NO IN (12,14) THEN INSERT INTO EMP SELECT * FROM NEW_EMP;`

   C. `INSERT FIRST WHEN DEPT_NO IN (12,14) THEN INTO EMP SELECT * FROM NEW_EMP;`

   D. `INSERT ALL WHEN DEPT_NO IN (12,14) THEN INTO EMP SELECT * FROM NEW_EMP;`

20. What will the salary of employee Arsinoe be at the completion of the following SQL statements?

```
UPDATE emp
  SET salary = 1000
  WHERE name = 'Arsinoe';
SAVEPOINT Point_A;

UPDATE emp
  SET  salary = salary * 1.1
  WHERE name = 'Arsinoe';
SAVEPOINT Point_B;

UPDATE emp
  SET  salary = salary * 1.1
  WHERE name = 'Berenike';
SAVEPOINT point_C;

ROLLBACK TO SAVEPOINT point_b;
COMMIT;
UPDATE emp
  SET salary = 1500
  WHERE name = 'Arsinoe';
SAVEPOINT point_d;

ROLLBACK TO point_d;

COMMIT;
```

   A. 1000

   B. 1100

   C. 1111

   D. 1500

Answers to Review Questions

1. **D.** When inserting from another table using a subquery, the VALUES clause should not be included. Options B and C are invalid syntaxes for the INSERT statement.

2. **E.** If a transaction is not currently open, any INSERT, UPDATE, MERGE, DELETE, SELECT FOR UPDATE, or LOCK statement will implicitly begin a transaction.

3. **B, C.** Option A will error out because when using columns in set, a subquery must be used as in option C. Option D is wrong because AND is used instead of a comma to separate columns in the SET clause.

4. **A, D.** COMMIT, ROLLBACK, and any DDL statement end a transaction—DDL is automatically committed. INSERT, UPDATE, and DELETE statements require a commit or rollback.

5. **A.** Option A uses a correlated subquery to match the correct employee. Option B selects all the rows in the subquery and hence will generate an error. Option C is not valid syntax. Option D will update all the rows in the table since the UPDATE statement does not have a WHERE clause. The WHERE clause preset belongs to the subquery.

6. **B.** In an UPDATE statement, the WHERE clause should come after the SET clause.

7. **D.** When deleting a row from a table, do not use column names. To change column values to NULL, use the UPDATE statement.

8. **C.** The FROM keyword in the DELETE statement is optional. Statement 3 is first building a subquery with the necessary condition and deleting the rows from the subquery.

9. **B.** When two savepoints are created with the same name, Oracle erases the older savepoint. In the code segment, the DELETE and the first INSERT are not rolled back.

10. **C.** When updating more than one column in a single UPDATE statement, separate the columns by a comma; do not use the AND operator.

11. **D.** Option A is updating the wrong table. Option B has the right syntax but will update all the rows in the EMPLOYEE table since there is no WHERE clause for the UPDATE statement. Since the WHERE clause is in the subquery, all the rows that do not belong to department 22 will be updated with a NULL. Options C and D are similar, except for the AND keyword instead of WHERE.

12. **D.** The first INSERT statement and the last INSERT statement will be saved in the database. The ROLLBACK TO A statement will undo the second and third inserts.

13. **B.** Option B will raise an exception because there are not enough column values for the implicit column list (all columns).

14. **B.** Since the location_id column is defined with a default value of 99, statement 1 will insert 99 for location_id. In statement 2, a NULL is explicitly inserted into the location_id column; Oracle will not replace the NULL with the default value defined.

15. B. The FIRST clause tells Oracle to execute only the first WHEN clause that evaluates to TRUE for each row. Since no rows have a channel_id of C, no rows would be inserted into the catalog_sales table; 24,000 rows have channel_id of I, so control would pass to the second WHEN clause 24,000 times, and the internet_sales table would get 24,000 rows. Since the second WHEN clause evaluates to TRUE and the INSERT FIRST option is specified, these rows would not make it to the third WHEN clause and would not be inserted into the new_channel_sales table. Had the INSERT ALL option been used, these 24,000 rows would also get inserted into the new_channel_sales table; 12,000 rows have a channel_id of T, so control would pass all the way to the third WHEN clause for these rows, and 12,000 rows would get inserted into new_channel_sales.

16. C. The TRUNCATE statement is DDL and performs an implicit commit. After the TRUNCATE statement on the employees table, there are 124 rows in the emp table. The one row that got inserted was removed when the ROLLBACK statement was executed.

17. D. You must have the SET keyword in an UPDATE statement. The BETWEEN operator and any other valid operators are allowed in the WHERE clause.

18. D. When DML operations are performed, Oracle automatically locks the rows. You can query (read) the rows, but no other DML operation is allowed on those rows. When you read the rows, Oracle constitutes a read-consistent view using the undo segments.

19. B. The keywords INSERT INTO are required in single-table INSERT statements but are not valid in multiple-table INSERT statements.

20. D. The final rollback (to point_d) will roll the changes back to just after setting the salary to 1500.

Chapter
6

Creating Tables and Constraints

ORACLE DATABASE 11*g*: SQL FUNDAMENTALS I EXAM OBJECTIVES COVERED IN THIS CHAPTER:

✓ **Using DDL Statements to Create and Manage Tables**

- Categorize the main database objects

- Review the table structure

- List the data types that are available for columns

- Create a simple table

- Explain how constraints are created at the time of table creation

- Describe how schema objects work

An Oracle database has many different types of objects. Related objects are logically grouped together in a schema, which consists of various types of objects. The basic types of objects in an Oracle Database are tables, indexes, constraints, sequences, and synonyms. Though this chapter discusses tables and constraints, I will start the chapter with an overview of the main database objects in Oracle.

The table is the basic structure of data storage in Oracle. A table has columns as part of the definition and stores rows of data. In a relational database, the data in various tables may be related. A constraint can be considered as a rule or policy defined in the database to enforce data integrity and business rules. In this chapter, I will discuss creating tables and using constraints. Since the table is the most important type of object in an Oracle Database, it is important to know how to create tables and constraints on tables.

Database Objects Overview

Data in the Oracle Database is stored in tables. A *table* is the main database object. Many other database objects, whether or not they store data, are generally based on the tables. Let's review the main database objects in Oracle that are relevant for this certification exam:

Table   A *table* is defined with columns and stores rows of data. A table should have at least one column. In Oracle, a table normally refers to a relational table. You can also create object tables. Object tables are created with user-defined datatypes. Temporary tables (called *global temporary tables* in Oracle) are used to hold temporary data specific to a transaction or session. A table can store a wide variety of data. Apart from storing text and numeric information, you can store date, timestamp, binary, or raw data (such as images, documents, and information about external files). A table can have *virtual columns*. As the name indicates, these types of columns do not consume storage space on disk; the database derives values in virtual columns from normal columns. Tables are discussed in the next sections of this chapter.

View   A *view* is a customized representation of data from one or more tables and/or views. Views are used as a window to show information from tables in a certain way or to restrict the information. Views are queries stored in the database that select data from one or more tables. They also provide a way to restrict data from certain users, thus providing an additional level of security.

Sequence   A *sequence* is a way to generate continuous numbers. Sequences are useful for generating unique serial numbers or key values. The sequence definition is stored in the data dictionary. Sequence numbers are generated independently of other database objects.

Synonym   A *synonym* is an alias for any table, view, sequence, or other accessible database object. Because a synonym is simply an alias, it requires no storage other than its definition in the data dictionary. Synonyms are useful because they hide the identity of the underlying object. The object can even be part of another database. A public synonym is accessible to all users of the database, and a private synonym is accessible only to its owner.

Index   An *index* is a structure associated with tables used to speed up the queries. An index is an access path to reach the desired row faster. Oracle has B-tree and bitmap indexes. Creating/dropping indexes does not affect the storage of data in the underlying tables. You can create unique or nonunique indexes. Unique indexes are created automatically by Oracle when you create a primary key or a unique key constraint in a table. A composite index has more than one column in the index.

Views, sequences, synonyms, and indexes are discussed in Chapter 7, "Creating Schema Objects."

Oracle 11*g* has a wide array of database objects to suit various application requirements. These objects are not discussed in this book because they are not part of the certification exam at this time. Some of the other database objects that may be used in application development are clusters, dimensions, directories, functions, Java sources/classes, libraries, materialized views, and types. To learn more about the various Oracle 11*g* database schema objects, please refer to the Oracle documentation called "Oracle Database Administrators Guide 11g Release 1 (11.) Part Number B28310-04," which is available online at `www.oracle`
`.com/pls/db111/db111.homepage`.

Schema Objects

A *schema* is a collection of related database objects grouped together. For example, a schema can have tables, views, triggers, synonyms, and PL/SQL programs such as procedures. A schema is owned by a database user and has the same name as the user. If the database user does not own any database objects, then no schema is associated with the user. A schema is a logical grouping of database objects.

A database user can have only one schema associated and is created when you create any database object. They may include any or all the basic database objects discussed earlier. Oracle 11*g* may also include the following types of structures in the schema. These objects are listed here only to give you an overview of schemas; creating and managing these objects are not part of the certification exam at this time. For the certification exam, prepare to know the schema objects discussed in this chapter and in Chapter 7.

Materialized view *Materialized views* are objects used to summarize and replicate data. They are similar to views but occupy storage space. Materialized views are mainly used in data-warehouse environments where data needs to be aggregated and stored so that queries and reports run faster. Materialized views can also be used to replicate data from another database.

Dimension A *dimension* is a logical structure to define the relationship between columns in a table. Dimensions are defined in the data dictionary and do not occupy any storage space. The columns in a dimension can be from a single table or from multiple tables. An example of a dimension would be the relationship between country, state, and city in a table that stores address information.

Cluster A *cluster* is a method of storing data from related tables at a common physical location. You can share the storage of rows in related tables for performance reasons if the access to the rows in the tables always involves join operations on the tables. For example, if you have an orders table and a customers table in the schema, you can query the orders table always joining the customers table, because that's where you get the customer name associated with the customer ID. A cluster may be created for the orders and customers tables so that the rows associated with the same customer are stored in the same physical storage area (block). Database storage and blocks are discussed in Chapter 8, "Introducing Oracle 11*g* Components and Architecture."

Database links A *database link* is a schema object that enables you to access an object from a different database. SQL queries can reference tables and views belonging to the remote database by appending `@db_link_name` to the table or view. For example, to access the `CUSTOMER_ORDERS` table using a database link named `LONDON_SALES`, you would use `CUSTOMER_ORDERS@LONDON_SALES`.

Triggers A *trigger* is a stored PL/SQL program that gets executed when a specified condition occurs. A trigger can be defined on a table to "fire" when an insert, update, or delete operation occurs on the table. A trigger may also be defined on the database to "fire" when certain database conditions occur, such as starting the database, or when a database error occurs.

Java objects Oracle Database 11*g* includes *Java objects* such as Java classes, Java sources, and Java resources. Java stored programs can be created using the different Java object types.

PL/SQL programs *PL/SQL stored programs* include procedures, functions, and packages. A *procedure* is a PL/SQL programmatic construct. A *function* is similar to a procedure but always returns a value. A *package* is a grouping of related PL/SQL objects.

Built-in Datatypes

When creating tables, you must specify a *datatype* for each column you define. Oracle 11*g* is rich with various datatypes to store different kinds of information. By choosing the appropriate datatype, you will be able to store and retrieve data without compromising its integrity. A datatype associates a predefined set of properties with the column.

The datatypes in Oracle 11*g* can be classified into five major categories. Figure 6.1 shows the categories and the datatype names.

FIGURE 6.1 Oracle built-in datatypes

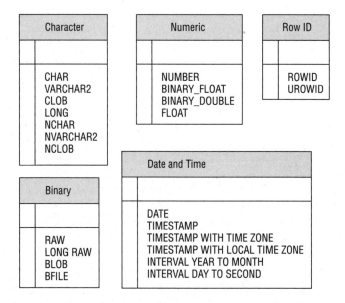

Chapter 1, "Introducing SQL," introduced four basic datatypes: CHAR, VARCHAR2, NUMBER, and DATE. Here, I will review those datatypes and describe the other datatypes that you can specify while creating a table.

Character Datatypes

Seven character datatypes can be used for defining columns in a table:

- CHAR
- NCHAR
- VARCHAR2
- NVARCHAR2
- CLOB
- NCLOB
- LONG

Character datatypes store alphanumeric data in the database character set or in the Unicode character set. You define the database character set when you create the database.

The character set determines which languages can be represented in the database. For example, US7ASCII is a 7-bit ASCII character set that can represent the English language and any other language that uses the English alphabet set. WE8ISO8859P1 is an 8-bit character set that can support multiple European languages such as English, German, French, Albanian, Spanish, Portuguese, Irish, and so on, because they all use a similar writing script. Unicode, the Universal Character Set, allows you to store any language character using a single character set. The Unicode character set supported by Oracle is either 16-bit encoding (UTF-16) or 8-bit encoding (UTF-8). You can choose the Unicode datatypes to be used in the database while creating the database. The default is the AL16UTF16 character set, which is UTF-16 encoding.

CHAR

The syntax for the CHAR datatype is as follows:

```
CHAR [(<size> [BYTE | CHAR ] ) ]
```

The CHAR datatype is fixed-length, with the maximum size of the column specified in parentheses. You can also include the optional keyword BYTE or CHAR inside the parentheses along with the size to indicate whether the size is in bytes or in characters. BYTE is the default.

For single-byte-database character sets (such as US7ASCII), the size specified in bytes and the size specified in characters are the same. If the column value is shorter than the size defined, trailing spaces are added to the column value. Specifying the size is optional, and the default size is 1 byte. The maximum allowed size in a CHAR datatype column is 2,000 bytes. Here are few examples of specifying a CHAR datatype column:

```
employee_id   CHAR (5)
employee_name CHAR (100 CHAR)
employee_sex  CHAR
```

NCHAR

The syntax for the NCHAR datatype is as follows:

```
NCHAR [ ( <size> ) ]
```

The NCHAR datatype is similar to CHAR, but it is used to store Unicode character-set data. The NCHAR datatype is fixed-length, with a maximum size of 2,000 bytes and a default size of a character.

The size in the NCHAR datatype definition is always specified in characters. Trailing spaces are added if the value inserted into the column is shorter than the column's maximum length. Here is an example of specifying an NCHAR datatype column:

```
emp_name NCHAR (100)
```

Several built-in Oracle 11*g* functions have options to represent NCHAR data. An NCHAR string may be represented by prefixing the string with N, as in this example:

```
SELECT  emp_name FROM employee_records
WHERE emp_name = N'John Smith';
```

VARCHAR2 or VARCHAR

The syntax for the VARCHAR2 datatype is as follows:

```
VARCHAR2 (<size> [BYTE | CHAR] )
```

VARCHAR2 and VARCHAR are synonymous datatypes. VARCHAR2 specifies variable-length character data. A maximum size for the column should be defined; Oracle 11*g* will not assume any default value. Unlike CHAR columns, VARCHAR2 columns are not blank-padded with trailing spaces if the column value is shorter than its maximum specified length. You can specify the size in bytes or characters; by default, the size is in bytes. The range of values allowed for size is from 1 to 4,000 bytes. For storing variable-length data, Oracle recommends using VARCHAR2 rather than VARCHAR, because the behavior of the VARCHAR datatype may change in a future release.

NVARCHAR2

The syntax for the NVARCHAR2 datatype is as follows:

```
NVARCHAR2 (<size>)
```

The NVARCHAR2 datatype is used to store Unicode variable-length data. The size is specified in characters, and the maximum size allowed is 4,000 bytes.

 WARNING   If you try to insert a value into a character datatype column that is larger than its maximum specified size, Oracle will return an error. Oracle will not chop or truncate the inserted value to store it in the database column.

CLOB

The syntax for the CLOB datatype is as follows:

```
CLOB
```

CLOB is one of the Large Object datatypes provided to store variable-length character data. The maximum amount of data you can store in a CLOB column is based on the block size of the database. CLOB can store up to (4GB–1)*(database block size). You do not specify the size with this datatype definition.

NCLOB

The syntax for the NCLOB datatype is as follows:

```
NCLOB
```

NCLOB is one of the Large Object datatypes and stores variable-length Unicode character data. The maximum amount of data you can store in a NCLOB column is (4GB–1)* (database block size). You do not specify the size with this datatype definition.

LONG

The syntax for the LONG datatype is as follows:

LONG

Using the LONG datatype is discouraged in Oracle Database 11g. It is provided only for backward compatibility. You should use the CLOB datatype instead of LONG. LONG columns can store up to 2GB of character data. There can be only one LONG column in the table definition. A LONG datatype column can be used in the SELECT clause of a query, the SET clause of the UPDATE statement, and the VALUES clause of the INSERT statement. You can also create a NOT NULL constraint on a LONG column.

LONG datatype columns cannot appear in the following:

- The WHERE, GROUP BY, or ORDER BY clauses
- A SELECT clause if the DISTINCT operator is used
- A SELECT list of subqueries used in INSERT statements
- A SELECT list of subqueries used with the UNION, INTERSECT, or MINUS operator
- A SELECT list of queries with the GROUP BY clause

Numeric Datatypes

Four built-in numeric datatypes can be used for defining numeric columns in a table:

- NUMBER
- BINARY_FLOAT
- BINARY_DOUBLE
- FLOAT

Numeric datatypes are used to store integer and floating-point numbers. The NUMBER datatype can store all types of numeric data, but BINARY_FLOAT and BINARY_DOUBLE give better performance with floating-point numbers. FLOAT is a subtype of NUMBER.

NUMBER

The syntax for the NUMBER datatype is as follows:

NUMBER [(<precision> [, <scale>])]

You can represent all non-Oracle numeric datatypes such as float, integer, decimal, double, and so on, using the NUMBER datatype. The NUMBER datatype can store both fixed-point and floating-point numbers. Oracle 11g introduced two new datatypes to support floating-point numbers—specifically, BINARY_FLOAT and BINARY_DOUBLE.

BINARY_FLOAT

The syntax for the BINARY_FLOAT datatype is as follows:

```
BINARY_FLOAT
```

The BINARY_FLOAT datatype represents a 32-bit floating-point number. There is no precision defined in the definition of this datatype because it uses binary precision. BINARY_FLOAT uses 5 bytes for storage.

A floating-point number can have a decimal point anywhere or can have no decimal point. Oracle stores NUMBER datatype values using decimal precision, whereas floating-point numbers (BINARY_FLOAT and BINARY_DOUBLE) are stored using binary precision. Oracle has three special values that can be used with floating-point numbers:

INF: Positive infinity

-INF: Negative infinity

NaN: Not a Number (NaN is not the same as NULL)

BINARY_DOUBLE

The syntax for the BINARY_DOUBLE datatype is as follows:

```
BINARY_DOUBLE
```

The BINARY_DOUBLE datatype represents a 64-bit floating-point number. BINARY_DOUBLE uses 9 bytes for storage. All the characteristics of BINARY_FLOAT are applicable to BINARY_DOUBLE.

FLOAT

The syntax for the FLOAT datatype is as follows:

```
FLOAT [(precision)]
```

The FLOAT datatype is a subtype of NUMBER and is internally represented as NUMBER. There is no scale for FLOAT numbers; only precision can be optionally included. The precision can range from 1 to default binary digits. In the NUMBER datatype the precision and scale are represented in decimal digits, whereas in FLOAT the precision is represented in binary digits. In Oracle 11g it is recommended you use BINARY_FLOAT or BINARY_DOUBLE instead of the FLOAT datatype.

Date and Time Datatypes

In pre–Oracle9i databases, the only datetime datatype available was DATE, which stores the date and time. Oracle9i Database introduced the TIMESTAMP and INTERVAL datatypes to enhance the storage and manipulation of date and time data. Six datetime datatypes in Oracle 11g can be used for defining columns in a table:

- DATE
- TIMESTAMP
- TIMESTAMP WITH TIME ZONE

- TIMESTAMP WITH LOCAL TIME ZONE
- INTERVAL YEAR TO MONTH
- INTERVAL DAY TO SECOND

The interval datatypes are used to represent a measure of time. They store the number of months or number of days/hours between two time points. All interval components are integers except the seconds, which may have fractional seconds represented.

DATE

The syntax for the DATE datatype is as follows:

DATE

The DATE datatype stores date and time information. You can store the dates from January 1, 4712 BC to December 31, 9999 AD. If you specify a date value without the time component, the default time is 12 a.m. (midnight, 00:00:00 hours). If you specify a date value without the date component, the default value is the first day of the current month. The DATE datatype stores century, year, month, date, hour, minute, and seconds internally. You can display the dates in various formats using the NLS_DATE_FORMAT parameter or by specifying a format mask with the TO_CHAR function. The various date-format masks are discussed in Chapter 2, "Using Single-Row Functions."

TIMESTAMP

The syntax for TIMESTAMP datatype is as follows:

TIMESTAMP [(<precision>)]

The TIMESTAMP datatype stores date and time information with fractional seconds precision. The only difference between the DATE and TIMESTAMP datatypes is the ability to store fractional seconds up to a precision of nine digits. The default precision is 6 and can range from 0 to 9.

TIMESTAMP WITH TIME ZONE

The syntax for the TIMESTAMP WITH TIME ZONE datatype is as follows:

TIMESTAMP [(<precision>)] WITH TIME ZONE

The TIMESTAMP WITH TIME ZONE datatype is similar to the TIMESTAMP datatype, but it stores the *time-zone displacement*. Displacement is the difference between the local time and the Coordinated Universal Time (UTC, also known as *Greenwich mean time*). The displacement is represented in hours and minutes. Two TIMESTAMP WITH TIME ZONE values are considered identical if they represent the same time in UTC. For example, 5 p.m. CST is equal to 6 p.m. EST or 3 p.m. PST.

TIMESTAMP WITH LOCAL TIME ZONE

The syntax for the TIMESTAMP WITH LOCAL TIME ZONE datatype is as follows:

TIMESTAMP [(<precision>)] WITH LOCAL TIME ZONE

The TIMESTAMP WITH LOCAL TIME ZONE datatype is similar to the TIME-STAMP datatype, but like the TIMESTAMP WITH TIME ZONE datatype, it also includes the time-zone displacement. TIMESTAMP WITH LOCAL TIME ZONE does not store the displacement information in the database but stores the time as a normalized form of the database time zone. The data is always stored in the database time zone, but when the user retrieves data, it is shown in the user's local-session time zone.

The following example demonstrates how the DATE, TIMESTAMP, TIMESTAMP WITH TIME ZONE, and TIMESTAMP WITH LOCAL TIME ZONE datatypes store data. The NLS_xx_FORMAT parameter is explicitly set to display the values in the nondefault format. The data is inserted at Central Daylight Time (CDT), which is seven hours behind UTC. (The output shown in the example was reformatted for better readability.)

```
CREATE TABLE date_time_demo (
r_no        NUMBER (2),
c_date      DATE DEFAULT SYSDATE,
c_timezone  TIMESTAMP DEFAULT SYSTIMESTAMP,
c_timezone2 TIMESTAMP (2) DEFAULT SYSTIMESTAMP,
c_ts_wtz    TIMESTAMP (0) WITH TIME ZONE
                          DEFAULT SYSTIMESTAMP,
c_ts_wltz   TIMESTAMP (9) WITH LOCAL TIME ZONE
                          DEFAULT SYSTIMESTAMP);

Table created.

INSERT INTO date_time_demo (r_no) VALUES (1);
1 row created.

ALTER SESSION SET NLS_DATE_FORMAT = 'YYYY-MM-DD HH24:MI:SS';
Session altered.

ALTER SESSION SET NLS_TIMESTAMP_FORMAT  = 'YYYY-MM-DD HH24:MI:SS.FF';
Session altered.

ALTER SESSION SET NLS_TIMESTAMP_TZ_FORMAT = 'YYYY-MM-DD HH24:MI:SS.FFTZH:TZM';
Session altered.

SELECT * FROM date_time_demo;

R_NO C_DATE               C_TIMEZONE
-------------------- ---------------------------
1 2008-10-24 13:09:14  2008-10-24 13:09:14. 000001
```

```
C_TIMEZONE2              C_TS_WTZ
---------------------    --------------------------
2008-10-24 13:09:14.00   2008-10-24 13:09:14.-07:00


C_TS_WLTZ
----------------------------
2008-10-24 13:09:14.000001000
```

INTERVAL YEAR TO MONTH

The syntax for the INTERVAL YEAR TO MONTH datatype is as follows:

```
INTERVAL YEAR [(precision)] TO MONTH
```

The INTERVAL YEAR TO MONTH datatype is used to represent a period of time as years and months. *precision* specifies the precision needed for the year field, and its default is 2. Valid precision values are from 0 to 9. This datatype can be used to store the difference between two datetime values, where the only significant portions are the year and month.

INTERVAL DAY TO SECOND

The syntax for the INTERVAL DAY TO SECOND datatype is as follows:

```
INTERVAL DAY [(precision)] TO SECOND
```

The INTERVAL DAY TO SECOND datatype is used to represent a period of time as days, hours, minutes, and seconds. *precision* specifies the precision needed for the day field, and its default is 6. Valid precision values are from 0 to 9. Larger precision values allow a greater difference between the dates; for example, a precision of 2 allows values from 0 through 99, and a precision of 4 allows values from 0 through 9999. This datatype can be used to store the difference between two datetime values, including seconds.

The following example demonstrates the INTERVAL datatypes. It creates a table with the INTERVAL datatypes, inserts data to it, and selects data from the table.

```
CREATE TABLE interval_demo (
ts1    TIMESTAMP (2),
iy2m   INTERVAL YEAR (3) TO MONTH,
id2s   INTERVAL DAY (4) TO SECOND);
Table created.

INSERT INTO interval_demo VALUES (
TO_TIMESTAMP('080101-102030.45', 'YYMMDD-HH24MISS.FF'),
TO_YMINTERVAL('3-7'),
TO_DSINTERVAL('4 02:20:30.30'));
1 row created.
```

```
SELECT * FROM interval_demo;
TS1                      IY2M     ID2S
------------------------ -------- ---------------------
2008-01-01 10:20:30.45    +003-07 +0004 02:20:30.300000
```

Date Arithmetic

Datetime datatypes can be used in expressions with the + or - operator. You can use the +, -, *, and / operators with the INTERVAL datatypes. Dates are stored in the database as Julian numbers with a fraction component for the time. A *Julian date* refers to the number of days since January 1, 4712 BC. Because of the time component of the date, comparing dates can result in fractional differences, even though the date is the same. Oracle provides a number of functions, such as TRUNC, that help you remove the time component when you want to compare only the date portions.

Adding 1 to the date simply moves the date ahead one day. You can add time to the date by adding a fraction of a day. One day equals 24 hours, or 24 × 60 minutes, or 24 × 60 × 60 seconds. Table 6.1 shows the numbers used to add or subtract time for a datetime datatype.

TABLE 6.1   Date Arithmetic

Time to Add or Subtract	Fraction	Date Difference
1 day	1	1
1 hour	1/24	1/24
1 minute	1/(24×60)	1/1440
1 second	1/(24×60×60)	1/86400

Subtracting two dates gives you the difference between the dates in days. This usually results in a fractional component that represents the time difference. If the time components are the same, there will be no fractional results.

A datetime value operation using a numeric value results in a datetime value. The following example adds 2 days and 12 hours to a date value:

```
ALTER SESSION SET NLS_DATE_FORMAT = 'YYYY-MM-DD HH24:MI:SS';

SELECT TO_DATE('2008-10-24 13:09:14') + 2.5 EXAMP
FROM dual;

EXAMP
-------------------
2008-10-27 01:09:14
```

This example subtracts six hours from a timestamp value:

```
SELECT TO_TIMESTAMP('2008-10-24 13:09:14.05') - 0.25 EXAMP
FROM dual;


EXAMP
-------------------
2008-10-24 07:09:14
```

A datetime value subtracted from another datetime value results in a numeric value (the difference in days). You cannot add two datetime values. Here is an example that results in the difference between dates as a fraction of a day:

```
SELECT SYSDATE,
       SYSDATE - TO_DATE('2007-10-24 13:09:14')
FROM dual;


SYSDATE             SYSDATE-TO_DATE('2007-10-2413:09:14')
------------------- ------------------------------------
2008-05-11 23:34:06                          200.433935
```

This example converts the fraction of days to hours, minutes, and seconds using the NUMTODSINTERVAL function:

```
SELECT SYSDATE,
       NUMTODSINTERVAL(SYSDATE - TO_DATE('2008-10-24 13:09:14'), 'DAY')
FROM DUAL;


SYSDATE             NUMTODSINTERVAL(SYSDATE
------------------- -----------------------------
2008-10-24 15:53:04   +000000000 02:43:49.999999999
```

A datetime value operation using an interval value results in a datetime value. The following example adds one year and three months to today's date:

```
SELECT TRUNC(SYSDATE),
       TRUNC(SYSDATE)+TO_YMINTERVAL('1-3')
FROM dual;
TRUNC(SYSDATE)      TRUNC(SYSDATE)+TO_Y
------------------- -------------------
2008-10-24 00:00:00 2010-01-24 00:00:00
```

An interval datatype operation on another interval or numeric value results in an interval value. You can use + and – between two interval datatypes and use * and / between interval and numeric values. The following example converts a string (which represents

1 day, 3 hours, and 30 minutes) to an INTERVAL DAY TO SECOND datatype and multiplies that value by 2, which results in 2 days and 7 hours:

```
SELECT TO_DSINTERVAL('1 03:30:00.0') * 2 FROM dual;


TO_DSINTERVAL('103:30:00.0')*2
-------------------------------
+000000002 07:00:00.000000000
```

The following example shows arithmetic between two INTERVAL DAY TO SECOND datatype values. The interval value of 3 hours and 30 minutes is subtracted from 1 day, 3 hours, and 30 minutes, resulting in 1 day.

```
SELECT TO_DSINTERVAL('1 03:30:00.0')
          - TO_DSINTERVAL('0 03:30:00.0')
FROM dual;


TO_DSINTERVAL('103:30:00.0')-TO_DSINTERVAL('003:30:00.0')
---------------------------------------------------------
+000000001 00:00:00.000000000
```

Binary Datatypes

Binary datatypes store information without converting it to the database's character set. This type of storage is required to store images, audio/video, executable files, and similar data. Four datatypes are available to store binary data:

- RAW
- LONG RAW
- BLOB
- BFILE

RAW

The syntax for the RAW datatype is as follows:

```
RAW (<size>)
```

RAW is used to store binary information up to 2,000 bytes. You must specify the maximum size of the column in bytes. RAW is a variable-length datatype.

LONG RAW

The syntax for the LONG RAW datatype is as follows:

```
LONG RAW
```

It's the same as RAW but with up to 2GB of storage and you can't specify a maximum size. LONG RAW is supported in Oracle 11*g* for backward compatibility. Use BLOB instead. You can have only one LONG RAW or LONG column in a table.

BLOB

The syntax for the BLOB datatype is as follows:

```
BLOB
```

BLOB can store binary data up to 4GB. There is no size specification for this datatype.

BFILE

The syntax for the BFILE datatype is as follows:

```
BFILE
```

BFILE is used to store information on external files. The external file size can be up to 4GB. Oracle stores only the file pointer in the database. The actual file is stored on the operating system. Of the four Large Object datatypes (CLOB, BLOB, NCLOB, and BFILE), only BFILE stores actual data outside the Oracle Database.

Row ID Datatypes

Physical storage of each row in a table can be represented using a unique value called the ROWID. Every table has a pseudocolumn called the ROWID. To store such values, Oracle provides two datatypes:

- ROWID
- UROWID

ROWID

The syntax for the ROWID datatype is as follows:

```
ROWID
```

ROWID can store the physical address of a row. Physical ROWIDs store the addresses of rows in ordinary tables (excluding index-organized tables), clustered tables, table partitions and subpartitions, indexes, and index partitions and subpartitions. Logical ROWIDs store the addresses of rows in index-organized tables. Physical ROWIDs provide the fastest possible access to a row of a given table.

UROWID

The syntax for the UROWID datatype is as follows:

```
UROWID
```

UROWID can store the logical ROWIDs of index-organized tables or non-Oracle Database tables. Oracle creates logical ROWIDs based on an index-organized table's primary key. The logical ROWIDs do not change as long as the primary key does not change.

Creating Tables

Now that you have learned about the various datatypes that you can use to store table data, you are ready to create a table. You can think of a table as a spreadsheet with columns and rows. It is a structure that holds data in a relational database. The table is created with a name to identify it and columns defined with valid column names and column attributes, such as the datatype and size. CREATE TABLE is a comprehensive statement with many options. The certification exam covers creating and managing a simple relational table only. Here is the simplest format to use to create a table:

```
CREATE TABLE products
( prod_id    NUMBER (4),
  prod_name  VARCHAR2 (20),
  stock_qty  NUMBER (15,3)
);
```

```
Table created.
```

You specify the table name following the keywords CREATE TABLE. The previous example creates a table named PRODUCTS under the user (schema) connected to the database. The table name can be qualified with the username; you must qualify the table when creating a table in another user's schema. Table and column names are discussed in more detail in the next section.

The column definitions are enclosed in parentheses. The table created by the previous code has three columns, each identified by a name and datatype. Commas separate the column definitions. This table has two columns with the NUMBER datatype and one column with the VARCHAR2 datatype. A datatype must be specified for each column.

When creating tables, you can specify the following:

- Default values for columns
- Constraints for the columns and/or table (discussed later in this chapter in the "Managing Constraints" section)
- The type of table: relational (heap), temporary, index-organized, external, or object (Index-organized and object tables are not covered on the certification exam.)
- Table storage, including any index storage and storage specification for the Large Object columns (LOBs) in the table
- The tablespace where the table/index should be stored
- Any partitioning and subpartitioning information

Naming Tables and Columns

Table names are used to identify each table. You should make table names as descriptive as possible. Table and column names are *identifiers* and can be up to 30 characters long. An identifier name should begin with a letter and can contain numeric digits. The only special characters allowed in an identifier name are the dollar sign ($), the underscore (_), and the number sign (#). The underscore can be used for meaningful separation of the words in an identifier name. These names are case insensitive. If, however, you enclose the identifier name in double quotation marks ("), it will be case sensitive in the Oracle dictionary.

WARNING   Creating table names enclosed in quotation marks with mixed case can cause serious problems when you query the database if you do not know the exact case of the table name.

You can use the DESCRIBE or DESC (SQL*Plus) command to list all the columns in the table, along with their datatype, size, nullity, and order. The syntax is DESCRIBE <*table name*>. The case sensitivity of names and describing tables are illustrated in the following examples:

```
CREATE TABLE MyTable (
 Column_1  NUMBER,
 Column_2  CHAR);
Table created.

DESC mytable
Name                     Null?      Type
-------------------- -------- --------
 COLUMN_1                            NUMBER
 COLUMN_2                            CHAR(1)

SELECT table_name FROM user_tables
WHERE  table_name = 'MyTable';
no rows selected

CREATE TABLE "MyTable" (
 "Column1" number,
 "Column2" char);
Table created.

DESC "MyTable"
Name                     Null?      Type
-------------------- -------- --------
 Column1                            NUMBER
 Column2                            CHAR(1)
```

```
SELECT table_name FROM user_tables
WHERE  upper(table_name) = 'MYTABLE';

TABLE_NAME
------------------------------

MYTABLE
MyTable
```

It is a good practice to give the other objects directly related to a table a name that reflects the table name. For example, consider the EMPLOYEE table. The primary key of the table may be named PK_EMPLOYEE, indexes might be named EMPLOYEE_NDX1 and EMPLOYEE_NDX2, a check constraint could be named CK_EMPLOYEE_STATUS, a trigger could be named TRG_ EMPLOYEE_HIRE, and so on.

Creating a Temporary Table

When you create a table without any specific keywords to indicate the type of the table, the table created is a relational table that is permanent. If you include the keywords GLOBAL TEMPORARY, Oracle creates a temporary relational table known as the *global temporary table* (GTT) whose definition is available to all sessions in the database, but the data is available only to the session that inserted data to it. The GTT is truly a temporary table. On other flavors of RDBMS, a permanent table created to hold temporary data is called a *temporary table*. You can do the same with Oracle, but Oracle provides true temporary tables with GTT.

The data inserted by a session is visible only to the session. Normally when you commit the data changes or new rows added to a table, the data is visible to all other sessions. When using GTTs, the data is truly temporary—it is not written permanently anywhere. The ON COMMIT clause can be included to specify whether the data in the temporary table is session-specific (ON COMMIT PRESERVE ROWS) or transaction-specific (ON COMMIT DELETE ROWS). ON COMMIT DELETE ROWS is the default. If the definition is for session-specific data, the inserted data will be available throughout the session. If the GTT is defined as transaction-specific, then when a COMMIT or ROLLBACK is performed, the data in the table is cleared. Here is an example of creating a temporary table whose inserted data will be available throughout the session:

```
CREATE GLOBAL TEMPORARY TABLE emp_bonus_temp  (
emp_id  NUMBER (10),
bonus   NUMBER (15,2))
ON COMMIT PRESERVE ROWS;
```

Specifying Default Values for Columns

When creating or altering a table, you can specify *default values* for columns. The default value specified will be used when you do not specify any value for the column while inserting data. The default value specified in the definition should satisfy the datatype and length of the column. If a default value is not explicitly set, the default for the column is implicitly set to NULL. Default values cannot refer to another column, and they cannot have the pseudo-columns LEVEL, NEXTVAL, CURRVAL, ROWNUM, or PRIOR. The default values can include SYSDATE, USER, USERENV, and UID.

In the following example, the table ORDERS is created with a column STATUS that has a default value of PENDING:

```
CREATE TABLE orders (
order_number NUMBER (8),
status       VARCHAR2 (10) DEFAULT 'PENDING');


Table created.


INSERT INTO orders (order_number) VALUES (4004);


1 row created.


SELECT * FROM orders;


ORDER_NUMBER STATUS
------------ ----------
        4004 PENDING
```

Here is an example of creating a table that includes default values for two columns:

```
CREATE TABLE emp_punch (
emp_id      NUMBER (6) NOT NULL,
time_in     DATE,
time_out    DATE,
updated_by  VARCHAR2 (30) DEFAULT USER,
update_time TIMESTAMP WITH LOCAL TIME ZONE
                            DEFAULT SYSTIMESTAMP
);


Table created.


DESCRIBE emp_punch
```

```
Name                      Null?     Type
------------------------- --------  ------------------
EMP_ID                    NOT NULL  NUMBER(6)
TIME_IN                             DATE
TIME_OUT                            DATE
UPDATED_BY                          VARCHAR2(30)
UPDATE_TIME                         TIMESTAMP(6) WITH
                                    LOCAL TIME ZONE


INSERT INTO emp_punch (emp_id, time_in)
VALUES (1090, TO_DATE('062801-2121','MMDDYY-HH24MI'));


1 row created.

SELECT * FROM emp_punch;


EMP_ID TIME_IN   TIME_OUT  UPDATED_BY  UPDATE_TIME
------ --------- --------- ----------  ------------------
1090   28-JUN-01           JOHN        02.55.58.000000 PM
```

This example uses a NOT NULL constraint in the table definition. A NOT NULL constraint prevents NULL values from being entered into the column. Constraints are discussed in detail in the "Managing Constraints" section later in this chapter.

If you explicitly insert a NULL value for a column with DEFAULT defined, the value in the DEFAULT clause will not be used. You can explicitly specify DEFAULT in the INSERT statement to use the DEFAULT value, as in the following example:

```
INSERT INTO emp_punch
VALUES (104, TO_DATE('062801-2121','MMDDYY-HH24MI'),
        DEFAULT, DEFAULT, NULL);


1 row created.

SELECT * FROM emp_punch;
```

```
EMP_ID TIME_IN   TIME UPDATED UPDATE_TIME
                 _OUT _BY
------ --------- ---- ------- ---------------------------
1090   28-JUN-01      JOHN    29-JUN-01 02.55.58.000000 PM
 104   28-JUN-01      JOHN
SQL>
```

Adding Comments

It is a good practice to document the purpose and any information on the type of data stored in the table in the database itself so that developers and administrators working on the database know the importance of the table/data. Oracle provides the COMMENT statement to add documentation to a table or a column.

Comments on tables are added using the COMMENT ON TABLE statement, and comments on table columns are added using the COMMENT ON COLUMN statement. The following example provides comments for the sample table:

```
COMMENT ON TABLE mytable IS
    'Oracle 11g Study Guide Example Table';
Comment created.

COMMENT ON COLUMN mytable.column_1 is
   'First column in MYTABLE';
Comment created.
```

You can query the table and column information from the Oracle dictionary using the following views: USER_TABLES, ALL_TABLES, USER_TAB_COLUMNS, and ALL_TAB_COLUMNS.

Creating a Table from Another Table

You can create a table using a query based on one or more existing tables or views. The column datatype and width will be determined by the query result. A table created in this fashion can select all the columns from another table (you can use *) or a subset of columns or expressions and functions applied on columns (these are called *derived columns*). The syntax for creating a table using an existing table is as follows:

```
CREATE TABLE <table characteristics> AS SELECT <query>
```

This syntax is generally known as CTAS (the abbreviated form of CREATE TABLE AS SELECT). The table characteristics include the new table name and its storage properties.

For example, suppose you need to duplicate the structure and data of the EMP table in the EMPLOYEES table. You can use CTAS, like this:

```
CREATE TABLE employees
AS SELECT * FROM emp;


Table created.
```

You can have complex query statements in the CREATE TABLE statement. The table is created with no rows if the query returned no rows. If you just want to copy the structure of the table, make sure the query returns no rows:

```
CREATE TABLE Y AS SELECT * FROM X WHERE 1 = 2;
```

You can provide column alias names to have different column names in the newly created table. The following example shows a table structure, displays the data, and then creates a new table with the data and displays it:

```
DESCRIBE city

Name                Null?    Type
------------------- -------- -------------
CNT_CODE            NOT NULL NUMBER(4)
ST_CODE             NOT NULL VARCHAR2(2)
CTY_CODE            NOT NULL NUMBER(4)
CTY_NAME                     VARCHAR2(20)
POPULATION                   NUMBER

SELECT COUNT(*) FROM city;


  COUNT(*)
----------
         3
CREATE TABLE new_city AS
SELECT cty_code CITY_CODE, cty_name CITY_NAME
FROM city;


Table created.

SELECT COUNT(*) FROM new_city;
```

```
  COUNT(*)
----------
        3
DESC new_city
 Name                    Null?    Type
 ------------------- -------- -------------
 CITY_CODE              NOT NULL NUMBER(4)
 CITY_NAME                       VARCHAR2(20)
```

 The CREATE TABLE … AS SELECT … statement will not work if the query refers to columns of the LONG datatype.

 When you create a table using the subquery, only the NOT NULL constraints associated with the columns are copied to the new table. Other constraints and column default definitions are not copied. This almost certainly will be an OCA certification exam question.

Modifying Tables

After you've created a table, you might want to modify it for several reasons. You can modify a table to change its column definition or default values, add a new column, rename a column, or drop an existing column. You can also drop and rename tables.

You might also modify a table if you need to change or add constraint definitions. You can make a table read-only so that no modifications are possible on the data in the table. The ALTER TABLE statement is used to change table definitions. Similar to the CREATE TABLE statement, the ALTER TABLE statement has several options. In the following sections, I will concentrate on the options that are pertinent to the OCA certification exam.

Adding Columns

Sometimes it is necessary to add a column to an existing table because there may be enhancements made to the application or because the developer just did not plan it completely well. To add a column to an existing table, you don't need to drop and re-create the table. Using the ALTER TABLE statement, you can easily add a column to the table. All columns added to the table using the ALTER TABLE ADD statement are added to the end of the table definition. Here is the syntax to add a new column to an existing table:

```
ALTER TABLE [<schema>.]<table_name> ADD <column_definitions>;
```

When a new column is added, it is always at the bottom of the table. For the existing rows, the new column value will be NULL.

Let's add a new column, ORDER_DATE, to the ORDERS table. Notice that the column is added to the end of the table definition. You cannot insert a new column in between other columns in a table. If you have such a requirement, the table has to be dropped and re-created.

```
DESCRIBE orders
 Name                 Null?    Type
 ------------------- -------- -------------
 ORDER_NUMBER        NOT NULL NUMBER(8)
 STATUS                       VARCHAR2(10)


SELECT * FROM orders;

ORDER_NUMBER STATUS
------------ ----------
        4004 PENDING
        5005 COMPLETED


ALTER TABLE orders ADD order_date DATE;

Table altered.

DESC orders
 Name                 Null?    Type
 ------------------- -------- ---------------
 ORDER_NUMBER        NOT NULL NUMBER(8)
 STATUS                       VARCHAR2(10)
 ORDER_DATE                   DATE

SELECT * FROM orders;

ORDER_NUMBER STATUS      ORDER_DAT
------------ ---------- ---------
        4004 PENDING
        5005 COMPLETED
```

If you are adding more than one column, the column definitions should be enclosed in parentheses and separated by commas. If you specify a DEFAULT value for a newly added column, all the rows in the table will have the default value automatically assigned. The following example adds two more columns to the ORDERS table:

```
ALTER TABLE orders ADD
 (quantity NUMBER (13,3),
  update_dt DATE DEFAULT SYSDATE);


Table altered.


SELECT * FROM orders;


ORDER_NUMBER STATUS     ORDER_DAT  QUANTITY UPDATE_DT
------------ ---------- --------- ---------- ---------
        4004 PENDING                         23-MAR-02
        5005 COMPLETED                       23-MAR-02
```

When adding a new column, you cannot specify the NOT NULL constraint if the table already has rows. To add a NOT NULL column, you need to follow three steps:

1. Modify the table to add the column.

2. Update the column with values for all the existing rows.

3. Add a NOT NULL constraint.

You may add a NOT NULL constraint with a DEFAULT clause, even if the table has rows. Here is an example:

```
ALTER TABLE orders
        ADD updated_by VARCHAR2 (30) NOT NULL;


ERROR at line 1:
ORA-01758: table must be empty to add mandatory
(NOT NULL) column

ALTER TABLE orders ADD updated_by VARCHAR2 (30)
  DEFAULT 'JOHN' NOT NULL;


Table altered.
```

In Oracle 11g, when you add a column with the NOT NULL constraint and the DEFAULT value, Oracle 11g does not update all the existing rows in the table with the default value. Oracle 11g simply updates the dictionary and gets you the value from the dictionary when you query the newly added column.

Modifying Columns

On many occasions, you may be required to change the table definition. The common definition changes are to add or remove a NOT NULL constraint to/from a column, changing the datatype of a column or changing the length of the column. The syntax to modify an existing column in a table is as follows:

```
ALTER TABLE [<schema>.]<table_name>
MODIFY <column_name> <new_attributes>;
```

If you omit any of the parts of the column definition (datatype, default value, or column constraint), the omitted parts remain unchanged. If you are modifying more than one column at a time, enclose the column definitions in parentheses. For example, to modify the ORDERS table, increasing the STATUS column to 15 and reducing the QUANTITY column to 10,3, do this:

```
ALTER TABLE orders MODIFY (quantity NUMBER (10,3),
                    status VARCHAR2 (15));
```

You can add or drop constraints in the column and modify the DEFAULT values for the column. The DEFAULT value included using the MODIFY clause affects only the new rows inserted to the table; the existing rows with NULL column values are not affected. To remove the DEFAULT value for a column, redefine the DEFAULT clause with a NULL value. For example, the following statement removes the default SYSDATE value from the UPDATE_DT column of the ORDERS table:

```
ALTER TABLE orders
MODIFY update_dt DEFAULT NULL;
```

These are the rules for modifying column definitions:

- You can increase the length of the character column and precision of the numeric column. If your table has many rows, increasing the length of a CHAR column will require a lot of resources, because the column data for all the rows needs to blank-padded with the additional length.

- You can decrease the length of a VARCHAR2 column and reduce the precision or increase the scale of a numeric column if all the data in the column fits the new length.

- You can decrease the length of a nonempty CHAR column if the parameter BLANK_TRIMMING is set to TRUE.

- The column values must be NULL to change the column's datatype. If you do not reduce the length, you can change the datatype from CHAR to VARCHAR2, or vice versa, even if the column is not empty.

Renaming Columns

Renaming column is not a common task, but sometimes you may have to change the name of a column because there was a typo in the script or the developers decided to store different data in the column. Renaming a column does not affect its data or datatype. The syntax to rename an existing column in a table is as follows:

```
ALTER TABLE [<schema>.]<table_name>
RENAME COLUMN <column_name> TO <new_name>;
```

When renaming a column, the column name must not be the same as an existing column in the table. The following example renames the DATA_VALUE column of the SAMPLE_DATA table to SAMPLE_VALUE:

```
DESCRIBE sample_data
 Name                                    Null?    Type
 --------------------------------------- -------- ---------------
 DATA_VALUE                                       VARCHAR2(20)
 DATA_TYPE                                        VARCHAR2(10)


ALTER TABLE sample_data
RENAME COLUMN data_value to sample_value;

Table altered.

DESCRIBE sample_data
 Name                                    Null?    Type
 --------------------------------------- -------- ---------------
 SAMPLE_VALUE                                     VARCHAR2(20)
 DATA_TYPE                                        VARCHAR2(10)
```

Dropping Columns

Similar to renaming columns, dropping columns is not a common activity for the DBA, but you should know how to drop a column in case you need to do it. You can drop a column that is not used, or you can mark the column as not used and drop it later. Here is the syntax for dropping a column:

```
ALTER TABLE [<schema>.]<table_name>
DROP {COLUMN <column_name> | (<column_names>)}
[CASCADE CONSTRAINTS]
```

DROP COLUMN drops the column name specified from the table. You can provide more than one column name separated by commas inside parentheses. The indexes and constraints on the column are also dropped. You must specify CASCADE CONSTRAINTS if the dropped column is part of a multicolumn constraint; the constraint will be dropped.

The syntax for marking a column as unused is as follows:

```
ALTER TABLE [<schema>.]<table_name>
SET UNUSED {COLUMN <column_name> | (<column_names>)}
[CASCADE CONSTRAINTS]
```

You usually mark a column as unused instead of dropping it immediately, especially at peak hours, if the table is very large, because it takes a lot of resources. In such cases, you would mark the column as unused and drop it later. Once the column is marked as unused, you will not see it as part of the table definition. Let's mark the UPDATE_DT column in the ORDERS table as unused:

```
ALTER TABLE orders SET UNUSED COLUMN update_dt;
```

```
Table altered.
```

```
DESCRIBE orders
```

Name	Null?	Type
ORDER_NUMBER	NOT NULL	NUMBER(8)
STATUS		VARCHAR2(15)
ORDER_DATE		DATE
QUANTITY		NUMBER(10,3)

Here is the syntax for dropping a column already marked as unused:

```
ALTER TABLE [<schema>.]<table_name>
DROP {UNUSED COLUMNS | COLUMNS CONTINUE}
```

Use the COLUMNS CONTINUE clause to continue a DROP operation that was previously interrupted. The DROP UNUSED COLUMNS clause will drop all the columns that are marked as unused. You cannot selectively drop column names after marking them as unused. The following example clears data from the UPDATE_DT column in the ORDERS table:

```
ALTER TABLE orders DROP UNUSED COLUMNS;
```

The data dictionary views DBA_UNUSED_COL_TABS, ALL_UNUSED_COL_TABS, and USER_UNUSED_COL_TABS provide the names of tables in which you have columns marked as unused.

Dropping Tables

When application designs change, some tables become orphaned or unused. You can use the DROP TABLE statement to drop an existing table. The syntax of the DROP TABLE statement is as follows:

```
DROP TABLE [schema.]table_name [CASCADE CONSTRAINTS]
```

When you drop a table, you remove the data and definition of the table. The indexes, constraints, triggers, and privileges on the table are also dropped. Once you drop a table, you cannot undo the action.

Oracle does not drop the views, materialized views, or other stored programs that reference the table, but it marks them as invalid. You must specify the CASCADE CONSTRAINTS clause if there are referential integrity constraints referring to the primary key or unique key of this table. Here's how to drop the table TEST owned by the user SCOTT:

```
DROP TABLE scott.test;
```

A method for emptying a table of all rows is to use the TRUNCATE statement. This is different from dropping and re-creating a table, because TRUNCATE does not invalidate dependent objects or drop indexes, triggers, or referential integrity constraints. See Chapter 5 for more information about using TRUNCATE.

Renaming Tables

Tables and other database schema objects can be renamed in Oracle. The RENAME statement is used to rename a table and other database objects, such as views, private synonyms, or sequences. The syntax for the RENAME statement is as follows:

```
RENAME old_name TO new_name;
```

Here, old_name and new_name are the names of a table, view, private synonym, or sequence.

When you rename a table, Oracle automatically transfers integrity constraints, indexes, and grants on the old table to the new table. Oracle invalidates all objects that depend on the renamed table, such as views, synonyms, stored procedures, and functions.

The following example renames the ORDERS table to PURCHASE_ORDERS:

```
RENAME orders TO purchase_orders;

Table renamed.
```

```
DESCRIBE purchase_orders
Name                 Null?     Type
-------------------  --------  ---------------
ORDER_NUMBER         NOT NULL  NUMBER(8)
STATUS                         VARCHAR2(15)
ORDER_DATE                     DATE
QUANTITY                       NUMBER(10,3)
```

 You can use the RENAME statement to rename only the objects you own. You cannot rename an object owned by another user.

You can also use the RENAME TO clause of the ALTER TABLE statement to rename a table. Using this technique, you can qualify the table name with the schema. You must use the ALTER TABLE statement to rename a table owned by another user (and you need the ALTER privilege on the table or the ALTER ANY TABLE system privilege). Here is an example:

```
ALTER TABLE scott.purchase_orders
RENAME TO orders;

Table altered.
```

Making Tables Read-Only

Often the DBA gets requests from users to make a table read-only. Many configuration tables can be made read-only after the initial application setup is completed so that accidental changes can be avoided. To place a table in read-only mode, use the READ ONLY clause of the ALTER TABLE statement.

The following statement makes the PRODUCTS table read-only:

```
ALTER TABLE products READ ONLY;

Table altered.
```

Once the table is marked as read-only, any operation on the table that changes its data is not allowed. Many DDL operations on the table are allowed. The following operations on the read-only table are not allowed:

- INSERT, UPDATE, DELETE, or MERGE statements
- The TRUNCATE operation
- Adding, modifying, renaming, or dropping a column
- Flashing back a table
- SELECT FOR UPDATE

The following operations are allowed on the read-only table:

- SELECT
- Creating or modifying indexes
- Creating or modifying constraints
- Changing the storage characteristics of the table
- Renaming the table
- Dropping the table

The following examples demonstrate some operations that are not allowed on a read-only table:

```
TRUNCATE TABLE products;
TRUNCATE TABLE products
                *
ERROR at line 1:
ORA-12081: update operation not allowed on table "HR"."PRODUCTS"


DELETE FROM products;
DELETE FROM products
            *
ERROR at line 1:
ORA-12081: update operation not allowed on table "HR"."PRODUCTS"


INSERT INTO products VALUES (200, 'TESTING', 'X1',0);
INSERT INTO products VALUES (200, 'TESTING', 'X1',0)
            *
ERROR at line 1:
ORA-12081: update operation not allowed on table "HR"."PRODUCTS"
```

To change a read-only table to read-write, use the READ WRITE clause of the ALTER TABLE statement. The following example makes the PRODUCTS table writable:

```
ALTER TABLE products READ WRITE;

Table altered.
```

Managing Constraints

Constraints are created in the database to enforce a business rule in the database and to specify relationships between various tables. You can also enforce business rules using database triggers and application code. *Integrity constraints* prevent bad data from being entered into the database. Oracle supports five types of integrity constraints, as shown in Table 6.2.

TABLE 6.2   Integrity Constraints

Constraint	Description
NOT NULL	Prevents NULL values from being entered into the column. These types of constraints are defined on a single column. By default, Oracle allows NULL values in any column.
CHECK	Checks whether the condition specified in the constraint is satisfied.
UNIQUE	Ensures that there are no duplicate values for the column(s) specified. Every value or set of values is unique within the table.
PRIMARY KEY	Uniquely identifies each row of the table and prevents NULL values. A table can have only one primary key constraint.
FOREIGN KEY	Establishes a parent-child relationship between tables by using common columns. The foreign key defined on a table refers to the primary key or unique key of another table.

Creating Constraints

Constraints are created using the CREATE TABLE or ALTER TABLE statements. You can specify the constraint definition at the column level if the constraint is defined on a single column. Multiple-column constraints must be defined at the table level; the columns should be specified in parentheses and separated by commas.

If you do not provide a name for the constraints, Oracle assigns a system-generated unique name that begins with SYS_. A name is provided for the constraint by specifying the keyword CONSTRAINT followed by the constraint name.

WARNING   You should not rely on system-generated names for constraints. If you want to compare table characteristics, such as between production and test databases, the inconsistent system-generated names will make this comparison difficult.

In the following sections, I will define the rules for each constraint type and provide examples of creating constraints.

NOT NULL Constraint

A NOT NULL constraint is defined at the column level; it cannot be defined at the table level. The syntax for a NOT NULL constraint is as follows:

```
[CONSTRAINT <constraint name>] [NOT] NULL
```

The following example creates a table with two columns that have NOT NULL constraints:

```
CREATE TABLE orders (
 order_num   NUMBER (4) CONSTRAINT nn_order_num NOT NULL,
 order_date  DATE NOT NULL,
 product_id  NUMBER (6))
```

The example provides a name for the constraint on the ORDER_NUM column. Since no name is specified for the constraint on the ORDER_DATE column, it will get a system-generated name.

Use ALTER TABLE MODIFY to add or remove a NOT NULL constraint on the columns of an existing table. The following examples remove a constraint and add a constraint to an existing table:

```
ALTER TABLE orders MODIFY order_date NULL;
ALTER TABLE orders MODIFY product_id NOT NULL;
```

Check Constraints

You can define a check constraint at the column level or table level. For both the column and table levels, the syntax is as follows:

```
[CONSTRAINT <constraint name>] CHECK ( <condition> )
```

The condition specified in the CHECK clause should evaluate to a Boolean result and can refer to values in other columns of the same row; the condition cannot use queries. Environment functions (such as SYSDATE, USER, USERENV, and UID) and pseudocolumns (such as ROWNUM, CURRVAL, NEXTVAL, and LEVEL) cannot be used to evaluate the check condition. One column can have more than one check constraint defined.

The following are examples of check constraints defined at the table level:

```
CREATE TABLE bonus (
 emp_id    VARCHAR2 (40) NOT NULL,
 salary    NUMBER (9,2),
 bonus     NUMBER (9,2),
CONSTRAINT ck_bonus check (bonus > 0));


ALTER TABLE bonus
ADD CONSTRAINT ck_bonus2 CHECK (bonus < salary);
```

The check constraint can be defined at the column level if the constraint refers to only that column.

You cannot use the ALTER TABLE MODIFY clause to add or modify check constraints (only NOT NULL constraints can be modified this way). Column-level constraints can be defined when using the CREATE TABLE statement or when using the ALTER TABLE statement with the ADD clause. Here is an example:

```
ALTER TABLE orders ADD cust_id number (5)
CONSTRAINT ck_cust_id CHECK (cust_id > 0);
```

You can use the check constraint to implement a NOT NULL constraint also. This is especially useful if you need to disallow NULL values in multiple columns together. For example, the following constraint definition for the BONUS table allows a NULL value for the BONUS and SALARY columns if both column values are NULL, or else both columns should have a valid non-NULL value.

```
ALTER TABLE bonus ADD CONSTRAINT ck_sal_bonus
CHECK ((bonus IS NULL AND salary IS NULL) OR
       (bonus IS NOT NULL AND salary IS NOT NULL));
```

Unique Constraints

A unique constraint protects one or more columns in a table, ensuring that no two rows contain duplicate data in the protected columns. Unique constraints can be defined at the column level for single-column unique keys. Here is the column-level syntax:

```
[CONSTRAINT <constraint name>] UNIQUE
```

For a multiple-column unique key (a *composite* key; the maximum number of columns specified can be 32), the constraint should be defined at the table level. Here is the table-level syntax:

```
[CONSTRAINT <constraint name>]
UNIQUE (<column>, <column>, …)
```

Oracle creates a unique index on the unique key columns to enforce uniqueness. If a unique index or nonunique index already exists on the table with the same column-order prefix, Oracle uses the existing index. To use the existing nonunique index for enforcing uniqueness, there must not be any duplicate values in the unique key columns.

Unique constraints allow NULL values in the constraint columns. The following example defines a unique constraint with two columns:

```
ALTER TABLE employee
ADD CONSTRAINT uq_emp_id UNIQUE (dept, emp_id);
```

The next example adds a new column to the EMP table and creates a unique key at the column level:

```
ALTER TABLE employee ADD
ssn VARCHAR2 (11) CONSTRAINT uq_ssn unique;
```

Primary Key Constraints

All characteristics of the unique key are applicable to the primary key constraint, except that NULL values are not allowed in the primary key columns. A table can have only one primary key. The column-level syntax is as follows:

```
[CONSTRAINT <constraint name>] PRIMARY KEY
```

Here is the table-level syntax:

```
[CONSTRAINT <constraint name>]
PRIMARY KEY (<column>, <column>, …)
```

Oracle creates a unique index and NOT NULL constraints for each column in the key. The following example defines a primary key when creating the table:

```
CREATE TABLE employee (
 dept_no VARCHAR2 (2),
 emp_id  NUMBER (4),
 name    VARCHAR2 (20) NOT NULL,
 ssn     VARCHAR2 (11),
 salary  NUMBER (9,2) CHECK (salary > 0),
CONSTRAINT pk_employee primary key (dept_no, emp_id),
CONSTRAINT uq_ssn unique (ssn))
```

To add a primary key to an existing table, use the ALTER TABLE statement. Here is an example:

```
ALTER TABLE employee
ADD CONSTRAINT pk_employee PRIMARY KEY (dept_no, emp_id);
```

Indexes created to enforce unique keys and primary keys can be managed in the same way as any other index. However, these indexes cannot be dropped explicitly using the DROP INDEX statement.

Foreign Key Constraints

A foreign key constraint protects one or more columns in a table by ensuring that for each non-NULL value there is data available elsewhere in the database with a primary or unique key. The foreign key is the column or columns in the table (child table) where the constraint is created. The referenced key is the primary key or unique key column or columns in the table (parent table) that is referenced by the constraint. The column datatypes in the parent table and the child table should match.

You can define a foreign key constraint at the column level or table level. Here is the syntax for the column-level constraint:

```
[CONSTRAINT <constraint name>]
REFERENCES [<schema>.]<table> [(<column>, <column>, …]
[ON DELETE {CASCADE | SET NULL}]
```

Multiple-column foreign keys should be defined at the table level. Here is the table-level syntax:

```
[CONSTRAINT <constraint name>]
FOREIGN KEY (<column>, <column>, …)
REFERENCES [<schema>.]<table> [(<column>, <column>, …]
[ON DELETE {CASCADE | SET NULL}]
```

The foreign key column(s) and referenced key column(s) can be in the same table (self-referential integrity constraint). NULL values are allowed in the foreign key columns.

The following is an example of creating a foreign key constraint on the COUNTRY_CODE and STATE_CODE columns of the CITY table, which refers to the COUNTRY_CODE and STATE_CODE columns of the STATE table (the composite primary key of the STATE table).

```
ALTER TABLE city ADD CONSTRAINT fk_state
FOREIGN KEY (country_code, state_code)
REFERENCES state (country_code, state_code);
```

You can omit the column listing of the referenced table if referring to the primary key of the table. For example, if the COUNTRY_CODE and STATE_CODE columns are the primary key of the STATE table, the previous statement could be written like this:

```
ALTER TABLE city ADD CONSTRAINT fk_state
FOREIGN KEY (country_code, state_code)
REFERENCES state;
```

The ON DELETE clause specifies the action to be taken when a row in the parent table is deleted and child rows exist for the deleted parent primary key. You can delete the child rows (CASCADE) or set the foreign key column values to NULL (SET NULL). If you omit this clause, Oracle will not allow you to delete from the parent table if child records exist. You must delete the child rows first and then delete the parent row. The following are two examples of specifying the delete action in a foreign key:

```
ALTER TABLE city ADD CONSTRAINT fk_state
 FOREIGN KEY (country_code, state_code)
 REFERENCES state (country_code, state_code)
 ON DELETE CASCADE;

ALTER TABLE city ADD CONSTRAINT fk_state
 FOREIGN KEY (country_code, state_code)
 REFERENCES state (country_code, state_code)
 ON DELETE SET NULL;
```

You can query the constraint information from the Oracle dictionary using the following views: USER_CONSTRAINTS, ALL_CONSTRAINTS, USER_CONS_COLUMNS, and ALL_CONS_COLUMNS.

Disabled Constraints

When a constraint is created, it is enabled automatically. You can create a *disabled* constraint by specifying the DISABLE keyword after the constraint definition. Here is an example:

```
ALTER TABLE city ADD CONSTRAINT fk_state
 FOREIGN KEY (country_code, state_code)
 REFERENCES state (country_code, state_code) DISABLE;

ALTER TABLE bonus
ADD CONSTRAINT ck_bonus CHECK (bonus > 0) DISABLE;
```

Dropping Constraints

Dropping a constraint defined on a table may be necessary if you find out that business data does not always meet strict data validations using constraints. In such instances it may be necessary to drop a constraint. Constraints are dropped using the `ALTER TABLE` statement. Any constraint can be dropped by specifying the constraint name, as in this example:

```
ALTER TABLE bonus DROP CONSTRAINT ck_bonus2;
```

To drop the `NOT NULL` constraint, use the `ALTER TABLE MODIFY` statement, like this:

```
ALTER TABLE employee MODIFY employee_name NULL;
```

To drop unique key constraints with referenced foreign keys, specify the `CASCADE` clause to drop the foreign key constraints and the unique constraint. Specify the unique key columns(s). Here is an example:

```
ALTER TABLE employee DROP UNIQUE (emp_id) CASCADE;
```

To drop primary key constraints with referenced foreign key constraints, use the `CASCADE` clause to drop all foreign key constraints and then the primary key. Here is an example:

```
ALTER TABLE bonus DROP PRIMARY KEY CASCADE;
```

Enabling and Disabling Constraints

When you create a constraint, the constraint is automatically enabled (unless you specify the `DISABLE` clause). You can disable a constraint by using the `DISABLE` clause of the `ALTER TABLE` statement. When you disable unique or primary key constraints, Oracle drops the associated unique index. When you reenable these constraints, Oracle builds the index.

You can disable any constraint by specifying the clause `DISABLE CONSTRAINT` followed by the constraint name. Specifying `UNIQUE` and the column name(s) can disable unique keys, and specifying `PRIMARY KEY` can disable the table's primary key. You cannot disable a primary key or unique key if foreign keys that are enabled reference it. To disable all the referenced foreign keys and the primary or unique key, specify `CASCADE`. The following three examples demonstrate disabling constraints:

```
ALTER TABLE bonus DISABLE CONSTRAINT ck_bonus;
```

```
ALTER TABLE employee DISABLE CONSTRAINT uq_employee;
```

```
ALTER TABLE state DISABLE PRIMARY KEY CASCADE;
```

Using the `ENABLE` clause of the `ALTER TABLE` statement enables a constraint. When you enable a disabled unique or primary key, Oracle creates an index if an index with the unique or primary key columns does not already exist. You can specify storage for the unique or primary key while enabling these constraints, as in this example:

```
ALTER TABLE state ENABLE PRIMARY KEY USING INDEX
TABLESPACE user_INDEX STORAGE (INITIAL 2M NEXT 2M);
```

Validated Constraints

You have seen how to enable and disable a constraint. ENABLE and DISABLE affect only future data that will be added or modified in the table. In contrast, the VALIDATE and NOVALIDATE keywords in the ALTER TABLE statement act on the existing data. Therefore, a constraint can have four states, as shown in Table 6.3.

TABLE 6.3 Constraints

Constraint	Description
ENABLE VALIDATE	This is the default for the ENABLE clause. The existing data in the table is validated to verify that it conforms to the constraint.
ENABLE NOVALIDATE	This does not validate the existing data but enables the constraint for future constraint checking.
DISABLE VALIDATE	The constraint is disabled (any index used to enforce the constraint is also dropped), but the constraint is kept valid. No DML operation is allowed on the table because future changes cannot be verified.
DISABLE NOVALIDATE	This is the default for the DISABLE clause. The constraint is disabled, and no checks are done on future or existing data.

Suppose you have a large data-warehouse table, where bulk data loads are performed every night. The primary key of this table is enforced using a nonunique index because Oracle does not drop the nonunique index when disabling the constraint. When you do batch loads, you can disable the primary key constraint as follows:

```
ALTER TABLE wh01 MODIFY CONSTRAINT pk_wh01
DISABLE NOVALIDATE;
```

After the batch load completes, you can enable the primary key like this:

```
ALTER TABLE wh01 MODIFY CONSTRAINT pk_wh01
ENABLE NOVALIDATE;
```

Oracle does not allow any INSERT, UPDATE, or DELETE operations on a table with a DISABLE VALIDATE constraint. This is a quick way to make a table read-only in releases prior to Oracle 11g. In Oracle 11g, you can use the READ ONLY clause of the ALTER TABLE statement to make a table read-only.

Deferring Constraint Checks

By default, Oracle checks whether the data conforms to the constraint when the statement is executed. Oracle allows you to change this behavior if the constraint is created using the DEFERRABLE clause (NOT DEFERRABLE is the default). It specifies that the transaction can set the constraint-checking behavior.

INITIALLY IMMEDIATE specifies that the constraint should be checked for conformance at the end of each SQL statement (this is the default). INITIALLY DEFERRED specifies that the constraint should be checked for conformance at the end of the transaction.

The DEFERRABLE status of a constraint cannot be changed using ALTER TABLE MODIFY CONSTRAINT; you must drop and re-create the constraint. You can change the INITIALLY {DEFERRED|IMMEDIATE} clause using ALTER TABLE.

If the constraint is DEFERRABLE, you can set the behavior by using the SET CONSTRAINTS command or by using the ALTER SESSION SET CONSTRAINT command. You can enable or disable deferred constraint checking by listing all the constraints or by specifying the ALL keyword. The SET CONSTRAINTS command is used to set the constraint-checking behavior for the current transaction, and the ALTER SESSION command is used to set the constraint-checking behavior for the current session.

As an example, let's create a primary key constraint on the CUSTOMER table and a foreign key constraint on the ORDERS table as DEFERRABLE. Although the constraints are created as DEFERRABLE, they are not deferred because of the INITIALLY IMMEDIATE clause.

```
ALTER TABLE customer ADD CONSTRAINT pk_cust_id
PRIMARY KEY (cust_id) DEFERRABLE
INITIALLY IMMEDIATE;

ALTER TABLE orders ADD CONSTRAINT fk_cust_id
FOREIGN KEY (cust_id)
REFERENCES customer (cust_id)
ON DELETE CASCADE DEFERRABLE;
```

If you try to add a row to the ORDERS table with a CUST_ID value that is not available in the CUSTOMER table, Oracle returns an error immediately, even though you plan to add the CUSTOMER row soon. Since the constraints are verified for conformance as each SQL statement is executed, you must insert the row in the CUSTOMER table first and then add it to the

ORDERS table. Since the constraints are defined as DEFERRABLE, you can change this behavior by using this command:

```
SET CONSTRAINTS ALL DEFERRED;
```

Now you can insert rows to these tables in any order. Oracle checks the constraint conformance only at commit time.

If you want deferred constraint checking as the default, create or modify the constraint by using INITIALLY DEFERRED, as in this example:

```
ALTER TABLE customer MODIFY CONSTRAINT pk_cust_id
INITIALLY DEFERRED;
```

 Real World Scenario

Creating Tables and Constraints for an Application

Here's a scenario you may find yourself in one day. You have been provided the following information to create tables and constraints for an application developed in your company to maintain geographic information:

- The COUNTRY table stores the country name and country code. The country code uniquely identifies each country. The country name must be present.

- The STATE table stores the state code, name, and its capital. The country code in this table refers to a valid entry in the COUNTRY table. The state name must be present. The state code and country code together uniquely identify each state.

- The CITY table stores the city code, name, and population. The city code uniquely identifies each city. The state and country where the city belongs are also stored in the table, which refers to the STATE table. The city name must be present.

- Each table should have a column identifying the created-on timestamp, with the system date as the default.

- The user should not be able to delete from the COUNTRY table if there are records in the STATE table for that country.

- The records in the CITY table should be automatically removed when their corresponding state is removed from the STATE table.

- All foreign and primary key constraints should be provided with meaningful names.

Let's start by creating the COUNTRY table:

```
SQL> CREATE TABLE country (
  2  code   NUMBER (4) PRIMARY KEY,
  3  name   VARCHAR2 (40));
Table created.
SQL>
```

Oops—CODE and NAME are not very descriptive column names, and you also have other columns in tables to store codes and names. Let's rename the columns to COUNTRY_CODE and COUNTRY_NAME:

```
SQL> ALTER TABLE country RENAME COLUMN
  2   code TO country_code;
Table altered.

SQL> ALTER TABLE country RENAME COLUMN
  2   name TO country_name;
Table altered.

SQL>
```

You also forgot to provide a name for the primary key constraint. Since the table was created with a system-generated name, you have to find the name first to rename the constraint:

```
SQL> SELECT constraint_name, constraint_type
  2   FROM user_constraints
  3   WHERE table_name = 'COUNTRY';

CONSTRAINT_NAME                 C
------------------------------- -
SYS_C0010893                    P

SQL> ALTER TABLE country RENAME CONSTRAINT SYS_C0010893 TO pk_country;
Table altered.

SQL>
```

Oops again—the table should include a column to store the created-on date, and the country name cannot be NULL.

Before you continue, realize that if you have a good logical and physical design before you start creating tables, you will not have any of these problems. This is not the typical or recommended approach to creating tables for the application. The objective here is to demonstrate the various options available.

```
SQL> ALTER TABLE country MODIFY country_name NOT NULL
  2   ADD created  DATE DEFAULT SYSDATE;
Table altered.
SQL>
```

Review the table created:

```
SQL> DESCRIBE country
 Name                   Null?     Type
 ------------------     --------  ------------
 COUNTRY_CODE           NOT NULL  NUMBER(4)
 COUNTRY_NAME           NOT NULL  VARCHAR2(40)
 CREATED                          DATE
SQL>
```

Let's create the STATE table. Notice that multiple column constraints can be defined only at the table level.

```
SQL> CREATE TABLE state (
  2   state_code    VARCHAR2 (3),
  3   state_name    VARCHAR2 (40) NOT NULL,
  4   country_code  NUMBER (4) REFERENCES country,
  5   capital_city  VARCHAR2 (40),
  6   created       DATE DEFAULT SYSDATE,
  7   CONSTRAINT pk_state PRIMARY KEY
  8     (country_code, state_code));
Table created.
SQL>
```

Since you did not provide a name for the COUNTRY_CODE foreign key, Oracle assigns a name. To rename this constraint to provide a meaningful name, you can use the ALTER TABLE statement as you did before. To demonstrate dropping a constraint and re-creating it using ALTER TABLE, let's drop this constraint and then add it. So, find the constraint name from the USER_CONSTRAINTS view to drop and re-create it:

```
SQL> SELECT constraint_name, constraint_type
  2   FROM   user_constraints
  3   WHERE  table_name = 'STATE';
CONSTRAINT_NAME                  C
------------------------------   -
SYS_C002811                      C
PK_STATE                         P
SYS_C002813                      R
SQL> ALTER TABLE state DROP CONSTRAINT SYS_C002813;
Table altered.
SQL> ALTER TABLE state ADD CONSTRAINT fk_state
  2   FOREIGN KEY (country_code) REFERENCES country;
Table altered.
SQL>
```

Now you'll create the CITY table. Notice the foreign key constraint is created with the ON DELETE CASCADE clause:

```
SQL> CREATE TABLE city (
  2  city_code    VARCHAR2 (6),
  3  city_name    VARCHAR2 (40) NOT NULL,
  4  country_code NUMBER (4) NOT NULL,
  5  state_code   VARCHAR2 (3) NOT NULL,
  6  population   NUMBER (15),
  7  created      DATE DEFAULT SYSDATE,
  8  constraint   pk_city PRIMARY KEY (city_code),
  9  constraint   fk_cigy FOREIGN KEY
 10               (country_code, state_code)
 11               REFERENCES state ON DELETE CASCADE);
Table created.
SQL>
```

Summary

Tables are the basic structure of data storage. A table comprises columns and rows, as in a spreadsheet. Each column has a characteristic that restricts and verifies the data it stores. You can use several datatypes to define columns. CHAR, NCHAR, VARCHAR2, CLOB, and NCLOB are the character datatypes. BLOB, BFILE, and RAW are the binary datatypes. DATE, TIMESTAMP, and INTERVAL are the date datatypes. TIMESTAMP datatypes can store the time-zone information also. NUMBER, BINARY_FLOAT, and BINARY_DOUBLE are the numeric datatypes.

You use the CREATE TABLE statement to create a new table. A table should have at least one column, and a datatype should be assigned to the column. The table name and column name should begin with a letter and can contain letters, numbers, or special characters. You can create a new table from an existing table using the CREATE TABLE...AS SELECT... (CTAS) statement. You can add, modify, or drop columns from an existing table using the ALTER TABLE statement.

Constraints are created in the database to enforce a business rule and to specify relationships between various tables. NOT NULL constraints can be defined only with a column definition and are used to prevent NULL values (an absence of data). Check constraints are used to verify whether the data conforms to certain conditions. Primary key constraints uniquely identify a row in the table. There can be only one primary key for a table, and the columns in the primary key cannot have NULL values. A unique key is similar to a primary key, but you can have more than one unique key in a table, as well as NULL values in the unique key columns.

You can enable and disable constraints using the ALTER TABLE statement. The constraint can be in four different states. ENABLE VALIDATE is the default state.

Exam Essentials

Understand datatypes.   Know each datatype's limitations and accepted values. Concentrate on the new TIMESTAMP and INTERVAL datatypes.

Know how date arithmetic works.   Know the resulting datatype of date arithmetic, especially between INTERVAL and DATE datatypes.

Know how to modify column characteristics.   Understand how to change datatypes, add and modify constraints, and make other modifications.

Understand the rules associated with changing datatype definitions of columns with rows in a table.   When the table is not empty, you can change a datatype only from CHAR to VARCHAR2, and vice versa. Reducing the length is allowed only if the existing data fits in the new length specified.

Understand the DEFAULT clause on the column definition.   The DEFAULT clause provides a value for the column if the INSERT statement omits a value for the column. When modifying a column to have default values, the existing rows with NULL values in the table are not updated with the default value.

Know the actions permitted on read-only tables   Understand the various actions that are permitted on a read-only table. Any operation that changes the data in the table is not allowed on a read-only table. Most DDL statements are allowed, including DROP TABLE.

Understand constraints.   Know the difference between a primary key and a unique key constraint, and understand how to use a nonunique index for primary/unique keys.

Know how a constraint can be defined.   You can use the CREATE TABLE or ALTER TABLE statement to define a constraint on the table.

Review Questions

1. The STATE table has the following constraints (the constraint status is shown in parentheses):

Primary key	pk_state (enabled)
Foreign key	COUNTRY table: fk_state (enabled)
Check constraint	ck_cnt_code (disabled)
Check constraint	ck_st_code (enabled)
NOT NULL constraint	nn_st_name (enabled)

   You execute the following SQL:

   ```
   CREATE TABLE STATE_NEW AS SELECT * FROM STATE;
   ```

   How many constraints will there be in the new table?
   - **A.** 0
   - **B.** 1
   - **C.** 3
   - **D.** 5
   - **E.** 2

2. Which line of code has an error?
   ```
   1   CREATE TABLE FRUITS_VEGETABLES
   2   (FRUIT_TYPE VARCHAR2,
   3    FRUIT_NAME CHAR (20),
   4    QUANTITY   NUMBER);
   ```
   - **A.** 1
   - **B.** 2
   - **C.** 3
   - **D.** 4

3. Which statement successfully adds a new column, ORDER_DATE, to the table ORDERS?
   - **A.** ALTER TABLE ORDERS ADD COLUMN ORDER_DATE DATE;
   - **B.** ALTER TABLE ORDERS ADD ORDER_DATE (DATE);
   - **C.** ALTER TABLE ORDERS ADD ORDER_DATE DATE;
   - **D.** ALTER TABLE ORDERS NEW COLUMN ORDER_DATE TYPE DATE;

4. What are the special characters allowed in a table name? (Choose all that apply.)

    A. &

    B. #

    C. @

    D. $

5. Consider the following statement:
    ```
    CREATE TABLE MY_TABLE (
    1ST_COLUMN   NUMBER,
    2ND_COLUMN   VARCHAR2 (20));
    ```

    Which of the following best describes this statement?

    A. Tables cannot be created without a defining a primary key. The table definition here is missing the primary key.

    B. The reserved word COLUMN cannot be part of the column name.

    C. The column names are invalid.

    D. There is no maximum length specified for the first column definition. You must always specify a length for character and numeric columns.

    E. There is no error in the statement.

6. Which dictionary view would you query to list only the tables you own?

    A. ALL_TABLES

    B. DBA_TABLES

    C. USER_TABLES

    D. USR_TABLES

7. The STATE table has six rows. You issue the following command:
    ```
    ALTER TABLE STATE ADD UPDATE_DT DATE DEFAULT SYSDATE;
    ```

    Which of the following is correct?

    A. A new column, UPDATE_DT, is added to the STATE table, and its contents for the existing rows are NULL.

    B. Since the table is not empty, you cannot add a new column.

    C. The DEFAULT value cannot be provided if the table has rows.

    D. A new column, UPDATE_DT, is added to STATE and is populated with the current system date and time.

8. The HIRING table has the following data:

```
EMPNO       HIREDATE
---------   ----------
1021        12-DEC-00
3400        24-JAN-01
2398        30-JUN-01
```

What will be result of the following query?
SELECT hiredate+1 FROM hiring WHERE empno = 3400;

A. 4-FEB-01

B. 25-JAN-01

C. N-02

D. None of the above

9. What is the default length of a CHAR datatype column if no length is specified in the table definition?

A. 256

B. 1,000

C. 64

D. 1

E. You must always specify a length for CHAR columns.

10. Which statement will remove the column UPDATE_DT from the table STATE?

A. ALTER TABLE STATE DROP COLUMN UPDATE_DT;

B. ALTER TABLE STATE REMOVE COLUMN UPDATE_DT;

C. DROP COLUMN UPDATE_DT FROM STATE;

D. ALTER TABLE STATE SET UNUSED COLUMN UPDATE_DT;

E. You cannot drop a column from the table.

11. Which actions are allowed on a table that is marked as read-only? (Choose all that apply.)

A. Truncating a table

B. Inserting new data

C. Dropping a constraint

D. Dropping an index

E. Dropping a table

12. Which of the following statements will create a primary key for the CITY table with the columns STATE_CD and CITY_CD?

   A. CREATE PRIMARY KEY ON CITY (STATE_CD, CITY_CD);

   B. CREATE CONSTRAINT PK_CITY PRIMARY KEY ON CITY (STATE_CD, CITY_CD);

   C. ALTER TABLE CITY ADD CONSTRAINT PK_CITY PRIMARY KEY (STATE_CD, CITY_CD);

   D. ALTER TABLE CITY ADD PRIMARY KEY (STATE_CD, CITY_CD);

   E. ALTER TABLE CITY ADD PRIMARY KEY CONSTRAINT PK_CITY ON (STATE_CD, CITY_CD);

13. Which of the following check constraints will raise an error? (Choose all that apply.)

   A. CONSTRAINT ck_gender CHECK (gender IN ('M', 'F'))

   B. CONSTRAINT ck_old_order CHECK (order_date > (SYSDATE - 30))

   C. CONSTRAINT ck_vendor CHECK (vendor_id IN (SELECT vendor_id FROM vendors))

   D. CONSTRAINT ck_profit CHECK (gross_amt > net_amt)

14. Consider the datatypes DATE, TIMESTAMP (TS), TIMESTAMP WITH LOCAL TIME ZONE (TSLTZ), INTERVAL YEAR TO MONTH (IY2M), and INTERVAL DAY TO SECOND (ID2S). Which operations are not allowed by Oracle Database 11g? (Choose all that apply.)

   A. DATE+DATE

   B. TSLTZ–DATE

   C. TSLTZ+IY2M

   D. TS*5

   E. ID2S/2

   F. IY2M+IY2M

   G. ID2S+IY2M

   H. DATE–IY2M

15. A constraint is created with the DEFERRABLE INITIALLY IMMEDIATE clause. What does this mean?

   A. Constraint checking is done only at commit time.

   B. Constraint checking is done after each SQL statement is executed, but you can change this behavior by specifying SET CONSTRAINTS ALL DEFERRED.

   C. Existing rows in the table are immediately checked for constraint violation.

   D. The constraint is immediately checked in a DML operation, but subsequent constraint verification is done at commit time.

16. What is the default precision for fractional seconds in a TIMESTAMP datatype column?

   A. 0

   B. 2

   C. 6

   D. 9

17. Which datatype shows the time-zone information along with the date value?

    A. TIMESTAMP

    B. TIMESTAMP WITH LOCAL TIME ZONE

    C. TIMESTAMP WITH TIME ZONE

    D. DATE

    E. Both options B and C

18. You have a large job that will load many thousands of rows into your ORDERS table. To speed up the loading process, you want to temporarily stop enforcing the foreign key constraint FK_ORDERS. Which of the following statements will satisfy your requirement?

    A. `ALTER CONSTRAINT FK_ORDERS DISABLE;`

    B. `ALTER TABLE ORDERS DISABLE FOREIGN KEY FK_ORDERS;`

    C. `ALTER TABLE ORDERS DISABLE CONSTRAINT FK_ORDERS;`

    D. `ALTER TABLE ORDERS DISABLE ALL CONSTRAINTS;`

19. You are connected to the database as user JOHN. You need to rename a table named NORDERS to NEW_ORDERS, owned by SMITH. Consider the following two statements:

1. `RENAME SMITH.NORDERS TO NEW_ORDERS;`

2. `ALTER TABLE SMITH.NORDERS RENAME TO NEW_ORDERS;`

Which of the following is correct?

    A. Statement 1 will work; statement 2 will not.

    B. Statements 1 and 2 will work.

    C. Statement 1 will not work; statement 2 will work.

    D. Statements 1 and 2 will not work.

20. Tom executed the following SQL statement.

```
create table xx (n number, x long, y clob);
```

Choose the best option.

    A. A table named xx will be created.

    B. Single-character column names are not allowed in table definitions.

    C. When using the LONG datatype, other LOB datatypes cannot be used in table definitions.

    D. One of the datatypes used in the column definition needs the size specified.

Answers to Review Questions

1.   B. When you create a table using CTAS (CREATE TABLE AS SELECT), only the NOT NULL constraints are copied.

2.   B. A VARCHAR2 datatype should always specify the maximum length of the column.

3.   C. The correct statement is C. When adding only one column, the column definition doesn't need to be enclosed in parentheses.

4.   B, D. Only three special characters ($, _, and #) are allowed in table names along with letters and numbers.

5.   C. All identifiers (column names, table names, and so on) must begin with an alphabetic character. An identifier can contain alphabetic characters, numbers, and the special characters $, #, and _.

6.   C. The USER_TABLES view provides information on the tables owned by the user who has logged on that session. DBA_TABLES will have all the tables in the database, and ALL_TABLES will have the tables owned by you as well as the tables to which you have access. USR_TABLES is not a valid dictionary view.

7.   D. When a default value is specified in the new column added, the column values for the existing rows are populated with the default value. If you include the NOT NULL constraint with the DEFAULT value, only the dictionary is updated.

8.   B. In date arithmetic, adding 1 is equivalent to adding 24 hours. To add 6 hours to a date value with time, add 0.25.

9.   D. If you do not specify a length for a CHAR datatype column, the default length of 1 is assumed.

10.   A. You can use the DROP COLUMN clause with the ALTER TABLE statement to drop a column. There is no separate DROP COLUMN statement or a REMOVE clause in the ALTER TABLE statement. The SET UNUSED clause is used to mark the column as unused. This column can be dropped later using the DROP UNUSED COLUMNS clause.

11.   C, D, E. All actions that do not modify the data in the table are permitted on a read-only table. The actions of creating/dropping a constraint, creating/dropping an index, and dropping a table are allowed. Though truncating is a DDL action, it is not permitted since the data in the table is affected.

12.   C, D. The ALTER TABLE statement is used to create and remove constraints. CREATE PRIMARY KEY and CREATE CONSTRAINT are invalid statements. A constraint is always added to an existing table using the ALTER TABLE statement.

13.   B, C. Check constraints cannot reference the SYSDATE function or other tables.

14. A, D, G. You cannot add two DATE datatypes, but you can subtract to find the difference in days. Multiplication and division operators are permitted only on INTERVAL datatypes. When adding or subtracting INTERVAL datatypes, both INTERVAL datatypes should be of the same category.

15. B. DEFERRABLE specifies that the constraint can be deferred using the SET CONSTRAINTS command. INITIALLY IMMEDIATE specifies that the constraint's default behavior is to validate the constraint for each SQL statement executed.

16. C. The default precision is 6 digits. The precision can range from 0 to 9.

17. C. Only TIMESTAMP WITH TIME ZONE stores the time-zone information as a displacement from UTC. TIMESTAMP WITH LOCAL TIME ZONE adjusts the time to the database's time zone before storing it.

18. C. You can disable a constraint by specifying its constraint name. You may enable the constraint after the load and avoid the constraint checking while enabling using the ALTER TABLE ORDERS MODIFY CONSTRAINT FK_ORDERS ENABLE NOVALIDATE; command.

19. C. RENAME can be used to rename objects owned by the user. ALTER TABLE should be used to rename tables owned by another user. To do so, you must have the ALTER privilege on the table or the ALTER ANY TABLE privilege.

20. A. The table will be created without error. A table cannot have more than one LONG column, but LONG and multiple LOB columns can exist together. If a LONG or LONG RAW column is defined, another LONG or LONG RAW column cannot be used.

Chapter

7

Creating Schema Objects

ORACLE DATABASE 11*g*: SQL FUNDAMENTALS I EXAM OBJECTIVES COVERED IN THIS CHAPTER:

✓ **Creating Other Schema Objects**

- Create simple and complex views

- Retrieve data from views

- Create, maintain, and use sequences

- Create and maintain indexes

- Create private and public synonyms

An Oracle database can contain far more objects than simply tables. Chapter 6, "Creating Tables and Constraints," gave you an overview of all the major objects that can be in an Oracle schema. In this chapter, you will learn in detail some of the schema objects, concentrating of course on the OCP certification exam objectives. You will be learning about creating and managing four types of schema objects in this chapter: views, sequences, indexes, and synonyms. These four types of objects with tables are the most commonly used schema objects in an Oracle Database.

A view is a logical representation of data from one or more tables or views. You can think of a view as a query stored in the database. You can consider it a logical table, with rows and columns. Oracle 11*g* allows you to create constraints on the views and restrict the operations on views. In this chapter, I will discuss the uses of views, how they are created and managed, and how to retrieve data from views.

You can use a sequence to generate artificial keys or serial numbers. Synonyms provide aliases for objects. Indexes provide an access path to the table data. Several types of indexes can be deployed to enhance the performance of queries. Views, sequences, synonyms, and indexes are basic database objects that you'll need to understand for the certification exam, as well as for your database administration work.

Creating and Modifying Views

A *view* is a customized representation of data from one or more tables and/or views. The tables that the view is referencing are known as *base tables*. A view can be considered as a stored query or a virtual table. Only the query is stored in the Oracle data dictionary; the actual data is not copied anywhere. This means that creating views does not take any storage space other than the space in the dictionary.

Use the CREATE VIEW statement to create a view. The query that defines the view can refer to one or more tables, to materialized views, or to other views. Let's begin by creating a simple view. This example will use the EMPLOYEES table of the HR schema as the base table:

```
SQL> DESCRIBE employees
 Name                          Null?    Type
 ----------------------------- -------- -------------
 EMPLOYEE_ID                   NOT NULL NUMBER(6)
 FIRST_NAME                             VARCHAR2(20)
```

LAST_NAME	NOT NULL	VARCHAR2(25)
EMAIL	NOT NULL	VARCHAR2(25)
PHONE_NUMBER		VARCHAR2(20)
HIRE_DATE	NOT NULL	DATE
JOB_ID	NOT NULL	VARCHAR2(10)
SALARY		NUMBER(8,2)
COMMISSION_PCT		NUMBER(2,2)
MANAGER_ID		NUMBER(6)
DEPARTMENT_ID		NUMBER(4)

The following code creates a view named ADMIN_EMPLOYEES, with the employee information for employees who belong to the administration department (department 10). Notice that the LAST_NAME and FIRST_NAME columns are combined to display just a NAME column. You can rename columns by using alias names in the view definition. The datatype of the view's columns is derived by Oracle.

```
CREATE VIEW admin_employees AS
SELECT first_name || last_name NAME,
       email, job_id POSITION
FROM    employees
WHERE   department_id = 10;

View created.

SQL> DESCRIBE admin_employees
```

Name	Null?	Type
NAME		VARCHAR2(45)
EMAIL	NOT NULL	VARCHAR2(25)
POSITION	NOT NULL	VARCHAR2(10)

```
SQL>
```

If you qualify the view name with a schema name, the view will be created in that schema. You must have the CREATE ANY VIEW privilege to create a view in someone else's schema.

The views that actually copy data from base tables and take up storage are called *materialized* views. Materialized views are commonly used in data-warehouse environments. In earlier versions of Oracle, materialized views were called *snapshots*, and they are sometimes still called snapshots.

When numeric operations are performed using numeric datatypes in the view definition, the resulting column will be a floating datatype, which is NUMBER without any precision or scale. The following example uses SALARY (defined NUMBER (8,2)) and COMMISSION_PCT (defined NUMBER (2,2)) in an arithmetic operation. The resulting column value is the NUMBER datatype.

```
CREATE VIEW emp_sal_comm AS
SELECT employee_id, salary,
       salary * NVL(commission_pct,0) commission
FROM   employees;

View created.

SQL> DESCRIBE emp_sal_comm
 Name                      Null?    Type
 ----------------------    -------- ----------
 EMPLOYEE_ID               NOT NULL NUMBER(6)
 SALARY                             NUMBER(8,2)
 COMMISSION                         NUMBER
SQL>
```

The maximum number of columns that can be defined in a view is 1,000, just as for a table.

Using Defined Column Names

You can also specify the column names immediately following the view name to have different column names in the view. Let's create another view using defined column names. This view joins the DEPARTMENTS table to the EMPLOYEES table, uses a function on the HIRE_DATE column, and also derives a new column named COMMISSION_AMT. Notice the ORDER BY clause in the view definition. The derived column COMMISSION_AMT is the NUMBER datatype, so there is no maximum length.

```
CREATE VIEW emp_hire
(employee_id, employee_name, department_name,
 hire_date, commission_amt)
AS SELECT employee_id, first_name || ' ' || last_name,
    department_name, TO_CHAR(hire_date,'DD-MM-YYYY'),
    salary * NVL(commission_pct, .5)
```

```
FROM employees JOIN departments USING (department_id)
ORDER BY first_name || ' ' || last_name;

View created.

SQL> DESC emp_hire
 Name                            Null?     Type
 ------------------------------  --------  ------------
 EMPLOYEE_ID                     NOT NULL  NUMBER(6)
 EMPLOYEE_NAME                             VARCHAR2(46)
 DEPARTMENT_NAME                 NOT NULL  VARCHAR2(30)
 HIRE_DATE                                 VARCHAR2(10)
 COMMISSION_AMT                            NUMBER
SQL>
```

 If you use an asterisk (*) to select all columns from a table in the query to create a view and you later modify the table to add columns, you should re-create the view to reflect the new columns. When * is used, Oracle expands it to the column list and stores the definition in the database.

Creating Views with Errors

If the CREATE VIEW statement generates an error, the view will not be created. You can create views with errors using the FORCE option (NO FORCE is the default). Normally, if the base tables do not exist, the view will not be created. If, however, you need to create the view with errors, you can do so. The view will be INVALID. Later, you can fix the error, such as creating the underlying table, and then the view can be recompiled. Oracle recompiles invalid views automatically when the view is accessed.

As an example, suppose you try to create a new view named TEST_VIEW on a nonexistent base table named TEST_TABLE:

```
CREATE VIEW test_view AS
SELECT c1, c2 FROM test_table;
SELECT c1, c2 FROM test_table
               *
ERROR at line 2:
ORA-00942: table or view does not exist
```

Since you did not use the FORCE option, the view was not created. When you use the FORCE option, Oracle creates the view. However, trying to access the view gives an error, because the table TEST_TABLE does not exist yet:

```
CREATE FORCE VIEW test_view AS
SELECT c1, c2 FROM test_table;

Warning: View created with compilation errors.

SELECT * FROM test_view;
SELECT * FROM test_view
               *
ERROR at line 1:
ORA-04063: view "HR.TEST_VIEW" has errors
```

Now, let's create the TEST_TABLE and access the view:

```
CREATE TABLE test_table (
 c1 NUMBER (10),
 c2 VARCHAR2 (20));

Table created.

SQL> SELECT * FROM test_view;

no rows selected
SQL>
```

This time, it works!

WARNING   The subquery that defines the view cannot contain the FOR UPDATE clause, and the columns should not reference the CURRVAL or NEXTVAL pseudo-column. These pseudocolumns are discussed later in the chapter in the "Creating and Managing Sequences" section.

Creating Read-Only Views

You can create a view as read-only using the WITH READ ONLY option. Such views can be used only in queries; no DML operations can be performed on such views. Let's create a read-only view:

```
CREATE VIEW all_locations
AS SELECT country_id, country_name, location_id, city
FROM   locations NATURAL JOIN countries
WITH READ ONLY;

View created.
```

Creating Constraints on Views

Oracle 11*g* allows you to create constraints on views. Constraints on views are not enforced—they are *declarative constraints*. To enforce constraints, you must define them on the base tables. When creating constraints on views, you must always include the DISABLE NOVALIDATE clause. You can define primary key, unique key, and foreign key constraints on views. The syntax for creating constraints on views is the same as for creating constraints on a table (see Chapter 6).

The following example creates a view with constraints. Line 2 defines a column-level foreign key constraint, line 5 defines a column-level unique constraint, and line 7 defines a view-level foreign key constraint. The column-level constraint is called an *inline* constraint, and the view-level constraint is called an *out-of-line* constraint.

```
SQL> CREATE VIEW emp_details
  2  (employee_no CONSTRAINT fk_employee_no
  3             REFERENCES employees DISABLE NOVALIDATE,
  4   manager_no,
  5   phone_number CONSTRAINT uq_email unique
  6             DISABLE NOVALIDATE,
  7   CONSTRAINT fk_manager_no FOREIGN KEY (manager_no)
  8             REFERENCES employees DISABLE NOVALIDATE)
  9  AS SELECT employee_id, manager_id, phone_number
 10  FROM    employees
 11  WHERE   department_id = 40
SQL> /

View created.
SQL>
```

Modifying Views

To change the definition of the view, use the CREATE VIEW statement with the OR REPLACE option. The ALTER VIEW statement can be used to compile an invalid view or to add and drop constraints. Sometimes views become invalid when their underlying objects change.

Changing a View's Definition

When using the OR REPLACE option, if the view exists it will be replaced with the new definition; otherwise, a new view will be created. When you use the CREATE OR REPLACE option instead of dropping and re-creating the view, the privileges granted on the view are preserved. The dependent stored programs and views become invalid if the column list in the old view definition differs from the new view definition and the dependent object is using the changed/dropped column.

In the ADMIN_EMPLOYEES view defined earlier, you didn't include a space between the first name and last name of the employee. Let's fix that now using the OR REPLACE option:

```
CREATE OR REPLACE VIEW admin_employees AS
 SELECT first_name ||' '|| last_name NAME,
        email, job_id
 FROM    employees
 WHERE   department_id = 10;


View created.
```

Recompiling a View

Views become invalid when the base tables are altered. Oracle automatically recompiles the view when it is accessed, but you can explicitly recompile the view using the ALTER VIEW statement. When the view is recompiled, the objects dependent on the view become invalid.

Let's change the length of a column in the TEST_TABLE table created earlier. The TEST_VIEW view is dependent on this table. You can see the status of the database objects in the USER_OBJECTS view. The following example queries the status of the view, modifies the table, queries the status of the view, compiles the view, and again queries the status of the view:

```
SQL> SELECT last_ddl_time, status FROM user_objects
  2  WHERE   object_name = 'TEST_VIEW';


LAST_DDL_TIME             STATUS
------------------------  -------
25-OCT-2001 11:17:24 AM VALID


SQL> ALTER TABLE test_table MODIFY c2 VARCHAR2 (8);
Table altered.


SQL> SELECT last_ddl_time, status FROM user_objects
  2  WHERE   object_name = 'TEST_VIEW';
```

```
LAST_DDL_TIME            STATUS
----------------------- -------
25-OCT-2001 11:17:24 AM INVALID

SQL> ALTER VIEW test_view compile;
View altered.

SQL> SELECT last_ddl_time, status FROM user_objects
  2  WHERE  object_name = 'TEST_VIEW';

LAST_DDL_TIME            STATUS
----------------------- -------
25-OCT-2001 05:47:46 PM VALID
SQL>
```

The syntax for adding or dropping constraints on a view is similar to that for modifying the constraints on a table, but you use the ALTER VIEW statement instead of the ALTER TABLE statement. The following example adds a primary key constraint on the TEST_VIEW view:

```
ALTER VIEW hr.test_view
ADD CONSTRAINT pk_test_view
PRIMARY KEY (C1) DISABLE NOVALIDATE;

View altered.
```

The next example drops the constraint you just added:

```
ALTER VIEW test_view DROP CONSTRAINT pk_test_view;

View altered.
```

Dropping a View

To drop a view, use the DROP VIEW statement. The view definition is dropped from the dictionary, and the privileges and grants on the view are also dropped. Other views and stored programs that refer to the dropped view become invalid.

```
SQL> DROP VIEW test_view;

View dropped.
SQL>
```

Once a view is dropped, there is no rollback, and the view is not available in the Recycle Bin. So, be sure before dropping the view.

Using Views

You can use a view in most places where a table is used, such as in queries and in DML operations. If certain conditions are met, most single-table views and many join views can be used to insert, update, and delete data from the base table. All operations on views affect the data in the base tables; therefore, they should satisfy any integrity constraints defined on the base tables.

The following are some common uses of views:

To represent a subset of data For security reasons, you may not want certain users to see all the rows of your table. You may create a view on the columns that the users need to access with a WHERE clause to limit the rows and then grant privileges on the view.

To represent a superset of data You can use views to represent information from multiple normalized tables in one unnormalized view.

To hide complex joins Since views are stored queries, you can have complex queries defined as views, where the end user doesn't need to worry about the relationship between tables or know SQL.

To provide more meaningful names for columns If your tables are defined with short and cryptic column names, you may create a view and provide more meaningful column names that the users will understand better.

To minimize application and data-source changes You may develop an application refer-ring to views, and if the data source changes or the data is derived in a different manner, only the view needs to be changed.

Using Views in Queries

You can use views in queries and subqueries. You can use all SQL functions and all the clauses of the SELECT statement when querying against a view, as you would when querying against a table.

When you issue a query against a view, most of the time Oracle merges the query with the query that defines the view and then executes the resulting query as if the query were issued directly against the base tables. This helps you use the indexes, if there are any defined on the table.

Let's query the results of the EMPLOYEE_DETAILS view created earlier:

```
SQL> SELECT * FROM emp_details;


EMPLOYEE_NO MANAGER_NO PHONE_NUMBER
----------- ---------- --------------
        203        101 515.123.7777
```

Let's consider another example using a WHERE clause and a GROUP BY clause. This example finds the total commission paid for each department from the EMP_HIRE view for all commissions greater than $100:

```
SELECT department_name, SUM(commission_amt) comm_amt
FROM    emp_hire
WHERE   commission_amt > 100
GROUP BY department_name;
```

DEPARTMENT_NAME	COMM_AMT
Accounting	10150
Administration	2200
Executive	29000
Finance	25800
Human Resources	3250
IT	14400
Marketing	9500
Public Relations	5000
Purchasing	12450
Sales	72640
Shipping	78200

Inserting, Updating, and Deleting Data through Views

You can update, insert, and delete rows through a view, but with some restrictions. You can perform DML statements on a view only if the view definition does not have the following:

- A DISTINCT clause
- A GROUP BY clause
- A START WITH clause
- A CONNECT BY clause
- A ROWNUM clause
- Set operators (UNION, UNION ALL, INTERSECT, or MINUS)
- A subquery in the SELECT clause

All DML operations on the view are performed on the base tables.

Let's create a simple view based on the DEPARTMENTS table. The following view includes all the columns that are part of any constraint in the DEPARTMENTS table, so you can insert a row through the view without violating any constraints:

```
CREATE OR REPLACE VIEW dept_above_250
AS SELECT department_id DID, department_name
```

```
FROM    departments
WHERE   department_id > 250;

View created.

SELECT * FROM dept_above_250;

        DID DEPARTMENT_NAME
---------- ------------------
        260 Recruiting
        270 Payroll
```

Let's insert a new department through the view and verify that the department is added to the DEPARTMENTS table. (The SET NULL * SQL*Plus command displays an asterisk whenever the column value is NULL.)

```
SET NULL *
INSERT INTO dept_above_250
VALUES (199, 'Temporary Dept');

1 row created.

SELECT * FROM departments
WHERE   department_id = 199;

DEPARTMENT_ID DEPARTMENT_NAME       MANAGER_ID LOCATION_ID
------------- -------------------- ---------- -----------
          199 Temporary Dept           *           *
```

Although the view is defined with a WHERE clause to verify DEPARTMENT_ID is greater than 250, Oracle did not enforce this condition when you inserted a new row. If you want the DML statements through the view to conform to the view definition, use the WITH CHECK OPTION clause. The WITH CHECK OPTION clause creates a check constraint on the view to enforce the condition (such constraints will have the constraint type "V" when you query the USER_CONSTRAINTS view).

Let's re-create the DEPT_ABOVE_250 view to include the WITH CHECK OPTION clause. The CONSTRAINT keyword can be followed by a constraint name. If you do not provide a constraint name, Oracle creates a constraint whose name begins with SYS_C, followed by a unique string.

```
CREATE OR REPLACE VIEW dept_above_250
AS SELECT department_id DID, department_name
```

```
FROM    departments
WHERE   department_id > 250
WITH CHECK OPTION;

View created.

INSERT INTO dept_above_250
VALUES (199, 'Temporary Dept');
INSERT INTO dept_above_250
            *
ERROR at line 1:
ORA-01402: view WITH CHECK OPTION where-clause violation

SELECT constraint_name, table_name
FROM    user_constraints
WHERE   constraint_type = 'V';

CONSTRAINT_NAME                 TABLE_NAME
------------------------------ ----------------
SYS_C002779                     DEPT_ABOVE_250
```

Let's provide a name for the constraint and query the USER_CONSTRAINTS view again:

```
CREATE OR REPLACE VIEW dept_above_250
AS SELECT department_id DID, department_name
FROM    departments
WHERE   department_id > 250
WITH CHECK OPTION CONSTRAINT check_dept_250;

View created.

SELECT constraint_name, table_name
FROM    user_constraints
WHERE   constraint_type = 'V';

CONSTRAINT_NAME                 TABLE_NAME
------------------------------ ----------------
CHECK_DEPT_250                  DEPT_ABOVE_250
SQL>
```

Real World Scenario

Controlling Access Using a View

Say you have an HR application that has a requirement: an employee can see only their own record; all other records must be invisible. You can use a view to control access to personal records.

The EMPLOYEE_INFO table in the HRMS schema holds the personal information of employees. The business requirement is for the employees to be able to view or update their own address information. EMPLOYEE_ID is the primary key of this table.

The SQL variable USER gives the username used to connect to the database. Use this variable to restrict the rows available to the user. The EMPLOYEE_INFO table has a column named LOGIN_ID. The view is defined as follows:

```
CREATE OR REPLACE VIEW employee_address AS
SELECT employee_id, first_name, last_name, middle_initial,
       street, city, zip, home_phone, email
FROM   employee_info
WHERE  login_id = USER
WITH CHECK OPTION;
```

For updating the address, the user is given UPDATE privileges on the view, not on the base table. You add the WITH CHECK OPTION clause so that the user cannot add new records to the base table.

Using Join Views

A *join view* is a view with more than one base table in the top-level FROM clause. An *updatable join view* (or modifiable join view) is a view that can be used to update the base tables through the view. Any INSERT, UPDATE, or DELETE operation on the join view can modify data from only one base table in any single SQL operation.

A table in the join view is *key-preserved* if the primary and unique keys of the table are unique on the view's result set. For example, let's create a view using the base tables COUNTRIES and REGIONS:

```
CREATE OR REPLACE VIEW country_region AS
SELECT a.country_id, a.country_name, a.region_id,
       b.region_name
FROM   countries a, regions b
WHERE  a.region_id = b.region_id;
```

View created.

```
SQL> DESC country_region
 Name                          Null?    Type
 ---------------------------   -------- ------------
 COUNTRY_ID                    NOT NULL CHAR(2)
 COUNTRY_NAME                           VARCHAR2(40)
 REGION_ID                              NUMBER
 REGION_NAME                            VARCHAR2(25)
SQL>
```

In the COUNTRY_REGION view, the COUNTRIES table is key-preserved because it is the primary key in the COUNTRIES table and its uniqueness is kept in the view also. The REGIONS table is not key-preserved because its primary key REGION_ID is duplicated several times for each country.

You can update only a key-preserved table through a view. If the view is defined with the WITH CHECK OPTION clause, you cannot update the columns that join the base tables. For example, if you define the COUNTRY_REGION view with the WITH CHECK OPTION clause, even though the COUNTRY table is key-preserved, you will not be able to update the REGION_ID column.

INSERT statements cannot refer to any columns of the non–key-preserved table. If the view is created with the WITH CHECK OPTION clause, no INSERT operation is permitted on the view.

Let's try a few examples. Updating the REGION_NAME column in the COUNTRY_REGION view produces an error:

```
UPDATE country_region
SET    region_name = 'Testing Update'
WHERE  region_id = 1;
SET    region_name = 'Testing Update'
       *
ERROR at line 2:
ORA-01779: cannot modify a column which maps to a non key-preserved table
```

Updating the REGION_ID column does not cause an error because the column belongs to a key-preserved table:

```
UPDATE country_region
SET    region_id = 1
WHERE  country_id = 'EG';

1 row updated.
```

Let's redefine the COUNTRY_REGION view with the WITH CHECK OPTION clause and try the same UPDATE statement again:

```
CREATE OR REPLACE VIEW country_region AS
SELECT a.country_id, a.country_name, a.region_id,
       b.region_name
FROM   countries a, regions b
WHERE  a.region_id = b.region_id
WITH CHECK OPTION;

View created.

UPDATE country_region
SET    region_id = 1
WHERE  country_id = 'EG';
SET    region_id = 1
       *
ERROR at line 2:
ORA-01733: virtual column not allowed here
```

Viewing Allowable DML Operations

Oracle provides data dictionary views with information about what DML operations are allowed on each column of the view: the USER_UPDATABLE_COLUMNS view has information on columns of the views owned by the user, the ALL_UPDATABLE_COLUMNS view has information on the columns of views to which the user has access, and the DBA_UPDATABLE_COLUMNS view has information on columns of all the views in the database.

Let's query the USER_UPDATABLE_COLUMNS view to see what information is available on the COUNTRY_REGION view:

```
SELECT column_name, updatable, insertable, deletable
FROM   user_updatable_columns
WHERE  owner = 'HR'
AND    table_name = 'COUNTRY_REGION';

COLUMN_NAME                     UPD INS DEL
------------------------------- --- --- ---
COUNTRY_ID                      YES YES YES
COUNTRY_NAME                    YES YES YES
REGION_ID                       YES YES YES
REGION_NAME                     NO  NO  NO
```

You can query information on the views from the data dictionary using USER_VIEWS (or DBA_VIEWS or ALL_VIEWS). This view contains the view definition SQL. The column names of the view can be queried from USER_TAB_COLUMNS.

Using Inline Views

A subquery can appear in the FROM clause of the SELECT statement. This is similar to defining and using a view, which is why it's called an inline view. The subquery in the FROM clause is enclosed in parentheses and may be given an alias name. The columns selected in the subquery can be referenced in the parent query, just as you would select from any normal table or view.

Inline views can be considered temporary views; you don't need to create these views to use them in queries. You access the columns of the inline-view result set in the same way you access the columns of a view in DML statements.

Let's consider an example using the EMPLOYEES table of the sample HR schema. You can use the following query to report the employee names, their salaries, and the average salary in their department. I'll limit the result set to the employees whose names begin with *B*:

```
SELECT first_name, salary, avg_salary
FROM   employees, (SELECT department_id,
       AVG(salary) avg_salary FROM employees e2
       GROUP BY department_id) dept
WHERE  employees.department_id = dept.department_id
AND    first_name like 'B%';


FIRST_NAME             SALARY AVG_SALARY
-------------------- ---------- ----------
Britney                  3900 3475.55556
Bruce                    6000       5760
```

The same query written using the ANSI syntax is as follows:

```
SELECT first_name, salary, avg_salary
FROM   employees
NATURAL JOIN (SELECT department_id,
       AVG(salary) avg_salary FROM employees e2
       GROUP BY department_id) dept
WHERE  first_name like 'B%';


FIRST_NAME             SALARY AVG_SALARY
-------------------- ---------- ----------
Britney                  3900 3475.55556
Bruce                    6000       5760
```

WARNING You cannot have an ORDER BY clause in the subquery appearing in a WHERE clause. A FROM clause subquery (inline view) can have an ORDER BY clause.

As another example, suppose you want to find the newest employee in each department. You need to get the MAX(HIRE_DATE) value for all employees in each department and get the name of employee, as follows:

```
SELECT department_name, first_name, last_name,
       hire_date
FROM   employees JOIN departments
       USING (department_id)
JOIN   (SELECT department_id, max(hire_date) hire_date
        FROM    employees
        GROUP BY department_id)
USING  (department_id, hire_date);
```

DEPARTMENT_NAME	FIRST_NAME	LAST_NAME	HIRE_DATE
Administration	Jennifer	Whalen	17-SEP-87
Marketing	Pat	Fay	17-AUG-97
Purchasing	Karen	Colmenares	10-AUG-99
Human Resources	Susan	Mavris	07-JUN-94
Shipping	Steven	Markle	08-MAR-00
IT	Diana	Lorentz	07-FEB-99
Public Relations	Hermann	Baer	07-JUN-94
Sales	Sundita	Kumar	21-APR-00
Sales	Amit	Banda	21-APR-00
Executive	Lex	De Haan	13-JAN-93
Finance	Luis	Popp	07-DEC-99
Accounting	William	Gietz	07-JUN-94
Accounting	Shelley	Higgins	07-JUN-94

The same query written using standard Oracle join syntax looks like this:

```
SELECT d.department_name, e.first_name, e.last_name,
       mhd.hire_date
FROM   employees e, departments d,
       (SELECT department_id, max(hire_date) hire_date
        FROM    employees
        GROUP BY department_id) mhd
WHERE  e.department_id = d.department_id
AND    e.department_id = mhd.department_id
AND    e.hire_date     = mhd.hire_date;
```

DEPARTMENT_NAME	FIRST_NAME	LAST_NAME	HIRE_DATE
Executive	Lex	De Haan	13-JAN-93
IT	Diana	Lorentz	07-FEB-99
Finance	Luis	Popp	07-DEC-99
Purchasing	Karen	Colmenares	10-AUG-99
Shipping	Steven	Markle	08-MAR-00
Sales	Amit	Banda	21-APR-00
Sales	Sundita	Kumar	21-APR-00
Administration	Jennifer	Whalen	17-SEP-87
Marketing	Pat	Fay	17-AUG-97
Human Resources	Susan	Mavris	07-JUN-94
Public Relations	Hermann	Baer	07-JUN-94
Accounting	Shelley	Higgins	07-JUN-94
Accounting	William	Gietz	07-JUN-94

Performing Top-*n* Analysis

Using an inline view, you can write queries to find top-*n* values. This is possible because Oracle allows an ORDER BY clause in the inline view. So, you sort the rows in the inline view and retrieve the top rows using the ROWNUM variable. The ROWNUM variable gives the row number; the row number is assigned only when the query is fetched. For example, here is a query intended to find the top five highest-paid employees:

```
SELECT last_name, salary
FROM   employees
WHERE  rownum <= 5
ORDER BY salary DESC ;
```

LAST_NAME	SALARY
King	24000
Kochhar	17000
De Haan	17000
Hunold	9000
Ernst	6000

Since the ROWNUM is assigned only when each row is returned, the result set is not right. What you got is just five rows from the table sorted by salary. The following query will return the top five highest-paid employees:

```
SELECT * FROM
  (SELECT last_name, salary
   FROM    employees
   ORDER BY salary DESC)
WHERE ROWNUM <= 5;
```

LAST_NAME	SALARY
King	24000
Kochhar	17000
De Haan	17000
Russell	14000
Partners	13500

The Oracle 11g Optimizer recognizes the top-*n* analysis queries and hence does not sort all the rows in the subquery.

Creating and Managing Sequences

An Oracle *sequence* is a named sequential-number generator. Sequence numbers are serial numbers incremented with a specific interval. Sequences are often used for artificial keys or to order rows that otherwise have no order. Like constraints (discussed in Chapter 6), sequences exist only in the data dictionary. They do not take up any storage space. Sequences can be configured to increase or decrease without bounds or to repeat (cycle) upon reaching a boundary value.

Creating and Dropping Sequences

Sequences are created with the CREATE SEQUENCE statement. The following statement creates a sequence in the HR schema:

```
CREATE SEQUENCE hr.employee_identity START WITH 2001;
```

You can use the following keywords in the CREATE SEQUENCE statement when creating a sequence:

START WITH Defines the first number that the sequence will generate. The default is MAXVALUE for descending sequences, which is −1, and MINVALUE for ascending sequences, which is 1.

INCREMENT BY Defines the increase or decrease amount for subsequently generated numbers. To specify a decreasing sequence, use a negative INCREMENT BY value. The default is 1.

MINVALUE Defines the lowest number the sequence will generate. This is the bounding value in a decreasing sequence. The default MINVALUE is NOMINVALUE, which evaluates to 1 for an increasing sequence and to -10^{26} for a decreasing sequence.

MAXVALUE Defines the largest number that the sequence will generate. This is the bounding value in the default, increasing sequence. The default MAXVALUE is the NOMAXVALUE, which evaluates to 10^{27} for an increasing sequence and to -1 for a decreasing sequence.

CYCLE Configures the sequence to repeat numbers after reaching the bounding value.

NOCYCLE Configures the sequence to not repeat numbers after reaching the bounding value. This is the default. When you try to generate MAXVALUE+1, an exception will be raised.

CACHE Defines the size of the block of sequence numbers held in memory. The default is 20.

NOCACHE Forces the data dictionary to be updated for each sequence number generated, guaranteeing no gaps in the generated numbers but decreasing the performance of the sequence.

When you create the sequence, the START WITH value must be equal to or greater than MINVALUE. Sequence numbers can be configured so that a set of numbers is fetched from the data dictionary and cached or held in memory for use. Caching the sequence improves its performance because the data dictionary table does not need to be updated for each generated number, only for each set of numbers. Sequences are removed with the DROP SEQUENCE statement:

```
DROP SEQUENCE sequence_name;
```

When the database instance terminates abnormally or the DBA performs SHUTDOWN ABORT on the database instance, the sequence numbers cached are lost. Hence, you could have gaps in the sequence.

Using Sequences

To access the next number in the sequence, you simply select from it, using the pseudocolumn NEXTVAL. To get the last sequence number your session has generated, you select from it using the pseudocolumn CURRVAL. If your session has not yet generated a new sequence number, CURRVAL will be undefined.

The syntax for accessing the next sequence number is as follows:

```
sequence_name.nextval
```

Here is the syntax for accessing the last-used sequence number:

```
sequence_name.currval
```

Sequence Initialization

The sequence is initialized in the session when you select the NEXTVAL from the sequence. One problem that you may encounter using sequences involves selecting CURRVAL from the sequence before initializing it within your session by selecting NEXTVAL from it. Here is an example:

```
CREATE SEQUENCE emp_seq NOMAXVALUE NOCYCLE;

Sequence created.

SELECT emp_seq.currval FROM dual;

ERROR at line 1:
ORA-08002: sequence POLICY_SEQ.CURRVAL is not yet defined
in this session
```

Make sure your code initializes a sequence within your session by selecting its NEXTVAL before you try to reference CURRVAL:

```
SELECT emp_seq.nextval FROM dual;

   NEXTVAL
----------
         1

SELECT emp_seq.currval FROM dual;

   CURRVAL
----------
         1
```

Sequences can be used in the SET clause of the UPDATE statement to assign a value to a column in an existing row. They can be used in the VALUES clause of the INSERT statement also. In Oracle 11g, you can also assign the value of a sequence to a variable. Here is an example using a small PL/SQL block:

```
SQL> VARIABLE v1 NUMBER
SQL> begin
  2    :v1 := emp_seq.nextval;
  3  end;
SQL> /

PL/SQL procedure successfully completed.
```

```
SQL> print v1

        V1
----------
         3

SQL>
```

Missing Sequence Values

Another potential problem in the use of sequences involves "losing" sequence values when a rollback occurs. A sequence's NEXTVAL increments outside any user transactions, so a rollback will not put the selected sequence values back into the sequence. These rolled-back values simply disappear and may create a gap in the use of the sequence numbers. This is not a bad thing—you don't want one session's use of a sequence to block others until it commits. However, you do need to understand how gaps happen. To demonstrate this, suppose you have a table with the old Acme employee identifiers and you need to assign new employee IDs to them using your new EMP_SEQ sequence:

```
SELECT * FROM old_acme_employees;

EMP_ID ACME_ID          HOLDER_NAME
------- ---------------- -----------
       C23              Joshua
       C24              Elizabeth
       D31              David
       D34              Sara
       A872             Jamie
       A891             Jeff
       A884             Jennie

UPDATE old_acme_employees SET emp_id = emp_seq.nextval;

7 rows updated.

SELECT * FROM old_acme_employees;

  EMP_ID ACME_ID          HOLDER_NAME
---------- ---------------- -----------
       5 C23              Joshua
       6 C24              Elizabeth
```

```
 7 D31          David
 8 D34          Sara
 9 A872         Jamie
10 A891         Jeff
11 A884         Jennie
```

Now suppose you encounter an error, such as a rollback segment unable to extend, before you commit these changes, and this error causes the process to roll back. You can simulate the error and rollback by simply executing a rollback before the update is committed:

```
ROLLBACK;
```

After you fix the problem and run the update again, you find that there are "missing" sequence values (values 5, 6, 7, and so on):

```
UPDATE old_acme_employees SET emp_id = emp_seq.nextval;


7 rows updated.


SELECT * FROM old_acme_employees;

    EMP_ID ACME_ID           HOLDER_NAME
---------- ----------------- ------------
        12 C23               Joshua
        13 C24               Elizabeth
        14 D31               David
        15 D34               Sara
        16 A872              Jamie
        17 A891              Jeff
        18 A884              Jennie


COMMIT;
```

Maximum and Minimum Values

Another potential pitfall occurs when you reach MAXVALUE on an ascending sequence (or MINVALUE on a descending sequence). If the sequence is set to NOCYCLE, Oracle will raise an exception if you try to select NEXTVAL after the sequence reaches MAXVALUE:

```
CREATE SEQUENCE emp_seq MAXVALUE 10 NOCYCLE;


Sequence created.
```

```
SELECT  emp_seq.nextval
FROM hr.employees;
```

```
ERROR:
ORA-08004: sequence EMP_SEQ.NEXTVAL exceeds MAXVALUE
and cannot be instantiated
```

Altering Sequences

A common problem with sequences is how to go about altering them to change the NEXTVAL. You cannot simply alter the sequence and set the NEXTVAL. If you use a sequence to generate keys in your table and reload the development table from production, your sequence may be out of sync with the table. You may get primary-key violations when you run the application in development and it tries to insert key values that already exist.

You cannot directly alter the sequence and change its NEXTVAL. Instead, you can take one of the following approaches:

- Drop and re-create it (invalidating all dependent objects and losing the grants).

- Select NEXTVAL from it enough times to bring the sequence up to a desired value.

- Alter the sequence by changing the INCREMENT BY value to a large number, select NEXTVAL from the sequence to make it increment by the large number, and then alter the INCREMENT BY value back down to the original small value.

The following session log shows an example of the third technique. Start with the sequence SALE_SEQ that has a LAST_NUMBER value of 441:

```
SELECT sequence_name, cache_size, last_number
FROM user_sequences;
```

```
SEQUENCE_NAME   CACHE_SIZE LAST_NUMBER
-------------- ---------- -----------
SALE_SEQ               20         441
```

The SALES table needs this sequence to be larger than 111555888. So, you alter the sequence's INCREMENT BY value, increment it with a SELECT of its NEXTVAL, and then alter the INCREMENT BY value back to 1. Now the program won't try to generate duplicate keys and will work fine in development:

```
SELECT sequence_name, cache_size, last_number
FROM user_sequences;
```

```
SEQUENCE_NAME   CACHE_SIZE LAST_NUMBER
-------------- ---------- -----------
SALE_SEQ               20         441
```

```
ALTER SEQUENCE sale_seq INCREMENT BY 111555888;

Sequence altered.

SELECT sale_seq.nextval FROM dual;

   NEXTVAL
----------
 111556309

ALTER SEQUENCE sale_seq INCREMENT BY 1;

Sequence altered.

SELECT sequence_name, cache_size, last_number
FROM user_sequences;

SEQUENCE_NAME  CACHE_SIZE LAST_NUMBER
-------------- ---------- -----------
SALE_SEQ               20   111556310
```

The sequence can be dropped using the DROP SEQUENCE statement. Once dropped, the sequence definition is permanently deleted from the data dictionary. The following example shows dropping sale_seq from the database:

```
DROP SEQUENCE hr.sale_seq;
```

Creating and Managing Synonyms

A *synonym* is an alias for another database object. A *public synonym* is available to all users, while a *private synonym* is available only to the owner or to the accounts to whom that owner grants privileges. Both of these are discussed more fully later in this section.

A synonym can point to a table, view, sequence, procedure, function, or package in the local database or, via a database link, to an object in another database. Synonyms are frequently used to simplify SQL by giving a universal name to a local or remote object. Synonyms also can be used to give different or multiple names to individual objects. Like views or stored SQL, synonyms in 11*g* become invalid if the objects they point to are dropped. Likewise, you can create a synonym that points to an object that does not exist or for which the owner does not have privileges.

For example, the user SCOTT owns a table named EMP. All users log in to the database under their own username and so must reference the table with the owner as SCOTT.EMP.

But when you create a public synonym EMP for SCOTT.EMP, then anyone who has privileges on the table can simply reference it in their SQL (or PL/SQL) as EMP, without needing to specify the owner. When the statement is parsed, Oracle will resolve the name EMP via the synonym to SCOTT.EMP.

Creating and Dropping Synonyms

You can create private synonyms with the CREATE SYNONYM statement. Public synonyms are created using the CREATE PUBLIC SYNONYM statement. Public synonyms are owned by the PUBLIC user. PUBLIC is not a regular database user but is an internal user-like structure, similar to a group. Every user in the database is a member of PUBLIC.

The syntax for creating a private synonym is as follows:

```
CREATE SYNONYM [schema.]synonym_name
FOR [schema.]object[@db_link];
```

The syntax for creating a public synonym is as follows:

```
CREATE PUBLIC SYNONYM synonym_name
FOR [schema.]object[@db_link];
```

To create a public synonym called EMPLOYEES for the table HR.EMPLOYEES, execute the following statement:

```
CREATE PUBLIC SYNONYM employees FOR hr.employees;
```

Alternatively, to create a private synonym called EMPLOYEES for the table HR.EMPLOYEES, you simply remove the keyword PUBLIC, as in the following statement. The synonym will be created in the user's schema. It is called private because the synonym is available only to that user. Let's run the following SQL as the SCOTT user:

```
CREATE SYNONYM employees FOR hr.employees;
```

To remove a synonym, use the DROP SYNONYM statement. For a public synonym, you need to make sure you include the keyword PUBLIC, as in this example:

```
DROP PUBLIC SYNONYM employees;
```

To drop a private synonym, issue the DROP SYNONYM statement without the PUBLIC keyword:

```
DROP SYNONYM employees;
DROP SYNONYM scott.employees;
```

Public Synonyms

Public synonyms are used to identify objects such as tables, views, materialized views, sequences, Java classes, procedures, functions, and packages. The data dictionary views are good examples of public synonyms. These synonyms are created when you run `catalog` `.sql` at database-creation time. When you write SQL code that references the dictionary view ALL_TABLES, you do not need to select from SYS.ALL_TABLES; you can simply select from ALL_TABLES. Your code can use the fully qualified SYS.ALL_TABLES or the unqualified ALL_TABLES and resolve to the same view, owned by user SYS. When you reference SYS .ALL_TABLES, you explicitly denote the object owned by user SYS. When you reference ALL_ TABLES, you actually denote the public synonym ALL_TABLES, which then resolves to SYS .ALL_TABLES. Sound confusing? Let's look at some examples to help clarify this concept.

Suppose the DBA creates a public synonym EMPLOYEES for the HR table EMPLOYEES:

```
CREATE PUBLIC SYNONYM employees FOR hr.employees;
```

Now the user SCOTT, who does not own an EMPLOYEES table but has SELECT privileges on the HR.EMPLOYEES table, can reference that table without including the schema owner (HR):

```
SELECT COUNT(*) FROM employees;


  COUNT(*)
----------
       107
```

As another example, suppose you want to create a public synonym NJ_EMPLOYEES for the HR.EMPLOYEES table in the New_Jersey database (using the database link New_Jersey). To create this synonym, execute the following statement:

```
CREATE PUBLIC SYNONYM nj_employees for hr.employees@new_jersey;
```

> **NOTE** When the object referenced by the synonym is dropped, the synonym will remain in the data dictionary. Its status will be changed from VALID to INVALID. When a synonym is dropped, all objects that reference the synonym will become INVALID.

Private Synonyms

Private synonyms can be created for objects that you own or objects that are owned by other users. You can even create a private synonym for an object in another database by incorporating a database link.

Private synonyms can be useful when a table is renamed and both the old and new names are needed. The synonym can be either the old or new name, with both the old and new names referencing the same object.

Private synonyms are also useful in a development environment. A developer can own a modified local copy of a table, create a private synonym that points to this local table, and test code and table changes without affecting everyone else. For example, a developer named Derek runs the following statements to set up a private version of the HR.EMPLOYEES

table so he can test some new functionality without affecting anyone else using the
HR.EMPLOYEES table:

```
CREATE TABLE my_employees AS SELECT * FROM hr.employees;
ALTER TABLE my_employees ADD pager_nbr VARCHAR2(10);
CREATE SYNONYM employees FOR my_employees;
```

Now Derek can test changes to his program that will use the new PAGER_NBR column. The
code in the program will reference the table as EMPLOYEES, but Derek's private synonym will
redirect Derek's access to the MY_EMPLOYEES table. When the code is tested and then promoted,
the code won't need to change, but the reference to EMPLOYEES will resolve via the public
synonym to the HR.EMPLOYEES table.

Use of a private synonym is not restricted to the owner of that synonym. If another user
has privileges on the underlying object, she can reference the private synonym as if it were
an object itself. For example, the user HR grants SELECT privileges on the EMPLOYEES table to
both ALICE and CHACKO:

```
GRANT SELECT ON employees TO alice, chacko;
```

Then user CHACKO creates a private synonym to alias this HR-owned object:

```
CREATE SYNONYM emp_tbl FOR hr.employees;
```

User ALICE can now reference CHACKO's private synonym:

```
SELECT COUNT(*) FROM chacko.empl_tbl;
```

```
  COUNT(*)
----------
       107
```

This redirection can be a useful technique to change the objects that SQL code references, without changing the code itself. At the same time, this kind of redirection can add
layers of obfuscation to code. Exercise care in the use of private synonyms.

Resolving Object References

Assume you have a table and a public synonym with the same name. When you select
from this object name, is Oracle going to use the table referenced in the public synonym, or
is it going to get the data from the table owned by the user? The key to avoiding confusion
is to know the order that Oracle follows when trying to resolve object references. When
your code references an unqualified table, view, procedure, function, or package, Oracle
will look in three places for the referenced object, in this order:

1. An object owned by the current user

2. A private synonym owned by the current user

3. A public synonym

Creating Database Links

An Oracle Database link is an object that gives you visibility into another database. Unlike other objects, a database link cannot be used by itself. Instead, it acts as a modifier for a table or view reference in a remote database. The syntax for creating a database link is as follows:

```
CREATE [SHARED] [PUBLIC] DATABASE LINK link_name
[CONNECT TO username IDENTIFIED BY password] USING 'tns_name';
```

Synonyms can be used to mask the location of the table or view. The source data can reside in a totally different database. Data from another database is accessed using a database link.

Like a synonym, the keyword PUBLIC makes the database link available to all users in the database. When the CONNECT TO clause is used, it specifies the username and password that will be used to establish a session in the remote database. This password is stored in the data dictionary in an unencrypted form, which is visible only in the data dictionary view USER_DB_LINKS or directly in the SYS.LINK$ table. By default, only user SYS has SELECT privileges on SYS.LINK$. The tns_name parameter specifies the service name for the remote database. The keyword SHARED tells Oracle that all users of a public database link should share a single network connection to the remote database.

To create a public database link called NEW_JERSEY that connects as the HOME_OFFICE user with the password SECRET in the NJ database, execute the following:

```
CREATE PUBLIC DATABASE LINK new_jersey
 CONNECT TO home_office IDENTIFIED BY secret USING 'NJ';
```

If you don't want everyone to share the same username in the remote database, create the database link without the CONNECT TO clause, like this:

```
CREATE PUBLIC DATABASE LINK new_jersey USING 'NJ';
```

This will tell Oracle that each user should connect to the NJ database via their own username and password. Each user that references the database link must then have an account in both the local and remote databases.

Unlike a private synonym, a private database link really is private and is not available to other users. So if user SYSTEM created a private database link to the NJ database that specifically connected to user SYSTEM in the NJ database, the DBA would not need to worry about non-DBA user BERNICE accessing the NJ database with DBA privileges. She could not use SYSTEM's private database link.

Creating and Managing Indexes

Indexes are data structures that can offer improved performance in obtaining specific rows over the default full-table scan. Indexes do not always improve performance, however. You may create many indexes on a table, as long as the combination of columns differs. You may also use the same column in many indexes as long as the combination of columns differs. In the following sections, I will review the indexing technologies covered on the certification exam: B-tree and bitmap. I'll also cover when and how indexes can improve performance.

You can create and drop indexes without affecting the base data in the table—indexes and table data are independent. Oracle maintains the indexes automatically when new rows are added to the table or existing rows are updated or deleted.

You can create indexes using a single column from the table (simple index), or you can use multiple columns from the table to create a concatenated or *composite index*.

How Indexes Work

Indexes are used to access data more quickly than reading the whole table, and they reduce disk I/O considerably when the queries use the available indexes. Oracle retrieves rows from a table in only one of two ways:

- By ROWID
- By full-table scan

Both B-tree and bitmap indexes map column data to ROWIDs for the columns of interest, but they do so in different ways. When one or more indexes are accessed, Oracle will use the known column values to find the corresponding ROWIDs. The rows can then be retrieved by ROWID.

Indexes may improve the performance of SELECT, UPDATE, and DELETE operations. You can use an index if a subset of the indexed columns appear in the SELECT or WHERE clause. Additionally, if all the columns needed to satisfy a query appear in an index, Oracle can access only the index and not the table. As an example, consider the HR.EMPLOYEES table, which has an index on the columns (LAST_NAME and FIRST_NAME). If you run the following query to get a count of the employees named Taylor, Oracle needs to access only the index, not the table, because all the necessary columns are in the index:

```
SELECT COUNT(*)
FROM hr.employees
WHERE last_name = 'Taylor';
```

Although indexes can improve the performance of data retrieval, they degrade performance for data changes (DML). This is because the indexes must be updated in addition to the table.

Using B-Tree Indexes

B-tree indexes are the most common index type, as well as the default. The B-tree indexes include index column values and the ROWID of the row. The ROWID uniquely identifies a row in the table.

B-tree indexes provide the best performance on *high-cardinality* columns, which are columns that have many distinct values. For example, in the HR.EMPLOYEES table, the columns LAST_NAME and PHONE_NUMBER are high-cardinality columns. JOB_ID is a low-cardinality column.

B-tree indexes offer an efficient method to retrieve a small number of interesting rows. However, if more than about 10 percent of the table must be examined, a full-table scan may be the preferred method, depending on the data. You can create the following types of B-tree indexes:

Nonunique This is the default B-tree index; the column values are not unique.

Unique Create this type of B-tree index by specifying the UNIQUE keyword in the CREATE INDEX statement. In unique indexes, each column value entry is unique. Oracle guarantees that the combination of all index column values in the composite index is unique. Oracle returns an error if you try to insert two rows with the same index column values.

 Oracle does not include the rows with all NULL values in the indexed columns when storing a B-tree index. Bitmap indexes store NULL values.

The CREATE INDEX statement creates a nonunique B-tree index on the columns specified. You must specify a name for the index, and the table name on which the index should be built. For example, to create an index on the ORDER_DATE column of the ORDERS table, specify the following SQL:

```
CREATE INDEX orders_ind1
ON orders (order_date);
```

To create a unique index, you must specify the keyword UNIQUE immediately after the CREATE. Here's an example:

```
CREATE UNIQUE INDEX orders_ind2
ON oe.orders (order_num);
```

You can create an index with multiple columns. Such an index is called a *composite* index. Specify the column names separated by comma. The following SQL creates a nonunique composite index on the OE.ORDERS table:

```
CREATE INDEX oe.order_ind4 ON oe.orders
  (customer_id, sales_rep_id);
```

Using Bitmap Indexes

Bitmap indexes are primarily used for decision-support systems or static data, because they do not support row-level locking. Bitmap indexes can be *simple* (one column) or *concatenated* (multiple columns), but in practice, bitmap indexes are almost always simple.

Bitmap indexes are best used for low- to medium-cardinality columns where multiple bitmap indexes can be combined with AND and OR conditions. Each key value has a bitmap, which contains a TRUE, FALSE, or NULL value for every row in the table. The bitmap index is constructed by storing the bitmaps in the leaf nodes of a B-tree structure. The B-tree structure makes it easy to find the bitmaps of interest quickly. Additionally, the bitmaps are stored in a compressed format, so they take up significantly less disk space than regular B-tree indexes.

To create a bitmap index, you must specify the keyword BITMAP immediately after CREATE. Bitmap indexes cannot be unique. The following SQL creates a bitmap index named ORDERS_IND3 on the ORDERS table using the STATUS column:

```
CREATE BITMAP INDEX orders_ind3
ON oe.orders (status);
```

Dropping Indexes

You can drop an index using the DROP INDEX statement. Use this statement to drop unique, nonunique, or bitmap indexes. Oracle frees up all the space used by the index when the index is dropped. When a table is dropped, the indexes built on the table are automatically dropped. The following SQL drops the ORDERS_IND3 index:

```
DROP INDEX oe.orders_ind3;
```

You cannot drop indexes used to enforce uniqueness or the primary key of the table. Such indexes can be dropped only after disabling the primary or unique key.

How to Find Out Whether the Index Is Being Used by the Optimizer

Oracle provides multiple ways to see how a query is being executed—the execution plan decided by the Oracle Optimizer. For this demonstration, you will use the tracing features of SQL*Plus.

The SET statement in SQL*Plus has an option to turn on tracing. The SET AUTOTRACE statement is used to turn on or off tracing. SET AUTOTRACE ON will show the query results, the execution plan, and the statistics associated with the execution. Since you are interested only in the execution plan here to verify index usage, you are interested in the result of the query. Hence, you can use SET AUTOTRACE TRACEONLY.

First, let's examine the columns and indexes on the OE.INVENTORIES table. You can query the DBA_INDEXES dictionary view to see the indexes on the table. The UNIQUENESS column tells whether the index is unique. The INDEX_TYPE column indicates the type of index—NORMAL is a B-tree index. For bitmap indexes, you will see BITMAP in this column.

```
SQL> DESCRIBE oe.inventories
 Name                          Null?    Type
 ------------------------- -------- -------------
 PRODUCT_ID                    NOT NULL NUMBER(6)
 WAREHOUSE_ID                  NOT NULL NUMBER(3)
 QUANTITY_ON_HAND              NOT NULL NUMBER(8)

SQL> SELECT index_name, uniqueness, index_type
  2  FROM dba_indexes
  3  WHERE table_owner = 'OE'
  4  AND table_name = 'INVENTORIES'
SQL> /


INDEX_NAME             UNIQUENES INDEX_TYPE
-------------------- --------- ------------------
INVENTORY_IX           NONUNIQUE NORMAL
INV_PRODUCT_IX         NONUNIQUE NORMAL

SQL>
```

You have two indexes on the table. You can query the DBA_IND_COLUMNS dictionary view to get the index name and index columns:

```
SQL> SELECT index_name, column_name, column_position
  2  FROM dba_ind_columns
  3  WHERE table_name = 'INVENTORIES'
  4  AND table_owner = 'OE'
  5  ORDER BY index_name, column_position
SQL> /


INDEX_NAME           COLUMN_NAME          COLUMN_POSITION
-------------------- -------------------- ----------------
INVENTORY_IX         WAREHOUSE_ID                        1
INVENTORY_IX         PRODUCT_ID                          2
INV_PRODUCT_IX       PRODUCT_ID                          1

SQL>
```

INVENTORY_IX is a composite index with two columns: WAREHOUSE_ID and PRODUCT_ID. WAREHOUSE_ID is the leading column in this index (position 1). INV_PRODUCT_IX is an index on the PRODUCT_ID column. The third column in the table, QUANTITY_ON_HAND, does not have any index.

There is one more piece of information you need to know before running the queries. Let's find out whether there is a primary key constraint defined on this table and which index is used to enforce the primary key. From the DESCRIBE you did earlier, you know that all the columns have a NOT NULL constraint defined. You can query the DBA_CONSTRAINTS diction-ary view, as in the following SQL:

```
SQL> SELECT constraint_name, index_name
  2  FROM dba_constraints
  3  WHERE table_name = 'INVENTORIES'
  4  AND owner = 'OE'
  5  AND constraint_type = 'P';


CONSTRAINT_NAME        INDEX_NAME
---------------------  ----------------
INVENTORY_PK           INVENTORY_IX

SQL>
```

Let's run a few SQL statements against the OE.INVENTORIES table and learn when indexes are used:

```
SQL> SET AUTOTRACE TRACEONLY
SQL> SELECT COUNT(*) FROM oe.inventories;

Execution Plan
----------------------------------------------------------
Plan hash value: 2210865566


----------------------------------------------------------
| Id | Operation              | Name         | Rows |
----------------------------------------------------------
|  0 | SELECT STATEMENT       |              |    1 |
|  1 |  SORT AGGREGATE        |              |    1 |
|  2 |   INDEX FAST FULL SCAN | INVENTORY_IX | 1112 |
----------------------------------------------------------
```

Oracle used the INVENTORY_IX index to get the result. You can see here that Oracle did not read the table to get the result; only the index is read. Let's look at another SQL statement:

```
SQL> SELECT * FROM oe.inventories
  2  WHERE product_id = 12345;
```

```
Execution Plan
---------------------------------------------------------
Plan hash value: 751505330


---------------------------------------------------------
| Id  | Operation                    | Name          |
---------------------------------------------------------
|   0 | SELECT STATEMENT             |               |
|   1 |   TABLE ACCESS BY INDEX ROWID| INVENTORIES   |
|*  2 |    INDEX RANGE SCAN          | INV_PRODUCT_IX |
---------------------------------------------------------
```

Since PRODUCT_ID is in the WHERE clause, Oracle used the index on the PRODUCT_ID column. If you change the columns in the SELECT clause and include only the columns that are in the INVENTORY_IX index, Oracle will not read the table, as in the following example:

```
SQL> SELECT warehouse_id FROM oe.inventories
  2  WHERE product_id = 12345;
```

```
Execution Plan
-----------------------------------------------
Plan hash value: 253941387


-----------------------------------------------
| Id  | Operation           | Name          |
-----------------------------------------------
|   0 | SELECT STATEMENT    |               |
|*  1 |   INDEX FAST FULL SCAN| INVENTORY_IX |
-----------------------------------------------
```

What if you did not have the single column index on the PRODUCT_ID column? Oracle 11*g* provides option to hide the index from the Optimizer using the INVISIBLE clause of the ALTER INDEX statement (this was not discussed in the main section of the chapter because it is not one of the test objectives). Let's try the same SQL and watch how the Optimizer behaves:

```
SQL> alter index oe.inv_product_ix invisible;

Index altered.

SQL> SELECT * FROM oe.inventories
  2  WHERE product_id = 12345;
```

```
Execution Plan
-------------------------------------------
Plan hash value: 3778774871


-------------------------------------------
| Id | Operation        | Name         |
-------------------------------------------
|  0 | SELECT STATEMENT |              |
|* 1 |  TABLE ACCESS FULL| INVENTORIES |
-------------------------------------------


SQL> SELECT warehouse_id FROM oe.inventories
  2  WHERE product_id = 12345;

Execution Plan
--------------------------------------------
Plan hash value: 253941387


--------------------------------------------
| Id | Operation         | Name          |
--------------------------------------------
|  0 | SELECT STATEMENT  |               |
|* 1 |  INDEX FAST FULL SCAN| INVENTORY_IX |
--------------------------------------------
```

Though PRODUCT_ID is part of the INVENTORY_IX index, Oracle did not use the index in the first SQL. It is doing a full-table scan. Optimizer compared the cost of accessing the index and table vs. accessing the table alone and decided to go with full-table scan, whereas when you included only the columns part of the index in the SELECT clause, Oracle uses the index.

This chapter completes the Oracle Database 11g: SQL Fundamentals I OCP certification exam materials. Chapters 8 through 17 will cover the Oracle Database 11g: Administration I test objectives. Good luck with your SQL certification exam. You are halfway through obtaining the prestigious Oracle 11g OCA certification.

Summary

In this chapter, you learned about four types of Oracle Database objects: views, sequences, synonyms, and indexes.

A view is a tailored representation of data from one or more tables or views. The view is a stored query. Views can be used to present a different perspective of data, to limit the data access, or to hide a complex query. Views can be used as you would use tables in queries. You can update, delete, and insert into the base tables through the view (with restrictions), but the operation can affect only one table at a time if there is more than one table in the view definition.

To change the definition of the view, you must re-create the view using the CREATE OR REPLACE statement. To recompile a view or add or drop constraints, use the ALTER VIEW statement. An inline view is a query that can be used instead of a table or view in the FROM clause of a query. By using the ORDER BY clause in views (and inline views), you can perform top-*n* analysis.

Sequences are number generators, and you can use them with the NEXTVAL and CURRVAL keywords. Sequences can be used in queries, or you can directly assign a sequence value to a variable. The sequence is created using a CREATE SEQUENCE statement. The next value of the sequence cannot be altered, but its increment value can be altered.

Oracle synonyms are a mechanism to alias other objects, either locally or in another database accessed through database links. Synonyms can be globally available (public) or restricted to limited users (private). Synonyms are widely used in Oracle Databases to ease data access so that the user does not have to know which schema or which database the data is coming from.

Indexes are used to get to the table row quickly. The two main types of Oracle indexes are B-tree and bitmap indexes. B-tree indexes are suitable for high-cardinality columns, whereas bitmap indexes are suitable for low-cardinality columns with mostly static data. B-tree indexes are the default and are widely used. Bitmap indexes are used in data warehouse environments.

This chapter completes the lessons for the OCA certification exam Oracle 11*g*: SQL Fundamentals I. I hope you have learned a lot from these chapters and have tried the review questions in each chapter. Do not forget to try the practice tests on the CD before taking the test. Good luck!

You will start learning the materials relevant to Oracle 11*g*: Administration I certification exam in the next chapter.

Exam Essentials

Understand how join views work.   Know the restrictions on the columns that can be updated in a join view.

Understand how constraints are used with views.   Understand the type of constraints that can be defined on a table.

Understand how inline views are used.   Inline views are subqueries used in the FROM clause. These subqueries can have an ORDER BY clause.

Know how to change the definition of a view.   The CREATE OR REPLACE VIEW statement is used to change the definition of the view. The ALTER VIEW statement is used to recompile a view or to manage constraints on a view.

Know the precise syntax for obtaining sequence values.   You should understand how to use *sequence_name*.NEXTVAL and *sequence_name*.CURRVAL to obtain the next and most recently generated number from a sequence.

Understand when indexes degrade performance.   Know that indexes degrade the performance of DML operations (INSERT, UPDATE, and DELETE).

Know when a bitmap index is more appropriate than a B-tree index.   Bitmap indexes work best on low- to medium-cardinality columns where row-level locking is not needed. In contrast, B-tree indexes work best on high- to medium-cardinality columns and do support row-level locking.

Know how Oracle will resolve table references.   Oracle will first search for a table or view that matches the referenced name. If no table or view is found, private synonyms are then examined. Finally, public synonyms are examined. If no matching name is found, Oracle will raise an exception.

Review Questions

1. How do you remove the view USA_STATES from the schema?

   A. ALTER VIEW USA_STATES REMOVE;

   B. DROP VIEW USA_STATES;

   C. DROP VIEW USA_STATES CASCADE;

   D. DROP USA_STATES;

2. In a join view, on how many base tables can you perform a DML operation (UPDATE/ INSERT/DELETE) in a single step?

   A. One

   B. The number of base tables in the view definition

   C. The number of base tables minus one

   D. None

3. The following code is used to define a view. The EMP table does not have a primary key or any other constraints.

   ```
   CREATE VIEW MYVIEW AS
   SELECT DISTINCT ENAME, SALARY
   FROM    EMP
   WHERE   DEPT_ID = 10;
   ```

   Which operation is allowed on the view?

   A. SELECT, INSERT, UPDATE, DELETE

   B. SELECT, UPDATE

   C. SELECT, INSERT, DELETE

   D. SELECT

   E. SELECT, UPDATE, DELETE

4. Which statements are used to modify a view definition? (Choose all that apply.)

   A. ALTER VIEW

   B. CREATE OR REPLACE VIEW

   C. REPLACE VIEW

   D. CREATE FORCE VIEW

   E. CREATE OR REPLACE FORCE VIEW

5. You create a view based on the EMPLOYEES table using the following SQL.
CREATE VIEW MYVIEW AS SELECT * FROM EMPLOYEES;

You modify the table to add a column named EMP_SSN. What do you need to do to have this new column appear in the view?

A. Nothing. Since the view definition is selecting all columns, the new column will appear in the view automatically.

B. Recompile the view using ALTER VIEW MYVIEW RECOMPILE.

C. Re-create the view using CREATE OR REPLACE VIEW.

D. Add the column to the view using ALTER VIEW MYVIEW ADD EMP_SSN.

6. Which is a valid status of a constraint created on a view?

A. DISABLE VALIDATE

B. DISABLE NOVALIDATE

C. ENABLE NOVALIDATE

D. All of the above

7. The SALARY column of the EMPLOYEE table is defined as NUMBER(8,2), and the COMMIS-SION_PCT column is defined as NUMBER(2,2). A view is created with the following code:
CREATE VIEW EMP_COMM AS
SELECT LAST_NAME,
SALARY * NVL(COMMISSION_PCT,0) Commission
FROM   EMPLOYEES;

What is the datatype of the COMMISSION column in the view?

A. NUMBER (8,2)

B. NUMBER (10,2)

C. NUMBER

D. FLOAT

8. Which clause in the SELECT statement is not supported in a view definition subquery?

A. GROUP BY

B. HAVING

C. CUBE

D. FOR UPDATE OF

E. ORDER BY

9. The EMPLOYEE table has the following columns:

```
EMP_ID      NUMBER (4)
EMP_NAME    VARCHAR2 (30)
SALARY      NUMBER (6,2)
DEPT_ID     VARCHAR2 (2)
```

Which query will show the top five highest-paid employees?

A.
```
SELECT * FROM
   (SELECT EMP_NAME, SALARY
    FROM   EMPLOYEE
    ORDER BY SALARY ASC)
   WHERE ROWNUM <= 5;
```

B.
```
SELECT EMP_NAME, SALARY FROM
   (SELECT *
    FROM   EMPLOYEE
    ORDER BY SALARY DESC)
   WHERE ROWNUM < 5;
```

C.
```
SELECT * FROM
   (SELECT EMP_NAME, SALARY
    FROM   EMPLOYEE
    ORDER BY SALARY DESC)
   WHERE ROWNUM <= 5;
```

D.
```
SELECT EMP_NAME, SALARY
   (SELECT *
    FROM   EMPLOYEE
    ORDER BY SALARY DESC)
   WHERE ROWNUM = 5;
```

10. The EMPLOYEE table has the following columns:

```
EMP_ID       NUMBER (4) PRIMARY KEY
EMP_NAME     VARCHAR2 (30)
SALARY       NUMBER (6,2)
DEPT_ID      VARCHAR2 (2)
```

A view is defined using the following SQL:
```
CREATE VIEW EMP_IN_DEPT10 AS
SELECT * FROM EMPLOYEE
WHERE  DEPT_ID = 'HR';
```

Which INSERT statement will succeed through the view?

A. INSERT INTO EMP_IN_DEPT10 VALUES (1000, 'JOHN',1500,'HR');

B. INSERT INTO EMP_IN_DEPT10 VALUES (1001, NULL,1700,'AM');

C. INSERT INTO EMP_IN_DEPT10 VALUES (1002, 'BILL',2500,'AC');

D. All of the above

11. To be able to modify a join view, the view definition should not contain which of the following in the top-level query? (Choose all that apply.)

A. A DISTINCT operator

B. An ORDER BY clause

C. Aggregate functions such as SUM, AVG, and COUNT

D. A WHERE clause

E. A GROUP BY clause

F. A ROWNUM pseudocolumn

12. Which statement will create a sequence that starts with 0 and gets smaller one whole number at a time?

A. create sequence desc_seq start with 0 increment by -1 maxvalue 1;

B. create sequence desc_seq increment by -1;

C. create sequence desc_seq start with 0 increment by -1;

D. Sequences can only increase.

13. Which statement is most correct in describing what happens to a synonym when the underlying object is dropped?

A. The synonym's status is changed to INVALID.

B. You can't drop the underlying object if a synonym exists unless the CASCADE clause is used in the DROP statement.

C. The synonym is automatically dropped with the underlying object.

D. Nothing happens to the synonym.

14. There is a public synonym named PLAN_TABLE for SYSTEM.PLAN_TABLE. Which of the following statements will remove this public synonym from the database?

   A. `drop table system.plan_table;`

   B. `drop synonym plan_table;`

   C. `drop table system.plan_table cascade;`

   D. `drop public synonym plan_table;`

15. A developer reports that she is receiving the following error:
`SELECT key_seq.currval FROM dual;`

```
ERROR at line 1:
ORA-08002: sequence KEY_SEQ.CURRVAL is not yet defined
```

Which of the following statements does the developer need to run to fix this condition?

   A. `create sequence key_seq;`

   B. `create synonym key_seq;`

   C. `select key_seq.nextval from dual;`

   D. `grant create sequence to public;`

16. Bitmapped indexes are best suited to which type of environment?

   A. High-cardinality columns

   B. Online transaction processing (OLTP) applications

   C. Full-table scan access

   D. Low- to medium-cardinality columns

17. Which clauses in a SELECT statement can an index be used for? (Choose all that apply.)

   A. SELECT

   B. FROM

   C. WHERE

   D. HAVING

18. You need to generate artificial keys for each row inserted into the PRODUCTS table. You want the first row to use a sequence value of 1000, and you want to make sure that no sequence value is skipped. Which of the following statements will meet these requirements?

    A. CREATE SEQUENCE product_key2

    START WITH 1000

    INCREMENT BY 1

    NOCACHE;

    B. CREATE SEQUENCE product_key2

    START WITH 1000

    NOCACHE;

    C. CREATE SEQUENCE product_key2

    START WITH 1000

    NEXTVAL 1

    NOCACHE;

    D. Options A and B meet the requirements.

    E. None of the above statements meet all the requirements.

19. Which statement will display the last number generated from the EMP_SEQ sequence?

    A. select emp_seq.curr_val from dual;

    B. select emp_seq.currval from dual;

    C. select emp_seq.lastval from dual;

    D. select last_number from all_sequences where sequence_name ='EMP_SEQ';

    E. You cannot get the last sequence number generated.

20. Which statement will create a sequence that will rotate through 100 values in a round-robin manner?

    A. create sequence roundrobin cycle maxvalue 100;

    B. create sequence roundrobin cycle to 100;

    C. create sequence max_value 100 roundrobin cycle;

    D. create rotating sequence roundrobin min 1 max 100;

Answers to Review Questions

1. B. A view is dropped using the DROP VIEW *view_name*; command.

2. A. You can perform an INSERT, UPDATE, or DELETE operation on the columns involving only one base table at a time. There are also some restrictions on the DML operations you perform on a join view.

3. D. Since the view definition includes a DISTINCT clause, only queries are allowed on the view.

4. B, E. The OR REPLACE option in the CREATE VIEW statement is used to modify the definition of the view. The FORCE option can be used to create the view with errors. The ALTER VIEW statement is used to compile a view or to add or modify constraints on the view.

5. C. When you modify the base table, the view becomes invalid. Oracle will recompile the view the first time it is accessed. Recompiling the view will make it valid, but the new column will not be available in the view. This is because when you create the view using *, Oracle expands the column names and stores the column names in the dictionary.

6. B. Since the constraints on the view are not enforced by Oracle, the only valid status of a constraint can be DISABLE NOVALIDATE. You must specify this status when creating constraints on a view.

7. C. When numeric operations are performed using numeric datatypes in the view definition, the resulting column will be a floating datatype, which is NUMBER without any precision or scale.

8. D. The FOR UPDATE OF clause is not supported in the view definition. The FOR UPDATE clause locks the rows, so it is not allowed.

9. C. You can find the top five salaries using an inline view with the ORDER BY clause. The Oracle 11*g* Optimizer understands the top-*n* rows query. Option B would have been correct if you had ROWNUM <= 5 in the WHERE clause.

10. D. The view is based on a single table, and the only constraint on the table is the primary key. Although the view is defined with a WHERE clause, you have not enforced that check while using DML statements through the WITH CHECK OPTION clause.

11. A, C, E, F. To be able to update a base table using the view, the view definition should not have a DISTINCT clause, a GROUP BY clause, a START WITH clause, a CONNECT BY clause, ROWNUM, set operators (UNION, UNION ALL, INTERSECT, or MINUS), or a subquery in the SELECT clause.

12. A. For a descending sequence, the default START WITH value is −1, and the default MAXVALUE value is −1. To start the sequence with 0, you must explicitly override both of these defaults.

13. A. When the underlying object is dropped, the synonym will become INVALID. You can see the status of the synonym by querying the USER_OBJECTS dictionary view.

14. D. To remove a public synonym, use the DROP PUBLIC SYNONYM statement. The DROP TABLE statement will remove a table from the database but will not drop any synonyms on the table. The synonym will become invalid.

15. C. A sequence is not yet initialized if NEXTVAL has not yet been selected from it within the current session. It has nothing to do with creating a sequence, creating a synonym, or granting privileges.

16. D. Bitmapped indexes are not suited for high-cardinality columns (those with highly selective data). OLTP applications tend to need row-level locking, which is not available with bitmap indexes. Full-table scans do not use indexes. Bitmap indexes are best suited to multiple combinations of low- to medium-cardinality columns.

17. A, C. The obvious answer is C, but an index also can be used for the SELECT clause. If an index contains all the columns needed to satisfy the query, the table does not need to be accessed.

18. D. Both options A and B produce identical results, because the INCREMENT BY 1 clause is the default if it is not specified. Option C is invalid because NEXTVAL is not a valid keyword within a CREATE SEQUENCE statement.

19. B. Option D is close, but it shows the greatest number in the cache, not the latest generated. The correct answer is from the sequence itself, using the pseudocolumn CURRVAL.

20. A. The keyword CYCLE will cause the sequence to wrap and reuse numbers. The keyword MAXVALUE will set the largest value the sequence will cycle to. The name roundrobin is there to confuse to you.

Oracle Database 11*g*: Administration I

Chapter

8

Introducing Oracle Database 11*g* Components and Architecture

---

**ORACLE DATABASE 11*g*:
ADMINISTRATION I EXAM OBJECTIVES
COVERED IN THIS CHAPTER:**

✓ **Exploring the Oracle Database Architecture**

- Explain the Memory Structures

- Describe the Process Structures

- Overview of Storage Structures

✓ **Preparing the Database Environment**

- Identify the tools for Administering an Oracle Database

- Plan an Oracle Database installation

- Install the Oracle software by using Oracle Universal Installer (OUI)

With this chapter, you'll start learning Oracle Database 11g (Oracle 11g) database administration. This chapter and the remaining chapters of the book will discuss the objectives for the Oracle 11g Administration I OCA certification exam.

With the release of Oracle 11g, Oracle Corporation has delivered a powerful and feature-rich database that can meet the performance, availability, recoverability, application-testing, and security requirements of any mission-critical application. As the Oracle DBA, you are responsible for managing and maintaining the Oracle Database 11g throughout its life cycle, from initial installation, creation, and configuration to final deployment. Performing these tasks requires a solid understanding of Oracle's product offerings so that you can apply the proper tools and features to the application. You must also use relational database concepts to design, implement, and maintain the tables that store the application data. At the heart of these activities is the need for a thorough understanding of the Oracle architecture and the tools and techniques used to monitor and manage the components of this architecture.

I will begin the chapter by reviewing the Oracle Database basics. You will learn what constitutes the Oracle Database 11g—an overview of the memory structures, the processes that manage the database, and how data is stored in the database. I will also discuss the tools used to administer the Oracle Database 11g and how to install the Oracle 11g software.

Exam objectives are subject to change at any time without prior notice and at Oracle's sole discretion. Please visit Oracle's Training and Certification website at http://education.oracle.com/pls/web_prod-plq-dad/db_pages.getpage?page_id=41&p_exam_id=1Z0_052 for the most current exam-objectives listing.

Oracle Database Fundamentals

Databases store data. The data itself is composed of related logical units of information. The *database management system* (DBMS) facilitates the storage, modification, and retrieval of this data. Some early database technologies used flat files or hierarchical file structures to store application data. Others used networks of connections between sets of data to store and locate information. The early DBMS architecture mixed the physical manipulation of data with its logical manipulation. When the location of data changed, the application referencing the data had to be updated. Relational databases brought a revolutionary change to this architecture. Relational DBMS introduced data independence, which separated the physical model of the data from its logical model. Oracle is a relational DBMS.

All releases of Oracle's database products have used a relational DBMS model to store data in the database. This relational model is based on the groundbreaking work of Dr. Edgar Codd, which was first published in 1970 in his paper "A Relational Model of Data for Large Shared Data Banks." IBM Corporation, which was then an early adopter of Dr. Codd's model, helped develop the computer language that is used to access all relational databases today—Structured Query Language (SQL). The great thing about SQL is that you can use it to easily interact with relational databases without having to write complex computer programs and without needing to know where or how the data is physically stored on disk. You saw several SQL statements in the previous chapters.

Relational Databases

The concept of a *relational database management system* (RDBMS) is that the data consists of a set of relational objects. The basic storage of data in a database is a table. The relations are implemented in tables, where data is stored in rows and columns. Figure 8.1 shows such a relationship.

FIGURE 8.1 Relational tables

EMP (Employee Table)

EMPNO	ENAME	JOB	MGR	HIREDATE	SAL	COMM	DEPTNO
7369	SMITH	CLERK	7902	17-DEC -8	0800		20
7499	ALLEN	SALESMAN	7698	20-FEB-8	11600	300	30
7521	WARD	SALESMAN	7698	22-FEB-8	11250	500	30
7566	JONES	MANAGER	7839	02-APR-8	12975		20
7654	MARTIN	SALESMAN	7698	28-SEP-8	11250	1400	30
7698	BLAKE	MANAGER	7839	07-MAY-8	12850		30
7844	URNER	SALESMAN	7698	08-SEP-8	11500		30

Primary Key Column

Foreign Key Column

DEPT (Department Table)

DEPTNO	DNAME	LOC
10	ACCOUNTING	NEW YORK
20	RESEARCH	DALLAS
30	SALES	CHICAGO
40	OPERATIONS	BOSTON

Primary Key Column

The DEPT table in the lower part of the figure stores information about departments in the company. Each department is identified by the department ID. Along with the ID, the name and location of the department are also stored in the table. The EMP table stores information about the employees in the company. Each employee is identified by a unique employee ID. This table includes employee information such as hire date, salary, manager, and so on. The DEPTNO column in both tables then provides a relationship between the tables. A department may have many employees, but an employee can work for only one department.

Since the user accessing this data doesn't need to know how or where the row is stored in the database, there must be a way to uniquely identify the rows in the tables. In our example, the department is uniquely identified by department number, and an employee is identified by an employee ID. The column (or set of columns) that uniquely identifies a row is known as the *primary key*. According to relational theory, each table in a relational database must have a primary key.

When relating tables together, the primary key of one table is placed in another table. For example, the primary key of the DEPT table is a column in the EMP table. In RDBMS terminology, this is known as a *foreign key*. A foreign key states that the data value in the column exists in another table and should continue to exist in the other table to keep the relationship between tables. The table where the column is a primary key is known as the *parent table*, and the table where the foreign key column exists is known as the *child table*. Oracle enforces the parent-child relationship between tables using *constraints*.

Oracle Database 11*g* Objects

Every RDBMS supports a variety of database objects. Oracle 11*g* supports the entire set of database objects required for a relational database, such as tables, views, constraints, and so on. It also supports a wide range of objects specific to the Oracle Database 11*g*, such as packages, sequences, materialized views, and so on. Table 8.1 lists the objects available in Oracle 11*g*. I also discussed many of these in Chapter 6, "Creating Tables and Constraints," and Chapter 7, "Creating Schema Objects."

TABLE 8.1   Oracle Database 11*g* Objects

Object Type	Description
Table	A table is the basic form of data storage. A table has columns and stores rows of data.
View	A view is a stored query. No data-storage space is occupied for view data.
Index	An index is an optional structure that is useful for locating data faster.
Materialized view	Materialized views are used to summarize and store data. They are similar to views but take up storage space to store data.

TABLE 8.1   Oracle Database 11*g* Objects *(continued)*

Object Type	Description
Index-organized table	An index-organized table use a primary key and stores the table data in the index segment.
Cluster	A cluster is a group of tables that share the same storage blocks.
Constraint	A constraint is a stored rule to enforce data integrity.
Sequence	A sequence provides a mechanism for the continuous generation of numbers.
Synonym	A synonym is an alias for a database schema object.
Triggers	A trigger is a PL/SQL program unit that gets executed when an event occurs.
Stored function	Stored functions are PL/SQL programs that can be used to create user-defined functions to return a value.
Stored procedure	Stored procedures are PL/SQL programs to define a business process.
Package	A package is a collection of procedures, functions, and other program constructs.
Java	Stored Java procedures can be created in Oracle to define business processes.
Database link	Database links are used to communicate between databases to share data.

You use SQL to create database objects and to interact with application data. In the next section, I will discuss the tools available to access and administer Oracle 11*g* database.

Interacting with Oracle 11*g*

SQL is the language used to interact with the Oracle 11*g* database. Many tools are available for the DBA to administer an Oracle 11*g* database. The common tools are as follows:

- SQL*Plus, which is a command-line interface utility
- SQL Developer, a GUI tool
- Oracle Enterprise Manager Database Control, a GUI tool

Using SQL*Plus and SQL Developer, you interact directly with the Oracle 11*g* database using SQL statements and a superset of commands such as STARTUP, SHUTDOWN, and so on. Using Enterprise Manager, you interact indirectly with the Oracle 11*g* database.

SQL*Plus

SQL*Plus is the primary tool for an Oracle DBA to administer the database using SQL commands. Before you can run SQL statements, you must connect to the Oracle 11*g* database. You can start SQL*Plus from a Windows command prompt using the SQLPLUS.EXE executable or using the $ORACLE_HOME/bin/sqlplus executable on the Unix/Linux platform. Figure 8.2 shows connecting to SQL*Plus from a Linux workstation.

FIGURE 8.2 SQL*Plus login in Linux

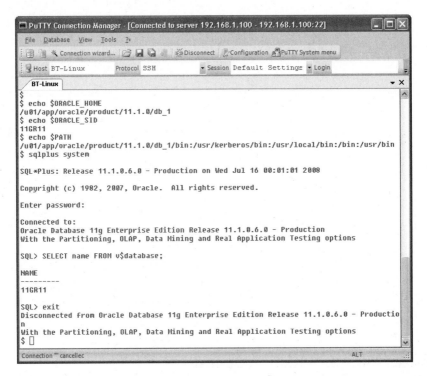

To get an overview of SQL*Plus and how to connect to the database using SQL*Plus, please refer to Chapter 1, "Introducing SQL."

SQL Developer

SQL Developer is a free GUI database-development tool. With SQL Developer, you can create and view the database objects, make changes to the objects, run SQL statements, run PL/SQL programs, create and edit PL/SQL programs, and perform PL/SQL debugging.

SQL Developer also includes a migration utility to migrate Microsoft Access and Microsoft SQL Server databases to Oracle 11g. Figure 8.3 shows the object browser screen of SQL Developer.

FIGURE 8.3   SQL Developer screen

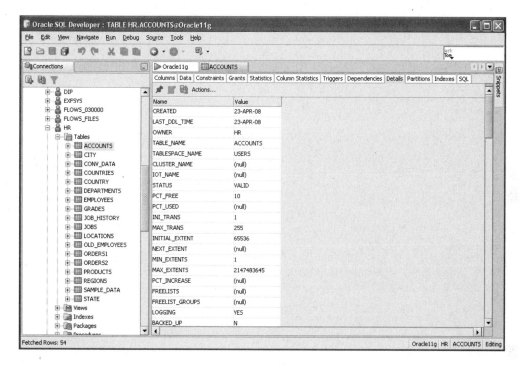

   You can download and learn more about SQL Developer on the OTN website (http://www.oracle.com/technology/products/database/sql_developer/index.html).

Enterprise Manager Database Control

Oracle Enterprise Manager Database Control is a web-based database management tool that is bundled with the Oracle 11g database. This is a graphical tool specifically designed to administer the Oracle database. The Enterprise Manager Database Control is used to manage a single database, whereas the Enterprise Manager Grid Control can manage multiple databases and other services and applications, such as OAS, and even non-Oracle applications at the same time. Figure 8.4 shows the Enterprise Manager Database Control home screen, where an overview of the database is shown.

FIGURE 8.4   Enterprise Manager home screen

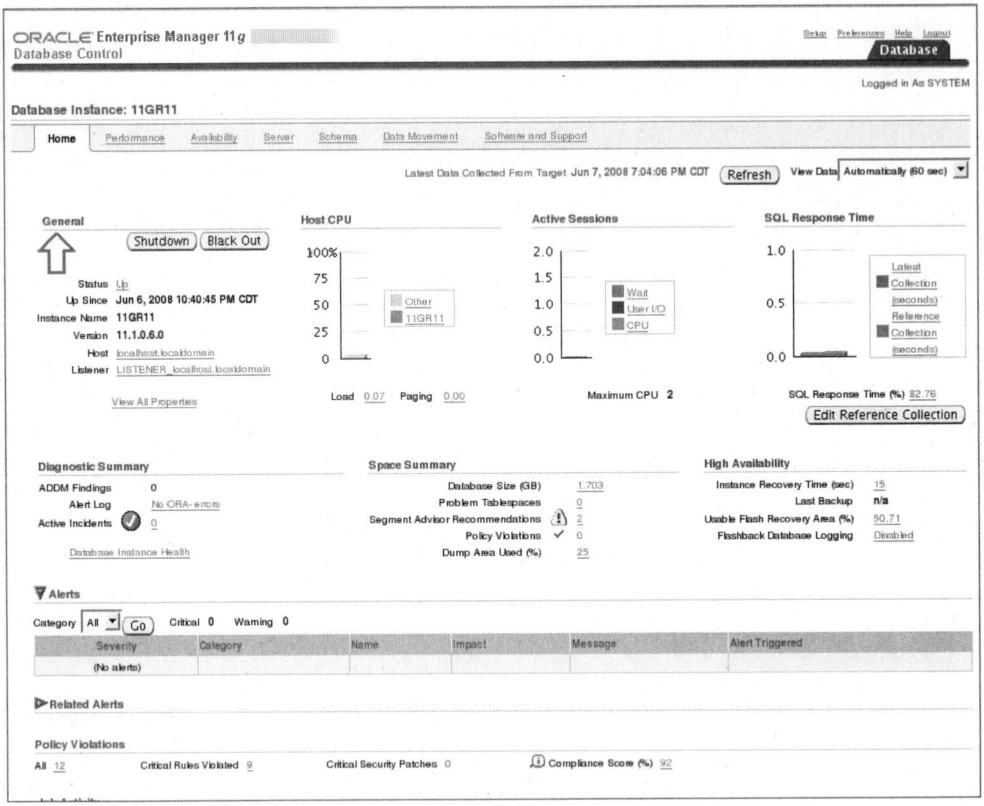

ORACLE Enterprise Manager 11*g*
Database Control

Setup   Preferences   Help   Logout
Database

Logged in As SYSTEM

Database Instance: 11GR11

| Home | Performance | Availability | Server | Schema | Data Movement | Software and Support |

Latest Data Collected From Target Jun 7, 2008 7:04:06 PM CDT   (Refresh)   View Data Automatically (60 sec) ▾

General

(Shutdown) (Black Out)

Status Up
Up Since Jun 6, 2008 10:40:45 PM CDT
Instance Name 11GR11
Version 11.1.0.6.0
Host localhost.localdomain
Listener LISTENER_localhost.localdomain

View All Properties

Host CPU

100%
75
50 Other
25 11GR11
0

Load 0.07   Paging 0.00

Active Sessions

2.0
1.5 Wait
1.0 User I/O
0.5 CPU
0.0

Maximum CPU 2

SQL Response Time

1.0 Latest
Collection
0.5 (seconds)
Reference
Collection
0.0 (seconds)

SQL Response Time (%) 82.76

(Edit Reference Collection)

Diagnostic Summary

ADDM Findings 0
Alert Log No ORA- errors
Active Incidents 0

Database Instance Health

Space Summary

Database Size (GB) 1.703
Problem Tablespaces 0
Segment Advisor Recommendations 2
Policy Violations 0
Dump Area Used (%) 25

High Availability

Instance Recovery Time (sec) 15
Last Backup n/a
Usable Flash Recovery Area (%) 50.71
Flashback Database Logging Disabled

▼ **Alerts**

Category All ▾ (Go)   Critical 0   Warning 0

Severity	Category	Name	Impact	Message	Alert Triggered
(No alerts)					

▶ **Related Alerts**

Policy Violations

All 12   Critical Rules Violated 9   Critical Security Patches 0   Compliance Score (%) 92

For all the database-administration examples in this chapter, you may use either SQL*Plus to perform the SQL command line or use the GUI tool Enterprise Manager (EM) Database Control. Before learning to administer the Oracle 11*g* database, let's start with the basics. In the next section, you'll learn about Oracle 11*g* architecture.

Oracle 11*g* Architecture

Each database-administration and -development tool described previously allows a user to interact with the database. Using these tools requires that user accounts be created in the database and that connectivity to the database be in place across the network. Users must also have adequate storage capacity for the data they insert, and they need recovery mechanisms for restoring the transactions they are performing in the event of a hardware failure. As the DBA, you take care of each of these tasks, as well as others, which include the following:

- Selecting the server hardware on which the database software will run
- Installing and configuring the Oracle 11*g* software on the server hardware
- Creating the Oracle 11*g* database
- Creating and managing the tables and other objects used to manage the application data
- Creating and managing database users
- Establishing reliable backup and recovery processes for the database
- Monitoring and tuning database performance

The remainder of this book is dedicated to helping you understand how to perform these and other important Oracle database-administration tasks. But first, to succeed as an Oracle DBA, you need to completely understand Oracle's underlying architecture and its mechanisms. Understanding the relationship between Oracle's memory structures, background processes, and I/O activities is critical before learning how to manage these areas.

The Oracle server architecture can be described in three categories:

- User-related processes
- Logical memory structures that are collectively called an *Oracle instance*
- Physical file structures that are collectively called a *database*

You will also see how the physical structures map to the logical structures of the database you are familiar with, such as tables and indexes.

Database is a confusing term that is often used to represent different things on different platforms; the only commonality is that it is something related to storing data. In Oracle, however, the term *database* represents the physical files that store data. An instance is composed of the memory structures and background processes. Each database should have at least one instance associated with it. It is possible for multiple instances to access a single database; such a configuration is known as Real Application Clusters (RAC). In this book, however, you'll concentrate only on single-instance databases because RAC is not part of the certification exam.

Figure 8.5 shows all the parts of an Oracle instance and database.

Although the architecture in Figure 8.5 may at first seem complex, each of these architecture components is described in more detail in the following sections, beginning with the user-related processes, and is actually fairly simple. This figure is an important piece of fundamental information when learning about the Oracle 11*g* architecture.

The key database components are memory structures, process structures, and storage structures. Process and memory structures together are called an *instance*; the storage structure is called a *database*. Taken together, the instance and the database are called an *Oracle server*.

FIGURE 8.5 The Oracle 11*g* architecture

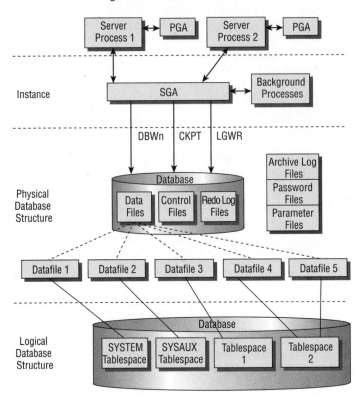

User Processes

At the user level, two types of processes allow a user to interact with the instance and, ultimately, with the database: the *user process* and the *server process*.

Whenever a user runs an application, such as a human-resources or order-taking application, Oracle starts a user process to support the user's connection to the instance. Depending on the technical architecture of the application, the user process exists either on the user's own computer or on the middle-tier application server. The user process then initiates a connection to the instance. Oracle calls the process of initiating and maintaining communication between the user process and the instance a *connection*. Once the connection is made, the user establishes a *session* in the instance.

After establishing a session, each user starts a server process on the host server itself. It is this server process that is responsible for performing the tasks that actually allow the user to interact with the database.

Examples of these interactions include sending SQL statements to the database, retrieving needed data from the database's physical files, and returning that data to the user.

> Server processes generally have a one-to-one relationship with user processes—in other words, each user process connects to one and only one server process. However, in some Oracle configurations, multiple user processes can share a single server process. We will discuss Oracle connection configurations in Chapter 11, "Understanding Network Architecture."

In addition to the user and server processes that are associated with each user connection, an additional memory structure called the *program global area* (PGA) is also created for each user. The PGA stores user-specific session information such as bind variables and session variables. Every server process on the server has a PGA memory area. Figure 8.6 shows the relationship between a user process, server processes, and the PGA.

FIGURE 8.6   The relationship between user and server processes and the PGA

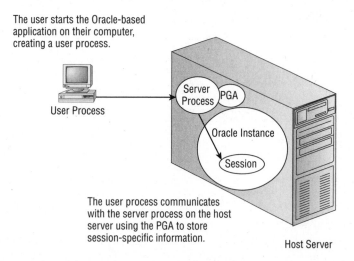

PGA memory is not shared. Each server process has a PGA associated with it and is exclusive. As a DBA, you set the total memory that can be allocated to all the PGA memory allocated to all server and background processes.

The server process communicates with the Oracle instance on behalf of the user. The Oracle instance is examined in the next section.

The Oracle Instance

An Oracle database instance consists of Oracle's main memory structure, called the *system global area* (SGA), and several Oracle background processes. It is with the SGA that the server process communicates when the user accesses the data in the database. Figure 8.7 shows the components of the SGA.

FIGURE 8.7 SGA components

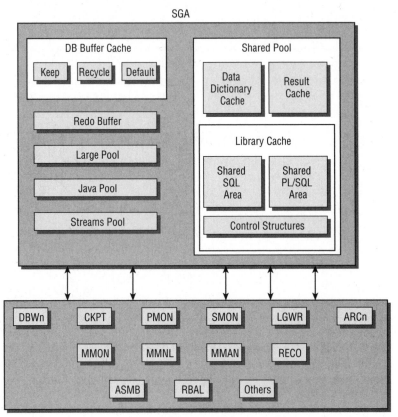

Background Processes

The components of the instance are described in the following sections.

Oracle Memory Structures

The SGA is a shared memory area. All the users of the database share the information maintained in this area. Oracle allocates memory for the SGA when the instance is started and deallocates it when the instance is shut down. The SGA consists of three required components and four optional components. Table 8.2 describes the required components.

TABLE 8.2   Required SGA Components

SGA Component	Description
Shared pool	Caches the most recently used SQL statements that have been issued by database users
Database buffer cache	Caches the data that has been most recently accessed by database users
Redo log buffer	Stores transaction information for recovery purposes

Table 8.3 describes the optional components.

TABLE 8.3   Optional SGA Components

SGA Component	Description
Java pool	Caches the most recently used Java objects and application code when Oracle's JVM option is used.
Large pool	Caches data for large operations such as Recovery Manager (RMAN) backup and restore activities and Shared Server components.
Streams pool	Caches the data associated with queued message requests when Oracle's Advanced Queuing option is used.
Result cache	This new area is introduced in the Oracle 11*g* database and stores results of SQL queries and PL/SQL functions for better performance.

Oracle 11*g* can manage the components of the SGA dynamically, without exceeding the value specified by the DBA for the parameter SGA_MAX_SIZE, but only for ASMM. Memory in the SGA is allocated in units of contiguous memory called *granules*. The size of a granule depends on the parameter MEMORY_MAX_TARGET. If MEMORY_MAX_TARGET is larger than 1024MB, the granule size is either 16MB or 4MB. MEMORY_MAX_TARGET is discussed in detail in Chapter 14, "Maintaining the Database and Managing Performance." A minimum of three granules must be allocated to SGA—one each for the required components in Table 8.2.

The sizes of these SGA components can be managed in two ways: manually or automatically. If you choose to manage these components manually, you must specify the size of each SGA component and then increase or decrease the size of each component according to the needs of the application. If these components are managed automatically, the instance itself will monitor the utilization of each SGA component and adjust their sizes accordingly, relative to a predefined maximum allowable aggregate SGA size.

Oracle 11*g* provides several dynamic performance views to see the components and sizes of SGA; you can use V$SGA and V$SGAINFO, as shown here:

```
SQL> SELECT * FROM v$sga;

NAME                      VALUE
-------------------- ----------
Fixed Size              1303916
Variable Size         570428052
Database Buffers      377487360
Redo Buffers            4935680
SQL>
```

Alternatively, you may use the SHOW SGA command from SQL*Plus, as shown here:

```
SQL> SHOW SGA

Total System Global Area  954155008 bytes
Fixed Size                  1303916 bytes
Variable Size             570428052 bytes
Database Buffers          377487360 bytes
Redo Buffers                4935680 bytes
SQL>
```

The output from this query shows that the total size of the SGA is 954,155,008 bytes. This total size is composed of the variable space that is composed of the shared pool, the large pool, the Java pool (570428052 bytes), the database buffer cache (377487360 bytes), the redo log buffer (4935680 bytes), and some additional space (1,303,916 bytes) that stores information used by the instance's background processes. The V$SGAINFO view displays additional details about the allocation of space within the SGA, as shown in the following query:

```
SQL> SELECT * FROM v$sgainfo;

NAME                                  BYTES RESIZEABLE
------------------------------- ---------- ----------
Fixed SGA Size                      1303916 No
Redo Buffers                        4935680 No
Buffer Cache Size                 352321536 Yes
Shared Pool Size                  339738624 Yes
Large Pool Size                     4194304 Yes
Java Pool Size                     12582912 Yes
Streams Pool Size                         0 Yes
Shared IO Pool Size                       0 Yes
```

```
Granule Size                        4194304 No
Maximum SGA Size                  954155008 No
Startup overhead in Shared Pool    46137344 No
Free SGA Memory Available         239075328
```

12 rows selected.

SQL>

The results of this query show in detail how much space is occupied by each component in the shared pool. The components with the RESIZEABLE column with a value of Yes can be managed dynamically by Oracle 11*g*.

You can also use EM Database Control to view the sizes of each of the SGA components, as shown in Figure 8.8. From the home screen, go to the Server tab and click Memory Advisors to see this.

FIGURE 8.8   EM Database Control showing SGA components

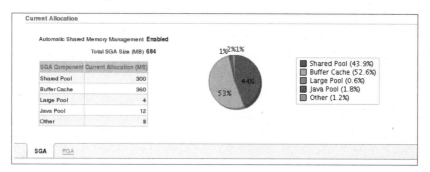

You'll learn more about the components in the SGA in the next sections.

Database Buffer Cache

The *database buffer cache* is the area in SGA that caches the database data, holding blocks from the data files that have been read recently. The database buffer cache is shared among all the users connected to the database. There are three types of buffers:

- *Dirty buffers* are the buffer blocks that need to be written to the data files. The data in these buffers has changed and has not yet been written to the disk.

- *Free buffers* do not contain any data or are free to be overwritten. When Oracle reads data from the disk, free buffers hold this data.

- *Pinned buffers* are the buffers that are currently being accessed or explicitly retained for future use.

Oracle uses a *least recently used algorithm* (LRU algorithm) to manage the contents of the shared pool and database buffer cache. When a user's server process needs to put a SQL statement into the shared pool or copy a database block into the buffer cache, Oracle uses the space in memory that is occupied by the least recently accessed SQL statement or buffer to hold the requested SQL or block copy. Using this technique, Oracle keeps frequently accessed SQL statements and database buffers in memory longer, improving the overall performance of the server by minimizing parsing and physical disk I/O.

> The background process DBW*n* writes the database blocks from the database buffer cache to the data files. Dirty buffers contain data that changed and must be written to disk.

To manage the buffer cache better, Oracle 11g provides three buffer caches. The DEFAULT cache is the default and is required. The KEEP cache and the RECYCLE cache can be optionally configured. By default all the data read from the disk is written to the DEFAULT pool. If you want certain data not to be aged from memory, you can configure the KEEP pool and use the ALTER TABLE statement to specify which tables should use the KEEP pool. Similarly, if you do not want to age out good data from the default cache for temporary data, you may specify such tables to have the RECYCLE pool instead of the default. The blocks in the KEEP pool also follow the LRU algorithm to age out blocks when new blocks need space in the KEEP pool. By sizing the KEEP pool appropriately, you can hold frequently used blocks longer in the KEEP pool. The RECYCLE cache removes the buffers from memory as soon as they are not needed.

> The DB_CACHE_SIZE parameter specifies the size of the database buffer cache default pool. To configure the keep and recycle pools, use the DB_KEEP_CACHE_SIZE and DB_RECYCLE_CACHE_SIZE parameters.

Redo Log Buffer

The *redo log buffer* is a circular buffer in the SGA that holds information about the changes made to the database data. The changes are known as *redo entries* or *change vectors* and are used to redo the changes in case of a failure. DML and DDL statements are used to make changes to the database data. The parameter LOG_BUFFER determines the size of the redo log buffer cache.

> The background process LGWR writes the redo log information to the online redo log files.

Shared Pool

The *shared pool* portion of the SGA holds information such as SQL, PL/SQL procedures and packages, the data dictionary, locks, character-set information, security attributes, and so on. The shared pool consists of the library cache and the data dictionary cache.

The *library cache* contains the shared SQL areas, private SQL areas, PL/SQL programs, and control structures such as locks and library cache handles.

The *shared SQL area* is used for maintaining recently executed SQL statements and their execution plans. Oracle divides each SQL statement that it executes into a shared SQL area and a private SQL area. When two users are executing the same SQL, the information in the shared SQL area is used for both. The shared SQL area contains the parse tree and execution plan, whereas the private SQL area contains values for the bind variables (persistent area) and runtime buffers (runtime area). Oracle creates the runtime area as the first step of an execute request. For INSERT, UPDATE, and DELETE statements, Oracle frees the runtime area after the statement has been executed. For queries, Oracle frees the runtime area only after all rows have been fetched or the query has been canceled.

Oracle processes PL/SQL program units the same way it processes SQL statements. When a PL/SQL program unit is executed, the code is moved to the *shared PL/SQL area*, and the individual SQL commands within the program unit are moved to the shared SQL area. Again, the shared program units are maintained in memory with an LRU algorithm.

The third area in the library cache is used to store control information and is maintained internally by Oracle. Various locks, latches, and other control structures reside here, and any server process that requires this information can access it.

The *data dictionary cache* holds the most recently used database dictionary information. The data dictionary cache is also known as the *row cache* because it holds data as rows instead of buffers (which hold entire blocks of data).

The *result cache* is new in Oracle 11*g* and is used to hold the SQL and PL/SQL function results. Executions of similar SQL statements can use the cached results to answer query requests. Because retrieving results from the SQL query result cache is faster than rerunning a query, frequently run queries experience a significant performance improvement when their results are cached.

 The parameter SHARED_POOL_SIZE determines the size of the shared pool.

Large Pool

The *large pool* is an optional area in the SGA that the DBA can configure to provide large memory allocations for specific database operations such as an RMAN backup or restore. The large pool allows Oracle to request large memory allocations from a separate pool to prevent contention from other applications for the same memory. The large pool does not have an LRU list. The parameter LARGE_POOL_SIZE determines the size of the large pool.

Java Pool

The *Java pool* is another optional area in the SGA that the DBA can configure to provide memory for Java operations, just as the shared pool is provided for processing SQL and PL/SQL statements. The parameter JAVA_POOL_SIZE determines the size of the Java pool.

Streams Pool

The *streams pool* is exclusively used by Oracle streams. The parameter STREAMS_POOL_SIZE determines the size of the streams pool.

> If any SGA component size is set smaller than the granule size, the size of the component is rounded to the nearest granule size.

> Oracle 11*g* can manage all the components of the SGA and PGA automatically; there is no need for the DBA to configure each pool individually. You will learn more about automatic memory management in Chapter 14.

Oracle Processes Structures

Many types of Oracle background processes exist. Each performs a specific job in helping to manage an instance. Five Oracle background processes are required by the Oracle instance, and several background processes are optional. The required background processes are found in all Oracle instances. Optional background processes may or may not be used, depending on the features that are being used in the database. Table 8.4 describes the required background processes.

TABLE 8.4   Required Oracle Background Processes

Process Name	OS Process	Description
Database Writer	DBW*n*	Writes modified database blocks from the SGA's database buffer cache to the data files on disk
Checkpoint	CKPT	Updates the data file headers following a checkpoint event
Log Writer	LGWR	Writes transaction recovery information from the SGA's redo log buffer to the online redo log files on disk
Process Monitor	PMON	Cleans up failed user database connections
System Monitor	SMON	Performs instance recovery following an instance crash, coalesces free space in the database, and manages space used for sorting

Table 8.5 describes some of the optional background processes.

TABLE 8.5   Optional Oracle Background Processes

Process Name	OS Process	Description
Archiver	ARC*n*	Copies the transaction recovery information from the redo log files to the archive location. Nearly all production databases use this optional process. You can have up to 30 archival processes (ARC0–ARC9, ARCa–ARCt).
Recoverer	RECO	Recovers failed transactions that are distributed across multiple databases when using Oracle's distributed database feature.
ASM Disk	ASMB	Present on databases using Automatic Storage Management disks.
ASM Balance	RBAL	Coordinates rebalance activity of disks in an ASM disk group.
Job Queue Monitor	CJQ*n*	Assigns jobs to the job queue processes when using Oracle's job scheduling feature.
Job Queue	J*nnn*	Executes database jobs that have been scheduled using Oracle's job-scheduling feature.
Queue Monitor	QMN*n*	Monitors the messages in the message queue when Oracle's Advanced Queuing feature is used.
Diagnosability	DIAG	Performs diagnostic dumps.
Diagnosablilty	DIA0	Diagnostic process responsible for hang detection and deadlock resolution.
Event Monitor	EMNC	Process responsible for event-management coordination and notification.
Flashback Data Archive	FBDA	Archives historical records from table when the flashback data archive feature is used.
Parallel Query Slave	Q*nnn*	Carries out portions of a larger overall query when Oracle's Parallel Query feature is used.
Dispatcher	D*nnn*	Assigns user's database requests to a queue where they are then serviced by shared server processes when Oracle's Shared Server feature is used. See Chapter 11 for details on using shared servers.
Shared Server	S*nnn*	Server processes that are shared among several users when Oracle's Shared Server feature is used. See Chapter 11 for details on using shared servers.

TABLE 8.5 Optional Oracle Background Processes *(continued)*

Process Name	OS Process	Description
Memory Manager	MMAN	Manages the size of each individual SGA component when Oracle's Automatic Shared Memory Management feature is used. See Chapter 14 for more information on using this feature.
Memory Monitor	MMON	Gathers and analyzes statistics used by the Automatic Workload Repository feature. See Chapter 14 for more information on using this feature.
Memory Monitor Light	MMNL	Gathers and analyzes statistics used by the Automatic Workload Repository feature. See Chapter 14 for more information on using this feature.
Recovery Writer	RVWR	Writes recovery information to disk when Oracle's Flashback Database feature is used. See Chapter 15, "Implementing Database Backups," for details on how to use the Flashback Database feature.
Change Tracking Writer	CTWR	Keeps track of which database blocks have changed when Oracle's incremental Recovery Manager feature is used. See Chapter 15 for details on using Recovery Manager to perform backups.

On Unix systems, you can view these background processes from the operating system using the ps command, as shown here:

```
$ ps -ef | grep 11GR11
oracle    2517    1  0 20:22 ?        00:00:00 ora_j000_11GR11
oracle    3436    1  0 Jun06 ?        00:00:01 ora_pmon_11GR11
oracle    3438    1  0 Jun06 ?        00:00:00 ora_vktm_11GR11
oracle    3442    1  0 Jun06 ?        00:00:00 ora_diag_11GR11
oracle    3444    1  0 Jun06 ?        00:00:00 ora_dbrm_11GR11
oracle    3446    1  0 Jun06 ?        00:00:01 ora_psp0_11GR11
oracle    3450    1  0 Jun06 ?        00:00:24 ora_dia0_11GR11
oracle    3452    1  0 Jun06 ?        00:00:00 ora_mman_11GR11
oracle    3454    1  0 Jun06 ?        00:00:03 ora_dbw0_11GR11
oracle    3456    1  0 Jun06 ?        00:00:10 ora_lgwr_11GR11
oracle    3458    1  0 Jun06 ?        00:00:02 ora_ckpt_11GR11
oracle    3460    1  0 Jun06 ?        00:00:05 ora_smon_11GR11
oracle    3462    1  0 Jun06 ?        00:00:00 ora_reco_11GR11
oracle    3464    1  0 Jun06 ?        00:00:05 ora_mmon_11GR11
oracle    3466    1  0 Jun06 ?        00:00:01 ora_mmnl_11GR11
oracle    3468    1  0 Jun06 ?        00:00:00 ora_d000_11GR11
```

```
oracle    3470    1   0 Jun06 ?       00:00:00 ora_s000_11GR11
oracle    3482    1   0 Jun06 ?       00:00:01 ora_arc0_11GR11
oracle    3484    1   0 Jun06 ?       00:00:01 ora_arc1_11GR11
oracle    3486    1   0 Jun06 ?       00:00:00 ora_arc2_11GR11
oracle    3488    1   0 Jun06 ?       00:00:00 ora_arc3_11GR11
oracle    3490    1   0 Jun06 ?       00:00:00 ora_smco_11GR11
oracle    3492    1   0 Jun06 ?       00:00:00 ora_fbda_11GR11
oracle    3494    1   0 Jun06 ?       00:00:00 ora_qmnc_11GR11
oracle    3510    1   0 Jun06 ?       00:00:00 ora_q000_11GR11
oracle    3512    1   0 Jun06 ?       00:00:00 ora_q001_11GR11
oracle    3744    1   0 Jun06 ?       00:00:02 ora_cjq0_11GR11
oracle    9616    1   0 14:01 ?       00:00:00 ora_w000_11GR11
$
```

This output shows that several background processes are running on the Linux server for the 11GR11 database.

The dynamic view V$BGPROCESS shows the background processes available. The following query lists multiple child processes only once to save space. To see all the processes, remove the WHERE clause and execute.

```
SQL> SELECT name, description
  2  FROM v$bgprocess
  3  WHERE SUBSTR(name, 4, 1) NOT BETWEEN '1' AND '9'
  4  AND SUBSTR(name, 4, 1) NOT BETWEEN 'a' AND 'z'
  5  ORDER BY name;


NAME  DESCRIPTION
----- -------------------------------------------------
ACMS  Atomic Controlfile to Memory Server
ARB0  ASM Rebalance 0
ARBA  ASM Rebalance 10
ARC0  Archival Process 0
ASMB  ASM Background
CJQ0  Job Queue Coordinator
CKPT  checkpoint
CTWR  Change Tracking Writer
DBRM  Resource Manager process
DBW0  db writer process 0
DIA0  diagnosibility process 0
DIAG  diagnosibility process
DMON  DG Broker Monitor Process
DSKM  slave DiSKMon process
EMNC  EMON Coordinator
```

```
FBDA   Flashback Data Archiver Process
FMON   File Mapping Monitor Process
FSFP   Data Guard Broker FSFO Pinger
GMON   diskgroup monitor
GTX0   Global Txn process 0
INSV   Data Guard Broker INstance SlaVe Process
KATE   Konductor of ASM Temporary Errands
LCK0   Lock Process 0
LGWR   Redo etc.
LMD0   global enqueue service daemon 0
LMON   global enqueue service monitor
LMS0   global cache service process 0
LNS0   Network Server 0
LSP0   Logical Standby
MARK   mark AU for resync koordinator
MMAN   Memory Manager
MMNL   Manageability Monitor Process 2
MMON   Manageability Monitor Process
MRP0   Managed Standby Recovery
NSV0   Data Guard Broker NetSlave Process 0
OFSC   OFS CSS
PING   interconnect latency measurement
PMON   process cleanup
PSP0   process spawner 0
QMNC   AQ Coordinator
RBAL   ASM Rebalance master
RCBG   Result Cache: Background
RECO   distributed recovery
RMS0   rac management server
RSM0   Data Guard Broker Resource Guard Process 0
RSMN   Remote Slave Monitor
RVWR   Recovery Writer
SMCO   Space Manager Process
SMON   System Monitor Process
VBG0   Volume BG 0
VDBG   Volume Driver BG
VKTM   Virtual Keeper of TiMe process

52 rows selected.
SQL>
```

Knowing the purpose of the required background processes is a must for the OCA certification exam. Let's discuss them in the next subsections.

Database Writer (DBW*n*)

The purpose of the *database writer process* (DBW*n*) is to write the contents of the dirty buffers to the data files. By default, Oracle starts one database writer process when the instance starts. For multiuser and busy systems, you can have up to 20 database writer processes (DBW0-9, DBWa-j) to improve performance. The parameter DB_WRITER_PROCESSES determines the additional number of database writer processes to be started. Having more DBW*n* processes than the number of CPUs is normally not beneficial.

The DBW*n* process writes the modified buffer blocks to disk, so more free buffers are available in the buffer cache. Writes are always performed in bulk to reduce disk contention; the number of blocks written in each I/O is operating system-dependent.

When Does Database Writer Write?

The DBW*n* background process writes to the data files whenever one of the following events occurs:

- A user's server process has searched too long for a free buffer when reading a buffer into the buffer cache.

- The number of modified and committed, but unwritten, buffers in the database buffer cache is too large.

- At a database checkpoint event. See Chapter 15 for information on checkpoints.

- The instance is shut down using any method other than a shutdown abort.

- A tablespace is placed into backup mode.

- A tablespace is taken offline to make it unavailable or is changed to READ ONLY.

- A segment is dropped.

Checkpoint (CKPT)

A *checkpoint* is when the DBW*n* process writes all the dirty buffers to the data files. When a checkpoint occurs, Oracle must update the headers of all data files as well as the control file to record the checkpoint. This update is done by the *checkpoint process* (CKPT); the DBW*n* process writes the actual data blocks to the data files.

Checkpoints help reduce the time required for instance recovery. If checkpoints occur too frequently, disk contention becomes a problem with the data file updates. If checkpoints occur too infrequently, the time required to recover a failed database instance can be significantly longer. Checkpoints occur automatically when an online redo log file is full (a log switch happens).

Log Writer (LGWR)

The *log writer process* (LGWR) writes the blocks in the redo log buffer of the SGA to the online redo log files. When the LGWR writes log buffers to disk, Oracle server processes can write new entries in the redo log buffer. LGWR writes the entries to the disk fast enough to ensure that room is available for the server process to write redo entries.

If the redo log files are multiplexed, LGWR writes simultaneously to all the members of the redo log group. Even if one of the log files in the group is damaged, LGWR writes the redo information to the available files. LGWR writes to the redo log files sequentially so that transactions can be applied in order in the event of a failure.

When Does Log Writer Write?

The LGWR background process writes to the current redo log group under any of the following conditions:

- Every three seconds

- When a user commits a transaction

- When the redo log buffer is a third full

- When the redo log buffer contains 1MB worth of redo information

- Whenever a database checkpoint occurs

As soon as a transaction commits, the information is written to redo log files. By writing the committed transaction immediately to the redo log files, the change to the database is never lost. Even if the database crashes, committed changes can be recovered from the online redo log files and applied to the data files.

Process Monitor (PMON)

The *process monitor process* (PMON) cleans up failed user processes and frees up all the resources used by the failed process. It resets the status of the active transaction table and removes the process ID from the list of active processes. It reclaims all the resources held by the user and releases all locks on tables and rows held by the user. PMON wakes up periodically to check whether it is needed. Other processes can call PMON if they detect a need for a PMON process.

PMON also checks on some optional background processes and restarts them if any have stopped.

System Monitor (SMON)

The *system monitor process* (SMON) performs instance or crash recovery at database startup by using the online redo log files. SMON is also responsible for cleaning up temporary segments in the tablespaces that are no longer used and for coalescing the contiguous free space in the dictionary-managed tablespaces. If any dead transactions were skipped during instance recovery because of file-read or offline errors, SMON recovers them when the tablespace or data file is brought back online. SMON wakes up regularly to check whether it is needed. Other processes can call SMON if they detect a need for an SMON process.

 In Windows environments, a Windows service called `OracleServiceInstanceName` is also associated with each instance. This service must be started in order to start up the instance in Windows environments.

Oracle Storage Structures

An instance is a memory structure, but the Oracle database consists of a set of physical files that reside on the host server's disk drives. The physical storage structures include three types of files. These files are called *control files*, *data files*, and *redo log files*. The additional physical files that are associated with the Oracle Database but are not technically part of the database are as follows: the *password file*, the *parameter file*, and any *archived redo log files*. The Oracle Net configuration files are also required for connectivity to the Oracle database. Table 8.6 summarizes the role that each of these files plays in the database architecture.

TABLE 8.6 Oracle Physical Files

File Type	Information Contained in Files
Control	Locations of other physical files, database name, database block size, database character set, and recovery information. These files are required to open the database.
Data	All application data and internal metadata.
Redo log	Record of all changes made to the database; used for instance recovery.
Parameter (pfile or spfile)	Configuration parameters for the SGA, optional Oracle features, and background processes.
Archived redo log	Copy of the contents of online redo logs, used for database recovery.
Password	Optional file used to store names of users who have been granted the SYSDBA and SYSOPER privileges. See Chapter 12, "Implementing Security and Auditing," for details on SYSDBA and SYSOPER privileges.
Oracle Net	Entries that configure the database listener and client-to-database connectivity. See Chapter 11 for details.

The three files that make up a database—the control file, the data file, and the redo log file—are described in the following sections.

Control Files

Control files are critical components of the database because they store important information that is not available anywhere else. This information includes the following:

- The name of the database
- Database-creation timestamp
- The names, locations, and sizes of the data files and redo log files
- Tablespace information
- Redo log information used to recover the database in the case of a disk failure or user error
- Archived log information
- RMAN backup information
- Checkpoint information

The control files are created when the database is created in the locations specified in the control_files parameter in the parameter file. Because a loss of the control files negatively impacts the ability to recover the database, most production databases multiplex their control files to multiple locations. Oracle uses the CKPT background process to automatically update each of these files as needed, keeping the contents of all copies of the control synchronized. You can use the dynamic performance view V$CONTROLFILE to display the names and locations of all the database's control files. A sample query on V$CONTROLFILE is shown here:

```
SQL> SELECT name FROM v$controlfile;


NAME
--------------------------------------------
/u02/oradata/PROD/control01.ctl
/u03/oradata/PROD/control02.ctl
/u05/oradata/PROD/control03.ctl


SQL>
```

This query shows that the database has three control files, called control01.ctl, control02.ctl, and control03.ctl, which are stored in the directories /u02/oradata/PROD/, /u03/oradata/PROD/, and /u05/oradata/PROD/, respectively. The control files can be stored in any directory; /u02, /u03, and /u05 used in the example shows that they are physically stored on different disks. You can also monitor control files using EM Database Control (on the Server tab, choose Control Files under Storage, as shown in Figure 8.9).

Control files are usually the smallest files in the database, generally between 1MB and 5MB in size. However, they can be larger depending on the PFILE/SPFILE setting for CONTROLFILE_RECORD_KEEP_TIME when the Recovery Manager feature is used.

FIGURE 8.9   EM Database Control showing control files

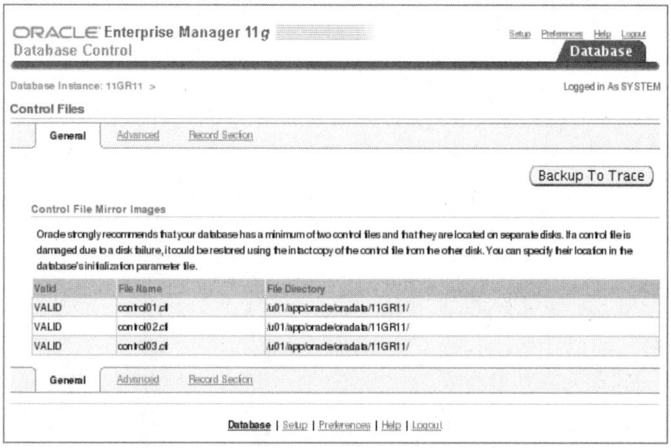

In the database, the control files keep track of the names, locations, and sizes of the database data files. Data files, and their relationship to another database structure called a *tablespace*, are examined in the next section.

Data Files

Data files are the physical files that actually store the data that has been inserted into each table in the database. The size of the data files is directly related to the amount of table data that they store. Data files are the physical structure behind another database storage area called a *tablespace*. A tablespace is a logical storage area within the database. Tablespaces group logically related segments. For example, all the tables for the Accounts Receivable application might be stored together in a tablespace called AR_TAB, and the indexes on these tables might be stored in a tablespace called AR_IDX.

By default, every Oracle 11*g* database must have at least three tablespaces. Table 8.7 describes these tablespaces.

TABLE 8.7   Required Tablespaces in Oracle 11*g*

Tablespace Name	Description
SYSTEM	Stores the data dictionary tables and PL/SQL code.
SYSAUX	Stores segments used for database options such as the Automatic Workload Repository, Online Analytical Processing (OLAP), and Spatial.
TEMP	Used for performing large sort operations. TEMP is required when the SYSTEM tablespace is created as a locally managed tablespace; otherwise, it is optional. See Chapter 10, "Allocating Database Storage and Creating Schema Objects," for details.

In addition to these three required tablespaces, most databases have tablespaces for storing other database segments such as undo and application data. Many production databases often have many more tablespaces for storing application segments. Either you or the application vendor determines the total number and names of these tablespaces. Tablespaces are discussed in detail in Chapter 10.

For each tablespace in the database, there must be at least one data file. Some tablespaces may be composed of several data files for management or performance reasons. The data dictionary view `DBA_DATA_FILES` shows the data files associated with each tablespace in the database. The following SQL statement shows a sample query on the `DBA_DATA_FILES` data dictionary view:

```
SQL> SELECT tablespace_name, file_name
  2  FROM dba_data_files
  3  ORDER BY tablespace_name;


TABLESPACE_N FILE_NAME
------------ --------------------------------------------
APPL_DATA    /u01/app/oracle/oradata/11GR11/appl_data01.dbf
APPL_DATA    /u01/app/oracle/oradata/11GR11/appl_data02.dbf
EXAMPLE      /u01/app/oracle/oradata/11GR11/example01.dbf
SYSAUX       /u01/app/oracle/oradata/11GR11/sysaux01.dbf
SYSTEM       /u01/app/oracle/oradata/11GR11/system01.dbf
UNDOTBS1     /u01/app/oracle/oradata/11GR11/undotbs01.dbf
USERS        /u01/app/oracle/oradata/11GR11/users01.dbf

7 rows selected.
SQL>
```

The output shows that the `APPL_DATA` tablespace is comprised of two data files; all other tablespaces have one data file. You can also monitor data files using EM, as shown in Figure 8.10.

Data files are usually the largest files in the database, ranging from megabytes to gigabytes or terabytes in size.

When a user performs a SQL operation on a table, the user's server process copies the affected data from the data files into the database buffer cache in the SGA. If the user has performed a committed transaction that modifies that data, the database writer process (DBW*n*) ultimately writes the modified data back to the data files.

FIGURE 8.10   EM Database Control showing data files

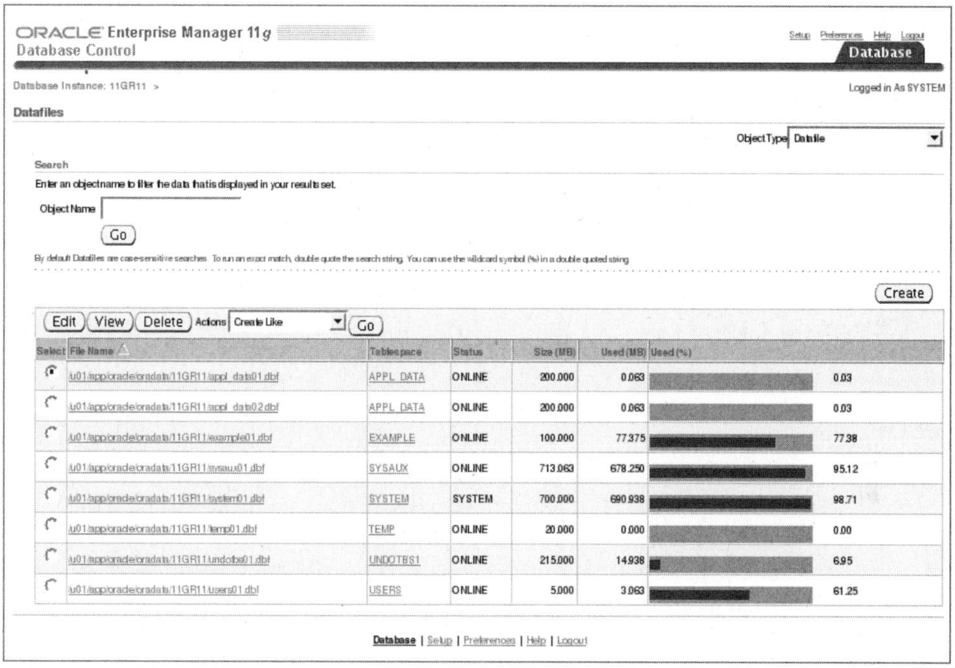

Redo Log Files

Whenever a user performs a transaction in the database, the information needed to reproduce this transaction in the event of a database failure is written to the redo log files and the user does not get a confirmation of the COMMIT until the transaction is successfully written to the redo log files.

Because of the important role that redo logs play in Oracle's recovery mechanism, they are usually multiplexed. This means that each redo log contains one or more copies of itself in case one of the copies becomes corrupt or is lost because of a hardware failure. Collectively, these sets of redo logs are referred to as *redo log groups*. Each multiplexed file within the group is called a *redo log group member*. Oracle automatically writes to all members of the redo log group to keep the files in sync. Each redo log group must be composed of one or more members. Each database must have a minimum of two redo log groups because redo logs are used in a circular fashion.

You can use the V$LOGFILE dynamic performance view to view the names of the redo log groups and the names and locations of their members, as shown here:

```
SQL> SELECT group#, member
  2  FROM v$logfile
  3  ORDER BY group#;
```

```
GROUP# MEMBER
---------- --------------------------------------------
         1 /u01/app/oracle/oradata/11GR11/redo01.log
         1 /u02/app/oracle/oradata/11GR11/redo01.log
         2 /u02/app/oracle/oradata/11GR11/redo02.log
         2 /u01/app/oracle/oradata/11GR11/redo02.log
         3 /u02/app/oracle/oradata/11GR11/redo03.log
         3 /u01/app/oracle/oradata/11GR11/redo03.log
```

6 rows selected.
SQL>

This output shows that the database has a total of three redo log groups and that each group has two members. Each of the members is located in a separate directory on the server's disk drives so that the loss of a single disk drive will not cause the loss of the recovery information stored in the redo logs. You can also monitor redo logs using EM Database Control, as shown in Figure 8.11.

FIGURE 8.11   EM Database Control showing redo logs

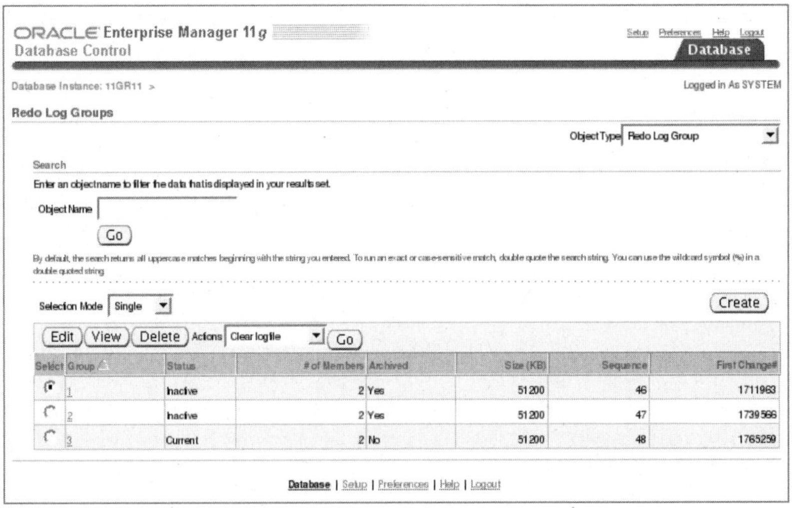

When a user performs a DML activity on the database, the recovery information for this transaction is written to the redo log buffer by the user's server process. LGWR eventually writes this recovery information to the active redo log group until that log group is filled. Once the current log fills with transaction information, LGWR switches to the next redo log until that log group fills with transaction information, and so on, until all available redo logs are used. When the last redo log is used, LGWR wraps around and starts using the first redo log again. As shown in the following query, you can use the V$LOG dynamic the first redo log again. As shown in the following query, you can use the V$LOG dynamic performance view to display which redo log group is currently active and being written to by LGWR:

```
SQL> SELECT group#, members, status
  2  FROM v$log
  3  ORDER BY group#;

   GROUP#    MEMBERS STATUS
---------- ---------- ----------------
        1          2 CURRENT
        2          2 INACTIVE
        3          2 INACTIVE
```

This output shows that redo log group number 1 is currently active and being written to by LGWR. Once redo log group 3 is full, LGWR switches to redo log group 1.

When LGWR wraps around from the last redo log group back to the first redo log group, any recovery information previously stored in the first redo log group is overwritten and therefore no longer available for recovery purposes. However, if the database is operating in *archive log mode*, the contents of these previously used logs are copied to a secondary location before the log is reused by LGWR. If this archiving feature is enabled, it is the job of the ARC*n* background process described in the previous section to copy the contents of the redo log to the archive location. These copies of old redo log entries are called *archive logs*. Figure 8.12 shows this process graphically.

FIGURE 8.12   How ARC*n* copies redo log entries to disk

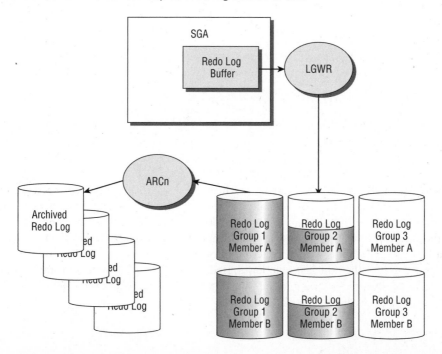

In Figure 8.12, the first redo log group has been filled, and LGWR has moved on to redo log group 2. As soon as LGWR switches from redo log group 1 to redo log group 2, the ARC*n* process starts copying the contents of redo log group 1 to the archive log file location. Once the first redo log group is safely archived, LGWR is free to wrap around and reuse the first redo log group once redo log group 3 is filled.

> Nearly all production databases run in archive-log mode because they need to be able to redo all transactions since the last backup in the event of a hardware failure or user error that damages the database.

A database can have multiple archive processes and multiple archive destinations. I will discuss more about archiving and how the archived redo logs are used for database recovery in Chapter 15.

> If LGWR needs to write to the redo log group that ARC*n* is trying to copy but cannot because the destination is full, the database hangs until space is cleared on the drive.

The Logical Structure

In the previous section, you saw how the Oracle database is configured physically. The obvious question is where and how your table is stored in a database. Let's now try to relate the physical storage to the logical structures you know, such as tables and indexes.

Oracle logically divides the database into smaller units to manage, store, and retrieve data efficiently. The following paragraphs give you an overview of the logical structures:

Tablespaces The database is logically divided into smaller units at the highest level, called *tablespaces*. A tablespace has a direct relation to the physical structure—a data file can belong to one and only one tablespace. A tablespace could have more than one data file associated with it.

A tablespace commonly groups related logical structures together. For example, you might group data specific to an application in a tablespace. This will ease the management of the application from the DBA's point of view. This logical division helps administer a portion of the database without affecting the rest of it. Each Oracle 11*g* database must have at least three tablespaces: SYSTEM, SYSAUX, and TEMP.

Tablespaces are discussed in detail in Chapter 10.

Blocks A *block* is the smallest unit of storage in Oracle. A block is usually a multiple of the operating-system block size. A data block corresponds to a specific number of bytes of storage space. The block size is based on the parameter DB_BLOCK_SIZE and determined when the database is created.

Extents   An *extent* is the next level of logical grouping. It is a grouping of contiguous blocks, allocated in one chunk.

Segments   A *segment* is a set of extents allocated for logical structures such as tables, indexes, clusters, table partitions, materialized views, and so on. Whenever you create a logical structure that stores data, Oracle allocates a segment, which contains at least one extent, which in turn has at least one block. A segment can be associated to only one tablespace.

Figure 8.13 shows the relationship between data files, tablespaces, segments, extents, and blocks.

FIGURE 8.13   Logical database structure

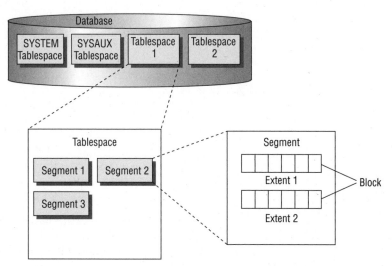

A schema is a logical structure that groups the database objects. A schema is not directly related to a tablespace or to any other logical storage structure. The objects that belong to a schema can reside in different tablespaces, and a tablespace can have objects that belong to multiple schemas. Schema objects include structures such as tables, indexes, synonyms, procedures, triggers, database links, so on.

The next section talks about how to install and configure the Oracle 11g software on your server so that you can then create a database. Creating a database is described in detail in Chapter 9, "Creating an Oracle 11g Database."

Installing Oracle 11*g*

One of your duties as an Oracle DBA is to install and configure the Oracle 11*g* software on the server so that a database can be created to store application data. This section discusses each of the steps that you must perform in order to successfully install Oracle 11*g*.

> The examples in this section are for a Linux server, but most of the concepts apply equally to Windows platforms. Any significant differences between Linux and Windows are noted.

Review the Documentation

Before beginning an installation of Oracle 11*g*, you need to review several documents so that you completely understand the installation requirements. These documents include the following:

- The installation guide for your operating system
- The general release notes for the version of Oracle you are installing
- The operating system–specific release notes for the version of Oracle you are installing
- Any "quick start" installation guides

Before you begin, review each of these documents so that you are thoroughly familiar with the install process and any known associated issues.

> All these documents are available on Oracle's Technology Network website located at http://otn.oracle.com/index.html.

Review the System Requirements

The next task is to review your server-hardware specifications to see whether they meet or exceed the specifications in the install documentation. Minimally, this means you must confirm that your server meets the installation requirements in these four areas:

- The operating system is of the proper release level.
- The server has adequate memory to perform the install and run an instance.
- The server has adequate CPU resources to perform the install and run an instance.
- The server has adequate disk storage space to perform the install and run a database.

Table 8.8 shows the recommended minimum hardware requirements for an Oracle 11*g* installation.

TABLE 8.8   Recommended Minimum Hardware Requirements for Oracle 11*g*

Hardware Component	Recommended Requirement
Memory	1GB.
Swap space	1.5GB or equal to the amount of RAM.
Temp space	200MB of free space in the /tmp directory on Unix systems.
Free disk space	1.5GB to 3.5GB of disk space is required for the base Oracle 11*g* installation.

The Oracle Universal Installer, which is described in the subsequent section "Using the Oracle Universal Installer," will perform a quick system check prior to starting an installation to see whether your system meets the specific requirements for your operating system. If your system does not meet the minimum requirements, the installer returns an error and aborts.

On Unix systems, you must examine one critical system requirement before installation: Unix kernel parameters. Unix kernel parameters are used to configure the Unix operating-system settings for operating system–level operations that impact Oracle-related activities such as the following:

- The maximum size allowed for a sharable memory segment on the server, which can impact the SGA size
- The maximum number of files that can be open on the server at one time, which impacts the total number of users and files in the database
- The number of processes that can run concurrently on the server, which impacts the number of users and the ability to use some optional features

The systems administrator usually makes Unix kernel changes, which may require a server reboot in order to take effect. The install guide and/or release notes provide details on the appropriate kernel setting for your operating system. In addition to kernel settings, the system administrator may have to configure the server's disk storage system and backup hardware before installing the Oracle software.

Plan Your Install

Once you review the documentation and system requirements, you are ready to begin planning your installation. This is the last step before actually running the Oracle Universal Installer.

One way to simplify installation planning is to adopt the Optimal Flexible Architecture (OFA) model that Oracle recommends as a best-practice methodology for managing Oracle installations in Unix environments (and to a lesser extent, Windows environments). Cary Millsap designed the OFA model to produce database installations that are easier to manage, upgrade, and back up, while at the same time minimizing problems associated with database growth. The OFA model addresses four areas:

- Naming conventions for Unix file systems and mount points

- Naming conventions for directory paths

- Naming conventions for database files

- Standardized locations for Oracle-related files

In addition to using the OFA model, planning your install also means answering the following questions:

- Which operating-system user will own the installed Oracle software?

- On which disk drive and directory will the Oracle software be installed?

- What directory structure will be used to store the Oracle software, its related configuration files, and the database itself?

- How should the database files be laid out so that the maximum performance benefits will be realized?

- How should the database files be laid out so that the maximum recoverability benefits will be realized?

Creating the Oracle User Account

On Unix systems, every file is owned by an operating-system user account. Therefore, before you can install the Oracle software, you must create a Unix user account that will own the Oracle binaries. The username for this account can be anything, but common Oracle usernames include `oracle`, `ora11g`, and `ora111`. Each Unix user is also in one or more operating-system groups. Create a new operating-system group for the Oracle Unix user. This group is usually called `dba`, and you will be prompted for it later during the installation.

On Windows systems, you can choose an account that has administrative privileges on the server.

Naming Volumes and Mount Points

Unless Oracle's Automatic Storage Management feature or raw devices are used, almost all files on a Unix server are stored on logical storage areas called *volumes* that are attached, or *mounted*, to directories, or *mount points*, by the Unix system administrator. The OFA model suggests that these mount points be given a name that consists of a combination of a character and numeric values. Common OFA mount points for Unix systems include the following:

- /u01
- /mnt01
- /du01
- /d01

Notice that the naming convention for these mount points is generic. The mount point's name has no relationship to what type of file it will ultimately hold. The OFA model recommends this generic naming convention because it provides the greatest flexibility for future management of the server's file systems.

 The concept of mount points does not apply directly to Windows environments. Windows environments assign a standard Windows drive letter (for example, C:, D:) to each volume.

Creating OFA Directory Paths

The OFA model prescribes that the directory structures under the mount points use a consistent and meaningful naming convention. In addition to this naming convention, the OFA model also assigns standard operating-system environment variable names to some of these directory paths as "nicknames" to aid in navigation and to ensure the portability of the directory structures in the event that they need to be moved to new file systems.

Table 8.9 shows the two operating-system environment variables used in the OFA model, along with the directories with which the variables are associated, for Unix systems.

TABLE 8.9   Comparison of Unix Directory Paths and Variables

Environment Variable	Directory Path	Description
$ORACLE_BASE	/u01/app/oracle	Top-level directory for Oracle software on the host server
$ORACLE_HOME	/u01/app/oracle/product/11.1.0/db_1	Directory into which the Oracle 11*g* software will be installed

Table 8.10 shows the variables and directories used in the OFA model for Windows systems.

TABLE 8.10   Comparison of Windows Directory Paths and Variables

Environment Variable	Directory Path	Description
%ORACLE_BASE%	D:\ORACLE	Top-level directory for Oracle soft-ware on the host server
%ORACLE_HOME%	D:\ORACLE\ORA111\DB_1	Directory into which the Oracle 11*g* software will be installed

These environment variables are used extensively when installing, patching, upgrading, and managing Oracle systems. Table 8.11 shows several examples of how these variables define the locations of other Oracle directories.

TABLE 8.11   Common Uses of ORACLE_BASE and ORACLE_HOME

Directory	Description
$ORACLE_HOME/dbs	Default location for pfiles and spfiles on Unix systems
%ORACLE_HOME%\database	Default location for pfiles and spfiles on Windows systems
$ORACLE_BASE/admin/PROD/pfile	Location of the pfile for a database called PROD on Unix systems
%ORACLE_BASE%\admin\PROD\pfile	Location of the pfile for a database called PROD on Windows systems
$ORACLE_HOME/network/admin	Default location for Oracle Net configuration files on Unix systems
%ORACLE_HOME%\network\admin	Default location for Oracle Net configuration files on Windows systems
$ORACLE_HOME/rdbms/admin	Location of many Oracle database-configuration scripts on Unix systems
%ORACLE_HOME%\rdbms\admin	Location of many database-configuration scripts on Windows systems

For Unix systems, Table 8.11 says $ORACLE_HOME/dbs is the default location for the pfile and spfile but then says that pfiles should be stored in $ORACLE_BASE/admin/<instance>/pfile. Windows systems are similar. This implies that the same file needs to be in two locations at the same time. You can accomplish this using two tricks. Which you use depends on your operating system.

The following examples use 11GR11 as the database (and instance) name. On Unix systems, you can create the pfile in the $ORACLE_BASE/admin/11GR11/pfile directory and then create a symbolic link in $ORACLE_HOME/dbs that points to the file in $ORACLE_BASE/admin/11GR11/pfile using this syntax:

```
ln -s $ORACLE_BASE/admin/11GR11/pfile/init11GR11.ora
    $ORACLE_HOME/dbs/init11GR11.ora
```

On Windows systems, you can create the pfile in the %ORACLE_BASE%\admin\11GR11\pfile directory and then put another pfile in %ORACLE_HOME%\dbs that contains a single entry that points to the other pfile in %ORACLE_BASE%\admin\11GR11\pfile like this:

```
ifile=D:\oracle\admin\11GR11\pfile\init11GR11.ora
```

Using these techniques allows you to put the initialization parameter files in their default locations under $ORACLE_HOME but also in their desired location under $ORACLE_BASE.

Why should the "real" copy of the pfiles be stored under $ORACLE_BASE instead of $ORACLE_HOME? Well, it is a good idea to keep only version-specific files under $ORACLE_HOME. That way, when you eventually uninstall the software from an old $ORACLE_HOME, you won't lose your carefully tailored initialization files.

In addition to $ORACLE_BASE and $ORACLE_HOME, a few other non-OFA-related operating-system environment variables on Unix and Windows systems are important to be aware of. These are described in Table 8.12.

TABLE 8.12   Common Non-OFA Environment Variables

Operating-System Variable	Description
$ORACLE_SID	Defines which instance a Unix user session should be connecting to on the server.
%ORACLE_SID%	Defines which instance a Windows user session should connect to on the server.
$TNS_ADMIN	Specifies where the Oracle Net configuration files are stored on Unix systems—if they are to be stored outside their default location of $ORACLE_HOME/network/admin.
%TNS_ADMIN%	Specifies where the Oracle Net configuration files are stored on Windows systems—if they are to be stored outside their default location of %ORACLE_HOME%\network\admin.

TABLE 8.12   Common Non-OFA Environment Variables *(continued)*

Operating-System Variable	Description
$TWO_TASK	Establishes a default Oracle Net connection string that will be used if none is specified by the user.
%LOCAL%	Establishes a default Oracle Net connection string that will be used if none is specified by the user.
$LD_LIBRARY_PATH	Specifies the locations of the Oracle shared object libraries. This variable usually points to $ORACLE_HOME/lib or $ORACLE_HOME/lib32 on Unix systems.
$PATH	Tells the operating system in which directories to look for executable files on Unix systems.
%PATH%	Tells the operating system in which directories to look for executable files on Windows systems.

There is no need to set any of these variables for an Oracle 11*g* install, except for ORACLE_BASE. These variables are important when you're ready to create a database.

For complete preinstallation checks and detailed commands to create Oracle software owner and groups on the Linux platform, please read the Oracle documentation's Oracle Database Installation Guide 11*g* Release 1 for Linux, specifically, Chapter 2, "Oracle Database Pre-installation Requirements." As mentioned earlier, all Oracle documentation is available at http://tahiti .oracle.com.

Using the Oracle Universal Installer

You use the Oracle Universal Installer (OUI) to install and configure the Oracle 11*g* software. The OUI is a Java-based application that provides the same installation look and feel no matter which operating system the install is being run on. The OUI process consists of seven primary operations:

- Mounting the CD and starting the OUI
- Performing preinstallation checks
- Responding to server-specific prompts for file locations, names, and so on
- Selecting the products you want to install

- Copying the files from the install media to $ORACLE_HOME
- Compiling the Oracle binaries
- Performing post-install operations using configuration assistants

Mounting the CD and Starting the OUI

To begin the install process, insert the Oracle 11*g* CD in the server. On some Unix systems, you may have to use the appropriate operating-system command to mount the CD in your server before it is accessible.

After mounting the CD, you may want to copy its contents to a staging directory so that you can install from there instead of from the CD. If you download software from the OTN, you don't need to mount the CD. You can start the install from the disk.

OUI installations on Unix systems must also set the X Windows DISPLAY environment variable; otherwise, the OUI will not appear.

Performing Preinstallation Checks

Start the OUI using the runInstaller.sh command, as shown in Figure 8.14.

FIGURE 8.14 Invoking Oracle 11*g* install

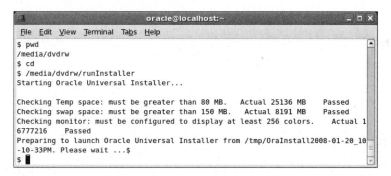

Notice that the output shows that the OUI checked the server's operating-system version, available RAM, temporary and swap space, and so on.

If needed, you can turn off the system verification that occurs prior to the installation by using the -ignoreSysPrereqs option of the runInstaller command.

Once the preinstallation tests are completed and passed, the OUI displays the initial OUI screen shown in Figure 8.15.

Choose the Oracle Database 11g option, and click the Next button on the OUI screen to proceed with the installation.

FIGURE 8.15   The initial OUI installation screen

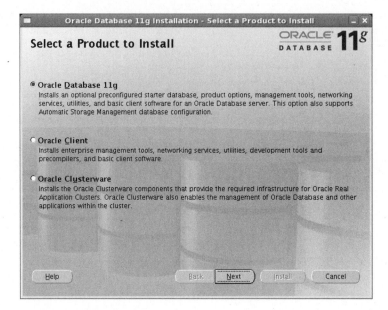

Responding to OUI Prompts

The next OUI screen, Select Installation Method, provides the option to perform a basic or advanced installation. In the basic installation, no more questions are asked, and the OUI takes all the default values to install the software. If you select the Create Starter Database check box and provide a name for the database, OUI will create a database along with the software install.

For this example, choose Advanced installation on this screen, as shown in Figure 8.16.

The next OUI screen, Specify Inventory Directory and Credentials, prompts you for two pieces of information:

- The location for the inventory files that the OUI uses to keep track of which Oracle products are installed on the server

- The name of the operating-system group of which the user doing the install is a member

  You can see both items in Figure 8.17.

FIGURE 8.16   Select Installation Method screen

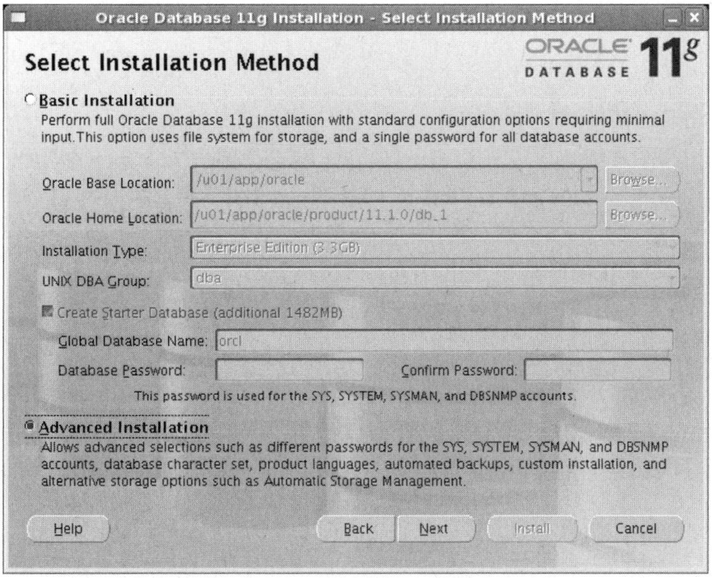

FIGURE 8.17   Specify Inventory Directory and Credentials screen

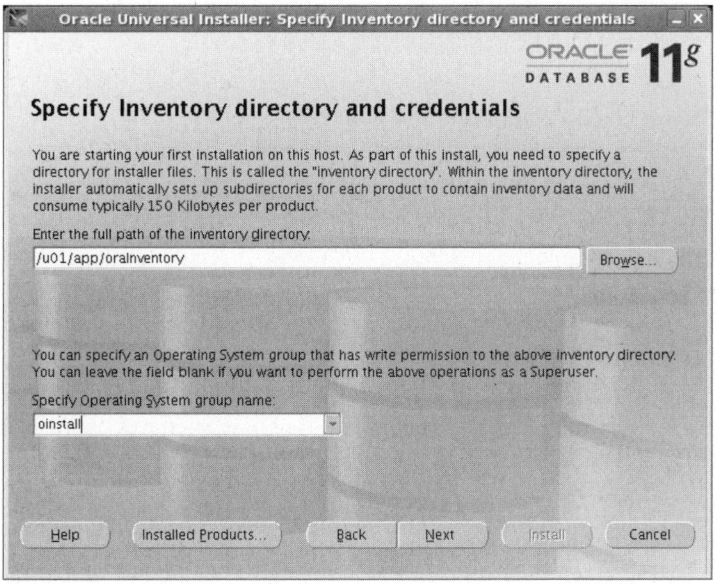

The value suggested for the oraInventory location, /u01/app/oraInventory, was selected based on the $ORACLE_BASE environment variable. The value suggested for the operating-system group, oinstall, is the Oracle default value. Because both settings are correct for our example environment, click the Next button to continue the installation.

Selecting Products to Install

The next screen, Select Installation Type, prompts you to select the type of installation to perform. In this example, I selected the Enterprise Edition option, as shown in Figure 8.18. Choose Enterprise Edition or Standard Edition based on the license you purchased. You may also choose Custom, if you want to pick and choose the products.

FIGURE 8.18 Select Installation Type screen

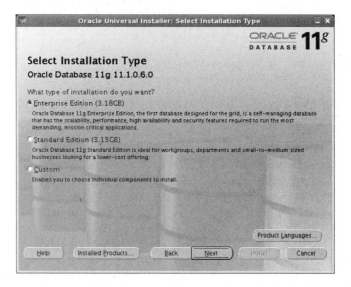

The next screen, Install Location, sets the software installation locations, as shown in Figure 8.19.

On the screen shown in Figure 8.19, the default values are populated based on the ORACLE_BASE variable. Click the Next button to open the next screen, which is shown in Figure 8.20.

The OUI goes through a second round of installation checks that confirm that the server's operating-system version and configuration are appropriate for the Enterprise Edition installation of Oracle 11*g*. If all the verification checks complete successfully, click the Next button to open the Select Configuration Option screen, as shown in Figure 8.21.

If these operating-system checks do not succeed, you must correct the areas that are failing the checks before continuing.

FIGURE 8.19   Install Location screen

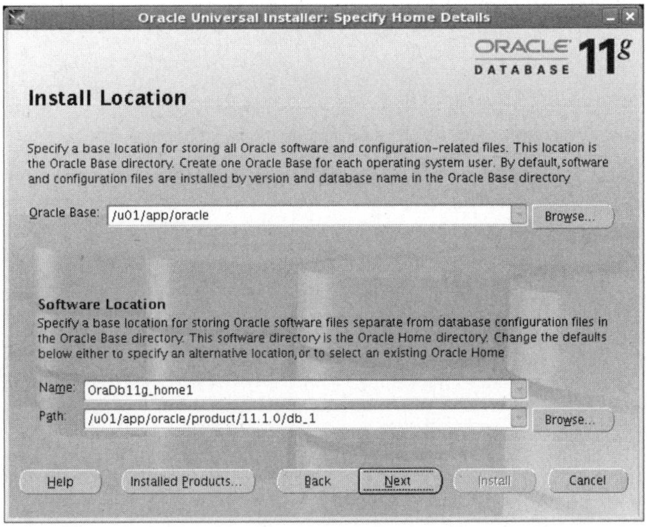

FIGURE 8.20   Prerequisite checks

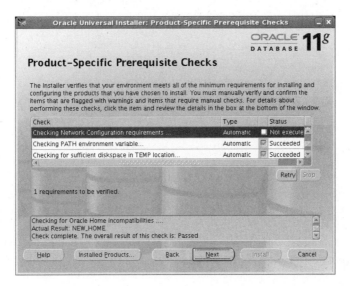

FIGURE 8.21   Select Configuration Option screen

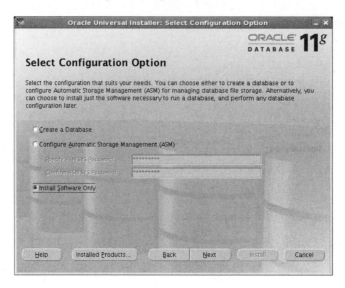

The next screen, Privileged Operating System Groups, asks whether you want to create a database following the installation process. Because creating a database is covered in Chapter 2, you'll skip this step for now. Choose the Install Software Only option, and then click Next to specify the privileged OS groups, as shown in Figure 8.22.

FIGURE 8.22   Privileged Operating System Groups screen

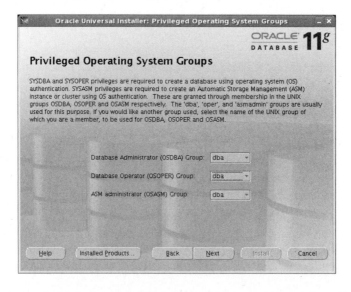

You can choose the defaults or specify specific OS groups for each function. Click Next to open the Summary screen, as shown in Figure 8.23.

FIGURE 8.23   The Summary screen

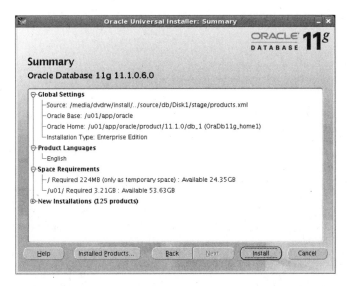

This screen summarizes all the options you selected and all the components that will be installed. If you need to make changes, click the Back button to modify your previous selections. If you are satisfied with your selections, click the Next button to start copying the Oracle binaries to the $ORACLE_HOME directory.

Copying and Compiling Files

The OUI displays status information while the installation and setup is in progress. Once the file-copy portion of the installation is complete, the OUI begins linking the binaries to create the executable files needed to make the Oracle 11*g* software run on the server. On Unix systems, after the linking process, you are prompted to execute configuration scripts as the superuser root from the Unix command line, as shown in Figure 8.24.

FIGURE 8.24   Running the script as root

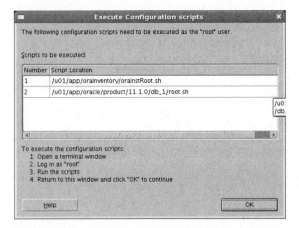

The orainstRoot.sh script creates the inventory location and necessary inventory directory. The following example shows this orainstRoot.sh script being executed from another session:

```
$ su -
Password:
# cd /u01/app/oraInventory
./orainstRoot.sh
Creating the Oracle inventory pointer file (/etc/oraInst.loc)
Changing permissions of /u01/app/oraInventory to 770.
Changing groupname of /u01/app/oraInventory to oinstall.
The execution of the script is complete
$
```

Running the script creates some directory structures that are used to support the Oracle installation and sets the proper file permissions on those directories as well as other files. Once the orainstRoot.sh script executes, click the Continue button to choose the installation type.

On Unix and Linux platforms, the orainstRoot.sh script creates a file named /etc/oraInst.loc, which has information about the Oracle Inventory location and the software installation owner name. The content of the /etc/oraInst.loc is as follows:

```
$ cat /etc/oraInst.loc
inventory_loc=/u01/app/oraInventory
inst_group=oinstall
$
```

The root.sh script should be executed as root. Executing the root.sh script copies some files to a location outside $ORACLE_HOME and sets the permissions on several files inside and outside $ORACLE_HOME. Once the root.sh script executes successfully, click OK to continue the installation.

One important file created by the root.sh script is the /etc/oratab file (the /var/opt/oracle/oratab file on Solaris). When databases are created on this server, this file will have information about the database and which oracle home directory is used by the database.

If you have multiple installations to perform, you can speed up the process and minimize errors by building an OUI response file. This text file contains all the necessary responses to the OUI prompts so that an unattended, silent install is possible.

Performing Postinstall Tasks

Once the `root.sh` script has completed, the OUI will perform some brief postinstallation configuration activities before displaying the End of Installation screen, as shown in Figure 8.25.

FIGURE 8.25 End of Installation screen

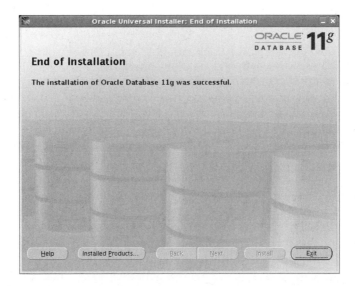

Click the Exit button and then the OK button on the pop-up screen to exit the OUI and return to the Unix prompt.

The OUI on Windows systems also offers a Basic Installation mode in which only a few installation questions are asked before the file copying begins. If you select the Advanced Installation mode, the prompts will closely follow those shown for Unix in this section.

Once the OUI is complete, you should have a completely installed and configured $ORACLE_HOME. You'll use this software to create your first database in Chapter 9, "Creating and Oracle 11*g* Database."

Summary

This chapter introduced you to the Oracle 11*g* database architecture and installing the Oracle 11*g* software. First I covered the Oracle database fundamentals and the Oracle database components, and then I showed how to create the database by installing the Oracle 11*g* software.

Most popular databases today are relational databases. Relational databases consist of data composed of a set of relational objects. Data is stored in tables as rows and columns. Oracle is a relational database. SQL is the language used to manage and administer Oracle databases. Several tools are available to administer an Oracle 11*g* database. The most common ones used by DBAs are SQL*Plus and Oracle Enterprise Manager. SQL Developer is a GUI tool that can be used to interact with the Oracle 11*g* database.

The Oracle 11*g* database architecture consists of three major components: memory, processes, and storage. A user process initiates a connection with the Oracle database and starts a server process. The server process is responsible for performing the tasks on the database. The memory structures and background processes together are an Oracle instance. The server process communicates with the memory structure known as the system global area. The SGA consists of a shared pool, database buffer cache, and redo log buffer. The shared pool also includes components such as a Java pool, large pool, result cache, and streams pool.

There are many types of background processes, each performing a specific job to maintain and manage the database instance. All databases have five background processes: database writer, checkpoint writer, log writer, process monitor, and system monitor. Depending on the configuration of the database, there may be other background processes such as archiver, ASM balancing, and so on.

The physical data structure consists of several files stored on disk. The most important file is the control file, which keeps track of several important pieces of information such as database name, names of data files and redo log files, backup information, so on. The CKPT process is responsible for keeping the control file updated. Redo log files contain information from the redo log buffer. The LGWR process is responsible for writing the redo log buffer contents to the redo log files. Oracle metadata and application data are stored in data files. The DBW*n* process is responsible for writing dirty blocks from the database buffer cache to the data files.

Looking at the logical structure of the database, a tablespace is the highest level of logical unit. A tablespace consists of several segments. A segment consists of one or more extents. An extent is a contiguous allocation of blocks. A block is the smallest unit of storage in an Oracle database.

Installing the Oracle 11*g* software is a relatively easy task once the preinstall checks and hardware requirements are met. Installing Oracle 11*g* is a joint task between the system administrator and DBA, because certain scripts need to be run as root on Linux/Unix platforms.

Exam Essentials

Describe the Oracle tools and what they are used for.   Know which tools are available for connecting to and interacting with an Oracle database. Understand how these tools differ from one another.

Understand the Oracle architecture components.   Be able to describe the logical and physical components of the Oracle architecture and the components that make up each. Know the relationship between segments, extents, database blocks, and operating-system blocks.

Know the background processes   Understand the Oracle 11g background processes and how they are used. The important ones to know are DBWn, SMON, CKPT, PMON, LGWR, ARCn, RBAL, and ASMB.

Identify the three types of database files that constitute the database.   Understand the purpose and key differences between the control files, data files, and redo log files.

Explain and categorize the SGA memory structures.   Identify the SGA areas along with the subcomponents contained within each of these areas.

Explain Oracle 11g system requirements.   Know what the requirements are for available server disk space and memory prior to performing an Oracle 11g installation.

Describe the Optimal Flexible Architecture.   Be able to explain the concepts associated with the OFA model and how to implement an OFA-compliant installation and database directory structure.

Describe the steps for installation and configuration.   Know how to set up the Oracle installation environment so that the OUI can be used to install and configure the Oracle 11g software.

Review Questions

1. What are the benefits of using the OFA standard for installing Oracle 11*g*? (Choose all that apply.)

   A. Helps eliminate fragmentation of free space in the SYSTEM tablespace

   B. Helps improve the database performance

   C. Facilitates routine administrative tasks such as software backups

   D. Helps avoid data-block corruption

2. You are trying to install Oracle 11*g* and the OUI prerequisite check failed. What should you do?

   A. Ignore the error, and proceed with installation.

   B. Cancel the installation, and try to install on a different server.

   C. Correct the underlying issue, and retry the installation.

   D. Cancel the installation, correct the underlying issue, and restart the installation.

3. When installing Oracle 11*g* on the Linux platform, which file is created by executing the `orainstRoot.sh` script as root?

   A. `/etc/oratab`

   B. `/etc/oraInst.loc`

   C. `$ORACLE_HOME/root.sh`

   D. None—the `orainstRoot.sh` script starts background processes required to start the OUI.

4. Which component is not part of the Oracle instance?

   A. System global area

   B. Process monitor

   C. Control file

   D. Shared pool

   E. None

5. Which background process guarantees that committed data is saved even when the changes have not been recorded in data files?

   A. DBW*n*

   B. PMON

   C. LGWR

   D. CKPT

   E. ARC*n*

6. You've just been hired as a DBA for a large company. During the interview process, you were shown the job description for the position. Which of the following tasks might have been included in this job description?

   A. Install and configure Oracle 11*g* software.

   B. Implement database installations according to OFA guidelines.

   C. Use OFA-compliant naming conventions for database files and directories.

   D. Any of the above may have been included on the DBA job description.

7. Which of the following best describes a RAC configuration?

   A. One database, multiple instances

   B. One instance, multiple databases

   C. Multiple databases on multiple servers

   D. Multiple shared server processes catering one database

8. Which component of the SGA contains the parsed SQL code?

   A. Database buffer cache

   B. Dictionary cache

   C. Library cache

   D. Parse cache

9. Which are the tasks accomplished by the SMON process? (Choose all that apply.)

   A. Performs recovery at instance startup

   B. Performs cleanup after a user session is terminated

   C. Starts any server process that stopped running

   D. Coalesces contiguous free space in dictionary-managed tablespaces

10. Choose the best statement from the options related to segments.

    A. A contiguous set of blocks constitutes a segment.

    B. A nonpartitioned table can have only one segment.

    C. A segment can belong to more than one tablespace.

    D. All of the above are true.

11. The Oracle Universal Installer prompts for which variable if not set?

    A. ORACLE_HOME

    B. ORACLE_SID

    C. ORACLE_BASE

    D. ORACLE_INSTALL_BASE

12. Which SGA component will you increase or configure so that RMAN backups are not using area from the shared pool?

   A. Java pool

   B. Streams pool

   C. Recovery pool

   D. Large pool

13. When a user session is terminated, which processes are responsible for cleaning up and releasing locks? (Choose all that apply.)

   A. DBW*n*

   B. LGWR

   C. MMON

   D. PMON

   E. SMON

14. The LRU algorithm is used to manage what part of the Oracle architecture?

   A. Users who log on to the database infrequently and may be candidates for being dropped

   B. The data file that stores the least amount of information and will need the least frequent backup

   C. The tables that users rarely access so that they can be moved to a less active tablespace

   D. The shared pool and database buffer cache portions of the SGA

15. Two structures make up an Oracle server: an instance and a database. Which of the following best describes the difference between an Oracle instance and a database?

   A. An instance consists of memory structures and processes, whereas a database is composed of physical files.

   B. An instance is used only during database creation; after that, the database is all that is needed.

   C. An instance is started whenever the demands on the database are high, but the database is used all the time.

   D. An instance is configured using a pfile, whereas a database is configured using an spfile.

16. Which of the following is the proper order of Oracle's storage hierarchy, from smallest to largest?

   A. Operating-system block, database block, segment, extent

   B. Operating-system block, database block, extent, segment

   C. Segment, extent, database block, operating-system block

   D. Segment, database block, extent, operating-system block

17. You've been asked to install Oracle 11*g* on a new Unix server. You're likely to ask the Unix system administrator to do all but which of the following for you in order to get the new server ready for Oracle?

    A. Modify the server's kernel parameters.

    B. Create a new Unix user to own the Oracle software.

    C. Create the mount points and directory structure using the OFA model.

    D. Determine which directory will be used for $ORACLE_HOME.

18. Oracle's OFA model specifies a naming convention for all but which of the following?

    A. Database name

    B. Mount points

    C. Directory paths

    D. Database filenames

19. The Oracle Universal Installer is started by executing which program?

    A. `emctl`

    B. `runInstaller`

    C. `ouistart`

    D. `isqlplusctl`

20. On Unix systems, the script `root.sh` must be executed during the installation process. What is the purpose of this script?

    A. It creates the root user in the database.

    B. It creates the root directory for the server.

    C. It grants root superuser privileges to the Oracle Unix account.

    D. It copies files and sets permissions on files outside $ORACLE_HOME.

Answers to Review Questions

1. A, C. The OFA standard helps in administering the Oracle software installation and all related Oracle files, such as alert logs and data files. OFA recommends that separate tablespaces be created to store application data; the SYSTEM tablespace should be used only for the data dictionary. By separating the software from database files, backups are made easy.

2. C. On the prerequisite check screen, you have the option to retry a failed test. So, you can fix the underlying issue and let OUI perform the test again to continue the installation.

3. B. If an Oracle installation is performed the first time on a server, the orainstRoot.sh script needs to be executed to create the /etc/oraInst.loc file. The oraInst.loc file specifies the Oracle inventory location.

4. C. Control file, data file, and redo log files are part of the Oracle database. The Oracle instance constitutes the memory structures and background processes.

5. C. The log writer (LGWR) process writes the redo log buffer information to the online redo log files. A commit operation is completed only after the redo buffer is written to online redo log files.

6. D. The tasks that a DBA performs encompass all these areas plus managing database storage, security, and availability.

7. A. With Real Application Clusters, multiple instances (known as *nodes*) can mount one database. One instance can be associated with only one database.

8. C. The shared SQL area is stored in the library cache in a shared pool and is shared between users. If a query is executed again before it is aged out of the library cache, Oracle will use the parsed code and execution plan from the library cache. The database buffer cache has the data blocks cached. The dictionary cache caches data dictionary information. There is no SGA component called the parse cache.

9. A, D. SMON is responsible for performing instance recovery using the online redo log files and for coalescing contiguous free space in tablespaces. The PMON is responsible for session cleanup and for freeing up all resources after a user session is terminated.

10. B. A table or index has a segment. A segment consists of one or more extents. A segment can belong to only one tablespace, but it can span across multiple data files.

11. C. To better conform to the OFA standard, the Oracle 11*g* OUI prompts for the ORACLE_BASE value if the ORACLE_BASE environment variable is not already set. The ORACLE_HOME value is derived from ORACLE_BASE, but you have the option to change the derived value.

12. D. The large pool is configured to have RMAN not use the shared pool; hence, the shared pool is totally dedicated to application space.

13. D. PMON is responsible for cleaning up failed user processes. It reclaims all the resources held by the user and releases all locks on tables and rows held by the user. No other process is involved in the session cleanup.

14. D. The LRU mechanism ensures that each user's server process can find free space in the shared pool and database buffer cache whenever they need it, but it also keeps frequently used objects cached in those memory areas.

15. A. The instance consists of the SGA and all the Oracle background processes. The database is composed of the control files, data files, and redo logs.

16. B. Multiple operating-system blocks make up database blocks, contiguous chunks of which make up extents. A segment consists of one or more extents.

17. D. Although the Unix system administrator is responsible for creating volume groups and mount points, the DBA generally decides where the Oracle binaries will be installed—the location derived from $ORACLE_BASE or designated by the $ORACLE_HOME environment variable.

18. A. The OFA model does not include any reference to naming conventions for the database or things inside the database, such as users, tables, or tablespaces.

19. B. The runInstaller executable performs a preinstall check of the operating system and hardware resources before starting the OUI graphical tool.

20. D. The root.sh script copies configuration files to directories outside $ORACLE_HOME and sets the permissions on those files accordingly.

Chapter

9

Creating an
Oracle 11*g* Database

**ORACLE DATABASE 11*g*:
ADMINISTRATION I EXAM OBJECTIVES
COVERED IN THIS CHAPTER:**

✓ **Creating an Oracle Database**

- Create a database by using the Database Configuration
  Assistant (DBCA)

✓ **Managing the Oracle Instance**

- Setting database initialization parameters

- Describe the stages of database startup and shutdown

- Using alert log and trace files

- Using data dictionary and dynamic performance views

As a DBA, you are responsible for creating and managing Oracle databases and services within your organization. Oracle provides a comprehensive and cohesive set of tools to help DBAs perform these tasks. It is important for you to understand these tools and how to use them properly.

Oracle has been using Java-based tools to manage the Oracle Database because Java gives the same look and feel for the tools across all platforms. In this chapter, I will cover how to use the Oracle Database Configuration Assistant tool, which creates and removes Oracle Databases, and how you can use templates to create databases.

After creating the database using DBCA, the database will be up and running. I will then cover how to shut down and restart the database for some configuration changes, apply patches, perform server maintenance, and so on. I'll describe the various database startup and shutdown options and explain the circumstances under which you use these options.

You will also learn more about the Oracle data dictionary, including how the dictionary is created, where it is created, and so on. Finally, I will cover initialization parameter files and discuss how you can use them to manage, locate, and view the database alert log.

Using DBCA to Create Oracle 11*g* Databases

The Oracle Database Configuration Assistant (DBCA) is a Java-based tool used to create Oracle Databases. If you've been a DBA for a few years, you probably remember the days of writing and maintaining scripts to create databases. Although it is still possible to manually create a database, the DBCA provides a flexible and robust environment in which you not only can create databases but also can generate templates containing the definitions of the databases created. This provides you with the ease of using a GUI-based interface with the flexibility of Oracle-generated XML-based templates that you can use to maintain a library of database definitions.

You can also use the DBCA to add options to a running database or to remove a database. In recent years, I have seen many diehard command-line DBAs switching to the DBCA tool to create databases, mainly because of its flexibility and ease of use.

You can also use the DBCA to create a database while the Oracle software is installed, or you can invoke the DBCA later to manually create a database. In the following sections, I will show you the steps necessary to create an Oracle Database using the DBCA tool.

Invoking the Database Configuration Assistant

You can invoke the DBCA from a command line in the Unix environment or as an application in a Windows 2000 environment. If you are using the Windows XP environment, choose Start ➢ All Programs ➢ Oracle *Oracle Home* ➢ Configuration and Migration Tools ➢ Database Configuration Assistant.

If you are in a Unix environment or would prefer to work from the command line in Windows, type **dbca** from the $ORACLE_HOME/bin location.

After you open the DBCA, you should see the Welcome screen, as shown in Figure 9.1. The Welcome screen will be different on a node that belongs to a RAC cluster, where you will have the option to create a single-instance database or a RAC database. Since RAC is not part of the certification exam, you will be using a node that is not part of the RAC.

FIGURE 9.1   DBCA Welcome screen

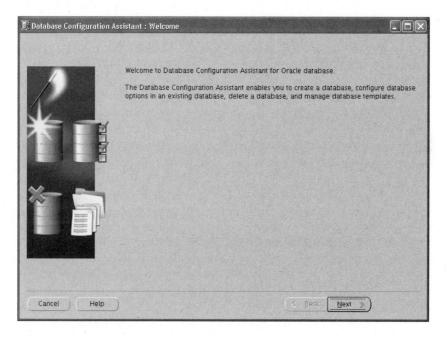

Click Next to open the Operations screen, as shown in Figure 9.2. You can create a database, configure database options, delete a database, manage templates, and configure automatic storage management.

FIGURE 9.2 DBCA Operations screen

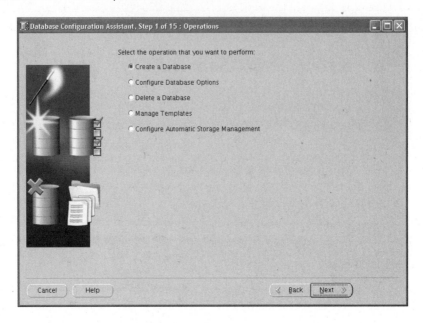

Table 9.1 lists and describes the DBCA database-management options.

TABLE 9.1 DBCA Database Management Options

Option	Description
Create a Database	Allows for the step-by-step creation of a database. The database can be created based on an existing template or customized for the specific needs of the organization.
Configure Database Options	Performs the necessary changes to move from a dedicated server to a shared server. You can also add database options that have not been previously configured for use with your database.
Delete a Database	Completely removes a database and all associated files.
Manage Templates	Manages database templates. The database templates are definitions of your database configuration saved in an XML file format on your local hard disk. You can choose from several predefined templates, or you can create customized templates.

TABLE 9.1   DBCA Database Management Options *(continued)*

Option	Description
Configure Automatic Storage Management (ASM)	Using ASM, Oracle manages the file placement and naming automatically. You provide a set of disks to the Oracle 11*g* database to use, and the provisioning and optimization are automatically handled by ASM. ASM is not covered in this book. When you're ready to take the OCP certification exam, refer to *OCP: Oracle Database 11g Administrator Certified Professional Study Guide* (Sybex, 2009).

Choose Create a Database, and click Next to open the Database Templates screen. In the coming sections, I will discuss database templates and the various screens in the DBCA to create a database.

Database Templates

The DBCA comes with two preconfigured database templates. These XML-based documents contain the information necessary to create the Oracle Database. You can choose one of these predefined templates, or you can build a custom database definition. The predefined database templates are Data Warehouse and General Purpose or Transaction Processing (see Figure 9.3). These templates were designed to create databases that are optimized for a particular type of workload. When you choose Custom Database, you will have more flexibility to create tablespaces and decide which components to install. The screens that are different when choosing the Custom Database option are identified later in the section.

FIGURE 9.3   DBCA Database Templates screen

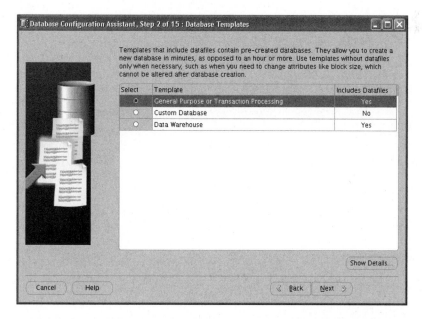

To display the configuration definitions for these preconfigured databases, click Show Details. Figure 9.4 shows the details of the General Purpose or Transaction Processing template. You have the option of saving the details as an HTML file using the button at the bottom-right corner. Before creating the database, you will get the summary information, and you will have the option to save the database create scripts as well as a similar HTML file with all the options and parameter values.

FIGURE 9.4   DBCA Templates Details screen

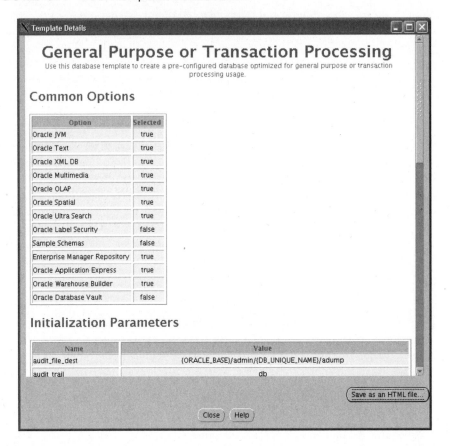

Table 9.2 displays information about what is contained in the template definition shown in Figure 9.4. When you scroll down, you'll see multiple sections on the page. Each section of the page gives further information about the template. For example, under the Common Options section, you will see a list of each of the database options that gets installed for the template definition you have chosen.

TABLE 9.2   Template Definition Details

Section	Description
Common Options	Displays which databases options will be installed
Initialization Parameters	Displays the common initialization parameters and their settings
Character Sets	Displays character sets to be used
Control Files	Displays filenames and locations for control files
Tablespaces	Displays names and types of tablespace
Datafiles	Displays filenames and size for each tablespace
Redo Log Groups	Displays group number and size

Choosing the Custom Database template option on the DBCA Database Templates screen gives you the fullest flexibility. For other templates, the database data files are pre-built with certain Oracle options. Also, the database block size cannot be changed from 8KB. A No value in the Includes Datafiles column in the Database Templates screen shows which templates are fully customizable.

After you have chosen the appropriate template to use, click Next. You will then be presented with the Database Identification screen.

Database Identification

The Database Identification screen (see Figure 9.5) allows you to enter the global database name and Oracle system identification name (commonly referred to as the *Oracle SID*).

The global database name is the fully qualified name of the database in the enterprise. It is composed of a database name and a database domain and takes the format *database_name.database_domain*; for example, `sales.company.com`.

In this example, the first part of the global database name, `OCA11G`, is the name of your database. Since I have not specified the domain name, there is no default domain name assigned. Normally, the database domain is the same as the network domain within the enterprise. A global database name must be unique within a given network domain. The database name can be up to eight characters and can include letters, numbers, and the special characters $, _, and #.

FIGURE 9.5 DBCA Database Identification screen

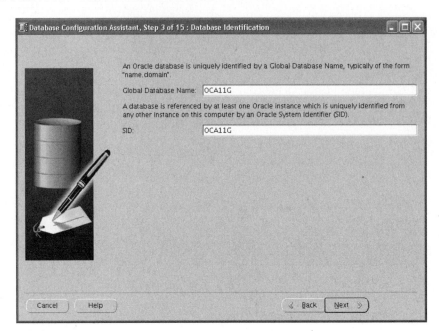

The Oracle SID is the name of the instance associated with the database. Usually this name is the same as the database name. For RAC databases where you have multiple instances associated with the database, the instance name is usually different from the database name. The Oracle SID can be a maximum of 12 characters and must be unique on the server. For example, you cannot have two Oracle SIDs called PROD on a single server.

Management Options

After you choose the database name, you can configure Enterprise Manager to monitor and manage your database using the DBCA Management Options screen (see Figure 9.6).

You can choose from two options: you can centrally manage all your databases from a single management console if the Management Agent is installed on the database server, or you can manage each database individually.

If the Oracle Management *Agent* is installed, the DBCA detects its presence and lists the name of the agent service. You can select this name if you want this existing agent to manage this database. Your new database then becomes one of the managed targets for the existing agent.

If you don't have an agent installed or are not doing centralized database management, you can still use Enterprise Manager to monitor and maintain the database. Choose the Use Database Control for Database Management radio button if you want to install Enterprise Manager and configure it locally.

FIGURE 9.6   DBCA Management Options screen

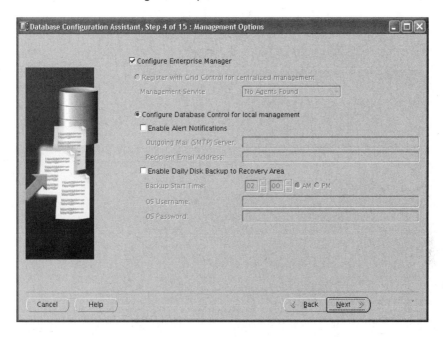

On the Management Options screen, you can also configure email notifications from Enterprise Manager. Email notifications are generated when certain database thresholds are reached, such as the maximum number of database sessions or low free space on a tablespace. After installing Enterprise Manager, you can configure notification of these database thresholds. To get these email notifications, you'll need the name of your SMTP mail server and the email address to which you want the email notifications sent.

Finally, using the Management Options screen, you can configure backups of your database. If you select Enable Daily Backup, Enterprise Manager backs up your database based on the start time you enter. The database is backed up to a designated area on your system that is specified later in the configuration process. You have to supply an operating-system username and password that Enterprise Manager will log in as to perform the backup. This user should have the proper write authorization to the area of the disk where you want the backup stored.

Database Credentials

You use the Database Credentials screen (see Figure 9.7) to configure passwords for the various administrative accounts that are set up automatically when the database is configured. You can select the same password for all the critical accounts, or you can elect to have a different password for each of the preconfigured accounts. How you elect to set your passwords may depend on the policies of your particular organization. Typically, the same critical passwords are set for these accounts, and the accounts that you won't need to access are selectively locked.

FIGURE 9.7 DBCA Database Credentials screen

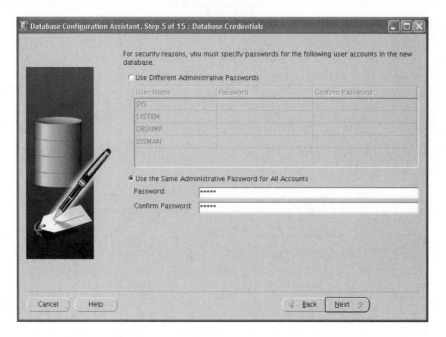

Four accounts are preconfigured when you set up your database:

SYS The SYS user owns all the internal Oracle tables that constitute the data dictionary. Normally, you should not perform any actions as the SYS user and should ensure that this account password is properly protected. Also, don't manually modify the underlying objects owned by the SYS user.

SYSTEM SYSTEM is an administrative user that contains additional administrative tables and views. Many DBAs use this account to administer the database, but ideally this account also should be locked and secured.

DBSNMP DBSNMP is a login used by the Enterprise Manager facility to monitor and gather performance statistics about the database.

SYSMAN SYSMAN is the equivalent of the SYS user for the Enterprise Manager facility. This Enterprise Manager administrator can create and modify other Enterprise Manager administrator accounts, as well as administer the database instance.

Once you have completed the Database Credentials page, click Next. You will now be presented with the Storage Options screen.

Storage Options

The Storage Options screen (see Figure 9.8) is used to define how you want to configure the disk storage areas used by the database. You have three choices:

- File System
- Automatic Storage Management (ASM)
- Raw Devices

FIGURE 9.8   DBCA Storage Options screen

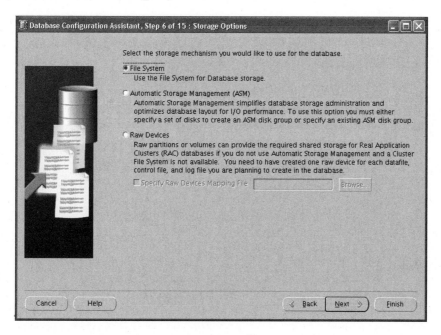

Let's take a look at these options in more detail.

File System Storage

File system storage is the most common type of storage configuration for many Oracle Databases. This type of storage definition relies on the underlying operating system to maintain and manage the actual files you as the DBA define. When you choose this option, the DBCA suggests a set of data filenames and directory locations for those files. You can modify this information at the database-storage step later in the database-creation process.

The DBCA uses the Optimal Flexible Architecture (OFA) directory design for laying out the suggested file locations. The OFA is an Oracle-recommended method for designing a flexible directory structure and naming convention for your Oracle Database files.

ASM Storage

Automatic Storage Management (ASM) is a newer type of storage mechanism available since Oracle 10*g*. ASM is designed to relieve the burden of disk and storage management and relies on Oracle to maintain your database storage. Instead of managing many individual database files, ASM allows you to define disk groups for file management.

Using disk groups, you can define one or more groups of disks as a logical unit that Oracle views as a single unit of storage. This concept is similar in nature to the way that some operating systems, including various flavors of Unix, define volume groups.

Oracle manages the storage definitions of the database within a second instance used exclusively by ASM to keep track of the diskgroup allocations. When you create a database and select the ASM option in the Storage Options screen, a series of screens guides you through the process of defining the secondary ASM database instance. Every server using ASM storage should have an ASM instance running.

For more information on ASM storage, see the Oracle documentation "Oracle Database Storage Administrator's Guide 11*g* Release 1 (11.1) Part Number B31107-04." You can find this and other Oracle 11*g* documentation at www.oracle.com/pls/db111.

Raw Devices

You can also select Raw Devices as your storage definition. *Raw devices* are disks that are not managed by the underlying operating system. Instead of the underlying operating system controlling disk reading and writing activities, Oracle performs the actions directly on the underlying hardware without handing the responsibilities off to the operating system.

Typically, the systems administrator predefines the raw disk partitions that will constitute the specific raw devices. Then you as the DBA map the raw devices to specific data files and redo log files. It is better to use ASM storage instead of raw devices, because you have better load-balancing options and monitoring features available with ASM.

Since the OCA certification exam is based on databases created using file-system storage, I will not be discussing ASM and raw devices in this book. Choose File System on the DBCA Storage Options screen, and click Next to specify the file locations.

Database File Locations

After you define the type of storage you want to use for your database, you need to define where you want to put the files that will constitute the database. Depending on the type of storage option you choose, you may have more or fewer location options available. Figure 9.9 shows the DBCA screen accepting the file locations.

FIGURE 9.9   DBCA Database File Locations screen

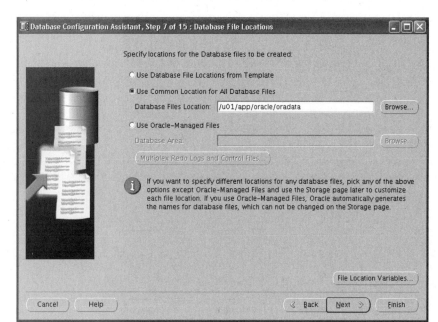

You are presented with three options on the Database File Locations screen:

- Use Database File Locations from Template
- Use Common Location for All Database Files
- Use Oracle-Managed Files

The following are descriptions of each of these options.

Use Database File Locations from Template

If you chose one of the predefined database templates to use for this database, Oracle uses the previously defined locations from the template as the basis for the database file locations. You still have the opportunity later in the database-definition process to review and modify the filenames and locations even if you choose this option.

Use Common Location for all Database Files

If you choose this option, you can specify a new directory for all your database files. Again, even if you choose this option, you can change the filenames and locations later in the database-definition process.

Use Oracle-Managed Files

If you choose Use Oracle-Managed Files, you let the Oracle Database manage the operating-system files comprising the database. As a DBA, you just specify the location of the database files. The tasks of creating and deleting files as required by the database are automatically managed—the DBA doesn't need to specify a data file's location when creating a new tablespace or specify the size or filename. Since you will not be presented with an option to change the storage characteristics of the data files later when the Use Oracle-Managed Files option is chosen, you can have multiplexed redo log files and control files by clicking the Multiplex Redo Logs and Control Files button. In the pop-up window, specify the location of the redo log and control files.

Once you have chosen the appropriate storage option for your database, click Next to get to the Recovery Configuration screen.

Recovery Configuration

You use the Recovery Configuration screen, as shown in Figure 9.10, to set up your database backup and recovery strategy. Oracle provides robust mechanisms for full point-of-failure recovery. As a DBA, it is critical to understand the backup and recovery requirements of your application so that you can choose the appropriate backup strategy.

FIGURE 9.10 DBCA Recovery Configuration screen

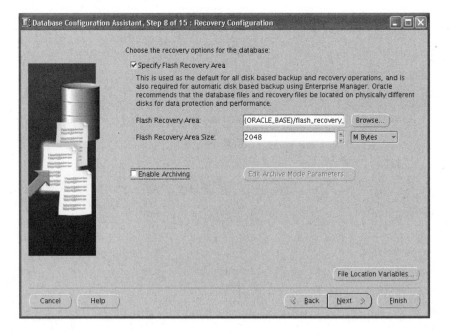

You can configure several options on this screen, including specifying the flash recovery area and size. You can also enable archive-log mode for the database and specify archive-log parameters. Let's take a look at each of these options.

Flash Recovery

Oracle flash recovery is an option available since Oracle 10*g*. It is the foundation of the new automated disk-based recovery feature. Flash recovery is designed to simplify your life in terms of Oracle backups by providing a centralized location to maintain and manage all the files related to database backups.

The flash recovery area is an area of the disk dedicated to the storage and management of files needed for recovering an Oracle Database. This area is completely separate from the other components of the Oracle Database, such as the data files, redo logs, and control files.

Oracle uses the flash recovery area to store and manage the archive logs. Enterprise Manager can store its backups in the flash recovery area and use it when restoring files during media recovery. The Oracle Recovery Manager (RMAN) uses the flash recovery area and ensures that the database is recoverable based on the files being stored in the flash recovery area. All files necessary to recover the database following a media failure are part of the flash recovery area.

You will explore the flash recovery area in more detail in Chapter 15, "Implementing Database Backups."

You can specify the directory location and the size of the disk area you want to dedicate to the flash recovery area. The default location of the directory provided by DBCA is ORACLE_BASE\flash_recovery_area. You can click File Location Variables on the Recovery Configuration screen to display a summary of the Oracle file location parameters, including the current setting of the ORACLE_BASE parameter. The size of the flash recovery area defaults to 2048MB and can be set larger or smaller by changing the Flash Recovery Size setting.

Enable Archive Logging

On the Recovery Configuration screen, you also have the ability to enable the Oracle archive-logging feature. Archive logging is the mechanism Oracle uses to enable you to perform a point-of-failure recovery of a database. To enable archive logging, select the Enable Archiving check box. Once you do so, the button Edit Archive Mode Parameters will be enabled. If you click this button, you are presented with a screen that enables you to set the various parameters that are used to configure archive logging (see Figure 9.11).

We will explore archive logging in more detail in Chapter 15.

FIGURE 9.11 DBCA Edit Archive Mode Parameters dialog box

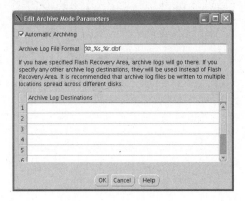

After completing the Recovery Configuration screen, click Next. You will then be presented with the Database Content screen.

Database Content

If you chose a predefined template (OLTP or Data Warehouse), you will be presented with the Database Content screen shown in Figure 9.12. You will then have the option to add sample schemas to the database, which is explored in the next section, "Sample Schemas and Custom Scripts."

FIGURE 9.12 DBCA Database Content Screen for predefined database template

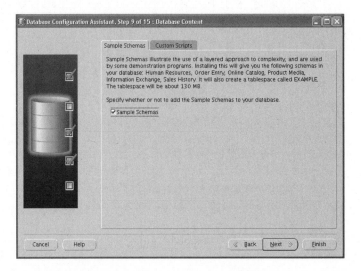

If you chose to create a custom database on the Database Templates screen, you will be presented with the Database Content screen shown in Figure 9.13.

FIGURE 9.13   The DBCA Database Content screen for custom database template

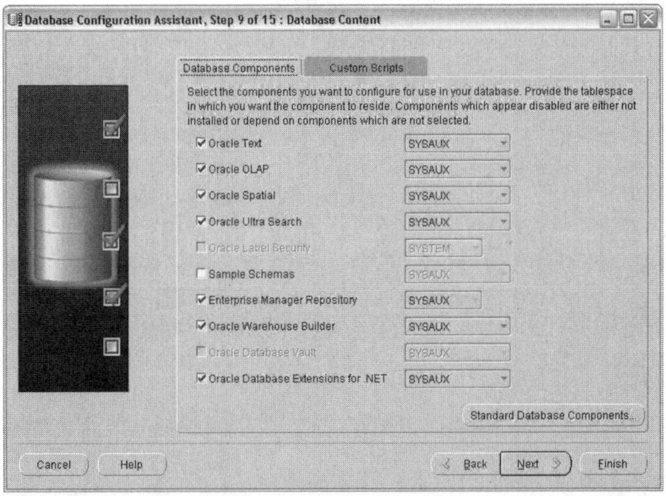

You use the options on this screen to specify which Oracle Database components you want to install. Table 9.3 describes the components that can be included and configured automatically by the DBCA.

TABLE 9.3   Oracle Optional Components

Component	Description
Oracle Text	Provides support for multimedia content such as audio and video.
Oracle OLAP	Provides facilities for creating and deploying online analytical processing applications.
Oracle Spatial	Provides the components and infrastructure for Oracle to manage and maintain geographic and spatial information such as map coordinates.
Oracle Ultra Search	Provides capabilities to perform extended text and searches within the Oracle Database.
Oracle Label Security	Manages and controls access to sensitive information within the database. This option will be enabled if the Label Security option is installed in the Oracle software home.
Sample Schemas	Installs some example data that can be used for learning purposes.

TABLE 9.3 Oracle Optional Components *(continued)*

Component	Description
Enterprise Manager Repository	Specifies the location of the schema used to manage the content of the OEM repository. If you chose to do local management of your database, this schema is required.
Oracle Warehouse Builder	Enables the ETL process and integrates various application data.
Oracle Database Vault	Addresses a security solution for regulatory compliance and security controls. This option will be enabled if the database vault option is installed in the Oracle software home.

Click the Standard Database Components button to display any additional standard features that Oracle will automatically configure for you and recommend as part of a standard database installation (see Figure 9.14). These features are the Oracle JVM, Oracle XML DB, Oracle Multimedia, and Oracle Application Express.

FIGURE 9.14 DBCA standard database components

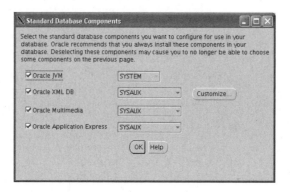

What Is a Schema?

When you are working with Oracle, you will often hear the words *schema* and *user* used interchangeably. Is there a difference between the two? Yes and no. A user is a defined database entity that has a set of abilities to perform activities based on their granted rights. A schema, which is associated with a user entity, is more appropriately defined as a collection of database objects. Some examples of database objects are tables, indexes, and views.

A schema can be related to a real person, such as a user of your Sales database who may have a user ID and password that they use to access the database. This user may or may not own any schema objects.

Because a schema is a collection of objects, DBAs often define a schema to represent a collection of objects associated with an application. For example, a DBA might create a schema called SALES and create objects owned by that schema. Then, they can grant access to other database users who need the ability to access the SALES schema.

In this way, the schema becomes a logical collection of objects associated with an application and is not tied to any specific user. This ability makes it easy to logically group common objects that are related to specific applications or tasks using a common schema name.

The main difference is that users are the entities that perform work, and schemas are the collections of objects that users perform work on.

Sample Schemas and Custom Scripts

The DBCA also lets you install examples of actual working databases. Oracle provides a set of example schemas and applications that use these schemas. You can install these sample schemas now or later by running a series of SQL scripts.

These sample schemas include the following:

- Human Resources (HR)
- Order Entry (OE)
- Product Media (PM)
- Sales History (SH)
- Queued Shipping (QS)

These schemas are designed to provide you with working examples of how to use and implement a variety of features within Oracle. For example, the Product Media schema shows how to use the Oracle Intermedia option, which is used to manage binary large objects (BLOBs) such as images and sound clips.

If you choose to create the sample schemas, Oracle creates a tablespace called EXAMPLE and stores all the necessary tables within that tablespace. Be aware that this adds about 130MB to your database definition. The examples shown in Chapters 1 through 7 mostly used the tables that belonged to the sample schema HR.

You can also run custom scripts as part of the database-creation process. Click the Custom Scripts tab on the Database Content screen to enter the names and locations of the custom scripts that you want to run at database creation (see Figure 9.15).

FIGURE 9.15 DBCA Database Content screen's Custom Scripts tab

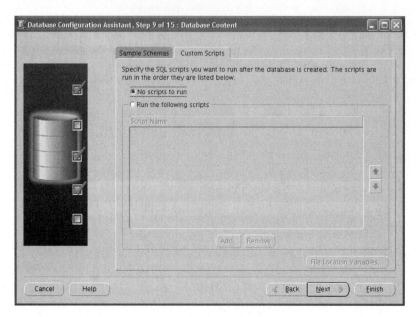

For example, you might want the DBCA to automatically create the schema and define the tables that you will use for this database. You can create a script that performs all the necessary work and have the DBCA run the script as part of the database-creation process. The custom scripts are run using the command-line utility SQL*Plus, so you will have to define a user ID and password within the body of the script. For example, your script might contain the following line:

```
connect some_userid/some_password
```

This line directs Oracle to connect to the current Oracle Database, which is determined by your ORACLE_SID environment variable using the supplied user ID and password.

After completing the Database Content screen, click Next. You will then be presented with the Initialization Parameters screen.

Initialization Parameters

You use the Initialization Parameters screen to define the various initialization-parameter settings used to configure size and set up the characteristics of the Oracle instance. The following four tabs are categorized according to the parameters used to manage the Oracle instance:

- Memory
- Sizing
- Character Sets
- Connection Mode

Let's take a look at each of these tabs and what settings you can manage on each one.

The Memory Tab

You use the options on the Memory tab to control the size of the database parameters that configure the overall memory footprint of the Oracle instance (see Figure 9.16). There are two general approaches to managing the memory database parameters: Oracle can set and manage most of the parameters for you, or you can customize each of the initialization parameters for your specific database.

If you choose the Typical setting, Oracle allocates memory to the various components within the Oracle system global area (SGA) and process global area (PGA). This memory allocation is automatic and is a percentage of the overall physical memory available on the server. The default is 30 percent of the total memory available, but you can change this setting by specifying the memory size or by sliding the bar to appropriate size. If you choose this setting, click the Show Memory Distribution button to see how Oracle will allocate the memory between the SGA and the PGA (see Figure 9.17).

FIGURE 9.16   Memory tab on the Initialization Parameters screen

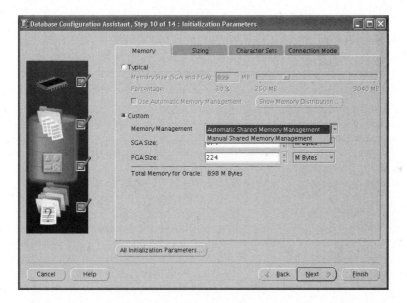

FIGURE 9.17   Memory distribution for SGA and PGA for the Typical setting

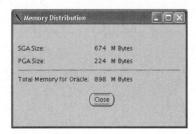

If you choose the Use Automatic Memory Management option under Typical, Oracle will manage the total memory automatically, including the SGA and PGA. The memory distribution will show differently, as in Figure 9.18, if this option is selected.

FIGURE 9.18   Memory distribution for Automatic Memory Management

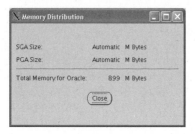

If you choose the Custom option, you will again have two options: Automatic Shared Memory Management and Manual Shared Memory Management. With automatic shared memory management, you specify only the SGA size and the PGA size. Each component inside the SGA is configured automatically by Oracle. With manual shared memory management, you have full control over how much each of the specific areas of the SGA will take. The main areas that you will configure are the shared pool, buffer cache, Java pool, large pool, and PGA size. Each of the settings maps to a specific Oracle parameter. Figure 9.19 shows the options.

FIGURE 9.19   DBCA showing manual shared memory management options

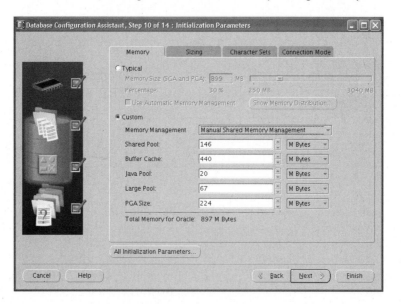

Memory management and the parameters associated with memory are discussed in detail in Chapter 14, "Maintaining the Database and Managing Performance."

The Sizing Tab

You use the options on the Sizing tab (see Figure 9.20) to configure the block size of your database and the number of processes that can connect to this database. The Block Size setting corresponds to the smallest unit of storage within the Oracle Database. All storage of database objects (tables, indexes, and so on) is governed by the block size. The block size defaults to 8KB, but you can modify it in the custom template only. Once the database is created, you cannot modify the database block size.

FIGURE 9.20   Sizing tab on the Initialization Parameters screen

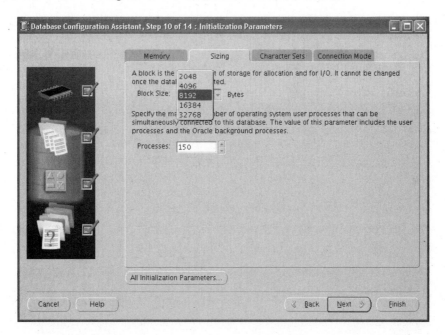

The maximum and minimum size of an Oracle block depends on the operating system. Generally, 8KB is sufficient for most transaction-oriented applications, and larger block sizes, such as 16KB and higher, are used in data warehouse–type applications. The block size can be 2KB, 4KB, 8KB, 16KB, or 32KB.

The Processes setting specifies the maximum number of simultaneous operating-system processes that can be connected to this Oracle Database. If you are not sure of the number of processes needed, you can start with the default value of 150. This parameter does have a bearing on the overall size of your Oracle instance. The larger you make this number, the more room Oracle must reserve in the SGA to track the processes.

The Character Sets Tab

You use the options on the Character Sets tab to configure the character sets you will use within your database (see Figure 9.21). You will determine the database character set, the national character set, the default language, and the default date format.

Specifying a database character set defines the type of encoding scheme that Oracle uses to determine how characters are displayed and stored within your Oracle environment. The character set you choose determines the languages that can be represented in your environment. It also controls other nuances, such as how your database interacts with your operating system and how much storage is required for your data. The default character set is based on the language setting of the operating system.

FIGURE 9.21   Character Sets tab on the Initialization Parameters screen

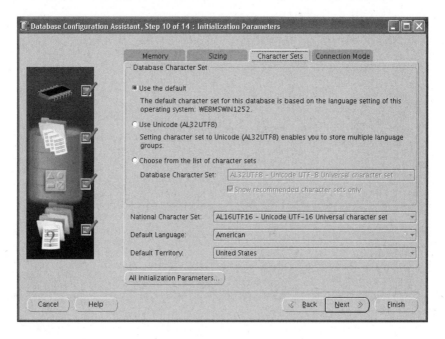

Specifying a national character set defines how your database represents Unicode characters in a database that does not use a Unicode-enabled character set.

You use the Default Language setting to manage certain aspects of how your database represents information pertaining to different locales. For example, this setting determines how your database displays time and monetary values.

You use the Default Date setting to specify how Oracle displays dates by default. For example, the AMERICA setting shows dates in the DD-MON-YYYY format by default.

The Connection Mode Tab

You use the options on the Connection Mode tab to specify the type of connections to use for this database (see Figure 9.22). You can choose Dedicated Server Mode or Shared Server Mode. The default connection mode is Dedicated Server Mode.

FIGURE 9.22   The Connection Mode tab on the Initialization Parameters screen

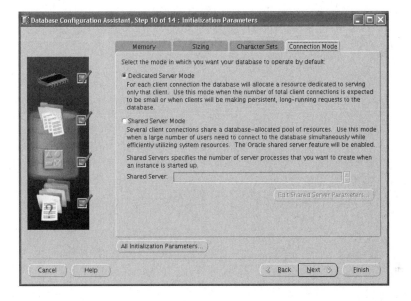

The dedicated server and shared server modes are covered in more detail in Chapter 11, "Understanding Network Architecture."

In the dedicated server mode, each user process will have a dedicated server process. In the shared process mode, many user processes share a server process.

If you want to review the initialization parameters and make any changes, click the All Initialization Parameters button. The screen shown in Figure 9.23 details the basic parameters. From this screen, you can view/edit the advanced parameters using the Show Advanced Parameters button. You have the option to edit a value on this screen.

After completing the Initialization Parameters screen, click Next. You will then be presented with the Security Settings screen.

FIGURE 9.23   DBCA Initialization Parameters screen

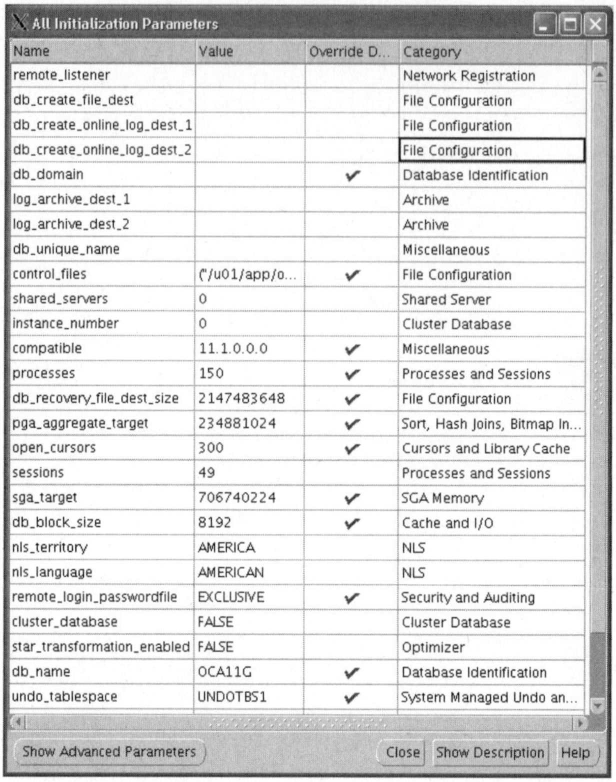

Name	Value	Override D...	Category
remote_listener			Network Registration
db_create_file_dest			File Configuration
db_create_online_log_dest_1			File Configuration
db_create_online_log_dest_2			File Configuration
db_domain		✓	Database Identification
log_archive_dest_1			Archive
log_archive_dest_2			Archive
db_unique_name			Miscellaneous
control_files	("/u01/app/o...	✓	File Configuration
shared_servers	0		Shared Server
instance_number	0		Cluster Database
compatible	11.1.0.0.0	✓	Miscellaneous
processes	150	✓	Processes and Sessions
db_recovery_file_dest_size	2147483648	✓	File Configuration
pga_aggregate_target	234881024	✓	Sort, Hash Joins, Bitmap In...
open_cursors	300	✓	Cursors and Library Cache
sessions	49		Processes and Sessions
sga_target	706740224	✓	SGA Memory
db_block_size	8192	✓	Cache and I/O
nls_territory	AMERICA		NLS
nls_language	AMERICAN		NLS
remote_login_passwordfile	EXCLUSIVE	✓	Security and Auditing
cluster_database	FALSE		Cluster Database
star_transformation_enabled	FALSE		Optimizer
db_name	OCA11G	✓	Database Identification
undo_tablespace	UNDOTBS1	✓	System Managed Undo an...

Show Advanced Parameters   Close Show Description Help

Security and Maintenance Settings

Oracle 11*g* has new and improved security settings such as case-sensitive passwords, more rigorous profile options, and so on. If you're not ready to use the Oracle 11*g* security options, choose the Revert to Pre-11g Default Security Settings option. Figure 9.24 shows the DBCA Security Settings screen.

When you click Next on the Security Settings screen, you will be presented with an option to configure automatic maintenance tasks, as shown in Figure 9.25.

On the next screen, you will be presented with options to review storage specifications for tablespaces, data files, control files, and redo log files.

FIGURE 9.24   DBCA Security Settings screen

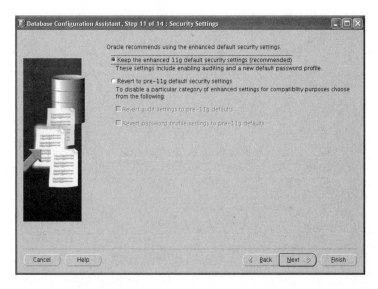

FIGURE 9.25   DBCA Automatic Maintenance Tasks screen

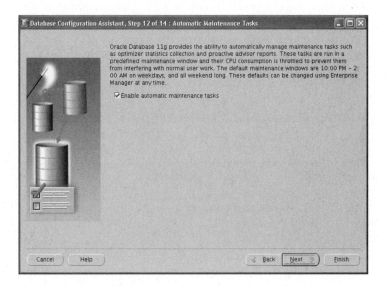

Database Storage

The Database Storage screen provides you with the opportunity to review and change the locations of the actual objects that compose the Oracle Database; namely, the data files, control files, and redo logs (see Figure 9.26).

FIGURE 9.26   The DBCA Database Storage initial screen

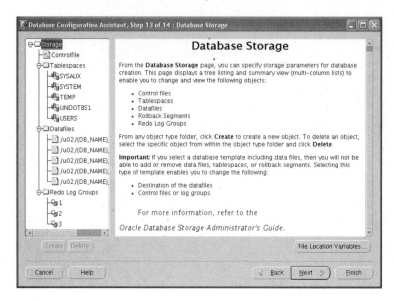

This screen displays a tree structure in the left pane. You can click the various elements within the tree to expand and display the details of each component. As with many of the other screens in the DBCA, you can click the File Location Variables button to display the settings for the various Oracle file location parameters, such as the ORACLE_BASE and ORACLE_HOME settings (see Figure 9.27).

FIGURE 9.27   DBCA File Location Variables dialog box

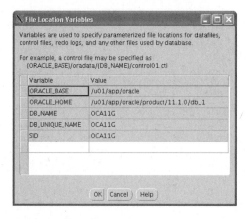

Selecting an element displays details about the element in the pane on the right. For example, clicking Controlfile displays a summary of the controlfile names and locations in the right pane. You can make manual changes to the names and locations of the control files in the right pane. Figure 9.28 shows the storage options available to configure a tablespace.

FIGURE 9.28　DBCA Database Storage tablespace storage screen

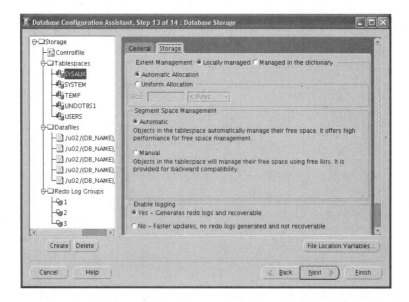

If you are creating a custom database definition that does not use a template, you can add new objects to a particular group. For example, clicking the Tablespaces folder and then clicking Create lets you add new tablespaces to your database definition. If you selected a database template that included data file definitions, you cannot add or remove data files, tablespaces, or rollback segments, but you can modify the location of the data files, control files, and redo log groups.

Chapter 10, "Allocating Database Storage and Creating Schema Objects," covers configuring and managing tablespaces and data files in detail.

After completing the Database Storage screen, click Next to create your database.

Creation Options

The Creation Options screen (see Figure 9.29) provides you with three options, and you can choose all three if needed.

Create Database　Use this option to have the DBCA immediately create your database.

Save as a Database Template　You actually have two choices with this option. You can elect to save your database definition to a template and create the database at a later time, or you can have the DBCA create the template and immediately create your database.

Generate Database Creation Scripts　This option will generate scripts for you to create the database at a later time without using the DBCA.

FIGURE 9.29   The DBCA Creation Options screen

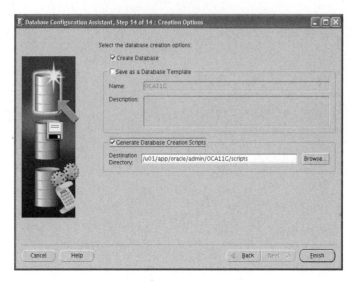

If you elect to create your database immediately, the DBCA uses the information you have provided in the previous screens to create all the necessary components of your database, populate the database with sample schemas if they were chosen, start your database, and allow you to configure the network components of your database, such as the Oracle Net listener.

I will discuss the listener component in more detail in Chapter 11.

If you elect to save your database to a template definition, this definition is added to the list of database definitions that you can select on subsequent executions of the DBCA.

You can also let the DBCA create a set of scripts that you can run manually to create the database. You can choose a location to store your scripts, and then you can run the scripts manually to generate your database. If you choose a manual creation process, you will also have to manually configure several items, including the Oracle Internet Directory Service if you elect to use centralized naming and your listener. Also, depending on your operating system, you will have to configure or modify the `oratab` file (under `/etc` or `/var/opt/oracle` depending on the platform) on Unix or create a service in the Windows environment.

When preparing for the test, create the database using a predefined template as well as a custom template. Save the database-creation scripts, and go through the scripts to understand what statements are executed behind the scenes by the DBCA to create the database. When using a custom template, a new database will be created using the `CREATE DATABASE` statement, whereas when using a predefined template, Oracle does not create a new database from scratch; instead, it clones an existing database from the template.

If you elect to have the DBCA create the database immediately, click Finish. You will see the Confirmation screen that summarizes the configuration options that you chose for this database (see Figure 9.30).

FIGURE 9.30   The DBCA Confirmation screen

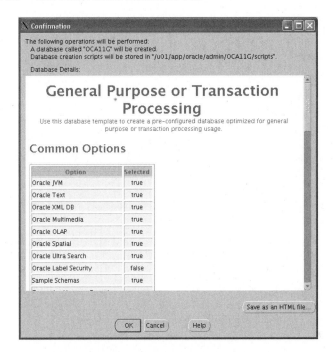

You can scroll down the window to examine the following:

- Options to install into the database
- The initialization-parameter settings
- Character-set settings
- Names and locations for data files
- Names and locations for redo logs
- Names and locations for control files

You can save this summary screen as an HTML file for later reference.

Once you start the database-creation process, Oracle creates the database as you have specified. It starts the instance, creates all the necessary database components, and configures all the database options you specified. Depending on how large a database you create and how many options you are installing, the process can take anywhere from several minutes to an hour or more.

After the database creation is complete, DBCA shows a summary screen, as shown in Figure 9.31. Note the information on this screen, especially the URL to invoke Enterprise Manager Database Control and the server parameter file location.

FIGURE 9.31   DBCA result summary screen

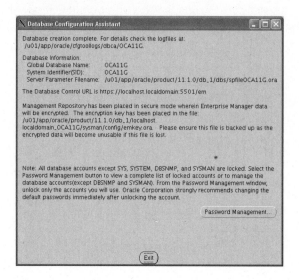

On this screen, you have the option to do password management. By default, all the accounts except SYS, SYSTEM, SYSMAN, and DBSNMP are locked. You can change the password and unlock selective accounts. Figure 9.32 shows the Password Management dialog box.

FIGURE 9.32   DBCA Password Management dialog box

When the creation process is complete, connect to the database with one of the tools such as SQL*Plus or Enterprise Manager to ensure that all the database options and components were installed properly. Logging into Enterprise Manager will give you an overview of the new database. By using the URL specified in Figure 9.31, you can invoke the Database Control home page. Log in using the SYSMAN account with the password you supplied in Figure 9.7. Figure 9.33 shows the home screen of Enterprise Manager Database Control.

FIGURE 9.33   Enterprise Manager Database Control home page

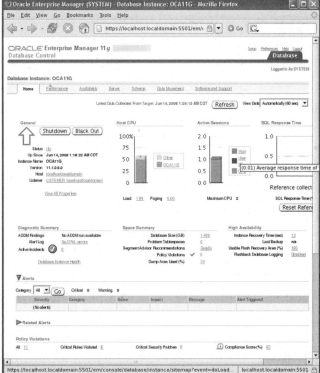

Configuring an Oracle Database Using the DBCA

The DBCA lets you change various aspects of an existing database. To change the database configuration, select Configure Database Options on the DBCA Operations screen (shown earlier in this chapter in Figure 9.2). If the database is not started, the DBCA starts it for you automatically. You must connect to the database as a user who has DBA authority.

Once you have selected and started the database, you can add options that may not have been previously included in the database. Using DBCA you can perform the following changes to database configuration:

- Add database components (refer to Figure 9.13).

- Change database security settings from pre-11*g* default security setting to 11*g* enhanced security settings, or vice versa (refer Figure 9.24).

- Change the default connection mode for the database. You can change from dedicated server mode to shared server mode, or vice versa (refer Figure 9.22).

Deleting an Oracle Database Using the DBCA

You can also delete a database using the DBCA. On the Operations screen (Figure 9.2), choose Delete a Database, and click Next to open the Database screen. The DBCA lists all the databases available for deletion. Choose the database you want to delete.

If you click Finish, the DBCA removes all files on the disk associated with the database you have chosen. If you are using Windows, the DBCA also removes the service associated with the database.

Exercise 9.1 shows you how to delete a database manually using SQL*Plus.

EXERCISE 9.1

Delete or Remove an Oracle Database Manually

Some DBAs prefer to use a command-line interface to perform their tasks. You can delete a database using the command-line tool SQL*Plus.

To do so, first connect to SQL*Plus as an administrator who has the ability to start up the database; that is, an administrator with either the SYSOPER or SYSDBA privilege.

Here's an example:

/u01/app/oracle>**sqlplus sys/**** as sysdba**

Once you are connected, you need to put the database in MOUNT mode. Issue the following command if the database is not running:

Startup mount;

Next, issue the following command:

Drop database;

This command deletes all the files associated with the database. If you are using raw disk devices, the special files created for these devices are not deleted. Also, you may have to remove any archived logs from the database archive area using the appropriate operating-system command.

Managing Database Templates Using the DBCA

As I explained earlier in this chapter, the DBCA can store and use XML-based templates to create your Oracle Database. As the DBA, you can manage these database-definition templates. Saving a definition of your database in a template format makes it easier to perform various tasks. For example, you can copy a preexisting template to modify new database definitions. The template definition is normally stored in the $ORACLE_HOME/assistants/dbca/templates directory on Unix and in the %ORACLE_HOME%\assistants\dbca\templates directory on Windows systems.

The DBCA can use two types of templates: seed and nonseed. *Seed* templates are template definitions that contain database-definition information and the actual data files and redo log files. The advantage of a seed template is that the DBCA makes a copy of the data files and redo logs included in the definition file. These prebuilt data files include all schema information, which makes for a faster database-creation process. The seed templates carry a .dbc extension. The associated predefined data files are stored as files having a .dfb extension. When you use a seed template, you can change the database name, the data-file locations, the number of control files and redo log groups, and the initialization parameters.

Nonseed templates contain custom-defined database definitions. Unlike seed templates, they do not come with preconfigured data files and redo logs. Nonseed templates carry a .dbt extension.

Now I'll cover the various options you have to manage templates.

Creating Template Definitions Using the DBCA

You can use the DBCA interface to create new database templates. When you connect to the DBCA, select Manage Templates on the Operations screen (see Figure 9.2, shown earlier in this chapter), and click Next to open the Template Management screen, as shown in Figure 9.34.

FIGURE 9.34   The DBCA Template Management screen

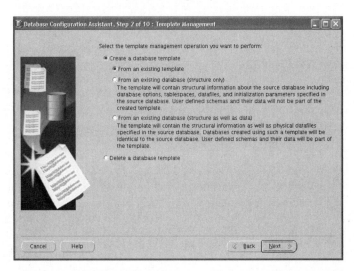

You have three choices for creating templates. Table 9.4 summarizes your options.

TABLE 9.4 Template-Creation Options

Selection	Description
From an Existing Template	Creates a new template definition from a preexisting template. This allows you to modify a variety of template settings, including parameters and data file storage characteristics.
From an Existing Database (Structure Only)	Creates a new template based on the structural characteristics of an existing database. The data files are created from scratch and will not include data from the original database. Choose this option when you want a database that is structurally like another database but does not contain any data. The database you are copying from can reside anywhere in your network.
From an Existing Database (Structure As Well As Data)	Creates a new template based on the structural characteristics of an existing database. The data files and all corresponding user data are included in the new database. Choose this option when you want an exact copy of an existing database. The database you are copying must reside on the same physical server as the new database you are creating.

Depending on the option selected, you are presented with a set of forms to save your template definition. If you elect to create a template from an existing database, you will have to connect to the database so that the DBCA can obtain information about the database. You must connect to the database as a user who has DBA credentials to perform this task.

If you are copying a definition from an existing template, you can configure the template by following a series of screens that are similar to those used to create a database. These screens allow you to configure the various aspects of the template, including initialization parameters and data file and redo log locations.

Deleting Template Definitions Using the DBCA

You can also delete an existing template definition. On the Operations screen (see Figure 9.2, shown earlier in this chapter), click Manage Templates. You will be presented with the Template Management screen (see Figure 9.34). Select the option Delete a Database Template. You can then choose the template to delete. When you remove the template, the DBCA removes the XML file from the system.

Working with Oracle 11*g* Metadata

In addition to tables such as DEPARTMENTS and EMPLOYEES that store important business data, Oracle Databases also contain system tables that store data about the database. Examples of the type of information in these system tables include the names of all the tables in the database, the column names and datatypes of those tables, the number of rows those tables contain, and security information about which users are allowed to access those tables. This "data about the database" is referred to as *metadata*. As a DBA, you will frequently use this metadata when performing your administration tasks.

An Oracle 11*g* database contains two types of metadata views:

- Data dictionary views
- Dynamic performance views

The SYS user owns the data dictionary and dynamic performance views in the Oracle 11*g* database, and they are stored in the SYSTEM tablespace. During normal database operation, Oracle uses the data dictionary frequently and updates the dictionary with the current status of the database components. The dictionary is also immediately updated when a DDL statement is executed.

Data dictionary views and dynamic performance views are described in the next section.

Data Dictionary Views

Data dictionary views provide information about the database and its objects. Depending on which features are installed and configured, an Oracle 11*g* database can contain more than 1,600 data dictionary views. Data dictionary views have names that begin with DBA_, ALL_, and USER_. Oracle creates public synonyms on many data dictionary views so users can access the views conveniently.

The difference between the DBA_, ALL_, and USER_ views can be illustrated using the DBA_TABLES data dictionary view as an example. The DBA_TABLES view shows information on all the tables in the database. The corresponding ALL_TABLES view, despite its name, shows only the tables that a particular database user owns or can access. For example, if you were logged into the database as a user named SCOTT, the ALL_TABLES view would show all the tables owned by the user SCOTT and the tables to which SCOTT has been granted access by other users. The USER_TABLES view shows only those objects owned by a user. If the user SCOTT were to examine the USER_TABLES view, only those tables he owns would be displayed. Figure 9.35 shows a graphical representation of the relationship between the DBA_, ALL_, and USER_ views.

Because the DBA_ views provide the broadest metadata information, they are generally the data dictionary views used by DBAs. Table 9.5 provides examples of DBA_ data dictionary views.

FIGURE 9.35 A comparison of data dictionary views

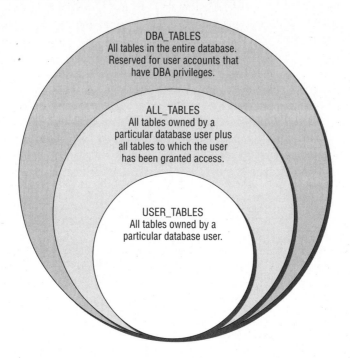

TABLE 9.5 Examples of Data Dictionary Views

Dictionary View	Description
DBA_TABLES	Shows the names and physical storage information about all the tables in the database
DBA_USERS	Shows information about all the users in the database
DBA_VIEWS	Shows information about all the views in the database
DBA_TAB_COLUMNS	Shows all the names and datatypes of the table columns in the database
DATABASE_PROPERTIES	Displays database properties such as NLS parameters, default temporary and permanent tablespace names, database time zone, so on
GLOBAL_NAME	Shows the global database name

You can find a complete list of the Oracle 11*g* data dictionary views in Part II of the "Oracle Database Reference 11*g* Release 1 (11.1) Part Number B28320-01" document available at http://tahiti.oracle.com.

Dynamic Performance Views

Throughout database operation, Oracle updates a set of virtual tables to record the current database activity and status. These tables are called *dynamic performance tables*. Views are created on top of the dynamic performance tables for better grouping of information and to have names in a user-friendly format. The dynamic performance views are sometimes called *fixed views*, because they cannot be altered or removed by the database administrator.

The dynamic performance tables begin with X$. The dynamic performance view names begin with V_$. Public synonyms are created on these views, and they begin with V$. For example, the dynamic performance view with data file information is v_$datafile, whereas the public synonym is v$datafile.

Depending on which features are installed and configured, an Oracle 11*g* database can contain approximately 480 dynamic performance views. Most of these views have names that begin with V$. Table 9.6 describes a few of these dynamic performance views.

TABLE 9.6   Examples of Dynamic Performance Views

Dynamic Performance View	Description
V$DATABASE	Contains information about the database, such as the database name and when the database was created
V$VERSION	Shows which software version the database is using
V$OPTION	Displays which optional components are installed in the database
V$SQL	Displays information about the SQL statements that database users have been issuing

You can find a complete list of the Oracle 11*g* data dictionary views in Part III of the "Oracle Database Reference 11*g* Release 1 (11.1) Part Number B28320-01" document available at http://tahiti.oracle.com.

Although the contents of the DBA_ and V$ metadata views are similar, there are some important differences between the two types. Table 9.7 compares these two types.

TABLE 9.7   Data Dictionary vs. Dynamic Performance Views

Data Dictionary Views	Dynamic Performance Views
The DBA_ views usually have plural names (for example, DBA_DATA_FILES).	The names of the V$ views are generally singular (for example, V$DATAFILE).
The DBA_ views are available only when the database is open and running.	Some V$ views are available even when the database is not fully open and running.
The data contained in the DBA_ views is static and is not cleared when the database is shut down.	The V$ views contain dynamic statistical data that is lost each time the database is shut down.

The data dictionary view DICTIONARY shows information about the data dictionary and dynamic performance views in the database. DICT is a synonym for the DICTIONARY view. The COMMENTS column shows the purpose or contents of the view. The V$FIXED_TABLE view lists the dynamic performance tables and views in the database.

The Oracle data dictionary and dynamic performance views are created while creating the database. The scripts to create the metadata are stored in the $ORACLE_HOME/rdbms/admin directory. Several scripts are in this directory, and the script that creates the base dictionary objects is called catalog.sql. The catproc.sql script creates the PL/SQL packages and functionality to support PL/SQL in the database.

You are not allowed to log in as SYS and modify the data dictionary views or update information directly using SQL. The only SYS-owned table you are allowed to delete records from is AUD$. This table is used to keep database audit information.

Managing Initialization-Parameter Files

Oracle uses initialization-parameter files to store information about initialization parameters used when an Oracle instance starts. Oracle reads the parameter file to obtain information about how the Oracle instance should be sized and configured upon startup.

The parameter file can be a plain text file, commonly referred to as a *pfile*, or it can be a binary parameter file, commonly referred to as an *spfile*. You can use either type of file to configure instance and database options; however, there are some important differences between the two types of configuration files, as shown in Table 9.8.

TABLE 9.8   Pfiles vs. Spfiles

Pfile	Spfile
Text file that can be edited using a text editor.	Binary file that cannot be edited directly.
When changes are made to the pfile, the instance must be shut down and restarted before it takes effect.	Parameter changes made to the database using ALTER SYSTEM are updated in the spfile.
Is called init*instance_name*.ora.	Is called spfile*instance_name*.ora.
Oracle instance reads only from pfile.	Oracle instance reads and writes to the spfile.
Can be created from an spfile using the create pfile from spfile command.	Can be created from a pfile using the create spfile from pfile command.

You can specify more than 285 documented configuration parameters in the pfile or spfile. Oracle 11*g* divides these parameters into two categories: basic and advanced. Oracle recommends you set only the basic initialization parameters manually. Oracle also recommends you do not modify the remaining parameters unless directed to do so by Oracle Support or to meet the specific needs of your application. Table 9.9 describes the basic initialization parameters . A "Yes" in the Static column indicates that the parameter is static and cannot be modified dynamically without a database restart.

TABLE 9.9   Oracle 11*g* Basic Initialization Parameters

Parameter Name	Static	Description
CLUSTER_DATABASE	Yes	Tells the instance whether it is part of a clustered environment.
COMPATIBLE	Yes	Specifies the release level and feature set you want to be active in the instance.
CONTROL_FILES	Yes	Designates the physical location of the database control files.
DB_BLOCK_SIZE	Yes	Specifies the default database block size. The database block size specified at database creation cannot be changed.

TABLE 9.9 Oracle 11*g* Basic Initialization Parameters *(continued)*

Parameter Name	Static	Description
DB_CREATE_FILE_DEST	No	Specifies the directory location where database data files will be created if the Oracle-Managed Files feature is used.
DB_CREATE_ONLINE_LOG_ DEST_*n*	No	Specifies the location(s) where the database redo log files will be created if the Oracle-Managed Files feature is used.
DB_DOMAIN	Yes	Specifies the logical location of the database on the network.
DB_NAME	Yes	Specifies the name of the database that is mounted by the instance.
DB_RECOVERY_FILE_DEST	No	Specifies the location where recovery files will be written if the flash recovery feature is used.
DB_RECOVERY_FILE_ DEST_SIZE	No	Specifies the amount of disk space available for storing flash recovery files.
DB_UNIQUE_NAME	Yes	Specifies a globally unique name for the database within the enterprise.
INSTANCE_NUMBER	Yes	Identifies the instance in a Real Application Clusters (RAC) environment.
LDAP_DIRECTORY_ SYSAUTH	Yes	Enables or disables Oracle Internet directory–based authentication for SYSDBA and SYSOPER connections to the database.
LOG_ARCHIVE_DEST_*n*	No	Specifies as many as nine locations where archived redo log files are to be written.
LOG_ARCHIVE_DEST_ STATE_*n*	No	Indicates how the specified locations should be used for log archiving.
NLS_LANGUAGE	Yes	Specifies the default language of the database.
NLS_TERRITORY	Yes	Specifies the default region or territory of the database.
OPEN_CURSORS	No	Sets the maximum number of cursors that an individual session can have open at one time.
PGA_AGGREGATE_TARGET	No	Establishes the overall amount of memory that all PGA processes are allowed to consume.
PROCESSES	Yes	Specifies the maximum number of operating-system processes that can connect to the instance.
REMOTE_LISTENER	No	Specifies a network name that points to the address or list of addresses of remote Oracle Net listeners.

TABLE 9.9   Oracle 11*g* Basic Initialization Parameters *(continued)*

Parameter Name	Static	Description
REMOTE_LOGIN_ PASSWORDFILE	Yes	Determines whether the instance uses a password file and what type.
ROLLBACK_SEGMENTS	Yes	Specifies the rollback-segment names, only if Automatic Undo Management is not being used.
SESSIONS	Yes	Determines the maximum number of sessions that can connect to the database.
SGA_TARGET	No	Establishes the maximum size of the SGA, within which space is automatically allocated to each SGA component when Automatic Memory Management is used.
SHARED_SERVERS	No	Specifies the number of shared server processes to start when the instance is started. See Chapter 11 for details.
STAR_TRANSFORMATION_ ENABLED	No	Determines whether the optimizer will consider star transformations when queries are executed. See Chapter 14 for details on the optimizer.
UNDO_MANAGEMENT	Yes	Establishes whether system undo is automatically or manually managed. See Chapter 8, "Introducing Oracle 11*g* Components and Architecture," for details on undo segments.
UNDO_TABLESPACE	No	Specifies which tablespace stores undo segments if the Automatic Undo Management option is used. See Chapter 13, "Managing Data and Undo," for details on undo management.

Any parameters not specified in the pfile or spfile take on their default values. The following is an example of the contents of a typical Oracle 11*g* pfile that contains both basic and advanced parameters:

```
audit_file_dest='/u01/app/oracle/admin/OCA11G/adump'
audit_trail='db'
compatible='11.1.0.0.0'
control_files=('/u01/app/oracle/oradata/OCA11G/control01.ctl'
,'/u01/app/oracle/oradata/OCA11G/control02.ctl'
,'/u01/app/oracle/oradata/OCA11G/control03.ctl')
db_block_size=8192
db_domain=''
db_name='OCA11G'
db_recovery_file_dest='/u01/app/oracle/flash_recovery_area'
```

```
db_recovery_file_dest_size=2147483648
diagnostic_dest='/u01/app/oracle'
dispatchers='(PROTOCOL=TCP) (SERVICE=OCA11GXDB)'
memory_target=1G
open_cursors=300
processes=150
remote_login_passwordfile='EXCLUSIVE'
undo_tablespace='UNDOTBS1'
```

In this sample pfile, the sizes of the shared pool, database buffer cache, large pool, and Java pool are not individually specified. Instead, Oracle 11*g*'s Automatic Memory Management features allow you to simply set one configuration parameter—MEMORY_TARGET—to establish the total amount of memory allocated to the SGA and PGA. I will discuss this parameter in Chapter 14.

On production databases, if your Oracle license is based on the number of named users, you can enforce the license compliance by setting the LICENSE_MAX_USERS parameter. The default for this parameter is 0, which means you can create any number of users in the database and the license compliance is not enforced.

 Real World Scenario

Handle with Care: Undocumented Configuration Parameters

You've just read a performance-tuning tip posted to the Oracle newsgroup at comp .databases.oracle.server. The person posting the tip suggests setting the undocumented pfile parameter _dyn_sel_est_num_blocks to a value of 200 in order to boost your database's performance. Should you implement this suggestion?

More than 1,000 undocumented configuration parameters are available in Oracle 11*g*. Undocumented configuration parameters are distinguished from their documented counterparts by the underscore that precedes their name, as with the parameter described in the newsgroup posting.

I do not recommend utilizing undocumented pfile or spfile parameters on any of your systems because knowing the appropriate reasons to use these parameters, and the appropriate values to set these parameters to, is almost pure speculation because of their undocumented nature. Although some undocumented parameters are relatively harmless (such as _trace_files_public), using others incorrectly can cause unforeseen database problems. What does the _dyn_sel_est_num_blocks parameter do, and what value should you set it to? Only the engineers of the Oracle 11*g* kernel code know for sure.

One exception to this suggestion is when you are directed to use an undocumented configuration parameter by Oracle Support. Oracle Support occasionally uses these parameters to enhance the generation of debug information or to work around a bug in the kernel code.

Locating the Default Parameter File

The default location that Oracle searches to find the pfile and spfile parameter files is $ORACLE_HOME/dbs on Unix systems and %ORACLE_HOME%\database on Windows systems.

Oracle uses a search hierarchy when a startup command is issued without specifying either a pfile or an spfile. Oracle looks for files with the following names in the default directory to start the instance:

- spfile$ORACLE_SID.ora
- spfile.ora
- init$ORACLE_SID.ora

Oracle first looks for a parameter file called spfile$ORACLE_SID.ora. If it doesn't find that, it searches for spfile.ora. Finally, it searches for a traditional text pfile with the default name of init$ORACLE_SID.ora.

If the parameter files do not exist in the default location or you want to use a different parameter file to start your database, you can specify a parameter file to use when you issue a startup command to start the Oracle Database.

> You will see examples of how database startup is performed later in this chapter in the section "Starting Up and Shutting Down an Oracle Instance."

Modifying Initialization-Parameter Values

In some instances, you may need to change the initialization parameters. For example, you might need to increase the number of sessions allowed to connect to the database because you are adding users. Whatever the case, you need to know how to make these changes. There are a few options to change the initialization-parameter value, based on the type of parameter file used. Here they are:

- If PFILE is used, edit the pfile using an OS editor, and make appropriate changes.
- If SPFILE is used, connect to the instance, and make changes using the ALTER SYSTEM SET parameter_name = value statement.
- Use EM Database Control to make changes.

Using EM Database Control

To use the EM Database Control tool to modify existing database parameters, navigate to the Server menu. In the Database Configuration section, you can modify your initialization parameters. The SPFile tab shows the parameters as set in the spfile. You can also use the filters to find the exact parameter that needs to be modified. The Category drop-down is a very useful feature. Figure 9.36 shows the EM screen to change initialization parameters.

The Initialization Parameters screen has two tabs:

Current tab   This tab displays all the currently active settings for initialization parameters for the database instance. If a parameter is marked Dynamic, you can modify it, and this modification immediately affects the parameter that affects the currently running instance without stopping the database. The changes you make on the Current tab are not permanent, so the next time the database is stopped and restarted, the settings revert to their original values.

SPFile tab   If you are using a server parameter file, you will see the SPFile tab. This tab also lets you change existing database parameters. The difference between changing parameters on this tab and changing parameters on the Current tab is that changes to the spfile are persistent across database startups and shutdowns because the changes are saved to the spfile definition. You can also apply your changes to the spfile only or to the spfile and the currently running instance.

FIGURE 9.36   The EM Database Control Initialization Parameters screen

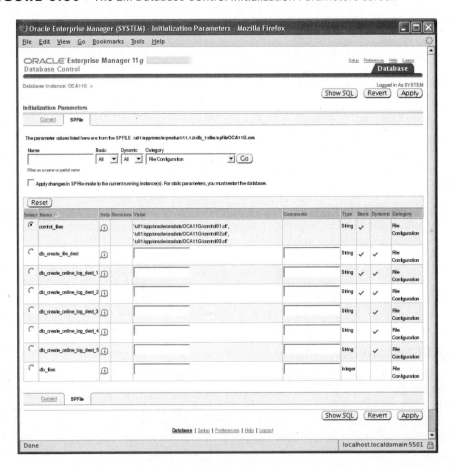

Using SQL*Plus

Though EM Database Control is a handy tool to modify the initialization parameters, sometimes it is convenient to use SQL*Plus and make changes to the parameters. You should know about two dynamic performance views: V$PARAMETER and V$SPPARAMETER.

V$PARAMETER

The V$PARAMETER view shows information about the initialization parameters that are currently in effect. This view has several useful columns. Table 9.10 lists some of the columns in V$PARAMETER and how they can be used in queries.

TABLE 9.10   V$PARAMETER Columns

Column Name	Description
NAME	This specifies the name of the initialization parameter.
VALUE	This specifies the current value of the parameter.
DISPLAY_VALUE	This specifies the current value in a more user-friendly format.
DESCRIPTION	This gives a short description about the parameter.
ISBASIC	TRUE indicates that the parameter is categorized as a basic parameter.
ISDEFAULT	FALSE indicates that the parameter was specified in the pfile or spfile during instance startup.
ISMODIFIED	FALSE indicates that the parameter has not been modified since the instance started.
ISSES_MODIFIABLE	TRUE indicates that the parameter can be modified using an ALTER SESSION statement.
ISSYS_MODIFIABLE	FALSE indicates that the parameter cannot be modified using an ALTER SYSTEM statement. Such parameters can be changed only using the SCOPE=SPFILE clause.

V$SPPARAMETER

The V$SPPARAMETER view shows the contents of the spfile used to start the instance. A TRUE value for the ISSPECIFIED column shows whether the parameter was specified in the spfile. If a pfile was used to start the instance, all the rows will have FALSE for the ISSPECIFIED column. Sometimes, querying the V$SPPARAMETER can produce readable output for parameters that take multiple values.

V$PARAMETER vs. V$SPPARAMETER

The following SQL example shows the difference in the result from the V$PARAMETER and V$SPPARAMETER views:

```
SQL> SELECT name, value
  2  FROM v$parameter
  3  WHERE name LIKE 'control%'
  4  AND isdefault = 'FALSE';


NAME                  VALUE
-------------------- -----------------------------------------------
control_files        /u01/app/oracle/oradata/OCA11G/control01.ctl, /u
                     01/app/oracle/oradata/OCA11G/control02.ctl,/u01/
                     app/oracle/oradata/OCA11G/control03.ctl


SQL> SELECT name, value
  2  FROM v$spparameter
  3  WHERE name LIKE 'control%'
  4  AND isspecified = 'TRUE';


NAME                  VALUE
-------------------- -----------------------------------------------
control_files        /u01/app/oracle/oradata/OCA11G/control01.ctl
control_files        /u01/app/oracle/oradata/OCA11G/control02.ctl
control_files        /u01/app/oracle/oradata/OCA11G/control03.ctl

SQL>
```

You can use the ALTER SESSION statement to change the value of a parameter in the current session. For example, if you want to change the default date-display format for the session only, use the following statement:

```
SQL> ALTER SESSION SET NLS_DATE_FORMAT = 'DD-MON-YYYY HH24:MI:SS';

Session altered.

SQL>
```

You can use the ALTER SYSTEM statement to change the value of a parameter system-wide or in the spfile, or both. You use the SCOPE clause to define where you want to change the parameter value: MEMORY, SPFILE, and BOTH are the valid values for the SCOPE clause.

A value of DEFERRED or IMMEDIATE in the ISSYS_MODIFIABLE column shows that the parameter can be dynamically changed using ALTER SYSTEM. The DEFERRED value indicates that the change you make does not take effect until a new session is started; the existing sessions will use the current value. IMMEDIATE indicates that as soon as you change the value of the parameter, it is available to all sessions in the instance. A *session* is a job or task that Oracle manages. When you log in to the database using SQL*Plus or any other tool, you start a session.

If you want to change a parameter value for the current instance but do not want the change to persist across database shutdowns, you can specify SCOPE=MEMORY, as in the following example:

```
SQL> ALTER SYSTEM SET UNDO_RETENTION = 3600 SCOPE=MEMORY;

System altered.
SQL>
```

Some parameters values can be set only at instance startup; they are not modifiable when the instance is running. Such parameter changes can be made with the SCOPE=SPFILE clause. Oracle will make the change only to the spfile, which takes effect after you restart the database:

```
SQL> ALTER SYSTEM SET UNDO_MANAGEMENT = MANUAL;
ALTER SYSTEM SET UNDO_MANAGEMENT = MANUAL
                     *
ERROR at line 1:
ORA-02095: specified initialization parameter cannot be modified

SQL> ALTER SYSTEM SET UNDO_MANAGEMENT = MANUAL SCOPE=SPFILE;

System altered.
SQL>
```

Most of the times when you make a parameter change, you want it to take effect immediately in memory as well as persist the change across database shutdowns. You can use the SCOPE=BOTH clause, which is the default, for this purpose. So if you omit the SCOPE clause, Oracle will make changes to the memory and to the spfile. If a pfile is used to start the instance, the change will be in memory only for the current running instance.

```
SQL> ALTER SYSTEM SET SGA_TARGET=500M SCOPE=BOTH;

System altered.
SQL>
```

You can use the SQL*Plus command SHOW PARAMETER to view the current value of an initialization parameter. You can specify the full parameter name or part of the name. For example, to view all parameters related to undo, you can do this:

```
SQL> SHOW PARAMETER undo

NAME                                TYPE          VALUE
----------------------------------- ----------- -----------
undo_management                     string        AUTO
undo_retention                      integer       3600
undo_tablespace                     string        UNDOTBS1
SQL>
```

In the next section, I will discuss the options to start up and shut down a database.

Starting Up and Shutting Down an Oracle Instance

As a DBA, you are responsible for the startup and shutdown of the Oracle instance. Oracle gives authorized administrators the ability to perform this task using a variety of interfaces. It is important to understand the options that are available to you to start up and shut down the Oracle instance and when the various options can or should be used. The stages of instance startup and the startup options appear frequently on OCA certification exams.

To start up or shut down an Oracle instance, you need to be connected to the database with the appropriate privileges. Two special connection account authorizations are available for startup and shutdown: SYSDBA and SYSOPER. The SYSDBA authorization is an all-empowering authorization that allows you to perform any database task. The SYSOPER authorization is a less powerful authorization that allows startup and shutdown abilities but restricts other administrative tasks, such as access to nonadministrative schema objects. These authorizations are managed either through a passwords file or via operating-system control.

When a database is initially installed, only the SYS schema can connect to the database with the SYSDBA authorization. You can grant this authorization and the SYSOPER authorization to give others the ability to perform these tasks without connecting as the SYS user.

Now I will discuss how to perform a database startup.

Starting Up an Oracle 11*g* Database

As described in Chapter 8, the Oracle instance is composed of a set of logical memory structures and background processes that users interact with to communicate with the Oracle Database. When Oracle is started, these memory structures and background processes are initialized and started so that users can communicate with the Oracle Database.

Whenever an Oracle Database is started, it goes through a series of steps to ensure database consistency. When it starts up, a database passes through three modes: NOMOUNT, MOUNT, and OPEN. I will review each of these *startup* modes and other special startup options such as FORCE and RESTRICT and discuss when you need to use these options. I'll then discuss how to use the available interfaces to start up an Oracle instance.

STARTUP NOMOUNT   This starts the instance without mounting the database. When a database is started in this mode, the parameter file is read, and the background processes and memory structures are initiated, but they are not attached or communicating with the disk structures of the database. When the instance is in this state, the database is not available for use.

If a database is started in NOMOUNT mode, only the background processes and instance are started. The instance is not associated with any database. This state is used to create a database or to create a database control file.

At times, a database may not be able to go to the next mode (called MOUNT mode) and remains in NOMOUNT mode. For example, this can occur if Oracle has a problem accessing the control file structures, which contain important information to continue with the startup process. If these structures are damaged or not available, the database startup process cannot continue until the problem is resolved.

 If STARTUP NOMOUNT fails, the most likely cause is that the parameter file cannot be read or is not in the default location. Other causes include OS resource limits that prevent memory or process allocation.

STARTUP MOUNT   This performs all the work of the STARTUP NOMOUNT option but also attaches and interacts with the database structures. At this point, Oracle obtains information from the control files that it uses to locate and attach to the main database structures. The control file contains the name of the database, all the data file names, and the redo log files associated with the database.

Certain administrative tasks can be performed while the database is in this mode, including renaming data files, enabling or disabling archive logging, renaming and adding redo log files, and recovering the database.

STARTUP OPEN   This is the default startup mode if no mode is specified on the STARTUP command line. STARTUP OPEN performs all the steps of the STARTUP NOMOUNT and STARTUP MOUNT options. This option makes the database available to all users.

When opening the database, you can use a couple of options. STARTUP OPEN READ ONLY opens the database in read-only mode. STARTUP OPEN RECOVER opens the database and performs a database recovery.

Although you typically use the STARTUP NOMOUNT, STARTUP MOUNT, and STARTUP OPEN options, a few other startup options are available that you can use in certain situations: STARTUP FORCE and STARTUP RESTRICT. These are discussed next.

STARTUP FORCE You can use the STARTUP FORCE startup option if you are experiencing difficulty starting the database in a normal fashion. For example, if a database server lost power and the database stopped abruptly, it can leave the database in a state in which a STARTUP FORCE startup is necessary. This type of startup should not normally be required but can be used if a normal startup does not work. What is also different about STARTUP FORCE is that it can be issued no matter what mode the database is in. STARTUP FORCE does a shutdown abort and then restarts the database.

STARTUP RESTRICT The STARTUP RESTRICT option starts up the database and places it in OPEN mode but gives access only to users who have the RESTRICTED SESSION privilege. You might want to open a database using the RESTRICTED option when you want to perform maintenance on the database while it is open but ensure that users cannot connect and perform work on the database. You might also want to open the database using the RESTRICTED option to perform database exports or imports and guarantee that no users are accessing the system during these activities. After you are done with your work, you can disable the restricted session, ALTER SYSTEM DISABLE RESTRICTED SESSION, so everyone can connect to the database.

Starting Up Oracle Using EM Database Control

Now that you understand the various startup options, let's look at how to use the EM Database Control to start up the Oracle instance.

When you invoke the Enterprise Manager console, you are notified that the database instance is down (see Figure 9.37).

FIGURE 9.37 The EM Database Control database status screen

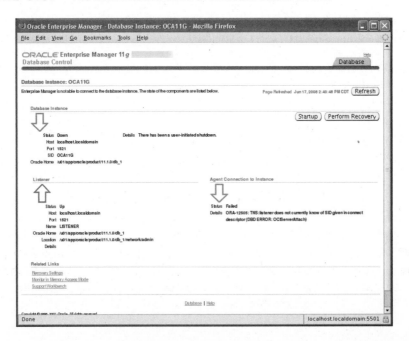

Perform the following steps to start the Oracle instance:

1. Click the Startup button located on the Database Control screen to open the Startup/Shutdown: Specify Host and Target Database Credentials screen (see Figure 9.38).

2. On the Startup/Shutdown: Specify Host and Target Database Credentials screen, you need to supply an operating-system username and password and an Oracle user ID and password that has either the SYSDBA or SYSOPER account authentication. After you enter the appropriate user ID and password information, click OK to open the Startup/Shutdown: Confirmation screen.

3. On the Startup/Shutdown: Confirmation screen, you can click Yes to continue, No to cancel, or Advanced Options to select advanced startup options.

If you click Advanced Options, you can select the type of startup you want. You can choose your startup mode (NOMOUNT, MOUNT, or OPEN), you can choose the parameter file to use, and you can choose to force database startup or to start the database in RESTRICTED mode. Click OK to return to the previous screen. By default, Oracle starts with the OPEN option and uses the default initialization file.

FIGURE 9.38   Startup/Shutdown: Specify Host and Target Database Credentials screen

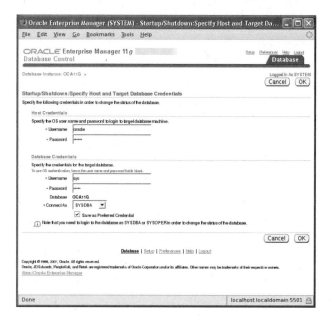

 You can also click Show SQL to see the actual startup command that will be executed.

After you choose the type of startup, click Yes. The startup process may take some time to complete, depending on the system speed and whether Oracle has to perform any recovery operations during the startup process. You will be presented with a screen indicating that the database is being started. If Oracle does not encounter any problems with the startup process, you will be notified that the database is now open and available.

Starting Oracle Using SQL*Plus

You can also use the command-line facility SQL*Plus to start the Oracle Database. You will need to connect to SQL*Plus as a user with SYSOPER or SYSDBA privileges. Here is the syntax of the startup options available:

STARTUP [NOMOUNT|MOUNT|OPEN] [PFILE/SPFILE=] [RESTRICT]

Table 9.11 shows some examples of startup commands that you can use from within SQL*Plus.

TABLE 9.11   SQL*Plus DB Startup-Command Examples

Command	Description
STARTUP NOMOUNT pfile= /u01/oracle/init.ora	Starts Oracle in NOMOUNT mode using a nondefault parameter file
STARTUP MOUNT	Starts Oracle in MOUNT mode using a default spfile or pfile
STARTUP OPEN	Starts Oracle in OPEN mode using a default spfile or pfile
STARTUP RESTRICT	Starts Oracle in OPEN mode and allows only users with restricted session privileges to connect to the database
STARTUP FORCE	Forces database startup using the default pfile or spfile
STARTUP OPEN PFILE= /u01/sp01.ora	Starts Oracle in OPEN mode using a nondefault parameter file

Here is an example of how you can use the STARTUP FORCE command with a nondefault parameter file to start an Oracle Database using SQL*Plus:

```
$ sqlplus / as sysdba
SQL*Plus: Release 11.1.0.6.0 - Production on Tue Jun 17 15:00:42 2008
Copyright (c) 1982, 2007, Oracle.  All rights reserved.
Connected to an idle instance.
SQL> startup force pfile=/home/oracle/pfile1.ora
ORACLE instance started.
Total System Global Area  707244032 bytes
```

```
Fixed Size                  1302260 bytes
Variable Size             306184460 bytes
Database Buffers          394264576 bytes
Redo Buffers                5492736 bytes
Database mounted.
Database opened.
SQL>
```

 If you are running Oracle on Windows, you can also start the database when you start the associated Oracle service. Starting the Oracle service automatically starts the Oracle Database.

Changing Database Startup States Using SQL

When the database is in the NOMOUNT or MOUNT state, you can go to the next state by using the ALTER DATABASE statement instead of shutting down the database and starting with the appropriate state option. The following SQL statements show how to perform database-availability state changes.

- To mount a database to an instance, use ALTER DATABASE MOUNT;.

- To open a database from nomount or mount state, use ALTER DATABSE OPEN;.

- To open a database in read-only mode, use ALTER DATABASE OPEN READ ONLY;.

- To enable restricted mode, use ALTER SYSTEM ENABLE RESTRICTED SESSION;.

- To disable restricted mode, use ALTER SYSTEM DISABLE RESTRICTED SESSION;.

 If the database is already open, you cannot return to the MOUNT or NOMOUNT state. You have to shut down the database and start with the appropriate state.

Shutting Down an Oracle 11*g* Database

In some instances, you will need to shut down a database, such as to perform regularly scheduled cold backups of the database, to perform database upgrades, or to change a non-dynamic initialization parameter. Just as with starting the database, several options as well as a variety of interfaces are available for database shutdown:

SHUTDOWN NORMAL   A normal shutdown is the default type of shutdown that Oracle performs if no shutdown options are provided. You need to be aware of the following when doing a normal shutdown:

- No new Oracle connections are allowed from the time the SHUTDOWN NORMAL command is issued.

- The database will wait until all users are disconnected to proceed with the shutdown process.

Because Oracle waits until all users are disconnected before shutting down, you can find yourself waiting indefinitely for a client who may be connected but is no longer doing any work or may have left for the day. This can require extra work, identifying which connections are still active and either notifying the users to disconnect or forcing the client disconnections by killing their session. This type of shutdown is also known as a *clean* shutdown because when you start Oracle again, no recovery is necessary.

SHUTDOWN TRANSACTIONAL   A transactional shutdown of the database is a bit more aggressive than a normal shutdown. The characteristics of the transactional shutdown are as follows:

- No new Oracle connections are allowed from the time the SHUTDOWN TRANSACTIONAL command is issued.

- No new transactions are allowed to start from the time the SHUTDOWN TRANSACTIONAL command is issued.

- Once all active transactions on the database have completed, all client connections are disconnected.

A transactional shutdown does allow client processes to complete prior to the disconnection. This can prevent a client from losing work and can be valuable especially if the database has long-running transactions that need to be completed prior to shutdown. This type of shutdown is also a clean shutdown and does not require any recovery on a subsequent startup.

SHUTDOWN IMMEDIATE   The immediate shutdown method is the next most aggressive option. An immediate shutdown is characterized as follows:

- No new Oracle connections are allowed from the time the SHUTDOWN IMMEDIATE command is issued.

- Any uncommitted transactions are rolled back. Thus, a user in the middle of a transaction will lose all the uncommitted work.

- Oracle does not wait for clients to disconnect. Any unfinished transactions are rolled back, and their database connections are terminated.

This type of shutdown works well if you want to perform unattended or scripted shutdowns of the database and you need to ensure that the database will shut down without getting hung up during the process by clients who are connected. Even though Oracle is forcing transactions to roll back and disconnecting users, an immediate shutdown is still a clean shutdown. No recovery activity takes place when Oracle is subsequently restarted.

SHUTDOWN ABORT   A shutdown abort is the most aggressive type of shutdown and has the following characteristics:

- No new Oracle connections are allowed from the time the SHUTDOWN ABORT command is issued.

- Any SQL statements currently in progress are terminated, regardless of their state.

- Uncommitted work is not rolled back.

- Oracle disconnects all client connections immediately upon the issuance of the SHUTDOWN ABORT command.

Do not use SHUTDOWN ABORT regularly. Use it only if the other options for database shutdown fail or if you are experiencing some type of database problem that is preventing Oracle from performing a clean shutdown. This type of shutdown is not a clean shutdown and requires instance recovery when the database is subsequently started. Instance recovery is performed automatically when you do the startup—no manual intervention required. During instance recovery the uncommitted changes are rolled back from the database, and committed changes are written to the data files. Oracle uses the redo log files and undo segments to construct the instance recovery information.

Shutting Down Oracle Using EM Database Control

You can use the EM Database Control to shut down the Oracle Database. To do so, invoke the EM Database Control from your web browser:

1. Click the Shutdown button in the Database Control home screen, next to the green up arrow.

2. After you click Shutdown, you are presented with the Startup/Shutdown: Specify Host and Target Database Credentials screen (similar to the screen you had when doing startup in Figure 9.37). You must supply an OS user ID and password to log into the target database machine. If you are not using operating-system authentication, you must also enter an Oracle user ID and password that has SYSDBA authority.

3. After you authenticate, the Startup/Shutdown: Confirmation screen appears. The default shutdown selected when you are using the EM Database Control is SHUTDOWN IMMEDIATE. Oracle also displays the current status of the database on this form.

To perform a nondefault type of shutdown, click the Advanced Options button. On the Startup/Shutdown: Advanced Shutdown Options screen (see Figure 9.39), you can select the type of shutdown.

FIGURE 9.39   The Startup/Shutdown: Advanced Shutdown Options screen

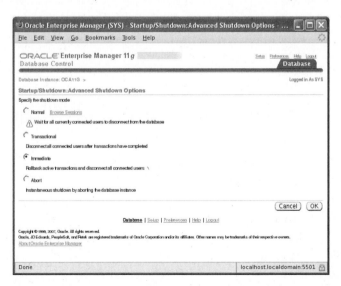

After you select the type of shutdown, click OK, and then click Yes on the Startup/Shutdown: Confirmation screen to open a screen informing you that the database shutdown is in progress. Once the process has completed, click the Refresh button, and you will see that the database is now shut down. On this EM Database Control status screen, you can start the database.

Shutting Down Oracle Using SQL*Plus

You can also use the command-line facility SQL*Plus to shut down the Oracle Database. You will need to connect to SQL*Plus as a user with the SYSOPER or SYSDBA privilege. Here is the syntax of the shutdown options available to you:

```
SHUTDOWN [NORMAL|TRANSACTIONAL|IMMEDIATE|ABORT]
```

Here is an example of how to use the SHUTDOWN IMMEDIATE command to shut down an Oracle Database using SQL*Plus:

```
$ sqlplus / as sysdba
SQL*Plus: Release 11.1.0.6.0 - Production on Tue Jun 17 15:00:04 2008
Copyright (c) 1982, 2007, Oracle.  All rights reserved.
Connected to:
Oracle Database 11g Enterprise Edition Release 11.1.0.6.0 - Production
With the Partitioning, OLAP, Data Mining and Real Application Testing options
SQL> shutdown immediate;
Database closed.
Database dismounted.
ORACLE instance shut down.
SQL>
```

If you are running in a Windows environment and shut down the database using either the Database Control or SQL*Plus tool, the Oracle service will continue to run. Even though the Oracle Windows service is running, the database is not available until a subsequent startup command is issued.

Monitoring the Database Alert Log

The database *alert log*, sometimes referred to as the *alert file*, contains information about certain activities and errors that occur within your database. The alert log contains a chronological summary of these events. The alert log contains a wealth of information that you can use to diagnose system problems and review the history of activities that have occurred on the system. Some of the events and actions recorded in the alert log include the following:

- Startup and shutdown information, including a record of every time a database is started or shut down
- Certain types of administrative actions, such as the ALTER SYSTEM and ALTER DATABASE commands
- Certain types of database errors, such as internal Oracle errors (ORA-600 errors) or space errors (ORA-1542, for example)
- Messages that are errors about shared servers and dispatchers
- Errors during materialized view refreshes
- The values of initialization parameters that have values different from their default values at instance startup

Here is an excerpt from an Oracle 11*g* alert log:

```
Tue Jun 17 11:50:48 2008
ALTER SYSTEM SET memory_target='1G' SCOPE=SPFILE;
Tue Jun 17 12:43:37 2008
ALTER SYSTEM SET undo_retention=3600 SCOPE=MEMORY;
Tue Jun 17 12:47:07 2008
ALTER SYSTEM SET sga_target='500M' SCOPE=BOTH;
Tue Jun 17 15:00:46 2008
… … …
Tue Jun 17 16:32:20 2008
Starting ORACLE instance (normal)
LICENSE_MAX_SESSION = 0
LICENSE_SESSIONS_WARNING = 0
Picked latch-free SCN scheme 2
Using LOG_ARCHIVE_DEST_1 parameter default value as
  /u01/app/oracle/product/11.1.0/db_1/dbs/arch
Using LOG_ARCHIVE_DEST_10 parameter default value as USE_DB_RECOVERY_FILE_DEST
Autotune of undo retention is turned on.
IMODE=BR
ILAT =18
LICENSE_MAX_USERS = 0
SYS auditing is disabled
Starting up ORACLE RDBMS Version: 11.1.0.6.0.
Using parameter settings in server-side spfile
  /u01/app/oracle/product/11.1.0/db_1/dbs/spfileOCA11G.ora
```

```
System parameters with non-default values:
  processes               = 150
  sga_target              = 676M
  control_files           = "/u01/app/oracle/oradata/OCA11G/control01.ctl"
  control_files           = "/u01/app/oracle/oradata/OCA11G/control02.ctl"
  control_files           = "/u01/app/oracle/oradata/OCA11G/control03.ctl"
  db_block_size           = 8192
  compatible              = "11.1.0.0.0"
  db_recovery_file_dest    = "/u01/app/oracle/flash_recovery_area"
  db_recovery_file_dest_size= 2G
  undo_tablespace         = "UNDOTBS1"
  remote_login_passwordfile= "EXCLUSIVE"
  db_domain               = ""
  dispatchers             = "(PROTOCOL=TCP) (SERVICE=OCA11GXDB)"
  audit_file_dest         = "/u01/app/oracle/admin/OCA11G/adump"
  audit_trail             = "DB"
  db_name                 = "OCA11G"
  open_cursors            = 300
  pga_aggregate_target    = 224M
  diagnostic_dest         = "/u01/app/oracle"
Tue Jun 17 16:32:20 2008
PMON started with pid=2, OS id=1353
Tue Jun 17 16:32:20 2008
VKTM started with pid=3, OS id=1355 at elevated priority
VKTM running at (20)ms precision
Tue Jun 17 16:32:20 2008
… … …
RECO started with pid=13, OS id=1379
Tue Jun 17 16:32:20 2008
MMON started with pid=14, OS id=1381
starting up 1 dispatcher(s) for network address
  '(ADDRESS=(PARTIAL=YES)(PROTOCOL=TCP))'...
Tue Jun 17 16:32:20 2008
MMNL started with pid=15, OS id=1383
starting up 1 shared server(s) ...
ORACLE_BASE from environment = /u01/app/oracle
Tue Jun 17 16:32:20 2008
ALTER DATABASE   MOUNT
Setting recovery target incarnation to 2
Successful mount of redo thread 1, with mount id 3172855255
```

```
Database mounted in Exclusive Mode
Lost write protection disabled
Completed: ALTER DATABASE   MOUNT
Tue Jun 17 16:32:27 2008
ALTER DATABASE OPEN
Beginning crash recovery of 1 threads
 parallel recovery started with 2 processes
Started redo scan
Completed redo scan
 636 redo blocks read, 107 data blocks need recovery
Started redo application at
 Thread 1: logseq 46, block 18524
Recovery of Online Redo Log: Thread 1 Group 1 Seq 46 Reading mem 0
  Mem# 0: /u01/app/oracle/oradata/OCA11G/redo01.log
Completed redo application
Completed crash recovery at
 Thread 1: logseq 46, block 19160, scn 1756449
 107 data blocks read, 107 data blocks written, 636 redo blocks read
Thread 1 advanced to log sequence 47
Thread 1 opened at log sequence 47
   Current log# 2 seq# 47 mem# 0: /u01/app/oracle/oradata/OCA11G/redo02.log
Successful open of redo thread 1
MTTR advisory is disabled because FAST_START_MTTR_TARGET is not set
SMON: enabling cache recovery
Successfully onlined Undo Tablespace 2.
Verifying file header compatibility for 11g tablespace encryption..
Verifying 11g file header compatibility for tablespace encryption completed
SMON: enabling tx recovery
Database Characterset is WE8MSWIN1252
Opening with internal Resource Manager plan
Starting background process SMCO
Tue Jun 17 16:32:28 2008
SMCO started with pid=21, OS id=1401
Starting background process FBDA
replication_dependency_tracking turned off (no async multimaster replication
found)
Tue Jun 17 16:32:29 2008
FBDA started with pid=23, OS id=1408
Starting background process QMNC
Tue Jun 17 16:32:29 2008
```

```
QMNC started with pid=22, OS id=1416
db_recovery_file_dest_size of 2048 MB is 0.00% used. This is a
user-specified limit on the amount of space that will be used by this
database for recovery-related files, and does not reflect the amount of
space available in the underlying filesystem or ASM diskgroup.
```

Completed: ALTER DATABASE OPEN

This excerpt shows a successful startup of a database. Notice the section that lists the nondefault initialization parameters. Also notice that Oracle performed an automatic recovery of the database. This indicates that the database was not shut down cleanly prior to this startup. You can also see that Oracle is starting dispatcher processes, which indicates I am running Oracle Shared Server.

The parameter that governs the location of the alert log is DIAGNOSTIC_DEST. This parameter is set to a path that designates where Oracle should place the log. The default value for DIAGNOSTIC_DEST is the ORACLE_BASE environment value, if set when starting the database. If ORACLE_BASE is not set, DIAGNOSTIC_DEST will default to the directory of ORACLE_HOME/log.

Oracle 11*g* supports two types of alert log files. The XML version of the file is located in the DIANOSTIC_DEST/rdbms/dbname/instancename/alert directory. The text file is in the DIANOSTIC_DEST/rdbms/*dbname*/*instancename*/trace directory. The alert log file is always named *alert_<instancename>.log*. For example, the alert log file name for the OCA11G database would be alert_oca11g.log.

The dictionary view V$DIAG_INFO shows the exact location of the alert log file for the instance. Here is an example from the OCA11G database running on a Linux server:

```
SQL> SELECT name, value FROM v$diag_info;
```

NAME	VALUE
Diag Enabled	TRUE
ADR Base	/u01/app/oracle
ADR Home	/u01/app/oracle/diag/rdbms/oca11g/OCA11G
Diag Trace	/u01/app/oracle/diag/rdbms/oca11g/OCA11G/trace
Diag Alert	/u01/app/oracle/diag/rdbms/oca11g/OCA11G/alert
Diag Incident	/u01/app/oracle/diag/rdbms/oca11g/OCA11G/incident
Diag Cdump	/u01/app/oracle/diag/rdbms/oca11g/OCA11G/cdump
Health Monitor	/u01/app/oracle/diag/rdbms/oca11g/OCA11G/hm
Default Trace File	/u01/app/oracle/diag/rdbms/oca11g/OCA11G/trace/OCA11G_ora_9018.trc
Active Problem Count	0
Active Incident Count	0

The ADR Base value is the directory specified (or derived by the instance using ORACLE_BASE or ORACLE_HOME) for DIGNOSTIC_DEST. The Diag Trace location is where the text version of the alert log file located.

The alert log is continuously appended to, so it is a good idea to periodically purge it. Many DBAs do so daily or weekly, saving a copy of the current alert log to a backup and clearing the current alert log. It is a good idea to save the log contents. You can use it to review when any initialization parameters have changed and to review database errors or problems recorded in the log.

You can view the alert log content using the EM Database Control. From the Server screen, click on the alert log contents link at the bottom under Related Links. Figure 9.40 shows the contents of alert log from EM.

The alert log file of an Oracle database 11*g* is part of the advanced fault diagnosability infrastructure known as the Automatic Diagnostic Repository (ADR). To learn more about ADR, read Chapter 8 of the "Oracle Database Administrator's Guide 11*g* Release 1 (11.1) Part Number B28310-03" document. All Oracle documentation can be accessed online at http://tahiti .oracle.com.

FIGURE 9.40   EM View Alert Log Contents screen

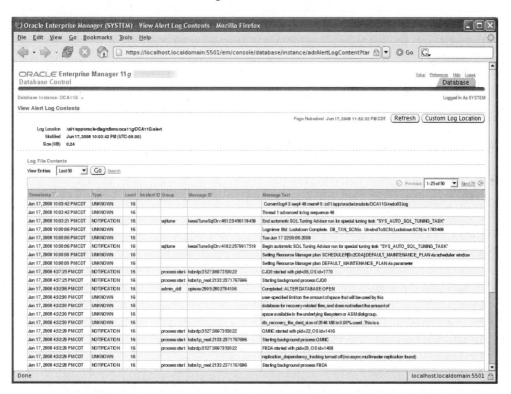

In Exercise 9.2, you'll learn to create an Oracle Database 11*g* without using DBCA.

EXERCISE 9.2

Creating an Oracle 11*g* database

You have learned to use the DBCA to create a database, learned to start and stop a database, and learned about alert log files and Oracle dictionary. Though the DBCA does all the background work and creates a database for you, it's good to know the stages in database creation and any relevant scripts needed if you decide to create the database manually. Here are the steps to create an Oracle 11*g* database on the Linux platform:

1. Set up the relevant environment variables before creating the database. The three important variables are ORACLE_SID, ORACLE_BASE, and ORACLE_HOME. The ORACLE_SID variable is the instance identifier, which can be up to 12 characters. On Unix platforms, the instance identifier is case sensitive. The ORACLE_BASE parameter decides where the trace file and dump file directories will be located. ORACLE_HOME is the location where the Oracle 11*g* software is installed.

    ```
    export ORACLE_SID=OCA11G2
    export ORACLE_BASE=/u01/app/oracle
    export ORACLE_HOME=/u01/app/oracle/product/11.1.0
    ```

2. Create a password file using the ORAPWD utility. This allows administrative logins to the Oracle 11*g* database from tools such as EM Database Control.

    ```
    cd $ORACLE_HOME/dbs
    orapwd file=orapwOCA11G2
    ```

3. Create an initialization-parameter file. You can create a text-based pfile, and using SQL*Plus you can create the spfile from the pfile.

    ```
    cd $ORACLE_HOME/dbs
    sqlplus / as sysdba
    SQL> create spfile from pfile;
    ```

4. Start the instance in NOMOUNT mode:

    ```
    SQL> startup nomount;
    ```

5. Create the database using the CREATE DATABASE statement. This statement creates the database with SYSTEM, SYSAUX, TEMP, and UNDOTBS1 tablespaces. It creates control files specified in the location of CONTROL_FILES parameter and redo log files. It also sets a password for SYS and SYSTEM users.

    ```
    CREATE DATABASE "OCA11G2"
    DATAFILE '/u01/app/oracle/oradata/OCA11G2/system01.dbf'
    SIZE 300M REUSE AUTOEXTEND ON NEXT  10240K MAXSIZE UNLIMITED
    EXTENT MANAGEMENT LOCAL
    ```

```
SYSAUX DATAFILE '/u01/app/oracle/oradata/OCA11G2/sysaux01.dbf'
SIZE 120M REUSE AUTOEXTEND ON NEXT  10240K MAXSIZE UNLIMITED
SMALLFILE DEFAULT TEMPORARY TABLESPACE TEMP TEMPFILE '/u01/app/oracle/
oradata/OCA11G2/temp01.dbf'
SIZE 20M REUSE AUTOEXTEND ON NEXT  640K MAXSIZE UNLIMITED
SMALLFILE UNDO TABLESPACE "UNDOTBS1" DATAFILE '/u01/app/oracle/oradata/
OCA11G2/undotbs01.dbf'
SIZE 200M REUSE AUTOEXTEND ON NEXT  5120K MAXSIZE UNLIMITED
CHARACTER SET WE8MSWIN1252
LOGFILE GROUP 1 ('/u01/app/oracle/oradata/OCA11G2/redo01.log') SIZE
51200K,
GROUP 2 ('/u01/app/oracle/oradata/OCA11G2/redo02.log') SIZE 51200K
USER SYS IDENTIFIED BY mypwd USER SYSTEM IDENTIFIED BY mypwd;
```

6. Create additional tablespaces if any are needed:

```
CREATE TABLESPACE "USERS"
DATAFILE '/u01/app/oracle/oradata/OCA11G2/users01.dbf' SIZE 5M;
```

7. Build data dictionary views and public synonyms (? in SQL*Plus refers to the ORACLE_ HOME directory):

```
SQL> @?/rdbms/admin/catalog.sql
```

8. Build the PL/SQL packages:

```
SQL> @?/rdbms/admin/catproc.sql
```

9. If you want to install additional options such as JVM or Oracle Ultra Search, run the relevant scripts:

```
SQL> @?/javavm/install/initjvm.sql;
```

10. Create an EM repository in the database:

```
SQL> @?/sysman/admin/emdrep/sql/emreposcre $ORACLE_HOME SYSMAN mypwd
TEMP ON
```

11. Configure EM Database Control:

```
$ORACLE_HOME/bin/emca -config dbcontrol db
```

Summary

In this chapter, you started off by learning how to create an Oracle 11*g* database using the Database Configuration Assistant. Then I discussed the Oracle metadata dictionary and parameter files. You also learned about database startup and shutdown as well as the alert log file.

You can use the DBCA to create databases. You can choose from preexisting database definitions stored as XML templates or create a database definition from a custom template. All aspects of the database, including database name, file location, sizing, and initialization-parameter settings, are defined within the DBCA. You can create a database after completing the database definition, or you can save the definition as a template or series of scripts to be run at a later time. You can also use the DBCA to remove databases or add options to existing databases.

You can manage and create new template definitions using the DBCA interface. This is advantageous because it serves as a way to centrally manage all your database definitions. You can also create new databases from existing databases with the DBCA by using templates.

Oracle uses initialization-parameter files to store information about initialization parameters used when an Oracle instance starts. Oracle reads the parameter file to obtain information about how the Oracle instance should be sized and configured upon startup. The parameter file can be either a plain-text file, commonly referred to as a pfile, or a binary file that is referred to as an spfile. You can use the EM Database Control facility to change existing database parameters.

The data dictionary contains information about the database and database objects. The data dictionary is created when the database is created using the script `catalog.sql`. The data dictionary views have static data, whereas the dynamic performance views have data that does not persist across database shutdowns.

The database needs to be started in order for work to be done against it. You can start up the database in one of several modes: MOUNT, NOMOUNT, and OPEN. You can also start up the database with the RESTRICT option to restrict general access to the database. You can also start up a database using the FORCE option if other startup methods fail.

You can shut down the database using one of several options: NORMAL, TRANSACTIONAL, IMMEDIATE, and ABORT. The NORMAL, TRANSACTIONAL, and IMMEDIATE options are considered clean shutdowns because no recovery is necessary upon a subsequent startup. You can start up and shut down the database using a variety of interfaces, including the EM Database Control utility and SQL*Plus.

The alert log contains information about certain activities and errors that occur within your database. The alert log contains a chronological summary of these events and a wealth of information that you can use to diagnose system problems and review histories of activities that occurred on the system. The DIGNOSTIC_DEST parameter determines the location of the alert log.

Exam Essentials

Be able to create a database using the DBCA. Describe the steps involved in creating a database using the Oracle Database Configuration Assistant (DBCA). Understand how the DBCA uses templates to store information about databases and how templates are used by the DBCA to create databases. Be familiar with the various options available to you when creating an Oracle Database using the DBCA.

Know how to manage DBCA templates. Understand how to use the DBCA to manage templates and the various options available when creating new database templates. Understand what each option is and when it should be used.

Describe the database startup modes. Understand the various modes of database startup. Understand what each database startup option is and when you might use the option.

Recognize how to start up an Oracle Database. Understand how to use the database tools to start up an Oracle Database.

Describe the database-shutdown modes. Understand the various modes of database shutdown. Understand what each database-shutdown option is and when you might use the option.

Be able to shut down an Oracle Database. Understand how to use the database tools to shut down an Oracle Database.

Know how to manage the Oracle parameter file. Be able to identify the Oracle parameter file and the different types of parameter files. Also understand how you can change the parameter files.

View and understand the contents of the Oracle alert log. Be able to identify the Oracle alert log and the kinds of information Oracle writes to the alert log. Be able to identify the database initialization parameter that provides the location of the alert log.

Be familiar with the metadata dictionary. Understand the difference between the static data dictionary and dynamic performance views.

Review Questions

1. You noticed that the current value of the UNDO_RETENTION parameter is 900 and is too low for some of your transactions. You issue the following statement:

   ALTER SYSTEM SET UNDO_RETENTION=4800;

   Which option is true?

   A. UNDO_RETENTION is a static parameter and hence cannot be changed using ALTER SYSTEM.

   B. The change will be available to the instance only after a database cycle.

   C. The value is changed in memory, and when the database restarts the next time, the new value will be preserved when using the spfile.

   D. The value is changed only in memory, and the server parameter file needs to be updated for the change to persist across database shutdowns.

2. You need to find the directory where the Oracle alert log is being written. Which initialization parameter contains this information?

   A. ALERT_LOG_DEST

   B. BACKGROUND_DUMP_DEST

   C. DIAGNOSTIC_DEST

   D. INIT_LOG_DUMP_DEST

3. Which data dictionary view is used to view the current values of parameters?

   A. V$DATABASE

   B. V$SPPARAMETER

   C. V$PARAMETER

   D. V$SYSPARAMETER

4. Which startup options must be used to start the instance when you're creating a new database?

   A. STARTUP FORCE

   B. STARTUP MOUNT

   C. STARTUP RESTRICT

   D. STARTUP NOMOUNT

5. The `DIAGNOSTIC_DEST` parameter is not set up in the initialization-parameter file. The value of the `ORACLE_HOME` environment variable is `/u01/app/oracle/product/11.1.0`, and the value of `ORACLE_BASE` is `/u01/app/oracle`. The database name is xyz, so what is the location of the text-alert log file for the xyz database?

A. `/u01/app/oracle/product/11.1.0/log/rdbms/xyz/xyz/trace`

B. `/u01/app/oracle/diag/rdbms/xyz/xyz/trace`

C. `/u01/app/oracle/diag/rdbms/xyz/xyz/alert`

D. `/u01/app/oracle/product/11.1.0/diag/rdbms/xyz/xyz/trace`

E. `/u01/app/oracle/log/rdbms/xyz/xyz/trace`

6. You want to create a database using the DBCA with `DB_BLOCK_SIZE` as 32KB. Which statement is true?

A. A block size of 32KB is not allowed in Oracle 11*g*.

B. You must choose the Data Warehouse template in the DBCA.

C. You must choose the Custom template in the DBCA.

D. You must set the environment variable `DB_BLOCK_SIZE` to 32768.

7. All the following are database-management options within the Database Configuration Assistant except which one?

A. Change Database Initialization Parameters

B. Create a Database

C. Manage Templates

D. Delete a Database

8. Which of the following is another term for the fully qualified name of a database?

A. ORACLE SID

B. Global database name

C. Global identifier

D. Oracle global name

E. ORACLE ID

9. Which of the following Oracle accounts is not automatically configured by the DBCA?

A. SYS

B. SYSTEM

C. SYSMAN

D. DBSNMP

E. All these accounts are configured automatically by DBCA.

10. Your database name is OCA11G. The options show the files that are available in the $ORACLE_HOME/dbs directory. Which file is used to start up the database instance when you issue the STARTUP command?

    A. initOCA11G.ora

    B. OCA11Gspfile.ora

    C. spfile.ora

    D. init.ora

11. Which initialization parameter cannot be changed after creating the database?

    A. DB_BLOCK_SIZE

    B. DB_NAME

    C. CONTROL_FILES

    D. None. All parameters can be changed as and when required.

12. Which script creates the database dictionary?

    A. dictionary.sql

    B. catdict.sql

    C. catproc.sql

    D. catalog.sql

13. If your database name is PROD and your instance name is PROD1, what would be the name of the text-alert log file?

    A. alertPROD.log

    B. alert_PROD1.log

    C. PROD1alert.log

    D. PROD_alert.log

14. Your database is not responding and is in a hung state. You want to shut down and start the database to release all resources. Which statements would you use?

    A. STARTUP AFTER SHUTDOWN

    B. STARTUP FORCE

    C. SHUTDOWN FORCE

    D. SHUTDOWN ABORT and STARTUP

15. Which of the following startup options does not perform a database recovery?

    A. STARTUP

    B. STARTUP FORCE RESTRICT

    C. STARTUP NOMOUNT

    D. STARTUP OPEN

    E. STARTUP RESTRICT

16. Which of the following shutdown statements does not perform a clean shutdown?

    A. SHUTDOWN ABORT

    B. SHUTDOWN TRANSACTIONAL

    C. SHUTDOWN

    D. SHUTDOWN IMMEDIATE

    E. All of these are considered clean shutdowns.

17. You would like to export the system and limit access to only the DBA staff during the export process. Which of the following startup options should you use?

    A. STARTUP NOMOUNT RESTRICT

    B. STARTUP RESTRICT

    C. STARTUP MOUNT RESTRICT

    D. STARTUP MOUNT FORCE RESTRICT

18. You want to start up the database using a binary initialization file. What is another name for this file?

    A. Configfile

    B. Pfile

    C. Spfile

    D. init_pfile.ora

19. Under normal circumstances, which of the following actions or events is not found in the Oracle alert log?

    A. Database startup and shutdown information

    B. Nondefault initialization parameters

    C. ORA-00600 errors

    D. New columns added to a user table

20. Which of the following is true about EM Database Control? (Choose all that apply.)

    A. You can start up and shut down a database using Database Control.

    B. You can read the contents of the alert log file.

    C. You can modify static initialization parameters.

    D. The CREATE DATABASE statement creates the Database Control repository in the database.

Answers to Review Questions

1. C. When using ALTER SYSTEM to change parameter values, the change is made to the server parameter file (spfile) too, because the default for the SCOPE clause is BOTH. Option D would have been correct, if the pfile was used to start up the database.

2. C. DIAGNOSTIC_DEST is the initialization parameter that determines where the Automatic Diagnostic Repository home is. The alert log file would be in the *<diagnostic_dest>*/ diag/rdbms/*<dbname>*/*<instancename>*/alert directory. A text version of the alert log is in the *<diagnostic_dest>*/diag/rdbms/*<dbname>*/*<instancename>*/trace directory.

3. C. V$PARAMETER shows information about the parameters and their current value in the database. V$SPPARAMTER shows the information as read from the spfile.

4. D. When creating a new database or creating a control file, the database should be in the NOMOUNT state.

5. B. The alert log file in Oracle 11g is saved in the $ORACLE_BASE/diag/rdbms/*<dbname>*/ *<instancename>*/trace directory. The XML version of the alert-log file is in the $ORACLE_BASE/diag/rdbms/*<dbname>*/*<instancename>*/alert directory.

6. C. The Custom template lets you choose the database block size in the DBCA. If the template includes data files, the block size of the template cannot be changed. The predefined templates that come with data files have the block size at 8KB.

7. A. The Database Configuration Assistant lets you create databases, manage templates, add database options, and delete databases. Although you can change initialization parameters when you are defining a database, this is not one of the management options available.

8. B. The *global database name* is another term for the fully qualified name of a database. The global database name is composed of the database name and database domain.

9. E. The DBCA configures the SYS, SYSTEM, SYSMAN, and DBSNMP accounts by default. You can unlock the accounts and set the initial password.

10. C. When starting the instance, Oracle looks for spfileOCA11G.ora file. If it could not find that file, it looks for spfile.ora. If that file is not found, Oracle looks for the initOCA11G .ora file.

11. A. The block size of the database cannot be changed after database creation. The database name can be changed after re-creating the control file with a new name, and the CONTROL_ FILES parameter can be changed after copying the control files to the new location.

12. D. The catalog.sql script creates the data dictionary views, dynamic performance views, and synonyms.

13. B. The text-alert log file has the name alert_<instancename>.log. For most non-RAC databases, the instance name and database name would be the same.

14. B, D. STARTUP FORCE will perform a SHUTDOWN ABORT and STARTUP of the database. SHUTDOWN ABORT will terminate all sessions and processes and shut down the instance.

15. C. The recovery of a database occurs when the database moves from the MOUNT mode to the OPEN mode. All these options attempt to start up and open the database except for option C, which only puts the database in NOMOUNT mode.

16. A. Any time you perform a SHUTDOWN ABORT, Oracle does not perform a clean shutdown. All other types of shutdowns are considered clean shutdowns because Oracle will not have to perform recovery on a subsequent database startup.

17. B. The STARTUP RESTRICT choice opens the database and allows only users with RESTRICTED database access to connect and use it.

18. C. A pfile is another term for a server-side binary file that Oracle reads when a database startup is performed. This binary file contains all the nondefault initialization parameters used at startup.

19. D. The Oracle alert log contains a chronological history of administrative events and actions and certain types of database errors that occur within the database. Adding a column to a user table is not an administrative action and is not recorded in the alert log.

20. A, B, C. The Database Control repository is not created when the CREATE DATABASE statement is executed. DBCA creates the Database Control repository and configures Database Control for you.

Chapter

10

Allocating Database Storage and Creating Schema Objects

ORACLE DATABASE 11g: ADMINISTRATION I EXAM OBJECTIVES COVERED IN THIS CHAPTER:

✓ **Managing Database Storage Structures**

- Overview of tablespace and datafiles
- Create and manage tablespaces
- Space management in tablespaces

✓ **Managing Schema Objects**

- Create and Modify tables
- Manage Constraints
- Create indexes
- Create and use temporary tables

In this chapter, you will learn more about the physical and logical storage structures. To start, you'll explore how a tablespace is the highest level of logical structure in an Oracle Database 11*g*, whereas a data file is a physical structure that is associated with a tablespace. I will also discuss how tables and indexes are logical structures that reside in a tablespace.

Additionally, you will learn about creating and managing tablespaces and how space is allocated and managed within tablespaces. I discussed creating tables and indexes in Chapter 6, "Creating Tables and Constraints," and Chapter 7, "Creating Schema Objects." Finally, you will learn how to create these structures specifying storage attributes.

Tablespaces and Data Files Overview

The database's data is stored logically in tablespaces and physically in data files that correspond to the tablespaces. The logical storage management is independent of the physical storage of the data files. A tablespace can have more than one data file associated with it, whereas one data file belongs to only one tablespace. A database has more than one tablespace. Figure 10.1 shows the relationship between the database, tablespaces, data files, and objects within the tablespace. Any object (such as a nonpartitioned table or index) created in the database is stored on a single tablespace, but the object's physical storage can be on multiple data files belonging to that tablespace. A segment is created when a table or index is created and is stored on a single tablespace.

I discussed the logical structures block, extent, and segment in Chapter 8, "Introducing Oracle Database 11*g* Components and Architecture." Here is a brief refresher of what you learned in Chapter 8. Starting with the highest level of Oracle disk-space management are tablespaces. Drilling down, you find *segments* that can reside in only one tablespace. Each segment is constructed from one or more *extents*. Each of these extents can reside in only one *data file*. Thus, for a segment to straddle multiple data files, it must be constructed from multiple extents that are located in separate data files. An extent is composed of a contiguous set of *data blocks*, which is at the lowest level of space management. A data block is a fixed number of bytes of disk space.

The size of the tablespace is the total size of all the data files belonging to that tablespace. The size of the database is the total size of all tablespaces in the database, which is the total size of all data files in the database. Changing the size of the data files belonging to a tablespace can change the size of that tablespace. You can add more space to a tablespace by adding more data files to the tablespace. You can then add more space to the database either by adding more tablespaces, by adding more data files to the existing tablespaces, or by increasing the size of the existing data files.

FIGURE 10.1   Tablespaces and data files

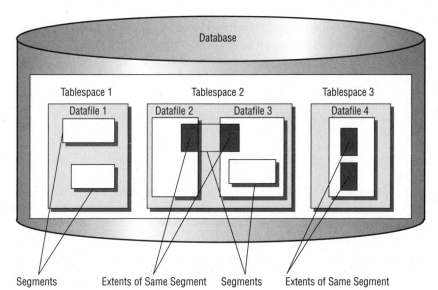

When you create a database, Oracle creates the SYSTEM tablespace. All the data dictionary objects are stored in this tablespace. You can add more space to the SYSTEM tablespace after you create the database by adding more data files or by increasing the size of the data files. The PL/SQL program units (such as procedures, functions, packages, or triggers) created in the database are also stored in the SYSTEM tablespace.

 The SYSTEM tablespace is a special tablespace that is required to be online all the time for the database to function properly. SYSAUX is an auxiliary tablespace always created when an Oracle 11*g* database is created. The SYSAUX and SYSTEM tablespaces cannot be renamed or dropped.

Oracle recommends not creating any objects other than the Oracle data dictionary in the SYSTEM tablespace. By having multiple tablespaces, you can do the following:

- Separate the Oracle dictionary from other database objects. Doing so reduces contention between dictionary objects and database objects for the same data file.
- Control I/O by allocating separate physical storage disks for different tablespaces.
- Manage space quotas for users on tablespaces.
- Have separate tablespaces for temporary segments (TEMP) and undo management (rollback segments). You can also create a tablespace for a specific activity; for example, you can place high-update tables in a separate tablespace. When creating the database, you can specify tablespace names for temporary tablespaces and undo tablespaces.

- Group application-related or module-related data together so that when maintenance is required for the application's tablespace, only that tablespace need be taken offline, and the rest of the database is available for users.
- Back up the database one tablespace at a time.
- Make part of the database read-only.

When you create a tablespace, Oracle creates the data files with the size specified. The space reserved for the data file is formatted but does not contain any user data. Whenever spaces for objects are needed, extents are allocated from this free space.

The tablespace name cannot exceed 30 characters. The name should begin with an alphabetic character and can contain alphabetic characters, numeric characters, and the special characters #, _, and $.

Managing Tablespaces

Tablespaces logically group schema objects for administration convenience. Tablespaces can store zero or more segments. *Segments* are schema objects that require storage outside the data dictionary. Tables and indexes are examples of segments. *Constraints* and sequences are examples of schema objects that do not store data outside the data dictionary and are therefore not segments.

You can place the tables and indexes associated with an application into a set of tablespaces in order to manage that data more easily. You can take a tablespace offline and recover it (potentially to a different point in time), separate from the rest of the database. You can also move it to another database and configure it as read-only so that you do not have to make additional backups of static data.

In the following sections, you will learn how to create and manage tablespaces in your database.

Identifying Default Tablespaces

The SYSTEM tablespace is used for the data dictionary and should not be used to store schema objects other than those that the installation places there. The SYSAUX tablespace stores schema objects associated with Oracle-provided features, such as the spatial data option, Extended Markup Language Database (XMLDB), or Oracle Multimedia (formerly known as Intermedia).

The SYSTEM and SYSAUX tablespaces are always created when the database is created. One or more temporary tablespaces are usually created in a database as well as an undo tablespace and several application tablespaces. Because SYSTEM and SYSAUX are the only tablespaces always created with the database, SYSTEM is the default tablespace for temporary and user data if another tablespace is not defined. You should not, however, continue to use them as the default tablespace for your users or applications. In the following sections, you will learn how to create additional tablespaces and enable their use as better defaults.

Creating and Maintaining Tablespaces

You create tablespaces using either the CREATE DATABASE or CREATE TABLESPACE statement. You must make several choices when creating a tablespace:

- Whether to make the tablespace bigfile or smallfile

- Whether to manage extents locally or with the dictionary

- Whether to manage segment space automatically or manually

Additionally, there are specialized tablespaces for temporary segments and undo segments.

A tablespace is created with the CREATE TABLESPACE statement. The following statement creates a tablespace named HR_DATA. The data file associated with the tablespace is physically stored on the disk at /u02/oradata/11GR11/hr_data01.dbf and has a size of 20MB.

```
SQL> CREATE TABLESPACE HR_DATA
  2   DATAFILE '/u02/oradata/11GR11/hr_data01.dbf'
  3   SIZE 20M;

Tablespace created.
SQL>
```

In the following sections, I will discuss the various options available when creating a tablespace.

Creating Bigfile and Smallfile Tablespaces

Bigfile tablespaces are built on a single data file (or temp file), which can be as many as 2^{32} data blocks in size. So, a bigfile tablespace that uses 8KB data blocks can be as much as 32TB in size (the maximum size is 128TB for a 32KB block size).

Bigfile tablespaces are intended for very large databases. When a very large database has thousands of read-write data files, operations that must update the data file headers, such as checkpoints, can take a relatively long time. If you reduce the number of data files, these operations can complete faster.

To create a bigfile tablespace, use the keyword BIGFILE in the CREATE statement, like this:

```
CREATE BIGFILE TABLESPACE PO_ARCHIVE
DATAFILE '/u02/oradata/11GR11/po_archive.dbf' size 25G;
```

Smallfile tablespace is the new name for the old Oracle tablespace data file option. With a smallfile tablespace, you can have multiple data files for a tablespace. Each data file can be as many as 2^{22} data blocks in size. So, data files in a smallfile tablespace that uses 8KB data blocks are limited to 32GB. The smallfile tablespace can have as many as 1,022 data files, limiting the 8KB data block tablespace to slightly less than 32TB—about the same as a bigfile tablespace.

To create a smallfile tablespace, either omit the keyword BIGFILE or explicitly use the keyword SMALLFILE, like this:

```
CREATE SMALLFILE TABLESPACE PO_DETAILS
DATAFILE '/u02/oradata/11GR11/po_details.dbf' size 2G;
```

> By default, Oracle Database 11*g* creates SMALLFILE tablespaces so that you do not have to specify SMALLFILE in the CREATE TABLESPACE statement. The DATABASE_PROPERTIES dictionary view shows what is the default tablespace type for your Oracle 11*g* database (look for the property name DEFAULT_TBS_TYPE). You can use the ALTER DATABASE statement to change the default behavior.

Working with Oracle Managed File Tablespaces

The Oracle Managed Files (OMF) feature can ease the administration of files used by an Oracle 11*g* database. Using the OMF feature, you specify operations in terms of tablespaces and not operating-system files. You don't explicitly name data files or temp files; the database does this for you.

To enable the OMF feature, set the initialization parameter DB_CREATE_FILE_DEST to the directory where you want the database to create and manage your data and temp files, like this:

```
ALTER SYSTEM SET
  db_create_file_dest = '/u02/oradata/'  SCOPE=BOTH;
```

When creating a tablespace using the OMF feature, you simply omit the filename:

```
CREATE TABLESPACE hr_data;
```

Oracle creates a tablespace using a unique filename, such as o1_mf_hr_data_46n3ck5t_ .dbf under the /u02/oradata/11GR11/datafile directory. Notice that Oracle 11*g* adds the subdirectories DBNAME/datafile in the DB_CREATE_FILE_DEST directory. This data file will have autoextend enabled and be 100MB unless you specify a different size. By default, the tablespace is a smallfile tablespace, but you can specify a bigfile tablespace by including the keyword BIGFILE.

The OMF feature is discussed later in the chapter.

Choosing Extent Management

When Oracle allocates space to an object in a tablespace, it is allocated in chunks of contiguous database blocks known as *extents*. Each object is allocated a segment, which has one or more extents. Oracle maintains the extent information such as extents free, extent size, extents allocated, and so on, either in the data dictionary or in the tablespace itself.

If you store the *extent management* information in the dictionary for a tablespace, that tablespace is called a *dictionary-managed tablespace*. Whenever an extent is allocated or freed, the information is updated in the corresponding dictionary tables. Such updates also generate undo information.

With dictionary extent management, the database tracks free and used extents in the data dictionary, changing the FET$ and UET$ tables with recursive SQL. With local extent management, the free/used extent information is maintained in a bitmap pattern in the header of the data file. So, Oracle has to check in the local bitmap instead of making trips to the UET$ or FET$ table. Local extent management is the default if not specified and is generally the preferred technique.

A simple example of a dictionary-managed tablespace creation command is as follows:

```
CREATE TABLESPACE APPL_DATA
DATAFILE '/disk3/oradata/DB01/appl_data01.dbf' SIZE 100M
EXTENT MANAGEMENT DICTIONARY;
```

This statement creates a tablespace named APPL_DATA; the data file specified is created with a size of 100MB. You can specify more than one file under the DATAFILE clause separated by commas; you may need to create more files if there are any operating-system limits on the file size. For example, if you need to have 6GB allocated for the tablespace and the operating system allows only 2GB as the maximum file size, you need three data files for the tablespace. The statement will be as follows:

```
CREATE TABLESPACE APPL_DATA
DATAFILE '/disk3/oradata/DB01/appl_data01.dbf' SIZE 2000M,
         '/disk3/oradata/DB01/appl_data02.dbf' SIZE 2000M,
         '/disk4/oradata/DB01/appl_data03.dbf' SIZE 2000M
EXTENT MANAGEMENT DICTIONARY;
```

The options available when creating and reusing a data file are discussed in the section "Managing Data Files" later in this chapter.

If you store the management information in the tablespace by using bitmaps in each data file, such a tablespace is known as a *locally managed tablespace*. Each bit in the bitmap corresponds to a block or a group of blocks. When an extent is allocated or freed for reuse, Oracle changes the bitmap values to show the new status of the blocks. These changes do not generate rollback information because they do not update tables in the data dictionary.

With locally managed tablespaces, you have two options for how extents are allocated: UNIFORM and AUTOALLOCATE. The UNIFORM option tells the database to allocate and deallocate extents in the tablespace with the same unvarying size that you can specify or let extents default to 1MB. UNIFORM is the default for temporary tablespaces and cannot be specified for undo tablespaces. To create consistent 10MB extents, use the clause EXTENT MANAGEMENT LOCAL UNIFORM SIZE 10M in the CREATE TABLESPACE statement. Here is an example:

```
CREATE TABLESPACE hr_index
DATAFILE '/u02/oradata/11GR11/hr_index01.dbf' SIZE 2G
EXTENT MANAGEMENT LOCAL UNIFORM SIZE 10M;
```

The minimum extent size for a locally managed tablespace with
AUTOALLOCATE is 64KB.

AUTOALLOCATE, on the other hand, tells the database to vary the size of extents for each segment. For example, on Windows and Linux with 8KB data blocks, each segment starts out with 64KB extents for the first 16 extents, and then the extents increase in size to 1MB for the next 63 extents. The size then increases to 8MB for the next 120 extents, then 64MB, and so on, as the segment grows. This algorithm allows small segments to remain small and large segments to grow without gaining too many extents. AUTOALLOCATE is best used for a general-purpose mixture of small and large tables. Here is an example of creating a tablespace using AUTOALLOCATE:

```
CREATE TABLESPACE hr_index
DATAFILE '/u02/oradata/11GR11/hr_index01.dbf' SIZE 2G
EXTENT MANAGEMENT LOCAL AUTOALLOCATE;
```

Bigfile tablespaces are created as locally managed; you cannot specify the EXTENT MANAGEMENT DICTIONARY clause for bigfile tablespaces. You can convert a smallfile tablespace from dictionary extent management to local extent management and back with the Oracle-supplied PL/SQL package DBMS_SPACE_ADMIN.

When the SYSTEM tablespace is created as a locally managed tablespace,
you cannot create dictionary-managed tablespaces in the database. The
Oracle 11g DBCA tool by default creates the SYSTEM tablespace as locally
managed.

Choosing Segment Space Management

For tablespaces that have local extent management, you can use either manual or automatic *segment space management*. Manual segment space management exists for backward compatibility and uses free-block lists to identify the data blocks available for inserts together with the parameters PCTFREE and PCTUSED, which control when a block is made available for inserts.

After each INSERT or UPDATE, the database compares the remaining free space in that data block with the segment's PCTFREE setting. If the data block has less than PCTFREE free space (meaning it is almost full), it is taken off the free-block list and is no longer available for inserts. The remaining free space is reserved for update operations that may increase the size of rows in that data block. After each UPDATE or DELETE, the database compares the used space in that data block with that segment's PCTUSED setting. If the data block has less than PCTUSED used space, the data block is deemed empty enough for inserts and is placed on the free block list.

To specify manual segment space management, use the SEGMENT SPACE MANAGEMENT MANUAL clause of the CREATE TABLESPACE statement, or simply omit the SEGMENT SPACE

MANAGEMENT AUTO clause. Oracle strongly recommends AUTOMATIC segment space management for permanent locally managed tablespaces, and the default behavior of Oracle 11*g* is AUTO. Here is a statement that creates a tablespace with manual segment space management:

```
CREATE TABLESPACE hr_index
DATAFILE '/u02/oradata/11GR11/hr_index01.dbf'  SIZE 2G
EXTENT MANAGEMENT LOCAL AUTOALLOCATE
SEGMENT SPACE MANAGEMENT MANUAL;
```

When automatic segment space management is specified, bitmaps are used instead of free lists to identify which data blocks are available for inserts. The parameters PCTFREE and PCTUSED are ignored for segments in tablespaces with automatic segment space management. Automatic segment space management is available only on tablespaces configured for local extent management; it is not available for temporary or system tablespaces. Automatic segment space management performs better and reduces your maintenance tasks, making it the preferred technique.

To specify automatic segment space management, use the SEGMENT SPACE MANAGEMENT AUTO clause of the CREATE TABLESPACE statement like this or do not include the SEGMENT SPACE MANAGEMENT clause (it is the default):

```
CREATE TABLESPACE hr_index
DATAFILE '/u02/oradata/11GR11/hr_index01.dbf'  SIZE 2G
EXTENT MANAGEMENT LOCAL AUTOALLOCATE
SEGMENT SPACE MANAGEMENT AUTO;
```

When automatic segment space management is used, Oracle ignores the storage parameters PCTUSED, FREELISTS, and FREELIST GROUPS when creating objects.

Although the name *segment space management* sounds similar to extent management, it is quite different and can be more accurately regarded as block space management.

Choosing Other Tablespace Options

Several options are available to use when creating a tablespace. You learned to create BIGFILE or SMALLFILE tablespaces and use the EXTENT MANAGEMENT and SEGMENT SPACE MANAGEMENT options in the previous sections. In this section, you will learn the other options available while creating a tablespace:

- Specifying nondefault block size
- Specifying default storage characteristics
- Specifying logging and flashback clauses
- Creating offline tablespaces

The following example shows the optional clauses you can use while creating a dictionary-managed tablespace:

```
CREATE TABLESPACE APPL_DATA
    DATAFILE '/disk3/oradata/DB01/appl_data01.dbf'
        SIZE 100M
    DEFAULT STORAGE (
                    INITIAL 256K
                    NEXT 256K
                    MINEXTENTS 2
                    PCTINCREASE 0
                    MAXEXTENTS 4096)
    BLOCKSIZE 16K
    MINIMUM EXTENT 256K
    LOGGING
    ONLINE
    FORCE LOGGING
    FLASHBACK ON
    EXTENT MANAGEMENT DICTIONARY
    SEGMENT SPACE MANAGEMENT MANUAL;
```

The following example shows the optional clauses you can use while creating a locally managed tablespace:

```
CREATE TABLESPACE APPL_DATA
    DATAFILE '/disk3/oradata/DB01/appl_data01.dbf'
        SIZE 100M
    DEFAULT STORAGE COMPRESS
    BLOCKSIZE 16K
    LOGGING
    ONLINE
    FORCE LOGGING
    FLASHBACK ON
    EXTENT MANAGEMENT LOCAL
    SEGMENT SPACE MANAGEMENT AUTO;
```

Though Oracle manages the tablespace characteristics very efficiently with its default values, you can specify several clauses to a finer level of control. The clauses in the CREATE TABLESPACE command can specify the following:

DEFAULT STORAGE clause The DEFAULT STORAGE clause specifies the default storage parameters for new objects that are created in the tablespace. If an explicit storage clause is specified when creating an object, the tablespace defaults are not used for the specified storage parameters. The storage parameters are specified within parentheses; no parameter is mandatory, but if you specify the DEFAULT STORAGE clause, you must specify at least one parameter inside the parentheses. The storage parameters are valid only for dictionary-managed tablespaces; for locally managed tablespaces, you can specify only the COMPRESS option. I will discuss the storage parameters later in the chapter in the section "Creating a Table."

BLOCKSIZE clause   Oracle allows a tablespace to have a different block size than the default standard database block size. The database block size is specified when you create the database using the initialization parameter DB_BLOCK_SIZE. This is the block size used for the SYSTEM tablespace and is known as the *standard block size*. The valid sizes of the nonstandard block size are 2KB, 4KB, 8KB, 16KB, and 32KB. If you do not specify a block size for the tablespace, the database block size is assumed. Multiple block sizes in the database are beneficial for large databases with OLTP and Decision Support System (DSS) data stored together and for storing large tables. The restrictions on specifying nonstandard block sizes along with the tablespace creation are discussed in the section "Using Nonstandard Block Sizes."

MINIMUM EXTENT clause   The MINIMUM EXTENT clause specifies that the extent sizes should be a multiple of the size specified. You can use this clause to control fragmentation in the tablespace by allocating extents of at least the size specified; this clause is always a multiple of the size specified. In the CREATE TABLESPACE example, all the extents allocated in the tablespace would be a multiple of 256KB. The INITIAL and NEXT extent sizes specified should be a multiple of MINIMUM EXTENT. This clause is valid only for dictionary-managed tablespaces.

LOGGING/NOLOGGING clause   The LOGGING/NOLOGGING clause specifies that the DDL operations and direct-load INSERT should be recorded in the redo log files. This is the default, and the clause can be omitted. When you specify NOLOGGING, data is modified with minimal logging, and hence the commands complete faster. Since the changes are not recorded in the redo log files, you need to apply the commands again in the case of a media recovery. You can specify LOGGING or NOLOGGING in the individual object creation statement, and it overrides the tablespace default.

FORCE LOGGING clause   You must specify this clause to log all changes irrespective of the LOGGING mode for individual objects in the tablespace. You can specify the NOLOGGING clause and FORCE LOGGING clause together when creating a tablespace. If you do so, the objects will be created in NOLOGGING mode and will be overridden by the FORCE LOGGING mode. When you take the tablespace out of the FORCE LOGGING mode, the NOLOGGING attribute for objects goes into effect.

ONLINE/OFFLINE clause   This clause specifies that the tablespace should be made online or available as soon as it is created. This is the default, and hence the clause can be omitted. If you do not want the tablespace to be available, you can specify OFFLINE.

FLASHBACK ON/OFF clause   FLASHBACK ON puts the tablespace in the flashback mode and is the default. The OFF option turns flashback off, and hence Oracle will not save any flashback data. I will discuss flashback operations in Chapter 15, "Implementing Database Backups."

The clauses related to encrypting the tablespace are not discussed here because they are beyond the scope for this book.

Using Nonstandard Block Sizes

The block size used while creating the database is specified in the initialization parameter using the DB_BLOCK_SIZE parameter. This is known as the *standard block size* for the database. You must choose a block size that suits most of your tables as the standard block size. In most databases, this is the only block size you will ever need. Oracle gives you the option of having multiple block sizes, which is especially useful when you're transporting tablespaces from another database with a different block size.

The DB_CACHE_SIZE parameter defines the buffer cache size that is associated with the standard block size. To create tablespaces with nonstandard block size, you must set the appropriate initialization parameter to define a buffer cache size for the block size. The initialization parameter is DB_*n*K_CACHE_SIZE, where *n* is the nonstandard block size. *n* can have values 2, 4, 8, 16, or 32 but cannot have the size of the standard block size. For example, if your standard block size is 8KB, you cannot set the parameter DB_8K_CACHE_SIZE. If you need to create a tablespace that uses a different block size, say 16KB, you must set the DB_16K_CACHE_SIZE parameter. By default, the value for DB_*n*K_CACHE_SIZE parameters is 0MB.

The temporary tablespaces created should have the standard block size.

The DB_*n*K_CACHE_SIZE parameter is dynamic; you can alter its value using the ALTER SYSTEM statement.

Creating Temporary Tablespaces

Oracle can manage space for sort operations more efficiently by using *temporary tablespaces*. By exclusively designating a tablespace for temporary segments, Oracle eliminates the allocation and deallocation of temporary segments in a permanent tablespace. A temporary tablespace can be used only for sort segments. A temporary tablespace is used for temporary segments, which are created, managed, and dropped by the database as needed. These temporary segments are most commonly generated during sorting operations such as ORDER BY, GROUP BY, and CREATE INDEX. They are also generated during other operations such as hash joins or inserts into temporary tables.

You create a temporary tablespace at database creation time with the DEFAULT TEMPORARY TABLESPACE clause of the CREATE DATABASE statement or after the database is created with the CREATE TEMPORARY TABLESPACE statement, like this:

```
CREATE TEMPORARY TABLESPACE temp
TEMPFILE '/u01/oradata/11GR1/temp01.dbf' SIZE 1G;
```

Notice that the keyword TEMPFILE is used instead of DATAFILE. Temp files are available only with temporary tablespaces, they never need to be backed up, and they do not log data changes in the redo logs. The EXTENT MANAGEMENT LOCAL clause is optional and can be omitted; you can provide it to improve readability. If you do not specify the extent size by using the UNIFORM SIZE clause, the default size used will be 1MB.

Although it is always good practice to create a separate temporary tablespace, it is required when the SYSTEM tablespace is locally managed.

Temporary tablespaces are created using temp files instead of data files. Temp files are allocated slightly differently than data files. Although data files are completely allocated and initialized at creation time, temp files are not always guaranteed to allocate the disk space specified. This means that on some Unix systems a temp file will not actually allocate disk space until a sorting operation requires it. Although this delayed allocation approach allows rapid file creation, it can cause problems down the road if you have not reserved the space that may be needed at runtime.

Each user is assigned a temporary tablespace when the user is created. By default, the default tablespace (where the user creates objects) and the temporary tablespace (where the user's sort operations are performed) are both the SYSTEM tablespace. No user should have SYSTEM as their default or temporary tablespace. This will unnecessarily increase fragmentation in the SYSTEM tablespace.

When creating a database, you can also create a temporary tablespace using the DEFAULT TEMPORARY TABLESPACE clause of the CREATE DATABASE statement. If the default temporary tablespace is defined in the database, all new users will have that tablespace assigned as the temporary tablespace by default if you do not specify another tablespace for the users' temporary tablespace. You can also designate a data tablespace for application tables during database creation using the DEFAULT TABLESPACE clause.

If there are multiple temporary tablespaces in a database and if you want to utilize the space in multiple temporary tablespaces to a user's sort operation, you can use the temporary tablespace groups. When creating the temporary tablespace, use the TABLESPACE GROUP clause as in the following example:

```
CREATE TEMPORARY TABLESPACE TEMP01
TEMPFILE '/u01/oradata/11GR1/temp01a.dbf' size 200M
EXTENT MANAGEMENT LOCAL UNIFORM SIZE 5M
TABLESPACE GROUP ALL_TEMPS;
```

In this example, the tablespace is made part of the ALL_TEMPS temporary tablespace group. Tablespace groups are applicable only to temporary tablespaces. If the group does not exist, Oracle creates the group and adds the tablespace to the group.

When creating a temporary tablespace, you can use only the EXTENT MANAGEMENT and TABLESPACE GROUP clauses along with TEMPFILE clause. All other options are invalid for temporary tablespaces.

Creating Undo Tablespaces

An undo tablespace stores undo segments, which are used by the database for several purposes, including the following:

- Rolling back a transaction explicitly with a ROLLBACK statement
- Rolling back a transaction implicitly (for example, through the recovery of a failed transaction)
- Reconstructing a read-consistent image of data
- Recovering from logical corruptions

To create an undo tablespace at database creation time, set the initialization parameter UNDO_MANAGEMENT=AUTO (default), and include an UNDO TABLESPACE clause in your CREATE DATABASE statement, like this:

```
CREATE DATABASE "TEST1"
DATAFILE '/u01/app/oracle/oradata/TEST1/system01.dbf'
    SIZE 300M REUSE AUTOEXTEND ON NEXT 10240K MAXSIZE UNLIMITED
    EXTENT MANAGEMENT LOCAL
SYSAUX DATAFILE '/u01/app/oracle/oradata/TEST1/sysaux01.dbf'
    SIZE 120M REUSE AUTOEXTEND ON NEXT  10240K MAXSIZE UNLIMITED
SMALLFILE DEFAULT TEMPORARY TABLESPACE TEMP
    TEMPFILE '/u01/app/oracle/oradata/TEST1/temp01.dbf'
    SIZE 20M REUSE AUTOEXTEND ON NEXT  640K MAXSIZE UNLIMITED
SMALLFILE UNDO TABLESPACE "UNDOTBS1"
    DATAFILE '/u01/app/oracle/oradata/TEST1/undotbs01.dbf'
    SIZE 200M REUSE AUTOEXTEND ON NEXT  5120K MAXSIZE UNLIMITED
DEFAULT TABLESPACE "USERS"
    DATAFILE '/u01/app/oracle/oradata/TEST1/users01.dbf'
    SIZE 5M REUSE AUTOEXTEND ON NEXT  1280K MAXSIZE UNLIMITED
    EXTENT MANAGEMENT LOCAL SEGMENT SPACE MANAGEMENT  AUTO
CHARACTER SET WE8MSWIN1252
NATIONAL CHARACTER SET AL16UTF16
LOGFILE
    GROUP 1 ('/u01/app/oracle/oradata/TEST1/redo01.log') SIZE 51200K,
    GROUP 2 ('/u01/app/oracle/oradata/TEST1/redo02.log') SIZE 51200K,
    GROUP 3 ('/u01/app/oracle/oradata/TEST1/redo03.log') SIZE 51200K
SET DEFAULT SMALLFILE TABLESPACE
USER SYS IDENTIFIED BY mysupersekret
USER SYSTEM IDENTIFIED BY supersekret;
```

You can create an undo tablespace after database creation with the CREATE UNDO TABLESPACE statement, like this:

```
CREATE UNDO TABLESPACE undo
DATAFILE '/ORADATA/PROD/UNDO01.DBF' SIZE 2G;
```

When creating undo tablespace, you can specify the undo retention clause. The RETENTION GUARANTEE option specifies that Oracle should preserve unexpired undo data until the period of time specified by the UNDO_RETENTION initialization parameter. This setting is useful for flashback query operations. RETENTION NOGUARANTEE is the default.

The only tablespace clauses available to specify are EXTENT MANAGEMENT LOCAL and DATAFILE when creating undo tablespaces. Undo management and retention are discussed in Chapter 13, "Managing Data and Undo."

> Although it is always good practice to create a separate undo tablespace, it is required when the SYSTEM tablespace is locally managed.

Removing Tablespaces

Tablespaces that are not needed in the database can be dropped. Once a tablespace is dropped, there is no rollback. Though you can drop a tablespace with objects in it, it may be safer to drop the objects first and then drop the tablespace. To remove a tablespace from the database, use the DROP TABLESPACE statement:

```
DROP TABLESPACE USER_DATA;
```

If the tablespace is not empty, you should specify the optional clause INCLUDING CONTENTS to recursively remove any segments (tables, indexes, and so on) in the tablespace, like this:

```
DROP TABLESPACE dba_sandbox INCLUDING CONTENTS;
```

If there are referential integrity constraints from the objects on other tablespaces referring to the objects in the tablespace that is being dropped, you must specify the CASCADE CONSTRAINTS clause:

```
DROP TABLESPACE USER_DATA INCLUDING CONTENTS CASCADE CONSTRAINTS;
```

When you drop a tablespace, the control file is updated with the tablespace and data file information.

Dropping a tablespace does not automatically remove the data files from the file system. Use the additional clause INCLUDING CONTENTS AND DATAFILES to remove the underlying data files as well as the stored objects, like this:

```
DROP TABLESPACE hr_data INCLUDING CONTENTS AND DATAFILES;
```

If the Oracle Managed Files feature is used for the tablespace, such files will be removed automatically when you drop the tablespace. For files that are not Oracle managed, if you need to free up the disk space, you can either use OS commands to remove the data files belonging to the dropped tablespace or use the AND DATAFILES clause.

You cannot drop the SYSTEM tablespace.

Modifying Tablespaces

Use an ALTER TABLESPACE statement to modify the attributes of a tablespace. These are some of the actions you can perform on tablespaces:

- Change the default storage clauses and the MINIMUM_EXTENT of a dictionary-managed tablespace.

- Change the extent allocation and LOGGING/NOLOGGING modes.

- Change the availability of the tablespace.

- Make the tablespace read-only or read-write.

- Coalesce the contiguous free space.

- Add more space by adding new data files or temporary files.

- Resize the data files or temporary files.

- Rename a tablespace or rename files belonging to the tablespace.

- Shrink temporary files or shrink space in the tablespace.

- Change flashback on or off and change retention guarantee.

- Begin and end a backup.

The following sections detail common modifications you can perform on the tablespaces.

Changing Storage Defaults

Changing the default storage or MINIMUM_EXTENT or LOGGING/NOLOGGING does not affect the existing objects in the tablespace. The DEFAULT STORAGE and LOGGING/NOLOGGING clauses are applied to the newly created segments if such a clause is not explicitly specified when creating new objects. For example, to change the storage parameters, use the following statement:

```
ALTER TABLESPACE APPL_DATA
DEFAULT STORAGE (INITIAL 2M NEXT 2M);
```

Only the INITIAL and NEXT values of the storage STORAGE are changed; the other storage parameters such as PCTINCREASE or MINEXTENTS remain unaltered.

Adding a Data File to a Tablespace

Smallfile tablespaces can have multiple data files and can thus be spread over multiple file systems without engaging a logical volume manager. To add a data file to a smallfile tablespace, use an ADD clause with the ALTER TABLESPACE statement. For example, the following statement adds a 2GB data file on the /u02 file system to the receivables tablespace:

```
ALTER TABLESPACE receivables ADD DATAFILE
  '/u02/oradata/ORA10/receivables01.dbf'
  SIZE 2G;
```

Taking a Tablespace Offline or Online

You can control the availability of certain tablespaces by altering the tablespace to be offline or online. When you make a tablespace offline, the segments in that tablespace are not accessible. The data stored in other tablespaces is available for use. When making a tablespace unavailable, you can use these four options:

NORMAL   This is the default. Oracle writes all the dirty buffer blocks in the SGA to the data files of the tablespace and closes the data files. All data files belonging to the tablespace must be online. You need not do a media recovery when bringing the tablespace online. For example:

```
ALTER TABLESPACE USER_DATA ONLINE;
```

TEMPORARY   Oracle performs a checkpoint on all online data files. It does not ensure that the data files are available. You may need to perform a media recovery on the offline data files when the tablespace is brought online. For example:

```
ALTER TABLESPACE USER_DATA OFFLINE TEMPORARY;
```

IMMEDIATE   Oracle does not perform a checkpoint and does not make sure that all data files are available. You must perform a media recovery when the tablespace is brought back online. For example:

```
ALTER TABLESPACE USER_DATA OFFLINE IMMEDIATE;
```

FOR RECOVER   This makes the tablespace offline for point-in-time recovery. You can copy the data files belonging to the tablespace from a backup and apply the archive log files. For example:

```
ALTER TABLESPACE USER_DATA OFFLINE FOR RECOVER;
```

You cannot make the SYSTEM tablespace offline because the data dictionary must always be available for the functioning of the database. If a tablespace is offline when you shut down the database, it remains offline when you start up the database. You can make a tablespace offline by using the following statement:

```
ALTER TABLESPACE USER_DATA OFFLINE
```

When a tablespace is taken offline, SQL statements cannot reference any objects contained in that tablespace. If there are unsaved changes when you take the tablespace offline, Oracle saves rollback data corresponding to those changes in a deferred rollback segment in the SYSTEM tablespace. When the tablespace is brought back online, Oracle applies the rollback data to the tablespace, if needed.

Making a Tablespace Read-Only

If a tablespace contains static data, it can be marked read-only. Tablespaces that contain historic or reference data are typical candidates for read-only. When a tablespace is read-only, it does not have to be backed up with the nightly or weekly database backups. One backup after being marked read-only is all that is needed for future recoveries. Tables in a read-only tablespace can only be selected from; their rows cannot be inserted, updated, or deleted.

You cannot make the SYSTEM tablespace read-only. When you make a tablespace read-only, all the data files must be online, and the tablespace can have no active transactions. You can drop objects such as tables or indexes from a read-only tablespace, but you cannot create new objects in a read-only tablespace.

Use a READ ONLY clause with an ALTER TABLESPACE statement to mark a tablespace read-only. For example, to mark the SALES2007 tablespace read-only, execute the following:

```
ALTER TABLESPACE sales2007 READ ONLY;
```

If you need to make changes to a table in a read-only tablespace, make it read writable again with the keywords READ WRITE, like this:

```
ALTER TABLESPACE sales2007 READ WRITE;
```

Oracle normally checks the availability of all data files belonging to the database when starting up the database. If you are storing your read-only tablespace on offline storage media or on a CD-ROM, you might want to skip the data file availability checking when starting up the database by setting the parameter READ_ONLY_OPEN_DELAYED to TRUE. Oracle checks the availability of data files belonging to read-only tablespaces only at the time of access to an object in the tablespace. A missing or bad read-only file will not be detected at database startup time.

Putting a Tablespace in Backup Mode

If you perform non-RMAN online backups, sometimes called *user-managed backups*, you need to put a tablespace in backup mode before you begin to copy the data files using an operating-system program. While the tablespace is in backup mode, the database continues to write data to the data files (checkpoints occur), but the occurrences of these checkpoints are not recorded in the header blocks of the data files. This omission tells the database that recovery may be needed if the database instance gets terminated abruptly.

While a tablespace is in backup mode, some additional information is written to the redo logs to assist with recovery, if needed.

 See Chapter 15 for more information on backups, and see Chapter 16, "Recovering the Database," for more information about recovery.

Some companies perform backups by splitting a third mirror, mounting these mirrored file systems onto another server, and then copying them to tape. To safely split the mirror, alter all your tablespaces into backup mode, make the split, and then alter all the tablespaces out of backup mode. Put them into backup mode like this:

```
ALTER TABLESPACE system BEGIN BACKUP;
```

Use the keywords END BACKUP to take a tablespace out of backup mode, like this:

```
ALTER TABLESPACE system END BACKUP;
```

If you forget to take a tablespace out of backup mode, the next time you bounce your database, it will see that the checkpoint number in the control file is later than the one in the data file headers and report that media recovery is required.

Obtaining Tablespace Information

DBAs often need to find the space used and available in a tablespace as well as query the tablespace characteristics. The data dictionary is the place to go for obtaining tablespace information. You can use the command-line utility SQL*Plus to query the information from data dictionary tables, or you can use Enterprise Manager Grid Control. We will review both in this section.

Obtaining Tablespace Information Using SQL*Plus

Many data dictionary views can provide information about tablespaces in a database, such as the following:

- DBA_TABLESPACES
- DBA_DATA_FILES
- DBA_TEMP_FILES
- V$TABLESPACE

The DBA_TABLESPACES view has one row for each tablespace in the database and provides the following information:

- The tablespace block size
- The tablespace status: online, offline, or read-only
- The contents of the tablespace: undo, temporary, or permanent
- Whether it uses dictionary-managed or locally managed extents
- Whether the segment space management is automatic or manual
- Whether it is a bigfile or smallfile tablespace

To get a listing of all the tablespaces in the database, their status, contents, extent management policy, and segment management policy, run the following query:

```
SELECT tablespace_name, status,contents
     ,extent_management extents
     ,segment_space_management free_space
FROM dba_tablespaces
```

TABLESPACE_NAME	STATUS	CONTENTS	EXTENTS	FREE_SPACE
SYSTEM	ONLINE	PERMANENT	LOCAL	MANUAL
UNDOTBS1	ONLINE	UNDO	LOCAL	MANUAL

SYSAUX	ONLINE	PERMANENT	LOCAL	AUTO
TEMP	ONLINE	TEMPORARY	LOCAL	MANUAL
USERS	ONLINE	PERMANENT	LOCAL	AUTO
EXAMPLE	ONLINE	PERMANENT	LOCAL	AUTO
DATA	ONLINE	PERMANENT	LOCAL	AUTO
INDX	ONLINE	PERMANENT	LOCAL	AUTO

The V$TABLESPACE view also has one row per tablespace, but it includes some information other than DBA_TABLESPACES, such as whether the tablespace participates in database flashback operations:

```
SELECT name, bigfile, flashback_on
FROM v$tablespace;
```

```
NAME        BIGFILE   FLASHBACK_ON
----------  --------  ------------
SYSTEM      NO        YES
UNDOTBS1    NO        YES
SYSAUX      NO        YES
USERS       NO        YES
TEMP        NO        YES
EXAMPLE     NO        YES
DATA        NO        YES
INDX        NO        YES
```

See Chapter 15 for more information on flashback operations.

The DBA_DATA_FILES and DBA_TEMP_FILES views contain information on data files and temp files, respectively. This information includes the tablespace name, filename, file size, and autoextend settings.

```
SELECT tablespace_name, file_name, bytes/1024 kbytes
FROM dba_data_files
UNION ALL
SELECT tablespace_name, file_name, bytes/1024 kbytes
FROM dba_temp_files;
```

TABLESPACE	FILE_NAME	KBYTES
USERS	C:\ORACLE\ORADATA\ORA11\USERS01.DBF	102400
SYSAUX	C:\ORACLE\ORADATA\ORA11\SYSAUX01.DBF	256000

```
UNDOTBS1   C:\ORACLE\ORADATA\ORA11\UNDOTBS01.DBF      51200
SYSTEM     C:\ORACLE\ORADATA\ORA11\SYSTEM01.DBF      460800
EXAMPLE    C:\ORACLE\ORADATA\ORA11\EXAMPLE01.DBF     153600
INDX       C:\ORACLE\ORADATA\ORA11\INDX01.DBF        102400
TEMP       C:\ORACLE\ORADATA\ORA11\TEMP01.DBF         51200
```

In addition to in the data dictionary, you can obtain tablespace information from several sources. Some of these sources are the DDL and the Enterprise Manager.

Generating DDL for a Tablespace

Another way to quickly identify the attributes of a tablespace is to ask the database to generate DDL to re-create the tablespace. The CREATE TABLESPACE statement that results contains the attributes for the tablespace. Use the PL/SQL package DBMS_METADATA to generate DDL for your database objects. For example, to generate the DDL for the USERS tablespace, execute this:

```
SELECT DBMS_METADATA.GET_DDL('TABLESPACE','USERS')
FROM dual;
```

The output from this statement is a CREATE TABLESPACE statement that contains all the attributes for the USERS tablespace:

```
CREATE TABLESPACE "USERS" DATAFILE
'/u01/app/oracle/oradata/11GR11/users01.dbf' SIZE 5242880
AUTOEXTEND ON NEXT 1310720 MAXSIZE 32767M
LOGGING ONLINE PERMANENT BLOCKSIZE 8192
EXTENT MANAGEMENT LOCAL AUTOALLOCATE SEGMENT SPACE MANAGEMENT AUTO;
```

Obtaining Tablespace Information Using the EM Database Control

Instead of querying the data dictionary views with a command-line tool such as SQL*Plus, you can use the interactive GUI tool EM Database Control to monitor and manage database structures, including tablespaces. The EM Database Control is an alternative to a command-line interface.

To use the Database Control, follow these steps:

1. Point your browser to the Enterprise Manager URL for your database (similar to https://*hostname*:5500/em/console).

2. Log in to EM, and navigate to the Server tab of the main screen, which is shown in Figure 10.2.

3. Click the Tablespaces link under the heading Storage to display a list of tablespaces like that shown in Figure 10.3.

FIGURE 10.2   The Enterprise Manager Server tab

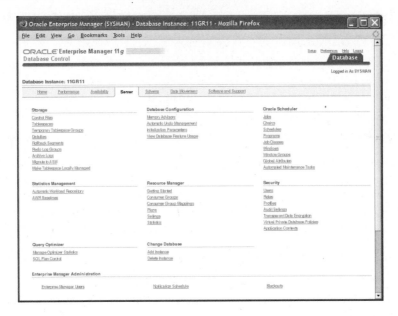

FIGURE 10.3   The Enterprise Manager Tablespaces screen

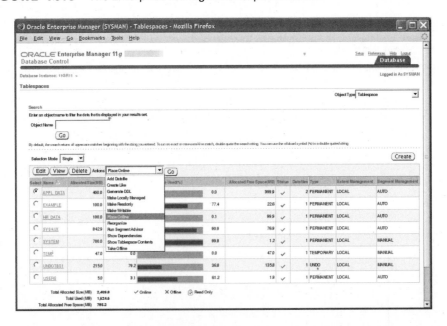

4. Click the radio button next to the tablespace you want to work with, and then click the Edit button. You can navigate to the tablespace General, Storage, and Thresholds edit screens, as shown in Figure 10.4.

FIGURE 10.4   The Enterprise Manager tablespace editor

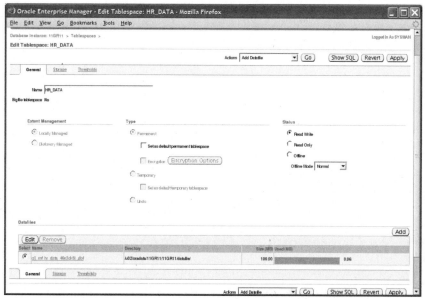

You use the screens and options in the EM Database Control to manipulate and change your tablespaces with many of the same options that the command-line interface supports. For example, to increase the size of the data file in the HR_DATA tablespace, click the Edit button next to the data file. The EM Database Control displays the tablespace edit screen, as shown in Figure 10.5.

FIGURE 10.5   Editing the data file size

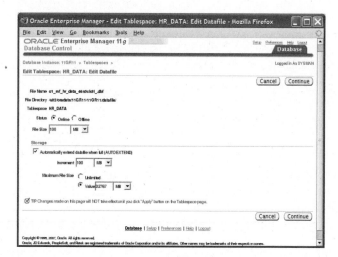

Edit the File Size field, increasing it to 100MB. The change will be applied when you click Continue.

Managing Data Files

Data files (or temporary files) are made when you create a tablespace or when you alter a tablespace to add files. If you are not using the OMF feature, you will need to manage data files yourself. The database will create or reuse one or more data files in the sizes and locations that you specify whenever you create a tablespace. A data file belongs to only one tablespace and only one database at a time. Temp files are a special variety of data file that are used in temporary tablespaces. When the database creates or reuses a data file, the operating-system file is allocated and initialized—filled with a regular pattern of mostly binary zeros. This initialization will not occur with temp files.

Performing Operations on Data Files

Operations that you may need to perform on data files include the following:

- Resizing them
- Taking them offline or online
- Moving (renaming) them

Sizing Files

You can specify that the data file (or temporary file) will grow automatically whenever space is needed in the tablespace. This is accomplished by specifying the AUTOEXTEND clause for the file. This functionality enables you to have fewer data files per tablespace and can simplify the administration of data files. The AUTOEXTEND clause can be ON or OFF; you can also specify file size increments. You can set a maximum limit for the file size; by default, the file size limit is UNLIMITED. You can specify the AUTOEXTEND clause for files when you run the CREATE DATABASE, CREATE TABLESPACE, ALTER TABLESPACE, and ALTER DATAFILE commands. For example:

```
CREATE TABLESPACE APPL_DATA
DATAFILE '/disk2/oradata/DB01/appl_data01.dbf'
SIZE 500M
AUTOEXTEND ON NEXT 100M MAXSIZE 2000M;
```

The AUTOEXTEND ON clause specifies that the automatic file-resize feature should be enabled for the specified file; NEXT specifies the size by which the file should be incremented, and MAXSIZE specifies the maximum size for the file. When Oracle tries to allocate an extent in the tablespace, it looks for a free extent. If a large enough free extent cannot be located (even after coalescing), Oracle increases the data file size by 100MB and tries to allocate the new extent.

The following statement disables the automatic file-extension feature:

```
ALTER DATABASE
DATAFILE '/disk2/oradata/DB01/appl_data01.dbf'
AUTOEXTEND OFF;
```

If the file already exists in the database, and you want to enable the autoextension feature, use the ALTER DATABASE command. For example, you can use the following statement:

```
ALTER DATABASE
DATAFILE '/disk2/oradata/DB01/appl_data01.dbf'
AUTOEXTEND ON NEXT 100M MAXSIZE 2000M;
```

You can increase or decrease the size of a data file or temporary file (thus increasing or decreasing the size of the tablespace) by using the RESIZE clause of the ALTER DATABASE DATAFILE command. For example, to redefine the size of a file, use the following statement:

```
ALTER DATABASE
DATAFILE '/disk2/oradata/DB01/appl_data01.dbf'
RESIZE 1500M;
```

When decreasing the file size, Oracle returns an error if it finds data beyond the new file size. You cannot reduce the file size below the high-water mark in the file. Reducing the file size helps reclaim unused space.

Making Files Online and Offline

Sometimes you may have to make data files unavailable to the database if there is a file corruption. You can use the ONLINE and OFFLINE clauses of the ALTER DATABASE statement to take a data file online or offline. You can specify the filename or specify the unique identifier number that represents the data file. This identifier can be found in the FILE# column of V$DATAFILE or the FILE_ID column of the DBA_DATA_FILES view.

To take a data file offline, use the OFFLINE clause. If the database is in NOARCHIVELOG mode, then you must specify the FOR DROP clause along with the OFFLINE clause. The data file will be taken offline and marked with status OFFLINE. You can remove the data file using OS commands, if you want to get rid of the data file. If the database is in ARCHIVELOG mode, you don't need to specify the FOR DROP clause when taking a data file offline. When you're ready to bring the data file online, Oracle performs media recovery on the data file to make it consistent with the database. Also, the FOR DROP clause is ignored if the database is in ARCHIVELOG mode. Here is an example of taking a data file offline:

```
ALTER DATABASE DATAFILE '/u01/oradata/11gr1/tools02.dbf' OFFLINE;
```

The following statement brings the data file online:

```
ALTER DATABASE DATAFILE '/u01/oradata/11gr1/tools02.dbf' ONLINE;
```

Renaming Files

You can rename data files using the RENAME FILE clause of the ALTER DATABASE command. You can also rename data files by using the RENAME DATAFILE clause of the ALTER
TABLESPACE command. The RENAME functionality is used to logically move tablespaces
from one location to another. To rename or relocate data files belonging to a non-SYSTEM
tablespace, you should follow certain steps. Consider the following example.

Your tablespace USER_DATA has three data files named, such as the following:

- /disk1/oradata/DB01/user_data01.dbf
- /disk1/oradata/DB01/userdata2.dbf
- /disk1/oradata/DB01/user_data03.dbf

Renaming a Data File

If you need to rename one of these, say the second file, follow these steps:

1. Take the tablespace offline:

   ALTER TABLESPACE USER_DATA OFFLINE;

2. Copy or move the file to the new location, or rename the file by using operating-system
   commands.

3. Rename the file in the database by using one of the following two commands:

   ALTER DATABASE RENAME FILE
   '/disk1/oradata/DB01/userdata2.dbf' TO
   '/disk1/oradata/DB01/user_data02.dbf';

   or

   ALTER TABLESPACE USER_DATA RENAME DATAFILE
   '/disk1/oradata/DB01/userdata2.dbf' TO

   '/disk1/oradata/DB01/user_data02.dbf';

4. Bring the tablespace online:

   ALTER TABLESPACE USER_DATA ONLINE;

Relocating a Tablespace

You may also determine that you need to relocate the tablespace from disk 1 to disk 2. If
so, you should follow the same steps. You can also rename all the files in the tablespace by
using a single command. The steps are as follows:

1. Take the tablespace offline:

   ALTER TABLESPACE USER_DATA OFFLINE;

2. Copy the file to the new location by using OS commands on the disk.

3. Rename the files in the database by using one of the following two commands. The number of data files specified before the keyword TO should be equal to the number of files specified after the keyword.

```
ALTER DATABASE RENAME FILE
'/disk1/oradata/DB01/user_data01.dbf',
'/disk1/oradata/DB01/userdata2.dbf',
'/disk1/oradata/DB01/user_data03.dbf'
 TO
'/disk2/oradata/DB01/user_data01.dbf',
'/disk2/oradata/DB01/user_data02.dbf',
'/disk2/oradata/DB01/user_data03.dbf';
```

or

```
ALTER TABLESPACE USER_DATA RENAME DATAFILE
'/disk1/oradata/DB01/user_data01.dbf',
'/disk1/oradata/DB01/userdata2.dbf',
'/disk1/oradata/DB01/user_data03.dbf'
 TO
'/disk2/oradata/DB01/user_data01.dbf',
'/disk2/oradata/DB01/user_data02.dbf',
'/disk2/oradata/DB01/user_data03.dbf';
```

4. Bring the tablespace online:

```
ALTER TABLESPACE USER_DATA ONLINE;
```

Renaming or Relocating Files Belonging to Multiple Tablespaces

If you need to rename or relocate files belonging to multiple tablespaces or if the file belongs to the SYSTEM tablespace, you must follow these steps:

1. Shut down the database. A complete backup is recommended before making any structural changes.
2. Copy or rename the files on the disk by using OS commands.
3. Start up and mount the database (STARTUP MOUNT).
4. Rename the files in the database by using the ALTER DATABASE RENAME FILE command.
5. Open the database by using ALTER DATABASE OPEN.

Moving Read-Only Tablespaces

If you need to move read-only tablespaces to a CD-ROM or any write-once read-many device, follow these steps:

1. Make the tablespace read-only.
2. Copy the data files belonging to the tablespace to the read-only device.
3. Rename the files in the database by using the ALTER DATABASE RENAME FILE command.

Real World Scenario

Moving a Data File from the H Drive to the G Drive

Your operating-system administrator informed you that he is seeing lot of contention on the H drive and is seeking options to move some of the reads off the H drive and to G drive. As a DBA, you can move one of the hot files belonging to the receivables tablespace to the G drive.

You need to take a tablespace offline to perform some maintenance operations, such as recovering the tablespace or moving the data files to a new location. Use the OFFLINE clause with an ALTER TABLESPACE statement to take a tablespace offline. Follow these steps to rename or move a data file:

1. Take the receivables tablespace offline:

```
ALTER TABLESPACE receivables OFFLINE;
```

2. Use an operating-system program to physically move the file, such as Copy in Microsoft Windows or cp in Unix.

3. Tell the database about the new location:

```
ALTER TABLESPACE receivables RENAME DATAFILE
    'H:\ORACLE\ORADATA\ORA10\RECEIVABLES02.DBF'
  TO 'G:\ORACLE\ORADATA\ORA10\RECEIVABLES02.DBF' ;
```

4. Bring the tablespace back online:

```
ALTER TABLESPACE receivables ONLINE;
```

Using the Oracle Managed Files Feature

The Oracle Managed Files feature is appropriate for smaller nonproduction databases or databases on disks using Logical Volume Manager (LVM). LVM is software available with most disk systems to combine partitions of multiple physical disks to one logical volume. LVM can use mirroring, striping, RAID 5, and so on. Using the OMF feature has the following benefits:

Error prevention Since Oracle removes the files associated with the tablespace, the DBA cannot make a mistake by removing a file belonging to an active tablespace.

A standard naming convention The files created using the OMF method have unique and standard filenames.

Space retrieval When tablespaces are removed, Oracle removes the files associated with the tablespace, thus freeing up space immediately on the disk. The DBA may forget to remove the file from disk.

Easy script writing   Application vendors need not worry about the syntax of specifying directory names in the scripts when porting the application to multiple platforms. The same script can be used to create tablespaces on different OS platforms.

The OMF feature can be used to create files and to remove them when the corresponding object (redo log group or tablespace) is dropped from the database. For managing OMF-created files, such as renaming or resizing, you need to use the traditional methods.

Enabling the Oracle Managed Files Feature

To enable the creation of Oracle-managed data files, you need to set the parameter DB_CREATE_FILE_DEST. You can specify this parameter in the initialization-parameter file or set/change it using the ALTER SYSTEM or ALTER SESSION statement. The DB_CREATE_FILE_DEST parameter defines the directory where Oracle can create data files. Oracle must have read-write permission on this directory. The directory must exist on the server where the database is located. Oracle will not create the directory; it will create create only the data file.

You can use the OMF feature to create data files when using the CREATE DATABASE, CREATE TABLESPACE, and ALTER TABLESPACE statements. In the CREATE DATABASE statement, you don't need to specify the filenames for the SYSTEM, UNDO, or TEMPORARY tablespaces. In the CREATE TABLESPACE statement, you can omit the DATAFILE clause. In the ALTER TABLESPACE ADD DATAFILE statement, you can omit the filename.

The data files created using the OMF feature will have a standard format. For data files, the format is ora_%t_%u.dbf, and for temp files, the format is ora_%t_%u.tmp, where %t is the tablespace name and %u is a unique eight-character string derived by Oracle. If the tablespace name is longer than eight characters, only the first eight characters are used. The filenames generated by Oracle are reported in the alert log file.

You can also use the OMF feature for the control files and redo log files of the database. Since these two types of files can be multiplexed, Oracle provides another parameter to specify the location of files, DB_CREATE_ONLINE_LOG_DEST_*n*, where *n* can be 1, 2, 3, 4, or 5. These initialization parameters also can be altered using ALTER SYSTEM or ALTER SESSION. If you set the parameters DB_CREATE_ONLINE_LOG_DEST_1 and DB_CREATE_ONLINE_LOG_DEST_2 in the parameter file when creating a database, Oracle creates two control files (one in each directory) and creates two online redo log groups with two members each (one member each in both directories).

The redo log file names created will have the format ora_%g_%u.log, where %g is the log group number and %u is an eight-character string. The control file will have a format of ora_%u.ctl, where %u is an eight-character string.

In the following sections, you will see examples of using the OMF feature while creating a database as well as creating additional tablespaces in a database.

Creating Databases Using the OMF Feature

Let's consider an example of creating a database. The following parameters are set in the initialization-parameter file:

```
UNDO_MANAGEMENT = AUTO
DB_CREATE_ONLINE_LOG_DEST_1 = '/ora1/oradata/MYDB'
```

```
DB_CREATE_ONLINE_LOG_DEST_2 = '/ora2/oradata/MYDB'
DB_CREATE_FILE_DEST = '/ora1/oradata/MYDB'
```

You do not have the CONTROL_FILES parameter set. Create the database using the following statement:

```
CREATE DATABASE MYDB
DEFAULT TEMPORARY TABLESPACE TEMP;
```

The following files will be created: the SYSTEM tablespace data file in /ora1/oradata/MYDB, the TEMP tablespace temp file in /ora1/oradata/MYDB, one control file in /ora1/oradata/MYDB and another control file in /ora2/oradata/MYDB, one member of the first redo log group in /ora1/oradata/MYDB and a second member in /ora2/oradata/MYDB, and one member of second redo log group in /ora1/oradata/MYDB and a second member in /ora2/oradata/MYDB. Since you specified the UNDO_MANAGEMENT clause and did not specify a name for the undo tablespace, Oracle creates the SYS_UNDOTBS tablespace as an undo tablespace and creates its data file in /ora1/oradata/MYDB. If you omit the DEFAULT TEMPORARY TABLESPACE clause, Oracle will not create a temporary tablespace.

> When using the OMF feature to create control files, you must get the names of control files from the alert log and add them to the initialization-parameter file using the CONTROL_FILES parameter for the instance to start again.

The data files and temp files created by the OMF feature will have a default size of 100MB, be autoextensible, and have no maximum file size. Each redo log member will be 100MB in size by default.

Creating Tablespaces Using the OMF Feature

Let's consider another example that creates two tablespaces. The data file for the APP_DATA tablespace will be stored in the directory /ora5/oradata/MYDB. The data file for the APP_INDEX tablespace will be stored in the directory /ora6/oradata/MYDB.

```
ALTER SESSION SET DB_CREATE_FILE_DEST = '/ora5/oradata/MYDB';
CREATE TABLESPACE APP_DATA
EXTENT MANAGEMENT DICTIONARY;
ALTER SESSION SET DB_CREATE_FILE_DEST = '/ora6/oradata/MYDB';
CREATE TABLESPACE APP_INDEX;
```

> If you do not specify the DB_CREATE_ONLINE_LOG_DEST_n parameter when creating a database or when adding a redo log group, the OMF feature creates one control file and two groups with one member each for redo log files in the DB_CREATE_FILE_DEST directory. If the DB_CREATE_FILE_DEST parameter is also not set and you did not provide filenames for data files and redo logs, Oracle creates the files in a default directory (mostly $ORACLE_HOME/dbs), but they will not be Oracle managed. This is the default behavior of the database.

Overriding the Default File Size

If you want to have different sizes for the files created by the OMF feature, you can do so by specifying the DATAFILE clause without a filename. You can also turn off the autoextensible feature of the data file. The following statement creates a tablespace of size 10MB and turns off the autoextensible feature:

```
CREATE TABLESPACE PAY_DATA DATAFILE SIZE 10M
AUTOEXTEND OFF;
```

Here is another example that creates multiple data files for the tablespace. The second and third data files are autoextensible.

```
CREATE TABLESPACE PAY_INDEX
DATAFILE SIZE 20M AUTOEXTEND OFF,
SIZE 30M AUTOEXTEND ON MAXSIZE 1000M,
SIZE 1M;
```

The following example adds files to an existing tablespace:

```
ALTER SYSTEM SET DB_CREATE_FILE_DEST = '/ora5/oradata/MYDB';
ALTER TABLESPACE USERS ADD DATAFILE;
ALTER SYSTEM SET DB_CREATE_FILE_DEST = '/ora8/oradata/MYDB';
ALTER TABLESPACE APP_DATA
ADD DATAFILE SIZE 200M AUTOEXTEND OFF;
```

Once created, Oracle Managed Files are treated like other database files. You can rename and resize them and must back them up. Archive log files cannot be managed by OMF.

How Do You Create a Database and its Associated Tablespaces with OMF?

You have been asked by your manager to create a test database for a new application your company just bought. The database is for testing the functionality of the application. The vendor told you it needs four tablespaces, namely, SJC_DATA, SJC_INDEX, WKW_DATA, and WKW_INDEX. The index tablespaces must be uniform extent sizes of 512KB and should have minimum sizes of 500MB. The vendor needs the SJC_DATA tablespace to be dictionary managed with the minimum and extent size multiple to be 128KB and the tablespace size to be 1GB. The SJC_DATA tablespace should be 250MB.

Since this is a test database for testing the functionality of the application, you decide to use the Oracle Managed Files feature, which makes your life easier by creating and cleaning the files belonging to the database.

Let's create the database. Your system administrator has given you four disks—namely, /ora1, /ora2, /ora3, and /ora4—each with 900MB of space.

Make sure you include the following in the parameter file:

```
UNDO_MANAGEMENT = AUTO
DB_CREATE_FILE_DEST = /ora1
```

```
DB_CREATE_ONLINE_LOG_DEST_1 = /ora1
DB_CREATE_ONLINE_LOG_DEST_2 = /ora2
```

Create the database using the following statement:

```
CREATE DATABASE SJCTEST
LOGFILE SIZE 20M
DEFAULT TEMPORARY TABLESPACE TEMP
TEMPFILE SIZE 200M
EXTENT MANAGEMENT LOCAL UNIFORM SIZE 2M
UNDO TABLESPACE UNDO_TBS SIZE 200M;
```

The previous statement creates a database named SJCTEST. The SYSTEM tablespace, undo tablespace, and temporary tablespace are created in /ora1. The SYSTEM tablespace has the default size of 100MB, and the undo tablespace and temporary tablespace will have the size of 200MB. Since you do not want each log file member to be 100MB, you specify a smaller size for online redo log members.

Two control files are created, and redo log files with two members are created. Each member is stored in /ora1 and /ora2.

After running the necessary scripts to create the catalog and packages, you create the tablespaces for the application:

```
ALTER SYSTEM SET DB_CREATE_FILE_DEST = "/ora2";
CREATE TABLESPACE SJC_DATA
EXTENT MANAGEMENT DICTIONARY
MINIMUM EXTENT 128K
DATAFILE SIZE 800M;
ALTER SYSTEM SET DB_CREATE_FILE_DEST = "/ora3";
ALTER TABLESPACE SJC_DATA ADD DATAFILE SIZE 200M;
CREATE TABLESAPCE WKW_INDEX
EXTENT MANAGEMENT LOCAL UNIFORM SIZE 512K
DATAFILE SIZE 500M;
ALTER SYSTEM SET DB_CREATE_FILE_DEST = "/ora4";
CREATE TABLESPACE WKW_DATA;
CREATE TABLESPACE SJC_INDEX
EXTENT MANAGEMENT LOCAL UNIFORM SIZE 512K
DATAFILE SIZE 500M;
```

Since you have only 900MB in each file system, to allocate 1GB to the SJC_DATA tablespace, you needed two data files. This is accomplished in two steps.

Querying Data File Information

Similar to gathering tablespace information, you can use SQL*Plus as well as the EM Grid Control to get information about data files and temporary files. In the following sections, you will query a few dictionary views that hold data file and temporary-file information. You can obtain the same information using the EM Grid Control by drilling down the tablespaces shown in Figure 10.5. You can query data file and temporary-file information by using the following views.

V$DATAFILE

This view shows data file information from the control file:

```
SELECT FILE#, RFILE#, STATUS, BYTES, BLOCK_SIZE
FROM V$DATAFILE;
```

FILE#	RFILE#	STATUS	BYTES	BLOCK_SIZE
1	1	SYSTEM	734003200	8192
2	2	ONLINE	883818496	8192
3	3	ONLINE	225443840	8192
4	4	ONLINE	5242880	8192
5	5	ONLINE	104857600	8192
6	6	ONLINE	209715200	8192
7	7	ONLINE	209715200	8192
8	8	ONLINE	104857600	8192

V$TEMPFILE

Similar to V$DATAFILE, this view shows information about the temporary files:

```
SELECT FILE#, RFILE#, STATUS, BYTES, BLOCK_SIZE
FROM V$TEMPFILE;
```

FILE#	RFILE#	STATUS	BYTES	BLOCK_SIZE
1	1	ONLINE	49283072	8192

DBA_DATA_FILES

This view shows information about the filenames, associated tablespace names, size, status, and so on:

```
SELECT TABLESPACE_NAME, FILE_NAME, BYTES,
        AUTOEXTENSIBLE
FROM DBA_DATA_FILES;
```

TABLESPACE	FILE_NAME	BYTES	AUT
USERS	/u01/app/oracle/oradata/11GR11/users01.dbf	5242880	YES
UNDOTBS1	/u01/app/oracle/oradata/11GR11/undotbs01.dbf	225443840	YES
SYSAUX	/u01/app/oracle/oradata/11GR11/sysaux01.dbf	883818496	YES
SYSTEM	/u01/app/oracle/oradata/11GR11/system01.dbf	734003200	YES
EXAMPLE	/u01/app/oracle/oradata/11GR11/example01.dbf	104857600	YES
APPL_DATA	/u01/app/oracle/oradata/11GR11/appl_data01.dbf	209715200	NO
APPL_DATA	/u01/app/oracle/oradata/11GR11/appl_data02.dbf	209715200	NO
HR_DATA	/u02/oradata/11GR11/11GR11/datafile/o1_mf_hr_data_46n3ck5t_.dbf	104857600	YES

DBA_TEMP_FILES

This view shows information similar to that of DBA_DATA_FILES for the temporary files in the database:

```
SELECT TABLESPACE_NAME, FILE_NAME, BYTES,
       AUTOEXTENSIBLE
FROM DBA_TEMP_FILES;
```

TABLESPACE	FILE_NAME	BYTES	AUT
TEMP	/u01/app/oracle/oradata/11GR11/temp01.dbf	49283072	NO

The maximum number of data files per tablespace is OS dependent, but on most operating systems, it is 1,022. The maximum number of data files per database is 65,533. The MAXDATAFILES clause in the CREATE DATABASE and CREATE CONTROLFILE statements also limits the number of data files per database. The maximum data file size is OS dependent. There is no limit on the number of tablespaces per database. Because only 65,533 data files are allowed per database, you cannot have more than 65,533 tablespaces, because each tablespace needs at least one data file.

A useful technique for managing disk space used by data files is to enable AUTOEXTEND for application tablespaces, which tells the database to automatically enlarge a data file when the tablespace runs out of free space. The AUTOEXTEND attribute applies to individual data files and not to the tablespace.

To resize a data file manually, use the `ALTER DATABASE DATAFILE` statement, like this:

```
ALTER DATABASE DATAFILE
  '/u01/app/oracle/oradata/11GR11/example01.dbf' RESIZE 2000M;
```

To configure a data file to automatically enlarge as needed by adding 100MB at a time up to a maximum of 8000MB, execute the following:

```
ALTER DATABASE DATAFILE
  'C:\ORACLE\ORADATA\ORA10\DATA01.DBF'
AUTOEXTEND ON NEXT 100M MAXSIZE 8000M;
```

If you plan to use the AUTOEXTEND option for the data files, use MAXSIZE to limit the file size to the disk space available. Also, it is not advised to enable AUTOEXTEND for temporary and undo tablespaces because user error can fill up the available disk space.

Working with Schema Objects

A *schema* is collection of database objects owned by a specific database user. In an Oracle 11*g* database, the schema has the same name as the database user, so the two terms are synonymous. Schema objects include the segments (tables, indexes, and so on) you have seen in tablespaces as well as nonsegment database objects owned by a user. These nonsegment objects include constraints, views, synonyms, procedures, and packages. Database objects that are not owned by one user and thus are not schema objects include roles, tablespaces, and directories. The schema objects you need to learn for the certification exam are tables, indexes, and constraints.

In Chapter 6, you learned to create tables, what datatypes can be used, and how to modify the table structure. In the following sections, you will learn to create tables with the storage clause. You also learned in Chapter 6 the various types of constraints and how constraints are used. In Chapter 7, you learned to create indexes and learned that they are similar to tables in that you can specify storage parameters when creating them. In this chapter, you will take this a step further, creating indexes that specify storage clauses. To fully prepare for the OCA certification exam, you must understand Chapters 6 and 7 before moving on in this one.

A Little Background on Creating Tables

Tables are the primary data storage containers in an Oracle Database. You can think of a table as a spreadsheet having column headings and many rows of information. A schema or a user in the database owns the table. The table columns have a defined datatype—the data stored in the columns should satisfy the characteristics of the column. You can also define rules for storing data in the columns using integrity constraints.

Data in a table is organized into rows and columns. Each column is named and has a specific datatype and size, such as CHAR(16), VARCHAR2(50), TIMESTAMP(6), or NUMBER. A row is a single occurrence of this set of columns. You can think of columns as fields, and you can think of rows as records.

When you create a table, you must give it a name as well as specify the column names and datatypes. You can optionally specify many additional attributes, such as column default values, extent sizes, which tablespace to use, and so on. Table and column names have the following requirements:

- They must be from 1 to 30 bytes in length.

- They must begin with a letter.

- They can include letters, numbers, the underscore symbol (_), the number symbol (#), and the dollar symbol ($). (However, Oracle discourages the use of number and dollar symbols in names.)

- They cannot be a reserved word such as NUMBER or INDEX.

Table names in Oracle are not case sensitive. This is good so you do not have to keep track of case. If you enclose the table name in double quotation marks, the case of the table name is preserved. You must enclose the table name in double quotation marks if the table name contains characters that are not uppercase.

If the name is enclosed in double quotation marks (" "), the only requirement is that the name be from 1 to 30 bytes long and not contain an embedded double quotation mark. Each column name must be unique within a table. The table name must be unique within the schema; you cannot have same name for a table and a view in a schema. The following are the types of tables available in Oracle 11*g*:

Heap table   Simply known as a table, this is the most common method of storing data. These tables are permanent and can be partitioned for easy storage management. Partitioning allows the table to be broken into multiple smaller pieces for easy management and better performance. The CREATE TABLE … ORGANIZATION HEAP statement is used to create a relational table. Since ORGANIZATION HEAP is the default, it can be omitted.

Temporary table   Temporary tables store private data or data that is specific to a session. This data cannot be shared with other users in the database. They're used for temporary data manipulation or for storing intermediary results. The CREATE GLOBAL TEMPORARY TABLE statement is used to create a temporary table.

Index-organized table (IOT)   Index-organized tables store the data in a structured primary key sorted manner. Each IOT must have a primary key defined. These tables are similar to a relational table with a primary key, but they do not use separate storage for the table and primary key like the relational tables do. The `CREATE TABLE … ORGANIZATION INDEX` statement is used to create an index-organized table.

External table   As the name indicates, data is stored outside the Oracle Database in flat files. External tables are read-only. No indexes are allowed on external tables. Column names defined in the Oracle Database are mapped to the columns in the external file. The default driver used to read an external table is SQL*Loader. The `CREATE TABLE … ORGANIZATION EXTERNAL` statement is used to create an external table.

Object table   Object tables are special kind of tables that support the object-oriented features of the Oracle 11g database. In an object table, each row represents an object.

In the following sections, you will see how to create and manage tables.

Creating a Table

To create a table, use the `CREATE TABLE` statement. At a minimum, you need to list the column names and datatypes for the table. You can create a table under the username used to connect to the database, or with proper privileges you can create a table under another username. A database user can be referred to as a *schema*, or as an *owner* when the user owns objects in the database. The simplest form of creating a table is as follows:

```
CREATE TABLE ORDERS (
ORDER_NUM      NUMBER,
ORDER_DATE     DATE,
PRODUCT_CD     VARCHAR2 (10),
QUANTITY       NUMBER (10,3),
STATUS         CHAR);
```

ORDERS is the table name; the columns in the table are specified in parentheses separated by commas. The table is created under the username used to connect to the database; to create the table under another schema, you need to qualify the table with the schema name. For example, if you want to create the ORDERS table as being owned by SCOTT, create the table by using `CREATE TABLE SCOTT.ORDERS ( )`, you must have the `CREATE ANY TABLE` privilege to do so.

A column name and a datatype identify each column. For certain datatypes, you can specify a maximum width. You can specify any Oracle built-in datatype or user-defined datatype for the column definition. When specifying user-defined datatypes, the user-defined type must exist before creating the table. You can add several attributes to your table definition such as the tablespace in which you want your table stored.

If you create a table without specifying the storage parameters and tablespace, the table will be created in the default tablespace of the user, and the storage parameters used will be those of the default specified for the tablespace. It is always better to estimate the size of the table and specify appropriate storage parameters when creating the table. If the table is too large, you might need to consider partitioning or creating the table in a separate tablespace. This helps you manage the table.

What Is Partitioning?

When tables are very large, you can manage them better by using partitioning. *Partitioning* is breaking a large table into manageable pieces based on the values in a column (or multiple columns) known as the *partition key*. If you have a very large table spread across many data files and one disk fails, you have to recover the entire table. However, if the table is partitioned, you need to recover only that partition. SQL statements can access the required partition(s) rather than reading the entire table. Partitioning improves performance and makes managing tables easier. Partitioning is not part of the certification exam. To learn more about partitioning, read "Oracle 11*g* Administrators Guide" in the Oracle documentation (http://tahiti.oracle.com).

Oracle allocates a segment to the table when the table is created. This segment will have the number of extents specified by the storage parameter MINEXTENTS. Oracle allocates new extents to the table as required. Though you can have an unlimited number of extents for a segment, a little planning can improve the performance of the table. Having numerous extents affects the operations on the table, such as when the table is truncated or full table scans are performed. A larger number of extents may cause additional I/Os in the data file and therefore may affect performance.

To create the ORDERS table using explicit storage parameters in the USER_DATA tablespace, use the following:

```
CREATE TABLE JAKE.ORDERS (
ORDER_NUM      NUMBER,
ORDER_DATE     DATE,
PRODUCT_CD     VARCHAR2 (10),
QUANTITY       NUMBER (10,3),
STATUS         CHAR)
TABLESPACE USER_DATA
PCTFREE    5
PCTUSED    75
INITRANS   1
STORAGE    (INITIAL 512K    NEXT 512K    PCTINCREASE 0
            MINEXTENTS 1    MAXEXTENTS 100
            FREELISTS 1     FREELIST GROUPS 1
            BUFFER_POOL KEEP);
```

The table will be owned by JAKE and will be created in the USER_DATA tablespace (JAKE should have appropriate space quota privileges in the tablespace). None of the storage parameters is mandatory to create a table; Oracle assigns default values if you omit them. Let's discuss the clauses used in the table creation.

TABLESPACE specifies the location where the table should be created. If you omit the STORAGE clause or any parameters in the STORAGE clause, the default will be taken from the tablespace's default storage (if applicable). If you omit the TABLESPACE clause, the table will be created in the default tablespace of the user.

PCTFREE and PCTUSED are block storage parameters. PCTFREE specifies the amount of free space that should be reserved in each block of the table for future updates. In this example, you specify a low PCTFREE for the ORDERS table, because there are not many updates to the table that increase the row length. PCTUSED specifies when the block should be considered for inserting new rows once the PCTFREE threshold is reached. Here you specified 75, so when the used space falls to less than 75 (because of updates or deletes), new rows will be added to the block.

INITRANS specifies the number of concurrent transactions that can update each block of the table. Oracle reserves space in the block header for the INITRANS number of concurrent transactions. For each additional concurrent transaction, Oracle allocates space from the free space—which has an overhead of dynamically allocating transaction entry space. If the block is full and no space is available, the transaction waits until a transaction entry space is available.

The STORAGE clause specifies the extent sizes, free lists, and buffer pool values. The INITIAL, NEXT, MINEXTENTS, MAXEXTENTS, and PCTINCREASE parameters control the size of the extents allocated to the table. If the table is created on a locally managed uniform extent tablespace, these storage parameters are ignored.

FREELIST GROUPS specifies the number of free list groups that should be created for the table. The default and minimum value is 1. Each free list group uses one data block (that's why the minimum value for INITIAL is two database blocks) known as the *segment header*, which has information about the extents, free blocks, and high-water mark of the table.

FREELISTS specifies the number of lists for each free list group. The default and minimum value is 1. The free list manages the list of blocks that are available to add new rows. A block is removed from the free list if the free space in the block is less than PCTFREE. The block remains out of the free list as long as the used space is greater than PCTUSED. Create more free lists if the volume of inserts to the table is great. An appropriate number would be the number of concurrent transactions performing inserts to the table. Oracle recommends having FREELISTS and INITRANS be the same value. The FREELIST GROUPS parameter is mostly used for RAC configuration, where you can specify a group for each instance.

The BUFFER_POOL parameter of the STORAGE clause specifies the area of the database buffer cache to keep the blocks of the table when read from the data file while querying or for update/delete. There are three buffer pools: KEEP, RECYCLE, and DEFAULT. The default value is DEFAULT. Specify KEEP if the table is small and is frequently accessed. The blocks in the KEEP pool are always available in the SGA, so I/O will be faster. The blocks assigned to the RECYCLE buffer pool are removed from memory as soon as they are not needed. Specify RECYCLE for large tables or tables that are seldom accessed. If you do not specify KEEP or RECYCLE, the blocks are assigned to the DEFAULT pool, where they will be aged out using an LRU algorithm.

> **NOTE** If the tablespace is created with the SEGMENT SPACE MANAGEMENT AUTO clause, the parameters PCTUSED, FREELISTS, and FREELIST GROUPS are ignored.

When a table is created, you can specify several optional clauses to improve efficiency of the table based on the purpose for which the table is created. You can specify storage parameters for the table, for its indexes, and for its LOB structures. In the following sections, you will learn how to specify storage for LOB structures and the various clauses available to specify table storage.

Storing LOB Structures

A table can contain columns of type CLOB, BLOB, or NCLOB. These internal LOB columns can have different storage settings than those of the table and can be stored in a different tablespace for easy management and performance improvement. The following example specifies storage for a LOB column when creating the table:

```
CREATE TABLE LICENSE_INFO
(DRIVER_ID    VARCHAR2 (20),
 DRIVER_NAME VARCHAR2 (30),
 DOB          DATE,
 PHOTO        BLOB)
TABLESPACE APP_DATA STORAGE (INITIAL 4M NEXT 4M PCTINCREASE 0)
LOB (PHOTO) STORE AS PHOTO_LOB
    (TABLESPACE APP_LARGE_DATA
    DISABLE STORAGE IN ROW
    STORAGE (INITIAL 128M NEXT 128M PCTINCREASE 0)
    CHUNK 4000
    PCTVERSION 20
    NOCACHE LOGGING);
```

The table LICENSE_INFO is created with a BLOB datatype column. The table is stored in the APP_DATA tablespace, and the BLOB column PHOTO is stored in the APP_LARGE_DATA tablespace. I'll now discuss the various clauses specified for the LOB storage.

The LOB segment is given the name PHOTO_LOB. If a name is not given, Oracle generates a name. You can specify multiple LOB columns in parentheses following the LOB keyword, if they all have the same storage characteristics. In such cases, you cannot specify a name for the LOB segment. For example, if the table has three LOB columns and all the LOB columns have the same characteristics, you may specify the following:

```
LOB (PHOTO, VIDEO, AUDIO) STORE AS
(TABLESPACE APP_LARGE_DATA
 CACHE READS NOLOGGING);
```

TABLESPACE specifies the tablespace where the LOB segment(s) should be stored. The tablespace can be locally or dictionary managed. If the LOB column is larger than 4,000 bytes, data is stored in the LOB segment. Storing data in the LOB segment is known as *out-of-line* storage. If the LOB column data is less than 4,000 bytes, it is stored *inline*, along with the other column data of the table. If the TABLESPACE clause is omitted, the LOB segment is created in the table's tablespace.

DISABLE/ENABLE STORAGE IN ROW specifies whether LOB data should be stored inline or out of line. ENABLE is the default and stores LOB data along with the other columns if the LOB data is smaller than 4,000 bytes. DISABLE stores the LOB data in the LOB segment irrespective of its size. Whether the LOB data is stored inline or out of line, the LOB locator is always stored along with the row.

STORAGE specifies the extent sizes and growth parameters. These parameters are the same as you would use with a table.

CHUNK specifies the total bytes of data that will be read or written during LOB manipulation. CHUNK must be a multiple of the database block size. If you specify a value other than a multiple of the block size, Oracle uses the next higher value that is a multiple of the block size. For example, if you specify 4000 for CHUNK and the database block size is 2048, Oracle will take the value of 4096. The default value for CHUNK is the database block size, and the maximum value is 32KB. The INITIAL and NEXT values specified in the STORAGE clause must be higher than the value for CHUNK.

PCTVERSION specifies the percentage of all used LOB data space that can be occupied by old versions of LOB data pages. Since LOB data changes are not written to the rollback segments, PCTVERSION specifies the percentage of old information that should be kept in the LOB segment for consistent reads. The default is 10 and can range from 0 through 100.

CACHE/NOCACHE/CACHE READS specifies whether to cache the LOB reads. If the LOB is read and updated frequently, use the CACHE clause. NOCACHE is the default, and it is useful for a LOB that is read infrequently and never updated. CACHE READS caches only the read operation. This is useful for a LOB that is read frequently but never updated.

LOGGING / NOLOGGING specifies whether redo information should be generated for LOB data. NOLOGGING does not write redo and is useful for faster data loads. You cannot specify CACHE and NOLOGGING together.

Using Other Create Clauses

The other clauses you can specify while creating a table (which may appear on the certification exam) are listed here. These clauses help you manage various types of operations on the table.

LOGGING/NOLOGGING   LOGGING is the default for the table and tablespace, but if the tablespace is defined as NOLOGGING, then the table uses NOLOGGING. LOGGING specifies that table creation and direct-load inserts should be logged to the redo log files. Creating the table by using a subquery and the NOLOGGING clause can improve the table creation time dramatically for large tables. If the table creation, initial data population (using a subquery), and direct-load inserts are not logged to the redo log files when using the NOLOGGING clause, you must back up the table (or better yet, the entire tablespace) after such operations are performed. Media recovery will not create or load tables created with the NOLOGGING attribute. You can also specify a separate LOGGING or NOLOGGING attribute for indexes and LOB storage of the table, independent of the table's attribute. The following example creates a table with the NOLOGGING clause:

```
CREATE TABLE MY_ORDERS (    )
TABLESPACE USER_DATA STORAGE (    )
NOLOGGING;
```

PARALLEL/NOPARALLEL   NOPARALLEL is the default. PARALLEL causes the table creation (if created using a subquery) and the DML statements on the table to execute in parallel. Normally, a single-server process performs operations on tables in a transaction (serial operation). When the PARALLEL attribute is set, Oracle uses multiple processes to complete the operation for a full-table scan. You can specify a degree for the parallelism; if not specified, Oracle calculates the optimum degree of parallelism. The parameter PARALLEL_THREADS_PER_CPU determines the number for parallel degree per CPU; usually the default is 2. If you do not specify the degree, Oracle calculates the degree based on this parameter and the number of CPUs available. The following example creates a table by using a subquery. The table creation will not be logged in the redo log file, and multiple processes will query the JAKE.ORDERS table and create the MY_ORDERS table.

```
CREATE TABLE MY_ORDERS (    )
TABLESPACE USER_DATA STORAGE (    )
NOLOGGING PARALLEL
AS SELECT * FROM JAKE.ORDERS;
```

CACHE/NOCACHE   NOCACHE is the default. For small lookup tables that are frequently accessed, you can specify the CACHE clause to have the blocks retrieved using a full table scan placed at the MRU end of the LRU list in the buffer cache; the blocks are not aged out of the buffer cache immediately. The default behavior (NOCACHE) is to place the blocks from a full-table scan at the tail end of the LRU list, where they are moved out of the list as soon as a different process or query needs these blocks for storing another table's blocks in the cache.

Creating a Table Using a Subquery

You can create a table using existing tables or views by specifying a subquery instead of defining the columns. The subquery can refer to more than one table or view. The table will be created with the rows returned from the subquery. You can specify new column names for the table, but Oracle derives the datatype and maximum width based on the query result—you cannot specify the datatype with this method. You can specify the storage parameters for the tables created by using the subquery.

For example, let's create a new table from the ORDERS table for the orders that are accepted. Notice that the new column names are specified.

```
CREATE TABLE ACCEPTED_ORDERS
  (ORD_NUMBER, ORD_DATE, PRODUCT_CD, QTY)
  TABLESPACE USERS
  PCTFREE 0
  STORAGE (INITIAL 128K NEXT 128K PCTINCREASE 0)
AS
  SELECT ORDER_NUM, ORDER_DATE, PRODUCT_CD, QUANTITY
  FROM   ORDERS
  WHERE  STATUS = 'A';
```

The CREATE TABLE…AS SELECT… will not work if the query refers to columns of the LONG datatype. When you create a table using the subquery, only the NOT NULL constraints associated with the columns are copied to the new table. Other constraints and column default definitions are not copied.

Creating a Temporary Table

Temporary tables hold information that is available only to the session that created the data. The definition of the temporary table is available to all sessions. A temporary table is created using the CREATE GLOBAL TEMPORARY TABLE statement. The data in the table can be session specific or transaction specific. The ON COMMIT clause specifies this. The following statement creates a temporary table that is transaction specific:

```
CREATE GLOBAL TEMPORARY TABLE INVALID_ORDERS
(ORDER#   NUMBER (8),
 ORDER_DT DATE,
 VALUE    NUMBER (12,2))
ON COMMIT DELETE ROWS
TABLESPACE TEMP_TABLES;
```

Oracle deletes rows or truncates the table after each commit. To define the table as session specific, use the ON COMMIT PRESERVE ROWS clause.

Storage for temporary tablespace is allocated in the temporary tablespace of the user if the TABLESPACE clause is omitted. Segments are created only when the first insert statement is performed on the table. The temporary segments allocated to temporary tables are deallocated at the end of the transaction for transaction-specific tables and at the end of session for session-specific tables.

You can create indexes on temporary tables. DML statements on temporary tables do not generate redo information, but undo information is generated. Programs can manipulate data in temporary tables or join them to permanent tables in the same manner as any other table.

Refer to Chapter 6 to learn about setting default values, modifying tables, renaming tables, and dropping tables.

Reorganizing Tables

You can use the MOVE clause of the ALTER TABLE command on a nonpartitioned table to reorganize or to move from one tablespace to another. The table is reorganized to reduce the number of extents by specifying larger extent sizes or to prevent row migration. When you move a table, Oracle creates a new segment for the table, copies the data, and drops the old segment. The new segment can be in the same tablespace or in a different tablespace. Since the old segment is dropped only after creating the new segment, you need to make sure you have sufficient space in the tablespace if you're not changing to a different tablespace. The MOVE clause can specify a new tablespace, new storage parameters for the table, new free-space management parameters, and new transaction-entry parameters. You can use the NOLOGGING clause to speed up the reorganization by not writing the changes to the redo log file.

The following example moves the ORDERS table to another tablespace named NEW_DATA. New storage parameters are specified, and the operation is not logged in the redo log files (NOLOGGING).

```
ALTER TABLE ORDERS MOVE
TABLESPACE NEW_DATA
STORAGE (INITIAL 50M NEXT 5M PCTINCREASE 0)
PCTFREE 0 PCTUSED 50
INITRANS 2 NOLOGGING;
```

Queries are allowed on the table while the move operation is in progress, but no insert, update, or delete operations are allowed. The granted permissions on the table are retained.

 The DROP TABLE statement can include the PURGE clause, which will not place the table in the Recycle Bin.

Truncating a Table

The TRUNCATE statement is similar to the DROP statement, but it does not remove the structure of the table, so none of the indexes, constraints, triggers, and privileges on the table are dropped. By default, the space allocated to the table and indexes is freed. If you do not want to free up the space, include the REUSE STORAGE clause. You cannot roll back a truncate operation. Also, you cannot selectively delete rows using the TRUNCATE statement. The syntax of TRUNCATE statement is as follows:

```
TRUNCATE {TABLE|CLUSTER} [<schema>.]<name>
[{DROP|REUSE} STORAGE]
```

You cannot truncate the parent table of an enabled referential integrity constraint. You must first disable the constraint and then truncate the table, even if the child table has no rows. The following example demonstrates this:

```
SQL> CREATE TABLE t1 (
  2    t1f1 NUMBER CONSTRAINT pk_t1 PRIMARY KEY);
```

```
Table created.

SQL> CREATE TABLE t2 (t2f1 NUMBER CONSTRAINT fk_t2
                              REFERENCES t1 (t1f1));
Table created.

SQL> TRUNCATE TABLE t1;
truncate table t1
              *
ERROR at line 1:
ORA-02266: unique/primary keys in table referenced by enabled foreign keys

SQL> ALTER TABLE t2 DISABLE CONSTRAINT fk_t2;
Table altered.

SQL> TRUNCATE TABLE t1;
Table truncated.

SQL>
```

Use the TRUNCATE statement to delete all rows from a large table; it does not write the undo entries and is much faster than the DELETE statement when deleting large number of rows.

Using Namespaces

When you refer an object in the SQL statement, Oracle locates the object in the appropriate namespace. A table can have the same name as an index or a constraint. The namespace is simply the domain of allowable names for the set of schema objects that it serves. The following are the namespaces available in Oracle 11*g*:

- Tables, views, private synonyms
- Constraints
- Indexes
- Clusters
- Database triggers
- Private database links
- Dimensions
- Roles
- Public synonyms

- Public database links
- Tablespaces
- Profiles

For example, if you have a view named BOOKS, you cannot name a table BOOKS (tables and views share a namespace), although you can create an index named BOOKS (indexes and tables have separate namespaces) and a constraint named BOOKS (constraints and tables have separate namespaces).

Working with Constraints

Constraints enforce business rules in the database. In other words, they limit the acceptable data values for a table. Constraints are optional schema objects that depend on tables. Although you can have a table without any constraints, you cannot create a constraint without a table.

Oracle lets you create several types of constraints on your tables to enforce your business rules, including the following:

- NOT NULL
- CHECK
- UNIQUE
- PRIMARY KEY
- FOREIGN KEY

You can create constraints together with the table in the CREATE TABLE statement. After you create a table, you add or remove a constraint from a table with an ALTER TABLE statement. You specify the constraint information with either the inline syntax as a column attribute or the out-of-line syntax as part of the table definition. Constraints do not require a name; if you do not name the constraint, Oracle generates one for you. However, the generated names are simply numbers prefixed with SYS_C and may not be very meaningful.

In the following sections, I will discuss the rules for each constraint type and show examples of creating constraints.

NOT NULL

NOT NULL constraints have the following characteristics:

- The constraint is defined at the column level.
- Use CREATE TABLE to define constraints when creating the table. The following example shows a named constraint on the ORDER_NUM column; for ORDER_DATE, Oracle generates a name:

```
CREATE TABLE ORDERS (
 ORDER_NUM   NUMBER (4) CONSTRAINT NN_ORDER_NUM NOT NULL,
```

```
   ORDER_DATE  DATE NOT NULL,
   PRODUCT_ID)
```

- Use ALTER TABLE MODIFY to add or remove a NOT NULL constraint on the columns of an existing table. The following code shows examples of removing a constraint and adding a constraint:

```
ALTER TABLE ORDERS MODIFY ORDER_DATE NULL;
ALTER TABLE ORDERS MODIFY PRODUCT_ID NOT NULL;
```

CHECK

CHECK constraints have the following characteristics:

- The constraint can be defined at the column level or the table level.
- The condition specified in the CHECK clause should evaluate to a Boolean result and can refer to values in other columns of the same row; the condition cannot use queries.
- Environmental functions such as SYSDATE, USER, USERENV, UID, and pseudocolumns such as ROWNUM, CURRVAL, NEXTVAL, and LEVEL cannot be used to evaluate the check condition.
- One column can have more than one CHECK constraint defined. The column can have a NULL value.
- The constraint can be created using CREATE TABLE or ALTER TABLE:

```
CREATE TABLE BONUS (
  EMP_ID    VARCHAR2 (40) NOT NULL,
  SALARY    NUMBER (9,2),
  BONUS     NUMBER (9,2),
CONSTRAINT CK_BONUS CHECK (BONUS > 0));

ALTER TABLE BONUS
ADD CONSTRAINT CK_BONUS2 CHECK (BONUS < SALARY);
```

UNIQUE

UNIQUE constraints have the following characteristics:

- The constraint can be defined at the column level for single-column unique keys. For a multiple-column unique key (for a composite key, the maximum number of columns specified can be 32), the constraint should be defined at the table level.
- Oracle creates a unique index on the unique key columns to enforce uniqueness. If a unique index or nonunique index already exists on the table with the same columns in the index, Oracle uses the existing index. To use the existing nonunique index, there must not be any duplicate keys in the table.
- Unique constraints allow NULL values in the constraint columns.

- Storage can be specified for the implicit index created when creating the key. If no storage is specified, the index is created on the default tablespace with the default storage parameters of the tablespace. You can specify the LOGGING and NOSORT clauses, as you would when creating an index. The index created can be a local or global partitioned index. The index will have the same name as the unique constraint. The following are two examples. The first one defines a unique constraint with two columns and specifies the storage parameters for the index. The second example adds a new column to the EMP table and creates a unique key at the column level.

```
ALTER TABLE BONUS
ADD CONSTRAINT UQ_EMP_ID UNIQUE (DEPT, EMP_ID)
USING INDEX TABLESPACE INDX
STORAGE (INITIAL 32K NEXT 32K PCTINCREASE 0);


ALTER TABLE EMP ADD
SSN VARCHAR2 (11) CONSTRAINT UQ_SSN UNIQUE;
```

PRIMARY KEY

PRIMARY KEY constraints have the following characteristics:

- All characteristics of the UNIQUE key are applicable except that NULL values are not allowed in the primary key columns.

- A table can have only one primary key.

- Oracle creates a unique index and NOT NULL constraints for each column in the key. Oracle can use an existing index if all the columns of the primary key are in the index. The following example defines a primary key when creating the table. Storage parameters are specified for both the table and the primary key index.

```
CREATE TABLE EMPLOYEE (
 DEPT_NO VARCHAR2 (2),
 EMP_ID  NUMBER (4),
 NAME    VARCHAR2 (20) NOT NULL,
 SSN     VARCHAR2 (11),
 SALARY  NUMBER (9,2) CHECK (SALARY > 0),
CONSTRAINT PK_EMPLOYEE PRIMARY KEY (DEPT_NO, EMP_ID)
 USING INDEX TABLESPACE INDX
 STORAGE (INITIAL 64K NEXT 64K)
 NOLOGGING,
CONSTRAINT UQ_SSN UNIQUE (SSN)
 USING INDEX TABLESPACE INDX)
TABLESPACE USERS
STORAGE (INITIAL 128K NEXT 64K);
```

- Indexes created to enforce unique keys and primary keys can be managed as any other index. However, these indexes cannot be dropped explicitly.

FOREIGN KEY

The foreign key is the column or columns in the table (child table) where the constraint is created; the referenced key is the primary key or unique key column or columns in the table (parent table) that is referenced by the constraint. The following rules are applicable to foreign key constraints:

- A foreign key constraint can be defined at the column level or the table level. Multiple-column foreign keys should be defined at the table level.

- The foreign key column(s) and referenced key column(s) can be in the same table (self-referential integrity constraint).

- NULL values are allowed in the foreign key columns. The following is an example of creating a foreign key constraint on the COUNTRY_CODE and STATE_CODE columns of the CITY table, which refers to the COUNTRY_CODE and STATE_CODE columns of the STATE table (the composite primary key of the STATE table).

  ```
  ALTER TABLE CITY ADD CONSTRAINT FK_STATE
    FOREIGN KEY (COUNTRY_CODE, STATE_CODE)
    REFERENCES STATE (COUNTRY_CODE, STATE_CODE);
  ```

- The ON DELETE clause specifies the action to be taken when a row in the parent table is deleted and child rows exist with the deleted parent primary key. You can delete the child rows (CASCADE) or set the foreign key column values to NULL (SET NULL). If you omit this clause, Oracle will not allow you to delete from the parent table if child records exist. You must delete the child rows first and then the parent row. The following are two examples of specifying the delete action in a foreign key:

  ```
  ALTER TABLE CITY ADD CONSTRAINT FK_STATE
    FOREIGN KEY (COUNTRY_CODE, STATE_CODE)
    REFERENCES STATE (COUNTRY_CODE, STATE_CODE)
    ON DELETE CASCADE;

  ALTER TABLE CITY ADD CONSTRAINT FK_STATE
    FOREIGN KEY (COUNTRY_CODE, STATE_CODE)
    REFERENCES STATE (COUNTRY_CODE, STATE_CODE)
    ON DELETE SET NULL;
  ```

  Refer to Chapter 6 to learn more about constraints.

Deferred Constraint Checking

By default, Oracle checks whether the data conforms to the constraint when the statement is executed. Oracle allows you to change this behavior if the constraint is created using the DEFERRABLE clause (NOT DEFERRABLE is the default). It specifies that the transaction can set the constraint-checking behavior. INITIALLY IMMEDIATE specifies that the constraint should be checked for conformance at the end of each SQL statement (this is the default). INITIALLY DEFERRED specifies that the constraint should be checked for conformance at the end of the transaction. The DEFERRABLE status of a constraint cannot be changed using ALTER TABLE MODIFY CONSTRAINT; you must drop and re-create the constraint, and you can change the INITIALLY [DEFERRED/IMMEDIATE] clause using ALTER TABLE.

If the constraint is DEFERRABLE, you can set the behavior by using the SET CONSTRAINTS command or by using the ALTER SESSION SET CONSTRAINT command. You can enable or disable deferred constraint checking by listing all the constraints or by specifying the ALL keyword. The SET CONSTRAINTS command is used to set the constraint-checking behavior for the current transaction, and the ALTER SESSION command is used to set the constraint-checking behavior for the current session.

For example, if you hire a new employee and create a new department for that person to manage, you need to add a row to both the EMPLOYEES table (which references the new department) and the DEPARTMENTS table (which references the new employee). Although this temporary violation will not go against the intent of the business rule, you will need to create the constraints with some additional options, like this:

```
ALTER TABLE employees
  ADD CONSTRAINT emp_dept_fk FOREIGN KEY (dept_nbr)
    REFERENCES departments(dept_nbr) ON DELETE CASCADE
    DEFERRABLE;


ALTER TABLE departments ADD CONSTRAINT
  dept_mgr_fk FOREIGN KEY (manager_id) REFERENCES
    employees(employee_id) ON DELETE SET NULL
    DEFERRABLE INITIALLY DEFERRED;
```

By default, the database checks that a FOREIGN KEY constraint is satisfied at the end of each statement. You define this behavior with the keywords INITIALLY IMMEDIATE. Also, by default, the database will not allow programs to defer constraint checking to the end of the transaction. You define this behavior with the keywords NOT DEFERRABLE.

When you create a constraint, you can tell the database to allow either immediate or deferred constraint checking by specifying the keyword DEFERRABLE. If you normally want a DEFERRABLE constraint to be deferred, create it with the INITIALLY DEFERRED option. Only DEFERRABLE constraints can be set to INITIALLY DEFERRED. Once you create a constraint, you cannot change its deferability (for example, from NOT DEFERRABLE to DEFERRABLE); instead, you must drop and re-create the constraint with the new specification.

Working with Indexes

Indexes are optional data structures built on tables. Indexes can improve data retrieval performance by providing a direct access method instead of the default full-table scan retrieval method. You can build B-tree or bitmap indexes on one or more columns in a table. An *index key* is defined as one data value stored in the index. A B-tree index sorts the keys into a binary tree and stores these keys together with the table's ROWIDs. In a bitmap index, a bitmap is created for each key. There is a bit in each bitmap for every ROWID in the table, forming the equivalent of a two-dimensional matrix. The bits are set if the corresponding row in the bitmap exists.

B-tree indexes are the default index type and are appropriate for medium- to high-cardinality columns (*high cardinality* means those having many distinct values). B-tree indexes support row-level locking and so are appropriate for multiuser, transactional applications. The indexes supporting PRIMARY KEY and UNIQUE constraints are B-tree indexes. The following are the types of B-tree indexes you can create:

Nonunique index   This is the default; the index column values are not unique.

Unique index   This is created by specifying the UNIQUE keyword: each column value entry of the index is unique. For composite indexes, Oracle guarantees that the combination of all index column values in the composite index is unique. Oracle returns an error if you try to insert two rows with the same index column values.

Reverse key index   The reverse key index is created by specifying the REVERSE keyword. The bytes of each column indexed are reversed, while keeping the column order. For example, if column ORDER_NUM has value 54321, Oracle reverses the bytes to 12345 and then adds it to the index. This type of indexing can be used for unique indexes when inserts to the table are always in the ascending order of the indexed columns. This helps distribute the adjacent valued columns to different leaf blocks of the index and as a result improves performance by retrieving fewer index blocks. *Leaf blocks* are the blocks at the lowest level of the B-tree.

Function-based index   The function-based index can be created on columns with expressions. For example, creating an index on the SUBSTR(EMPID, 1,2) can speed up the queries using SUBSTR(EMPID, 1, 2) in the WHERE clause.

Bitmap indexes, on the other hand, are best for multiple combinations of low- to medium-cardinality columns (you cannot create a unique bitmap index), and they do not support row-level locking. Bitmap indexes are best in environments in which changes to data are limited and controlled, such as many data warehousing applications. Because bitmap indexes cannot efficiently make changes to the indexed data, they are often dropped prior to data loading and then re-created after a data load.

 NOTE   Oracle does not include the rows with NULL values in the index columns when storing the index.

Refer to Chapter 7 to learn more about creating and modifying indexes.

Specifying Storage

If you do not specify the TABLESPACE clause in the CREATE INDEX statement, Oracle creates the index in the default tablespace of the user. If the STORAGE clause is not specified, Oracle inherits the default storage parameters defined for the tablespace. All the storage parameters discussed in the "Creating a Table" section are applicable to indexes and have the same meaning except for PCTUSED. The PCTUSED parameter cannot be specified for indexes. Keep the INITRANS parameter for the index more than the INITRANS specified for the corresponding table, because the index blocks can hold a larger number of rows than a table.

Here is an example of creating an index and specifying the storage:

```
CREATE UNIQUE INDEX IND2_ORDERS
ON ORDERS (ORDER_NUM)
TABLESPACE USER_INDEX
PCTFREE    25
INITRANS   2
MAXTRANS   255
STORAGE    (INITIAL 128K    NEXT 128K    PCTINCREASE 0
            MINEXTENTS 1    MAXEXTENTS 100
            FREELISTS 1     FREELIST GROUPS 1
            BUFFER_POOL KEEP);
```

When creating indexes for a table with rows, Oracle writes the data blocks with index values up to PCTFREE. The free space reserved by specifying PCTFREE is used when inserting into the table a new row (or updating a row that changes the corresponding index key column value) that needs to be placed between two index key values of the leaf node. If no free space is available in the block, Oracle uses a new block. If many new rows are inserted into the table, keep the PCTFREE parameter of the index high.

Using Other Create Clauses

You can specify NOLOGGING to make the index creation faster and therefore not write information to the redo log files. The default is LOGGING.

It is possible to collect statistics about the index while creating the index by specifying the COMPUTE STATISTICS clause. This avoids another ANALYZE on the index later.

The ONLINE clause specifies that the table will be available for DML operations when the index is built.

If data is loaded to the table in the order of an index, you can specify the NOSORT clause. Oracle does not sort the rows, but if the data is not sorted, Oracle returns an error. Specifying this clause saves time and temporary space.

For multicolumn indexes, eliminating the repeating key columns can save storage space. Specify the COMPRESS clause when creating the index. NOCOMPRESS is the default. This clause can be used only with nonpartitioned indexes. Index performance may be affected when using this clause.

Specify PARALLEL to create the index using multiple server processes. NOPARALLEL is the default.

The following is an example of creating an index by specifying some of the miscellaneous clauses:

```
SQL> CREATE INDEX IND5_ORDERS ON ORDERS
  2  (ORDER_NUM, ORDER_DATE)
  3  TABLESPACE INDX
```

```
4  NOLOGGING
5  NOSORT
6  COMPRESS
7  SORT
8  COMPUTE STATISTICS;
```

Index created.

SQL>

Reverse Key Indexes

Specifying the REVERSE keyword creates a reverse key index. Reverse key indexes improve performance of certain OLTP applications using the parallel server. The following example creates a reverse key index on the ORDER_NUM and ORDER_DATE columns of the ORDERS table:

```
CREATE UNIQUE INDEX IND2_ORDERS
ON ORDERS (ORDER_DATE, ORDER_NUM)
TABLESPACE USER_INDEX
REVERSE;
```

Function-Based Indexes

Function-based indexes are created as regular B-tree or bitmap indexes. Specify the expression or function when creating the index. Oracle precalculates the value of the expression and creates the index. For example, this creates a function based on

```
SUBSTR(PRODUCT_ID,1,2):
CREATE INDEX IND4_ORDERS
ON ORDERS (SUBSTR(PRODUCT_ID,1,2))
TABLESPACE USER_INDEX;
```

To use the function-based index, you must set the instance initialization parameter QUERY_REWRITE_ENABLED to TRUE and QUERY_REWRITE_INTEGRITY to TRUSTED. Also, the COMPATIBLE parameter should be set to 8.1.0 or higher. A query can use this index if its WHERE clause specifies a condition by using SUBSTR(PRODUCT_ID,1,2), as in the following example:

```
SELECT * FROM ORDERS
WHERE SUBSTR(PRODUCT_ID,1,2) = 'BT';
```

Index-Organized Tables

You can store index and table data together in a structure known as an *index-organized table*. IOTs are suitable for tables in which the data access is mostly through its primary key, such as lookup tables, where you have a code and a description. An IOT is a B-tree index, and instead of storing the ROWID of the table where the row belongs, the entire row is stored as part of the index. You can build additional indexes on the columns of an IOT. The data in an IOT is accessed the same way you would access the data in a table.

Since the row is stored along with the B-tree index, there is no physical ROWID for each row. The primary key identifies the rows in an IOT. Oracle "guesses" the location of the row and assigns a logical ROWID for each row, which permits the creation of secondary indexes. You can partition an IOT, but the partition columns should be a subset of the primary key columns.

To build additional indexes on the IOT, Oracle uses a logical ROWID, which is derived from the primary key values of the IOT. The logical ROWID can include a guessed physical location of the row in the data files. This guessed location is not valid when a row is moved from one block to another. If the logical ROWID does not include the guessed location of the ROWID, Oracle has to perform two index scans when using the secondary index. The logical ROWIDs can be stored in columns with the datatype UROWID.

An index-organized table is created using the CREATE TABLE command with the ORGANIZATION INDEX keyword. You must specify the primary key for the table when creating the table.

```
SQL> CREATE TABLE IOT_EXAMPLE (
  2  PK_COL1   NUMBER (4),
  3  PK_COL2   VARCHAR2 (10),
  4  NON_PK_COL1 VARCHAR2 (40),
  5  NON_PK_COL2 DATE,
  6  CONSTRAINT PK_IOT PRIMARY KEY
  7        (PK_COL1, PK_COL2))
  8  ORGANIZATION INDEX
  9  TABLESPACE INDX
 10  STORAGE (INITIAL 32K NEXT 32K PCTINCREASE 0);

Table created.

SQL>
```

 Real World Scenario

Creating Tables, Indexes, and Constraints for a Customer-Maintenance Application

Let's consider an example of creating tables that are needed to manage a customer database. The objective of this example is to give you the various options available when defining tables, indexes, and constraints. The DBA is given the physical structure of the tables and the relationship between tables by the development team:

- The DBA reviews the columns of the CUSTOMER_MASTER table and the type of data stored. CUST_ID is the unique identifier of the table, the primary key. This table contains the customer name, email address, date of birth, primary contact address type, and status flag.

- The CUSTOMER_ADDRESS table keeps the addresses of the customer. The customer can have up to four different addresses: business1, business2, home1, and home2.

- The CUSTOMER_REFERENCES table keeps information about the new customers introduced by a customer. This table simply keeps the customer ID of the referring and new customers.

- Each table has a record creation date, created username, update date, and update username.

The DBA decided to keep the tables and indexes in separate tablespaces and is using the uniform-extent feature of the tablespace. This helps manage the space on the tablespace more effectively. Data is kept in the CUST_DATA tablespace, and indexes are maintained in the CUST_INDX tablespace. Let's create the tablespaces:

```
CREATE TABLESPACE CUST_DATA DATAFILE
'C:\ORACLE\ORADATA\CUST_DATA01.DBF' SIZE 512K
AUTOEXTEND ON NEXT 128K MAXSIZE 2000K
EXTENT MANAGEMENT LOCAL UNIFORM SIZE 256K
SEGMENT SPACE MANAGEMENT AUTO;
CREATE TABLESPACE CUST_INDX DATAFILE
'C:\ORACLE\ORADATA\CUST_INDX.DBF' SIZE 256K
AUTOEXTEND ON NEXT 128K MAXSIZE 2000K
EXTENT MANAGEMENT LOCAL UNIFORM SIZE 128K
SEGMENT SPACE MANAGEMENT AUTO;
```

Now create the CUSTOMER_MASTER table. The table needs to have the primary key CUST_ID and the unique key EMAIL. A nonunique index is created on the EMAIL column and is used for the UNIQUE key enforcement. The DBA also wants to create an index on the DOB column because the firm sends out birthday greetings to all its customers every week. The check constraint on the ADD_TYPE makes sure no other values get inserted into the column.

```
CREATE TABLE CUSTOMER_MASTER (
CUST_ID      VARCHAR2 (10),
CUST_NAME    VARCHAR2 (30),
EMAIL        VARCHAR2 (30),
DOB          DATE,
ADD_TYPE     CHAR (2) CONSTRAINT CK_ADD_TYPE
             CHECK (ADD_TYPE IN ('B1','B2','H1','H2')),
CRE_USER     VARCHAR2 (5) DEFAULT USER,
CRE_TIME     TIMESTAMP (3) DEFAULT SYSTIMESTAMP,
MOD_USER     VARCHAR2 (5),
MOD_TIME     TIMESTAMP (3),
CONSTRAINT PK_CUSTOMER_MASTER PRIMARY KEY (CUST_ID)
  USING INDEX TABLESPACE CUST_INDX)
```

```
TABLESPACE CUST_DATA;
CREATE INDEX CUST_EMAIL ON CUSTOMER_MASTER (EMAIL)
TABLESPACE CUST_INDX;
ALTER TABLE CUSTOMER_MASTER ADD CONSTRAINT UQ_CUST_EMAIL
UNIQUE (EMAIL) USING INDEX CUST_EMAIL;
```

Create the CUSTOMER_ADDRESSES table. Let's create the table first and then add the primary key and foreign key. The foreign key is created with an option to defer its checking until commit time.

```
CREATE TABLE CUSTOMER_ADDRESSES (
CUST_ID     VARCHAR2 (10),
ADD_TYPE    CHAR (2),
ADD_LINE1   VARCHAR2 (40) NOT NULL,
ADD_LINE2   VARCHAR2 (40),
CITY        VARCHAR2 (40) NOT NULL,
STATE       VARCHAR2 (2) NOT NULL,
ZIP         NUMBER (5) NOT NULL)
TABLESPACE CUST_DATA;
ALTER TABLE CUSTOMER_ADDRESSES ADD CONSTRAINT
PK_CUST_ADDRESSES PRIMARY KEY (CUST_ID, ADD_TYPE)
USING INDEX TABLESPACE CUST_INDX;
ALTER TABLE CUSTOMER_ADDRESSES ADD CONSTRAINT
FK_CUST_ADDRESSES FOREIGN KEY (CUST_ID)
REFERENCES CUSTOMER_MASTER;
ALTER TABLE CUSTOMER_ADDRESSES ADD CONSTRAINT
CK_ADD_TYPE2 CHECK (ADD_TYPE IN ('B1','B2','H1','H2'));
```

The DBA forgot to enable the constraint DEFERRABLE clause and to delete records from the CUSTOMER_ADDRESSES table when the row was deleted from the CUSTOMER_MASTER table.

```
ALTER TABLE CUSTOMER_ADDRESSES
DROP CONSTRAINT FK_CUST_ADDRESSES;
ALTER TABLE CUSTOMER_ADDRESSES ADD CONSTRAINT
FK_CUST_ADDRESSES FOREIGN KEY (CUST_ID)
REFERENCES CUSTOMER_MASTER
ON DELETE CASCADE DEFERRABLE INITIALLY IMMEDIATE;
```

Create the CUSTOMER_REFERENCES table. Since this table row never grows with updates, the DBA sets the PCTFREE parameter of the table to 0.

```
CREATE TABLE CUSTOMER_REFERENCES (
CUST_ID     VARCHAR2 (10) REFERENCES CUSTOMER_MASTER,
CUST_REF_ID VARCHAR2 (10) REFERENCES CUSTOMER_MASTER,
```

```
CRE_USER      VARCHAR2 (5),
CRE_TIME      TIMESTAMP (3) DEFAULT SYSTIMESTAMP,
MOD_USER      VARCHAR2 (5) DEFAULT USER,
MOD_TIME      TIMESTAMP (3),
CONSTRAINT PK_CUST_REFS PRIMARY KEY (CUST_ID, CUST_REF_ID))
TABLESPACE CUST_DATA
PCTFREE 0;
```

By reviewing the creating, the DBA found that the CUSTOMER_ADDRESSES table does not have the created and modified user information and the CUSTOMER_REFERENCES table has a DEFAULT value assigned to the wrong column. Let's fix these problems:

```
ALTER TABLE CUSTOMER_ADDRESSES ADD (
CRE_USER      VARCHAR2 (5) DEFAULT USER,
CRE_TIME      TIMESTAMP (3) DEFAULT SYSTIMESTAMP,
MOD_USER      VARCHAR2 (5),
MOD_TIME      TIMESTAMP (3));
ALTER TABLE CUSTOMER_REFERENCES MODIFY
MOD_USER DEFAULT NULL;
ALTER TABLE CUSTOMER_REFERENCES MODIFY
CRE_USER DEFAULT USER;
```

Also, the primary key for the CUSTOMER_REFERENCES table did not specify a tablespace for the primary key index, so it got created in the default tablespace of the table.

```
SQL> SELECT TABLESPACE_NAME FROM DBA_INDEXES WHERE
  2   INDEX_NAME = 'PK_CUST_REFS';
TABLESPACE_NAME
------------------------------
CUST_DATA
SQL> ALTER INDEX PK_CUST_REFS REBUILD TABLESPACE CUST_INDX;
Index altered.
SQL> SELECT TABLESPACE_NAME FROM DBA_INDEXES WHERE
  2   INDEX_NAME = 'PK_CUST_REFS';
TABLESPACE_NAME
------------------------------
CUST_INDX
SQL>
```

Query the dictionary views to see the table information:

```
SQL> SELECT TABLE_NAME, TABLESPACE_NAME
  2   FROM    USER_TABLES
  3   WHERE   TABLE_NAME LIKE 'CUST%';
```

```
TABLE_NAME                      TABLESPACE_NAME
------------------------------  ------------------------
CUSTOMER_ADDRESSES              CUST_DATA
CUSTOMER_MASTER                 CUST_DATA
CUSTOMER_REFERENCES             CUST_DATA
SQL> SELECT SEGMENT_NAME, SEGMENT_TYPE, TABLESPACE_NAME, BYTES
  2  FROM    DBA_SEGMENTS
  3  WHERE   OWNER = 'CM'
  4  AND     SEGMENT_NAME LIKE '%CUST%';
SEGMENT_NAME          SEGMENT_TYPE         TABLESPACE      BYTES
--------------------  -------------------  ----------  ----------
CUSTOMER_MASTER       TABLE                CUST_DATA       65536
CUSTOMER_ADDRESSES    TABLE                CUST_DATA       65536
CUSTOMER_REFERENCES   TABLE                CUST_DATA       65536
PK_CUSTOMER_MASTER    INDEX                CUST_INDX       32768
CUST_EMAIL            INDEX                CUST_INDX       32768
PK_CUST_ADDRESSES     INDEX                CUST_INDX       32768
PK_CUST_REFS          INDEX                CUST_INDX       65536
7 rows selected.
SQL>
SQL> SELECT INDEX_NAME, COLUMN_NAME, COLUMN_POSITION
  2  FROM    USER_IND_COLUMNS
  3  WHERE   INDEX_NAME LIKE '%CUST%'
  4  ORDER BY 1,3;
INDEX_NAME            COLUMN_NAME          COLUMN_POSITION
--------------------  --------------------  ---------------
CUST_EMAIL            EMAIL                              1
PK_CUSTOMER_MASTER    CUST_ID                            1
PK_CUST_ADDRESSES     CUST_ID                            1
PK_CUST_ADDRESSES     ADD_TYPE                           2
PK_CUST_REFS          CUST_ID                            1
PK_CUST_REFS          CUST_REF_ID                        2
6 rows selected.
SQL>
```

Query the dictionary views to see the constraint information. Notice that the two foreign key constraints on the CUSTOMER_REFERENCES table and the NOT NULL constraints in the CUSTOMER_ADDRESSES table have system-generated names.

```
SQL> SELECT CONSTRAINT_NAME, CONSTRAINT_TYPE, TABLE_NAME,
  2          R_CONSTRAINT_NAME
```

```
   3  FROM    USER_CONSTRAINTS
   4  WHERE   TABLE_NAME LIKE 'CUST%';
CONSTRAINT_NAME         C TABLE_NAME              R_CONSTRAINT_NAME
--------------------    - --------------------    --------------------
SYS_C002792             C CUSTOMER_ADDRESSES
SYS_C002793             C CUSTOMER_ADDRESSES
SYS_C002794             C CUSTOMER_ADDRESSES
SYS_C002795             C CUSTOMER_ADDRESSES
PK_CUST_ADDRESSES       P CUSTOMER_ADDRESSES
FK_CUST_ADDRESSES       R CUSTOMER_ADDRESSES     PK_CUSTOMER_MASTER
CK_ADD_TYPE2            C CUSTOMER_ADDRESSES
CK_ADD_TYPE             C CUSTOMER_MASTER
PK_CUSTOMER_MASTER      P CUSTOMER_MASTER
UQ_CUST_EMAIL           U CUSTOMER_MASTER
PK_CUST_REFS            P CUSTOMER_REFERENCES
SYS_C002804             R CUSTOMER_REFERENCES    PK_CUSTOMER_MASTER
SYS_C002805             R CUSTOMER_REFERENCES    PK_CUSTOMER_MASTER
13 rows selected.
SQL>
SQL> SELECT CONSTRAINT_NAME, GENERATED, INDEX_NAME
   2  FROM    USER_CONSTRAINTS
   3  WHERE   TABLE_NAME LIKE 'CUST%';
CONSTRAINT_NAME         GENERATED        INDEX_NAME
--------------------    --------------   --------------------
SYS_C002792             GENERATED NAME
SYS_C002793             GENERATED NAME
SYS_C002794             GENERATED NAME
SYS_C002795             GENERATED NAME
PK_CUST_ADDRESSES       USER NAME        PK_CUST_ADDRESSES
FK_CUST_ADDRESSES       USER NAME
CK_ADD_TYPE2            USER NAME
CK_ADD_TYPE             USER NAME
PK_CUSTOMER_MASTER      USER NAME        PK_CUSTOMER_MASTER
UQ_CUST_EMAIL           USER NAME        CUST_EMAIL
PK_CUST_REFS            USER NAME        PK_CUST_REFS
SYS_C002804             GENERATED NAME
SYS_C002805             GENERATED NAME
13 rows selected.
SQL>
```

Summary

This chapter discussed the most important aspect of the Oracle Database: storing data. You learned to create both tablespaces and data files as well as to create schema objects that store the data. You found out how to create and manage tablespaces as well as how Oracle stores some schema objects as segments that are comprised of extents and data blocks. In addition, you learned how to create and modify tables, indexes, and constraints. I also covered deferred constraint checking and how to configure foreign key constraints to support either deferrable or not deferrable implementations.

A data file belongs to one tablespace, and a tablespace can have one or more data files. The size of the tablespace is the total size of all the data files belonging to that tablespace. The size of the database is the total size of all tablespaces in the database, which is the same as the total size of all data files in the database. Tablespaces are logical storage units used to group data depending on their type or category. Understand the relationship between data files and tablespaces because that is important information to know for the certification.

Tablespaces can handle the extent management through the Oracle dictionary or locally in the data files that belong to the tablespace. Locally managed tablespaces can have uniform extent sizes; this reduces fragmentation and wasted space. You can also make Oracle do the entire extent sizing for locally managed tablespaces.

A temporary tablespace is used only for sorting; no permanent objects can be created in a temporary tablespace. Only one sort segment will be created for each instance in the temporary tablespace. Multiple transactions can use the same sort segment, but one transaction can use only one extent. Although temporary files are part of the database, they do not appear in the control file, and the block changes do not generate any redo information because all the segments created on locally managed temporary tablespaces are temporary segments.

You learned about tables, indexes, and constraints in this chapter. Also study Chapters 6 and 7 before taking the certification exam. Tables are created using the CREATE TABLE command. By default, the table will be created in the current schema. To create the table in another schema, you should qualify the table with the schema name. Storage parameters can be specified when creating the table. Tables can be moved or reorganized using the MOVE clause.

Indexes can be created as B-tree or bitmap. Bitmap indexes save storage space for low-cardinality columns. You can create reverse key or function-based indexes. An index-organized table stores the index and row data in the B-tree structure. Tablespace and storage should be specified when creating indexes. Indexes can be created ONLINE; that is, the table will be available for insert/update/delete operations while the indexing is in progress. The REBUILD clause of the ALTER INDEX command can be used to move the index to a different tablespace or to reorganize the index.

Constraints are created on the tables to enforce business rules. There are five types of constraints: NOT NULL, CHECK, UNIQUE, PRIMARY KEY, and FOREIGN KEY.

The constraints can be created to check the conformance at each SQL statement or when committing the changes—checking for conformance at each statement is the default. You can enable and disable constraints. Constraints can be enabled with the NOVALIDATE clause to save time after large data loads.

Exam Essentials

Know the relationship of data files to tablespaces.   Tablespaces are built on one or more data files—bigfile tablespaces on a single data file and smallfile tablespaces on one or more data files.

Understand the statements needed to create, modify, and drop tablespaces.   Use a CREATE TABLESPACE, ALTER TABLESPACE, and DROP TABLESPACE statement to create, modify, and drop a tablespace, respectively.

Know how to take tablespaces offline and what consequences the OFFLINE IMMEDIATE option poses.   Use an ALTER TABLESPACE statement to take a tablespace offline or bring it online. If you use the OFFLINE IMMEDIATE option, you must perform media recovery when you bring it back online.

Understand the default tablespaces for the database.   When the database is created, if you do not specify the DEFAULT TABLESPACE and DEFAULT TEMPORARY TABLESPACE clauses, the SYSTEM tablespace will be the default for user objects and temporary segments.

Know how to use the EM Database Control to view tablespace information.   The EM Database Control can be used to view tablespace information as well as perform various administrative tasks. A working knowledge of this tool is required.

Know the difference between segment space management and extent management.   Extent management deals with segment-level space allocations, and segment space management deals with data block-level space allocations.

Know which initialization parameter controls OMF placement.   The DB_CREATE_FILE_ DEST parameter tells the database where to place Oracle Managed Files.

Know the different types of constraints and which have dependencies with others.   There are the CHECK, NOT NULL, UNIQUE, PRIMARY KEY, and FOREIGN KEY constraints. A PRIMARY KEY constraint implicitly includes NOT NULL and UNIQUE constraints. A FOREIGN KEY constraint must refer to a PRIMARY KEY or UNIQUE constraint.

Know the types of indexes and when they are appropriate.   B-tree indexes are medium- to high-cardinality columns in applications in which data can change frequently. Bitmap indexes are best for low- to medium-cardinality columns in applications that control data changes, usually in batches.

Review Questions

1. Which of the following statements about tablespaces is true?

   A. A tablespace is the physical implementation of logical structure called a namespace.

   B. A tablespace can hold the objects of only one schema.

   C. A bigfile tablespace can have only one data file.

   D. The SYSAUX tablespace is an optional tablespace created only if you install certain database options.

2. Automatic segment space management on the tablespace causes which of the following table attributes in that tablespace to be ignored?

   A. The whole storage clause

   B. NEXT and PCTINCREASE

   C. BUFFERPOOL and FREEPOOL

   D. PCTFREE and PCTUSED

3. Which is not a type of segment that is stored in a tablespace?

   A. Undo

   B. Redo

   C. Permanent

   D. Temporary

4. Can a table name ever include the special metacharacter dollar sign ($)?

   A. No

   B. Yes

   C. Only if the table name is enclosed in double quotes

   D. Only if the table name is enclosed in single quotes

5. Which operation can you not do to a table that is created with the following SQL statement?

```
CREATE TABLE properties
("Location"  NUMBER primary key
,value       NUMBER(15)
,lot         varchar2(12)
,constraint positive_value check
   (value > 0)
);
```

    A. Rename the primary key to `properties`.

    B. Insert a `null` into the `value` column.

    C. Add a column named `owner`.

    D. Rename the index-supporting primary key to `properties`.

    E. None of the above.

6. Which constraint-checking model is the default?

    A. Initially immediate and deferrable

    B. Initially immediate and not deferrable

    C. Initially deferred and not immediately

    D. Initially deferrable and not immediate

7. Which allocation unit is the smallest?

    A. Data file

    B. Extent

    C. Data block

    D. Segment

8. Which of the following is not a valid Oracle 11*g* datatype?

    A. TIMESTAMP WITH LOCAL TIMEZONE

    B. BINARY

    C. BLOB

    D. UROWID

9. How do you specify that a temporary table will be emptied at the end of a user's session?

    A. Create the temporary table with the `ON COMMIT PRESERVE ROWS` option.

    B. Create the temporary table with the `ON DISCONNECT PRESERVE ROWS` option.

    C. Create the temporary table with the `ON DISCONNECT PURGE ROWS` option.

    D. Create the temporary table with the `ON COMMIT DELETE ROWS` option.

10. You performed the following statement in the database. What actions can you perform on the table CUST_INFO in the CUST_DATA tablespace. (Choose all that apply.)

```
ALTER TABLESPACE CUST_DATA READ ONLY;
```

    A. `ALTER TABLE CUST_INFO DROP COLUMN xx;`

    B. `TRUNCATE TABLE CUST_INFO;`

    C. `INSERT INTO CUST_INFO VALUES (…);`

    D. `DROP TABLE CUST_INFO;`

    E. `RENAME CUST_INFO TO CUSTOMER_INFO;`

11. Which statements should be executed to make the USERS tablespace read-only, if the tablespace is offline? (Choose all that apply.)

    A. ALTER TABLESPACE USERS READ ONLY

    B. ALTER DATABASE MAKE TABLESPACE USERS READ ONLY

    C. ALTER TABLESPACE USERS ONLINE

    D. ALTER TABLESPACE USERS TEMPORARY

12. How would you add more space to a tablespace? (Choose all that apply.)

    A. ALTER TABLESPACE *<TABLESPACE NAME>* ADD DATAFILE SIZE *<N>*

    B. ALTER DATABASE DATAFILE *<FILENAME>* RESIZE *<N>*

    C. ALTER DATAFILE *<FILENAME>* RESIZE *<N>*

    D. ALTER TABLESPACE *<TABLESPACE NAME>* DATAFILE *<FILENAME>* RESIZE *<N>*

13. The database is using automatic memory management. The standard block size for the database is 8KB. You need to create a tablespace with a block size of 16KB. Which initialization parameter should be set?

    A. DB_8K_CACHE_SIZE

    B. DB_16K_CACHE_SIZE

    C. DB_CACHE_SIZE

    D. None of the above

14. Which data dictionary view can be queried to obtain information about the files that belong to locally managed temporary tablespaces?

    A. DBA_DATA_FILES

    B. DBA_TABLESPACES

    C. DBA_TEMP_FILES

    D. DBA_LOCAL_FILES

15. How would you drop a tablespace if the tablespace were not empty?

    A. Rename all the objects in the tablespace, and then drop the tablespace.

    B. Remove the data files belonging to the tablespace from the disk.

    C. Use ALTER DATABASE DROP *<TABLESPACE NAME>* CASCADE.

    D. Use DROP TABLESPACE *<TABLESPACE NAME>* INCLUDING CONTENTS.

16. Which command is used to enable the autoextensible feature for a file if the file is already part of a tablespace?

    A. ALTER DATABASE.

    B. ALTER TABLESPACE.

    C. ALTER DATA FILE.

    D. You cannot change the autoextensible feature once the data file created.

17. Which statement is true regarding the SYSTEM tablespace?

   A. It can be made read-only.

   B. It can be offline.

   C. Data files can be renamed.

   D. Data files cannot be resized.

18. The following statement is issued against the primary key constraint (PK_BONUS) of the BONUS table. Which statements are true? (Choose all that apply.)

   `ALTER TABLE BONUS MODIFY CONSTRAINT PK_BONUS DISABLE VALIDATE;`

   A. No new rows can be added to the BONUS table.

   B. Existing rows of the BONUS table are validated before disabling the constraint.

   C. Rows can be modified, but the primary key columns cannot change.

   D. The unique index created when defining the constraint is dropped.

19. Which clause in the ALTER TABLE command is used to reorganize a table?

   A. REORGANIZE

   B. REBUILD

   C. RELOCATE

   D. MOVE

20. Which keyword should be used in the CREATE INDEX command to create a function-based index?

   A. CREATE FUNCTION INDEX

   B. CREATE INDEX   ORGANIZATION INDEX

   C. CREATE INDEX   FUNCTION BASED

   D. None of the above

Answers to Review Questions

1. C. Bigfile tablespaces can have only a single data file. The traditional or smallfile tablespace can have many data files.

2. D. Segment space management refers to free-space management, with automatic segment space management using bitmaps instead of FREELISTS, PCTFREE, and PCTUSED.

3. B. Redo information is not stored in a segment; it is stored in the redo logs. Undo segments are stored in the undo tablespace, temporary segments are in the temporary tablespace, and permanent segments go into all the other tablespaces.

4. B. Objects in an Oracle 11g database can always include letters, numbers, and the characters $, _, and # (dollar sign, underscore, and number sign). Names can include any other character only if they are enclosed in double quotes. The character dollar sign is not a special metacharacter in an Oracle 11g database.

5. E. You can rename both a constraint and an index to the same name as a table—they are in separate namespaces. Columns can be added, and owner is a valid column name. If the check constraint condition evaluates to FALSE, the data value will not be allowed; if the condition evaluates to either TRUE or NULL, the value is allowed.

6. B. Constraints can be created as deferrable and initially deferred, but deferred constraint checking is not the default.

7. C. An extent is composed of two or more data blocks; a segment is composed of one or more extents, and a data file houses all these.

8. B. Although BINARY_FLOAT and BINARY_DOUBLE are valid datatypes, BINARY is not.

9. A. The options for temporary tables are either ON COMMIT DELETE ROWS, which causes the table to flush at the end of each transaction, or ON COMMIT PRESERVE ROWS, which causes the table to flush at the end of each session.

10. B, D, E. When a tablespace is read-only, DML operations and operations that affect data in the table are not allowed. Truncate and drop operations are allowed, and you can also rename the table using the RENAME statement or the ALTER TABLE statement.

11. C, A. To make a tablespace read-only, all the data files belonging to the tablespace must be online and available. So, bring the tablespace online and then make it read-only.

12. A, B. You can add more space to a tablespace either by adding a data file or by increasing the size of an existing data file. Option A does not have a file name specified; it uses the OMF feature to generate filename.

13. B. DB_CACHE_SIZE doesn't need to be set for the standard block size since automatic memory management is used. If you set DB_CACHE_SIZE, its value will be used as the minimum. DB_16K_CACHE_SIZE should be set for the nonstandard block size. You must not set the DB_8K_CACHE_SIZE parameter because the standard block size is 8KB.

14. C. Locally managed temporary tablespaces are created using the CREATE TEMPORARY TABLESPACE command. The data files (temporary files) belonging to these tablespaces are in the DBA_TEMP_FILES view. The EXTENT_MANAGEMENT column of the DBA_TABLESPACES view shows the type of the tablespace. The data files belonging to locally managed permanent tablespaces and dictionary-managed (permanent and temporary) tablespaces can be queried from DBA_DATA_FILES. Locally managed temporary tablespaces reduce contention on the data dictionary tables.

15. D. The INCLUDING CONTENTS clause is used to drop a tablespace that is not empty. Oracle does not remove the data files that belong to the tablespace if the files are not Oracle managed; you need to do it manually using an OS command. Oracle updates only the control file. To remove the files, you can include the INCLUDING CONTENTS AND DATAFILES clause.

16. A. You can use the ALTER TABLESPACE command to rename a file that belongs to the tablespace, but all other file-management operations are done through the ALTER DATABASE command. To enable autoextension, use ALTER DATABASE DATAFILE *<FILENAME>* AUTOEXTEND ON NEXT *<INTEGER>* MAXSIZE *<INTEGER>*.

17. C. The data files belonging to the SYSTEM tablespace can be renamed when the database is in the MOUNT state by using the ALTER DATABASE RENAME FILE statement.

18. A, D. DISABLE VALIDATE disables the constraint and drops the index but keeps the constraint valid. No DML operations are allowed on the table.

19. D. The MOVE clause is used to reorganize a table. You can specify new tablespace and storage parameters. Queries are allowed on the table, but no DML operations are allowed during the move.

20. D. No keyword needs to be specified to create a function-based index other than to specify the function itself. To permit the Oracle optimizer to use a function-based index, you must set the parameter QUERY_REWRITE_ENABLED to TRUE and QUERY_REWRITE_INTEGRITY to TRUSTED.

Chapter

11

Understanding Network Architecture

**ORACLE DATABASE 11*g*:
ADMINISTRATION I EXAM OBJECTIVES
COVERED IN THIS CHAPTER:**

✓ **Configuring the Oracle Network Environment**

  ▪ Configure and Manage the Oracle Network

  ▪ Using the Oracle Shared Server architecture

Networks have evolved from simple terminal-based systems to complex multi-tiered systems. Today's networks can comprise many computers on multiple operating systems using a wide variety of protocols and communicating across wide geographic areas. Although networks have become increasingly complex, they also have become easier to use and manage. For instance, we all take advantage of the Internet without knowing or caring about the components that make this communication possible, because the complexity of this huge network is completely hidden from us.

The experienced Oracle database administrator has seen this maturation process in the Oracle network architecture as well. From the first version of SQL*Net to the latest releases of Oracle Net, Oracle has evolved its network strategy and infrastructure to meet the demands of the rapidly changing landscape of network communications.

This chapter highlights the areas you need to consider when implementing an Oracle network strategy and when managing an Oracle 11g network. I'll also discuss the most common network configurations. The chapter introduces the features of Oracle Net—the connectivity-management software that is the backbone of the Oracle network architecture. I'll explain how to configure the main client- and server-side components of Oracle Net, and I'll discuss the tools you have at your disposal to perform these tasks.

As the number of users connecting to Oracle Databases in the enterprise grows, the system requirements of the servers increase—particularly the memory and process requirements. When a system starts to encounter these capacity issues, you need to know which alternatives are available within the Oracle environment that can address the problem. One configuration alternative that may help to overcome this capacity problem is Oracle Shared Server.

This chapter also discusses Oracle Shared Server and its benefits. You will learn about the client connection process and how Oracle Shared Server processes user requests. You will also learn how to configure Oracle Shared Server.

Introducing Network Configurations

You can select from three basic types of network configurations when designing an Oracle infrastructure:

- Single-tier
- Two-tier
- *n*-tier

Single-tier is the simplest type. It has been around for years and is characterized by the use of terminals for serial connections to the Oracle server. The two-tier configuration is also referred to as the *client/server* architecture, and more recently the *n*-tier architecture has been introduced. Let's take a look at each of these configuration alternatives.

Single-Tier Architecture

Single-tier architecture was the standard for many years before the birth of the personal computer. Applications using single-tier architecture are sometimes referred to as *green-screen* applications because most of the terminals that used them, such as the IBM 3270, had green screens. Single-tier architecture is commonly associated with mainframe-type applications.

This architecture is still in use today for many mission-critical applications, such as order processing and fulfillment and inventory control, because it is the simplest architecture to configure and administer. Because the terminals are directly connected to the host computer, the complexities of network protocols and multiple operating systems don't exist.

When single-tier architecture is used—for example, in mainframes—users interact with the database using terminals, which are nongraphical, character-based devices. In this type of architecture, client terminals are directly connected to larger server systems such as mainframes. All the intelligence exists on the mainframe, and all the processing takes place there. Simple serial connections also exist on the mainframe. Although no complex network architecture is necessary, a single-tier architecture is somewhat limiting in terms of scalability and flexibility (see Figure 11.1).

FIGURE 11.1   Single-tier architecture

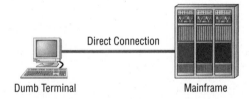

Dumb Terminal   Mainframe

Two-Tier Architecture

Two-tier architecture gained popularity with the introduction of the personal computer and is commonly referred to as *client/server* computing. In a two-tier environment, clients connect to servers over a network using a network protocol, which is the agreed-upon method for the client to communicate with the server. Transmission Control Protocol/Internet Protocol (TCP/IP) is a popular network protocol and has become the de facto standard of network computing. Whether you choose TCP/IP or some other network protocol, both the client and the server must be able to understand it. Figure 11.2 shows an example of two-tier architecture.

FIGURE 11.2 Two-tier architecture

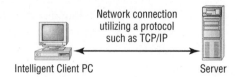

This architecture has definite benefits over single-tier architecture. First, client/server computing introduces the graphical user interface (GUI). This interface is easier to understand and learn, and it offers more flexibility than the traditional character-based interfaces of the single-tier architecture. Also, two-tier architecture allows the client computer to share the application process load. To a certain degree, this reduces the processing requirements of the server.

The two-tier architecture does have some faults, even though at one time, this configuration was thought to be the panacea of all networking architectures. Unfortunately, the main problem—that being scalability—persists. Notice that the term *client/server* contains a slash (/). The slash represents the invisible component of the two-tier architecture and the one that is often overlooked: the network! The limitation of client/server computing is one of scalability.

When prototyping projects, many developers fail to consider the network component and soon find out that what worked well in a small environment does not scale effectively to larger, more complex systems. The two-tier architecture model was subject to a great deal of redundancy because application software was required on every desktop. As a result, many companies end up with bloated computers and large servers that still do not perform adequately. What is needed is a more scalable model for network communications. That is what *n*-tier architecture provides.

n-Tier Architecture

n-*tier architecture* is the next logical step after two-tier architecture. Instead of dividing application processing work between a client and a server, you divide the work among three or more machines. The *n*-tier architecture introduces *middleware* components, such as application servers or web servers, situated between the client and the database server, which can be used for a variety of tasks, including the following:

- Moving data between machines that work with different network protocols
- Serving as firewalls that can control client access to the servers
- Offloading processing of the business logic from the clients and servers to the middle tier
- Executing transactions and monitoring activity between clients and servers to balance the load among multiple servers
- Acting as a gateway to bridge existing systems to new systems

The Internet is an example of the ultimate *n*-tier architecture, with the user's browser providing a consistent presentation interface. This common interface means less training of staff and also increases the potential reuse of client-side application components.

n-tier architecture is rapidly becoming the architecture of choice for enterprise networks. This model is scalable and divides the tasks of presentation, business logic and routing, and database processing among many machines, which means that this model accommodates large applications. Many factors are driving *n*-tier computing, such as the Internet and Oracle grid computing, which uses a large number of back-end processors to scale database services and connectivity.

By reducing the processing load on the database servers, those servers can do more work with the same number of resources. Also, the transaction servers can balance the flow of network transactions intelligently, and application servers can reduce the processing and memory requirements of the client (see Figure 11.3).

FIGURE 11.3   Connection requests in *n*-tier architecture

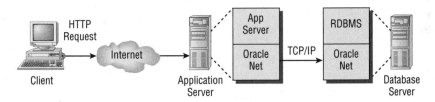

An Overview of Oracle Net Features

Oracle Net is the glue that bonds the Oracle network together. It is responsible for handling client-to-server and server-to-server communications, and it can be configured on the client, the middle-tier application, web servers, and the Oracle server.

Oracle Net manages the flow of information in the Oracle network infrastructure. First it establishes the initial connection to the Oracle server, and then it acts as the messenger, passing requests from the client back to the server or passing them between two Oracle servers. Oracle Net handles all negotiations between the client and server during the client connection.

In addition to functioning as an information manager, Oracle Net supports the use of middleware products such as Oracle Application Server and Oracle Connection Manager. These products allow *n*-tier architectures to be used in the enterprise, which increases the flexibility and performance of application designs.

To provide a further understanding of the features of Oracle Net, the following sections discuss in detail the five categories of networking solutions that Oracle Net addresses:

- Connectivity
- Manageability
- Scalability

- Security
- Accessibility

Connectivity

A client can interact with an Oracle Database in many ways. A client can be running a PC-based application or a dumb terminal application, or perhaps the client is connecting to the database via the Internet. Let's take a look at how Oracle supports connectivity to the database through these and other interfaces:

Multiprotocol support   Oracle Net supports a wide range of industry-standard protocols such as TCP/IP and named pipes. This support is handled transparently and allows Oracle Net to connect to a wide range of computers and a wide range of operating environments.

Multiple operating systems   Oracle Net can run on many operating systems, from Windows XP to all variants of Unix to large mainframe-based operating systems. This range allows users to bridge existing systems to other Unix or PC-based systems, which increases the data access flexibility of the organization without making wholesale changes to the existing systems.

Java and JDBC   Applications written in Java can take advantage of the Java Database Connectivity (JDBC) drivers provided with Oracle to connect to an Oracle server. The two basic types of JDBC drivers are JDBC Oracle Call Interface (OCI) and JDBC thin.

The JDBC OCI driver is a client-side installed driver that is used if the Java application is resident on a client computer. This driver is also called a *type II* driver because the driver software is installed on the computer that is using the application. It uses OCI to interact with the Oracle Net infrastructure. Figure 11.4 shows how a client and server communicate when using a JDBC OCI connection.

FIGURE 11.4   Oracle JDBC OCI connection

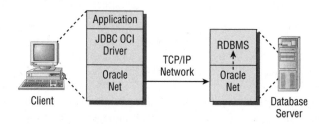

In this example, the Java application installed on the client uses the JDBC OCI driver and Oracle Database server. When an application makes a database request, it uses the JDBC OCI driver to translate the JDBC calls and send them to Oracle Net. Oracle Net is used on both the client and the server to broker all communications between the two end points.

The JDBC thin driver is written entirely in Java and, as such, is platform independent. It does not have to be installed on a client computer (which is why it's called a *thin driver*). The driver interfaces directly with a layer of the Oracle Net infrastructure called the *two-task common layer*.

Manageability

Oracle Net provides a variety of features that allow you to manage the components of an Oracle network. Let's review the key manageability features of Oracle Net.

Web Applications

Oracle Net supports a variety of connectivity solutions from a web browser interface. Connections can be made through a middle-tier web or application server or directly from a web browser to an Oracle service.

When a middle-tier solution is used, the web browser uses HTTP to contact a database service and request information. Typically, an application or web server receives this request and hands it off to Oracle Net, which manages the connection between the web server and the database server. Once the database server receives the connection request, the request is processed and passed back to the web server. The web server then sends the response to the client's web browser. This type of request fulfillment requires that the middle-tier application server be loaded with the Oracle Net software, but the client does not require any additional software.

Oracle also supports web connectivity directly from a web client. For example, a Java applet running within a web browser can use a JDBC driver to connect directly to an Oracle server without the need for an application or web server.

Location Transparency

Oracle Net provides the infrastructure to manage the database location. This is important especially in large organizations that support many databases and clients. Each database in the organization is represented as one or more services. Database services are defined by one or more service names. The actual definition of the service names is managed within Oracle Net. The definition holds information about the type and location of the service on the network. This layer of abstraction provides location transparency to the client and centralizes the management of connection information within Oracle Net, which simplifies the job of managing the network.

Directory Naming

Directory naming allows service names to be resolved through a centralized naming repository. The central repository takes the form of a Lightweight Directory Access Protocol (LDAP)–compliant server. LDAP is a protocol and language that defines a standard method for storing, identifying, and retrieving services. It provides a simplified way to manage directories of information, whether this information is about users in an organization or Oracle services connected to a network. The LDAP server allows for a standard form of managing and resolving names in an Oracle environment. The quality of these services excels because LDAP provides a single, industry-standard interface to a directory service such as Oracle Internet Directory (OID). By using OID, you ensure the security and reliability of the directory information because information is stored in the Oracle Database.

Scalability

Many enterprise systems are growing rapidly, supporting larger and larger databases and user communities. Your network capabilities need to be able to support this growth. Oracle Net provides features that allow you to expand your network reach and maximize your system resources to meet these demands.

Oracle Shared Server

Oracle Shared Server is an optional configuration of the Oracle server that allows support for a large number of concurrent connections without increasing physical resource requirements. This is accomplished by sharing resources among groups of users.

Oracle Shared Server is discussed in detail later in the chapter in the section "An Overview of Oracle Shared Server."

Connection Manager

Oracle Connection Manager is a middleware solution that provides three additional scalability features:

Multiplexing   Connection Manager can group many client connections and send them as a single multiplexed network connection to the Oracle server. This reduces the total number of network connections that the server has to manage.

Network access   You can configure Connection Manager with rules that restrict access by IP address. You can set up this rules-based configuration to accept or reject client connection requests. Also, connections can be restricted by point of origin, destination server, or Oracle server.

Cross-protocol connectivity   This feature allows clients and servers that use different network protocols to communicate. Connection Manager acts as a translator, providing two-way protocol conversion.

Oracle Connection Manager is controlled by a set of background processes that manage the communications between clients and servers. Figure 11.5 provides an overview of the Connection Manager architecture.

Security

The threat of data tampering and database security is an issue of major concern in many organizations as network systems continue to grow in number and complexity and as users gain increasing access to systems. Sensitive business transactions are being conducted with greater frequency and, in many cases, are not protected from unauthorized tampering or message interception. Oracle Net is capable of providing organizations with a secure network environment to conduct business transactions. I'll now discuss the tools available in Oracle 11*g* to protect sensitive information.

FIGURE 11.5   Connection Manager architecture

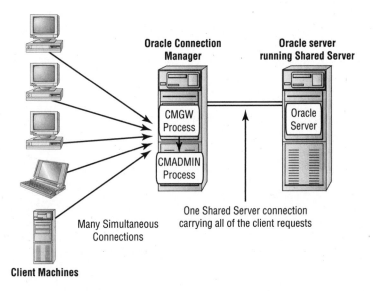

Advanced Security

Oracle Advanced Security, formerly known as the Advanced Security Option and the Advanced Networking Option, not only provides the tools necessary to ensure secure transmissions of sensitive information, but it also provides mechanisms to confidently identify and authenticate users in the Oracle enterprise.

When configured on the client and the Oracle server, Oracle Advanced Security supports secured data transmissions by encrypting and optionally checksumming the transmission of information that is sent in a transaction. Oracle supports encryption and checksumming by taking advantage of industry-standard algorithms, such as RSA RC4, Standard DES and Triple DES, and MD5 checksumming. These security features ensure that data transmitted from the client has not been altered during transmission to the Oracle server.

Oracle Advanced Security also gives you the ability to authenticate users connecting to the Oracle servers. In fact, a number of authentication features ensure that users really are who they claim to be. These are offered in the form of token cards, which use a physical card and a user-identifying PIN to gain access to the system; retina scans also supported now, which uses fingerprint technology to authenticate user connection requests; public key; and certificate-based authentication.

Firewall Support

Firewalls are an important security mechanism in corporate networks. Firewalls are generally a combination of hardware and software that is used to control network traffic and prevent intruders from compromising corporate network security. Firewalls fall into two broad categories:

IP-filtering firewalls   IP-filtering firewalls monitor the network packet traffic on IP networks and filter out packets that either originated or did not originate from specific groups of machines. The information contained in the IP packet header is interrogated to obtain this information. Vendors of this type of firewall include Network Associates and Axent Communications.

Proxy-based firewalls   Proxy-based firewalls prevent information from outside the firewall from flowing directly into the corporate network. The firewall acts as a gatekeeper, inspecting packets and sending only the appropriate information to the corporate network. This prevents any direct communication between clients outside the firewall and applications inside the firewall. Check Point Software Technologies and Cisco are examples of vendors that market proxy-based firewalls.

Oracle works closely with the vendors of both types of firewalls to ensure support of database traffic through these types of mechanism. Oracle supplies the Oracle Net Application Proxy Kit to the firewall vendors. This product can be incorporated into the firewall architecture to allow database packets to pass through the firewall and still maintain a high degree of security.

 Real World Scenario

Know Thy Firewall

It is important to understand your network infrastructure, the network routes you are using to obtain database connections, and the type of firewall products you are using. In more than one situation, I've seen firewalls cause connectivity issues between a client and an Oracle server.

For instance, a small patch was applied to a firewall when a friend of mine was working as a DBA for one of his former employers. In this case, employees started experiencing intermittent disconnects from the Oracle Database. After many days of investigation and network tracing, the team pinned down the exact problem. The database team then contacted the firewall vendor, who sent a new patch that corrected the problem.

In another instance, the development staff started experiencing a similar connection problem. It turned out that the networking routes for the development staff had been modified to connect through a new firewall, with connections timing out after 20 minutes. This timeout was too short for this department. Increasing the timeout parameter solved the problem.

These are examples of the types of network changes you need to be aware of to avoid unnecessary downtime and to avoid wasting staff time and resources.

Accessibility

In many organizations, workers need to be able to communicate across a variety of systems and databases. They spend a lot of time bringing together data from different systems. The accessibility features of Oracle Net have capabilities that allow you to communicate with nondatabase data sources. This ability opens up new opportunities to provide customers with accurate and timely information. I'll now discuss the options available in Oracle 11*g* to access data that resides in a non-Oracle database and to execute programs that are not SQL or PL/SQL.

Heterogeneous Services

The Heterogeneous Services component provides the ability to communicate with non-Oracle databases and services. These services allow organizations to leverage and interact with their existing data stores without having to necessarily move the data to an Oracle server.

The suite of Heterogeneous Services comprises the Oracle Transparent Gateway and Generic Connectivity. These products allow Oracle to communicate with non-Oracle data sources in a seamless configuration. Heterogeneous Services also integrates existing systems with the Oracle environment, which allows you to leverage your investment in those systems. These services also allow for two-way communication and replication from Oracle data sources to non-Oracle data sources.

External Procedures

In some development efforts, interfacing with procedures that reside outside the database may be necessary. These procedures are typically written in a third-generation language, such as C. Oracle Net provides the ability to invoke such external procedures from Oracle PL/SQL callouts. When a call is made, a process is started that acts as an interface between Oracle and the external procedure. This callout process defaults to the name `extproc`. The listener is then responsible for supplying information, such as a library or procedure name and any parameters, to the called procedure. These programs are then loaded and executed under the control of the `extproc` process.

Configuring Oracle Net on the Server

Now that you understand the basic features Oracle Net provides, you need to understand how to configure the major components of Oracle Net. You must configure Oracle Net on the server in order for client connections to be established. The following sections will focus on how to configure the network elements of the Oracle server. It will also describe the types of connection methods that Oracle Net supports. We will then discuss how to manage Oracle Net on the server and troubleshoot connections from the server if clients experience connection problems.

Understanding the Oracle Listener

The Oracle *listener* is the main server-side Oracle networking component that allows connections to be established between client computers and an Oracle Database. You can think of the listener as a big ear that listens for connection requests to Oracle services.

The type of Oracle service being requested is part of the connection descriptor information supplied by the process requesting a connection, and the service name resolves to an Oracle Database. The listener can listen for any number of databases configured on the server, and it is able to listen for requests being transported on a variety of protocols. A client connection can be initiated from the same machine that the listener resides on, or it may come from some remote location.

The listener is controlled by a centralized file called `listener.ora`. Though only one `listener.ora` file is configured per machine, there may be numerous listeners on a server, and this file contains all the configuration information for every listener configured on the server. If multiple listeners are configured on a single server, they are usually set up for failover purposes or to balance connection requests and minimize the burden of connections on a single listener.

The content and structure of the `listener.ora` file is discussed later in this chapter in the section "Managing Oracle Listeners."

Every listener is a named process that runs on either a middle-tier server or the database server. The default name of the Oracle listener is LISTENER, and it is typically created when you install Oracle. If you configure multiple listeners, each has a unique name.

Now that you have a basic understanding of the Oracle listener, let's explore the main function of the listener, which is responding to client connection requests.

How Do Listeners Respond to Connection Requests?

A listener can respond to a client request for a connection in several ways. The response depends on several factors, such as how the server-side network components are configured and what type of connection the client is requesting. The listener then responds to the connection request in one of two ways.

The listener can spawn a new process and pass control of the client session to the process. In a *dedicated server* environment, every client connection is serviced by its own server-side process. Server-side processes are not shared among clients. Two types of dedicated connection methods are possible: direct and redirect. Each method results in a separate process that handles client processing, but the mechanics of the actual connection-initiation process are different. For remote clients to use dedicated connections, the listener process must be running on the same physical server as the database or databases for which it is listening.

The listener can also pass control of a connection request to a dispatcher. This type of connection takes place in an Oracle Shared Server environment. There are also two types of connection methods when using Oracle Shared Server: direct and redirect.

Let's take a look at each of these connection-method types.

Dedicated Connections: Direct Handoff Method

Direct handoff connections are possible when the client and database exist on the same server. For example, a direct handoff method is used when the client connection request originates from the same machine on which the listener and database are running.

 Another name for direct handoff connections is *bequeath connections*.

The following steps, which show the connection process for the bequeath connections, are illustrated in Figure 11.6:

1. The client contacts the Oracle listener after resolving the service name.

2. The listener starts a dedicated process, and the client connection inherits the dedicated server process network connect end point from the listener.

3. The client now has an established connection to the dedicated server process.

FIGURE 11.6 Dedicated connections: direct handoff method

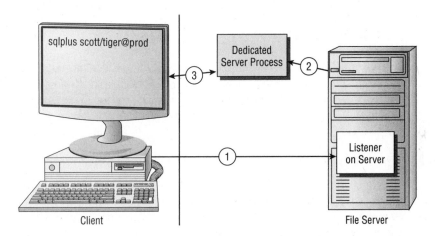

Dedicated Connections: Redirect Method

Redirect connections occur in a dedicated server environment when the client exists on a machine that is separate from the listener and database server. The listener must inform the client of the address of the spawned process in order for the process to contact the newly created dedicated server process.

The following steps, which show the connection process for redirect connections in a dedicated server environment, are illustrated in Figure 11.7:

1. The client contacts the Oracle listener after resolving the service name.

2. The listener starts a dedicated process.

3. The listener sends an acknowledgment back to the client with the address of the dedicated server connect end point on the database server to which the client will connect.

4. The client establishes a connection to the dedicated server connect end point.

FIGURE 11.7 Dedicated connections: redirect method

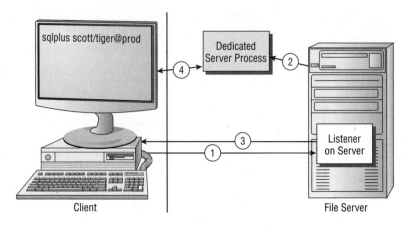

Oracle Shared Server: Direct Handoff Method

When you are using Oracle Shared Server, the client connection can also be established using a direct handoff method. This would be the case, for example, when the client request originates from the same machine on which the listener and database are running. Figure 11.8 outlines the connection steps when using Oracle Shared Server and the direct handoff method:

1. The client contacts the Oracle listener after resolving the service name.

2. The Oracle listener passes the connection request to the dispatcher with least load.

3. The client now has an established connection to the dispatcher process.

4. PMON (process monitor) sends information to the listener about the number of connections being serviced by the dispatchers.

FIGURE 11.8 Oracle Shared Server: direct handoff method

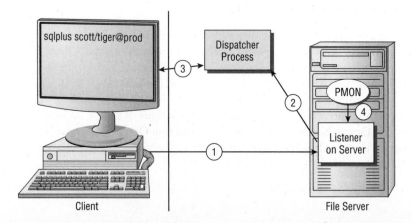

Oracle Shared Server: Redirect Method

The listener can also redirect the user to a server process or a dispatcher process when using Oracle Shared Server. This type of connection can occur when the operating system does not directly support direct handoff connections or the listener is not on the same physical machine as the Oracle server.

The following steps are illustrated in Figure 11.9:

1. The client contacts the Oracle server after resolving the service name.

2. The listener sends information to the client, redirecting the client to the dispatcher port. The original network connection between the listener and the client is disconnected.

3. The client then sends a connect signal to the server or dispatcher process to establish a network connection.

4. The dispatcher or server process sends an acknowledgment to the client.

5. PMON sends information to the listener about the number of connections being serviced by the dispatchers. The listener uses this information to maintain consistent loads between the dispatchers.

FIGURE 11.9   Oracle Shared Server: redirect connection method

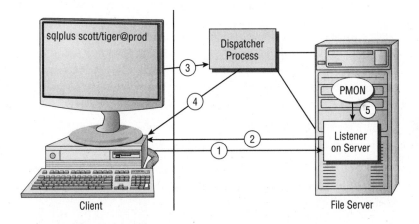

Managing Oracle Listeners

You can configure the server-side listener files in a number of ways. As part of the initial Oracle installation process, the installer prompts you to create a default listener. If you choose this method, the installer uses the set of screens that are part of the Oracle Net Configuration Assistant to do the initial listener configuration. Figure 11.10 shows an example of the opening screen for this assistant.

If you want to set up more than just basic configurations of Oracle network files, you will have to use Oracle Net Manager, the web-based tool Oracle Enterprise Manager (EM), or the command-line facility lsnrctl. In the next few sections, you will learn how to use these tools to configure the server-side network files.

FIGURE 11.10   Oracle Net Configuration Assistant opening screen

Managing Listeners with Oracle Net Manager

Oracle Net Manager is a tool you can use to create and manage most client- and server-side configuration files. Oracle Net Manager has evolved from the Oracle 7 tool, Network Manager, to the latest Oracle 11g version. Throughout this evolution, Oracle has continued to enhance the functionality and usability of the tool.

If you are using a Windows environment, you can start Oracle Net Manager by choosing Start ➢ Programs ➢ *Your Oracle 11g Programs choice* ➢ Configuration and Migration Tools ➢ Net Manager. In a Unix environment, you can start it by running `netmgr` from your `$ORACLE_HOME/bin` directory.

Figure 11.11 shows an example of the Oracle Net Manager opening screen.

FIGURE 11.11   The opening screen for Oracle Net Manager

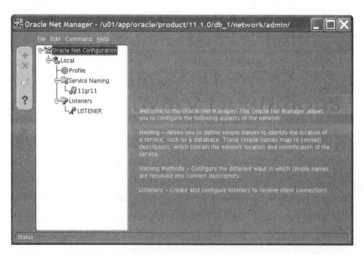

Configuring Listener Services Using Oracle Net Manager

Oracle Net Manager provides an easy-to-use graphical interface for configuring most of the network files you will be using. By using Oracle Net Manager, you can ensure that the files are created in a consistent format, which will reduce the potential for connection problems.

When you first start Oracle Net Manager, the opening screen displays a tree structure with a top level called Oracle Net Configuration. If you click the plus (+) sign next to this icon, you will see the Local folder. The choices under the Local folder relate to different network configuration files. Here are the network file choices and what each configures:

Icon	File Configured
Profile	sqlnet.ora
Service Naming	tnsnames.ora
Listeners	listener.ora

Creating the Listener

Earlier I said that, by default, Oracle creates a listener called LISTENER when it is initially installed. The default settings that Oracle uses for the listener.ora file are as follows:

Section of the File	Setting
Listener name	LISTENER
Port	1521
Protocols	TCP/IP and IPC
Hostname	Default Host Name
SID name	Default Instance

You can use Oracle Net Manager to create a nondefault listener or change the definition of existing listeners. Oracle Net Manager has a wizard interface for creating most of the basic network elements, such as the listener.ora and tnsnames.ora files.

Follow these steps to create the listener:

1. Click the plus (+) sign next to the Local icon.
2. Click the Listeners folder.
3. Click the plus sign icon, or choose Edit ➢ Create to open the Choose Listener Name dialog box.
4. Oracle Net Manager defaults to LISTENER or to LISTENER1 if the default listener is already created. Click OK if this is correct, or enter a new name and then click OK to open the Listening Locations screen, as shown in Figure 11.12.

FIGURE 11.12 The Listening Locations screen

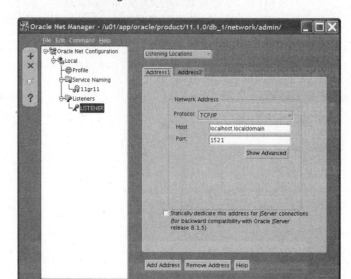

5. To configure the listening locations, click the Listening Locations drop-down list, and make your selection. Then click the Add Address button at the bottom of the screen to open a new window.

   The prompts on this screen depend on your protocol. By default, TCP/IP information is displayed. If you are using TCP/IP, the Host and Port fields are filled in for you. The *host* is the name of the machine in which the listener is running, and the *port* is the listening location for TCP/IP connections. The default value for the port is 1521.

6. To save your information, choose File ➢ Save Network Configuration, and then look in the directory where the file was saved.

   You can also add listeners by following these steps. Listeners must have unique names and listen on separate ports, so assign the listener a new name and a new port (1522, for example). You also must assign service names to the listener. You'll see how to add service information in the next section.

   Oracle Net Manager actually creates three files in this process: listener.ora, tnsnames.ora, and sqlnet.ora. The tnsnames.ora file does not contain any information. The sqlnet.ora file may contain a few entries at this point, but you can ignore them for the time being. The listener.ora file contains information, as shown in the following code:

```
# listener.ora Network Configuration File:
# /u01/app/oracle/product/11.1.0/db_1/network/admin/listener.ora
# Generated by Oracle configuration tools.

LISTENER =
  (DESCRIPTION_LIST =
```

```
(DESCRIPTION =
  (ADDRESS = (PROTOCOL = TCP)(HOST = localhost.localdomain)(PORT = 1521))
  (ADDRESS = (PROTOCOL = IPC)(KEY = EXTPROC1521))
)
)
```

To figure out where the files are stored, just look at the top banner of the Oracle Net Manager screen.

Adding Service-Name Information to the Listener

After you create the listener with the name, protocol, and listening location information, you can define the network services to which the listener is responsible for connecting. This is called *static service registration*, because Oracle is not automatically registering the service with the listener. In releases of Oracle prior to Oracle8*i*, static service registration was the only method to associate services with a listener.

A listener can listen to an unlimited number of network service names. Follow these steps to add the service-name information:

1. To select the listener to configure, click the Listeners icon, and highlight the name of the listener that you want to configure.

2. From the drop-down list at the top right of the screen, select Database Services.

3. Click the Add Database button at the bottom of the screen. This opens the window that allows you to add the database (see Figure 11.13).

FIGURE 11.13   The Database Services screen

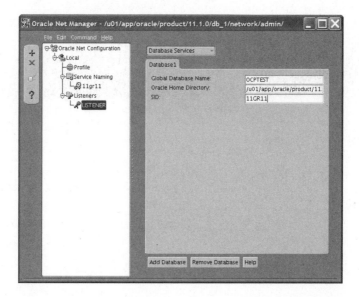

4. Enter values in the Global Database Name, Oracle Home Directory, and SID fields. The entries for SID and Global Database Name are the same if you are using a flat naming convention.

5. Choose File ➢ Save to save your configuration.

Here is an example of the completed listener.ora file:

```
# listener.ora Network Configuration File:
# /u01/app/oracle/product/11.1.0/db_1/network/admin/listener.ora
# Generated by Oracle configuration tools.

SID_LIST_LISTENER =
  (SID_LIST =
    (SID_DESC =
      (GLOBAL_DBNAME = OCPTEST)
      (ORACLE_HOME = /u01/app/oracle/product/11.1.0/db_1)
      (SID_NAME = 11GR11)
    )
  )


LISTENER =
  (DESCRIPTION_LIST =
    (DESCRIPTION =
      (ADDRESS = (PROTOCOL = TCP)(HOST = localhost.localdomain)(PORT = 1521))
    )
    (DESCRIPTION =
      (ADDRESS = (PROTOCOL = IPC)(KEY = EXTPROC1521))
    )
  )
```

Table 11.1 describes each of the listener.ora parameters for the Listening Location section of the listener.ora file.

TABLE 11.1   Parameters for the Listening Location Section of listener.ora

Parameter	Description
LISTENER	Indicates the starting point of a listener definition. This is actually the name of the listener being defined. The default name is LISTENER.
DESCRIPTION	Describes each of the listening locations.

TABLE 11.1   Parameters for the Listening Location Section of listener.ora *(continued)*

Parameter	Description
ADDRESS	Contains address information about the locations where the listener is listening.
PROTOCOL	Designates the protocol for this listening location.
HOST	Holds the name of the machine on which the listener resides.
PORT	Contains the address on which the listener is listening.
SID_LIST_*LISTENER*	Defines the list of Oracle services for which the listener (named LISTENER) is configured.
SID_DESC	Describes each Oracle SID.
GLOBAL_DBNAME	Identifies the global database name. This entry should match the SERVICE_NAMES entry in the init.ora file for the Oracle service.
ORACLE_HOME	Shows the location of the Oracle executables on the server.
SID_NAME	Contains the name of the Oracle SID for the Oracle instance.

Understanding Service Registration

Oracle 11*g* allows two types of service registration. Static service registration occurs when entries are added to the listener.ora file manually by using one of the Oracle tools. It is static because you are adding this information manually. Static service registration is necessary if you will be connecting to pre-Oracle8*i* instances using Oracle Enterprise Manager or if you will be connecting to external services.

Another way to manage listeners that does not require manual updating of service information in the listener.ora file is called *dynamic service registration*. Dynamic service registration allows an Oracle instance to automatically register itself with an Oracle listener. The benefit of this feature is that it does not require you to perform any updates of server-side network files when new Oracle instances are created. Dynamic service registration will be covered in more detail later in this chapter in the section "Dynamically Registering Services."

Optional *listener.ora* Parameters

You can set optional parameters that add functionality to the listener. To do so, select a parameter from the General Parameters drop-down list at the top right of the screen. Table 11.2 describes these parameters and where you can find them in Oracle Net Manager.

TABLE 11.2   Optional `listener.ora` Parameter Definitions

Net Manager Prompt	`listener.ora` Parameter	Description
Startup Wait Time	STARTUP_WAIT_TIME	Defines how long a listener will wait before it responds to a STATUS command in the `lsnrctl` command-line utility.
Save Configuration On Shutdown	CONNECT_TIMEOUT	Defines how long a listener will wait for a valid response from a client once a session is initiated. The default is 10 seconds.
Unavailable from Net Manager	SAVE_CONFIG_ON_STOP	Specifies whether modifications made during an `lsnrctl` session should be saved when exiting.
Log File	LOG_FILE. Will not be in the `listener.ora` file if the default setting is used. By default, listener logging is enabled with the log created in the default location	Specifies where a listener will write log information. This is ON by default and defaults to $ORACLE_HOME/network/log/listener.log.
Trace Level	TRACE_LEVEL. Not present if tracing is disabled. The default is OFF	Sets the level of detail if listener connections are being traced. Valid values include Off, User, Support, and Admin.
Trace File	TRACE_FILE	Specifies the location of listener trace information. Defaults to $ORACLE_HOME/network/trace/listener.trc.
Require A Password For Listener Operations	PASSWORDS	Specifies password required to perform administrative tasks in the `lsnrctl` command-line utility.

As you will see, you cannot add some parameters directly from the Oracle Net Manager and must do so manually. These optional parameters also have the listener name appended to them so that you can identify the listener definition to which they belong. For example, if the parameter STARTUP_WAIT_TIME is set for the default listener, the parameter created is STARTUP_WAIT_TIME_LISTENER.

Managing Listeners with Oracle Enterprise Manager

Oracle Enterprise Manager (EM) is a web-based tool that allows you to manage many aspects of an Oracle 11g server. Being able to perform administrative functions via a web interface lets you administer the database from any location where a web browser is available.

You can also manage Oracle Net using EM. On the Database Control home page, notice under the General section a list of listeners that are available to manage. Click a listener to display a screen (see Figure 11.14) that gives you details about that listener, including when the listener was started, the Oracle Net address and port information for the listener, and the listening location information.

FIGURE 11.14   The Oracle Enterprise Manager listener console

You can also add and edit listeners using the Database Control interface. Let's take a look at how to do so using the Oracle Enterprise Manager Database Control console.

Adding a Listener Using Enterprise Manager Database Control

You can use Enterprise Manager Database Control to add a listener by following these steps:

1. To add a new listener using the Database Control, select the Net Services Administration option listed under the Related Links section to open the Net Services Administration screen, as shown in Figure 11.15.

FIGURE 11.15 The Oracle Enterprise Manager Net Services Administration screen

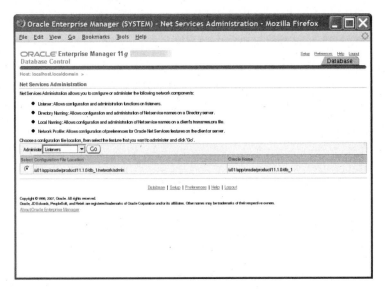

2. From the Administer drop-down list, select the listener, and click Go to open a login screen. Connect to the server with a valid operating-system user ID and password to open the listener control screen. In this example, a listener is already configured and named LISTENER. To create an additional listener, click the Create button to open the Create Listener screen, as shown in Figure 11.16.

3. Choose a name for the listener. Oracle will choose a new name for you and place that in the Listener Name field. In Figure 11.16, LISTENER0 is the new listener to be created.

You can fully configure the new listener using this interface. At a minimum, the listener needs listening address information. Click the Add button to open the Add Address screen. You can choose a protocol, such as TCP/IP, for which the listener will be listening. You also need to designate a listening port and host where the listener will be listening for connections. The other parameters, the send and receive buffer size, are optional advanced parameters. Click OK to save your information.

FIGURE 11.16   The Oracle Enterprise Manager Create Listener screen

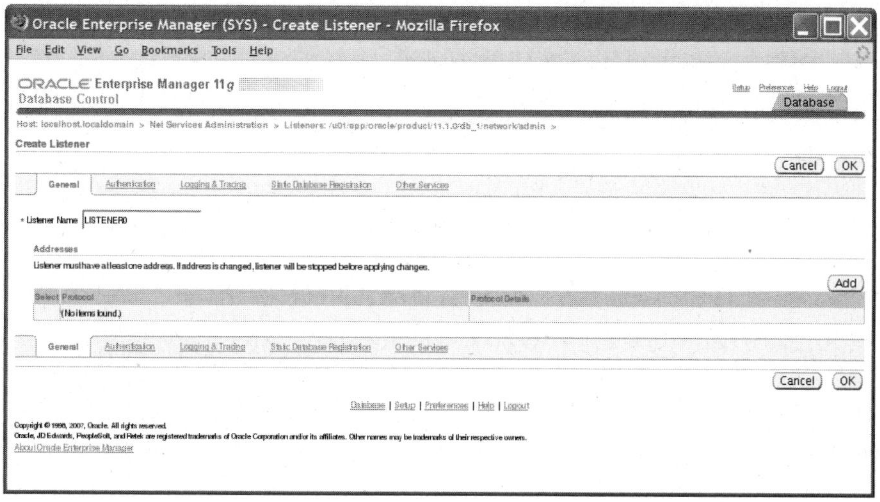

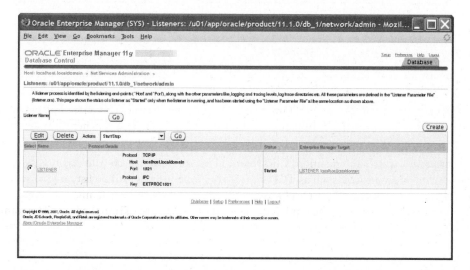

Editing Existing Listeners Using EM Database Control

From the Oracle Enterprise Manager Listener console, you can also make changes to an existing listener. Choose Edit to modify the `listener.ora` parameters, and save this information to the existing `listener.ora` file. To perform these functions, you must be logged in to the machine on which the listener file is located. From the login screen, enter the appropriate user ID and password for the machine and choose Login.

Once you are connected to the machine, you can administer all aspects of the listener. Figure 11.17 shows the main Oracle Enterprise Manager Listeners administration screen.

FIGURE 11.17   The Oracle Enterprise Manager Listeners administration screen

Use the Actions drop-down list to start or stop the listener as well as perform other actions such as tracing. Click the Edit button to configure the listener (see Figure 11.18). You use the tabs across the top of the listener administration screen to configure various aspects of the listener. You can manage logging and tracing, add listener services, and enter service-name information to statically register new services with the listener. You can also manage the listening location and port information. If you choose to edit the port or listening location of the listener, click the Edit button to open the Edit Address screen. You can change the hostname and port. Once you make a change, the listener is stopped and restarted with the new configuration information.

FIGURE 11.18 The Oracle Enterprise Manager Edit Listener screen

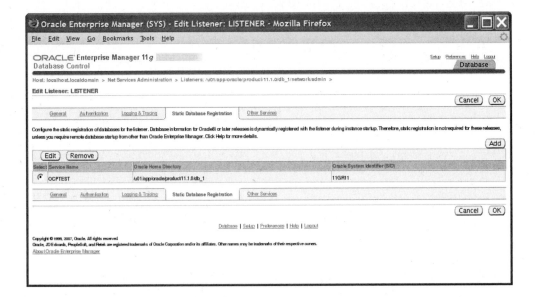

Managing Listeners with *lsnrctl*

You can also use a command-line interface, lsnrctl, to administer the listener. This tool gives you full configuration and administration capabilities. If you have been using Oracle, this tool should be familiar. This command-line interface has been around since the early releases of the Oracle product. Other Oracle network components, such as Connection Manager, also have command-line tools that are used to administer their associated processes.

In Windows, the listener runs as a service. Services are programs that run in the background in Windows. You can start the listener from the Windows Services panel. Choose Start ➢ Settings ➢ Control Panel ➢ Services. Then select the name of the listener service from the list of services. If the name of your listener is Listener, for example, look for an entry such as OracleOra11gListener. Select the listener name, and click Start.

To invoke the command-line utility, type **lsnrctl** at the command line. The following code shows a resulting login screen:

```
$ pwd
/u01/app/oracle/product/11.1.0/db_1/bin
$ ./lsnrctl

LSNRCTL for Linux: Version 11.1.0.6.0 - Production on 17-AUG-2008 20:50:36

Copyright (c) 1991, 2007, Oracle.  All rights reserved.

Welcome to LSNRCTL, type "help" for information.

LSNRCTL>
```

You can perform a variety of functions from within the lsnrctl utility. Let's take a look at the most common functions you'll perform on the listener using this utility.

Starting the Listener

The listener has commands to perform various functions. You can type **help** at the LSNRCTL> prompt to display a list of these commands. To start the default listener named LISTENER, type **start** at the prompt. To start a different listener, type **start** and then that listener name. For example, typing **start listener1** starts the LISTENER1 listener.

The following code shows the results of starting the default listener:

```
$ lsnrctl start

LSNRCTL for Linux: Version 11.1.0.6.0 - Production on 17-AUG-2008 20:51:49

Copyright (c) 1991, 2007, Oracle.  All rights reserved.

Starting /u01/app/oracle/product/11.1.0/db_1/bin/tnslsnr: please wait...

TNSLSNR for Linux: Version 11.1.0.6.0 - Production
System parameter file is /u01/app/oracle/product/11.1.0/db_1/network/admin/
listener.ora
Log messages written to /u01/app/oracle/diag/tnslsnr/localhost/listener/alert/
log.xml
Listening on: (DESCRIPTION=(ADDRESS=(PROTOCOL=tcp)(HOST=localhost.localdomain)
(PORT=1521)))
Listening on: (DESCRIPTION=(ADDRESS=(PROTOCOL=ipc)(KEY=EXTPROC1521)))

Connecting to (DESCRIPTION=(ADDRESS=(PROTOCOL=TCP)(HOST=localhost.localdomain)
(PORT=1521)))
```

```
STATUS of the LISTENER
------------------------
Alias                    LISTENER
Version                  TNSLSNR for Linux: Version 11.1.0.6.0 - Production
Start Date               17-AUG-2008 20:51:49
Uptime                   0 days 0 hr. 0 min. 0 sec
Trace Level              off
Security                 ON: Local OS Authentication
SNMP                     OFF
Listener Parameter File  /u01/app/oracle/product/11.1.0/db_1/network/admin/
listener.ora
Listener Log File        /u01/app/oracle/diag/tnslsnr/localhost/listener/
alert/log.xml
Listening Endpoints Summary...
  (DESCRIPTION=(ADDRESS=(PROTOCOL=tcp)(HOST=localhost.localdomain)(PORT=1521)))
  (DESCRIPTION=(ADDRESS=(PROTOCOL=ipc)(KEY=EXTPROC1521)))
Services Summary...
Service "OCPTEST" has 1 instance(s).
  Instance "11GR11", status UNKNOWN, has 1 handler(s) for this service...
The command completed successfully
$
```

This listing shows a summary of information, including the services that the listener is listening for, the log locations, and whether tracing is enabled for the listener.

Reloading the Listener

If the listener is running and modifications are made to the listener.ora file manually, with Oracle Net Manager or with Enterprise Manager, you must reload the listener to refresh the listener with the most current information. The reload command rereads the listener.ora file for the new definitions. As you can see, it is not necessary to stop and start the listener to reload it. Although stopping and restarting the listener can also accomplish a reload, using the reload command is better because the listener is not actually stopped, which makes this process more efficient. The following code shows an example of the reload command:

```
$ lsnrctl reload

LSNRCTL for Linux: Version 11.1.0.6.0 - Production on 17-AUG-2008 20:53:45

Copyright (c) 1991, 2007, Oracle.  All rights reserved.

Connecting to (DESCRIPTION=(ADDRESS=(PROTOCOL=TCP)(HOST=localhost.localdomain)
(PORT=1521)))
The command completed successfully
$
```

Reloading the listener has no effect on clients connected to the Oracle server.

In the previous code example, Oracle has reread the listener.ora file and applied any changes you made to the file against the currently running listener process. You can see the address, protocol, and port designation of the default listener. Notice that this listener is listening on the default port of 1521.

Showing the Status of the Listener

You can display the status of the listener by using the status command. The status command shows whether the listener is active, the locations of the logs and trace files, how long the listener has been running, and the services for the listener. This is a quick way to verify that the listener is up and running with no problems.

The following code shows the result of the lsnrctl status command:

```
$ lsnrctl status

LSNRCTL for Linux: Version 11.1.0.6.0 - Production on 17-AUG-2008 20:54:58

Copyright (c) 1991, 2007, Oracle.  All rights reserved.

Connecting to (DESCRIPTION=(ADDRESS=(PROTOCOL=TCP)(HOST=localhost.localdomain)
(PORT=1521)))
STATUS of the LISTENER
------------------------
Alias                     LISTENER
Version                   TNSLSNR for Linux: Version 11.1.0.6.0 - Production
Start Date                17-AUG-2008 20:51:49
Uptime                    0 days 0 hr. 3 min. 8 sec
Trace Level               off
Security                  ON: Local OS Authentication
SNMP                      OFF
Listener Parameter File   /u01/app/oracle/product/11.1.0/db_1/network/admin/
listener.ora
Listener Log File         /u01/app/oracle/diag/tnslsnr/localhost/listener/
alert/log.xml
Listening Endpoints Summary...
  (DESCRIPTION=(ADDRESS=(PROTOCOL=tcp)(HOST=localhost.localdomain)(PORT=1521)))
  (DESCRIPTION=(ADDRESS=(PROTOCOL=ipc)(KEY=EXTPROC1521)))
Services Summary...
Service "11GR11" has 1 instance(s).
  Instance "11GR11", status READY, has 1 handler(s) for this service...
Service "11GR11XDB" has 1 instance(s).
  Instance "11GR11", status READY, has 1 handler(s) for this service...
```

```
Service "11GR11_XPT" has 1 instance(s).
  Instance "11GR11", status READY, has 1 handler(s) for this service...
Service "O10GR21" has 1 instance(s).
  Instance "O10GR21", status READY, has 1 handler(s) for this service...
Service "O10GR21XDB" has 1 instance(s).
  Instance "O10GR21", status READY, has 1 handler(s) for this service...
Service "O10GR21_XPT" has 1 instance(s).
  Instance "O10GR21", status READY, has 1 handler(s) for this service...
Service "OCPTEST" has 1 instance(s).
  Instance "11GR11", status UNKNOWN, has 1 handler(s) for this service...
The command completed successfully
$
```

This code example depicts a listener that has recently been started. You also see what the log file and parameter file locations are for the listener. This is a good facility to use to get a quick listing of vital information for the listener.

   Use lsnrctl status to see how long the listener was up. Look for Uptime.

Listing the Services for the Listener

The lsnrctl services command displays information about the services, such as whether the services have any dedicated, prespawned server processes or dispatched processes associated with them, and how many connections have been accepted and rejected per service. Use this method to check whether a listener is listening for a particular service.

The following code shows an example of running the services command:

```
$ lsnrctl services

LSNRCTL for Linux: Version 11.1.0.6.0 - Production on 17-AUG-2008 20:56:05

Copyright (c) 1991, 2007, Oracle.  All rights reserved.

Connecting to (DESCRIPTION=(ADDRESS=(PROTOCOL=TCP)(HOST=localhost.localdomain)
(PORT=1521)))
Services Summary...
Service "11GR11" has 1 instance(s).
  Instance "11GR11", status READY, has 1 handler(s) for this service...
    Handler(s):
      "DEDICATED" established:0 refused:0 state:ready
        LOCAL SERVER
Service "11GR11XDB" has 1 instance(s).
  Instance "11GR11", status READY, has 1 handler(s) for this service...
```

```
    Handler(s):
        "D000" established:0 refused:0 current:0 max:1022 state:ready
            DISPATCHER <machine: localhost.localdomain, pid: 3375>
            (ADDRESS=(PROTOCOL=tcp)(HOST=localhost.localdomain)(PORT=30767))
Service "OCPTEST" has 1 instance(s).
  Instance "11GR11", status UNKNOWN, has 1 handler(s) for this service...
    Handler(s):
        "DEDICATED" established:0 refused:0
            LOCAL SERVER
The command completed successfully
$
```

In this example, you can see that the listener is listening for connections to the service OCPTEST. The line "DEDICATED" established:0 refused:0 shows you how many connections to this service have been accepted or rejected by the listener. One reason why a listener may reject servicing a request is if the database is not available.

Other Commands in lsnrctl

You can run other commands in lsnrctl. Table 11.3 summarizes these other commands. Type the command at the LSNRCTL> prompt to execute it.

TABLE 11.3   A Summary of the lsnrctl Commands

Command	Definition
change_password	Allows a user to change the password needed to stop the listener.
Exit	Exits the lsnrctl utility.
Quit	Performs the same function as exit.
save_config	Copies the listener.ora file called listener.bak when changes are made to the listener.ora file from lsnrctl.
Services	Lists a summary of services and details information about the number of connections established and the number of connections refused for each protocol service handler.
start listener	Starts the named listener.
status listener	Shows the status of the named listener.
stop listener	Stops the named listener.
Trace	Turns on tracing for the listener.
Version	Displays the version of the Oracle Net software and protocol adapters.

Using the set Commands in lsnrctl

The lsnrctl utility also has commands called set commands. To issue these commands, type **set** *commandname* at the LSNRCTL> prompt. You use the set commands to modify the listener.ora file. For example, you can use this command to set up logging and tracing. You can set most of these parameters using the Oracle Net Manager.

To display the current setting of a parameter, use the show command, which displays the current settings of the parameters set using the set command. Table 11.4 summarizes the lsnrctl set commands. Type **set** or **show** to display a listing of all the commands.

TABLE 11.4   A Summary of the lsnrctl set Commands

Command	Description
current_listener	Sets the listener to modify or shows the name of the current listener.
displaymode	Sets display for the lsnrctl utility to RAW, COMPACT, NORMAL, or VERBOSE.
log_status	Shows whether logging is on or off for the listener.
log_file	Shows the name of listener log file.
log_directory	Shows the log directory location.
rawmode	Shows more detail on STATUS and SERVICES when set to ON. Values are ON or OFF.
startup_waittime	Sets the length of time that a listener will wait to respond to a status command in the lsnrctl command-line utility.
spawn	Starts external services that the listener is listening for and that are running on the server.
save_config_on_stop	Saves changes to the listener.ora file when exiting lsnrctl.
trc_level	Sets the trace level to OFF, USER, ADMIN, or SUPPORT.
trc_file	Sets the name of the listener trace file.
trc_directory	Sets the name of the listener trace directory.

Stopping the Listener

To stop the listener, you must issue the lsnrctl stop command. This command stops the default listener. To stop a nondefault listener, include the name of the listener. For example, to stop LISTENER1, type `lsnrctl stop listener1`. If you are in the `lsnrctl>` facility, you will stop the current listener defined by the `current_listener` setting. To see what the current listener is set to, use the `show` command. The default value is `LISTENER`.

Stopping the listener does not affect clients connected to the database. It only means that no new connections can use this listener until the listener is restarted.

The following code shows what the `stop` command looks like:

```
$ lsnrctl stop

LSNRCTL for Linux: Version 11.1.0.6.0 - Production on 17-AUG-2008 20:59:32

Copyright (c) 1991, 2007, Oracle.  All rights reserved.

Connecting to (DESCRIPTION=(ADDRESS=(PROTOCOL=TCP)(HOST=localhost.localdomain)
(PORT=1521)))
The command completed successfully
$
```

Dynamically Registering Services

Oracle 11*g* databases can automatically register their presence with an existing listener. The instance registers with the listener defined on the local machine. Dynamic service registration allows you to take advantage of other features, such as load balancing and automatic failover. The PMON process is responsible for registering this information with the listener.

When dynamic service registration is used, you will not see the service listed in the `listener.ora` file. To see the service listed, run the `lsnrctl services` command. Be aware that if the listener is started after the Oracle instance, there may be a time lag before the instance actually registers information with the listener.

For an instance to automatically register with a listener, the listener must be configured as a default listener, or you must specify the `init.ora` parameter `LOCAL_LISTENER`. The `LOCAL_LISTENER` parameter defines the location of the listener with which you want the Oracle server to register. This is a default listener definition:

```
Listener Name = LISTENER
Port = 1521
Protocol = TCP/IP
```

You must configure two other `init.ora` parameters to allow an instance to register information with the listener. Two parameters are used to allow automatic registration: `INSTANCE_NAME` and `SERVICE_NAMES`.

The `INSTANCE_NAME` parameter is set to the name of the Oracle instance you want to register with the listener. The `SERVICE_NAMES` parameter is a combination of the instance name and the domain name. The domain name is set to the value of the `DB_DOMAIN` initialization parameter. For example, if your DB_DOMAIN is set to BJS.COM and your Oracle instance is DBA, set the parameters as follows:

```
Instance_name = DBA
Service_names = DBA.BJS.COM
```

If you are not using domain names, set the INSTANCE_NAME and SERVICE_NAMES parameters to the same values.

Oracle Net Logging and Tracing on the Server

If a network problem persists, you can use *logging* and *tracing* to help resolve it. Oracle generates information into log files and trace files that can assist you in tracking down network connection problems. You can use logging to find out general information about the success or failure of certain components of the Oracle network. You can use tracing to get in-depth information about specific network connections.

 By default, Oracle produces logs for clients and the Oracle listener.

- *Logging* records significant events, such as starting and stopping the listener, along with certain kinds of network errors. Errors are generated in the log in the form of an error stack. The listener log records information such as the version number, connection attempts, and the protocols for which it is listening. You can enable logging at the client, middle-tier, and server locations.

- *Tracing*, which you can also enable at the client, middle-tier, or server location, records all events that occur on a network, even when an error does not occur. The trace file provides a great deal of information that logs do not, such as the number of network round-trips made during a network connection or the number of packets sent and received during a network connection. Tracing enables you to collect a thorough listing of the actual sequence of the statements as a network connection is being processed. This gives you a much more detailed picture of what is occurring with connections that the listener is processing.

 Real World Scenario

Use Tracing Sparingly

Use tracing only as a last resort if you are having connectivity problems between the client and server. Complete all the server-side checks described earlier before you resort to tracing. The tracing process generates a significant amount of overhead, and depending on the trace level set, it can create some rather large files. This activity will impede system I/O performance because of all the information that is written to the logs, and if left unchecked, it could fill your disk or file system.

> I was once involved with a large project that was using JDBC to connect to the Oracle server. We were having difficulty with connections being periodically dropped between the JDBC client and the Oracle server. We enabled tracing to try to find the problem. We did eventually correct the problem (it was with how our DNS names server was config-ured), but the tracing was left on inadvertently. When the system eventually went into production, the trace files grew so large that they filled the disk where tracing was being collected. To prevent this from happening, periodically ensure that the trace parameters are not turned on, and if they are, turn them off.

Use Oracle Net Manager to enable most logging and tracing parameters. Many of the logging and tracing parameters are found in the `sqlnet.ora` file. Let's take a look at how to enable logging and tracing for the various components in an Oracle network.

Server Logging

By default, the listener is configured to enable the generation of a log file. The log file records information about listener startup and shutdown, successful and unsuccessful connection attempts, and certain types of network errors. Here's what everything means by default:

- The listener log location is *<DIAGNOSTIC_DEST>*/diag/tnslsnr/*<hostname>*/listener/ trace on Unix.

- The default name of the file is listener.log.

- The XML version of the listener log is under *<DIAGNOSTIC_DEST>*/diag/tnslsnr/ *<hostname>*/listener/alert, and the filename is log.xml.

- If the DIAGNOSTIC_DEST parameter is not defined, Oracle defaults it to $ORACLE_BASE.

Information in the listener.log file contains information about connection attempts, the name of the program executing the request, and the name of the client attempting to connect. The last field contains a zero if a request was successfully completed.

Server Tracing

As mentioned earlier, tracing gathers information about the flow of traffic across a network connection. Data is transmitted back and forth in the form of packets. A packet contains sender information, receiver information, and data. Even a single network request can gen-erate a large number of packets.

In the trace file, each line starts with the name of the procedure executed in one of the Oracle Net layers and is followed by a set of hexadecimal numbers. The hexadecimal num-bers are the actual data transmitted. If you are not encrypting the data, sometimes you will see the actual data after the hexadecimal numbers.

If you are doing server-to-server communications and have a sqlnet .ora file on the server, you can enter information in the Server Informa-tion section located on the Tracing tab of the Profile screen in Oracle Net Manager tracing. This provides tracing information for server-to-server communications.

Enabling Server Tracing

You can enable server tracing from the same Oracle Net Manager screens shown earlier. Simply click the Tracing Enabled radio button. The default trace file location is $DIAGNOSTIC_ DEST/diag/tnslsnr/*hostname*/listener/trace in Unix. You can set the trace level to OFF, USER, ADMIN, or SUPPORT. The USER level detects specific user errors. The ADMIN level contains all the user-level information along with installation-specific errors. SUPPORT is the highest level and can produce information that might be beneficial to Oracle Support personnel. This level also can produce large trace files.

The following example shows a section of the listener.ora file with the logging and tracing parameters enabled:

```
TRACE_LEVEL_LISTENER = ADMIN
TRACE_FILE_LISTENER = LISTENER.trc
LOGGING_LISTENER = ON
LOG_FILE_LISTENER = LISTENER.log
```

Configuring Oracle Net for the Client

Once the Oracle server is properly configured, you can focus on configuring the clients to allow for connectivity to the Oracle server. It is important to understand how to configure Oracle clients because without proper knowledge of how to do this, you are limited in your connection choices to the server. As a DBA, you must understand the network needs of the organization, the type of connectivity that is required, and client/server connections vs. *n*-tier connectivity, for example, in order to make the appropriate choices about client-side configuration. This section should help clarify the client-side connectivity options available to you and show you how to troubleshoot client connection problems.

Client-Side Names Resolution Options

When a client needs to connect to an Oracle server, the client must supply three pieces of information: their user ID, password, and net service name. The net service name provides the necessary information, in the form of a connect descriptor, to locate an Oracle service in a network.

This connect descriptor describes the path to the Oracle server and its service name, which is an alias for an Oracle Database. The location where this information is kept depends on the names resolution method you choose. The five methods of net service name resolution are Oracle Internet Directory, external naming, host naming, Oracle Easy Connect, and local naming. Normally, you choose just one of these methods, but you can use any combination.

Oracle Internet Directory is advantageous when you are dealing with complex networks that have many Oracle servers. When you choose this method, you can configure and manage net service names and connect descriptor information in a central location.

External naming uses a non-Oracle facility to manage and resolve Oracle service names. For example, if an organization uses an external names resolution method such as Network Information Service (NIS), the database service information could be stored in this external location and used by clients to resolve service names.

You need to be only casually familiar with the Oracle Internet Directory and the external naming resolution options. For a more detailed description of how to configure and use external naming, please consult "Oracle Database Net Services Administrator's Guide 11*g* Release 1 (11.1) Part Number B28316-04." You can find the Oracle documentation at `http://tahiti .oracle.com`.

In the following sections, we will take a closer look at the host naming, Oracle Easy Connect, and local naming methods.

The Host Naming Method

In small networks with few Oracle servers to manage, you can take advantage of the *host naming method*. Host naming is advantageous when you want to reduce the amount of configuration work necessary. Host naming saves you from configuring the clients, although it does have limitations. The following are the four prerequisites to using host naming:

- You must use TCP/IP as your network protocol.

- You must not use any advanced networking features, such as Oracle Connection Manager.

- You must have an external naming service, such as DNS, or a `HOSTS` file available to the client.

- The listener must be set up with the `GLOBAL_DBNAME` parameter equal to the name of the machine.

Now let's discuss how to configure this naming method.

Configuring the Host Naming Method

By default, Oracle attempts to use the host naming method from the client only after it attempts connections using local naming. To override this default search path for resolving names, set the `NAMES.DIRECTORY_PATH` parameter in the `sqlnet.ora` file on the client so that it searches for host naming only. The following is an example of the `sqlnet.ora` file:

```
# SQLNET.ORA Network Configuration File:
# Generated by Oracle configuration tools.

NAMES.DEFAULT_DOMAIN = bjs.com
NAMES.DIRECTORY_PATH= (HOSTNAME)
```

The host naming and the Oracle Easy Connect methods do not require any client-side configuration files. We'll discuss these connection methods later in this section.

You can check TCP/IP connectivity from the client using the TCP/IP utility ping. The ping utility attempts to contact the server by sending a small request packet. The server responds in kind with an acknowledgment.

The server must be configured with a listener running TCP/IP, and the listener must be listening on the default port of 1521. If the instance has not been dynamically registered with the listener, you must configure the listener with the GLOBAL_DBNAME parameter.

The Oracle Easy Connect Method

The Oracle Easy Connect method is a connection resolution technique introduced in Oracle 10*g*. This method is similar to the host naming method described in the previous section but adds parameters that allow for a port and service-name specification. By default, the Oracle Easy Connect names resolution method is configured when Oracle Net is installed.

Like the host naming method, the Oracle Easy Connect method eliminates the need for any connection information to be configured on the client. This makes for less setup and administrative work. It enhances the host naming method by allowing for a port and service specification. Remember from the previous section that the host naming method requires a listener to be listening on the default port of 1521. Allowing a port specification addresses one of the limitations of the host naming method. Using the Oracle Easy Connect method requires that certain conditions be met:

- Oracle Net Services 10*g* or 11*g* must be installed on the client.
- Oracle Net TCP/IP services must be enabled and supported on both the client and the server.
- No advanced connection descriptor features are allowed such as connection pooling or external procedure calls.

Table 11.5 describes the connect descriptor components when you are using the Oracle Easy Connect method.

TABLE 11.5 Easy Connect Components

Syntax Component	Description
//	Optional: Used when you are connecting via a URL.
Host	Required: The host or IP address to connect to.
Port	Optional: The port to connect to. The default is 1521.

TABLE 11.5   Easy Connect Components *(continued)*

Syntax Component	Description
Service name	The service name for the database. The default is the hostname of the computer on which the database resides. If the database name is different from the hostname, enter the service name.

Here is an example of how to connect to a database using the Easy Connect method:

```
CONNECT scott/tiger@myhostname:1521/11GR11
```

The example shows how a user connects to the database service 11GR11 that is running on the myhostname server and has an Oracle listener listening for TCP/IP connections on port 1521. As stated previously, this method is configured automatically when you install Oracle Net. If you want the Oracle Easy Connect method to be the first method chosen by a client when a connection request is made, you can modify the NAMES.DIRECTORY_PATH parameter in the sqlnet.ora file. The following discussion shows how to do this.

You can use the Oracle Net Manager tool to configure the Easy Connect method as the default names resolution method. Start the Oracle Net Manager tool, and then follow these steps:

1. Choose Local ➤ Profile Pane in the Navigator pane.
2. Select Naming from the panel on the right.
3. Select the Methods tab.
4. Select EZCONNECT in the Selected Methods list. You can click the promote arrows to move EZCONNECT to the top of the Selected Methods list.
5. Choose File ➤ Save Network Configuration to save your changes.

   When you check your sqlnet.ora file, you should see the following entry:

   ```
   NAMES.DIRECTORY_PATH=(EZCONNECT,TNSNAMES)
   ```

The Local Naming Method

The *local naming method* is probably the most widely used and well-known method for resolving net service names. Most users know this method as the tnsnames.ora method because it uses the tnsnames.ora file.

To use the local naming method, you must configure the tnsnames.ora file, which can be in any location, as long as the client can get to it. The default location for the tnsnames.ora file and the sqlnet.ora file is %ORACLE_HOME%\network\admin in Windows and $ORACLE_HOME/network/admin in Unix systems. If you want to change the location of this file, set the environmental variable TNS_ADMIN. In Unix-based systems, you can export TNS_ADMIN to the user's shell environment or in the user's profile. In Windows, this setting is in the registry. The Windows registry key that stores the TNS_ADMIN depends on your particular setup. Generally, it is somewhere under Hkey_local_machine/software/oracle, but it may be at a lower level depending on your configuration.

Most installations probably keep the files in these default locations on the client and server. Some users create shared disks and place the tnsnames.ora and sqlnet.ora files in this shared location to take a centralized approach to managing these files. If server-to-server communication is necessary, these files need to be on the server. The default location on the server is the same as the default location on the client.

Now that you have an understanding of the local naming method, I will discuss how to configure this method using Oracle Net Manager.

Configuring the Local Naming Method Using Oracle Net Manager

To configure the local naming method, you use Oracle Net Manager. To start this configuration, open Net Manager, and select Service Naming on the Local tab. Click the plus sign on the left side of the screen, or choose Edit ➢ Create.

The Oracle Net Manager starts the net service name wizard, which guides you through the process of creating the net service names definition. The following steps detail how to configure the local naming method:

1. When you configure a client to use the local naming method, you must first choose a *net service name*. This is the name that users enter when they are referring to the location to which they want to connect. The name you supply here should not include the domain portion if you are using the hierarchical naming mode. Figure 11.19 shows an example of choosing the net service name. Click the Next button to continue.

FIGURE 11.19 Choosing a net service name

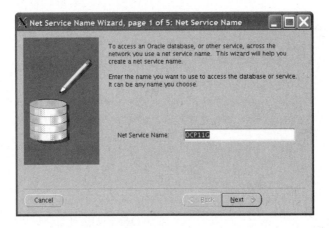

2. The next step is to enter the type of protocol that the client should use when they connect to the server for this net service name. By default, TCP/IP is chosen (see Figure 11.20). The list of protocols depends on your platform. Click the Next button to continue.

FIGURE 11.20   Choosing a network protocol

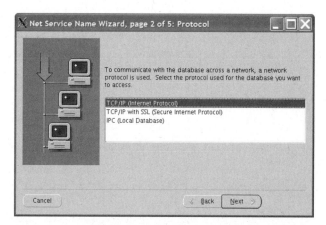

3.   The next step is to choose the hostname and port. This step depends on the protocol you chose in the previous step. If you chose TCP/IP, you are prompted for the hostname and the port number. The hostname is the name of the machine on which the listener process is running. The port number is the listening location for the listener. The default port is 1521 (see Figure 11.21).

FIGURE 11.21   Choosing a hostname and a port

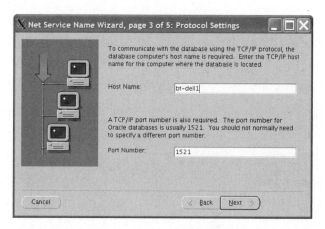

4.   The next step is to define the service name. For Oracle 11*g*, the service name does not have to be the same as the ORACLE_SID because a database can have multiple service names. In Oracle 11*g*, the service name is normally the same as the global database name. This is the service name that is supplied to the listener, so the listener has to be listening for this service. You can also choose whether this service is for Oracle8*i* or

later databases or Oracle8*i* and previous databases. You can also select the connection type from one of these choices:

- Database Default
- Shared Server
- Dedicated Server

Figure 11.22 shows an example of the Oracle Net Manager service name screen.

5. The last step is to test the net service name and verify that all the connection information entered is correct. Click the Test button to test the network connection.

Click Finish button to create the `tnsnames.ora` entry. You can edit the entry, as shown in Figure 11.23.

FIGURE 11.22 Choosing the service name

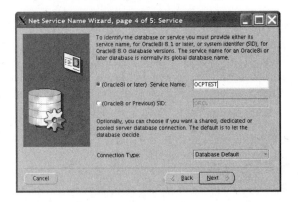

FIGURE 11.23 The Oracle Net Manager `tnsnames.ora` wizard

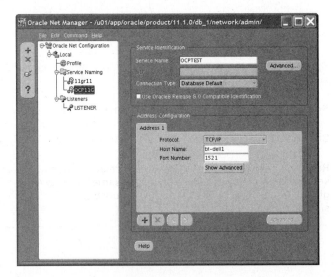

After you complete all this, save your changes by choosing File ➤ Save Network Configuration. This creates and saves the tnsnames.ora file.

Contents and Structure of the *tnsnames.ora* File

You created the tnsnames.ora file using the Oracle Net Manager, so open the tnsnames.ora file to view its contents. The tnsnames.ora file is located at the location the TNS_ADMIN variable is set to, which defaults to the $ORACLE_HOME/network/admin directory. Here is an example of the tnsnames.ora file:

```
OCP11G =
  (DESCRIPTION =
    (ADDRESS_LIST =
      (ADDRESS = (PROTOCOL = TCP)(HOST = bt-dell1)(PORT = 1521))
    )
    (CONNECT_DATA =
      (SERVICE_NAME = OCPTEST)
    )
  )
```

Table 11.6 summarizes the parameters in the tnsnames.ora file.

TABLE 11.6   The tnsnames.ora Parameters

Parameter	Description
DESCRIPTION	Starts the connect descriptor section of the file.
ADDRESS_LIST	Starts a list of all connect descriptor address information.
ADDRESS	Specifies the connect descriptor for the net service name.
PROTOCOL	Specifies the protocol used, such as TCP/IP.
HOST	Specifies the name of the machine on which the listener is running. An IP address can also be specified in TCP/IP.
PORT	Specifies the listening location of the listener specific to TCP/IP.
CONNECT_DATA	Starts the services section for this net service name.
SERVICE_NAME	Replaces the SID parameter from older releases of Oracle. Defines which service to connect to, which can be the same as the ORACLE_SID or the global database name. Databases can now be referred to by more than a single service name.

Configuring Local Naming Using Enterprise Manager

You can also use Oracle Enterprise Manager to configure local naming. You do so from the Net Services Administration screen as described in the "Adding a Listener Using Enterprise Manager Database Control" section earlier in this chapter. You will see the screen shown in Figure 11.15. Choose Local Naming from the Administer drop-down list, and click Go to open the Local Naming screen, as shown in Figure 11.24.

FIGURE 11.24   Using Enterprise Manager to configure local naming

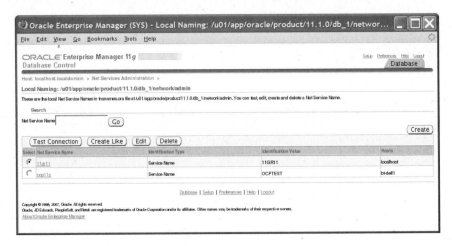

1. Click the Create button to open the Create Net Service Name page. Here you can enter the unique service name that you want users to use to connect to this Oracle service. This can also be the Oracle SID.

2. Select the type of connection to use for this service: a dedicated server, shared server, or the database default.

3. Specify the address information. This includes the protocol, port, and host used by the service being connected to.

4. Click the Add button under Addresses to open the Add Address screen to fill in the appropriate information.

On the Create New Service Name page, there is a section to configure failover and load balancing options. Five choices are listed under the Connect Time Failover and Load Balancing section. Table 11.7 summarizes these prompts. If you have multiple listeners listening for this service or are using Oracle Connection Manager, you can select from this list. The default is to use the first address only; this is the case where a single listener is being used.

Source routing is used with Oracle Connection Manager. Oracle passes control from the first address listed to the next address, and so on, until the ultimate destination is reached. Every address listed is used in the case of source routing.

TABLE 11.7   Advanced-Features Summary

Option	Advanced Feature
Try each address, in order, until one succeeds.	Failover
Try each address, randomly, until one succeeds.	Failover Load Balancing
Try one address, selected at random.	Load Balancing
Use each address in order until you reach the destination.	Source Routing
Use only the first address.	None

Troubleshooting Client-Side Connection Problems

Connection problems can also occur from the Oracle client. Several areas affect the ability of a client to connect successfully to the server. The client must be able to contact both the computer on which the Oracle server is located and the listener listening for connections to the Oracle server. The client must also be able to resolve the net service name. Let's look at the checks to perform on the client to verify connectivity to the Oracle server and to detect and troubleshoot client-side connection problems. Use the following list to help you systematically check various aspects of the client connection process:

- Verify that the client can contact the server.
- Determine the network route that the client is taking to the server.
- Verify local naming configuration files.
- Check for multiple-client network configuration files.
- Check network file locations.
- Check the NAMES.DIRECTORY_PATH parameter.
- Check the NAMES.DEFAULT_DOMAIN parameter.
- Check the client protocol adapters installed.
- Check for any common client-side error codes.

Oracle provides the tnsping utility to verify that the local naming entry defined in the tnsnames.ora file can talk to the service name defined in the listener.ora file. You can find tnsping in the $ORACLE_HOME/bin directory. It also provides the time it took to reach the listener in milliseconds.

Checking Network File Locations

One of the most common problems encountered is clients moving network files and not setting the TNS_ADMIN environmental variable to the new file location. Oracle expects the tnsnames.ora and sqlnet.ora files to be in the default location. If it cannot locate the files and you have not set TNS_ADMIN, you receive an ORA-12154 error message. You also receive this error if the supplied net service name is invalid or the NAMES.DEFAULT_DOMAIN value is mismatched in tnsnames.ora and sqlnet.ora files. The following code shows an example of this error message:

```
$ sqlplus system@ocp11r1

SQL*Plus: Release 11.1.0.6.0 - Production on Sun Aug 17 23:47:17 2008

Copyright (c) 1982, 2007, Oracle.  All rights reserved.

Enter password:
ERROR:
ORA-12154: TNS: could not resolve the connect identifier specified
```

 If you decide to move network files, be sure to set the TNS_ADMIN environmental variable to the location of the files. Oracle first searches the default location for the files and then searches the TNS_ADMIN location for the files.

Checking NAMES.DIRECTORY_PATH

Make sure the client has the proper names resolution setting. The NAMES.DIRECTORY_PATH parameter in the sqlnet.ora file controls the order in which the client resolves net service names. If the parameter is not set, the default is local naming, OID, and then host naming.

If this parameter is set incorrectly, the client may never check the appropriate names resolution type. For example, if you are using local naming and the parameter is set to HOSTNAMES, the tnsnames.ora file will never be used to resolve the net service name. You will receive an ORA-12154 "Could Not Resolve the Connect Identifier Specified" error message.

Checking NAMES.DEFAULT_DOMAIN

NAMES.DEFAULT_DOMAIN is another common error. It was more common in older releases of Oracle because the parameter defaulted to the value WORLD. Check the client sqlnet.ora file to see whether the parameter is set. If the parameter has a value and you are using unqualified net service names, the parameter value is appended to the end of the net service name. An unqualified service name is a service name that does not contain domain information.

For example, if you entered **sqlplus matt/casey@PROD** and the NAMES.DEFAULT_DOMAIN is set to WORLD, Oracle appends .WORLD to the net service name; as a result, Oracle passes the command as `sqlplus matt/casey@PROD.WORLD`. You will receive an ORA-12154 "Could Not Resolve the Connect Identifier Specified" error message if the service name should not include the `.WORLD` domain extension. You use this parameter only if you are using a hierarchical naming convention.

Checking for Client-Side Error Codes

You should next check for client-side error codes. Here is a summary of some of the common client-side Oracle error messages you might encounter. They are discussed in detail in the following sections.

```
ORA-12154 "TNS: could not resolve connect identifier specified"
ORA-12198 "TNS: could not find path to destination"
ORA-12203 "TNS: Unable to connect to destination"
ORA-12533 "TNS: illegal address parameters"
ORA-12541 "TNS: No listener"
```

ORA-12154   This indicates that the client cannot find the service listed in the `tnsnames.ora` file. Some of the causes of this were previously described, such as the file is not in the proper directory or the `TNS_ADMIN` variable is not specified or specified incorrectly.

ORA-12198 and ORA-12203   This indicates that the client found an entry for the service in the `tnsnames.ora` file but the service specified was not found. Check to make sure the service specified in the `tnsnames.ora` file actually points to a valid database service.

ORA-12533   This indicates that you have configured the `ADDRESS` section of the `tnsnames.ora` file incorrectly. Check to make sure the syntax is correct, or re-create the definition using the Oracle Net Manager tool.

ORA-12541   This indicates that the client contacted a server that does not have a listener running on the specified port. Make sure the listener is started on the server and that the listening port specifications on the client and the server match.

An Overview of Oracle Shared Server

Oracle Shared Server is an optional configuration of Oracle Server that allows the server to support a larger number of concurrent connections without increasing physical resource requirements. It does so by sharing resources among groups of users.

Shared Server is suitable for *high-think* applications. High-think applications are composed of small transactions with natural pauses in the transaction patterns, which makes them good candidates for Oracle Shared Server connections. Many web-based applications fit this model. These types of applications are typically form-based and involve submissions of small amounts of information to the database with small result sets returned to the client.

Oracle manages dedicated server and shared server connections differently. As a DBA, you need to be able to identify these differences. This knowledge will help you better understand the advantages and disadvantages of Oracle Shared Server and when it might be advantageous to use Oracle Shared Server in your environment.

Dedicated Server vs. Shared Server

If you have ever gone to an upscale restaurant, you may have had your own personal waitperson. That waitperson is there to greet you and escort you to your seat. They take your order for food and drinks and even help prepare your order. No matter how many other patrons enter the restaurant, your waitperson is responsible for serving only your requests. Therefore, your service is consistent—if the person is a good waitperson.

A *dedicated server* environment works in much the same way. Every client connection is associated with a dedicated server process, sometimes called a *shadow process,* on the machine where the Oracle server exists. No matter how many other connections are made to the server, the same dedicated server is always responsible for processing only your requests. You use the services of that server process until you disconnect from the Oracle server.

Most restaurants operate more like shared servers. When you walk in, you are assigned a waitperson, but they may be responsible for serving many other tables. This is good for the restaurant because they can serve more customers without increasing the staff. It may be fine for you as well, if the restaurant is not too busy and the waitperson is not responsible for too many tables. Also, if most of the orders are small, the staff can keep up with the requests, and the service will be as good as if you had your own waitperson.

In a diner, things work slightly different; the waitperson takes your order and places it on a turnstile. If the diner has multiple cooks, the order is picked up from the turnstile and prepared by one of the available cooks. When the cook completes the preparation of the dinner, it is placed in a location where the waitperson can pick it up and bring it to your table.

This is how an Oracle Shared Server environment works. In an Oracle Shared Server environment, *dispatcher* processes are responsible for servicing client requests. These processes are capable of handling requests from many clients. This is different from the dedicated server environment, where a single client process is handled by a single server process. Like the waitperson in the diner, a dispatcher can be responsible for taking the orders of many clients.

 When using Oracle Shared Server, idle connections can be reused and allow several users to connect to the database, thus improving scalability.

When you request something from the server, it is the dispatcher's responsibility to take your request and place it in a location called a *request queue*. The request queue functions like the turnstile in the diner analogy. All dispatcher processes place their client requests in one request queue, which is a structure contained in the system global area (SGA).

Shared Server *processes*, like cooks in a diner, are responsible for fulfilling the client requests. The Oracle Shared Server process executes the request and places the result into an area of the SGA called a *response queue*. Every dispatcher has its own response queue. The dispatcher picks up the completed request from the response queue and returns the results to the client. Figure 11.25 illustrates the following processing steps for a Shared Server request:

1. The client passes a request to the dispatcher serving it.

2. The dispatcher places the request on a request queue in the SGA.

3. One of the Shared Server processes executes the request.

4. The Shared Server places the completed request on the dispatchers' response queue of the SGA.

5. The dispatcher picks up the completed request from the response queue.

6. The completed request is passed back to the client.

FIGURE 11.25   Request processing in Shared Server

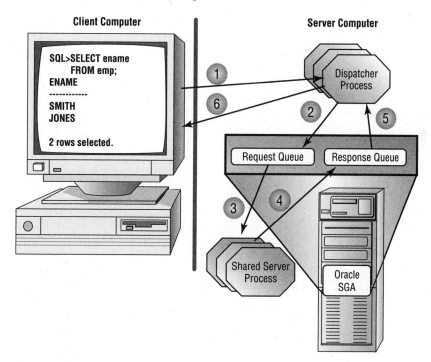

Requests placed in the request queue are processed on a first-in, first-out basis (FIFO). Currently, there is no way to prioritize requests within the queue.

Advantages and Disadvantages of Shared Server

Oracle Shared Server is used when server resources, such as memory and active processes, become constrained. People tend to throw more hardware at problems such as these; this will likely remedy the problem, but it may be an unnecessary expense.

If your system is experiencing these problems, Oracle Shared Server allows you to support the same number or a greater number of connections without requiring additional hardware. As a result, Oracle Shared Server tends to decrease the overall memory and process requirements on the server. Because clients are sharing processes, the total number of processes is reduced. This translates into resource savings on the server.

Shared Server also allows for connection pooling. Connection pooling enables the database server to disconnect an idle Oracle Shared Server connection to service an incoming request. The idle connection is still active and is reenabled once the client makes the next request. The connection pooling feature of Oracle Shared Server allows it to handle a larger number of requests without having to start additional dispatcher processes. You configure connection pooling by adding attributes to one of the Oracle Shared Server parameters.

See the section "Configuring Connection Pooling with the Dispatchers Parameter" later in this chapter to see how connection pooling is configured.

Shared Server is also required to take advantage of certain network options, such as connection multiplexing and client access control, which are features of Oracle Connection Manager. Oracle Connection Manager is a facility provided by Oracle that controls access to database services and multiplex connections in an Oracle environment. The access control component of Oracle Connection Manager allows you to configure rules that allow or disallow fulfillment of a connection request. The multiplexing component acts as a concentrator feature. It funnels multiple client sessions through a shared network connection from the Oracle Connection Manager server to the database server.

You can find out more about Oracle Connection Manager in "Oracle Database Net Services Administrators Guide 11*g* Release 1 (11.1) Part Number B28316-04."

Oracle Shared Server also has some disadvantages. Applications that generate a significant amount of network traffic or result in large result sets are not good candidates for Shared Server connections. Think of the earlier diner analogy. Your service is fine until two parties of twelve people show up. All of a sudden, the waitperson is overwhelmed with work from these two other tables, and your service begins to suffer. The same thing would happen in a Shared Server environment. If requests for large quantities of information start going to the dispatchers, the dispatchers can become overwhelmed, and you can see performance suffer for the other clients connected to the dispatcher. This, in turn, increases your response times. Dedicated processes better serve these types of applications.

Some functions are not allowed when you are using an Oracle Shared Server connection. You cannot start up, shut down, or perform certain kinds of recovery of an Oracle server when you are connected via a shared server.

Also, you should not perform certain administrative tasks using Oracle Shared Server connections, including bulk loads of data, index and table rebuilds, and table analysis. These types of tasks deal with manipulating large data sets and should use dedicated connections.

Oracle Shared Server is a scalability enhancement option, not a performance enhancement option. If you are looking for a performance increase, Shared Server is not what you should be configuring. Use Shared Server only if you are experiencing the system constraint problems discussed earlier in this chapter. You will always have equal or better performance in a dedicated server environment.

Oracle Shared Server Infrastructure

As described in the previous section, you manage client connections quite differently when using Oracle Shared Server as opposed to using a dedicated server. To accommodate the change, several modifications take place inside the internal memory structures of the Oracle server. The way in which the database and listener interact is also affected when using Oracle Shared Server. It is important to understand these changes when configuring and managing Oracle Shared Server.

Certain changes are necessary to the memory structures within Oracle to provide the Shared Server capability. Let's see what changes within the Oracle infrastructure are necessary to provide this support.

PGA and SGA Changes When Using Oracle Shared Server

When Oracle Shared Server is configured, Oracle adds two new types of structures to the SGA: request queues and response queues. These structures do not exist in a dedicated server environment. There is one request queue for all dispatchers, but each dispatcher has its own response queue. Therefore, if you have four dispatchers, you will have one request queue and four response queues. The request queue is located in the SGA where the dispatcher places client requests. A Shared Server process executes each request and places the completed request in the dispatcher's response queue.

In a dedicated server environment, each server has a memory segment called a *program global area* (PGA). The PGA is an area of memory where information about each client session is maintained. This information includes bind variables, cursor information, and the client's sort area. In an Oracle Shared Server environment, this information is moved from the PGA to an area of the SGA called the *user global area* (UGA). You can configure a special area of the SGA called the *large pool* to accommodate the bulk of the UGA.

Figure 11.26 shows how the SGA and PGA structures differ between a dedicated server and an Oracle Shared Server environment.

Each connection being serviced by a dispatcher is bound to a shared memory segment and forms a *virtual circuit*. The dispatcher uses the shared memory segment to manage communications between the client and the Oracle Database. The Oracle Shared Server processes use the virtual circuits to send and receive information to the appropriate dispatcher process.

To limit the amount of UGA memory a session can allocate, set the PRIVATE_SGA resource limit in the user's profile.

The Role of the Listener in an Oracle Shared Server Environment

The listener plays an important role in the Oracle Shared Server environment. The listener supplies the client with the address of the dispatcher to connect to when a user requests connections to an Oracle Shared Server. The listener maintains a list of dispatchers available from the Oracle Shared Server. The Oracle background process PMON notifies the listener as to which dispatcher is responsible for servicing each virtual circuit. The listener is then aware of the number of connections that the dispatcher is managing. This information allows the listener to take advantage of dispatcher load balancing.

Load balancing allows the listener to make intelligent decisions about which dispatcher to redirect client connections to so that no one dispatcher becomes overburdened. When the listener receives a connection request, it looks at the current connection load for each dispatcher and redirects the client connection request to the least-loaded dispatcher. The listener determines the least-loaded dispatcher for all nodes if Real Application Clusters (RAC) are being used, followed by the least-loaded instance for the node, and finally by the least-loaded dispatcher for the instance. By doing so, the listener ensures that connections are evenly distributed across dispatchers.

The listener can either redirect the client connection to an available dispatcher or directly hand off the request to the dispatcher. The latter is performed whenever possible and is done typically when the listener and database service exist on the same node. When the listener and database service exist on different nodes, the redirection method is used.

FIGURE 11.26   SGA/PGA comparison of dedicated server and shared server

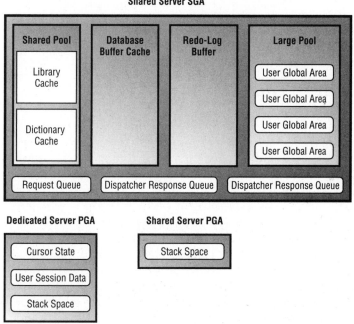

When a client connection terminates, the listener is updated to reflect the change in the number of connections that the dispatcher is handling.

Figure 11.27 illustrates the following steps in the Oracle Shared Server connection process after the database has been started and the dispatcher processes have been started:

1. The client contacts the Oracle Database server after resolving the service name.

2. The listener validates the Oracle service name supplied by the client and hands off or redirects the client connection to the least-busy dispatcher.

3. The listener sends information to the client so the client can redirect the connection to the appropriate dispatcher process.

4. The dispatcher process manages the client server request.

5. PMON registers connection information with the listener.

FIGURE 11.27   The Shared Server connection process

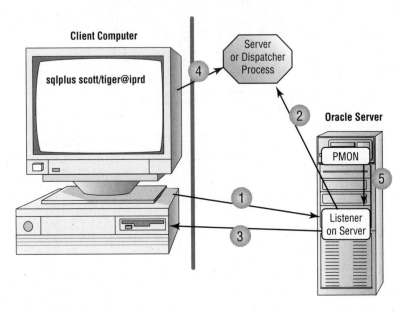

Configuring the Oracle Shared Server

You can configure Oracle Shared Server in a number of ways. You can configure it at the time the database is created, you can use Enterprise Manager to configure it after the database has been created, or you can manually configure it by editing initialization parameters. I'll discuss the parameters necessary to configure Oracle Shared Server. I'll also give examples of how to configure Shared Server at database creation or after the database is created using EM.

Defining the Shared Server Parameters

You configure Oracle Shared Server by adding parameters to the Oracle initialization file. These parameters identify the number and type of dispatchers, the number of shared servers, and the name of the database you want to associate with Shared Server.

One advantage of Oracle 11g is that all the parameters necessary to manage Oracle Shared Server can be changed dynamically. This fulfills one of your primary goals of ensuring the highest degree of database availability possible. Let's take a look at the parameters used to manage Oracle Shared Server.

Using the *DISPATCHERS* Parameter

The DISPATCHERS parameter defines the number of dispatchers that should start when the instance is started. This parameter specifies the number of dispatchers and the type of protocol to which the dispatchers can respond. If you configured your database using the Database Configuration Assistant, this parameter may already be configured.

You can add dispatchers dynamically using the ALTER SYSTEM command.

The DISPATCHERS parameter has a number of optional attributes. Table 11.8 describes several of them. You need to specify only ADDRESS, DESCRIPTION, or PROTOCOL for a DISPATCHERS definition. All the attributes for this parameter can be abbreviated.

TABLE 11.8   Summary of DISPATCHER Attributes

Attribute	Abbreviations	Description
ADDRESS	ADD or ADDR	Specifies the network protocol address of the end point on which the dispatchers listen.
CONNECTIONS	CON or CONN	The maximum number of network connections per dispatcher. The default value varies by operating system.
DESCRIPTION	DES or DESC	The network description of the end point where the dispatcher is listening, including the protocol being listened for.
DISPATCHERS	DIS or DISP	The number of dispatchers to start when the instance is started. The default is 1.
LISTENER	LIS or LIST	The address of the listener to which PMON sends connection information. This attribute needs to be set only when the listener is nonlocal, it uses a port other than 1521, the default port and the LOCAL_LISTENER parameter have not been specified, or the listener is resident on a different network node.
PROTOCOL	PRO or PROT	The network protocol for the dispatcher to listen for. This is the only required attribute.
SESSIONS	SES or SESS	The maximum number of network sessions allowable for this dispatcher. This will vary by operating system but predominantly defaults to 16KB.
SERVICE	SER or SERV	The Oracle net service name that the dispatcher registers with the listener. If it is not supplied, the dispatcher registers with the services listed in the SERVICE_NAMES initialization parameter.
POOL	POO	Provides connection pooling capabilities to provide the ability to handle a larger number of connections.

The two main attributes are DISPATCHERS and PROTOCOL. For example, if you want to configure three TCP/IP dispatchers and two IPC dispatchers, you set the parameter as follows:

```
DISPATCHERS = "(PRO=TCP)(DIS=3)(PRO=IPC)(DIS=2)"
```

You must consider several factors (discussed in the following section) when determining the appropriate setting for the DISPATCHERS parameter.

DETERMINING THE NUMBER OF DISPATCHERS TO START

The number of dispatchers you start depends on your particular configuration. Your operating system may place a limit on the number of connections that one dispatcher can handle. Consult your operating-system documentation to obtain this information.

When determining the number of dispatchers to start, consider the type of work that the database sessions will be performing and the number of concurrent connections that your database will be supporting. The more data-intensive the operations and the larger the number of concurrent connections, the fewer sessions each dispatcher should handle. Generally speaking, a starting point is to allow 50 concurrent sessions for each dispatcher.

You can use the following formula to determine the number of dispatchers to configure initially:

```
Number of Dispatchers = CEIL  (maximum number of concurrent sessions /
   connections per dispatcher)
```

For example, if you have 500 concurrent TCP/IP connections and you want each dispatcher to manage 50 concurrent connections, you need 10 dispatchers. You set your DISPATCHERS parameter as follows:

```
DISPATCHERS = "(PRO=TCP)(DIS=10)"
```

You can determine the number of concurrent connections by querying the V$SESSION view. This view shows you the number of clients currently connected to the Oracle server. Here is an example of the query:

```
SQL> select sid,serial#,username,server,program from v$session
  2  where username is not null;
    SID   SERIAL# USERNAME   SERVER    PROGRAM
--------- --------- ---------- --------- ----------------
       7       13     SCOTT   DEDICATED SQLPLUS.EXE
       8       12     SCOTT   DEDICATED SQLPLUS.EXE
       9        4    SYSTEM   DEDICATED SQLPLUS.EXE
```

In this example, three users are connected to the server. You can ignore any sessions that do not have a username because these would be the Oracle background processes such as PMON and SMON. If you take a sampling of this view over a typical work period, you get an idea of the average number of concurrent connections for your system. You can then use this number as a guide when you establish the starting number of dispatchers.

MANAGING THE NUMBER OF DISPATCHERS

You can start additional dispatchers or remove dispatchers dynamically using the ALTER SYSTEM command. You can start any number of dispatchers up to the MAX_DISPATCHERS setting, which is discussed next. Here is an example of adding three TCP/IP dispatchers to a system configured with two TCP/IP dispatchers:

```
ALTER SYSTEM SET DISPATCHERS="(PRO=TCP)(DIS=5)";
```

Notice that you set the number to the total number of dispatchers you want, not to the number of dispatchers you want to add.

You use additional attributes to the DISPATCHERS parameter to configure connection pooling.

CONFIGURING CONNECTION POOLING WITH THE DISPATCHERS PARAMETER

Connection pooling gives Oracle Shared Server the ability to handle a larger volume of connections by automatically disconnecting idle connections and using the idle connections to service incoming client requests. If the idle connections become active again, the connection to the dispatchers is automatically reestablished. This provides added scalability to Oracle Shared Server. If you manage applications that have a large number of possible client connections but also have a large number of idle connections, you might want to consider configuring this Oracle Shared Server option. Web applications are good candidates for connection pooling because they are typically composed of a large client base with small numbers of concurrent connections.

You enable connection pooling by adding attributes to the DISPATCHERS parameter. The POOL attribute specifies that a dispatcher is allowed to perform connection pooling. Set this attribute to the value ON to enable connection pooling for a dispatcher. You also need to specify the TICK attribute, which sets the number of 10-minute increments of inactivity for a connection to be considered idle.

Here is an example that turns on connection pooling:

```
DISPATCHERS="(PROTOCOL=tcp)(DISPATCHERS=1)(POOL=on)(TICK=1)
  (CONNECTIONS=500)(SESSIONS=1000)"
```

In this example, you want to turn on connection pooling. An idle connection is considered any connection with 10 minutes of inactivity. You want the TCP/IP dispatcher to handle a maximum of 500 concurrent connections and a maximum of 1,000 sessions per dispatcher.

Using the *MAX_DISPATCHERS* Parameter

You set the MAX_DISPATCHERS parameter to the maximum number of dispatchers you anticipate needing for Oracle Shared Server. In Oracle 11g, this parameter can be set dynamically using the ALTER SYSTEM command. The maximum number of processes that a dispatcher can run concurrently is operating system–dependent. Use the following formula to set this parameter:

```
MAX_DISPATCHERS = (maximum number of concurrent sessions/connections
    per dispatcher)
```

Here is an example of the parameter and adjusting the parameter using the ALTER SYSTEM command:

```
ALTER SYSTEM SET MAX_DISPATCHERS=10;
```

In the ALTER SYSTEM example, the MAX_DISPATCHERS parameter is being set to 10. This will be the maximum number of dispatchers that Oracle Shared Server can start simultaneously.

Using the *SHARED_SERVERS* Parameter

The SHARED_SERVERS parameter specifies the minimum number of shared servers to start and retain when the Oracle instance is started. A setting of 0 or no setting means that shared servers will not be used. If dispatchers have been configured, the default value of SHARED_SERVERS is 1. This parameter can be changed dynamically, so even if shared servers are not configured when the instance starts, they can be configured without bringing the Oracle instance down and restarting it.

The number of servers necessary depends on the type of activities your users are performing. Oracle monitors the response queue loads, starts additional shared servers as needed, and removes these shared servers when the servers are no longer needed. Generally, for the types of high-think applications that will be using shared server connections, 25 concurrent connections per shared server should be adequate. If the users are going to require larger result sets or are doing more intensive processing, you'll want to reduce this ratio.

Here is an example of setting the SHARED_SERVERS parameter:

```
SHARED_SERVERS = 3
```

You can start additional Oracle shared servers or reduce the number of Oracle shared servers dynamically using the ALTER SYSTEM command. You can start any number of Oracle shared servers up to the MAX_SERVERS setting. Here is an example of adding three additional Oracle shared servers to a system initially configured with two shared servers:

```
ALTER SYSTEM SET SHARED_SERVERS = 5;
```

Notice that you set the number to the total number of Oracle shared servers you want, not to the number of Oracle shared servers you want to add.

Using the *SHARED_SERVER_SESSIONS* Parameter

The SHARED_SERVER_SESSIONS parameter specifies the total number of Oracle Shared Server sessions that are allowed for the Oracle instance. If the number of Oracle Shared Server client connections reaches this limit, any clients that attempt to connect via an Oracle Shared Server connection will receive the following error message:

```
ERROR:
ORA-00018 maximum number of sessions exceeded
```

Once the number of Oracle Shared Server connections falls below this number, additional Shared Server connections can be established. Using this parameter limits the total number of Shared Server sessions. Dedicated server connections are still allowed if this limit is reached. This parameter can be set in the Oracle initialization file and can be modified dynamically using the ALTER SYSTEM command. Here is an example of how you specify the initialization parameter:

SHARED_SERVER_SESSIONS = 2

Here is an example of how to dynamically modify the parameter using the ALTER SYSTEM command:

ALTER SYSTEM SET SHARED_SERVER_SESSIONS = 5;

Using the *MAX_SHARED_SERVERS* Parameter

The MAX_SHARED_SERVERS parameter sets the maximum number of Oracle shared servers that can be running concurrently. This number can be modified dynamically using the ALTER SYSTEM command. Generally, you should set this parameter to accommodate your heaviest work times. If no value is specified for MAX_SHARED_SERVERS, the number of Oracle shared servers that can be started is unlimited, which is also the default setting.

The V$SHARED_SERVER_MONITOR view can assist in determining the maximum number of Oracle shared servers that have been started since the Oracle instance was started.

Here is an example of the parameter and the ALTER SYSTEM command that will change the value MAX_SHARED_SERVER to 20:

ALTER SYSTEM SET MAX_SHARED_SERVERS = 20;

Using the *CIRCUITS* Parameter

The CIRCUITS parameter manages the total number of virtual circuits allowed for all incoming and outgoing network sessions. There is no default value for this parameter, and it does influence the total size of the SGA at system startup. Generally, you do not manually configure this parameter unless there is a need to specifically limit the number of virtual circuits.

Here is an example of the parameter:

CIRCUITS = 200

You can also use the ALTER SYSTEM command to change the parameter as follows:

ALTER SYSTEM SET CIRCUITS = 300;

Now that you understand the parameters that are needed to use the Oracle Shared Server, you need to know how to configure these parameters.

Managing a Shared Server

If the Oracle Shared Server parameters were configured dynamically using the ALTER SYSTEM command or at database creation, it isn't necessary to stop and start the server. After you configure the Oracle Shared Server parameters, you need to understand how to view information about Oracle Shared Server. Oracle provides a set of dynamic performance views that you can use to gather information about the Oracle Shared Server configuration and the performance of Oracle Shared Server. You can also gather information about Oracle Shared Server connections by using the lsnrctl utility.

In the following sections, I will explain how to display information about Oracle Shared Server connections using the listener utility and discuss the various dynamic performance views used to manage Shared Server.

Displaying Information about Shared Server Connections Using the Listener Utility

You can use the lsnrctl command-line listener utility to display information about the dispatcher processes. Remember from the previous section that the Oracle background process PMON registers dispatcher information with the listener. The listener keeps track of the current connection load for all the dispatchers.

Use the lsnrctl services query to view information about dispatchers. The following example shows a listener listening for two TCP/IP dispatchers:

```
$ lsnrctl services

LSNRCTL for Linux: Version 11.1.0.6.0 - Production on 18-AUG-2008 00:01:47

Copyright (c) 1991, 2007, Oracle.  All rights reserved.

Connecting to (DESCRIPTION=(ADDRESS=(PROTOCOL=TCP)(HOST=localhost.localdomain)
(PORT=1521)))
Services Summary...
Service "11GR11" has 1 instance(s).
  Instance "11GR11", status READY, has 2 handler(s) for this service...
    Handler(s):
      "DEDICATED" established:21 refused:0 state:ready
         LOCAL SERVER
      "D000" established:0 refused:0 current:0 max:1000 state:ready
         DISPATCHER <machine: localhost.localdomain, pid: 3375>
         (ADDRESS=(PROTOCOL=tcp)(HOST=localhost.localdomain)(PORT=30767))
Service "11GR11XDB" has 1 instance(s).
  Instance "11GR11", status READY, has 0 handler(s) for this service...
```

Notice that the listing displays how many connections each dispatcher is managing, the listening location of the dispatcher, and the process ID of the dispatcher. The display also shows how many total client connections were established and how many were refused by each dispatcher since the time it was started. This summary information can be helpful when looking at how well the connections are balanced across all the dispatchers. It also can be helpful to see how many connections were refused. A connection can be refused if a user supplies an invalid user ID or password or reaches the MAX_SHARED_SERVER limit.

Requesting a Dedicated Connection in a Shared Server Environment

You can configure Oracle Shared Server connections and dedicated server connections to connect to a single Oracle server. This is advantageous if you have a mix of database activity. Some types of activities are well suited to Oracle Shared Server connections, and other types of activities are better suited to dedicated connections.

By default, if Oracle Shared Server is configured, a client is connected to a dispatcher unless the client explicitly requests a dedicated connection. As part of the connection descriptor, the client has to send information requesting a dedicated connection. Clients can request dedicated connections if the names resolution method is local naming. You cannot use this option with host naming. If local naming is being used, you can make the necessary changes to the tnsnames.ora file to allow dedicated connections. You can make these changes manually, or you can use Oracle Net Manager.

Configuring Dedicated Connections Manually

If you are using local naming, you can add a parameter to the service-name entry in the tnsnames.ora file. The parameter (SERVER=DEDICATED) is added to the DBA net service name. Here is an example of the entry in the tnsnames.ora file:

```
ORCL =
  (DESCRIPTION =
    (ADDRESS = (PROTOCOL = TCP)(HOST = XYZ01)(PORT = 1521))
    (CONNECT_DATA =
      (SERVICE_NAME = orcl)
      (SERVER = DEDICATED)  # Request a dedicated connection for DBA
    )
  )
```

Configuring Dedicated Connections Using Oracle Net Manager

You can use Oracle Net Manager to modify the connection type for a service. In Windows, Oracle Net Manager is a tool; in Unix, you open Oracle Net Manager by executing netmgr.
After you start Oracle Net Manager, follow these steps:

1. Under Service Naming in the left pane, select the service name you want to modify.

2. Click the Connection Type drop-down list in the Service Identification section, and choose Dedicated Server.

 **Real World Scenario**

Choosing the Appropriate Connection Method Makes a Difference

As a DBA, you've configured Oracle Shared Server and are monitoring the dispatchers and shared server performance daily. The Shared Server environment has been running smoothly for months, but your monitoring starts to indicate that the wait times have increased significantly over the past week. You are also starting to receive complaints from the user community regarding system response time.

You start to investigate whether there have been any significant changes to the hardware, the network, or the database application. You confer with the systems administration and network group and find that no changes have taken place. Then your discussion with the applications group reveals that a new ad hoc reporting utility has been installed and a small number of administrators are starting to use the tool. These users are connecting via Oracle Shared Server and are requesting large data sets via the ad hoc reporting tool.

You suggest to the applications team that the administrators connect to the database using dedicated connections to alleviate the load on the shared servers. After modifying the appropriate network files, you again monitor the shared server wait times and discover that the waits have fallen back in line with what you were seeing prior to the deployment of the ad hoc reporting tool.

Summary

This chapter provided the foundation of knowledge you will need when you are designing, configuring, and managing the Oracle network infrastructure. Oracle Net manages the flow of information from client computers to Oracle servers and forms the foundation of all networked computing in the Oracle environment. Oracle Net provides services that can be divided into five main categories: connectivity, directory services, scalability, security, and accessibility.

Oracle Net provides support to *n*-tier architecture, where middleware components such as application servers are situated between the client and database server.

The listener is the main server-side component in the Oracle Net environment. Listener configuration information is stored in the `listener.ora` file, and you manage the listener using the `lsnrctl` command-line utility. You configure the listener by using the Oracle Net Manager. The Oracle Net Manager provides a graphical interface for creating most of the Oracle Net files you will use for Oracle, including the `listener.ora` file. If multiple listeners are configured, each one has a separate entry in the `listener.ora` file.

Depending on your network environment, the client configuration setups can vary from no work to configuring a number of files on the client. Local naming is the most popular of the names resolution methods, and it uses the `tnsnames.ora` file, which is typically located on each client, to resolve net service names. The client looks up the net service name in the `tnsnames.ora` file and uses the resulting connect descriptor information to connect to the Oracle server.

Shared Server is a configuration of the Oracle server that allows you to support a greater number of connections without the need for additional resources. In this configuration, user connections share processes called *dispatchers*. Dispatchers replace the dedicated server processes in a dedicated server environment. The Oracle Server is also configured with shared server processes that can process the requests of many clients. You add a number of parameters to the `init.ora` file to configure Shared Server. You can add dispatchers and shared servers dynamically after the Oracle server is started. You can add more shared servers and dispatchers up to the maximum value specified.

Exam Essentials

Understand what Oracle Net is and the functionality it provides.   Be able to list the five categories of functionality that Oracle Net provides and explain the functionality that falls into each category. Also understand what functionality the Oracle Shared Server and Oracle Connection Manager options provide. In addition, be able to define Oracle Advanced Security and know when to use it.

Be able to define the main responsibilities of the Oracle listener.   To fully understand the function of the Oracle listener, you should understand how the listener responds to client connection requests. In addition, know the difference between bequeath connections and redirect connections, and know under what circumstances the listener will use each. Also, be able to outline the steps involved in using each of these connection types.

Be able to define the `listener.ora` file and the ways in which the file is created.   To understand the purpose of this file, know its default contents and how to change it using the various Oracle tools. In addition, be able to define the sections of the file and know the definitions of the optional parameters it contains. Also understand the structure of the `listener.ora` file when one or more listeners are configured.

Understand how to use the `lsnrctl` command-line utility.   To start up and shut down the listener, know how to use the `lsnrctl` command-line utility. Be able to explain the command-line options for the `lsnrctl` utility, such as `services`, `status`, and `reload`. When using this utility, also know the options available to you, and be able to define the various `set` commands.

Understand the concepts of static and dynamic service registration.   Be able to define the difference between static service registration and dynamic service registration and know the advantages of using dynamic service registration over static service registration. Also, be aware of the situations in which you have to use static service registration. Lastly, be familiar with the initialization parameters that you will need to set in order to enable dynamic service registration.

Define the Oracle client-side names resolution options.   Be able to define the Oracle client-side names resolution options. Know in which situations to use local naming, Oracle Easy Connect, host naming, and OID.

Define the local naming method.   In addition to knowing the meaning of the local naming method and what it does, understand how to use the Oracle Net Manager to configure this names resolution method. Understand the primary file used in the local naming method, the `tnsnames.ora` file.

Define the contents and structure of the `tnsnames.ora` file. Be able to describe the tnsnames.ora file and the various sections of the file and to explain how the file is used. Understand the contents of the tnsnames.ora file so that you can identify syntax problems with the structure of entries in the file. Be familiar with the common locations of this file and how to set the TNS_ADMIN parameter to override the default location of this and the other client-side network files.

Define and correct client-side errors. Understand the types of client-side connection errors that can occur. Be able to define these errors and understand the situations in which a client might encounter them.

Define Oracle Shared Server. Be able to list the advantages of Shared Server vs. a dedicated server and when it is appropriate to consider both options.

Understand the architecture of Oracle Shared Server. Be able to summarize the steps that a client takes to initiate a connection with a shared server and the processes behind those steps. Understand what happens during client request processing, and outline the steps.

Understand the changes that are made in the SGA and the PGA. Make sure you understand that in a Shared Server environment, many PGA structures are moved in the large pool inside the SGA. This means the SGA will become larger and that the large pool will need to be configured in the init.ora file.

Know how to configure Oracle Shared Server. Be able to define each of the parameters involved in the configuration of Oracle Shared Server. Know what parameters can be dynamically modified and what parameters require the Oracle instance to be restarted to take effect.

Know how to configure clients running in Shared Server mode. Be able to configure clients that need a dedicated connection to Oracle if it is running in Shared Server mode.

Review Questions

1. All of the following are examples of networking architectures except which one?

    A. Client/server.

    B. *n*-tier.

    C. Single-tier.

    D. Two-tier.

    E. All the above are examples of network architectures.

2. Which of the following files must be present on the Oracle server to start a nondefault Oracle listener?

    A. `listener.ora`

    B. `lsnrctl.ora`

    C. `sqlnet.ora`

    D. `tnsnames.ora`

3. Which of the following is the correct way to start a listener called LISTENER?

    A. `lsnrctl startup listener`

    B. `lsnrctl start`

    C. `listener start`

    D. `listener start listener`

4. When dynamic service registration is used, you will not see the service listed in which of the following files where it would normally be located?

    A. `sqlnet.ora`

    B. `tnsnames.ora`

    C. `listener.ora`

    D. None of the above

5. What are the ways in which a client can resolve a net service name? (Choose all that apply.)

    A. Local naming

    B. Host naming

    C. Easy Connect

    D. Oracle Global Naming

    E. All the above

6. Connection Manager provides which of the following?

    A. Multiplexing

    B. Cross-protocol connectivity

    C. Network access control

    D. All the above

7. Which is a requirement for using host naming?

    A. You must use `tnsnames.ora` on the client.

    B. You must be using TCP/IP.

    C. You must have an OID present.

    D. You must have a `sqlnet.ora` file present on the client.

    E. None of the above.

8. Which of the following statements about `tnsnames.ora` is false?

    A. It is used to resolve an Oracle service name.

    B. It can exist on the client.

    C. It is used for local naming.

    D. It does not support TCP/IP.

9. A client receives the following error message:

    `"ORA-12154 TNS:could not resolve the connect identifier specified"`

    Which of the following could be possible causes of the error? (Choose all that apply.)

    A. The listener is not running on the Oracle server.

    B. The user entered an invalid net service name.

    C. The user supplied the correct net service name, but the net service name is misspelled in the `tnsnames.ora` on the client file.

    D. The listener is not configured to listen for this service.

10. What portion of the `tnsnames.ora` file specifies the name or IP address of the server where the listener process is listening?

    A. CONNECT_DATA

    B. PORT

    C. SERVICE_NAME

    D. HOST

11. A client wants to connect to the database `dbprod.com` located on the `dbprod.com` server to a nondefault port using Oracle Easy Connect. Which of the following connect strings is the best choice for the client use?

    A. CONNECT scott/tiger@dbprod.com:1522

    B. CONNECT scott/tiger@1521:dbprod.com/dbprod.com

    C. CONNECT scott/tiger@dbprod.com/1522:dbprod.com

    D. CONNECT scott/tiger@dbprod.com:1521/dbprod.com

    E. CONNECT scott/tiger@dbprod.com:1522/dbprod.com

12. All the following are reasons to configure the server using Shared Server *except* which one?

- **A.** Overall memory utilization is reduced.
- **B.** The system is predominantly used for decision support with large result sets returned.
- **C.** The system is predominantly used for small transactions with many users.
- **D.** The number of idle connections on the server is reduced.

13. Which of the following is true about Shared Server?

- **A.** Dedicated connections cannot be made when Shared Server is configured.
- **B.** It is recommended that index rebuilds be performed when connected via Shared Server.
- **C.** The database can be started when connected via Shared Server.
- **D.** The database cannot be stopped when connected via Shared Server.

14. The administrator wants to allow a user to connect via a dedicated connection into a database configured in Shared Server mode. Which of the following lines accomplishes this?

- **A.** (SERVER=DEDICATED)
- **B.** (CONNECT=DEDICATED)
- **C.** (INSTANCE=DEDICATED)
- **D.** (MULTITHREADED=FALSE)
- **E.** None of the above

15. In which of the following files would you find the Shared Server configuration parameters?

- **A.** listener.ora
- **B.** mts.ora
- **C.** init.ora
- **D.** tnsnames.ora
- **E.** sqlnet.ora

16. What is the first step that the dispatcher performs after it receives a request from the user?

- **A.** Pass the request to a shared server.
- **B.** Place the request in a request queue in the PGA.
- **C.** Place the request in a request queue in the SGA.
- **D.** Process the request.

17. When configured in Shared Server mode, which of the following is contained in the PGA?

- **A.** Cursor state
- **B.** Sort information
- **C.** User session data
- **D.** Stack space
- **E.** None of the above

18. Which of the following is false about request queues?

    A. They reside in the SGA.

    B. They are shared by all the dispatchers.

    C. Each dispatcher has its own request queue.

    D. The shared server processes remove requests from the request queue.

19. What is the process that notifies the listener after a database connection is established?

    A. SMON

    B. DBWR

    C. PMON

    D. LGWR

20. Which command can you execute to get details about the number of sessions connected via Shared Server?

    A. `lsnrctl sessions`

    B. `lsnrctl conn`

    C. `lsnrctl status`

    D. `lsnrctl services`

    E. None of the above

Answers to Review Questions

1.   E. All these are examples of network connectivity configurations. Networking can be as simple as a dumb terminal connected directly to a server via a serial connection. It can also be as complex as an *n*-tier architecture that involves clients, middleware, the Internet, and database servers.

2.   A. The listener is the process that manages incoming connection requests. The `listener` `.ora` file is used to configure the listener and must be configured to start a nondefault listener. The `sqlnet.ora` file is an optional client- and server-side file. The `tnsnames.ora` file is used for doing local naming resolution. There is no such file as `lsnrctl.ora`. You do not need the `listener.ora` file to start a default listener on port 1521.

3.   B. Because the default listener name is LISTENER, simply enter `lsnrctl start`. The name LISTENER is assumed to be the listener to start in this case.

4.   C. When services are dynamically registered with the listener, their information is not present in the `listener.ora` file.

5.   A, B, C. Oracle uses service names in networks in much the same way it uses synonyms in the database. Service names provide location transparency and hide the complexity of connect string information. You can configure Oracle Net to connect in several ways, including host naming, local naming, OID, and Oracle Easy Connect. Oracle Global Naming is not a valid Oracle option.

6.   D. Connection Manager is a middleware solution that provides for the multiplexing of connections, cross-protocol connectivity, and network access control. All the answers describe Connection Manager.

7.   B. Host naming is typically used in small installations that have few Oracle Databases. This is an attractive option when you want to minimize client-side configuration. TCP/IP is a requirement when you use host naming.

8.   D. A `tnsnames.ora` file is configured when you want to use local naming, and it typically exists on the client workstation. It is also used to resolve a service name. The `tnsnames.ora` file used in local naming does indeed support TCP/IP.

9.   B, C. Supplying a net service name that is not contained in the `tnsnames.ora` file can cause this error. Problems with the `tnsnames.ora` file can cause this error too. Listener problems will not cause this error.

10. D. The HOST portion specifies the name of the server to contact. CONNECT_DATA specifies the database service to connect to. The PORT portion specifies the location where the listener is listening on the HOST. Option C, SERVICE_NAME, is the name of the actual database service.

11. A. The correct syntax to use with the Oracle Easy Connect method when you are connecting to a non-URL location is *connect username/password@host:port/service_name*. If the service name and the host are identical, you do not have to include the service name. If the port is any port other than the default port of 1521, it must be specified. Because you want to connect to a nondefault port where the database name and the hostname are the same, the best answer is A.

12. B. Shared Server is a scalability option of Oracle. It provides a way to increase the number of supported user processes while reducing the overall memory usage. This configuration is well suited to high-volume, small-transaction–oriented systems with many users connected. Because users share processes, the number of overall idle processes is also reduced. It is not well suited for large data retrieval type applications such as decision support.

13. D. Users can still request dedicated connections in a Shared Server configuration. Bequeath and dedicated connections are one and the same. The database cannot be stopped or started by the DBA when connected over a Shared Server connection.

14. A. A user must explicitly request a dedicated connection when a server is configured in Shared Server mode. Otherwise, the user gets a Shared Server connection. The correct parameter is (SERVER=DEDICATED).

15. C. The Shared Server configuration parameters exist in the init.ora or the SPFILE file on the Oracle Server machine.

16. C. Once a dispatcher receives a request from the user process, it places the request on the request queue. Remember that in a Shared Server environment, a request can be handled by a shared server process. This is made possible by placing the request and user information in the SGA.

17. D. A small PGA is maintained even though most of the user-specific information is moved to the SGA (specifically called the UGA in the shared pool or the large pool). The only information left in the reduced PGA is stack space.

18. C. Request queues reside in the SGA, and there is one request queue per instance. This is where shared server processes pick up requests that are made by users. Dispatchers have their own response queues, but they *share* a single request queue.

19. C. The PMON process notifies the listener after a client connection is established. This is so that the listener can keep track of the number of connections being serviced by each dispatcher.

20. D. Dispatchers register with listeners so that when a listener redirects a connection to a dispatcher, the listener knows how many active connections the dispatcher is serving. The lsnrctl services command summarizes the number of connections established, connections currently active, and other valuable information regarding Shared Server. The lsnrctl status command summarizes only dispatchers and does not display any details about connections.

Chapter

12

Implementing Security and Auditing

ORACLE DATABASE 11*g*: ADMINISTRATION I EXAM OBJECTIVES COVERED IN THIS CHAPTER:

✓ **Administering User Security**

- Create and manage database user accounts
- Grant and revoke privileges
- Create and manage roles
- Create and manage profiles

✓ **Implementing Oracle Database Security**

- Database security and principle of least privilege
- Work with standard database auditing

One of the key functions of a DBA is to protect your data and database by controlling database access; DBAs must also keep track of key database activities. They must maintain the security, integrity, performance, and availability of their databases. In this chapter, you will learn about managing database security, including how to manage user accounts; implement password expiration and complexity rules; and configure security policies using object, system, and role privileges. To further enhance your ability to monitor and manage database access, you will also learn how to use auditing mechanisms to fine-tune your security policy, identify attempts to access areas of your database that a user is not authorized to visit, and identify intrusion attempts.

Creating and Managing User Accounts

One of the most basic administrative requirements for a DBA is to identify and manage the users. The first step to doing this is to make sure that each user who connects to the Oracle Database 11*g* has an *account*. An account shared between many users is difficult to trouble-shoot and audit and is therefore a poor security practice that should be avoided.

You create a new database account with the CREATE USER statement. When you create a new account, at a minimum the user should have a unique username and authentication method. You can optionally assign additional attributes to the user account with the CREATE USER statement. To change or assign new attributes to an existing user account, use the ALTER USER statement.

The terms *user account*, *account*, *user*, and *schema* are all interchangeable and refer to a database user account. A *schema* is a user who owns objects. All schemas are users, but not all users are schemas.

The following is an example of the CREATE USER statement with all the optional clauses available:

```
SQL> CREATE USER james
  2   IDENTIFIED BY mia0101
  3   DEFAULT TABLESPACE users
  4   TEMPORARY TABLESPACE temp
  5   QUOTA UNLIMITED ON users
  6   PROFILE default
```

```
7  PASSWORD EXPIRE
8  ACCOUNT UNLOCK
SQL> /
```

User created.

SQL>

In the following sections, you'll learn about the clauses presented in the CREATE USER statement.

Configuring Authentication

When a user connects to an Oracle Database instance, the user account must be authenticated. *Authentication* involves validating the identity of the user and confirming that the user has the authority to use the database. Oracle offers three authentication methods for your user accounts: password authentication (the most common), external authentication, and global authentication.

I'll cover each of these authentication methods in the following sections.

Password-Authenticated Users

When a user with password authentication attempts to connect to the database, the database verifies that the username is a valid database account and that the password supplied matches that user's password as stored in the database.

Password-authenticated user accounts are the most common and are sometimes referred to as *database-authenticated* accounts. With a password-authenticated account, the database stores the encrypted password in the data dictionary. For example, to create a password-authenticated user named rajesh with a password of welcome, you execute the following:

```
CREATE USER rajesh IDENTIFIED BY welcome;
```

The keywords IDENTIFIED BY *password* (in this case, *password* is welcome) tell the database that this user account is a password-authenticated account.

> The user password in the Oracle 11*g* database is case sensitive. In earlier releases of Oracle, user passwords were case insensitive.

Externally Authenticated Users

When an externally identified user attempts to connect to the database, the database verifies that the username is a valid database account and trusts that the operating system has performed authentication.

Externally authenticated user accounts do not store or validate a password in the database. These accounts are sometimes referred to as *OPS$ accounts*, because when Oracle introduced them in Oracle 6, the account had to be prefixed with the keyword OPS$. With all releases of the database since then, including Oracle 11g, you can configure this OS_AUTHENT_PREFIX in the initialization file or spfile. For example, to create an externally authenticated user named oracle using the default OS_AUTHENT_PREFIX, you execute the following:

```
CREATE USER ops$oracle IDENTIFIED EXTERNALLY;
```

The keywords IDENTIFIED EXTERNALLY tell the database that this user account is an externally authenticated account. If you log in to the server as user **oracle**, you can log in to the database without providing a username or password, as shown here:

```
$ sqlplus /

SQL*Plus: Release 11.1.0.6.0 - Production on Mon Sep 1 17:07:46 2008
Copyright (c) 1982, 2007, Oracle.  All rights reserved.
Connected to:
Oracle Database 11g Enterprise Edition Release 11.1.0.6.0 - Production
With the Partitioning, OLAP, Data Mining and Real Application Testing options

SQL>
```

Externally authenticated accounts are frequently used for administrative scripts so that a password does not have to be embedded in a human-readable script.

Globally Authenticated Users

When a globally identified user attempts to connect to the database, the database verifies that the username is valid and passes the connection information to the advanced security option for authentication. The advanced security option supports several mechanisms for authentication, including biometrics, X.509 certificates, Kerberos, and RADIUS.

Globally authenticated user accounts do not store or validate a password in the database as a password-authenticated account does. These accounts rely on authentication provided by a service supported through the advanced security option.

The syntax for creating a globally authenticated account depends on the service called, but all use the keywords IDENTIFIED GLOBALLY, which tells the database to engage the advanced security option for authentication. Here is an example:

```
CREATE USER spy_master IDENTIFIED GLOBALLY AS 'CN=spy_master, OU=tier2,
   O=security, C=US';
```

Assigning Tablespaces and Quotas

Every user is assigned a default tablespace. When a user creates tables or indexes, they are created on the tablespace specified by the TABLESPACE clause. If the TABLESPACE clause is not provided, the segments will be created on the user's *default tablespace*. If you execute a CREATE TABLE statement and do not explicitly specify a tablespace, the database uses your default tablespace.

If you do not explicitly assign a default tablespace to a user at the time you create the user, the database assigns the database's default tablespace to the new user account. To assign a default tablespace to either a new user via a CREATE USER statement or an existing user, use the keywords DEFAULT TABLESPACE *tablespace_name*, like this:

```
CREATE USER rajesh IDENTIFIED BY welcome
DEFAULT TABLESPACE users;
```

Or use an ALTER USER statement:

```
ALTER USER rajesh
DEFAULT TABLESPACE users;
```

By default, the database default tablespace is SYSTEM. To change the database default tablespace (the value that users inherit if no default tablespace is provided), use the ALTER DATABASE statement, like this:

```
ALTER DATABASE DEFAULT TABLESPACE users;
```

Assigning a Temporary Tablespace

Every user is assigned a temporary tablespace in which the database stores temporary segments. Temporary segments are created during large sorting operations, such as ORDER BY, GROUP BY, SELECT DISTINCT, MERGE JOIN, or CREATE INDEX.

Temporary segments are also used when a temporary table is used. The database creates and drops temporary segments transparently to the user. Because of the transitory nature of temporary segments, you must use a dedicated tablespace of type TEMPORARY for your user's temporary tablespace setting.

If you do not explicitly assign a temporary tablespace at user creation time, the database assigns the database default temporary tablespace to the new user account. Use the keywords TEMPORARY TABLESPACE *tablespace_name* to assign a temporary tablespace either to a new user via the CREATE USER statement:

```
CREATE USER rajesh IDENTIFIED BY welcome
DEFAULT TABLESPACE users
TEMPORARY TABLESPACE temp;
```

or to an existing user via an ALTER USER statement:

```
ALTER USER rajesh
TEMPORARY TABLESPACE temp;
```

If the SYSTEM tablespace is locally managed at the time of database creation, you're required to provide a non-SYSTEM temporary-type tablespace as the database default temporary tablespace. To change the database default temporary tablespace, use the ALTER DATABASE statement, like this:

```
ALTER DATABASE DEFAULT TEMPORARY TABLESPACE temp;
```

 You can query the data dictionary view DATABASE_PROPERTIES to view the current default tablespace and temporary tablespace assignment for the database.

Assigning Space Quotas

By default, Oracle 11*g* does not allocate any *space quota* in any tablespace when the user is created. To create segments (tables, indexes, and so on) in any tablespace, the user must have space quota granted on the tablespace. Tablespace quotas limit the amount of disk space that a user can consume. The default quota is none. You can assign a space usage quota at the same time you create a user, with the CREATE USER statement:

```
CREATE USER chip IDENTIFIED BY "Seek!r3t" QUOTA 100M ON USERS;
```

Or you can assign it after the user has been created with the ALTER USER statement:

```
ALTER USER bart QUOTA UNLIMITED ON USERS;
```

The special keyword UNLIMITED tells the database that the user should not have a preset limit on the amount of space that their objects can consume.

The user can create objects in any tablespace if the user has the UNLIMITED TABLESPACE system privilege. You will learn system privileges later in the chapter in the section "Granting System Privileges."

In 11*g* Release 2, a new feature called deferred segment creation is introduced. So when a new table is created, no space quota is needed as the segment is created only when the first row is inserted. This means that a quota of zero does not automatically prevent the creation of tables in a schema as it was in previous releases.

Assigning a Profile and Account Settings

In addition to default and temporary tablespaces, every user is assigned a profile. A profile serves two purposes:

- It can limit the resource usage of some resources.
- It can enforce password-management rules.

The default profile is appropriately named default. To explicitly assign a profile to a user, include the keywords PROFILE *profile_name* in the CREATE USER or ALTER USER statement. For example, to assign the profile named resource_profile to the new user jiang as well as to the existing user hamish, execute the following SQL:

```
CREATE USER jiang IDENTIFIED BY "kneehow.ma"
DEFAULT TABLESPACE users
TEMPORARY TABLESPACE temp
PROFILE resource_profile;


ALTER USER hamish
PROFILE resource_profile;
```

If you want users to change the password the first time they log in to the database, you can set the PASSWORD EXPIRE option. Each user will be forced to change the password at the first login. Here is an example of creating the user with an expired password:

```
SQL> CREATE USER shelly IDENTIFIED BY welcome
  2  PASSWORD EXPIRE;
```

```
User created.

SQL> GRANT CONNECT TO shelly;
SQL> connect shelly/welcome
ERROR:
ORA-28001: the password has expired

Changing password for shelly
New password:
Retype new password:
SQL> SHOW user
SQL> USER is "SHELLY"
```

By default, the user account is unlocked at creation. To lock the user account, use the ACCOUNT LOCK option.

To create and manage user accounts using EM Database Control, click the Server tab, and choose Users under the Security heading, as shown in Figure 12.1.

FIGURE 12.1   Database Control's server-administration screen

Click the Users link to get a listing of all users in the database. Clicking the Create button on this screen opens the screen to create the user, as shown in Figure 12.2.

FIGURE 12.2 Grid Control's Create User screen

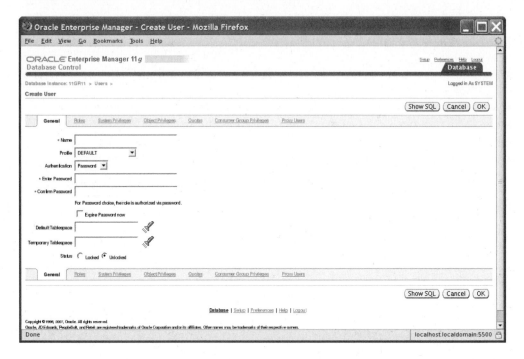

Removing a User from the Database

You use the DROP USER statement to remove a user from the database. You can optionally include the keyword CASCADE to tell the database to recursively drop all objects owned by that user.

To drop both user rajesh and all the objects he owns, execute the following:

```
DROP USER rajesh CASCADE;
```

Dropping a user implicitly drops any object privileges (but not role or system privileges) in which the user was the grantor. The data dictionary records both grantee and grantor for object privileges, but only the grantee is recorded for role and system privileges.

Managing Default User Accounts

The SYS and SYSTEM user accounts are always created with an Oracle 11*g* database. Additionally, the SYSMAN and DBSNMP accounts are created together with a database via the Database Configuration Assistant (DBCA).

Other special accounts can be created to support installed products, such as Recovery Manager (RMAN) or XMLDB. When created via the DBCA, these special accounts are locked and expired, leaving only SYS, SYSTEM, SYSMAN, and DBSNMP open. The SYS and SYSTEM accounts are the data dictionary owner and an administrative account, respectively. SYSMAN and DBSNMP are used by Enterprise Manager.

If your database is created via any means other than the DBCA, ensure that the accounts are locked and expired and that the default passwords are changed. You expire and lock an account using the ALTER USER statement like this:

```
ALTER USER mdsys PASSWORD EXPIRE ACCOUNT LOCK;
```

Depending on the functionality installed in your Oracle 11*g* database, you may need to lock and expire several default user accounts. Your database-created user accounts may include the following:

- ANONYMOUS
- APEX_PUBLIC_USER
- BI
- CTXSYS
- DBSNMP
- DIP
- EXFSYS
- FLOWS_030000
- FLOWS_FILES
- HR
- IX
- MDDATA
- MDSYS
- MGMT_VIEW
- OE
- OLAPSYS
- ORACLE_OCM
- ORDPLUGINS
- ORDSYS
- OUTLN
- OWBSYS
- PM
- SCOTT
- SH
- SI_INFORMTN_SCHEMA
- SPATIAL_CSW_ADMIN_USR
- SPATIAL_WFS_ADMIN_USR
- SYS
- SYSMAN
- SYSTEM
- TSMSYS
- WKPROXY
- WKSYS
- WK_TEST
- WMSYS
- XDB
- XS$NULL

Granting and Revoking Privileges

Privileges allow a user to access database objects or execute stored programs that are owned by another user. Privileges also enable a user to perform system-level operations, such as connecting to the database, creating a table, or altering the database.

Privileges are assigned to a user, to the special user PUBLIC, or to a role with the GRANT statement and can be rescinded with the REVOKE statement.

The Oracle 11*g* database has three types of privileges:

Object privileges   These include permissions on schema objects such as tables, views, sequences, procedures, and packages. To use a schema object owned by another user, you need privileges on that object.

System privileges   These include permissions on database-level operations, such as connecting to the database, creating users, altering the database, consuming unlimited amounts of tablespace, and querying all tables in the database.

Role privileges   These include permissions granted to a user by way of a role. A *role* is a named group of privileges. Object and system privileges can be granted to a role.

I'll cover each of these privileges and how to grant them in the following sections.

Granting Object Privileges

Object privileges bestow upon the grantee the permission to use a schema object owned by another user in a particular way. As you'll see, there are several types of object privileges, some of which apply only to certain schema objects. For example, the INDEX privilege applies only to tables, and the SELECT privilege applies to tables, views, and sequences.

The following object privileges can be granted individually, can be granted grouped in a list, or can be granted with the keyword ALL to implicitly grant all available object privileges for a particular schema object.

 Be careful when using ALL. It may implicitly grant powerful privileges.

Table Object Privileges

Oracle 11*g* provides several object privileges for tables. These privileges give the table owner considerable flexibility in controlling how schema objects are used and by whom.

Commonly Granted Privileges

The following privileges are commonly granted, and you should know them well:

SELECT   This is the most commonly used privilege for tables. With this privilege, the table owner permits the grantee to query the specified table with a SELECT statement.

INSERT This permits the grantee to create new rows in the specified table with an INSERT statement.

UPDATE This permits the grantee to modify existing rows in the specified table with an UPDATE statement.

DELETE This permits the grantee to remove rows from the specified table with a DELETE statement.

Powerful Administrative Privileges on Tables

The following are powerful administrative privileges on tables; grant them cautiously:

ALTER This permits the grantee to execute an ALTER TABLE statement on the specified table. This privilege can be used to add, modify, or rename columns in the table, to move the table to another tablespace, or even to rename the specified table.

DEBUG This permits the grantee to access, via a debugger, the PL/SQL code in any triggers on the specified table.

INDEX This permits the grantee to create new indexes on the table. These new indexes will be owned by a different user than the table, which is an unusual practice. In most cases, the indexes on a table are owned by the same user who owns the table.

REFERENCES This permits the grantee to create foreign key constraints that reference the specified table.

View Object Privileges

Oracle 11g offers a smaller set of object privileges for views than it does for tables:

SELECT This is the most commonly used privilege for views. With this privilege, the view owner permits the grantee to query the view.

INSERT This permits the grantee to execute an INSERT statement on the specified view to create new rows.

UPDATE This permits the grantee to modify existing rows in the specified view with an UPDATE statement.

DELETE This permits the grantee to execute a DELETE statement on the specified view to remove rows.

DEBUG This permits the grantee to access, via a debugger, the PL/SQL code in the body of any trigger on this view.

REFERENCES This permits the grantee to create foreign key constraints on the specified view.

Sequence Object Privileges

Oracle 11g provides only two object privileges for sequences:

SELECT This permits the grantee to access the current and next values (CURRVAL and NEXTVAL) of the specified sequence.

ALTER   This permits the grantee to change the attributes of the specified sequence with an ALTER statement.

Stored Functions, Procedures, Packages, and Java Object Privileges

Oracle 11*g* provides only two object privileges for stored PL/SQL programs:

DEBUG   This permits the grantee to access, via a debugger, all the public and private variables and types declared in the specified program. If the specified object is a package, both the specification and the body are accessible to the grantee. The grantee can also use a debugger to place breakpoints in the specified program.

EXECUTE   This permits the grantee to execute the specified program. If the specified object is a package, any program, variable, type, cursor, or record declared in the package specification is accessible to the grantee.

How to Grant Privileges

You use the GRANT statement to confer object privileges on either a user or a role. The optional keywords WITH GRANT OPTION additionally allow the grantee to confer these privileges on other users and roles. For example, to give SELECT, INSERT, UPDATE, and DELETE privileges on the table CUSTOMERS to the role SALES_MANAGER, execute the following statement while connected as the owner of table CUSTOMERS:

```
GRANT SELECT,INSERT,UPDATE,DELETE ON customers TO sales_manager;
```

If you grant privileges to the special user PUBLIC, you make them available to all current and future database users. For example, to give all database users the SELECT privilege on table CUSTOMERS, execute the following while connected as the owner of the table:

```
GRANT SELECT ON customers TO public;
```

When you extend a privilege to another user or role, you can also extend the ability for that grantee to turn around and grant the privilege to others. To extend this extra option, include the keywords WITH GRANT OPTION in the GRANT statement. For example, to give the SELECT privilege on table SALES.CUSTOMERS to the user SALES_ADMIN together with the permission for SALES_ADMIN to grant the SELECT privilege to others, execute the following:

```
GRANT SELECT ON sales.customers TO sales_admin WITH GRANT OPTION;
```

You can include the WITH GRANT OPTION keywords only when the grantee is a user or the special account PUBLIC. You cannot use WITH GRANT OPTION when the grantee is a role.

If you grant an object privilege using the WITH GRANT OPTION keywords and later revoke that privilege, the revoke cascades, and the privileges created by the grantee are also revoked. For example, Mary grants SELECT privileges on her table clients to Zachary with the WITH GRANT OPTION keywords. Zachary then creates a view based on the table mary.clients and grants the SELECT privilege on it to Rex. If Mary revokes the SELECT privilege from Zachary, the revoke cascades and removes the privilege from Rex. See Figure 12.3 for an illustration of this example.

FIGURE 12.3   The revoking of object privilege cascades.

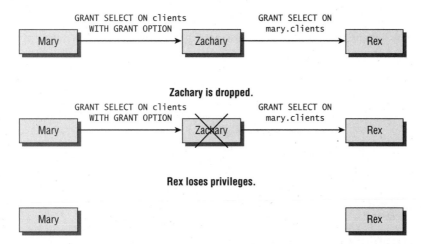

Zachary is dropped.

Rex loses privileges.

With object privileges, the database records both the grantor and the grantee. Therefore, a grantee can obtain a privilege from more than one grantor. When this multiple grant of the same privilege occurs, revoking one of these grants does not remove the privilege. To remove the privilege, all grants must be revoked, as shown in Figure 12.4.

FIGURE 12.4   The revoking of an object privilege with multiple grant paths

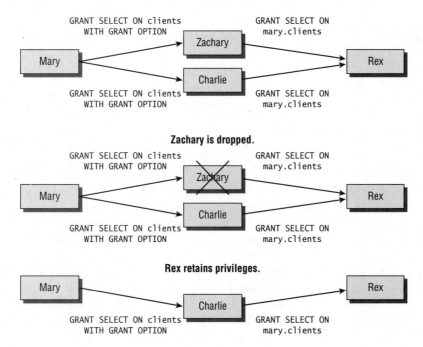

Zachary is dropped.

Rex retains privileges.

Continuing with our example, Mary has granted SELECT on her table clients to Zachary using WITH GRANT OPTION. Zachary has then granted SELECT on mary.clients to Rex. Mary has also granted SELECT on her table clients to Charlie, who has in turn granted to Rex. Rex now has the SELECT privilege from more than one grantee. If Zachary leaves and his account is dropped, the privilege from Charlie remains and Rex can still select from mary.clients.

The data dictionary view DBA_TAB_PRIVS lists all the object privileges granted in the database. It shows the grantor and the grantee along with the privilege.

Granting System Privileges

In general, *system privileges* permit the grantee to execute Data Definition Language (DDL) statements—such as CREATE, ALTER, and DROP—or Data Manipulation Language (DML) statements system-wide. Oracle 11*g* has more than 200 system privileges, all of which are listed in the data dictionary view SYSTEM_PRIVILEGE_MAP.

You will not be required to know all these privileges for the certification exam (thank goodness!), because many are for features that fall outside the scope of the exam. Pay attention to the database-related and table-related system privileges.

You should be familiar with the following groups.

Database

Oracle 11*g* gives you four database-oriented system privileges:

ALTER DATABASE   This permits the grantee to execute the ALTER DATABASE statement.

ALTER SYSTEM   This permits the grantee to execute the ALTER SYSTEM statement.

AUDIT SYSTEM   This permits the grantee to execute AUDIT and NOAUDIT statements to perform statement auditing.

AUDIT ANY   This permits the grantee to execute AUDIT and NOAUDIT statements to perform object auditing on objects in any schema.

Debugging

Oracle 11*g* gives you two debugging-oriented system privileges.

DEBUG CONNECT SESSION   This permits the grantee to connect the current session to a debugger.

DEBUG ANY PROCEDURE   This permits the grantee to debug all PL/SQL and Java code in the database. This system privilege is equivalent to granting the object privilege DEBUG for every applicable object in the database.

Indexes

Oracle 11*g* gives you three system privileges related to indexes:

CREATE ANY INDEX   This permits the grantee to create an index in any schema.

ALTER ANY INDEX   This permits the grantee to alter indexes in any schema.

DROP ANY INDEX   This permits the grantee to drop indexes from any schema.

Job Scheduler

Oracle 11*g* gives you several system privileges related to the job scheduler:

CREATE JOB   This permits the grantee to create jobs, programs, or schedules in their own schema.

CREATE ANY JOB   This permits the grantee to create jobs, programs, or schedules in any schema.

WARNING   The CREATE ANY JOB privilege gives the grantee the ability to execute programs using any other user's credentials. Grant it cautiously.

EXECUTE ANY PROGRAM   This permits the grantee to use any program in a job in their own schema.

EXECUTE ANY CLASS   This permits the grantee to specify any job class for jobs in their own schema.

MANAGE SCHEDULER   This permits the grantee to create, alter, or delete any job class, window, or window group.

Procedures

Oracle 11*g* gives you several system privileges related to stored procedures:

CREATE PROCEDURE   This permits the grantee to create procedures in their own schema.

CREATE ANY PROCEDURE   This permits the grantee to create procedures in any schema.

ALTER ANY PROCEDURE   This permits the grantee to recompile any procedure in the database.

DROP ANY PROCEDURE   This permits the grantee to remove procedures from any schema.

EXECUTE ANY PROCEDURE   This permits the grantee to run any procedure in any schema.

Profiles

Oracle 11*g* gives you three system privileges related to user profiles:

CREATE PROFILE   This permits the grantee to create profiles. Causing a profile to be used requires an ALTER USER statement (which requires the ALTER USER privilege).

ALTER PROFILE   This permits the grantee to modify existing profiles.

DROP PROFILE   This permits the grantee to drop profiles from the database.

Roles

Oracle 11*g* gives you several system privileges related to roles. Because roles deal with security, some of these privileges are very powerful.

CREATE ROLE   This permits the grantee to create new roles.

ALTER ANY ROLE   This permits the grantee to change the password for any role in the database.

DROP ANY ROLE   This permits the grantee to remove any role from the database.

GRANT ANY ROLE   This permits the grantee to grant any role to any user or revoke any role from any user or role.

> The GRANT ANY ROLE privilege permits grantees to assign or rescind powerful administrative roles, such as SCHEDULER_ADMIN and IMP_FULL_DATABASE, to or from any user, including themselves or other DBAs. Grant it cautiously.

Sequences

Oracle 11*g* gives you several system privileges to manage sequences:

CREATE SEQUENCE   This permits the grantee to create new sequences in their own schema.

CREATE ANY SEQUENCE   This permits the grantee to create new sequences in any schema.

ALTER ANY SEQUENCE   This permits the grantee to change the characteristics of any sequence in the database.

DROP ANY SEQUENCE   This permits the grantee to remove any sequence from any schema in the database.

SELECT ANY SEQUENCE   This permits the grantee to select from any sequence.

Sessions

Oracle 11*g* gives you four session-oriented system privileges:

CREATE SESSION This permits the grantee to connect to the database. This privilege is required for user accounts but may be undesirable for application owner accounts.

ALTER SESSION This permits the grantee to execute ALTER SESSION statements.

ALTER RESOURCE COST This permits the grantee to change the way that Oracle calculates resource cost for resource restrictions in a profile.

> For more information on managing resource consumption, see the section "Controlling Resource Usage by Users" later in this chapter.

RESTRICTED SESSION This permits the grantee to connect when the database has been opened in RESTRICTED SESSION mode, typically for administrative purposes. User accounts should not normally be granted this privilege.

Synonyms

Oracle 11*g* gives you several system privileges related to synonyms:

CREATE SYNONYM This permits the grantee to create new synonyms in their own schema.

CREATE ANY SYNONYM This permits the grantee to create new synonyms in any schema.

CREATE PUBLIC SYNONYM This permits the grantee to create new public synonyms, which are accessible to all users in the database.

DROP ANY SYNONYM This permits the grantee to remove any synonyms in any schema.

DROP PUBLIC SYNONYM This permits the grantee to remove any public synonym from the database.

Tables

Oracle 11*g* gives you several system privileges for managing tables:

CREATE TABLE This permits the grantee to create new tables in their own schema.

CREATE ANY TABLE This permits the grantee to create new tables in any schema.

ALTER ANY TABLE This permits the grantee to alter existing tables in any schema.

DROP ANY TABLE This permits the grantee to drop tables from any schema.

COMMENT ANY TABLE This permits the grantee to assign table or column comments to any table or view in any schema.

SELECT ANY TABLE This permits the grantee to query any table or view in any schema.

INSERT ANY TABLE   This permits the grantee to insert new rows into any table in any schema.

UPDATE ANY TABLE   This permits the grantee to modify rows in any table in any schema.

DELETE ANY TABLE   This permits the grantee to delete rows from tables in any schema.

LOCK ANY TABLE   This permits the grantee to execute a LOCK TABLE statement to explicitly lock a table in any schema.

FLASHBACK ANY TABLE   This permits the grantee to execute a SQL flashback query, using the AS OF syntax, on any table or view in any schema.

See Chapter 15, "Implementing Database Backups," for more information on using flashback queries.

Tablespaces

Oracle 11g gives you four system privileges to control tablespace management:

CREATE TABLESPACE   This permits the grantee to create new tablespaces.

ALTER TABLESPACE   This permits the grantee to alter existing tablespaces with the ALTER TABLESPACE statement.

DROP TABLESPACE   This permits the grantee to delete tablespaces from the database.

MANAGE TABLESPACE   This permits the grantee to alter a tablespace ONLINE, OFFLINE, BEGIN BACKUP, or END BACKUP.`

UNLIMITED TABLESPACE   This permits the grantee to consume unlimited disk quota in any tablespace. This system privilege is equivalent to granting unlimited quota in each tablespace to the specified grantee.

Triggers

Oracle 11g gives you several system privileges to control trigger management:

CREATE TRIGGER   This permits the grantee to create new triggers on tables in their own schema.

CREATE ANY TRIGGER   This permits the grantee to create new triggers on tables in any schema.

ALTER ANY TRIGGER   This permits the grantee to enable, disable, or compile existing triggers on tables in any schema.

DROP ANY TRIGGER   This permits the grantee to remove triggers from tables in any schema.

ADMINISTER DATABASE TRIGGER   This permits the grantee to create new ON DATABASE triggers. The grantee must also have the CREATE TRIGGER or CREATE ANY TRIGGER privilege before they can create an ON DATABASE trigger.

Users

Oracle 11*g* gives you several system privileges to control who can manage user accounts:

CREATE USER   This permits the grantee to create new database users.

ALTER USER   This permits the grantee to change the authentication method or password and assign quotas, temporary tablespaces, default tablespaces, or profiles for any user in the database. All users can change their own password without this privilege.

> The ALTER USER privilege allows the grantee to change the authentication method or password for any user (and also change it back). This makes it possible for the grantee to masquerade as another user. Grant this privilege cautiously.

DROP USER   This permits the grantee to remove users together with any objects they own from a database.

Views

Oracle 11*g* gives you several system privileges to manage views. Note that some of these privileges include the word TABLE and not VIEW. These privileges apply to either tables or views.

CREATE VIEW   This permits the grantee to create new views in their own schema.

CREATE ANY VIEW   This permits the grantee to create new views in any schema.

DROP ANY VIEW   This permits the grantee to remove views from any schema.

COMMENT ANY TABLE   This permits the grantee to assign table or column comments to any table or view in any schema.

FLASHBACK ANY TABLE   This permits the grantee to execute a SQL flashback query, using the AS OF syntax, on any table or view in any schema.

Others

Oracle 11*g* gives you several system privileges for managing your database that don't fit into the other categories. These privileges include powerful administrative capabilities and should not be granted lightly.

ANALYZE ANY   This permits the grantee to execute an ANALYZE statement on tables, indexes, or clusters in any schema.

GRANT ANY OBJECT PRIVILEGE   This permits the grantee to assign object privileges on any object in any schema.

GRANT ANY PRIVILEGE   This permits the grantee to assign any system privilege to other users or roles.

GRANT ANY ROLE   This permits the grantee to assign any role to other users or roles. This privilege also gives the grantee permission to revoke any role.

SELECT ANY DICTIONARY   This permits the grantee to select from the SYS-owned data dictionary tables, such as TAB$ or SYSAUTH$.

SYSDBA   The most powerful system privilege, this permits the grantee to create, alter, start up, or shut down databases; enable ARCHIVELOG and NOARCHIVELOG mode; recover a database; and create an spfile; in addition to having all the system privileges the database has to offer, including RESTRICTED SESSION.

SYSOPER   Only slightly less powerful than SYSDBA, this privilege permits the grantee to start up, shut down, alter, mount, back up, and recover a database. The grantee can create or alter an spfile and enter restricted session mode.

SYSASM   Similar to the SYSDBA privilege, this gives the grantee privilege to manage an ASM instance. This privilege is new to Oracle 11*g*.

How to Grant System Privileges

As with object privileges, you use the GRANT statement to confer system privileges on either a user or a role. Unlike object privileges, the optional keywords WITH ADMIN OPTION are required to additionally allow the grantee to confer these privileges on other users and roles. For example, to give the CREATE USER, ALTER USER, and DROP USER privileges to the role APPL_DBA, you execute the following statement:

```
GRANT create user, alter user, drop user TO appl_dba;
```

System and role privileges require the wording WITH ADMIN OPTION; object privileges require the wording WITH GRANT OPTION. Because the function is so similar but the syntax is different, be sure you know when to use ADMIN and when to use GRANT—a question involving this subtle difference may appear on the exam.

As with object privileges, you can grant system privileges to the special user PUBLIC. Granting privileges to PUBLIC allows anyone with a database account and the CONNECT privilege to exercise this privilege. In general, because system privileges are more powerful than object privileges, take care when granting a system privilege to PUBLIC. For example, to give all current and future database users the FLASHBACK ANY TABLE privilege, execute the following:

```
GRANT flashback any table TO public;
```

To give the INDEX ANY TABLE privilege to the role APPL_DBA together with the permission to allow anyone with the role APPL_DBA to grant this privilege to others, execute the following:

```
GRANT index any table TO appl_dba WITH ADMIN OPTION;
```

If you grant a system privilege WITH ADMIN OPTION and later revoke that privilege, the privileges created by the grantee will not be revoked. Unlike object privileges, the revocation of system privileges does not cascade. Think of it this way: WITH GRANT OPTION includes the keyword GRANT and so implies that a revoke cascades, but WITH ADMIN OPTION does not mention GRANT, so a revoke has no effect. Here's an example. Mary grants the SELECT ANY TABLE privilege to new DBA Zachary with ADMIN OPTION. Zachary then grants this privilege to Rex. Later, Zachary gets promoted and leaves the department, so Mary revokes the SELECT ANY TABLE privilege from Zachary. Rex's privilege remains unaffected. You can see this in Figure 12.5.

FIGURE 12.5   The revoking of system privileges

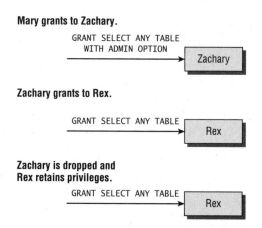

The database records only the privilege granted, not who granted it.

This behavior differs from object privileges, because the database does not record both grantor and grantee for system privileges—only the grantee is recorded.

 The data dictionary view DBA_SYS_PRIVS lists all the system privileges granted in the database.

Role Privileges

Role privileges confer on the grantee a group of system, object, and other role privileges. Users who have been granted a role inherit the privileges that have been granted to that role. Roles can be password protected, so users may have a role granted to them yet not be able to use that role in all database sessions. I'll cover roles and role privileges—including how to grant them—in the following section, "Creating and Managing Roles."

Creating and Managing Roles

A *role* is a tool for administering privileges. Privileges can be granted to a role, and then that role can be granted to other roles and users. Users can thus inherit privileges via roles. Roles serve no other purpose than to administer privileges.

To create a role, use the CREATE ROLE statement. You can optionally include an IDENTIFIED BY clause that requires users to authenticate themselves before enabling the role. Roles requiring authentication are typically used inside an application, where a user's activities are controlled by the application. To create the role APPL_DBA, execute the following:

```
CREATE ROLE appl_dba;
```

To enable a role, execute a SET ROLE statement, like this:

```
SET ROLE appl_dba IDENTIFIED BY seekwrit;
```

The data dictionary view DBA_ROLE_PRIVS lists all the role privileges granted in the database.

Granting Role Privileges

As with object and system privileges, you use the GRANT statement to confer role privileges on either a user or another role. Also, like system privileges, the optional keywords WITH ADMIN OPTION allow the grantee to confer these privileges on other users and roles. For example, to give the OEM_MONITOR role to user charlie, execute the following:

```
GRANT oem_monitor TO charlie;
```

As with the other privileges, you can grant role privileges to the special user PUBLIC. Granting privileges to PUBLIC allows anyone with a database account to exercise this privilege. For example, to give all current and future database users use of the plustrace role, execute the following:

```
GRANT plustrace TO public;
```

To give the INDEX ANY TABLE privilege to the role APPL_DBA together with the permission to allow anyone with the role APPL_DBA to grant this privilege to others, execute the following:

```
GRANT index any table TO appl_dba WITH ADMIN OPTION;
```

When it comes to granting a role WITH ADMIN OPTION, roles behave like system privileges, and subsequent revocations do not cascade.

If the role granted to a user is not the default role, the user must enable the role in the session to be able to use the role. In the following sections, you will learn to work with roles in a session.

Enabling Roles

Roles can be enabled—or disabled, for that matter—selectively in each database session. If you have two concurrent sessions, the roles in effect for each session can be different.

Use the SET ROLE *role_list* statement to enable one or more roles. *role_list* is a comma-delimited list of roles to enable. This list can include the keyword ALL, which enables all the roles granted to the user. You can optionally append a list of roles to exclude from the ALL list by specifying ALL EXCEPT *exclusion_list*.

If a role has a password associated with it, the keywords IDENTIFIED BY *password* must immediately follow the role name in the *role_list*.

For example, to enable the password-protected role HR_ADMIN, together with the unprotected role EMPLOYEE, execute the following:

```
SET ROLE hr_admin IDENTIFIED BY "my!seekrit", employee;
```

To enable all roles except HR_ADMIN, run this:

```
SET ROLE ALL EXCEPT hr_admin;
```

You can enable as many roles as have been granted to you, up to the MAX_ENABLED_ROLES initialization parameter.

Identifying Enabled Roles

The roles that are enabled in your session are listed in the data dictionary view SESSION_ROLES. To identify these enabled roles for your session, run the following:

```
SELECT role FROM session_roles;
```

These roles include the roles that have been granted to you, the roles that have been granted to the special user PUBLIC, and the roles that you have inherited by way of other roles. To identify the roles granted to either user or the special user PUBLIC, run the following:

```
SELECT granted_role FROM user_role_privs
WHERE username IN (USER, 'PUBLIC');
```

The role DBA includes the role SCHEDULER_ADMIN, which in turn has system privileges (such as CREATE ANY JOB). A user who has been granted the DBA role inherits the SCHEDULER_ADMIN role indirectly. To identify the roles that are both enabled in your session and granted directly to you or PUBLIC but not those roles that you inherited, run this:

```
SELECT role FROM session_roles
INTERSECT
SELECT granted_role FROM user_role_privs
WHERE username IN (USER, 'PUBLIC');
```

In your sessions, you can disable only these directly granted and public roles.

Disabling Roles

Roles can be disabled in a database session either en masse or by exception. Use the SET ROLE NONE statement to disable all roles. Use the SET ROLE ALL EXCEPT *role_list* statement to enable all roles except those in the comma-delimited *role_list*.

There is no way to selectively disable a single role. Also, you cannot disable roles that you inherit by way of another role without disabling the parent role. For example, if you have been granted the DBA, RESOURCE, and CONNECT roles, you inherit several roles through the DBA role when it is enabled. If you want to disable the SCHEDULER_ADMIN role you inherited through the DBA role, you cannot do that. The options you have are that you can disable the DBA role or you can create a new role similar to the DBA role without the SCHEDULER_ADMIN role and use that role.

Setting Default Roles

Roles that are enabled by default when you log on are called *default roles*. You do not need to specify a password for default roles and do not have to execute a SET ROLE statement to enable a default role. Change the default roles for a user account with an ALTER USER DEFAULT ROLE *role_list* statement. The *role_list* can include the keywords ALL, NONE, and EXCEPT, in the same manner as with a SET ROLE statement.

Including a password-protected role in the *role_list* defeats the purpose of password protecting the role because it is automatically enabled without the password. When you create a role, you are implicitly granted that role with the admin option, and it is configured as a default role for your account.

For example, to create the role EMPLOYEE, grant it to user scott, and configure all of scott's roles except PLUSTRACE as default roles, run the following:

```
CREATE ROLE employee;
GRANT employee TO scott;
ALTER USER scott DEFAULT ROLE ALL EXCEPT plustrace;
```

Because the creator of a role automatically has that role assigned as a default role, administrative users (such as SYS or SYSTEM) who create many roles may need to alter their default role list. If you attempt to log on with more default roles than allowed by the MAX_ENABLED_ROLES initialization parameter, you will raise an exception, and your logon will fail.

 Real World Scenario

A Password-Protected Role

Lucinda works in HR and needs to be able to modify an employee's salary after they have a review and their raise is approved. The HR application ensures that the raise is approved and falls within corporate guidelines. Although Lucinda needs to be able to change employee salaries, she should be allowed to do so only from within the HR application, because it ensures that business rules are followed.

You wisely choose to use a password-protected role to satisfy these requirements. Update privilege on the salary table is granted to the password-protected role salary_admin. Lucinda is then granted the salary_admin role, but she is not told the password for it. The HR application has the password encoded within it, so when Lucinda runs the HR application, unknown to her, a SET ROLE salary_admin IDENTIFY BY *password* statement is executed, enabling the role and allowing her to change the salary.

If Lucinda tries to execute an UPDATE statement on the salary table from SQL*Plus, she will get an insufficient privileges error.

Default Database Roles

When you create a new Oracle 11g database, Oracle creates several roles in the database based on the options you chose at the database creation. The following are few of the important roles that are created automatically during database creation:

CONNECT   This role has only one privilege, CREATE SESSION.

RESOURCE   This role has the privileges required to create common objects in the user's schema.

DBA   This is the most powerful role in the database. Only database administrators should be given this role. This role has all the system privileges and several administrative privileges.

SELECT_CATALOG_ROLE   This role gives the user access to query the data dictionary views.

EXECUTE_CATALOG_ROLE   This role gives the user privileges to execute the packages and procedures in the data dictionary.

DELETE_CATALOG_ROLE   This role gives the user the ability to delete records from the system audit table (SYS.AUD$).

To list all the roles defined in the database, query the data dictionary view DBA_ROLES. To view the system privileges granted to a role, query the DBA_SYS_PRIVS dictionary view. For example, the following query lists the system privileges granted to the RESOURCE role:

```
SQL> SELECT grantee, privilege, admin_option
  2  FROM dba_sys_privs
  3  WHERE grantee = 'RESOURCE'
SQL> /


GRANTEE              PRIVILEGE             ADM
-------------------- --------------------- ---
RESOURCE             CREATE TRIGGER        NO
RESOURCE             CREATE SEQUENCE       NO
RESOURCE             CREATE TYPE           NO
RESOURCE             CREATE PROCEDURE      NO
RESOURCE             CREATE CLUSTER        NO
RESOURCE             CREATE OPERATOR       NO
RESOURCE             CREATE INDEXTYPE      NO
RESOURCE             CREATE TABLE          NO

8 rows selected.
SQL>
```

Applying the Principle of Least Privilege

The principle of least privilege states that each user should be given only the minimal privileges needed to perform their job. This principle is a central tenet to the *initially closed philosophy* whereby all access is initially closed or unavailable and access is opened on a need-to-know basis. Highly secure environments typically operate under an initially closed philosophy. The contrasting philosophy is an initially open philosophy, whereby all access is by default open to all users and only sensitive areas are closed. Academic or learning environments typically operate under an initially open philosophy.

Many IT organizations want the most secure policies for production systems, which calls for the initially closed approach to security. To support the need for administrators and programmers to quickly learn new technology, these shops frequently create "sandbox" systems that follow the initially open philosophy. These sandbox systems afford their limited users the learning benefit of the initially open approach, while not storing or giving gateway access to any sensitive information elsewhere in the enterprise.

To implement the principle of least privilege on your production or development systems, you should take several actions, or best practices, while setting up or locking down the database. Let's take a look at these:

Protect the data dictionary   Ensure that users with the SELECT ANY TABLE privilege cannot access the tables that underlie the data dictionary by setting 07_DICTIONARY_ACCESSIBILITY = FALSE. This is the default setting.

Revoke unnecessary privileges from PUBLIC   By default, several packages and roles are granted to the special user PUBLIC. Review these privileges, and revoke the EXECUTE privilege from PUBLIC if these packages are not necessary. Some of these packages include the following:

UTL_TCP   This permits the grantee to establish a network connection to any waiting TCP/IP network service. Once a connection is established, arbitrary information can be sent and received directly from the database to and from the other TCP services on your network. If your organization is concerned about information exchange over TCP/IP, revoke the EXECUTE privilege on this package from PUBLIC. Grant privileges on this package only to those users who need it.

UTL_SMTP   This permits the grantee to send arbitrary email. If your organization is concerned about information exchange via email, revoke the EXECUTE privilege on this package from PUBLIC. Grant privileges on this package only to those users who need it.

UTL_HTTP   This permits the grantee to send and receive arbitrary data via the HTTP protocol. If your organization is concerned about information exchange via HTTP, revoke the EXECUTE privilege on this package from PUBLIC. Grant privileges on this package only to those users who need it.

UTL_FILE   This permits the grantee to read and write text data to and from arbitrary operating-system files that are in the designated directories. UTL_FILE does not manage concurrency, so multiple user sessions can step on each other, overwriting changes via UTL_FILE. Consider revoking the EXECUTE privilege on this package from PUBLIC.

DBMS_OBFUSCATION_TOOLKIT and DBMS_CRYPTO These permit the grantee to employ encryption technologies. In a managed environment using encryption, the keys are stored and managed. If encryption keys are lost, the encrypted data is undecipherable. Consider revoking the EXECUTE privilege on these packages from PUBLIC.

You can revoke the EXECUTE privileges like this:

```
REVOKE EXECUTE ON utl_tcp FROM PUBLIC;
REVOKE EXECUTE ON utl_smtp FROM PUBLIC;
REVOKE EXECUTE ON utl_http FROM PUBLIC;
REVOKE EXECUTE ON utl_file FROM PUBLIC;
REVOKE EXECUTE ON dbms_obfuscation_toolkit
    FROM PUBLIC;
REVOKE EXECUTE ON dbms_crypto FROM PUBLIC;
```

You can query the data dictionary to see what other packages may need to be locked down by revoking the EXECUTE privilege from PUBLIC. Here is a query to list the packages, owned by user SYS, that have the EXECUTE privilege granted to PUBLIC:

```
SELECT table_name
FROM dba_tab_privs p
    ,dba_objects   o
WHERE p.owner=o.owner
AND    p.table_name = o.object_name
AND    p.owner = 'SYS'
AND    p.privilege = 'EXECUTE'
AND    p.grantee = 'PUBLIC'
AND    o.object_type='PACKAGE';
```

Limit the users who have administrative privileges Grant administrative privileges to user accounts cautiously. Some powerful administrative privileges and roles to exercise caution with include the following:

SYSDBA This gives the grantee the highest level of privileges with the Oracle Database software. A clever user with the SYSDBA role can circumvent most database security measures. There is usually no good reason to grant this role to any account except SYS, and the SYS password should be both cautiously guarded and changed regularly. Also, guard operating-system accounts carefully. If you are logged on to the database server using a privileged operating-system account, you might be able to connect to the database with SYSDBA authority and no password by entering **connect / as sysdba** in SQL*Plus.

DBA This permits the grantee to assign privileges and manipulate data throughout the database. A clever user with the DBA role can circumvent most database security measures. Grant this role only to those users who need it.

The ANY system privileges SELECT ANY TABLE, GRANT ANY ROLE, DELETE ANY TABLE, and so on, permit the grantee to assign privileges and manipulate data throughout the database. A malicious user with the one of these roles can wreak havoc in your database. Grant these privileges only to those users who need them.

Do not enable REMOTE_OS_AUTHENT   The default setting for the initialization parameter REMOTE_OS_AUTHENT is FALSE. There is rarely a reason to enable this feature. When set to TRUE, this parameter tells the database to trust any client to authenticate externally authenticated accounts. For example, if you have an externally identified account named ORACLE that has DBA privileges for use in administrative scripts running on the database server (a common practice), setting this parameter to TRUE will allow someone with a notebook or desktop PC with a locally created ORACLE account to connect to your database with DBA credentials and no password.

Controlling Resource Usage by Users

An Oracle 11g database lets you limit some resources that your user accounts consume. Disk-space limits are governed by tablespace quotas (discussed in "Assigning Tablespace and Quotas" earlier in the chapter); CPU and memory limits are implemented with *profiles*.

CPU and session-oriented resource limits are managed through profiles. Profiles let you set limits for several resources, including CPU time, memory, and the number of logical reads performed during a user session or database call. A database call is either a parse, an execute, or a fetch. Usually, the database implicitly performs these calls for you. You can explicitly make these database calls from Java, PL/SQL, or Oracle Call Interface (OCI) programs.

A logical read is a measure of the amount of work that the database performs while executing SQL statements. Statements that generate more logical reads require the database to perform more work than statements generating fewer logical reads. Technically, a logical read is counted for each row accessed via ROWID (index access) and for each data block accessed via a multiblock read (full-table scan or index fast full scan).

To enable resource limit restrictions with profiles, first enable them in the database by setting the initialization parameter resource_limit to TRUE, like this:

```
ALTER SYSTEM SET resource_limit = TRUE SCOPE = BOTH;
```

To assign resource limits to a profile, use the CREATE PROFILE or ALTER PROFILE statement with one or more of the kernel resource parameters. The following is an example of the CREATE PROFILE statement, with all the resources that can be controlled. A resource value of DEFAULT indicates that the value is derived from the DEFAULT profile. Initially, the DEFAULT profile has all the system resources set to UNLIMITED.

```
CREATE PROFILE "TEST1" LIMIT
CPU_PER_SESSION DEFAULT
CPU_PER_CALL DEFAULT
CONNECT_TIME DEFAULT
IDLE_TIME 10
```

```
SESSIONS_PER_USER DEFAULT
LOGICAL_READS_PER_SESSION DEFAULT
LOGICAL_READS_PER_CALL 250000
PRIVATE_SGA 25000
COMPOSITE_LIMIT DEFAULT;
```

Each resource is explained here:

CONNECT_TIME   This limits any session established by a user having this profile set to the specified number of minutes. Connection time is sometimes called *wall clock time* to differentiate it from CPU time. When a session exceeds the specified number of minutes, the database rolls back any uncommitted changes and terminates the session. The next call to the database raises an exception. You can use the special value UNLIMITED to tell the database that there is no limit to a session's duration. Set this parameter in a CREATE PROFILE or ALTER PROFILE statement like this:

```
CREATE PROFILE agent LIMIT CONNECT_TIME 10;
ALTER PROFILE data_analyst LIMIT CONNECT_TIME UNLIMITED;
```

CPU_PER_CALL   This limits the amount of CPU time that can be consumed by any single database call in any session established by a user with this profile. The specified value is in hundredths of a second and applies to a parse, an execute, or a fetch call. These calls are implicitly performed by the database for any SQL statement executed in SQL*Plus and can be explicitly called from OCI, Java, and PL/SQL programs. When this limit is breached, the statement fails and is automatically rolled back, and an exception is raised. The user can then commit or roll back any uncommitted changes in the transaction. Set this parameter in a CREATE PROFILE or ALTER PROFILE statement like this:

```
CREATE PROFILE agent LIMIT CPU_PER_CALL 3000;
ALTER PROFILE data_analyst LIMIT CPU_PER_CALL UNLIMITED;
```

CPU_PER_SESSION   This limits the amount of CPU time that can be consumed in any session established by a user with this profile. The specified value is in hundredths of a second and applies to a parse, an execute, or a fetch. When this limit is breached, the current statement fails, the transaction is automatically rolled back, and an exception is raised. The user can then commit or roll back any uncommitted changes in the transaction before logging off. Set this parameter in a CREATE PROFILE or ALTER PROFILE statement like this:

```
CREATE PROFILE agent LIMIT CPU_PER_CALL 30000;
ALTER PROFILE data_analyst LIMIT CPU_PER_CALL UNLIMITED;
```

IDLE_TIME   This limits the duration of time between database calls to the specified number of minutes. If a user having this profile exceeds this setting, the next statement fails, and the user is allowed to either commit or roll back any uncommitted changes before logging off. Long-running statements are not affected by this setting. Set IDLE_TIME in a CREATE PROFILE or ALTER PROFILE statement like this:

```
CREATE PROFILE agent LIMIT IDLE_TIME 10;
ALTER PROFILE daemon LIMIT IDLE_TIME UNLIMITED;
```

LOGICAL_READS_PER_CALL This caps the amount of work that any individual database call performs to the specified number of logical reads. The database call is either a parse, an execute, or a fetch. If the limit is exceeded, the database rolls back the statement, returns an error to the calling program, and allows the user to either commit or roll back any uncommitted changes. Logical reads are computed as the sum of consistent gets plus current mode gets. Set this parameter in a CREATE PROFILE or ALTER PROFILE statement like this:

```
CREATE PROFILE agent LIMIT LOGICAL_READS_PER_CALL 2500;
ALTER PROFILE data_analyst LIMIT LOGICAL_READS_PER_CALL 1000000;
```

LOGICAL_READS_PER_SESSION This limits the amount of database work that a user's session can consume to the specified number of logical reads. When the limit is exceeded, the current statement fails and an exception is raised, and the user must either commit or roll back the transaction and end the session. Logical reads are computed as the sum of consistent gets plus current mode gets. Set this parameter in a CREATE PROFILE or ALTER PROFILE statement like this:

```
CREATE PROFILE agent LIMIT LOGICAL_READS_PER_SESSION 250000;
ALTER PROFILE data_analyst
    LIMIT LOGICAL_READS_PER_SESSION 35000000;
```

PRIVATE_SGA This limits the amount of system global area (SGA) memory in bytes that a user connecting with shared servers (via a multithreaded server [MTS]) can allocate to the persistent area in the program global area (PGA). This area contains bind information among other items. Set this parameter in a CREATE PROFILE or ALTER PROFILE statement like this:

```
CREATE PROFILE agent LIMIT PRIVATE_SGA 2500;
ALTER PROFILE data_analyst LIMIT PRIVATE_SGA UNLIMITED;
```

SESSIONS_PER_USER This restricts a user with this profile to the specified number of database sessions. This setting can be useful to discourage DBAs from all connecting to a shared administrative account to do their work when corporate policy indicates that they should be connecting to their individual accounts. Set this parameter in a CREATE PROFILE or ALTER PROFILE statement like this:

```
CREATE PROFILE admin_profile LIMIT SESSIONS_PER_USER 2;
ALTER PROFILE data_analyst LIMIT SESSIONS_PER_USER 6;
```

COMPOSITE_LIMIT This limits the number of service units that can be consumed during a user session. Service units are calculated as the weighted sum of CPU_PER_SESSION, LOGICAL_READS_PER_SESSION, CONNECT_TIME, and PRIVATE_SGA values. The weightings are established with the ALTER RESOURCE COST statement and can be viewed from the RESOURCE_COST data dictionary view. This COMPOSITE_LIMIT allows you to cap the resource consumption of user groups in more complex ways than a single resource limit. Set this parameter in a CREATE PROFILE or ALTER PROFILE statement like this:

```
CREATE PROFILE admi_profile LIMIT COMPOSITE_LIMIT UNLIMITED;
ALTER PROFILE data_analyst LIMIT COMPOSITE_LIMIT 100000;
```

To enforce the resource limits established with profiles, you must enable them by setting the initialization parameter RESOURCE_LIMIT to TRUE. The default setting is FALSE. Set this parameter with the ALTER SYSTEM statement, like this:

```
ALTER SYSTEM SET resource_limit = TRUE SCOPE=BOTH;
```

You can also use profiles to manage passwords, which is discussed in the next section.

Implementing Password Security Features

For users who are configured for database authentication, password-security rules are enforced with profiles and password complexity rules with verification functions. Profiles have a set of standard rules that define how long a password can remain valid, the elapsed time, the number of password changes before a password can be reused, the number of failed login attempts that will lock the account, and how long the account will remain locked.

If you want a parameter to inherit the setting from the DEFAULT profile, set the parameter's value to the keyword DEFAULT. Explicitly assign password rules to a profile using the CREATE PROFILE or ALTER PROFILE statement. The following is an example of the CREATE PROFILE statement, with all the password features that can be controlled:

```
CREATE PROFILE "TEST2" LIMIT
PASSWORD_LIFE_TIME 60
PASSWORD_GRACE_TIME 7
PASSWORD_REUSE_MAX 2
PASSWORD_REUSE_TIME 4
PASSWORD_LOCK_TIME DEFAULT
FAILED_LOGIN_ATTEMPTS 5
PASSWORD_VERIFY_FUNCTION DEFAULT;
```

Each option is discussed in detail here with examples:

FAILED_LOGIN_ATTEMPTS and PASSWORD_LOCK_TIME   The FAILED_LOGIN_ATTEMPTS parameter specifies how many times in a row the user can fail password authentication. If this limit is breached, the account is locked for PASSWORD_LOCK_TIME days. If the PASSWORD_LOCK_TIME parameter is set to UNLIMITED and a user exceeds FAILED_LOGIN_ATTEMPTS, the account must be manually unlocked. You can set these parameters in a CREATE PROFILE or ALTER PROFILE statement like this:

```
    -- lock account for 10 minutes if 3 consecutive logins fail
    CREATE PROFILE agent LIMIT
       FAILED_LOGIN_ATTEMPTS 3
       PASSWORD_LOCK_TIME 10/1440;

    -- remove failed login restrictions
    ALTER PROFILE student LIMIT FAILED_LOGIN_ATTEMPTS UNLIMITED;
```

```
-- manually unlock an account
ALTER USER scott ACCOUNT UNLOCK;
```

The default value for `FAILED_LOGIN_ATTEMPTS` **in Oracle 11g is 10 and for** `PASSWORD_LOCK_TIME` **is 1 day.**

PASSWORD_LIFE_TIME and PASSWORD_GRACE_TIME The `PASSWORD_LIFE_TIME` parameter specifies the maximum number of days that a password can remain in force, and `PASSWORD_GRACE_TIME` is the number of days after the first successful login following password expiration during which the user will be reminded to change their password but allowed to log in. After the `PASSWORD_GRACE_TIME` limit is reached, the user must change their password. If you set `PASSWORD_LIFE_TIME` to a value and set `PASSWORD_GRACE_TIME` to `UNLIMITED`, users will be reminded to change their password every time they log in but never forced to actually do so. You can set these two parameters in a `CREATE PROFILE` or `ALTER PROFILE` statement like this:

```
-- limit the password lifetime to 90 days
-- during the last 14 days the user will be reminded
-- to change the password
CREATE PROFILE agent LIMIT
    PASSWORD_LIFE_TIME 90 - 14
    PASSWORD_GRACE_TIME 14;


-- set no limit to password lifetime
ALTER PROFILE student LIMIT
    PASSWORD_LIFE_TIME UNLIMITED
    PASSWORD_GRACE_TIME DEFAULT;
```

The default value for `PASSWORD_LIFE_TIME` **in Oracle 11g is 180 days and for** `PASSWORD_GRACE_TIME` **is 7 days.**

PASSWORD_REUSE_TIME and PASSWORD_REUSE_MAX The `PASSWORD_REUSE_TIME` parameter specifies the minimum number of days that must transpire before a password can be reused. `PASSWORD_REUSE_MAX` specifies the minimum number of password changes that must occur before a password can be reused. If you specify a value for one of these two parameters and `UNLIMITED` for the other, passwords can never be reused. If you set both `PASSWORD_REUSE_TIME` and `PASSWORD_REUSE_MAX` to `UNLIMITED` (the default), these parameters are essentially disabled. You can set these password parameters in a `CREATE PROFILE` or `ALTER PROFILE` statement like this:

```
-- require at least 4 password changes and 1 year
-- before a password may be reused.
CREATE PROFILE agent LIMIT
    PASSWORD_REUSE_TIME 365
    PASSWORD_REUSE_MAX 4;
```

```
-- remove password reuse constraints
ALTER PROFILE student LIMIT
   PASSWORD_REUSE_TIME UNLIMITED
   PASSWORD_REUSE_MAX UNLIMITED;
```

 Real World Scenario

Setting Password Lock Time to Two Hours

Several password attributes are durations expressed in days. These durations are normally set with integer values, such as 1, 15, 30, 90, or 365 days.

The default password lock time for Oracle 11*g* is 1 day, and the unit used to express the lock time is in days. A few of the clients I worked for needed the password lock to go away after two hours if the user tried to enter incorrect password too many times. How do you set the value in hours or minutes when the unit is in days?

All these password profile attributes take fractional values as well; hence, you can represent hours and minutes. Since there are 1,440 minutes in a day, you can represent 5 minutes as 5/1440 days and represent 5 seconds as 5/86400 days. The following code sets the password lock time to two hours:

ALTER PROFILE student LIMIT PASSWORD_LOCK_TIME 2/24;

You can represent the value using decimal numbers; for example, the following code sets the password lock time to six hours:

ALTER PROFILE student LIMIT PASSWORD_LOCK_TIME .25;

Using a fractional number of days is a great way to try combinations of values and observe the results of setting these password rules.

PASSWORD_VERIFY_FUNCTION   The PASSWORD_VERIFY_FUNCTION parameter lets you codify additional rules that will be verified when a password is changed. These rules usually verify password complexity such as minimal password length or check that a password does not appear in a dictionary. The PL/SQL function used in the PASSWORD_VERIFY_FUNCTION parameter must be created under the user SYS and must have three parameters of type VARCHAR2. These parameters must contain the username in the first parameter, the new password in the second, and the old password in the third. You can set this parameter in a CREATE PROFILE or ALTER PROFILE statement like this:

```
-- use a custom password function
CREATE PROFILE agent LIMIT PASSWORD_VERIFY_FUNCTION my_function;
```

```
-- disable use of a custom function
ALTER PROFILE student LIMIT PASSWORD_VERIFY_FUNCTION DEFAULT;
```

 **Real World Scenario**

Implementing a Corporate Password-Security Policy

Many companies have security policies requiring that several password complexity rules be followed. For your Oracle 11*g* database, these rules can be incorporated into a password verify function. This real-world scenario highlights an example of three password complexity requirements and how they are satisfied through a password verify function named MY_PASSWORD_VERIFY.

The first rule specifies that the password must be at least six characters in length. The second rule disallows passwords containing some form of either the username or the word *password*. The third rule requires the password to contain at least one alphabetic character, at least one digit, and at least one punctuation character. If the new password fails any of these tests, the function raises an exception, and the password change fails.

After creating this function as user SYS, assign it to a profile, like this:

ALTER PROFILE student LIMIT password_verify_function my_password_verify;

Any user having the student profile will need to abide by the password rules enforced by the my_password_verify function:

```
CREATE OR REPLACE FUNCTION my_password_verify
    (username VARCHAR2
    ,password VARCHAR2
    ,old_password VARCHAR2
    ) RETURN BOOLEAN
IS

BEGIN
    -- Check for the minimum length of the password
    IF LENGTH(password) < 6 THEN
        raise_application_error(-20001
            ,'Password must be at least 6 characters long');
    END IF;

    -- Check that the password does not contain any
    -- upper/lowercase version of either the user name
    -- or the keyword PASSWORD
```

```
     IF (    regexp_like(password,username,'i')
        OR regexp_like(password,'password','i')) THEN
        raise_application_error(-20002
           ,'Password cannot contain username or PASSWORD');
     END IF;

     -- Check that the password contains at least one letter,
     -- one digit and one punctuation character
     IF NOT(    regexp_like(password,'[[:digit:]]')
           AND regexp_like(password,'[[:alpha:]]')
           AND regexp_like(password,'[[:punct:]]')
           ) THEN
        raise_application_error(-20003
           ,'Password must contain at least one digit '||
            'and one letter and one punctuation character');
     END IF;

     -- password is okey dokey
     RETURN(TRUE);
END;
/
```
Oracle 11*g* provides the PL/SQL code to create a password complexity verify function. The script is called utlpwdmg.sql and is in the $ORACLE_HOME/rdbms/admin directory. The name of the function created using this script is called verify_function_11g.

Auditing Database Activity

Auditing involves monitoring and recording specific database activity. An Oracle 11*g* database supports four levels of auditing:

- Statement
- Privilege
- Object
- Fine-grained access

These afford you two locations for recording these activities. Audit records can be stored in either of these locations.

- Database
- Operating-system files

You tell the Oracle Database where to record audit trail records by setting the initialization parameter audit_trail. The default is DB, as in AUDIT_TRAIL=DB, which tells the database to record audit records in the database. AUDIT_TRAIL=DB,EXTENDED tells the database to record audit records in the database together with bind variables (SQLBIND) and the SQL statement triggering the audit entry (SQLTEXT). AUDIT_TRAIL=OS tells the database to record audit records in operating-system files. You cannot change this parameter in memory, only in your pfile or spfile. For example, the following statement will change the location of audit records in the spfile:

```
ALTER SYSTEM SET audit_trail=DB SCOPE=SPFILE;
```

The audit_trail parameter can also have values XML and XML,EXTENDED. With these two options, audit records are written to OS files in XML format. The value of NONE disables auditing.

After changing the audit_trail parameter, you will need to bounce (shut down and start up) your database instance for the change to take effect.

When recorded in the database, most audit entries are recorded in the SYS.AUD$ table. On Unix systems, operating-system audit records are written into files in the directory specified by the initialization parameter audit_file_dest (which is set to $ORACLE_BASE/admin/$ORACLE_SID/adump if the database is created using DBCA). On Windows systems, these audit records are written to the Event Viewer log file.

The four levels of auditing are described in the following sections.

> **NOTE** Certain database activities are always recorded in the OS audit files. Database connections using administrator privileges such as SYSDBA and SYSOPER are recorded. Database startup and shutdown are also recorded in the OS audit files.

Managing Statement Auditing

Statement auditing involves monitoring and recording the execution of specific types of SQL statements. In the following sections, you will learn how to enable and disable statement auditing as well as identify what statement auditing options are enabled.

Enabling Statement Auditing

You enable auditing of specific SQL statements with an AUDIT statement. For example, to audit the SQL statements CREATE TABLE, DROP TABLE, and TRUNCATE TABLE, use the TABLE audit option like this:

```
AUDIT table;
```

To record audit entries for specific users only, include a BY *USER* clause in the AUDIT statement. For example, to audit CREATE, DROP, and TRUNCATE TABLE statements for user juanita only, execute the following:

AUDIT table BY juanita;

Frequently, you want to record only attempts that fail—perhaps to look for users who are probing the system to see what they can get away with. To further limit auditing to only these unsuccessful executions, use a WHENEVER clause like this:

AUDIT table BY juanita WHENEVER NOT SUCCESSFUL;

You can alternately specify WHENEVER SUCCESSFUL to record only successful statements. If you do not include a WHENEVER clause, both successful and unsuccessful statements trigger audit records.

You can further configure non-DDL statements to record one audit entry for the triggering session or one entry for each auditable action during the session. Specify BY ACCESS or BY SESSION in the AUDIT statement, like this:

AUDIT INSERT TABLE BY juanita BY ACCESS;

There are many auditing options other than TABLE or INSERT TABLE. Table 12.1 shows all the statement-auditing options.

TABLE 12.1   Statement-Auditing Options

Statement-Auditing Option	Triggering SQL Statements
ALTER SEQUENCE	ALTER SEQUENCE
ALTER TABLE	ALTER TABLE
COMMENT TABLE	COMMENT ON TABLE COMMENT ON COLUMN
DATABASE LINK	CREATE DATABASE LINK DROP DATABASE LINK
DELETE TABLE	DELETE
EXECUTE PROCEDURE	Execution of any procedure or function or access to any cursor or variable in a package
GRANT PROCEDURE	GRANT on a function, package, or procedure
GRANT SEQUENCE	GRANT on a sequence
GRANT TABLE	GRANT on a table or view

TABLE 12.1 Statement Audit Options *(continued)*

Statement-Auditing Option	Triggering SQL Statements
INDEX	CREATEINDEX
INSERT TABLE	INSERT into table or view
LOCK TABLE	LOCK
NOT EXISTS	All SQL statements
PROCEDURE	CREATE FUNCTION DROP FUNCTION CREATE PACKAGE CREATE PACKAGE BODY DROP PACKAGE CREATE PROCEDURE DROP PROCEDURE
PROFILE	CREATE PROFILE ALTER PROFILE DROP PROFILE
ROLE	CREATE ROLE ALTER ROLE DROP ROLE SET ROLE
SELECT SEQUENCE	SELECT on a sequence
SELECT TABLE	SELECT from table or view
SEQUENCE	CREATE SEQUENCE DROP SEQUENCE
SESSION	LOGON
SYNONYM	CREATE SYNONYM DROP SYNONYM
SYSTEM AUDIT	AUDIT NOAUDIT
SYSTEM GRANT	GRANT REVOKE

TABLE 12.1 Statement Audit Options *(continued)*

Statement-Auditing Option	Triggering SQL Statements
TABLE	CREATE TABLE DROP TABLE TRUNCATE TABLE
TABLESPACE	CREATE TABLESPACE ALTER TABLESPACE DROP TABLESPACE
TRIGGER	CREATE TRIGGER ALTER TRIGGER (to enable or disable) ALTER TABLE (to enable all or disable all)
UPDATE TABLE	UPDATE on a table or view
USER	CREATE USER ALTER USER DROP USER
VIEW	CREATE VIEW DROP VIEW

Identifying Enabled Statement-Auditing Options

You can identify the statement-auditing options that have been enabled in your database by querying the DBA_STMT_AUDIT_OPTS data dictionary view. For example, the following example shows that SESSION auditing is enabled for all users, NOT EXISTS auditing is enabled for all users, and TABLE auditing WHENEVER NOT SUCCESSFUL is enabled for user juanita:

```
SELECT audit_option, failure, success, user_name
FROM dba_stmt_audit_opts
ORDER BY audit_option, user_name;


AUDIT_OPTION          FAILURE      SUCCESS     USER_NAME
--------------------  ----------  ----------  -------------
CREATE SESSION        BY ACCESS   BY ACCESS
NOT EXISTS            BY ACCESS   BY ACCESS
TABLE                 BY ACCESS   NOT SET      JUANITA
```

Oracle Database 11*g* comes with the following auditing enabled by default:

- ALTER ANY PROCEDURE
- ALTER ANY TABLE
- ALTER DATABASE
- ALTER PROFILE
- ALTER SYSTEM
- ALTER USER
- CREATE ANY JOB
- CREATE ANY LIBRARY
- CREATE ANY PROCEDURE
- CREATE ANY TABLE
- CREATE EXTERNAL JOB
- CREATE PUBLIC DATABASE LINK

- CREATE SESSION
- CREATE USER
- DROP ANY PROCEDURE
- DROP ANY TABLE
- DROP PROFILE
- DROP USER
- EXEMPT ACCESS POLICY
- GRANT ANY OBJECT PRIVILEGE
- GRANT ANY PRIVILEGE
- GRANT ANY ROLE
- ROLE
- SYSTEM AUDIT

You can enable administrator auditing by setting the initialization parameter AUDIT_SYS_OPERATIONS=TRUE. All the activities performed connected as SYS or SYSDBA/SYSOPER privileges are recorded in the OS audit trail.

Disabling Statement Auditing

To disable auditing of a specific SQL statement, use a NOAUDIT statement, which allows the same BY and WHENEVER options as the AUDIT statement. If you enable auditing for a specific user, specify that user in the NOAUDIT statement as well. However, it is not necessary to include the WHENEVER NOT SUCCESSFUL clause in the NOAUDIT statement.

For example, to disable the three audit options in the previous section, execute the following three statements:

```
NOAUDIT session;
NOAUDIT not exists;
NOAUDIT table BY juanita;
```

Examining the Audit Trail

Statement, privilege, and object audit records are written to the SYS.AUD$ table and made available via the data dictionary views DBA_AUDIT_TRAIL and USER_AUDIT_TRAIL. These data dictionary views cannot contain values for every record because this view is used for three different types of audit records. For example, you can view the user, time, and type of statement audited for user juanita by executing the following:

```
SELECT username, timestamp, action_name
FROM dba_audit_trail
WHERE username = 'JUANITA';
```

```
ORA USER          TIMESTAMP               ACTION_NAME
----------------  ----------------------  -------------
JUANITA           15-Jun-2004 18:43:52    LOGON
JUANITA           15-Jun-2004 18:44:19    LOGOFF
JUANITA           15-Jun-2004 18:46:01    LOGON
JUANITA           15-Jun-2004 18:46:40    CREATE TABLE
```

If you enable AUDIT SESSION, the database creates one audit record when a user logs on and updates that record when the user logs off successfully. These session audit records contain some valuable information that can help you narrow the focus of your tuning efforts. Among the information recorded in the audit records are the username, logon time, logoff time, and the number of physical reads and logical reads performed during the session. By looking for sessions with high counts of logical or physical reads, you can identify high-resource-consuming jobs and narrow the focus of your tuning efforts.

Managing Privilege Auditing

Privilege auditing involves monitoring and recording the execution of SQL statements that require a specific system privilege, such as SELECT ANY TABLE or GRANT ANY PRIVILEGE. You can audit any system privilege. In the following sections, you will learn how to enable and disable privilege auditing as well as identify which privilege-auditing options are enabled in your database.

Enabling Privilege Auditing

You enable privilege auditing with an AUDIT statement, specifying the system privilege that you want to monitor. For example, to audit statements that require the system privilege CREATE ANY TABLE, execute the following:

```
AUDIT create any table;
```

To record audit entries for specific users only, include a BY *USER clause* in the AUDIT statement. For example, to audit SQL statements made by user juanita that require the CREATE ANY TABLE privilege, execute the following:

```
AUDIT create any table BY juanita;
```

Just as you do with statement auditing, you can further configure non-DDL privileges to record one audit entry for the triggering session or one for each auditable action during the session by specifying BY ACCESS or BY SESSION in the AUDIT statement, like this:

```
AUDIT DELETE ANY TABLE BY juanita BY ACCESS;
```

Identifying Enabled Privilege-Auditing Options

You can report on the privilege auditing that has been enabled in your database by querying the DBA_PRIV_AUDIT_OPTS data dictionary view. For example, the following report shows that ALTER PROFILE auditing is enabled for all users and that ALTER USER and DELETE ANY TABLE auditing is enabled for user juanita:

```
SELECT privilege, user_name
FROM dba_priv_audit_opts
ORDER BY privilege, user_name;


PRIVILEGE            USER_NAME
-------------------- ----------------
ALTER PROFILE
DELETE ANY TABLE     JUANITA
ALTER USER           JUANITA
```

Disabling Privilege Auditing

To disable auditing of a system privilege, use a NOAUDIT statement. The NOAUDIT statement allows the same BY options as the AUDIT statement. If you enable auditing for a specific user, you need to specify that user in the NOAUDIT statement. For example, to disable the three audit options in the previous section, execute the following three statements:

```
NOAUDIT alter profile;
NOAUDIT delete any table BY juanita;
NOAUDIT alter user BY juanita;
```

Managing Object Auditing

Object auditing involves monitoring and recording the execution of SQL statements that require a specific object privilege, such as SELECT, INSERT, UPDATE, DELETE, or EXECUTE.

Unlike either statement or system privilege auditing, schema object auditing cannot be restricted to specific users—it is enabled for all users or no users. In the following sections, you will learn how to enable and disable object-auditing options as well as identify which object-auditing options are enabled.

Enabling Object Auditing

You enable object auditing with an AUDIT statement, specifying both the object and object privilege that you want to monitor. For example, to audit SELECT statements on the HR.EMPLOYEE_SALARY table, execute the following:

```
AUDIT select ON hr.employee_salary;
```

You can further configure these audit records to record one audit entry for the triggering session or one for each auditable action during the session by specifying BY ACCESS or BY SESSION in the AUDIT statement. This access/session configuration can be defined differently for successful or unsuccessful executions. For example, to make one audit entry per auditable action for successful SELECT statements on the HR.EMPLOYEE_SALARY table, execute the following:

```
-- one audit entry for each trigging statement
AUDIT select ON hr.employee_salary
   BY ACCESS WHENEVER SUCCESSFUL;


-- one audit entry for the session experiencing one or more
-- triggering statements
AUDIT select ON hr.employee_salary
   BY SESSION WHENEVER NOT SUCCESSFUL;
```

Identifying Enabled Object-Auditing Options

The object-auditing options that are enabled in the database are recorded in the DBA_OBJ_AUDIT_OPTS data dictionary view. Unlike the statement and privilege _AUDIT_OPTS views, the DBA_OBJ_AUDIT_OPTS data dictionary view always has one row for each auditable object in the database. There are columns for each object privilege that auditing can be enabled on, and in each of these columns, a code is reported that shows the auditing options. For example, the following report on the HR.EMPLOYEES table shows that no auditing is enabled for the INSERT object privilege and that the SELECT object privilege has auditing enabled with one audit entry for each access when the access is successful and one audit entry for each session when the access is not successful:

```
SELECT owner, object_name, object_type, ins, sel
FROM dba_obj_audit_opts
WHERE owner='HR'
AND   object_name='EMPLOYEE_SALARY';
```

```
OWNER          OBJECT_NAME                OBJECT_TY INS SEL
------------   --------------------------  ---------  --- ---
HR             EMPLOYEE_SALARY            TABLE      -/-  A/S
```

The coding for the object privilege columns contains one of three possible values: a hyphen (-) to indicate no auditing is enabled, an A to indicate BY ACCESS, or an S to indicate BY SESSION. The first code (preceding the slash) denotes the action for successful statements, and the second code (after the slash) denotes the action for unsuccessful statements.

Disabling Object Auditing

To disable object auditing, use a NOAUDIT statement, which allows the same WHENEVER options as the AUDIT statement. For example, to disable the auditing of unsuccessful SELECT statements against the HR.EMPLOYEES table, execute the following:

```
NOAUDIT select ON hr.employee_salary  WHENEVER NOT SUCCESSFUL;
```

Purging the Audit Trail

Database audit records for statement, privilege, and object auditing are stored in the table SYS.AUD$. Depending on how extensive your auditing and retention policies are, you will need to periodically delete old audit records from this table. The database does not provide an interface to assist in deleting rows from the audit table, so you will need to do so yourself. To purge audit records older than 90 days, execute the following as user SYS:

```
DELETE FROM sys.aud$ WHERE timestamp# < SYSDATE -90;
```

You might want to copy the audit records into a different table for historical retention or export them to an operating-system file before removing them. It is a good practice to audit changes to the AUD$ table so that you can identify when changes were made.

Only the user SYS, a user with the DELETE ANY TABLE privilege, or a user to whom SYS granted the DELETE privilege on SYS.AUD$ can delete the audit trail records from the SYS.AUD$ table.

Oracle 11*g* audits all DML statements against the SYS.AUD$ table. The INSERT, UPDATE, MERGE, and DELETE statements against the SYS.AUD$ table are not deleted from the SYS.AUD$ table. You have to truncate the SYS.AUD$ table to remove such records.

You can also use EM Grid Control to enable and disable auditing. On the Server tab (as shown earlier in Figure 12.1), click the Audit Settings link under Security. As shown in Figure 12.6, the Audit Settings screen shows the audit location, enabled audits, and audit trail information.

FIGURE 12.6   EM Grid Control Audit Settings screen

Managing Fine-Grained Auditing

Fine-grained auditing (FGA) lets you monitor and record data access based on the content of the data. With FGA, you define an audit policy on a table and optionally a column. When the specified condition evaluates to TRUE, an audit record is created, and an optional event-handler program is called. You use the PL/SQL package DBMS_FGA to configure and manage FGA.

In the following sections, you will learn how to create, drop, enable, and disable fine-grained auditing policies.

Creating an FGA Policy

To create a new FGA policy, use the packaged procedure DBMS_FGA.ADD_POLICY. This procedure has the following parameters:

object_schema This is the owner of the object to be audited. The default is NULL, which tells the database to use the current user.

object_name This is the name of the object to be monitored.

policy_name   This is a unique name for the new policy

audit_condition   This is a SQL expression that evaluates to a Boolean. When this condition evaluates to either TRUE or NULL (the default), an audit record can be created. This condition cannot directly use the SYSDATE, UID, USER, or USERENV functions, it cannot use subqueries or sequences, and it cannot reference the pseudocolumns LEVEL, PRIOR, and ROWNUM.

audit_column   This is a comma-delimited list of columns that the database will look to access. If a column in audit_column is referenced in the SQL statement and the audit_condition is not FALSE, an audit record is created. Columns appearing in audit_column do not have to also appear in the audit_condition expression. The default value is NULL, which tells the database that any column being referenced should trigger the audit record.

handler_schema   This is the owner of the event handler procedure. The default is NULL, which tells the database to use the current schema.

handler_module   This is the name of the event handler procedure. The default NULL tells the database to not use an event handler. If the event handler is a packaged procedure, the handler_module must reference both the package name and the program, using dot notation, like this:

```
UTL_MAIL.SEND_ATTACH_RAW
```

enable   This is a Boolean that tells the database whether this policy should be in effect. The default is TRUE.

statement_types   This tells the database which types of statements to monitor. Valid values are a comma-delimited list of SELECT, INSERT, UPDATE, and DELETE. The default is SELECT.

audit_trail   This parameter tells the database whether to record the SQL statement and bind variables for the triggering SQL in the audit trail. The default value DBMS_FGA.DB_EXTENDED indicates that the SQL statement and bind variables should be recorded in the audit trail. Set this parameter to DBMS_FGA.DB to save space by not recording the SQL statement or bind variables in the audit trail.

audit_column_ops   This parameter has only two valid values: DBMS_FGA.ALL_COLUMNS and DBMS_FGA.ANY_COLUMNS. When set to DBMS_FGA.ALL_COLUMNS, this parameter tells the database that all columns appearing in the audit_column parameter must be referenced in order to trigger an audit record. The default is DBMS_FGA.ANY_COLUMNS, which tells the database that if any column appearing in the audit_column also appears in the SQL statement, an audit record should be created.

To create a new disabled audit policy named COMPENSATION_AUD that looks for SELECT statements that access the HR.EMPLOYEES table and references either SALARY or COMMISSION_PCT, execute the following:

```
DBMS_FGA.ADD_POLICY(object_schema=>'HR'
    ,object_name=>'EMPLOYEES'
    ,policy_name=>'COMPENSATION_AUD'
    ,audit_column=>'SALARY, COMMISSION_PCT'
    ,enable=>FALSE
    ,statement_types=>'SELECT');
```

Enabling an FGA Policy

Use the procedure `DBMS_FGA.ENABLE_POLICY` to enable an FGA policy. This procedure will not raise an exception if the policy is already enabled. For example, you can enable the `COMPENSATION_AUD` policy added in the previous section like this:

```
DBMS_FGA.ENABLE_POLICY(object_schema=>'HR'
    ,object_name=>'EMPLOYEES'
    ,policy_name=>'COMPENSATION_AUD');
```

WARNING If you use direct path inserts, be careful with FGA. If an FGA policy is enabled on a table participating in a direct path insert, the auditing overrides the hint, disabling the direct path access and causing conventional inserts. As with all hints, the database does not directly tell you that your hint is being ignored.

Disabling an FGA Policy

To turn off an FGA, use the `DBMS_FGA.DISABLE_POLICY` procedure. Here is an example:

```
DBMS_FGA.DISABLE_POLICY(object_schema=>'HR'
    ,object_name=>'EMPLOYEES'
    ,policy_name=>'COMPENSATION_AUD');
```

Dropping an FGA Policy

To remove an FGA policy, use the `DBMS_FGA.DROP_POLICY` procedure. For example, to drop the `COMPENSATION_AUD` policy used in this section, run this:

```
DBMS_FGA.DROP_POLICY(object_schema=>'HR'
    ,object_name=>'EMPLOYEES'
    ,policy_name=>'COMPENSATION_AUD');
```

Identifying FGA Policies in the Database

Query the `DBA_AUDIT_POLICIES` data dictionary view to report on the FGA policies defined in your database. For example, the following report shows that the policy named `COMPENSATION_AUD` on the column `SALARY` in the table `HR.EMPLOYEES` is defined but not enabled:

```
SELECT policy_name ,object_schema||'.'||
       object_name object_name
       ,policy_column
       ,enabled ,audit_trail
FROM dba_audit_policies;
```

```
POLICY_NAME       OBJECT_NAME   POLICY ENABLED AUDIT_TRAIL
----------------  ------------  ------ ------- -----------
COMPENSATION_AUD  HR.EMPLOYEES  SALARY NO      DB_EXTENDED
```

Audit records from this policy, when enabled, capture the standard auditing information as well as the text of the SQL statement that triggered the auditing (DB_EXTENDED).

Reporting on the FGA Audit Trail Entries

The DBA_FGA_AUDIT_TRAIL data dictionary view is used in reporting on the FGA audit entries that have been recorded in the database. The following example shows audit trail entries for the COMPENSATION_AUD policy, listing the database username and the timestamp of the audit record and computer from which the database connection was made:

```
SELECT db_user, timestamp, userhost
FROM dba_fga_audit_traiL
WHERE policy_name='COMPENSATION_AUD'


DB_USER       TIMESTAMP             USERHOST
------------  --------------------  ---------------------
CHIPD         10-Jun-2004 09:48:14  XYZcorp\CHIPNOTEBOOK
JUANITA       19-Jun-2004 14:50:47  XYZcorp\HR_PC2
```

Summary

Oracle 11g gives you a well-stocked toolkit for managing users and securing the database. You create and manage user accounts with the CREATE, ALTER, and DROP USER statements. User passwords in Oracle 11g are case sensitive. You can assign tablespace resources to be used for sorting that are different than those for tables or indexes. You can limit the disk, CPU, and memory resources that your users consume by employing tablespace quotas and kernel resource limits in user profiles.

To protect data from unwanted access or manipulation, you can employ object and system privileges. You can create and use roles to make managing these database privileges easier. You can enable object, statement, privilege, and fine-grained auditing to help you monitor and record sensitive database activity. By default, DBCA enables several key auditing features when you create an Oracle 11g database.

The Oracle 11g database has several powerful features (user accounts and packages) that will need to be locked down in your production systems, and in this chapter you learned which user accounts need to be locked, as well as which standard packages should be locked down to better protect your company's data.

Exam Essentials

Be familiar with the authentication methods.   Database accounts can be authenticated by the database (identified by password), by the operating system (identified externally), or by an enterprise security service (identified globally).

Know how to assign default and temporary tablespace to users.   Assign default and temporary tablespaces with either a CREATE USER statement or an ALTER USER statement. Understand which tablespace would be assigned if you omitted the DEFAULT TABLESPACE clause when creating a user.

Be able to identify and grant object, system, and role privileges.   Know the difference between these types of privileges and when to use each type.

Know the differences between the WITH ADMIN OPTION and WITH GRANT OPTION keywords. The ADMIN option applies to role or system privileges, but the GRANT option applies to object privileges.

Know how to enable roles.   Know when a role needs to be enabled and how to enable it.

Be able to secure your database.   Make sure you know how to lock down your database. Know which packages should be secured and how to secure them.

Know how to implement password security.   An Oracle 11g database gives you several standard password-security settings. Know what is available in a profile and what needs to be implemented in a password-verifying function.

Know how to enable, disable, and identify enabled auditing options.   Be able to describe the types of auditing, how to enable them, and how to report on the audit trail.

Review Questions

1. Which of the following statements creates an Oracle account but lets the operating system authenticate logons?

    A. `create user ops$admin identified by os;`

    B. `create user ops$admin identified externally;`

    C. `create user ops$admin nopassword;`

    D. `create user ops$admin authenticated by os;`

2. If you want to capture the SQL statement and bind variables when performing statement auditing, which value should the AUDIT_TRAIL parameter have?

    A. NONE

    B. DB

    C. DB,EXTENDED

    D. OS

    E. OS,EXTENDED

3. Which of the following statements gives user desmond the ability to alter table `gl.accounts`?

    A. `grant alter on gl.accounts to desmond;`

    B. `grant alter to desmond on gl.accounts;`

    C. `grant alter table to desmond;`

    D. `allow desmond to alter table gl.accounts;`

4. Which of the following statements gives user desmond the ability to alter table `gl.accounts` as well as give this ability to other accounts?

    A. `grant alter any table with grant option to desmond;`

    B. `grant alter on gl.accounts to desmond with admin option;`

    C. `grant alter any table to desmond with grant option;`

    D. `grant alter any table to desmond with admin option;`

5. Examine the CREATE USER statement, and choose which of the following options best applies.

    ```
    CREATE USER JOHN IDENTIFIED BY JOHNNY
    DEFAULT TABLESPACE INDEX01
    PASSWORD EXPIRE
    QUOTA UNLIMITED ON DATA01
    QUOTA UNLIMITED ON INDEX01;
    GRANT CONNECT TO JOHN;
    ```

    A. JOHN will not be able to log in to the database using SQL*Plus until the DBA changes his password.

    B. JOHN is authenticated by the database.

    C. When creating tables, if JOHN did not specify the TABLESPACE clause, the table will be created on the DATA01 tablespace.

    D. Specifying unlimited space quota on INDEX01 is a redundant step since INDEX01 is JOHN's default tablespace.

6. User system granted SELECT on sh.products to user ian using WITH GRANT OPTION. Ian then granted SELECT on sh.products to user stuart. Ian has left the company, and his account has been dropped. What happens to Stuart's privileges on sh.products?

    A. Stuart loses his SELECT privilege on sh.products.

    B. Stuart retains his SELECT privilege on sh.products.

    C. Stuart loses his SELECT privilege if Ian was dropped with the CASCADE REVOKE option.

    D. Stuart retains his SELECT privilege if Ian was dropped with the NOCASCADE REVOKE option.

7. User system granted SELECT ANY TABLE to user ian using WITH ADMIN OPTION. Ian then granted SELECT ANY TABLE to user stuart. Ian has left the company, and his account has been dropped. What happens to Stuart's privileges?

    A. Stuart loses his privileges.

    B. Stuart retains his privileges.

    C. Stuart loses his privileges if Ian was dropped with the CASCADE REVOKE option.

    D. Stuart retains his privileges if Ian was dropped with the NOCASCADE REVOKE option.

8. Which of the following system privileges can allow the grantee to masquerade as another user and therefore should be granted judiciously?

    A. CREATE ANY JOB

    B. ALTER USER

    C. CREATE ANY PROCEDURE

    D. All of the above

9. Which of the following statements enables the role user_admin in the current session?

    A. alter session enable role user_admin;

    B. alter session set role user_admin;

    C. alter role user_admin enable;

    D. set role user_admin;

10. Which of the following SQL statements allows user `augustin` to use the privileges associated with the password-protected role `info_czar` that has been granted to him?

    A. `set role all;`

    B. `alter user augustin default role all;`

    C. `alter session enable role info_czar;`

    D. `alter session enable info_czar identified by brozo`

11. By default, how much space can any account use for a new table?

    A. None

    B. Up to the current free space in the tablespace

    C. Unlimited space, including autoextends

    D. Up to the default quota established at tablespace creation time

12. Which of the following SQL statements results in a disconnection after a session is idle for 30 minutes?

    A. `alter session set idle_timeout=30;`

    B. `alter session set idle_timeout=1800;`

    C. `alter profile default limit idle_time 30;`

    D. `alter profile default set idle_timeout 30;`

13. Which of the following prevents a user from reusing a password when they change their password?

    A. Setting the initialization parameter NO_PASSWORD_REUSE to TRUE

    B. Altering that user's profile to UNLIMITED for PASSWORD_REUSE_TIME and 1 for PASSWORD_REUSE_MAX

    C. Altering that user's profile to UNLIMITED for both PASSWORD_REUSE_TIME and PASSWORD_REUSE_MAX

    D. Using a password verify function to record the new password and comparing the new passwords to those recorded previously

14. Examine the code, and choose the best option that describes the reason for error.

```
CREATE USER JOHN IDENTIFIED BY JOHN1;
CREATE ROLE HR_QUERY;
GRANT CONNECT, OEQUERY, SELECT ANY TABLE TO HR_QUERY;
ALTER USER JOHN DEFAULT ROLE ALL EXCEPT HR_QUERY;
GRANT HR_QUERY TO JOHN;
CONNECT JOHN/JOHN1
SELECT COUNT(*) FROM HR.EMPLOYEES;
Error: ORA-01031: insufficient privileges
```

A. John needs the SELECT_CATALOG_ROLE privilege.

B. HR_QUERY is not a default role for John.

C. The SELECT privilege on the HR.EMPLOYEES table is not granted to JOHN or HR_QUERY.

D. John should enable the role using the SET ROLE statement and a password.

15. You created a database user using the following statement. Which option will connect the user successfully to the database?

```
CREATE USER JOHN IDENTIFIED BY John1;
GRANT CONNECT TO JOHN;
```

A. CONNECT JOHN/JOHN1

B. CONNECT JOHN/john1

C. CONNECT john/John1

D. All of the above

16. What is the default value for the AUDIT_TRAIL parameter?

A. NONE

B. DB

C. DB,EXTENDED

D. XML

17. Which of the following SQL statements limits attempts to guess passwords by locking an account after three failed logon attempts?

A. alter profile default limit failed_login_attempts 3;

B. alter system set max_logon_failures = 3 scope=both;

C. alter user set failed_login_attempts = 3;

D. alter system set failed_login_attempts = 3 scope=both;

18. Where can the database write audit_trail records?

A. In a database table

B. In a file outside the database

C. Both in the database and in an operating-system file

D. Either in the database or in an operating-system file

19. User JAMES has a table named JOBS created on the tablespace USERS. When you issue the following statement, what effect will it have on the JOBS table?

ALTER USER JAMES QUOTA 0 ON USERS;

   A. No more rows can be added to the JOBS table.

   B. No new blocks can be allocated to the JOBS table.

   C. No new extents can be allocated to the JOBS table.

   D. The table JOBS cannot be accessed.

   E. The table is truncated.

20. How do you manage fine-grained auditing?

   A. With the AUDIT and NOAUDIT statements

   B. With the DBMS_FGA package

   C. With the GRANT and REVOKE statements

   D. With the CREATE, ALTER, and DROP statements

Answers to Review Questions

1. B. Authentication by the operating system is called external authentication, and the Oracle account name must match the operating-system account name prefixed with the OS_AUTHENT_PREFIX string.

2. C. The AUDIT_TRAIL parameter with the value DB,EXTENDED enables capturing SQL statements and bind variables in auditing. OS,EXTENDED is not a valid value for AUDIT_TRAIL.

3. A. Altering a table in another user's schema requires either the object privilege ALTER on that object or the system privilege ALTER ANY TABLE. Option A has the correct syntax for granting the object privilege on ALTER gl.accounts to user desmond. Although option C would allow user desmond to alter his own tables, he would need the ALTER ANY TABLE privilege to alter another user's table.

4. D. Either the ALTER ANY TABLE system privilege or the ALTER object privilege is required. Conferring the ability to further grant the privilege requires the keywords WITH ADMIN OPTION for system or role privileges or the keywords WITH GRANT OPTION for object privileges. Only option D has both the correct syntax and the correct keywords.

5. B. JOHN will be able to log in to the database using SQL*Plus, and Oracle will prompt for new password when John logs in the first time. Since John's default tablespace is INDEX01, the tables and indexes created will be on the INDEX01 tablespace if the TABLESPACE clause is omitted. Though INDEX01 is the default tablespace, to create objects on INDEX01 or any other tablespace, a specific space quota needs to be defined, or the user should have the UNLIMITED TABLESPACE system privilege.

6. A. When object privileges are granted through an intermediary, they are implicitly dropped when the intermediary is dropped. CASCADE REVOKE and NOCASCADE REVOKE are not part of the GRANT statement syntax.

7. B. When system privileges are granted through an intermediary, they are not affected when the intermediary is dropped. CASCADE REVOKE and NOCASCADE REVOKE are not part of the GRANT statement syntax.

8. D. The CREATE ANY JOB and CREATE ANY PROCEDURE system privileges allow the grantee to create and run programs with the privileges of another user. The ALTER USER privilege allows the grantee to change a user's password, connect as that user, and then change the password back. These are all powerful system privileges and should be restricted to as few administrative users as practical.

9. D. The SET ROLE statement enables or disables roles in the current session.

10. B. To enable a password-protected role, you need to either execute a SET ROLE statement specifying the password or alter the user to make the role a default role. Default roles do not require a set role statement or a password to become enabled.

11. A. By default, user accounts have no quota in any tablespace. Before a user can create a table or an index, you need to either give the user a quota in one or more specific tablespaces or grant the UNLIMITED TABLESPACE system privilege to give an unlimited quota (including autoextends) in all tablespaces.

12. C. Profiles limit the amount of idle time, CPU time, logical reads, or other resource-oriented session limits. Option C uses the correct syntax to limit idle time for a session to 30 minutes.

13. B. Although option D could also work, it involves storing the passwords in a table in the database, which could be a security concern. It also takes a lot more effort to configure and maintain. The better technique is to use the standard database profile features PASSWORD_REUSE_TIME and PASSWORD_REUSE_MAX. Setting one of these profile parameters to UNLIMITED and the other to a specific value prevents passwords from being reused. If both of these profile parameters are set to UNLIMITED, these parameters are essentially disabled. There is no initialization parameter called NO_PASSWORD_REUSE.

14. B. Since HR_QUERY has the SELECT ANY TABLE privilege, no other privilege is required to query user tables in the database. To avoid the error, HR_QUERY must be defined as a default role for John, or John should use the SET ROLE statement. A password is not needed for SET ROLE because the role is not password protected.

15. C. In Oracle 11g user passwords are case sensitive. The username is not case sensitive if you did not enclose it in double quotes.

16. B. In Oracle 11g, the default value for AUDIT_TRAIL parameter is DB. By default, Oracle 11g enables several key database-auditing features.

17. A. You limit the number of failed logon attempts with a profile.

18. D. The destination of audit_trail records is controlled by the initialization parameter audit_trail. Setting this parameter to DB or DB,EXTENDED causes the audit trail to be written to a database table. Setting the parameter to OS or XML causes the audit trail to be written to an operating-system file.

19. C. When a space quota is exceeded or quota is removed from a user on a tablespace, the tables remain in the tablespace, but no new extents can be allocated. New rows can be inserted into the table as long as the table does not require Oracle to allocate a new extent in the table.

20. B. Fine-grained auditing is managed using the DBMS_FGA package. The AUDIT and NOAUDIT statements are used to manage statement, privilege, and object auditing. The GRANT and REVOKE statements are used to manage system, object, and role privileges. The CREATE, ALTER, and DROP statements are used to manage several types of database objects and settings.

Chapter

13

Managing Data and Undo

ORACLE DATABASE 11*g***: ADMINISTRATION I EXAM OBJECTIVES COVERED IN THIS CHAPTER:**

✓ **Managing Data and Concurrency**

- Manage data using DML

- Identify and administer PL/SQL objects

- Monitor and resolve locking conflicts

✓ **Managing Undo Data**

- Overview of Undo

- Transactions and undo data

- Managing undo

Oracle supports manipulating data via several interfaces, but the most common are SQL and PL/SQL. Understanding how to use and manage PL/SQL programs is an important skill for any DBA. Some database functionality is delivered only as PL/SQL programs, such as fine-grained auditing, and other functionality is available in both a command-line version and as a PL/SQL program, such as Data Pump export and Data Pump import. As you gain experience, you will increasingly rely on using PL/SQL to manage your databases. So, you need to have a solid grasp of SQL and PL/SQL fundamentals to be a successful Oracle DBA.

In Chapter 5, "Manipulating Data," you learned to add, change, and remove information from an Oracle Database using SQL DML statements. In this chapter, you will review DML statements and learn how to administer PL/SQL stored objects. You will also understand what "undo" is in Oracle and how Oracle uses undo information to build consistent results.

Manipulating Data through SQL

The Structured Query Language (SQL) includes Data Definition Language (DDL) statements, Data Control Language (DCL) statements, and Data Manipulation Language (DML) statements. You learned to add, modify, and delete information from the Oracle Database using DML statements in Chapter 5. You also learned how to create, alter, and delete objects using DDL statements in Chapters 6, 7, and 10. In Chapter 12, "Implementing Security and Auditing," you learned how to use the DCL statements GRANT and REVOKE to give and take privileges on database objects. To provide complete coverage of the main OCP objective "Managing Data and Concurrency," in this chapter I will explain the DML statements INSERT, UPDATE, and DELETE for adding, modifying, and removing data from your tables.

After using DML statements to add rows to a table, update rows in a table, or delete rows from a table, you must make these changes permanent by executing a COMMIT command. Alternatively, you can undo the DML changes with a ROLLBACK command. Until you commit the changes, other database sessions will not be able to see your changes.

Read Chapter 5 to understand DML statements completely. This chapter reviews only the INSERT, UPDATE, and DELETE statements.

Using the INSERT Statement

You use the INSERT statement to add rows in one or more tables. You can create these rows with specific data values or copy them from existing tables using a subquery.

Inserting into a Single Table

When using SQL, the only way to add rows in an Oracle 11*g* table is with an INSERT statement, and the most common variety of INSERT statement is the single table insert. The syntax for a simple INSERT statement is as follows:

```
INSERT INTO [schema.]table_name [(column_list)]
VALUES (data_values)
```

In the syntax, *table_name* is the name of the table where you want to add new rows, and it can be qualified with the schema name. *column_list* is the name of columns in the table, each separated by a comma, that you want to populate. The *data_values* are the corresponding values for each column in the *column_list*, each separated by a comma. Using this syntax you add one row at a time to the table.

column_list is optional, with the default being a list of all columns in the table in COLUMN_ID order. See the data dictionary views USER_TAB_COLUMNS, ALL_TAB_COLUMNS, or DBA_TAB_COLUMNS for the COLUMN_ID. Although inserting into a table is more common, you can also insert into a view, as long as the view does not contain one of the following:

- A DISTINCT operator
- A set operator (UNION, MINUS, and so on)
- An aggregate function (SUM, COUNT, AVG, and so on)
- A GROUP BY, ORDER BY, or CONNECT BY clause
- A subquery in the SELECT list

Here are some examples of using the INSERT statement to insert rows into a single table. The following inserts one row, channel 3, in the channels table:

```
INSERT INTO channels (channel_id ,channel_desc
   ,channel_class ,channel_class_id
   ,channel_total ,channel_total_id)
VALUES (3 ,'Direct Sales' ,'Direct'
   ,12 ,'Channel total' ,1);
```

The following inserts one row, channel 5, in the channels table:

```
INSERT INTO channels VALUES
   (5 ,'Catalog' ,'Indirect' ,13 ,'Channel total' ,1);
```

You can also add rows to a table based on the result from a subquery. The following example copies zero or more rows from the `territories` table in the `home_office` database to the `regions` table. `home_office` is the name of the database link.

```
INSERT INTO regions (region_id ,region_name)
   SELECT region_seq.NEXTVAL , terr_name
   FROM territories@home_office
WHERE class = 'R';
```

The number and datatypes of values in the `VALUES` list must match the number and datatypes in the column list. The database will perform implicit datatype conversion if necessary to convert the values into the datatype of the target.

To understand database links, read the sidebar "Creating Database Links" in Chapter 7, "Creating Schema Objects."

Inserting into Multiple Tables

Most `INSERT` statements are the single-table variety, but Oracle also supports a multiple-table `INSERT` statement. You'll most frequently use multitable inserts in data warehouse Extract, Transform, and Load (ETL) routines.

With a multitable insert, you can make a single pass through the source data and load the data into more than one table. By reducing the number of passes through the source data, you can reduce the overall work and thus achieve faster throughput.

The syntax for the multiple-table `INSERT` statement is as follows:

```
INSERT [ALL | FIRST] {WHEN <condition>
THEN INTO <insert_clause> … … …}
[ELSE <insert_clause>]
```

If a `WHEN` condition evaluates to `TRUE`, the corresponding `INTO` clause is executed. If no `WHEN` condition evaluates to `TRUE`, the `ELSE` clause is executed. The keyword `ALL` tells the database to check each `WHEN` condition. On the other hand, the keyword `FIRST` tells the database to stop checking `WHEN` conditions after finding the first `TRUE` condition.

In the following example, an insurance company has policies for both property and casualty in the `policy` table, but in its data mart, the company might break out these policy types into separate fact tables. During the monthly load, new policies are added to both the `property_premium_fact` and `casualty_premium_fact` tables. You can use a multitable `INSERT` to add these rows more efficiently than two separate `INSERT` statements. A multitable `INSERT` looks like this:

```
INSERT FIRST
WHEN policy_type = 'P' THEN
   INTO property_premium_fact(policy_id ,
       policy_nbr ,premium_amt)
```

```
VALUES (property_premium_seq.nextval ,
        policy_number ,gross_premium)
WHEN p.policy_type = 'C' THEN
  INTO property_premium_fact(policy_id ,
      policy_nbr ,premium_amt)
  VALUES (property_premium_seq.nextval ,
          policy_number ,gross_premium)
SELECT policy_nbr ,gross_premium ,policy_type
FROM policies
WHERE policy_date >=
      TRUNC(SYSDATE,'MM') - TO_YMINTERVAL('00-01');
```

By using this multitable INSERT statement instead of two separate statements, the code makes a single pass through the policy table instead of two and thus saves a significant amount of I/O and processing time.

Using the UPDATE Statement

You use an UPDATE statement to change existing rows in a table. The basic syntax for the UPDATE statement is as follows:

```
UPDATE <table_name>
SET <column_list> = <values>
  [,<column_list> = <values> … … …]
[WHERE <condition>]
```

The column list can be either a single column or a comma-delimited list of columns. A single list of columns lets you assign single values—either literals or from a subquery. The following updates customer XYZ's phone and fax numbers and sets their quantity based on their orders:

```
UPDATE order_rollup r
SET phone = '3125551212'
  ,fax   = '7735551212'
  ,qty   = (SELECT SUM(d.qty)
              FROM order_details d
              WHERE d.customer_id = r.customer_id)
WHERE r.customer_id = 'XYZ';
```

When you use a comma-delimited list of columns, you must enclose them in parentheses. The comma-delimited list lets you assign multiple values from a subquery. The following updates both the quantity and the price for customer XYZ for the order they placed on October 1, 2008:

```
UPDATE order_rollup
SET (qty, price) = (SELECT SUM(qty), SUM(price)
```

```
                          FROM order_details
                          WHERE customer_id = 'XYZ')
WHERE customer_id = 'XYZ'
 AND  order_period = TO_DATE('01-Oct-2008');
```

Assigning multiple values from a single subquery can save you from having to perform multiple subqueries, thus improving the efficiency of your SQL.

Using the MERGE Statement

The MERGE statement is used to both update and insert rows in a table. The MERGE statement has a join specification that describes how to determine whether an update or insert should be executed. The syntax of a simple MERGE statement is as follows:

```
MERGE INTO <table>
USING <subquery or table>
ON <condition>
[WHEN MATCHED THEN UPDATE SET <column> = <expression> [WHERE <condition>]]
[WHEN NOT MATCHED THEN INSERT <column_list> VALUES <values_list> [WHERE
<condition>]]
[WHERE <condition>]
```

The WHEN MATCHED predicate specifies how to update the existing rows. The WHEN NOT MATCHED predicate specifies how to create rows that do not exist.

The following example has a new pricing sheet for products in category 33. This new pricing data has been loaded into the NEW_PRICES table. You need to update the PRODUCT_INFORMATION table with these new prices. The NEW_PRICES table contains updates to existing rows in the PRODUCT_INFORMATION table as well as new products. The new products need to be inserted, and the existing products need to be updated.

```
SELECT product_id,category_id,list_price,min_price
FROM oe.product_information
WHERE category_id=33;


PRODUCT_ID CATEGORY_ID LIST_PRICE  MIN_PRICE
---------- ----------- ----------  ----------
      2986          33        125         111
      3163          33         35          29
      3165          33         40          34
      3167          33         55          47
      3216          33         30          26
      3220          33         45          36


SELECT *
FROM new_prices;
```

```
PRODUCT_ID LIST_PRICE  MIN_PRICE
---------- ---------- ----------
      2986        135        121
      3163         40         32
      3164         40         35
      3165         40         37
      3166         50         45
      3167         55         50
      3216         30         26
      3220         45         36
```

You can use the MERGE statement to perform an update/insert of the new pricing data into the PRODUCT_INFORMATION table, as follows:

```
MERGE INTO oe.product_information pi
USING (SELECT product_id, list_price, min_price
    FROM new_prices) NP
ON (pi.product_id = np.product_id)
WHEN MATCHED THEN UPDATE SET pi.list_price =np.list_price
                            ,pi.min_price = np.min_price
WHEN NOT MATCHED THEN INSERT (pi.product_id,pi.category_id
                            ,pi.list_price,pi.min_price)
   VALUES (np.product_id, 33,np.list_price, np.min_price);
```

```
PRODUCT_ID CATEGORY_ID LIST_PRICE  MIN_PRICE
---------- ----------- ---------- ----------
      2986          33        135        121 (updated)
      3163          33         40         32 (updated)
      3164          33         40         35 (inserted)
      3165          33         40         37 (updated)
      3166          33         50         45 (inserted)
      3167          33         55         50 (updated)
      3216          33         30         26 (updated)
      3220          33         45         36 (updated)
```

Using the DELETE Statement

You use the DELETE statement to remove rows from a table. The syntax for a basic DELETE statement is as follows:

```
DELETE [FROM] <table>
[WHERE <condition>]
```

Here are some examples of a DELETE statement. The following removes orders from certain states:

```
DELETE FROM orders
WHERE state IN ('TX','NY','IL')
 AND  order_date < TRUNC(SYSDATE) - 90
```

The following removes customer GOMEZ:

```
DELETE FROM customers
WHERE customer_name = 'GOMEZ';
```

The following removes duplicate line_detail_id values. Note that the keyword FROM is not needed.

```
DELETE line_details
WHERE rowid NOT IN (SELECT MAX(rowid)
                    FROM line_detail
                    GROUP BY line_detail_id)
```

The following example removes all rows from table order_staging:

```
DELETE FROM order_staging;
```

The WHERE clause is optional, and when it is not present, all rows from the table are removed. If you need to remove all rows from a table, consider using the TRUNCATE statement. TRUNCATE is a DDL statement and, unlike the DELETE statement, does not support a ROLLBACK. Using TRUNCATE, unlike using DELETE, does not generate undo and executes much faster for a large table.

When you perform the TRUNCATE operation, Oracle performs an implicit commit since it is a DDL and also requires an exclusive lock on the table. To read more about the difference between DELETE and TRUNCATE, see the section "Truncating a Table" in Chapter 5.

Identifying PL/SQL Objects

PL/SQL is Oracle's procedural language extension to SQL. This Oracle proprietary language was derived from Ada and has evolved to include a robust feature set, including sequential and conditional controls, looping constructs, exception handling, records, and collections, as well as object-oriented features such as methods, overloading, upcasting, and type inheritance.

Full knowledge of the PL/SQL language is well beyond the scope of the OCA/OCP exams, and more developers than DBAs create PL/SQL programs. But a significant number of database features are delivered as PL/SQL programs, and knowing how to identify and work with these programs is crucial to your effectiveness. In this section, you will learn what kinds of PL/SQL programs are available, when each is appropriate, and what configuration options are applicable to working with PL/SQL programs.

The exam covers five types of named PL/SQL programs, which are usually stored in the database: functions, procedures, packages, package bodies, and triggers. Each of these program types is covered in the following sections. The name and source code for each stored PL/SQL program is available from the data dictionary views DBA_SOURCE and DBA_TRIGGERS, although some packages are supplied *wrapped*, which means that the source code is a binary form. You can wrap your programs as well with the wrap utility.

> Wrap is an Oracle-provided utility used to hide the PL/SQL source code, which helps protect your intellectual property. See Appendix A in the Oracle documentation "Oracle Database PL/SQL Language Reference 11*g* Release 1 (11.1) Part Number B28370-02" for details on using Wrap. You can access the Oracle documentation at http://tahiti.oracle.com. You can also use the subprograms available in the DBMS_DDL package to wrap code.

Working with Functions

Functions are PL/SQL programs that execute zero or more statements and return a value through a RETURN statement. Functions can also receive or return zero or more values through their parameters. Oracle provides several built-in functions such as the commonly used SYSDATE, COUNT, and SUBSTR functions. Several SQL functions and hundreds of PL/SQL functions come with Oracle Database 11g. We discussed several of the SQL functions in Chapter 2, "Using Single-Row Functions," and Chapter 3, "Using Group Functions." Because functions have a return value, a datatype is associated with them. Functions can be invoked anywhere an expression of the same datatype is allowed. Here are some examples:

- As a default value:
  ```
  DECLARE
     today   DATE DEFAULT SYSDATE;
  ```

- In an assignment:
  ```
  today := SYSDATE;
  ```

- In a Boolean expression:
  ```
  IF TO_CHAR(SYSDATE,'Day') = 'Monday'
  ```

- In a SQL expression:
  ```
  SELECT COUNT(*)
  FROM employees
  WHERE hire_date > SYSDATE-30;
  ```

- In the parameter list of another procedure or function:
  ```
  SELECT TRUNC(SYSDATE)
  ```

Create a function with the CREATE FUNCTION statement, like this:

```
CREATE OR REPLACE FUNCTION is_weekend(
  check_date IN DATE DEFAULT SYSDATE)
  RETURN VARCHAR2 AS
BEGIN
  CASE TO_CHAR(check_date,'DY')
  WHEN 'SAT' THEN
      RETURN 'YES';
  WHEN 'SUN' THEN
      RETURN 'YES';
  ELSE
      RETURN 'NO';
  END CASE;
END;
```

Functions, like all named PL/SQL, have the OR REPLACE keywords available in the CREATE statement. When present, OR REPLACE tells the database to not raise an exception if the object already exists. This behavior differs from a DROP and CREATE, in that privileges are not lost during a REPLACE operation and any objects that reference this object will not become invalid.

Working with Procedures

Procedures are PL/SQL programs that execute one or more statements. Procedures can receive and return values only through their parameter lists. You create a procedure with the CREATE PROCEDURE statement, like this:

```
CREATE OR REPLACE PROCEDURE archive_orders
   (cust_id   IN NUMBER
   ,retention IN NUMBER) IS
BEGIN

   INSERT INTO orders_archive
   SELECT * FROM orders
   WHERE customer = cust_id
   AND   order_date < SYSDATE - retention;

   DELETE orders
   WHERE customer = cust_id
   AND   order_date < SYSDATE - retention;

   INSERT INTO maint_log
```

```
  (action, action_date, who) VALUES
  ('archive orders '||retention||' for '||cust_id
  ,SYSDATE ,USER);
END;
```

The keyword IS, in the third line, is synonymous with the keyword AS, shown in the third line of the last example function in the previous section. Both are syntactically valid for all named SQL.

You invoke a procedure as a stand-alone statement within a PL/SQL program or by using the CALL or EXEC command. Here is an example:

```
EXEC DBMS_OUTPUT.PUT_LINE('Hello world!');
Hello world!

PL/SQL procedure successfully completed.

CALL  DBMS_OUTPUT.PUT_LINE('Hello world!');
Hello world!

Call completed.
```

 A function or procedure by default is executed with the privileges of its owner, not of its invoker. If you create the procedure or function with a clause AUTHID CURRENT_USER, then the procedure or function will be executed with the privileges of the invoker. To be able to execute a procedure or function owned by another user, you must have been given the EXECUTE privilege or should have the EXECUTE ANY system privilege.

Working with Packages

A *package* is a container for functions, procedures, and data structures such as records, cursors, variables, and constants. A package has a publicly visible portion, called the *specification* (or *spec* for short) and a private portion called the *package body*. The package spec describes the programs and data structures that can be accessed from other programs. The package body contains the implementation of the procedures and functions. The package spec is identified in the data dictionary as the type PACKAGE, and the package body is identified as the type PACKAGE BODY.

To create a package spec, use the CREATE PACKAGE statement. In the following example, the package spec table_util contains one function and one procedure:

```
CREATE OR REPLACE PACKAGE table_util IS
  FUNCTION version RETURN VARCHAR2;
  PROCEDURE truncate (table_name IN VARCHAR2);
```

```
END table_util;
```

Privileges on a package are granted at the package-spec level. The EXECUTE privilege on a package allows the grantee to execute any program or use any data structure declared in the package specification. You cannot grant the EXECUTE privilege on only some of the programs declared in the spec.

Creating a Package Body

A package body depends on a package spec having the same name. The package body can be created only after the spec. The package body implements the programs that were declared in the package spec and can optionally contain private programs and data accessible only from within the package body.

To create a package body, use the CREATE PACKAGE BODY statement:

```
CREATE OR REPLACE PACKAGE BODY table_util IS
```

Here is an example of a private variable that can be referenced only in the package body:

```
version_string VARCHAR2(8) := '1.0.0';
```

Here is the code for the version function:

```
FUNCTION version RETURN VARCHAR2 IS
  BEGIN
     RETURN version_string;
  END;
```

Here is the code for the truncate procedure:

```
PROCEDURE truncate (table_name IN VARCHAR2) IS
  BEGIN
     IF  UPPER(table_name) = 'ORDER_STAGE'
      OR UPPER(table_name) = 'SALES_ROLLUP'
     THEN
        EXECUTE IMMEDIATE 'truncate table ' ||
           UPPER(table_name);
     ELSE
        RAISE_APPLICATION_ERROR(-20010
           ,'Invalid table for truncate: '|| table_name);
     END IF;
  END;
END table_util;
```

The package name following the END statement is optional but encouraged because it improves readability.

Working with Triggering Events and Managing Triggers

Triggers are PL/SQL programs that are invoked in response to an event in the database. Three sets of events can be hooked, allowing you to integrate your business logic with the database in an event-driven manner. Triggers can be created on DML events, DDL events, and database events. These three trigger event classes provide developers and you, the DBA, with a robust toolkit with which to design, build, and troubleshoot systems.

I will cover each of these events in more detail in the following sections. I will also discuss how to enable and disable triggers.

DML Trigger Events

DML triggers are invoked, or *fired*, when the specified DML events occur. If the keywords FOR EACH ROW are included in the trigger definition, the trigger fires once for each row that is changed. If these keywords are missing, the trigger fires once for each statement that causes the specified change. If the DML event list includes the UPDATE event, the trigger can be further restricted to fire only when updates of specific columns occur.

The following example creates a trigger that fires before any insert and before an update to the HIRE_DATE column of the EMPLOYEE table:

```
CREATE OR REPLACE TRIGGER employee_trg
 BEFORE INSERT OR UPDATE OF hire_date
 ON employees FOR EACH ROW
BEGIN
   log_update(USER,SYSTIMESTAMP);
   IF INSERTING THEN -- if fired due to insert
     :NEW.create_user :=  USER;
     :NEW.create_ts   :=  SYSTIMESTAMP;
   ELSIF UPDATING THEN -- if fired due to update
     IF :OLD.hire_date <> :NEW.hire_date THEN
        RAISE_APPLICATION_ERROR(-20013,
          'update of hire_date not allowed');
     END IF;
   END IF;
END;
```

This trigger will fire once for each row affected, because the keywords FOR EACH ROW are included. When the triggering event is an INSERT, two columns are forced to the specific values returned by USER and SYSTIMESTAMP. DML triggers cannot be created on SYS-owned objects. Table 13.1 shows the DML trigger events.

TABLE 13.1 DML Trigger Events

Event	When It Fires
INSERT	When a row is added to a table or a view.
UPDATE	When an UPDATE statement changes a row in a table or view. Update triggers can also specify an OF clause to limit the scope of changes that fire this type of trigger.
DELETE	When a row is removed from a table or a view.

Multiple triggers on a table fire in the following order:

1. Before statement triggers
2. Before row triggers
3. After row triggers
4. After statement triggers

 Until Oracle 11*g*, if you had two or more triggers defined for the same statement for the same timing point, the order of trigger execution was unpredictable. In Oracle 11*g*, the FOLLOWS clause removes that restriction.

DDL Trigger Events

DDL triggers fire either for DDL changes to a specific schema or to all schemas in the database. The keywords ON DATABASE specify that the trigger will fire for the specified event on any schema in the database.

The following is an example of a trigger that fires for a DDL event in only one schema:

```
CREATE OR REPLACE TRIGGER NoGrantToPublic
BEFORE GRANT ON engineering.SCHEMA
DECLARE
    grantee_list    dbms_standard.ora_name_list_t;
    counter         BINARY_INTEGER;
BEGIN
    -- get the list of grantees
    counter := GRANTEE(grantee_list);
    FOR loop_counter IN
      grantee_list.FIRST..grantee_list.LAST
    LOOP
        -- if PUBLIC is on the grantee list, stop the action
        IF REGEXP_LIKE(grantee_list(loop_counter)
            ,'public','i') THEN
            RAISE_APPLICATION_ERROR(-20113
```

```
          ,'No grant to PUBLIC allowed for '
          ||DICTIONARY_OBJ_OWNER||'.'
          ||DICTIONARY_OBJ_NAME);
      END IF;
    END LOOP;
END;
```

In the preceding example, the DDL event is a GRANT statement issued by user engineering. The code examines the grantee list, and if it finds the special user/role PUBLIC, an exception is raised, causing the grant to fail. Table 13.2 shows the DDL trigger events.

TABLE 13.2   DDL Trigger Events

Event	When It Fires
[BEFORE/AFTER] ALTER	When an ALTER statement changes a database object
[BEFORE/AFTER] ANALYZE	When the database gathers or deletes statistics or validates the structure of an object
[BEFORE/AFTER] ASSOCIATE STATISTICS	When the database associates a statistic with a database object with an ASSOCIATE STATISTICS statement
[BEFORE/AFTER] AUDIT	When the database records an audit action (except FGA)
[BEFORE/AFTER] COMMENT	When a comment on a table or column is modified
[BEFORE/AFTER] CREATE	When the database object is created
[BEFORE/AFTER] DDL	In conjunction with any of the following: ALTER, ANALYZE, ASSOCIATE STATISTICS, AUDIT, COMMENT, CREATE, DISASSOCIATE STATISTICS, DROP GRANT, NOAUDIT, RENAME, REVOKE, or TRUNCATE
[BEFORE/AFTER] DISASSOCIATE STATISTICS	When a database disassociates a statistic type from a database object with a DISASSOCIATE STATISTICS statement
[BEFORE/AFTER] DROP	When a DROP statement removes an object from the database
[BEFORE/AFTER] GRANT	When a GRANT statement assigns a privilege
[BEFORE/AFTER] NOAUDIT	When a NOAUDIT statement changes database auditing
[BEFORE/AFTER] RENAME	When a RENAME statement changes an object name
[BEFORE/AFTER] REVOKE	When a REVOKE statement rescinds a privilege
[BEFORE/AFTER] TRUNCATE	When a TRUNCATE statement purges a table

Database Trigger Events

Database event triggers fire when the specified database-level event occurs. Most of these triggers are available only before or after the database event, but not both.

The following example creates an after-server error trigger that sends an email notification when an ORA-01555 error occurs:

```
CREATE OR REPLACE TRIGGER Email_on_1555_Err
AFTER SERVERERROR ON DATABASE
DECLARE
    mail_conn           UTL_SMTP.connection;
    smtp_relay          VARCHAR2(32) := 'mailserver';
    recipient_address   VARCHAR2(64) := 'DBA@hotmail.com';
    sender_address      VARCHAR2(64) := 'oracle@sybex.com';
    mail_port           NUMBER := 25;
    msg                 VARCHAR2(200);
BEGIN
   IF USER = 'SYSTEM' THEN
      -- Ignore this error
      NULL;
   ELSIF IS_SERVERERROR (1555) THEN
      -- compose the message
      msg := 'Subject: ORA-1555 error';
      msg := msg||'Snapshot too old err at '||systimestamp;
      -- send email notice
      mail_conn := UTL_SMTP.open_connection(smtp_relay
            ,mail_port);
      UTL_SMTP.HELO(mail_conn, smtp_relay);
      UTL_SMTP.MAIL(mail_conn, sender_address);
      UTL_SMTP.RCPT(mail_conn, recipient_address);
      UTL_SMTP.DATA(mail_conn, msg);
      UTL_SMTP.QUIT(mail_conn);
   END IF;
END;
```

Be careful when using database triggers. Fully test them in development before deploying them to production. Table 13.3 shows the database trigger events.

TABLE 13.3 Database Trigger Events

Event	When It Fires
AFTER LOGON	When a database session is established—only the AFTER trigger is allowed
BEFORE LOGOFF	When a database session ends normally—only the BEFORE trigger is allowed

TABLE 13.3   Database Trigger Events *(continued)*

Event	When It Fires
AFTER STARTUP	When the database is opened—only the AFTER trigger is allowed
BEFORE SHUTDOWN	When the database is closed—only the BEFORE trigger is allowed
AFTER SERVERERROR	When a database exception is raised—only the AFTER trigger is allowed
AFTER SUSPEND	When a server error causes a transaction to be suspended—only the AFTER trigger is allowed

Enabling and Disabling Triggers

The database automatically enables a trigger when you create it. After creating a trigger, you can disable (temporarily prevent it from firing) or reenable it. You can disable and enable triggers by name with an ALTER TRIGGER statement. Here are two examples:

```
ALTER TRIGGER after_ora60 DISABLE;
```

```
ALTER TRIGGER load_packages ENABLE;
```

Alternatively, you can enable and disable multiple DML triggers with an ALTER TABLE statement, like this:

```
ALTER TABLE employees DISABLE ALL TRIGGERS;
ALTER TABLE employees ENABLE ALL TRIGGERS;
```

You can also create a trigger with the ENABLE or DISABLE clause. ENABLE is the default.

You can query the STATUS column of the DBA_TRIGGERS view to find out whether a trigger is enabled or disabled.

Using and Administering PL/SQL Programs

Oracle 11*g* comes bundled with hundreds of built-in packages that give you significant capabilities for administering your database. Many features in the database are implemented through one or more of these built-in packages. To use the job scheduler, collect and manage optimizer statistics, implement fine-grained auditing, send email from the database, and use Data Pump or Log Miner, you must engage built-in packages. As you gain experience, you will use these built-in packages more extensively.

These are some of the commonly used built-in catalog packages:

- DBMS_STATS
- DBMS_METADATA
- DBMS_MONITOR

- UTL_FILE

- UTL_MAIL

To view the names and parameter lists for stored programs (except triggers), use the SQL*Plus DESCRIBE command like this:

```
describe dbms_monitor
-- some output is deleted for brevity


PROCEDURE SESSION_TRACE_DISABLE
Argument Name    Type                 In/Out Default?
---------------  -------------------  ------ --------
SESSION_ID       BINARY_INTEGER       IN     DEFAULT
SERIAL_NUM       BINARY_INTEGER       IN     DEFAULT


PROCEDURE SESSION_TRACE_ENABLE
Argument Name    Type                 In/Out Default?
---------------  -------------------  ------ --------
SESSION_ID       BINARY_INTEGER       IN     DEFAULT
SERIAL_NUM       BINARY_INTEGER       IN     DEFAULT
WAITS            BOOLEAN              IN     DEFAULT
BINDS            BOOLEAN              IN     DEFAULT
PLAN_STAT        VARCHAR2             IN     DEFAULT
```

You can see in this output from DESCRIBE that the packaged procedure DBMS_MONITOR contains several procedures, including SESSION_TRACE_DISABLE and SESSION_TRACE_ENABLE. Furthermore, you can see the names, datatypes, and in/out mode for each parameter (SESSION_ID, SERIAL_NUM, and so on).

 An extensive list of Oracle built-in PL/SQL packages is available in the manual "Oracle Database PL/SQL Packages and Types Reference 11*g* Release 1 (11.1) Part Number B28419-03." Fortunately, you don't have to know all these programs for the certification exam!

A PL/SQL program may be invalidated when a dependent object is changed through the ALTER command. The database automatically recompiles the package body the next time it is called, but you can choose to compile invalid PL/SQL programs yourself and thus eliminate the costly recompile during regular system processing. To explicitly compile a named SQL program, use the ALTER...COMPILE statement, like this:

```
ALTER PROCEDURE archive_orders COMPILE;
ALTER FUNCTION is_weekend COMPILE;
ALTER PACKAGE table_util COMPILE;
```

```
ALTER PACKAGE table_util COMPILE BODY;
ALTER TRIGGER fire_me COMPILE;
```

Other objects, such as views or types, are similarly compiled.

Oracle 11*g* implements a finer-grained dependency control; hence, if the package specification is not changed, the PL/SQL objects that reference the functions and procedures of the package are not invalidated when only the package body is changed.

Monitoring Locks and Resolving Lock Conflicts

In any database with many users, you will eventually have to deal with locking conflicts when two or more users try to change the same row in the database. In the following sections, I'll present an overview of how locking works in the Oracle Database, how users are queued for a particular resource once it is locked, and how Oracle classifies lock types in the database. Then, I'll show you a number of ways to detect and resolve locking issues; I'll also cover a special type of lock situation: the deadlock.

Understanding Locks and Transactions

Locks prevent multiple users from changing the same data at the same time. Before one or more rows in a table can be changed, the user executing the DML statement must obtain a lock on the row or rows; a *lock* gives the user exclusive control over the data until the user has committed or rolled back the transaction that is changing the data.

In Oracle 11*g*, a transaction can lock one row, multiple rows, or an entire table. Although you can manually lock rows, Oracle can automatically lock the rows needed at the lowest possible level to ensure data integrity and minimize conflicts with other transactions that may need to access other rows in the table.

In Table 13.4, both updates to the EMPLOYEES table return to the command prompt immediately after the UPDATE because the locks are on different rows in the EMPLOYEES table and neither session is waiting for the other lock to be released.

TABLE 13.4   Concurrent Transactions on Different Rows of the Same Table

Session 1	Time	Session 2
update employees set salary = salary * 1.2 where employee_id = 102;	11:29	update employees set manager = 100 where employee_id = 109;
commit;	11:30	commit;

Real World Scenario

Packaged Applications and Locking

The HR department recently purchased a benefits-management package that interfaced well with our existing employee-management tables; however, once HR started using the application, other users who accessed the employee tables started complaining of severe slowdowns in updates to the employee information.

Reviewing the CPU and I/O usage of the instance did not reveal any problems, and it wasn't until we looked at the locking information that we noticed a table lock on the employees table whenever the benefits-management features were being used! The benefits-management application was written to work on a number of database platforms, and the least capable of those platforms did not support row locking. As a result, no one could make changes to the employees table whenever an employee's benefits were being changed, and everyone had to wait for the benefits changes to complete. Fortunately, the parameter file for the benefits-management package had an option to specify Oracle as the target platform; after setting the specific database version in the package's parameter file, the package was smart enough to use row locking instead of table locking whenever the employee table needed to be updated.

Queries never require a lock. Even if another transaction has locked several rows or an entire table, a query always succeeds, using the prelock image of the data stored in the undo tablespace.

If multiple users require a lock on a row or rows in a table, the first user to request the lock obtains it, and the remaining users are enqueued using a first-in, first-out (FIFO) method. At a SQL> command prompt, a DML statement (INSERT, UPDATE, DELETE, or MERGE) that is waiting for a lock on a resource appears to hang, unless the NOWAIT keyword is used in a LOCK statement.

The WAIT and NOWAIT keywords are explained in the next section, "Maximizing Data Concurrency."

At the end of a transaction, when either a COMMIT or a ROLLBACK is issued (either explicitly by the user or implicitly when the session terminates normally or abnormally), all locks are released.

Maximizing Data Concurrency

Rows of a table are locked either explicitly by the user at the beginning of a transaction or implicitly by Oracle, usually at the row level, depending on the operation. If a table must be locked for performance reasons (which is rare), you can use the LOCK TABLE command, specifying the level at which the table should be locked.

In the following example, you lock the EMPLOYEES and DEPARTMENTS tables at the highest possible level, EXCLUSIVE:

```
SQL> lock table hr.employees, hr.departments
     in exclusive mode;
Table(s) Locked.
```

Until the transaction with the LOCK statement either commits or rolls back, only queries are allowed on the EMPLOYEES or DEPARTMENTS table.

In the sections that follow, I will review the lock modes, as well as show you how to avoid the lock enqueue process and terminate the command if the requested resource is already locked.

Lock Modes

Lock modes provide a way for you to specify how much and what kinds of access other users have on tables that you are using in DML commands. In Table 13.5, you can see the types of locks that can be obtained at the table level.

TABLE 13.5   Table Lock Modes

Table Lock Mode	Description
ROW SHARE	Permits concurrent access to the locked table but prohibits other users from locking the entire table for exclusive access.
ROW EXCLUSIVE	Same as ROW SHARE but also prohibits locking in SHARE mode. This type of lock is obtained automatically with standard DML commands such as UPDATE, INSERT, or DELETE.
SHARE	Permits concurrent queries but prohibits updates to the table; this mode is required to create an index on a table and is automatically obtained when using the CREATE INDEX statement.
SHARE ROW EXCLUSIVE	Used to query a whole table and to allow other users to query the table but to prevent other users from locking the table in SHARE mode or updating rows.
EXCLUSIVE	The most restrictive locking mode; permits queries on the locked table but prohibits DML by any other users. This mode is required to drop the table and is automatically obtained when using the DROP TABLE statement.

Manual lock requests wait in the same queue as implicit locks and are satisfied in a FIFO manner as each request releases the lock with an implicit or explicit COMMIT or ROLLBACK.

You can explicitly obtain locks on individual rows by using the SELECT ... FOR UPDATE statement, as you can see in the following example:

```
SQL> select * from hr.employees
     where manager_id = 100
     for update;
```

Not only does this query show the rows that satisfy the query conditions, but it also locks the selected rows and prevents other transactions from locking or updating these rows until a COMMIT or ROLLBACK occurs.

NOWAIT Mode

Using NOWAIT in a LOCK TABLE statement returns control to the user immediately if any locks already exist on the requested resource, as you can see in the following example:

```
SQL> lock table hr.employees
     in share row exclusive mode
     nowait;
lock table hr.employees
               *
ERROR at line 1:
ORA-00054: resource busy and acquire with NOWAIT specified or timeout expired

SQL>
```

This is especially useful in a PL/SQL application if an alternate execution path can be followed if the requested resource is not yet available. NOWAIT can also be used in the SELECT ... FOR UPDATE statement.

WAIT Mode

You can tell Oracle 11g to wait a specified number of seconds to acquire a DML lock. If you do not specify a NOWAIT or WAIT clause, then the database waits indefinitely if the table is locked by another user. In the following example, Oracle will wait for 60 seconds to acquire the lock. If the lock is not acquired within 60 seconds, an error is returned.

```
SQL> lock table hr.employees
     in share row exclusive mode
     wait 60;
```

DDL Lock Waits

When DML statements have rows locked in a table or if the table is manually locked by a user, DDL statements on the table fail with the ORA-00054 error. To have the DDL statements wait for a specified number of seconds before throwing the ORA-00054 error, you can set the initialization parameter DDL_LOCK_TIMEOUT. The default value is 0, which means the error is issued immediately. You can specify a value up to 1,000,000 seconds.

```
SQL> alter table hr.employees modify salary number (15,2);
alter table hr.employees modify salary number (15,2)
                 *
ERROR at line 1:
ORA-00054: resource busy and acquire with NOWAIT specified or timeout expired

SQL> show parameter ddl_lock
NAME                                 TYPE        VALUE
------------------------------------ ----------- ------------------------------
ddl_lock_timeout                     integer     0
SQL>
```

Detecting and Resolving Lock Conflicts

Although locks are a common and sometimes unavoidable occurrence in many databases, they are usually resolved by waiting in the queue. In some cases, you may need to resolve the lock problem manually (such as if a user makes an update at 4:59 p.m. and does not perform a COMMIT before leaving for the day).

In the next few sections, I will describe in more detail some of the reasons that lock conflicts occur and how to detect lock conflicts, and I'll discuss a more specific and serious type of lock conflict: a deadlock.

Understanding Lock Conflicts

In addition to the proverbial user who makes a change at 4:59 p.m. and forgets to perform a COMMIT before leaving for the day, other more typical lock conflicts are caused by long-running transactions that perform hundreds, thousands, or even hundreds of thousands of DML commands in the overnight batch run but are not finished updating the tables when the normal business day starts. The uncommitted transactions from the overnight batch jobs may lock tables that need to be updated by clerical staff during the business day, causing a lock conflict.

Another typical cause of lock conflicts is using unnecessarily high locking levels. In the "Packaged Applications and Locking" sidebar earlier in this chapter, we described a third-party application that routinely locked resources at the table level instead of at the row level to be compatible with every SQL-based database on the market. Developers may unnecessarily code updates to tables with higher locking levels than required by Oracle 11*g*.

Detecting Lock Conflicts

Detecting locks in Oracle 11*g* using EM Database Control makes your job easy; you don't need to query against V$SESSION, V$TRANSACTION, V$LOCK, and V$LOCKED_OBJECT to see who is locking what resource. You can click the Instance Locks link on the Performance tab of EM Grid Control. In Figure 13.1, you can see the tables locked by the user SCOTT after executing the following statement:

```
SQL> lock table hr.employees, hr.departments
     in exclusive mode;
Table(s) Locked.
```

FIGURE 13.1 The Instance Locks screen in EM Database Control

SCOTT has an EXCLUSIVE lock on both the EMPLOYEES and DEPARTMENTS tables. You can drill down on the locked object by clicking one of the links in the Object Name column; similarly, you can review other information about SCOTT's session by clicking one of the links in the Session ID column.

If the HR user performs the following SQL, HR's session will wait until the SCOTT user releases the locks:

```
SQL> UPDATE employees SET salary = 0 WHERE salary IS NULL;
```

On the EM Grid Control screen, choose Blocking Locks from the drop-down view, and you can see that user SCOTT is blocking the HR user, as shown in Figure 13.2.

FIGURE 13.2   The blocking locks shown in EM Database Control

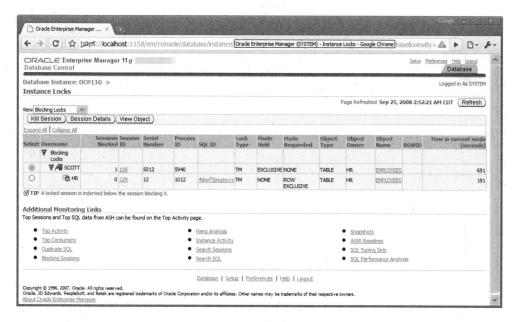

The data dictionary view DBA_LOCK is very handy for the DBA to look for locks and whether any session is blocking other users. A session with value of Blocking in the BLOCKING_OTHERS column may have to be manually terminated using the ALTER SYSTEM KILL SESSION statement. DBA_WAITERS is another view that shows only the sessions that are waiting on a lock. This view shows the holding session and the waiting session.

Understanding and Resolving Deadlocks

Resolving a lock conflict, the user can either COMMIT or ROLLBACK the current transaction. If you cannot contact the user and it is an emergency, you can select the session holding the lock and click the Kill Session button on the Instance Locks screen of the EM Database Control (refer to Figure 13.1, earlier in this chapter). The next time the user whose session has been killed tries to execute a command, the error message "ORA-00028: Your session has been killed" is returned. Again, this is an option of last resort: you'll lose all the statements executed in the session since the last COMMIT.

A more serious type of lock conflict is a deadlock. A *deadlock* is a special type of lock conflict in which two or more users are waiting for a resource locked by the other users. As a result, neither transaction can complete without some kind of intervention: the session that first detects a deadlock rolls back the statement waiting on the resource with the error message "ORA-00060: Deadlock detected while waiting for resource." Oracle automatically resolves deadlocks without user/DBA intervention.

In Table 13.6, two sessions are attempting to update a row locked by the other session.

TABLE 13.6 Deadlock Scenario

Session 1	Time	Session 2
update employees set salary = salary * 1.2 where employee_id = 102;	11:29	update employees set manager = 100 where employee_id = 109;
update employees set salary = salary * 1.2 where employee_id = 109;	11:44	
	11:50	update employees set manager = 100 where employee_id = 102;

Prior to 11:44, session 1 and session 2 updated two different rows in the database and did not commit the transaction. At 11:44, session 1 issued an UPDATE statement against the same row locked by session 2. This causes session 1 to hang, waiting for the lock to be released by session 2. The lock held by session 2 will be released only when session 2 performs a commit or rollback. At 11:50, when session 2 is trying to update a row already locked by session 1, you have a deadlock situation: session 1 waiting on session 2 and session 2 waiting on session 1. When this situation forms, Oracle throws out the ORA-00060 error and fails the statement. Remember, the transaction is not rolled back, because only the statement is in error. In our example, session 2 will get the ORA-00060 error when the update at 11:50 is issued, but session 1 will wait until session 2 commits or rolls back.

Leveraging Undo Management

Whenever a process or a user session changes data in the database, Oracle saves the old value as it existed before it was modified as undo data. This provides a number of benefits to the database user:

- It lets the user change their minds and roll back, or undo, the change to the database.

- It supports read-consistent queries. Once a query starts, any changes to the query's underlying tables are not reflected in the query's results.

- It supports flashback query, an Oracle feature introduced in Oracle9*i*. Flashback query allows a user to see how a table looked at some point in the past. As long as the undo data still exists for the requested point of time, flashback queries are possible.

In the following sections, I present all aspects of undo management. First, I will show how transactions are related to undo management and how undo records are stored in an undo tablespace along with some of the features supported by undo records. Next, I will show you how to set up the initialization parameters to specify a target for how much undo is retained in the undo tablespace; in addition, I will show you the commands needed to guarantee that undo space is available for SELECT statements at the expense of DML commands.

Monitoring an undo tablespace is not unlike monitoring any other tablespace: you want to make sure you have enough undo space in the tablespace to satisfy all types of user transactions but not so much that you're wasting space that can be used for objects in other tablespaces. Therefore, I will present some methods to accurately calculate the optimal amount of undo space you will need. Finally, I will review the notification methods you can use to proactively alert you to problems with the undo tablespace.

Understanding Undo Segments

Undo segments, also known as *rollback segments*, are similar to other segments in the database, such as table or index segments, in that an undo segment consists of extents, which in turn consist of data blocks. Also, an undo segment contains data similar to that stored in a table. However, that is where the similarity ends. Undo segments must be stored in a special type of tablespace called an *undo tablespace*. Although a database can have more than one undo tablespace, only one undo tablespace can be active at any one time. Undo segments contain undo information about one or many tables involved in a transaction. Also, undo segments automatically grow and shrink as needed, acting as a circular buffer—transactions that fill up the extents in an undo segment can wrap around to the beginning of the segment if the first extent is not being used by an active transaction.

At the beginning of a transaction—in other words, when the first DML command is issued after a previous COMMIT or a user first connects to the database—the transaction is assigned to an undo segment in the undo tablespace. Any changes to any table in the transaction are recorded in the assigned undo segment. The names of the current active undo segments can be retrieved from the dynamic performance view V$ROLLNAME, as you can see in the following query:

```
SQL> select * from v$rollname;

       USN NAME
---------- ----------------------
         0 SYSTEM
         1 _SYSSMU1_1192467665$
         2 _SYSSMU2_1192467665$
         3 _SYSSMU3_1192467665$
         4 _SYSSMU4_1192467665$
         5 _SYSSMU5_1192467665$
         6 _SYSSMU6_1192467665$
         7 _SYSSMU7_1192467665$
         8 _SYSSMU8_1192467665$
         9 _SYSSMU9_1192467665$
        10 _SYSSMU10_1192467665$

11 rows selected.
```

The data dictionary view DBA_ROLLBACK_SEGS shows both active (online) and inactive (offline) undo segments in both the SYSTEM and undo tablespaces.

The undo segment with an undo segment number (USN) of 0 is an undo segment reserved for exclusive use by system users such as SYS or SYSTEM or if no other undo segments are online and the data being changed resides in the SYSTEM tablespace. In this example, nine other undo segments are available in the undo tablespace for user transactions.

The dynamic performance view V$TRANSACTION shows the relationship between a transaction and the undo segments. In the following query, you begin a transaction and then join V$TRANSACTION to V$ROLLNAME to find out the name of the undo segment assigned to the transaction:

```
SQL> set transaction name 'Update clerk salaries';
Transaction set.

SQL> update hr.employees set salary = salary * 1.25
    where job_id like '%CLERK';
44 rows updated.
```

```
SQL> select xid, status, start_time, xidusn seg_num,
          r.name seg_name
     from v$transaction t join v$rollname r
          on t.xidusn = r.usn
     where t.name = 'Update clerk salaries';
```

```
XID              STATUS  START_TIME        SEG_NUM SEG_NAME
---------------- ------- ----------------- ------- --------------------
05001100DD020000 ACTIVE  09/25/08 03:03:34       5 _SYSSMU5_1192467665$
```

```
1 row selected.
```

The column XID is the internally assigned, unique transaction number assigned to this transaction, and it is assigned the undo segment _SYSSMU5_1192467665$. The column XIDUSN (aliased as SEG_NUM in the query) is the undo segment number for _SYSSMU5_1192467665$. A transaction can reside in only one undo segment; it cannot be moved to another undo segment. However, many different transactions can use the same undo segment.

If an extent in the assigned undo segment fills up and more space is required, the next available extent is used; if all extents in the segment are needed for current transactions, a new extent is allocated for the undo segment.

All undo segments are owned by SYS, regardless of who is making changes in a transaction. Each segment must have a minimum of two extents; the maximum number of extents in an undo segment is high: for an undo tablespace with a block size of 8KB, the default maximum number of extents per undo segment is 32,765.

During a media failure with an undo tablespace, the tablespace can be recovered using archived and online redo log files just as with any other tablespace; however, the instance must be in a MOUNT state to recover an undo tablespace.

Tablespace recovery is discussed in Chapter 16, "Recovering the Database."

Using Undo Data

Undo data is the old value of data when a process or user changes data in a table or an index. Undo data serves four purposes in an Oracle Database:

- User rollback of a transaction
- Read consistency of DML operations and queries
- Database recovery operations
- Flashback functionality

User Transaction Rollback

In Chapter 8, "Introducing Oracle Database 11g Components and Architecture," you learned about transactions and how they are managed within the database architecture. At the user level, you might have one or hundreds of DML commands (such as DELETE, INSERT, UPDATE, or MERGE) within a particular transaction that need to be undone by a user or a process that is making changes to one or more tables. Undoing the changes within a transaction is called *rolling back* part or all of the transaction. The undo information needed to roll back the changes is called, appropriately, the *rollback information* and is stored in a special type of tablespace called an *undo tablespace*.

When an entire transaction is rolled back, Oracle undoes all the changes since the beginning of the transactions, using the saved undo information in the undo tablespace, releases any locks on rows involved in the transaction, and ends the transaction.

If a failure occurs on the client or a network, abnormally terminating the user's connection to the database, undo information is used in much the same way as if the user explicitly rolled back the transaction, and Oracle undoes all the changes since the beginning of the transaction, using information saved in the undo tablespace.

Read Consistency

Undo also provides read consistency for users who are querying rows involved in a DML transaction by another user or session. When one user starts to make changes to a table after another user has already begun a query against the table, the user issuing the query will not see the changes to the table until after the query has completed and the user issues a new query against the table. Undo segments in an undo tablespace are used to reconstruct the data blocks belonging to the table to provide the previous values of the rows for any user issuing SELECT statements against the table before the DML statements' transaction commits.

For example, the user KELSIEJ begins a transaction at 3 p.m. that contains several long-running DML statements against the EMPLOYEES table; the statements aren't expected to finish until 3:15 p.m. As each DML command is issued, the previous values of each row are saved in the transaction's undo segment. At 3:05 p.m., the user SARAHCR issues a SELECT against the EMPLOYEES table; none of the changes made so far by KELSIEJ are visible to SARAHCR. The undo tablespace provides the previous values of the EMPLOYEES table to SARAHCR and any other users querying the EMPLOYEES table between 3 p.m. and 3:15 p.m. Even if SARAHCR's query is still running at 3:20 p.m., the query still appears as it did at 3 p.m. before KELSIEJ started making changes.

INSERT statements use little space in an undo segment; only the pointer to the new row is stored in the undo tablespace. To undo an INSERT statement, the pointer locates the new row and deletes it from the table if the transaction is rolled back.

In a few situations, either SARAHCR's query or KELSIEJ's DML statements might fail, because the undo tablespace is not sized correctly or because the undo retention period is too short.

You can also apply read consistency to an entire transaction instead of just a single SELECT statement by using the SET TRANSACTION statement as follows:

```
SQL> set transaction read only;
Transaction set.
```

Until the transaction is either rolled back or committed, all queries in the transaction see only those changes to other tables that were committed before the transaction began. Only the following statements are permitted in a read-only transaction:

- SELECT statements without the FOR UPDATE clause
- LOCK TABLE
- SET ROLE
- ALTER SESSION
- ALTER SYSTEM

In other words, a read-only transaction cannot contain any statement that changes data in a table, regardless of where the table resides. For example, although an ALTER USER command does not change data in the USERS or any other non-SYSTEM tablespace, it does change the data dictionary tables and therefore cannot be used in a read-only transaction.

Monitoring, Configuring, and Administering Undo

Compared with configuring rollback operations in releases previous to Oracle9i, managing undo in later versions of Oracle requires little intervention. However, two particular situations will trigger intervention: either not enough undo space to handle all active transactions or not enough undo space to satisfy long-running queries that need undo information for read consistency. Running out of undo space for transactions generates messages such as "ORA-01650: Unable to extend rollback segment"; long-running queries whose undo entries have been reused by current transactions typically receive the "ORA-01555: Snapshot too old" message.

In the following sections, I will show you how to configure the undo tablespace using two initialization parameters: UNDO_MANAGEMENT and UNDO_TABLESPACE. I will also present the methods available for monitoring the health of the undo tablespace, as well as using EM Database Control's Undo Advisor to size or resize the undo tablespace. Using the dynamic performance view V$UNDOSTAT, you can calculate an optimal size for the undo tablespace if the Undo Advisor is not available. Finally, I will show you how to guarantee that long-running queries will have undo entries available, even if it means that a DML transaction fails, by using the RETENTION GUARANTEE option.

Configuring the Undo Tablespace

Manual undo management is not recommended, although it is still available in Oracle 11g. Instead, use manual undo management only for compatibility with Oracle8i or earlier. Automatic undo management is the default for the Oracle 11g database. To configure automatic undo management, use the initialization parameters UNDO_MANAGEMENT, UNDO_TABLESPACE, and UNDO_RETENTION.

UNDO_MANAGEMENT

The parameter UNDO_MANAGEMENT specifies the way in which undo data is managed in the database: either manually using rollback segments or automatically using a single tablespace to hold undo information.

The allowed values for UNDO_MANAGEMENT are MANUAL and AUTO. To change the undo-management mode, you must restart the instance. This parameter is not dynamic, as you can see in the following example:

```
SQL> alter system
     set undo_management = manual;


set undo_management = manual
    *
ERROR at line 2:
ORA-02095: specified initialization parameter cannot be modified
```

If you are using an spfile, you can change the value of this parameter in the spfile only and then restart the instance for the parameter to take effect, as follows:

```
SQL> alter system
     set undo_management = manual scope=spfile;
System altered.
```

UNDO_TABLESPACE

The parameter UNDO_TABLESPACE specifies the name of the undo tablespace to use for read consistency and transaction rollback.

You can create an undo tablespace when the database is created; you can resize it later or create a new one later. In any case, only one undo tablespace can be active at any given time, unless the value of UNDO_TABLESPACE is changed while the old undo tablespace still contains active transactions. In this case, the old undo tablespace remains active until the last transaction using the old undo tablespace either commits or rolls back; all new transactions use the new undo tablespace.

If UNDO_TABLESPACE is not defined but at least one undo tablespace exists in the database, the first undo tablespace discovered by the Oracle instance at startup is assigned to

UNDO_TABLESPACE. You can find out the name of the current undo tablespace with the SHOW PARAMETER command, as in the following example:

```
SQL> show parameter undo_tablespace

NAME                        TYPE          VALUE
--------------------------  -----------   --------------------
undo_tablespace             string        UNDOTBS1
```

For most platforms, if an undo tablespace is not explicitly created in the CREATE DATABASE command, Oracle automatically creates one with the name SYS_UNDOTBS.

Here is an example of how you can switch the undo tablespace from UNDOTBS1 to UNDO_BATCH:

```
SQL> show parameter undo_tablespace

NAME                        TYPE          VALUE
--------------------------  -----------   --------------------
undo_tablespace             string        UNDOTBS1

SQL> alter system set undo_tablespace=undo_batch;
System altered.

SQL> show parameter undo_tablespace

NAME                        TYPE          VALUE
--------------------------  -----------   --------------------
undo_tablespace             string        UNDO_BATCH
```

UNDO_RETENTION

The parameter UNDO_RETENTION specifies, in seconds, how long undo information that has already been committed should be retained until it can be overwritten. This is not a guaranteed limit: if the number of seconds specified by UNDO_RETENTION has not been reached and if a transaction needs undo space, already committed undo information can be overwritten.

```
SQL> show parameter undo

NAME                                 TYPE          VALUE
----------------------------------   -----------   ----------
undo_management                      string        AUTO
undo_retention                       integer       900
undo_tablespace                      string        UNDOTBS1
```

To guarantee undo retention, you can use the RETENTION GUARANTEE keywords for the undo tablespace, as you will see later in this chapter in the section "Guaranteeing Undo Retention."

Setting UNDO_RETENTION to zero turns on automatic undo retention tuning. Oracle continually adjusts this parameter to retain just enough undo information to satisfy the longest-running query to date. If the undo tablespace is not big enough for the longest-running query, automatic undo retention retains as much as possible without extending the undo tablespace. In any case, automatic undo retention attempts to maintain at least 900 seconds, or 15 minutes, of undo information.

Regardless of how long undo information is retained, it falls into one of three categories:

Uncommitted undo information   This is undo information that is still supporting an active transaction and is required in the event of a ROLLBACK or a transaction failure. This undo information is never overwritten.

Committed undo information   Also known as *unexpired undo*, this is undo information that is no longer needed to support an active transaction but is still needed to satisfy the undo retention interval, as defined by UNDO_RETENTION. This undo can be overwritten, however, if an active transaction needs undo space.

Expired undo information   This is undo information that is no longer needed to support an active transaction and is overwritten when space is required by an active transaction.

Here is an example of how you can change undo retention from its current value to 12 hours:

```
SQL> show parameter undo_retention

NAME                 TYPE          VALUE
-------------------- ------------- -----------------------
undo_retention       integer       600

SQL> alter system set undo_retention = 43200;
System altered.

SQL> show parameter undo_retention

NAME                 TYPE          VALUE
-------------------- ------------- -----------------------
undo_retention       integer       43200
```

Unless you use the SCOPE parameter in the ALTER SYSTEM command, the change to UNDO_RETENTION takes effect immediately and stays in effect the next time the instance is restarted.

Monitoring the Undo Tablespace

Undo tablespaces are monitored just like any other tablespace: if a specific set of space thresholds is not defined, the database default values are used; otherwise, a specific set of thresholds can be assigned. When an undo tablespace's data files do not have the AUTOEXTEND attribute set, transactions can fail because too many transactions are vying for too little undo space.

Although you can allow the data files in your undo tablespace to autoextend initially, turn off autoextend on its data files once you believe that the undo tablespace has been sized correctly. This prevents a single user from accidentally using up large amounts of disk space in the undo tablespace by neglecting to commit transactions as frequently as possible.

Figure 13.3 shows the Automatic Undo Management screen in EM Database Control (click the Server tab and choose Automatic Undo Management under Database Configuration). The current size of the undo tablespace is 270MB, and during the last seven days, the size of this undo tablespace has been sufficient to support the maximum undo generation.

FIGURE 13.3   The Automatic Undo Management screen in EM Database Control

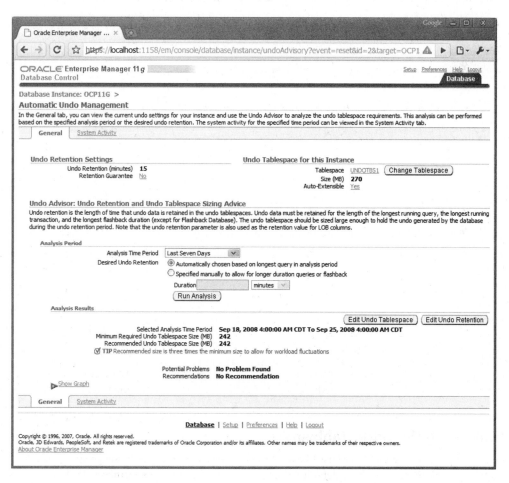

EM Database Control uses the data dictionary view V$UNDOSTAT to calculate the undo usage rate and provide recommendations. V$UNDOSTAT collects 10-minute snapshots of the undo space consumption and, in conjunction with UNDO_RETENTION and the database block size, can provide an optimal undo tablespace size.

Running out of space in an undo tablespace can also trigger an "ORA-01555: Snapshot too old" error. Long-running queries that need a read-consistent view of one or more tables can be at odds with ongoing transactions that need undo space. Unless the undo tablespace is defined with the RETENTION GUARANTEE parameter (described later in this chapter in the section "Guaranteeing Undo Retention"), ongoing DML can use undo space that is needed for long-running queries. As a result, a "Snapshot too old" error is returned to the user executing the query, and an alert is generated. This alert is also known as a *long query warning alert*.

The long query warning alert can be triggered independently of the space available in the undo tablespace if the UNDO_RETENTION initialization parameter is set too low.

Regardless of how often the "Snapshot too old" error occurs, the alert is generated at most once during a 24-hour period. Increasing the size of the undo tablespace or changing the value of UNDO_RETENTION does not reset the 24-hour timer. For example, an alert is generated at 10 a.m., and you add undo space at 11 a.m. The undo tablespace is still too small, and users are still receiving "Snapshot too old" errors at 2 p.m. You will not receive a long query warning alert until 10 a.m. the next day, but chances are you will get a phone call before then!

Sizing the Undo Tablespace Using the Undo Advisor

The EM Database Control Undo Advisor helps you determine how large an undo tablespace should be, given adjustments to the undo retention setting.

In Figure 13.3, the Undo Advisor screen shows analysis of the undo tablespace based on the longest-running query in the analysis period. If you don't expect your undo usage to increase or you don't expect to need to retain undo information longer than the current longest one, you can drop the size of the undo tablespace to 242MB from the current size of 270MB.

On the other hand, if you expect to need undo information for more than the current longest-running query, you can see the impact of this increase by entering a new value for undo retention and clicking the Run Analysis button. You can click the Edit Undo Tablespace button to increase or decrease the size of the tablespace, as shown in Figure 13.4.

FIGURE 13.4   Edit Tablespace screen in EM Database Control

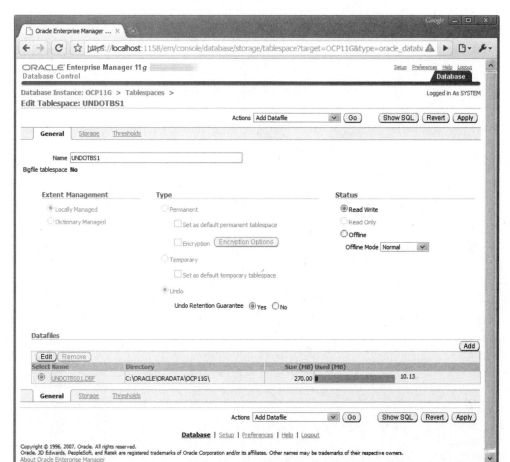

Guaranteeing Undo Retention

By default, undo information from committed transactions (unexpired undo) is overwritten before a transaction fails because of a lack of expired undo. If your database requirements are such that you want long-running queries to succeed at the expense of DML in a transaction, such as in a data warehouse environment where a query can run for hours or even days, you can set the RETENTION GUARANTEE parameter for the undo tablespace.

This parameter is not available as an initialization parameter. You can set retention guarantee using the Edit Tablespace EM Database Control screen shown in Figure 13.4

by choosing Yes for Undo Retention Guarantee. You can also use ALTER TABLESPACE at the command line to set it, as in the following example:

```
SQL> alter tablespace undotbs1 retention guarantee;
Tablespace altered.
```

Turning off the parameter is just as easy, as you can see in the next example:

```
SQL> alter tablespace undotbs1 retention noguarantee;
Tablespace altered.
```

Different undo tablespaces can have different settings for RETENTION. As expected, you cannot set RETENTION for a tablespace that is not an undo tablespace. The following example is attempting to change the RETENTION setting for the USERS tablespace and receives an error message:

```
SQL> select tablespace_name, contents,
  2      retention from dba_tablespaces;


TABLESPACE_NAME                    CONTENTS  RETENTION
------------------------------     --------- -----------
SYSTEM                             PERMANENT NOT APPLY
UNDOTBS1                           UNDO      NOGUARANTEE
SYSAUX                             PERMANENT NOT APPLY
TEMP                               TEMPORARY NOT APPLY
USERS                              PERMANENT NOT APPLY
EXAMPLE                            PERMANENT NOT APPLY
OE_TRANS                           PERMANENT NOT APPLY


SQL> alter tablespace users retention guarantee;


alter tablespace users retention guarantee
*
ERROR at line 1:
ORA-30044: 'Retention' can only be specified for undo tablespace
```

Summary

In this chapter, you learned how to use the SQL DML statements to manipulate data as well as how to identify, execute, and compile PL/SQL programs, including triggers. You also learned how locks work in Oracle 11g database and how undo is managed.

To create, change, and remove data from an Oracle Database, use the INSERT, UPDATE, MERGE, and DELETE statements.

Although Oracle usually manages locks at the minimum level to ensure that two sessions do not try to simultaneously update the same row in a table, you can explicitly lock a table at a number of levels. In addition, you can lock a subset of rows in a table to prevent updates or locks from other transactions with the FOR UPDATE clause in the SELECT statement.

You learned some reasons that lock conflicts occur and how to resolve them; a special kind of lock conflict, a deadlock, occurs when two users are waiting on a resource locked by the other user. Deadlocks, unlike other types of lock conflicts, are resolved quickly and automatically by Oracle long before any manual lock resolution is attempted.

I presented the undo tablespace and its importance for the two types of database users: those who want to query a table and receive consistent results and those who want to make changes to a table and have the option to roll back the data to its state when the transaction started.

You can configure an undo tablespace with a handful of initialization parameters. UNDO_MANAGEMENT defines the mode in which undo is managed and can be either MANUAL or AUTO. UNDO_TABLESPACE identifies the current undo tablespace, which can be switched while the database is open to users; however, only one undo tablespace can be active at a time.

You can use EM Database Control to both proactively monitor and resize the undo tablespace. For databases whose long-running queries have priority over successful DML transactions, you can specify that an undo tablespace retain expired undo information at the expense of failed transactions.

Exam Essentials

Know the syntax for how to insert data with either a list of values or a subquery. A list of values requires the keyword VALUES, while a subquery does not.

Know that PL/SQL functions have a RETURN clause. Functions have a datatype and a RETURN clause. The other PL/SQL programs do not.

Know how to enable and disable triggers. Use the ALTER TRIGGER statement to enable or disable any individual trigger and the ALTER TABLE ENABLE ALL TRIGGERS or ALTER TABLE DISABLE ALL TRIGGERS statement to enable or disable triggers en masse. You can also specify the ENABLE or DISABLE clause at the time of trigger creation.

Know the purpose of the Undo Advisor. Optimize the UNDO_RETENTION parameter as well as the size of the undo tablespace by using Undo Advisor. Use the graph on the Undo Advisor screen to perform what-if analyses given the undo retention requirements.

Be able to monitor locking and resolve lock conflicts. Identify the reasons for database lock conflicts, and explain how to resolve them. Show an example of a more serious type of lock conflict, a deadlock.

Understand the options to wait for acquiring a lock. The LOCK TABLE statement includes the WAIT clause to specify how long to wait to acquire a lock. You can set the initialization parameter DDL_LOCK_TIMEOUT to specify the number of seconds to wait when trying to acquire a DDL lock.

List the features supported by undo data in an undo tablespace. Enumerate the four primary uses for undo data: rollback, read consistency, database recovery, and flashback operations. Show how the rollback requirements for users who perform long transactions can interfere with read consistency required for query users. Be able to identify and use the method to preserve expired undo at the expense of transactions.

Summarize the steps for monitoring, configuring, and administering the undo tablespace. Set the initialization parameters required to use an undo tablespace. Be able to review the status of the undo tablespace using EM Database Control, and use the Undo Advisor to resize the undo tablespace when conditions warrant it. Alter the initialization parameter UNDO_RETENTION to configure how long undo information needs to be retained for long-running queries.

List the types of lock modes available when locking a table. Identify the locks available, from least restrictive to most restrictive. Be able to request a lock with either a LOCK or SELECT statement and return immediately if the lock is not available.

Review Questions

1. Changes made with an UPDATE statement are permanent in the database after what occurs?

   A. DBWR flushes the changes to disk.

   B. You issue a SAVEPOINT statement.

   C. You issue a COMMIT statement.

   D. A checkpoint occurs.

2. Why would you execute a CREATE OR REPLACE PROCEDURE statement instead of a DROP PROCEDURE statement and a CREATE PROCEDURE statement?

   A. It is less typing.

   B. There is no difference between the two.

   C. CREATE OR REPLACE PROCEDURE does not invalidate dependent objects.

   D. DROP PROCEDURE and CREATE PROCEDURE require regranting of privileges.

3. Which of the following is not a trigger event?

   A. UPDATE

   B. SELECT

   C. NOAUDIT

   D. SERVERERROR

4. You need to let an application role execute the SLEEP procedure in the DBMS_LOCK package but do not want to let an application role have access to the other more powerful capabilities of the DBMS_LOCK package. How can you satisfy these requirements best?

   A. Grant EXECUTE on dbms_lock to the user system. Then create a procedure in the system schema that calls DBMS_LOCK.SLEEP. Finally, grant EXECUTE on this procedure to the application role.

   B. Grant EXECUTE on DBMS_LOCK to the application role.

   C. Grant EXECUTE on DMBS_LOCK.SLEEP to the application role.

   D. Write your own procedure to mimic the functionality of the DBMS_LOCK.SLEEP procedure.

5. Which of the following INSERT statements raises an exception?

   A. INSERT INTO ORDERS SELECT * FROM STANDING_ORDERS

   B. INSERT FIRST WHEN ORDER_TYPE IN (2,5,12) THEN INSERT INTO ORDERS SELECT * FROM STANDING_ORDERS

   C. INSERT FIRST WHEN ORDER_TYPE IN (2,5,12) THEN INTO ORDERS SELECT * FROM STANDING_ORDERS

   D. INSERT INTO ALL WHEN ORDER_TYPE IN (2,5,12) THEN INTO ORDERS SELECT * FROM STANDING_ORDERS

6. What will be the salary of employee number 189 at the completion of the following SQL statements?

```
update emp set salary = 1000 where employee_num = 189;
savepoint save_1;
update emp set salary = salary * 1.1 where employee_num = 189;
savepoint save_2;
update emp set salary = salary * 1.1 where employee_num = 189;
savepoint save_3;
rollback to savepoint save_2;
commit;
update emp set salary = 1500 where employee_num = 189;
savepoint save_4;
rollback to save_4;
commit;
```

A. 1,000

B. 1,100

C. 1,111

D. 1,500

7. Which of the following commands returns an error if the transaction starts with SET TRANSACTION READ ONLY?

A. ALTER SYSTEM

B. SET ROLE

C. ALTER USER

D. None of the above

8. Guaranteed undo retention can be specified for which of the following objects?

A. A tablespace

B. A table

C. The database

D. A transaction

E. The instance

9. Which of the following lock modes permits concurrent queries on a table but prohibits updates to the locked table?

A. ROW SHARE

B. ROW EXCLUSIVE

C. EXCLUSIVE

D. SHARE ROW EXCLUSIVE

E. SHARE

10. Select the statement that is *not* true regarding undo tablespaces.

    A. Undo tablespaces will not be created if they are not specified in the CREATE DATABASE command.

    B. Two undo tablespaces can be active if a new undo tablespace was specified and the old one contains pending transactions.

    C. You can switch from one undo tablespace to another while the database is online.

    D. UNDO_MANAGEMENT cannot be changed dynamically while the instance is running.

11. To resolve a lock conflict, which of the following methods can you use? (Choose all that apply.)

    A. Oracle automatically resolves the lock after a short but predefined time period by killing the session that is holding the lock.

    B. The DBA can kill the session holding the lock.

    C. The user can either roll back or commit the transaction that is holding the lock.

    D. Oracle automatically resolves the lock after a short but predefined period by killing the session that is requesting the lock.

12. If all extents in an undo segment fill up, which of the following occurs next? (Choose all that apply.)

    A. A new extent is allocated in the undo segment if all existing extents still contain active transaction data.

    B. Other transactions using the segment are moved to another existing segment with enough free space.

    C. A new undo segment is created, and the transaction that filled up the undo segment is moved in its entirety to another undo segment.

    D. The first extent in the segment is reused if the undo data in the first extent is not needed.

    E. The transaction that filled up the undo segment spills over to another undo segment.

13. Which of the following commands returns control to the user immediately if a table is already locked by another user?

    A. `LOCK TABLE HR.EMPLOYEES IN EXCLUSIVE MODE WAIT DEFERRED;`

    B. `LOCK TABLE HR.EMPLOYEES IN SHARE MODE NOWAIT;`

    C. `LOCK TABLE HR.EMPLOYEES IN SHARE MODE WAIT DISABLED;`

    D. `LOCK TABLE HR.EMPLOYEES IN EXCLUSIVE MODE NOWAIT DEFERRED;`

14. Two transactions occur at the wall clock times in the following table. What happens at 10:05?

Session 1	Time	Session 2
update customer set region = 'H' where state='WI' and county='GRANT';	9:51	
	9:59	update customer set mgr=201 where state='IA' and county='JOHNSON';
update customer set region='H' where state='IA' and county='JOHNSON';	10:01	
	10:05	update customer set mgr=201 where state='WI' and county='GRANT';

    A. Session 2 will wait for session 1 to commit or roll back.

    B. Session 1 will wait for session 2 to commit or roll back.

    C. A deadlock will occur, and both sessions will hang unless one of the users cancels their statement or the DBA kills one of the sessions.

    D. A deadlock will occur, and Oracle will cancel one of the statements.

    E. Neither session is updating the same column, so no waiting or deadlock will occur.

15. Undo information falls into all the following categories except for which one?

    A. Uncommitted undo information

    B. Undo information required in case an instance crash requires a rollforward operation when the instance is restarted

    C. Committed undo information required to satisfy the undo retention interval

    D. Expired undo information that is no longer needed to support a running transaction

16. Undo segments are owned by which user?

    A. SYSTEM

    B. The user who initiated the transaction

    C. SYS

    D. The user who owns the object changed by the transaction

17. The EM Database Control Undo Advisor uses _____ to recommend the new size of the undo tablespace.

A. the value of the parameter UNDO_RETENTION

B. the number of "Snapshot too old" errors

C. the current size of the undo tablespace

D. the desired amount of time to retain undo data

E. the most recent undo generation rate

18. A developer wants to write a PL/SQL program that inserts new data into the cust_trans table, for which cust_id is the primary key. The data is to read from the new_cust_info table, which is populated daily. If cust_id already exists in the cust_trans table, he wants to update the row with new information. Which option would you recommend?

A. Include the EXCEPTION clause in the PL/SQL program.

B. Use the UPSERT SQL statement instead of PL/SQL.

C. Use the MERGE SQL statement instead of PL/SQL.

D. Delete the rows from the cust_trans table that exist in the new_cust_info table, and then perform an insert from the new_cust_info table.

19. Choose the option that is true regarding locks in the Oracle 11g database.

A. When session 1 has a table locked using the LOCK TABLE...EXCLUSIVE MODE statement, all DML statements and queries wait until session1 does a COMMIT or ROLLBACK.

B. When SELECT...FOR UPDATE is performed, the table is locked.

C. The DDL_LOCK_TIMEOUT parameter can be set to TRUE to not return the ORA-00054 error.

D. The LOCK TABLE statement can include the WAIT clause to specify the number of seconds to wait for acquiring the lock.

20. Which can be used to execute a user-defined PL/SQL function named IS_CREDIT_OK? (Choose all that apply.)

A. X := IS_CREDIT_OK

B. SELECT IS_CREDIT_OK INTO X FROM DUAL

C. EXECUTE IS_CREDIT_OK

D. RUN IS_CREDIT_OK

Answers to Review Questions

1. C. A commit makes pending DML changes permanent. When a checkpoint occurs, DBWR flushes dirty buffers to disk, which is independent of transaction boundaries.

2. D. Using CREATE OR REPLACE PROCEDURE is less typing, but, more important, when you drop an object, all privileges granted on that object are dropped as well. When you perform a CREATE OR REPLACE PROCEDURE, you do not lose privileges granted on that object. When you drop and create a procedure, it invalidates all dependent objects, whereas if you re-create, the dependent objects are invalidated only if the procedure specification is changed.

3. B. You can create a trigger for just about any database event that involves a change to data, but you cannot create a SELECT trigger in Oracle 11g.

4. A. You cannot grant privileges on only one packaged procedure. You can grant EXECUTE only on the whole package. To be more restrictive in granting privileges, you need to create an intermediate procedure that calls the single procedure you want and grant EXECUTE on that intermediate procedure to the grantee. Granting a privilege to a role does not allow the role grantee to use that privilege in a PL/SQL program.

5. D. Single-table inserts must begin with the keywords INSERT INTO and cannot contain the keywords THEN INTO. Multitable INSERT statements cannot begin with the keywords INSERT INTO and may contain the keywords THEN INTO. Option D contains an invalid combination of keywords and will thus raise an exception.

6. D. The last ROLLBACK statement rolls back all DML statements since SAVEPOINT SAVE_4. The last UPDATE was executed before the SAVEPOINT to SAVE_4; therefore, the change made by the last UPDATE is unchanged, and the salary remains 1,500.

7. D. When you use SET TRANSACTION READ ONLY, no data changes can be made in the transaction. You can do DDL changes though. DDL statements does an implicit COMMIT and ends the transaction. ALTER USER is a DDL statement.

8. A. Guaranteed undo retention can be set at the tablespace level by using the RETENTION GUARANTEE clause with either the CREATE TABLESPACE or ALTER TABLESPACE command. Only undo tablespaces can have this attribute.

9. E. SHARE mode permits concurrent queries but prohibits updates to the locked table. SHARE mode is required to create an index on the table.

10. A. If an undo tablespace is not explicitly created in the CREATE DATABASE command, Oracle automatically creates one with the name SYS_UNDOTBS.

11. B, C. Locks are resolved at the user level by either committing or rolling back the transaction holding the lock. Also, the DBA can kill the session holding the lock as a last resort.

12. A, D. If a transaction fills up an undo segment, either a new extent is allocated for the undo segment or other extents in the segment are reused if the undo data in those extents is no longer needed by other transactions using the same undo segment. Transactions cannot cross segment boundaries in an undo tablespace, and they cannot move to another segment.

13. B. Regardless of the type of lock requested, NOWAIT is required if you want the command with the lock request to terminate immediately if a lock is already held on the table.

14. D. At 10:01, session 1 waits for session 2. At 10:05, a deadlock will occur; Oracle detects the deadlock and cancels one of the statements.

15. B. Undo information is required for instance recovery but only to roll back uncommitted transactions after the online redo logs roll forward.

16. C. Undo segments are always owned by SYS.

17. D. The Undo Advisor uses the desired time period for undo data retention and analyzes the impact of the desired undo retention setting.

18. C. Though options A and D can be used to achieve the same result, they are not the most efficient. There is no UPSERT statement in Oracle 11*g*. The MERGE statement is used to conditionally update or insert rows into a table.

19. D. In Oracle, locks never block readers. Option A is true, if it did not include the word *queries* in it. Only DML statements wait when the table is locked in exclusive mode. SELECT...FOR UPDATE locks only the rows returned by the SELECT clause; it does not lock the table. The DDL_LOCK_TIMEOUT parameter is used to specify the number of seconds to wait when DDL statements on locked objects are executed. The LOCK TABLE statement can include the WAIT clause to specify the number of seconds to wait to acquire the lock.

20. A, B. A function always returns a value; hence, the function can be used in the SELECT statements and assignments. Functions can also be used in PL/SQL constructs such as IF statements. EXECUTE is used to run a procedure. RUN is used to execute a SQL or PL/SQL script file.

Chapter

14

Maintaining the Database and Managing Performance

**ORACLE DATABASE 11*g*:
ADMINISTRATION I EXAM OBJECTIVES
COVERED IN THIS CHAPTER:**

✓ **Database Maintenance**

- Use and manage Optimizer Statistics
- Use and manage Automatic Workload Repository (AWR)
- Use Advisory Framework
- Manage Alerts and Thresholds

✓ **Performance Management**

- Use Automatic Memory Management
- Use Memory Advisors
- Troubleshoot invalid and unusable objects

Successful database administrators are always on the lookout for potential database problems that could adversely impact the availability or performance of the systems they manage. Fortunately, Oracle 11*g* comes with an array for proactive performance monitoring and an alert mechanism to help you do this.

The Oracle Database 11*g* periodically collects statistics on the database objects and uses the statistics to find the best execution plan for a SQL statement. The Automatic Workload Repository collects, analyzes, and maintains the performance statistics of the database. Oracle 11*g* also offers several advisors that help DBAs fine-tune the database components. One new tool is Automatic Memory Management, which greatly simplifies memory management. In this chapter, you will learn about all the database-management and performance-management tools available to DBAs for better database administration.

Proactive Database Maintenance

You can monitor your systems for management and performance problems in essentially two ways:

- *Reactive monitoring* involves monitoring a database environment after a performance or management issue has arisen. For example, you start gathering performance statistics using third-party tools, EM, or homegrown scripts after users call to tell you that the system is slow. Obviously, this type of monitoring leaves a lot to be desired because a problem has already arisen and the users of the system are already impacted. You can use the techniques discussed in this chapter for reactive monitoring, but they are most effective when used to perform proactive monitoring.

- *Proactive monitoring* allows you to identify and respond to common database-performance and -management issues before they occur. Most of the features in Enterprise Manager Database Control are geared toward proactive monitoring.

The database-maintenance framework in Oracle 11*g* consists of these proactive tool sets:

- Automated tasks, such as collecting optimizer statistics

- Automatic Workload Repository

- Advisory Framework

- Server alerts and thresholds

Automatic Diagnostic Repository, where the alert log and trace information are kept, is used for reactive database maintenance.

The monitoring tools available in EM Database Control collect their information from a variety of sources including data dictionary views, dynamic performance views, and the operating system. Oracle 11*g* also makes extensive use of the cost-based optimizer statistics for its proactive monitoring. But discussing all the database-maintenance options available in Oracle 11*g* is not in the scope of this book; it is a large topic that warrants its own book. In the following section, you will instead learn the database-maintenance options available in Oracle 11*g* that are relevant to the OCP certification exam.

Managing Optimizer Statistics

Optimizer statistics are a collection of important statistical data that describe the contents of the database. The query optimizer uses the optimizer statistics to find the best way to get to the row of data the query wants to find. The database collects statistics on objects that have segments allocated as well as overall system statistics. The optimizer uses the statistics to decide how to do the following:

- Access data and determine which indexes to use
- Join tables
- Evaluate expressions and conditions

The *cost-based optimizer* (CBO) uses these statistics to formulate efficient execution plans for each SQL statement that is issued by application users. For example, the CBO may have to decide whether to use an available index when processing a query. The CBO can only make an effective guess at the proper execution plan when it knows the number of rows in the table, the size and type of indexes on that table, and how many rows the CBO expects to be returned by a query. Because of this, the statistics gathered and stored in the data dictionary views are sometimes called optimizer statistics.

The following are some of the statistics collected:

- Table and index statistics
  - Total number of rows in table and average row length
  - Total number of blocks used
  - Levels and number of leaf blocks for indexes
- Column statistics
  - Number of distinct values in a column
  - Number of NULL values
  - Low value and high value for a column
  - Data distribution and data skew
- System statistics
  - Disk I/O performance
  - CPU performance

You can use the DBMS_STATS package to collect optimizer statistics in the database. DBMS_STATS has several subprograms (procedures and functions) to collect and manage statistics. In the following sections, you will learn how to collect optimizer statistics and what management options are available to maintain the statistics.

 NOTE   Optimizer statistics are a snapshot of statistical information at a specific point in time. They are persistent across instance restarts because they are stored in the data dictionary tables.

Collecting Statistics

In an Oracle 11g database, you'll rarely need to manually collect statistics. The default collection frequency and options are good for most of the database environments. You may have to collect statistics manually when you bulk load data into a table or when you delete several rows from the table. Sometimes you may have to create histograms for the optimizer to be able to make better execution plans based on the query.

When you create the Oracle 11g database using DBCA, gathering optimizer statistics is automatically set up and enabled using the Automated Maintenance Tasks (AutoTask) infrastructure. AutoTask schedules maintenance tasks to run automatically, using the Oracle Scheduler, during maintenance windows. Automatic optimizer statistics are collected using the procedure DBMS_STATS.GATHER_DATABASE_STATS_JOB_PROC. This procedure collects statistics on objects that have no statistics collected or have stale statistics. Oracle Database considers statistics stale when more than 10 percent of data in the table has changed since statistics were gathered on the table. This procedure also prioritizes the objects that need the statistics collected and processes them first.

You can enable and disable the automatic optimizer statistics gathering by using the DBMS_AUTO_TASK package. To disable the automatic statistics gathering, use the DISABLE subprogram as shown here:

```
BEGIN
  DBMS_AUTO_TASK_ADMIN.DISABLE (
       client_name=>'auto optimizer stats collection',
       operation=>NULL, window_name=>NULL);
END;
```

If you disable the automatic statistics gathering, make sure you collect statistics manually so that the optimizer produces intelligent execution plans. To enable automatic statistics gathering, use the ENABLE subprogram as follows:

```
BEGIN
  DBMS_AUTO_TASK_ADMIN.ENABLE (
       client_name=>'auto optimizer stats collection',
       operation=>NULL, window_name=>NULL);
END;
```

To view the status of AutoTask jobs, you can run the following query:

```
SQL> SELECT client_name, status FROM dba_autotask_client;
```

CLIENT_NAME	STATUS
auto optimizer stats collection	ENABLED
auto space advisor	ENABLED
sql tuning advisor	ENABLED

You can collect the statistics manually using the DBMS_STATS procedure from SQL*Plus or using EM Database Control.

Manually Collecting Stats Using SQL*Plus

Collecting manual statistics is useful for tables and indexes whose storage characteristics change frequently or that need to be analyzed outside the normal analysis window. Manual statistics may also need to be collected if the data in the table is highly volatile, such as when you truncate and load the table often. For such tables, you can collect the statistics when the table is fully loaded and lock the statistics so that subsequent statistics-gathering jobs do not override the statistics. The following example shows collecting statistics on a table and locking the statistics:

```
BEGIN
  DBMS_STATS.GATHER_TABLE_STATS('HR','EMPLOYEES', cascade=>TRUE);
  DBMS_STATS.LOCK_TABLE_STATS('HR','EMPLOYEES');
END;
```

Procedures are available to collect optimizer statistics at the database, schema, table, or index level. Table 14.1 shows the optimizer's statistics-gathering procedures.

TABLE 14.1   DBMS_STATS Statistics-Gathering Procedures

Procedure Name	Purpose
GATHER_TABLE_STATS	Collects table, column, and index stats
GATHER_INDEX_STATS	Collects index stats
GATHER_SCHEMA_STATS	Collects stats on all objects in the schema
GATHER_DATABASE_STATS	Collects stats on all objects in all schemas of the database
GATHER_DICTIONARY_STATS	Collects statistics on SYS-owned dictionary objects

The following example collects statistics on all objects owned by the HR schema, sampling 10 percent of rows for the statistics gathering:

```
SQL> EXEC DBMS_STATS.GATHER_SCHEMA_STATS('HR',estimate_percent=>10);
PL/SQL procedure successfully completed.
SQL>
```

For complete details of the many options available in the DBMS_STATS package, see Chapter 127 of the "Oracle Database PL/SQL Packages and Types Reference 11*g* Release 1 (11.1) Part Number B28419-03" documentation, available at http://tahiti.oracle.com.

Manually Collecting Stats Using EM Grid Control

You can use the EM Gather Statistics Wizard to manually collect statistics for individual segments, schemas, or the database as a whole. To start the wizard, click the Server tab on the EM Database Control screen, and click the Manage Optimizer Statistics link under Query Optimizer (Figure 14.1).

FIGURE 14.1 Server tab in EM Grid Control

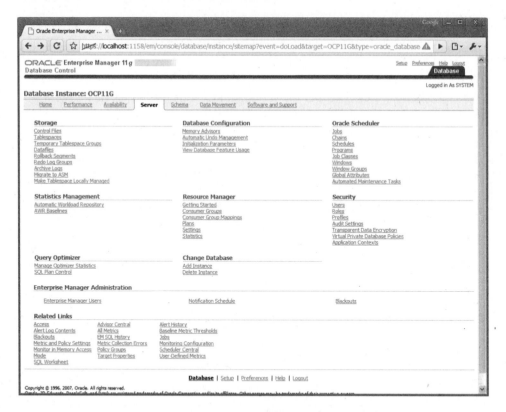

You can choose from several options in addition to gathering optimizer statistics, as shown on the Manage Optimizer Statistics screen (Figure 14.2). Whenever you collect statistics, existing statistics are saved to history tables and preserved for 31 days. You can click the Restore Optimizer Statistics link to restore old statistics. You can also lock, unlock, and delete statistics.

FIGURE 14.2 Manage Optimizer Statistics screen in EM Grid Control

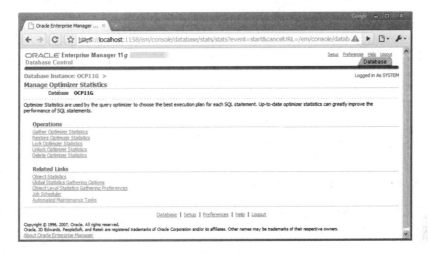

Click the Gather Optimizer Statistics link on the Manage Optimizer Statistics screen. You can collect statistics at the database, schema, object, or system level. Choose the options needed to collect statistics, as shown in Figure 14.3.

FIGURE 14.3 Gather Optimizer Statistics screen in EM Database Control

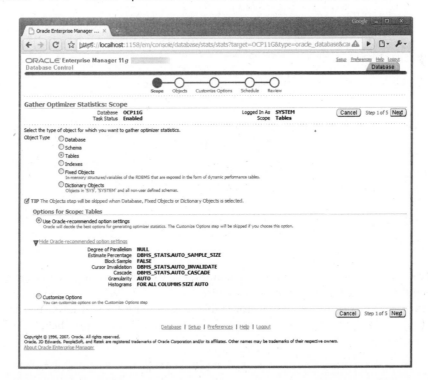

You will be taken through scope, objects, options, schedule, and review screens. Provide the options needed for the statistics collection. If you have chosen to customize the options shown in Figure 14.3, you will get a screen similar to Figure 14.4 for choosing options.

FIGURE 14.4   Customize Options for the Gather Optimizer Statistics screen in EM Database Control

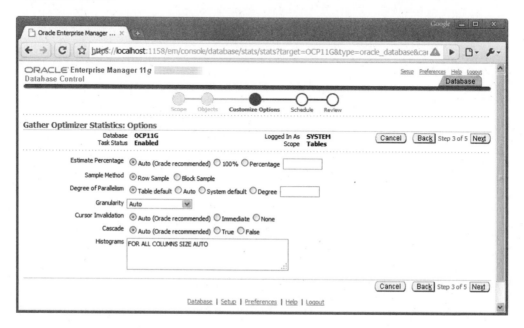

You can also view the SQL behind the options you have chosen by clicking the Show SQL button. Figure 14.5 shows the code behind a statistics-gathering job for two HR-owned tables.

> To read more about collecting and managing optimizer statistics, read Chapter 13 from the "Oracle Database Performance Tuning Guide 11*g* Release 1 (11.1) Part Number B28274-01" Oracle documentation.

In the next section, you will learn how to set preferences for statistics gathering.

FIGURE 14.5 Show SQL for the Gather Optimizer Statistics screen in EM Grid Control

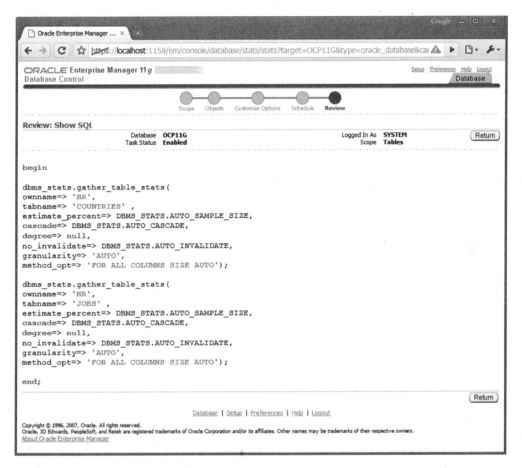

Defining Statistics Preferences

The default staleness percentage for statistics gathering is 10; if you want to change this and other default options, you can set the preferences for statistics gathering using EM Grid Control or using DBMS_STATS directly. In this section, you will learn how to set preferences using EM Database Control, and using the Show SQL option, you can see the DBMS_STATS code behind it.

On the EM Database Control Manage Optimizer statistics screen (shown earlier in Figure 14.2), you can click the Global Statistics Gathering and Object Level Statistics Gathering Preferences links.

Figure 14.6 shows the Global Statistics Gathering Options screen. Using this screen, you set the preferences at a global level, which is applicable to all the objects in all the schemas, unless specific schema or object level preferences are set.

FIGURE 14.6   Global Statistics Gathering Options screen in EM Grid Control

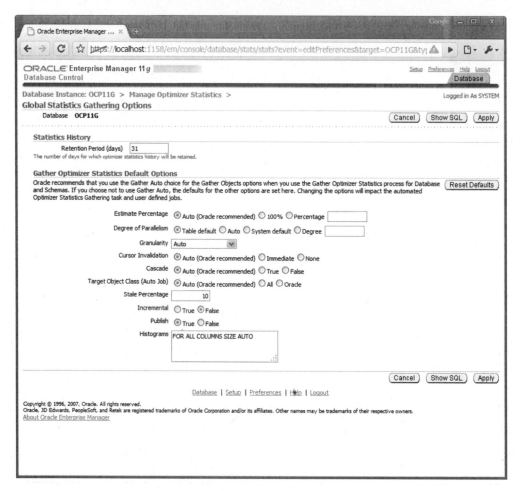

Here you can change the retention period for how long optimizer statistics history is kept in the database (DBMS_STATS.ALTER_STATS_HISTORY_RETENTION), as well as other default options (DBMS_STATS.SET_GLOBAL_PREFS). Table 14.2 shows the EM Grid Control option and its corresponding preference name when using DBMS_SQL.

If you want to minimize the time required to collect table statistics for partitioned tables, you can set the global preference INCREMENTAL to TRUE, where only statistics on a (new) partition are gathered and the table statistics are adjusted accordingly:

```
EXEC DBMS_STATS.SET_GLOBAL_PREFS ('INCREMENTAL', 'TRUE');
```

TABLE 14.2 `DBMS_STATS.SET_GLOBAL_PREFS` Preferences

Preference Parameter	EM Database Control Option	Purpose
ESTIMATE_PERCENT	Estimate Percent	Sets the percentage of rows in the table to consider when estimating statistics
DEGREE	Degree of Parallelism	Specifies how many parallel processes are used to gather stats
GRANULARITY	Granularity	Determines granularity of statistics to collect for partitioned tables
NO_INVALIDATE	Cursor Invalidation	Determines whether dependent cursors should be made invalid
CASCADE	Cascade	Determines whether index statistics should be gathered when table statistics are gathered
AUTOSTATS_TARGET	Target Object Class	Determines which objects are considered for automatic statistics collection
STALE_PERCENT	Stale Percent	Sets the percentage of rows that need to change before statistics are gathered again
INCREMENTAL	Incremental	Gives global stats on the partitioned table maintained without doing a full scan
PUBLISH	Publish	Determines whether newly gathered stats are published immediately
METHOD_OPT	Histograms	Sets options for collecting histograms

Similar to global stats preferences, you can also set preferences on a table or schema. Click the Object Level Statistics Gathering Preferences link on the Manage Optimizer Statistics screen (Figure 14.2). Figure 14.7 shows the Object Level Statistics Gathering Preferences screen.

FIGURE 14.7 Object Level Statistics Gathering Preferences screen in EM Grid Control

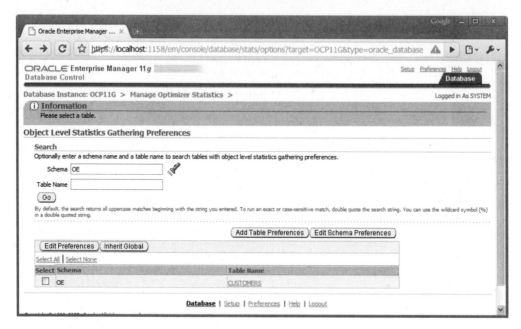

To view the tables where preferences are set, enter the filters, if any (schema and/or table name), and click Go. You have the following options on this screen:

- Select existing tables, and click Edit Preferences to edit (this runs DBMS_STATS.SET_TABLE_PREFS).

- Select existing tables, and click Inherit Global to remove preferences (this runs DBMS_STATS.DELETE_TABLE_PREFS).

- Click Add Table Preferences to set table preferences on a new table (this runs DBMS_STATS.SET_TABLE_PREFS).

- Click Edit Schema Preferences to add/edit schema preferences (this runs DBMS_STATS.SET_SCHEMA_PREFS).

The data dictionary view DBA_TAB_STAT_PREFS (or ALL_ or USER_) gives the tables with a preference set. Remember, when you use the SET_SCHEMA_PREFS procedure, DBMS_STATS adds an entry to this view for each table under the schema. When you use the SET_DATABASE_PREFS procedure, DBMS_STATS adds an entry to this view for each table in the database except system tables. To include system tables, set the third parameter to TRUE.

Let's explore two important features of Oracle 11g statistics gathering using the table preferences.

Changing the Default Staleness Threshold

Since Oracle10*g*, tables have had the default MONITORING enabled. The statistics-collection job looks for staleness of 10 percent or more for it to reanalyze the table. In Oracle 11*g*, you can specify the threshold value for each table if you want to override the 10 percent default using SET_TABLE_PREFS. Here's an example:

```
SQL> exec dbms_stats.set_table_prefs('SH','CUSTOMERS','STALE_PERCENT','20');
PL/SQL procedure successfully completed.

SQL> DESCRIBE dba_tab_stat_prefs
 Name                            Null?    Type
 ------------------------- -------- ---------------------------
 OWNER                     NOT NULL VARCHAR2(30)
 TABLE_NAME                NOT NULL VARCHAR2(30)
 PREFERENCE_NAME                    VARCHAR2(30)
 PREFERENCE_VALUE                   VARCHAR2(1000)

SQL> SELECT table_name, preference_name, preference_value
     FROM dba_tab_stat_prefs;

TABLE_NAME     PREFERENCE_NAME         PREFERENCE_VALUE
-------------- ---------------------- --------------------
CUSTOMERS      STALE_PERCENT           20
```

You can also use the function GET_PREFS to verify the preference value. The function returns the custom defined preference value. And if no such value is defined, it returns the default.

```
SQL> SELECT dbms_stats.get_prefs('STALE_PERCENT','SH','CUSTOMERS')
     FROM dual;

DBMS_STATS.GET_PREFS('STALE_PERCENT','SH','CUSTOMERS')
----------------------------------------------------------------
20

SQL> SELECT dbms_stats.get_prefs('STALE_PERCENT','HR','EMPLOYEES')
     FROM dual;

DBMS_STATS.GET_PREFS('STALE_PERCENT','HR','EMPLOYEES')
----------------------------------------------------------------
10
```

Pending Statistics

In Oracle 11*g*, the statistics gathering is divided into two steps—collect statistics and publish. By default, the behavior is like pre–Oracle 11*g* databases; the statistics will be available (published) to all users as soon as the stats are gathered. If you want to test the implications of the new statistics before making it available to all users in the database, you can do so. This is helpful to test the new statistics to make sure they do not affect the database negatively.

To test with the new statistics before making them available to all users, perform these steps:

1. Set the table preference parameter PUBLISH to FALSE. If you're messing with many tables, you can use the SET_SCHEMA_PREFS, SET_DATABASE_PREFS, or SET_GLOBAL_PREFS procedure. For demonstrating the example, the statistics on table HR.EMPLOYEES are deleted:

```
SQL> select table_name, num_rows, last_analyzed from dba_tables
  2  where owner = 'HR' and table_name = 'EMPLOYEES';
TABLE_NAME NUM_ROWS    LAST_ANAL
---------- ---------- ---------
EMPLOYEES


SQL> select dbms_stats.get_prefs('PUBLISH','HR','EMPLOYEES')
     from dual;
DBMS_STATS.GET_PREFS('PUBLISH','HR','EMPLOYEES')
------------------------------------------------------------
TRUE


SQL> exec dbms_stats.set_table_prefs('HR','EMPLOYEES','PUBLISH','FALSE');
PL/SQL procedure successfully completed.
```

2. Gather table statistics as you normally would using the DBMS_STATS package. Since the PUBLISH preference is set to FALSE, you do not see the statistics:

```
SQL> exec dbms_stats.gather_table_stats('HR','EMPLOYEES');
PL/SQL procedure successfully completed.


SQL> select num_rows, last_analyzed from dba_tables
  2  where owner = 'HR' and table_name = 'EMPLOYEES';
  NUM_ROWS LAST_ANAL
---------- ---------
```

3. You can verify the pending statistics by querying DBA_TAB_PENDING_STATS:

```
SQL> select table_name, num_rows, blocks, sample_size
  2  from dba_tab_pending_stats;
```

TABLE_NAME	NUM_ROWS	BLOCKS	SAMPLE_SIZE
EMPLOYEES	107	5	107

4. Test your SQL by making the pending statistics visible:

```
SQL> alter session set optimizer_use_pending_statistics = true;
```

5. When you're ready to publish the statistics, perform the following:

```
SQL> exec dbms_stats.publish_pending_stats('HR','EMPLOYEES');
PL/SQL procedure successfully completed.

SQL> select num_rows, last_analyzed from dba_tables
  2  where owner = 'HR' and table_name = 'EMPLOYEES';
  NUM_ROWS LAST_ANAL
---------- ---------
       107 15-FEB-08

SQL> select table_name, num_rows, blocks, sample_size
  2  from dba_tab_pending_stats;
no rows selected
```

The PUBLISH_PENDING_STATS procedure accepts the schema name and table name as the first two parameters. If you specify NULL for the schema name, the default user's schema will be used. If you specify NULL for the table name, all pending stats on all tables in the schema are published.

Extended Statistics

In Oracle 11*g*, you can tell the optimizer the relationship between columns by using the *extended statistics* feature (multicolumn statistics). The extended statistics feature also includes statistics on columns where a function is applied (function-based statistics). By collecting extended statistics on columns, the optimizer will be able to estimate the selectivity better.

To collect multicolumn statistics (extended histograms), use the GATHER_TABLE_STATS procedure with the METHOD_OPT option like you would collect normal histogram statistics.

To create multicolumn statistics and function-based statistics, follow these two steps:

1. Create an extended statistics group using the DBMS_STATS.CREATE_EXTENDED_STATS function. The function returns the name of the extended stat group created. This function has three arguments: the owner, the table name, and the extension. The "extension" could be a combination of columns, up to 32 or expression on column (for function-based statistics, discussed later).

2. Collect histogram statistics on the table using the GATHER_TABLE_STATS procedure. FOR ALL COLUMNS SIZE SKEWONLY is a good option because Oracle collects histograms only on columns with large data distribution.

Real World Scenario

Collecting Extended Table Statistics: An Example

I'll now demonstrate the extended statistics feature of Oracle 11g with an example. The CUSTOMERS table is populated and has about 91,000 rows. Statistics are collected on the table with the FOR ALL ROWS SIZE AUTO option:

```
SQL> select column_name, num_distinct, histogram
  2  from dba_tab_col_statistics
  3  where owner = 'BTHOMAS' and table_name = 'CUSTOMERS';


COLUMN_NAME                        NUM_DISTINCT HISTOGRAM
------------------------------ ------------ ---------------
CUST_COUNTRY                               3 FREQUENCY
CUST_STATE                                6 FREQUENCY
CUST_NAME                             47692 NONE

SQL>
SQL> select * from customers where cust_country = 'India' and cust_state =
'TN';


-------------------------------------------------------------------------------
| Id  | Operation          | Name      | Rows  | Bytes | Cost (%CPU)| Time     |
-------------------------------------------------------------------------------
|   0 | SELECT STATEMENT   |           |  1447 | 41963 |   137   (1)| 00:00:02 |
|*  1 |  TABLE ACCESS FULL | CUSTOMERS |  1447 | 41963 |   137   (1)| 00:00:02 |
-------------------------------------------------------------------------------


Predicate Information (identified by operation id):
---------------------------------------------------
   1 - filter("CUST_STATE"='TN' AND "CUST_COUNTRY"='India')



SQL> SELECT dbms_stats.create_extended_stats('BTHOMAS','CUSTOMERS',
               '(CUST_COUNTRY, CUST_STATE)') EXTSTAT
     FROM dual;
```

```
EXTSTAT
-------------------------------
SYS_STUZVS6GX30A0GN_5YRYSD2LPM


SQL>
SQL> exec dbms_stats.gather_table_stats(null, 'customers',
        method_opt=>'for all columns size skewonly');

PL/SQL procedure successfully completed.

SQL> select column_name, num_distinct, histogram
  2  from user_tab_col_statistics
  3* where table_name = 'CUSTOMERS'
SQL> /


COLUMN_NAME                        NUM_DISTINCT HISTOGRAM
------------------------------ ------------ ---------------
CUST_NAME                              47692 HEIGHT BALANCED
CUST_STATE                                 6 FREQUENCY
CUST_COUNTRY                               3 FREQUENCY
SYS_STUZVS6GX30A0GN_5YRYSD2LPM             8 FREQUENCY

SQL> select * from customers where cust_country = 'India' and cust_state =
'TN';


--------------------------------------------------------------------------------
| Id  | Operation           | Name       | Rows  | Bytes | Cost (%CPU)| Time     |
--------------------------------------------------------------------------------
|   0 | SELECT STATEMENT    |            |    86 |  2580 |   137   (1)| 00:00:02 |
|*  1 |  TABLE ACCESS FULL| CUSTOMERS  |    86 |  2580 |   137   (1)| 00:00:02 |
--------------------------------------------------------------------------------


Predicate Information (identified by operation id):
---------------------------------------------------
   1 - filter("CUST_STATE"='TN' AND "CUST_COUNTRY"='India')
```

As you can see in the example, before extended statistics were collected, the estimated number of rows was 1447, whereas after the extended statistics collection, the number of rows optimizer estimated to return is 86.

To drop the extend statistics, use the DROP_EXTENDED_STATISTICS procedure:

```
SQL> exec dbms_stats.drop_extended_stats(null,'CUSTOMERS',
         '(CUST_COUNTRY, CUST_STATE)');
PL/SQL procedure successfully completed.
SQL>
```

To define the extension and collect statistics in one step, you can do the following:

```
SQL> exec dbms_stats.gather_table_stats(null, 'customers',
         method_opt=>'for all columns size skewonly
         for columns (cust_country, cust_state)');
PL/SQL procedure successfully completed.

SQL> select extension_name, extension from user_stat_extensions
  2  where table_name = 'CUSTOMERS';

EXTENSION_NAME                        EXTENSION
-----------------------------------   -----------------------------
SYS_STUZVS6GX30A0GN_5YRYSD2LPM        ("CUST_COUNTRY","CUST_STATE")
```

In the next section, you'll learn to enable and disable the automatic statistics collection as well as perform other AutoTask jobs.

Configuring Automated Maintenance Tasks Using EM

The following are three default automated maintenance tasks:

- Gathering optimizer statistics
- Running the Segment Advisor
- Running the SQL Tuning Advisor

You can also enable and disable the AutoTask jobs using EM Grid Control. On the Server tab, choose Automated Maintenance Tasks under Oracle Scheduler. Figure 14.8 shows the Automated Maintenance Tasks screen.

By clicking the Configure button, you can enable or disable the default AutoTask jobs, as well as adjust the days on which these tasks are run, as shown in Figure 14.9.

To learn more about Automated Maintenance Tasks and Oracle Scheduler, read the "Oracle Database Administrator's Guide 11*g* Release 1 (11.1) Part Number B28310-04" Oracle documentation.

FIGURE 14.8   Automated Maintenance Tasks screen

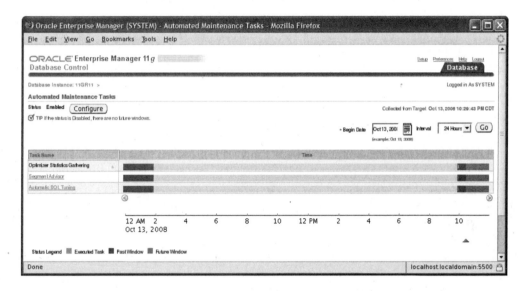

FIGURE 14.9   Configure Automated Maintenance Tasks screen

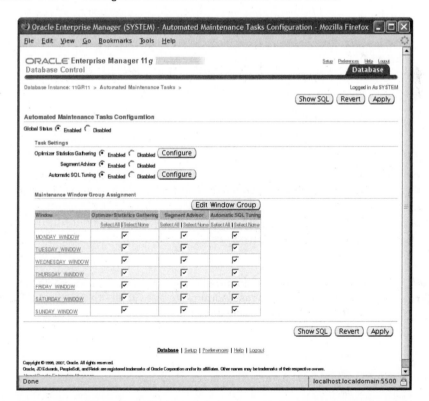

Gathering Performance Statistics

Oracle Database generates several performance statistics that are used for self-tuning purposes and are available for administrators to better tune the database. Most of the performance statistics information is available through V$ dictionary views (also known as *dynamic performance views*). The information in the V$ views are not persistent; that is, information is lost when the database is shut down. Automatic Workload Repository (AWR) saves the performance information in system tables and is made available for analysis through EM Database Control and other third-party tools. AWR information is persistent across database shutdowns.

The AWR data is captured at a system or database level, and session-level information is captured using another mechanism called the Active Session History (ASH). You will learn about AWR and ASH in the following sections.

Using Automatic Workload Repository

Two background processes are responsible for collecting the performance statistics: Memory Monitor (MMON) and Memory Monitor Light (MMNL). These processes work together to collect performance statistics directly from the system global area (SGA). The MMON process does most of the work by waking up every 60 minutes and gathering statistical information from the data dictionary views, dynamic performance views, and optimizer and then storing this information in the database. The tables that store these statistics are the Automatic Workload Repository. These tables are owned by the user SYSMAN and are stored in the SYSAUX tablespace.

To activate the AWR feature, you must set the pfile/spfile's parameter STATISTICS_LEVEL to the appropriate value. The values assigned to this parameter determine the depth of the statistics that the MMON process gathers. Table 14.3 shows the values that can be assigned to the STATISTICS_LEVEL parameter.

TABLE 14.3 Specifying Statistics Collection Levels

Collection Level	Description
BASIC	Disables the AWR and most other diagnostic monitoring and advisory activities. Few database statistics are gathered at each collection interval when operating the instance in this mode.
TYPICAL	Activates the standard level of collection activity. This is the default value for AWR and is appropriate for most environments.
ALL	Captures all the statistics gathered by the TYPICAL collection level, plus the execution plans and timing information from the operating system.

Once gathered, the statistics are stored in the AWR for a default duration of eight days. However, you can modify both the frequency of the snapshots and the duration for which they are saved in the AWR. One way to modify these intervals is by using the Oracle-supplied package DBMS_WORKLOAD_REPOSITORY. The following SQL command shows the DBMS_WORKLOAD_ REPOSITORY package being used to change the AWR collection interval to 1 hour and the retention period to 30 days:

```
SQL> execute dbms_workload_repository.modify_snapshot_settings
          (interval=>60,retention=>43200);
PL/SQL procedure successfully completed.
```

 The 30-day retention value shown here is expressed in minutes: 60 minutes per hour × 24 hours per day × 30 days = 43,200 minutes.

You can also change the AWR collection interval, retention period, and collection depth using EM Database Control. Choose the Server tab, and click Automatic Workload Repository under Statistics Management (see Figure 14.10).

FIGURE 14.10 AWR statistics collection and retention using EM

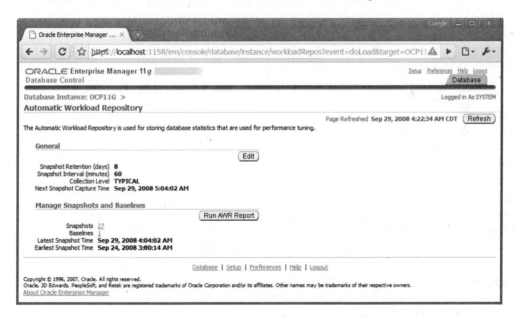

Click the Edit button to change the settings, as shown in Figure 14.11.

FIGURE 14.11   Changing AWR statistics collection and retention using EM

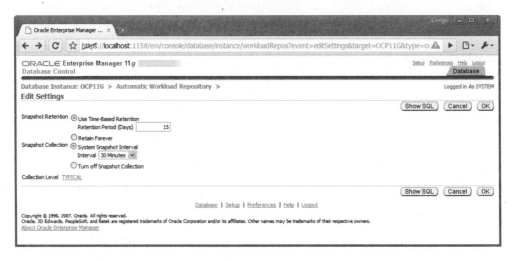

In Figure 14.11, the retention period for statistics gathered by the MMON process is set to 15 days, and statistics are collected every 30 minutes. You can also modify the depth at which statistics are collected by the AWR by clicking the Collection Level link. Clicking this link opens the Initialization Parameters screen where you can specify any of the three predefined collection levels shown in Table 14.3. Figure 14.12 shows the AWR collection level being changed from TYPICAL to ALL.

FIGURE 14.12   Changing the AWR statistics collection level

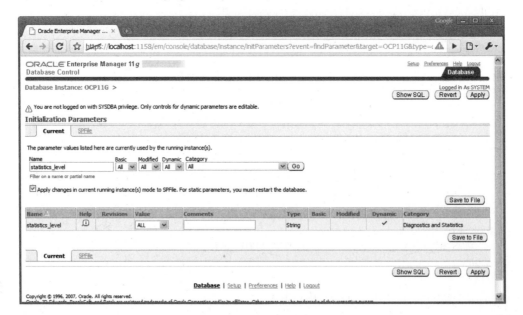

Take care when specifying the AWR statistics collection interval. Gathering snapshots too frequently requires additional space in the SYSAUX tablespace and adds database overhead each time the statistics are collected. AWR does not use any space in the SGA.

Using EM Database Control, you can view the AWR report. Click the Run AWR Report button on the Automatic Workload Repository screen shown earlier in Figure 14.10. You can get the same report using SQL*Plus by running the script $ORACLE_HOME/rdbms/admin/awrrpt.sql.

You can manage the AWR snapshots with SQL*Plus by utilizing the DBMS_WORKLOAD_REPOSITORY package, as described in the next section.

Managing AWR Snapshots Manually

You can create AWR snapshots by using the CREATE_SNAPSHOT procedure, as shown here:

```
SQL> EXECUTE DBMS_WORKLOAD_REPOSITORY.CREATE_SNAPSHOT ();
PL/SQL procedure successfully completed.
SQL>
```

You can use the DROP_SNAPSHOT_RANGE procedure to delete a range of snapshots, and you can query valid snapshot IDs from the DBA_HIST_SNAPSHOT view. The following example shows how to query the DBA_HIST_SNAPSHOT view:

```
SQL> SELECT snap_id, begin_interval_time, end_interval_time
  2  FROM dba_hist_snapshot
  3  ORDER BY snap_id;

  SNAP_ID BEGIN_INTERVAL_TIME              END_INTERVAL_TIME
---------- ------------------------------  ------------------------------
        1 24-SEP-08 02.06.11.000 AM        24-SEP-08 03.00.14.156 AM
        2 25-SEP-08 12.06.26.000 AM        25-SEP-08 12.17.55.437 AM
        3 25-SEP-08 12.17.55.437 AM        25-SEP-08 01.00.51.296 AM
        4 25-SEP-08 01.00.51.296 AM        25-SEP-08 02.00.22.109 AM
... ... ...
       27 27-SEP-08 07.03.17.375 PM        29-SEP-08 04.03.47.687 AM
       28 29-SEP-08 04.03.47.687 AM        29-SEP-08 05.00.39.437 AM
       29 29-SEP-08 05.00.39.437 AM        29-SEP-08 05.42.13.718 AM
```

To delete snapshots in the range 5–15, you can execute the following code. Note that the ASH (discussed in the next section) data is also purged between the time periods specified by the snapshot range.

```
SQL> BEGIN
  2    DBMS_WORKLOAD_REPOSITORY.DROP_SNAPSHOT_RANGE (5, 15);
  3  END;
  4  /
PL/SQL procedure successfully completed.
SQL>
```

Once AWR snapshots are taken and stored in the database, the Automatic Database Diagnostic feature uses the AWR data, as described in the "Automatic Database Diagnostic Monitoring" section.

Active Session History

ASH is sampled data at specified intervals from the current state of all active sessions. The data is collected in memory and can be accessed by V$ views. The ASH information is also written to a persistent store by the AWR snapshots.

The V$ACTIVE_SESSION_HISTORY provides the information collected by the ASH sampler. The sessions are sampled every second and are stored in a circular buffer in SGA. Each session is stored as a row. The current and historical information is available in the data dictionary view DBA_HIST_ACTIVE_SESS_HISTORY. ASH information also includes the execution plan for each SQL captured.

Oracle provides a script to generate an ASH report, $ORACLE_HOME/rdbms/admin/ashrpt.sql. You will be prompted for the report type (HTML or text), the begin time in minutes prior to SYSDATE, the duration in minutes for the report, and a name for the report. You can also use EM Database Control to generate the ASH report.

On the EM Database Control home screen, click the Performance tab, and click the Run ASH Report button, as shown in Figure 14.13.

FIGURE 14.13 Performance screen in EM Database Control

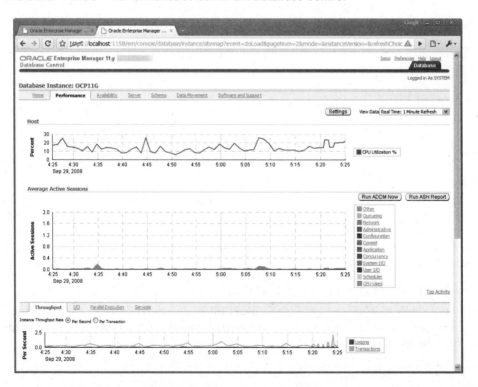

The screen shown in Figure 14.14 captures parameters for the ASH report. Specify the start time and end time for the report, and click the Generate Report button.

FIGURE 14.14 ASH report parameters

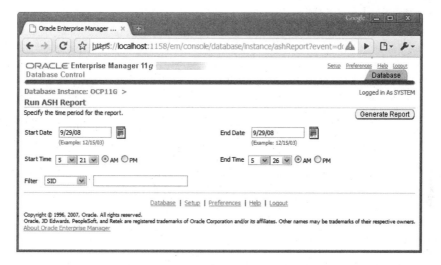

Any session that is connected to the database and does not wait for a wait event that belongs to the idle wait class is considered as an active session.

AWR Baselines

It is a good practice to baseline your database when everything is working as expected. When things go south, you can use this baseline to compare system statistics and performance metrics. *AWR baselines* contain performance data from a specific time period that is preserved for comparison when problems occur. This baseline data is excluded from the AWR purging process.

You can create two types of baselines: a *single* baseline and a *repeating* baseline. A single baseline is captured at a single fixed-time interval, such as October 5 between 10 a.m. and 1 p.m. A repeating baseline repeats during a time interval for a specific period, such as every Friday between 10 a.m. and 1 p.m. You can create and delete AWR baselines using EM Database Control or SQL*Plus.

Managing AWR Baselines Using SQL*Plus

To create a single baseline, use the CREATE_BASELINE procedure as shown in the following code. You can include the optional expiration parameter to automatically delete the snapshot after the specified number of days.

```
SQL> BEGIN
  2    DBMS_WORKLOAD_REPOSITORY.CREATE_BASELINE(
  3      start_snap_id => 27,
  4      end_snap_id => 29,
  5      baseline_name => 'OCP Example',
  6      expiration => 21);
  7  END;
SQL> /
PL/SQL procedure successfully completed.
SQL>
```

To drop a baseline, use the DROP_BASELINE procedure as shown in the following code. The **cascade** parameter specifies that only the baseline should be dropped, not the snapshots associated with the baseline.

```
SQL> BEGIN
  2    DBMS_WORKLOAD_REPOSITORY.DROP_BASELINE(
  3      baseline_name => 'OCP Example',
  4      cascade => FALSE);
  5  END;
SQL> /
PL/SQL procedure successfully completed.
SQL>
```

You can create a baseline for the future date and time. These are called *baseline templates*. The following code creates a baseline template:

```
SQL> BEGIN
  2    DBMS_WORKLOAD_REPOSITORY.CREATE_BASELINE_TEMPLATE(
  3      start_time => TO_DATE('01-JAN-09 05.00.00','DD-MON-YY HH.MI.SS'),
  4      end_time => TO_DATE('01-JAN-09 08.00.00','DD-MON-YY HH.MI.SS'),
  5      baseline_name => 'baseline_090101',
  6      template_name => 'template_090101',
  7      expiration => 21);
  8  END;
SQL> /
PL/SQL procedure successfully completed.
SQL>
```

AWR baselines and baseline templates are never dropped automatically (or purged) from the database unless explicitly dropped by the DBA or the expiration period ends.

Managing AWR Baselines Using EM Database Control

Using EM Database Control to create, rename, and drop AWR baselines is easier than using SQL*Plus and error-free. From the database home page, click the Server tab (shown earlier in Figure 14.1). Click the AWR Baselines link under Statistics Management. The current baselines are displayed, as shown in Figure 14.15.

FIGURE 14.15   AWR Baselines screen

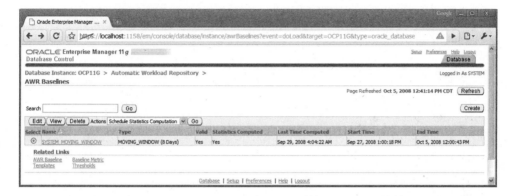

Click the Create button to create a new baseline. You will be presented with the option to create a single baseline or a repeating baseline. If you choose a single baseline, you will be presented with the screen shown in Figure 14.16. Enter the name of the baseline. You can specify the snapshots to include in the baseline by using the snapshot IDs or using a time range.

FIGURE 14.16   AWR Create Single Baseline screen

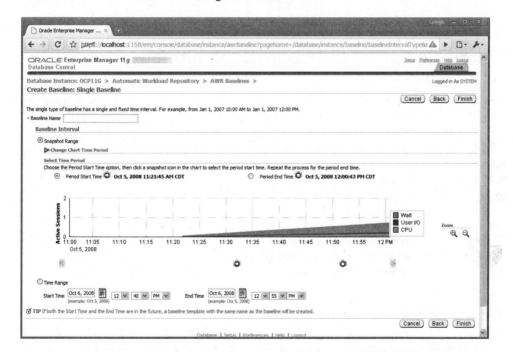

If you choose to create a repeating baseline, you'll see the screen shown in Figure 14.17. Enter a baseline name, and specify the frequency.

FIGURE 14.17 AWR Create Repeating Baseline screen

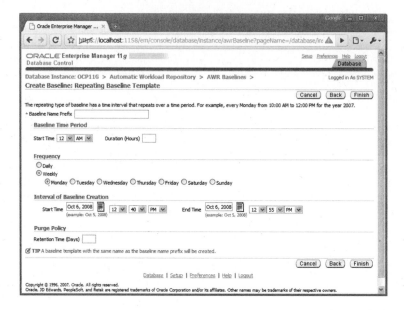

You can drop a baseline by choosing the baseline and clicking the Delete button on the AWR Baselines screen (Figure 14.15).

Automatic Database Diagnostic Monitoring

Following each AWR statistics-collection process, the Automated Database Diagnostic Monitoring (ADDM) feature automatically analyzes the gathered statistics and compares them to the statistics gathered by the previous two AWR snapshots. By comparing the current statistics to these two previous snapshots, the ADDM can easily identify potential database problems such as these:

- CPU and I/O bottlenecks
- Resource-intensive SQL or PL/SQL or Java execution
- Lock contention
- Utilization of Oracle's memory structures within the SGA
- RAC-specific issues
- Issues with Oracle Net configuration
- Data-concurrency issues

Based on these findings, the ADDM may recommend possible remedies. The goal of these recommendations is to minimize DB Time. DB Time is composed of two types of time measures for nonidle database users: CPU time and wait time. This information is stored as the cumulative time that all database users have spent either using CPU resources or waiting for access to resources such as CPU, I/O, or Oracle's memory structures. High or increasing values for DB Time indicate that users are requesting increasingly more server resources and may also be experiencing waits for those resources, which can lead to less than optimal performance. In this way, minimizing DB Time is a much better way to measure overall database performance than Oracle's old ratio-based tuning methodologies.

DB Time is calculated by combining all the times from all nonidle user sessions into one number. Therefore, it is possible for the DB Time value to be larger than the total time that the instance has been running.

Once ADDM completes its comparison of the newly collected statistics to the previously collected statistics, the results are stored in the AWR. You can use these statistics to establish baselines against which future performance will be compared, and you can use deviations from these baseline measures to identify areas that need attention. In this manner, ADDM allows you to not only better detect and alert yourself to potential management and performance problems in the database but also allows you to automatically take corrective actions to rectify those problems quickly and with little or no manual intervention.

The following sections introduce the interfaces, features, and functionality of ADDM and explain how you can use this utility to monitor and manage database storage, security, and performance. We'll begin by examining the EM Database Control tools you can use to view the results of ADDM analysis.

Using EM Database Control to View ADDM Analysis

EM Database Control graphically displays the results of the ADDM analysis on several screens, including the following:

- The Performance Findings link under the Diagnostic Summary section of the EM Database Control main screen

- The Performance tab of the EM Database Control main screen

- The ADDM screen located by clicking the Advisor Central link at the bottom of the EM Database Control main screen

You'll see sample output from each of the EM Database Control screens in the following sections.

The EM Database Control Performance Findings Link

The EM Database Control home screen contains a section called Diagnostic Summary. One of the links under this section is ADDM Findings. Figure 14.18 shows this section.

FIGURE 14.18 The Diagnostic Summary section of the EM Database Control home screen

The output in Figure 14.18 shows that ADDM discovered four performance-related findings. Clicking the link for these four performance findings displays the ADDM summary screen, at the bottom of which is the Performance Analysis section, as shown in Figure 14.19.

The Findings section on this screen shows the ADDM analysis and the recommendation to resolve the issue.

FIGURE 14.19 ADDM summary screen

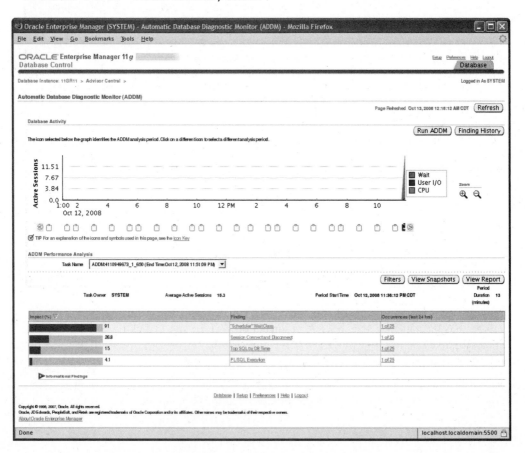

The EM Database Control Performance Tab

You can also click the Performance tab on the EM Database Control main screen to view performance data collected by AWR and analyzed by ADDM. You can click the Run ADDM Now button to take an AWR snapshot and perform ADDM analysis. Figure 14.20 shows the Performance tab of EM Database Control.

FIGURE 14.20   EM Database Control Performance tab

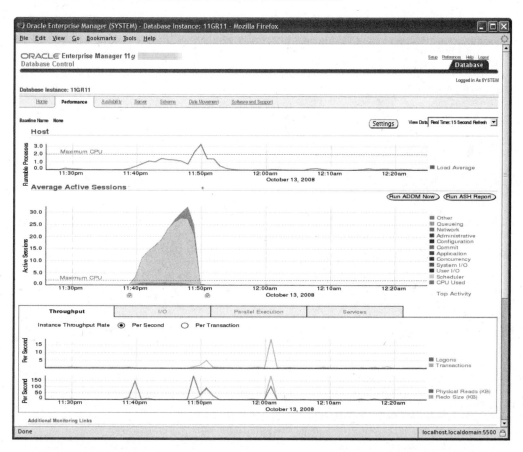

Using Active Sessions of the Performance tab, you can drill down into detailed information that has been identified as having an impact on performance. Click the Scheduler link, which will take you to the screen shown in Figure 14.21.

FIGURE 14.21 Detailed performance information

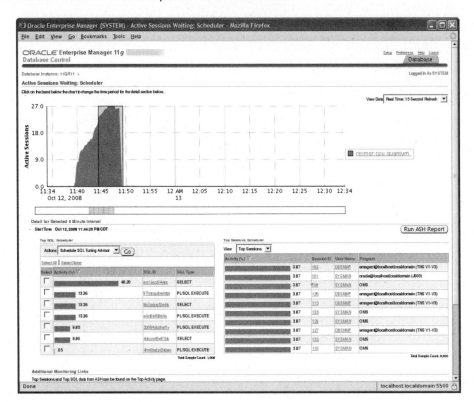

The Advisor Central Screen

The Advisor Central screen also contains ADDM findings. The link for the Advisor Central screen is at the bottom of the EM Database Control home screen. Click this link to display the Advisor Central screen, shown in Figure 14.22.

Click the ADDM link in the Advisors section of this screen to display a graph that shows all the recent AWR snapshots taken by the MMON process.

As stated earlier, the ADDM automatically compares the most recent AWR snapshot with the last two AWR snapshots when formulating its recommendations. However, you can use this Create ADDM Task screen to manually select any two AWR snapshot times and formulate ADDM recommendations for activity that occurred between those two points in time. To start this process, click the Period Start Time radio button, and then select a start date and time by clicking the point in the graph's timeline that corresponds to the beginning period that you want to use. Repeat this process to specify the end-process timestamp.

You can also manually perform an ADDM analysis without EM Database Control by using the addmrpt.sql script located in the $ORACLE_HOME/ rdbms/admin directory.

FIGURE 14.22 The Advisor Central screen

You can use the DBMS_ADDM package to manually analyze AWR snapshots. Table 14.4 shows some of the subprograms in DBMS_ADDM that can be used to manually manage ADDM analysis.

TABLE 14.4 Partial List of DBMS_ADDM Subprograms

Procedure Name	Description
ANALYZE_DB	Creates an ADDM analysis by specifying the begin and end AWR snapshot IDs
DELETE	Deletes an ADDM task
INSERT_FINDING_DIRECTIVE	Excludes certain findings from ADDM reporting
INSERT_SEGMENT_DIRECTIVE	Excludes a certain schema, object, or segment from ADDM reporting (do not run Segment Advisor on these segments)
INSERT_SQL_DIRECTIVE	Excludes certain SQL from ADDM reporting

The DBA_ADVISOR_FINDINGS, DBA_ADVISOR_RECOMMENDATIONS, and DBA_ADVISOR_ACTIONS dictionary views have a column named FILTERED. If the value for this column is Y, the row in the view is filtered by a directive and is not reported.

Although using EM Database Control to create and view ADDM results is by far the simplest way to review ADDM recommendations, you can also query the ADDM data dictionary views directly. I'll discuss some of these data dictionary views in the following section.

Using Data Dictionary Views to View ADDM Analysis

You can use more than 20 data dictionary views to examine the results of ADDM's activities. Table 14.5 describes five commonly used ADDM views that store the recommendation information you saw in the EM Database Control pages.

TABLE 14.5 ADDM Data Dictionary Views

View Name	Description
DBA_ADDM_TASKS	Displays executed advisor tasks
DBA_ADDM_FINDINGS	Describes the findings identified by the ADDM analysis
DBA_ADVISOR_OBJECTS	Describes the objects that are referenced in the ADDM findings and recommendations
DBA_ADVISOR_RECOMMENDATIONS	Describes the recommendations made based on ADDM findings
DBA_ADVISOR_RATIONALE	Describes the rationale behind each ADDM finding

DBA_ADDM_TASKS, DBA_ADDM_INSTANCES, and DBA_ADDM_FINDINGS are extensions of the corresponding DBA_ADVISOR_ views but are specific for ADDM tasks and findings.

The following SQL statement shows a sample query on the DBA_ADVISOR_FINDINGS data dictionary view that identifies the type of performance problem that is causing the most impact on the database:

```
SQL> SELECT task_id, type, message
  2  FROm dba_advisor_findings
  3  WHERE impact= (select MAX(impcat) FROM dba_advisor_findings);
```

```
TASK_ID TYPE        MESSAGE
------- ---------   ------------------------------------------------
    164 PROBLEM     SQL statements consuming significant database time
                    were found.
```

The output from this query shows that SQL statements being executed in the database are contributing to the poor database performance. By itself, the DBA_ADVISOR_FINDINGS table does not identify which SQL statements are consuming the database time. Instead, these are shown in the DBA_ADVISOR_OBJECTS data dictionary view and are identified by the TASK_ID value shown in the query on DBA_ADVISOR_FINDINGS. A query on that view, using the TASK_ID of 164 returned by the ADDM session that had the potential for the greatest database impact, returns the SQL statements shown here:

```
SQL> SELECT attr4
  2  FROM dba_advisor_objects
  3  WHERE task_id = 164;


ATTR4
-----------------------------------------------------------------------
UPDATE customers SET credit_limit=credit_limit*1.15 WHERE cust_id = :B1

DELETE FROM sales WHERE time_id BETWEEN '01-JAN-00' and '01-JAN-01';

UPDATE sales_history SET quantity_sold = quantity_sold+10 WHERE
   CHANNEL_ID := B1

SELECT COUNT(*) FROM Sales_history;

SELECT DISTINCT channel_id FROM sales_history;
```

This query shows all the SQL statements that were captured by the AWR during the snapshot period and that were used in the ADDM analysis for that same period.

The DBA_ADVISOR_ACTIONS data dictionary view shows the ADDM recommendations for each finding. The following query shows the recommendations for correcting the performance issues associated with TASK_ID 164, which was identified earlier as being the costliest database activity:

```
SQL> SELECT TRIM(attr1) ATTR1, TRIM(attr2) ATTR2, TRIM(attr3) ATTR3
  2  FROM dba_advisor_actions
  3  WHERE task_id = 164;


ATTR1           ATTR2     ATTR3
----------      ------    ----------
log_buffer      262144    15728640
db_cache_size   25165824  50331648

undo_retention  900       363
```

This output indicates that ADDM recommends that the values for LOG_BUFFER, DB_ CACHE_SIZE, and UNDO_RETENTION all be changed from their current values to 15,728,640 bytes; 50,331,648 bytes; and 363 seconds, respectively.

If you want to see the rationale behind each of the actions shown in DBA_ADVISOR_ACTIONS, query the DBA_ADVISOR_RATIONALE data dictionary view. The DBA_ADVISOR_RATIONALE view stores the ADDM recommendations that ADDM has formulated based on the AWR data like those stored in DBA_ADVISOR_FINDINGS and DBA_ADVISOR_OBJECTS. The following example shows a sample query on the DBA_ADVISOR_RATIONALE view using the TASK_ID of 164 identified earlier:

```
SQL> SELECT message
  2  FROM dba_advisor_rationale
  3  WHERE task_id = 164;


MESSAGE
----------------------------------------------------------------------
Buffer cache writes due to small log files were consuming significant
   database time.

The buffer cache was undersized causing significant read I/O.

The value of "undo retention" was 900 seconds and the longest running
   query lasted only 330 seconds. This extra retention caused
   unnecessary I/O.
```

As you can see from the complexity of these examples, examining the ADDM results via EM Database Control is much easier than accessing the data dictionary views via SQL. From a practical standpoint, you would run SQL queries against these ADDM views only if EM Database Control were unavailable.

To gain further insight into the recommendations and information gathered by the ADDM, Oracle 11g also provides several advisor utilities in EM Database Control. I will discuss these advisors in the next section.

The Advisory Framework

Oracle 11g comes with several advisors to help proactively manage the database. The top portion of Figure 14.22 shows the advisors available in Oracle 11g and how to invoke them.

Advisors provide recommendations that are key for a DBA to manage the database effectively. The advisors can be classified into various categories. The following are the advisors:

- Memory
  - SGA Advisor
  - PGA Advisor
  - Shared Pool Advisor
  - Buffer Cache Advisor
- SQL
  - SQL Tuning Advisor
  - SQL Access Advisor
- Automatic Undo Management
  - Undo Advisor
- Recovery
  - MTTR Advisor
  - Data Recovery Advisor
- Space
  - Segment Advisor

The purpose of each advisor is explained next. Since the OCA certification exam expects you to only be familiar with the general purpose of the advisors, I won't go into detail of each advisor in this book. You can click each advisor's link on the Advisor Central screen and familiarize yourself with the contents.

Memory advisors   Memory advisors provide the optimal size for various memory parameters. If AMM is enabled, the advisor provides the target amount of memory to allocate to the instance. If AMM is disabled but ASMM is enabled, the advisor provides recommendations on the optimal sizes for SGA and PGA. If no automatic memory features are enabled, you can get the sizes for individual SGA components such as shared pool and buffer cache. AMM and ASMM are discussed later in the chapter.

SQL Tuning Advisor   This provides SQL tuning advice. You may use the top activity or current session's graphs to drill down to the SQL statement to tune. You can tune one statement or multiple statements. The advice includes restructuring SQL statements, creating additional indexes, using materialized views, partitioning tables, refreshing the optimizer statistics, and so on.

SQL Access Advisor   The SQL Access Advisor provides recommendations on schema modifications. It recommends indexes and materialized views to optimize SQL queries.

Undo Advisor   The Undo Advisor recommends the optimal size for the undo tablespace based on the undo retention and flashback requirements.

MTTR Advisor   The MTTR Advisor provides the optimal value for the FAST_START_ MTTR_TARGET initialization parameter. This parameter determines the amount of time required by the instance to start in the event of an instance crash. Instance failure can occur when the host server crashes, when any critical SGA background process fails, or if the instance is shut down using the ABORT option. Instance recovery occurs automatically on the first startup following the instance failure. During instance recovery, Oracle uses the online redo logs to roll back any uncommitted transactions that were "in flight" when the instance crashed to ensure that all committed transactions are written to disk. As a DBA, you often try to minimize the time it takes to perform this instance recovery so that you can bring up the database quickly.

Data Recovery Advisor   The Data Recovery Advisor helps diagnose and repair data failures and corruptions. It analyzes the failure based on the symptoms and determines the repair strategies.

Segment Advisor   The Segment Advisor identifies whether a segment is a good candidate for a shrink operation based on the level of fragmentation within the segment. The advisor also keeps historical growth of the segment, which can be used for capacity planning. Segments that can be shrunk are those that the Segment Advisor has found to need less space than they are currently allocated. By shrinking or compressing these segments, space is returned to the database for use by other objects, and the total number of I/Os needed to access these objects is reduced, potentially improving the performance of SQL statements that access these objects.

In the next section, you'll learn about another tool in the Oracle 11g database that helps you proactively monitor the database with timely alerts.

Monitoring Server-Generated Alerts

In addition to monitoring and making recommendations on SQL, memory, mean time to recover, segments, and undo activity, an Oracle 11g database can also proactively monitor itself for other types of problems related to configuration, security, and space management. To do so, you use the server-generated alerts feature.

A *server-generated alert* is an alert from the Oracle 11g database that says it suspects a problem with the database. These alerts are also an integral part of the ADDM architecture. They notify you when a management or performance issue occurs and begin taking corrective actions—if you configured such actions. By default, the alert notifications are sent to a predefined persistent queue named ALERT_QUE owned by SYS. EM Grid Control reads this queue.

There are two types of server-generated alerts: threshold based and event based. *Threshold* alerts are triggered when a specified threshold is met, such as when a tablespace has reached certain capacity. Threshold alerts can be fired at a warning level (for example, 85 percent tablespace capacity) or at a critical level (for example, 97 percent tablespace capacity). *Event* alerts are triggered when a specified event occurs, such as a database error.

Viewing and Configuring Alerts Using EM Database Control

The EM Database Control home page displays the alerts when they are triggered. Figure 14.23 shows the Alerts section of the Database Control home page.

FIGURE 14.23   Alerts section of the Database Control home page

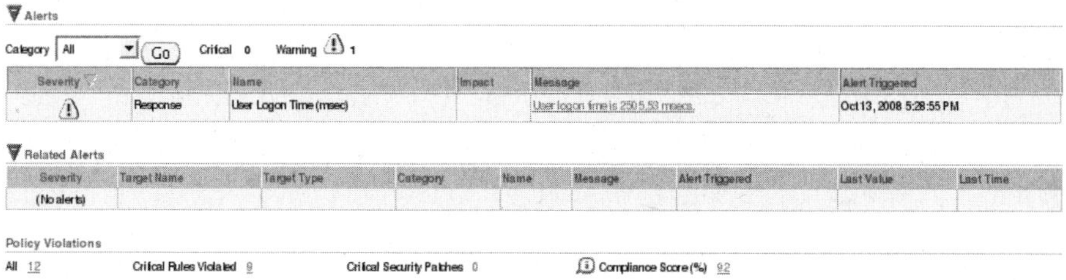

You can see the alert history by clicking the Alert link. You can configure the alerts by clicking the Metric and Policy Settings link under Related Links. Figure 14.24 shows the top portion of the Metric and Policy Settings screen.

FIGURE 14.24   Metric and Policy Settings screen

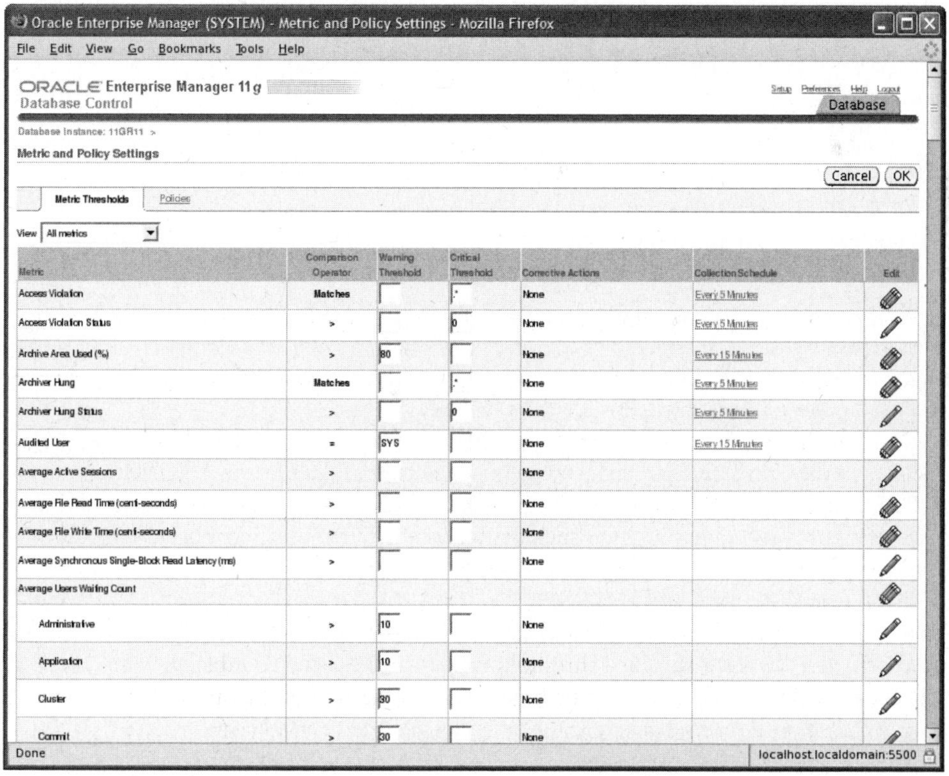

As you can see in Figure 14.24, each alert can have two levels of severity: Warning and Critical. These two alert levels allow you to achieve greater granularity. For example, you might want two thresholds set up with regard to the archive destination. One might be a warning threshold that triggers an alert when the archive destination is 80 percent full— causing a message to be displayed on the EM Database Control main screen. In addition, you might want to set up a critical threshold so that you receive an email whenever the archive destination device is 90 percent full. In this manner, you can escalate a potential problem from an EM Database Control console message to an email alert as the problem gets worse.

You can also use warning and critical alerts to distinguish between lower-severity problems, such as statistics indicating temporary poor performance, and higher-severity problems, such as ORA-0600 error messages in the database alert log. You can achieve this by defining warning thresholds only for lower-severity alerts and defining warning and critical alerts for higher-severity problems.

Viewing and Configuring Alerts Using SQL

You can use SQL*Plus to configure the alert thresholds and to view the alerts. The DBMS_ SERVER_ALERT package has the subprograms to define and query the thresholds. The SET_ THRESHOLD procedure is used to define the threshold, and the GET_THRESHOLD procedure is used to retrieve threshold information.

You can also query the thresholds from the DBA_THRESHOLDS dictionary view. The following is an example:

```
SQL> SELECT metrics_name, warning_value, critical_value
  2  FROM dba_thresholds
  3  WHERE metrics_name like 'Tablespace%'
SQL> /
METRICS_NAME                         WARNING_VA CRITICAL_V
----------------------------------- ---------- ----------
Tablespace Bytes Space Usage         0          0
Tablespace Space Usage               85         97
SQL>
```

Threshold alerts are written to DBA_OUTSTANDING_ALERTS. Nonthreshold alerts are written only to DBA_ALERT_HISTORY. Entries from DBA_OUTSTANDING_ALERTS are cleared when the alert condition is cleared. The following is a query from the DBA_OUTSTANDING_ALERTS view:

```
SQL> SELECT reason FROM dba_outstanding_alerts;
REASON
--------------------------------------------------------
db_recovery_file_dest_size of 4395630592 bytes is 97.27%
used and has 119794176 remaining bytes available.
```

```
Metrics "Database Time Spent Waiting (%)" is at 36.84571
for event class "Concurrency"
```

The V$METRIC view shows system-level metric values. Metric history is saved in the V$METRIC_HISTORY view.

So far, you have seen several tools that help DBAs proactively monitor the database. I cannot possible identify all the potential issues and how to proactively avoid them. Errors and database corruptions do happen. The Oracle 11*g* database has a reporting mechanism to analyze the problem reactively and take measures to avoid it in the future. You'll learn about the Automatic Diagnostic Repository in the next section.

Understanding Automatic Diagnostic Repository

The Automatic Diagnostic Repository (ADR) is a file-based repository for database diagnostic data such as alert log files, trace files, core dump files, health monitor reports, and so on. In prior releases of Oracle, the trace and dump files were traditionally saved in directories specified by the _DUMP_DIRECTORY parameters. Starting with Oracle 11*g*, these files and much more are saved under the ADR framework.

ADR replaces the BACKGROUND_DUMP_DEST, CORE_DUMP_DEST, and USER_DUMP_DEST locations. A new parameter, DIAGNOSTIC_DEST, specifies the base directory for the ADR. The default for DIAGNOSTIC_DEST is $ORACLE_BASE if available; otherwise, it's $ORACLE_HOME/log. ADR is a vast topic and is not covered here in its entirety.

Within ADR base, there can be multiple ADR homes. Each ADR home is the base directory for all the files belonging to an instance. The ADR home directory for an instance is $DIAGNOSTIC_DEST/diag/rdbms/<dbname>/<instance name>.

The subdirectories under the DIAGNOSTIC_DEST are as follows:

```
DIAGNOSTIC_DEST/diag                    DIAGNOSTIC_DEST/diag
    rdbms                                   tnslsnr
        <db_name>                               <machine_name>
            <instance_name>                         <listener_name>
                alert                                   alert
                cdump                                   cdump
                hm                                      incident
                incident                                incpkg
                incpkg                                  lck
                ir                                      metadata
                lck                                     stage
                metadata                                sweep
                stage                                   trace
                sweep
                trace
```

In Oracle 11g, an alert log file is written in XML format as well as in text format. The XML-format file is under the `alert` directory, whereas the text-format file is under the `trace` directory. Table 14.6 shows where to look for log and trace files in Oracle 11g.

TABLE 14.6 Alert File and Trace File Locations

Type of File	Pre–Oracle 11g Location	Oracle 11g Location
Alert log (text)	BACKGROUND_DUMP_DEST	`<ADR_HOME>/trace`
Alert log (XML)	None	`<ADR_HOME>/alert`
Server trace files	BACKGROUND_DUMP_DEST	`<ADR_HOME>/trace`
User trace files	USER_DUMP_DEST	`<ADR_HOME>/trace`
Core dump files	CORE_DUMP_DEST	`<ADR_HOME>/cdump`
Incident dumps	USER_DUMP_DEST, BACKGROUND_DUMP_DEST	`<ADR_HOME>/incident/incdir_n`

The values for _DUMP_DEST parameters are ignored by Oracle 11g. The new view **V$DIAG_INFO** gives file locations:

```
SQL> SELECT name, value FROM v$diag_info;

NAME                         VALUE
------------------------     ---------------------------------------------
Diag Enabled                 TRUE
ADR Base                     c:\oracle
ADR Home                     c:\oracle\diag\rdbms\w11gr1\w11gr1
Diag Trace                   c:\oracle\diag\rdbms\w11gr1\w11gr1\trace
Diag Alert                   c:\oracle\diag\rdbms\w11gr1\w11gr1\alert
Diag Incident                c:\oracle\diag\rdbms\w11gr1\w11gr1\incident
Diag Cdump                   c:\oracle\diag\rdbms\w11gr1\w11gr1\cdump
Health Monitor               c:\oracle\diag\rdbms\w11gr1\w11gr1\hm
Default Trace File           c:\...\w11gr1\trace\w11gr1_ora_6036.trc
Active Problem Count         0
Active Incident Count        0
```

The standard directory structure and diagnostic framework enables DBAs to package and send trace-file and log information to Oracle Support for timely resolution to issues. The ADR command interface (ADRCI) is a command-line tool available to view the ADR information and to package incident and problem information into a zip file.

Using ADRCI to View the Alert Log File

You invoke the ADRCI command-line tool with the executable adrci, and you use the show alert command to view the alert log file. You can use options such as -tail to view the end of the file or -P to filter the output. You can also use the SPOOL command similar to SQL*Plus to write the output to a file.

The help command in adrci displays all the available commands in ADRCI. Invoke ADRCI using the adrci.exe executable on Windows or using the adrci executable on Unix/Linux platforms.

```
$ adrci

ADRCI: Release 11.1.0.6.0 - Beta on Wed Oct 15 06:53:26 2008
Copyright (c) 1982, 2007, Oracle.  All rights reserved.
ADR base = "/u01/app/oracle"

adrci> help
 HELP [topic]
   Available Topics:
        CREATE REPORT
        ECHO
        EXIT
        HELP
        HOST
        IPS
        PURGE
        RUN
        SET BASE
        SET BROWSER
        SET CONTROL
        SET ECHO
        SET EDITOR
        SET HOMES | HOME | HOMEPATH
        SET TERMOUT
        SHOW ALERT
        SHOW BASE
        SHOW CONTROL
        SHOW HM_RUN
        SHOW HOMES | HOME | HOMEPATH
        SHOW INCDIR
```

```
SHOW INCIDENT
SHOW PROBLEM
SHOW REPORT
SHOW TRACEFILE
SPOOL
```

There are other commands intended to be used directly by Oracle, type "HELP EXTENDED" to see the list
adrci>

To find out the purpose and get detailed syntax information on a specific command, do help <command>:

adrci> help show alert

```
Usage: SHOW ALERT [-p <predicate_string>]  [-term]
                  [ [-tail [num] [-f]] | [-file <alert_file_name>] ]
Purpose: Show alert messages.
Options:
  [-p <predicate_string>]: The predicate string must be double quoted.
  The fields in the predicate are the fields:
        ORIGINATING_TIMESTAMP        timestamp
        NORMALIZED_TIMESTAMP         timestamp
        ORGANIZATION_ID              text(65)
        COMPONENT_ID                 text(65)
        HOST_ID                      text(65)
        HOST_ADDRESS                 text(17)
        MESSAGE_TYPE                 number
        MESSAGE_LEVEL                number
        MESSAGE_ID                   text(65)
        MESSAGE_GROUP                text(65)
        CLIENT_ID                    text(65)
        MODULE_ID                    text(65)
        PROCESS_ID                   text(33)
        THREAD_ID                    text(65)
        USER_ID                      text(65)
        INSTANCE_ID                  text(65)
        DETAILED_LOCATION            text(161)
        UPSTREAM_COMP_ID             text(101)
        DOWNSTREAM_COMP_ID           text(101)
```

```
EXECUTION_CONTEXT_ID              text(101)
EXECUTION_CONTEXT_SEQUENCE        number
ERROR_INSTANCE_ID                 number
ERROR_INSTANCE_SEQUENCE           number
MESSAGE_TEXT                      text(2049)
MESSAGE_ARGUMENTS                 text(129)
SUPPLEMENTAL_ATTRIBUTES           text(129)
SUPPLEMENTAL_DETAILS              text(129)
PROBLEM_KEY                       text(65)
```

[-tail [num] [-f]]: Output last part of the alert messages and output latest messages as the alert log grows. If num is not specified, the last 10 messages are displayed. If "-f" is specified, new data will append at the end as new alert messages are generated.

[-term]: Direct results to terminal. If this option is not specified, the results will be open in an editor.
By default, it will open in emacs, but "set editor" can be used to set other editors.

[-file <alert_file_name>]: Allow users to specify an alert file which may not be in ADR. <alert_file_name> must be specified with full path. Note that this option cannot be used with the -tail option

```
Examples:
  show alert
  show alert -p "message_text like '%incident%'"
  show alert -tail 20
```

```
adrci>
```

Using EM to View the Alert Log File

You can also use EM Database Control to view the alert log contents. On the Database Control home page, click the Alert Log Contents link under Related Links. You can view the last 50, 100, or up to 2,000 lines of the alert log. See Figure 14.25.

FIGURE 14.25 View Alert Log Contents screen in Database Control

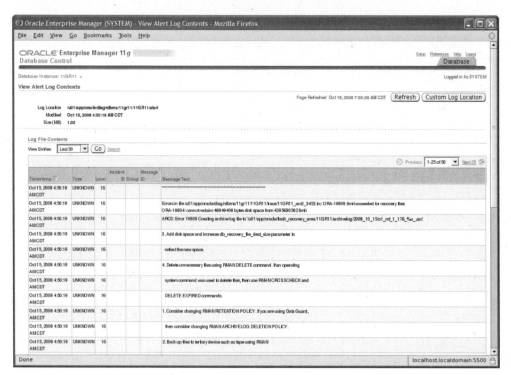

In the next section, you will learn the tools available to monitor the performance of the database.

Managing Performance

Although AWR, ADDM, advisors, and ADR all help you proactively monitor and manage your databases, you can use additional performance-specific features of EM Database Control to further enhance the performance of your database. When thinking about tuning, you should consider the following areas:

- Memory-allocation issues
- I/O contention (disk/SAN configuration)
- CPU contention
- Network issues
- SQL problems (bad SQL, optimizer plans)

Several dictionary and dynamic performance views are available in Oracle 11*g* that help you tune and gather system information. When it comes to tuning, managing the instance memory is very important. How much memory should you allocate for all the various SGA components? In the following sections, you will learn how Oracle 11*g* can help you take the guesswork out of database administration and tune the database.

Sources of Tuning Information

EM Database Control provides a wealth of information for improving database monitoring and management, but you also need to be aware of several other sources of information about database performance, including the following:

- The alert log
- Background and user trace files
- Dynamic performance views
- Data dictionary views

The Alert Log

The Oracle alert log records informational and error messages for a variety of activities that have occurred against the database during its operation. These activities are recorded in chronological order from the oldest to most recent. You can find the alert log in the ADR directory that you learned about earlier.

The alert log frequently indicates whether gross tuning problems exist in the database. Tables that are unable to acquire additional storage, sorts that are failing, and problems with rollback segments are all examples of tuning problems that can show up as messages in the alert log. Most of these messages are accompanied by an Oracle error message.

Background and User Trace Files

Oracle trace files are text files that contain session information for the process that created them. Trace files can be generated by the Oracle background processes, through the use of trace events, or by user server processes. These trace files can contain useful information for performance tuning and system troubleshooting. Trace files are also located in the ADR directories.

You can generate user trace files for a particular session by using the DBMS_MONITOR package. Many subprograms are available in this package to enable and disable trace; the most common ones are SESSION_TRACE_ENABLE to start the tracing and SESSION_TRACE_DISABLE to stop the tracing.

To use the SESSION_TRACE_ENABLE procedure, you must know the SID and SERIAL# on the session, which you can get by querying the V$SESSION view. The third argument to the procedure is waits, which is TRUE by default. The fourth argument is binds, which is FALSE by default. By enabling the waits, the wait information is written to the trace file. By enabling the binds, the bind variable values are also written to the trace file. Once you have the SID and SERIAL#, you can enable trace for the session by doing the following:

```
SQL> BEGIN
        DBMS_MONITOR.SESSION_TRACE_ENABLE(session_id=>324,
                                          serial_num=>54385,
                                          waits=>TRUE,
                                          binds=>TRUE);
    END;
```

To stop tracing, you have to pass in the SID and SERIAL# as parameters:

```
SQL> BEGIN
        DBMS_MONITOR.SESSION_TRACE_DISABLE(session_id=>324,
                                           serial_num=>54385);
    END;
```

You can also use EM Database Control to enable and disable trace. To see the sessions in the instance, you can choose any of the following links under the Additional Monitoring Links on the Performance tab in Database Control (see Figure 14.26):

- Top Consumers
- Blocking Sessions
- Instance Locks
- Search Sessions

FIGURE 14.26 Additional Monitoring Links section on the Performance tab

When you click Top Consumers, you will get an overview of the consumers. Click Top Sessions to view the sessions in the instance, as shown in Figure 14.27.

You can use the Enable SQL Trace and Disable SQL Trace buttons on this screen to enable and disable tracing.

The 10046 trace event, which can be activated at the instance or session level, is particularly useful for finding performance bottlenecks. See Note 171647.1 at http://metalink.oracle.com for a discussion of using the 10046 trace event as a tuning technique.

FIGURE 14.27   Top Sessions screen on EM

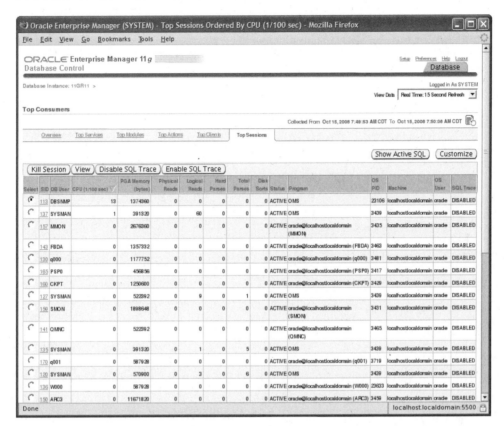

Dynamic Performance Views

As described in Chapter 8, "Introducing Oracle Database 11g Components and Architecture," Oracle Database 11g contains several dynamic performance views. Table 14.7 contains a partial listing of some of the V$ views that are frequently used in performance tuning and troubleshooting.

TABLE 14.7   A Partial Listing of Dynamic Performance Views

Name	Description
V$SGAINFO	Shows information about the size of the SGA's components
V$PGASTAT	Shows information about PGA memory usage

TABLE 14.7   A Partial Listing of Dynamic Performance Views   *(continued)*

Name	Description
V$EVENT_NAME	Shows database events that may require waits when requested by the system or by an individual session
V$SYSTEM_EVENT	Shows events for which waits have occurred for all sessions accessing the system
V$SESSION_EVENT	Shows events for which waits have occurred, individually identified by session
V$SESSION_WAIT	Shows events for which waits are currently occurring, individually identified by session
V$STATNAME	Matches the name to the statistics listed only by number in V$SESSTAT and V$SYSSAT
V$SYSSTAT	Shows overall system statistics for all sessions, both currently and previously connected
V$SESSTAT	Shows statistics on a per-session basis for currently connected sessions
V$SESSION	Shows current connection information on a per-session basis
V$WAITSTAT	Shows statistics related to block contention
V$LOCK	Lists the locks currently in the database
V$PARAMETER	Shows the initialization-parameter values that are currently in effect
V$SPPARAMETER	Shows the contents of the server parameter file (spfile); look for value TRUE in column ISSPECIFIED to see if the parameter was explicitly specified in the spfile, as opposed to default values.
V$FILESTAT	Shows number of reads/writes and timing statistics for data files
V$DATAFILE	Shows data file properties
V$TEMPFILE	Shows temporary file properties
V$TEMPSEG_USAGE	Displays temporary segment usage by session

In general, queries that incorporate V$SYSSTAT show statistics for the entire instance since the time it was started. By joining this view to the other relevant views, you get the overall picture of performance in the database. Alternatively, queries that incorporate V$SESSTAT show statistics for a particular session. These queries are better suited for examining the performance of an individual operation or process. EM Database Control makes extensive use of these views when creating performance-related graphs.

Data Dictionary Views

Depending on the features and options installed, an Oracle 11g database has hundreds of data dictionary views. Table 14.8 contains a partial listing of some of the DBA views that are used when you tune performance on a database.

TABLE 14.8   A Partial Listing of Data Dictionary Views for Tuning and Troubleshooting

Name	Description
DBA_TABLES	Table storage, row, and block information
DBA_INDEXES	Index storage, row, and block information
INDEX_STATS	Index depth and dispersion information
DBA_DATA_FILES	Data file location, naming, and size information
DBA_SEGMENTS	General information about any space-consuming segment in the database
DBA_HISTOGRAMS	Table and index histogram definition information
DBA_OBJECTS	General information about all objects in the database, including tables, indexes, triggers, sequences, and partitions
DBA_WAITERS	Shows sessions that are waiting for another session to release a lock
DBA_TABLESPACES	Shows tablespaces in the database and their properties
DBA_FREE_SPACE	Shows the free space available in all tablespaces in the database

The DBA_OBJECTS data dictionary view contains a STATUS column that indicates, through the use of a VALID or INVALID value, whether a database object is valid and ready to be used or is invalid and in need of some attention before it can be used. Invalid and unusable objects are discussed in the next section.

Compiling Invalid and Unusable Objects

Invalid PL/SQL objects and unusable indexes have an impact on database performance. Common examples of invalid objects are PL/SQL code that contains errors or references to other invalid objects and indexes that are unusable because of maintenance operations or failed direct-path load processes. Some invalid objects, such as PL/SQL stored procedures and functions, dynamically recompile the next time they are accessed, and they then take on a status of VALID again. This approach has a cost associated, because users experience a slight delay while the object is being recompiled. But you must manually correct other invalid objects, such as unusable indexes. Therefore, proactive database-management techniques dictate that you identify and remedy invalid objects before they cause problems for database users.

Identifying Unusable Objects Using the Data Dictionary

One way to identify invalid PL/SQL objects is to query the DBA_OBJECTS data dictionary view and then correct them using the commands shown here. The following query identifies the invalid objects in the database:

```
SQL> SELECT owner, object_name, object_type
  2  FROM dba_objects
  3  WHERE status = 'INVALID';
```

OWNER	OBJECT_NAME	OBJECT_TYPE
SH	P_UPDATE_SALES_HISTORY	PROCEDURE
WHSE	LOAD_DATASTAGE	PACKAGE BODY
OE	SAMPLE_VIEW	VIEW

As you can see in the query, few objects are invalid in the database. To compile these invalid objects, you can use the ALTER *object_name* command. For example, to compile the view and procedure, do the following:

```
SQL> ALTER VIEW oe.sample_view COMPILE;
```

```
View altered.
```

```
SQL> ALTER PROCEDURE sh.p_update_sales_history COMPILE;
```

```
Procedure altered.
```

You can use the same syntax to compile a view, procedure, function, package specification, or trigger. To compile a package body, the syntax is slightly different:

```
SQL> ALTER PACKAGE whse.load_datastage COMPILE BODY;
```

```
Package body altered.
```

Indexes may be left in the unusable state, where direct-load operations on the table fail for some reason. Unusable indexes are ignored by the optimizer. You can identify such indexes by querying the DBA_INDEXES view. If the index is partitioned, you must query DBA_INDEX_PARTITIONS:

```
SQL> SELECT owner, index_name, index_type
  2  FROM dba_indexes
  3  WHERE status = 'UNUSABLE';
```

OWNER	INDEX_NAME	INDEX_TYPE
HR	JOB_ID_PK	NORMAL

To fix the issue, you can rebuild the index:

```
SQL> ALTER INDEX hr.job_id_pk REBUILD;
```

When rebuilding an index using the REBUILD command, the amount of space used by the index is temporarily larger than the actual space needed to store the index. Make sure that adequate space exists in the tablespace before starting the rebuild process. This is because when you rebuild the index, Oracle builds a new index at a new location and drops the unusable index after the new index is built. You may specify the TABLESPACE clause and ONLINE clause for the index rebuild. By specifying the TABLESPACE clause, you can rebuild the index to a new tablespace. The ONLINE clause makes sure that users can perform DML operations on the table while the index is rebuilt. If ONLINE is not specified, users wait for the index rebuild to complete.

By default, Oracle 11*g* checks for invalid object metrics every 24 hours.

Identifying Unusable Objects Using EM

EM Database Control also offers a mechanism for fixing invalid database objects. Figure 14.28 shows the Schema tab in EM Database Control. You can see various types of objects under the Database Objects group and the Programs group.

FIGURE 14.28   Schema tab in EM Database Control

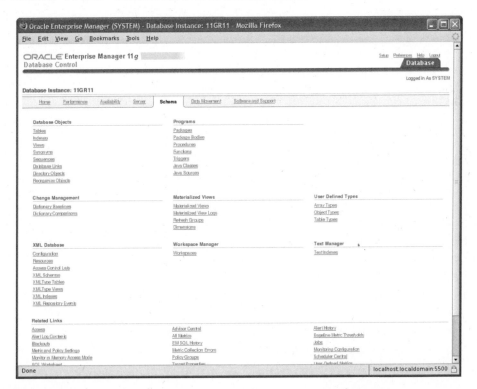

You can get a list of PL/SQL objects and their status by clicking any of the PL/SQL object types under Programs. To list the views and their status, click the Views link under Database Objects. Figure 14.29 shows that the object list is filtered by the HR schema, and you can see that the view is invalid. To compile the view, choose Compile in the Actions drop-down, and click Go.

FIGURE 14.29   Compile Invalid View using EM Database Control

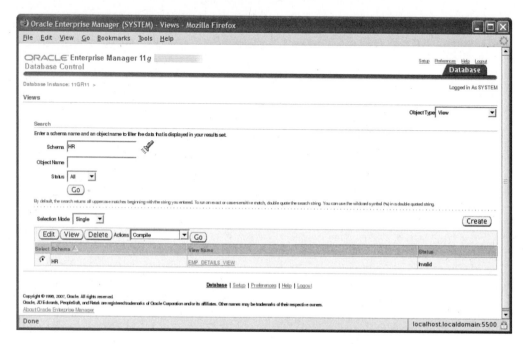

Using the same screen, you can choose a different object type by using the Object Type drop-down, rather than going back and forth on the EM screen.

To rebuild an index, choose the Reorganize action after picking the index you want to rebuild. EM guides you through a six-step interview process to set new attributes for the index when rebuilt. EM provides an impact report in step 4, which is particularly useful in analyzing the space requirements, as shown in Figure 14.30.

EM Database Control will generate a job to rebuild the index and submit it at a time specified by you in step 5. The summary screen will show the SQL statements used to rebuild the index as well as the procedures submitted to schedule the rebuild task.

FIGURE 14.30   Impact Report for rebuilding the index

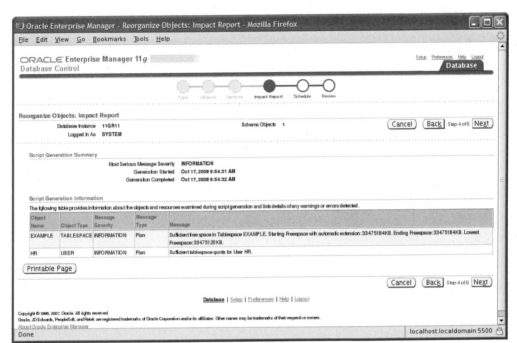

Tuning Memory

In Chapter 8 you learned about the architecture of Oracle 11g. An Oracle instance consists of memory structures and background processes. The memory structure comprises SGA and PGA, and it is important to size the SGA and PGA appropriately for better database performance.

Fortunately, Oracle 11g provides a variety of automatic options to tune memory so that DBAs don't need to worry about tuning the individual memory components such as the Java pool and the shared pool. In the following sections, you will revisit the memory components and learn the options available to tune and manage.

Memory Components

The two primary memory components are SGA and PGA. SGA consists of the following components. The parameters that control these pools are also provided for your reference.

- Shared pool: SHARED_POOL_SIZE
- Database buffer cache: DB_CACHE_SIZE

- Large pool: LARGE_POOL_SIZE
- Java pool: JAVA_POOL_SIZE
- Streams pool: STREAMS_POOL_SIZE
- Log buffer: LOG_BUFFER_SIZE
- Result Cache: RESULT_CACHE_SIZE
- Database keep buffer cache: DB_KEEP_CACHE_SIZE
- Database recycle buffer cache: DB_RECYCLE_CACHE_SIZE
- Buffer cache for nonstandard block size: DB_nK_CACHE_SIZE

The parameters that can be configured to manage the PGA are as follows:

- SORT_AREA_SIZE
- HASH_AREA_SIZE
- BITMAP_MERGE_AREA_SIZE
- CREATE_BITMAP_AREA_SIZE

As you can see from the previous components and parameters, it can get complicated to correctly size these pools and memory parameters. Oracle 11g takes the pain away from DBAs by providing these automatic memory-tuning options:

- Automatic SGA tuning using SGA_TARGET
- Automatic PGA tuning using PGA_AGGREGATE_TARGET
- Automatic Memory tuning (PGA and SGA) using MEMORY_TARGET

The following advisors views are available in Oracle 11g to tune the individual components of memory:

- V$DB_CACHE_ADVICE to size the database buffer cache
- V$SHARED_POOL_ADVICE to size the shared pool
- V$JAVA_POOL_ADVICE to size the Java pool
- V$STREAMS_POOL_ADVICE to size the streams pool

Automatic Shared Memory Management

Automatic Shared Memory Management (ASMM) was introduced in Oracle 10g and can automatically tune five important SGA components as well as the area required (fixed size) for internal allocations:

- SHARED_POOL_SIZE
- DB_CACHE_SIZE
- LARGE_POOL_SIZE
- JAVA_POOL_SIZE
- STREAMS_POOL_SIZE

To enable ASMM, you set the SGA_TARGET parameter, where you specify the total size for the SGA. You still have to manually size the other SGA components, which in most cases do not need much tuning. These components are as follows:

- LOG_BUFFER
- DB_KEEP_CACHE_SIZE
- DB_RECYCLE_CACHE_SIZE
- DB_nK_CACHE_SIZE

SGA_TARGET is a dynamic parameter; you can increase it to the maximum size specified by the static parameter SGA_MAX_SIZE.

You can change a dynamic initialization parameter by using the ALTER SYSTEM statement, whereas you should change static parameters in the spfile or init.ora first. The instance needs to be restarted for the new value to take effect.

You can still specify sizes for the five pools when using ASMM. Oracle will use the values specified as the minimum size for the components. To get full automatic tuning, the five SGA components must be set to zero or not specified in the initialization file.

The parameter STATISTICS_LEVEL must be set to TYPICAL or ALL for the Automatic Shared Memory Management feature to function.

You can tune the appropriate size of SGA_TARGET using the advisor view V$SGA_TARGET_ ADVICE. The V$SGAINFO view shows the sizes of various SGA components.

```
SQL> SELECT * FROM v$sgainfo;
```

NAME	BYTES	RES
Fixed SGA Size	1303916	No
Redo Buffers	4935680	No
Buffer Cache Size	318767104	Yes
Shared Pool Size	352321536	Yes
Large Pool Size	25165824	Yes
Java Pool Size	12582912	Yes
Streams Pool Size	0	Yes
Shared IO Pool Size	0	Yes
Granule Size	4194304	No
Maximum SGA Size	954155008	No
Startup overhead in Shared Pool	46137344	No
Free SGA Memory Available	239075328	

```
SQL> SELECT * FROM v$sga_target_advice;
```

SGA_SIZE	SGA_SIZE_FACTOR	ESTD_DB_TIME	ESTD_DB_TIME_FACTOR	ESTD_PHYSICAL_READS
684	1	301	1	27924
342	.5	323	1.0731	31035
513	.75	301	1	27924
855	1.25	278	.9236	24657
1026	1.5	278	.9236	24657
1197	1.75	278	.9236	24657
1368	2	278	.9236	24657

Automatic SQL Execution Memory Management

You can use Automatic SQL Execution Memory Management to tune the PGA using the PGA_AGGREGATE_TARGET and WORKAREA_SIZE_POLICY parameters. Both parameters can be dynamically modified.

PGA_AGGREGATE_TARGET specifies the target amount of memory available to the instance (PGA memory) for all server processes. Setting a nonzero value for PGA_AGGREGATE_TARGET automatically sets the WORKAREA_SIZE_POLICY parameter to AUTO, which means the _AREA_SIZE parameters are automatically sized.

WARNING If you set PGA_AGGREGATE_TARGET=0 and set WORKAREA_SIZE_POLICY to AUTO, Oracle 11*g* will throw an ORA-04032 error at startup.

You can tune PGA performance by using the advisor view V$PGA_TARGET_ADVICE. The advice is generated by simulating past workload.

Automatic Memory Management

Automatic Memory Management (AMM) is new to Oracle 11*g* and further eases the memory management. AMM automatically tunes the SGA and PGA components. All you have to do is to specify the total memory available to the instance by using the MEMORY_TARGET parameter.

When AMM is used, Oracle automates the sizing of SGA and PGA, and it causes the indirect transfer of memory from SGA to PGA, and vice versa, as required by the workload. The default for SGA is 60 percent and the default for PGA is 40 percent allocation when the instance is started.

MEMORY_TARGET is a dynamic parameter; you can increase it up to the maximum specified by the static parameter MEMORY_MAX_TARGET. By default, AMM is not enabled in Oracle 11*g*—the default value for MEMORY_TARGET is zero.

You still can set SGA_TARGET, PGA_AGGREGATE_TARGET, and the various SGA pool parameters in the initialization file. Oracle 11*g* will use these values as the minimum when configuring the various pools. Table 14.9 shows some rules when you have configured the AMM and ASMM memory parameters.

TABLE 14.9 Memory-Tuning Parameters Dependency

MEMORY_TARGET (MT)	SGA_TARGET (ST)	Result
MT=0 AMM is disabled	AMM is disabled ASMM is disabled	ST=0 Must specify values for individual pools.
MT=0	AMM is disabled ASMM is enabled	ST>0 Individual pools will be automatically tuned. SGA and PGA memory will be treated separately.
MT>0	AMM is enabled ASMM is disabled	ST=0 Full automatic tuning of SGA and PGA.
MT>0	AMM is enabled ASMM is enabled	ST>0 Automatic tuning of SGA and PGA, but SGA will keep the minimum value specified by ST.

You can adjust the MEMORY_TARGET parameter size after reviewing the advisor view V$MEMORY_TARGET_ADVICE:

```
SQL> SELECT * FROM v$memory_target_advice;

MEMORY_SIZE MEMORY_SIZE_FACTOR ESTD_DB_TIME ESTD_DB_TIME_FACTOR    VERSION
----------- ------------------ ------------ -------------------- ----------
        912                  1          303                    1          0
        456                 .5          304                    1          0
        684                .75          304                    1          0
       1140               1.25          304                    1          0
       1368                1.5          304                    1          0
       1596               1.75          304                    1          0
       1824                  2          304                    1          0
```

If you want to know the size of all the AMM memory components, you can query the V$MEMORY_DYNAMIC_COMPONENTS view:

```
SQL> SELECT component, current_size, min_size, max_size
  2  FROM v$memory_dynamic_components;
```

COMPONENT	CURRENT_SIZE	MIN_SIZE	MAX_SIZE
shared pool	352321536	352321536	352321536
large pool	25165824	8388608	25165824
java pool	12582912	12582912	12582912
streams pool	0	0	0
SGA Target	717225984	717225984	717225984
DEFAULT buffer cache	318767104	318767104	335544320
KEEP buffer cache	0	0	0
RECYCLE buffer cache	0	0	0
DEFAULT 2K buffer cache	0	0	0
DEFAULT 4K buffer cache	0	0	0
DEFAULT 8K buffer cache	0	0	0
DEFAULT 16K buffer cache	0	0	0
DEFAULT 32K buffer cache	0	0	0
Shared IO Pool	0	0	0
PGA Target	239075328	239075328	239075328
ASM Buffer Cache	0	0	0

The V$MEMORY_RESIZE_OPS view has a circular history of the last 800 SGA resize requests, both manual and automatic.

Managing Memory Using EM Database Control

You can use EM Database Control to enable and disable various memory-tuning options as well as monitor the memory components and their performance. You can use the information on this screen to decide whether your Oracle 11g database needs more memory allocated for better performance. On the Server tab, click the Memory Advisors link on the Database Configuration section. This takes you to the Memory Advisors screen, as shown in Figure 14.31.

This screen shows the current status of memory usage as well as gives you the option to enable or disable Automatic Memory Management. Click the Advice button, and you can view the memory size advice.

FIGURE 14.31   Memory Advisors screen in EM

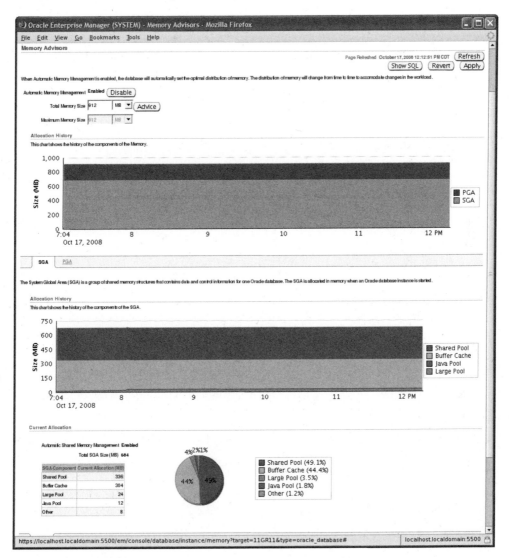

If you disable AMM using the Disable button, EM automatically enables ASMM, as shown in Figure 14.32.

FIGURE 14.32   ASMM screen in EM

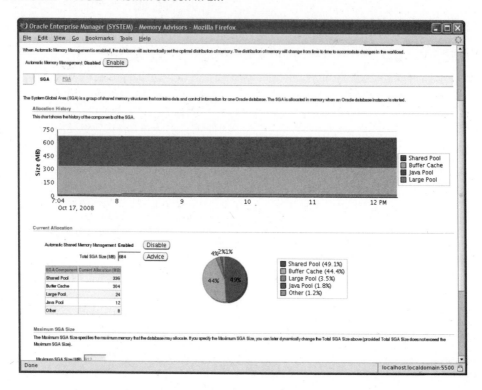

If you disable ASMM, EM will prompt you to provide the sizes for individual components, as shown in Figure 14.33.

FIGURE 14.33   Memory Components screen in EM

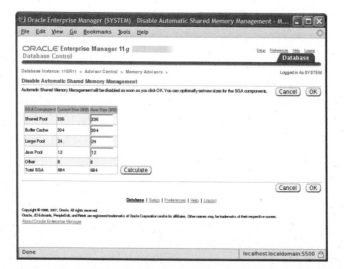

You can also get to the Memory Advisor screen from Advisor Central. EM also shows several important performance metrics, discussed in the next section.

Important Performance Metrics

Throughput is another example of a statistical performance metric. *Throughput* is the amount of processing that a computer or system can perform in a given amount of time, for example, the number of customer deposits that can be posted to the appropriate accounts in four hours under regular workloads. Throughput is an important measure when considering the scalability of the system. *Scalability* refers to the degree to which additional users can be added to the system without system performance declining significantly. New features such as Oracle Database 10*g*'s Grid Computing capabilities make Oracle one of the most scalable database platforms on the market.

Performance considerations for transactional systems usually revolve around throughput maximization.

Another important metric related to performance is response time. *Response time* is the amount of time it takes for a single user's request to return the desired result when using an application, for example, the time it takes for the system to return a listing of all the customers who purchased products that require service contracts.

Performance-tuning considerations for decision-support systems usually revolve around response time minimization.

You can use EM Database Control to both monitor and react to sudden changes in performance metrics such as throughput and response time.

Using EM Database Control to View Performance Metrics

EM Database Control provides a graphical view of throughput, response time, I/O, and other important performance metrics. The Performance tab in EM Database Control gives a good overview of database performance, as shown earlier in this chapter in Figure 14.13. On this screen you can see session performance and host performance, as well as throughput, I/O, and concurrency. The Additional Monitoring Links section on this screen takes you to various performance-tuning screens, shown earlier in Figure 14.26.

Click Top Activity to view the top sessions in the instance. You can drill down to a particular wait category. This screen is useful to figure out whether there was a performance problem and if you want to know what happened in the last few minutes, as shown in Figure 14.34.

FIGURE 14.34   Top Activity screen on EM

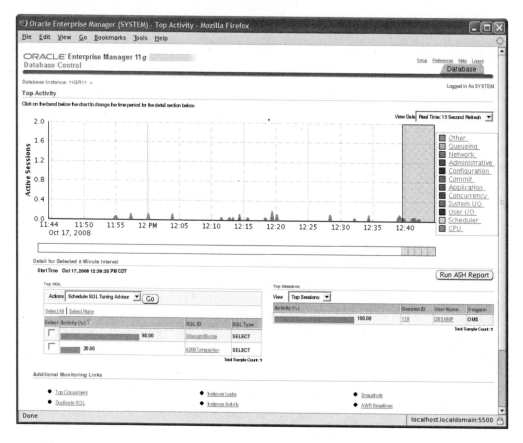

The Top Consumers link is another very useful tool. When you click this link, an Overview tab is displayed, as shown in Figure 14.35.

FIGURE 14.35   Top Consumers overview on EM

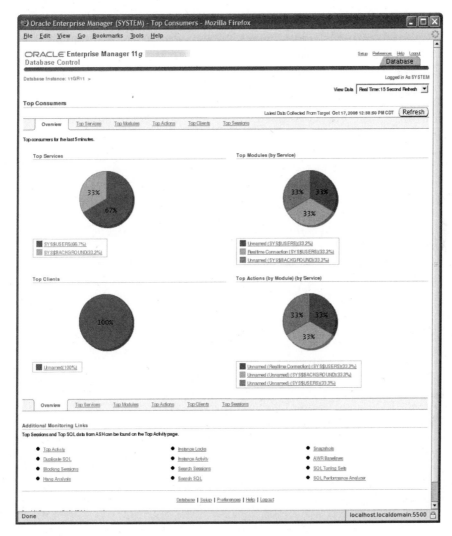

This tab shows the following sections:

- Top Services

- Top Modules

- Top Actions

- Top Clients

- Top Sessions

The Top Sessions area shows the CPU usage and I/O operations for each session, as shown previously in Figure 14.27.

Summary

Oracle 11g provides many tools for proactively identifying and fixing potential performance and management problems in the database. In this chapter, you learned about tools such as AWR, ADDR, ADR, AMM, and ASMM.

At the core of the monitoring system is the Automatic Workload Repository, which uses the MMON background process to gather statistics from the SGA and store them in a collection of tables owned by the user SYSMAN.

Following each AWR statistics collection interval, the Automatic Database Diagnostic Monitoring feature examines the newly gathered statistics and compares them with the two previous AWR statistics to establish baselines in an attempt to identify poorly performing components of the database. The ADDM then summarizes these findings on the EM Database Control main screen and Performance tab. Using these screens, you can identify and examine the SQL statements that are contributing the most to DB Time. You can further explore the opportunities for improving the performance or manageability of your database using the EM Database Control advisors, which include the SQL Tuning Advisor, SQL Access Advisor, Memory Advisor, Mean Time To Recover Advisor, Segment Advisor, and Undo Management Advisor.

In addition to alerts, you can find indicators of database performance in the database alert log, user and background trace files, data dictionary views, and dynamic performance views. Some data dictionary views do not contain accurate information about the segments in the database until after statistics are collected on those objects. Therefore, you can automatically collect segment statistics through the use of EM Database Control jobs.

Invalid and unusable database objects also have a negative impact on performance and manageability. You can monitor and repair invalid and unusable objects using the data dictionary and the EM Database Control Administration screen.

Memory tuning is simplified in Oracle 11g using Automatic Memory Management. AMM is configured using the MEMORY_TARGET parameter. If other memory parameters are specified, they will be considered as the minimum for those components.

EM Database Control summarizes several important performance metrics on the EM Database Control main screen. These metrics include performance statistics for the host server, user sessions, and instance throughput.

Exam Essentials

Understand the Automatic Workload Repository.   Describe the components of the AWR and how they are used to collect and store database performance statistics.

Describe the role of Automatic Database Diagnostic Monitor.   Know how ADDM uses the AWR statistics to formulate tuning recommendations using historical and baseline metrics.

Explain how each advisor is used to improve performance.   Describe how you can use each of the EM Database Control advisors shown on the Advisor Central screen to improve database performance and manageability.

Describe how alerts are used to monitor performance.   Show how you can configure the EM Database Control alert system to alert you via the console or via email whenever a monitored event occurs in the database.

Remember the location of alert log file.   Starting in Oracle 11g, the alert log file location is determined by the DIAGNOSTIC_DEST parameter. Learn the location of the text alert log file and XML alert log file.

Identify and fix invalid or unusable objects.   Understand the techniques you can use to identify invalid procedures, functions, triggers, and views and how to validate them. Know how to find unusable indexes and how to fix them.

Understand Automatic Memory Management.   Know the parameters that control the memory management and how the pools are allocated.

Understand sources of tuning information.   Know in which dynamic performance views, data dictionary views, and log files tuning information can be found outside the EM Database Control monitoring system.

Review Questions

1. Which of the following components of the Oracle architecture stores the statistics gathered by the MMON process?

    A. ADDM

    B. AWR

    C. ASMM

    D. ADR

2. Which of the following options for the pfile/spfile's STATISTICS_LEVEL parameter turns off AWR statistics gathering and ADDM advisory services?

    A. OFF

    B. TYPICAL

    C. ALL

    D. BASIC

3. Which parameter is used to enable Automatic Memory Management?

    A. AMM_TARGET

    B. MEMORY_TARGET

    C. SGA_TARGET

    D. All of the above

4. Which statement about an index with the status UNUSABLE in DBA_INDEXES is true?

    A. The index will be automatically fixed the next time it is used.

    B. The Oracle optimizer throws an error when it tries to use the index.

    C. The index must be recompiled using the ALTER INDEX…RECOMPILE statement.

    D. The index must be reorganized using the ALTER INDEX…REBUILD statement before it can be used again.

5. Suppose you have used EM Database Control to drill down into ADDM findings and have found that a single SQL statement is causing the majority of I/O on your system. Which of the following advisors is best suited to troubleshoot this SQL statement?

    A. SQL Tuning Advisor

    B. SQL Access Advisor

    C. Both A and B

    D. Neither A nor B

6. You found out that few procedures in the APPS schema have an INVALID status in the DBA_ OBJECTS view. What are your options to fix the issue? (Choose the best two answers.)

   A. Do nothing. When the procedure is accessed the next time, Oracle will try to recompile.

   B. Drop the procedure so that users get a valid error.

   C. Recompile the procedure using ALTER PROCEDURE...COMPILE.

   D. Contact the developer or vendor to get the source code and re-create the procedure.

7. Which procedure is used to tell Oracle that the statistics gathered should not be published?

   A. DBMS_STATS.PUBLISH_STATS

   B. DBMS_STATS.SET_TABLE_PREFS

   C. DBMS_STATS.PENDING_STATS

   D. DBMS_STATS.GATHER_TABLE_STATS

8. Which data dictionary view contains information explaining why ADDM made its recommendations?

   A. DBA_ADVISOR_FINDINGS

   B. DBA_ADVISOR_OBJECTS

   C. DBA_ADVISOR_RECOMMENDATIONS

   D. DBA_ADVISOR_RATIONALE

9. Which of the following advisors determines whether the space allocated to the shared pool, large pool, or buffer cache is adequate?

   A. SQL Tuning Advisor

   B. SGA Tuning Advisor

   C. Memory Advisor

   D. Pool Advisor

10. Which of the following advisors determines whether the estimated instance-recovery duration is within the expected service-level agreements?

   A. Undo Management Advisor

   B. SQL Access Advisor

   C. SQL Tuning Advisor

   D. MTTR Advisor

11. If no email address is specified, where will alert information be displayed?

   A. In the DBA_ALERTS data dictionary view.

   B. In the V$ALERTS dynamic performance view.

   C. In the EM Database Control main screen.

   D. No alert information is sent or displayed.

12. When you configure an alert, which of the following types of alert thresholds can you use to monitor a tablespace for diminishing free space?

A. Warning threshold

B. Critical threshold

C. Both A and B

D. Neither A nor B

13. Multiple baseline metrics can be gathered and stored in the AWR. Why might you want more than one metrics baseline?

A. You might want a separate baseline metric for each user.

B. You might want a separate baseline metric for daytime usage vs. off-hours usage.

C. You might want a separate baseline metric for each schema.

D. You would never want more than one baseline metric, even though it is possible to gather and store them.

14. Using EM Database Control, you discover that two application PL/SQL functions and a view are currently invalid. Which of the following might you use to fix these objects? (Choose two.)

A. Shut down and restart the database.

B. Use EM Database Control to recompile the object.

C. Export the invalid objects, drop them, and then import them.

D. Use the ALTER FUNCTION...COMPILE and ALTER VIEW...COMPILE commands.

15. Which statement about MEMORY_TARGET parameter is not true?

A. It is a dynamic initialization parameter.

B. It represents the total maximum memory that can be allocated to the instance memory (PGA and SGA combined).

C. Its default value is zero.

D. You will not get an error when SGA_TARGET and PGA_AGGREGATE_TARGET parameters are set to nonzero values.

16. Which of the following is a performance metric that could be defined as "the amount of work that a system can perform in a given amount of time"?

A. Response time

B. Uptime

C. Throughput

D. Runtime

17. Which of the following is typically not one of the three primary sources of performance metric information on the EM Database Control Performance tab?

   A. Host

   B. Session

   C. Instance

   D. Network

18. By default, how long will database statistics be retained in the AWR?

   A. 7 days

   B. 30 days

   C. 7 hours

   D. Indefinitely

19. Your users have called to complain that system performance has suddenly decreased markedly. Where would be the most likely place to look for the cause of the problem in EM Database Control?

   A. Main screen

   B. Performance tab

   C. Administration tab

   D. Maintenance tab

20. Using EM Database Control, you've identified that the following SQL statement is the source of a high amount of disk I/O:

`SELECT NAME, LOCATION, CREDIT_LIMIT FROM CUSTOMERS`

What might you do first to try to improve performance?

   A. Run the SQL Tuning Advisor.

   B. Run the SQL Access Advisor.

   C. Check the EM Database Control main screen for alerts.

   D. Click the Alert Log Content link in the EM Database Control main screen.

Answers to Review Questions

1. B. The MMON process gathers statistics from the SGA and stores them in the AWR. The ADDM process then uses these statistics to compare the current state of the database with baseline and historical performance metrics before summarizing the results on the EM Database Control screens.

2. D. Setting STATISTICS_LEVEL = BASIC disables the collection and analysis of AWR statistics. TYPICAL is the default setting, and ALL gathers information for the execution plan and operating-system timing. OFF is not a valid value for this parameter.

3. B. Automatic Memory Management is enabled by setting a nonzero value for the MEMORY_TARGET parameter. The default value for this parameter is zero. SGA_TARGET enables the ASSM (Automatic Shared Memory Management) feature.

4. D. Unusable indexes must be manually rebuilt by the DBA, or the user owning the index can rebuild or drop/recreate as well, before the index can be used. The Oracle optimizer ignores the unusable index.

5. C. You can use the SQL Tuning Advisor and SQL Access Advisor together to determine whether I/O can be minimized and overall DB Time reduced to the targeted SQL statement.

6. A, C. Invalid PL/SQL objects will be automatically recompiled the next time they are accessed. The DBA can manually recompile the procedure. Manual recompilation is the recommended approach.

7. B. The DBMS_STATS.SET_TABLE_PREFS procedure is used to set the PUBLISH preference to FALSE. To be able to use the pending statistics, the OPTIMIZER_USE_PENDING_STATISTICS parameter must be set to TRUE in the session.

8. D. DBA_ADVISOR_RATIONALE provides the rationale for each ADDM recommendation. The ADDM findings are stored in DBA_ADVISOR_FINDINGS. The objects related to the findings are shown in DBA_ADVISOR_OBJECTS. The actual ADDM recommendations are found in DBA_ADVISOR_RECOMMENDATIONS.

9. C. The Memory Advisor can help determine whether the overall size of the SGA is appropriate and whether memory is properly allocated to the SGA components.

10. D. The Mean Time To Recover (MTTR) Advisor provides recommendations that you can use to configure the database so that the instance-recovery time fits within the service levels that you specified.

11. C. By default, alerts are displayed in the Alerts section of the EM Database Control main screen, even when email notifications are not configured.

12. C. You can specify both warning and critical thresholds for monitoring the available free space in a tablespace. In this situation, the warning threshold is generally a lower number than the critical threshold.

13. B. Because many transactional systems run batch processing during off-hours, having a relevant baseline for each type of usage pattern yields better results in terms of alerts and ADDM recommendations.

14. B, D. After fixing the issue that originally caused the invalid status, you can use both EM Database Control and SQL to compile an invalid object. Starting and stopping the database will not fix invalid objects. Export/import is also not an appropriate technique for recompiling invalid objects.

15. B. MEMORY_TARGET represents the total size allocated for SGA and PGA components. The maximum that can be allocated for these structures is determined by the MEMORY_MAX_ TARGET parameter. You still can set the SGA_TARGET and PGA_AGGREGATE_TARGET parameters; Oracle will use these as the minimums.

16. C. Throughput is an important performance metric because it is an overall measure of performance that can be compared against similar measures taken before and after tuning changes are implemented.

17. D. Network information may be contained in the Session Information section of the EM Database Control Performance screen, but only if network issues contributed to session wait times.

18. A. By default, database statistics are retained in the AWR for seven days. You can change the default duration using the EM Database Control Automatic Workload Repository link on the Performance tab or using the DBMS_WORKLOAD_REPOSITORY PL/SQL package.

19. B. The Performance tab of EM Database Control provides a quick overview of how the host system, user sessions, and throughput are impacted by the system slowdown. You can also drill down into any of these three areas to take a look at details about this slowdown.

20. A. Running the SQL Tuning Advisor provides the most information about how the performance of this SQL statement might be improved. The SQL Access Advisor is run only after the output from the SQL Tuning Advisor indicates that it will be useful. EM Database Control does not store detailed information about I/O activity in either its alerts or the alert log.

Chapter

15

Implementing Database Backups

ORACLE DATABASE 11*g*:
ADMINISTRATION I EXAM OBJECTIVES
COVERED IN THIS CHAPTER:

✓ **Backup and Recovery Concepts**

- Identify the importance of checkpoints, redo log files, and archived log files

- Overview of flash recovery area

- Configure ARCHIVELOG mode

✓ **Performing Database Backups**

- Create consistent database backups

- Back up your database without shutting it down

- Create incremental backups

- Automate database backups

- Manage backups, view backup reports and monitor the flash recovery area

Oracle's administration tool, Enterprise Manager Database Control, makes configuring and performing backups easier. Most, if not all, of the functionality available with the command-line interface is available in a graphical user interface to save time and make backup operations less error-prone.

Oracle Database 11*g* makes it easy for you to configure your database to be highly available and reliable. In other words, you want to configure your database to minimize the amount of downtime while at the same time being able to recover quickly and without losing any committed transactions when the database becomes unavailable for reasons that may be beyond your control.

In this chapter, I will first describe the components you will use to minimize or eliminate data loss in your database while at the same time keeping availability high. Specifically, I will cover the following:

- Checkpoints
- Redo log files
- Archived redo log files
- The flash recovery area

Next, you will learn how to configure your database for recovery. This will include a discussion of ARCHIVELOG mode and other required initialization parameters. Once your environment is configured, you will need to know how to actually back it up, using both operating-system commands and the RMAN utility. You will also learn how to automate and manage your backups as well as how to monitor one of the key components in your backup strategy: the flash recovery area. In Chapter 16, "Recovering the Database," you will then learn how to use the files created and maintained during your backups to quickly recover the database in the event of a database failure.

Understanding and Configuring Recovery Components

As a database administrator, your primary goal is to keep the database open and available for users, usually 24 hours a day, 7 days a week. Your partnership with the server's system administrator includes the following tasks:

- Proactively solving common causes of failures
- Increasing the mean time between failure (MTBF)

- Ensuring a high level of hardware redundancy

- Increasing availability by using Oracle options such as Real Application Clusters (RAC) and Oracle Streams (an advanced replication technology)

- Decreasing the mean time to recover (MTTR) by setting the appropriate Oracle initialization parameters and ensuring that backups are readily available in a recovery scenario

- Minimizing or eliminating loss of committed transactions by using archived redo logs, standby databases, and Oracle Data Guard

A number of structures and events in the database directly support backup and recovery operations. The control files maintain the list of database files in the database, along with a record of the most recent database backups (if you are using RMAN for your backups). The checkpoint (CKPT) background process works in concert with the database writer (DBW*n*) process to manage the amount of time required for instance recovery; during instance recovery, the redo log files are used to synchronize the data files. For more serious types of failures, such as media failures, archived redo log files are applied to a restored backup copy of a data file to synchronize the data files and ensure that no committed transactions are lost. Finally, the flash recovery area, introduced in Oracle 10*g*, is a common area for all recovery-related files that makes your job much easier when backing up or recovering your database.

To maximize your database's availability, it almost goes without saying that you want to perform regularly scheduled backups. Most media failures require some kind of restoration of a data file from a disk or tape backup before you can initiate media recovery.

In addition to regularly scheduled backups (see the section "Performing Backups" later in this chapter), you can configure a number of other features to maximize your database's availability and minimize recovery time, such as multiplexing control files, multiplexing redo log files, configuring the database in ARCHIVELOG mode, and using a flash recovery area.

Understanding Control Files

The control file is one of the smallest, yet also one of the most critical, files in the database. Recovering from the loss of one copy of a control file is relatively straightforward; recovering from the loss of your only control file or all control files is more of a challenge and requires more-advanced recovery techniques.

In the following section, you will get an overview of the control file architecture. You will then learn how maximize the recoverability of the control file in the section "Multiplexing Control Files."

Control File Architecture

The control file is a relatively small (in the megabyte range) binary file that contains information about the structure of the database. You can think of the control file as a metadata repository for the physical database. It has the structure of the database, meaning the data files and redo log files constitute a database. The control file is created when the database is created and is updated with the physical changes, for example, whenever you add or rename a file.

The control file is updated continuously and should be available at all times. Don't edit the contents of the control file; only Oracle processes should update its contents. When you start up the database, Oracle uses the control file to identify and to open the data files and redo log files. Control files play a major role when recovering a database.

The contents of the control file include the following:

- The database name to which the control file belongs. A control file can belong to only one database.

- The database-creation timestamp.

- The name, location, and online/offline status information of the data files.

- The name and location of the redo log files.

- Redo log archive information.

- Tablespace names.

- The current log sequence number, which is a unique identifier that is incremented and recorded when an online redo log file is switched.

- The most recent checkpoint information.

- The beginning and ending of undo segments.

- Recovery Manager's backup information. Recovery Manager (RMAN) is the Oracle utility you use to back up and recover databases.

The control file size is determined by the MAX clauses you provide when you create the database:

- MAXLOGFILES

- MAXLOGMEMBERS

- MAXLOGHISTORY

- MAXDATAFILES

- MAXINSTANCES

Oracle preallocates space for these maximums in the control file. Therefore, when you add or rename a file in the database, the control file size does not change.

When you add a new file to the database or relocate a file, an Oracle server process immediately updates the information in the control file. Back up the control file after any structural changes. The log writer (LGWR) process updates the control file with the current log sequence number. The CKPT process updates the control file with the recent checkpoint information. When the database is in ARCHIVELOG mode, the archiver (ARC*n*) process updates the control file with information such as the archive log filename and log sequence number.

The control file contains two types of record sections: reusable and not reusable. RMAN information is kept in the reusable section. Items such as the names of the backup data files are kept in this section, and once this section fills up, the entries are reused in a circular fashion after the number of days specified by the initialization parameter CONTROL_FILE_RECORD_KEEP_TIME is reached. Therefore, the control file can continue to grow because of new RMAN backup information recorded in the control file before CONTROL_FILE_RECORD_KEEP_TIME.

You can query the control file names and their status by using EM Database Control. On the Server tab, click the Control Files link under Storage. You will see the Control Files screen, as shown in Figure 15.1.

FIGURE 15.1   Control Files screen of EM

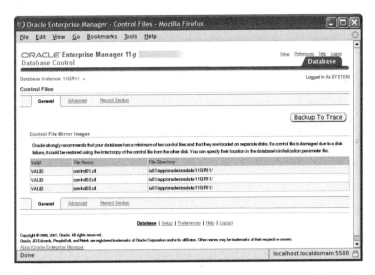

The Record Section tab on this screen shows the record information from the control file, as shown in Figure 15.2. It shows the size used in the control file for each section, the total number of records that can be saved with the current size of the control file, and the number or records used.

FIGURE 15.2   Control Files screen's Record Section tab

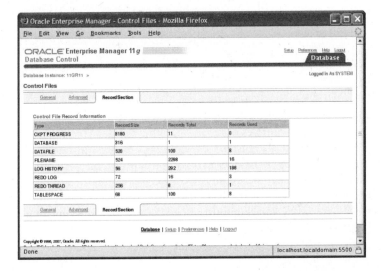

Multiplexing Control Files

Because the control file is critical for database operation, at a minimum you must have two copies of the control file; Oracle recommends a minimum of three copies. You duplicate the control file on different disks either by using the multiplexing feature of Oracle or by using the mirroring feature of your operating system. If you have multiple disk controllers on your server, at least one copy of the control file should reside on a disk managed by a different disk controller.

If you use the Database Configuration Assistant (DBCA) to create your database, three copies of the control files are multiplexed by default.

The next two sections discuss the two ways that you can implement the multiplexing feature: using an init.ora and using the server-side spfile.

Multiplexing Control Files Using init.ora

Multiplexing means keeping a copy of the same control file on different disk drives and ideally on different controllers too. To multiplex a control file, copy the control file to multiple locations and change the CONTROL_FILES parameter in the text-based initialization file init.ora to include all control filenames. The following syntax shows three multiplexed control files:

```
CONTROL_FILES = ('/ora01/oradata/MYDB/ctrlMYDB01.ctl',
                 '/ora02/oradata/MYDB/ctrlMYDB02.ctl',
                 '/ora03/oradata/MYDB/ctrlMYDB03.ctl')
```

By storing the control file on multiple disks, you avoid the risk of a single point of failure. When multiplexing control files, updates to the control file can take a little longer, but that is insignificant when compared with the benefits. If you lose one control file, you can restart the database after copying one of the other control files or after changing the CONTROL_FILES parameter in the initialization file.

When multiplexing control files, Oracle updates all the control files at the same time but uses only the first control file listed in the CONTROL_FILES parameter for reading.

When creating a database, you can list the control file names in the CONTROL_FILES parameter, and Oracle creates as many control files as are listed. You can have a maximum of eight multiplexed control file copies.

If you need to add more control file copies, follow these steps:

1. Shut down the database.

   ```
   SQL> SHUTDOWN NORMAL
   ```

2. Copy the control file to more locations by using an operating-system command:

   ```
   $ cp /u02/oradata/ord/control01.ctl /u05/oradata/ord/control04.ctl
   ```

3. Change the initialization-parameter file to include the new control file name(s) in the parameter CONTROL_FILES by changing this:

   ```
   CONTROL_FILES=('/u02/oradata/ord/control01.ctl',
   '/u03/oradata/ord/control02.ctl',
   '/u04/oradata/ord/control03.ctl')
   ```

to this:

```
CONTROL_FILES=('/u02/oradata/ord/control01.ctl',
'/u03/oradata/ord/control02.ctl',
'/u04/oradata/ord/control03.ctl',
'/u05/oradata/ord/control04.ctl')
```

4. Start the instance:

```
SQL> STARTUP
```

This procedure is somewhat similar to the procedure for recovering from the loss of a control file.

 You can find examples of control file recovery in Chapter 16.

After creating the database, you can change the location of the control files, rename the control files, or drop certain control files. You must have at least one control file for each database. To add, rename, or delete control files, you need to follow the preceding steps. Basically, you shut down the database, use the operating-system copy command (copying, renaming, or deleting the control files accordingly), modify the init.ora parameter file, and start up the database.

Multiplexing Control Files Using an Spfile

Multiplexing using a binary spfile is similar to multiplexing using init.ora. The major difference is in how the CONTROL_FILES parameter is changed. Follow these steps:

1. Alter the spfile while the database is still open:

```
SQL> ALTER SYSTEM SET CONTROL_FILES =
        '/ora01/oradata/MYDB/ctrlMYDB01.ctl',
        '/ora02/oradata/MYDB/ctrlMYDB02.ctl',
        '/ora03/oradata/MYDB/ctrlMYDB03.ctl',
        '/ora04/oradata/MYDB/ctrlMYDB04.ctl' SCOPE=SPFILE;
```

This parameter change takes effect only after the next instance restart by using the SCOPE=SPFILE qualifier. The contents of the binary spfile are changed immediately, but the old specification of CONTROL_FILES is used until the instance is restarted.

2. Shut down the database:

```
SQL> SHUTDOWN NORMAL
```

3. Copy an existing control file to the new location:

```
$ cp /ora01/oradata/MYDB/ctrlMYDB01.ctl /ora04/oradata/MYDB/ctrlMYDB04.ctl
```

4. Start the instance:

```
SQL> STARTUP
```

Understanding Checkpoints

The CKPT process controls the amount of time required for instance recovery. During a checkpoint, CKPT updates the control file and the header of the data files to reflect the last successful transaction by recording the last system change number (SCN). The SCN, which is a number sequentially assigned to each transaction in the database, is also recorded in the control file against the data file name that is taken offline or made read-only.

A checkpoint occurs automatically every time a redo log file switch occurs, either when the current redo log file fills up or when you manually switch redo log files. The DBW*n* processes in conjunction with CKPT routinely write new and changed buffers to advance the checkpoint from where instance recovery can begin, thus reducing the MTTR.

 You can find more information on tuning the MTTR and how often checkpointing occurs in Chapter 16.

Understanding Redo Log Files

A redo log file records all changes to the database, in most cases before the changes are written to the data files.

To recover from an instance or a media failure, redo log information is required to roll data files forward to the last committed transaction. Ensuring that you have at least two members for each redo log file group dramatically reduces the likelihood of data loss because the database continues to operate if one member of a redo log file is lost.

In the following sections, I will give you an architectural overview of redo log files, as well as show you how to add redo log groups, add or remove redo log group members, and clear a redo log group in case one of the redo log group's members becomes corrupted.

Redo Log File Architecture

Online redo log files are filled with redo records. A redo record, also called a *redo entry*, consists of a group of change vectors, each of which describes a change made to a single block in the database. Redo entries record data that you can use to reconstruct all changes made to the database, including the undo segments. When you recover the database by using redo log files, Oracle reads the change vectors in the redo records and applies the changes to the relevant blocks.

The LGWR process writes redo information from the redo log buffer to the online redo log files under a variety of circumstances:

- When a user commits a transaction, even if this is the only transaction in the log buffer
- When the redo log buffer becomes one-third full
- When the buffer contains approximately 1MB of *changed* records; this total does not include deleted or inserted records
- When a database checkpoint is performed

LGWR always writes its records to the online redo log file *before* DBW*n* writes new or modified database buffer cache records to the data files.

Each database has its own set of online redo log groups. A redo log group can have one or more redo log members (each member is a single operating-system file). If you have a RAC configuration, in which multiple instances are mounted to one database, each instance has one online redo thread. That is, the LGWR process of each instance writes to the same online redo log files, and hence Oracle has to keep track of the instance from where the database changes are coming. Single-instance configurations will have only one thread, and that thread number is 1. The redo log file contains both committed and uncommitted transactions. Whenever a transaction is committed, a system change number is assigned to the redo records to identify the committed transaction.

The redo log group is referenced by an integer; you can specify the group number when you create the redo log files—either when you create the database or when you create a redo log group after you create the database. You can also change the redo log configuration (adding, dropping, or renaming files) by using database commands. The following example shows a CREATE DATABASE command:

```
CREATE DATABASE "MYDB01"
... ... ...
LOGFILE '/ora02/oradata/MYDB01/redo01.log' SIZE 10M,
        '/ora03/oradata/MYDB01/redo02.log' SIZE 10M;
```

This example creates two log-file groups; the first file is assigned to group 1, and the second file is assigned to group 2. You can have more files in each group; this practice is known as the *multiplexing* of redo log files, which I'll discuss later in this chapter in the section "Multiplexing Redo Log Files." You can specify any group number—the range will be between 1 and the initialization parameter MAXLOGFILES. Oracle recommends that all redo log groups be the same size. The following is an example of creating the log files by specifying the group number:

```
CREATE DATABASE "MYDB01"
... ... ...
LOGFILE GROUP 1 '/ora02/oradata/MYDB01/redo01.log' SIZE 10M,
        GROUP 2 '/ora03/oradata/MYDB01/redo02.log' SIZE 10M;
```

Log Switch Operations

The LGWR process writes to only one redo log file group at any time. The file that is actively being written to is known as the *current* log file. The log files that are required for instance recovery are known as the *active* log files. The other log files are known as *inactive*. Oracle automatically recovers an instance when starting up the instance by using the online redo log files. Instance recovery can be needed if you do not shut down the database cleanly or if your database server crashes.

The log files are written in a circular fashion. A log switch occurs when Oracle finishes writing to one log group and starts writing to the next log group. A log switch always occurs when the current redo log group is completely full and log writing must continue. You can force a log switch by using the ALTER SYSTEM command. A manual log switch can be necessary when performing maintenance on the redo log files by using the ALTER SYSTEM SWITCH LOGFILE command.

Whenever a log switch occurs, Oracle allocates a sequence number to the new redo log group before writing to it. As stated earlier, this number is known as the *log sequence number*. If there are lots of transactions or changes to the database, the log switches can occur too frequently. Size the redo log files appropriately to avoid frequent log switches. Oracle writes to the alert log file whenever a log switch occurs.

Redo log files are written sequentially on the disk, so the I/O will be fast if there is no other activity on the disk. (The disk head is always properly positioned.) Keep the redo log files on a separate disk for better performance. If you have to store a data file on the same disk as the redo log file, do not put the SYSTEM, UNDOTBS, SYSAUX, or any very active data or index tablespace file on this disk. A commit cannot complete until a transaction's information has been written to the redo logs, so maximizing the throughput of the redo log files is a top priority.

Database checkpoints are closely tied to redo log file switches. You learned about checkpoints earlier in the chapter in the section "Understanding Checkpoints." A checkpoint is an event that flushes the modified data from the buffer cache to the disk and updates the control file and data files. The CKPT process updates the headers of data files and control files; the actual blocks are written to the file by the DBW*n* process. A checkpoint is initiated when the redo log file is filled and a log switch occurs; when the instance is shut down with NORMAL, TRANSACTIONAL, or IMMEDIATE; when a tablespace status is changed to read-only or put into BACKUP mode; or when other values specified by certain parameters (discussed later in this section) are reached.

You can force a checkpoint if needed, as shown here:

ALTER SYSTEM CHECKPOINT;

Forcing a checkpoint ensures that all changes to the database buffers are written to the data files on disk.

Another way to force a checkpoint is by forcing a log-file switch:

ALTER SYSTEM SWITCH LOGFILE;

The size of the redo log affects the checkpoint performance. If the size of the redo log is smaller and the transaction volume is high, a log switch occurs often, and so does the checkpoint. The DBW*n* process writes the dirty buffer blocks whenever a checkpoint occurs. This situation might reduce the time required for instance recovery, but it might also affect the runtime performance. You can adjust checkpoints primarily by using the initialization parameter FAST_START_MTTR_TARGET. It is used to ensure that recovery time at instance startup (if required) will not exceed a certain number of seconds.

> You can use the FAST_START_MTTR_TARGET parameter to tune checkpoint frequency; its value determines how long an instance can take to start after an instance crash.

Multiplexing Redo Log Files

You can keep multiple copies of the online redo log file to safeguard against damage to these files. When multiplexing online redo log files, LGWR concurrently writes the same redo log information to multiple identical online redo log files, thereby eliminating a single point of redo log failure. All copies of the redo file are the same size and are known as a *redo group,* which is identified by an integer. Each redo log file in the group is known as a *redo member.* You must have at least two redo log groups for normal database operation.

When multiplexing redo log files, keeping the members of a group on different disks is preferable so that one disk failure will not affect the continuing operation of the database. If LGWR can write to at least one member of the group, database operation proceeds as normal; an entry is written to the alert log file. If all members of the redo log file group are not available for writing, Oracle hangs, crashes, or shuts down. An instance recovery or media recovery can be needed to bring up the database, and you can lose committed transactions.

You can create multiple copies of the online redo log files when you create the database. For example, the following statement creates two redo log file groups with two members in each:

```
CREATE DATABASE "MYDB01"
... ... ...
LOGFILE
  GROUP 1 ('/ora02/oradata/MYDB01/redo0101.log',
           '/ora03/oradata/MYDB01/redo0102.log') SIZE 50M,
  GROUP 2 ('/ora02/oradata/MYDB01/redo0201.log',
           '/ora03/oradata/MYDB01/redo0202.log') SIZE 50M;
```

The maximum number of log file groups is specified in the clause MAXLOGFILES, and the maximum number of members is specified in the clause MAXLOGMEMBERS. You can separate the filenames (members) by using a space or a comma.

In the following sections, you will learn how to create a new redo log group, add a new member to an existing group, rename a member, and drop a member from an existing group. In addition, I'll show you how to drop a group and clear all members of a group in certain circumstances.

Redo Log Troubleshooting

In the case of redo log groups, it's best to be generous with the number of groups and the number of members for each group. After estimating the number of groups that would be appropriate for your installation, add one more. The slight additional work involved in maintaining either additional or larger redo logs is small in relation to the time needed to fix a problem when the number of users and concurrent active transactions increase.

The space needed for additional log file groups is minimal and is well worth the effort up front to avoid the undesirable situation in which writes to the redo log file are waiting on the completion of writes to the database files or the archived log file destination.

Creating New Groups

You can create and add more redo log groups to the database by using the ALTER DATABASE command. The following statement creates a new log file group with two members:

```
ALTER DATABASE ADD LOGFILE
   GROUP 3 ('/ora02/oradata/MYDB01/redo0301.log',
             '/ora03/oradata/MYDB01/redo0302.log') SIZE 10M;
```

If you omit the GROUP clause, Oracle assigns the next available number. For example, the following statement also creates a multiplexed group:

```
ALTER DATABASE ADD LOGFILE
     ('/ora02/oradata/MYDB01/redo0301.log',
      '/ora03/oradata/MYDB01/redo0302.log') SIZE 10M;
```

To create a new group without multiplexing, use the following statement:

```
ALTER DATABASE ADD LOGFILE
     '/ora02/oradata/MYDB01/redo0301.log' REUSE;
```

You can add more than one redo log group by using the ALTER DATABASE command—just use a comma to separate the groups.

If the redo log files you create already exist, use the REUSE option, and don't specify the size. The new redo log size will be the same as that of the existing file.

Adding a new redo log group is straightforward using EM Database Control. To do so, click the Server tab, and then click the Redo Log Groups link under Storage. You can view the current redo log groups and add another redo log group using the Create button, as you can see in Figure 15.3 on the Redo Log Groups screen.

FIGURE 15.3   The Redo Log Groups maintenance screen

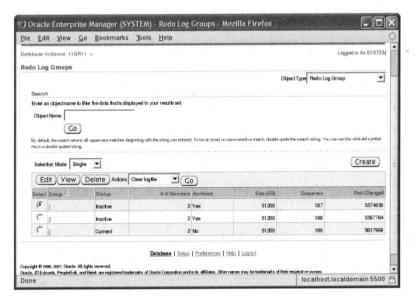

Adding New Members

If you forgot to multiplex the redo log files when creating the database (multiplexing redo log files is the default when you use DBCA) or if you need to add more redo log members, you can do so by using the ALTER DATABASE command. When adding new members, you do not specify the file size, because all group members will have the same size.

If you know the group number, use the following statement to add a member to group 2:

```
ALTER DATABASE ADD LOGFILE MEMBER
'/ora04/oradata/MYDB01/redo0203.log' TO GROUP 2;
```

You can also add group members by specifying the names of other members in the group, instead of specifying the group number. Specify all the existing group members with this syntax:

```
ALTER DATABASE ADD LOGFILE MEMBER
 '/ora04/oradata/MYDB01/redo0203.log' TO
('/ora02/oradata/MYDB01/redo0201.log',
 '/ora03/oradata/MYDB01/redo0202.log');
```

You can add a new member to a group in EM Database Control by clicking the Edit button shown in Figure 15.3 and then clicking Add. Figure 15.4 shows the Edit Redo Log Group screen, where you can add or remove redo log group members.

FIGURE 15.4   The Edit Redo Log Group screen

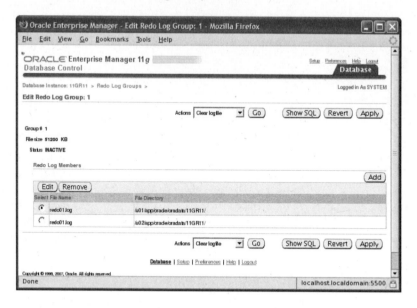

Renaming Log Members

If you want to move the log file member from one disk to another or just want a more meaningful name, you can rename a redo log member. Before renaming the online redo log members, the new (target) online redo files should exist. The SQL commands in Oracle change only the internal pointer in the control file to a new log file; they do not change or rename the operating-system file. You must use an operating-system command to rename or move the file. Follow these steps to rename a log member:

1. Shut down the database.

2. Copy/rename the redo log file member to the new location by using an operating-system command.

3. Start up the instance, and mount the database (STARTUP MOUNT).

4. Rename the log file member in the control file. Use ALTER DATABASE RENAME FILE 'old_redo_file_name' TO 'new_redo_file_name'; .

5. Open the database (ALTER DATABASE OPEN).

6. Back up the control file.

Another way to achieve the same result is to add a new member to the group and then drop the old member from the group, as discussed in the "Adding New Members" section earlier in this chapter and the "Dropping Redo Log Groups" section, which is next.

You can rename a log-group member in EM Database Control by clicking the Edit button shown in Figure 15.4 and then changing the filename in the File Name box.

Dropping Redo Log Groups

You can drop a redo log group and its members by using the ALTER DATABASE command. Remember that you should have at least two redo log groups for the database to function normally. The group that is to be dropped should not be the active group or the current group—that is, you can drop only an inactive log-file group. If the log file to be dropped is not inactive, use the ALTER SYSTEM SWITCH LOGFILE command.

To drop the log-file group 3, use the following SQL statement:

```
ALTER DATABASE DROP LOGFILE GROUP 3;
```

When an online redo log group is dropped from the database, the operating-system files are not deleted from disk. The control files of the associated database are updated to drop the members of the group from the database structure. After dropping an online redo log group, make sure the drop is completed successfully, and then use the appropriate operating-system command to delete the dropped online redo log files.

You can delete an entire redo log group in EM Database Control by clicking the Delete button (see Figure 15.3, shown earlier) and then confirming the delete by clicking the Yes button.

Dropping Redo Log Members

In much the same way that you drop a redo log group, you can drop only the members of an inactive redo log group. Also, if there are only two groups, the log member to be dropped should not be the last member of a group. Each redo log group can have a different number of members, though this is not advised. For example, say you have three log groups, each with two members. If you drop a log member from group 2 and a failure occurs to the sole member of group 2, the instance will hang, crash, and potentially cause the loss of committed transactions when attempts are made to write to the missing redo log group, as I discussed earlier in this chapter. Even if you drop a member for maintenance reasons, ensure that all redo log groups have the same number of members.

To drop a redo log member, use the DROP LOGFILE MEMBER clause of the ALTER DATABASE command:

```
ALTER DATABASE DROP LOGFILE MEMBER
'/ora04/oradata/MYDB01/redo0203.log';
```

The operating-system file is not removed from the disk; only the control file is updated. Use an operating-system command to delete the redo log file member from disk.

 NOTE If a database is running in ARCHIVELOG mode, redo log members cannot be deleted unless the redo log group has been archived.

You can drop a member of a redo log group in EM Database Control by clicking the Edit button (see Figure 15.4, shown earlier), selecting the member to be dropped, and then clicking the Remove button.

Clearing Online Redo Log Files

Under certain circumstances, a redo log group member (or all members of a log group) can become corrupted. To solve this problem, you can drop and add the log-file group or group member again. It is much easier, however, to use the ALTER DATABASE CLEAR LOGFILE command. The following example clears the contents of redo log group 3 in the database:

```
ALTER DATABASE CLEAR LOGFILE GROUP 3;
```

Another distinct advantage of this command is that you can clear a log group even if the database has only two log groups and only one member in each group. Additionally, by using the UNARCHIVED keyword, you can clear a log-group member even if it has not been archived. In this case, it is advisable to do a full database backup at the earliest convenience, because the unarchived redo log file is no longer usable for database recovery.

You can clear the redo logs by choosing Clear Logfile from the Actions drop-down box and clicking Go (as shown earlier in Figure 15.3). The other options available in the drop-down box are as follows:

- Create Like
- Force Checkpoint
- Generate DDL
- Sizing Advice
- Switch Logfile

Understanding Archived Redo Log (ARCHIVELOG) Files

If you use only online redo log files, your database is protected against instance failure but not media failure. Although saving the redo log files before they are overwritten takes additional disk space and management, the increased recoverability of the database outweighs the slight additional overhead and maintenance costs.

In the following sections, I will present an overview of how archived redo log files work, how to set the location for saving the archived redo log files, and how to enable archiving in the database.

Archived Redo Log File Architecture

An archived redo log file is a copy of a redo log file before it is overwritten by new redo information. Because the online redo log files are reused in a circular fashion, you have no way of bringing a backup of a data file up to the latest committed transaction unless you configure the database in ARCHIVELOG mode.

The process of copying is called *archiving*. The ARC*n* background processes do this archiving. By archiving the redo log files, you can use them later to recover a database, update a standby database, or use the LogMiner utility to audit the database activities.

When an online redo log file is full and LGWR starts writing to the next redo log file, ARC*n* copies the completed redo log file to the archive destination. It is possible to specify more than one archive destination. The LGWR process waits for the ARC*n* process to complete the copy operation before overwriting any online redo log file. As with LGWR, the failure of one of the ARC*n* backup processes will cause instance failure, but no committed transactions will be lost because the "Commit Complete" message is not returned to the user or calling program until LGWR successfully records the transaction in the online redo log file group.

When the archiver process is copying the redo log files to another destination, the database is said to be in ARCHIVELOG mode. If archiving is not enabled, the database is said to be in NOARCHIVELOG mode. In production systems, you cannot afford to lose data and should therefore run the database in ARCHIVELOG mode so that in the event of a failure, you can recover the database to the time of failure or to a point in time. You can achieve this ability to recover by restoring the database backup and applying the database changes by using the archived log files.

 Real World Scenario

Archive-Logging Space Issues

After you configure the database for ARCHIVELOG mode, your job is only half complete. You need to continually make sure there is enough room for the archived log files. Otherwise, the database will hang. At least once in your DBA career, you will get a phone call from some users saying that the database is "hung." It's not until you check the alert log that you discover the archiving process cannot find disk space for a newly filled log file in the archiving destinations.

There should be enough space available for online archived redo log files to recover and roll forward from the last full backup of each data file that is also online; the remaining archived logs and any previous data file backups can be moved to another disk or to tape.

Remembering your zero-transaction-loss strategy (which should be every DBA's strategy), make sure you do not misplace or delete an archived log file before it is backed up to tape; otherwise, you will not be able to perform a complete recovery because of a media failure.

If you use RMAN and the flash recovery area for all your backup files, then you can further automate this process by directing RMAN to maintain enough backups to satisfy a recovery-window policy (number of days) or a redundancy policy (multiple copies of each backup). Once an archived log or other backup file is no longer needed for the policy, the files are automatically deleted from the flash recovery area.

Setting the Archive Destination

You specify the archive destination in the initialization-parameter file. To change the archive destination parameters during normal database operation, you use the ALTER SYSTEM command. The following sections cover some of the parameters associated with archive-log destinations and the archiver process. You can find a complete list of initialization parameters in the Oracle documentation "Oracle 11g Reference" at http://tahiti.oracle.com.

LOG_ARCHIVE_DEST_n

Using this parameter, you can specify at most 10 archiving destinations. These locations can be on the local machine or on a remote machine where the standby database is located. The syntax for specifying this parameter in the initialization file is as follows:

```
LOG_ARCHIVE_DEST_n =  "null_string" |
((SERVICE = tnsnames_name |
  LOCATION = 'directory_name')
 [MANDATORY | OPTIONAL]
 [REOPEN [= integer]])
```

For example, the following specifies a location for the archive-log files on the local machine at /archive/MYDB01. The MANDATORY clause specifies that writing to this location must succeed.

```
LOG_ARCHIVE_DEST_1 = ((LOCATION='/archive/MYDB01') MANDATORY)
```

Here is another example, which applies the archive logs to a standby database on a remote computer:

```
LOG_ARCHIVE_DEST_2 = (SERVICE=STDBY01) OPTIONAL REOPEN 60;
```

In this example, STDBY01 is the Oracle Net connect string used to connect to the remote database. Because writing is optional, the database activity continues even if ARCn could not write the archive-log file. It tries the writing operation again because the REOPEN clause is specified. The REOPEN clause specifies when the next attempt to write to this location should be made if the first attempt does not succeed. The default value is 300 seconds.

You can also use the EM Database Control web pages to configure the backup and recovery settings by choosing the Availability tab of EM Database Control. Figure 15.5 shows the Backup/Recovery section on the Availability tab.

FIGURE 15.5 Backup/Recovery section options in EM

By clicking the Recovery Settings link, you can configure the archive-log destinations using the Media Recovery section. For the database shown in the example, only one archive location is set up, as shown in Figure 15.6.

FIGURE 15.6   The log-archive destinations

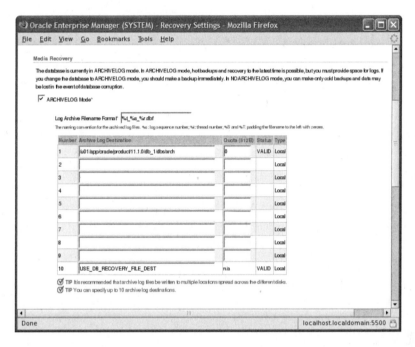

Destination 10 is the flash recovery area using the string USE_DB_RECOVERY_FILE_DEST.

 The flash recovery area is discussed in the section "Understanding the Flash Recovery Area," later in this chapter.

LOG_ARCHIVE_MIN_SUCCEED_DEST

This parameter specifies the number of destinations that the ARC*n* process should successfully write at a minimum to proceed with overwriting the online redo log files. The default value of this parameter is 1. This parameter cannot exceed the total number of enabled destinations. If this parameter value is less than the number of MANDATORY destinations, the parameter is ignored.

LOG_ARCHIVE_FORMAT

This parameter specifies the format in which to write the filename of the archived redo log files. To ensure that the log files are not overwritten, you use predefined substitution variables to construct the name of each archived redo log file. You can provide a text string and any of the predefined substitution variables. The variables are as follows:

- %s: This is the log sequence number.

- %t: This is the thread number.

- %r: This is the reset log's ID, which ensures uniqueness even after using advanced recovery techniques that reset the log sequence numbers.

- %d: This is the database ID.

The format you provide must include at least %s, %t, and %r. If you use the same archived redo log location for multiple databases, you must also use %d. In Figure 15.6, shown previously, the log-archive filename format is defined as %t_%s_%r.dbf.

Setting ARCHIVELOG

Specifying these parameters does not start writing the archive-log files. To enable archiving of the redo log files, place the database in ARCHIVELOG mode. You can specify the ARCHIVELOG clause while creating the database. However, you might prefer to create the database first and then enable ARCHIVELOG mode. To enable ARCHIVELOG mode, follow these steps:

1. Shut down the database.

2. Set up the appropriate initialization parameters.

3. Start up and mount the database; you can change ARCHIVELOG mode only when the database is in the MOUNT state.

4. Enable ARCHIVELOG mode by using the command ALTER DATABASE ARCHIVELOG.

5. Open the database by using ALTER DATABASE OPEN.

6. Back up the database.

To disable ARCHIVELOG mode, follow these steps:

1. Shut down the database.

2. Start up and mount the database.

3. Disable ARCHIVELOG mode by using the command ALTER DATABASE NOARCHIVELOG.

4. Open the database by using ALTER DATABASE OPEN.

The dynamic performance view V$DATABASE tells you whether you are in ARCHIVELOG mode, as you can see in this query:

```
SQL> SELECT dbid, name, created, log_mode
     FROM v$database;


     DBID NAME      CREATED   LOG_MODE
---------- --------- --------- ------------
1387044942 ORD       03-MAR-04 ARCHIVELOG
```

Understanding the Flash Recovery Area

As the price of disk space drops, the difference in its price compared with tape is offset by the advantages of using a disk as the primary backup medium. Even a slow disk can be accessed randomly faster than a tape drive. This rapid access means that any database-recovery operation takes only minutes instead of hours.

Using disk space as the primary medium for all database-recovery operations is the key component of the Oracle 11g database's flash recovery area. The flash recovery area is a single, unified storage area for all recovery-related files and recovery activities in an Oracle database.

The flash recovery area can be a single directory, an entire file system, or an Automatic Storage Management (ASM) disk group. To further optimize the use of disk space for recovery operations, a flash recovery area can be shared by more than one database.

In the following sections, I will cover all the major aspects of a flash recovery area: what can and should be kept in the flash recovery area and how to set up a flash recovery using initialization parameters and SQL commands. Also, as with other aspects of Oracle 11g, I will show how you can manage most parts of the flash recovery area using EM Database Control, and I'll introduce some of the more advanced management techniques.

Flash Recovery Area Occupants

All the files needed to recover a database from a media failure or a logical error are contained in the flash recovery area. The flash recovery area can contain the following:

Control files   A copy of the control file is created in the flash recovery area when the database is created. This copy of the control file can be used as one of the mirrored copies of the control file to ensure that at least one copy of the control file is available after a media failure.

Archived log files   When the flash recovery area is configured, the initialization parameter LOG_ARCHIVE_DEST_10 is automatically set to the flash recovery area location. The corresponding ARC*n* processes create archived log files in the flash recovery area and any other defined LOG_ARCHIVE_DEST_*n* locations.

Flashback logs   If the flashback database is enabled, its flashback logs are stored in the flash recovery area.

Control file and spfile autobackups   The flash recovery area holds control file and spfile autobackups generated by RMAN if RMAN is configured for control file autobackup. When RMAN backs up data file 1, which is part of the SYSTEM tablespace, the control file is automatically included in the RMAN backup.

Data file copies   For RMAN BACKUP AS COPY image files, the default destination for the data file copies is the flash recovery area.

RMAN backup sets   By default, RMAN uses the flash recovery area for both backup sets and image copies. In addition, RMAN puts restored archived log files from tape into the flash recovery area in preparation for a recovery operation.

The Flash Recovery Area and SQL Commands

You must define two initialization parameters to set up the flash recovery area: DB_RECOVERY_FILE_DEST_SIZE and DB_RECOVERY_FILE_DEST. Because both of these are dynamic parameters, the instance doesn't need to be shut down and restarted for the flash recovery area to be usable.

DB_RECOVERY_FILE_DEST_SIZE, which must be defined before DB_RECOVERY_FILE_DEST, defines the size of the flash recovery area. To maximize the benefits of the flash recovery area, it should be large enough to hold a copy of all data files, incremental backups, online redo logs, archived redo logs not yet backed up to tape, control files, and control file autobackups. At a bare minimum, you need enough space to hold the archived log files not yet copied to tape.

Here is an example of configuring DB_RECOVERY_FILE_DEST_SIZE:

```
SQL> ALTER SYSTEM SET
     db_recovery_file_dest_size = 8g SCOPE=both;
```

The size of the flash recovery area will be 8GB, and because this example uses the SCOPE=BOTH parameter in the ALTER SYSTEM command, the initialization parameter takes effect immediately and stays in effect even after a database restart.

The parameter DB_RECOVERY_FILE_DEST specifies the physical location where all flash recovery files are stored. The ASM disk group or file system must have at least as much space as the amount specified with DB_RECOVERY_FILE_DEST_SIZE, and it can have significantly more. DB_RECOVERY_FILE_DEST_SIZE, however, can be increased on the fly if more space is needed and the file system where the flash recovery area resides has the space available.

The following example uses the directory /OraFlash for the flash recovery area, like so:

```
SQL> ALTER SYSTEM SET
     db_recovery_file_dest = '/OraFlash' SCOPE=both;
```

Clearing the value of DB_RECOVERY_FILE_DEST disables the flash recovery area; the parameter DB_RECOVERY_FILE_DEST_SIZE cannot be cleared until the DB_RECOVERY_FILE_DEST parameter has been cleared.

The Flash Recovery Area and EM Database Control

You can create and maintain the flash recovery area using EM Database Control. Click the Availability tab, and then click the Recovery Settings link to display the Configure Recovery Settings screen. Figure 15.7 shows the Flash Recovery section.

In the Flash Recovery section, the flash recovery area has been configured for a database in the file system /u01/app/oracle/flash_recovery_area, with a maximum size of 15,000MB (15GB). Just more than 4GB of space is currently used in the flash recovery area. Flashback logging has not yet been enabled for this database.

FIGURE 15.7   Flash Recovery section of the Recovery Settings screen

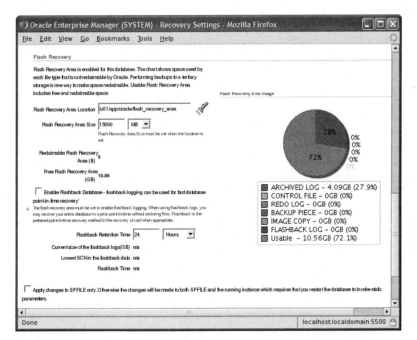

You can enable flashback logging by selecting the Enable Flashback Database box. Oracle's flashback features complement the media-recovery options in the database. Using the FLASHBACK DATABASE command in RMAN, you can revert the data file contents to a state at a prior time. This operation is much faster than recovering from a full database backup and applying the archive logs to recover the database to a point in time. The flashback logs contain the past versions of the data blocks.

You can enable flashback database using SQL*Plus. The steps needed are as follows:

1.   Make sure the database is in ARCHIVELOG mode and the flash recovery area is configured using the DB_RECOVERY_FILE_DEST and DB_RECOVERY_FILE_DEST_SIZE parameters.

2.   Specify the length of desired flashback window using the DB_FLASHBACK_RETENTION_TARGET parameter.

3.   Shut down the database, and start in MOUNT state.

4.   Enable the flashback database feature using the ALTER DATABASE FLASHBACK ON statement.

5.   Open the database.

You can find more information about configuring and using flashback logs with flashback database in *OCP: Oracle Database 11g Administrator Certified Professional Study Guide* (Sybex, 2009).

Flash Recovery Area Management

Because the space in the flash recovery area is limited by the initialization parameter DB_RECOVERY_FILE_DEST_SIZE, the Oracle database keeps track of which files are no longer needed on disk so that they can be deleted when there is not enough free space for new files. Each time a file is deleted from the flash recovery area, a message is written to the alert log.

A message is also written to the alert log in other circumstances. If no files can be deleted and the recovery area's used space is at 85 percent, a warning message is issued. When the space used is at 97 percent, a critical warning is issued. These warnings are recorded in the alert log file, can be viewed in the data dictionary view DBA_OUTSTANDING_ALERTS, and are available on the main screen of EM Database Control.

When you receive these alerts, you have a number of options. If your retention policy can be adjusted to keep fewer copies of data files or reduce the number of days in the recovery window, this can help alleviate the space problems in the flash recovery area. Assuming your retention policy is sound, you should instead add more disk space or back up some of the files in the flash recovery area to another destination such as another disk or a tape device.

 If the flash recovery area is full, Oracle 11*g* will write ORA-19809 and ORA-19804 errors to the alert log file. The flash recovery area is automatically cleared based on the retention specified. To manually clear the flash recovery area, you must perform BACKUP RECOVERY AREA to back up the flash recovery area files and to delete the files.

Performing Backups

Your backup strategy depends on the activity of your database, the level of availability required by your service-level agreements (SLAs), and how much downtime you can tolerate during a recovery effort.

In this section, I'll first review some terminology, and then I will show you a way to back up the control file to a text file that you can edit and use in case of the loss of all control files. I will then discuss how to back up the database using OS utilities. Finally, I will introduce Recovery Manager and show you how to make some of the backups described in the terminology review.

Understanding Backup Terminology

You can make a *whole* backup, which backs up the entire database, or you can back up only part of the database, which is called a *partial* backup. Whole backups and partial backups are known as Oracle *backup strategies*. The backup type can be divided into two general categories: *full* backups and *incremental* backups. Depending on whether you make your database backups when the database is open or closed, backups can be further categorized into the backup modes known as *consistent* backup and *inconsistent* backup.

Your backups can be managed using operating-system and SQL commands or entirely by RMAN. Many backup types are available using RMAN only, such as incremental backups; unless you have some specific requirements, it is highly recommended that you use RMAN to implement your backup strategy.

The following are definitions for whole database backups, partial database backups, full backups, incremental backups, consistent backups, and inconsistent backups:

Whole database　A whole database backup includes all data files and at least one control file. Online redo log files are never backed up; restoring backed-up redo log files and replacing the current redo log files will result in loss of data during media recovery. Only one of the control files needs to be backed up; all copies of the control file are identical.

Partial database　A partial database backup includes zero or more tablespaces, which in turn includes zero or more data files; a control file is optional in a partial database backup. As you may infer, a partial database backup that includes no tablespaces and does not include the control file backs up 0 bytes of data to the backup destination.

Full　A full backup includes all blocks of every data file backed up in a whole or partial database backup.

Incremental　An incremental backup makes a copy of all data blocks that have changed since a previous backup. Though Oracle11*g* supports five levels of incremental backups from 0 to 4, 0 and 1 are most commonly used. An incremental backup at level 0 is considered a baseline backup; it is the equivalent of a full backup and contains all data blocks in the data file(s) that are backed up. Although incremental backups can take less time, the potential downside is that you must first restore the baseline backup and then apply all incremental backups performed since the baseline backup.

Consistent　A consistent backup, also known as an *offline backup*, is performed while the database is not open. These backups are consistent because the SCN in the control file matches the SCN in every data file's header. Although recovering using a consistent backup requires no additional recovery operation after a failure, you reduce your database's availability during a consistent backup as well as risk the loss of committed transactions performed since the consistent backup.

Inconsistent　Although the term *inconsistent backup* may sound like something you might avoid in a database, it is a way to maintain the availability of the database while performing backups. An inconsistent backup, also known as an *online backup*, is performed while the database is open and available to users. The backup is inconsistent because the SCN in the control file is most likely out of sync with the SCN in the header of the data files. Inconsistent backups require recovery when they are used for recovering from a media failure, but they keep availability high because the database is open while the backup is performed.

Backups can be performed using two methods: using user-managed backup or using Oracle's backup and recovery tool called Recovery Manager. RMAN backups are easier to create, and the recovery operations are pretty much automated. I discuss RMAN backups in the section "Using RMAN to Create Backups."

In the next sections, you will learn to back up the control file, back up the database, and use Recovery Manager.

Backing Up the Control File

In addition to multiplexing the control file, you can guard against the loss of all control files by backing up the control file. You can back up the control using three methods:

- An editable text file; this backup is called a *backup to trace*.
- A binary backup of the control file.
- RMAN backup of the control file.

Text Backup of Control File

The text backup is created using the ALTER DATABASE BACKUP CONTROLFILE TO TRACE statement, and the file is created in the trace directory under <ADR_HOME>/trace. The trace file format is *sid_ora_pid*.trc, where *sid* is the session database ID and *pid* is the process ID of the user creating the trace backup. This special backup of the control file is not a trace file per se; in other words, it is not a dump file or an error report for a failed user or system process. It is a proactive rather than reactive report of the contents of the control file, and the report happens to end up in a directory with other trace files.

Back up the control file to trace after any change to the structure of the database, such as adding or dropping a tablespace or creating a new redo log file group. Using the command line to create a backup of the control file is almost as easy as clicking the Backup to Trace button within EM Database Control (see Figure 15.1 earlier in the chapter):

```
SQL> alter database backup controlfile to trace;
Database altered.
```

If you want to create the control file create statement in a named file, rather than an Oracle-generated trace file name, you can do this:

```
SQL> alter database backup controlfile to trace as '/tmp/mydbcontrol.txt';
Database altered.
```

The control file create statements are created in the file */tmp/mydbcontrol.txt*.

Here is an excerpt from the output of the command; note that a lot of editing might be required before using this file to re-create the control file:

```
--
-- The following are current System-scope REDO Log Archival related
-- parameters and can be included in the database initialization file.
--
-- LOG_ARCHIVE_DEST=''
```

```
--  LOG_ARCHIVE_DUPLEX_DEST=''
--
--  LOG_ARCHIVE_FORMAT=%t_%s_%r.dbf
--
--  DB_UNIQUE_NAME="11GR11"
--
--  LOG_ARCHIVE_CONFIG='SEND, RECEIVE, NODG_CONFIG'
--  LOG_ARCHIVE_MAX_PROCESSES=4
--  STANDBY_FILE_MANAGEMENT=MANUAL
--  STANDBY_ARCHIVE_DEST=?/dbs/arch
--  FAL_CLIENT=''
--  FAL_SERVER=''
--
--  LOG_ARCHIVE_DEST_10='LOCATION=USE_DB_RECOVERY_FILE_DEST'
--  LOG_ARCHIVE_DEST_10='OPTIONAL REOPEN=300 NODELAY'
--  LOG_ARCHIVE_DEST_10='ARCH NOAFFIRM NOEXPEDITE NOVERIFY SYNC'
--  LOG_ARCHIVE_DEST_10='REGISTER NOALTERNATE NODEPENDENCY'
--  LOG_ARCHIVE_DEST_10='NOMAX_FAILURE NOQUOTA_SIZE NOQUOTA_USED NODB_UNIQUE_
NAME'
--  LOG_ARCHIVE_DEST_10='VALID_FOR=(PRIMARY_ROLE,ONLINE_LOGFILES)'
--  LOG_ARCHIVE_DEST_STATE_10=ENABLE
--
--  LOG_ARCHIVE_DEST_1='LOCATION=/u01/app/oracle/product/11.1.0/db_1/dbs/arch'
--  LOG_ARCHIVE_DEST_1='MANDATORY NOREOPEN NODELAY'
--  LOG_ARCHIVE_DEST_1='ARCH NOAFFIRM EXPEDITE NOVERIFY SYNC'
--  LOG_ARCHIVE_DEST_1='NOREGISTER NOALTERNATE NODEPENDENCY'
--  LOG_ARCHIVE_DEST_1='NOMAX_FAILURE NOQUOTA_SIZE NOQUOTA_USED NODB_UNIQUE_
NAME'
--  LOG_ARCHIVE_DEST_1='VALID_FOR=(PRIMARY_ROLE,ONLINE_LOGFILES)'
--  LOG_ARCHIVE_DEST_STATE_1=ENABLE
--
-- The following commands will create a new control file and use it
-- to open the database.
-- Data used by Recovery Manager will be lost.
-- The contents of online logs will be lost and all backups will
-- be invalidated. Use this only if online logs are damaged.
-- After mounting the created controlfile, the following SQL
-- statement will place the database in the appropriate
-- protection mode:
--  ALTER DATABASE SET STANDBY DATABASE TO MAXIMIZE PERFORMANCE
```

```
STARTUP NOMOUNT
CREATE CONTROLFILE REUSE DATABASE "11GR11" RESETLOGS  ARCHIVELOG
    MAXLOGFILES 16
    MAXLOGMEMBERS 3
    MAXDATAFILES 100
    MAXINSTANCES 8
    MAXLOGHISTORY 292
LOGFILE
  GROUP 1 (
    '/u01/app/oracle/oradata/11GR11/redo01.log',
    '/u02/app/oracle/oradata/11GR11/redo01.log'
  ) SIZE 50M,
  GROUP 2 (
    '/u01/app/oracle/oradata/11GR11/redo02.log',
    '/u02/app/oracle/oradata/11GR11/redo02.log'
  ) SIZE 50M,
  GROUP 3 (
    '/u01/app/oracle/oradata/11GR11/redo03.log',
    '/u02/app/oracle/oradata/11GR11/redo03.log'
  ) SIZE 50M
-- STANDBY LOGFILE
DATAFILE
  '/u01/app/oracle/oradata/11GR11/system01.dbf',
  '/u01/app/oracle/oradata/11GR11/sysaux01.dbf',
  '/u01/app/oracle/oradata/11GR11/undotbs01.dbf',
  '/u01/app/oracle/oradata/11GR11/users01.dbf',
  '/u01/app/oracle/oradata/11GR11/example01.dbf',
  '/u01/app/oracle/oradata/11GR11/appl_data01.dbf',
  '/u01/app/oracle/oradata/11GR11/appl_data02.dbf'
CHARACTER SET WE8MSWIN1252
;
-- Commands to re-create incarnation table
-- Below log names MUST be changed to existing filenames on
-- disk. Any one log file from each branch can be used to
-- re-create incarnation records.
-- ALTER DATABASE REGISTER LOGFILE '/u01/app/oracle/ ⤶
flash_recovery_area/11GR11/archivelog/2008_10_26/o1_mf_1_1_%u_.arc';
-- ALTER DATABASE REGISTER LOGFILE '/u01/app/oracle/ ⤶
flash_recovery_area/11GR11/archivelog/2008_10_26/o1_mf_1_1_%u_.arc';
-- Recovery is required if any of the datafiles are restored backups,
```

```
-- or if the last shutdown was not normal or immediate.
RECOVER DATABASE USING BACKUP CONTROLFILE
-- Database can now be opened zeroing the online logs.
ALTER DATABASE OPEN RESETLOGS;
-- Files in read-only tablespaces are now named.
ALTER DATABASE RENAME FILE 'MISSING00008'
  TO '/u02/oradata/11GR11/11GR11/datafile/o1_mf_hr_data_46n3ck5t_.dbf';
-- Online the files in read-only tablespaces.
ALTER TABLESPACE "HR_DATA" ONLINE;
-- Commands to add tempfiles to temporary tablespaces.
-- Online tempfiles have complete space information.
-- Other tempfiles may require adjustment.
ALTER TABLESPACE TEMP ADD TEMPFILE '/u01/app/oracle/oradata/11GR11/temp01.dbf'
     SIZE 400M  REUSE AUTOEXTEND ON NEXT 100M  MAXSIZE 4000M;
-- End of tempfile additions.
--
```

Binary Backup of Control File

Another way to back up your control file is to make a binary copy of it using the similar ALTER DATABASE command, as in the following example:

```
SQL> alter database backup controlfile to
                  '/ora_backup/11GR11/ctlfile20040911.bkp';
Database altered.
```

You can then copy the binary backup of the control file to a backup device.

RMAN Backup of Control File

Using RMAN, you can back up the control file using the BACKUP CURRENT CONTROLFILE statement, as shown here. This backup is also a binary backup.

```
RMAN> BACKUP CURRENT CONTROLFILE;

Starting backup at 26-OCT-08
using target database control file instead of recovery catalog
allocated channel: ORA_DISK_1
channel ORA_DISK_1: SID=123 device type=DISK
channel ORA_DISK_1: starting full datafile backup set
channel ORA_DISK_1: specifying datafile(s) in backup set
including current control file in backup set
channel ORA_DISK_1: starting piece 1 at 26-OCT-08
channel ORA_DISK_1: finished piece 1 at 26-OCT-08
```

```
piece handle=/u01/app/oracle/flash_recovery_area/ ⤶
11GR11/backupset/2008_10_26/o1_mf_ncnnf_TAG20081026T225337_4jbgtcgs_.bkp ⤶
tag=TAG20081026T225337 comment=NONE
channel ORA_DISK_1: backup set complete, elapsed time: 00:00:02
Finished backup at 26-OCT-08

RMAN>
```

Backing Up the Database

An Oracle 11g database can be backed using different modes, depending on the ARCHIVELOG setting of the database. If the database is in ARCHIVELOG mode, you can perform an online database backup (also known as an *inconsistent* or *hot* backup) or offline database backup (also known as a *consistent* or *cold* backup). If the database is in NOARCHIVELOG mode, you can perform an offline backup only.

You can use OS utilities to perform the database backup or use the RMAN. Using RMAN is the preferred and easier method of backup. In the following sections, you will learn how to back up the database using OS utilities (user-managed backups). RMAN backups are discussed in the next section.

User-Managed Cold Backups

Cold backups are performed after shutting down the database. Shut down the database cleanly using the SHUTDOWN IMMEDIATE or SHUTDOWN TRANSACTIONAL statement, and copy all control files and data files to another location or to your tape management system using OS commands. You can also copy the redo logs, but this is not needed if the database shutdown is clean. You also need to back up the parameter file (init file or spfile) and password file.

You can identify the control files in the database using the dynamic performance view V$CONTROLFILE. The data files that need to be backed up can be identified by using the view V$DATAFILE.

User-Managed Hot Backups

To perform a hot backup, the database must be in ARCHIVELOG mode. Before starting to copy the data files belonging to a tablespace, you must place the tablespace in backup mode using the BEGIN BACKUP clause. For example, if you want to back up the USERS tablespace, perform the following:

```
SQL> ALTER TABLESPACE user BEGIN BACKUP;
```

When a tablespace is placed in the backup mode, data-block changes are written to the redo log files. After you take the tablespace out of the backup mode, the database advances the data file checkpoint SCN to the current database-checkpoint SCN.

When a tablespace is in backup mode, use OS utilities to copy the data files belonging to the tablespace to another location or to the tape management system. To take the tablespace out of the backup mode, use the END BACKUP clause as in the following example:

```
SQL> ALTER TABLESPACE user END BACKUP;
```

If your database is small or if you plan to place all the tablespaces in backup mode for the hot backup, instead of placing each tablespace in backup mode, you can use the ALTER DATABASE statement to make the whole database in backup mode, as in the following example:

```
SQL> ALTER DATABASE BEGIN BACKUP;
```

> You cannot perform incremental backups using user-managed backups. You must use RMAN for incremental backups.

Using RMAN to Create Backups

RMAN is the primary component of the Oracle database used to perform backup and recovery operations. You can use RMAN to back up all types: whole or partial databases, full or incremental, and consistent or inconsistent. RMAN is closely integrated with EM Database Control.

RMAN has a command-line interface for advanced configuration and backup operations; the most common backup functions are available via a GUI within EM Database Control. It includes a scripting language to make it easy to automate backups, and it can back up the most critical types of files in your database except for online redo log files (which you should not back up anyway), password files, and text-based init.ora files. Data files, control files, archived log files, and spfiles can be backed up using RMAN. In other words, RMAN is a "one-stop shopping" solution for all your backup and recovery needs. In the rare circumstance that you have to back up outside RMAN, you can register the file created during this backup with RMAN for future use in an RMAN recovery scenario.

> Because of the relatively static nature of password files and text-based init.ora files, these can be included in the regular operating-system backups, or you can back them up manually whenever they are changed.

In the following sections, I will explain the difference between image copies and backup sets and how RMAN handles each of these backup types. After learning some of the RMAN configuration settings, I will show you some examples of how RMAN performs full and incremental backups, using both the command line and the graphical user interface.

Configuring RMAN Backup Settings

Configuring RMAN backup settings is straightforward using EM Database Control. On the Availability tab, click Backup Settings to open the Device tab screen, as shown in Figure 15.8.

FIGURE 15.8 The Backup Settings: Device screen

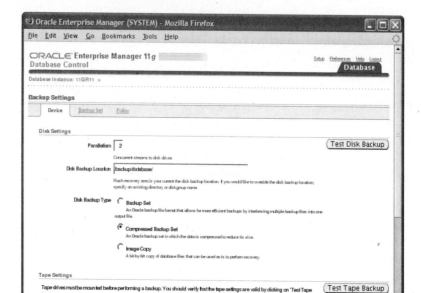

There is a separate section in this screen for your disk device and any tape devices. Under the Disk Settings section, you can control the following parameters:

Parallelism To take advantage of multiple CPUs or disk controllers, increase the value of this parameter to reduce the overall backup time by performing different portions of the backup in parallel.

Disk Backup Location If you are not backing up to the flash recovery area, change this value to the location where you want the backups stored.

Disk Backup Type You can choose image copy, backup set, or compressed backup set.

Under the Tape settings, you can specify whether you want the backups to be written directly to the tape or media management tool. You also have the option to configure the Oracle Secure Backup (OSB) tool on this screen. OSB is a separately licensed product from Oracle to manage the backups and tape libraries. Using OSB, you can back up any type of OS files anywhere on the network.

Click the Backup Set tab, and specify the maximum size for a backup-set piece (a single file), as shown in Figure 15.9. In this case, set the maximum backup-set piece size to 2GB to make it easier to move files around on file systems whose file-size limit is 2GB.

FIGURE 15.9   The Backup Settings: Backup Set screen

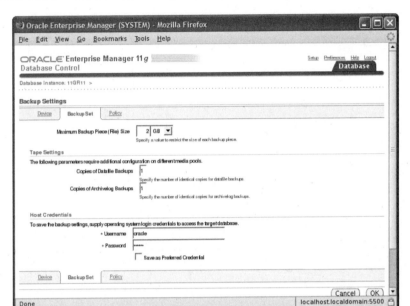

You use the last tab on the Backup Settings screen, the Policy tab, to set a number of other default backup settings, such as automatically backing up the control file with each backup, skipping read-only and offline data files, and using a block-change tracking file. A block-change tracking file keeps track of changed blocks in each tablespace so that incremental backups need not read every block in every data file to determine which blocks need to be backed up during an incremental backup. Figure 15.10 shows an example of the Policy tab with a block-change tracking file specified.

Always enable the automatic backup of control files and spfiles. This is an Oracle-recommended best practice.

Infrequently used parameters, such as the control file autobackup filename format and the snapshot control file destination filename, are not available from the graphical user interface; you must use the RMAN command-line interface to change these values.

You can invoke the RMAN command line by using the executable `rman`. RMAN can optionally use a catalog database where the backup information is kept. If a catalog database is not used, RMAN uses the database control file to perform the backup and recovery operations.

FIGURE 15.10   The Backup Settings: Policy screen

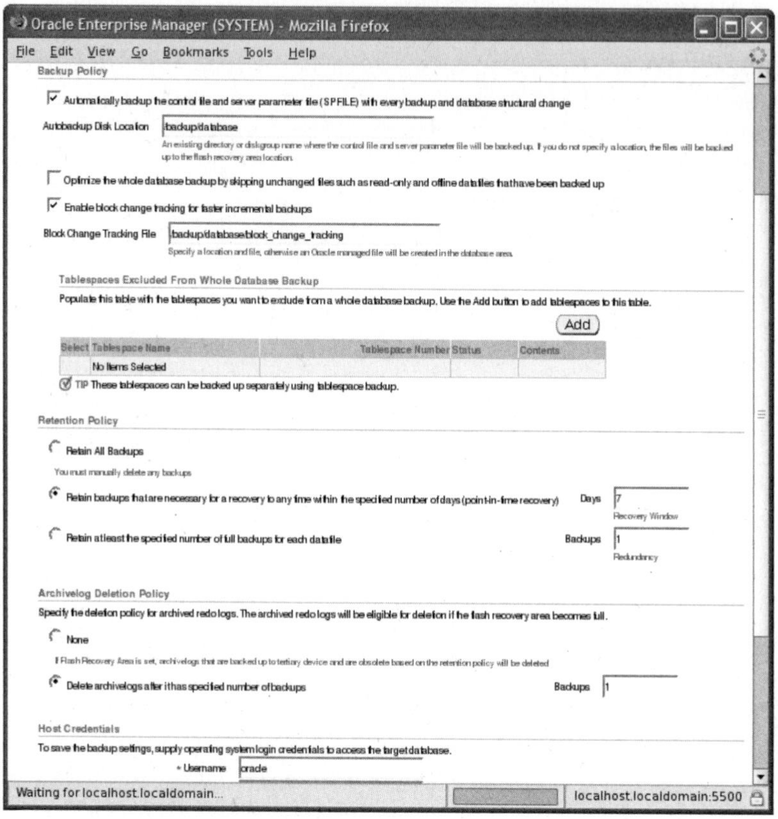

The following RMAN command-line session uses the RMAN SHOW ALL command to display all default RMAN backup settings:

```
$ rman target / nocatalog
Recovery Manager: Release 11.1.0.6.0 - Production on Sun Oct 26 23:51:53 2008
Copyright (c) 1982, 2007, Oracle.  All rights reserved.
connected to target database: 11GR11 (DBID=4110949673)
using target database control file instead of recovery catalog

RMAN> SHOW ALL;

RMAN configuration parameters for database with db_unique_name 11GR11 are:
CONFIGURE RETENTION POLICY TO RECOVERY WINDOW OF 7 DAYS;
CONFIGURE BACKUP OPTIMIZATION OFF; # default
CONFIGURE DEFAULT DEVICE TYPE TO DISK; # default
```

```
CONFIGURE CONTROLFILE AUTOBACKUP ON;
CONFIGURE CONTROLFILE AUTOBACKUP FORMAT
FOR DEVICE TYPE DISK TO '/backup/database/%F';
CONFIGURE DEVICE TYPE DISK BACKUP TYPE TO COMPRESSED BACKUPSET PARALLELISM 2;
CONFIGURE DATAFILE BACKUP COPIES FOR DEVICE TYPE DISK TO 1; # default
CONFIGURE ARCHIVELOG BACKUP COPIES FOR DEVICE TYPE DISK TO 1; # default
CONFIGURE CHANNEL DEVICE TYPE DISK FORMAT
    '/backup/database/%U' MAXPIECESIZE 2 G;
CONFIGURE MAXSETSIZE TO UNLIMITED; # default
CONFIGURE ENCRYPTION FOR DATABASE OFF; # default
CONFIGURE ENCRYPTION ALGORITHM 'AES128'; # default
CONFIGURE COMPRESSION ALGORITHM 'BZIP2'; # default
CONFIGURE ARCHIVELOG DELETION POLICY TO BACKED UP 1 TIMES TO 'SBT_TAPE';
CONFIGURE SNAPSHOT CONTROLFILE NAME TO
'/u01/app/oracle/product/11.1.0/db_1/dbs/snapcf_11GR11.f'; # default

RMAN>
```

 You can enable block-change tracking in the database by using the SQL statement ALTER DATABASE ENABLE BLOCK CHANGE TRACKING.

Understanding Image Copies and Backup Sets

Image copies are duplicates of data files or archived redo log files, which means that every block of every file is backed up; you can use RMAN or operating-system commands to make image copies. In contrast, backup sets are copies of one or more data files or archived redo log files that are stored in a proprietary format readable only by RMAN; backup sets consist of one or more physical files and do not include never-used blocks in the data files being backed up. Backup sets can save even more space by using a compression algorithm designed specifically for the type of data found in an Oracle data file.

   Another difference between image copies and backup sets is that image copies can be copied only to a disk location; backup sets can be written to disk or directly to a tape or other secondary storage device.

Creating Full and Incremental Backups

The Oracle-recommended backup strategy uses RMAN to make a one-time, whole-database, baseline incremental level-zero online backup weekly and then a level-one incremental backup for the other days of the week. You can easily fine-tune this strategy for your own needs by making, for example, a level-two incremental backup at noon during the weekdays if heavy Data Manipulation Language (DML) is occurring in the database.

Using RMAN, you can accomplish this backup strategy with just a couple of the RMAN commands that follow. First, here is the baseline level-one backup at the RMAN command prompt:

```
RMAN> backup incremental level 0
      as compressed backupset database;
```

This backs up the entire database using compression to save disk space in addition to the space savings already gained by using backup sets instead of image copies.

Starting with a baseline level-zero incremental backup, you can make level-one incremental backups during the rest of the week, as in the following example:

```
RMAN> backup incremental level 1

      as compressed backupset database;
```

The options are the same as in the previous example, except that only the blocks that have changed since the last backup are copied to the backup set.

Another variation is to make an incrementally updated backup. An incrementally updated backup uses an incremental backup and updates the changed blocks in an existing image copy as if the entire image copy were backed up. In a recovery scenario, you can restore the image copy of the data file(s) without using an incremental backup; the incremental backup is already applied, saving a significant amount of time during a recovery operation. The following RMAN script shows how an incrementally updated backup works at the command line:

```
run
{
   recover copy of database with tag 'inc_upd_img';
   backup incremental level 1 for
      recover of copy with tag 'inc_upd_img' database;
}
```

This short and cryptic script demonstrates the advantages of using a graphical user interface to perform incrementally updated backups. As you can see in Figure 15.11, on the Schedule Backup: Options screen, you can click a check box to perform an incrementally updated backup in addition to the full backup or incremental backup discussed previously in this section. The Schedule backup link is under the Manage section on the Availability screen (see Figure 15.5 earlier in the chapter).

The Oracle-suggested backup is provided on the right side of the screen. If you want to enable this policy for backups, click the Schedule Oracle-Suggested Backup button. To customize the backups according to your company policy, click the Schedule Customized Backup button. You will be provided with four screens to schedule the backup. The first screen is to specify the backup options, as shown in Figure 15.12.

FIGURE 15.11 Scheduling the backup and specifying the backup type

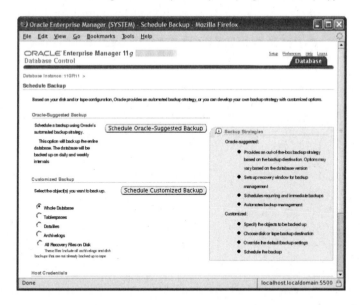

FIGURE 15.12 Customized backup schedule: Options screen

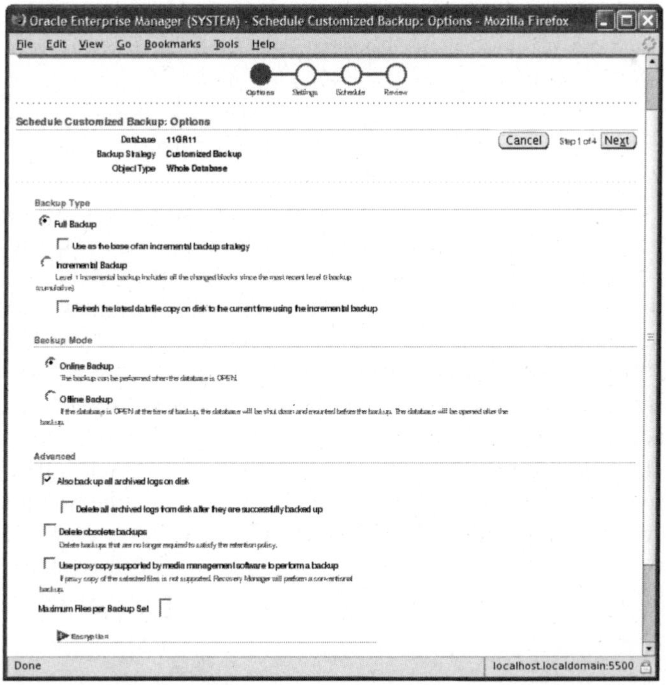

On this screen, you can specify the backup type (full backup or incremental), backup mode (online or offline), and whether to back up archive logs. Click the Next button to advance to the next screen, where you specify the backup settings. Specify whether you want to back up to disk or tape (see Figure 15.13). If you click the View Default Settings button, you will be taken to the screen shown in Figure 15.8.

FIGURE 15.13 Customized backup schedule: Settings screen

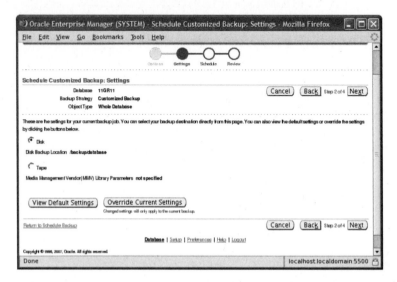

If you do not want to change the default settings but do not want to use the default location for backups, you can click the Override Current Settings button. The Schedule screen gives you the option to perform the backup one time or on a repeating basis. If you choose Repeating, you will be provided with the options to specify the backup repeating schedules, as shown in Figure 15.14.

On the Review screen, you will be provided with a summary of all the options you chose in the previous screens and the RMAN script that will be used to back up the database, as shown in Figure 15.15. You also have the option to edit the RMAN script before scheduling the job.

After reviewing the backup settings, click the Submit Job button to schedule the backup. In the next section, you will learn about managing RMAN backups.

Managing Backups

Managing your database backups is straightforward using EM Database Control. In the following sections, you will get an overview of the RMAN backup- and catalog-maintenance commands and learn how to monitor the flash recovery area and automate backups using the Scheduler.

FIGURE 15.14   Customized backup schedule: Schedule screen

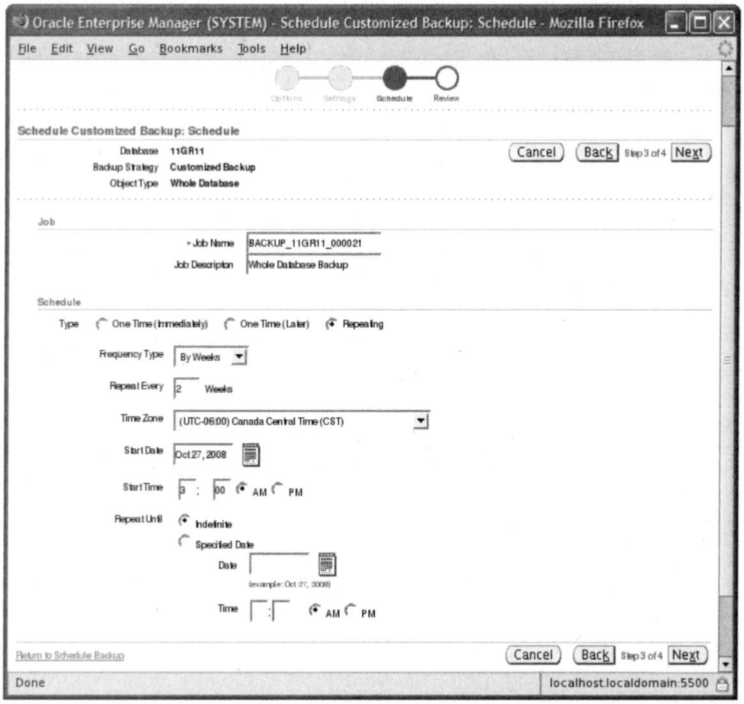

FIGURE 15.15   Customized backup schedule: Review screen

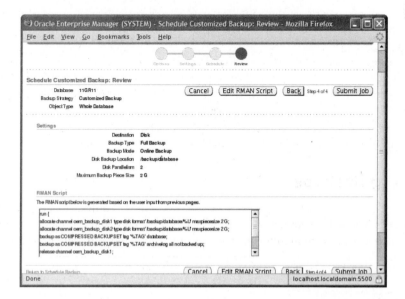

Catalog Maintenance

A number of backup-management functions are available on the Manage Current Backups screen in EM Database Control (see Figure 15.16). To get there, from the screen shown in Figure 15.5, click the Manage Current Backups link.

FIGURE 15.16 The Manage Current Backups screen

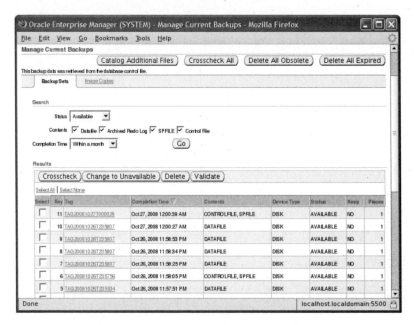

This screen shows you the current backups based on the search criteria entered. The four buttons at the top perform the following functions:

Catalog Additional Files This button adds any image-copy backups made outside RMAN to the RMAN catalog.

Crosscheck All This button double-checks the backup files listed in the catalog (or control file) against the actual files on disk (or tape) to make sure they are all available.

Delete All Obsolete This button deletes all backup files not needed to satisfy the existing retention policy.

Delete All Expired This button deletes the catalog entry for any backups not found when a crosscheck was performed.

Viewing Backup Reports

On the screen shown in Figure 15.5, click the Backup Reports link to show the View Backup Report screen, as shown in Figure 15.17.

FIGURE 15.17   View Backup Report screen

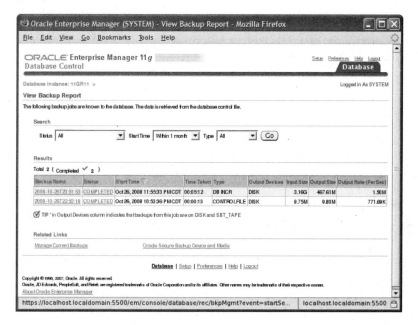

Click the name of the backup in the Backup Name column to display a detailed status report of the backup, including what is being backed up (data files, control files, spfiles), the size of the backup, the backup start and end times, and the backup pieces.

Summary

In this chapter, you learned the database structures that are key elements to ensure a smooth recovery in the event of a database failure: control files, online redo log files, and archived redo log files. You learned to back up the various pieces of the database and learned how to schedule and manage backups using EM Database Control.

The control files contain the metadata about every other structure in the database. The online redo log files provide performance benefits to ongoing transactions and ensure that no committed transactions are lost after an instance failure; being able to change the number of redo log groups and the number of members in each group enhances both the availability and performance of the database. Archived redo log files make copies of online redo log files to one or more destinations before they are overwritten by new transactions. The common thread through all three of these structures is multiplexing: creating redundant copies of database components or redundant archival locations to minimize the impact of a media failure.

You learned about the flash recovery area and how it can be used as the central location for backups of all database files, control files, initialization-parameter files, and archived redo log files in the database. You can manage the flash recovery area via the EM Database Control interface or by using a SQL command-line interface to set or change database initialization parameters that control its location and size.

Before making database backups, you must understand backup strategies, types, and modes. ARCHIVELOG mode provides many benefits and few downsides, especially in a production environment; NOARCHIVELOG mode, in many ways, restricts the types of backups you can make.

Recovery Manager, or RMAN, provides a number of benefits over manual backup methods using a combination of SQL and operating-system commands. You can access most RMAN functionality via EM Database Control or with a command-line version for advanced backup and recovery techniques. One of RMAN's many benefits is the ability to create compressed backup sets, which not only skips unused blocks in database data files but also compresses the blocks before writing to the backup set, saving I/O bandwidth and disk space.

Exam Essentials

Identify the purpose of the redo log files.   Describe the redo log file architecture. Provide details about how to create new redo log file groups and add new members to redo log file groups. Be able to drop redo log group members. Know how to clear online redo log file groups when a log file member becomes corrupted.

Be able to multiplex a control file.   List the steps required to create additional copies of the control file, for both an init.ora file and an spfile.

Describe the basic differences between operating a database in ARCHIVELOG mode and in NOARCHIVELOG mode.   Identify the initialization parameters and commands that control the archive process. Briefly describe how archive-log information is recorded in the control file.

Identify and discuss backup terminology.   Enumerate the backup strategies, the backup types, and the backup modes. Give examples of how you can combine the strategies, types, and modes in different scenarios.

List the benefits of using RMAN to create backups.   Show how to configure RMAN backup settings via the EM Database Control interface. Differentiate image copies from backup sets. Provide examples of an incremental backup strategy.

Explain the benefits of the flash recovery area.   Show how you can access the characteristics and status of the flash recovery area using EM Database Control as well as via dynamic performance views. Describe the database components that can be stored in the flash recovery area. Enumerate the initialization parameters that control the location and size of the flash recovery area.

Know how flashback database option works. The flashback database option can greatly reduce the time required to rewind the database to a prior point in time. Understand the parameters associated with flashback database.

Understand backup catalog maintenance. Show how the EM Database Control interface simplifies cataloging, crosschecking, and cleaning up.

Review Questions

1. Among the failure events, which is the most serious?

    A. The loss of an entire redo log file group but no loss in any other group

    B. The loss of one member of each redo log file group

    C. The failure of the ARC0 background process

    D. The failure of the LGWR background process

2. To enable the flashback database option, the database must be in which of the following modes?

    A. NOARCHIVELOG mode

    B. ARCHIVELOG mode

    C. FLASHBACK LOG mode

    D. BEGIN BACKUP mode

3. When the database is in ARCHIVELOG mode, database recovery is possible up to which event or time?

    A. The last redo log file switch

    B. The last checkpoint position

    C. The last commit

    D. The last incremental backup using RMAN

4. From the following, choose the true statement regarding image copies and backup sets.

    A. An image copy stores one data file per image copy, and a backup set can store all data files in a single file.

    B. An image copy stores one data file per image copy, and a backup set consists of one file per data file backed up.

    C. Both image copies and backup sets use a single file to store all objects to be backed up.

    D. A backup set stores each data file in its own backup file, but an image copy places all data files into a single output file.

5. The option on the EM Database Control backup-scheduling options screen that allows you to refresh an image copy on disk with an incremental backup is known as which RMAN feature?

    A. Incrementally updated backups

    B. Incremental level-zero backups

    C. Compressed image-copy refresh

    D. Compressed incremental backups

6. When should the DBA make a trace copy of the control file using ALTER DATABASE BACKUP CONTROLFILE TO TRACE?

    A. After every backup

    B. After multiplexing the control files

    C. Whenever restarting the instance

    D. Whenever the physical structure of the database changes

7. Which of the following is not a step in configuring your database to archive redo log files?

    A. Place the database in ARCHIVELOG mode.

    B. Multiplex the online redo log files.

    C. Specify a destination for archived redo log files.

    D. Specify a naming convention for your archived redo log files.

8. Why are online backups known as inconsistent backups?

    A. Because not all control files are synchronized to the same SCN until the database is shut down

    B. Because both committed and uncommitted transactions are included in a backup when the database is online

    C. Because a database failure while an online backup is in progress can leave the database in an inconsistent state

    D. Because online backups make copies of data files while they are not consistent with the control files

9. Which parameter is used to specify the archive-log destination?

    A. ARCHIVE_LOG_DEST_*n*

    B. LOG_ARCHIVE_DEST_*n*

    C. DB_CREATE_FILE_DEST

    D. DB_RECOVERY_FILE_DEST_*n*

10. Which of the following initialization parameters specifies the location where the control file trace backup is sent?

    A. DIAGNOSTIC_DEST

    B. BACKGROUND_DUMP_DEST

    C. LOG_ARCHIVE_DEST

    D. CORE_DUMP_DEST

11. Which of the following pieces of information is not available in the control file?

    A. Instance name

    B. Database name

    C. Tablespace names

    D. Log sequence number

12. Which data dictionary view shows that the database is in ARCHIVELOG mode?

    A. V$INSTANCE

    B. V$LOG

    C. V$DATABASE

    D. V$THREAD

13. Which file records all changes made to the database and is used only when recovering an instance?

    A. Archive-log file

    B. Redo log file

    C. Control file

    D. Alert log file

14. Which initialization parameter contains the value used as the default for archived log file destination 10?

    A. LOG_ARCHIVE_DEST

    B. STANDBY_ARCHIVE_DEST

    C. LOG_ARCHIVE_DUPLEX_DEST

    D. DB_RECOVERY_FILE_DEST

    E. USE_DB_RECOVERY_FILE_DEST

15. Which of the following commands is a key step in multiplexing control files using an spfile?

    A. ALTER SYSTEM SET CONTROL_FILES= '/u01/oradata/PRD/cntr101.ctl', '/u01/oradata/PRD/cntr102.ctl' SCOPE=SPFILE;

    B. ALTER SYSTEM SET CONTROL_FILES= '/u01/oradata/PRD/cntr101.ctl', '/u01/oradata/PRD/cntr102.ctl' SCOPE=MEMORY;

    C. ALTER SYSTEM SET CONTROL_FILES= '/u01/oradata/PRD/cntr101.ctl', '/u01/oradata/PRD/cntr102.ctl' SCOPE=BOTH;

    D. The number of control files is fixed when the database is created.

16. Which statement adds a member /logs/redo22.log to redo log file group 2?

    A. ALTER DATABASE ADD LOGFILE '/logs/redo22.log' TO GROUP 2;

    B. ALTER DATABASE ADD LOGFILE MEMBER '/logs/redo22.log' TO GROUP 2;

    C. ALTER DATABASE ADD MEMBER '/logs/redo22.log' TO GROUP 2;

    D. ALTER DATABASE ADD LOGFILE '/logs/redo22.log';

17. What is the biggest advantage of having the control files on different disks?

    A. Database performance.

    B. Guards against failure.

    C. Faster archiving.

    D. Writes are concurrent, so having control files on different disks speeds up control file writes.

18. To place the database into ARCHIVELOG mode, in which state must you start the database?

    A. MOUNT

    B. NOMOUNT

    C. OPEN

    D. SHUTDOWN

    E. Any of the above

19. Which of the following commands places the database in ARCHIVELOG mode?

    A. ALTER SYSTEM ARCHIVELOG;

    B. ALTER DATABASE ARCHIVELOG;

    C. ALTER SYSTEM SET ARCHIVELOG=TRUE;

    D. ALTER DATABASE ENABLE ARCHIVELOG MODE;

    E. ALTER DATABASE ARCHIVELOG MODE;

20. Which of the following substitution-variable formats are always required for specifying the names of the archived redo log files? (Choose all that apply.)

    A. %d

    B. %s

    C. %r

    D. %t

Answers to Review Questions

1. A. Losing an entire redo log file group can result in losing committed transactions that may not yet have been written to the database files. Losing all members of a redo log file group except for one does not affect database operation and does not result in lost data. A message is placed in the alert log file. The failure of LGWR or ARC0 causes an instance failure, but you do not lose any committed transaction data.

2. B. To enable the flashback database option, the database must be in ARCHIVELOG mode. FLASHBACK LOG mode is not a valid mode of database operation. BEGIN BACKUP mode is used to perform hot backups without using RMAN.

3. C. In ARCHIVELOG mode, recovering the database is possible up to the last COMMIT statement; in other words, no committed transactions are lost in ARCHIVELOG mode.

4. A. Image copies are duplicate data and log files in OS format. Backup sets are binary compressed files in Oracle proprietary format. In addition to storing multiple data files in a single output file, backup sets do not contain unused blocks.

5. A. Incrementally updated backups save time during a recovery operation because fewer incremental backups need to be applied to the restored image copy.

6. D. In the rare event that all multiplexed copies of the control file are lost, having a trace copy of the control file reduces the possibility of data loss and reduces downtime during a recovery operation. The preferred and recommended way to back up a control file is to enable control file autobackup using RMAN.

7. B. Although it is recommended that you multiplex your online redo log files, it is not required to enable ARCHIVELOG mode of the database.

8. D. During an online backup, even if all data files are backed up at the same time, they are rarely, if ever, in sync with the control file.

9. B. LOG_ARCHIVE_DEST_*n* specifies the archive-log location. You can configure up to 10 archive-log destinations. LOG_ARCHIVE_DEST_10 is reserved for the flash recovery area, which is specified by the parameter DB_RECOVERY_FILE_DEST.

10. A. The trace backup is created in a subdirectory under the location specified by the DIAGNOSTIC_DEST parameter—$DIAGNOSTIC_DEST/diag/<dbname>/<instancename>/ trace directory.

11. A. The instance name is not in the control file. The control file has information about the physical database structure.

12. C. The V$DATABASE view in the column LOG_MODE shows whether the database is in ARCHIVELOG mode or in NOARCHIVELOG mode.

13. B. The redo log file records all changes made to the database. The LGWR process writes the redo log buffer entries to the redo log files. These entries are used to roll forward, or to update, the data files during an instance recovery. Archive log files are used for media recovery.

14. D. DB_RECOVERY_FILE_DEST points to the flash recovery area, and this is the default for archived log-file destination number 10.

15. A. The location of the new control files is not valid until an operating-system copy is made of the current control file to the new location(s) and the instance is restarted. The SCOPE=SPFILE option specifies that the parameter change will not take place until a restart. Specifying either MEMORY or BOTH causes an error, because CONTROL_FILES is not a dynamic parameter.

16. B. When adding log-file members, specify the group number, or specify all the existing group members.

17. B. Having the control files on different disks ensures that even if you lose one disk, you lose only one control file. If you lose one of the control files, you can shut down the database and copy a control file, or you can change the CONTROL_FILES parameter and restart the database.

18. A. To put the database into ARCHIVELOG mode, the database must be in the MOUNT state; the control files and all data files that are not offline must be available to change the database to ARCHIVELOG mode.

19. B. You use the ALTER DATABASE ARCHIVELOG command while the database is in the MOUNT state to enable archiving of online redo log files.

20. B, C, D. The substitution variable %d, which represents the database ID, is required only if multiple databases share the same archive-log destination.

Chapter

16

Recovering the Database

ORACLE DATABASE 11g: ADMINISTRATION I EXAM OBJECTIVES COVERED IN THIS CHAPTER:

✓ **Backup and Recovery Concepts**

- Identify the types of failure that can occur in an Oracle database

- Describe ways to tune instance recovery

✓ **Performing Database Recovery**

- Overview of Data Recovery Advisor

- Use Data Recovery Advisor to Perform recovery (Control file, Redo log file, and Data file)

Oracle Database 11*g* makes it easy for you to recover from a number of database failures. In Chapter 15, "Implementing Database Backups," I emphasized the importance of checkpoints, redo log files, and archived log files to maintain a high level of availability and recoverability. I also showed you how to use the flash recovery area and several ways to back up your database. In this chapter, I'll show you how to use those backups effectively when some kind of failure inevitably occurs.

First, you'll understand the kinds of failures that can occur in an Oracle database and explore how they can occur because of mistakes by users or DBAs or because of hardware or software failures that are out of your direct control. Each of these failures can require little or no action whatsoever, as in the case of an instance failure, but at the other end of the spectrum, a crash of the disk containing the SYSTEM tablespace requires a recovery effort.

To balance performance with recoverability, you will learn how to tune instance recovery to minimize the amount of time Oracle will require to recover from an instance failure while still providing a reasonable response time for ongoing transactions. In a nutshell, your job is to increase the mean time between failures (MTBF) by providing redundant components where possible and leveraging other Oracle high-availability features such as Real Application Clusters (RAC) and Streams (an advanced replication technology). Hand in hand with increasing MTBF is decreasing the mean time to recovery (MTTR) to ensure compliance with any service-level agreements you have in place. Last, but certainly not least, these efforts should help you minimize data loss in such a way that committed transactions are never lost.

In this chapter, you will also learn the steps required to recover from the loss of both system-critical and non-system-critical data files for databases that are operating in both ARCHIVELOG and NOARCHIVELOG modes. I'll also show you how to recover from the loss of a control file or a redo log file.

The Data Recovery Advisor was introduced in Oracle 11*g*, which automates most of the recovery tasks and is integrated with Enterprise Manager (EM) Database Control. As with most DBA operations in the database, EM Database Control makes many of these administration tasks easier and less error-prone.

Understanding Types of Database Failure

Database-related failures fall into six general categories. Understanding which category a failure belongs in will help you more quickly understand the nature of the recovery effort you need to use to reverse the effects of the failure and maintain a high level of availability and performance in your database. The six general categories of failures are as follows:

Statement   A single database operation fails, such as a Data Manipulation Language (DML) statement—INSERT, UPDATE, and so on.

User process   A single database connection fails.

Network   A network component between the client and the database server fails, and the session is disconnected from the database.

User error   An error message is not generated, but the operation's result, such as dropping a table, is not what the user intended.

Instance   The database instance crashes unexpectedly.

Media   One or more of the database files is lost, deleted, or corrupted.

In the next six sections, I'll provide details on these failure types and suggest some possible solutions for each one. For one particular type of failure, media failure, I'll provide more detailed solutions for recovery later in this chapter.

Statement Failures

Statement failures occur when a single database operation fails, such as a single INSERT statement or the creation of a table. Table 16.1 shows the most common problems that occur when a statement fails, along with their solutions.

TABLE 16.1   Common Problems and Solutions for When a Statement Fails

Problem	Solution
Attempts to access tables without the appropriate privileges	Provide the appropriate privileges, or create views on the tables and grant privileges on the view.
Running out of space	Add space to the tablespace, increase the user's quota on the tablespace, or enable resumable-space allocation.
Entering invalid data	If constraints and triggers are not in place to enforce data integrity, entering bad data may succeed and cause application issues. DBAs need to work with users to validate and correct data.
Logic errors in applications	Work with developers to correct program errors or provide additional logic in the application to recover gracefully from unavoidable errors.

Although granting user privileges or additional quotas within a tablespace solves many of these problems, also consider whether there are any gaps in the user education process that might lead to some of these problems in the first place.

User-Process Failures

The abnormal termination of a user session is categorized as a *user-process failure*. After a user-process failure, any uncommitted transaction must be cleaned up. The PMON (process monitor) background process periodically checks all user processes to ensure that the session is still connected. If the PMON finds a disconnected session, it rolls back the uncommitted transaction and releases all locks held by the disconnected process. Causes for user-process failures typically fall into one of these categories:

- A user closes their SQL*Plus window without logging out.

- The workstation reboots suddenly before the application can be closed.

- The application program causes an exception and closes before the application can be terminated normally.

A small percentage of user-process failures is generally no cause for concern unless it becomes chronic. A failure may be a sign that user education is lacking—for example, training users to terminate the application gracefully before shutting down their workstation. A DBA intervention is not needed for user-process failures, but administrators must watch for trends, and if happens too often, they need to investigate because there may be application problems or network issues that cause an excessive number of user-process failures. More information may be available in the alert log file showing whether the user process is hitting a bug and whether there are any trace files written.

Network Failures

Depending on the locations of your workstation and your server, getting from your workstation to the server over the network might involve a number of hops; for example, you might traverse several local switches and WAN routers to get to the database. From a network perspective, this configuration provides a number of points where failure can occur. These types of failures are called *network failures*.

In addition to hardware failures between the server and client, a listener process on the Oracle server can fail, or the network card on the server itself can fail. To guard against these kinds of failures, you can provide redundant network paths from your clients to the server, as well as additional listener connections on the Oracle server and redundant network cards on the server.

User-Error Failures

Even if all your redundant hardware is at peak performance and your users have been trained to disconnect from their Oracle sessions properly, users can still inadvertently delete or modify data in tables or drop an index. This is known as a *user-error failure*. Although these operations succeed from a statement point of view, they might not be logically correct: the DROP TABLE command worked fine, but you really didn't want to drop that table!

If data was inadvertently deleted from a table and not yet committed, a ROLLBACK statement will undo the damage. If a COMMIT has already been performed, you have a number of options at your disposal, such as using data in the undo tablespace for a flashback query or using data in the archived and online redo logs with the LogMiner utility, available as a command-line interface or a graphical user interface.

You can recover a dropped table using Oracle's recycle-bin functionality. A dropped table is stored in a special structure in the tablespace and is available for retrieval as long as the space occupied by the table in the tablespace is not needed for new objects. Even if the table is no longer in the tablespace's recycle bin, depending on the criticality of the dropped table, you can use either tablespace point-in-time recovery (TSPITR) or flashback database recovery to recover the table, taking into consideration the potential data loss for other objects stored in the same tablespace for TSPITR or in the database if you use flashback database recovery.

 TSPITR and flashback database recovery are beyond the scope of this book but are covered in more detail in *OCP: Oracle Database 11g Administrator Certified Professional Study Guide* (Sybex, 2009).

If the inadvertent changes are limited to a small number of tables that have few or no interdependencies with other database objects, flashback-table functionality is most likely the right tool to bring back the table to a certain point in time.

Later in this chapter, in the section "Performing Recovery Operations," I'll show you how to recover dropped tables from the recycle bin using the flashback drop functionality, retrieve deleted rows from a table using the flashback query functionality, use the flashback table functionality to bring a table back to a specific point in time along with its dependent objects, and use LogMiner to query online and archived redo logs for the previous state of modified rows.

 The Oracle 11*g* database provides flashback technology, which is aimed to recover from user errors.

Instance Failures

An *instance failure* occurs when the instance shuts down without synchronizing all the database files to the same system change number (SCN), requiring a recovery operation the next time the instance is started. Many of the reasons for an instance failure are out of your direct control; in these situations, you can minimize the impact of these failures by tuning instance recovery. You will learn how to tune instance recovery later in this chapter, in the section "Tuning Instance Recovery."

Here are a few causes for instance failure:

- A power outage

- A server-hardware failure

- Failure of an Oracle background process

- Emergency shutdown procedures (intentional power outage or SHUTDOWN ABORT)

In all these scenarios, the solution is easy: run the STARTUP command, and let Oracle automatically perform instance recovery using the online redo logs and undo data in the undo tablespace. If the cause of the instance failure is related to an Oracle background-process failure, you can use the alert log and process-specific trace files to debug the problem. EM Database Control makes it easy to review the contents of the alert log and any other alerts generated right before the point of failure.

Media Failures

Another type of failure that is somewhat out of your control is media failure. A *media failure* is any type of failure that results in the loss of one or more database files: data files, control files, or redo log files. Although the loss of other database-related files such as an init.ora file or a server-parameter file (spfile) is of great concern, Oracle Corporation does not consider it a media failure. The database file can be lost or corrupted for a number of reasons:

- Failure of a disk drive

- Failure of a disk controller

- Inadvertent deletion or corruption of a database file

Following the best practices defined in Chapter 15—in other words, adequately mirroring control files and redo log files and ensuring that full backups and their subsequent archived redo log files are available—will keep you prepared for any type of media failure.

In the next section, I will show you how to recover from the loss of control files, data files, and redo log files.

Performing Recovery Operations

Once the inevitable database failure occurs, you can perform a relatively quick and painless recovery operation if you have followed the backup guidelines presented in Chapter 15 and clearly understand the types of failures presented earlier in this chapter.

Before I show you how to perform recovery, however, it is important for you to understand how an Oracle instance starts up and what kinds of failures can occur at each startup phase. Understanding the startup phases is important, because some types of recovery operations must occur in a particular phase. Once a database is started, the instance will fail under a number of conditions that I will describe in detail.

Next, I will describe how instance recovery works and how to tune instance recovery, and then show you ways to easily recover from several types of user errors. Finally, I will show you how to recover from media failures due to the loss of both critical and non–system-critical data files.

Understanding Instance Startup

Starting up a database involves several phases, from being shut down to being open and available to users. If certain prerequisites are not present, the database startup halts, and you must take some kind of remedial action to permit the startup to proceed. In the following list are the four basic database states along with their prerequisites after you type the STARTUP command at the SQL*Plus prompt:

SHUTDOWN   No background processes are active. A STARTUP command is used when the database is in this state; the STARTUP command fails if you are in any other state unless you are using STARTUP FORCE to restart an instance.

NOMOUNT   Also known as the STARTED state, the instance must be able to access the initialization-parameter file, either as a text-based init.ora file or as an spfile.

MOUNT   In this state, the instance checks that all control files listed in the initialization-parameter file are present and identical. Even if one of the multiplexed control files is unavailable or corrupted, the instance does not enter the MOUNT state and stays in the NOMOUNT state.

OPEN   Most of the time spent in the instance startup occurs during this phase. All redo log groups must have at least one member available, and all data files that are marked as online must be available.

You are notified in a number of ways that a redo log group member is missing or a data file is missing. If a data file is missing or corrupted, you will get a message while you are running the STARTUP command, as in this example:

```
SQL> startup

ORACLE instance started.

Total System Global Area  197132288 bytes
Fixed Size                   778076 bytes
Variable Size             162537636 bytes
Database Buffers           33554432 bytes
Redo Buffers                 262144 bytes
Database mounted.
```

```
ORA-01157: cannot identify/lock data file 4 - see DBWR trace file
ORA-01110: data file 4: '/u05/oradata/ord/users01.dbf'
```

SQL>

The message in SQL*Plus shows only the first data file that needs attention. You will have to use the dynamic performance view V$RECOVER_FILE to list all the files that need attention. Here is a query against the view V$RECOVER_FILE and a second query joining V$RECOVER_FILE and V$DATAFILE given the previous STARTUP command:

```
SQL> select file#, error from v$recover_file;

    FILE# ERROR
---------- -------------------------------------------------
        4 FILE NOT FOUND
       11 FILE NOT FOUND

SQL> select file#, name from
  2         v$datafile join v$recover_file using (file#);

    FILE# NAME
---------- ---------------------------------------
        4 /u05/oradata/ord/users01.dbf
       11 /u08/oradata/ord/idx02.dbf
SQL>
```

If a data file is offline or taken offline, the instance can still start as long as the data file does not belong to the SYSTEM or UNDO tablespace. Once the instance is started, you can proceed to recover the missing or corrupted data file and subsequently bring it online. If all files are available but out of sync, automatic instance recovery is performed as long as the online redo log files can bring all data files to the same SCN. Otherwise, media recovery is required using archived redo log files.

If a redo log group member is missing, a message is generated in the alert log, but the database will still open.

Keeping an Instance from Failing

Media failures are not always critical, depending on which type of data file is lost. If any of the multiplexed copies of the control file are lost, an entire redo log group is lost, or any data file from the SYSTEM or UNDO tablespace is lost, the instance will fail.

In some cases, the instance becomes unavailable to users but will not shut down; in this case, you can use SHUTDOWN ABORT to force the instance to shut down without resynchronizing the data files with the control file. The next time the instance is started, instance recovery will be performed. If you plan on starting up the instance right after using SHUTDOWN ABORT, you can instead use STARTUP FORCE as shorthand for a SHUTDOWN ABORT and a STARTUP.

 Later in this chapter, I will show you how to recover from the loss of a control file, a redo log file member, or one or more data files.

Recovering from Instance Failure

As I discussed earlier, in the section "Instance Failures," an instance failure is any kind of failure that prevents the synchronization of the database's data files and control files before the instance is shut down.

Oracle automatically recovers from instance failure during *instance recovery*. Instance recovery is initiated by simply starting up the database with the STARTUP command.

 Instance recovery is also known as *crash recovery*.

During a STARTUP operation, Oracle first attempts to read the initialization file, and then it mounts the control file and attempts to open the data files referenced in the control files. If the data files are not synchronized, instance recovery is initiated.

Instance recovery occurs in phases:

Phase 1 Find data files that are out of sync with the control file.

Phase 2 Use the online redo log files to restore the data files to the state before instance failure in a rollforward operation. After the rollforward, data files have committed and uncommitted data.

Phase 3 Open the database. Once the rollforward operation completes, the database is open to users.

Phase 4 Oracle then uses the undo segments to roll back any uncommitted transactions. The rollback operation uses data in the undo tablespace; without a consistent undo tablespace, the rollback operation cannot succeed. After the rollback phase, the data files contain only committed data.

Tuning Instance Recovery

Before a user receives a "Commit complete" message, the new or changed data must be successfully written to a redo log file. At some point in the future, the same information must be used to update the data files; this operation usually lags behind the redo log file write because sequential writes to the redo log file are by nature faster than random writes to one or more data files on disk.

As I discussed in Chapter 15, checkpoints keep track of what still needs to be written from the redo log files to the data files. Any transactions not yet written to the data files are at an SCN after the last checkpoint.

The amount of time required for instance recovery depends on how long it takes to bring the data files up-to-date from the last checkpoint position to the latest SCN in the control file. To prevent performance problems, the distance between the checkpoint position and the end of the redo log group cannot be more than 90 percent of the size of the redo log group.

You can tune instance recovery by setting an MTTR target, in seconds, using the initialization parameter FAST_START_MTTR_TARGET. The default value for this parameter is zero; the maximum is 3,600 seconds (1 hour).

A setting of zero disables the target, which reduces the likelihood of redo logs waiting for writes to the data files. However, if FAST_START_MTTR_TARGET is set to a low nonzero value, writes to the redo logs most likely have to wait for writes to the data files. Although this reduces the amount of time it takes to recover the instance in the case of an instance failure, it affects performance and response time. Setting this value too high can result in an unacceptable amount of time needed to recover the instance after an instance failure.

Two other parameters control instance recovery time:

LOG_CHECKPOINT_TIMEOUT   This is the maximum number of seconds that any new or modified block in the buffer cache waits until it is written to disk.

FAST_START_IO_TARGET   This is similar to FAST_START_MTTR_TARGET, except that the recovery operation is specified as the number of I/Os instead of the number of seconds to finish instance recovery.

Setting either of these parameters overrides FAST_START_MTTR_TARGET. As part of the enhanced manageability features introduced with Oracle9*i*, setting FAST_START_MTTR_TARGET is the easiest and most straightforward way to define your database's recovery time given the time-based constraints included in most typical SLAs.

The EM Database Control interface makes it easy to adjust FAST_START_MTTR_TARGET. On the Availability screen of Database Control, choose Recovery Settings. Figure 16.1 shows the Instance Recovery setting, which you can find in the top section of the Recovery Settings screen.

FIGURE 16.1   Adjusting MTTR for instance recovery

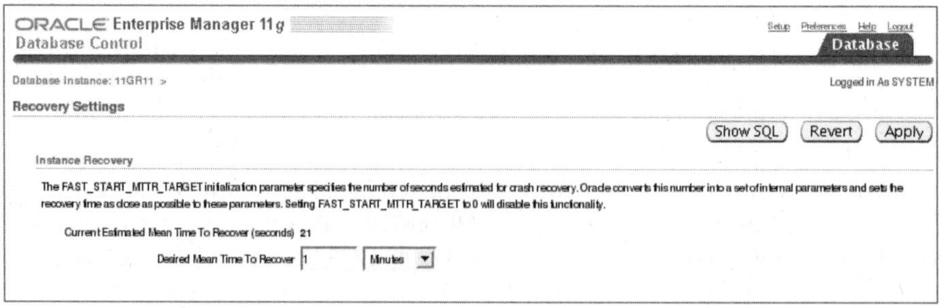

Enter the desired value using seconds or minutes. When you click the Apply button, the new value for FAST_START_MTTR_TARGET goes into effect immediately and stays in effect when the instance is restarted.

Using the SQL*Plus command line, you can accomplish this task by using the ALTER SYSTEM command, as in this example:

```
SQL> alter system set fast_start_mttr_target=60 scope=both;
System altered.
```

Using SCOPE=BOTH, the new value of the parameter takes effect immediately and stays in effect the next time the instance is restarted.

Recovering from User Errors

Earlier in this chapter, in the section "User-Error Failures," you learned a number of scenarios in which a user's data was inadvertently changed or deleted or a table was dropped. In the following sections, you'll learn quite a few helpful tasks, such as how to do the following:

- Use flashback query to retrieve selected rows from a previous state of a table

- Recover a table using flashback drop and a tablespace's recycle bin

- Bring an entire table and its dependent objects (such as indexes) back to a specific point in time using flashback table

- Roll back a specific transaction and its dependent transactions using flashback transaction

- Query previous transactions in the online and archived redo logs using the LogMiner utility

Using Flashback Query

One of the features introduced in Oracle9*i* was called *flashback query*. It allows a user to "go back in time" and view the contents of a table as it existed at some point in the recent past. A flashback query looks a lot like a standard SQL SELECT statement, with the addition of the AS OF TIMESTAMP clause.

Before users can take advantage of the flashback query feature, you, the DBA, must perform two tasks:

- Make sure there is an undo tablespace in the database that is large enough to retain changes made by all users for a specified period of time. This is the same tablespace that is used to support COMMIT and ROLLBACK functionality (discussed in Chapter 13, "Managing Data and Undo").

- Specify how long the undo information will be retained for use by flashback queries by using the initialization parameter UNDO_RETENTION. This parameter is specified in seconds; therefore, if you specify UNDO_RETENTION=172800 (default is 900), the undo information for flashback queries can be available for up to two days.

The key to the flashback query functionality is using the AS OF TIMESTAMP clause in the SELECT statement; you can specify the timestamp as any valid expression that evaluates to a date or timestamp value. In the following example, you want to query the EMPLOYEES table as it existed 15 minutes ago:

```
SQL> SELECT employee_id, last_name, email
     FROM hr.employees
     AS OF TIMESTAMP (systimestamp - interval '15' minute)
     WHERE employee_id = 101;


EMPLOYEE_ID LAST_NAME                EMAIL
----------- --------------------- --------------------
        101 Kochhar                  NKOCHHAR
```

You can just as easily specify an absolute time of day to retrieve the contents of the row at that time, as in this example:

```
SQL> SELECT employee_id, last_name, email
     FROM hr.employees
     AS OF TIMESTAMP
        (to_timestamp ('01-Sep-04 16:18:57.845993',
                       'DD-Mon-RR HH24:MI:SS.FF'))
     WHERE employee_id = 101;


EMPLOYEE_ID LAST_NAME                EMAIL
----------- --------------------- --------------------
        101 Kochhar                  NTKOCHHAR
```

If your flashback query requires undo data that is no longer available in the undo tablespace, you will receive an error message:

```
SQL> SELECT employee_id, last_name, email
     FROM hr.employees
     AS OF TIMESTAMP (systimestamp - interval '10' month)
     WHERE employee_id = 101;


select employee_id, last_name, email
       *
ERROR at line 1:
ORA-08180: no snapshot found based on specified time
```

Real World Scenario

Using Flashback Query to Retrieve Missing Rows

Recently an application administrator in my company inadvertently deleted a bunch of rows from a database table and committed the transaction. He learned about the deletion with the wrong WHERE clause only when users started calling him about the missing data on their screens and the various errors they were getting.

Panicked, the application administrator called his manager and told her about what happened, and they planned an outage for the affected application and a couple of other applications hosted in the same database.

In our company, the DBA is the last person to know about issues, but by the time a problem comes to the DBA, it is a crisis.

The application administrator told the DBA team that there was a recovery situation and that he had arranged for all the outages and notifications. One of our DBAs asked the application administrator the time of the data deletion and the table name. The DBA did a query similar to the following to show the records the administrator deleted. Luckily, there were not many transactions going on in the database, because users were getting errors and the changed rows were still available in the undo. If there were many transactions, Oracle could have overwritten the committed transaction's rollback space (depending on the UNDO_RENTENTION setting):

```
SELECT * FROM vms.dvbt606a
AS OF TIMESTAMP to_timestamp ('12-Sep-08 12:20', 'DD-Mon-RR HH24:MI');
```

Then the DBA got the WHERE clause from the administrator to filter out the rows that the administrator deleted and inserted those rows into the original table using the following SQL statement:

```
INSERT INTO vms.dvbt606a
SELECT * FROM vms.dvbt606a
AS OF TIMESTAMP to_timestamp ('12-Sep-08 12:20', 'DD-Mon-RR HH24:MI')
WHERE TRANS_DATE BETWEEN TO_DATE('01-MAY-08','DD-MON-YY')
      AND TO_DATE('31-MAY-08','DD-MON-YY');
```

We did not have to take any applications offline, and the whole recovery operation took less than 15 minutes after coming to the DBA. We could have also used the FLASHBACK TABLE feature, which would have made the recovery sooner (and there would be no need to know the WHERE clause used for deletion), but nobody thought of it.

Using Flashback Drop and the Recycle Bin

Another user-recovery flashback feature, *flashback drop*, lets you restore a dropped table without using tablespace point-in-time recovery. Although tablespace point-in-time recovery could effectively restore a table and its contents to a point in time before it was dropped, it is potentially time-consuming and has the side effect of losing work from other transactions that occurred within the same tablespace after the table was dropped.

In the following sections, I will talk about the new logical structure available in each tablespace—the recycle bin—and how you can query the recycle bin and retrieve dropped objects from it. I will also describe some minor limitations involved in using the recycle bin.

Recycle-Bin Concepts

The *recycle bin* is a logical structure within each tablespace that holds dropped tables and objects related to the tables, such as indexes. The space associated with the dropped table is not immediately available but shows up in the data dictionary view DBA_FREE_SPACE. When space pressure occurs in the tablespace, objects in the recycle bin are deleted in a first-in, first-out (FIFO) fashion, maximizing the amount of time that the most recently dropped object remains in the recycle bin.

The dropped object still belongs to the owner and still counts against the quota for the owner in the tablespace; in fact, the table itself is still directly accessible from the recycle bin, as you will see in subsequent examples.

Retrieving Dropped Tables from the Recycle Bin

You retrieve a dropped table from the recycle bin at the SQL command line by using the FLASHBACK TABLE...TO BEFORE DROP command. In the following example, the user retrieves the table ORDER_ITEMS from the recycle bin after discovering that the table was inadvertently dropped:

```
SQL> select order_id, line_item_id, product_id
  2  from order_items
  3  where rownum < 5;
from order_items
     *
ERROR at line 2:
ORA-00942: table or view does not exist


SQL> flashback table order_items to before drop;

Flashback complete.

SQL> select order_id, line_item_id, product_id
  2  from order_items
  3  where rownum < 5;
```

```
ORDER_ID LINE_ITEM_ID PRODUCT_ID
---------- ------------ ----------
      2355            1       2289
      2356            1       2264
      2357            1       2211
      2358            1       1781
```

SQL>

If the table ORDER_ITEMS was re-created after it was dropped, Gary would add the RENAME TO clause in the FLASHBACK TABLE command to give the restored table a new name, as in the following example:

```
SQL> drop table order_items;

Table dropped.

SQL> flashback table order_items to before drop
  2        rename to order_items_old_version;

Flashback complete.

SQL> select order_id, line_item_id, product_id
  2  from order_items_old_version
  3  where rownum < 5;

ORDER_ID LINE_ITEM_ID PRODUCT_ID
---------- ------------ ----------
      2355            1       2289
      2356            1       2264
      2357            1       2211
      2358            1       1781
```

SQL>

If the table to be retrieved from the recycle bin was dropped more than once and you want to retrieve an incarnation of the table before the most recent one, you can use the name of the table in the recycle bin; you can query the view RECYCLEBIN or use the SHOW RECYCLEBIN command.

Recycle-Bin Considerations and Limitations

A few limitations are associated with the recycle bin:

- Only non-SYSTEM locally managed tablespaces can have a recycle bin. However, dependent objects in a dictionary-managed tablespace are protected if the dropped object is in a locally managed tablespace.

- A table's dependent objects are saved in the recycle bin when the table is dropped, except for bitmap join indexes, referential integrity constraints (foreign key constraints), and materialized view logs.

- Indexes are protected only if the table is dropped first; explicitly dropping an index does not place the index into the recycle bin.

Using Flashback Table

Flashback table allows you to recover one or more tables to a specific point in time without having to use more time-consuming recovery operations such as tablespace point-in-time recovery or flashback database that can also affect the availability of the rest of the database. Flashback table works in place by rolling back only the changes made to the table or tables and their dependent objects, such as indexes. Flashback table is different from flashback drop; flashback table undoes recent transactions to an existing table, whereas flashback drop recovers a dropped table. Flashback table uses data in the undo tablespace, whereas flashback drop uses the recycle bin.

The FLASHBACK TABLE command brings one or more tables back to a point in time before any number of logical corruptions have occurred on the tables. To be able to flash back a table, you must enable row movement for the table. Because DML operations are used to bring the table back to its former state, the row IDs in the table change. As a result, flashback table is not a viable option for applications that depend on the table's row IDs to remain constant.

In the following example, you find out that someone in the HR department has accidentally deleted all the employees in department 60, the IT department, along with the row for IT in the DEPARTMENTS table. Because this happened less than 15 minutes ago, you are sure that there is enough undo information to support a flashback table operation.

Before running the FLASHBACK TABLE command, you confirm that the row in DEPARTMENTS for the IT department is still missing using this query:

```
SQL> SELECT * FROM hr.departments
     WHERE department_name = 'IT';


no rows selected
```

Next, you flash back the table to 15 minutes ago, specifying both tables in the same command, as follows:

```
SQL> FLASHBACK TABLE hr.employees, hr.departments
     TO TIMESTAMP systimestamp - interval '15' minute;


Flashback complete.
```

Finally, you check to see whether the IT department is truly back in the table:

```
SQL> SELECT * FROM hr.departments
    WHERE department_name = 'IT';


DEPARTMENT_ID DEPARTMENT_NAME    MANAGER_ID LOCATION_ID
------------- ------------------ ---------- -----------
          60 IT                        103        1400
```

If you flash back either too far or not far enough, you can simply rerun the FLASHBACK TABLE command with a different timestamp or SCN, as long as the undo data is still available.

Although the rest of the database is unaffected by a flashback table operation, the FLASHBACK TABLE command acquires exclusive DML locks on the tables involved in the flashback. This is usually not an availability issue, because the users who would normally use the table are waiting for the flashback operation to complete anyway!

Integrity constraints are not violated when one or more tables are flashed back; this is why you typically group tables related by integrity constraints or parent-child relationships in the FLASHBACK TABLE command. When a flashback operation is in progress, the triggers on the table are disabled. If you want the triggers to fire during the flashback operation, add the ENABLE TRIGGERS clause to the FLASHBACK TABLE statement, as in the following example.

```
SQL> FLASHBACK TABLE hr.employees
    TO TIMESTAMP TO_TIMESTAMP('02NOV08 22:00'. 'DDMONYY HH24:MI')
    ENABLE TRIGGERS;
```

 WARNING To be able to perform a flashback table operation, the table must have ROW MOVEMENT enabled. Enable row movement using ALTER TABLE <name> ENABLE ROW MOVEMENT.

Using EM Database Control to Perform Table Recovery

You can perform recovery operations using EM Database Control. On the Availability screen, choose Perform Recovery under the Manage section of Backup/Recovery. On the Perform Recovery screen, choose Tables as the recovery scope. As you can see in Figure 16.2, choosing Tables as the recovery scope gives you two options:

- Flashback Existing Tables
- Flashback Dropped Tables

FIGURE 16.2 Table recovery screen

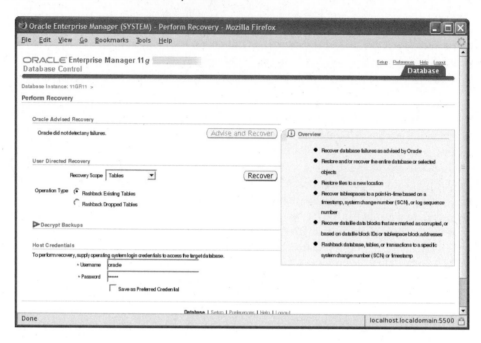

Choose Flashback Existing Tables to roll back the table to a previous state. Click Recover to get to the Perform Object Level Recovery screen, as shown in Figure 16.3. Here you have four options to choose from:

- Evaluate Row Changes and Transactions to Decide on a Point in Time
- Flashback to a Timestamp
- Flashback to a Restore Point
- Flashback to a Known SCN

Based on the option you choose, you will be presented with one of three screens. Choose Flashback to a Timestamp for this example. You will be presented with a screen to choose the tables that you want to flash back, as shown in Figure 16.4.

Choose the tables you want to perform flashback on, and click Next. A summary screen will be shown for you to review the specifications such as timestamp, corresponding SCNs, and table names. Click Submit to perform the flashback operation.

To retrieve a dropped table, choose Flashback Dropped Tables from the screen shown earlier, in Figure 16.2. You will be presented with all the tables that are in the recycle bin, as shown in Figure 16.5. Choose the table(s) you want to restore, and click Next.

FIGURE 16.3   Perform Object Level Recovery screen

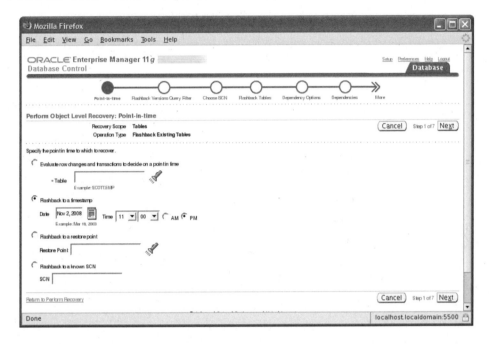

FIGURE 16.4   Perform Object Level Recovery: Flashback Tables screen

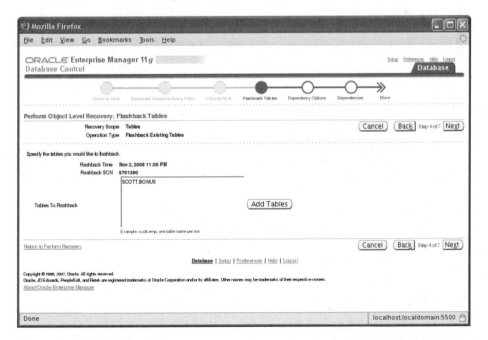

FIGURE 16.5   Perform Object Level Recovery: Dropped Objects Selection screen

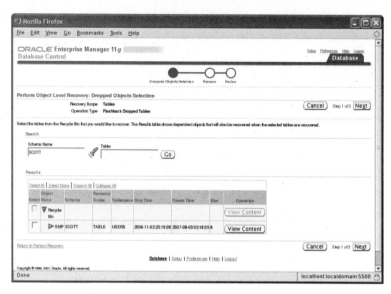

On the next screen, you will have the option to rename the restored table or to keep the original name. A summary screen, as shown in Figure 16.6, will be displayed with the impact analysis.

FIGURE 16.6   Perform Object Level Recovery: Review screen

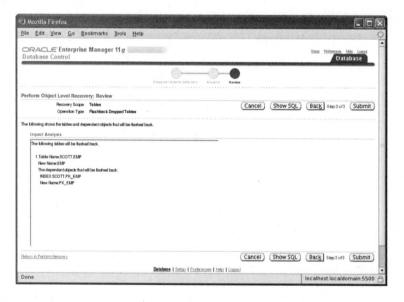

Click Submit to retrieve the dropped table from the recycle bin.

Using Flashback Transaction

You can use the flashback transaction technology to undo a transaction and its dependent transactions. The DBMS_FLASHBACK.TRANSACTION_BACKOUT procedure is used to accomplish this task.

You must meet the following prerequisites to perform a flashback transaction on an Oracle 11*g* database:

- The database must be in ARCHIVELOG mode.

- Supplemental logging must be enabled in the database using ALTER DATABASE ADD SUPPLEMENTAL LOG DATA.

- A supplemental log data primary key should be created using the statement ALTER DATA-BASE ADD SUPPLEMENTAL LOG DATA (PRIMARY KEY) COLUMNS.

- The user performing the flashback transaction must have the SELECT ANY TRANSACTION privilege.

- The user should have the EXECUTE privilege on DBMS_FLASHBACK.

- The user also should have appropriate DML privileges on the tables (such as INSERT/ UPDATE/DELETE).

Using EM Database Control, you can perform the flashback transaction. In the Perform Recovery screen (shown earlier, in Figure 16.2), choose Transactions as the recovery scope. You will be presented with the screen shown in Figure 16.7.

FIGURE 16.7   Flashback Transaction: Perform Query screen

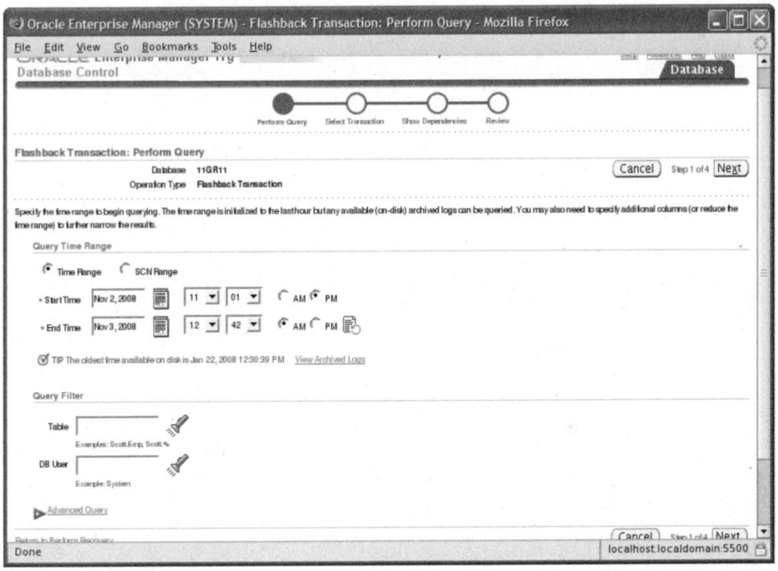

Specify the time range of transactions you want to recover. If your database is very active, you will be able to restrict the number of transactions retrieved for the time range by specifying a query filter using the table name or username. When you click Next, Oracle will mine the transactions that happened between the time range and give you the screen shown in Figure 16.8.

FIGURE 16.8 Flashback Transaction: Select Transaction screen

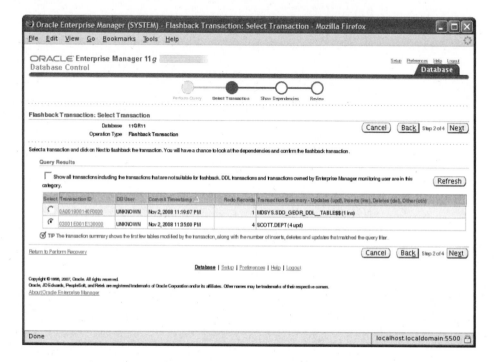

Here you can select the transaction you want to revert. To see the SQL statements that made the change, click the transaction ID. Click Next to see the summary screen, as shown in Figure 16.9.

Here clicking the Show Undo SQL Script button will show you the statements that are run to undo the changes made in the transaction. Click Finish to complete the flashback-transaction operation.

FIGURE 16.9 Flashback Transaction: Review screen

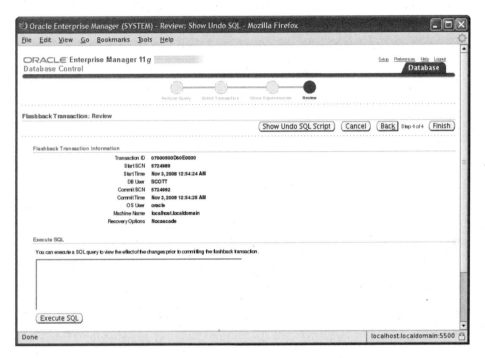

Using LogMiner

Oracle LogMiner is another tool you can use to view past activity in the database. The LogMiner tool can help find changed records in redo log files by using a set of PL/SQL procedures and functions. LogMiner extracts all DDL and DML activity from the redo log files for viewing via the dynamic performance view V$LOGMNR_CONTENTS. In addition to extracting the DDL and DML statements used to change the database, the V$LOGMNR_CONTENTS view also contains the DML statements needed to reverse the change made to the database. This is a good tool for not only pinpointing when changes were made to a table but also for automatically generating the SQL statements needed to reverse those changes.

LogMiner works differently from Oracle's flashback query feature. The flashback query feature allows a user to see the contents of a table at a specified time in the past, while Log-Miner can search a time period for all changes against the table. A flashback query uses the undo information stored in the undo tablespace; LogMiner uses redo logs, both online and archived. Both tools can be useful for tracking down how and when changes to database objects took place.

You can configure and use LogMiner either by using a SQL command line or by using EM Database Control (choose View and Manage Transactions from the Availability screen). Figure 16.10 shows the Log Miner screen.

FIGURE 16.10 LogMiner screen

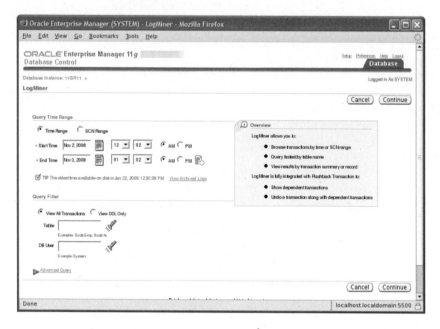

Specify the time range to mine the transactions. When you click Next, the screen shown in Figure 16.11 will be displayed with all the SQL statements that went into the database during the time range. Click the transaction ID to see all the related SQL statements in the transaction.

FIGURE 16.11 LogMiner Results screen

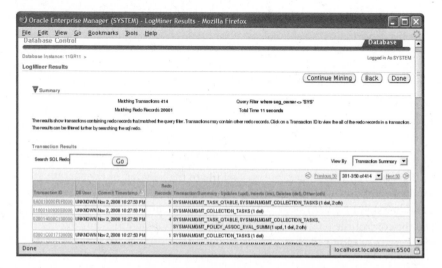

When you click a transaction, you can see all the related transactions and have the option to flash back the transaction. Click the Flashback Transaction button to undo the changes made in that transaction. You can view the SQL statements that are executed in that transaction using the SQL Redo column, as shown in Figure 16.12.

FIGURE 16.12   LogMiner's Transaction Details screen

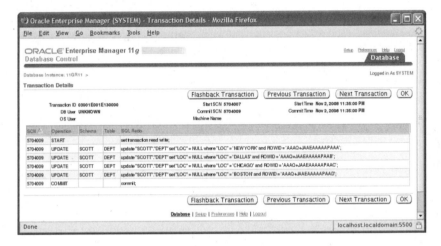

 LogMiner does not actually undo the change; it only provides the statements that you can use to undo the change. You can extract and run any or all DML commands you find in the redo logs, keeping in mind any integrity constraints in place for the tables you are modifying. The Flashback Transaction button on the LogMiner screen invokes the flashback transaction feature of the database discussed earlier in the chapter.

Recovering from Loss of a Control File

Losing one of the multiplexed control files immediately aborts the instance. Assuming you have not lost every control file, recovering from this failure is fairly straightforward.

Here are the steps to recover from the loss of a control file:

1. If the instance is not shut down, use SHUTDOWN ABORT to force a complete shutdown.

2. Copy one of the good copies of the control file to the location of the corrupted or missing control file. If the corrupted or missing control file resided on a failed disk, copy it to another suitable location instead, and update the initialization-parameter file to update the control-file reference. Alternatively, you can temporarily remove the reference from the initialization-parameter file until you find a suitable location. However, it is

highly desirable to maintain at least two, if not more, copies of the control file available in the case of another media failure.

3. Start the instance with STARTUP.

In the following example, you use a server-parameter file (spfile) for initialization parameters, and you decide to temporarily do without a third multiplexed control file until the disk containing the lost control file is repaired. You'll change the initialization-parameter CONTROL_FILES using the ALTER SYSTEM … SCOPE=SPFILE command when the instance is started in NOMOUNT mode. You cannot start in MOUNT mode because that mode checks for the existence of all copies of the control file, and as far as the spfile is concerned, you are still missing a control file.

The first step is to start the database in NOMOUNT mode, as you can see in this example:

```
SQL> startup nomount

ORACLE instance started.

Total System Global Area   188743680 bytes
Fixed Size                    778036 bytes
Variable Size              162537676 bytes
Database Buffers            25165824 bytes
Redo Buffers                  262144 bytes
SQL>
```

Looking at the dynamic performance view V$SPPARAMETER, you can see that you still have three copies of the control file referenced, but the disk containing the third copy has failed:

```
SQL> select name, value from v$spparameter
     where name = 'control_files';

NAME             VALUE
---------------  -----------------------------------------------------------
control_files    /u02/oradata/ord/control01.ctl
control_files    /u06/oradata/ord/control02.ctl
control_files    /u07/oradata/ord/control03.ctl
```

In the next step, you change the value of CONTROL_FILES in the spfile and restart the instance, as you can see here:

```
SQL> alter system set control_files =
     '/u02/oradata/ord/control01.ctl',
     '/u06/oradata/ord/control02.ctl'
     scope = spfile;

System altered.
```

```
SQL> shutdown immediate
ORA-01507: database not mounted
ORACLE instance shut down.

SQL> startup
ORACLE instance started.

Total System Global Area  188743680 bytes
Fixed Size                   778036 bytes
Variable Size             162537676 bytes
Database Buffers           25165824 bytes
Redo Buffers                 262144 bytes
Database mounted.
Database opened.
SQL>
```

Once the instance is restarted successfully, you confirm that the control file is no longer being referenced, as you can see in this query:

```
SQL> select name, value from v$spparameter
     where name = 'control_files';
```

```
NAME            VALUE
--------------- --------------------------------------
control_files   /u02/oradata/ord/control01.ctl
control_files   /u06/oradata/ord/control02.ctl
```

You still have two multiplexed copies of the control file; therefore, you are covered in case of a media failure of the disk containing one of the remaining control files.

Using the Data Recovery Advisor

The Data Recovery Advisor (DRA) is a new tool introduced in the Oracle 11*g* database that automatically diagnoses database failures and determines the appropriate recovery options. In addition to recommending the recovery options available, it can perform the recovery after the DBA confirms the operation. DRA can proactively check for failures, before the database process detects corruption and signals an error.

DRA has user interfaces through the GUI of EM Database Control and through the command-line utility RMAN. DRA in Oracle 11*g* Release 1 supports only single-instance databases; it does not support RAC databases.

You can invoke the Data Recovery Advisor from EM Database Control using any of the following methods:

- Using the Perform Recovery screen shown earlier in Figure 16.2. If there are any failures detected, the Advise and Recover button will be enabled, as shown in Figure 16.13. It will also display a summary of failures with the failure description.

FIGURE 16.13 Invoking DRA from Perform Recovery screen

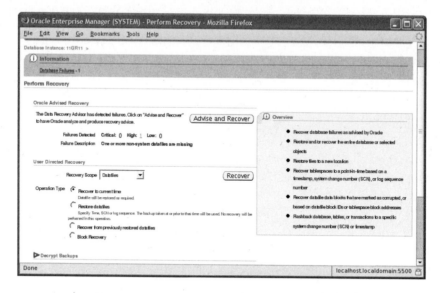

- Using the Support Workbench. Support Workbench is invoked from the Software and Support tab of EM Database Control. The Checker Findings tab in Support Workbench shows the failures in the database, as shown in Figure 16.14. By clicking the Launch Recovery Advisor button, you can invoke DRA.

- Using the Advisor Central page by clicking the Data Recovery Advisor link under Advisors.

FIGURE 16.14 Invoking DRA from the Support Workbench screen

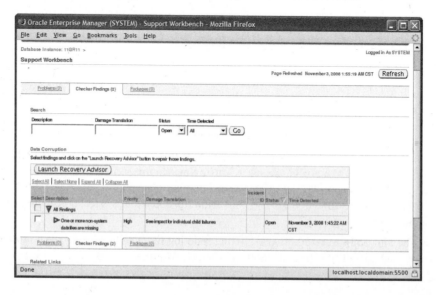

The Health Monitor (HM) tool in the Oracle 11*g* database proactively monitors the health of the database. It assesses data failures and reports to the Data Recovery Advisor. DRA consolidates the findings of HM into failures and assigns a priority based on the failure.

Failure checks in the database can be reactive or proactive. When an error occurs in the database, reactive checks are automatically executed. The following are examples of data failures where the DRA can analyze and suggest repair options:

- Missing data files
- Data files with incorrect OS permissions
- Offline tablespaces
- Corrupted data files (physical corruption)
- Corrupt index entry or dictionary entry (logical corruption)
- I/O failures
- Number of open files exceeded

In the following sections, you will look at the various scenarios of media-failure errors and see how DRA can help analyze and fix errors.

Recovering from the Loss of a Redo Log File

A database instance stays up as long as at least one member of a redo log group is available. The alert log records the loss of a redo log group member; as with most database status information, EM Database Control allows you to easily review the contents of the alert log.

The dynamic performance view V$LOGFILE provides the status of each member of each redo log file member of each redo log group; the STATUS column is defined as follows:

INVALID The file is corrupted or missing.

STALE This redo log file member is new and has never been used.

DELETED The file is no longer being used.

<blank> The redo log file is in use and is not corrupted.

When you are aware of a missing or deleted redo log group member, follow these three steps to ensure that you maintain a maximum level of redundancy. Losing the remaining member(s) of the redo log group will cause the instance to fail.

1. Verify which redo log group member is missing.

2. Archive the redo log group's contents; if you clear this redo log group before archiving it, you must back up the full database to ensure maximum recoverability of the database in case of the loss of a data file. Use the command ALTER SYSTEM ARCHIVE LOG GROUP *groupnum*; to force the archive operation. (*groupnum* refers to the redo log group that you want to archive.)

3. Clear the log group to re-create the missing redo log file members using the command ALTER DATABASE CLEAR LOGFILE GROUP *groupnum*;. Alternatively, you can replace the missing member by copying one of the good group members to the location of the

missing member; using ALTER DATABASE CLEAR LOGFILE GROUP has the advantage of being platform-independent.

In this example, you lose a redo log file group member and check the status of the redo log file groups using V$LOGFILE:

```
SQL> select * from v$logfile
    order by group#;

    GROUP# STATUS  TYPE    MEMBER                          IS_
---------- ------- ------- ------------------------------- ---
         1         ONLINE  /u07/oradata/ord/redo01.log     NO
         1         ONLINE  /u08/oradata/ord/redo01.log     NO
         2         ONLINE  /u07/oradata/ord/redo02.log     NO
         2         ONLINE  /u08/oradata/ord/redo02.log     NO
         3         ONLINE  /u07/oradata/ord/redo03.log     NO
         3         ONLINE  /u08/oradata/ord/redo03.log     NO


SQL> ! rm /u08/oradata/ord/redo01.log


SQL> select * from v$logfile order by group#;

    GROUP# STATUS  TYPE    MEMBER                          IS_
---------- ------- ------- ------------------------------- ---
         1         ONLINE  /u07/oradata/ord/redo01.log     NO
         1 INVALID ONLINE  /u08/oradata/ord/redo01.log     NO
         2         ONLINE  /u07/oradata/ord/redo02.log     NO
         2         ONLINE  /u08/oradata/ord/redo02.log     NO
         3         ONLINE  /u07/oradata/ord/redo03.log     NO
         3         ONLINE  /u08/oradata/ord/redo03.log     NO
```

It appears that group number 1 has a missing member, so you want to archive group number 1 using the ALTER SYSTEM ARCHIVE command:

```
SQL> alter system archive log group 1;
```

Finally, you can re-create the missing redo log file group member using the ALTER DATA-BASE command mentioned in step 3:

```
SQL> alter database clear logfile group 1;

Database altered.
```

Checking the view V$LOGFILE again, you can see that the redo log group member is no longer invalid:

```
SQL> select * from v$logfile order by group#;
```

GROUP#	STATUS	TYPE	MEMBER	IS_
1		ONLINE	/u07/oradata/ord/redo01.log	NO
1		ONLINE	/u08/oradata/ord/redo01.log	NO
2		ONLINE	/u07/oradata/ord/redo02.log	NO
2		ONLINE	/u08/oradata/ord/redo02.log	NO
3		ONLINE	/u07/oradata/ord/redo03.log	NO
3		ONLINE	/u08/oradata/ord/redo03.log	NO

```
6 rows selected.
```

By reviewing the contents of the alert log using either the EM Database Control interface by clicking the Alert Log Content link at the bottom of the Database Control home page or by reviewing the file $ORACLE_BASE/admin/ord/bdump/alert_ord.log, you can see the failures associated with the missing redo log group member:

```
Sun Sep 12 17:31:43 2008
ARC1: Evaluating archive    log 1 thread 1 sequence 2500
Sun Sep 12 17:31:43 2008
Errors in file
/u01/app/oracle/diag/rdbms/11gr11/11GR11/trace/11GR11_ora_3506.trc:
ORA-00313: open failed for members of log group 1 of thread 1
ORA-00312: online log 1 thread 1: '/u02/app/oracle/oradata/11GR11/redo01.log'
ORA-27037: unable to obtain file status
Linux Error: 2: No such file or directory
Additional information: 3
```

The Database Recovery Advisor knows about the failure. You can see the error reported on the EM Database Control home page, as shown in Figure 16.15.

FIGURE 16.15 Critical errors in the Alerts section of home page

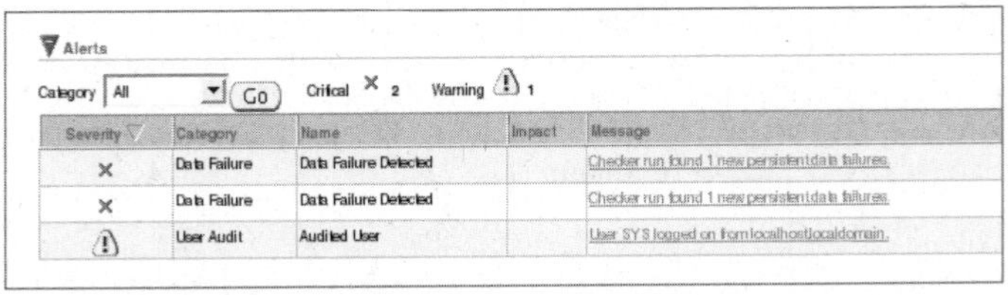

When you invoke DRA, you can see more details about these failures. As shown in Figure 16.16, you can click the Advise button to see more information about how this failure could have happened and how to remediate the failure.

FIGURE 16.16   View and Manage Failures screen

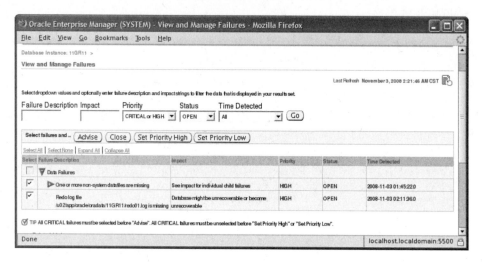

You can increase or decrease the priority of a failure by using the Set Priority High and Set Priority Low buttons. If you have taken care of the issue or if you do not want to resolve a noncritical failure, you can use the Close button to close the failure incident.

To fix a missing redo log group member, you can use the actions such as Switch Log File and Clear Log File on the Redo Log Groups screen.

Recovering from the Loss of a Non–System-Critical Data File

If you lose a non-system-critical data file (in other words, not the SYSTEM or UNDO tablespace), your options are similar to those when you lose a system-critical data file, except that most of your recovery effort in ARCHIVELOG mode can occur while the database is open to users, who can use tablespaces other than the one being recovered.

Loss of a Non-System-Critical Data File in NOARCHIVELOG Mode

The loss of a non-system-critical data file in NOARCHIVELOG mode requires the complete restoration of the database, including the control files and all data files, not just the missing data files. As a result, you must reenter any changes made to the database since the last backup.

Loss of a Non-System-Critical Data File in ARCHIVELOG Mode

The loss of a non-system-critical data file in ARCHIVELOG mode affects only objects that are in the missing file, and recovery can proceed while the rest of the database is online.

Because you are in ARCHIVELOG mode, no committed transactions in the lost data file will have to be reentered.

Recovering from the loss of a non–system-critical data file is not quite as complicated as the recovery from a system-critical data file, which I will cover in the next section; the database is continuously available to all users, except for the data files being recovered.

In the EM Database Control interface, invoke the Data Recovery Advisor. Choose the failure you want to fix, and click the Advice button. Figure 16.17 shows the Manual Actions screen.

FIGURE 16.17   Manual Actions screen of DRA

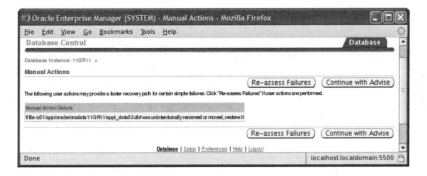

Click the Continue with Advise button to see the recovery advice. DRA generates a RMAN script to execute, as shown in Figure 16.18. You can run this script manually using the RMAN command line with no modification.

FIGURE 16.18   Recovery Advice screen of DRA

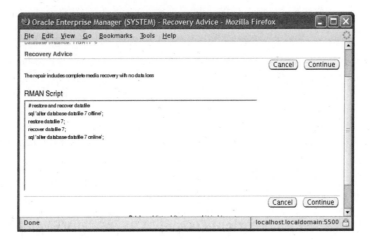

Click Continue to review and submit a job to start the restore and recovery.

You can also recover from the failure without using DRA. On the Perform Recovery screen, choose Datafiles as the recovery scope. You will be presented with four options to recover, as shown in Figure 16.19:

- **Recover to Current Time:** Restore the data file from backup, and recover the data file using archive log and redo log files.

- **Restore Datafiles:** No recovery is performed.

- **Recover from Previously Restored Datafile:** Continue recovery after the data file restore.

- **Block Recovery:** Recover the corrupted blocks in a data file.

FIGURE 16.19   User-directed recovery of a data file

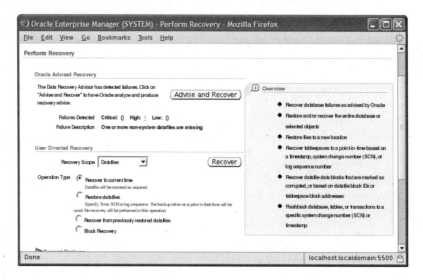

You have the option to restore the data file to its original location or to another location. You also have the option to edit the RMAN script generated. When you click Submit, the RMAN script is executed, and the data file is recovered. Because the database is in ARCHIVELOG mode, you will not lose any committed transactions in the USERS tablespace.

You can run the RMAN statement LIST FAILURE at the RMAN command prompt, and you will see output similar to the following:

```
$ rman target /

Recovery Manager: Release 11.1.0.6.0 - Production on Mon Nov 3 02:57:39 2008
Copyright (c) 1982, 2007, Oracle.  All rights reserved.
connected to target database: 11GR11 (DBID=4110949673)
```

```
RMAN> list failure;

using target database control file instead of recovery catalog
List of Database Failures
=========================


Failure ID Priority Status     Time Detected Summary
---------- -------- --------- ------------- -------
482        HIGH     OPEN       03-NOV-08
           One or more non-system datafiles are missing

RMAN>
```

The ADVISE FAILURE commands lists the failures. You can list all failures, or you can specify options such as CRITICAL, HIGH, so on. Here is some output from the ADVISE FAILURE statement:

```
RMAN> advise failure all;

List of Database Failures
=========================


Failure ID Priority Status     Time Detected Summary
---------- -------- --------- ------------- -------
482        HIGH     OPEN       03-NOV-08
           One or more non-system datafiles are missing

analyzing automatic repair options; this may take some time
using channel ORA_DISK_1
using channel ORA_DISK_2
analyzing automatic repair options complete

Mandatory Manual Actions
========================
no manual actions available

Optional Manual Actions
=======================
1. If file /u01/app/oracle/oradata/11GR11/appl_data02.dbf
was unintentionally renamed or moved, restore it
```

```
Automated Repair Options
========================
Option Repair Description
------ ------------------
1       Restore and recover datafile 7
  Strategy: The repair includes complete media recovery with no data loss
  Repair script: /u01/app/oracle/diag/rdbms/11gr11/11GR11/hm/reco_2087308400.hm

RMAN>
```

To fix the failures using DRA, you can use the command REPAIR FAILURE, as shown next. It asks for your confirmation before performing the restore and recovery. If you do not want the confirmation, include the NOPROMPT clause, which will automatically repair all HIGH and CRITICAL priority failures. The REPAIR FAILURE command can be executed only after performing the ADVISE FAILURE.

```
RMAN> repair failure;

Strategy: The repair includes complete media recovery with no data loss
Repair script: /u01/app/oracle/diag/rdbms/11gr11/11GR11/hm/reco_2087308400.hm

contents of repair script:
   # restore and recover datafile
   sql 'alter database datafile 7 offline';
   restore datafile 7;
   recover datafile 7;
   sql 'alter database datafile 7 online';

Do you really want to execute the above repair (enter YES or NO)? YES
executing repair script

sql statement: alter database datafile 7 offline

Starting restore at 03-NOV-08
using channel ORA_DISK_1
using channel ORA_DISK_2

channel ORA_DISK_1: starting datafile backup set restore
channel ORA_DISK_1: specifying datafile(s) to restore from backup set
channel ORA_DISK_1: restoring datafile 00007 to
/u01/app/oracle/oradata/11GR11/appl_data02.dbf
channel ORA_DISK_1: reading from backup piece /backup/database/0ejun1kq_1_1
```

```
channel ORA_DISK_1: piece handle=/backup/database/0ejun1kq_1_1
 tag=BACKUP_11GR11_0000_110208102644
channel ORA_DISK_1: restored backup piece 1
channel ORA_DISK_1: restore complete, elapsed time: 00:00:07
Finished restore at 03-NOV-08

Starting recover at 03-NOV-08
using channel ORA_DISK_1
using channel ORA_DISK_2

starting media recovery

archived log for thread 1 with sequence 193 is already on disk as file
 /flash_recovery_area/11GR11/archivelog/2008_11_02/o1_mf_1_193_4jwzm1yv_.arc
... ... ...
media recovery complete, elapsed time: 00:00:01
Finished recover at 03-NOV-08

sql statement: alter database datafile 7 online
repair failure complete

RMAN>
```

When you run REPAIR FAILURE, the Data Recovery Advisor closes the failure after successfully repairing the failure. As you saw in the Figure 16.16, you can increase or decrease the priority of a failure by using the CHANGE FAILURE command in RMAN. You can also close a failure using this command.

```
RMAN> CHANGE FAILURE 2 PRIORITY LOW;
RMAN> CHANGE FAILURE 5 CLOSE;
```

Data Recovery Advisor Views

The Data Recovery Advisor added four new views to the Oracle 11*g* data dictionary. These views start with V$IR_.

- V$IR_FAILURE: List of all the failures in the database (the same result you see with the LIST FAILURE command)

- V$IR_MANUAL_CHECKLIST: List of the manual-actions section of ADVISE FAILURE

- V$IR_REPAIR: Repair recommendations as provided by the ADVISE FAILURE command

- V$IR_FAILURE_SET: Link between V$IR_REPAIR and V$IR_FAILURE

Recovering from the Loss of a System-Critical Data File

When you lose a system-critical data file (in other words, a file from the SYSTEM or
UNDO tablespace), the kinds of recovery available depend on whether you are operating
in ARCHIVELOG mode or NOARCHIVELOG mode. Oracle strongly recommends operating in
ARCHIVELOG mode for any production database that is not read-only.

Loss of a System-Critical Data File in NOARCHIVELOG Mode

The loss of a system-critical data file in NOARCHIVELOG mode requires a complete restoration
of the database, including the control files and all data files, not just the missing data files.
As a result, you must reenter any changes made to the database since the last backup, which
must have been a cold backup.

Loss of a System-Critical Data File in ARCHIVELOG Mode

The loss of a system-critical data file in ARCHIVELOG mode cannot proceed while the database is open; recovery must be performed while the database is in the MOUNT state. Because
the database is operating in ARCHIVELOG mode, you will not have to reenter any committed
transactions in the database.

When a system-critical data file is lost, such as the data file for the SYSTEM tablespace,
the instance will abort; in the rare circumstance that this does not happen, shut down the
database, and start it in MOUNT mode, as in this example:

```
SQL> shutdown abort
ORACLE instance shut down.
SQL> startup mount
ORACLE instance started.

Total System Global Area  197132288 bytes
Fixed Size                   778076 bytes
Variable Size             162537636 bytes
Database Buffers           33554432 bytes
Redo Buffers                 262144 bytes
Database mounted.
SQL>
```

Once the database is mounted, you can restore and recover the missing data file. After
the recovery is completed, open the database.

To use the Data Recovery Advisor for the recovery, invoke Perform Recovery from the
Availability screen of EM Database Control. Select Datafiles as the recovery scope, choose
Restore to Current Time, and add the files that need recovery. Submit the job to complete
the recovery operation. After the recovery operation is completed, open the database using
ALTER DATABASE OPEN.

Users are not required to reenter any data because the recovery is up to the time of the
last commit in the database.

The difference between recovering from the loss of a system-critical data file and non–system-critical data file is the state of the database. To recover a system-critical data file, the database must be in MOUNT state, not OPEN.

Summary

In this chapter, you learned about the types of failures that can occur in the database. You learned the stages in instance startup and how to improve the instance recovery time. You also learned to recover from failures using the Data Recovery Advisor framework.

Understanding failure is critical to deciding the type of action required to recover from the failure. This chapter reviewed the six types of failures in a database: statement, user process, network, user error, instance, and media.

In addition to knowing how an instance fails, you need to know what is required to keep a database up and running: all control files, at least one member of each redo log group, and all data files for the SYSTEM and UNDO tablespaces. For instance failures, you want to know how long the database will take to recover. You can use the initialization parameter FAST_START_MTTR_TARGET to specify the target recovery time, making it easier to meet service-level agreements.

You learned ways to recover from three of the failure types: instance, user errors, and media. In the discussion on instance failures, you learned the steps required to successfully start up the database, identifying the prerequisites that must be in place for the startup phase to complete.

In many cases, users themselves can solve their errors; flashback query can retrieve rows that have been deleted from a table in the past, even after a COMMIT has been performed. Dropped tables are kept in the recycle bin, which lets a user bring back the entire table as long as the space occupied by the table in the tablespace was not overwritten by new objects. Flashback table brings a table back to a given point in time without affecting other objects or users in the database; flashback query and flashback table are often used as complementary tools when many rows or even a few rows in a table have been lost or inadvertently deleted. Flashback transaction is used to flash back an entire transaction and its dependent transactions. Finally, you can access previous transactions against a table from the online and archived redo logs when the self-service recovery tools are not successful in recovering user data.

Also in this chapter, I presented scenarios of media failures and how to recover from such failures using the Data Recovery Advisor. If the database is in ARCHIVELOG mode, you can recover the database from these failures without losing any committed transactions. If the database is in NOARCHIVELOG mode, you can recover only to the last good cold backup. RMAN includes several commands to support the Data Recovery Advisor.

Exam Essentials

Identify the initialization parameters used to tune instance recovery. Be able to define the possible values for FAST_START_MTTR_TARGET, FAST_START_IO_TARGET, and LOG_CHECKPOINT_ TIMEOUT. Show the relationship between these parameters and in which situations each is most appropriately used.

List the phases of instance startup. Show how the database instance moves from SHUTDOWN to NOMOUNT to MOUNT to OPEN, and describe the conditions required in each step before the instance can proceed to the next phase.

Be able to list the types of failures that can occur in a database. Identify the six types of failures: statement, user process, network, user error, instance, and media.

List the features supported by Oracle to help users fix their own errors. Describe each type of user-error recovery solution: flashback query, flashback table, flashback transaction, and flashback drop.

Be able to use flashback query to retrieve previous table data. Show how flashback query can help a user look at the contents of a table at some point in time in the past. Demonstrate the flexibility in specifying the date at which the flashback query is executed.

Describe how flashback drop is used. Describe the components of flashback drop, such as the recycle bin, and show how it can store a deleted table unless space pressure occurs in the tablespace. Be able to identify the restrictions on the types of objects that can be saved in the recycle bin.

Understand how many control files and redo log members are required for the database to function. When you use multiplexed control files and redo log files, Oracle Database 11g requires all control files to be available and at least one member of the redo log group to be available for the database to function.

Understand the failures that can be identified and repaired by the Data Recovery Advisor. The Data Recovery Advisor can detect and repair all types of media failures and logical corruption. It cannot detect user errors or network issues.

Identify the three types of database files affected by media failures. Compare and contrast the loss of control files, redo log file group members, and data files, and describe how to recover from the loss of each of these files. Understand how the loss of certain types of data files may have a larger impact on availability and recoverability than others.

Familiarize yourself with the commands you can use to identify and perform recovery using RMAN. RMAN commands such as LIST FAILURE, ADVISE FAILURE, REPAIR FAILURE, and CHANGE FAILURE are used to support the Data Recovery Advisor actions.

Review Questions

1. The distance between the checkpoint position in a redo log group and the end of the redo log group can never be what percentage of the smallest redo log group?

   A. 15

   B. 100

   C. 50

   D. 90

   E. None of the above; the distance is relative to the size of the largest redo log group.

2. A database user tries to add a new row to a table, but the tablespace where the table resides is out of space. This type of failure is considered a _____ failure, and the DBA can solve this problem by _____ .

   A. user error; providing additional user privileges

   B. user error; increasing the user's quota

   C. statement failure; enabling resumable-space allocation

   D. statement failure; changing the application logic

3. Which of the following initialization parameters controls the mean time to recover the database, in seconds, after an instance failure?

   A. FAST_START_IO_TARGET

   B. LOG_CHECKPOINT_TIMEOUT

   C. FAST_START_MTTR_TARGET

   D. MTTR_TARGET_ADVICE

   E. FAST_START_TARGET_MTTR

4. What background process frees up locks and rolls back uncommitted changes for an abnormally disconnected session?

   A. ORB0

   B. RBAL

   C. SMON

   D. PMON

5. Which of the following is not an example of a user-process failure?

   A. A user's PC suddenly reboots.

   B. The network or an application develops problems.

   C. The DBA kills the user session.

   D. Users terminate SQL*Plus without logging out.

6. Which of the following can help prevent database network failures? (Choose all that apply.)

   A. Configure a backup listener process on the server.

   B. Open more than one session when updating the database.

   C. Configure multiple network cards on the server.

   D. Create a standby database.

7. Identify the statement that is not true regarding the loss of a control file.

   A. A damaged control file can be repaired by using one of the remaining undamaged control files, assuming there are at least two copies of the control file.

   B. The missing or damaged control file can be replaced while the instance is still active.

   C. You can temporarily run the instance with one fewer control file, as long as you remove one of the references to the missing control file in the spfile or `init.ora` file.

   D. An instance typically fails when one of the multiplexed control files is lost or damaged.

8. Which failures can be detected by the Data Recovery Advisor, which then provides repair recommendations? (Choose all that apply.)

   A. Instance failure

   B. Accidental deletion of a data file

   C. Disk containing one redo log member is offline

   D. User accidentally dropped a table

9. The instance can still be started even if some data files are missing; this rule does not apply to which tablespaces? (Choose all that apply.)

   A. USERS

   B. SYSTEM

   C. TEMP

   D. SYSAUX

   E. UNDO

10. Select the statement that is *not* true regarding media failure. A media failure occurs when

   A. the network card on the server fails.

   B. the DBA accidentally deletes one of the data files for the SYSTEM tablespace.

   C. there is a head crash on all physical drives in the RAID controller box.

   D. a corrupted track on a CD containing a read-only tablespace causes a query to fail.

11. Choose the correct statement about the Data Recovery Advisor.

   A. The Data Recovery Advisor is a stand-alone tool.

   B. The Data Recovery Advisor does not support RAC databases.

   C. The `CHANGE FAILURE` command can be used in SQL*Plus session.

   D. The `REPAIR FAILURE` command works only after `LIST FAILURE`.

12. To recover a data file from the SYSTEM or UNDO tablespace, the instance must be in which database state?

   A. NOMOUNT

   B. OPEN

   C. ABORT

   D. MOUNT

13. The STATUS column of the dynamic performance view V$LOGFILE contains what value if one of the redo log file group members has been lost because of a media failure?

   A. INVALID

   B. STALE

   C. DELETED

   D. The column contains a NULL value.

14. Place the following events or actions leading up to and during instance recovery in the correct order.

   1. The database is opened and available.

   2. Oracle uses undo segments in the undo tablespace to roll back uncommitted transactions.

   3. The DBA issues the STARTUP command at the SQL*Plus prompt.

   4. Oracle applies the information in the online redo log files to the data files.

   A. 4, 3, 2, 1

   B. 3, 4, 1, 2

   C. 2, 1, 3, 4

   D. 2, 1, 4, 3

   E. 3, 2, 4, 1

   F. 3, 4, 2, 1

15. You noticed that when your instance crashes, it takes a long time to start up the database. Which advisor can be used to tune this situation?

   A. The Undo Advisor

   B. The SQL Tuning Advisor

   C. The Database Tuning Advisor

   D. The MTTR Advisor

   E. The Instance Tuning Advisor

16. If a data file is missing when the instance is started, where is the error message recorded?

   A. Only in the alert log.

   B. All missing files are returned directly to the administrator in the SQL*Plus session.

   C. The first missing file is returned directly to the administrator in the SQL*Plus session, and the rest of the missing files are identified in V$RECOVER_FILE.

   D. Only in the alert log and in the DBWR background-process trace files.

17. In ARCHIVELOG mode, the loss of a data file for any tablespace other than the SYSTEM or UNDO tablespace affects which objects in the database?

A. The loss affects only objects whose extents reside in the lost data file.

B. The loss affects only the objects in the affected tablespace, and work can continue in other tablespaces.

C. The loss will not abort the instance but will prevent other transactions in any tablespace other than SYSTEM or UNDO until the affected tablespace is recovered.

D. The loss affects only those users whose default tablespace contains the lost or damaged data file.

18. Which dynamic performance view shows the data files either needing media recovery or missing at instance startup?

A. V$RECOVER_FILE

B. V$DATAFILE

C. V$TABLESPACE

D. V$RECOVERY_FILE_DEST

E. V$RECOVERY_FILE_STATUS

19. A fire breaks out in the server room near the routers, and the operations manager cuts off power to all servers, including the database servers. Before the fire is put out, the disk drive containing the SYSTEM tablespace and both network cards on the Oracle Database 11g server are destroyed. The user SCOTT was about to create a new table, but the connection was dropped after the power was disconnected from the server. This scenario is primarily an example of what kind of failure?

A. Network

B. Instance

C. Statement

D. Media

E. User error

F. User process

20. Which of the following conditions prevents the instance from progressing through the NOMOUNT, MOUNT, and OPEN states?

A. One of the redo log file groups is missing a member.

B. The instance was previously shut down uncleanly with SHUTDOWN ABORT.

C. Either the spfile or init.ora file is missing.

D. One of the five multiplexed control files is damaged.

E. The USERS tablespace is offline, with one of its data files deleted.

Answers to Review Questions

1. D. The distance (in bytes) between the checkpoint position in a redo log group and the end of the current redo log group can never be more than 90 percent of the size of the smallest redo log group.

2. C. The failure of one statement is considered a statement failure, and one way to solve the problem is to enable resumable-space allocation. When resumable space is enabled, Oracle generates an alert and places the session in a suspended state.

3. C. The parameter FAST_START_MTTR_TARGET specifies the desired time, in seconds, to recover a single instance from a crash or instance failure. The parameters LOG_CHECKPOINT_ TIMEOUT and FAST_START_IO_TARGET can still be used in Oracle 11g but should be used only together with an advanced-tuning scenario or for compatibility with older versions of Oracle. MTTR_TARGET_ADVICE and FAST_START_TARGET_MTTR are not valid initialization parameters.

4. D. The PMON process periodically polls server processes to make sure their sessions are still connected.

5. C. A DBA's disconnection of a session is an intentional process termination, not a failure. If a user's PC reboots, the user does not get a chance to log off, and the session is cleaned up by PMON; similarly, disconnecting from the application or SQL*Plus before logging out is considered a user-process failure. A network problem can prematurely disconnect a user session, causing a user-process failure. In all cases, PMON performs the session cleanup, whether the disconnection was intentional or not.

6. A, C. In addition to configuring a backup listener process and installing multiple network cards, you can implement connect-time failover and a backup network connection to reduce the possibility of network failures.

7. B. The instance must be shut down, if it is not already down, to repair or replace the missing or damaged control file.

8. B, C. Media failure, physical corruption, logical corruption, and missing data files all can be identified by the Data Recovery Advisor, which also provides recommendations for repair.

9. B, E. If a tablespace is taken offline because a data file is missing, the instance can still be started as long as the missing data file does not belong to the SYSTEM or UNDO tablespace.

10. A. If a network card fails, the failure type is network; the actual media containing the database files are not affected.

11. B. The Data Recovery Advisor in Oracle 11g Release 1 does not support RAC databases. It is integrated with EM Database Control and with RMAN. CHANGE FAILURE and other commands can be executed using RMAN. The ADVISE FAILURE command must be run before you can perform REPAIR FAILURE.

12. D. Unlike recovery of non–system-critical tablespaces other than SYSTEM or UNDO that can be recovered with the database in OPEN state, the database must be in MOUNT state to recover either the SYSTEM or UNDO tablespace.

13. A. If the redo log file group member has been lost because of a media failure or inadvertent deletion, the STATUS column is set to INVALID when an attempt is made to write redo information to that member.

14. B. Instance recovery, also known as crash recovery, occurs when the DBA attempts to open the database but the files were not synchronized to the same SCN when the database was shut down. Once the DBA issues the STARTUP command, Oracle uses information in the redo log files to restore the data files (including the undo tablespace's data files) to the state before the instance failure. Oracle then uses undo data in the undo tablespace after the database has been opened and made available to users to roll back uncommitted transactions.

15. D. The MTTR Advisor can tell the DBA the most effective value for the FAST_START_MTTR_TARGET parameter. This parameter specifies the maximum time required in seconds to perform instance recovery.

16. C. In addition to reporting the first missing file to the administrator and listing all the missing files in the dynamic performance view V$RECOVER_FILE, the missing data file(s) are noted in the DBWR background-process trace files.

17. B. The loss of one or more of a tablespace's data files does not prevent other users from doing their work in other tablespaces. Recovering the affected data files can continue while the database is still online and available.

18. A. The dynamic performance view V$RECOVER_FILE contains a list of the data files that either need media recovery or are missing when the instance is started.

19. B. The primary failure in this scenario is instance. Subsequently, a network failure will occur when connections are attempted through the burned-out router. However, no connections are possible until the network card in the server is replaced; the instance cannot start because of a media failure on the disk containing the SYSTEM tablespace.

20. D. All copies of the control files as defined in the spfile or the init.ora file must be identical and available. If one of the redo log file groups is missing a member, a warning is recorded in the alert log, but instance startup still proceeds. If the instance was previously shut down with SHUTDOWN ABORT, instance recovery automatically occurs during startup. Only an spfile or an init.ora file is needed to enter the NOMOUNT state, not both. If a tablespace is offline, the status of its data files is not checked until an attempt is made to bring it online; therefore, it will not prevent instance startup.

Chapter

17

Moving Data and Using EM Tools

ORACLE DATABASE 11*g*: ADMINISTRATION I EXAM OBJECTIVES COVERED IN THIS CHAPTER:

✓ **Moving Data**

- Describe and use methods to move data (Directory objects, SQL*Loader, External Tables)

- Explain the general architecture of Oracle Data Pump

- Use Data Pump Export and Import to move data between Oracle databases

✓ **Intelligent Infrastructure Enhancements**

- Use the Enterprise Manager Support Workbench

- Managing Patches

As a DBA, you are often required to move data between databases, extract data, or load data received from external sources. Oracle 11*g* provides tools to move data. You can use these tools to back up data from a table or a schema before making changes for quick recovery. Oracle Data Pump is a high-performance data-movement tool that you can use to unload and load data between Oracle databases, and you can use the SQL*Loader tool to load data received from external sources such as flat files.

In this chapter you will also learn about contacting Oracle Support through Enterprise Manager Support Workbench. EM Support Workbench is new in Oracle 11*g* and can be used to examine a database problem and contact Oracle Support for a resolution. EM can also alert you when database patches are ready. You will learn to use EM to stage and apply a patch.

Understanding Data Pump

The Data Pump facility is a high-speed mechanism for transferring data or metadata from one database to another or from operating-system files. Data Pump employs direct path unloading and direct path loading technologies. Unlike the older export and import programs (exp and imp), which operated on the client side of a database session, the Data Pump facility runs on the server. Thus, you must use a database directory to specify dump-file and log-file locations.

You can use Data Pump to copy data from one schema to another between two databases or within a single database. You can also use it to extract a logical copy of the entire database, a list of schemas, a list of tables, or a list of tablespaces to portable operating-system files. Data Pump can also transfer or extract the metadata (DDL statements) for a database, schema, or table.

You can call Data Pump from the command-line programs expdp and impdp or through the DBMS_DATAPUMP PL/SQL package, or you can invoke it from EM.

Data Pump export extracts data and metadata from your database, and Data Pump import loads this extracted data into the same database or into a different database, optionally transforming metadata along the way. These transformations let you, for example, copy tables from one schema to another or remap a tablespace from one database to another.

These are some of the key features of Data Pump:

- A fine-grained object selection using INCLUDE and EXCLUDE options

- An option to specify a lower-compatibility version so only supported object types are exported

- The ability to perform export and import in using parallel processes

- The ability to detach and attach to a job from the client session, allowing the DBA to close the export/import session and yet have the ability to administer the jobs

- An option to change target table names, tablespace names, and schema names

- Another option to compress metadata or data or both during export

- A tablespace metadata export to support the transportable tablespace feature of the database

- An option to append data to an existing table or to truncate and load data to an existing table

- The automatic use of direct path export whenever possible

- The ability to copy data from one database to another using a network

- The ability to specify a sample percentage to unload only a subset of data

- The ability to monitor job progress; job status can be queried from the database or using EM

- An option to restart or terminate failed export and import jobs

Architecture of Data Pump

In Oracle 11*g* Data Pump, the database does all the work. This is a major deviation from the architecture of export/import utilities, which previously ran as clients and did the major part of the work. The dump files for export/import were stored at the client, whereas the Data Pump files are stored at the server. Figure 17.1 shows the Data Pump architecture.

Data Pump Components

Data Pump consists of the following components:

Data Pump API   DBMS_DATAPUMP is the PL/SQL API for Data Pump, which is the engine. Data Pump jobs are created and monitored using this API.

Metadata API   The DBMS_METADATA API provides the database object definition to the Data Pump processes.

Client Tools   Data Pump client tools expdp and impdp use the procedures provided by the DBMS_DATAPUMP package. These tools make calls to the Data Pump API to initiate and monitor Data Pump operations.

Data-movement APIs   Data Pump uses the Direct Path API (DPAPI) to move data. Certain circumstances do not allow the use of DPAPI; in those cases, the Oracle external table with the ORACLE_DATADUMP access driver API is used.

FIGURE 17.1 Data Pump architecture

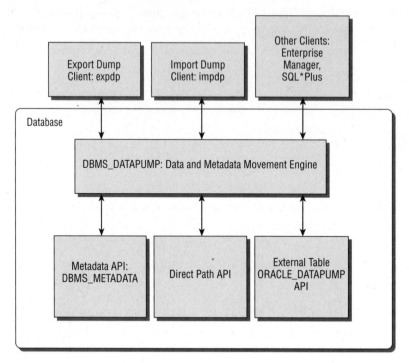

Data Pump Processes

Oracle Data Pump jobs, once started, are performed by various processes on the database server. The following are the processes involved in the Data Pump operation:

Client process This process is initiated by the client utility—expdp, impdp, or other clients—to make calls to the Data Pump API. Since Data Pump is completely integrated into the database, once the Data Pump job is initiated, this process is not necessary for the progress of the job.

Shadow process When a client logs into the Oracle Database, a foreground process is created (a standard feature of Oracle). This shadow process services the client data dump API requests. This process creates the master table and creates Advanced Queries (AQ) queues used for communication. Once the client process ends, the shadow process goes away too.

Master control process (MCP) The *master control process* controls the execution of the Data Pump job; there is one MCP per job. MCP divides the Data Pump job into various metadata and data-load or -unload jobs and hands them over to the worker processes. The MCP has a process name of the format <ORACLE_SID>_DMnn_<PROCESS_ID>. It maintains the job state, job description, restart information, and file information in the master table.

Worker process The MCP creates the worker processes based on the value of the PAR-ALLEL parameter. The workers perform the tasks requested by the MCP, mainly loading or unloading data and metadata. The worker processes have the format <ORACLE_SID>_DWnn_<PROCESS_ID>. The worker processes maintain the current status in the master table that can be used to restart a failed job.

Parallel query (PQ) processes The worker processes can initiate parallel-query processes if an external table is used as the data-access method for loading or unloading. These are standard parallel-query slaves of the parallel-execution architecture.

Oracle Data Pump cannot be used to load data into a database from data exported using the exp utility.

Let's consider the example of an export Data Pump operation and see all the activities and processes involved. Say user A invokes the expdp client, which initiates the shadow process. The client calls the DBMS_DATAPUMP.OPEN procedure to establish the kind of export to be performed. The OPEN call starts the MCP process and creates two AQ queues.

The first queue is the status queue, used to send the status of the job, which includes logging information and errors. Clients interested in the status of the job can query this queue. This is strictly a unidirectional queue—the MCP posts the information to the queue, and the clients consume the information. The second queue is the command-and-control queue, which is used to control the worker processes established by the MCP and to perform API commands and file requests. This is a bidirectional queue where the MCP listens and writes. The commands are sent to this queue by the DBMS_DATAPUMP methods or by using the parameters of the expdp client.

Once all the components (parameters and filters) of the job are defined, the client (expdp) invokes DBMS_DATAPUMP.START_JOB. Based on the number of parallel processes requested, the MCP starts the worker processes. The MCP directs one of the worker processes to do the metadata extraction using the DBMS_METADATA API.

During the operation, a master table is maintained in the schema of the user who initiated the Data Pump export. The master table has the same name as the name of the Data Pump job. This table maintains one row per object with status information. In the event of a failure, Data Pump uses the information in this table to restart the job. The master table is the heart of every Data Pump operation; it maintains all the information about the job. Data Pump uses the master table to restart a failed or suspended job. The master table is dropped (by default) when the Data Pump job finishes successfully.

The master table is written to the dump file set as the last step of the export dump operation and is removed from the user's schema. For an import dump operation, the master table is loaded from the dump file set to the user's schema as the first step and is used to sequence the objects being imported.

While the export job is underway, the original client who invoked the export job can detach from the job without aborting the job. This is especially useful when performing long-running data export jobs. Users can attach the job at any time using the DBMS_DATAPUMP methods and query the status or change the parallelism of the job.

WARNING   Since the master table is created in the Data Pump user's schema as a table, if there is an existing table in the schema with the Data Pump job name, the job fails. The user must have appropriate privileges to create the table and have appropriate tablespace quotas.

Data Access Methods

Data Pump chooses the most appropriate data-access method. Two methods are supported: direct path access and external table access. Direct path export has been supported since Oracle 7.3. External tables were introduced in Oracle9*i*, and support for writing to external tables has been available since Oracle 10*g*. Data Pump provides an external-tables access driver (ORACLE_DATAPUMP) that can be used to read and write files. The format of the file is the same as the direct path methods; hence, it's possible to load data that is unloaded in another method. Data Pump uses the Direct Load API whenever possible. The following are the exceptions when an external tables method will be used:

- Tables with fine-grained access control are enabled in insert and select operations.
- A domain index exists for a LOB column.
- A global index on multipartition table exists during a single-partition load.
- Clustered table or table has an active trigger during import.
- A table contains BFILE columns.
- A referential integrity constraint is present during import.
- A table contains a VARRAY column with an embedded opaque type.
- Loading and unloading very large tables and partitions, where the PARALLEL SQL clause can be used to an advantage.
- Loading tables that are partitioned differently at load time and unload time.

Using Data Pump Clients

Oracle 11*g* comes with the expdp utility to invoke Data Pump for export and comes with impdp for import. The Data Pump export utility (expdp) unloads data and metadata to a set of OS files called *dump files*. The Data Pump import utility (impdp) loads data and meta-data stored in an export dump file to a target database. expdp and impdp accept parameters that are then passed to the DBMS_DATAPUMP program. The command-line executable name for Data Pump export is expdp and for Data Pump import is impdp on Windows as well as Unix platforms. For a user to invoke expdp/impdp, they need to set up a directory where the dump files will be stored and they must have appropriate privileges to perform Data Pump export/import. In the next section, I will discuss how to set up the export dump location.

Setting Up the Dump Location

Since Data Pump is server-based, directory objects must be created in the database where the Data Pump files will be stored. Directory objects are named directory locations on the database server representing the physical location on the server's file system. Directories are used with several database features, including BFILEs, external tables, utl_file, SQL*Loader, and Data Pump.

The directory object contains the location of a specific operating-system directory. By using a named directory object, you do not have to hard-code the directory path in programs, and you get file-management flexibility.

Under Unix, you create directories with the CREATE DIRECTORY statement, like this:

```
CREATE DIRECTORY dump_dir AS '/oracle/data_pump/dumps';
CREATE DIRECTORY log_dir  AS '/oracle/data_pump/logs';
```

Under Windows, you create directories like this:

```
CREATE DIRECTORY dpump_dir  AS 'G:\datadumps';
```

Directories are not schema objects, like tables or synonyms, because they are not owned by a schema. Instead, directories are like profiles or roles in that they are owned by the database. To control access to a directory, you need to grant the READ or WRITE object privilege on that directory, like this:

```
GRANT read,write ON DIRECTORY dump_dir TO PUBLIC;
```

To create directories, you must have the CREATE ANY DIRECTORY system privilege. By default, only the users SYSTEM and SYS have this privilege. Be careful in granting this system privilege to users, because the database employs the operating-system credentials of the database-instance owner.

> Directory objects are owned by the SYS user; thus, the directory names must be unique across the database.

The user executing Data Pump must have been granted permissions on the directory. READ permission is required to import, and WRITE permission is required to export and to create log files or SQL files.

Note that the oracle user (who owns the software installation and database files) must have read and write OS privileges on the directory. The user SCOTT, for example, need not have any OS privileges on the directory for Data Pump to succeed.

A default directory can be created for Data Pump operations in the database. Privileged users (with the EXP_FULL_DATABASE or IMP_FULL_DATABASE privilege) need not specify a directory object name when performing the Data Pump operation. The name of the default directory must be DATA_PUMP_DIR. Also, the privileged users need not have explicit READ or WRITE permission on DATA_PUMP_DIR.

Using EM Database Control, you can create and edit directory objects. On the Database Control Schema page, click Directory Objects under Database Objects. Figure 17.2 shows the Directory Objects screen that appears.

FIGURE 17.2 Directory Objects screen of EM

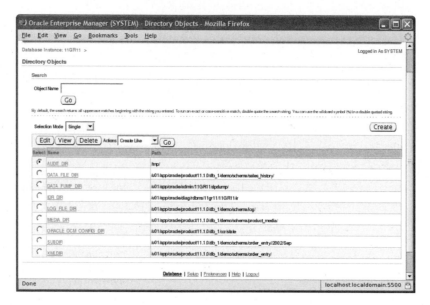

Click the Edit button to change the physical directory. You can also use the Delete button to delete an existing directory and the Create button to create a new directory.

Data Pump can write three types of files to the OS directory defined in the database. Remember that absolute paths are not supported; Data Pump can write only to a directory defined by a directory database object. The file types are as follows:

Dump files These contain data and metadata information.

Log files These record the standard output to a file and contain job progress and status information.

SQL files Data-dump import can extract the metadata information from a dump file, which can be used to create database objects without using the Data Pump import utility.

You can specify the location of the files to the Data Pump clients using three methods (given in the order of precedence):

- Prefix the filename with the directory name separated by a colon; for example, `DUMPFILE=dumplocation:myfile.dmp`.
- Use the `DIRECTORY` parameter on the OS environment.
- Define the `DATA_DUMP_DIR` directory in the database for privileged users.

The export and import done using the `expdp` and `impdp` tools can have different modes based on the requirement. The next section discusses this.

Specifying Export and Import Modes

Export and import using the Data Pump clients can be performed in five different modes to unload or load different portions of the database. When performing the dump-file import, specifying the mode is optional; when no mode is specified, the entire dump file is loaded with the mode automatically set to the one used for export.

Table 17.1 describes the export and import modes.

TABLE 17.1   Export and Import Modes in Data Pump

Mode	Description	Export	Import
Database	Performed by specifying the FULL=Y parameter	The export user requires the EXP_FULL_DATABASE role.	The import user requires the IMP_FULL_DATABASE role.
Tablespace	Performed by specifying the TABLESPACES parameter	Data and metadata for only those objects contained in the specified tablespaces are unloaded. The export user requires the EXP_FULL_DATABASE role.	All objects contained in the specified tablespaces are loaded. The import user requires the IMP_FULL_DATABASE privilege. The source dump file can be exported in database, tablespace, schema, or table mode.
Schema	Performed by specifying the SCHEMAS parameter. This is the default mode	Only objects belonging to the specified schema are unloaded. The EXP_FULL_DATABASE role is required to specify a list of schemas.	All objects belonging to the specified schema are loaded. The source can be a database or schema-mode export. The IMP_FULL_DATABASE role is required to specify a list of schema.
Table	Performed by specifying the TABLES parameter	Only the specified table, its partitions, and its dependent objects are unloaded. The export user must have the SELECT privilege on the tables.	Only the specified table, its partitions, and its dependent objects are loaded. This requires the IMP_FULL_DATABASE role to specify tables belonging to a different user.
Transport tablespace	Performed by specifying the TRANSPORT_TABLESPACES parameter	Only metadata for tables and their dependent objects within the specified set of tablespaces are unloaded. Use this mode to transport tablespaces from one database to another.	Metadata from a transport tablespace export is loaded.

In a database-mode export, the entire database is exported to operating-system files, including user accounts, public synonyms, roles, and profiles. In a schema-mode export, all data and metadata for a list of schemas is exported. At the most granular level is the table-mode export, which includes the data and metadata for a list of tables. A tablespace-mode export extracts both data and metadata for all objects in a tablespace list as well as any object dependent on those in the specified tablespace list. Therefore, if a table resides in your specified tablespace list, all its indexes are included whether or not they also reside in the specified tablespace list. In each of these modes, you can further specify that only data or only metadata be exported. The default is to export both data and metadata.

With some objects, such as indexes, only the metadata is exported; the actual internal structures contain physical addresses and are always rebuilt on import.

The files created by a Data Pump export are called *dump files*, and one or more of these files can be created during a single Data Pump export job. Multiple files are created if your Data Pump job has a parallel degree greater than 1 or if a single dump file exceeds the filesize parameter. All the export dump files from a single Data Pump export job are called a *dump-file set*.

Using expdp

You use the expdp utility to perform Data Pump exports. Any user can export objects or a complete schema owned by the user without any additional privileges. Nonprivileged users must have WRITE permission on the directory object and must specify the DIRECTORY parameter or specify the directory object name along with the dump filename.

Here is an example to perform an export by user SCOTT. Since Scott is not a privileged user, he must specify the DIRECTORY object name.

```
$ expdp scott/tiger

Export: Release 11.1.0.6.0 - Production on Saturday, 15 November, 2008
13:50:05
Copyright (c) 2003, 2007, Oracle.  All rights reserved.
Connected to: Oracle Database 11g Enterprise Edition Release 11.1.0.6.0 -
Production
With the Partitioning, OLAP, Data Mining and Real Application Testing options
ORA-39002: invalid operation
ORA-39070: Unable to open the log file.

ORA-39145: directory object parameter must be specified and non-null
```

Let's create a directory for user SCOTT and grant read and write privileges on this directory:

```
SQL> CREATE DIRECTORY dumplocation AS '/u02/dpump';
Directory created.
```

```
SQL> GRANT READ, WRITE on DIRECTORY dumplocation TO scott;
Grant succeeded.
```

Now, let's try the export specifying the directory:

```
$ expdp scott/tiger directory=dumplocation
Export: Release 11.1.0.6.0 - Production on Saturday, 15 November, 2008
16:04:22
Copyright (c) 2003, 2007, Oracle.  All rights reserved.
Connected to: Oracle Database 11g Enterprise Edition Release 11.1.0.6.0 -
Production
With the Partitioning, OLAP, Data Mining and Real Application Testing options
FLASHBACK automatically enabled to preserve database integrity.
Starting "SCOTT"."SYS_EXPORT_SCHEMA_01":  scott/********
directory=dumplocation
Estimate in progress using BLOCKS method...
Processing object type SCHEMA_EXPORT/TABLE/TABLE_DATA
Total estimation using BLOCKS method: 192 KB
Processing object type SCHEMA_EXPORT/PRE_SCHEMA/PROCACT_SCHEMA
Processing object type SCHEMA_EXPORT/TABLE/TABLE
Processing object type SCHEMA_EXPORT/TABLE/INDEX/INDEX
Processing object type SCHEMA_EXPORT/TABLE/CONSTRAINT/CONSTRAINT
Processing object type SCHEMA_EXPORT/TABLE/INDEX/STATISTICS/INDEX_STATISTICS
Processing object type SCHEMA_EXPORT/TABLE/COMMENT
Processing object type SCHEMA_EXPORT/TABLE/STATISTICS/TABLE_STATISTICS
Processing object type SCHEMA_EXPORT/POST_SCHEMA/PROCACT_SCHEMA
. . exported "SCOTT"."DEPT"                          5.914 KB       4 rows
. . exported "SCOTT"."EMP"                           8.570 KB      14 rows
. . exported "SCOTT"."SALGRADE"                      5.867 KB       5 rows
. . exported "SCOTT"."BONUS"                            0 KB        0 rows
Master table "SCOTT"."SYS_EXPORT_SCHEMA_01" successfully loaded/unloaded
******************************************************************************
Dump file set for SCOTT.SYS_EXPORT_SCHEMA_01 is:
  /u02/dpump/expdat.dmp
Job "SCOTT"."SYS_EXPORT_SCHEMA_01" successfully completed at 16:04:55
$
```

Since you did not specify any other parameters, expdp used default values for the file-names (expdat.dmp and export.log), did schema-level export (login schema), calculated job estimation using the blocks method, used a default job name (SYS_EXPORT_SCHEMA_01), and exported both data and metadata.

Data Pump Export Parameters

You can use various parameters while invoking expdp. You can obtain a list of parameters by specifying expdp help=y:

```
$ expdp help=y
Export: Release 11.1.0.6.0 - Production on Saturday, 15 November, 2008
16:54:49
Copyright (c) 2003, 2007, Oracle.  All rights reserved.


The Data Pump export utility provides a mechanism for transferring data
objects
between Oracle databases. The utility is invoked with the following command:

    Example: expdp scott/tiger DIRECTORY=dmpdir DUMPFILE=scott.dmp


You can control how Export runs by entering the 'expdp' command followed
by various parameters. To specify parameters, you use keywords:

    Format:  expdp KEYWORD=value or KEYWORD=(value1,value2,...,valueN)
    Example: expdp scott/tiger DUMPFILE=scott.dmp DIRECTORY=dmpdir
SCHEMAS=scott
            or TABLES=(T1:P1,T1:P2), if T1 is partitioned table


USERID must be the first parameter on the command line.


Keyword               Description (Default)
------------------------------------------------------------------------
ATTACH                Attach to existing job, e.g. ATTACH [=job name].
COMPRESSION           Reduce size of dumpfile contents where valid keyword.
                      values are: ALL, (METADATA_ONLY), DATA_ONLY and NONE.
CONTENT               Specifies data to unload where the valid keyword
                      values are: (ALL), DATA_ONLY, and METADATA_ONLY.
DATA_OPTIONS          Data layer flags where the only valid value is:
                      XML_CLOBS-write XML datatype in CLOB format
DIRECTORY             Directory object to be used for dumpfiles and logfiles.
DUMPFILE              List of destination dump files (expdat.dmp),
                      e.g. DUMPFILE=scott1.dmp, scott2.dmp, dmpdir:scott3.dmp.
ENCRYPTION            Encrypt part or all of the dump file where valid keyword
                      values are: ALL, DATA_ONLY, METADATA_ONLY,
                      ENCRYPTED_COLUMNS_ONLY, or NONE.
ENCRYPTION_ALGORITHM  Specify how encryption should be done where valid
                      keyword values are: (AES128), AES192, and AES256.
ENCRYPTION_MODE       Method of generating encryption key where valid keyword
                      values are: DUAL, PASSWORD, and (TRANSPARENT).
```

ENCRYPTION_PASSWORD	Password key for creating encrypted column data.
ESTIMATE	Calculate job estimates where the valid keyword values are: (BLOCKS) and STATISTICS.
ESTIMATE_ONLY	Calculate job estimates without performing the export.
EXCLUDE	Exclude specific object types, e.g. EXCLUDE=TABLE:EMP.
FILESIZE	Specify the size of each dumpfile in units of bytes.
FLASHBACK_SCN	SCN used to set session snapshot back to.
FLASHBACK_TIME	Time used to get the SCN closest to the specified time.
FULL	Export entire database (N).
HELP	Display Help messages (N).
INCLUDE	Include specific object types, e.g. INCLUDE=TABLE_DATA.
JOB_NAME	Name of export job to create.
LOGFILE	Log file name (export.log).
NETWORK_LINK	Name of remote database link to the source system.
NOLOGFILE	Do not write logfile (N).
PARALLEL	Change the number of active workers for current job.
PARFILE	Specify parameter file.
QUERY	Predicate clause used to export a subset of a table.
REMAP_DATA	Specify a data conversion function, e.g. REMAP_DATA=EMP.EMPNO:REMAPPKG.EMPNO.
REUSE_DUMPFILES	Overwrite destination dump file if it exists (N).
SAMPLE	Percentage of data to be exported;
SCHEMAS	List of schemas to export (login schema).
STATUS	Frequency (secs) job status is to be monitored where the default (0) will show new status when available.
TABLES	Identifies a list of tables to export - one schema only.
TABLESPACES	Identifies a list of tablespaces to export.
TRANSPORTABLE	Specify whether transportable method can be used where valid keyword values are: ALWAYS, (NEVER).
TRANSPORT_FULL_CHECK	Verify storage segments of all tables (N).
TRANSPORT_TABLESPACES	List of tablespaces from which metadata will be unloaded.
VERSION	Version of objects to export where valid keywords are: (COMPATIBLE), LATEST, or any valid database version.

The following commands are valid while in interactive mode.
Note: abbreviations are allowed

Command	Description
ADD_FILE	Add dumpfile to dumpfile set.
CONTINUE_CLIENT	Return to logging mode. Job will be re-started if idle.

EXIT_CLIENT	Quit client session and leave job running.
FILESIZE	Default filesize (bytes) for subsequent ADD_FILE commands.
HELP	Summarize interactive commands.
KILL_JOB	Detach and delete job.
PARALLEL	Change the number of active workers for current job. PARALLEL=<number of workers>.
REUSE_DUMPFILES	Overwrite destination dump file if it exists (N).
START_JOB	Start/resume current job.
STATUS	Frequency (secs) job status is to be monitored where the default (0) will show new status when available. STATUS[=interval]
STOP_JOB	Orderly shutdown of job execution and exits the client. STOP_JOB=IMMEDIATE performs an immediate shutdown of the Data Pump job.

$

FLASHBACK_SCN and FLASHBACK_TIME are mutually exclusive parameters.

The DUMPFILE parameter can specify more than one file. The filenames can be comma-separated, or you can use the %U substitution variable. If you specify %U in the DUMPFILE filename, the number of files initially created is based on the value of the PARALLEL parameter. Preexisting files that match the name of the files generated are not overwritten; an error is flagged. To forcefully overwrite the files, use the REUSE_DUMPFILES=Y parameter. The FILESIZE parameter determines the size of each file. Table 17.2 shows some examples.

You can specify all the parameters in a file and specify the filename with the PARFILE parameter. The only exception is the PARFILE parameter inside the parameter file. Recursive PARFILE is not supported.

The SAMPLE parameter is useful to get a subset of data unloaded from the source table. Specify the percentage of rows that need to be unloaded using this parameter. The SAMPLE parameter is not valid for network exports.

In the next section, I will discuss the impdp utility, which does the import from a dump file created using expdp.

TABLE 17.2   Data Pump DUMPFILE Examples

Parameter Examples	File Characteristics
DUMPFILE=exp%U.dmp FILESIZE=200M	Initially the exp01.dmp file will be created; once the file is 200MB, the next file will be created.
DUMPFILE=exp%U_%U.dmp PARALLEL=3	Initially three files will be created: exp01_01.dmp, exp02_02.dmp, and exp03_03.dmp. Notice that every occurrence of the substitution variable is incremented each time. Since there is no FILESIZE, no more files will be created.
DUMPFILE=DMPDIR1:exp%U.dmp, DMPDIR2:exp%U.dmp FILESIZE=100M	This method is especially useful if you do not have enough space in one directory to perform the complete export job. The dump files are stored in directories defined by DMPDIR1 and DMPDIR2.

Using impdp

The Data Pump import program impdp is the utility that can read and apply the dump file created by the expdp utility. The directory permission and privileges for using impdp are similar to those for expdp.

impdp has several modes of operation, including full, schema, table, and tablespace. In the full mode, the entire content of an export file set is loaded. In a schema-mode import, all content for a list of schemas in the specified file set is loaded. The specified file set for a schema-mode import can be from either a database or a schema-mode export. With a table-mode import, only the specified table and dependent objects are loaded from the export file set. With a tablespace-mode import, all objects in the export file set that were in the specified tablespace list are loaded.

With all these modes, the source can be a live database instead of a set of export files. Table 17.3 shows the supported mapping of export mode to import mode.

TABLE 17.3   Export to Import Modes

Source Export Mode	Import Mode
Database Schema Table	Full
Tablespace Live database	

TABLE 17.3 Export to Import Modes *(continued)*

Source Export Mode	Import Mode
Database Schema Live database	Schema
Database Schema Table Tablespace Live database	Table
Database Schema Table Tablespace Live database	Tablespace

The IMP_FULL_DATABASE role is required if the source is a live database or the export session required the EXP_FULL_DATABASE role.

Data Pump Import Parameters

You can use various parameters while invoking impdp. You can obtain a list of parameters by specifying impdp help=y:

```
$ impdp help=y

Import: Release 11.1.0.6.0 - Production on Saturday, 15 November, 2008
21:13:53

Copyright (c) 2003, 2007, Oracle.  All rights reserved.


The Data Pump Import utility provides a mechanism for transferring data
objects
between Oracle databases. The utility is invoked with the following command:

     Example: impdp scott/tiger DIRECTORY=dmpdir DUMPFILE=scott.dmp

You can control how Import runs by entering the 'impdp' command followed
by various parameters. To specify parameters, you use keywords:

     Format:  impdp KEYWORD=value or KEYWORD=(value1,value2,...,valueN)
     Example: impdp scott/tiger DIRECTORY=dmpdir DUMPFILE=scott.dmp

USERID must be the first parameter on the command line.
```

```
Keyword                   Description (Default)
------------------------------------------------------------------------
ATTACH                    Attach to existing job, e.g. ATTACH [=job name].
CONTENT                   Specifies data to load where the valid keywords are:
                          (ALL), DATA_ONLY, and METADATA_ONLY.
DATA_OPTIONS              Data layer flags where the only valid value is:
                          SKIP_CONSTRAINT_ERRORS-constraint errors are not fatal.
DIRECTORY                 Directory object to be used for dump, log, and sql
                          files.
DUMPFILE                  List of dumpfiles to import from (expdat.dmp),
                          e.g. DUMPFILE=scott1.dmp, scott2.dmp, dmpdir:scott3.dmp.
ENCRYPTION_PASSWORD       Password key for accessing encryptß  ed column data.
                          This parameter is not valid for network import jobs.
ESTIMATE                  Calculate job estimates where the valid keywords are:
                          (BLOCKS) and STATISTICS.
EXCLUDE                   Exclude specific object types, e.g. EXCLUDE=TABLE:EMP.
FLASHBACK_SCN             SCN used to set session snapshot back to.
FLASHBACK_TIME            Time used to get the SCN closest to the specified time.
FULL                      Import everything from source (Y).
HELP                      Display help messages (N).
INCLUDE                   Include specific object types, e.g. INCLUDE=TABLE_DATA.
JOB_NAME                  Name of import job to create.
LOGFILE                   Log file name (import.log).
NETWORK_LINK              Name of remote database link to the source system.
NOLOGFILE                 Do not write logfile.
PARALLEL                  Change the number of active workers for current job.
PARFILE                   Specify parameter file.
PARTITION_OPTIONS         Specify how partitions should be transformed where the
                          valid keywords are: DEPARTITION, MERGE and (NONE)
QUERY                     Predicate clause used to import a subset of a table.
REMAP_DATA                Specify a data conversion function,
                          e.g. REMAP_DATA=EMP.EMPNO:REMAPPKG.EMPNO
REMAP_DATAFILE            Redefine datafile references in all DDL statements.
REMAP_SCHEMA              Objects from one schema are loaded into another schema.
REMAP_TABLE               Table names are remapped to another table,
                          e.g. REMAP_TABLE=EMP.EMPNO:REMAPPKG.EMPNO.
REMAP_TABLESPACE          Tablespace object are remapped to another tablespace.
REUSE_DATAFILES           Tablespace will be initialized if it already exists (N).
SCHEMAS                   List of schemas to import.
SKIP_UNUSABLE_INDEXES     Skip indexes that were set to the Index Unusable state.
SQLFILE                   Write all the SQL DDL to a specified file.
STATUS                    Frequency (secs) job status is to be monitored where
                          the default (0) will show new status when available.
```

STREAMS_CONFIGURATION Enable the loading of Streams metadata
TABLE_EXISTS_ACTION   Action to take if imported object already exists.
                       Valid keywords: (SKIP), APPEND, REPLACE and TRUNCATE.
TABLES   Identifies a list of tables to import.
TABLESPACES   Identifies a list of tablespaces to import.
TRANSFORM   Metadata transform to apply to applicable objects.
                       Valid transform keywords: SEGMENT_ATTRIBUTES, STORAGE,
                       OID, and PCTSPACE.
TRANSPORTABLE   Options for choosing transportable data movement.
                       Valid keywords: ALWAYS and (NEVER).
                       Only valid in NETWORK_LINK mode import operations.
TRANSPORT_DATAFILES   List of datafiles to be imported by transportable mode.
TRANSPORT_FULL_CHECK   Verify storage segments of all tables (N).
TRANSPORT_TABLESPACES List of tablespaces from which metadata will be loaded.
                       Only valid in NETWORK_LINK mode import operations.
VERSION   Version of objects to export where valid keywords are:
                       (COMPATIBLE), LATEST, or any valid database version.
                       Only valid for NETWORK_LINK and SQLFILE.

The following commands are valid while in interactive mode.
Note: abbreviations are allowed

Command   Description (Default)

CONTINUE_CLIENT   Return to logging mode. Job will be re-started if idle.
EXIT_CLIENT   Quit client session and leave job running.
HELP   Summarize interactive commands.
KILL_JOB   Detach and delete job.
PARALLEL   Change the number of active workers for current job.
                       PARALLEL=<number of workers>.
START_JOB   Start/resume current job.
                       START_JOB=SKIP_CURRENT will start the job after skipping
                       any action which was in progress when job was stopped.
STATUS   Frequency (secs) job status is to be monitored where
                       the default (0) will show new status when available.
                       STATUS[=interval]
STOP_JOB   Orderly shutdown of job execution and exits the client.
                       STOP_JOB=IMMEDIATE performs an immediate shutdown of the
                       Data Pump job.

$

You must include one parameter to specify the mode, either `full`, `schemas`, `tables`, or `tablespaces`. You can include several other parameters on the command line or place them in a file and use the `parfile=` parameter to instruct `impdp` where to find them. Here are some examples of imports:

- Read the dump file `FULL.DMP` and extract all DDL, placing it in the file `FULL.SQL`. Do not write a log file.

  ```
  impdp system/password full=y dumpfile=dumplocation:FULL.DMP
     nologfile=y sqlfile= dumplocation:FULL.SQL
  ```

- Read the data accessed via the database link `PROD`, and import schema `HR` into schema `HR_TEST`, importing only metadata, writing the log file to the database directory `chap7`, and naming this log file `HR_TEST.imp`.

  ```
  impdp system/password network_link=prod schemas="HR"
     remap_schema="HR:HR_TEST" content=metadata_only
     logfile= dumplocation:HR_TEST.imp
  ```

- Read the dump file `HR.DMP`, and write to the SQL file `HR_proc_give.sql` all the DDL to create any procedures with the name `LIKE 'GIVE%'`. Do not write a log file.

  ```
  impdp system/password full=y dumpfile= dumplocation:HR.DMP
     nologfile=y sqlfile= dumplocation:HR_proc_give.SQL
     include=PROCEDURE:"LIKE 'GIVE%'"
  ```

The combinations of parameters you can use in copying data and metadata give you, the DBA, flexibility in administering your databases.

> When using the schema-level import with the SCHEMAS parameter, if the schema does not exist in the target database, the import operation creates it with the same attributes from the source. The schema created by the import operation will need to have the password reset.

You can use the CONTENT, INCLUDE, and EXCLUDE parameters in the `impdp` utility to filter the metadata objects. Their behavior is the same as in the `expdp` utility. I'll discuss them in detail in the "Data and Metadata Filters" section. In the next section, I will discuss methods to use a different target for tablespaces, schemas, and data files.

Import Transformations

While performing the import, you can specify a different target name for data files, tablespaces, or schemas. These transformations are possible because the object metadata is stored in the dump file as XML. The REMAP_ parameters are used to specify this. When any one of the three REMAP_ parameters is used, Data Pump makes transformations to the metadata DDL during import. The IMP_FULL_DATABASE role is required to use these parameters. You can use these parameters multiple times if there is more than one transformation to be made, but the same source cannot be repeated more than once. The following are the parameters you can use to specify a different target name for each type of object:

REMAP_DATAFILES Using this parameter, you can specify a different name for the data file. The filename referenced could be in a CREATE TABLESPACE, CREATE LIBRARY, or CREATE DIRECTORY statement. REMAP_DATAFILES is especially useful when performing a full database import, when the tablespaces are being created by impdp and the source directories do not exist in the target database server, or when the source and target platforms are different (VMS, Windows, Unix). The syntax is as follows:

```
REMAP_DATAFILE=source_datafile:target_datafile
```

REMAP_SCHEMA Using this parameter, you can load all the objects belonging to the source schema to a target schema. Multiple source schemas can map to the same target schema. If the target schema specified does not exist, the import operation creates the schema and performs the load. The syntax is as follows:

```
REMAP_SCHEMA=source_schema:target_schema
```

REMAP_TABLE Using this parameter, you can rename a table while performing the import. Only the table is renamed; its dependent indexes, triggers, constraints, and columns are not renamed. The syntax is as follows:

```
REMAP_TABLE=source_table:target_table
```

REMAP_TABLESPACE Using this parameter, you can create the objects that belong to a tablespace in the source to another in the target. The syntax is as follows:

```
REMAP_TABLESPACE=source_tablespace:target_tablespace
```

TRANSFORM Using the TRANSFORM parameter, you can specify that the storage clause should not be generated in the DDL for import. This is useful if the storage characteristics of the source and target databases are different. TRANSFORM has the following syntax:

```
TRANSFORM=name:boolean_value[:object_type]
```

The name of the transform can be either SEGMENT_ATTRIBUTES or STORAGE. STORAGE removes the STORAGE clause from the CREATE statement DDL, whereas SEGMENT_ATTRIBUTES removes physical attributes, tablespaces, logging, and storage attributes. boolean_value can be Y or N; the default is Y. The type of object is optional; the valid values are TABLE and INDEX.

For example, if you want to ignore the storage characteristics during the import and use the defaults for the tablespace, you can do the following:

```
impdp dumpfile=scott.dmp  transform=storage:N:table exclude=indexes
```

The next example will remove all the segment attributes; the import will use the user's default tablespace and its default storage characteristics:

```
impdp dumpfile=scott.dmp  transform=segment_attributes:N
```

In the next section, I will discuss how data can be copied from one database to another without using a dump file.

Network-Mode Import

NETWORK_LINK enables the network-mode import using a database link. The database link must be created before performing the import. Export is performed on the source database based on the various parameters; the data and metadata are passed to the source database using the database link and loaded. To get a consistent export from the source database, you can use the FLASHBACK_SCN or FLASHBACK_TIME parameter.

Using FLASHBACK_SCN, FLASHBACK_TIME, ESTIMATE, or TRANSPORT_TABLESPACES requires the NETWORK_LINK parameter to also be specified. Here is an example of how to copy the SCOTT schema in the source (remote) database to LARRY in the target (local) database. Scott's objects are stored in the USERS tablespace; in the target, you will create Larry's objects in the EXAMPLE tablespace. The database link name is NEW_DB.

```
$ impdp schemas=scott network_link=new_db remap_schema=scott:larry ⤶
   remap_tablespace=users:example
```

WARNING

The network mode import is different from using SQL*Net to perform the import: impdp username/password@database.

In the next example, data is read via the database link PROD, and it imports only the data from HR.DEPARTMENTS into schema HR_TEST.DEPARTMENTS. Write a log file to file DEPT_DATA.log.

```
impdp system/password network_link=prod schemas="HR"
    remap_schema="HR:HR_TEST" content=data_only
    include=TABLE:"= 'DEPARTMENTS'"
    logfile= dumplocation:HR_TEST.imp
```

Using Network Mode to Refresh Test Data from Production

Consider that you periodically refresh the Oracle10g test database with production data. Since you have to preserve all the grants on the test schema, you can perform the following steps using SQL*Plus and exp/imp tools to perform the data refresh:

1. Disable all the foreign keys.

2. Disable all the primary keys.

3. Drop the indexes so that the import goes faster.

4. Truncate the tables.

5. Export the data from the production database.

6. Import the data to the test database using parameters:

```
COMMIT=Y
BUFFERS=10485760
FROMUSER=SCHEMAPROD
TOUSER=SCHEMATEST
IGNORE=Y
GRANTS=N
```

You can achieve the same results in a single step using impdp with the following parameters (TEST_SCHEMA is the name of database link and must exist):

```
SCHEMAS=SCHEMAPROD
NETWORK_LINK=TEST_SCHEMA
REMAP_SCHEMA=SCHEMAPROD:SCHEMATEST
TABLE_EXISTS_ACTION=REPLACE
EXCLUDE=OBJECT_GRANT
```

Data and Metadata Filters

The Data Pump provides fine-grained object selection to filter the metadata objects during export and import. You can specify the EXCLUDE and INCLUDE parameters with expdp and impdp clients to filter metadata objects. You can use the CONTENT parameter to specify whether you need to export/import just data, just metadata, or both. You can use the QUERY parameter to filter data rows.

The EXCLUDE and INCLUDE parameters are mutually exclusive. Also, when you specify either parameter, you cannot specify CONTENT=DATA_ONLY. The QUERY, EXCLUDE, and INCLUDE parameters have the following syntax:

```
QUERY=[schema.][table_name:]"query clause"
EXCLUDE=object_type[:"object names"]

INCLUDE=object_type[:"object names"]
```

Table 17.4 shows examples of data and metadata filter usage. Though the explanations in the Accomplishes column refer to unloading, it is applicable to loading also.

TABLE 17.4   Data Pump Metadata Filter Examples

Parameter Examples	Accomplishes
schemas=traing content=metadata_only	Unloads the metadata information for all objects owned by the TRAING schema. No data row will be unloaded.

TABLE 17.4 Data Pump Metadata Filter Examples *(continued)*

Parameter Examples	Accomplishes
content=data_only schemas=traing query=traing.student:"where ee_dept = 'IST'"	No metadata will be unloaded; only data rows will be unloaded. All data rows will be unloaded for all tables owned by TRAING, except the STUDENT table, where only the rows that belong to the IST dept is unloaded.
content=data_only tables=traing.student query="where ee_dept = 'IST'"	Only rows in the STUDENT table that belong to the IST department are unloaded.
schemas=traing exclude=view,package,procedure, function,grant,trigger exclude=index:"like 'S%'"	Table rows will be unloaded. Metadata definitions for view, trigger, procedure, function, grants, packages, and indexes that begin with *S* are not unloaded.
Content=data_only schemas=hr include=table:"in ('EMPLOYEES','DEPARTMENTS')" query="where DEPARTMENT_ID = 10"	Only rows belonging to the department 10 are unloaded from the EMPLOYEES and DEPARTMENTS tables.

You can obtain the parameter values for INCLUDE and EXCLUDE by querying the OBJECT_PATH column from the following data dictionary views:

- DATABASE_EXPORT_OBJECTS for full-database export parameters
- SCHEMA_EXPORT_OBJECTS for schema-level export parameters
- TABLE_EXPORT_OBJECTS for table-level export parameters

The following query shows the values that can be used with the INCLUDE/EXCLUDE parameters when performing a schema-level export that is related to packages:

```
SQL> select object_path, comments
     from schema_export_objects
     where object_path like '%PACKAGE%';


OBJECT_PATH        COMMENTS
------------------ -------------------------------------------------
ALTER_PACKAGE_SPEC Recompile package specifications in the selected
                   schemas
PACKAGE            Packages (both specification and body) in sele-
                   cted schemas and their dependent grants and audits
```

```
PACKAGE_BODY        Package bodies in the selected schemas
PACKAGE_SPEC        Package specifications in the selected schemas
... ... ...
SQL>
```

Data Pump has the ability to monitor the jobs and make adjustments to the jobs. The jobs initiated by impdp and expdp can be monitored and modified by using the same clients. In the next section, I will discuss managing the jobs using expdp and impdp.

Managing Data Pump Jobs

Data Pump clients expdp and impdp provide an interactive command interface. Since each export and import operation has a job name, you can attach to that job from any computer and monitor the job or make adjustments to the job. Table 17.5 lists the parameters that can be used interactively.

TABLE 17.5 Data Pump Interactive Parameters

Parameter	Purpose
ADD_FILE	Adds another file or a file set to the DUMPFILE set.
CONTINUE_CLIENT	Changes mode from interactive client to logging mode.
EXIT_CLIENT	Leaves the client session and discontinues logging but leaves the current job running.
KILL_JOB	Detaches all currently attached client sessions and terminates the job.
PARALLEL	Increases or decreases the number of threads.
START_JOB	Starts (restarts) a job that is not currently running. The SKIP_CURRENT option can be used to skip the recent failed DDL statement that caused the job to stop.
STOP_JOB	Stops the current job; the job can be restarted later.
STATUS	Displays detailed status of the job; the refresh interval can be specified in seconds. The detailed status is displayed to the output screen but not written to the log file.

The data dictionary view DBA_DATAPUMP_JOBS shows the active job information along with its current state, the number of threads, and the number of client sessions attached. You can join this view with DBA_DATAPUMP_SESSIONS to get the SADDR column of the sessions attached and can join the SADDR column with V$SESSION to get more information. The

V$SESSION_LONGOPS view also has an entry showing the progress of the job. Use the SID and SERIAL# columns from V$SESSOIN to query V$SESSION_LONGOPS.

The following example should help you understand the parameters more clearly. Say you have an export dump job to be performed. You start the job with the following parameters in a parameter file:

```
DIRECTORY=DUMPLOCATION
DUMPFILE=volest.dmp
LOGFILE=volest.exp.log
SCHEMAS=volest
JOB_NAME=VOLEST_EXP_TEST
```

A table with name VOLEST_EXP_TEST is created in your schema. This is the master control table. Querying the DBA_DATAPUMP_JOBS view will show the status of the jobs running:

```
SQL> SELECT job_name, state
  2  FROM dba_datapump_jobs;


JOB_NAME                         STATE
-------------------------------- ----------------
VOLEST_EXP_TEST                  EXECUTING


SQL>
```

By pressing Ctrl+C, you can stop the logging screen, and you can enter interactive mode. If you find that the job is halfway through and is consuming resources on the server, you can suspend the job and restart it later when the server is less busy:

```
Export> stop_job
Are you sure you wish to stop this job ([y]/n): y
oracle@linux>
```

Let's say you went home and logged back in to your company network. From home, you see the status of the job; the job is in suspended mode. Now, you may use more processing power available in the server to resume the job, so the first step is to attach to the job:

```
oracle@linux:> expdp bill/billthedba attach=VOLEST_EXP_TEST


Export: Release 11.1.0.6.0 - Production on Saturday, 15 November, 2008
23:33:18
Copyright (c) 2003, 2007, Oracle.  All rights reserved.
Connected to: Oracle Database 11g Enterprise Edition Release 11.1.0.6.0 -
Production
With the Partitioning, OLAP, Data Mining and Real Application Testing options
```

```
Job: VOLEST_EXP_TEST
  Owner: BILL
  Operation: EXPORT
  Creator Privs: FALSE
  GUID: D8C25554B641EF14E030007F0200562C
  Start Time: Friday, 23 April, 2004 15:16
  Mode: SCHEMA
  Instance: BT10GNF1
  Max Parallelism: 1
  EXPORT Job Parameters:
  Parameter Name        Parameter Value:
      CLIENT_COMMAND        bill/******** parfile=volest.par
      DATA_ACCESS_METHOD    AUTOMATIC
      ESTIMATE              BLOCKS
      INCLUDE_METADATA      1
      LOG_FILE_DIRECTORY    DUMPLOCATION
      LOG_FILE_NAME         volest.exp.log
      TABLE_CONSISTENCY     0
      USER_METADATA         1
  State: IDLING
  Bytes Processed: 730,622,512
  Percent Done: 69
  Current Parallelism: 1
  Job Error Count: 0
  Dump File: /oradata/dumpfiles/volest.dmp
    bytes written: 733,958,144

Worker 1 Status:
  State: UNDEFINED

Export> parallel=4

Export> status=60

Job: VOLEST_EXP_TEST
  Operation: EXPORT
  Mode: SCHEMA
  State: IDLING
  Bytes Processed: 730,622,512
```

```
Percent Done: 69
Current Parallelism: 4
Job Error Count: 0
Dump File: /oradata/dumpfiles/volest.dmp
   bytes written: 733,958,144

Worker 1 Status:
  State: UNDEFINED

Export> start_job

Export> continue_client
```

After attaching to the job, you increased the threads to 4 from 1 (`parallel=4`), set up to display detailed status to the screen every minute (`status=60`), restarted the job (`start_job`), and let the output display on the screen (`continue_client`).

 Multiple clients (sessions) can attach to a job.

You can use Enterprise Manager Grid Control or Database Control to perform the Data Pump export and import. You can also do the job monitoring using OEM. The next section discusses using the Data Pump Wizard in EM.

 Real World Scenario

Using Fine-Grained Object Selection

The fine-grained object selection in Data Pump export came as a real boon for DBAs. As DBAs, we perform daily exports on the OLTP database excluding certain large (maybe I should say "huge") tables. This particular database includes tables that are DSS in nature in addition to the OLTP tables. In Oracle8*i* and Oracle9*i*, I had to re-create one of the dictionary views to exclude certain multimillion-row transaction tables. I'm not listing the view name here because changing SYS-owned data dictionary views isn't supported.

In Oracle 10*g* and Oracle 11*g*, you do not have to mess with the dictionary views anymore to perform a selective export excluding certain objects. After upgrading the database, I did a tablespace reorganization to better group the tables. I organized the tables into multiple tablespaces based on the expected size of the tables. The tablespaces have a naming convention of %LARGE, %MED, and %SMALL.

While performing the daily export dump using expdp, you simply use `EXCLUDE=TABLESPACE:"like '%LARGE'"`, which excludes all the objects created in the %LARGE tablespaces.

Using the Data Pump Wizard

You can use EM Database Control as a menu-driven interface to Data Pump export jobs. This program steps you through several options and then shows you the PL/SQL code that it will execute. Therefore, you can also use EM Database Control to learn more about using the PL/SQL interface. From the Database Control home page, click the Data Movement tab. Under Move Row Data, you will see links related to Data Pump operations:

- Export to Export Files
- Import from Export Files
- Import from Database
- Monitor Export and Import Jobs

Figure 17.3 shows the Data Movement tab in EM Database Control.

FIGURE 17.3 Data Movement tab in EM

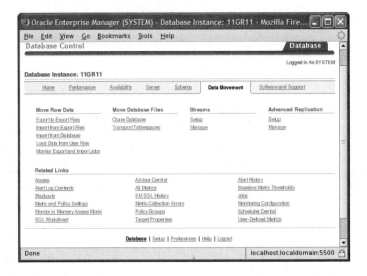

Click the Export to Export Files link to start a Data Pump export job. The export and import both support database, schema, table, and tablespace modes. On the first screen, you choose the mode of export. The screen shown on Figure 17.4 appears when you choose the Database export mode. Here you have the option to estimate the disk space required for the dump file as well as the number of threads (PARALLEL) required.

You can expand the Show Advanced Options link to specify whether you want data-only export or metadata-only export, to include or exclude objects, to export a consistent view of data as of a timestamp or SCN, and to filter rows using a query. On the next two screens, you can specify the location of the dump file and job schedule. You have the option to run the job immediately, to run the job at a later time, or to repeatedly run the job. The final screen shows a review of the Data Pump export, as shown in Figure 17.5. Click Submit Job to start the Data Pump export.

FIGURE 17.4   Data Pump Export: Options screen in EM

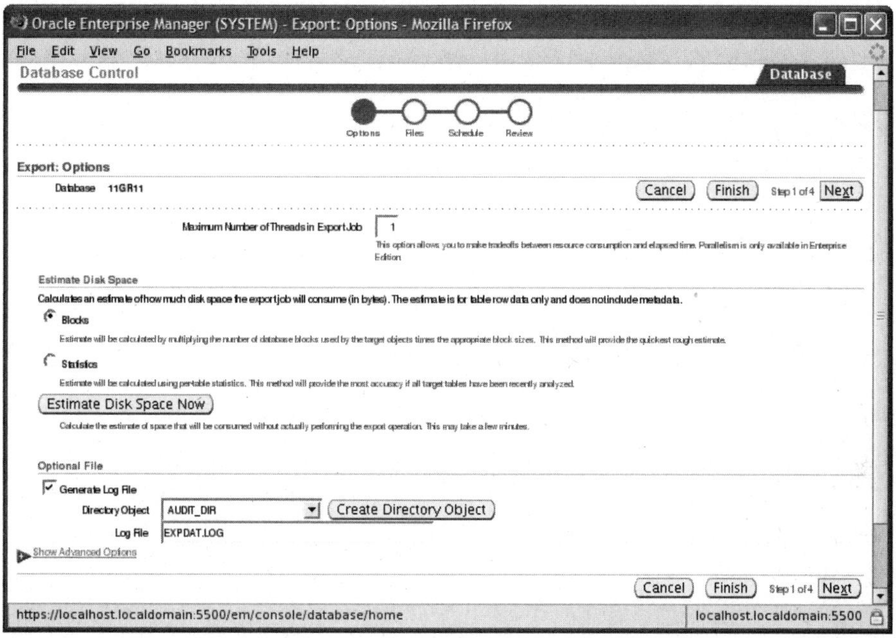

FIGURE 17.5   Data Pump Export: Review screen in EM

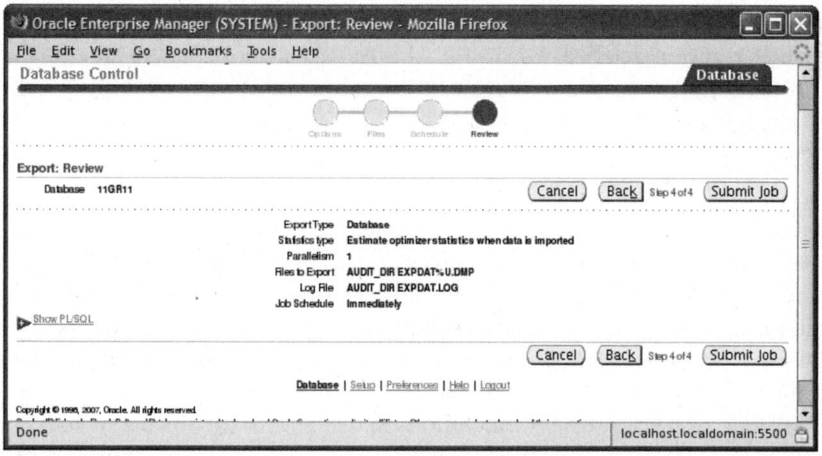

Click the Show PL/SQL link to see the PL/SQL code behind the export job. You can run this code using SQL*Plus to perform the export job. Here is an example:

```
declare
  h1    NUMBER;
begin
  h1 := dbms_datapump.open (
        operation => 'EXPORT',
        job_mode => 'FULL',
        job_name => 'EXPORT000041',
        version => 'COMPATIBLE');
  dbms_datapump.set_parallel(handle => h1, degree => 1);
  dbms_datapump.add_file(handle => h1,
        filename => 'EXPDAT.LOG',
        directory => 'AUDIT_DIR', filetype => 3);
  dbms_datapump.set_parameter(handle => h1,
        name => 'KEEP_MASTER', value => 0);
  dbms_datapump.add_file(handle => h1,
        filename => 'EXPDAT%U.DMP',
        directory => 'AUDIT_DIR', filetype => 1);
  dbms_datapump.set_parameter(handle => h1,
        name => 'INCLUDE_METADATA', value => 1);
  dbms_datapump.set_parameter(handle => h1,
        name => 'DATA_ACCESS_METHOD', value => 'AUTOMATIC');
  dbms_datapump.set_parameter(handle => h1,
        name => 'ESTIMATE', value => 'BLOCKS');
  dbms_datapump.start_job(handle => h1,
        skip_current => 0, abort_step => 0);
  dbms_datapump.detach(handle => h1);
end;
/
```

Once the Data Pump job is submitted, you can view its progress by clicking the Monitor Export and Import Jobs link on the Data Movement screen. A summary of the job appears, as shown in Figure 17.6.

Here you have the option to increase the parallelism of the job; use the Change Job State button to stop or suspend the job. You also have option to specify another location for the dump file.

Import Using EM Database Control

Click the Import from Export Files link on the Data Movement screen to invoke the Data Pump Import Wizard. Similar to export, import also has four modes: database, schema, table, and tablespace. After you choose the type of import, the next screen lets you choose the dump file to import from. On the next screen, you have the option to remap the schema and tablespace. On the import schema screen shown in Figure 17.7, HR schema objects are imported to the JAMES schema, and the objects in the EXAMPLE tablespace are moved to the USERS tablespace.

FIGURE 17.6   Data Pump export job run status

FIGURE 17.7   Data Pump Import: Re-mapping screen

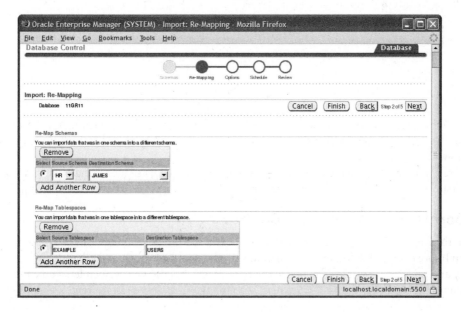

On the next screen, you can specify the number of parallel processes and the log-file destination directory. Similar to export, you can specify to run the job immediately or at a later time. By clicking the Submit Job button on the Review screen, as shown in Figure 17.8, you submit the import job.

FIGURE 17.8   Data Pump Import: Review screen

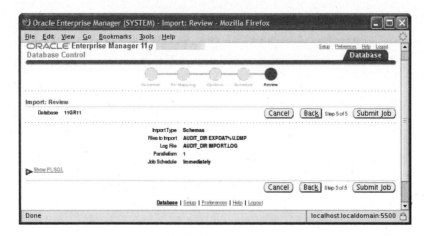

Similar to export, clicking the Show PL/SQL link shows the PL/SQL code behind the import:

```
declare
  h1    NUMBER;
begin
  h1 := dbms_datapump.open (operation => 'IMPORT',
        job_mode => 'SCHEMA', job_name => 'IMPORT000043',
        version => 'COMPATIBLE');
  dbms_datapump.set_parallel(handle => h1, degree => 1);
  dbms_datapump.add_file(handle => h1, filename => 'IMPORT.LOG',
        directory => 'AUDIT_DIR', filetype => 3);
  dbms_datapump.set_parameter(handle => h1,
        name => 'KEEP_MASTER', value => 0);
  dbms_datapump.add_file(handle => h1, filename => 'EXPDAT%U.DMP',
        directory => 'AUDIT_DIR', filetype => 1);
  dbms_datapump.metadata_remap(handle => h1, name => 'REMAP_SCHEMA',
        old_value => 'HR', value => 'JAMES');
  dbms_datapump.metadata_remap(handle => h1,
        name => 'REMAP_TABLESPACE',
        old_value => 'EXAMPLE', value => 'USERS');
```

```
  dbms_datapump.metadata_filter(handle => h1,
      name => 'SCHEMA_EXPR', value => 'IN(''HR'')');
  dbms_datapump.set_parameter(handle => h1,
      name => 'INCLUDE_METADATA', value => 1);
  dbms_datapump.set_parameter(handle => h1,
      name => 'DATA_ACCESS_METHOD', value => 'AUTOMATIC');
  dbms_datapump.set_parameter(handle => h1,
      name => 'SKIP_UNUSABLE_INDEXES', value => 0);
  dbms_datapump.start_job(handle => h1, skip_current => 0,
      abort_step => 0);
  dbms_datapump.detach(handle => h1);
end;
/
```

Loading Data with SQL*Loader

SQL*Loader is a program that reads data files in many possible formats, parses the data (breaks it into meaningful pieces), and loads the data into database tables. Like Data Pump, myriad options are available and a hefty book could be devoted to its use. The Oracle Database Utilities manual devotes several hundred pages of reference material to SQL*Loader alone. This section will not be so comprehensive or attempt to cram all possible uses of SQL*Loader into a few short pages. Instead, I will cover the basics and teach you what is necessary for the exam.

SQL*Loader uses the following file types:

Log   This is a mandatory file. If you do not specify a log file, SQL*Loader will try to create one in the current directory with the name of your control file and a .log filename extension. If SQL*Loader cannot create the log file, execution is aborted. The log file contains a summary of the SQL*Loader session, including any errors that were generated.

Control   This is a mandatory file. This file tells SQL*Loader where the other files are, how to parse and load the data, and which tables to load the data into, and this file can contain the data as well.

Data   Data files are optional and, if included, hold the data that SQL*Loader reads and loads into the database. The data can be located in the control file, so these files are optional.

Bad   This holds the "bad" data records—those that did not pass validation by either SQL*Loader or the database. Bad files are created only if one or more records fail validation. Just as with the log file, if you do not specify a bad file, the database will create one, with the name of your control file and a .bad filename extension.

Discard   This holds data records that did not get loaded because they did not satisfy the record-selection criteria in the control file. Discard files are created only if data records were discarded because they did not satisfy the selection criteria.

SQL*Loader provides a robust toolkit to build data-loading programs for your Oracle 11g database. It can operate either on the database server or on a client machine.

The following section will show you how to employ SQL*Loader to load data into your database tables.

Specifying SQL*Loader Command-Line Parameters

To invoke the SQL*Loader program, use the command sqlldr followed by one or more command-line parameters. These parameters can be identified positionally on the command line or with a *keyword=value* pair. You can mix positional and keyword notation provided that all the keyword-notation parameters appear after all the positional parameters.

For example, to invoke SQL*Loader, telling it to use the connect string system/password and use the control file regions.ctl, you can execute any of the following command lines:

```
sqlldr system/password regions.ctl
sqlldr control=regions.ctl userid=system/password
sqlldr system/password control=regions.ctl
```

The command-line parameters include those shown here, by executing the sqlldr command with no parameters:

```
$ sqlldr

SQL*Loader: Release 11.1.0.6.0 - Production on Sun Nov 16 00:46:00 2008
Copyright (c) 1982, 2007, Oracle.  All rights reserved.
Usage: SQLLDR keyword=value [,keyword=value,...]

Valid Keywords:
    userid -- ORACLE username/password
   control -- control file name
       log -- log file name
       bad -- bad file name
      data -- data file name
   discard -- discard file name
discardmax -- number of discards to allow       (Default all)
      skip -- number of logical records to skip  (Default 0)
      load -- number of logical records to load  (Default all)
    errors -- number of errors to allow          (Default 50)
```

```
         rows -- number of rows in conventional path bind array
                 or between direct path data saves
                 (Default: Conventional path 64, Direct path all)
     bindsize -- size of conventional path bind array in bytes  (Default 256000)
       silent -- suppress messages during run
                 (header,feedback,errors,discards,partitions)
       direct -- use direct path                      (Default FALSE)
      parfile -- parameter file: name of file that contains
                 parameter specifications
     parallel -- do parallel load                     (Default FALSE)
         file -- file to allocate extents from
skip_unusable_indexes -- disallow/allow unusable indexes or
                         index partitions  (Default FALSE)
skip_index_maintenance -- do not maintain indexes, mark affected
                          indexes as unusable  (Default FALSE)
commit_discontinued -- commit loaded rows when load
                       is discontinued  (Default FALSE)
readsize -- size of read buffer           (Default 1048576)
external_table -- use external table for load;
                  NOT_USED, GENERATE_ONLY, EXECUTE  (Default NOT_USED)
columnarrayrows -- number of rows for direct path column array  (Default 5000)
streamsize -- size of direct path stream buffer in bytes  (Default 256000)
multithreading -- use multithreading in direct path
resumable -- enable or disable resumable for current session  (Default FALSE)
resumable_name -- text string to help identify resumable statement
resumable_timeout -- wait time (in seconds) for RESUMABLE  (Default 7200)
date_cache -- size (in entries) of date conversion cache  (Default 1000)


PLEASE NOTE: Command-line parameters may be specified either by
position or by keywords.  An example of the former case is 'sqlldr
scott/tiger foo'; an example of the latter is 'sqlldr control=foo
userid=scott/tiger'.  One may specify parameters by position before
but not after parameters specified by keywords.  For example,
'sqlldr scott/tiger control=foo logfile=log' is allowed, but
'sqlldr scott/tiger control=foo log' is not, even though the
position of the parameter 'log' is correct.
$
```

Many of the command-line parameters can also appear in the control file. When they appear as both command-line parameters and in the control file, the command-line options take precedence.

Specifying Control File Options

The control file contains commands to tell SQL*Loader where to find the data, how to parse it, how to load it, what to do when errors occur, and what to do with records that fail validation. A control file has two or three main sections. The first contains session-wide information, such as log filename, bind size, and whether direct or conventional path loading will be used. The second section contains one or more INTO TABLE blocks. These blocks specify the target tables and columns. The third section, if present, is the actual data. Comments can appear anywhere in the control files (except in the data lines) and should be used liberally. The control file language can be somewhat cryptic, so generous use of comments is encouraged. Comments in a control file start with a double dash and end with a new line. The control file must begin with the line LOAD DATA or CONTINUE LOAD DATA and also have an INTO TABLE clause, together with directions on how to parse the data and load it into which columns.

The best way to learn how to construct a control file is to look at examples and then use variations of them to build your control file. This section gives you several examples but is certainly not a comprehensive sampling. Again, the intent is to present you with enough information to get you going.

For a comprehensive reference, see the Oracle manual "Oracle Database Utilities 11*g* Release 1."

The first example is rather simple and straightforward. The control file contains both control file commands and the data. The command line is as follows:

```
sqlldr hr/hr control=regions.ctl
```

The control file regions.ctl contains the following:

```
LOAD DATA
-- Control file begins with LOAD DATA
INFILE *
-- The * tells SQL*Loader the data is inline
INTO TABLE regions TRUNCATE
-- truncate the target table before loading
FIELDS TERMINATED BY ',' OPTIONALLY ENCLOSED BY '"'
-- how to parse the data
 (region_id, region_name)
-- positional mapping of data file fields to table columns
-- lines following BEGINDATA are loaded
-- no comments are allowed after BEGINDATA
BEGINDATA
1,"Europe"
2,"Americas"
3,"Asia"
4,"Middle East and Africa"
```

The LOAD DATA command tells SQL*Loader that you are beginning a new data load. If you are continuing a data load that was interrupted, specify CONTINUE LOAD DATA. The command INFILE * tells SQL*Loader that the data will appear in the control file. The table REGIONS is loaded. The keyword TRUNCATE tells SQL*Loader to truncate the table before loading it. Instead of TRUNCATE, you can specify INSERT (the default), which requires the table to be empty at the start of the load. APPEND tells SQL*Loader to add the data to any existing data in the table. REPLACE tells SQL*Loader to issue a DELETE to empty out the table before loading. DELETE differs from a TRUNCATE; for DELETE the DML triggers fire and DELETE can be rolled back.

The lines in the control file that follow the BEGINDATA contain the data to parse and load. The parsing specification tells SQL*Loader that the data fields are comma-delimited and that text data can be enclosed by double quotation marks. These double quotation marks should not be loaded as part of the data. The list of columns enclosed in parentheses are the table columns that will be loaded with the data fields.

In the second example, the same data is loaded into the same table, but it is located in a stand-alone file called regions.dat and is in the following pipe-delimited, fixed format:

```
1|Europe                 |
2|Americas                |
3|Asia                    |
4|Middle East and Africa |
```

The command line is as follows:

```
sqlldr hr/hr control=regions.ctl
```

The content of the control file is as follows:

```
LOAD DATA
INFILE  '/apps/seed_data/regions.dat'
BADFILE '/apps/seed_data/regions.bad'
DISCARDFILE '/apps/seed_data/regions.dsc'
OPTIONS (DIRECT=TRUE)
-- data file spec
INTO TABLE regions APPEND
-- add this data to the existing target table
(region_id   POSITION(1)    INTEGER EXTERNAL
,region_name POSITION(3:25) NULLIF region_name = BLANKS
) -- how to parse the data
```

The control file tells SQL*Loader where to find the data file (INFILE) as well as the bad and discard files (BADFILE and DISCARDFILE). The OPTIONS line specifies direct path loading. With fixed-format data, the column specification identifies the starting and ending positions. A numeric datatype can be identified as INTEGER EXTERNAL. The directive

NULLIF region_name = BLANKS tells SQL*Loader to set the region_name column to NULL if the data field contains only white space.

You shouldn't have to know the minutiae of how to tell SQL*Loader precisely how to parse data—the options are far too arcane to expect you to recite them off the top of your head for an exam—but knowing the SQL*Loader capabilities of reading fixed-format and variable-format data is essential. More important to your job is knowing about direct path loads and unusable indexes, which are discussed in the next section.

Using Direct Path Loading

Direct path loading is a SQL*Loader option that allows you, under certain conditions, to use the direct path interface to load data into a table. The direct path interface can be significantly faster than conventional path loading. With conventional loading, SQL*Loader loads data into a bind array and passes it to the database engine to process with an INSERT statement. Full undo and redo mechanisms operate on conventional path loads. Direct path loading is enabled by specifying the DIRECT=Y parameter.

With direct path loading, SQL*Loader reads data, passing it to the database via the direct path API. The API formats it directly into Oracle data blocks in memory and then flushes these blocks, en masse, directly to the data files using multiblock I/O, bypassing the buffer cache, as well as redo and undo mechanisms. Direct path loads always write to a table above the high-water mark; thus, always increase the number of data blocks that a table is actually using.

The important thing to remember about direct path load is that it is fast but has restrictions, including the following:

- Indexes are rebuilt at the end of a direct path load. If unique constraint violations are found, the unique index is left in an unusable state. To correct the index, you must find and remove the constraint violations and then rebuild the index.

NOTE   Unusable indexes are a possible result of direct path loading. Make sure you know what causes an unusable index and how to fix it.

- Direct path load cannot occur if there are active transactions against the table being loaded.
- Triggers do not fire during direct path loads.
- Direct path loading into clustered tables is not supported.
- During direct path loads, foreign key constraints are disabled at the beginning of the load and then reenabled after the load.

- Only primary key, unique, and NOT NULL constraints are enforced.

- Direct path load prevents other users from making changes to the table while the direct load operation is in progress.

Using EM to Load Data

You can invoke the SQL*Loader API from EM Database Control using the Load Data from User Files link on the Data Movement screen (shown earlier in Figure 17.3). You have the option to generate a control file using the wizard or to use an existing control file. The EM Wizard uses seven screens to collect information to build a control file.

Figure 17.9 shows the first screen, where you specify the file locations. You can specify the location on the database server (using directory objects) or on the local machine.

FIGURE 17.9   SQL*Loader data file location

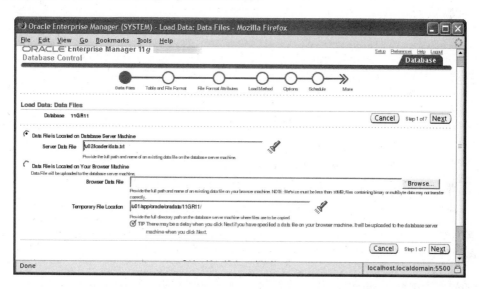

On the next screen, you specify the table to load data into as well as the file format. A sample of the data file appears for you to preview. On the File Format Attributes screen, you can specify the delimiter used to separate columns and have the option to verify the column mappings. On the next screen (Load Method), you specify whether you want to use conventional load or direct load. You can also choose Parallel Direct Load, which is the fastest of all loading options.

Figure 17.10 shows the loading options. Here you can specify the discard file, bad file, and log file. You can also specify a variety of other options.

FIGURE 17.10   SQL*Loader options

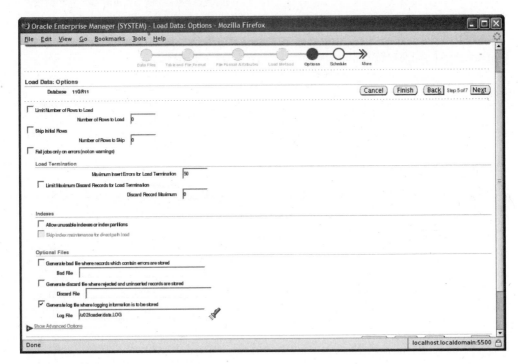

On the next screen, you can schedule the load operation for immediately or for later. Finally, you'll have a chance to review your options before submitting the load job.

Populating External Tables

External tables were introduced in Oracle9*i* and were read-only from the Oracle Database. In Oracle 10*g*, external tables were made writable. In Oracle9*i*, ORACLE_LOADER was the only access driver available for external tables; Oracle 10*g* introduced the ORACLE_DATAPUMP access driver. The external tables that use the ORACLE_LOADER access driver are read-only— they read ASCII flat files from the OS. Only the external tables created with the ORACLE_ DATAPUMP access driver can be written to. The resulting file is in proprietary format (Oracle native external representation, DPAPI), which only Data Pump can read. You can use this file to load to another Oracle Database.

You may ask how is this beneficial—why don't you use the Oracle Data Pump clients to generate the file? Well, though Oracle Data Pump can handle a certain level of filtering, join operations with another table are not possible. Using the external table ORACLE_DATAPUMP access driver, you can unload data that is derived from complex queries. This is useful in loading data marts from data warehouse or similar applications. Data from external tables can be used in SQL queries.

In the following sections, you will learn how to populate an external table using the ORACLE_DATAPUMP and ORACLE_LOADER DPAPI.

Loading External Tables Using Data Pump

You use the ORACLE_DATAPUMP access driver to unload data from an Oracle Database to a flat file (DPAPI format) using the external table method. The external table must be created using the CREATE TABLE...AS SELECT... (CTAS) method. You can specify the PARALLEL clause when creating the table; the ORACLE_DATAPUMP access driver unloads data into multiple flat files at the same time. One parallel execution server will write to only one file at a time. Unloading data in the context of an external table means creating an external table using the CTAS method.

During the unload (or populate) operation, the data goes from the subquery to the SQL engine for the data to be processed and is extracted in the DPAPI format to write to the flat file. The external table to unload data can be created only using the CTAS method with the ORACLE_DATAPUMP access driver. The unload operation does not include the metadata for the tables. You can use the VERSION clause when unloading the data to make sure it loads correctly on the target database.

I'll now demonstrate how to unload data using the ORACLE_DATAPUMP access driver. You will join the EMPLOYEES and DEPARTMENTS tables of the HR schema to unload data. The following statement creates the table in the database as well as creates two files, empl_comm1.dmp and empl_comm2.dmp, in the OS:

```
SQL> CREATE TABLE empl_commission
  2  ORGANIZATION EXTERNAL (TYPE ORACLE_DATAPUMP
  3  DEFAULT DIRECTORY work_dir
  4  LOCATION ('empl_comm1.dmp','empl_comm2.dmp'))
  5  PARALLEL 2
  6  AS
  7  SELECT employee_id,
  8         first_name || ' ' || last_name employee_name,
  9         department_name,
 10         TO_CHAR(hire_date,'DD-MM-YYYY') hire_date,
 11         salary * NVL(commission_pct, 0.5) commission
 12  FROM hr.employees JOIN hr.departments USING (department_id)
 13  ORDER BY first_name || ' ' || last_name
SQL> /

Table created.
```

```
SQL> SELECT department_name, sum(commission) total_comm
  2  FROM    empl_commission
  3  GROUP BY department_name;
```

DEPARTMENT_NAME	TOTAL_COMM
Accounting	10150
Finance	25800
Human Resources	3250
Marketing	9500
Purchasing	12450
Sales	72640
Shipping	78200
Administration	2200
Executive	29000
IT	14400
Public Relations	5000

```
11 rows selected.

SQL>
```

ORGANIZATION EXTERNAL specifies that the resulting table is an external table. TYPE ORACLE_DATAPUMP specifies that the Data Pump access driver should be used. DEFAULT DIRECTORY specifies the location of the dump files. The LOCATION parameter specifies the filenames. Most often when external tables are used, a very large amount of data is unloaded; hence, using the PARALLEL clause will speed up the operation. If the parallel clause is used, the number of files specified in the LOCATION clause must match the PARALLEL degree. If you did not specify enough files to match the degree of parallelism, Oracle decreases the parallelism to match the number of files provided.

The files created using the ORACLE_DATAPUMP access driver can be read-only by Oracle 11*g* because the data is unloaded in a proprietary format. You can use this method to move data from one database to another.

You can copy the dump files to another Oracle 10*g* or 11*g* database and load it using the Data Pump utility, or you can create an external table on these dump files and load from it. Let's create an external table using these dump files and query it:

```
SQL> CREATE TABLE new_empl_commission (
  2  employee_id  NUMBER (6),
  3  employee_name VARCHAR2 (40),
  4  department_name VARCHAR2 (30),
  5  hire_date VARCHAR2 (10),
```

```
 6    commission NUMBER)
 7    ORGANIZATION EXTERNAL (TYPE ORACLE_DATAPUMP
 8    DEFAULT DIRECTORY work_dir
 9    ACCESS PARAMETERS (
10    LOGFILE 'new_empl_commission.log')
11    LOCATION ('empl_comm1.dmp', 'expl_comm2.dmp'));

Table created.
```

 The data dictionary views DBA_EXTERNAL_TABLES and DBA_EXTERNAL_LOCA-
TIONS can be queried to view the characteristics, location, and filenames of
external tables.

Loading External Tables Using Loader

You use the ORACLE_LOADER access driver to load data to an Oracle database from a flat
file using the external table method. You can specify the PARALLEL clause when creating
the table; the ORACLE_LOADER access driver divides the large flat file into chunks that can
be processed separately. Loading data in the context of external table means reading data
from the external table (flat file) and loading to a table in the database using the INSERT
statement.

Let's create an external table using the ORACLE_LOADER access driver; say the user already
has privilege to read from and write to the directory WORK_DIR. The source data file is
employee.dat, which has fixed column data (name, title, and salary). The following code
shows the contents of the employee.dat file, creates the external table using the ORACLE_
LOADER driver, and queries the external table. You can use the data from this external table
to load other tables using INSERT statements.

```
linux:oracle>cat employee.dat
SMITH    CLERK      800
SCOTT    ANALYST    3000
ADAMS    CLERK      1100
MILLER   CLERK      1300
linux:oracle>
SQL> CREATE TABLE employees (
 2    ename   VARCHAR2 (10),
 3    title   VARCHAR2 (10),
 4    salary NUMBER (8))
 5    ORGANIZATION EXTERNAL (
 6    TYPE ORACLE_LOADER
```

```
  7  DEFAULT DIRECTORY WORK_DIR
  8  ACCESS PARAMETERS (RECORDS DELIMITED BY NEWLINE FIELDS (
  9  ename CHAR(10),
 10  title CHAR(10),
 11  salary CHAR(8)))
 12  LOCATION ('employee.dat'))
 13  PARALLEL
SQL> /

Table created.

SQL> SELECT * FROM employees;

ENAME       TITLE         SALARY
----------  ----------  ----------
SMITH       CLERK            800
SCOTT       ANALYST         3000
ADAMS       CLERK           1100
MILLER      CLERK           1300

SQL>
```

Only SELECT statements are allowed on external tables; no INSERT, UPDATE, or DELETE operation is permitted on external tables.

You have learned to move data to and from a database using various tools. Next, you will learn the infrastructure enhancements available in Enterprise Manager to contact Oracle Support and to manage patches.

Using EM Support Workbench

Oracle 11g comes with an advanced fault diagnostic infrastructure framework for detecting, diagnosing and resolving database problems. The problems that are targeted are critical errors that affect the health of the database (such as ORA-600, ORA-7445, and so on).

When a critical error occurs in the database, Oracle flags them as incidents and assigns an incident number. All the diagnostic data such as trace files, alert log information, and dumps related to the error are captured and tagged with the incident number. This data is then stored in the Automatic Diagnostic Repository, where it can be retrieved using the ADRCI utility or using EM Database Control.

The EM Database Control feature that enables you to interact with the fault diagnostic infrastructure of the database is called EM Support Workbench. With Support Workbench, you can investigate, report, diagnose, and repair the problem. In the following sections, you will learn how the Support Workbench works by going through the phases of a problem.

Identifying a Problem

The Health Check framework of Oracle 11g performs proactive checks on the database periodically. Upon detecting a critical error, the fault diagnostic infrastructure runs a few more checks to analyze the critical error. These errors are then tagged as incidents and reported. You can view active incident counts on the Database Control home page, as shown in Figure 17.11.

FIGURE 17.11   Database Control home page showing active incidents and alerts

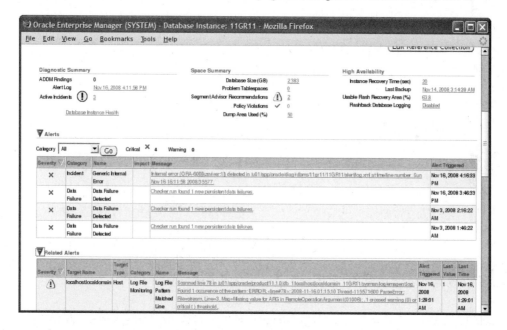

By clicking the Active Incidents count, you will be taken to the Support Workbench home page. You can also invoke the Support Workbench using the Software and Support page in Database Control. The Support Workbench groups similar incidents together and calls it a *problem*. As you can see in Figure 17.12, there are three incidents of the ORA-600 error, and they are grouped together as one problem.

FIGURE 17.12   Support Workbench Problems screen

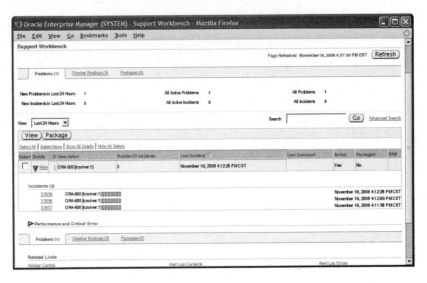

Select the problem by checking the box next to it, and click the View button to see more details about the problem, as shown in Figure 17.13.

FIGURE 17.13   Support Workbench Problem Details screen

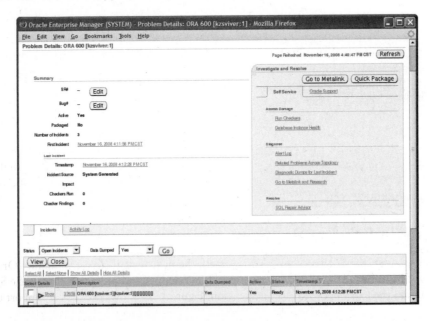

In the next section, you will learn how to gather more information about the problem.

Gathering Additional Diagnostic Information

On the Problem Details screen, under the Investigate and Resolve section, you have various options. On the Self Service tab, you have links available to gather more information about the problem. If you prefer self-service, you can run more checks on the database, diagnose the current problem, or resolve the issue by running the SQL Repair Advisor (if the error is caused by a SQL Statement). The following are your options on the Self Service tab:

- Assess Damage

    - Run Checkers: Run the database health check again to find more issues.

    - Database Instance Health: Show the database health screen, which shows the number of incidents and problems by hour for the last 24 hours.

- Diagnose

    - Alert Log: Shows the alert log entries related to the incident.

    - Related Problems Across Topology: Shows any other incidents that may be related to the current problem.

    - Diagnostic Dumps for Last Incident: Shows the dump and trace files associated with the incident.

    - Go to Metalink and Research: Metalink is Oracle's support site, where you can search and find solutions to the issue.

- Resolve:

    - SQL Repair Advisor: Since the problem is caused by a SQL statement, you can run the SQL Repair Advisor to fix the SQL issue.

You can use the tools under Diagnose to gather more information about the incident and problem. If you have identified the SQL causing the problem and you find an issue with the SQL, you can resolve the problem by yourself. You may also get an answer by searching Oracle's support website, Metalink. Contacting Metalink is discussed later in the chapter.

After self-service, if you could not resolve the problem or could not find more information about the problem of symptoms, you can contact Oracle Support. EM Support Workbench makes contacting Oracle Support easy without having to remember the URL or phone number and gathers all the information that would be of help to the support analyst. Let's go through the next steps of Support Workbench to contact Oracle Support for a resolution to the example problem.

Creating a Service Request

If you cannot identify or resolve the issue yourself, the next logical step is to contact Oracle Support for help. On the Problem Details page shown in Figure 17.13, click the Oracle Support tab under the Investigate and Resolve section. Figure 17.14 shows the Oracle Support tab.

FIGURE 17.14 Contacting the Oracle Support section of Support Workbench

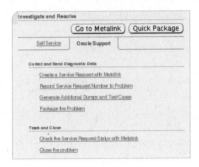

The Create a Service Request with Metalink link takes you to the Metalink login page, where you can log in and enter a service request. The URL for Metalink is https://metalink.oracle.com. Once the service request (SR) is created, you can use the Edit button on the Problem Details screen to update the SR number.

After you create the SR, the next step is to send relevant trace and dump files to Oracle for analysis. Support Workbench provides a packaging service to make this task easier for the DBA.

Oracle Support Services (OSS) is a 24/7 operation providing support to all Oracle customers throughout the world. The primary method of contacting OSS is using the web page at https://metalink.oracle.com. You have to register for an account first and provide information such as the customer service identifier (CSI) number, your contact information, so on.

Once you log in to Metalink, you can find a wealth of information, including the following:

- Searches for known issues
- Forum to discuss various issues
- Opening an SR
- Patches and updates
- Product certification
- Bug information
- Knowledge Base articles
- User documentation
- Electronic technical reference documents

The Metalink forums enable you to interact with other customers to share ideas and provide solutions. You can download patches and patch documentation.

See Metalink note 166650.1, "Global Customer Support Working Effectively with Support," for more information on using the Oracle Support Services.

Packaging Diagnostic Data

You can invoke packaging in two ways. On the Support Workbench page, you can select the problem and click the Package button. This gives you the option to create a quick package or a custom package. A *quick package* gathers information for a single problem with all the default options. With a *custom package*, you have the option to edit the package contents, remove any sensitive data, and add more traces and test cases. Another option to invoke packages is from the Problem Details screen, where you can invoke quick packaging for the problem. You can also optionally upload the packaged information to Oracle under the service request number. Figure 17.15 shows the Quick Packaging screen.

FIGURE 17.15   Quick Packaging screen

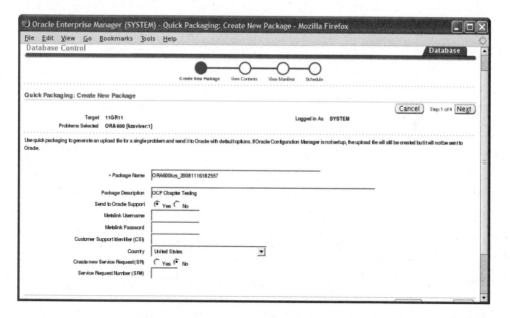

On this screen, you have the option to upload the created package to Oracle Support. If you want Support Workbench to upload the information, provide your Metalink username and password along with the CSI number. If you have not created an SR yet, you have the option to create a new SR from this screen. Enter the SR number for uploading diagnostic information for an existing SR.

If you choose custom packaging, the screen will look like Figure 17.16. Here Oracle will show you all the incidents to report and the files that are being packaged. You can exclude the files you do not want to send. Also, you have the option to add more incidents to the same package.

FIGURE 17.16 Customize Package screen

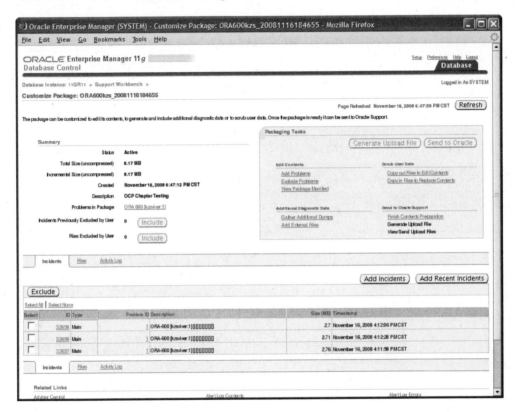

In the Packaging Tasks section, you have the option to add more problems or exclude problems. You can also edit the files you sent to Oracle. Once you have added all the necessary files, click the Finish Contents Preparation link. You will see a confirmation screen with all the files you choose to include in the packaging and an option to generate the upload file. After the file is generated, the Send to Oracle button will be enabled, and you can use it to send the information to Oracle.

Configuring Incident Packaging

You can customize the package-retention and -configuration rules by using the Incident Packaging Configuration link in the Related Links section of the Support Workbench screen. Figure 17.17 shows the default retention and packaging settings.

FIGURE 17.17   Incident packaging configuration

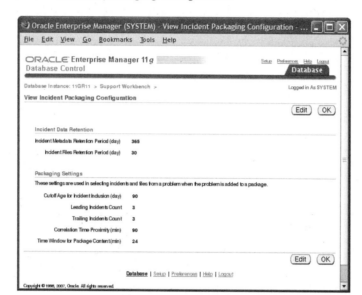

Click the Edit button to change the defaults. You can change the following values:

Incident Metadata Retention Period   Information such as the incident ID, time, and problem are known as the *metadata*. The default is to keep this information for 365 days.

Incident Files Retention Period   Specify how long you want to keep the files (data) related to an incident; the default is 30 days.

Cutoff Age for Incident Inclusion   Include the incidents that are not older than the value specified here in days.

Leading Incidents Count and Trailing Incidents Count   If a problem has several incidents, the packaging by default includes only three incidents from the time it started occurring and three incidents from the latest occurrence.

Correlation Time Proximity   Specify the interval in minutes that should be treated as "happened at the same time" for related incidents. The default is 90 minutes.

Time Window for Package Content   This is the time in minutes to include incidents in the package; the default is 24 minutes.

Tracking and Closing the Incident

You can track the progress of the incident by adding comments to the activity log. The activity log is available on the Problem Details screen as well as on the packaging screens. The Activity Log tab shows the system-generated operations that have occurred on the problem so far. This tab enables you to add your own comments while investigating the problem. Figure 17.18 shows the Activity Log tab.

FIGURE 17.18   Problem activity log

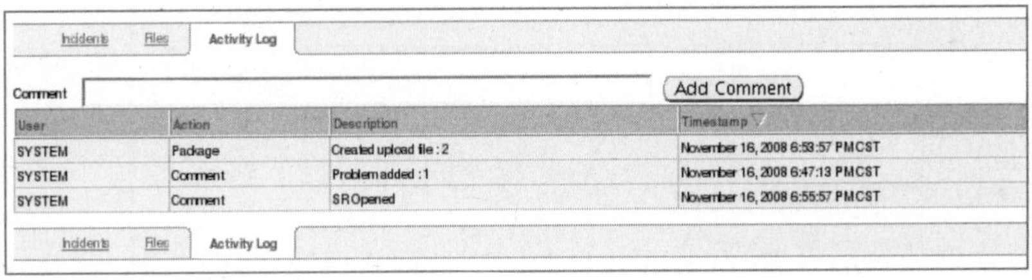

Incidents	Files	Activity Log		
Comment				Add Comment
User	**Action**	**Description**	**Timestamp**	
SYSTEM	Package	Created upload file : 2	November 16, 2008 6:59:57 PM CST	
SYSTEM	Comment	Problem added : 1	November 16, 2008 6:47:13 PM CST	
SYSTEM	Comment	SR Opened	November 16, 2008 6:55:57 PM CST	
Incidents	Files	Activity Log		

You can add an entry using the Add Comment button. If the problem is related to an Oracle bug, you can add the bug number on the Problem Details screen by clicking the Edit button (shown earlier in Figure 17.13).

As you saw on the Self Service tab of the Problem Details screen, the Oracle advisors that can help you repair critical errors are the SQL Repair Advisor and the Data Recovery Advisor.

When you have a resolution for the issue, you can close the incident by clicking the Close button on the Support Workbench screen or by clicking the Close the Problem link on the Problem Details screen.

 NOTE   By default closed incidents are not shown on the Problem Details screen. All incidents (open and closed) are purged after 30 days. You can disable the incident purging on the Incident Details page. You can get to the Incident Details page by clicking the incident ID on the Problem Details screen (shown earlier in Figure 17.13). Click the Disable Purging button to disable the purging of the incident.

In the next section, you will learn how Enterprise Manager can help DBAs manage patches.

Using EM to Manage Patches

As a DBA, you have several reasons to download and apply patches. In Oracle 11g, Oracle has made the patch research and application easier by integrating OSS with Enterprise Manager. Oracle Corporation releases the following types of patches for its database product:

Patch release   A patch release is a major patch that changes the version number of the database. Oracle release numbers have the format 11.1.0.6.0, where 11 is the major release number, 1 is the maintenance release number, 0 is the application-server release number, 6 is the component-specific release number, and 0 is the platform-specific release number. When a patch release is applied, the component-specific release number will change. Patch releases go through rigorous regression testing. Patch releases are cumulative, which means the latest patch release will include most interim patches and critical patch updates, as well as lower patch releases.

Interim patches   Interim patches are one-off patches to fix a specific issue on a platform. The Oracle release numbers do not change when applying interim patches. Interim patches do not go through regression testing.

Critical patch updates   Critical patch updates (CPUs) include security patches and other patches that depend on the security patches. CPUs are cumulative, which means previous CPUs are included. CPUs go through regression testing, and they do not advance the release numbers.

Patch releases are installed using the Oracle Universal Installer (OUI). You can install interim patches and CPUs using the OPatch utility. You can use opatch lsinventory to review all the patches applied to an Oracle Home installation:

```
$ $ORACLE_HOME/OPatch/opatch lsinventory
Invoking OPatch 11.1.0.6.0


Oracle Interim Patch Installer version 11.1.0.6.0
Copyright (c) 2007, Oracle Corporation.  All rights reserved.


Oracle Home       : /u01/app/oracle/product/11.1.0/db_1
Central Inventory : /u01/app/oraInventory
   from           : /etc/oraInst.loc
OPatch version    : 11.1.0.6.0
OUI version       : 11.1.0.6.0
OUI location      : /u01/app/oracle/product/11.1.0/db_1/oui
Log file location : /u01/app/oracle/product/11.1.0/db_1/ ↩
 cfgtoollogs/opatch/opatch2008-11-16_23-08-22PM.log
Lsinventory Output file location :
/u01/app/oracle/product/11.1.0/db_1/cfgtoollogs/opatch/ ↩
 lsinv/lsinventory2008-11-16_23-08-22PM.txt


--------------------------------------------------------------------------
Installed Top-level Products (1):
Oracle Database 11g                                        11.1.0.6.0
There are 1 products installed in this Oracle Home.
```

```
Interim patches (1) :

Patch  6529615      : applied on Sun Nov 16 23:08:05 CST 2008
   Created on 7 Nov 2008, 04:01:26 hrs US/Pacific
   Bugs fixed:
     6529615

-------------------------------------------------------------------------

OPatch succeeded.
$
```

To apply a patch using OPatch, first read the README.txt file accompanying each patch for instructions. Most of the patches are installed by using the opatch apply statement, from the patch staging directory. Enterprise Manager can be used to review, download, and apply patches. The patch-management links are in the Database Software Patching section on the Software and Support tab of Database Control, as shown in Figure 17.19.

FIGURE 17.19 Database Software Patching links on EM

I will discuss each link in the following sections.

Using the Patch Advisor

The Patch Advisor shows the critical patch updates and the recommended patches for the release of the database on your server. Before you can use the Patch Advisor, you must set up Metalink login credentials and perform Metalink integration with EM. You can do this in two steps:

1. Enter the Metalink username and password. Click the Setup link on the top-right corner of EM Database Control. Click Patching Setup on the left menu, as shown in Figure 17.20.

2. Run the Refresh from Metalink job. Under the Related Links section on the Database Control home page, click the Jobs link to invoke the Job Activity screen. Under the Create drop-down list, choose Refresh from Metalink, and click Go, as shown in Figure 17.21.

Click the Patch Advisor link on the screen shown in Figure 17.19. The Patch Advisor screen shows critical security patches that need to be applied to ORACLE_HOME and recommended patches, as shown in Figure 17.22. Oracle can show the recommended patches based on the features used in the database. Select All from the drop-down box to show all the recommended patches.

FIGURE 17.20 Software patching setup in EM

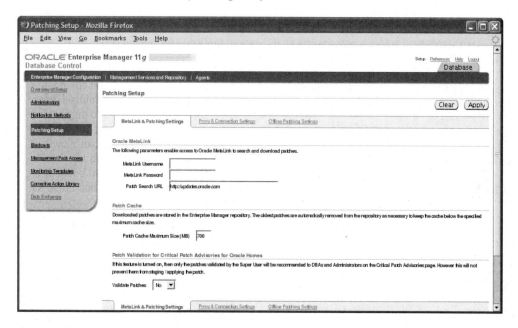

FIGURE 17.21 Refresh from Metalink job setup in EM

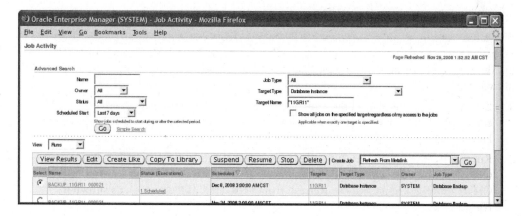

FIGURE 17.22 Patch Advisor screen on EM

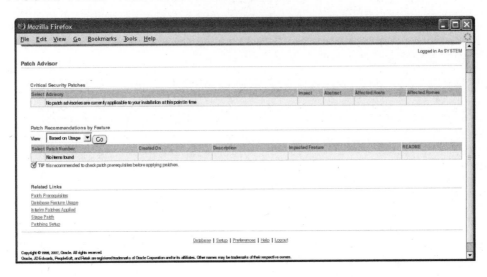

You can also invoke the patching setup screen by clicking the Patching Setup link in the Related Links section.

Viewing the Patch Cache

The patch cache is the location on the server where all your patches are downloaded and kept. One advantage of having the patch cache is that you can apply the patch to multiple Oracle Homes from one download. Figure 17.23 shows the Patch Cache screen.

FIGURE 17.23 Patch Cache screen in EM

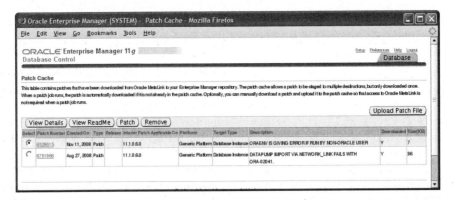

You can click the View ReadMe button to read the patch application details, and you can click the Patch button to apply the patch.

Finding the Patch Prerequisites

Click the Patch Prerequisite Check link to get the screen to evaluate the standard prerequisite checks on Oracle Home and Server with deployment-specific checks. Figure 17.24 shows the Patch prerequisite checker screen.

FIGURE 17.24   Patch Prerequisite Checker screen in EM

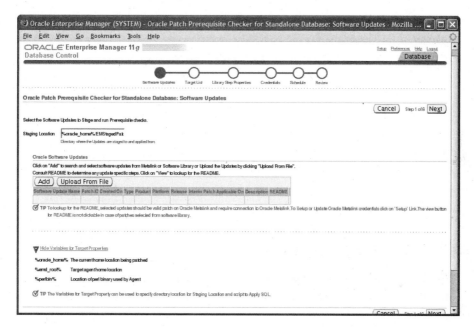

Staging a Patch

You can download patches from Metalink and stage them for later application. Figure 17.25 shows the staging patch screen.

You can select the patch to download by specifying the patch number or by specifying the product and release-number criteria. When the patches are displayed, choose the patch you want to stage. Click Next to prepare for staging or applying the patch.

On the next screen, specify the targets or destination of the patch. You can choose the Oracle Instance name or the Oracle home location. On the Set Credentials screen, specify the host operating-system username and password. On the Stage or Apply screen, you can choose to download the patch or to apply the patch after downloading. On the Schedule screen, specify whether you want the patch to be downloaded immediately or at a later time. Figure 17.26 shows the Summary screen. Review the patch sizes, where the patches will be applied, and so on, and click the Finish button to download the patch.

FIGURE 17.25 Staging patch screen in EM

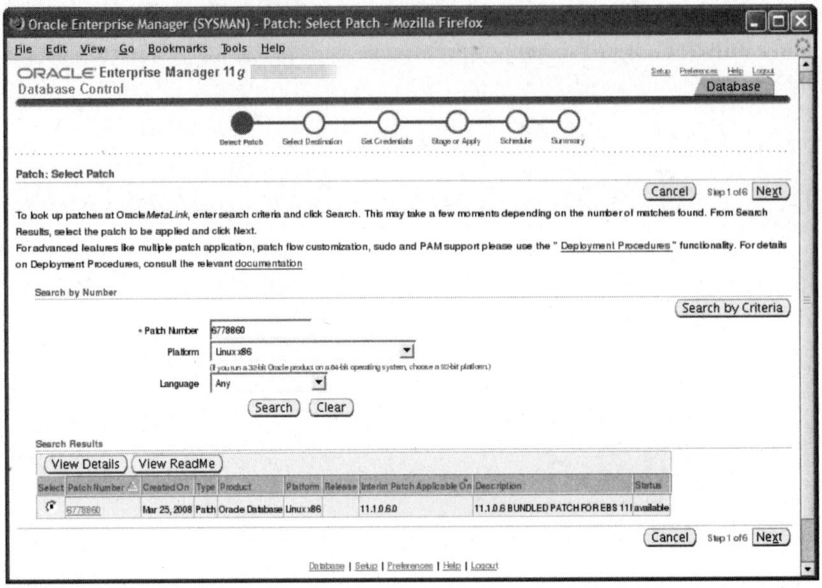

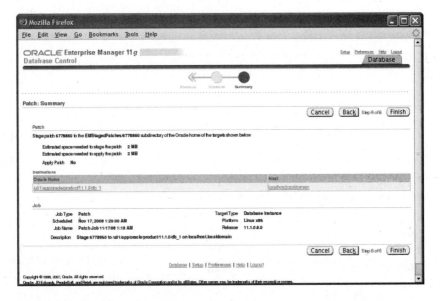

FIGURE 17.26 Patch: Summary screen in EM

Staged patches are stored under the $ORACLE_HOME/EMStagedPatches directory in this example.

Applying a Patch

When you click the Apply Patch link on the Software and Support page, you invoke the Patch Wizard. Figure 17.27 shows the first screen, where the wizard prompts you to select the patches.

FIGURE 17.27   Apply Patch Wizard in EM

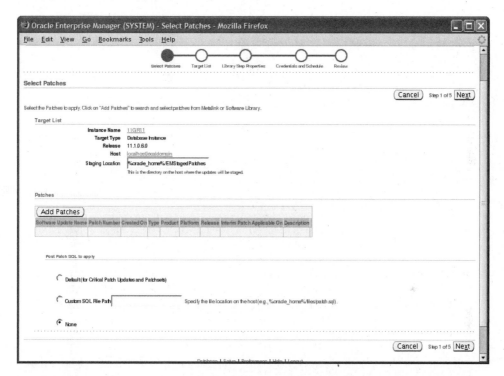

Click the Add Patches button to select the patches to apply. The Add Patches button brings you to the page shown in Figure 17.28, where you can search for patches and select the patch.

The Target List step is skipped for non-RAC instances; the Library Step Properties step is also skipped most of the time, unless you have customized the deployment procedures. The Credentials and Schedule screen prompts you to enter the Oracle software-owner username and password. For the schedule, you can specify one time (immediately), one time (later), or repeating.

FIGURE 17.28 Searching for and selecting patches in EM

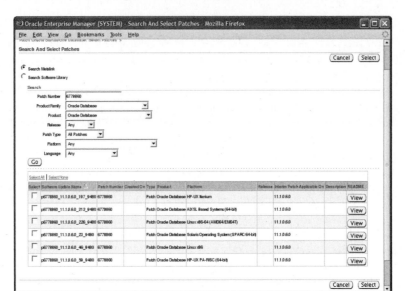

Figure 17.29 shows the review screen. The patch will be downloaded and applied when you click the Finish button.

FIGURE 17.29 Apply patch Summary screen in EM

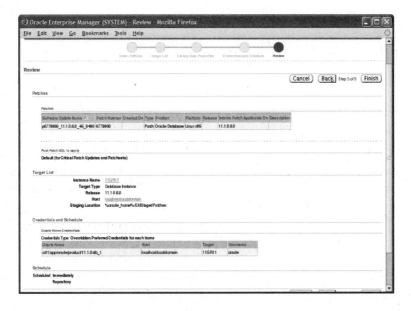

As you can see from the previous screens and options, EM Database Control helps DBAs be proactive about the critical and recommended patches they need.

Summary

In this chapter, I discussed how to move data using Oracle Data Pump, using SQL*Loader, and using external tables. You also learned how to use Enterprise Manger to diagnose and contact Oracle Support as well as manage patches.

Data Pump is a very high-speed infrastructure for data and metadata movement. The client utilities expdp and impdp are used to unload and load data and metadata. The Data Pump architecture includes the data and metadata movement engine DBMS_DATAPUMP, the Direct Path API that supports a stream interface, the metadata API DBMS_METADATA, the external tables API, and the client utilities.

Data Pump export and import are performed on the server. You can attach to a job from any computer and monitor its progress or make resource adjustments. In the interactive mode, you can add a file to export a dump-file set, kill a job, stop a job, change the parallelism, and enable detailed status logging.

SQL*Loader is used to load ASCII files to the Oracle database. You can invoke Data Pump and SQL*Loader using EM Database Control.

You can also use external tables to move data. You can use the ORACLE_DATAPUMP access driver to write data into an external table, and you can use the ORACLE_LOADER access driver to read flat files into Oracle Database.

EM Database Control infrastructure enhancements include Support Workbench and patch management. Using Support Workbench, you can identify, investigate, diagnose, and resolve incidents. The Patch Advisor provides the patches that are needed on the database and can be used to stage and apply patches.

Exam Essentials

Know how to create database directory objects.   Directory objects are required for use in the Data Pump export and Data Pump import programs.

Know that directory objects are not owned by individual schema.   Directory objects are not schema objects. Instead, they are owned by the database like roles or profiles.

Be aware of the Data Pump export and import modes.   Data Pump export has database, schema, table, and tablespace modes, and Data Pump import has full, schema, table, and tablespace modes. Although these modes sound similar, they differ between the two tools.

Be familiar with the Data Pump options that let you transfer both data and metadata from one schema to another.   The content= parameter controls whether data, metadata, or both are copied. The remap_schema parameter allows you to transfer data from one schema to another.

Be aware of the limitations of SQL*Loader direct-path mode, including unusable indexes. SQL*Loader direct-path mode has several limitations, the most prominent being that it locks the table in exclusive mode for the duration of the load. Unique indexes are marked unusable if unique violations are found after a direct path load. These unique violations must be resolved before the index can be rebuilt.

Know the external table access drivers. ORACLE_DATAPUMP and ORACLE_LOADER are the access drivers used with external tables. The ORACLE_DATAPUMP access driver can be used to read and write to an external table. The ORACLE_LOADER access driver is read-only.

Understand Support Workbench's capabilities. Support Workbench can identify, diagnose, and package an incident to contact Oracle Support Services for help.

Be familiar with the Patch Advisor and patch staging screens. EM Database Control makes patch management easy. You can get information about the patches relevant to the database, you can stage patches, and you can apply patches.

Review Questions

1. Which two PL/SQL packages are used by Oracle Data Pump?

   A. UTL_DATAPUMP

   B. DBMS_METADATA

   C. DBMS_DATAPUMP

   D. UTL_FILE

   E. DBMS_SQL

2. These options list the benefits of Oracle Data Pump; pick two that are not true.

   A. Data Pump supports fine-grained object selection using the EXCLUDE, INCLUDE, and CONTENT options.

   B. Data Pump has the ability to specify the target version of the database so that the objects exported are compatible. This is useful in moving data from Oracle 10*g* to Oracle9*i*.

   C. Data Pump has the ability to specify the maximum number of threads to unload data.

   D. The DBA can choose to perform the export using direct path or external tables.

   E. The Data Pump job can be monitored from another computer on the network.

3. The Data Pump job maintains a master control table with information about Data Pump. Choose the right statement.

   A. The master table is the heart of Data Pump operation and is maintained in the SYS schema.

   B. The master table contains one row for the operation that keeps track of the object being worked so that the job can be restarted in the event of failure.

   C. During the export, the master table is written to the dump file set at the beginning of export operation.

   D. The Data Pump job runs in the schema of the job creator with that user's rights and privileges.

   E. All of the above.

4. When using the expdp and impdp clients, the parameters LOGFILE, DUMPFILE, and SQLFILE need a directory object where the files will be written to or read from. Choose the non-supported method for non-privileged users.

   A. Specify the DIRECTORY parameter.

   B. Specify the filename parameters with directory:file_name.

   C. Use the initialization parameter DATA_PUMP_DIR.

   D. None of the above (all are supported).

5. Which command-line parameter of expdp and impdp clients connects you to an existing job?

   A. CONNECT_CLIENT

   B. CONTINUE_CLIENT

   C. APPEND

   D. ATTACH

6. Which option unloads the data and metadata of the SCOTT user, except the tables that begin with TEMP? The dump file also should have the DDL to create the user.

   A. CONTENT=BOTH TABLES=(not like 'TEMP%') SCHEMAS=SCOTT

   B. SCHEMAS=SCOTT EXCLUDE=TABLE:"LIKE 'TEMP%'"

   C. INCLUDE=METADATA EXCLUDE=TABLES:"NOT LIKE 'TEMP%'" SCHEMAS=SCOTT

   D. TABLES="NOT LIKE 'TEMP%'" SCHEMAS=SCOTT

7. Which parameter is not a valid one for using the impdp client?

   A. REMAP_INDEX

   B. REMAP_TABLE

   C. REMAP_SCHEMA

   D. REMAP_TABLESPACE

   E. REMAP_DATAFILE

8. When do you use the FLASHBACK_TIME parameter in the impdp utility?

   A. To load data from the dump file that was modified after a certain time.

   B. To discard data from the dump file that was modified after a certain time.

   C. When the NETWORK_LINK parameter is used.

   D. FLASHBACK_TIME is valid only with expdp, not with impdp.

9. To perform a Data Pump import from a live database, which parameter needs to be set?

   A. db_link

   B. network_link

   C. dumpfile

   D. directory

10. Choose two statements about EM Support Workbench that are true.

   A. It can identify problems, contact Oracle Support, and resolve problems automatically.

   B. It helps collect diagnostic data and package it to send to Oracle Support.

   C. Multiple incidents of similar nature are combined as a problem.

   D. It is primarily used to track service requests created with Oracle Support.

11. Which types of patches do not undergo rigorous testing?

  A. Interim patches

  B. Critical patch updates

  C. Patch releases

  D. None of the above

12. When is it most appropriate to use external table?

  A. When you need to read binary files (PDF and photos) into Oracle Database

  B. To query a large file without loading the data into the database

  C. When the `expdp` and `impdp` utilities are not licensed for use

  D. To load a large file into the database quickly

13. Which constraint is not enforced during the direct path load using SQL*Loader?

  A. Primary key.

  B. Unique key.

  C. Not null.

  D. Check.

  E. All the constraints are enforced.

  F. No constraints are enforced.

14. Which utility can be used to identify the patches applied to your Oracle Database home location?

  A. ADRCI

  B. OPatch

  C. Oracle Universal Installer (OUI)

  D. All of the above

15. Choose the correct statement about Oracle Support Services.

  A. Support can be contacted using the `metalink.oracle.com` web page.

  B. Anyone can register and search Oracle Support's Knowledge Base.

  C. There is no published phone number to contact OSS.

  D. Support analysts are available only during U.S. Pacific time zone work hours.

16. When using EM Database Control to load data into Oracle Database from a flat file, you should do which of the following?

  A. Cut and paste the file content into the data text box.

  B. Always build your own control file and specify it for the data load.

  C. Keep the log file, bad file, and data file in the same directory.

  D. Load the data file from the server or on your client machine.

  E. Load the data from the client machine.

17. Choose the statement that is *not* true from the following about direct path load.

   A. Direct path load cannot occur if active transactions against the table are being loaded.

   B. Triggers do not fire during direct path loads.

   C. During direct path loads, foreign key constraints are disabled at the beginning of the load and then reenabled after the load.

   D. Only primary key, unique, and NOT NULL constraints are enforced.

   E. Direct path load allows other users to perform DML operations on the table while the direct load operation is in progress.

18. Which two advisors can help you repair critical errors?

   A. SQL Tuning Advisor

   B. SQL Repair Advisor

   C. SQL Syntax Advisor

   D. Data Recovery Advisor

19. When using EM Support Workbench, how is a problem closed?

   A. When the error is no longer appearing

   B. When Oracle Support Services closes the SR in Metalink

   C. When the DBA manually closes the incident

   D. All of the above

20. To register for Oracle Support Services Metalink access, you must do which of the following? (Choose all that apply.)

   A. Have a valid driver's license

   B. Be an Oracle customer with a valid CSI number

   C. Get approval from the CSI administrator

   D. Be a member of the IOUG or OAUG user group

Answers to Review Questions

1. B, C. The DBMS_METADATA package provides the database object definitions to the export worker process in the proper order of their creation. The DBMS_DATAPUMP package has the API for high-speed export and import for bulk data and metadata loading and unloading.

2. B, D. Oracle Data Pump is known to versions 10*g* and newer; Oracle9*i* does not support Data Pump. Though Data Pump can perform data access using the direct-path or external-table method, Data Pump makes the decision automatically; the DBA cannot specify the data-access method. Data Pump also supports network mode to import directly from the source database and can estimate the space requirements for the dump file.

3. D. The master table is the heart of the Data Pump operation and is maintained in the schema of the job creator. It bears the name of the job, contains one row for each object and each operation, and keeps status. Using this information helps restart a failed job or suspend and resume a job. The master table is written to the dump file as the last step of the export and is loaded to the schema of the user as the first step of the import.

4. C. If a directory object is created with name DATA_PUMP_DIR, the privileged users can use this location as the default location for Data Pump files. Privileged users are users with EXP_FULL_DATABASE or IMP_FULL_DATABASE roles. Using %U in the filename generates multiple files for parallel unloads with each parallel process writing to one file.

5. D. The ATTACH parameter lets you attach or connect to an existing Data Pump job and places you in interactive mode. ATTACH without any parameters attaches to the currently running job, if there is only one job from the user. Otherwise, you must specify the job name when using the ATTACH parameter.

6. B. If the CONTENT parameter is not specified, both data and metadata will be unloaded. The valid values for CONTENT are METADATA_ONLY, DATA_ONLY, and ALL. If Scott is performing the export, SCHEMAS=SCOTT is optional.

7. A. REMAP_DATAFILE changes the name of the source data file to the target data filename in all DDL statements where the source data file is referenced. REMAP_SCHEMA loads all objects from the source schema into the destination schema. When using REMAP_TABLESPACE, all objects selected for import with persistent data in the source tablespace are remapped to be created in the destination tablespace. REMAP_TABLE changes the name of the table. Since the dump file is in XML format, Data Pump can make these transformations easily. REMAP_INDEX is an invalid parameter.

8. C. You can specify the FLASHBACK_TIME or FLASHBACK_SCN parameter only when performing a network import where the source is a database.

9. B. The network_link parameter specifies a database link to the source database.

10. B, C. Oracle Support Workbench can help DBAs diagnose the problem, collect more information and related traces, and dump files into a package to send to Oracle Support for analysis.

11. A. Interim patches are also known as one-off patches, created for a specific problem. CPU and patch releases undergo rigorous testing.

12. B. External tables can be used to read ASCII flat files without loading into the database. The external table must be created with the ORACLE_LOADER access driver.

13. D. Primary key, unique key, and not null constraints are enforced during direct path load. Check and foreign key constraints are not enforced.

14. B. OPatch is used to apply the CPU and interim patches. The lsinventory option of the $ORACLE_HOME/OPatch/opatch command is used to query patches.

15. A. OSS can be contacted via phone or the Web. The Web is the preferred method of contact.

16. D. The data file, log file, and bad file can be on the database server or on the client machine. When using a database server, you must specify the file location using directory objects.

17. E. While the direct path load is in progress, users cannot run any DML statements against the table. Only queries are allowed.

18. B, D. The SQL Repair Advisor can be invoked to diagnose issues arising out of SQL statements. The Data Recovery Advisor can be used to recover from block corruptions and missing data files.

19. C. Problems are closed manually by the DBA. If the retention periods are not changed, incident data will be purged from the Automatic Diagnostic Repository after 30 days, and Metadata will be kept for 1 year.

20. B, C. You must have a valid customer support identifier to register and use the OSS web page.

Appendix

About the Companion CD

IN THIS APPENDIX:

- What you'll find on the CD
- System requirements
- Using the CD
- Troubleshooting

What You'll Find on the CD

The following sections are arranged by category and summarize the software and other goodies you'll find on the CD. If you need help with installing the items provided on the CD, refer to the installation instructions in the "Using the CD" section of this appendix.

Some programs on the CD might fall into one of these categories:

Shareware programs are fully functional, free, trial versions of copyrighted programs. If you like particular programs, register with their authors for a nominal fee and receive licenses, enhanced versions, and technical support.

Freeware programs are free, copyrighted games, applications, and utilities. You can copy them to as many computers as you like—for free—but they offer no technical support.

GNU software is governed by its own license, which is included inside the folder of the GNU software. There are no restrictions on distribution of GNU software. See the GNU license at the root of the CD for more details.

Trial, demo, or *evaluation* versions of software are usually limited either by time or by functionality (such as not letting you save a project after you create it).

Sybex Test Engine

For Windows

The CD contains the Sybex test engine, which includes all the assessment test and chapter review questions in electronic format, as well as two bonus exams located only on the CD.

PDF of the Book

For Windows

We have included an electronic version of the text in .pdf format. You can view the electronic version of the book with Adobe Reader.

Adobe Reader

For Windows

We've also included a copy of Adobe Reader so you can view PDF files that accompany the book's content. For more information on Adobe Reader or to check for a newer version, visit Adobe's website at www.adobe.com/products/reader/.

Electronic Flashcards

For PC, Pocket PC, and Palm

These handy electronic flashcards are just what they sound like. One side contains a question or fill-in-the-blank question, and the other side shows the answer.

System Requirements

Make sure your computer meets the minimum system requirements shown in the following list. If your computer doesn't match up to most of these requirements, you may have problems using the software and files on the companion CD. For the latest and greatest information, please refer to the ReadMe file located at the root of the CD-ROM.

- A PC running Microsoft Windows 98, Windows 2000, Windows NT4 (with SP4 or later), Windows Me, Windows XP, or Windows Vista
- An Internet connection
- A CD-ROM drive

Using the CD

To install the items from the CD to your hard drive, follow these steps:

1. Insert the CD into your computer's CD-ROM drive. The license agreement appears.

2. Read the license agreement, and then click the Accept button if you want to use the CD.

The CD interface appears. The interface allows you to access the content with just one or two clicks.

Windows users: The interface won't launch if you have autorun disabled. In that case, click Start ➤ Run (for Windows Vista, Start ➤ All Programs ➤ Accessories ➤ Run). In the dialog box that appears, type `D:\Start.exe`. (Replace *D* with the proper letter if your CD drive uses a different letter. If you don't know the letter, see how your CD drive is listed under My Computer.) Click OK.

Troubleshooting

Wiley has attempted to provide programs that work on most computers with the minimum system requirements. Alas, your computer may differ, and some programs may not work properly for some reason.

The two likeliest problems are that you don't have enough memory (RAM) for the programs you want to use or you have other programs running that are affecting installation or running of a program. If you get an error message such as "Not enough memory" or "Setup cannot continue," try one or more of the following suggestions and then try using the software again:

Turn off any antivirus software running on your computer. Installation programs sometimes mimic virus activity and may make your computer incorrectly believe that it's being infected by a virus.

Close all running programs. The more programs you have running, the less memory is available to other programs. Installation programs typically update files and programs; so if you keep other programs running, installation may not work properly.

Have your local computer store add more RAM to your computer. This is, admittedly, a drastic and somewhat expensive step. However, adding more memory can really help the speed of your computer and allow more programs to run at the same time.

Customer Care

If you have trouble with the book's companion CD-ROM, please call the Wiley Product Technical Support phone number at (800) 762-2974. Outside the United States, call +1 (317) 572-3994. You can also contact Wiley Product Technical Support at `http://sybex.custhelp.com`. John Wiley & Sons will provide technical support only for installation and other general quality-control items. For technical support on the applications themselves, consult the program's vendor or author.

To place additional orders or to request information about other Wiley products, please call (877) 762-2974.

Glossary

A

Active Session History (ASH)   Sampled data at specified intervals from the current state of all active sessions. The data is collected in memory and can be accessed by V$ views.

ADDM   *See* Automated Database Diagnostic Monitoring (ADDM).

aggregate functions   Functions that operate on groups of rows, also known as group functions. The exact number of inputs for aggregate functions is not determined until the query is executed and all rows are fetched. This differs from *single-row functions*, in which the number of inputs is known at parse time, before the query is executed.

alert log file   A file where Oracle Database writes information about the database start-ups, shutdown, check points, redo log switches, errors, and warning information.

anonymous block   An unnamed PL/SQL program.

archived redo log file   A file that contains the contents of a previously used redo log file. It's created only when the database is operating in ARCHIVELOG mode.

ARCHIVELOG mode   A database configuration in which redo log files are copied to the archive log destination, which ensures that they won't be overwritten and lost. These archived logs are used primarily for media recovery.

ARC*n*   An Oracle background process that copies the online redo log files to an archived log destination.

arithmetic operators   Operators used to manipulate information in the arithmetic expressions. Addition (+), subtraction (–), multiplication (*), and division (/) are the arithmetic operators.

ASM   *See* Automated Storage Management (ASM).

auditing   The monitoring and recording of specific database activities.

Automated Database Diagnostic Monitoring (ADDM)
The process that analyzes the data in the Automatic Workload Repository (AWR) to identify sources of potential performance bottlenecks and that recommends solutions for correcting the problem. *See also* Automatic Workload Repository (AWR).

automated maintenance tasks   Tasks performed by Oracle Database to gather database statistics, run the segment-space advisor periodically, and so on.

Automated Storage Management (ASM)   A type of storage mechanism that is new in Oracle 10*g*. Oracle manages the storage definitions of the database within a second database used exclusively by ASM to keep track of the disk allocations for your databases.

Automatic Memory Management (AMM)   A mechanism to manage the memory requirement automatically by allocating the total memory to Oracle. Oracle will manage the SGA and PGA based on demand.

Automatic Shared Memory Management (ASMM)   A mechanism to manage the shared memory requirement automatically by allocating the memory to Oracle. Oracle will manage the individual pools in SGA based on demand.

Automatic Workload Repository (AWR)   The collection of tables, owned by the SYSMAN schema, that stores the performance statistics gathered from the system global area (SGA) by the Memory Monitor (MMON) background process.

AWR   *See* Automatic Workload Repository (AWR).

B

B-tree index   An index database object that organizes table data in a binary tree format.

back up to trace   A method of backing up the control file contents to a text file in the location specified.

backup sets   A set of Recovery Manager (RMAN) files that contains the saved data from a backup.

base tables   The tables used to define a view.

baseline metrics   A collection of performance statistics against which current or future database performance is measured to determine whether a significant performance deviation has occurred.

bigfile tablespace   A tablespace built on a single data file that can be up to 2^{32} data blocks in size.

binary operators   Operators that take two operands. All operators are binary, except the + or − used to represent the sign of a numeric value.

bitmap index   An index database object that organizes table data in a series of bitmaps. A bitmap index is analogous to a two-dimensional matrix, where index keys and table rows are the axes.

block   The smallest unit of data storage in the database.

block change tracking file   A file that tracks the blocks changed since the last incremental backup, saving time during an incremental backup because not all blocks in every data file need to be checked for changes.

C

cardinality   The number of distinct values. If a table has a cardinality of 1,000, it has 1,000 rows. If a column has a cardinality of 30, it has 30 distinct values (there may be 1,000 rows but only 30 distinct values).

Cartesian join   A join that joins two tables with no common condition, also known as a cross join. Each row from the first table is joined against every row in the second table.

CASE   An expression that can be used to derive IF...THEN...ELSE logic in SQL.

change vectors   A description of a change made to a single block in the database.

CHAR   Datatype used to store fixed-length character data.

checkpoint   An event during which the dirty data-block buffers are flushed to disk and database files are updated to reflect this action. The database is put into a consistent state.

checkpoint (CKPT) process   The Oracle background process that updates the control file and the data file headers to reflect the last successful transaction by recording the last system change number (SCN).

CKPT   *See* checkpoint (CKPT) process.

column   The vertical space in a table or a view that holds a specific domain of data. In the relational model, an entity has attributes. When this model is implemented in an Oracle Database, an entity becomes a table, and an attribute becomes a column.

column alias   Another name for the column to display with the query results. Alias names can provide meaningful names for the result set.

COMMIT   The SQL command for making permanent the changes made during a transaction.

comparison operators   Operators that compare two values or expressions and give a Boolean result of TRUE, FALSE, or NULL.

complex join   A join that includes additional filter criteria along with the join conditions in the WHERE clause.

compound query   A query that includes a set operator to join two or more queries.

concatenation operator   Operator used to join two text strings. The operator is ||.

concurrency   The condition where many users/sessions can access and modify data at the same time.

connection   The communication channel between the user process and the server process. *See also* server process; user process.

Connection Manager   *See* Oracle Connection Manager.

consistency   A state maintained by the database. A statement/transaction sees a time-consistent image of the data plus any uncommitted data from the statement/transaction.

consistent backup   A backup performed while the database is shut down and unavailable. This is also referred to as offline backup.

constraint An optional schema object that restricts values in the dependent table to a specified condition. Constraints enforce business rules about data.

control file A small binary file that contains metadata about the physical structure of the database, such as the database name, locations of the data files and redo logs, and recovery information.

conversion functions Single-row functions used to convert the datatype of input between numeric, character, and datetime values.

correlated subquery A subquery that references the column names of the parent query.

cost-based optimizer The Oracle optimizer mode that uses statistics about the size, selectivity, and dispersion of the tables and indexes in the database to formulate the most efficient execution plan.

cross join A join that joins two tables with no common condition, also known as a Cartesian join. Each row from the first table is joined against every row in the second table.

CURRVAL The sequence pseudocolumn that will return the last number generated from the sequence-number generator.

D

data block The smallest unit of disk allocation in data or temp files, composed of one or more file-system blocks.

Data Control Language (DCL) The category of SQL commands that control access to database objects, including the GRANT and REVOKE commands.

Data Definition Language (DDL) The category of SQL commands used to create objects in the database, including CREATE, ALTER, and DROP.

Data Manipulation Language (DML) The category of SQL commands used to create, modify, or remove data from a table, including INSERT, UPDATE, and DELETE.

Data Recovery Advisor A tool to identify failures, recommend resolution, and perform recovery action.

database A collection of control files, data files, and redo logs.

database buffer cache The portion of the system global area (SGA) where copies of the data blocks are cached in memory. *See also* system global area (SGA).

Database Configuration Assistant (DBCA)
A Java-based tool you can use to create Oracle databases. The DBCA can store and manage definitions of your databases in the form of templates that can be used to make copies of a database.

Database Control   A web-based component of the Enterprise Management Framework for managing Oracle Database 10g. Database Control allows you to monitor and administer a single Oracle Database instance or a single Real Application Clusters (RAC) environment.

database templates   XML-based documents that the DBCA creates to store information about database definitions. The documents contain everything the DBCA needs to create a database. *See also* Database Configuration Assistant (DBCA).

Database Writer (DBWn)   The Oracle background process that is responsible for writing changed data-block buffers from the database buffer cache back to the data files on disk.

data files   The physical database files that store the database's segments, such as tables, indexes, rollback, and partition.

datatype   A characteristic assigned to each column in a table that defines what type of data can be stored in the column and its valid values.

DATE   Datatype used to store date and time information.

DB Time   A cumulative measure of time spent by the database responding to user requests, including wait times for access to resources such as memory, disk, and CPU for all nonidle user sessions.

DBCA   *See* Database Configuration Assistant (DBCA).

DBMS_DATAPUMP   The Procedural Language SQL (PL/SQL) package that is an API to Data Pump.

DBWn   *See* Database Writer (DBWn).

DCL   *See* Data Control Language (DCL).

DDL   *See* Data Definition Language (DDL).

deadlock   A special kind of lock conflict that prevents two or more transactions from completing because each transaction has a lock on a resource needed by the other transaction.

declarative constraints   Constraints that are not enforced. These constraints will have a state of DISABLE NOVALIDATE.

dedicated server   A type of connection in which every client connection has an associated dedicated server process on the machine where the Oracle server exists. *See also* shared server process.

default role   A role initially enabled for every user session.

default tablespace   The tablespace where a user's tables and indexes are stored if not declared explicitly.

deferred constraint checking   Constraint checking that is deferred to a transaction level. By default, constraints are checked at the statement level.

DELETE   SQL statement used to remove rows from a table.

DIAGNOSTIC_DEST   Parameter specifying the location of the parent directory where all trace, log, and dump files will be written on the server.

directory object   A database object that identifies a file-system location. Directory objects are used by Data Pump jobs.

dispatcher   A process in an Oracle Shared Server environment that manages requests from one or more client connections.

DML   *See* Data Manipulation Language (DML).

DUAL   A dummy table in the Oracle Database. DUAL has one column and one row. It is mainly used to query the system variables such as SYSDATE and USER.

dynamic service registration   The ability of an Oracle instance to automatically register its existence with a listener.

E

Emctl   The command-line utility used to stop and start the Oracle Management agent.

Enterprise Manager (EM) Database Control   The web-based GUI tool for managing Oracle environments.

environment variables   Variables that define the SQL*Plus environment. These variables are set using the SET command. The SHOW command is used to display the value of the variables.

equality join (equijoin)   A join in which two tables are joined with an equality operator or an IN operator. Natural joins and JOIN...USING are examples of equality joins.

escape character   A character used to prefix a pattern-matching character, such as % or _, to allow the inclusion of the pattern-matching character in the string.

exclusive lock   A table lock that will block all changes to data and all other table locks.

expression   A combination of one or more values, operators, and SQL functions that result in a value.

extent management   Defines how free and used extents are managed in a tablespace.

extents   A group of contiguous data blocks allocated to a segment.

Extproc   The default name of the callout process that is used when executing external procedures from Oracle.

F

FAST_START_MTTR_TARGET   An initialization parameter that specifies the desired amount of time, in seconds, to perform instance recovery after an instance failure.

FGA   *See* fine-grained auditing (FGA).

fine-grained auditing (FGA)   Special auditing that allows custom rules to be used in monitoring and capturing audit records.

firewall   Generally, a combination of hardware and software that controls network traffic and prevents intruders from compromising corporate network security.

flash recovery area   A single, unified storage area for all recovery-related files and recovery activities in an Oracle database.

flashback database   A flashback feature that lets you recover the entire database to a specific point in time in the past.

flashback drop   A flashback feature that retrieves a table after it has been dropped without using other more complicated and disruptive recovery techniques such as point-in-time recovery or flashback database.

flashback query   A feature of the Oracle database that allows a user to view the contents of a table as of a user-specified point in time in the past. How far in the past a flashback query can retrieve rows depends on the size of the undo tablespace and on the setting of the UNDO_RETENTION system parameter.

flashback table   A flashback feature that allows you to recover one or more existing tables to a specific point in time. Flashback table is done in place by rolling back only the changes made to the table or tables and their dependent objects, such as indexes.

foreign key   A relationship between two tables. The foreign key defined on a table refers to the primary key or unique key of another table.

full backup   A backup that includes all blocks of every data file backed up in a whole or partial database backup.

full outer join   A join between two tables that returns rows based on the matching condition, as well as unmatched rows from the table on the right and left of the JOIN clause.

function   A PL/SQL program that returns a value and is called in an expression.

G

Generic Connectivity   One of the Heterogeneous Services offered by Oracle that allows for connectivity solutions based on third-party connection options such as OLEDB (a Microsoft standard) and Open Database Connectivity (ODBC). *See also* Heterogeneous Services.

granule   The unit of contiguous memory used within the system global area (SGA) for allocating space to the shared pool, database buffer cache, Java pool, and large pool.

grid computing   The concept of spreading Oracle's memory structures across two or more computers on an as-needed basis in order to maximize the performance of the application during peak usage and minimize the use of resources during low usage.

Grid Control
A web-based user interface that communicates with and centrally manages all the components within the Oracle enterprise. From a centralized location, Grid Control lets you monitor and administer the entire computing environment, including hosts, databases, listeners, application servers, HTTP servers, and web applications.

GROUP BY   Clause used in queries to group aggregate data.

H

HAVING   Clause used in queries to filter out aggregated results.

Health Monitor   Component of Oracle Database to proactively monitor the health of database.

Heterogeneous Services   The facility that lets you communicate with non-Oracle databases and services.

host   The physical machine on which the Oracle server is located. This can be an IP address or a real name that is resolved via some external naming solution, such as DNS.

host string   The database alias name used to connect to the Oracle database. You connect to the database by supplying a username, a password, and a host string. The host string can be omitted if the database is local.

hostnaming method   A name-resolution method for small networks that minimizes the amount of configuration work you must perform.

I

identifiers   Names used in the database, such as table names, column names, and so on. An identifier must begin with an alphabetic character and can contain alphabetic characters, digits, and three special characters: #, $, and _.

image copies   A bit-for-bit duplicate of data files or archived redo log files in a database. You can create image copies using operating-system commands or Recovery Manager (RMAN).

inconsistent backup   A backup performed when the database is open and the system change number (SCN) in the data files and the control file do not necessarily match. This is also referred to as an online backup.

incremental backup   A backup that makes a copy of all data blocks that have changed since a previous baseline backup.

incrementally updated backup   A backup that applies an incremental backup to an image copy, reducing the amount of time required in the event of media recovery.

index   A data structure that physically organizes data from a table in order to improve table access speed.

index key   A single occurrence of an index value.

inline view   A subquery that appears in the FROM clause. This type of subquery is similar to selecting from a view.

inner join   A join that selects only matching rows of both tables. This is the default type of join.

INSERT   SQL statement used to add rows to a table.

instance   The Oracle system global area (SGA) and all the Oracle background processes. *See also* system global area (SGA).

instance failure   A circumstance in which the database instance fails unexpectedly because of a power outage or the failure of an Oracle background process.

instance recovery   The process of synchronizing the contents of each data file with the control file during instance startup using the online redo log files and data in the undo tablespace.

integrity constraints   Constraints that protect the data integrity. They are business rules defined in the database.

IP-filtering firewalls   A type of firewall that monitors the network packet traffic on IP networks and filters out packets that either originated or did not originate from specific groups of machines.

J

Java pool   The system global area (SGA) memory structure where Java code is cached. *See also* system global area (SGA).

Java Virtual Machine (JVM)   The software that interprets and executes Java code inside the database.

join   A relationship between two tables specified by using common columns or a condition to join two tables together.

Julian date   A date that refers to the number of days since January 1, 4712 BC.

JVM   *See* Java Virtual Machine (JVM).

K

key   A distinct value in an index or a unique combination of columns in a table to identify the primary key.

key-preserved   A state of a table in a join view. A table in the join view is key-preserved if the primary and unique keys of the table are unique to the view's result set.

L

large pool   An optional area in the system global area (SGA) used for specific database operations such as backup or recovery. *See also* system global area (SGA); user global area (UGA).

least recently used (LRU) algorithm   The mechanism that the Oracle kernel uses to manage the shared pool and database buffer caches, whereby the SQL or buffers that have been least recently accessed are those that are overwritten to make room for new SQL or buffers when these requests are made by user server processes.

left outer join   A join between two tables that returns rows based on the matching condition, as well as unmatched rows from the table to the left of the JOIN clause.

LGWR   *See* log writer (LGWR).

listener   A server-side process that is responsible for listening and establishing connections to an Oracle server in response to a client connection request.

listener.ora   The configuration file for the Oracle listener located on the Oracle server.

literals   Values that represent a fixed value (constant). There are four types of literals: integer, character, number, and interval.

load balancing   The ability of the Oracle listener to balance the number of connections between a group of dispatcher processes in an Oracle Shared Server environment.

local naming method   A name-resolution method that relies on resolving an Oracle Net service name via the tnsnames.ora file.

log sequence number   An identifier unique to the database that is incremented and recorded when an online redo log file is switched.

log writer (LGWR)   The background process that writes redo log entries from the redo log buffer to the online redo logs. *See also* redo log buffer.

logging   The recording of the Data Manipulation Language (DML) statements, creation of new objects, and other changes in the redo logs. The process also records significant events, such as starting and stopping the listener, along with certain kinds of network errors. *See also* Data Manipulation Language (DML).

logical operators   Operators that are used to combine the results of two comparison conditions to produce a single result or to reverse the result of a single comparison. NOT, AND, and OR are the logical operators.

long query warning alert   An alert generated when a query issues an "ORA-01555: snapshot too old error" message. This error usually occurs either when there is not enough space in the undo tablespace to hold the previous values of changed data or when the undo retention period for the database is set too low.

lsnrctl   The command-line utility to manage the Oracle listener.

M

managed targets   Entities that can be monitored and managed within the Oracle Management Framework. These entities include databases, application servers, web servers, applications, and Oracle agents such as the Oracle Net listener and Connection Manager. *See also* Oracle Connection Manager.

mean time to recovery (MTTR)   The average amount of time it takes to recover the database and make it available after an instance failure occurs.

media failure   A failure in which one or more database files is damaged. Media failure applies to control files, redo log files, temp files, and data files.

metadata   Data that describes data. Metadata includes table definitions, stored PL/SQL program code, and privileges but not the information found in tables.

metric   A measurement that is collected and stored in the Automatic Workload Recovery (AWR) repository. *See also* Automatic Workload Recovery (AWR).

middleware   Software and hardware that sits between a client and the Oracle server. Middleware can provide a variety of functions, such as load balancing, security, and application-specific business-logic processing.

MTTR   *See* mean time to recovery (MTTR).

multiple-column subquery   A subquery that selects multiple columns in the subquery. Such subqueries are generally used in UPDATE statements or in the WHERE clause.

multiple-row subquery   A subquery that returns no rows or more than one row.

multiplexing   Creating multiple copies of a redo log file or control file in different locations so that the loss of one copy does not significantly affect your ability to recover a database.

multitable join   A join that joins more than two tables in a query.

N

NAMES.DIRECTORY_PATH   An entry found in the sqlnet.ora file that defines the net service name search method hierarchy for a client.

natural join   A join that joins two tables using the columns with the same name and datatype in both tables.

nested subquery   A subquery within another subquery.

Net Service Names   The name of an Oracle service on the network. This is the name the user enters when referring to an Oracle service.

network failure   A failure in the network connection between the client and the database; for example, a router reboot or a failure of a network card in the server.

NEXTVAL   The sequence pseudocolumn that will cause the generation of the next number from the sequence-number generator.

NOARCHIVELOG mode   A database mode in which redo log files are not written to an archive destination before they are overwritten. A database in NOARCHIVELOG mode can recover only from an instance failure.

nonequality join   A join that joins two tables with a nonequality operator.

_n_-tier architecture   A network architecture involving at least three computers, typically a client computer, a middle-tier computer, and a database server.

NULL   A value that represents unknown or missing data. Most functions return NULL when called with a NULL argument.

NUMBER   Datatype used to store numeric values in table.

O

object privilege   A database privilege that allows the grantee to perform a specific operation on a database object, such as a SELECT, an UPDATE, or a DELETE operation on a table.

OFA   _See_ Optimal Flexible Architecture (OFA).

Optimal Flexible Architecture (OFA)   A model for organizing mount points, directory structures, and files so that they will be easier to manage, maintain, and back up.

optimizer statistics Measures such as number of rows, average row length, number of leaf blocks, and degree of selectivity that are stored as metadata whenever statistics are automatically or manually collected for database tables and indexes.

Oracle Connection Manager A networking solution from Oracle with connection multiplexing, access control and multiprotocol support. It enables a large number of users to connect to a database with a minimal number of network connections.

Oracle flash recovery area A component of the new automated disk-based recovery mechanisms in Oracle 10g. Flash recovery is designed to simplify your life in terms of Oracle backups by providing a centralized location to maintain and manage all the files related to database backups.

Oracle Management Agent A process that identifies and collects data about entities of interest within the Oracle Management Framework.

Oracle Management Framework An integrated set of tools that lets you perform traditional tasks more easily and efficiently as well as provides an effective mechanism for monitoring components within the enterprise.

Oracle Net Networking software that establishes a connection between Oracle Database and a client session.

Oracle server The combination of an Oracle instance and database.

Oracle Services Oracle Corporation's nonsoftware offerings, such as education and consulting services.

Oracle Shared Server A connection configuration that enhances the scalability of the Oracle Server through the use of dispatcher processes and Shared Server resources. Shared Server allows the server to support a larger number of lightweight concurrent connections by allowing them to share resources.

Oracle Transparent Gateway A connectivity product that seamlessly extends the reach of Oracle to non-Oracle data stores and allows you to treat non-Oracle data sources as if they were part of the Oracle environment.

Oracle Universal Installer (OUI) The Java-based installation tool for installing Oracle software.

OUI *See* Oracle Universal Installer (OUI).

outer join A join used to select data from a table even if there is no matching row in the joined table. These are the rows that are not returned by using a simple join. An outer join is specified by the outer-join operator (+) or the FULL OUTER JOIN keywords.

P

package   A container for bundling procedures, functions, and data structures.

package body   The part of a package that contains the program implementation.

package specification   The part of a package that declares its external interface.

partial database backup   A backup that includes zero or more tablespaces, which in turn include zero or more data files; a control file is optional in a partial database backup.

password   A secret word associated with each user ID to authenticate a database connection.

password file   The encrypted file that contains the usernames and passwords of users who have been granted SYSDBA and SYSOPER privileges.

pfile   A plain-text file that contains database-initialization parameters. Oracle reads this file at startup and uses the information to configure various aspects of the Oracle instance and database.

PGA   *See* program global area (PGA).

ping   A TCP/IP utility that checks basic network connectivity between two computers.

PMON   *See* Process Monitor (PMON).

port   Used with TCP/IP to name the ends of logical connections, which carry conversations between two computers.

primary key   A column or combination of column values that can identify a row uniquely. Primary key columns cannot have NULL values.

principle of least privilege   Permits only the minimal set of privileges that are required for the situation.

private synonym   A restricted alias to another object.

privileges   The assigned permissions to create, modify, remove, or use a database object or a feature.

proactive monitoring   Monitoring the Oracle server for potential issues before they occur, thus avoiding the impact on the database's performance, availability, or manageability.

procedure   A PL/SQL program that is invoked as a stand-alone statement.

Process Monitor (PMON)   The background process that cleans up failed user connections.

profile   A set of limits on database resources or password characteristics.

program global area (PGA)   An area of memory in which information for each client session is maintained. PGA includes bind variable, cursor information, and the client's sort area.

proxy-based firewall   A firewall that prevents information from outside the firewall from flowing directly into the corporate network. The firewall acts as a gatekeeper, inspecting packets and sending only the appropriate information to the corporate network.

public synonym   A global alias to another object.

Q

query   A category of SQL statement that retrieves rows from database tables.

R

raw device   A disk that does not contain an operating system–managed file system. Instead of a file system managing the reading and writing activities, Oracle does so.

reactive monitoring   Monitoring the Oracle server for issues after they have occurred, too late to avoid impacting the database's performance, availability, or manageability.

read consistency   Oracle's read consistency uses undo data to ensure that a statement (or a transaction) sees a set of data that does not change during its execution.

recycle bin   A logical container in each tablespace holding dropped tables that can be retrieved by a database user as long as the space occupied by the deleted object is not required for new objects in the tablespace.

redo entry   A group of *change vectors*. Redo entries record data that you can use to reconstruct all changes made to the database, including the undo segments. This is also referred to as a redo record.

redo log   The physical files on disk that store the transaction recovery information written from the redo log buffer by the LGWR (log writer) process. *See also* log writer (LGWR).

redo log buffer   The portion of the system global area (SGA) where transaction recovery information is stored until it can be written to the redo log files. *See also* system global area (SGA).

redo log file   One of the files that constitutes a redo log group. This is also referred to as a redo log member.

redo log group   A collection of multiplexed (mirrored) redo log files that contain information about changes in the database.

redo log group member   One of the redo logs within a redo log group.

referential integrity   Enforcing business rules within or between tables using primary key constraints and foreign key constraints.

refuse packet   A packet sent via TCP/IP that acknowledges the refusal of some network request.

request queue   A location in the system global area (SGA) in an Oracle Shared Server environment in which the dispatcher process places client requests. The shared server process then processes these requests. See also system global area (SGA).

response queue   The location in the system global area (SGA) in an Oracle Shared Server environment where a shared server process places a completed client request. The dispatcher process then picks up the completed request and sends it back to the client.

response time   The time it takes for a single user's request to return the desired result while using an application. Frequently used as a performance measure in data warehouse systems.

right outer join   A join between two tables that returns rows based on the matching condition, as well as unmatched rows from the table to the right of the JOIN clause.

role   A mechanism for grouping privileges for ease in administering them.

role privilege   A database privilege that, by proxy, gives the grantee any combination of object, system, or other role privileges. Some role privileges that are included with all Oracle databases are DBA, resource, and java_admin.

rollforward   The first phase of instance recovery, during which information in the online redo log files is applied to the data files (including the undo tablespace) to bring the data files up to their state before the instance failed.

ROLLBACK   The SQL statement to undo a transaction.

rollback   The second phase of instance recovery, during which uncommitted transactions are backed out from the data files.

rollback segments   Manually managed segments for storing undo information. This information is used for read consistency and recovery purposes. Rollback segments were replaced by system-managed undo segments when automatic undo management was used.

rolling back   The process of undoing one or more changes to data within a transaction.

row   A single instance of data in a table. In the relational model, a row is analogous to a tuple.

row exclusive lock   A table lock that is implicitly acquired with an INSERT, an UPDATE, a MERGE, or a DELETE statement.

row share lock   A table lock that is implicitly acquired with a SELECT FOR UPDATE statement.

ROWID   A pseudocolumn in every table that is the physical address of a row in the database.

S

savepoint   An intermediate point within a transaction to which changes can be rolled back, without rolling back the entire transaction.

scalability   The ability of a system to continue to provide adequate performance as the amount of data, the number of users, or both increases.

scalar subquery   A subquery that returns one row and one column value. If the scalar subquery returns no rows, the resulting value is NULL.

SCN   *See* system change number (SCN).

script file   One or more SQL and/or SQL*Plus commands saved in a file for reuse.

segment   A schema object that stores data outside the data dictionary. Tables and indexes are segments, while constraints and sequences are not.

segment space management   Defines how free space within a segment is managed.

SELECT   The SQL statement used to query data. This is the most commonly used statement in Oracle.

self join   A join in which a table is joined to itself in a query.

self-referencing foreign key   A foreign key constraint that refers to the primary key column of the same table.

sequence   A named sequential-number generator.

server parameter file (spfile)   A binary, dynamically modifiable file that stores a list of instance configuration parameters.

server process   The operating-system process that executes on the host server on behalf of the user. The server process is responsible for parsing and placing SQL statements into the shared pool, copying database blocks into the database buffer cache, and placing transaction-recovery information into the redo log buffer.

session   The term used to describe a user's connection to an instance.

set operators   Operators used to write compound queries. UNION, UNION ALL, MINUS, and INTERSECT are the set operators.

SGA   *See* system global area (SGA).

shadow process   Another name for a dedicated server process. *See also* shared server process.

share lock   A table lock that will block all changes to data and exclusive locks but will allow other share locks.

share row exclusive lock   A table lock that will block all changes to data and other locks, except other row share locks.

shared server process   Processes in an Oracle Shared Server configuration that executes the client requests.

shared pool   The portion of the system global area (SGA) where cached SQL statements and supported metadata are stored.

single-row functions   Functions that operate on a single row at a time. These functions know how many arguments they will operate on at compile time, before any data is fetched.

single-row subquery   A subquery that returns only one row.

single-tier architecture   A network architecture in which the client and server processes all run on the same computer.

smallfile tablespace   A traditional tablespace that can have multiple data files, each limited to 2^{22} data blocks in size.

spfile   *See* server parameter file (spfile).

SQL   *See* Structured Query Language (SQL).

SQL buffer   A buffer where the previously executed SQL statement is stored. SQL in the buffer can be edited, or it can be run using the / command.

SQL*Loader   The Oracle bulk load program to load data from a flat file.

statement   A single SQL command that can include subqueries.

statement failure   The failure of a single database operation such as a Data Manipulation Language (DML) statement; for example, INSERT, UPDATE, and so on. *See also* Data Manipulation Language (DML).

static service registration   The inputting of service-name information directly into the listener.ora file.

Streams pool   The portion of the system global area (SGA) that is used to cache Oracle queuing information when the Oracle Streams feature is used. *See also* system global area (SGA).

Structured Query Language (SQL)   The English-like language developed to allow users to easily query and manipulate the data stored in relational databases.

subquery   A query within another query. A subquery answers queries that have multiple parts. The subquery answers one part of the question, and the parent query answers the other part.

substitution variable   A variable that will accept values from the user during execution of the SQL.

superaggregates   Summary rows (created by the ROLLUP and CUBE clauses) containing NULL in the grouped expressions. The GROUPING function returns a 1 for these summary rows and a 0 for the nonsummary rows, and it is used to distinguish the summary rows from the nonsummary rows.

Support Workbench   Support Workbench can be used to examine a database problem and contact Oracle Support for a resolution.

synonym   An alias to another object.

SYSASM   A special database authorization given to users to manage ASM instances.

SYSDATE   A built-in function to get the current system date and time.

SYSDBA   A special all-empowering database authorization assigned to users that allows them to perform any database task.

SYSOPER   A special database authorization assigned to users that allows them to perform a variety of database tasks, such as startup and shutdown. Its capabilities are not as encompassing as SYSDBA.

system change number (SCN)   A unique number sequentially assigned to each transaction in the database.

system global area (SGA)   The shared memory structure that Oracle uses to cache application users' SQL statements, data, index, and rollback buffers, Java, and redo information.

system monitor (SMON)   The background process that is responsible for instance recovery, temporary tablespace management, and space management.

system privilege   A database privilege that allows the grantee to perform a specific system operation, such as creating a session or altering any table.

T

table   The basic structure in the database to store data. Tables are defined with columns and contain rows of data.

table alias name   An alias name for a table in queries generally used to qualify ambiguous columns to tell Oracle specifically to which table the column belongs.

tablespace   A logical storage area for database segments.

temporary tablespace   The tablespace in which a user's temporary segments are stored.

throughput   The amount of work that an application or the database can perform in a specified amount of time. This is frequently used as a performance measure in systems.

time-zone displacement   The difference between the time zone and UTC (Coordinated Universal Time zone).

TIMESTAMP   Datatype used to storage datetime data with a fraction of seconds, and optional time-zone information.

tnsnames.ora   The name of the physical file that is used to resolve an Oracle Net service name when you are using the local naming resolution method.

tnsping   An Oracle-supplied utility used to test basic connectivity from an Oracle client to an Oracle listener.

tracing   A configuration that records all events that occur on a network, even when an error does not occur. This facility can be established at the client, the middle tier, or the server location.

transaction   A unit of work within a series of SQL statements. A statement begins with the user's first Data Manipulation Language (DML) statement and ends with a COMMIT or ROLLBACK command. *See also* Data Manipulation Language (DML).

trigger   A Procedural Language/SQL (PL/SQL) program that is invoked in response to a database event.

two-tier architecture   A network architecture that is characterized by a client computer and a back-end server that communicate using some type of network protocol, such as TCP/IP.

U

UGA   *See* user global area (UGA).

Undo Advisor   A tool within the Oracle advisory framework that uses past undo usage to recommend settings for the UNDO_RETENTION parameter as well as an optimal size for the undo tablespace.

undo data   The data blocks changed or updated, along with pointers to rows inserted that are stored in an undo tablespace to support read consistency, rolling back, and recovery from failed transactions or an instance crash. This is also referred to as rollback information.

undo segment   The segment that stores the before image of modified data. This is used for rollback or transaction-recovery purposes.

undo tablespace   A special type of tablespace that holds undo data. Only one undo tablespace can be active in the database at any given time.

Unicode   A multibyte character set that can represent characters from any language. Unicode can, for example, represent characters from English, Greek, Urdu, and Japanese within a single character set.

updatable join view   A view that queries from more than one table and can be used to update the base tables through the view.

UPDATE   SQL statement used to modify existing rows in a table.

user error   A user operation that does not generate an error message, but whose result was unintended, such as accidentally dropping a table.

user global area (UGA)   An area in either the system global area (SGA) or program global area (PGA) used to keep track of session-specific information. *See also* program global area (PGA); system global area (SGA).

user process   The process that runs on the client computer or application server and connects to the instance using a server process.

user-process failure   The failure of a single connection to the database.

username   A unique identification to connect to Oracle Database.

V

VARCHAR2   Datatype used to store variable-length character data.

view   A customized representation of data from one or more tables. Views can be used to present a different perspective of data, to limit the data access, or to hide a complex query.

W

WHERE   A clause used with SQL statements to limit the number of rows retrieved.

whole-database backup   A database backup that includes all data files and at least one control file.

Index

Note to the Reader: Throughout this index **boldfaced** page numbers indicate primary discussions of a topic. *Italicized* page numbers indicate illustrations.

C

G

Wiley Publishing, Inc.
End-User License Agreement

READ THIS. You should carefully read these terms and conditions before opening the software packet(s) included with this book "Book". This is a license agreement "Agreement" between you and Wiley Publishing, Inc. "WPI". By opening the accompanying software packet(s), you acknowledge that you have read and accept the following terms and conditions. If you do not agree and do not want to be bound by such terms and conditions, promptly return the Book and the unopened software packet(s) to the place you obtained them for a full refund.

1. License Grant. WPI grants to you (either an individual or entity) a nonexclusive license to use one copy of the enclosed software program(s) (collectively, the "Software," solely for your own personal or business purposes on a single computer (whether a standard computer or a workstation component of a multi-user network). The Software is in use on a computer when it is loaded into temporary memory (RAM) or installed into permanent memory (hard disk, CD-ROM, or other storage device). WPI reserves all rights not expressly granted herein.

2. Ownership. WPI is the owner of all right, title, and interest, including copyright, in and to the compilation of the Software recorded on the physical packet included with this Book "Software Media". Copyright to the individual programs recorded on the Software Media is owned by the author or other authorized copyright owner of each program. Ownership of the Software and all proprietary rights relating thereto remain with WPI and its licensers.

3. Restrictions On Use and Transfer.

(a) You may only (i) make one copy of the Software for backup or archival purposes, or (ii) transfer the Software to a single hard disk, provided that you keep the original for backup or archival purposes. You may not (i) rent or lease the Software, (ii) copy or reproduce the Software through a LAN or other network system or through any computer subscriber system or bulletin-board system, or (iii) modify, adapt, or create derivative works based on the Software.

(b) You may not reverse engineer, decompile, or disassemble the Software. You may transfer the Software and user documentation on a permanent basis, provided that the transferee agrees to accept the terms and conditions of this Agreement and you retain no copies. If the Software is an update or has been updated, any transfer must include the most recent update and all prior versions.

4. Restrictions on Use of Individual Programs. You must follow the individual requirements and restrictions detailed for each individual program in the About the CD-ROM appendix of this Book or on the Software Media. These limitations are also contained in the individual license agreements recorded on the Software Media. These limitations may include a requirement that after using the program for a specified period of time, the user must pay a registration fee or discontinue use. By opening the Software packet(s), you will be agreeing to abide by the licenses and restrictions for these individual programs that are detailed in the About the CD-ROM appendix and/or on the Software Media. None of the material on this Software Media or listed in this Book may ever be redistributed, in original or modified form, for commercial purposes.

5. Limited Warranty.

(a) WPI warrants that the Software and Software Media are free from defects in materials and workmanship under normal use for a period of sixty (60) days from the date of purchase of this Book. If WPI receives notification within the warranty period of defects in materials or workmanship, WPI will replace the defective Software Media.

(b) WPI AND THE AUTHOR(S) OF THE BOOK DISCLAIM ALL OTHER WARRANTIES, EXPRESS OR IMPLIED, INCLUDING WITHOUT LIMITATION IMPLIED WARRANTIES OF MERCHANTABILITY AND FITNESS FOR A PARTICULAR PURPOSE, WITH RESPECT TO THE SOFTWARE, THE PROGRAMS, THE SOURCE CODE CONTAINED THEREIN, AND/OR THE TECHNIQUES DESCRIBED IN THIS BOOK. WPI DOES NOT WARRANT THAT THE FUNCTIONS CONTAINED IN THE SOFTWARE WILL MEET YOUR REQUIREMENTS OR THAT THE OPERATION OF THE SOFTWARE WILL BE ERROR FREE.

(c) This limited warranty gives you specific legal rights, and you may have other rights that vary from jurisdiction to jurisdiction.

6. Remedies.

(a) WPI's entire liability and your exclusive remedy for defects in materials and workmanship shall be limited to replacement of the Software Media, which may be returned to WPI with a copy of your receipt at the following address: Software Media Fulfillment Department, Attn.: OCA Oracle Database 11g Administrator Certified Associate Study Guide, Wiley Publishing, Inc., 10475 Crosspoint Blvd., Indianapolis, IN 46256, or call 1-800-762-2974. Please allow four to six weeks for delivery. This Limited Warranty is void if failure of the Software Media has resulted from accident, abuse, or misapplication. Any replacement Software Media will be warranted for the remainder of the original warranty period or thirty (30) days, whichever is longer.

(b) In no event shall WPI or the author be liable for any damages whatsoever (including without limitation damages for loss of business profits, business interruption, loss of business information, or any other pecuniary loss) arising from the use of or inability to use the Book or the Software, even if WPI has been advised of the possibility of such damages.

(c) Because some jurisdictions do not allow the exclusion or limitation of liability for consequential or incidental damages, the above limitation or exclusion may not apply to you.

7. U.S. Government Restricted Rights. Use, duplication, or disclosure of the Software for or on behalf of the United States of America, its agencies and/or instrumentalities "U.S. Government" is subject to restrictions as stated in paragraph (c)(1)(ii) of the Rights in Technical Data and Computer Software clause of DFARS 252.227-7013, or subparagraphs (c) (1) and (2) of the Commercial Computer Software - Restricted Rights clause at FAR 52.227-19, and in similar clauses in the NASA FAR supplement, as applicable.

8. General. This Agreement constitutes the entire understanding of the parties and revokes and supersedes all prior agreements, oral or written, between them and may not be modified or amended except in a writing signed by both parties hereto that specifically refers to this Agreement. This Agreement shall take precedence over any other documents that may be in conflict herewith. If any one or more provisions contained in this Agreement are held by any court or tribunal to be invalid, illegal, or otherwise unenforceable, each and every other provision shall remain in full force and effect.

The Best OCA: Oracle Database 11*g* Book/CD Package on the Market!

Get ready for your Oracle Certified Administrator for Oracle Database 11g certification with the most comprehensive and challenging sample tests anywhere!

The Sybex Test Engine features:

- All the review questions, as covered in each chapter of the book.
- Challenging questions representative of those you'll find on the real exam.
- Four full-length bonus exams—two each for exams 1Z0-501 and 1Z0-502—available only on the CD.
- An Assessment Test to narrow your focus to certain objective groups.

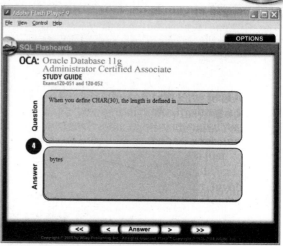

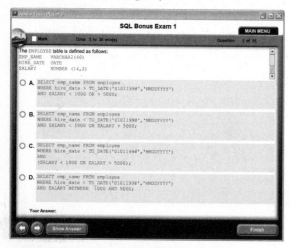

Copyright © 2008 by Wiley Publishing, Inc. All rights reserved. Flash™ Copyright © 1995-2008 Adobe Inc.

Use the Electronic Flashcards for PCs or Palm devices to jog your memory and prep last-minute for the exam!

- Reinforce your understanding of key concepts with these hardcore flashcard-style questions.
- Download the Flashcards to your Palm device and go on the road. Now you can study for the Oracle Database 11*g*: SQL Fundamentals I (1Z0-051) and Oracle Database 11*g*: Administration I (1Z0-052) exams anytime, anywhere.

Search through the complete book in PDF!

- Access the entire *OCA: Oracle Database 11g Administrator Certified Associate Study Guide* complete with figures and tables, in electronic format.
- Search the *OCA: Oracle Database 11g Administrator Certified Associate Study Guide* chapters to find information on any topic in seconds.

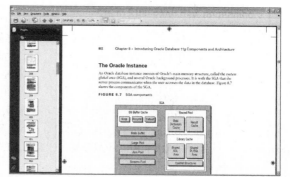